A Short History of the American Nation

A Short History of the American Nation

Seventh Edition

John A. Garraty
Gouverneur Morris Professor of History
Columbia University, Emeritus

 LONGMAN

An imprint of Addison Wesley Longman, Inc.

New York • Reading, Massachusetts • Menlo Park, California • Harlow, England
Don Mills, Ontario • Sydney • Mexico City • Madrid • Amsterdam

For Kathy, Jack, and Sarah

Executive Editor: Bruce Borland
Developmental Editor: Diane Colwyn
Director of Development: Betty Slack
Supplements Editor: Jessica Bayne
Project Coordination and Text Design: Ruttle, Shaw & Wetherill, Inc.
Cover Design: John Callahan
Cover Illustration: "Mission San Carlos del Rio Carmelo" by Orianna Day, The Fine Arts Museums of San Francisco, Gift of
    Mrs. Eleanor Martin
Photo Researcher: Leslie Coopersmith
Electronic Production Manager: Christine Pearson
Manufacturing Manager: Helene G. Landers
Electronic Page Makeup: Ruttle, Shaw & Wetherill, Inc.
Printer and Binder: R.R. Donnelley & Sons Company
Cover Printer: The Lehigh Press, Inc.

For permission to use copyright material, grateful acknowledgement is made to the copyright holders on page C-1, which are hereby made part of this copyright page.

Garraty, John Arthur, [date]
    A short history of the American nation/John A. Garraty.—7th ed.
        p.   cm.
    Includes bibliographical references and index.
    ISBN 0–673–98027–8
    1. United States—History.   I. Title.
E178.1.G242   1997   96–2468
973—dc20   CIP

ISBN 0-673-98027-8

12345678910—DOC—99989796

BRIEF CONTENTS

DETAILED CONTENTS vi
MAPS AND GRAPHS xv
PREFACE xvi
ABOUT THE AUTHOR xx

1 Europe Discovers America 1

2 American Society in the Making 24

3 America in the British Empire 47

4 The American Revolution 70

5 The Federalist Era:
   Nationalism Triumphant 89

6 Jeffersonian Democracy 109

7 National Growing Pains 124

8 Toward a National Economy 146

9 Jacksonian Democracy 162

10 The Making of Middle-Class America 178

11 A Democratic Culture 192

12 Expansion and Slavery 205

13 The Sections Go Their Ways 221

14 The Coming of the Civil War 237

15 The War to Save the Union 252

16 Reconstruction and the South 270

17 In the Wake of War 285

18 An Industrial Giant 303

19 American Society in the
    Industrial Age 319

20 Intellectual and Cultural Trends 335

21 Politics: Local, State, and National 348

22 The Age of Reform 363

23 From Isolation to Empire 383

24 Wodrow Wilson and the Great War 398

25 Postwar Society and Culture:
    Change and Adjustment 418

26 The New Era, 1921–1933 434

27 The New Deal, 1933–1941 450

28 War and Peace 470

29 The American Century 486

30 The Best of Times,
    The Worst of Times 506

31 Society in Flux, 1945–1980 527

32 Our Times 544

THE DECLARATION OF INDEPENDENCE A-1
THE CONSTITUTION OF THE UNITED STATES A-3
PICTURE CREDITS C-1
INDEX I-1

Detailed Contents

MAPS AND GRAPHS   xv
PREFACE   xvi
ABOUT THE AUTHOR   xx

CHAPTER 1
Europe Discovers America   1

Columbus and the Discovery of America   1
The Indian and the European   4
Native American Civilizations   6
The Spanish Decline   8
The Protestant Reformation   9
English Beginnings in America   9
The Settlement of Virginia   10
"Purifying" the Church of England   13
Of Plymouth Plantation   14
A Puritan Commonwealth   15
Troublemakers   16
Other New England Colonies   17
French and Dutch Settlements   17
Maryland and the Carolinas   18
The Middle Colonies   19
Indians and Europeans as "Americanizers"   20
Supplementary Reading   22

CHAPTER 2
American Society in the Making   24

What Is an American?   24
The Southern Colonies: A Hustling People   25
The Chesapeake: "Seasoning Time"   25
The Lure of Land   25
The Resort to Slavery   27
"Their Darling Tobacco"   28
Bacon's Rebellion   29
The Carolinas: "More Like a Negro Country"   30
Home and Family in the Colonial South   31
Georgia and the Back Country   33

Colonial New England: A Covenanted People   34
The Stamp of Puritanism: Family Bonds   34
Women and Children   34
Visible Saints and Others   36
Democracies Without Democrats   36
Dedham: A "Typical" Town   37
The Dominion of New England   37
Crisis in Salem Village   38
"To Advance Learning"   39
"The Serpent Prosperity"   40
A Merchant's World   41
The Middle Colonies: A Rising People   41
"This Promiscuous Breed"   43
"The Best Poor Man's Country"   44
The Politics of Diversity   44
Supplementary Reading   46

CHAPTER 3
America in the British Empire   47

The British Colonial System   47
Mercantilism   48
The Navigation Acts   49
The Effects of Mercantilism   50
The Great Awakening   51
The Rise and Fall of Jonathan Edwards   53
The Enlightenment in America   54
Colonial Scientific Achievements   55
Other People's Wars   55
The Great War for the Empire   56
The Peace of Paris   58
Putting the Empire Right   59
Tightening Imperial Controls   60
The Sugar Act   61
"Essential Rights and Liberties"   61
The Stamp Act: The Pot Set Boiling   62
Rioters or Rebels?   63
Taxation or Tyranny?   63

The Declaratory Act 64
The Townshend Duties 64
The Boston Massacre 65
The Tea Act Crisis 66
From Resistance to Revolution 67
Supplementary Reading 68

CHAPTER 4
The American Revolution 70

"The Shot Heard Round the World" 70
The Second Continental Congress 71
The Battle of Bunker Hill 71
The Great Declaration 72
1776: The Balance of Forces 74
Loyalists 74
Early Defeats 75
Saratoga and the French Alliance 76
The War Moves South 77
Victory at Yorktown 78
The Peace of Paris 79
Forming a National Government 80
Financing the War 80
State Republican Governments 80
Social Reform 81
The Effects of the Revolution on Women 83
Growth of a National Spirit 84
The Great Land Ordinances 85
National Heroes 86
A National Culture 86
Supplementary Reading 88

CHAPTER 5
The Federalist Era: Nationalism Triumphant 89

Border Problems 89
Foreign Trade 90
The Specter of Inflation 91
Daniel Shays's "Little Rebellion" 91
The Road to Philadelphia 92
The Great Convention 93
The Settlement 94
Ratifying the Constitution 95

Washington as President 97
Congress Under Way 97
Hamilton and Financial Reform 98
The Ohio Country: A Dark and Bloody Ground 100
The New Revolution: France 101
Federalists and Republicans: The Rise of Political Parties 102
1794: Crisis and Resolution 102
Jay's Treaty 103
1795: All's Well That Ends Well 103
Washington's Farewell 104
The Election of 1796 105
The XYZ Affair 105
The Alien and Sedition Acts 106
The Kentucky and Virginia Resolves 106
Supplementary Reading 108

CHAPTER 6
Jeffersonian Democracy 109

The Election of 1800 109
The Federalist Contribution 110
Thomas Jefferson: Political Theorist 110
Jefferson as President 111
Attack on the Judiciary 112
The Barbary Pirates 113
The Louisiana Purchase 114
Federalism Discredited 116
Lewis and Clark 116
Jeffersonian Democracy 117
Flies in the President's Ointment 118
The Burr Conspiracy 119
Napoleon and the British 119
The Impressment Controversy 120
The Embargo Act 121
Supplementary Reading 122

CHAPTER 7
National Growing Pains 124

Madison in Power 124
Tecumseh and the Prophet 125
Depression and Land Hunger 126
Resistance to War 126

The War of 1812   126
Britain Assumes the Offensive   128
The Treaty of Ghent   130
The Hartford Convention   130
The Battle of New Orleans   130
Fruits of "Victory"   131
Anglo-American Rapprochement   132
The Transcontinental Treaty   132
The Monroe Doctrine   133
The Era of Good Feelings   135
New Sectional Issues   136
Northern Leaders   138
Southern Leaders   139
Western Leaders   140
The Missouri Compromise   140
The Election of 1824   142
J. Q. Adams as President   143
Calhoun's *Exposition and Protest*   143
The Meaning of Sectionalism   144
Supplementary Reading   145

CHAPTER 8
Toward a National Economy   146

America's Industrial Revolution   146
Birth of the Factory   146
An Industrial Proletariat?   147
Francis Cabot Lowell's Waltham System   148
Strangers at the Door   149
The Persistence of the Household System   149
Corporations   150
Cotton Revolutionizes the South   150
Revival of Slavery   152
Roads to Market   153
Transportation and the Government   154
"Organs of Communication"   155
The Canal Boom   155
The Emporium of the Western World   157
Government Aid to Business   157
The Marshall Court   158
Supplementary Reading   161

CHAPTER 9
Jacksonian Democracy   162

The "Coronation" of King Mob   162
"Democratizing" Politics   162
1828: The New Party System in Embryo   164
The Jacksonian Appeal   164
The Spoils System   164
President of All the People   165
Sectional Tensions Revived   166
"The Bank . . . I Will Kill It!"   166
Jackson's Bank Veto   167
Jackson Versus Calhoun   168
Indian Removals   169
The Nullification Crisis   170
Boom and Bust   172
The Jacksonians   173
Rise of the Whigs   173
Martin Van Buren: Jacksonianism Without
    Jackson   174
The Log Cabin Campaign   175
Supplementary Reading   177

CHAPTER 10
The Making of Middle-Class America   178

Tocqueville and Beaumont in America   178
Tocqueville in Judgment   178
A Restless People   179
Off to Work   180
The Family Recast   181
The Second Great Awakening   182
The Era of Associations   183
Backwoods Utopias   183
The Age of Reform   185
"Demon Rum"   186
The Abolitionist Crusade   187
Women's Rights   189
Supplementary Reading   191

CHAPTER 11
A Democratic Culture   192

In Search of Native Grounds   192
The Romantic View of Life   193
Emerson and Thoreau   193
Edgar Allan Poe   194
Nathaniel Hawthorne   195
Herman Melville   195

Walt Whitman   196
The Wider Literary Renaissance   196
Domestic Tastes   197
Education for Democracy   198
Engines of Culture   200
The State of the Colleges   200
Civic Cultures   201
Scientific Stirrings   202
American Humor   202
Supplementary Reading   204

CHAPTER 12
Expansion and Slavery   205
Tyler's Troubles   205
The Webster-Ashburton Treaty   206
The Texas Question   206
Manifest Destiny   207
Life on the Trail   208
California and Oregon   208
The Election of 1844   209
Polk as President   211
War with Mexico   211
To the Halls of Montezuma   213
The Treaty of Guadalupe Hidalgo   213
Fruits of Victory   214
Slavery: The Fire Bell in the Night
    Rings Again   214
The Election of 1848   216
The Gold Rush   216
The Compromise of 1850   217
Supplementary Reading   219

CHAPTER 13
The Sections Go Their Ways   221
The South   221
The Economics of Slavery   221
Antebellum Plantation Life   222
The Sociology of Slavery   223
Psychological Effects of Slavery   224
Manufacturing in the South   225
The Northern Industrial Juggernaut   226
Self-Generated Expansion   227
A Nation of Immigrants   227
How Wage Earners Lived   228

Progress and Poverty   229
Foreign Commerce   229
Steam Conquers the Atlantic   230
Canals and Railroads   231
Financing the Railroads   231
Railroads and the Economy   233
Railroads and the Sectional Conflict   235
The Economy on the Eve of Civil War   236
Supplementary Reading   236

CHAPTER 14
The Coming of the Civil War   237
The Slave Power Comes North   237
Uncle Tom's Cabin   237
"Young America"   238
The Little Giant   239
The Kansas-Nebraska Act   240
Know-Nothings and Republicans   241
"Bleeding Kansas"   241
Making a Senator a Martyr   242
Buchanan Tries His Hand   243
The Court's Turn   243
The Lecompton Constitution   244
The Emergence of Lincoln   244
The Lincoln-Douglas Debates   245
John Brown's Raid   247
The Election of 1860   247
The Secession Crisis   248
Supplementary Reading   251

CHAPTER 15
The War to Save the Union   252
Fort Sumter: The First Shot   252
The Blue and the Gray   253
The Test of Battle: Bull Run   254
Paying for the War   255
Politics as Usual   255
Behind Confederate Lines   256
War in the West: Shiloh   257
McClellan: The Reluctant Warrior   258
Lee Counterattacks: Antietam   258
The Emancipation Proclamation   260
Negrophobia and the Draft Riots   261
The Emancipated People   261

Antietam to Gettysburg   262
Lincoln Finds His General:
    Grant Wins Vicksburg   263
Economic and Social Effects,
    North and South   264
Women in Wartime   264
Grant in the Wilderness   265
Sherman in Georgia   265
To Appomattox Court House   266
Costs and Prospects   266
Supplementary Reading   268

CHAPTER 16
Reconstruction and the South 270

Presidential Reconstruction   270
Republican Radicals   271
The Fourteenth Amendment   272
The Reconstruction Acts   273
Congress Takes Charge   274
The Fifteenth Amendment   274
"Black Republican" Reconstruction:
    Scalawags and Carpetbaggers   275
The Ravaged Land   276
Sharecropping and the Crop Lien System   278
The White Backlash   279
Grant as President   280
The Disputed Election of 1876   281
The Compromise of 1877   283
Supplementary Reading   284

CHAPTER 17
In the Wake of War 285

The American Commonwealth   285
"Root, Hog, or Die"   285
The Shape of Politics   286
Issues of the Gilded Age   287
Blacks After Reconstruction   288
Booker T. Washington and the Atlanta
    Compromise   289
The West After the Civil War   291
The Plains Indians   291
Indian Wars   292

The Destruction of Tribal Life   294
Exploiting Mineral Wealth in the West   295
The Land Bonanza   296
Western Railroad Building   297
The Cattle Kingdom   299
Open-Range Ranching   300
Barbed-Wire Warfare   301
Supplementary Reading   302

CHAPTER 18
An Industrial Giant 303

Industrial Growth: An Overview   303
Railroads: The First Big Business   304
Iron, Oil, and Electricity   305
Competition and Monopoly: The Railroads   307
Competition and Monopoly: Steel   308
Competition and Monopoly: Oil   309
Competition and Monopoly: Retailing and
    Utilities   310
Americans React to Big Business   310
Reformers: George, Bellamy, Lloyd   311
Reformers: The Marxists   312
The Government Reacts to Big Business:
    Railroad Regulation   312
The Government Reacts to Big Business:
    The Sherman Antitrust Act   313
The Union Movement   314
The American Federation of Labor   315
Labor Militancy Rebuffed   315
Whither America, Whither Democracy   316
Supplementary Reading   318

CHAPTER 19
American Society in the
Industrial Age 319

Middle-Class Life   319
Wage Earners   319
Working Women   320
Farmers   321
Working-Class Family Life   322
Working-Class Attitudes   322
Mobility: Social, Economic, and Educational   323

The "New" Immigration   324
The Old Immigrants and the New   325
The Expanding City and Its Problems   326
The Urban "Infrastructure"   327
The Cities Modernize   328
Leisure Activities: More Fun and Games   329
The Churches Respond to Industrial Society   331
The Settlement Houses   332
Civilization and Its Discontents   333
Supplementary Reading   334

Chapter 20
Intellectual and Cultural
Trends   335

The Pursuit of Knowledge   335
Magazine Journalism   336
Colleges and Universities   337
Scientific Advances   339
The New Social Sciences   339
Progressive Education   340
Law and History   341
Realism in Literature   342
Mark Twain   342
William Dean Howells   343
Henry James   344
Realism in Art   344
The Pragmatic Approach   345
Supplementary Reading   347

Chapter 21
Politics: Local, State, and
National   348

Political Strategy and Tactics   348
Political Decision Making: Ethnic and
    Religious Issues   348
City Government   349
Republicans and Democrats   350
The Men in the White House   351
Congressional Leaders   353
Agricultural Discontent   354
The Populist Movement   355
Showdown on Silver   356

The Election of 1896   359
The Meaning of the Election   361
Supplementary Reading   362

Chapter 22
The Age of Reform   363

Roots of Progressivism   363
The Muckrakers   364
The Progressive Mind   365
"Radical" Progressives:
    The Wave of the Future   366
Political Reform: Cities First   367
Political Reform: The States   367
State Social Legislation   368
Political Reform in Washington   370
Theodore Roosevelt: Cowboy
    in the White House   371
Roosevelt and Big Business   372
Square Dealing   373
TR: In His Own Right   373
Tilting Left   374
William Howard Taft:
    The Listless Progressive   375
Breakup of the Republican Party   376
The Election of 1912   376
Wilson: The New Freedom   377
The Progressives and Minority Rights   378
Black Militancy   379
Supplementary Reading   381

Chapter 23
From Isolation to Empire   383

America's Divided View of the World   383
Origins of the Large Policy   383
The Course of Empire in the Pacific   384
The Course of Empire in Latin America   385
The Cuban Revolution   386
The "Splendid Little" Spanish-American War   388
Developing a Colonial Policy   389
The Anti-Imperialists   389
The Philippine Insurrection   390
Cuba and the United States   390
The United States in the Caribbean   392

The Open Door Policy   392
The Isthmian Canal   394
"Noncolonial Imperial Expansion"   396
Supplementary Reading   397

CHAPTER 24
Woodrow Wilson and the
Great War   398

Missionary Diplomacy   398
Outbreak of the Great War   399
Freedom of the Seas   400
The Election of 1916   401
The Road to War   402
Mobilizing the Economy   403
Workers in Wartime   405
Paying for the War   405
Propaganda and Civil Liberties   406
Wartime Reforms   406
Women and Blacks in Wartime   407
"Over There"   408
Preparing for Peace   408
The Paris Peace Conference   411
The Senate and the League of Nations   412
Demobilization   414
The Red Scare   415
The Election of 1920   416
Supplementary Reading   417

CHAPTER 25
Postwar Society and Culture:
Change and Adjustment   418

Closing the Gates   418
New Urban Social Patterns   418
The Younger Generation   419
The "New" Woman   420
Popular Culture: Movies and Radio   421
The Golden Age of Sports   423
Urban–Rural Conflicts: Fundamentalism   424
Urban–Rural Conflicts: Prohibition   425
The Ku Klux Klan   426
Sacco and Vanzetti   426
Literary Trends   426

The "New Negro"   428
The "New Era"   430
The Age of the Consumer   430
Henry Ford   431
The Airplane   431
Supplementary Reading   433

CHAPTER 26
The New Era: 1921–1933   434

"Normalcy"   434
"Regulating" Business   435
The Harding Scandals   435
Coolidge Prosperity   436
Peace Without a Sword   437
The Peace Movement   439
The Good Neighbor Policy   439
The Totalitarian Challenge   440
War Debts and Reparations   440
The Election of 1928   441
Economic Problems   442
The Crash of 1929   443
Hoover and the Depression   443
The Economy Hits Bottom   445
The Depression and Its Victims   446
The Election of 1932   447
Supplementary Reading   449

CHAPTER 27
The New Deal: 1933–1941   450

The Hundred Days   450
The National Recovery Administration (NRA)   451
The Agricultural Adjustment Act (AAA)   452
The Tennessee Valley Authority (TVA)   452
The New Deal Spirit   453
The Unemployed   453
Literature in the Depression   454
The Extremists   455
The Second New Deal   457
The Election of 1936   458
Roosevelt and the "Nine Old Men"   459
The New Deal Winds Down   460
Significance of the New Deal   461

Women as New Dealers: The Network   462
Blacks During the New Deal   462
A New Deal for Indians   463
The Role of Roosevelt   464
The Triumph of Isolationism   464
War Again in Europe   465
A Third Term for FDR   467
The Undeclared War   467
Supplementary Reading   468

Chapter 28
War and Peace   470
The Road to Pearl Harbor   470
Mobilizing the Home Front   471
The War Economy   472
War and Social Change   473
Minorities in Time of War: Blacks,
    Hispanics, and Indians   473
The Treatment of German, Italian,
    and Japanese Americans   475
Women's Contribution to the War Effort   475
Allied Strategy: Europe First   476
Germany Overwhelmed   477
The Naval War in the Pacific   478
Island Hopping   480
"The Shatterer of Worlds"   481
Wartime Diplomacy   482
Mounting Suspicions   482
Yalta and Potsdam   483
Supplementary Reading   485

Chapter 29
The American Century   486
The Postwar Economy   486
Postwar Society: The Baby Boomers   487
The Containment Policy   488
The Marshall Plan   489
Dealing with Japan and China   490
The Election of 1948   491
Containing Communism Abroad   492
Hot War in Korea   492
The Communist Issue at Home   494

"McCarthyism"   495
Dwight D. Eisenhower   495
The Eisenhower-Dulles Foreign Policy   496
McCarthy Self-Destructs   497
Asian Policy After Korea   497
The Middle East Cauldron   498
Eisenhower and the Soviet Union   499
Latin America Aroused   500
The Politics of Civil Rights   500
The Election of 1960   502
Supplementary Reading   504

Chapter 30
The Best of Times, the Worst
of Times   506
John Fitzgerald Kennedy   506
The Cuban Crises   506
Kennedy's Domestic Program   507
Tragedy in Dallas   508
"We Shall Overcome"   509
The Great Society   511
War in Vietnam   512
Hawks and Doves   513
The Election of 1968   515
Nixon as President: "Vietnamizing" the War   516
The Cambodian "Incursion"   517
Détente   518
Nixon in Triumph   518
The Economy Under Nixon   520
The Watergate Break-in   521
More Troubles   522
The Oil Crisis   522
The Judgment: Expletive Deleted   523
The Meaning of Watergate   524
Supplementary Reading   526

Chapter 31
Society in Flux   527
A Changing Society   527
Television   528
"A Nation of Sheep"   528
Religion in Changing Times   528

Literature and Art	530
Two Dilemmas	531
The Costs of Prosperity	532
New Racial Turmoil	534
Native-Born Ethnics	535
Rethinking Public Education	536
Students in Revolt	537
The Counterculture	539
The Sexual Revolution	539
Women's Liberation	540
Supplementary Reading	543

CHAPTER 32
Our Times — 544

Ford as President	544
The Carter Presidency	545
Cold War or Détente?	545
A Time of Troubles	546
Double-Digit Inflation	547
The Carter Recession	547
The Iranian Crisis: Origins	547
The Iranian Crisis: Carter's Dilemma	548

The Election of 1980	549
Reagan as President	550
Four More Years	551
The "Reagan Revolution"	552
Change and Uncertainty	553
The Merger Movement	555
The Iran-Contra Arms Deals	555
The Election of 1988	556
The End of the Cold War	557
Domestic Problems and Possibilities	558
The War in the Persian Gulf	558
Things Go Wrong	559
The Election of 1992	560
A New Start	560
The Imponderable Future	561
Supplementary Reading	562

THE DECLARATION OF INDEPENDENCE	A-1
THE CONSTITUTION OF THE UNITED STATES	A-3
CREDITS	C-1
INDEX	I-1

MAPS AND GRAPHS

Voyages of Discovery, 1487–1610   5
Primary East Coast Indian Nations in the 1600s   8
The Southern Colonies   26
Colonial New England   35
Colonial Overseas Trade   42
The Middle Colonies   43
Pitt's Strategy, French and Indian War, 1758–1760   58
Eastern North America, 1763   60
New York-New Jersey Campaigns, 1776–1777   75
Yorktown and the War in the South, 1778–1781   78
The United States, 1787–1802   104
The Revolution of 1800   109
Exploring the Louisiana Purchase   115
The War of 1812   129
The United States, 1819   134
The Missouri Compromise, 1820–1821   141
Cotton Production and Slave Population, 1800–1860   151
Prices for Cotton and for Slaves, 1802–1860   152
Canals and Roads, 1820–1850   156
Election of 1824—Election of 1828—Election of 1832   165
Indian Removals   170
Election of 1832—Election of 1836—Election of 1840   174
Rural Versus Urban Population, 1820–1860   180

Trails West   210
Free and Slave Areas, 1850   215
The United States at Mid-Century   218
Ten Leading Manufactured Products, 1860   227
Primary Railroads, 1860   234
The Election of 1860   249
War in the West, 1862   257
War in the East, 1861–1862   259
War Ends in Virginia, 1864–1865   267
Casualties of the Civil War   267
The Compromise of 1877   282
The West: Cattle, Railroads, and Mining, 1850–1893   300
Primary Railroads, 1890   305
Rural and Urban Population, 1860–1910   326
The Election of 1896   360
The United States in the Caribbean   393
The Western Front, 1918   409
Casualties of the Great War   410
Unemployment of Non-Farm Workers   455
World War II, European Theater   478
World War II, Pacific Theater   480
The Korean War, 1950–1953   494
Southeast Asia, 1954–1975   514
The Middle East   549
Changing Living Standards, 1979–1994   555

This is the seventh edition of *A Short History of the American Nation,* the sixth time I have revised it, and the process remains for me both challenging and endlessly fascinating. Historians try to explain what happened in the past and of course "what happened" does not change. But what is important to point out about the past is that it changes constantly as more information about past events comes to light and as current events raise new questions about the events and people of earlier times. Year by year hundreds of new books and articles are published about various aspects of American history; when those dealing with any particular subject have been digested and synthesized and combined with already existing knowledge, a new, "up-to-date" description of that topic results. This process keeps authors like me who write American history textbooks very busy.

Goals of This Revision

The work of revising a survey of all American history takes many forms. First there are the small alterations involved in incorporating new details and examples, and in clarifying obscurities that have previously escaped notice. Then there is the matter of bringing the narrative as close to the present as possible, something that is relatively easy to do, but difficult to do well. Nearly always revision also involves changes in emphasis— some subjects need to be condensed or eliminated; others require more space either because more has been discovered about them or because recent developments make them seem more significant. Finally, and most important, are the larger changes made necessary because historians, responding to contemporary interests, to noteworthy work being done by colleagues and other specialists, and to the questions and interests of their students, have produced persuasive new interpretations and even opened up entirely new subjects. Dealing with this work, in turn, re-

quires more of the simpler kinds of revisions just mentioned.

This revision of *A Short History of the American Nation* contains many examples of all these types of change.

Organizational Changes

To improve the flow of topics and to readjust the amount of space devoted to various periods of American history, I have reorganized and condensed Chapters 7 through 10. Chapters 7 and 8, covering the political history of the Madison, Monroe, and John Quincy Adams administrations, have been tightened and combined, and a new section on the meaning of sectionalism added. The material in Chapter 11 of the sixth edition dealing with immigration and the lives of working people has been added to the chapter "Toward a National Economy," now Chapter 8.

New Coverage and Features

At many key points, especially when dealing with the colonial period and the American Revolution, more attention has been devoted to the impact of Spain and of Hispanic culture on American development. Chapter 1 contains a new section. "Spain's American Empire," and there are expanded discussions of Spain's role in the Revolution and on Spanish activities along the southern and western frontier of the United States in the 1780s and 1790s. Coverage of Indian-European interactions in the 16th and 17th centuries has also been revised.

As in every new edition of *A Short History of the American Nation,* I have paid a good deal of attention also to the "Supplementary Readings" at the end of each chapter. I have eliminated many older titles that, although valuable, are out of print, and I have substituted more recent and in most instances equally worthwhile volumes that are readily available, often in paperback.

Approach

In making all these changes and others less important, I have not, I trust, altered my basic approach to American history, which is to deal with the subject in narrative fashion and to use the political history of the nation as the frame or skeleton on which social, economic, and cultural developments depend. The American nation (the United States) is, after all, a political institution.

The people of the United States, in their infinite variety, also remain central to my account. The theory that a few great individuals, cut from larger cloth than the general run of human beings, have shaped the course of past events oversimplifies history. But the past becomes more comprehensible when attention is paid to how the major figures on the historical stage have reacted to events and to one another. Since generalizations require concrete illustration if they are to be grasped fully, readers will find many anecdotes and quotations on the following pages, along with the facts and dates and statistics every good history must contain. This illustrative material is interesting, and most of it is entertaining, but I believe it is instructive as well.

I also believe that one need not be an uncritical admirer of the American nation and its people to recognize that the history of the United States deserves to be treated with dignity and respect. Individually and as a society, we have rarely lived up perfectly to the principles enunciated in the Declaration of Independence and the Constitution, but recent events in Eastern Europe demonstrate how cherished these "American" values are by people who have been deprived of them. American values are not well served by patriotic hoopla or by slighting or excusing dark and discreditable aspects of the American past. The English radical Oliver Cromwell is said to have told an artist who was painting his picture to portray him "warts and all." Cromwell wanted to be remembered as he was, confident that, on balance, history would judge him fairly. This is another principle on which *A Short History of the American Nation* continues to be based.

Supplements

For Instructors

Instructor's Resource Manual. Written by Michael Mayer of the University of Montana, this volume has been designed to aid both the novice and experienced instructor in teaching American history. Each chapter includes a concise chapter overview, a list of points for student mastery, lecture supplements, and questions for class discussion. A special feature of each chapter is a set of documents with accompanying questions for student analysis.

Longman Comprehensive American History Transparency Set. This vast collection of American history map transparencies will soon become a necessary teaching aid. This set includes over 200 map transparencies ranging from the first Native Americans to the end of the Cold War, covering wars, social trends, elections, immigration, and demographics. Included are a reproducible set of student map exercises, teaching tips, and correlation charts. This extensive map package provides *complete* geographic coverage of American history.

Discovering American History Through Maps and Views. Created by Gerald Danzer of the University of Illinois at Chicago, the recipient of the AHA's 1990 James Harvey Robinson Prize for his work in the development of map transparencies, this set of 140 four-color acetates is a unique instructional tool. It contains an introduction on teaching history through maps and a detailed commentary on each transparency. The collection includes cartographic and pictorial maps, views and photos, urban plans, building diagrams, and works of art.

America Through the Eyes of Its People: A Collection of Primary Sources, Revised Edition. This one-volume collection of primary documents portrays the rich and varied tapestry of American life. It contains documents by women, Native Americans, African Americans, Hispanics, and others who helped to shape the course of U.S. history. These documents and accompanying student exercises are designed to be duplicated by instructors for student use. This revised edition includes more social history and regional materials and has been reformatted so that it is easier to use.

A Guide to Teaching American History Through Film. Written by Randy Roberts of Purdue University, this guide provides instructors with a creative and practical tool for stimulating classroom discussion. The sections include "American Films: A Historian's Perspective," a list of films, practical suggestions, and bibliography. The film listing is presented in narrative form, emphasizing connections between each film and the topics being discussed.

American Impressions: A CD-ROM for U.S. History. This unique and ground-breaking CD-ROM for the U.S. History course is organized in a topical and thematic framework which allows in-depth coverage with a media-centered focus. Hundreds of photos, maps, works of art, graphics, and historical film clips are organized into narrated vignettes and interactive activities to create a tool for both professors and students. The first volume includes: "The Encounter Period," "Revolution to Republic," "A Century of Labor and Reform," and "The Struggle for Equality." A Guide for Instructors provides teaching tips and suggestions for using advanced media in the classroom. The CD-ROM is available in both Macintosh and Windows formats.

Visual Archives of American History, Second Edition. This two-sided video laserdisc explores history from the meeting of three cultures to the present. It is an encyclopedic chronology of U.S. history offering hundreds of photographs and illustrations, a variety of source and reference maps—several of which are animated—plus 50 minutes of video. For ease in planning lectures, a manual listing barcodes for scanning and frame numbers for all the material is available.

Video Lecture Launchers. Prepared by Mark Newman of the University of Illinois at Chicago, these video lecture launchers (each two to five minutes in duration) cover key issues in American history from 1877 to the present. The launchers are accompanied by an Instructor's Manual.

"This Is America" Immigration Videos. Produced by the American Museum of Immigration, these two 20-minute videos tell the story of American immigrants, relating their personal stories and accomplishments. These videos show the richness and strength contributed to America by millions of immigrants.

Transparencies. A set of over 30 four-color map transparencies drawn from the text.

Test Bank. This test bank, prepared by Larry Peterson of North Dakota State University, contains more than 2,000 test items, including multiple-choice, true/false, essay questions and map exercises. The questions are keyed to topic, difficulty level, cognitive type, and relevant text page.

TestMaster Computerized Testing System. This flexible, easy-to-master computer test bank includes all the test items in the printed test bank. The TestMaster software allows you to edit existing questions and add your own items. Tests can be printed in several different formats and can include figures such as graphs and tables. Available for IBM and Macintosh computers.

QuizMaster. This new program enables you to design TestMaster generated tests that your students can take on a computer rather than in printed form. QuizMaster is available separately from TestMaster and can be obtained free through your sales representative.

Grades. A grade-keeping and classroom management software program that maintains data for up to 200 students.

For Students

Study Guide and Practice Tests. This two-volume study guide, co-authored by Ken L. Weatherbie of Del Mar College and Billy Hathorn of Laredo Community College, is designed to provide students with a comprehensive review of text material and to encourage application and critical analysis. Each chapter contains a chapter overview, learning objectives, important glossary terms, identification, map and critical thinking exercises, and multiple-choice and essay questions.

SuperShell II Computerized Tutorial. Prepared by Ken L. Weatherbie of Del Mar College, this interactive program for IBM computers helps students learn major facts and concepts through drill and practice exercises and diagnostic feedback. SuperShell II provides immediate correct answers, the text page number on which the material is discussed, and a running score of the student's performance.

Learning to Think Critically: Films and Myths About American History. Randy Roberts and Robert May of Purdue University use well-known films such as *Gone with the Wind* and *Casablanca* to explore some common myths about America and its past. Many widely held assumptions about our country's past come from or are perpetuated by popular films. Which are true? Which are patently not true? And how does a student of history approach documents, sources, and textbooks with a critical and discerning eye? This short handbook subjects some popular beliefs to historical scrutiny in order to help students develop a method of inquiry for approaching the subject of history in general.

Mapping American History: Student Activities. Written by Gerald Danzer of the University of Illinois at Chicago, this free map workbook for students features exercises designed to teach students to interpret and analyze cartographic materials as historical documents. The instructor is entitled to a free copy of the workbook for each copy of the text purchased from Longman.

TimeLink Computer Atlas of American History. This atlas, compiled by William Hamblin of Brigham Young University, is an introductory software tutorial and textbook companion. This Macintosh program presents the historical geography of the continental United States from colonial times to the settling of the West and the admission of the last continental state in 1912. The program covers territories in different time periods, provides quizzes, and includes a special Civil War module.

Acknowledgments

To the following reviewers who gave generously of their time and knowledge to read the manuscript and provide thoughtful evaluations and suggestions for revision of the text, I express my gratitude: Robert Calvert, Texas A&M University; Juan Garcia, University of Arizona; Robert M. Goldman, Virginia Union University; Greg Goodwin, Bakersfield College; Don Higginbotham, University of North Carolina; John McLaughlin, Mount Wachusett Community College; Louis Masur, City College of New York; Michael S. Mayer, University of Montana; Lester Rodney, Morehouse College; James R. Ward, Angelo State University.

John A. Garraty

John A. Garraty is Gouverneur Morris Professor of History Emeritus at Columbia University. He received his B.A. from Brooklyn College, an M.A. and a Ph.D. from Columbia, and an L.H.D. from Michigan State University, where he taught before joining the Columbia faculty. Professor Garraty is the author and editor of scores of books and articles, among them biographies of Silas Wright, Henry Cabot Lodge, Woodrow Wilson, and George W. Perkins. He contributed a volume, *The New Commonwealth,* to the New American Nation series. He edited *Quarrels That Have Shaped the Constitution,* Supplements 4 through 7 of the *Dictionary of American Biography,* and *The Reader's Companion to American History.* He is also the author of *1001 Things Everyone Should Know About American History.* Professor Garraty has served as vice president and head of the teaching division of the American Historical Association. His areas of special research interest include the Gilded Age, unemployment (in a historical sense), and the Great Depression of the 1930s.

A Short History of the American Nation

CHAPTER 1

Europe Discovers America

Columbus and the Discovery of America
The Indian and the European
Native American Civilizations
The Spanish Decline
The Protestant Reformation
English Beginnings in America
The Settlement of Virginia
"Purifying" the Church of England
Of Plymouth Plantation
A Puritan Commonwealth
Troublemakers
Other New England Colonies
French and Dutch Settlements
Maryland and the Carolinas
The Middle Colonies
Indians and Europeans as "Americanizers"

Who discovered America? This is not an easy question to answer. The first human beings to set foot on the continents of North and South America were the ancestors of the modern Indians. These people came from Asia; they entered the North American continent tens of thousands of years ago during the Ice Age, when a land bridge connected northeastern Asia with Alaska. Being hunters and herders, they were looking for game and green grass. Almost certainly the settlers were unaware that they were entering "new" territory. So we must look elsewhere

(and much later in time) for the "discoverer" of America as we use that word.

Columbus and the Discovery of America

Probably the first European to reach America was a Norseman, Leif Eriksson. He ventured before the day of the compass into the void of the North Atlantic and, around the year 1000, reached the shores of Labrador. But Eriksson's discovery passed practically unnoticed. It was roughly 500 years later, about two o'clock in the morning of October 12, 1492, that a sailor named Roderigo de Triana, clinging in a gale to the mast of the ship *Pinta,* saw a gleam of white on the moonlit horizon and shouted: *"Tierra! Tierra!"* The land he had spied was an island in the West Indies, a place distinguished for neither beauty nor size. Nevertheless, when Triana's master, Christopher Columbus, went ashore bearing the flag of Castile, he named it San Salvador, or Holy Savior. Columbus selected this imposing name for the island out of gratitude and wonder at having found it—he had sailed with three frail vessels more than 3,000 miles for 33 days without sight of land. The name was appropriate, too, from history's far larger viewpoint. Neither Columbus nor any of his men suspected it, but the discovery of San Salvador was probably the most important event in the history of Western civilization since the birth of Christ.

San Salvador was the gateway to two continents. Columbus did not know it, and he refused to learn the truth, but his voyage threw open to exploitation by the peoples of western Europe more than a quarter of all the land in the world, a region of more than 16 million square miles, an area lushly endowed with every imaginable resource. He made possible a mass movement from Europe (and later from Africa and to a lesser extent from other regions) into the New World. Gathering force rapidly, this movement has not slackened to this day. Something on the order of 70 million persons have been involved in the migration to the American continent.

Columbus was an intelligent as well as a dedicated and skillful mariner. However, he failed to grasp the significance of his accomplishment. He

1

was seeking a way to China and Japan and the Indies, the amazing countries described by the Venetian Marco Polo in the late 13th century.

Having read carefully Marco Polo's account of his adventures in the service of Kublai Khan, Columbus had decided that these rich lands could be reached by sailing directly west from Europe. The idea was not original, but while others merely talked about it, Columbus acted. If one could sail to Asia directly, the trading possibilities and the resulting profits would be limitless. Oriental products were highly valued all over Europe. Spices such as pepper, cinnamon, ginger, nutmeg, and cloves were of first importance, their role being not so much to titillate the palate as to disguise the taste of spoiled meats in regions that had little ice. Europeans also prized such tropical foods as rice, figs, and oranges, as well as perfumes (often used as a substitute for soap), silk and cotton, rugs, textiles such as muslin and damask, dyestuffs, fine steel products, precious stones, and various drugs.

These products flowed into western Europe by way of the Italian city-states. By the 11th century Venice had established a thriving trade with Constantinople, shipping large quantities of European foodstuffs to the great metropolis on the Bosporus. The Venetians also supplied young Slavs, captured or purchased along the nearby Dalmatian coast, to the markets of Egypt and Syria (the word *slave* originally meant a "Slav").

The Venetians brought back oriental products from these voyages, and the effect was like that of tossing a stone into a pond. Europeans bestirred themselves, searching for more goods to offer in exchange. They possessed surpluses of grain and food, but these bulky products were expensive to transport over long distances. However, in Flanders, in the Low Countries, woolen cloth of high quality was being manufactured. Other areas were producing furs and lumber. Demand led to increased output; thus the flow of commerce stimulated manufacturing, which in turn spurred the growth of towns. As towns became larger and more numerous, the market for food expanded and surrounding rural areas increased their agricultural output.

The resulting labor shortage in both town and country produced important changes in the structure of medieval society. The manorial system, based on serfdom, soon began to change. As their labor became more valuable, serfs won the right to pay off their traditional obligations in money rather than in service and to leave the manors and move to the towns or to newly opened farmland. The lords themselves often instituted this change, for they wished to increase agricultural output by draining swamps and clearing forests, and they willingly granted freedom to serfs who would move to the new lands. And they needed money rather than the services of serfs to buy the expensive oriental luxuries being dangled before their eyes by traders.

The Crusades further accelerated the tempo of this new activity. Genuine religious motives seem to have inspired these mighty efforts, protracted over two centuries from 1095 to about 1290, to drive the Muslims from the Holy Land. Once the crusading armies had won a foothold in Asia Minor, the commerce of Venice and of other Italian cities increased still more, and their merchant fleets expanded. The business of transporting and supplying the European armies was itself extremely profitable. Furthermore, when the waves of Crusaders returned home, they brought with them more oriental products and a taste for these things that persisted after the goods themselves had been consumed.

The volume of this trade cannot be exactly determined. It was large enough to keep the fleets of the thriving Italian cities busy, and it tended to grow with the years. Yet it was not impressive by modern standards. In the 1920s the Belgian historian Henri Pirenne estimated that the entire tonnage of the 13th-century Venetian fleet would scarcely fill a single freighter, the cargo of which, in turn, would scarcely serve as ballast for a modern supertanker. Nor did the increase in trade cause universal prosperity or even a steady economic expansion in western Europe. In fact, during the late 14th and early 15th centuries the West endured a serious economic depression.

This decline resulted principally from the terrible losses occasioned by the plague known as the Black Death, which ravaged Europe in the mid-14th century. Part of the difficulty, however, stemmed from the steady drain of precious metals to the Orient (because of the unfavorable balance of east-west trade) and from the high cost of oriental goods. It was easy to blame this on the greed of the Italians, who monopolized east-west trade. However, even if the Italians had labored only for the joy of serving their fellow human beings, or if other merchants had been able to break the Italian monopoly, the cost of eastern products would have remained high. To transport spices from the Indies, silk from China, or rugs, cloth, and steel from the Middle East was extremely costly. The routes were long and complicated, with pirates or highwaymen a constant threat. Every petty tyrant through whose domain the caravans passed levied taxes, a quasi-legal form of robbery.

But during the 15th century, Europe recovered from the losses of the plague years. By the 1450s strong rulers were consolidating countless small fiefs into nations. They established uniform laws, maintained internal order, and focused the resources and energies of their subjects in ways that led to the exploration of the world and the founding of European settlements in distant lands.

Merchants profited from this concentration of political and economic power, but overland trade with the east remained expensive and arduous. If oriental produce could be carried to Europe by water, the trip would be both cheaper and more comfortable. The goods would have to be loaded and unloaded only once. A small number of sailors could provide all the necessary labor, and the free wind would supply the power to move the cargo to its destination. By the 15th century, this idea was beginning to be transformed into action.

The great figure in the transformation was Prince Henry the Navigator, third son of John I, king of Portugal. Henry was deeply interested in navigation and exploration. Sailing a vessel out of sight of land was still, in Henry's day, more an art than a science and was extremely hazardous. Ships were small and clumsy. Primitive compasses and instruments for reckoning latitude existed, but under shipboard conditions they were very inaccurate. Navigators could determine longitude only by keeping track of direction and estimating speed; even the most skilled could place little faith in their estimates.

Henry attempted to improve and codify navigational knowledge. To his court at Sagres, hard by Cape St. Vincent, the extreme southwestern point of Europe, he brought geographers, astronomers, and mapmakers, along with Arab and Jewish mathematicians. He built an observatory and supervised the preparation of tables measuring the declination of the sun and other navigational data. Searching for a new route to the Orient, Henry's captains sailed westward to the Madeiras and the Canaries and south along the coast of Africa, seeking a way around that continent. In 1445 Dinis Dias reached Cape Verde, site of present-day Dakar.

Henry was interested in trade, but he cared more for the advancement of knowledge, for the glory of Portugal, and for spreading Christianity. When his explorers developed a profitable business in slaves, he tried to stop it. Nevertheless, the movement he began had, like the Crusades, important commercial overtones. Probably half of the Portuguese voyages were undertaken by private merchants. Without the gold, ivory, and other African goods, which brought great prosperity to Portugal, the explorers would probably not have been so bold and persistent. Yet, like Henry, they were idealists, by and large. The Age of Discovery was in a sense the last Crusade; its leaders displayed mixed religious and material motives along with a love of adventure. In any case, the Portuguese realized that if they could find a way around Africa, they might well sail directly to India and the Spice Islands.* The profits from such a voyage would surely be spectacular.

For 20 years after Henry's death in 1460, the Portuguese concentrated on exploiting his discoveries. In the 1480s King John II undertook systematic new explorations focused on reaching India. Gradually his caravels probed southward along the sweltering coast—to the equator, to the region of Angola, and beyond.

Into this bustling, prosperous, expectant little country in the corner of Europe came Christopher Columbus in 1476. Columbus was a weaver's son from Genoa, born in 1451. He had taken to the sea early, ranging widely in the Mediterranean. For a time he became a chartmaker in Lisbon. He married a local woman. Then he was again at sea. He cruised northward, perhaps as far as Iceland, south to the equator, westward in the Atlantic to

---

*The Moluccas, west of New Guinea. In the geography of the 15th century, the Spice Islands were part of "the Indies," a vague term that encompassed the southeast rim of Asia from India to what is now Indonesia.

the Azores. Had his interest lain in that direction, he might well have been the first person to reach Asia by way of Africa, for in 1488, in Lisbon, he met and talked with Bartholomeu Dias, just returned from his voyage around the southern tip of Africa, which had demonstrated that the way lay clear for a voyage to the Indies.

But by this time Columbus had committed himself to the westward route. When King John II refused to finance him, he turned to the Spanish court, where, after many disappointments, he finally persuaded Queen Isabella to equip his expedition. In August 1492 he set out from the port of Palos with his tiny fleet, the *Santa María,* the *Pinta,* and the *Niña.* A little more than two months later, after a stopover in the Canary Islands to repair the *Pinta*'s rudder, his lookout sighted land.

Columbus's success was due in large part to his single-minded conviction that the Indies could be reached by sailing westward for a relatively short distance and that a profitable trade would develop over this route. His conviction cost him dearly. He refused to accept the plain evidence, which everywhere confronted him, that this was an entirely new world. Searching for treasure, he pushed on to Cuba. When he heard the native word *Cubanocan,* meaning "middle of Cuba," he mistook it for *El Gran Can* (Marco Polo's "Grand Khan") and sent emissaries on a fruitless search through the tropical jungle for the khan's palace. He finally returned to Spain relatively empty-handed but certain that he had explored the edge of Asia. Three later voyages failed to shake his conviction.

Columbus died in 1506. By that time other captains had taken up the work, most of them more willing than he to accept the New World on its own terms. As early as 1493, Pope Alexander VI had divided the non-Christian world between Spain and Portugal. The next year, in the Treaty of Tordesillas, these powers negotiated an agreement about exploiting the new discoveries. In effect, Portugal continued to concentrate on Africa, leaving the New World, except for what eventually became Brazil, to the Spanish. Thereafter, from their base on Hispaniola (Santo Domingo), founded by Columbus, the Spaniards quickly fanned out through the Caribbean and then over large parts of the two continents that bordered it.

In 1513 Juan Ponce de León made the first Spanish landing on the mainland of North America, exploring the east coast of Florida. In the same year Vasco Núñez de Balboa crossed the Isthmus of Panama and discovered the Pacific Ocean. In 1519 Hernan Cortés landed an army in Mexico and overran the empire of the Aztecs, rich in gold and silver. That same year Ferdinand Magellan set out on his epic three-year voyage around the world. By discovering the strait that bears his name, at the southern tip of South America, he gave the Spanish a clear idea of the size of the continent. In the 1530s Francisco Pizarro subdued the Inca empire in Peru, providing the Spaniards with still more treasure, drawn chiefly from the silver mines of Potosì. In 1536 Buenos Aires was founded by Pedro de Mendoza. Within another decade Francisco Vasquez de Coronado had marched as far north as Kansas and west to the Grand Canyon, and Hernando de Soto had discovered the Mississippi River. Fifty years after Columbus's first landfall, Spain was master of a huge American empire.

What explains this mighty surge of exploration and conquest? Greed for gold and power, a sense of adventure, the desire to Christianize the Indians—mixed motives propelled the *conquistadores* onward. Some saw the New World as a reincarnation of the Garden of Eden, a land of infinite promise. Ponce de León and many others actually expected to find the Fountain of Youth in America. Their vision, at once so selfish and so exalted, reveals the central paradox of New World history. This immense land brought out both the best and the worst in the conquistadors. "Virgin" America inspired conflicting feelings in their hearts. They worshiped it for its purity and promise, yet they could not resist the opportunity to take advantage of its innocence.

The Indian and the European

The *conquistadores* were brave and imaginative men, well worthy of their fame. It must not, however, be forgotten that they wrenched their empire from innocent hands; in an important sense, the settlement of the New World, which the historian Francis Jennings has called "the invasion of America," ranks among the most flagrant exam-

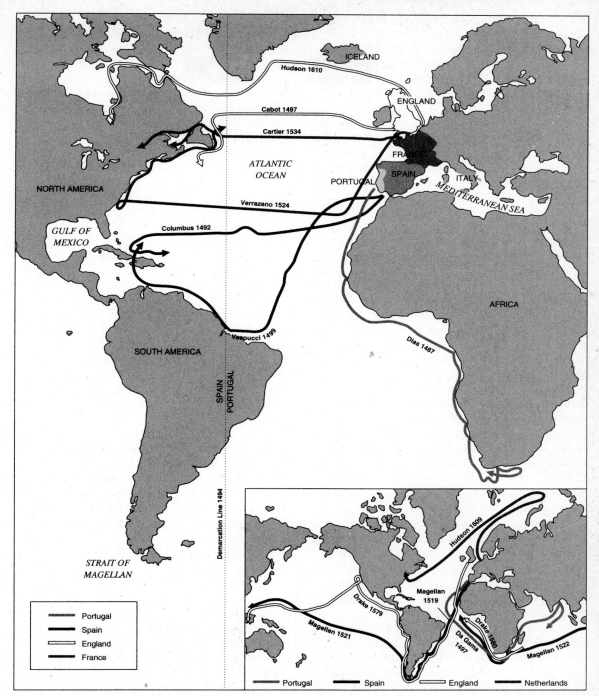

ICELAND

Hudson 1610

ENGLAND

Cabot 1497

Cartier 1534

FRANCE

ATLANTIC OCEAN

SPAIN

ITALY

PORTUGAL

MEDITERRANEAN SEA

NORTH AMERICA

Verrazano 1524

GULF OF MEXICO

Columbus 1492

AFRICA

SOUTH AMERICA

Vespucci 1499

Dias 1487

SPAIN
PORTUGAL

Demarcation Line 1494

STRAIT OF MAGELLAN

Portugal
Spain
England
France

Hudson 1609

Magellan 1519

Drake 1579

Magellan 1521

De Gama 1497

Drake 1580

Magellan 1522

Portugal   Spain   England   Netherlands

Voyages of Discovery, 1487–1610

ples of unprovoked aggression in human history. When Columbus landed on San Salvador he planted a cross, "as a sign," he explained to Ferdinand and Isabella, "that your Highnesses held this land as your own." Of the Lucayans, the native inhabitants of San Salvador, Columbus wrote:

The people of this island . . . are artless and generous with what they have, to such a degree as no one would believe. . . . If it be asked for, they never say no, but rather invite the person to accept it, and show as much lovingness as though they would give their hearts.

The Indians of San Salvador behaved this way because the Spaniards seemed the very gods. "All believe that power and goodness dwell in the sky," Columbus reported, "and they are firmly convinced that I have come from the sky." The products of Europe fascinated them. For a bit of sheet copper an inch square, they would part with a bushel of corn; knives, hatchets, and fishhooks made of metal were even more precious to a people whose own technology was still in the Stone Age.

But the Spaniards would not settle for the better of the bargain. Columbus also remarked of the Lucayans: "These people are very unskilled in arms . . . with fifty men they could all be subjected and made to do all that one wished." He and his compatriots tricked and cheated the Indians at every turn. Before entering a new area, Spanish generals customarily read a *Requerimiento* (requirement) to the inhabitants. This long-winded document recited a Spanish version of the history of the human race from the Creation to the division of the non-Christian world by Pope Alexander VI and then called on the Indians to recognize the sovereignty of the reigning Spanish monarch. ("If you do so. . . we shall receive you in all love and charity.") If this demand was rejected, the Spanish promised: "We shall powerfully enter into your country, and . . . shall take you, your wives, and your children, and shall make slaves of them. . . . The death and losses which shall accrue from this are your fault." This arrogant harangue was read in Spanish and often out of earshot of the Indians. When they responded by fighting, the Spaniards decimated them, drove them from their lands, and held the broken survivors in contempt. As Bar-

tolomé de las Casas, a priest among them, said, the *conquistadores* behaved "like the most cruel Tygres, Wolves, and Lions, enrag'd with a sharp and tedious hunger."

Wherever they went, the Europeans mistreated the people they encountered. When the Portuguese reached Africa, they carried off thousands into slavery. The Dutch behaved shamefully in the East Indies, as did the French in their colonial possessions—although, in North America at least, the French record was better than most.

English settlers described the Indians as being "of a tractable, free, and loving nature, without guile or treachery," yet in most instances they exploited and all but exterminated them. "Why should you take by force from us that which you can obtain by love?" one puzzled chief asked an early Virginia colonist, according to the latter's own account. The first settlers of New England dealt fairly with the local inhabitants. They made honest, if somewhat misguided, efforts to Christianize and educate them and to respect their rights. But within a few years their relations with the Indians deteriorated, and in King Philip's War (1675–1676), proportionately the bloodiest in American history, they destroyed the tribes as independent powers.

Native American Civilizations

Of course the victims of the Europeans' cruelty were not innocent "noble savages." Being human, Indians suffered from all the human failings in one form or another. During thousands of years they had multiplied, occupying the hemisphere from Alaska to Tierra del Fuego. By 1500 there were somewhere between 50 and 60 million Indians, 1 or 2 million living in what is now the United States.

In the course of many centuries the Indians' cultures had evolved in different ways. Climate, soil conditions, wars, and other factors, including pure chance, shaped their ways of life profoundly, just as these forces shaped the civilizations that had developed over the ages in Asia, Africa, and Europe. More than a thousand languages were spoken in North and South America at the time of Columbus.

Even in the relatively limited area that the first Spanish explorers visited, the native cultures displayed an extraordinary variety. If the people who greeted Columbus were relatively primitive, the civilizations of the Incas of Peru and the Aztecs of Mexico were in many respects as highly developed as any in Europe or Asia. The Incas built roads as enduring as those of the Romans. Montezuma, the Aztec emperor, lived in a great palace surrounded by courtiers and servants in a city as large as and far more impressive architecturally than Madrid, the home of Cortés's master, King Charles V.

North of Mexico no such imposing civilizations existed, but the number of different patterns of life was enormous. Some groups were nomads who lived by hunting and fishing. Others lived settled lives based on hunting and agriculture. "Political organization among Indians varied from the simple family groups of the remote Arctic and desert West to the complex confederacies of tribes in the East," Wilcomb Washburn writes in *The Indian in America.*

The Indians had certain traits in common, and many of these the Europeans shared. Cruelty and war, slavery and plunder existed in the New World long before Columbus. The priest who claimed that Indians were "without evil and without guile" was as far off the mark as the Spaniard who claimed that they indulged in "every kind of intemperance and wicked lust." Indian men were by current standards chauvinists, as indeed were most Europeans of that day. Hunting and fishing—which, again like many Europeans, the Indians regarded as sports as well as sources of food—were usually male occupations, as was warfare. In agricultural communities, men and women shared other tasks; in general, the men did the heavy work of clearing land and building shelters; the women did the planting, cultivating, and harvesting. When Indians observed European men planting seeds and weeding their fields, they scoffed at them for being effeminate.

Most of the terrible decimation that was everywhere the Indians' fate was caused by European diseases such as smallpox and measles. The population of Mexico was at least 20 million when Cortés invaded the country and only 2 million a century later. The population of Hispaniola fell from perhaps 8 million when Columbus first touched there to a couple of hundred 50 years later.

The Europeans could not be blamed for these deaths. They did not understand the diseases any better than the Indians did. The fact remains that in conflicts between Indians and whites, far more often than not, the whites were the main cause of the trouble.

Most Europeans simply assumed that non-Europeans were inferior beings. Apparently their prejudices were not always of racial origin; some early colonists considered Indians members of the white race whose skin had been darkened by exposure to the elements. The term *red man* did not become current until the 18th century.

The relativity of cultural values escaped all but a handful of the Europeans. If some of the natives were naive in thinking that the invaders, with their huge ships and their potent fire sticks, were gods, these "gods" were equally naive in their thinking. Since the Indians did not worship the Christian God and indeed worshiped a large number of other gods, the Europeans dismissed them as contemptible heathens.

Most Indians lived in close harmony with their surroundings. They adjusted to and took advantage of existing ecologies (for example, by trapping furbearing animals in winter and netting fish during spring spawning runs), whereas the Europeans sought to change ecologies to their advantage (as by plowing fields and building fences). Indians who lived nomadic lives had small use for personal property that was not easily portable. They had little interest in amassing wealth, as individuals or as tribes. Even the Aztecs, with their treasures of gold and silver, valued the metals for their durability and the beautiful things that could be made with them rather than as objects of commerce.

This lack of concern for material things led Europeans to conclude that the native people of America were childlike creatures, not to be treated as equals. Indians "do but run over the grass, as do also foxes and wild beasts," an Englishman wrote in 1622, "so it is lawful now to take a land, which none useth, and make use of it." In the sense that Indians lived in close harmony with nature, the first part of this statement contained a grain of truth, though of course the second did not follow from it logically.

The Europeans' inability to grasp the communal nature of land tenure among Indians also led to innumerable quarrels. Traditional tribal boundaries were neither spelled out in deeds or treaties nor marked by fences or any other sign of occupation. Often corn grown by a number of families was stored in a common bin and drawn upon by all as needed. Such practices were utterly alien to the European mind.

The Indians, writes the historian William Cronon, "moved from habitat to habitat to find maximum abundance through minimal work, and so reduce their impact on the land." The English colonists, Cronon goes on to say, "believed in and required permanent settlements." And he concludes: "English fixity sought to replace Indian mobility; here was the central conflict in the ways Indians and colonists interacted with their environments."

The Spanish Decline

While Spain waxed fat on the wealth of the Americas, the other nations of western Europe did little. In 1497 and 1498 King Henry VII of England sent John Cabot to the New World. Cabot visited Newfoundland and the northeastern coast of the continent. His explorations formed the basis for later British claims in North America, but they were not followed up for many decades. In 1524 Giovanni da Verrazano made a similar voyage for France, coasting the continent from Carolina to Nova Scotia. Some ten years later the Frenchman Jacques Cartier explored the St. Lawrence River as far inland as present-day Montreal. During the 16th century, fishermen from France, Spain, Portugal, and England began exploiting the limitless supplies of cod and other fish they found in the cold waters off Newfoundland. They landed at many points along the mainland coast from Nova Scotia to Labrador to collect water and wood and to dry their catches, but they made no permanent settlements until the next century.

There were many reasons for this delay, the most important probably being that Spain had achieved a large measure of internal tranquility by the 16th century, whereas France and England were still torn by serious religious and political conflicts. The Spanish also profited from having seized those areas in America best suited to producing quick returns. Reinforced by the treasure of the Aztecs and the Incas, Spain seemed too mighty to be challenged in either the New World or the Old. Under Philip II, who succeeded Charles in 1556, Spanish strength seemed at its peak, especially after Philip added Portugal to his

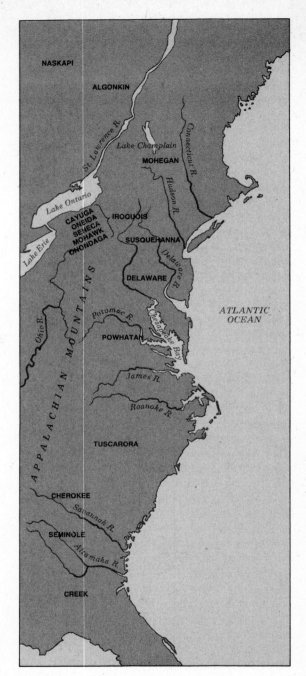

Primary East Coast Indian Nations in the 1600s

domain in 1580. But the great empire was in trouble. The corruption of the Spanish court had much to do with this. Even more important was the disruption of the Catholic church throughout Europe by the Protestant Reformation.

The Protestant Reformation

The spiritual lethargy and bureaucratic corruption besetting the Roman Catholic church in the early 16th century made it a fit target for reform. A thriving business in the sale of indulgences, payments that were supposed to win forgiveness of earthly sins for departed loved ones and thus release them from purgatory, was a public scandal. The luxurious lifestyle of the popes and the papal court in Rome was another. Yet the fact that the movement launched by Martin Luther in 1517 and carried forward by men like John Calvin addressed genuine shortcomings does not entirely explain why the Protestant Reformation led so directly to the rupture of Christendom. Probably more important were the political possibilities let loose by their challenge to Rome's spiritual authority. German princes seized upon Luther's campaign against the sale of indulgences to stop all payments to Rome and to confiscate church property. Swiss cities like Geneva and Zürich joined the Protestant revolt for spiritual reasons, but also to win independence from Catholic kings. The efforts of Spain to suppress Protestantism in the Low Countries stimulated nationalist movements there, especially among the Dutch.

The decision of Henry VIII of England to break with Rome was also political. The refusal of Pope Clement VII to agree to an annulment of Henry's marriage of 20 years to Catherine of Aragon, the daughter of Ferdinand and Isabella, provided the occasion. Catherine had given birth to six children, but all were girls; Henry was without a male heir. By repudiating the pope's spiritual authority and declaring himself head of the English (Anglican) church in 1534, Henry freed himself to divorce Catherine and to marry whomever—and however often—he saw fit. By the time of his death, five wives and 13 years later, England had become a Protestant nation.

The growing political and religious conflict had economic overtones. In some lands the business classes tended to support Protestant leaders, in part because the new sects, stressing simplicity, made fewer financial demands on the faithful than the Catholics did. And as the commercial classes rose to positions of influence, England, France, and the United Provinces of the Netherlands experienced a flowering of trade and industry. Dutch traders captured most of the Far Eastern business once monopolized by the Portuguese, and they infiltrated Spain's Caribbean stronghold. A number of English merchant companies, soon to play a vital role as colonizers, sprang up in the last half of the 16th century. These joint-stock companies, ancestors of the modern corporation, enabled groups of investors to pool their capital and limit their individual responsibilities to the sums actually invested—a very important protection in such risky enterprises.

English Beginnings in America

English merchants took part in many kinds of international activity. The Muscovy Company spent large sums searching for a passage to China around Scandinavia and dispatched six overland expeditions in an effort to reach the Orient by way of Russia and Persia. In the 1570s Martin Frobisher made three voyages across the Atlantic, hoping to discover a northwest passage to the Orient or new gold-bearing lands.

Such projects, particularly in the area of America, received strong but concealed support from the Crown. Queen Elizabeth I invested heavily in Frobisher's expeditions. England was still too weak to challenge Spain openly, but Elizabeth hoped to break the Spanish overseas monopoly just the same. She encouraged her boldest sea dogs to plunder Spanish merchant ships on the high seas. When Captain Francis Drake was about to set sail on his fabulous round-the-world voyage in 1577, the queen said to him: "Drake! . . . I would gladly be revenged on the King of Spain for divers injuries that I have received." Drake took her at her word. He sailed through the Strait of Magellan and terrorized the west coast of South America, capturing the Spanish treasure ship *Cacafuego,* heavily laden with Peruvian silver. After exploring the coast of California, which he claimed for England, Drake crossed the Pacific and went on to circumnavigate the globe, returning home in triumph in 1580. Although Elizabeth took pains to deny it to the Spanish ambassador, Drake's voyage was officially sponsored.

When schemes to place settlers in the New World began to mature at about this time, the queen again became involved. The first English effort was led by Sir Humphrey Gilbert, an Oxford educated soldier and courtier with a lifelong interest in far-off places. Gilbert owned a share of the Muscovy Company; as early as 1566, he was trying to get a royal grant for an expedition in search of a northeast passage to the Orient. But soon his interests concentrated on the northwest route. He read widely in navigational and geographical lore and in 1576 wrote a persuasive *Discourse . . . to prove a passage by the north west to Cathaia.* Two years later the queen authorized him to explore and colonize "heathen lands not actually possessed by any Christian prince."

We know almost nothing about Gilbert's first attempt except that it occurred in 1578–1579; in 1583 he set sail again with five ships and over 200 settlers. He landed them on Newfoundland, then evidently decided to seek a more congenial site farther south. However, no colony was established, and on his way back to England his ship went down in a storm off the Azores.

Gilbert's half brother, Sir Walter Raleigh, took up the work. Handsome, ambitious, and impulsive, Raleigh was a great favorite of Elizabeth. He sent a number of expeditions to explore the east coast of North America, a land he named Virginia in honor of his unmarried sovereign. In 1585 he settled about a hundred men on Roanoke Island, off the North Carolina coast, but these settlers returned home the next year. In 1587 Raleigh sent another group to Roanoke, including a number of women and children. Unfortunately, the supply ships sent to the colony in 1588 failed to arrive; when help did get there in 1590, not a soul could be found. The fate of these pioneers has never been determined.

One reason for the delay in getting aid to the Roanoke colonists was the attack of the Spanish Armada on England in 1588. Angered by English raids on his shipping and by the assistance Elizabeth was giving to the rebels in the Netherlands, King Philip II had decided to invade England. His motives were religious as well as political and economic, for England was now seemingly committed to Protestantism. His great fleet of some 130 ships bore huge crosses on the sails as if on an-

other crusade. The Armada carried 30,000 men and 2,400 guns, the largest naval force ever assembled up to that time. However, the English fleet badly mauled this armada, and a series of storms completed its destruction. Thereafter, although the war continued and Spanish sea power remained formidable, Spain could no longer block English penetration of the New World.

Experience had shown that the cost of planting settlements in a wilderness 3,000 miles from England was more than any individual purse could bear. (Raleigh lost about £40,000 in his overseas ventures; early on he began to advocate government support of colonization.) As early as 1584, Richard Hakluyt, England's foremost authority on the Americas, made a convincing case for royal aid. In his *Discourse on Western Planting,* Hakluyt stressed the military advantages of building "two or three strong fortes" along the Atlantic coast of North America. Ships operating from such bases would make life uncomfortable for "King Phillipe" by intercepting his treasure fleets—a matter, Hakluyt added coolly, "that toucheth him indeede to the quicke." Colonies in America would also enrich the mother country by expanding the market for English woolens, bringing in valuable tax revenues, and by providing employment for the swarms of "lustie youthes that be turned to no provitable use" at home. From the great American forests would come the timber and naval stores needed to build a bigger navy and merchant marine.

Queen Elizabeth read Hakluyt's essay, but she was too cautious and too devious to act boldly on his suggestions. Only after her death in 1603 did full-scale efforts to found English colonies in America begin, and even then the organizing force came from merchant capitalists, not from the Crown. This was unfortunate, because the search for quick profits dominated the thinking of these enterprisers. Larger national ends, although not neglected because the Crown was always involved, were subordinated. On the other hand, if private investors had not taken the lead, no colony would have been established at this time.

The Settlement of Virginia

In September 1605 two groups of English merchants petitioned the new king, James I, for a license to colonize Virginia, as the whole area claimed by England was then named. This was granted the following April, and two joint-stock companies were organized, one controlled by London merchants, the other by a group from the area around Plymouth and Bristol.*

This first charter revealed the commercial motivation of both king and company in the plainest terms. Although it spoke of spreading Christianity and bringing "the Infidels and Savages, living in those Parts, to human Civility," it stressed the right "to dig, mine, and search for all Manner of Mines of Gold, Silver, and Copper." On December 20, 1606, the London Company dispatched about 100 settlers aboard the *Susan Constant, Discovery,* and *Godspeed.* This little band reached the Chesapeake Bay area in May 1607 and founded Jamestown, the first permanent English colony in the New World.

From the start everything seemed to go wrong. The immigrants established themselves in what was practically a malarial swamp simply because it appeared easily defensible against Indian attack. They failed to get a crop in the ground because of the lateness of the season and were soon almost without food. Their leaders, mere deputies of the London merchants, did not respond to the challenges of the wilderness. The settlers lacked the skills that pioneers need. More than a third of them were "gentlemen" unused to manual labor, and many of the rest were the gentlemen's body servants, almost equally unequipped for the task of colony building. During the first winter more than half of the settlers died.

All the land belonged to the company, and aside from the gentlemen and their retainers, most of the settlers were only hired laborers who had contracted to work for it for seven years. This was most unfortunate. The situation demanded people skilled in agriculture, and such a labor force was available. In England times were bad. The growth of the textile industry had led to an increased demand for wool, and great landowners were dismissing laborers and tenant farmers and shifting from labor-intensive agriculture to sheep raising. Inflation, caused by a shortage of goods to supply the needs of a grow-

ing population and by the influx of large amounts of American silver into Europe, worsened the plight of the dispossessed. Many landless farmers were eager to migrate if offered a decent opportunity to obtain land and make new lives for themselves.

The merchant directors of the London Company, knowing little or nothing about Virginia, failed to provide the colony with effective guidance. They set up a council of settlers, but they kept all real power in their own hands. Instead of stressing farming and public improvements, they directed the energies of the colonists into such futile labors as searching for gold (the first supply ship devoted precious space to two goldsmiths and two "refiners"), glassblowing, silk raising, winemaking, and exploring the local rivers in hopes of finding a water route to the Pacific and the riches of China.

One colonist, Captain John Smith, tried to stop some of this foolishness. He quickly realized that building houses and raising food were essential to survival, and he soon became an expert forager and Indian trader. He did not hesitate to take advantage of the Indians when the opportunity arose, but he recognized the limits of the colonists' power and the vast differences between Indian customs and values and his own.

Smith pleaded with company officials in London to send over more people accustomed to working with their hands, such as farmers, fishermen, carpenters, masons, and "diggers up of trees." "A plaine soldier who can use a pickaxe and a spade is better than five knights," he said. Whether Smith was actually rescued from death at the hands of the Indians by the princess Pocahontas is not certain, but there is little doubt that without his direction the colony would have perished in the early days. However, he stayed in Virginia only two years.

Lacking competent leaders and faced with appalling hardships, the Jamestown colonists failed to develop a sufficient sense of common purpose. Each year they died in wholesale lots. The causes of death were disease, starvation, Indian attack, and above all, ignorance and folly. Between 1606 and 1622 the London Company invested more than £160,000 in Virginia and sent over about 6,000 settlers. Yet no dividends were ever earned, and of the settlers, fewer than 2,000 were still alive in 1622. In 1625 the population was down to about

---

*The London Company was to colonize south Virginia, whereas the Plymouth Company, the Plymouth-Bristol group of merchants, was granted northern Virginia.

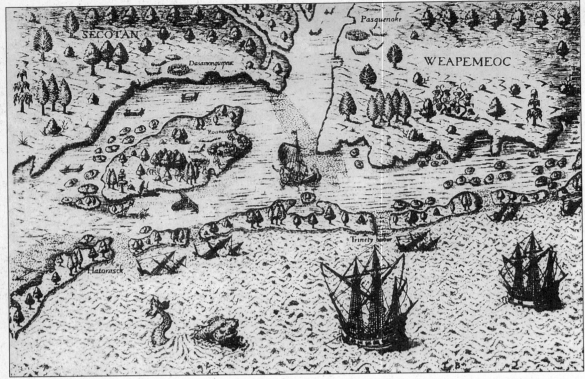

A 16-century engraving by John White shows English ships off the coast of Virginia. Wrecked vessels lie along the barrier islands near Hatteras ("Hatorask"). On Roanoke Island and the mainland beyond it are palisaded Indian villages and warriors armed with bows and arrows.

1,300. The only profits were those taken by certain shrewd investors who had organized a joint-stock company to transport women to Virginia "to be made wives" by the colonists.

One major problem, the mishandling of the local Indians, was largely the colonists' doing. It is quite likely that the settlement would not have survived if the Powhatan Indians had not given the colonists food in the first hard winters, taught them the ways of the forest, introduced them to valuable new crops such as corn and yams, and showed them how to clear dense timber by girdling the trees and burning them down after they were dead. The settlers accepted Indian aid, then took whatever else they wanted by force. They "conciliated the Powhatan people while they were of use," one historian has written, "and pressed them remorselessly, facelessly, mechanically, as innocent of conscious ill will as a turning wheel, when they became of less value than their

land." The Indians did not submit meekly to such treatment. They proved brave, skillful, and ferocious fighters, once they understood that their very existence was at stake. The burden of Indian fighting might easily have been more than the frail settlement could bear.

What saved the Virginians was not the brushing aside of the Indians but the realization that they must produce their own food, and the cultivation of tobacco, which flourished there and could be sold profitably in England. Once the settlers discovered tobacco, no amount of company pressure could keep them at wasteful tasks, like looking for gold. With money earned from the sale of tobacco, the colonists could buy the manufactured articles they could not produce in a raw new country; this freed them from dependence on outside subsidies. It did not mean profit for the London Company, however, for by the time tobacco caught on, the surviving original colonists had served their seven years and were no longer hired hands. To attract more settlers, the company had permitted first tenancy and then outright ownership of farms. Thus the profits of tobacco went largely to the planters, not to the "adventurers" who had organized the colony.

Important administrative reforms helped Virginia to forge ahead. A revised charter in 1612 extended the London Company's control over its own affairs in Virginia. Despite serious intracompany rivalry between groups headed by Sir Thomas Smythe and Sir Edwin Sandys, a somewhat more intelligent direction of Virginia's affairs resulted. First the merchants appointed a single resident governor and gave him sufficient authority to control the settlers. Then they made it much easier for settlers to obtain land of their own. In 1619 a rudimentary form of self-government was instituted: a House of Burgesses, consisting of delegates chosen in each district, met at Jamestown to advise the governor on local problems. The company was not bound by the actions of the burgesses, but from this seed sprang the system of representative government that became the American pattern.

These reforms, however, came too late to save the fortunes of the London Company. In 1619 the Sandys faction won control and started an extensive development program, but in 1622 a bloody Indian attack took the lives of 347 colonists. Morale sank and James I, who disliked Sandys, decided that the colony was being badly managed. In 1624 the charter was revoked and Virginia became a royal colony.

"Purifying" the Church of England

Although the prospect of a better material life brought most English settlers to America, for some, economic opportunity was not the only reason they abandoned what their contemporary, William Shakespeare, called "dead mother England." A profound unease with England's spiritual state explains why many colonists embarked on their "errand into the wilderness."

The Anglican church became once and for all the official Church of England during the long reign of Elizabeth I (1558–1603). Like her father, Henry VIII, Elizabeth took more interest in politics than religion. So long as England had its own church, with her at its head, she was content. The Anglican church under Elizabeth closely resembled the Catholic church it had replaced.

This middle way satisfied most, but not all, of Elizabeth's subjects. Steadfast Catholics could not accept it. Some left England; the rest practiced their faith in private. At the other extreme, more radical Protestants claimed that the Anglican church as still too much like the Church of Rome. They objected to the richly decorated vestments worn by the clergy and to the use of candles, incense, and music in church services. They insisted that emphasis should be put on reading and analyzing the Bible in order to encourage ordinary worshipers to truly understand their faith. Since they wanted to "purify" Anglicanism, these critics were called Puritans.

Puritans objected to the way Elizabeth's bishops interpreted the Protestant doctrine of predestination. The Anglican clergy did not come right out and say that good works could win a person admission to Heaven—that heresy was called Arminianism. But they implied that while God had already decided whether or not a person was saved, an individual's efforts to lead a good life could somehow cause God to change His mind.

Some Puritans—later called Congregationalists—favored a completely decentralized arrangement, with the members of each church and their chosen minister beholden only to one another. Others, called Presbyterians, favored some organization above the local level, but one controlled by elected laymen, not by the clergy.

Puritans were also of two minds as to whether reform could be accomplished within the Anglican church. During Elizabeth's reign most hoped that it could. After King James I succeeded Elizabeth I in 1603, however, their fears that the royal court might be backsliding into its old "popish" ways mounted. James was married to a Catholic, and the fact that he favored toleration for Catholics gave further substance to the rumor that he was himself a secret member of that church. This rumor proved to be false, but in his 22-year reign (1603–1625) James did little to advance the Protestant cause. His one contribution—which had a significance far beyond what he or anyone else anticipated—was to authorize a new translation of the Bible. The King James Version (1611) was both a monumental scholarly achievement and a literary masterpiece of the first order.

Of Plymouth Plantation

In 1606, worried about the future of their faith, members of the church in Scrooby, Nottinghamshire, "separated" from the Anglican church, declaring it corrupt beyond salvage. In 17th-century England, Separatists had to go either underground or into exile. Since only the second would permit them to practice their religious faith openly, exile it was. In 1608 some 125 members of the group departed England for the Low Countries. They were led by their pastor, John Robinson; church elder William Brewster; and a young man of 16, William Bradford. After a brief stay in Amsterdam, the group settled in the town of Leyden. In 1619, however, disheartened by the difficulties they had encountered in making a living and distressed because their children were being "subjected to the great licentiousness of the youth" in Holland, these "Pilgrims" decided to move again—to seek "a place where they might have liberty and live comfortably."

Negotiations with the head of the Virginia Company in London, Sir Edwin Sandys, raised the possibility of America. Although unsympathetic to their religious views, Sandys appreciated the Pilgrims' inherent worth and supported their request to establish a settlement in the Virginia Company's grant. Since the Pilgrims were short of money, they formed a joint-stock company with other prospective emigrants and some optimistic investors who agreed to pay the expenses of the group in return for half the profits of the venture. In September 1620 about 100 strong—only 35 of them Pilgrims from Leyden—the group set out from Plymouth, England, on the ship *Mayflower*.

Had the *Mayflower* reached their intended destination, the Pilgrims might have been soon forgotten. Instead their ship touched America slightly to the north, on Cape Cod Bay. Unwilling to remain longer at the mercy of storm-tossed December seas, they decided to settle where they were. Since they were outside the jurisdiction of the London Company, some members of the group claimed to be free of all governmental control. Therefore, before going ashore, the Pilgrims drew up the Mayflower Compact. "We whose names are underwritten," the Compact ran,

do by these Presents, solemnly and mutually in the presence of God and one another covenant and combine ourselves under into a civil Body Politick and by Virtue hereof do enact . . . such just and equal laws . . . as shall be thought most meet and convenient for the general Good of the Colony.

Thus early in American history the idea was advanced that a society should be based on a set of rules chosen by its members, an idea carried further in the Declaration of Independence. The Pilgrims chose William Bradford as their first governor. The story of the first 30 years of the colony has been preserved in his *Of Plymouth Plantation*. Having landed on the bleak Massachusetts shore in December, at a place called Plymouth, the Pilgrims had to endure a winter of desperate hunger. About half of them died.

But by great good luck there was an Indian in the area, named Squanto, who spoke English! Squanto had been kidnapped in 1615 by an English sea captain, Thomas Hunt, who took him to Spain and sold him as a slave. Squanto escaped, however, and somehow made his way to England. He fell in with people involved in colonization and exploring. He spent some time in Newfoundland in 1617–1618, returned to England, and in 1619 made another voyage to America as a pilot. This time he remained.

It is easy to understand why the Pilgrims believed that Squanto was "a special instrument sent of God for their good." In addition to serving as an interpreter, he showed them the best places to fish, and what to plant and how to cultivate it. They, in turn, worked hard, got their crops in the ground in good time, and after a bountiful harvest the following November, they treated themselves and their Indian neighbors to the first Thanksgiving feast. Although they grew neither rich nor numerous on the thin New England soil, their place in American history was assured. That place is one of honor for, among other reasons, the integrity that characterized their dealings with the Indians. Theirs were victories won not with sword and gunpowder like those of Cortés or with bull-

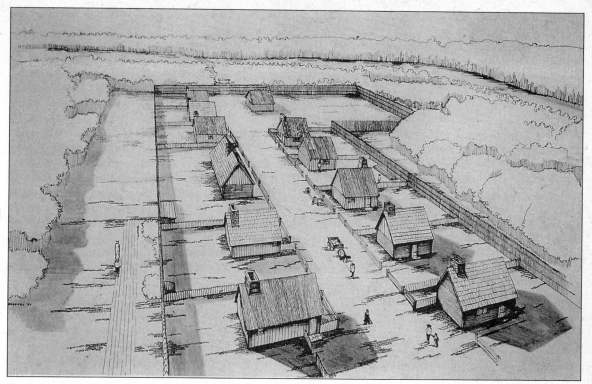

The story of the first 30 years of Pilgrim life in Plymouth, Massachusetts, is preserved in Governor William Bradford's account, *Of Plymouth Plantation*. A glimpse of the first colony is shown in this reconstruction drawing.

dozer and dynamite like those of modern pioneers, but with simple courage and practical piety.

A Puritan Commonwealth

The Pilgrims were not the first English colonists to inhabit the northern regions. The Plymouth Company had settled a group on the Kennebec River in 1607. These colonists gave up after a few months, but fishermen and traders continued to visit the area, which was christened New England by Captain John Smith after an expedition there in 1614.

In 1620 the Plymouth Company was reorganized as the Council for New England. More interested in real estate deals than in colonizing, the council disposed of a number of tracts in the area north of Cape Cod. The most significant of these grants was a small one made to a group of Puritans from Dorchester, who established a settlement at Salem in 1629. Later that year these

Dorchester Puritans organized the Massachusetts Bay Company and obtained a royal grant to the area between the Charles and Merrimack rivers. The Massachusetts Bay Company was organized like any other commercial venture, but with single-minded determination the Puritans made it a way of obtaining religious refuge in America.

Unlike the Separatists in Plymouth, most Puritans had managed to satisfy both Crown and conscience while James I was king. James had been content to keep Puritans at bay, but Charles, who succeeded to the throne in 1625, and his favorite Anglican cleric, William Laud, intended to bring them to heel. Laud tightened the central control that the Puritans found so distasteful and removed ministers with Puritan leanings from their pulpits. No longer able to remain within the Anglican fold in good conscience and now facing prison if they tried to worship in the way they thought right, the Puritans decided to migrate to America in force. In the summer of 1630 nearly 1,000 of them set out from England, carrying the charter of the Massachusetts Bay Company with them. By the fall, they had founded Boston and several other towns. The Puritan commonwealth was under way.

Massachusetts settlers suffered fewer hardships in the early years than had the early Jamestown and Plymouth colonists. Luck played a part in this, but so did careful planning. They also benefited from a constant influx of new recruits. Continuing bad times and the persecution of Puritans at home led to the Great Migration of the 1630s. Only a minority came to Massachusetts (many thousands more poured into new English colonies in the West Indies), but by 1640 well over 10,000 had arrived. This concentrated group of industrious, well-educated, and fairly prosperous colonists swiftly created a complex and distinct civilization on the very edge of what a pessimist among them called "a hideous and desolate wilderness, full of wild beasts and wild men."

The directors of the Massachusetts Bay Company believed their enterprise to be divinely inspired. Before leaving England, they elected John Winthrop, a 29-year-old lawyer, as governor of the colony. Winthrop spoke for the solid and sensible core of the Puritans. His lay sermon, "A Modelle of Christian Charity," made clear his sense of the momentousness of that experiment:

> Wee must Consider that wee shall be as a Citty upon a Hill, the eies of all people are upon us; soe that if wee shall deale falsely with our god . . . and soe cause him to withdrawe his present help from us, wee shall be made a story and a by-word through the world. . . .

The colonists also established an elected legislature, the General Court. Their system was not democratic in the modern sense because the right to vote and hold office was limited to church members. But this did not mean that the government was run by clergymen or that it was not sensitive to the popular will. Clergymen were influential, but since they were not allowed to hold public office, their authority was indirect and based on the respect of their parishioners, not on law or force. Until the mid-1640s, most families contained at least one adult male church member. Since these "freemen" soon secured the right to choose the governor and elect the representatives ("deputies")

to the General Court, a kind of practical democracy existed.

The Puritans had a clear sense of what their churches should be like. After getting permission from the General Court, a group of colonists who wished to form a new church could select a minister and conduct their spiritual affairs as they saw fit. Membership, however, was restricted to those who could present satisfactory evidence of their having experienced "saving grace," such as by a compelling recounting of some extraordinary emotional experience, some mystical sign of intimate contact with God. During the 1630s, however, few applicants were denied membership. Having removed oneself from England was considered in most cases sufficient proof of spiritual purity. Indeed, as Winthrop had more than one occasion to lament, most of the colony's early troublemakers came not from those of doubtful spiritual condition but from its "visible saints."

Troublemakers

The "godly and zealous" Roger Williams was a prime example, even by Plymouth's standards, of an extreme separatist. He arrived in Massachusetts in 1631 and was elected minister of the church in Salem in 1635. But his opposition to the alliance of church and civil government had turned both ministers and magistrates of the colony against him. Magistrates should have no voice in spiritual matters, he insisted—"forced religion stinks in God's nostrils." He also advanced the radical idea that it was "a Nationale sinne" for anyone, including the king, to take possession of any American land without buying it from the Indians. For these heresies he was banished by the General Court. Williams departed Massachusetts in January 1636, traveling south to the head of Narragansett Bay. There he worked out mutually acceptable arrangements with the local Indians and founded the town of Providence. In 1644, after obtaining a charter from Parliament, he established the colony of Rhode Island and Providence Plantations. The government was relatively democratic, all religions were tolerated, and church and state were rigidly separated. Whatever Williams's temperamental excesses, he was more than ready to practice what he preached when given the opportunity.

Anne Hutchinson, who arrived in Boston in 1631, was another "visible saint" who went too far. Hutchinson was not to be taken lightly. According to Governor Winthrop, her husband William was "a man of mild temper and weak parts, wholly guided by his wife." (He was not so weak as to be unable to father Anne's 15 children, however.) Where virtually all the ministers in the Bay Colony went wrong, she contended, was in emphasizing the obligation of the saved to lead morally pure lives. By taking the Puritan view that there was no necessary relationship between moral conduct and salvation to its extreme limits, she concluded that those possessed of saving grace were exempt from the rules of good behavior and the laws of the commonwealth. This was the heresy known as antinomianism, or "belief against the law."

In 1636 the General Court charged Hutchinson with defaming the clergy. At her trial she coolly announced that even the Ten Commandments must yield to one's own insights if these were directly inspired by God. When pressed for details, she acknowledged that she was a regular recipient of such divine insights. The General Court banished her from the commonwealth and she and her followers then moved to Rhode Island.

The banishment of dissenters like Roger Williams and Anne Hutchinson did not endear the Massachusetts Puritans to posterity. Yet Williams and Hutchinson posed genuine threats to the Puritan community. Could it accommodate such uncooperative spirits and remain intact? When forced to choose between the peace of the commonwealth and sending dissenters packing, Winthrop, the magistrates, and the ministers did not hesitate.

Other New England Colonies

From the successful Massachusetts Bay Colony, settlement radiated outward to other areas of New England, propelled by an expanding population and Puritan intolerance. What are now New Hampshire and Maine were gradually absorbed, New Hampshire becoming a separate colony in 1680.

Meanwhile, beginning in 1635, a number of Massachusetts congregations had pushed southwestward into the fertile valley of the Connecticut River. A group headed by the Reverend Thomas Hooker founded Hartford in 1636. Hooker was influential in the drafting of the Fundamental Orders, a sort of constitution creating a government for the valley towns, in 1639. The government resembled that of Massachusetts, except that it did not limit voting to church members. Other groups of Puritans came directly from England to settle towns in and around New Haven in the 1630s. These were incorporated into Connecticut shortly after the Hooker colony obtained a royal charter in 1662.

French and Dutch Settlements

While the English were settling Virginia and New England, other Europeans were challenging Spain's monopoly in the New World. French explorers had pushed up the St. Lawrence as far as the site of Montreal in the 1530s, and beginning in 1603, Samuel de Champlain made several voyages to the region. In 1608 he founded Quebec, having penetrated as far inland as Lake Huron before the Pilgrims left Leyden. The French also planted colonies in St. Christopher, Guadeloupe, Martinique, and other islands in the West Indies after 1625.

Through their West India Company, the Dutch also established themselves in the West Indies. On the mainland they founded New Netherland in the Hudson Valley, basing their claim to the region on the explorations of Henry Hudson in 1609. As early as 1624, there was a Dutch outpost, Fort Orange, on the site of present-day Albany. Two years later New Amsterdam was located at the mouth of the Hudson River, and Manhattan Island was purchased from the Indians by Peter Minuit, the director-general of the West India Company, for trading goods worth about 60 guilders.

The Dutch traded with the Indians for furs and plundered Spanish colonial commerce enthusiastically. Through the Charter of Privileges of Patroons, which authorized large grants of land to individuals who would bring over 50 settlers, they tried to encourage large-scale agriculture. Only one such estate—Rensselaerswyck, on the Hudson south of Fort Orange, owned by the rich Amsterdam merchant Kiliaen Van Rensselaer—was successful. Peter Minuit was removed from his post in New Amsterdam in 1631, but he organized a group of Swedish settlers several years later and founded the colony of New Sweden on the lower reaches of the Delaware River. New Sweden was in constant conflict with the Dutch, who finally overran it in 1655.

Maryland and the Carolinas

The Virginia and New England colonies were essentially corporate ventures. Most of the other English colonies in America were founded by individuals or by a handful of partners who obtained charters from the ruling sovereign. It was becoming easier to establish settlements in America, for experience had taught the English a great deal about the colonization process. Settlers knew better what to bring with them and what to do after they arrived. Moreover, the psychological barrier was much less formidable. Like a modern athlete seeking to run a mile in less than four minutes, colonizers knew after about 1630 that what they were attempting could be accomplished.

Numbers of influential Englishmen were eager to try their luck as colonizers. The grants they received made them "proprietors" of great estates which were, at least in theory, their personal property. By granting land to settlers in return for a small annual rent, they hoped to obtain a steadily increasing income while holding a valuable speculative interest in all undeveloped land.

One of the first of the proprietary colonies was Maryland, granted by Charles I to George Calvert, Lord Baltimore. Calvert had a deep interest in America, being a member of both the London Company and the Council for New England. He hoped to profit financially from Maryland but, since he was a Catholic, he also intended the colony to be a haven for his coreligionists. Calvert died shortly before Charles approved his charter, so the grant went to his son Cecilius. The first settlers arrived in 1634, founding St. Mary's just north of the Potomac. The presence of the now well-established Virginia colony nearby greatly aided the Marylanders; they had little difficulty in getting started and in developing an economy based, like Virginia's, on tobacco.

The Maryland charter resembled the charter of the old county palatine of Durham in the north of England, whose bishop-overlords had possessed almost regal authority. Lord Baltimore had the right to establish feudal manors, hold people in serfdom, make laws, and set up his own courts. He soon discovered, however, that to attract settlers he had to allow them to own their farms and that to maintain any political influence at all he had to give the settlers considerable say in local affairs. Other wise concessions marked his handling of the religious question. He would have preferred an exclusively Catholic colony, but while Catholics did go to Maryland, there existed from the beginning a large Protestant majority. Baltimore dealt with this problem by agreeing to a Toleration Act (1649) that guaranteed freedom of religion to anyone "professing to believe in Jesus Christ." Even so, there were constant religious conflicts in the early years. However, because the Calverts adjusted their pretensions to American realities, they made a fortune out of Maryland and maintained an influence in the colony until the Revolution.

During the period of the English Civil War and Oliver Cromwell's Protectorate, no important new colonial enterprises were undertaken. With the restoration of the monarchy in 1660 came a new wave of settlement. Most of the earlier colonies were organized by groups of merchants; those of the Restoration period reflected the concerns of great English landowners. They granted generous terms to settlers—easy access to land, religious toleration, and political rights—all far more extensive than those available in England.

The first new venture involved a huge grant south of Virginia to eight proprietors with large interests in colonial affairs, including the Earl of Clarendon, Sir Anthony Ashley Cooper, and Sir William Berkeley, a former governor of Virginia. These men did not intend to recruit large numbers of European settlers. Instead they depended on the "excess" population of New England, Virginia, and the West Indies. They (and the Crown) hoped for a diversified economy, the charter granting tax concessions to exporters of wine, silk, oil, olives, and other exotic products. The region was called Carolina in honor of Charles I.

The Carolina charter, like Maryland's, gave the proprietors wide authority. With the help of the political philosopher John Locke, they drafted a grandiose plan of government called the Fundamental Constitutions, which created a hereditary nobility and provided for huge paper land grants to a hierarchy headed by the lords proprietors and lesser "landgraves" and "caciques." The human effort to support the feudal society was to be supplied by peasants (what the Fundamental Constitutions called "leet-men.")

This pretentious system proved unworkable. The landgraves and caciques got grants, but they could not find leet-men willing to toil on their domains. Probably the purpose of all this elaborate feudal nonsense was promotional; the proprietor hoped to convince investors that they could make fortunes in Carolina rivaling those of English lords. Life followed a more mundane pattern similar to what was going on in Virginia and Maryland, with property relatively easy to obtain.

The first settlers arrived in 1670, most of them from the sugar plantations of Barbados, where slave labor was driving out small independent farmers. Charles Town (now Charleston) was founded in 1680. Another center of population sprang up in the Albemarle district, just south of Virginia, settled largely by individuals from that colony. Two quite different societies grew up in these areas. The Charleston colony, with an economy based on a thriving trade in furs and on the export of foodstuffs to the West Indies, was prosperous and cosmopolitan. The Albemarle settlement, where the soil was less fertile, was poorer and more primitive. Eventually, in 1712, the two were formally separated, becoming North and South Carolina.

The Middle Colonies

Gradually it became clear that the English would dominate the entire coast between the St. Lawrence Valley and Florida. After 1660 only the Dutch challenged their monopoly. The two nations, once allies against Spain, had fallen out because of the fierce competition of their textile

manufacturers and merchants. England's efforts to bar Dutch merchant vessels from its colonial trade also brought the two countries into conflict in America. Charles II precipitated a showdown by granting his brother James, Duke of York, the entire area between Connecticut and Maryland. This was tantamount to declaring war. In 1664 English forces captured New Amsterdam without a fight—there were only 1,500 people in the town—and soon the rest of the Dutch settlements capitulated. New Amsterdam became New York. The duke did not interfere much with the way of life of the Dutch settlers, and they were quickly reconciled to English rule. New York had no local assembly until the 1680s, but there had been no such body under the Dutch either.

In 1664, even before the capture of New Amsterdam, the Duke of York gave New Jersey, the region between the Hudson and the Delaware, to Lord John Berkeley and Sir George Carteret. To attract settlers, these proprietors offered land on easy terms and established freedom of religion and a democratic system of local government. A considerable number of Puritans from New England and Long Island moved to the new province.

In 1674 Berkeley sold his interest in New Jersey to two Quakers. Quakers believed that they could communicate directly with their Maker; their religion required neither ritual nor ministers. Originally a sect emotional to the point of fanaticism, by the 1670s the Quakers had come to stress the doctrine of the Inner Light—the direct, mystical experience of religious truth—which they believed possible for all persons. They were at once humble and fiercely proud, pacifistic yet unwilling to bow before any person or to surrender their right to worship as they pleased. They distrusted the intellect in religious matters and, although ardent proselytizers of their own beliefs, they tolerated those of others cheerfully. When faced with opposition, they resorted to passive resistance, a tactic that embroiled them in grave difficulties in England and in most of the American colonies. In Massachusetts Bay, for example, four Quakers were executed when they refused either to conform to Puritan ideas or to leave the colony.

The acquisition of New Jersey (when Sir George Carteret died in 1680, they purchased the rest of the colony) gave the Quakers a place where they could practice their religion in peace. The proprietors, in keeping with their principles, drafted an extremely liberal constitution for the colony, the Concessions and Agreements of 1677, which created an autonomous legislature and guaranteed settlers freedom of conscience, the right of trial by jury, and other civil rights.

The main Quaker effort at colonization came in the region immediately west of New Jersey, a fertile area belonging to William Penn, the son of a wealthy English admiral. Penn had early rejected a life of ease and had become a Quaker missionary. As a result, he was twice jailed. Yet he possessed qualities that enabled him to hold the respect and friendship even of people who found his religious ideas abhorrent. From his father, Penn had inherited a claim to £16,000 that the admiral had lent Charles II. The king, reluctant to part with that much cash, paid off the debt in 1681 by giving Penn the region north of Maryland and west of the Delaware River, insisting only that it be named Pennsylvania, in honor of the admiral. The Duke of York then added Delaware, the region between Maryland and Delaware Bay, to Penn's holdings.

William Penn considered his colony a "Holy Experiment." He treated the Indians fairly, buying title to their lands and trying to protect them in their dealings with settlers and traders. Anyone who believed in "one Almighty and Eternal God" was entitled to freedom of worship. Penn's political ideas were paternalistic rather than democratic—the assembly he established could only approve or reject laws proposed by the governor and council—but individual rights were as well protected in Pennsylvania as in New Jersey.

Penn's altruism, however, did not prevent him from taking excellent care of his own interests. He sold land to settlers large and small on easy terms but reserved huge tracts for himself and attached quitrents to the land he disposed of. He promoted Pennsylvania tirelessly, writing glowing, although perfectly honest, descriptions of the colony that were circulated widely in England and, in translation, on the Continent. These attracted many settlers, including large numbers of Germans—the Pennsylvania "Dutch" (a corruption of *deutsch,* meaning "German"). By 1685 there were almost 9,000 European settlers in Pennsylvania, by 1700 twice that number, a heart-ening contrast to the early history of Virginia and Plymouth. Pennsylvania produced wheat, corn, rye, and other crops and sold its surpluses in West Indian sugar islands.

Indians and Europeans as "Americanizers"

Interaction with the native peoples was characteristic of life in all the English settlements. Colonists learned a great deal about how to live in the American forest from the Indians: the names of plants and animals (hickory, pecan, raccoon, skunk, moose); what to eat in their new home and how to catch or grow it; what to wear (leather leggings and especially moccasins); how best to get from one place to another; how to fight; in some respects how to think.

Although the colonists learned from the Indians how to use many wild plants and animals for food and clothing, they would probably have discovered most of these on their own. Corn, however, was something the Indians had already domesticated. Its contribution to the success of English colonization was enormous. The colonists also took advantage of that marvel of Indian technology, the birchbark canoe. For their part, the Indians adopted European technology eagerly. All metal objects were indeed of great usefulness to them, though most of the products that metals replaced were neither crude nor inefficient in most cases. (To say that a gun is a more deadly weapon than a bow is true only of *modern* guns. A bowman could get off six times as many shots in a given time as a soldier armed with a clumsy 17th-century firelock and would probably hit the target more frequently.)

Indians also took on many of the whites' attitudes. Some tribes used the products of European technology to tyrannize over tribes in more remote areas. During wars, as we shall soon be pointing out, Indians fought almost as often with colonists against other Indians as with other Indians against colonists.

The fur trade illustrates the pervasiveness of Indian-white interaction. It was in some ways a perfect business arrangement. The colonists got "valuable" furs for "cheap" European products,

William Penn met with a group of Delaware Indians in the fall of 1683 to arrange the terms of a land transfer in eastern Pennsylvania. Goodwill between Indians and settlers lasted for about 50 years, until the latter began forcing the Indians westward. This re-creation of Penn's famous treaty is an engraving based on a painting by Benjamin West.

and the Indians got "priceless" tools, knives, and other trade goods in exchange for "cheap" beaver pelts and deerskins. The demand for furs caused the Indians to become more efficient hunters and trappers. Hunting parties became larger. Farming tribes shifted their villages in order to be nearer trade routes and waterways. In some cases small groups combined into confederations in order to control more territory. As one historian puts it, "the fur trade set off a chain reaction . . . within the Indian world."

Although the colonists learned much from the Indians, their objective was not to be like the Indians, whom they considered the epitome of savagery and barbarism. Their fear of becoming "Indianized," the historian James Axtell notes, is clear from the adage "It is very easy to make an

Indian out of a white man, but you cannot make a white man out of an Indian." Yet the constant conflicts with Indians forced the colonists to band together and in time gave them a sense of having shared a common history. And later, when they broke away from Great Britain, they used the image of the Indian to symbolize the freedom and independence they sought for themselves.

In sum, during the 200-odd years that followed Columbus's first landfall in the Caribbean, a complex development had taken place in the Americas, one that profoundly affected the civilizations of the people who preceded Columbus and those who followed him. We shall now turn to a more detailed look at how this happened in one part of that vast region, the part on which our own civilization has evolved.

Milestones

	Exploration		Settlement
c. 1000	Leif Eriksson reaches Newfoundland	c. 50,000 B.C.	First humans reach North America from Asia
1445–1488	Portuguese sailors explore west coast of Africa	1493	Columbus founds La Navidad Hispaniola
1492	First voyage of Christopher Columbus	1494	Treaty of Tordesillas divides theNew World between Spain and Portugal
1497	John Cabot explores east coast of North America	1576	Settlement of St. Augustine
1498	Vasco da Gama sails around Africa to India	1587	Founding of "Lost Colony" of Roanoke Island
1513	Ponce de Léon explores Florida	1607	Settlement of Jamestown
1519–1521	Hernán Cortés conquers Mexico	1608	Founding of Quebec
1519–1522	Ferdinand Magellan circumnavigates the globe	1620	Settlement of Plymount, signing of Mayflower Compact
1539–1542	Hernando de Soto explores the lower Mississippi River valley	1624	Settlement of New Amsterdam
1634	Settlement of Maryland	1630	Settlement of Massachusetts Bay
1540–1542	Francisco Vasquez de Coronado explores the Southwest	1636	Founding of Rhode Island
		1639	Founding of Connecticut
1579	Francis Drake explores the coast of California	1664	Conquest of New Amsterdam by the English
1609	Henry Hudson discovers the Hudson River	1670	Settlement of Charles Town (later Charleston)
		1681	Settlement of Philadelphia

Supplementary Reading

On the explorers see D. B. Quinn, **North America from Earliest Discovery to First Settlements*** (1977), and S. E. Morison's biography of Columbus, **Admiral of the Ocean Sea** (1942). The English background of colonization is treated in Wallace Notestein, **The English People on the Eve of Colonization*** (1954), and Carl Bridenbaugh, **Vexed and Troubled Englishmen*** (1968).

On French and Spanish colonization, see W. J. Eccles, **France in America*** (1972), and Charles Gibson, **Spain in America*** (1966). On

the interactions of European and Indian civilizations, consult A. W. Crosby, **The Columbian Exchange** (1972), James Axtell, **The European and the Indian** (1981), and William Cronon, **Changes in the Land** (1981). W. E. Washburn, **The Indian in America** (1975), contains a good discussion of the culture and history of North American Indian groups.

On the African slave trade see, J. A. Rawley, **The Trans-Atlantic Slave Trade** (1981), and H. S. Klein, **The Middle Passage** (1978).

A general account of the history of English colonization is W. F. Cravens, **The Colonies in Transition*** (1968). On Virginia, E. S. Morgan,

American Slavery, American Freedom (1975), is outstanding. For Maryland, consult G. T. Main, **Tobacco Colony** (1982).

D. R. Rutman, **Winthrop's Boston** (1965), is a good account of the Puritan colony. For the middle colonies, see Michael Kammen, **Colonial New York** (1975), and G. B. Nash, **Quakers and Politics** (1968). For Carolina consult A. R. Ekirch, **Poor Carolina** (1981).

Biographies worth noting include A. T. Vaughan, **American Genesis: Captain John Smith*** (1975), E. S. Morgan, **The Puritan Dilemma: The Story of John Winthrop*** (1958), Morgan's **Roger Williams** (1967), and M. M. Dunn, **William Penn** (1967).

*Available in paperback

CHAPTER 2

American Society in the Making

What Is an American?
The Southern Colonies: A Hustling People
The Chesapeake: "Seasoning Time"
The Lure of Land
The Resort to Slavery
"Their Darling Tobacco"
Bacon's Rebellion
The Carolinas: "More Like a Negro Country"
Home and Family in the Colonial South
Georgia and the Back Country
Colonial New England: A Convenanted People
The Stamp of Puritanism: Family Bonds
Women and Children
Visible Saints and Others
Democracies Without Democrats
Dedham: A "Typical" Town
The Dominion of New England
Crisis in Salem Village
"To Advance Learning"
The Serpent Prosperity
A Merchant's World
The Middle Colonies: A Rising People
"This Promiscuous Breed"
"The Best Poor Man's Country"
The Politics of Diversity

*T*he colonies were settled chiefly by English people at first, with a leavening of Germans, Scots, Scotch-Irish, Dutch, French, Swedes, Finns, a scattering of other nationalities, a handful of Sephardic Jews, and a gradually increasing number of black African slaves. The cultures these people brought with them varied according to the nationality, social status, intelligence, and taste of the individual. The newcomers never lost this heritage entirely, but they—and certainly their descendants—became something quite different from their relatives who remained in the Old World. They became what we call Americans.

But not right away.

What Is an American?

The subtle but profound changes that occurred when Europeans moved to the New World were hardly self-willed. Most of the settlers came, it is true, hoping for a more bountiful existence and sometimes also for nonmaterialistic reasons, such as the opportunity to practice their religions in ways barred to them at home. For some whose alternative was prison or execution, there was really no choice. Still, even the most rebellious or alienated seldom intended to develop an entirely new civilization; rather, they wished to reconstruct the old on terms more favorable to themselves. Nor did a single "American" type result from the careful selection of particular kinds of Europeans as colonizers. Settlers came from every walk of life and in rough proportion to their numbers in Europe (if we exclude the very highest social strata). Certainly there was no systematic selection of "the finest grain to provide seed for cultivating the wilderness."

Why then did America become something more than another Europe? Why was New England not merely a new England? The fact of physical separation provides part of the answer. America was isolated from Europe by 3,000 miles of ocean. The crossing took anywhere from a few weeks to several months, depending on wind and weather. No one undertook an ocean voyage lightly, and few who made the westward crossing ever thought seriously of returning. The modern mind can scarcely grasp the awful isolation that enveloped settlers. One had to construct a new life or perish—if not of hunger, then of loneliness.

Unlike separation from Europe, some factors affected some settlers differently than others.

Factors as material as the landscape encountered, as quantifiable as population patterns, as elusive as chance and calculation all shaped colonial social arrangements. Their cumulative impact did not at first produce anything like a uniform society throughout the 2,000-mile-long and 50-mile-wide corridor that contained England's American colonies. Two quite different societies developed, one at each end of the corridor. A third society in the middle shared elements of both. The "Americans" who evolved in these regional societies were in many ways as different from each other as all were from their European cousins. The process by which these identities merged into an American nation remained incomplete. It was—and is—ongoing.

The Southern Colonies: A Hustling People

The southern parts of English North America comprised three regions: the Chesapeake Bay, consisting of "tidewater" Virginia and Maryland; the "low country" of the Carolinas (and eventually Georgia); and the "back country," a vast territory that extended from the fall line in the foothills of the Appalachians where falls and rapids put an end to navigation on the tidal rivers to the farthest point of western settlement. Not until well into the 18th century would the emergence of common features—export-oriented agricultural economies, a labor force in which black slaves figured prominently, and the absence of towns of any size—prompt people to think of "the South" as a single region.

The Chesapeake: "Seasoning Time"

When the English philosopher Thomas Hobbes wrote in 1651 that human life tended to be "nasty, brutish, and short," he might well have had in mind the royal colony of Virginia. Although the colony grew from about 1,300 to nearly 5,000 in the decade after the crown took it over in 1624, the death rate remained appalling. Since more than 9,000 immigrants had entered the colony, nearly half the population died during that decade.

The climate helped make the Chesapeake area a death trap. "Hot and moist" is how Robert Beverly described the weather in *The History and Present State of Virginia* (1705), the dampness "occasioned by the abundance of low grounds, marshes, creeks, and rivers." Almost without exception newcomers underwent "seasoning," a period of illness which in its mildest form consisted of "two or three fits of a feaver and ague." Long after food shortages and Indian warfare had ceased to be serious problems, life in the Chesapeake remained precarious. Well into the 1700s a white male of 20 in Middlesex County could look forward to about 25 more years of life. Across Chesapeake Bay, in Charles County, Maryland, the average life expectancy was even lower.

Because of the persistent shortage of women in the Chesapeake region (men outnumbered women by three to two even in the early 1700s), widows easily found new husbands. Many men spent their entire lives alone or in the company of other men. Others married Indian women and became part of Indian society.

All Chesapeake settlers felt the psychological effects of their precarious and frustrating existence. Random mayhem and calculated violence posed a continuous threat to life and limb. Social arrangements were rude at best and often as "brutish" as Hobbes had claimed. "Success," writes Gloria T. Main in *Tobacco Colony: Life in Early Maryland*, "was primarily the product of good timing and good health." If a white man got started when tobacco prices were high and survived the seasoning period, he could "begin to amass the necessary capital with which to acquire land, a wife, and then a servant. . . . By rigorously saving and reinvesting his cash income, he could secure his own enterprise and help his children launch theirs."

The Lure of Land

Agriculture was the bulwark of life for the Chesapeake settlers and the rest of the colonial south; the tragic experiences of the Jamestown settlement revealed this quickly enough. Jamestown also suggested that a colony could not succeed unless its inhabitants were allowed to own their own land. The first colonists had agreed to work for seven years in return for a share of the profits. When their contracts expired there were few profits. To satisfy these settlers and to attract new cap-

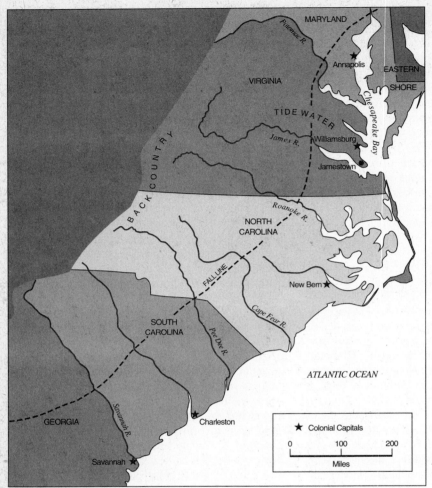

The Southern Colonies

ital, the company declared a "dividend" of land, its only asset. The surviving colonists each received 100 acres. Thereafter, as prospects continued poor, the company relied more and more on grants of land to attract both capital and labor. A number of wealthy Englishmen were given immense tracts, some running to several hundred thousand acres. Lesser persons willing to settle in Virginia received more modest grants. Whether dangled before a great tycoon, a country squire, or a poor farmer, the offer of land had the effect of encouraging immigration to the colony.

Soon what was known as the headright system became entrenched in both Virginia and Maryland. Behind the system lay the principle that land should be parceled out according to the availability of labor to cultivate it. For each "head" entering the colony the government issued a "right" to take any 50 acres of unoccupied land. To "seat" a claim and receive title to the property, the holder of the headright had to mark out its boundaries, plant a crop, and construct some sort of habitation. This system was adopted in all the colonies south of New York.

The first headrights were issued with no strings attached, but generally the grantor demanded a small annual payment called a "quitrent." A quitrent was actually a tax, perhaps a shilling for 50 acres, that provided a way for the proprietors to derive incomes from their colonies.

Quitrents were usually resented and difficult to collect.

The headright system encouraged landless Europeans to migrate to America. More often than not, however, those most eager to come could not afford passage across the Atlantic. To bring together those with money who sought land and labor and poor people who wanted to get to America, the indentured servant system was developed. Indenture resembled apprenticeship. In return for transportation, the indentured servants agreed to work for a stated period, usually about five years. During that time they received no compensation beyond their keep. Indentured women were forbidden to marry and if they became pregnant (as many did), the time lost from work was added to their terms of service.

Servants lacked any incentive to work hard, whereas masters tended to "abuse their servantes . . . with intollerable oppression." In this clash of wills, the advantage lay with the master; servants lacked full political and civil rights, and masters could administer physical punishment and otherwise abuse them. An indenture, however, was a contract; servants could and did sue when planters failed to fulfill their parts of the bargain.

Servants who completed their years of labor became free. Usually the ex-servant was entitled to an "outfit" (a suit of clothes, some farm tools, seed, and perhaps a gun). In the Carolinas and in Pennsylvania, servants also received small grants of land when their service was completed.

The headrights issued when indentured servants entered the colonies went to whoever paid their passage, not to the servants. Thus the system gave a double reward to capital—land and labor for the price of the labor alone. Since well over half of the white settlers of the southern colonies came as indentured servants, the effect on the structure of southern society was enormous.

Most servants eventually became landowners, but with the passage of time their lot became harder. The best land belonged to the large planters, and low tobacco prices and high local taxes combined to keep many ex-servants in dire poverty. Some were forced to become "squatters" on land along the fringes of settlement that no one had yet claimed. When someone turned up with a legal title to the land, the squatters demanded "squatters' rights," the privilege of buying the land from the legal owner without paying for the improvements they had made on it. This led to lawsuits and sometimes to violence.

In the 1670s conflicts between Virginians who owned choice land and ex-servants on the outer edge of settlement brought the colony to the brink of class warfare. The costs of meeting the region's ever-growing need for labor with indentured servants were becoming prohibitive. Some other solution was needed.

The Resort to Slavery

The first African blacks brought to English North America arrived on a Dutch ship and were sold at Jamestown in 1619. Early records are vague and incomplete, so it is not possible to say whether these Africans were treated as slaves or freed after a period of years like indentured servants. What is certain is that by about 1640 *some* blacks were slaves (a few, with equal certainty, were free) and that by the 1660s local statutes had firmly established the institution of slavery in Virginia and Maryland.

Whether slavery produced race prejudice in America or prejudice produced slavery is a hotly debated, important, and difficult-to-answer question. Most 17th-century Europeans were prejudiced against Africans; the usual reasons that led them to look down on "heathens" with customs other than their own were in the case of Africans greatly reinforced by their blackness, which the English equated with dirt, the Devil, danger, and death. Yet the English knew that the Portuguese and Spaniards had enslaved blacks—*negro* is Spanish for black. Since the English adopted the word as a name for Africans, their treatment of Africans in the New World may also have derived from the Spanish, which suggests that they treated blacks in their colonies as slaves from the start.

Probably the Africans' blackness lay at the root of the tragedy, but prejudice and existing enslavement interacted with each other as both cause and effect, bringing about the total debasement of the African. "The concept of Negro slavery," the historian Winthrop Jordan writes

*was neither borrowed from foreigners, nor ex-
tracted from books, nor invented out of whole
cloth, nor extrapolated for servitude, nor generated by English reaction to Negroes as such, nor
necessitated by the exigencies of the New World.
Not any one of these made the Negro a slave,*
but all.

Slavery soon spread throughout the colonies.
As early as 1626 there were 11 slaves in New
Netherland, and the Massachusetts Body of Liberties of 1641 provided that "there shall never be
any bond-slavery . . . amongst us; unlesse it be
lawful captives taken in just warrs [*i.e.*,Indians]
and such strangers as willingly sell themselves, or
are solde to us." However, relatively few blacks
were imported until late in the 17th century, even
in the southern colonies. In 1650 there were only
300 blacks in Virginia and as late as 1670 no more
than 2,000.

White servants were much more highly
prized. The African, after all, was almost entirely
alien to both the European and the American
ways of life. In a country starved for capital, the
cost of slaves—roughly five times that of servants—was another disadvantage. For these reasons, so long as white servants could be had in
sufficient numbers, there were few slaves in the
Chesapeake and those that were generally
worked alongside white servants and shared
roughly the same food, clothing, and quarters.

In the 1670s the flow of new servants slackened, the result of improving economic conditions
in England and the competition of other colonies
for labor. At the same time, the formation of the
Royal African Company (1672) made slaves more
readily available. The indenture system began to
give way to slavery as the "permanent" solution to
the region's chronic need for labor. An additional
inducement causing planters and politicians to
switch was the recognition that, unlike white servants, black slaves (and their offspring) would be
forever barred from competing with whites for
land or political power.

"Their Darling Tobacco"

Labor and land made agriculture possible, but it
was necessary to find a market for American
crops in the Old World if the colonists were to enjoy anything but the crudest sort of existence.
They could not begin to manufacture all the articles they required; to obtain from England such
items as plows and muskets and books and chi-
naware, they had to have cash crops, or what their
English creditors called "merchantable commodities." Here, at least, fortune favored the Chesapeake.

The founders of Virginia tried to produce all
sorts of things that were needed in the old country: grapes and silk in particular, indigo, cotton,
oranges, olives, sugar, and many other plants. But
it was tobacco, unwanted, even strongly opposed
at first, that became for farmers on both sides of
Chesapeake Bay "their darling."

Tobacco was unknown in Europe until Spanish explorers brought it back from the West Indies. It was not common in England until the time
of Sir Walter Raleigh. Then it quickly proved irresistible to thousands of devotees. At first the London Company discouraged its colonists from
growing tobacco. Since it clearly contained some
habit-forming drug, many people opposed its use.
King James I wrote a pamphlet attacking the
weed, saying that smoking was a "vile and stink-
ing" habit "dangerous to the Lungs." But English
smokers and partakers of snuff ignored their king,
and the Virginians ignored their company. By
1617 a pound of tobacco was worth more than 5
shillings in London. Company and Crown then
changed their tune, granting the colonists a monopoly and encouraging them in every way.

Unlike wheat, which required expensive
plows and oxen to clear the land and prepare the
soil, tobacco plants could be set on semicleared
land and cultivated with a simple hoe. Although
tobacco required lots of human labor, a single laborer working two or three acres could produce
as much as 1,200 pounds of cured tobacco, which,
in a good year, yielded a profit of more than 200
percent. Under these circumstances, production
in America leaped from 2,500 pounds in 1616 to
nearly 30 million pounds in the late 17th century,
or roughly 400 pounds of tobacco for every man,
woman, and child in the Chesapeake colonies.

The tidewater region was blessed with many
navigable rivers and the planters spread along
their banks, giving the Chesapeake a shabby, helter-skelter character of rough habitations and

stump-littered fields, surrounded by forest. There were no towns and almost no roads. English ships made their way up the rivers from farm to farm, gathering the tobacco at each planter's wharf. The vessels also served as general stores of a sort where planters could exchange tobacco for everything from cloth, shoes, tools, salt, and nails to such exotic items as tea, coffee, chocolate, and spices.

However, the tremendous expansion of tobacco caused the price to plummet in the late 17th century. This did not stop the expansion of the colonies, but it did alter their society. Small farmers found it more difficult to make a decent living. At the same time men with capital and individuals with political influence were engrossing large tracts of land. Tobacco was notorious for the speed with which it exhausted the fertility of the soil. Growers with a lot of land could shift frequently to new fields within their holdings, allowing the old fields to lie fallow and thus maintain high yields, but the only option that small farmers had when their land gave out was to move to unsettled land on the frontier. To do that in the 1670s was to risk trouble with properly indignant Indians. It might also violate colonial laws designed to slow westward migration and limit tobacco production.

Bacon's Rebellion

Chesapeake settlers showed little respect for constituted authority. The most serious challenge took place in Virginia in 1676. Planters in the outlying counties heartily disliked the officials in Jamestown who ran the colony. The royal governor, Sir William Berkeley, and his "Green Spring" faction (the organization took its name from the governor's plantation) had ruled Virginia for more than 30 years. Outsiders resented the way Berkeley and his henchmen used their offices to line their pockets. They also resented their social pretensions, for Green Springers made no effort to conceal their opinion, which had considerable basis in fact, that western planters were a crude and vulgar lot.

Early in 1676 planters on the western edge of settlement, always looking for excuses to grab land by doing away with the Indians who owned it,

asked Berkeley to authorize an expedition against Indians who had been attacking nearby plantations. Berkeley refused. The planters then took matters into their own hands. Their leader, Nathaniel Bacon, was (and remains today) a controversial figure. His foes described him as extremely ambitious and possessed "of a most imperious and dangerous hidden Pride of heart." But even his sharpest critics conceded that he was well qualified "to lead a giddy and unthinking multitude."

When Berkeley refused to authorize him to attack the Indians, Bacon promptly showed himself only too willing to lead that multitude not only against Indians but even against the governor. Without permission he raised an army of 500 men, described by the Berkeley faction as "rabble of the basest sort." Berkeley then declared him a traitor.

Several months of monumental confusion followed. Bacon murdered some peaceful Indians, marched on Jamestown and forced Berkeley to legitimize his authority, then headed west again to kill more Indians. In September he returned to Jamestown and burned it to the ground. Berkeley fled across Chesapeake Bay to the Eastern Shore. But a few weeks later Bacon came down with a "violent flux"—probably it was a bad case of dysentery—and he died. Soon thereafter an English naval squadron arrived with enough soldiers to restore order. Bacon's Rebellion came to an end.

On the surface, the uprising changed nothing. No sudden shift in political power occurred. Indeed, Bacon had not sought to change either the political system or the social and economic structure of the colony. But if the *rebellion* did not change anything, nothing was ever again quite the same after it ended. With seeming impartiality, the Baconites had warred against Indians and against other planters. But which was the real enemy of anyone interested in growing tobacco? Surely Baconites and Green Springers had no differences that could not be compromised. And their common interest extended beyond the question of how to deal with Indians. "For men bent on the maximum exploitation of labor," the historian Edmund S. Morgan wrote, "the implication should have been clear."

There is every reason to think that it was clear. In the quarter-century following Bacon's Rebellion the Chesapeake region became committed to black slavery. Large differences in the wealth and lifestyles of growers of tobacco resulted. The few who succeeded in accumulating 20 or more slaves and enough land to keep them occupied grew richer. The majority either grew poorer or at best had to struggle to hold their own.

Bacon's Rebellion, however, sealed an implicit contract between the inhabitants of the "great houses," and those who lived in more modest lodgings: southern whites might differ greatly in wealth and influence, but they stood as one and forever behind the principle that blacks must have neither. This was the basis—the price—of the harmony and prosperity achieved by those who survived "seasoning" in the Chesapeake colonies.

The Carolinas: "More Like a Negro Country"

The English and, after 1700, the Scotch-Irish settlers of the tidewater parts of the Carolinas turned to agriculture as enthusiastically as had their Chesapeake neighbors. In substantial sections of what became North Carolina, tobacco flourished. In South Carolina, Madagascar rice was introduced in the low-lying coastal areas in 1696. By 1700 almost 100,000 pounds were being exported annually; by the eve of the Revolution, rice exports from South Carolina and Georgia exceeded 65 million pounds a year.

In the 1740s another cash crop, indigo, was introduced in South Carolina by Eliza Lucas. Indigo did not compete with rice either for land or labor. It prospered on high ground and needed care in seasons when the slaves were not busy in the rice paddies. The British were delighted to have a new source of indigo because the blue dye was important in their woolens industry. Parliament quickly placed a bounty on it to stimulate production.

Their tobacco, rice, and indigo, along with furs and forest products such as lumber, tar, and resin, meant that the southern colonies had no difficulty in obtaining manufactured articles from abroad. Planters dealt with agents in England and Scotland, called factors, who managed the sale of their crops, filled their orders for manufactures, and supplied them with credit. This was a great convenience but not necessarily an advantage, for

it prevented the development of a diversified economy. Throughout the colonial era, while small-scale manufacturing developed rapidly in the north, it was stillborn in the south.

Reliance on European middlemen also retarded the development of urban life. Until the rise of Baltimore in the 1750s, Charleston was the only city of importance in the entire South. Despite its rich export trade, its fine harbor, and the easy availability of excellent lumber, Charleston's shipbuilding industry never remotely rivaled that of Boston, New York, or Philadelphia.

On the South Carolina rice plantations, slave labor predominated from the beginning, for free workers would not submit to its backbreaking and unhealthy regimen. The first quarter of the 18th century saw an enormous influx of Africans into all the southern colonies. By 1730 roughly three out of every ten people south of Pennsylvania were black, and in South Carolina the blacks were the majority. "Carolina," remarked a newcomer in 1737, "looks more like a negro country than like a country settled by white people."

Given the existing race prejudice and the degrading impact of slavery, this demographic change had an enormous impact on life wherever blacks were concentrated. In each colony regulations governing the behavior of blacks, both free and slave, increased in severity as the density of the black population increased. The South Carolina Negro Act of 1740 denied slaves "freedom of movement, freedom of assembly, freedom to raise [their own] food, to earn money, to learn to read English." The blacks had no civil rights under any of these codes, and punishments were sickeningly severe. Whipping was common for minor offenses, death by hanging or by being burned alive for serious crimes. Blacks were sometimes castrated for sexual offenses—even for lewd talk about white women—or for repeated attempts to escape.

That blacks resented slavery goes without saying, but since slavery did not mean the same thing to all of them, their reactions to it varied. Throughout the 18th century a constant stream of new slaves was arriving from Africa. These "outlandish" blacks tended to respond differently than American-born slaves. Among the latter, field hands experienced a different kind of slavery than did household servants, and slave artisans faced

This idealized view of slave life shows the black family when work for the master is finished, catching their own fish and harvesting fruits from their own garden plot. In reality, most slaves had time to pursue such tasks only at the end of an exhausting day in the master's fields.

still another set of circumstances. In short, the slaves' places in society influenced their behavior.

The master race sought to acculturate the slaves in order to make them more efficient workers. A slave who could understand English was easier to order about; one who could handle farm tools or wait on tables was more useful than one who could not; a carpenter or a mason was more valuable still. But acculturation increased the slave's independence and mobility, and this posed problems. Field hands seldom tried to escape; they expressed their dissatisfactions by pilferage and petty sabotage, by laziness, or by feigning stupidity. Most runaways were artisans who hoped to "pass" as free in a nearby town. It was one of the many paradoxes of slavery that the more valuable a slave became, the harder that slave was to control.

Yet few runaway slaves became rebels. Indeed, organized slave rebellions were rare, and although individual assaults by blacks on whites were common enough, personal violence was also common among whites, then and throughout American history. But the masters had sound reasons for fearing their slaves; the particular viciousness of the system lay in the fact that oppression bred resentment, which in turn produced still greater oppression.

What is superficially astonishing is that the whites grossly exaggerated the danger of slave revolts. They pictured the black as powerful, bestial, and lascivious, a caldron of animal emotions that had to be restrained at any cost. Probably the characteristics they attributed to the blacks were really projections of their own passions. The most striking illustration was the fear that if blacks were free, they would breed with whites. Yet in practice, the interbreeding, which indeed took place, was almost exclusively the result of white men using their power as masters to have sexual relations with female slaves.

Thus the "peculiar institution" was fastened upon America with economic, social, and psychic barbs. Ignorance and self-interest, lust for gold and for the flesh, primitive prejudices and complex social and legal ties, all combined to convince the whites that black slavery was not so much good as a fact of life. A few Quakers attacked the institution on the religious ground that all human beings are equal before God: "Christ dyed for all, both *Turks, Barbarians, Tartarians,* and *Ethyopians.*" Yet a few Quakers owned slaves, and even the majority who did not usually succumbed to color prejudice. Blackness was a defect, but it was no justification for enslavement, they argued.

Home and Family in the Colonial South

Life for all but the most affluent planters was by modern standards crude. Houses were mostly one- and two-room affairs, roughly built and unpainted. Furniture and utensils were sparse and crudely made. Chairs were rare; if a family possessed one it was reserved for the head of the house. People sat, slept, and ate on benches and planks. The typical dining table was made of two boards covered, if by anything, with a "board cloth." Toilets and plumbing of any kind were unknown; even chamber pots were beyond the reach of poorer families.

Clothes were equally crude and, since soap was expensive, rarely washed, therefore foul-smelling and often infested with vermin. Food was plentiful. Corn, served as bread, hominy, pancakes, and in various other forms, was the chief staple. But there was plenty of beef, pork, and game, usually boiled with vegetables over an open fire.

Women, even indentured ones, rarely worked in the fields. Household maintenance was their responsibility including tending to farm animals, making butter and cheese, pickling and preserving, spinning and sewing, and, of course, caring for children. For exceptional women, the labor shortage created opportunities. Some managed large plantations; Eliza Lucas ran three in South Carolina for her absent father while still in her teens, and after the death of her husband, Charles Pinckney, she managed his large properties.

Because of the high death rate, second and third marriages were common. Despite the likelihood that a widow would soon remarry, studies of wills reveal that most southern men took special pains to provide for their wives and expressed confidence in their ability to manage the inheritance effectively.

Southern children were not usually subjected to as strict discipline as children in New England were, but the difference was relative. Formal schooling for ordinary youngsters was nonexistent; the isolated rural character of society made the maintenance of schools prohibitively expensive. Whatever most children learned, they got from their parents or other relatives. A large percentage of southerners were illiterate. As in other regions, children were put to some kind of useful work at an early age.

More well-to-do, "middling" planters had more comfortable lifestyles, but they still lived in relatively crowded quarters, having perhaps three rooms to house a family and a couple of servants. Food in greater variety and abundance was another indication of a higher standard of living.

Until the early 18th century only a handful of colonists achieved real affluence. That fortunate few, masters of several plantations and many slaves lived in solid, two-story houses of six or more rooms, furnished with English and other imported furnishings. When the occasion warranted, the men wore fine broadcloth, the women the latest (or more likely the next-to-latest) fashions. Some even sent their children abroad for schooling. The founding of the College of William and Mary in Williamsburg, Virginia, in 1696 was an effort to provide the region with its own institution of higher learning. However, William and Mary was not much more than a grammar school for decades.

These large planters also held the commissions in the militia, the county judgships, and the

This restored kitchen of the Harlow House in Plymouth is typical of the interior of colonial houses. The stock of the musket over the fireplace is pointed to a "Betty lamp," an early type of lighting device containing a wick soaked in grease or some other oily substance.

seats in the colonial legislatures. The control that these "leading families" exercised over their neighbors was not entirely unearned. They were, in general, responsible leaders. And they recognized the necessity of throwing open their houses and serving copious amounts of punch and rum to ordinary voters when election time rolled around. Such gatherings served to acknowledge the representative character of the system.

No matter what their station, southern families led relatively isolated lives. Churches, which might be expected to serve as centers of community life, were few and far between. By the middle of the 18th century the Anglican church was the "established" religion, its ministers supported by public funds. The Virginia assembly had made attendance at Anglican services compulsory in 1619. In Maryland, Lord Baltimore's Toleration Act did not survive the invasion of the colony by militant Puritans. It was repealed in 1654, reenacted in 1657, then repealed again in 1692 when the Anglican church was established.

But for all its legal standing, the Anglican church was not a very powerful force in the south. Most of the ministers the Bishop of London sent to America were second-rate men. If they had intellectual or spiritual ambitions when they arrived, their rural circumstances provided little opportunity to develop them. Most people had few opportunities to attend formal services. One result was that marriages tended to become civil rather than religious ceremonies.

Social events of any kind were great occasions. Births, marriages, and especially funerals called for much feasting; if there were neither heirs nor debts to satisfy, it was possible to "consume" the entire contents of a modest estate in celebrating the deceased's passing. (At one Maryland funeral the guests were provided with 55 gallons of an alcoholic concoction composed of brandy, cider, and sugar.)

Other forms of entertainment and relaxation included hunting and fishing, cockfights, and horse racing—horses were widely owned, used for getting from place to place rather than as draft animals, since tobacco was transported by water and cultivated with hoes, not plows.

Even the most successful planters were hardworking, conserving types, not idle grandees chiefly concerned with conspicuous display. The vast, undeveloped country encouraged them to produce and then invest their savings in more production. William Byrd II (1674–1744), one of the richest men in Virginia, habitually rose before dawn. Besides his tobacco fields, he operated a sawmill and a grist mill, prospected for iron and coal, and engaged in the Indian trade.

Georgia and the Back Country

West of the fall line of the rivers that irrigated tidewater Chesapeake and Carolina lay the back country. This region included the Great Valley of Virginia, the Piedmont, and what became the final English colony, Georgia, founded in 1733 by a group of London philanthropists who were concerned over the plight of honest persons imprisoned for debt. They conceived of settling these unfortunates in the New World. (Many Europeans were still beguiled by the prospect of regenerating their society in the New World.) The government, eager to create a buffer between South Carolina and the hostile Spanish in Florida, readily granted a charter (1732) to the group, who agreed to manage the colony without profit to themselves for a period of 21 years.

In 1733 their leader, James Oglethorpe, founded Savannah. Oglethorpe was a complicated person, vain, high-handed, and straitlaced, yet hardworking and idealistic. He hoped to people the colony with sober and industrious yeoman farmers. Land grants were limited to 50 acres and made nontransferable. To insure sobriety, rum and other "Spirits and Strong Waters" were banned. To guarantee that the colonists would have to work hard, the entry of "any Black . . . Negroe" was prohibited. The Indian trade was to be strictly regulated in the interest of fair dealing.

Oglethorpe intended that silk, wine, and olive oil be the main products—none of which, unfortunately, could be profitably produced in Georgia. His noble intentions came to naught. The settlers swiftly found ways to circumvent all restrictions. Rum flowed, slaves were imported, large land holdings amassed. Georgia developed an economy much like South Carolina's. In 1752 the founders, disillusioned, abandoned their responsibilities. Georgia then became a royal colony.

It was only about this time that settlers in any numbers penetrated the rest of the southern back country. So long as cheap land remained available closer to the coast and Indians along the frontier remained a threat, only the most daring and foot-loose hunters or fur traders lived far inland. But once settlement began, it came with a rush. Chief among those making the trek were Scotch-Irish and German immigrants. By 1770 the back country contained about 250,000 settlers, 10 percent of the population of the colonies.

This internal migration did not proceed altogether peacefully. In 1771 frontiersmen in North Carolina calling themselves Regulators fought a pitched battle with 1,200 troops dispatched by the Carolina assembly, which was dominated by low-country interests. The Regulators were protesting their lack of representation in the assembly. They were crushed and their leaders executed. This was neither the last nor the bloodiest sectional conflict in American history.

Colonial New England: A Covenanted People

If survival in the Chesapeake required junking many European notions about social arrangements and submitting to the dictates of the wilderness, was this also true in Massachusetts and Connecticut? Ultimately it probably was, but in the early going, Puritan ideas certainly fought the New England reality to a draw.

Like other early New England towns and unlike these southern ones, Boston had a dependable water supply. The surrounding patchwork of forest, pond, dunes, and tidemarsh, was much more open than the malaria-infected terrain of the tidewater and low-country South. One consequence was that New Englanders escaped "the agues and fevers" that beset settlers to the south, leaving them free to attend to their spiritual, economic, and social well-being. "Seasoning" proceeded so imperceptibly as almost to escape notice.

The Stamp of Puritanism: Family Bonds

New England's Puritans were set apart from other English settlers by how much—and how long—they lived out of their baggage. The supplies the first arrivals brought with them eased their adjustment. The Puritans' baggage, however, included besides pots and pans, saws and shovels, a plan for the proper ordering of society.

At the center of the plan was a covenant, or agreement, to insure the upright behavior of all who took up residence. They sought to provide what John Winthrop described to the passengers on the *Arbella* as the two imperatives of human existence: "that every man might have need of other, and from hence they might be all knitt more nearly together in the Bond of brotherly affection."

The first and most important covenant governing Puritan behavior was that binding family members. The family's authority was backed by the Fifth Commandment: "Honor thy father and thy mother, that thy days may be long upon the land." In a properly ordered Puritan family, as elsewhere in the colonies, authority flowed downward. Sociologists describe such a family as nuclear and patriarchal; each household contained one family, and in it, the father was boss. His principal responsibilities consisted of providing for the physical welfare of the household, including any servants, and making sure they behaved properly. All economic dealings between the family and other parties were also transacted by him.

The Reverend John Cotton's outline of a woman's responsibilities clearly established her subordinate position: She should keep house, educate the children, and improve "what is got by the industry of the man." The poet Anne Bradstreet reduced the functions of a Puritan woman to two: "loving Mother and obedient Wife." Colonial New England, and the southern colonies as well, did have their female blacksmiths, silversmiths, shipwrights, gunsmiths, and butchers as well as shopkeepers and teachers. Such early examples of domestic "liberation," however, were mostly widows and the wives of incapacitated husbands. Even so, most widows, especially young ones, quickly remarried. According to the historian Laurel Thatcher Ulrich, colonial women generally, and New England women in particular, "were by definition basically domestic."

Women and Children

Dealings with neighbors and relatives and involvement in church activities marked the outer

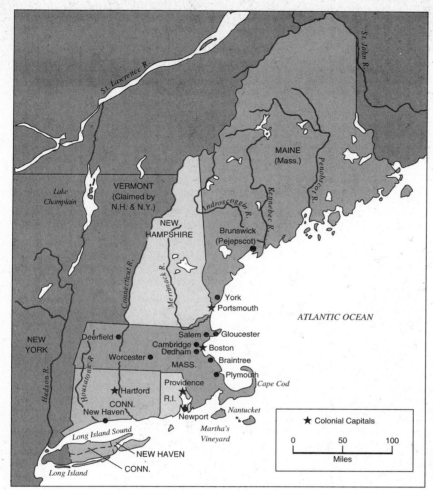

Colonial New England

limits of the social range of most Puritan women. Care of the children was a full-time occupation when broods of twelve or fourteen were more common than those of one or two. Fewer children died in New England than in the Chesapeake or in Europe. Childbearing and motherhood, therefore, likely extended over two decades of a woman's life. Meanwhile, she also functioned as the chief operating officer of the household. Cooking, baking, sewing, and supervising servants all fell to her. These jobs were physically demanding, though not so debilitating as to prevent large numbers of New England wives from seeing one or more husbands off to the hereafter.

As Puritan social standards required husbands to rule over wives, so parents ruled over children. The virtue most insistently impressed upon New England children was obedience; Cotton Mather's advice, "better whipt, than damned," graced many a New England rod taken up by a parent in anger, from there to be rapidly transferred to the afterparts of misbehaving offspring. But household chores kept children out of mischief. By age 6 or 7 girls did sewing and helped with housework, and boys were put to work outdoors. Older children might be sent to live with another family to work as servants or apprentices. Only when well into adulthood would children emerge from under parental control.

Such practices may convey the impression that Puritans hustled their young through childhood with as little love as possible. New Englanders harbored no illusions. "Innocent vipers" is how one minister described children, having 14 of his own to submit as evidence. Yet for all their acceptance of the doctrine of infant damnation, Puritan parents were not indifferent to the fate of their children. "I do hope," Cotton Mather confessed, "that when my children are gone they are not lost; but carried unto the Heavenly Feast with Abraham." Another minister assigned children who died in infancy "the easiest room in hell."

Population growth reinforced Puritan ideas about the family. When the outbreak of the English Civil War put an end to the Great Migration in the early 1640s, immigration slackened off sharply. Thereafter growth was chiefly due to the region's extraordinarily high birthrate, (more than three times the rate today) and strikingly low mortality rate. This resulted in a population much more evenly distributed by age and sex than that in the south.

Visible Saints and Others

When it came to religion, Puritans believed that church membership ought to be the joint decision of a would-be member and those already in the church. Obvious sinners and those ignorant of Christian doctrine were rejected out of hand. But what of "outwardly just" applicants who lacked compelling evidence that they had experienced God's saving grace? In the late 1630s, with the Great Migration in full swing and new arrivals clamoring for admission to the churches, such "merit-mongers" were excluded, thereby limiting church membership to the community's "visible saints." A decade later, the Great Migration over and applications down, some of the saints began to have second thoughts.

By the early 1650s fewer than half of all New England adults were church members, and so exacting had the examination for membership become that most young people refused to submit themselves to it. How these growing numbers of nonmembers could be compelled to attend church services was a problem ministers could not long defer. Meanwhile, the magistrates found it harder to defend the policy of not letting taxpayers vote because they were not church members. But what really forced reconsideration of the membership policy was the concerns of nonmember parents about the souls of their children, who could not be baptized.

At first the churches permitted baptism of the children of church members. Most Puritans approved this practice, which allowed them the hope that a child who died after receiving baptism might at least be spared Hell's hottest precincts. Since most of the first generation were church members, nearly all the second-generation New Englanders were baptized, whether they became church members or not. The problem began with the third generation, the offspring of parents who had been baptized but who did not become church members. By the mid-1650s it was clear that if nothing were done, soon a majority of the people would be living in a state of original sin. If that happened, how could the churches remain the dominant force in New England life?

Fortunately, a way out was at hand. In 1657 an assembly of Massachusetts and Connecticut ministers recommended a form of intermediate church membership that would permit the baptism of people who were not visible saints. Five years later, some 80 ministers and laymen met at Boston's First Church to hammer out what came to be called the Half-Way Covenant. It provided limited (halfway) membership for any applicant not known to be a sinner who was willing to accept the provisions of the church covenant. They and their children could be baptized, but the sacrament of communion and a voice in church decision making were reserved for full members.

Opponents of the Half-Way Covenant argued that it reflected a slackening of religious fervor. Some loss of religious intensity there may have been, but the rise in church memberships, the continuing prestige accorded ministers, and the lessening of the intrachurch squabbling in the decades after the Half-Way Covenant was adopted suggest that the secularization of New England society had a long way to go.

Democracies Without Democrats

Like the southern colonies, the New England colonies derived their authority from charters granted by the Crown or Parliament. Except for rare fits of meddling by London bureaucrats, they were largely left to their own devices where matters of purely local interest were concerned. This typically involved maintaining order by regulating how people behaved. According to Puritan theory, government was both a civil covenant, entered into by all who came within its jurisdiction, and the principal mechanism for policing the institutions on which the maintenance of the social order depended. When Massachusetts and Connecticut passed laws requiring church attendance, levying taxes for the support of the clergy, and banning Quakers from practicing their faith, they were acting as "shield of the churches." When they provided the death penalty both for adultery and for blaspheming a parent, they claimed they were defending the integrity of families. When they set the price a laborer might charge for his services or even the amount of gold braid that servants might wear on their jackets, they believed they were enforcing the Puritan principle that people must accept their assigned stations in life.

Laws like these have prompted historians and Americans generally to characterize New England colonial legislation as socially repressive and personally invasive. Yet a healthy respect for the backsliding ways of humanity obliged New Englanders not to depend too much on provincial governments. The primary responsibility for maintaining "Good Order and Peace" fell to the more than 500 towns of the region. These differed greatly in size and development. By the early 18th century the largest, Boston, Newport, and Portsmouth, were well along toward becoming urban centers. This was before "frontier" towns like Amherst, Kent, and Hanover had even been founded. Nonetheless, town life gave New England the distinctiveness it has still not wholly lost.

Dedham: A "Typical" Town

Dedham, Massachusetts, illustrates how this worked. In 1634 the heads of 30 households in Watertown, already feeling crowded in that then two-year-old village, petitioned the General Court for a grant of land to establish a new town. A year later they became the proprietors of a 200-square-mile tract west of Watertown on the condition that they all move there, "gather" a church, and organize a town government. These "proprietors" then drew up a town covenant, which committed all who signed it to conduct themselves "according to that most perfect rule, the foundation wherof is

everlasting love." Other clauses bound them to keep out the "contrary minded," to submit personal differences to the judgment of the town, and to conduct their business so as to create a "loving and comfortable society in our said town."

The covenant provided that town business be decided at semiannual town meetings, at which all male adults who had subscribed to the covenant could vote. At these meetings a representative to the General Court was to be elected and seven selectmen chosen to run the town between town meetings. In addition, matters relating to town lands were to be decided, taxes to pay the minister's salary set, and provisions for poor and incompetent people made. The next century brought many changes to Dedham. Yet when the town's 1,200 residents celebrated its centenary in 1736, they were governing themselves much as had their great-grandparents.

But was colonial New England democratic? To be democratic, a government must at least offer those subject to its authority a voice in its operations. With the possible exception of the 1670s and 1680s, when a stiff property-holding requirement (£80 of taxable estate) was in effect in Massachusetts and Connecticut, most adult male New Englanders could vote. Compared with England or with the southern colonies, where blacks had no political rights, the New England governments were relatively responsive to public opinion.

Relatively few voters, however, bothered to vote because most offices went uncontested. Those elected consistently came from the wealthiest and most established levels of the community. In Dedham, 5 percent of the adult males filled 60 percent of the town's positions. (Even in Rhode Island, widely regarded as almost too democratic, voters usually elected their wealthiest and longest-settled townsmen.) Ordinary voters tended to choose their "betters," and those they selected took seriously the responsibilities of public office. Together they created "a speaking aristocracy in the face of a silent democracy."

The Dominion of New England

The most serious threat to these arrangements occurred in the 1680s. Following the execution of Charles I in 1649, England was ruled by one man, the Lord Protector, Oliver Cromwell. Cromwell's death in 1658 led to the restoration of the Stuart monarchy in the person of Charles II (1660–1685). During his reign and the abbreviated one of his brother, James II (1685–1688), the government sought to bring the colonies under effective royal control.

Massachusetts seemed in particular need of supervision. Accordingly, in 1684 its charter was annulled and the colony, along with all those north of Pennsylvania, became part of the Dominion of New England, governed by Edmund Andros.

Andros arrived in Boston in late 1686 with orders to make the northern colonies behave like colonies, not like sovereign powers. He set out to abolish popular assemblies, to change the land-grant system so as to provide the king with quitrents, and to enforce religious toleration, particularly of Anglicans. Being a professional soldier and administrator, he scoffed at those who resisted his authority. "Knoweing no other government then their owne," he said, they "think it best, and are wedded to . . . it."

Fortunately for New Englanders, the Dominion fell victim two years later to yet another political turnabout in England, the Glorious Revolution. In 1688 Parliament decided it had had enough of the Catholic-leaning Stuarts and sent James II packing. In his place it installed a more resolutely Protestant Dutchman, William of Orange, and his wife, James's daughter Mary. When news of these events reached Boston in the spring of 1689, a force of more than 1,000 colonists led by a contingent of ministers seized Andros and lodged him in jail. Two years later Massachusetts was made a royal colony that also included Plymouth and Maine. As in all such colonies, the governor was appointed by the king. The new General Court was elected by property owners; church membership was no longer required for voting.

Crisis in Salem Village

Many New England towns resembled "peaceable kingdoms." But in some, tensions developed between generations when they ran out of land sufficient to support the grandchildren of the founders. Others allowed petty disputes to divide townspeople into rival camps. Still others seemed doomed to serious discord. Among these, Salem village provides a singular example.

In 1666, families living in the rural outback of the thriving town of Salem petitioned the General Court for the right to establish their own church. For political and economic reasons this was a questionable move, but in 1672 the General Court authorized the establishment of a separate parish.

Over the next 15 years three preachers came and went before, in 1689, one Samuel Parris became minister. Parris had spent 20 years in the Caribbean as a merchant and had taken up preaching only three years before coming to Salem. Accompanying him were his wife; a daughter, Betty; a niece, Abigail; and the family's West Indian slave, Tituba, who told fortunes and practiced magic on the side.

Parris proved as incapable of bringing peace to the feuding factions of Salem Village as had his predecessors. In January 1692 the church voted to dismiss him. At this point Betty and Abigail, now 9 and 11, along with Ann Putnam, a 12-year-old, started "uttering foolish, ridiculous speeches which neither they themselves nor any others could make sense of." A doctor diagnosed the girls' ravings as the work of the "Evil Hand" and declared them bewitched.

But who had done the bewitching? The first persons accused were three women whose unsavory reputations and frightening appearances made them likely candidates: Sarah Good, a pauper with a nasty tongue; Sarah Osborne, a bedridden widow; and the slave Tituba, who had brought suspicion on herself by volunteering to bake a "witch cake," made of rye meal and the girls' urine. The cake should be fed to a dog, Tituba said. If the girls were truly afflicted, the dog would show signs of bewitchment!

The three women were brought before the local deputies to the General Court. As each was questioned, the girls went into contortions; "their arms, necks and backs turned this way and that way . . . their mouths stopped, their throats choked, their limbs wracked and tormented." Tituba confessed to being a witch. Sarah Good and Sarah Osborne each claimed to be innocent. All three were sent to jail on suspicion of witchcraft.

These proceedings triggered new accusations. By the end of April, 24 more people had been charged with practicing witchcraft. Officials in neighboring Andover, lacking their own "bewitched," called in the girls to help with their investigations. By May the hunt had extended to Maine and Boston and up the social ladder to some of the colony's most prominent citizens, including Lady Mary Phips, whose husband, William, had just been appointed governor.

By June, when Governor Phips convened a special court consisting of members of his council, more than 150 persons (Lady Phips no longer among them) stood formally charged with practicing witchcraft. In the next four months the court convicted 28 of them. Five "confessed" and were spared. One woman won a reprieve because she was pregnant. Two others escaped. But 19 persons were hanged.

Anyone who spoke in defense of the accused was in danger of being charged with witchcraft, but some brave souls challenged both the procedures and the findings of the court. Finally, at the urging of the leading ministers of the Commonwealth, Governor Phips adjourned the court and forbade any further executions.

No one involved in these gruesome proceedings escaped with reputation intact, but those whose reputations suffered most were the ministers. Among the clergy only Increase Mather deserves any credit. He persuaded Phips to halt the executions, arguing that "it were better that ten witches should escape, than that one innocent person should be condemned." The behavior of his son Cotton defies apology. It was not that Cotton Mather accepted the existence of witches—at the time everyone did, which incidentally suggests that Tituba was not the only person in Salem who practiced witchcraft—or even that Mather took such pride in being the resident expert on demonology. It was rather his vindictiveness. He even stood at the foot of the gallows bullying hesitant hangmen into doing "their duty."

"To Advance Learning"

Along with the farmers and artisans who settled in New England with their families during the Great Migration came nearly 150 university-trained colonists. Nearly all had studied divinity. These men became the first ministers in Massachusetts and Connecticut, and a brisk "seller's market" existed for them. Larger churches began stockpiling candidates by hiring newly arrived Cambridge and Oxford graduates as assistants or teachers in

anticipation of the retirement of their senior ministers. But what to do when, as a 1643 promotional pamphlet, *New Englands First Fruits*, put it, "our present ministers shall lie in the dust"? Fear of leaving "an illiterate Ministry to the Churches" turned New Englanders to finding a way to "advance learning and perpetuate it to Posterity."

In 1636 the Massachusetts General Court appropriated £400 to found "a schoole or colledge." Two years later, just as the first freshmen gathered in Cambridge, John Harvard, a recent arrival who had died of tuberculosis, left the college £800 and his library. After a shaky start, during which students conducted a hunger strike against a sadistic and larcenous headmaster, Harvard settled into an annual pattern of admitting a dozen or so 14-year old boys, stuffing their heads with four years of theology, logic, and mathematics, and then sending them out into the wider world of New England.

Immediately below Harvard on the educational ladder came the grammar schools, where boys spent seven years learning Latin and Greek. Massachusetts and Connecticut soon passed education acts which required all towns of any size to establish such schools. New Englanders hoped, as the Massachusetts law of 1647 stated, to thwart "that old deluder, Satan," by insuring "that Learning may not be buried in the graves of our forefathers." But not every New England town required to maintain a school actually did so. Those that did often paid their teachers poorly. Only the most dedicated Harvard graduates took up teaching as a career. Some parents kept their children at their chores rather than at school.

Yet the cumulative effect of the Puritan community's educational institutions, the family and the church as well as the school, was impressive. A majority of men in 17th-century New England could read and write and by the middle of the 18th century, male literacy was almost universal. Literacy among women also improved steadily, despite the almost total neglect of formal education for girls.

Spreading literacy created a thriving market for the printed word. Many of the first settlers brought impressive libraries with them, and large numbers of English books were imported throughout the colonial period. The first printing press in the English colonies was founded in Cambridge in 1638, and by 1700 Boston was producing an avalanche of printed matter. Most of these publications were reprints of sermons, but modest amounts of history, poetry, reports of scientific investigations, and treatises on political theory also appeared.

By the early 18th century the intellectual life of New England had taken on a character potentially at odds with the ideas of the first Puritans. In the 1690s Harvard acquired a reputation for religious toleration. According to orthodox Puritans, its graduates were unfit for the ministry and its professors were no longer interested in training young men for the clergy. In 1701 several Connecticut ministers therefore founded a new "Collegiate School" designed to uphold the Puritan values that Harvard seemed ready to abandon. The new college was named after its first English benefactor, Elihu Yale. Nonetheless, as became all too clear at commencement ceremonies in 1722 when its president and six tutors announced themselves Anglicans, Yale quickly acquired purposes well beyond those assigned to it by its creators.

The assumption that the clergy had the last word on learned matters, still operative at the time of the witchcraft episode, came under direct challenge in 1721. When a smallpox epidemic swept through Boston that summer, Cotton Mather, the most prestigious clergyman in New England, recommended that the citizenry be inoculated. Instead of accepting Mather's authority, his heretofore silent critics seized on his support of the then-radical idea of inoculation to challenge his professional credentials. They filled the unsigned contributor columns of New England's first newspaper, the *Boston Gazette,* and the *New England Courant,* which opened in the midst of the inoculation controversy, with their views.

The *Courant* was published by James Franklin and his 16-year-old brother, Benjamin. The younger Franklin's "Silence Dogood" essays were particularly infuriating to members of the Boston intellectual establishment. Franklin described Harvard as an institution where rich and lazy "blockheads . . . learn little more than how to carry themselves handsomely . . . and from whence they return, after Abundance of Trouble, as Blockheads as ever, only more proud and conceited."

James Franklin was jailed in 1722 for criticizing the General Court, and shortly thereafter the *New England Courant* went out of business. Meanwhile, Ben had departed Boston for Philadelphia, where, as everyone knows, fame and fortune awaited him.

"The Serpent Prosperity"

Prior experience (and the need to eat) turned the first New Englanders to farming. They grew barley (used to make beer), rye, oats, green vegetables, and also native crops such as potatoes, pumpkins, and, most important, Indian corn, or maize. Corn was easily cultivated and its yield exceeded that of other grains. It proved versatile and tasty when prepared in a variety of ways and also made excellent fodder for livestock. In the form of corn liquor, it was easy to store, to transport, and, in a pinch, to imbibe.

The colonists also had plenty of meat. They grazed cattle, sheep, and hogs on the common pastures or in the surrounding woodlands. Deer, along with turkey, and other game birds abounded. The Atlantic provided fish, especially cod, which was easily preserved by salting. In short, New Englanders ate an extremely nutritious diet. Abundant surpluses of firewood kept the winter cold from their doors. The combination contributed significantly to their good health and longevity.

The trouble was that the shortness of the growing season, the rocky and often hilly terrain, and careless methods of cultivation, which exhausted the soil, meant that farmers did not produce large enough surpluses for trading.

The earliest Puritans accepted this economic marginality. The more pious positively welcomed it as insurance against "the serpent prosperity," which might otherwise deflect their spiritual mission into commercial opportunism. No prominent English merchants joined the Great Migration, though many were devoted Puritans and some had invested in the Massachusetts Bay Company. Settlers who turned to business upon arrival attracted suspicion, if not open hostility. Laws against usury (lending money at excessive rates) and profiteering in scarce commodities were in effect from the first days of settlement. Robert Keayne, a prosperous Boston merchant, was twice fined £200 by the General Court and admonished by his church for "taking above six-pence in the shilling profit." Keayne paid the fines, all the while convinced that "my goods and prices were cheap pennyworths."

Early Puritan leaders resisted the argument of people like Keayne that business was a calling no less socially useful than the ministry or public office. Differences in wealth should be modest and should favor those to whom the community looked for leadership. In the Puritan scheme of things, Governor Winthrop should stand higher than Keayne in all rankings, wealth included. But Winthrop died in 1649, broke and in debt, whereas Keayne died three years later in sufficient prosperity (despite those stiff fines) to leave the town of Boston and Harvard College impressive benefactions. The gap between the Puritan ideal and the emerging reality was becoming embarrassingly clear.

A Merchant's World

Winthrop's generation had tried to minimize dependence on European-manufactured goods by producing their own. When their efforts failed, they next pinned their hopes on establishing direct trade links with European suppliers by offering the skins of beaver and other such fur-bearing animals as otter, muskrat, and mink. Unfortunately, the beavers soon caught wind of what was going on and took off for points west and north. By the late 1650s the New Englanders were back where they started. As one English merchant wrote, as trading partners New Englanders "have noe returns." The colonists then turned to indirect trading schemes, in which merchants like Robert Keayne played a central role and from which they ultimately derived stature as well as wealth.

Fish, caught offshore on grounds that extended from Cape Cod to Newfoundland, provided merchants with their opening into the world of transatlantic commerce. In 1643 five New England vessels set out with their holds packed with fish, which they sold in Spain and the Canary Islands; they took payment in sherry and madeira, for which a market existed in England. One of these ships also had the dubious distinction of initiating New England into the business of trafficking in human beings when its captain took pay-

ment in African slaves, whom he subsequently sold in the West Indies.

This was the start of the famous "triangular trade." Only occasionally was the pattern truly triangular; more often, intermediate legs gave it a polygonal character. So long as their ships ended up with something that could be exchanged for English goods needed at home, it did not matter what they started out with or how many things they bought and sold along the way.

So maritime trade and those who engaged in it became the driving force of the New England economy. Because numerous merchants congregated in Portsmouth, Salem, Boston, Newport, and New Haven, these towns soon differed greatly from towns in the interior. They were larger and faster growing, and a smaller percentage of their inhabitants was engaged in farming.

The largest and most thriving town was Boston, which by 1720 had become the commercial hub of the region. It had a population of more than 10,000; in the entire British Empire, only London and Bristol were larger. More than one-quarter of Boston's male adults had either invested in shipbuilding or were directly employed in maritime commerce. Ship captains and merchants held most of the public offices.

Beneath this emergent mercantile elite lived a stratum of artisans and small shopkeepers, and beneath these a substantial population of mariners, laborers, and "unattached" people with little or no property and still less political voice. In the 1670s, at least a dozen prostitutes plied their trade in Boston. By 1720 crime and poverty had become serious problems; public relief rolls frequently exceeded 200 souls and dozens of criminals languished in the town jail. Boston bore little resemblance to what the first Puritans had in mind when they planted their "Citty upon a Hill." But neither was it like any European city of the time. It stood there on Massachusetts Bay, midway between its Puritan origins and its American future.

The Middle Colonies: A Rising People

New York, New Jersey, Pennsylvania, and Delaware owe their collective name, the Middle

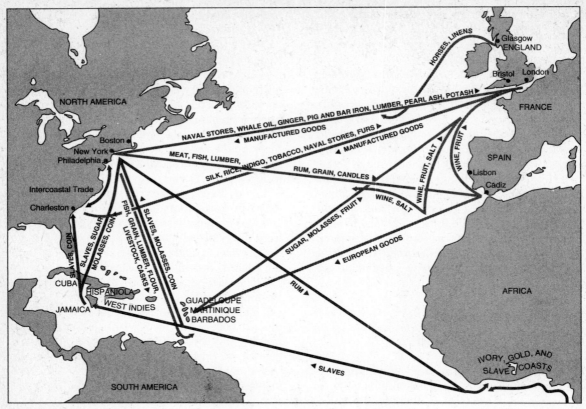

Colonial Overseas Trade

Colonies, to geography. Sandwiched between New England and the Chesapeake region, they often receive only passing notice in accounts of colonial America. The lack of a distinctive institution, such as slavery or the town meeting, explains part of this neglect.

Actually, both institutions existed there. Black slaves made up about 10 percent of the population; indeed, one New York county in the 1740s had proportionally more blacks than large sections of Virginia. And eastern Long Island was settled by people from Connecticut who brought the town meeting system with them.

This quality of "in-betweenness" extended to other economic and social arrangements. Like colonists elsewhere, most people in the Middle Colonies became farmers. But whereas northern farmers concentrated on producing crops for local consumption and southerners for export, Middle

Colony farmers did both. In addition to raising foodstuffs and keeping livestock, they grew wheat, which the thin soil and shorter growing season of New England did not permit but for which there existed an expanding market in the densely settled Caribbean sugar islands.

Social arrangements differed more in degree than in kind from those in other colonies. Unlike New England settlers, who clustered together in agricultural villages, families in the Hudson Valley of New York and in southeastern Pennsylvania lived on the land they cultivated, often as spatially dispersed as the tobacco planters of the Chesapeake. In contrast with Virginia and Maryland, however, substantial numbers congregated in the seaport centers of New York City and Philadelphia. They also settled interior towns like Albany, an important center of the fur trade on the upper Hudson, and Germantown, an "urban village"

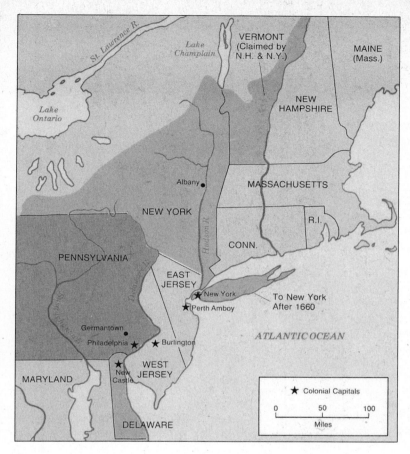

The Middle Colonies

northwest of Philadelphia where many people were engaged in trades like weaving and tailoring and flour milling.

"This Promiscuous Breed"

The Middle Colonists also possessed traits that later would be seen as distinctly "American." Their ethnic and religious heterogeneity is a case in point. Traveling through Pennsylvania in 1744, the Swedish botanist Peter Kalm encountered "a very mixed company of different nations and religions." In addition to "Scots, English, Dutch, Germans, and Irish," he reported, "there were Roman Catholics, Presbyterians, Quakers, Methodists, Seventh day men, Moravians, Anabaptists, and one Jew." In New York City one embattled English resident complained: "Our chiefest unhappi-ness here is too great a mixture of nations, & English the least part."

Scandinavian and Dutch settlers outnumbered the English in New Jersey and Delaware even after the English took over these colonies. William Penn's first success in attracting colonists was with German Quakers and other persecuted religious sects, among them Mennonites and Moravians from the Rhine Valley. The first substantial influx of immigrants into New York after it became a royal colony consisted of French Huguenots.

Early in the 18th century, hordes of Scotch-Irish settlers from Northern Ireland and Scotland descended on Pennsylvania. These colonists spoke English but felt little loyalty to the English government, which had treated them badly back home, and less to the Anglican church, since most of them were Presbyterians. Large numbers of them followed the valleys of the Appalachians south into the back country of Virginia and the Carolinas.

Why so few English in the Middle Colonies? Here, again, timing provides the best answer. The English economy was booming. There seemed to be work for all. Migration to North America, although never drying up, slowed to a trickle. The result was colonies in which English settlers were a minority.

The intermingling of ethnic groups gave rise to many prejudices. Benjamin Franklin, though generally complimentary toward Pennsylvania's hardworking Germans, thought them clannish to a fault. The French traveler Hector St. John de Crèvecoeur, while marveling at the adaptive qualities of "this promiscuous breed," complained that "the Irish . . . love to drink and to quarrel; they are litigious, and soon take to the gun, which is the ruin of everything." Yet by and large the various types managed to get along with each other successfully enough. Crèvecoeur attended a wedding in Pennsylvania where the groom's grandparents were English and Dutch and one of his uncles had married a Frenchwoman. The groom and his three brothers, Crèvecoeur added with some amazement, "now have four wives of different nations."

"The Best Poor Man's Country"

Ethnic differences seldom caused conflict in the Middle Colonies because they seldom limited opportunity. The promise of prosperity (promotional pamphlets proclaimed Pennsylvania "the best poor man's country in the world") had attracted all in the first place, and achieving prosperity was relatively easy, even for those who came with only a willingness to work. From its founding, Pennsylvania granted upwards of 500 acres of land to families on arrival, provided they would pay the proprietor an annual quitrent. Similar arrangements existed in New Jersey and Delaware. Soon travelers in the Middle Colonies were being struck by "a pleasing uniformity of decent competence."

New York was something of an exception to this favorable economic situation. When the English took over New York, they extended the Dutch patroon system by creating 30 manorial estates covering some 2 million acres. But ordinary New Yorkers never lacked ways of becoming landowners. A hundred acres along the Hudson River could be bought in 1730 for what an unskilled laborer could earn in three months. Even tenants on the manorial estates could obtain long-term leases that had most of the advantages of ownership but did not require the investment of any capital. "One may think oneself to be a great lord," one frustrated "lord" of a New York manor wrote a colleague, "but it does not amount to much, as you well know."

Mixed farming offered the most commonly trod path to prosperity in the Middle Colonies, but not the only one. Inland communities offered comfortable livelihoods for artisans. Farmers always needed barrels, candles, rope, horseshoes and nails, and dozens of other articles in everyday use. Countless opportunities awaited the ambitious settler in the shops, yards, and offices of New York and Philadelphia. Unlike Boston, New York and Philadelphia profited from navigable rivers that penetrated deep into the back country. Although founded half a century after New York and Boston, Philadelphia grew more rapidly than either. In the 1750s, when its population reached 15,000, it passed Boston to become the largest city in English America.

Most Philadelphians who stuck to their business, particularly if it happened to be maritime commerce, did well for themselves. John Bringhurst, a merchant, began his career as a clerk. At his death in 1751 he left an estate of several thousand pounds. According to the historian Gary Nash, the city's "leather-apron" artisans often accumulated estates of more than £400, a substantial sum at the time. By way of contrast, in Boston after 1710, economic stagnation made it much more difficult for a skilled artisan to rise in the world.

The Politics of Diversity

"Cannot more friendly and private courses be taken to set matters right in an infant province?" an exasperated William Penn asked the people of Pennsylvania in 1704. "For the love of God, me, and the poor country, be not so governmentish." However well-intentioned Penn's advice, however justified his annoyance, the Pennsylvanians ignored him. Instead, they and their fellows throughout the region constructed a political culture that diverged sharply from the patterns of New England and the south both in contentiousness and in the sophistication required of local politicians.

Superficially the governments of the Middle Colonies closely resembled those of earlier settlements. All had popularly elected representative assemblies and most male adults could vote. In Pennsylvania, where Penn had insisted that there be no religious test and where 50 acres constituted a freehold, something close to universal manhood suffrage existed. In New York even non-property-holding white male residents voted in local elections, and rural tenants with lifetime leases enjoyed full voting rights.

In Pennsylvania and most of New York, representatives were elected by counties. In this they resembled Virginia and Maryland. But unlike the southerners, voters did not tend to defer in politics to the landed gentry. In New York, in 1689, during the political vacuum following the abdication of King James II, Jacob Leisler, a disgruntled merchant and militia captain, seized control of the government. "Leisler's Rebellion" did not amount to much. He held power for less than two years before he was overthrown and sent to the gallows. Yet for two decades New York politics continued to be a struggle between the Leislerians, and other self-conscious "outs" who shared Leisler's dislike of English rule, and anti-Leislerians, who had in common only that they had opposed his takeover. Each group sought the support of a succession of ineffective governors, and the one that failed to get it invariably proceeded to make that poor man's tenure as miserable as possible.

New York lapsed into political tranquility during the governorship of Robert Hunter (1710–1719), but in the early 1730s conflict broke out over a claim for back salary by Governor William Cosby. When Lewis Morris, the chief justice of the supreme court, opposed Cosby's claim, the governor replaced him. Morris and his assembly allies responded by establishing the *New York Weekly Journal*. To edit the paper they hired an itinerant German printer, John Peter Zenger.

Governor Cosby might have tolerated the *Weekly Journal*'s front-page lectures on the right of the people to criticize their rulers had the back pages not contained advertisements referring to his supporters as spaniels and to him as a monkey. After submitting to two months of "open and implacable malice against me," he shut down the paper, arrested Zenger, and charged him with seditious libel. What began as a squalid salary dispute became one of the most celebrated tests of freedom of the press in the history of journalism. At the trial Zenger's attorney, James Hamilton, argued that the truth of his client's criticisms of Cosby constituted a proper defense against seditious libel. This reasoning (though contrary to English law at the time) persuaded the jury to acquit Zenger.

Politics in Pennsylvania turned on conflict between two interest groups, one clustered around the proprietor, the other around the assembly, which was controlled by a coalition of Quaker representatives from Philadelphia and the German speaking Pennsylvania Dutch.

Neither the proprietary party nor the Quaker party qualifies as a political party in the modern sense of being organized and maintained for the purpose of winning elections. Nor can they be categorized as standing for "democratic" or "aristocratic" interests. But their existence guaranteed that the political leaders had to take popular opinion into account. Moreover, having once appealed to public opinion, they had to be prepared to defer to it. Success turned as much on knowing how to follow as on knowing how to lead.

The 1763 uprising of the "Paxton Boys" of western Pennsylvania put this policy to a full test. The uprising was triggered by eastern indifference to Indian attacks on the frontier—an indifference made possible by the fact that the east outnumbered the west in the assembly, 26 to 10. Fuming because they could obtain no help from Philadelphia against the Indians, a group of Scotch-Irish from Lancaster county fell upon a village of peaceful Conestoga Indians and murdered them in cold blood. Then these Paxton Boys marched on the capital, several hundred strong.

Fortunately a delegation of burghers, headed by Benjamin Franklin, talked them out of attacking the town by acknowledging the legitimacy of their grievances about representation and by promising to vote a bounty on Indian scalps! It was just such fancy footwork that established Franklin, the leader of the assembly party, as Pennsylvania's consummate politician. "Tell me, Mr. Franklin," a testy member of the proprietary party asked, "how is it that you are always with the majority?" Soon thereafter, the assembly sent Franklin to London to defend local interests against the British authorities, a situation in which he would definitely not be "with the majority."

Milestones

1609–1611	"Seasoning time" in Jamestown	**1676**	Bacon's Rebellion
1612	Introduction of tobacco cultivation in Virginia	**1684–1688**	Dominion of New England
		1689	Leisler's Rebellion
1619	First Africans sold in Virginia	**1692**	Salem witchcraft trials
1630–1640	"Great Migration" of Puritans to America	**1693**	Founding of the College of William and Mary
1636	Founding of Boston Latin School and Harvard College	**1696**	Introduction of rice cultivation in South Carolina
1657	Half-Way Covenant	**1733**	Georgia settled

Supplementary Reading

Among general interpretations of colonial society, D. J. Boorstin, **The Americans: The Colonial Experience*** (1958), as well as H. M. Jones, **O Strange New World*** (1964), remain stimulating.

D. F. Hawke, **The Colonial Experience** (1966), provides a good survey of colonial history.

J. A. Henretta, **The Evolution of American Society*** (1973), and G. B. Nash, **The Urban Crucible*** (1979), present the results of social research on the period. On economic conditions, E. J. Perkins, **The Economy of Colonial America** (1980), is an up-to-date survey. On the institution of slavery generally, see D. B. Davis, **The Problem of Slavery in Western Culture** (1966), and W. D. Jordan, **White Over Black: American Attitudes Toward the Negro*** (1968). A. E. Smith, **Colonists in Bondage*** (1971), is a good study of indentured servitude, but see also W. D. Galenson, **White Servitude in Colonial America** (1981).

On life in the colonial south see T. W. Tate and David Ammerman, eds., **The Chesapeake in the Seventeenth Century** (1979), D. B. and A. H. Rutman, **A Place in Time** (1984), P. H. Wood, **Black Majority: Negroes in Colonial South Carolina** (1974), and T. H. Breen and Stephen Innes, **"Myne Owne Ground": Race and Freedom on Virginia's Eastern Shore*** (1980).

Family and community life are surveyed in D. F. Hawke, **Everyday Life in Early America** (1988), and E. S. Morgan, **The Puritan Family*** (1966). See also John Demos, **A Little Common-wealth*** (1970), R. L. Bushman, **From Puritan to Yankee*** (1967), K. A. Lockridge, **A New England Town*** (1970), and Philip Greven, **Four Generations*** (1970). The places of women and children are effectively presented in L. T. Ulrich, **Good Wives: Image and Reality in the Lives of Women in Northern New England** (1982), and Philip Greven, **The Protestant Temperament: Patterns of Child-Rearing, Religious Experience, and the Self in Early America** (1980).

On the Puritan way of life see Perry Miller, **Errand in the Wilderness** (1958), E. S. Morgan, **Visible Saints*** (1963), and R. G. Pope, **The Half-Way Covenant** (1969).

On the interplay of religion and social thought, see Stephen Foster, **Their Solitary Way** (1971), D. D. Hall, **Worlds of Wonder, Days of Judgment** (1989), and E. S. Morgan's biography of John Winthrop, **The Puritan Dilemma*** (1958). The disturbances in Salem Village are discussed in John Demos, **Entertaining Satan: Witchcraft and the Culture of Early New England*** (1982).

Educational and intellectual developments are treated in Bernard Bailyn, **Education in the Forming of American Society*** (1960), and L. A. Cremin, **American Education: The Colonial Experience*** (1970).

On the Middle Colonies see R. C. Ritchie, **The Duke's Province** (1977), Patricia Bonomi, **A Factious People: Politics and Society in Colonial New York** (1971), and G. B. Nash, **Quakers and Politics** (1968).

*Available in paperback.

CHAPTER 3

America in the British Empire

The British Colonial System

Mercantilism

The Navigation Acts

The Effects of Mercantilism

The Great Awakening

The Rise and Fall of Jonathan Edwards

The Enlightenment in America

Colonial Scientific Achievements

Other People's Wars

The Great War for the Empire

The Peace of Paris

Putting the Empire Right

Tightening Imperial Controls

The Sugar Act

"Essential Rights and Liberties"

The Stamp Act: The Pot Set Boiling

Rioters or Rebels?

Taxation or Tyranny?

The Declaratory Act

The Townshend Duties

The Boston Massacre

The Tea Act Crisis

From Resistance to Revolution

Since the colonies were founded piecemeal by persons with varying motives and backgrounds, common traditions and loyalties developed slowly. For the same reason, the British government was slow to think of its American possessions as a unit or to deal with them in any centralized way. The particular circumstances that led to its founding determined the specific form of each colony's government and the degree of local independence permitted it.

The British Colonial System

There was a pattern basic to all colonial governments and a general framework to the system of imperial control for all the king's overseas plantations. In the earliest days of any settlement, the need to rely on home authorities was so obvious that few questioned England's sovereignty. Thereafter, as the fledglings grew strong enough to think of using their own wings, distance and British political inefficiency combined to allow them a great deal of freedom. Although royal representatives in America tried to direct policy, the Crown generally yielded the initiative in local matters to the colonies while reserving the right to veto actions it deemed to be against the national interest. External affairs were controlled entirely in London.

Each colony had a governor. By the 18th century he was an appointed official, except in Rhode Island and Connecticut. Governors were chosen by the king in the case of the royal colonies and by the proprietors of Maryland, Delaware, and Pennsylvania. Their powers were much like those of the king in Great Britain. They executed the local laws, appointed many minor officials, summoned and dismissed the colonial assemblies, and proposed legislation to them. They possessed the right to veto colonial laws, but in most colonies, again like the king, they were financially dependent on their "subjects."

Each colony also had a legislature. Except in Pennsylvania, these assemblies consisted of two houses. The lower house, chosen by qualified voters, had general legislative powers, including control of the purse. In all the royal colonies members of the upper house, or council, were appointed by the king, except in Massachusetts, where they were elected by the General Court. The councils served primarily as advisors to the governors, but they also had some judicial and legislative powers. Judges were appointed by the king and served at his pleasure. Yet both councilors and judges were normally selected from among the leaders of the local communities; London had neither the time nor the will to investigate their political beliefs. The system, therefore, tended to strengthen the influence of entrenched colonials.

The lower houses of the legislatures tended to dominate the government in nearly every colony. Financial power, including the right to set the governor's salary, gave them some importance, and the fact that the assemblies usually had the backing of public opinion was significant. They extended their influence by slow accretion. Governors came and went, but the lawmakers remained, accumulating experience, building on precedent, widening decade by decade their control over colonial affairs.

Within the British government the king's Privy Council had the responsibility for formulating colonial policy. It did so on an ad hoc basis, treating each situation as it arose and seldom generalizing. Everything was decentralized: The treasury had charge of financial matters, the army and the admiralty of military and naval affairs, and so on. The Privy Council could disallow (annul) specific colonial laws, but it did not proclaim constitutional principles to which all colonial legislatures had to conform. It acted as a court of last appeal in colonial disputes and handled each case individually. One day the council might issue a set of instructions to the governor of Virginia, the next a different set to the governor of South Carolina. No one one person or committee thought broadly about the administration of the overseas empire.

At times the British authorities, uneasy about their lack of control over the colonies, attempted to create a more effective system. Whenever possible, the original, broadly worded charters were revoked. To transform proprietary and corporate colonies into royal colonies (whose chief officials were appointed by the king) seems to have been London's official policy by the late 17th century. The Privy Council appointed a number of subcommittees to advise it on colonial affairs at this time. The most important was the Lords of Trade, which had its own staff and archives and wielded great influence.

In 1696 a new Board of Trade took over the functions of the Lords of Trade and expanded them considerably. It nominated colonial governors and other high officials. It reviewed all the laws passed by the colonial legislatures, recommending the disallowance of those that seemed to conflict with imperial policy. The efficiency, assiduousness, and wisdom of the Board of Trade fluctuated over the years, but the Privy Council and the Crown nearly always accepted its recommendations.

Colonists naturally disliked having their laws disallowed, but London exercised this power with considerable restraint; only about 5 percent of the laws reviewed were rejected. Furthermore, the board served as an important intermediary for colonists seeking to influence king and Parliament. All the colonies in the 18th century maintained agents in London to present the colonial point of view before board members. The most famous colonial agent was Benjamin Franklin, who represented Pennsylvania, Georgia, New Jersey, and Massachusetts at various times during his long career. However, agents seldom had much influence on British policy.

The British never developed an effective, centralized government for the American colonies. By and large, their American "subjects" ran their own affairs. This fact more than any other explains our present federal system and the wide areas in which the state governments are sovereign and independent.

Mercantilism

The Board of Trade, as its name implies, was concerned with commerce as well as colonial administration. According to prevailing European opinion, colonies were important chiefly for economic reasons. The 17th century was a period of hard times. Many people were unemployed. Therefore some authorities saw the colonies as excellent dumping grounds for surplus people. If only two idlers in each parish were shipped overseas, one clergyman calculated in 1624, England would be rid of 16,000 undesirables.

Most 17th-century theorists, however, envisaged colonies as potential sources of raw materials. To obtain these, they developed a system that later economists called mercantilism. The most important raw materials in the eyes of mercantilists were gold and silver, which, being universally valued, could be exchanged at any time for anything the owner desired. How much gold and silver ("treasure" according to mercantilists) a nation possessed was considered the best barometer of its prosperity and power. Since there were no significant deposits of gold or silver in western Europe, every early colonist dreamed of finding *El Dorado*. The Spanish were the winners in this search; from the mines of Mexico and South America a rich treasure in gold and silver poured into the Iberian Peninsula. Failing to control the precious metals at the source, the other powers tried to obtain them by guile and warfare (witness the exploits of Francis Drake).

In the mid-17th century another method, less hazardous and in the long run far more profitable, called itself to the attention of the statesmen of western Europe. If a country could make itself as nearly self-sufficient as possible and at the same time keep all its citizens busy producing items marketable in other lands, it could sell more abroad than it imported. This state of affairs was known as "having a favorable balance of trade." The term is misleading; in reality, trade, which means exchange, always balances unless one party simply gives its goods away, a practice not recommended by mercantilists. A country with a favorable balance in effect made up the difference by "importing" money in the form of gold and silver. Nevertheless, mercantilism came to mean concentrating on producing for export and limiting imports of ordinary goods and services in every way possible. Colonies that did not have deposits of precious metals were well worth having if they supplied raw materials that would otherwise have to be purchased from foreign sources, or if their people bought substantial amounts of the manufactured goods produced in the mother country.

Of the English colonies in the New World, those in tropical and subtropical climes were valued for their raw materials. The more northerly ones were important as markets, but because they were small in the 17th century, in English eyes they took second place. In 1680 the sugar imported from the single West Indian island of Barbados was worth more than all the goods sent to England by the mainland colonies.

If the possession of gold and silver signified wealth, trade was the route that led to riches, with merchants as pilots to steer the ship of state to prosperity. "Trade is the Wealth of the World," Daniel Defoe wrote in 1728. One must, of course, have something to sell, so internal production must be stimulated.

The Navigation Acts

The nurture of commerce was fundamental. Toward this end Parliament enacted the Navigation Acts. These laws, put into effect over a period of half a century and more, were designed to bring money into the treasury, to develop the imperial merchant fleet, to channel the flow of colonial raw materials into England, and to keep foreign goods and vessels out of colonial ports (since the employment of foreign ships in the carrying trade was as much an import as the consumption of foreign wheat or wool).

The system originated in the 1650s in response to the stiff commercial competition offered by the Dutch. Before 1650 a large share of the produce of the English colonies in America reached Europe in Dutch vessels; the first slaves in Virginia, it will be recalled, arrived on a Dutch ship and were doubtless paid for in tobacco that was later burned in the clay pipes of the burghers of Amsterdam and Rotterdam.

Dismayed by this trend, Parliament in 1650 and 1651 barred foreign ships from the English colonies (except when specially licensed) and prohibited the importation into England of goods that were not carried in English ships or those of the country where the goods had been originally produced. All foreign vessels were excluded from the English coastal trade. Although phrased in general terms, this legislation struck primarily at the Dutch, and in 1652 the English provoked the first of three wars with the Dutch Republic that were only extensions of the policy laid down in the first Navigation Acts.

The laws of 1650–1651 were not rigidly enforced, because England did not have enough ships to supply its overseas possessions. The colonies protested vigorously and then ignored the regulations. Nevertheless, the English persisted. New laws were passed and as the merchant marine expanded (tonnage doubled between 1660 and 1688) and the Royal Navy gradually reduced Dutch power in the New World, enforcement became fairly effective.

The Navigation Act of 1660 reserved the entire trade of the colonies to English ships and required that the captain and three-quarters of his crew be English. (Colonists, of course, were English, and their ships were treated on the same terms as those sailing out of London or Liverpool.) The act also provided that certain colonial "enumerated articles"—sugar, tobacco, cotton, ginger, and dyes like indigo and fustic—could not be "shipped, carried, conveyed or transported" outside the empire. Three years later Parliament required that with trifling exceptions all European products destined for the colonies be brought to England before being shipped across the Atlantic. Since trade between England and the colonies was reserved to English vessels, this meant that the goods would have to be unloaded and reloaded in England. Legislation in 1673 and 1696 was concerned with enforcing these laws: it dealt with the posting of bonds, the registration of vessels, and the appointment of customs officials. Early in the 18th century the list of enumerated articles was expanded to include rice, molasses, naval stores, furs, and copper.

The English looked upon the empire broadly; they envisioned the colonies as part of an economic unit, not as servile dependencies to be exploited for England's selfish benefit. The growing of tobacco in England was prohibited, and valuable bounties were paid to colonial producers of indigo and naval stores. A planned economy, England specializing in manufacturing and the colonies in the production of raw materials, was the grand design. By and large, the system suited the realities of life in an underdeveloped country rich in raw materials and suffering from a chronic labor shortage.

Much has been made by some historians of the restrictions that the British placed on colonial manufacturing. The Wool Act of 1699 prohibited the export (but not the manufacture for local sale) of colonial woolen cloth. A similar law regarding hats was passed in 1732, and in 1750 an Iron Act outlawed the construction of new rolling and slitting mills in America. No other restrictions on manufacturing were imposed. At most the Wool Act stifled a potential American industry; the law was directed chiefly at Irish woolens rather than American. The hat industry cannot be considered a major one. Iron, however, was important; by 1775 the industry was thriving in Virginia, Mary-

land, New Jersey, and Pennsylvania, and America was turning out one-seventh of the world supply. Yet the Iron Act was designed to steer the American iron industry in a certain direction, not to destroy it. Eager for iron to feed English mills, Parliament eliminated all duties on colonial pig and bar iron entering England, a great stimulus to the basic industry. A similar system had been set up with regard to West Indian sugar as early as 1651, when the English fixed the duty on semirefined sugar at a level more than three times higher than that on raw sugar.

The Effects of Mercantilism

All the legislation reflected, more than it molded, the imperial economy. It made England to be the colonies' main customer and chief supplier of manufactures, but this would have happened in any case, and it remained the case after the Revolution, when the Navigation Acts no longer applied to America. Furthermore, important colonial products for which no market existed in England, such as fish, wheat, and corn, were never enumerated and moved freely and directly to foreign ports. Most colonial manufacturing was untouched by English law. Shipbuilding benefited from the Navigation Acts, since many English merchants bought vessels built in the colonies. Between 1769 and 1771, Massachusetts, New Hampshire, and Rhode Island yards constructed perhaps 250 ships of 100 to 400 tons for transatlantic commerce and twice that many sloops and schooners for fishermen and coastal traders. The manufacture of rum for local consumption and for the slave trade was significant; so were barrelmaking, flour milling, shoemaking, and dozens of other crafts that operated without restriction.

Two forces that worked in opposite directions must be considered before arriving at any judgment about English mercantilism. Although the theory presupposed a general imperial interest above that of both colony and mother country, when conflicts of interest arose, the latter nearly always predominated. Whenever Parliament or the Board of Trade resolved an Anglo-American disagreement, the colonists tended to lose out. The Hat Act, for example, may have been good mercantilism, but Parliament passed it because English feltmakers were concerned over the news that Massachusetts and New York were turning out 10,000 hats a year.

The requirement that foreign goods destined for the colonies must first be unloaded in England increased the cost of certain goods to Americans for the benefit of English merchants and dock-workers. The enumeration of tobacco and other colonial products meant that English merchants could profit by reexporting surpluses to the Continent; by 1700 this reexport trade amounted to 30 percent of the value of all of England's exports.

On the other hand, the restrictions of English mercantilism were greatly lessened by inefficiency. The English government was by modern standards incredibly cumbersome and corrupt. The king and his ministers handed out government posts to win political favor or to repay political debts, regardless of the recipient's ability to perform the duties of the office. Transported to remote America, this bumbling and cynical system scarcely functioned at all when local opinion resisted it. Smuggling became a respected profession, bribery of English officials standard practice. Despite a supposedly prohibitive duty of sixpence a gallon imposed by the Molasses Act of 1733, molasses from the French West Indies continued to be imported, for the duty was seldom collected. A customs officer in Salem offered to pass French molasses for 10 percent of the legal tax, and in New Jersey the collectors "entered into a composition with the Merchants and took a Dollar a Hogshead or some such small matter."

Mercantilistic policies hurt some colonists, such as the tobacco planters, who grew far more than British consumers could smoke. But the policies helped others, and most people proved adept at getting around those aspects of the system that threatened them. In any case, the colonies enjoyed almost continuous prosperity in the years between 1650 and the Revolution, as even so dedicated a foe of trade restrictions as Adam Smith admitted.

By the same token, England profited greatly from its overseas possessions. Despite all its inefficiencies, mercantilism worked. Prime Minister Sir Robert Walpole's famous policy of "salutary neglect," which involved looking the other way when Americans violated the Navigation Acts, was partly a bowing to the inevitable, partly the result of complacency. English manufactures were better and cheaper than those of other nations. This fact, together with ties of language and a common heritage, predisposed Americans toward doing business in England. All else followed naturally; the mercantilistic laws merely steered the American economy in a direction it had already taken. They were not a cause of serious discontent until after the French and Indian War.

The Great Awakening

Although a majority of the settlers were of English, Scotch, or Scotch-Irish descent, and their interests generally coincided with those of their cousins in the mother country, people in the colonies were beginning to recognize their common interests and character. Their interests and loyalties were still predominantly local, but by 1750 the word "American," used to describe something characteristic of all the British possessions in North America, had entered the language. Events in one part of America were beginning to have direct effects on other regions. One of the first of these developments was the so-called Great Awakening.

By the early 18th century, religious fervor had slackened in all the colonies. Prosperity turned many colonists away from their forebears' preoccupation with the rewards of the next world to the more tangible ones of this. John Winthrop invested his faith in God and his own efforts in the task of creating a spiritual community; his grandsons invested in Connecticut real estate.

The proliferation of religious denominations made it impracticable to enforce laws requiring regular religious observances. Even in South Carolina, the colony that came closest to having an "Anglican Establishment," only a minority of persons were churchgoers. Settlers in frontier districts lived beyond the reach of church or clergy. The result was a large and growing number of "persons careless of all religion."

This state of affairs came to an abrupt end with the Great Awakening of the 1740s. The Awakening began in the Middle Colonies as the result of religious developments that originated in Europe. In the late 1720s two newly arrived ministers, Theodore Frelinghuysen, a Calvinist from Westphalia, and William Tennent, an Irish-born Presbyterian, sought to instill in their sleepy Pennsylvania and New Jersey congregations the evangelical zeal and spiritual enthusiasm they had witnessed among the pietists in Germany and the Methodist followers of John Wesley in England. Their example inspired other clergymen, including Tennent's two sons.

A more significant surge of religious enthusiasm followed the arrival in 1738 in Georgia of the Reverend George Whitefield, a young Oxford-trained Anglican minister. Whitefield was a marvelous pulpit orator and no mean actor. He played on the feelings of his audience the way a conductor directs a symphony.

He undertook a series of fund-raising tours throughout the colonies. The most successful began in Philadelphia in 1739. Benjamin Franklin, not a very religious person and not easily moved by emotional appeals, heard one of these sermons. "I silently resolved he should get nothing from me", he later recalled.

> I had in my Pocket a Handful of Copper Money, three or four silver Dollars, and five Pistoles in Gold. As he proceeded I began to soften and concluded to give the Coppers. Another Stroke of his Oratory . . . determin'd me to give the Silver; and he finish'd so admirably that I empty'd my Pocket wholly into the Collector's Dish.

Whitefield's visit changed the "manners of our inhabitants," Franklin added.

Wherever Whitefield went, he filled the churches. If no local clergyman offered his pulpit, he attracted thousands to meetings out-of-doors. During a three-day visit to Boston, 19,000 people (more than the population of the town) thronged to hear him.

His oratorical brilliance aside, Whitefield succeeded in releasing an epidemic of religious emotionalism because his message was so well suited to American ears. By preaching a theology that one critic said was "scaled down to the comprehension of twelve-year olds," he spared his audiences the rigors of hard thought. Though he usually began by chastising his listeners as sinners, "half animals and half devils," he invariably took care to leave them with the hope that eternal salvation could be theirs. While not denying the doctrine of predestination, he preached a God responsive to good intentions. He disregarded sectarian differences and encouraged his listeners to do the same. "God help us to forget party

names and become Christians in deed and truth," he prayed.

Whitefield attracted some supporters among ministers with established congregations, but many more from among younger "itinerants," as preachers who lacked permanent pulpits were called. A visit from him or one of his followers inevitably prompted comparisons between this new, emotionally charged style and the more restrained "plaine style" favored by the typical settled minister. Parishioners who had heard a revivalist preacher listened the next Sunday to the droning of their regular minister with what one of Whitefield's imitators claimed was the fear that their souls were at risk because they had been "living under the ministry of dead men."

Of course not everyone found the Whitefield style edifying. When those who did not spoke up, churches sometimes split into factions. Those who supported the incumbent minister were called, among Congregationalists, "Old Lights," and among Presbyterians, "Old Sides," whereas those who favored revivalism were known as "New Lights" and "New Sides." These splits often ran along class lines. The richer, better-educated, and more influential members of the church tended to stay with the traditional arrangements.

The strains these divisions put on communities already struggling to maintain a sense of civic unity produced what the historian Richard Bushman has called a "psychological earthquake." Persons chafing under the restraints of Puritan authoritarianism and made guilt-ridden by their rebellious feelings now found release. For some the release was more than spiritual; Timothy Cutler, a conservative Anglican clergyman, complained that as a result of the Awakening "our presses are forever teeming with books and our women with bastards." Whether or not Cutler was correct, the Great Awakening helped some people to rid themselves of the idea that disobedience to authority entailed damnation. Anything that God justified, human law could not condemn.

Other institutions besides the churches were affected by the Great Awakening. In 1741 the president of Yale College criticized the theology of itinerant ministers. One of these promptly retorted that a Yale faculty member had no more divine grace than a chair! Other revivalists called upon the New Light churches of Connecticut to withdraw their support from Yale and endow a college of their own. The result was the College of New Jersey (now Princeton), founded in 1746 by New Side Presbyterians. Three other educational by-products of the Great Awakening followed: the College of Rhode Island (Brown), founded by Baptists in 1765; Queen's College (Rutgers), founded by Dutch Reformers in 1766; and Dartmouth, founded by New Light Congregationalists in 1769. These institutions promptly set about to refute the charge that the evangelical temperament was hostile to learning. Jonathan Edwards, the most famous native-born revivalist of the Great Awakening, was living proof that it need not be.

The Rise and Fall of Jonathan Edwards

Jonathan Edwards, though deeply pious, was passionately devoted to intellectual pursuits. But in 1725, four years after graduating from Yale, he was offered the position of assistant at his grandfather Solomon Stoddard's church in Northampton, Massachusetts. He accepted, and when Stoddard died two years later, Edwards became pastor.

During his six decades in Northampton, Stoddard had so dominated the ministers of the Connecticut Valley that some referred to him as

This Joseph Badger portrait shows a young Jonathan Edwards, probably the most famous revivalist of the Great Awakening. He is best known for his famous sermon, "Sinners in the Hands of an Angry God."

"pope." His prominence came in part from the "open enrollment" admission policy he adopted for his own church. Evidence of saving grace was neither required nor expected of members: mere good behavior sufficed. As a result, the grandson inherited a congregation whose members were possessed of an "inordinate engagedness after this world." How ready they were to meet their Maker in the next was another question.

Edwards set out to change this. When a 5-year-old girl begged her mother to take her to church so she could "hear Mr. Edwards preach," he knew he was on the right track.

For all his learning and intellectual brilliance, Edwards did not stick at dramatizing what unconverted listeners had to look forward to. The heat of Hell's consuming fires and the stench of brimstone became palpable at his rendering. In his most famous sermon, "Sinners in the Hands of an Angry God," delivered at Enfield, Connecticut, in 1741, he pulled out all the stops, depicting a "dreadfully provoked" God holding the unconverted over the pit of Hell, "much as one holds a spider, or some loathsome insect." Later, on the off chance that his listeners did not recognize themselves among the "insects" in God's hand, he declared that "this is the dismal case of every soul in this congregation that has not been born again, however moral and strict, sober and religious, they may otherwise be." A great moaning reverberated through the church. People cried out, "What must I do to be saved?"

Unfortunately for some church members, Edwards's warnings about the state of their souls caused much anxiety. One disconsolate member, Joseph Hawley, slit his throat. Edwards took the suicide calmly. "Satan seems to be in a great rage," he declared. But for some of Edwards's most prominent parishioners, Hawley's death aroused doubts. They began to miss the easy, Arminian ways of Solomon Stoddard.

Rather than soften his message, Edwards persisted and in 1749 his parishioners voted unanimously to dismiss him. He became a missionary to some Indians in Stockbridge, Massachusetts. In 1759 he was appointed president of Princeton, but he died of smallpox before he could take office.

By the early 1750s, a reaction had set in against religious "enthusiasm" in all its forms. Except in the religion-starved south, where traveling New Side Presbyterians and Baptists continued their evangelizing efforts, the Great Awakening had run its course. Whitefield's last tour of the colonies in 1754 attracted little notice.

Although it caused divisions, the Great Awakening also fostered religious toleration. If one group claimed the right to worship in its own way, how could it deny to other Protestant churches equal freedom? The Awakening was also the first truly national event in American history. It marks the time when the previously distinct histories of New England, the Middle Colonies, and the South began to intersect. Powerful links were being forged. As early as 1691 there was a rudimentary intercolonial postal system. In 1754, not long after the Awakening, the farsighted Benjamin Franklin advanced his Albany Plan for a colonial union to deal with common problems, such as defense against Indian attacks on the frontier. Thirteen once isolated colonies, expanding to the north and south as well as westward, were merging.

The Enlightenment in America

The Great Awakening pointed ahead to an America marked by religious pluralism; by the 1740s many colonists were rejecting the stern Calvinism of Jonathan Edwards in favor of a far less forbidding theology, one more in keeping with the ideas of the European Enlightenment.

The Enlightenment had an enormous impact in America. The founders of the colonies were contemporaries of the astronomer Galileo Galilei (1564–1642), the philosopher-mathematician René Descartes (1596–1650), and Sir Isaac Newton (1642–1727), the genius who revealed to the world the workings of gravity. American society developed amid the excitement generated by these great scientists. Their discoveries implied that impersonal, scientific laws governed the behavior of all matter, animate and inanimate. Earth and the heavens, human beings and the lower animals—all seemed parts of an immense, intricate machine. God had set it all in motion and remained the master technician (the divine watchmaker) overseeing it, but He took fewer and fewer occasions to interfere with its immutable operation. If human reasoning powers and direct observation of natural phenomena rather than God's

revelations provided the key to knowledge, it followed that knowledge of the laws of nature, by enabling people to understand the workings of the universe, would enable them to control their earthly destinies and to have at least a voice in their eternal destinies.

Most creative thinkers of the European Enlightenment realized that human beings were not entirely rational and that a complete understanding of the physical world was beyond their grasp. They did, however, believe that human beings were becoming more rational and would be able, by using their rational powers, to discover the laws governing the physical world. Their faith in these ideas produced the so-called Age of Reason.

Many churchgoing colonists, especially better educated ones, accepted the assumptions of the Age of Reason wholeheartedly. Some repudiated the doctrine of original sin and asserted the benevolence of God. Others came to doubt the divinity of Christ and eventually declared themselves Unitarians. Still others, among them Benjamin Franklin, embraced Deism, a faith that revered God for the marvels of His universe rather than for His power over humankind.

The impact of Enlightenment ideas went far beyond religion. The writings of John Locke and other political theorists found a receptive audience. Ideas generated in Europe often reached America with startling speed, where they were quoted in newspapers from Massachusetts to Georgia. No colonial political controversy really heated up in America until all involved had published pamphlets citing half a dozen European authorities. Radical ideas that in Europe were discussed only by an intellectual elite became almost commonplace in the colonies.

As the topics of learned discourse expanded, ministers lost their monopoly on intellectual life. By the 1750s only a minority of Harvard and Yale graduates were becoming ministers. The College of Philadelphia (later the University of Pennsylvania), founded in 1751, and King's College (later Columbia), founded in New York in 1754, added two institutions to the growing ranks of American colleges that were not primarily training grounds for clergymen. Lawyers, who first appeared in any number in colonial towns in the 1740s, swiftly asserted their intellectual authority in public affairs. Physicians and the handful of professors of natural history declared themselves better able to make sense of the new scientific discoveries than clergymen. And self-educated amateurs could also make useful contributions.

The most famous instances of popular participation occurred in Philadelphia. It was there, in 1727, that 21-year-old Benjamin Franklin founded the Junto, a club at which he and other young artisans gathered on Friday evenings to discuss "any point of morals, politics, or natural philosophy." In 1743 Franklin established an expanded version of the Junto, the American Philosophical Society, which he hoped would "cultivate the finer arts and improve the common stock of knowledge."

Colonial Scientific Achievements

America produced no Galileo or Newton, but colonists contributed significantly to the collection of scientific knowledge. The unexplored continent provided a laboratory for the study of natural phenomena. The Philadelphia Quaker, John Bartram, a "down right plain Country Man," ranged from Florida to the Great Lakes during the middle years of the 18th century, gathering and classifying hundreds of plants. Bartram also studied Indians closely, speculating about their origins and collecting information about their culture. Astronomy was another science to which 18th-century Americans were able to contribute by virtue of their distance from Europe. In 1761 Professor John Winthrop of Harvard, a descendant of the first governor of the Massachusetts Bay Colony, led a scientific expedition to Newfoundland, the only place in British North America from which the transit of the planet Venus could be observed. Another transit of Venus passed directly over several colonies in 1769. It attracted the attention of amateur astronomers from Massachusetts to Maryland. The most accurate observations were made by David Rittenhouse of Philadelphia. Thomas Jefferson later described Rittenhouse somewhat hyperbolically as "second to no astronomer living."

Jefferson was on firmer ground when he said of Benjamin Franklin that "no one of the present age has made more important discoveries." One of his biographers has called Franklin a "harmonious human multitude." His studies of electricity, which he capped in 1752 with his famous kite experiment, established him as a scientist of international stature. He also invented the lightning rod, the iron Franklin stove (a far more efficient way to heat a room than an open fireplace), bifocal spectacles, and several other ingenious devices. In addition he served 14 years (1751–1764) in the Pennsylvania assembly. He founded a circulating library and helped to get the first hospital in Philadelphia built.

Franklin wrote so much about the virtues of hard work and thrift that some historians have described him as stuffy and straitlaced. Nothing could be further from the truth. He recognized the social value of conventional behavior, but he was no slave to convention. He wrote satirical essays on such subjects as the advantage of having affairs with older and plain-looking women (who were, he claimed, more likely to appreciate the attention).

Franklin's international fame notwithstanding, the theoretical contributions of American thinkers and scientists were modest. No colony produced a Voltaire, or Gibbon, or Rousseau. Most were practical rather than speculative types, tinkerers rather than constructors of grand designs. Thomas Jefferson, for example, made no theoretical discovery of importance, but his range was almost without limit: linguist, bibliophile, political scientist, architect, inventor, scientific farmer, and—above all—apostle of reason. Involvement at even the most marginal level in the intellectual affairs of Europe gave influential New Englanders, Middle Colonists, and southerners a chance to get to know one another. Although their role in what Jefferson called "the Republic of Letters" was still minor, by midcentury their influence on the intellectual climate of the colonies was growing. That climate was one of eager curiosity, flexibility of outlook, and confidence.

Other People's Wars

The British colonies were part of a great empire that was part of a still larger world. Seemingly isolated in their remote communities, scattered like a broken string of beads between the wide Atlantic and the trackless Appalachian forests,

Americans were constantly affected by outside events both in the Old World and in the New. Under the spell of mercantilistic logic, the western European nations competed fiercely for markets and colonial raw materials. War—hot and cold, declared and undeclared—was almost a permanent condition of 17th- and 18th-century life, and when the powers clashed, they fought wherever they could get at one another, in America, in Europe, and elsewhere.

Although the American colonies were minor pieces in the game and were sometimes casually exchanged or sacrificed by the masterminds in London, Paris, and Madrid in pursuit of some supposedly more important objective, the colonists quickly generated their own international animosities. North America, a huge and, compared to densely populated Europe, an almost empty stage, evidently did not provide enough room for French, Dutch, Spanish, and English companies to perform. Frenchmen and Spaniards clashed savagely in Florida as early as the 16th century. Before the landing of the Pilgrims, Samuel Argall of Virginia was sacking French settlements in Maine and carrying off Jesuit priests into captivity at Jamestown. Instead of fostering tranquility and generosity, the abundance of America seemed to make the settlers belligerent and greedy.

The North Atlantic fisheries quickly became a source of trouble between Canadian and New England colonists, despite the fact that the waters of the Grand Banks teemed with cod and other fish. To dry and salt their catch, the fishermen needed land bases, and French and English Americans struggled constantly to possess the harbors of Maine, Nova Scotia, and Newfoundland.

Even more troublesome was the fur trade. The yield of the forest was easily exhausted by indiscriminate slaughter, and traders contended bitterly to control valuable hunting grounds. The French in Canada conducted their fur trading through tribes such as the Algonquins and the Hurons. This brought them into conflict with the Five Nations, the powerful Iroquois Confederation in central New York. As early as 1609, the Five Nations were at war with the French and their Indian allies. For decades this struggle flared sporadically, the Iroquois more than holding their own both as fighters and as traders. They combined, according to one terrified Frenchman, the stealth and craftiness of the fox, the ferocity and

courage of the lion, and the speed of a bird in flight. They brought quantities of beaver pelts to the Dutch at Albany, some obtained by their own trappers, others taken by ambushing the fur-laden canoes of their enemies. They preyed on and ultimately destroyed the Hurons in the land north of Lake Ontario and dickered with Indian trappers in far-off Michigan. When the English took over the New Amsterdam colony, they eagerly adopted the Iroquois as allies, buying their furs and supplying them with trading goods and guns. In the final showdown for control of North America, the friendship of the Iroquois was vitally important to the English.

By the last decade of the 17th century, it had become clear that the Dutch lacked the strength to maintain a big empire and that Spain was fast declining. The future, especially in North America, belonged to England and France. In the wars of the next 125 years, European alliances shifted dramatically, yet the English and what the Boston lawyer John Adams called "the turbulent Gallicks" were always on opposite sides.

These conflicts did not directly involve any considerable portion of the colonial populace, but they served to increase the bad feelings between settlers north and south of the St. Lawrence. Every Indian raid was attributed to French provocateurs, although more often than not the English colonists were responsible for the Indian troubles. Conflicting land claims further aggravated the situation. Massachusetts, Connecticut, and Virginia possessed overlapping claims to the Ohio Valley, and Pennsylvania and New York also had pretensions in the region. Yet the French, ranging broadly across the midcontinent, insisted that the Ohio country was exclusively theirs.

The Great War for the Empire

In this beautiful, almost untouched land, a handful of individuals determined the future of the continent. Over the years, the French had established a chain of forts and trading posts throughout the northwest. By the 1740s, however, Pennsylvania fur traders, led by George Croghan, a rugged Irishman, were setting up posts north of the Ohio River and dickering with Miami and Huron Indians who ordinarily sold their furs to the French. In 1748 Croghan built a fort at Pickawillany, deep in the Miami country, in what is now western Ohio. That same year agents of a group of Virginia land speculators, who had recently organized what they called the Ohio Company, reached this area.

With trifling exceptions, an insulating band of wilderness had always separated the French and English in America. Now the two powers came into contact. The immediate result was a showdown battle for control of North America, the "great war for the empire." Thoroughly alarmed by the presence of the English on land they had long considered their own, the French struck hard. Attacking suddenly in 1752, they wiped out Croghan's post at Pickawillany and drove his traders back into Pennsylvania. Then they built a string of barrier forts south from Lake Erie along the Pennsylvania line: Fort Presque Isle, Fort Le Boeuf, and Fort Venango. The Pennsylvania authorities chose to ignore this action, but Lieutenant Governor Robert Dinwiddie of Virginia (who was an investor in the Ohio Company) dispatched a 21-year-old surveyor named George Washington to warn the French that they were trespassing on Virginia territory.

Washington, a gangling, inarticulate, and intensely ambitious young planter, made his way northwest in the fall of 1753 and delivered Dinwiddie's message to the commandant at Fort Le Boeuf. It made no impression. "[The French] told me," Washington reported, "That it was their absolute Design to take Possession of the Ohio, and by G— they would do it." Governor Dinwiddie thereupon promoted Washington to lieutenant colonel and sent him back in the spring of 1754 with 150 men to seize a strategic junction south of the new French forts, where the Allegheny and Monongahela rivers join to form the Ohio.

Eager but inexperienced in battle, young Washington botched his assignment. As his force labored painfully through the tangled mountain country southeast of the fork of the Ohio, he received word that the French had already occupied the position and were constructing a powerful post, Fort Duquesne. Outnumbered by perhaps four to one, Washington foolishly pushed on. He surprised and routed a French reconnaissance party, but this brought upon him the main body of enemy troops.

Hastily he threw up a defensive position, aptly named Fort Necessity, but the ground was ill chosen; the French easily surrounded the fort and Washington had to surrender. After tricking the young officer, who could not read French, into signing an admission that he had "assassinated" the leader of the reconnaissance party, his captors, with the gateway to the Ohio country firmly in their hands, permitted him and his men to march off. Nevertheless, Washington returned to Virginia a hero, for although still undeclared, this was war, and he had struck the first blow against the hated French.

In the resulting conflict, which historians call the French and Indian War (the colonists simply "the French War"), the English outnumbered the French by about 1.5 million to 90,000. But the English were divided and disorganized, the French disciplined and united. The French controlled the disputed territory, and most of the Indians took their side. With an ignorance and arrogance typical of 18th-century colonial administration, the British mismanaged the war and failed to make effective use of local resources. For several years they stumbled from one defeat to another.

General Edward Braddock, a competent but uninspired soldier, was dispatched to Virginia to take command. In June 1755 he marched against Fort Duquesne with 1,400 Redcoats and a smaller number of colonials, only to be decisively defeated by a much smaller force of French and Indians.

Elsewhere Anglo-American troops fared little better in the early years of the war. Expeditions against Fort Niagara, key to all French defenses in the west, and Crown Point, gateway to Montreal, bogged down. Meanwhile Indians armed by the French bathed the frontier in blood. Venting the frustrations caused by 150 years of white advance, they attacked defenseless outposts with unrestrained brutality. They poured molten lead into their victims' wounds, ripped off the fingernails of captives, even drank the blood of those who endured their tortures stoically.

In 1756 the conflict spread to Europe to become the Seven Years' War. Prussia sided with Great Britain, Austria with the French. On the world stage too, things went badly for the British. Finally, in 1758, as defeat succeeded defeat, King George II was forced to allow William Pitt, whom he detested, to take over leadership of the war effort.

Pitt recognized, as few contemporaries did, the potential value of North America. Instead of relying on the tightfisted and shortsighted colonial assemblies for men and money, he poured regiment after regiment of British regulars and the full resources of the British Treasury into the contest, mortgaging the future recklessly to secure the prize. Grasping the importance of sea power in fighting a war on the other side of the Atlantic, he used the British navy to bottle up the enemy fleet and hamper French communications with Canada. He possessed a keen eye for military genius, and when he discovered it, he ignored seniority and the outraged feelings of mediocre generals and promoted talented young officers to top commands. His greatest find was James Wolfe, whom he made a brigadier at 31.

In the winter of 1758, as Pitt's grand strategy matured, Fort Duquesne fell. It was appropriately renamed Fort Pitt, the present Pittsburgh. The following summer Fort Niagara was overrun. General Jeffrey Amherst took Crown Point, and Wolfe sailed up the St. Lawrence to Quebec. There the French General, Louis Joseph de Montcalm, had prepared formidable defenses. But after months of probing and planning Wolfe found and exploited a chink in the city's armor and captured it. Both he and Montcalm died in the battle. In 1760 Montreal fell and the French abandoned all Canada to the British. Spain attempted to stem the British advance but failed utterly. A Far Eastern fleet captured Manila in 1762, and another British force took Cuba. The French sugar islands in the West Indies were also captured, while in India British troops reduced the French posts one by one.

The Peace of Paris

Peace was restored in 1763 by the Treaty of Paris. Its terms were moderate considering the extent of the British triumph. France abandoned all claim to North America except two small islands near Newfoundland; Great Britain took over Canada and the eastern half of the Mississippi Valley, Spain (in a separate treaty) the area west of the great river and New Orleans. Guadeloupe and Martinique, the French sugar islands, were re-

Pitt's Strategy, French and Indian War, 1758–1760

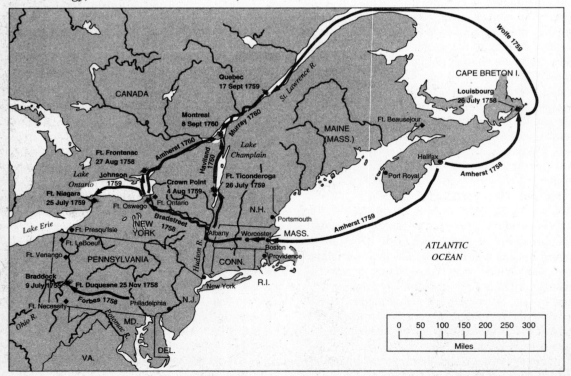

turned by the British, as were some of the captured French bases in India and Africa. Spain got back both the Philippine Islands and Cuba; in exchange the Spanish ceded East and West Florida to Great Britain. France and Spain thus remained important colonial powers.

"Half the continent," the historian Francis Parkman wrote, "had changed hands at the scratch of a pen." From the point of view of the English colonists in America, the victory was overwhelming. All threat to their frontiers seemed to have been swept away. Surely, they believed in the first happy moments of victory, their peaceful and prosperous expansion was assured for countless generations.

No honest American could deny that the victory had been won chiefly by British troops and with British gold. Colonial militiamen fought well in defense of their homes or when some highly prized objective seemed ripe for the plucking. They lacked discipline and determination when required to fight far from home and under commanders they did not know. Little wonder that the great victory produced a burst of praise for king and mother country throughout America. Parades, cannonading, fireworks, banquets, the pealing of churchbells—these were the order of the day in every colonial town. "Nothing," said Thomas Pownall, wartime governor of Massachusetts and a student of colonial administration, "can eradicate from [the colonists'] hearts their natural, almost mechanical affection to Great Britain." A young South Carolinian who had been educated in England claimed that the colonists were "more wrapped up in a king" than any people he had ever heard of.

Putting the Empire Right

In London peace proved a time for reassessment; that the empire of 1763 was not the same as the empire of 1754 was obvious. The new, far larger dominion would be much more expensive to maintain. Pitt had spent a huge sum winning and securing it, much of it borrowed money. Great Britain's national debt had doubled between 1754 and 1763. Now this debt had to be serviced and repaid, and the strain that this would place on the economy was clear to all. Furthermore, the day-to-day cost of administering an empire that extended

from Hudson Bay to India was far larger than that which the already burdened British taxpayer could be expected to bear. Before the great war for the empire, Britain's North American possessions were administered for about £70,000 a year; after 1763 the cost was five times as much.

The American empire had also grown far more complex. A system of administration that treated it as a string of separate plantations struggling to exist on the edge of the forest would no longer suffice. The war had been fought for control of the Ohio Valley. Now that the prize had been secured, ten thousand hands were eager to secure it. How best could their needs be satisfied now that peace had come? Colonial claims, based on charters drafted by men who thought the Pacific lay over the next hill, threatened to make the great valley a battleground once more. The Indians remained unpacified. Rival land companies contested for charters, while fur traders strove to hold back the wave of settlement that must inevitably destroy the world of the beaver and the deer. One Englishman who traveled through America at this time predicted that if the colonists were left to their own devices "there would soon be civil war from one end of the continent to the other."

Apparently only Great Britain could deal with these problems and rivalries, for when Franklin had proposed a rudimentary form of colonial union—the Albany Plan of 1754—it was rejected by almost everyone. Unfortunately, the British government did not rise to the challenge. Perhaps this was to be expected. A handful of aristocrats (fewer than 150 peers were active in government affairs) dominated British politics. Even the best educated English leaders were nearly all monumentally ignorant of American conditions. The British imperial system lacked effective channels of communication. Information about American attitudes came from royal officials in the colonies and others with special interests to protect or advance, or from the colonial agents and merchants in London, whose information was often out of date. Serene in their ignorance, most English leaders insisted that colonials were uncouth and generally inferior beings. During the French and Indian War, General Wolfe characterized colonial troops as "the dirtiest, most contemptible cowardly dogs you can conceive." The Britishers failed to understand that colonial soldiers were volunteers who had formally contracted to serve under specific conditions. Lord John Loudoun, the British commander in chief during the French War, was flabbergasted to discover that New England troops refused to obey one of his direct orders on the ground that it violated their contracts. Little wonder that any officer with a royal commission outranked all officers of the colonial militia, regardless of title.

Many English people resented Americans simply because the colonies were rapidly becoming rich and powerful. They were growing at an extraordinary rate. Between 1750 and 1770 the population of British America increased from 1 million to more than 2 million. As early as 1751, Benjamin Franklin predicted that in a century "the greatest number of Englishmen will be on this Side of the Water." (His guess was on the mark: In 1850 the population of the United States was 23.1 million, that of Great Britain about 20.8 million.) If the English did not say much about this possibility, they too considered it from time to time—without Franklin's complacency.

Tightening Imperial Controls

The attempt of the British to deal with the intricate colonial problems that resulted from the great war for the empire led to the American Revolution—a rebellion that was costly, but which produced excellent results for the colonists, for Great Britain, for the rest of the empire, and eventually for the entire world. Trouble began when the British decided after the war to intervene more actively in American affairs. Parliament had never attempted to raise revenue in America." "Compelling the colonies to pay money without their consent would be rather like raising contributions in an enemy's country than taxing Englishmen for their own benefit," Benjamin Franklin wrote. Nevertheless, the *legality* of parliamentary taxation, or of other parliamentary intervention in colonial affairs, had not been seriously contested.

In 1759 a general tightening of imperial regulations began. Royal control over colonial courts was strengthened. In Massachusetts the use of general search warrants (writs of assistance) was authorized in 1761. These writs authorized customs officers searching for smuggled goods to en-

ter homes and warehouses without evidence or specific court orders. Nearly all Americans resented the invasions of privacy that the writs caused. A Boston lawyer, James Otis, argued in a case involving 63 merchants that the writs were "against the Constitution" and therefore "void." Otis lost the case, but by boldly suggesting that Parliament's authority over the colonies was not absolute, he became a colonial hero.

After the signing of the peace treaty in 1763, events pushed the British authorities to still more vigorous activity in America. Freed of the restraint imposed by French competition, Englishman and colonist increased their pressure on the Indians. Fur traders now cheated them outrageously, while callous military men hoped to exterminate them like vermin. One British officer expressed the wish that they could be hunted down with dogs.

Led by an Ottawa chief named Pontiac, the tribes made one last effort to drive the whites back across the mountains. What the whites called Pontiac's Rebellion caused much havoc, but it failed. By 1764 most of the western tribes had accepted the peace terms offered by a royal commissioner, Sir William Johnson, one of the few

Eastern North America, 1763

whites who understood and sympathized with them. The British government then placed 15 regiments, some 6,000 soldiers, in posts along the frontier, as much to protect the Indians from the settlers as the settlers from the Indians. It proclaimed a new western policy: no settlers were to cross the Appalachian divide. Only licensed traders might do business with the Indians beyond that line. The purchase of Indian land was forbidden. In compensation, three new colonies—Quebec, East Florida, and West Florida—were created, but they were not permitted to set up local assemblies.

This Proclamation of 1763 excited much indignation in America. The frustration of dozens of schemes for land development in the Ohio Valley angered many influential colonists.

The Sugar Act

Americans disliked the new western policy but realized that the problems were knotty and that no simple solution existed. Their protests were somewhat muted. Great Britain's effort to raise money in America to help support the increased cost of colonial administration caused far more vehement complaints. George Grenville, who became prime minister in 1763, was a fairly able man, although long-winded and rather narrow in outlook. His reputation as a financial expert was based chiefly on his eagerness to reduce government spending. Under his leadership Parliament passed, in April 1764, the so-called Sugar Act. This law placed tariffs on sugar, coffee, wines, and other things imported into America in substantial amounts. Taxes on European products imported by way of Great Britain were doubled, and the enumerated articles list was extended to include iron, raw silk, and potash. The sixpence-per-gallon tax on foreign molasses, imposed in 1733 and designed to be prohibitively high, was reduced to threepence, at which level the foreign product could compete with molasses from the British West Indies.

At the same time, measures aimed at enforcing all the trade laws were put into effect. (A three-penny molasses duty would not produce much revenue if it were as easy to avoid as the old levy had been.) Those accused of violating the Sugar Act were to be tried before British naval officers in vice-admiralty courts. Grenville was determined to end smuggling, corruption, and inefficiency. Soon income from import duties soared.

The Sugar Act came at a bad time. During the war the seaports prospered. Shipbuilding boomed. Merchants earned fat profits supplying British troops with food and other goods. British soldiers and sailors spent most of their wages in the colonies. But when the fighting shifted to the Caribbean after the fall of Canada, most of this spending stopped. The soldiers "are gone to drink [rum] in a warmer Region, the place of its production," a New York merchant mourned. A depression increased the impact of the new laws. Hard-hit merchants and artisans found British policy alarming.

Few Americans were willing to concede that Parliament had the right to tax them. As *Englishmen*, they believed that no one should be deprived arbitrarily of his property and that, as James Otis put it in his stirring pamphlet *The Rights of the British Colonies Asserted and Proved* (1764), everyone should be "free from all taxes but what he consents to in person, or by his representative." The philosopher John Locke had made clear in his *Second Treatise of Government* (1690) that property ought never be taken from people without their consent, not because material values transcend all others, but because human liberty can never be secure when arbitrary power of any kind exists. "If our Trade may be taxed why not our Lands?" the Boston town meeting asked when news of the Sugar Act reached America. "Why not the produce of our Lands and every Thing we possess or make use of?"

"Essential Rights and Liberties"

To most people in Great Britain the colonial protest against taxation without representation seemed a hypocritical quibble (and it is probably true that many protesters had not thought the argument through). The distinction between tax laws and other types of legislation was artificial, the British reasoned. Either Parliament was sovereign in America or it was not, and only a fool or a traitor would argue that it was not. If the colonists were loyal subjects of George III, as they claimed, they should bear cheerfully their fair share of the cost of governing his widespread dominions. As to representation, the colonies *were* represented in Parliament; every member of that body stood for the interests of the entire empire. If Americans had no say in the election of members of Commons, neither did most Englishmen.

This concept of "virtual" representation accurately described the British system. It made no sense in America, where from the time of the first settlements members of the colonial assemblies had represented the people of the districts in which they stood for office. The confusion between virtual and geographically based representation revealed the extent to which colonial and British political practices had diverged over the years.

The British were correct in concluding that selfish motives influenced colonial objections to the Sugar Act. The colonists denounced taxation without representation, but they would have rejected the offer of a reasonable number of seats in Parliament if it had been made, and they would probably have complained about paying taxes to support imperial administration even if imposed by their own assemblies. American abundance and the simplicity of colonial life had enabled them to prosper without assuming any considerable tax burden. Now their maturing society was beginning to require communal rather than individual solutions to the problems of existence. Not many of them were prepared to face up to this hard truth.

Over the course of colonial history, Americans had taken a narrow view of imperial concerns. They had avoided complying with the Navigation Acts whenever they could profit by doing so. Colonial militiamen had compiled a sorry record when asked to fight for Britain or even for the inhabitants of colonies other than their own. True, most Americans professed loyalty to the Crown, but not many would voluntarily open their purses except to benefit themselves. In short, they were provincials, in attitude and in fact.

But the colonists were opposed in principle to taxation without representation. They failed, however, to agree on a common plan of resistance. Many of the assemblies drafted protests, but these varied in force as well as in form. Merchant groups that tried to organize boycotts of products subject to the new taxes met with indifferent success. Then, in 1765, Parliament provided the flux necessary for welding colonial opinion by passing the Stamp Act.

The Stamp Act: The Pot Set Boiling

The Stamp Act placed stiff excise taxes on all kinds of printed matter—newspapers, legal documents, licenses, even playing cards. Stamp duties were intended to be relatively painless to pay and cheap to collect; in England similar taxes brought in about £100,000 annually. Grenville hoped the Stamp Act would produce £60,000 a year in America, and the law provided that all revenue should be applied to "defraying the necessary expenses of defending, protecting, and securing, the . . . colonies."

Hardly a farthing was collected. The Sugar Act had been related to Parliament's uncontested power to control colonial trade, but the Stamp Act was a direct tax. When Parliament ignored the politely phrased petitions of the colonial assemblies, more vigorous protests quickly followed. Virginia took the lead. In late May of 1765, Patrick Henry introduced resolutions asserting redundantly that the burgesses possessed "the only and sole and exclusive right and power to lay taxes" on Virginians and suggesting that Parliament had no legal authority to tax the colonies at all. The more extreme of his resolutions failed of enactment, but the debate they occasioned attracted wide and favorable attention. On June 6, 1765, the Massachusetts assembly proposed an intercolonial Stamp Act Congress, which, when it met in New York City in October, passed another series of resolutions of protest. The Stamp Act was "burthensome and grievous," the delegates declared. People should not be taxed without "their own consent."

During the summer irregular organizations known as Sons of Liberty began to agitate against the act. Far more than anyone realized, this marked the start of the revolution. For the first time extra-legal organized resistance was taking place. Although led by men of character and position, the "Liberty Boys" frequently resorted to violence to achieve their aims. In Boston they looted the houses of the stamp master and his brother-in-law, Lieutenant Governor Thomas Hutchinson. In Connecticut stamp master Jared Ingersoll, faced an angry mob demanding his resignation. When threatened with death if he refused, he coolly replied that he was prepared to die "perhaps as well now as another Time." Probably his life was not really in danger, but the crowd convinced him that resistance was useless, and he capitulated.

The fate of most of the other stamp masters was little different. For a time no business requiring stamped paper was transacted; then, gradually, people began to defy the law by issuing and accepting unstamped documents. Threatened by mob action should they resist, British officials stood by helplessly. The law was a dead letter.

The looting associated with this crisis alarmed many colonists, including some prominent opponents of the Stamp Act. "When the pot is set to boil," the lawyer John Adams remarked, "the scum rises to the top." This does not mean that people like Adams disapproved of crowd protests or even the destruction of property. What Adams called "state-quakes" were similar in his opinion to earthquakes, a kind of natural violence.

Rioters or Rebels?

In many cases the rioting had a social as well as a political character. Times were hard and once roused, laborers and artisans may well have directed their energies toward righting what they considered local wrongs.

Yet the mass of the people were not social revolutionaries. They might envy and resent the wealthy landowners and merchants, but there is no evidence that they wished to overthrow the established order.

The British were not surprised that Americans disliked the Stamp Act. They had not, however, anticipated that they would react so violently and so unanimously. Americans did so for many reasons. Business continued to be poor in 1765, and at a time when 3 shillings was a day's wage for an urban laborer, the stamp tax was 2 shillings for an advertisement in a newspaper, 5 shillings for a will, and 20 shillings for a license to sell liquor. The taxes would also hurt the business of lawyers, merchants, newspaper editors, and tavernkeepers. Even clergymen dealt with papers requiring

stamps. The protests of such influential and articulate people had powerful impact on public opinion.

The greatest cause of concern to the colonists was Great Britain's flat rejection of the principle of no taxation without representation. This alarmed them because *as Americans* they objected to being taxed by a legeslative body they had not been involved in choosing. To buy a stamp was to surrender all claim to self-government. Furthermore, as *British subjects* they valued what they called "the rights of Englishmen." They saw the Stamp Act as only the worst in a series of arbitrary invasions of these rights.

Already Parliament had passed another measure, the Quartering Act, requiring local legislatures to house and feed new British troops sent to the colonies. Besides being a form of indirect taxation, a standing army seemed a threat to liberty. Why were Redcoats necessary in Boston and New York where there was no foreign enemy for miles around? In hard times, soldiers were particularly unwelcome because being miserably underpaid, they took any job they could get in their off hours, thus competing with unemployed colonists.

Reluctantly, many Americans were beginning to fear that the London authorities had organized a conspiracy to subvert the liberties of all British subjects.

Taxation or Tyranny?

There was no such conspiracy; yet to the question, Were American rights actually in danger? no certain answer can be made. Grenville and his successors were English politicians, not tyrants. They looked down on bumptious colonials but surely had no wish to destroy either them or their prosperity. The British attitude was like that of a parent making a recalcitrant youngster swallow a bitter medicine: Protests were understandable, but in the patient's own interest they must be ignored.

At the same time, British leaders felt challenged to assert royal authority and centralize imperial power at the expense of colonial autonomy. The need to maintain a substantial British army in America to control the western Indians tempted the government to use some of the troops to "control" white Americans as well. This attitude flew in the face of the fact that the colonies were no longer entirely dependent on "the mother country." Indeed, many colonists believed that America would soon become what Franklin called "a great country, populous and mighty . . . able to shake off any shackles that may be imposed on her." This view of the future surely meant dealing with Great Britain on terms approaching equality. But psychologically, British leaders were not ready to deal with Americans as equals or to consider American interests on a par with their own. In the long run, American liberty would be destroyed if this attitude was not changed.

Besides refusing to use stamps, Americans responded to the Stamp Act by boycotting British goods. Nearly 1,000 merchants signed nonimportation agreements. These struck British merchants hard in their pocketbooks, and they in turn began to bring pressure on Parliament for repeal. After a hot debate the hated law was repealed in March 1766. In America there was jubilation at the news, and the ban on British goods was lifted and the colonists congratulated themselves on having stood fast in defense of principle.

The Declaratory Act

The great controversy over the constitutional relationship of colony to mother country was only beginning. The same day that it repealed the Stamp Act, Parliament passed a Declaratory Act stating that the colonies were "subordinate" and that Parliament could enact any law it wished "to bind the colonies and people of *America*."

To most Americans this bold statement of parliamentary authority seemed unconstitutional—a flagrant violation of their conception of how the British imperial system worked. Actually, the Declaratory Act highlighted the degree to which British and American views of the system had drifted apart. The parties were using the same words but giving them different meanings. Their conflicting definitions of the word *representation* was a case in point. Another involved the word *constitution*. To the British, the constitution meant the totality of laws, customs, and institutions that had developed over time and under which the nation functioned. In America, partly because governments were based on specific charters, the same word meant a written document or contract

spelling out, and thus limiting, the powers of government. If in England Parliament passed an "unconstitutional" law, the result might be rebellion, but that the law existed none would deny." "If the parliament will positively enact a thing to be done which is unreasonable," the great 18th-century English legal authority Sir William Blackstone wrote, "I know of no power that can control it." In America people were beginning to think that an unconstitutional law simply had no force.

Even more basic were the differing meanings that English and Americans were giving to the word *sovereignty*. As Bernard Bailyn has explained in *The Ideological Origins of the American Revolution,* 18th-century English political thinkers believed that sovereignty (ultimate political power) could not be divided. Government and law being based ultimately on force, some "final, unqualified, indivisible" authority had to exist if social order were to be preserved. The Glorious Revolution in England had settled the question of where sovereignty resided—in Parliament. The Declaratory Act, so obnoxious to Americans, seemed to the English the mere explication of the obvious.

Given these ideas and the long tradition out of which they had sprung, one can sympathize with the British failure to follow the colonists' reasoning (which had not yet evolved into a specific proposal for constitutional reform). But most responsible British officials refused even to listen to the American argument.

The Townshend Duties

Despite the repeal of the Stamp Act, the British did not abandon the policy of taxing the colonies. If direct taxes were inexpedient, indirect ones like the Sugar Act certainly were not. The government was hard pressed for funds to cover an annual budget of over £8.5 million. Therefore, in June 1767, the chancellor of the exchequer, Charles Townshend, introduced a series of levies on glass, lead, paints, paper, and tea imported into the colonies. Townshend was a charming man experienced in colonial administration, but he was something of a playboy (his nickname was Champagne Charlie), and he lacked both integrity and common sense. He liked to think of Americans as ungrateful children; he once said he would rather see the colonies turned into "Primitive Desarts" than treat them as equals. Townshend thought it "perfect nonsense" to draw a distinction between direct and indirect taxation, yet in his arrogance he believed the colonists were stupid enough to do so.

By this time the colonists were thoroughly on guard, and they responded quickly to the Townshend levies with a new boycott of British goods. In addition they made elaborate efforts to stimulate colonial manufacturing. By the end of 1769 imports from the mother country had been almost halved. Meanwhile, administrative measures enacted along with the Townshend duties were creating more ill will. A Board of Customs Commissioners, with headquarters in Boston, took charge of enforcing the trade laws, and new vice-admiralty courts were set up to handle violations. These courts operated without juries, and many colonists considered the new commissioners rapacious racketeers who systematically attempted to obtain judgments against honest merchants in order to collect the huge forfeitures—one-third of the value of ship and cargo—that were their share of all seizures.

The struggle forced Americans to do some deep thinking about both American and imperial political affairs. In 1765 the Stamp Act Congress (another extralegal organization) had brought the delegates of nine colonies to New York. Now, in 1768, the Massachusetts General Court took the next step. It sent the legislatures of the other colonies a "Circular Letter" expressing the "humble opinion" of the people that the Townshend Acts were "Infringements of their natural & constitutional Rights." The limit of British power in America was much debated, and this too was no doubt inevitable, again because of change and growth. As the colonies matured, the balance of Anglo-American power *had* to shift or the system would become tyrannical. Even in the late 17th century the assumptions that led Parliament to pass the Declaratory Act would have been unrealistic. In 1766 they were absurd.

After the passage of the Townshend Acts, John Dickinson, a Philadelphia lawyer, published *Letters from a Farmer in Pennsylvania to the Inhabitants of the British Colonies*. Dickinson considered himself a loyal British subject. "Let us behave like dutiful children, who have received unmerited blows from a beloved parent," he wrote. Nevertheless, he insisted that although Parliament was sovereign and might collect inci-

dental revenues in the process of regulating commerce, it had no right to tax the colonies. Another moderate Philadelphian, John Raynell, put it this way: "If the Americans are to be taxed by a Parliament where they are not . . . Represented, they are no longer Englishmen but Slaves."

Some Americans were far more radical than Dickinson. Samuel Adams of Boston, a genuine revolutionary agitator, believed by 1768 that Parliament had no right at all to legislate for the colonies. If few were ready to go that far, fewer still accepted the reasoning behind the Declaratory Act.

The British ignored American thinking. When news of the Massachusetts Circular Letter reached England, the secretary of state for the colonies, Lord Wills Hillsborough, ordered the governor to dissolve the legislature. Two regiments of British troops were transferred from the frontier to Boston, part of a general plan to bring the army closer to the centers of colonial unrest.

The Boston Massacre

These acts convinced more Americans that the British were conspiring to destroy their liberties. Resentment was particularly strong in Boston, where the postwar depression had come on top of twenty years of economic stagnation. Crowding 4,000 British soldiers into a town of 16,000 people was a formula for trouble and on March 5, 1770, trouble erupted. Late that afternoon a crowd of idlers began tossing snowballs at Redcoats guarding the Custom House. Some of these missiles had been carefully wrapped around suitably sized rocks. Gradually the crowd grew larger, its mood meaner. The soldiers panicked and began firing their muskets. When the smoke cleared, five Bostonians lay dead or dying on the bloody ground.

This so-called Boston Massacre played into the hands of radicals like Samuel Adams. But cooler heads again prevailed. Announcing that he was "defending the rights of man and unconquerable truth," John Adams volunteered his services to make sure the soldiers got a fair trial. Most were acquitted, the rest treated leniently by the standards of the day. In Great Britain, confrontation also gave way to adjustment. In April 1770 all the Townshend duties except the threepenny tax

Paul Revere's engraving of the Boston Massacre, which shows British Redcoats firing on unarmed citizens, fanned colonial outrage over the incident.

on tea were repealed. The tea tax was maintained as a matter of principle. "A peppercorn in acknowledgment of the right was of more value than millions without it," one British peer declared smugly—a glib fallacy. At this point the nonimportation movement collapsed; although the boycott on tea was continued, many merchants imported British tea and paid the tax too. During the next two years no serious crisis erupted. Imports of British goods were nearly 50 percent higher than before the nonimportation agreement.

In 1772 new troubles broke out. The first was plainly the fault of the colonists involved. Early in June the British patrol boat *Gaspee* ran aground in Narragansett Bay, south of Providence, while pursuing a suspected smuggler. That night a gang of local people boarded the helpless *Gaspee* and put it to the torch. Then Thomas Hutchinson, now governor of Massachusetts, suddenly announced that henceforth the Crown rather than the local legislature would pay his salary. Since control over the salaries of royal officials gave the legislature a powerful hold on them, this development was disturbing. Groups of radicals formed "com-

mittees of correspondence," and stepped up communications with one another, planning joint action in case of trouble. This was another monumental step toward revolution; a resistance movement lacking in "legitimate" authority, but ready to act in the name of the public interest, was taking shape.

The Tea Act Crisis

In the spring of 1773 an entirely unrelated event precipitated the final crisis. The British East India Company held a monopoly of all trade between India and the rest of the empire. This monopoly had yielded fabulous returns, but decades of corruption and inefficiency together with heavy military expenses in recent years had weakened the company until it was almost bankrupt.

Among the assets of this venerable institution were some 17 million pounds of tea stored in English warehouses. Normally, East India Company tea was sold to English wholesalers. They in turn sold it to American wholesalers, who distributed it to local merchants for sale to the consumer. A substantial British tax was levied on the tea as well as the threepenny Townshend duty. Now Lord Frederick North, the new prime minister, decided to remit the British tax and to allow the company to sell directly in America through its own agents. The savings would permit a sharp reduction of the retail price and at the same time yield a nice profit to the company. The Townshend tax was retained, however, to preserve (as Lord North said when the East India Company directors suggested its repeal) the principle of Parliament's right to tax the colonies.

The company then shipped 1,700 chests of tea to colonial ports. Though the idea of buying this high-quality tea at bargain prices was tempting, after a little thought nearly everyone in America appreciated the grave dangers involved in buying it. If Parliament could grant the East India Company a monopoly of the tea trade, it could parcel out all or any part of American commerce to whomever it pleased.

Public indignation was so great in New York and Philadelphia that when the tea ships arrived, the authorities ordered them back to England without attempting to unload. The situation in

Boston was different. The tea ship *Dartmouth* arrived on November 27. The radicals, marshaled by Sam Adams, were determined to prevent it from landing its cargo; Governor Hutchinson was equally determined to collect the tax and enforce the law. For days the town seethed, while the *Dartmouth* and two later arrivals swung with the tides on their moorings. Then, on the night of December 16, a band of colonists disguised as Indians rowed out to the ships and dumped the hated tea chests in the harbor.

The destruction of the tea was a serious crime for which many persons, aside from the painted "Patriots" who jettisoned the chests, were responsible. The British burned with indignation when news of the "Tea Party" reached London. People talked (fortunately it was only talk) of flattening Boston with heavy artillery. Nearly everyone agreed that the colonists must be taught a lesson. George III himself said: "We must master them or totally leave them to themselves."

From Resistance to Revolution

Parliament responded in the spring of 1774 by passing the Coercive Acts. The Boston Port Act closed the harbor of Boston to all commerce until its citizens paid for the tea. The Administration of Justice Act provided for the transfer of cases to courts outside Massachusetts when the governor felt that an impartial trial could not be had within the colony. The Massachusetts Government Act revised the colony's charter drastically, strengthening the power of the governor, weakening that of the local town meetings, making the council appointive rather than elective, and changing the method by which juries were selected. These were unwise laws—they cost Great Britain an empire. All of them, and especially the Port Act, were unjust laws as well. Parliament was punishing the community for the crimes of individuals, abandoning persuasion and conciliation in favor of coercion and punishment.

The Americans named the Coercive Acts (together with a new Quartering Act and the Quebec Act, an unrelated measure that attached the area north of the Ohio River to Canada and gave the region an authoritarian, centralized government) the "Intolerable" Acts. That the British answer to

the crisis was coercion the Americans found unendurable. The American Revolution had begun.

In the course of a decade the people of the colonies, loyal subjects of Great Britain, had been forced by new British policies to take power into their own hands and to unite in order to exercise that power effectively. Ordinary working people, not just merchants, lawyers, and other well-to-do people, played increasingly more prominent roles in public life as crisis after crisis roused their indignation. This did not yet mean that most Americans wanted to be free from British rule. Parliament, however—and in the last analysis George III and most Britons—insisted that their authority over the colonies was unlimited. Behind their stubbornness lay the arrogant psychology of the European: "Colonists are inferior. . . . We own you."

Lord North directed the Coercive Acts only at Massachusetts, but the colonies began at once to act in concert. In June 1774 Massachusetts called for a meeting of delegates from all the colonies to consider common action. This First Continental Congress met at Philadelphia in September; only Georgia failed to send delegates. Many points of view were represented, but even the so-called conservative proposal introduced by Joseph Galloway of Pennsylvania, called for a thorough overhaul of the empire. Galloway suggested an *American* government, consisting of a president general appointed by the king and a grand council chosen by the colonial assemblies that would manage intercolonial affairs and possess a veto over parliamentary acts affecting the colonies.

This was not what the majority wanted. If taxation without representation was tyranny, so was all legislation. Therefore Parliament had no right to legislate in any way for the colonies. John Adams, although prepared to *allow* Parliament to regulate colonial trade, now believed that Parliament had no inherent right to control it.

Propelled by the reasoning of Adams and others, the Congress passed a declaration of grievances and resolves that amounted to a complete condemnation of Britain's actions since 1763. A Massachusetts proposal that the people take up arms to defend their rights was endorsed. The delegates also organized a "Continental Association" to boycott British goods and to stop all exports to the empire. To enforce this boycott, committees were appointed locally "to observe the conduct of all persons touching this association" and to expose violators to public scorn.

If the Continental Congress reflected the views of the majority—there is no reason to suspect that it did not—it is clear that the Americans had decided that drastic changes must be made. It was not merely a question of mutual defense against the threat of British power, not only, in Franklin's aphorism, a matter of hanging together lest they hang separately. A nation was being born.

Looking back many years later, one of the delegates to the First Continental Congress made just these points. He was John Adams of Massachusetts, and he said: "The revolution was complete, in the minds of the people, and the Union of the colonies, before the war commenced."

Milestones

1650–1696	Navigation Acts enacted by Parliament	1760	George III becomes king of England
1689–1697	King William's War (War of the League of Augsburg)	1763	Proclamation of 1763
1699–1750	Parliament enacts laws regulating colonial manufacturing	1764	Sugar Act
		1765	Stamp Act, leading to the Stamp Act Congress
1702–1713	Queen Anne's War (War of the Spanish Succession)	1766	Repeal of Stamp Act and passage of the Declaratory Act
1733	Molasses Act		
1738–1742	Height of the Great Awakening	1767	Townshend Duties, leading to the Massachusetts Circular Letter
1740–1748	King George's War (War of the Austrian Succession)		
1743	Franklin founds the American Philosophical Society	1770	Boston Massacre
		1772	Burning of the *Gaspee*
1752	Franklin discovers the nature of lightning	1773	Tea Act, leading to the Boston Tea Party
1754	Albany Congress	1774	Coercive Acts, leading to the First Continental Congress
1754–1763	French and Indian War (Seven Years' War)		

Supplementary Reading

The fullest analysis of the British imperial system can be found in the early volumes of L. H. Gipson, **British Empire Before the American Revolution** (1936–1968). See also J. A. Henretta, **Salutary Neglect** (1972), J. P. Greene, **Peripheries and Center** (1989), and Michael Kammen, **Empire and Interest** (1974).

On the colonial economy see R. R. Menard, **The Economy of British America** (1985), and E. J. Perkins, **The Economy of Colonial America** (1980).

On the Great Awakening, see J. M. Bumsted and J. E. Van Wetering, **What Can I Do to Be Saved: The Great Awakening** (1976), and P. V. Bonami, **Religion, Society, and Politics in Colonial America** (1986). For the Enlightenment, see H. F. May, **The Enlightenment in America** (1976).

The colonial wars are described in H. H. Peckham, **The Colonial Wars*** (1963), and Fred Anderson, **A People's Army** (1984). On the causes of the Revolution, see Pauline Maier, **From Resistance to Revolution** (1972), E. S. Morgan, **The Birth of the Republic** (1977), and

Edward Countryman, **The American Revolution** (1985). Bernard Bailyn's **The Ideological Origins of the American Revolution*** (1967) and **The Origins of American Politics*** (1968) are brilliant analyses of the political thinking and political structure of 18th-century America. G. B. Nash, **The Urban Crucible*** (1979), is good on the internal causes of conflict in the colonies. Other important studies include Pauline Maier, **The Old Revolutionaries** (1980), B. W. Labaree, **The Boston Tea Party*** (1964), John Shy, **Toward Lexington: The Role of the British Army in the Coming of the American Revolution*** (1965), and M. G. Kammen, **A Rope of Sand: The Colonial Agents, British Politics, and the American Revolution** (1968).

* Available in paperback.

CHAPTER 4

The American Revolution

"The Shot Heard Round the World"
The Second Continental Congress
The Battle of Bunker Hill
The Great Declaration
1776: The Balance of Forces
Loyalists
Early Defeats
Saratoga and the French Alliance
The War Moves South
Victory at Yorktown
The Peace of Paris
Forming a National Government
Financing the War
State Republican Governments
Social Reform
The Effects of the Revolution on Women
Growth of a National Spirit
The Great Land Ordinances
National Heroes
A National Culture

*T*he actions of the First Continental Congress led the British authorities to force a showdown with their bumptious colonial offspring. "The New England governments are in a state of rebellion," George III announced. "Blows must decide whether they are to be subject to this country or independent." Already General Thomas Gage, commander in chief of all British forces in North America, had been appointed governor of Massachusetts. Some 4,000 Redcoats were concentrated in Boston, camped on the town common once peacefully reserved for the citizens' cows. Parliament echoed with demands for a show of strength in America.

"The Shot Heard Round the World"

The London government decided to use troops against Massachusetts in January 1775, but the order did not reach General Gage until April. In the interim, Parliament voted new troop levies and declared Massachusetts to be in a state of rebellion. The Massachusetts Patriots, as they were now calling themselves, formed an extralegal provincial assembly, reorganized the militia, and began training "Minute Men" and other fighters.

When Gage received his orders on April 14, he acted swiftly. The Patriots had been accumulating arms at Concord, some 20 miles west of Boston. On the night of April 18, Gage dispatched 700 crack troops to seize these supplies. The Patriots were forewarned. Paul Revere and other horsemen rode off to alert the countryside and warn John Hancock and Sam Adams, leaders of the provincial assembly, whose arrest had been ordered. When the Redcoats reached Lexington early the next morning, they found the common occupied by about 70 Minute Men. After an argument, the Americans began to withdraw. Then someone fired a shot. There was a flurry of gunfire and the Minute Men fled, leaving eight dead.

The British then marched on to Concord, where they destroyed whatever supplies the Patriots had been unable to carry off. But militiamen were pouring into the area from all sides. A hot skirmish at Concord's North Bridge forced the Redcoats to yield that position. Becoming alarmed, they began to march back to Boston. Soon they were being subjected to a withering fire from American irregulars along their line of march. A strange battle developed on a "field" 16 miles long and only a few hundred yards wide. Gage was obliged to send out an additional 1,500 soldiers to avoid total disaster. When the first day of the Revolutionary War ended, the British had sustained 273 casualties, the Americans less than 100. "The Rebels are not the despicable rabble too many have supposed them to be," General Gage admitted.

In this engraving by Amos Doolittle, made from a sketch by Ralph Earle, British forces at North Bridge in Concord fight a rearguard action. A line of riflemen holds off the Massachusetts militia on the left, while the mass of the Redcoats retreats toward Boston.

For a brief moment of history, tiny Massachusetts stood alone at arms against an empire that had humbled France and Spain. Yet Massachusetts assumed the offensive! The provincial government organized an expedition that captured Fort Ticonderoga and Crown Point on Lake Champlain. The other colonies rallied quickly to the cause, sending reinforcements to Cambridge. When the news reached Virginia, George Washington wrote sadly: "A brothers' sword has been sheathed in a brother's breast, and the once-happy and peaceful plains of America are either to be drenched in blood or inhabited by a race of slaves." And then Washington added: "Can a virtuous man hesitate in his choice?"

The Second Continental Congress

On May 10, the day Ticonderoga fell, the Second Continental Congress met in Philadelphia. It was a distinguished group, more radical than the First Congress. Besides John and Sam Adams, Patrick Henry and Richard Henry Lee of Virginia, and Christopher Gadsden of South Carolina, all holdovers from the First Congress, there was Thomas Jefferson, a quiet young planter from Virginia, who was an indifferent speaker but a brilliant writer. Jefferson had recently published *A Summary View of the Rights of British America*, an essay criticizing the institution of monarchy and warning George III that "Kings are the servants, not the proprietors of the people." The Virginia convention had also sent George Washington, who could neither write well nor make good speeches, but who knew more than any other colonist about commanding men. He wore his buff-and-blue colonel's uniform, a not-too-subtle indication of his willingness to place his skill at the disposal of the Congress. The renowned Benjamin Franklin was also a delegate. The Boston merchant John Hancock was chosen president of the Congress.

This Congress, like the first, had no legal authority, yet it had to make agonizing decisions under the pressure of rapidly unfolding military events, with the future of every American depending on its actions. It naturally dealt first with the military crisis. It organized the forces gathering around Boston into a Continental Army and appointed George Washington commander in chief. After Washington and his staff left for the front on June 23, the Congress turned to the task of requisitioning men and supplies.

The Battle of Bunker Hill

Meanwhile, in Massachusetts the first major battle of the war had been fought. The British position on the peninsula of Boston was impregnable to direct assault, but high ground north and south, at Charlestown and Dorchester Heights, could be used to pound the city with artillery. When the Patriots seized Bunker Hill and Breed's Hill at Charlestown, Gage determined at once to drive them off. This was accomplished on June 17. Twice the Redcoats marched up Breed's Hill, each time being thrown back. On the third assault they carried the position, for the defenders had run out of ammunition. However, more than 1,000 Redcoats fell in a couple of hours, out of a force of 2,500. The Patriots lost only 400 men. The British had cleared the Charlestown peninsula, but the victory was really the Americans'. They had proved themselves against professional soldiers and exacted a terrible toll. "The day ended in glory," a British officer wrote, "but the loss was uncommon in officers for the number engaged."

The Battle of Bunker Hill, as it was called for no good reason, greatly reduced whatever hope remained for a negotiated settlement. The spilling of so much blood left each side determined to force the other's submission. The British recalled General Gage, replacing him with General William Howe, a veteran of the French and Indian War, and George III proclaimed the colonies to be "in open rebellion." The Continental Congress dispatched one last plea to the king (the Olive Branch Petition), but this was a sop to the moderates. Immediately thereafter it adopted the "Declaration of the Causes and Necessity of Taking Up Arms," which condemned everything the British had done since 1763. Americans were "a people attacked by unprovoked enemies"; the time had come to choose between "submission" and "resistance by force." The Congress then ordered an attack on Canada and created committees to seek foreign aid and buy munitions abroad. It authorized the outfitting of an American navy.

The Great Declaration

Congress (and the bulk of the people) still hung back from a break with the Crown. It was sobering to think of casting off everything that being English meant: love of king, the traditions of a great nation, pride in the power of a mighty empire. Then, too, rebellion might end in horrors worse than submission to *British* tyranny. The disturbances following the Stamp Act and the Tea Act had revealed an alarming fact about American society. The organizers of those protests, mostly persons of wealth and status, had thought in terms of "ordered resistance." They countenanced violence only as a means of forcing the British authorities to pay attention to their complaints. But protest meetings and mob actions had brought thousands of ordinary citizens into the struggle for self-government. Some upper-class Patriots resented the pretensions of these people. In addition, not all the property that had been destroyed belonged to Loyalists and British officials. Talk about "rights" and "liberties" might well give the poor (to say nothing of the slaves) an exaggerated impression of their importance. Finally, in a world where every country had some kind of monarch, could common people *really* govern themselves? The most ardent defender of American rights might well hesitate after considering all the implications of independence.

Two events in January 1776 pushed the colonies a long step toward independence. First came the news that the British were sending hired Hessian soldiers to fight against them. Colonists associated mercenary soldiers with looting and rape and feared that the German-speaking Hessians would run amok among them. Such callousness on the part of Britain made reconciliation seem out of the question.

The second decisive event was the publication of *Common Sense*. This tract was written by Thomas Paine, a onetime English corsetmaker and civil servant turned pamphleteer, a man who had been in America scarcely a year. *Common Sense* called boldly for complete independence. It attacked not only George III but also the idea of monarchy itself. Paine called George the "sullen tempered Pharaoh of England" and a "Royal Brute." "A government of our own is our natural right," he insisted. "O! ye that love mankind! Ye that dare oppose not only tyranny but the tyrant, stand forth!" Virtually everyone in the colonies must have read *Common Sense* or heard it explained and discussed. About 150,000 copies were sold in the critical period between January and July.

The tone of the debate changed sharply as Paine's slashing attack had its effect. The Continental Congress unleashed privateers against British commerce, opened American ports to foreign shipping, and urged the extralegal provincial conventions that had been set up by the Patriots to frame constitutions and establish state governments.

On June 7, Richard Henry Lee of Virginia introduced a resolution of the Virginia Convention:

> RESOLVED: That these United Colonies are, and of right ought to be, free and independent States, that they are absolved from all allegiance to the British Crown, and that all political connection between them and the State of Great Britain is, and ought to be, totally dissolved.

This resolution was not passed at once; Congress first appointed Thomas Jefferson, Benjamin Franklin, John Adams, Roger Sherman, and Robert Livingston to frame a suitable justification of independence. Jefferson wanted John Adams to prepare a draft, but Adams refused, saying: "You can write ten times better than I can." Jefferson's draft, with a few amendments made by Franklin and Adams and somewhat toned down by the whole Congress, was officially adopted by the delegates on July 4, 1776.

A detail from John Trumbull's *Declaration of Independence* **portrays the five-man drafting committee presenting its handiwork to the Congress: from left, Massachusetts, John Adams, Connecticut's Roger Sherman, New York's Robert Livingston, Virginia's Thomas Jefferson, and Pennsylvania's Benjamin Franklin. Trumbull's skillful composition "ranks" the contributors, with Jefferson dominating.**

Jefferson's Declaration consisted of two parts. The first was by way of introduction: It justified the abstract right of any people to revolt and described the theory on which the Americans based their creation of a new, republican government. The second, much longer, section was a list of the "injuries and usurpations" of George III, a bill of indictment explaining why the colonists felt driven to exercise the rights outlined in the first part of the document. Here Jefferson stressed George's interference with the functioning of representative government in America, his harsh administration of colonial affairs, his restrictions on civil rights, and his maintenance of troops in the colonies without their consent.

Jefferson sought to marshal every possible evidence of British perfidy and to make the king, rather than Parliament, the villain. He held George III responsible for Parliament's efforts to tax the colonies and restrict their trade, for many actions by subordinates that George had never deliberately authorized, and for some things that never happened. He even blamed the king for the existence of slavery in the colonies, a charge that Congress cut from the document, not entirely because it was untrue. The long bill of particulars reads more like a lawyer's brief than a careful analysis, but it was intended to convince the world that the Americans had good reasons for exercising their right to form a government of their own.

Jefferson's general statement of the right of revolution has inspired oppressed peoples all over the world for more than 200 years:

> We hold these truths to be self-evident, that all men are created equal, that they are endowed by their Creator with certain unalienable Rights, that among these are Life, Liberty and the pursuit of Happiness. That to secure these rights, Governments are instituted among Men, deriving their just powers from the consent of the governed. That whenever any Form of Government becomes destructive of these ends, it is the Right of the People to alter or to abolish it, and to institute new Government. . . .

The Declaration was intended to influence foreign opinion, but it had little effect outside Great Britain, and there it only made people determined to subdue the rebels. Why, then, has it had so much influence on modern history? As John Adams later pointed out—Adams viewed his great contemporary with a mixture of affection, respect, and jealousy—the basic idea was commonplace among 18th-century liberals. But if the idea lacked originality, it had never before been put into practice on such a scale. Revolution was not new, but the spectacle of a people solemnly explaining and justifying their right, in an orderly manner, to throw off their oppressors and establish a new system on their own authority was almost without precedent. Soon the French would be drawing upon this example in their revolution, and rebels everywhere have since done likewise. And if Jefferson did not create the concept, he gave it a nearly perfect form.

1776: The Balance of Forces

A formal declaration of independence merely cleared the way for tackling the problems of founding a new nation and maintaining it in defiance of Great Britain. Lacking both traditions and authority based in law, the Congress had to create political institutions and a new national spirit—all in the midst of war.

The military situation took precedence over other tasks because one disastrous battle might make everything else meaningless. At the start, the Americans had what we might call the "home court advantage." They already possessed their lands except for the few square miles occupied by British troops. Although thousands of colonists fought for George III, the British soon learned that to put down the American rebellion they would have to bring in men and supplies from bases on the other side of the Atlantic, a formidable task.

Certain long-run factors operated in America's favor. Although His Majesty's soldiers were brave and well disciplined, the army was as inefficient and ill-directed as the rest of the British government. Whereas nearly everyone in Great Britain wanted to crack down on Boston after the Tea Party, many boggled at engaging in a full-scale war against all the colonies. Aside from a reluctance to spill so much blood, there was the question of expense. Finally, the idea of dispatching the cream of the British army to America while powerful European enemies still smarted

from past defeats seemed dangerous. For all these reasons, the British approached gingerly the task of subduing the rebellion. When Washington fortified Dorchester Heights overlooking Boston, General Howe withdrew his troops to Halifax rather than risk another Bunker Hill. On March 17, 1776, Washington marched his troops into Boston. For the moment the 13 colony-states were clear of Redcoats.

Awareness of Britain's problems undoubtedly spurred the Continental Congress to the bold actions of the spring of 1776. However, on the very day that Congress voted for independence (July 2), General Howe was back on American soil, landing in force on Staten Island in New York harbor in preparation for an assault on the city. Soon Howe had at hand 32,000 well-equipped troops and a powerful fleet commanded by his brother, Richard, Lord Howe. As Washington realized, British control of New York City and the Hudson River would split the new nation in two.

The demonstration of British might accentuated American military and economic weaknesses: Both money and the tools of war were continually in short supply in a predominantly agricultural country. Many of Washington's soldiers were armed with weapons no more lethal than spears and tomahawks. Few had proper uniforms. Almost no one knew anything about such mundane but vital matters as how to construct and maintain proper sanitary facilities when large numbers of soldiers were camped at one place for extended periods of time. What was inelegantly known as "the Itch" afflicted soldiers throughout the war.

Loyalists

Whereas nearly all colonists had objected to British policies, many still hesitated to take up arms against the mother country. Even Massachusetts harbored many Loyalists, or Tories, as they were called; about 1,000 Americans fled Boston with General Howe, abandoning their homes rather than submitting to the rebel army.

No one knows exactly how the colonists divided on the question of independence. John Adams's off-the-cuff estimate was that a third of the people were pro-revolution, a third loyal to Britain, the rest more or less neutral, but most historians today think about two-fifths of the people supported the war, only one-fifth the king. The divisions cut across geographic, social, and economic lines. Many, in Tom Paine's famous phrase, were summer soldiers and sunshine patriots— they supported the Revolution when all was going well and lost their enthusiasm in difficult hours.

A high proportion of those holding royal appointments and many Anglican clergymen remained loyal to King George, as did numbers of merchants with close connections in Britain. There were pockets of Tory strength among persons of non-English origin and other minority groups who tended to count on London for protection against the local majority.

Many became Tories because they were pessimistic about the condition of society and the possibility of improving it. "What is the whole history of human life," wrote Jonathan Boucher of Virginia, "but a series of disappointments?" Still others, knowing that they already possessed a remarkably free system of government, could not stomach shedding blood merely to avoid paying more taxes or to escape from what they considered minor restrictions on their activities.

The Tories lacked organization. While Patriot leaders worked closely together, many Tory "leaders" did not even know one another. They had no central committee to lay plans or coordinate their efforts. When the revolutionaries took over a colony, some Tories fled; others sought the protection of the British army; others took up arms; others accommodated themselves silently to the new regime.

If the differences separating Patriot from Loyalist are unclear, feelings were nonetheless bitter. Individual Loyalists were often tarred and feathered, and otherwise abused. Some were thrown into jail, others exiled, their property confiscated. Battles between Tory units and the Continental Army were often exceptionally bloody. "Neighbor was against neighbor, father against son and son against father," one Connecticut Tory reported. "He that would not thrust his own blade through his brother's heart was called an infamous villain."

Early Defeats

General Howe's campaign against New York brought to light another American weakness—the lack of military experience. Washington, expecting Howe to attack New York, had moved south to meet the threat, but both he and his men failed badly in this first major test. Late in August Howe crossed from Staten Island to Long Island, where he easily outflanked and defeated Washington's army. Had he then acted decisively, he could probably have ended the war on the spot, but Howe could not make up his mind whether to be a peacemaker or a conqueror. When he hesitated, Washington managed to withdraw his troops to Manhattan Island.

Howe could still have trapped Washington simply by using his fleet to land troops on the northern end of Manhattan; instead he attacked New York City directly, leaving the Americans an escape route to the north. Again Patriot troops proved no match for British regulars. Though Washington, in a rage, threatened to shoot cowardly Connecticut soldiers as they fled the battlefield, he had to fall back on Harlem Heights in upper Manhattan.

New York–New Jersey Campaigns, 1776–1777

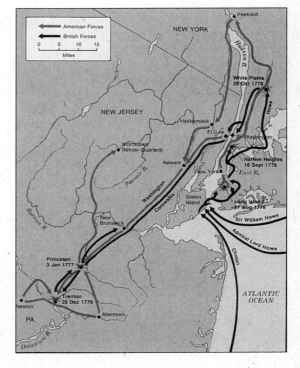

Still Washington refused to see the peril in remaining on an island while the enemy commanded the surrounding waters. Only when Howe shifted a powerful force to Westchester, directly threatening his rear, did Washington move north to the mainland. Finally, after several narrow escapes, he crossed the Hudson River to New Jersey, where the British could not use their naval superiority against him.

The battles in and around New York City seemed to presage an easy British triumph. Yet somehow Washington salvaged a moral victory from these ignominious defeats. He learned rapidly; seldom thereafter did he place his troops in such vulnerable positions. And his men, in spite of repeated failure, had become an army. In November and December 1776 they retreated across New Jersey and into Pennsylvania. General Howe then abandoned the campaign, going into winter quarters in New York but posting garrisons at Trenton, Princeton, and other strategic points.

The troops at Trenton were hated Hessian mercenaries. Washington decided to attack them. He crossed the ice-clogged Delaware River with 2,400 men on Christmas night during a wild storm. This force reached Trenton at daybreak in the midst of a sleet storm. The Hessians were taken completely by surprise. A few escaped in disorder, the rest—900 men—surrendered. The victory gave a boost to American morale. A few days later Washington won another battle at Princeton. These engagements had little strategic importance. Without them, however, there might not have been an American army to resume the war in the spring.

Saratoga and the French Alliance

When spring came to New Jersey in April 1777, Washington had fewer than 5,000 men under arms. Great plans—far too many and too complicated, as it turned out—were afoot in the British camp. The strategy called for General John Burgoyne to lead a large army from Canada down Lake Champlain toward Albany, while a smaller force under Lieutenant Colonel Barry St. Leger pushed eastward toward Albany from Fort Oswego on Lake Ontario. General Howe was to lead a third force north up the Hudson. Patriot resistance would be smashed between these three armies and the New England states isolated from the rest.

As a venture in coordinated military tactics the British campaign of 1777 was a fiasco. "Gentleman Johnny" Burgoyne, a charming character, part politician, part poet, part gambler, part ladies' man, yet also a brave soldier, had begun his march from Canada in mid-June. By early July his army, which consisted of about 7,000 men, had captured Fort Ticonderoga at the southern end of Lake Champlain. He quickly pushed beyond Lake George, but then bogged down. Burdened by a huge baggage train that included 138 pieces of generally useless artillery, more than 30 carts laden with his personal wardrobe and supply of champagne, and his mistress, he could advance at but a snail's pace through the dense woods north of Saratoga. Patriot forces, mainly militia, impeded his way by felling trees across the forest trails.

St. Leger was also slow in carrying out his part of the grand design. He did not leave Fort Oswego until July 26, and when he stopped to besiege a Patriot force at Fort Stanwix, General Benedict Arnold had time to march west from the army resisting Burgoyne with 1,000 men and drive him back to Oswego.

Meanwhile, Howe wasted time trying to trap Washington into exposing his army in New Jersey. This enabled Washington to send some of his regulars to buttress the militia units opposing Burgoyne. Then, just as St. Leger was setting out for Albany, Howe took the bulk of his army off by sea to attack Philadelphia, leaving only a small force commanded by General Sir Henry Clinton to aid Burgoyne.

When Washington moved south to oppose Howe, the Britisher taught him a series of lessons in tactics, defeating him at the Battle of Brandywine, then feinting him out of position, and moving unopposed into Philadelphia. But by that time it was late September, and disaster was about to befall General Burgoyne.

The American forces under Philip Schuyler and later under Horatio Gates and Benedict Arnold had erected formidable defenses immediately south of Saratoga. Burgoyne struck at this position twice and was thrown back each time with heavy losses. Each day more local militia swelled the American forces. Soon Burgoyne was under siege, his troops pinned down by withering fire from every direction, unable even to bury their dead. The only hope was General Clinton, who had finally started up the Hudson from New York. Clinton got as far as Kingston, about 80 miles below Saratoga, but on October 16 he decided to return to New York for reinforcements. The next day, at Saratoga, Burgoyne surrendered. Some 5,700 British prisoners were marched off to Virginia.

This overwhelming triumph changed the course and character of the war, for when news of the victory reached France, Louis XVI immediately recognized the United States. The French were eager to weaken Great Britain, and helping the rebellious Americans was an obvious way to do so. In May 1776 the Comte de Vergennes, France's foreign minister, had persuaded Louis XVI to authorize the expenditure of 1 million livres for munitions for America, and more was added the next year. Spain also contributed, not out of sympathy for the revolution but because of its desire to injure Great Britain. By February 1778 Vergennes and three American commissioners in Paris—Benjamin Franklin, Arthur Lee, and Silas Deane—had drafted a commercial treaty and a formal treaty of alliance. The help of Spain and France, Washington declared when he heard the news, "will not fail of establishing the Independence of America in a short time."

When the news of Saratoga reached England, Lord North realized that a Franco-American alliance would probably follow. To forestall it he was ready to give in on all the issues that had agitated the colonies before 1775. Both the Coercive Acts and the Tea Act would be repealed. Parliament would promise never to tax the colonies. But instead of implementing this proposal promptly, Parliament delayed until March 1778. Royal peace commissioners did not reach Philadelphia until June, a month after Congress had ratified the French treaty. The British proposals were icily rejected, and while the peace commissioners were still in Philadelphia war broke out between France and Great Britain.

The Revolution, however, was far from won. After the loss of Philadelphia, Washington had settled his army for the winter at Valley Forge, 20 miles to the northwest. The army's supply system collapsed. Often the men had nothing to eat but "Fire Cake," a mixture of ground grain and water baked in the campfire. According to the Marquis de Lafayette, one of the Europeans who volunteered to fight on the American side, "the unfortunate soldiers . . . had neither coats, nor hats, nor shirts, nor shoes; their feet and legs froze till they grew black, and it was often necessary to amputate them." To make matters worse, there was grumbling in Congress over Washington's failure to win victories, and talk of replacing him as commander in chief with Horatio Gates, the "hero" of Saratoga.

As the winter dragged on, so many officers resigned that Washington was heard to say that he was afraid of "being left Alone with the Soldiers only." Since enlisted men could not legally resign, they deserted by the hundreds. Yet the army survived. Gradually the soldiers who remained became a tough, professional fighting force. Their spirit has been described by the historian Charles Royster as "a mixture of patriotism, resentment, and fatalism."

The War Moves South

Spring brought a revival of American hopes in the form of more supplies, new recruits, and, above all, word of the French alliance. In May the British replaced General Howe with General Clinton, who decided to transfer his base back to New York. Thereafter British strategy changed. Fighting in the northern states degenerated into skirmishing and other small-unit clashes. Instead, relying on sea power and the supposed presence of many Tories in the south, the British concentrated their efforts in South Carolina and Georgia. Savannah fell late to them in 1778, and most of the settled parts of Georgia were overrun during 1779. In 1780 Clinton led a massive naval expedition against Charleston. When the city surrendered in May, more than 3,000 soldiers were captured, the most overwhelming American defeat of the war. Leaving General Cornwallis and some 8,000 men to carry on the campaign, Clinton then sailed back to New York.

in June 1780 Congress placed the highly regarded Gates in charge of southern resistance.

Gates encountered Cornwallis at Camden, South Carolina. Foolishly, he entrusted a key sector of his line to untrained militiamen, who panicked when the British charged with fixed bayonets. Gates suffered heavy losses and had to fall back. Congress then recalled him, sensibly permitting Washington to replace him with General Nathanael Greene, a first-rate officer.

Greene, avoiding a major engagement with Cornwallis' superior numbers, divided his troops and staged raids on scattered points. In January 1781, at the Battle of Cowpens in northwestern South Carolina, General Daniel Morgan inflicted a costly defeat on Colonel Banastre Tarleton, one of Cornwallis' best officers. Cornwallis pursued Morgan hotly, but the American rejoined Greene and at Guilford Court House they again inflicted heavy losses on the British. Then Cornwallis withdrew to Wilmington, North Carolina, where he could rely on the fleet for support and reinforcements. Greene's Patriots quickly regained control of the Carolina back country.

Victory at Yorktown

Seeing no future in the Carolinas and unwilling to vegetate at Wilmington, Cornwallis marched north into Virginia, where he joined forces with troops under Benedict Arnold. (Disaffected by what he considered unjust criticism of his generalship, Arnold had sold out to the British in 1780. He intended to betray the bastion of West Point on the Hudson River. The scheme was foiled when incriminating papers were found on the person of a British spy, Major John André. Arnold fled to the British and André was hanged.) As in the Carolina campaign, the British had numerical superiority at first but lost it rapidly when local militia and Continental forces concentrated against them. Cornwallis soon discovered that Virginia Tories were of little help in such a situation. "When a Storm threatens, our friends disappear," he grumbled.

General Clinton ordered Cornwallis to establish a base at Yorktown, where he could be supplied by sea. It was a terrible mistake. The British navy in American waters far outnumbered American and French vessels, but the Atlantic is wide, and in those days communication was slow. The

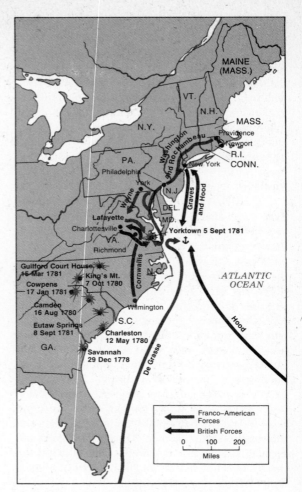

Yorktown and the War in the South, 1778–1781

French had a fleet in the West Indies under Admiral De Grasse and another squadron at Newport, Rhode Island, where a French army was stationed. In the summer of 1781, Washington, De Grasse, and the Comte de Rochambeau, commander of the French land forces, designed and carried out with an efficiency unparalleled in 18th-century warfare a complex plan to bottle up Cornwallis.

The British navy in the West Indies and at New York might have forestalled this scheme had it moved promptly and in force. But Admiral Sir George Rodney sent only part of his Indies fleet.

As a result, De Grasse, after a battle with a British fleet commanded by Admiral Thomas Graves, won control of the Chesapeake and cut Cornwallis off from the sea.

The next move was up to Washington, and this was his finest hour as a commander. Acting in conjunction with Rochambeau, he tricked Clinton into thinking he was going to strike at New York and then pushed boldly south. In early September he reached Yorktown and joined up with French troops. He soon had nearly 17,000 French and American veterans in position.

Cornwallis was helpless. He held out until October 17 and then asked for terms. Two days later more than 7,000 British soldiers marched out of their lines and laid down their arms.

The Peace of Paris

The British gave up trying to suppress the rebellion after Yorktown, but the event that confirmed the existence of the United States was the signing of a peace treaty with Great Britain. The negotiations were complicated. The United States and France had solemnly pledged not to make a separate peace. Spain, at war with Great Britain since 1779, was allied with France but not with America. Although eager to profit at British expense, the Spanish hoped to limit American expansion beyond the Appalachians, for they had ambitions of their own in the Mississippi Valley. France, although ready enough to see America independent, did not want the new country to become *too* powerful. In a conflict of interest between America and Spain, France tended to support Spain.

The Continental Congress appointed John Adams, Benjamin Franklin, John Jay, Thomas Jefferson, and Henry Laurens as a commission to conduct peace talks in Paris. Franklin and Jay did most of the negotiating. Congress had instructed the commissioners to rely on the advice of France's foreign minister, the Comte de Vergennes, subject only to the limitation that they must hold out at all costs for independence.

The commissioners soon discovered that Vergennes was not the perfect friend that Congress had assumed. He was, after all, a French official, and France had interests far more important than its concern for its American ally. Vergennes

"means to keep his hand under our chin to prevent us from drowning," Adams complained, "but not to lift our head out of the water." They therefore hinted to the British representative, Richard Oswald, that they would consider making a separate peace. They suggested that Great Britain would be far better off with America, a nation that favored free trade, in control of the trans-Appalachian region than with a mercantilist power like Spain. Soon the Americans were deep in negotiations with Oswald. They told Vergennes what they were doing but did not discuss details. Oswald was friendly and cooperative, and the Americans drove a hard bargain.

By the end of November 1782 a preliminary treaty had been signed. "His Britannic Majesty," Article 1 began, "acknowledges the said United States . . . to be free, sovereign and independent States." Other terms were equally in line with American objectives. The boundaries of the nation were set at the Great Lakes, the Mississippi River, and 31 degrees north latitude (roughly the northern boundary of Florida, which the British turned over to Spain). Britain recognized the right of Americans to fish on the Grand Banks off Newfoundland and—far more important—to dry and cure their catch on unsettled beaches in Labrador and Nova Scotia. The British agreed to withdraw their troops from American soil "with all convenient speed."

Where the touchy problem of Tory property seized during the Revolution was concerned, the Americans agreed only that Congress would "earnestly recommend" that the states "provide for the restitution of all estates, rights and properties." They promised to prevent further property confiscation and prosecutions of Tories—certainly a wise as well as a humane policy—and they agreed not to impede the collection of debts owed British subjects. Vergennes was flabbergasted by the success of the Americans. "The English buy the peace more than they make it," he wrote. "Their concessions . . . exceed all that I should have thought possible."

The American commissioners obtained such favorable terms because they were shrewd diplomats, and because of the rivalries that existed among the European powers. In the last analysis, Britain preferred to have a weak nation of English-speaking people in command of the Mississippi

Valley rather than France or Spain. From their experience at the peace talks, the Americans learned the importance of playing one power against another without committing themselves completely to any. This policy demanded constant contact with European affairs and skill at adjusting policies to changes in the European balance of power. And it enabled the United States, a young and relatively feeble country, to grow and prosper.

Forming a National Government

Independence was won on the battlefield and at the Paris Peace Conference, but it could not have been achieved without the work of the Continental Congress and the new state governments. Congress was essentially a legislative body rather than a complete government and from the start its members struggled to create a workable central authority. But they were handicapped by much confusion and bickering. In July 1776, John Dickinson prepared a draft of a national constitution, but it could not command much support. The larger states objected to equal representation of all the states, and the states with large western land claims were reluctant to cede them to the central government. It was not until November 1777 that the Articles of Confederation were submitted to the states for ratification.

The Articles merely provided a legal basis for authority that the Continental Congress had already been exercising. Each state, regardless of size, was to have but one vote; the union was only a "league of friendship." Article 11 defined the limit of national power: "Each state retains its sovereignty, freedom, and independence, and every Power, Jurisdiction, and right, which is not by this confederation expressly delegated to the United States, in Congress assembled." Time would prove this an inadequate arrangement, chiefly because the central government lacked the authority to impose taxes and had no way of enforcing the powers that it did possess. As the historian David Ramsay explained in 1789: "No coercive power was given to the general government, nor was it invested with any legislative power over individuals."

Financing the War

In practice, Congress and the states carried on the war cooperatively. General officers were appointed by Congress, lesser ones locally. The Continental Army, small but increasingly effective, was the backbone of Washington's force. The states raised militia chiefly for short-term service.

The fact that Congress's requisitions of money often went unhonored by the states does not mean that the states failed to contribute heavily to the war effort. Altogether they spent about $5.8 million in hard money, and they met Congress's demands for beef, corn, rum, fodder, and other military supplies. In addition, Congress raised large sums by borrowing. Americans bought bonds worth between $7 and $8 million during the war. Foreign governments lent another $8 million, most of this furnished by France. Congress issued more than $240 million in paper money, the states over $200 million more. This currency fell rapidly in value, resulting in an inflation that caused hardship and grumbling. The people, in effect, paid much of the cost of the war through the depreciation of their savings, but it is hard to see how else the war could have been financed, given the prejudice of the populace against paying taxes to fight a war against British taxation.

State Republican Governments

However crucial the role of Congress, in an important sense the real revolution occurred when the individual colonies broke their ties with Great Britain. Using their colonial charters as a basis, the states began framing new constitutions even before the Declaration of Independence. By early 1777 all but Connecticut and Rhode Island had taken this decisive step.

On the surface the new governments were not drastically different from those they replaced. The most significant change was the removal of outside control. Gone were the times when a governor could be maintained in office by orders from London. The new constitutions varied in details, but all provided for an elected legislature, an executive, and a system of courts. In general, the powers of the governor and of judges were limited—a natural result of past experience, if somewhat illogical now that these officials were no longer appointed by an outside authority. The theory appeared to be that elected rulers no less than those appointed by kings were subject to the temptations of authority, that, as one Patriot put it, all men are "tyrants enough at heart." The typical governor had no voice in legislation and little in appointments. Pennsylvania went so far as to eliminate the office of governor, replacing it with an elected council of 12.

Power was concentrated in the legislature, which the people had come to count on to defend their interests. In addition to the lawmaking authority exercised by the colonial assemblies, the state constitutions gave the legislatures the power to declare war, conduct foreign relations, control the courts, and perform many other essentially executive functions. While continuing to require that voters be property owners or taxpayers, the constitution makers remained suspicious even of the legislature. They saw legislators as *representatives,* that is, agents carrying out the wishes of the voters of a particular district rather than superior persons chosen to decide public issues according to their own best judgment. Most of the constitutions contained bills of rights protecting the people's civil liberties against all branches of the government. In Britain such checks were imposed only on the Crown; the Americans invoked them against their elected representatives as well.

The state governments combined the best of the British system, including its respect for fairness and due process, with the uniquely American stress on individualism and a healthy dislike of too much authority. The idea of drafting written frames of government—contracts between the people and their representatives that carefully spelled out the powers and duties of the latter—grew out of the experience of the colonists after 1763, when the vagueness of the unwritten British Constitution had caused so much controversy, and from the compact principle, the heart of republican government, as described so eloquently in the Declaration of Independence. This constitutionalism represented one of the most important innovations of the Revolutionary era: a peaceful method for altering the political system. In the midst of violence the states changed their frames

of government in an orderly, legal manner—a truly remarkable achievement that became a beacon of hope to future reformers everywhere.

Social Reform

Back in 1909 the historian Carl Becker wrote that the American Revolution was not merely a fight for "home rule," that is, for independence from Great Britain. It was also, Becker insisted, a fight to determine "who should rule at home."

Many states seized the occasion of constitution making to introduce important reforms. In Pennsylvania, Virginia, North Carolina, and other states the seats in the legislature were reapportioned in order to give the western districts their fair share. Primogeniture, entail (the right of an owner of property to prevent his heirs from ever disposing of it), and quitrents were abolished wherever they had existed. Steps toward greater freedom of religion were taken, especially in states where the Anglican church had enjoyed a privileged position. "Our civil rights have no dependence on our religious opinions," Jefferson's Virginia Statute of Religious Liberty (1786) stated. "Truth is great and will prevail if left to herself." Therefore "no man shall be compelled to frequent or support any religious worship . . . nor shall otherwise suffer on account of his religious opinions."

Many of the states continued to support religion after independence was won, but they usually distributed the money roughly in accordance with the numerical strength of the various Protestant denominations.

A number of states moved tentatively against slavery. In attacking British policy after 1763, colonists had frequently claimed that Parliament was trying to make slaves of them. No less a personage than George Washington wrote in 1774: "We must assert our rights, or submit to every imposition, that can be heaped upon us, till custom and use shall make us tame and abject slaves." However exaggerated the language, such reasoning led to denunciations of slavery, often vague but significant in their effects on public opinion. Then, too, the forthright statements in the Declaration of Independence about liberty and equality seemed impossible to reconcile with slaveholding. Gradually some Americans began to realize that blacks were not inherently inferior to whites and that the degrading environment of slavery was responsible for their low state.

The war opened direct paths to freedom for some slaves. In November 1775, Lord Dunmore, the royal governor of Virginia, proclaimed that all slaves "able and willing to bear arms" for the British would be liberated. But the British treated most slaves in territories they controlled as captured property. Probably more of them who became free achieved their independence by running away during the confusion that accompanied the British invasion of the south. Still, about 5,000 blacks served in the Patriot army and navy. Most of them were assigned noncombat duties, but some fought in every major battle from Lexington to Yorktown.

Beginning with Pennsylvania in 1780, the northern states all did away with slavery. In most cases, slaves born after a certain date were to become free on reaching maturity. Since New York did not pass a gradual emancipation law until 1799 and New Jersey until 1804, there were numbers of slaves in the so-called free states well into the 19th century—more than 3,500 as late as 1830. But the institution as such was on its way toward extinction. Except for Georgia and South Carolina, the southern states removed restrictions on the right of individual owners to free their slaves. The greatest success of voluntary emancipation came in Virginia, where 10,000 blacks were freed between 1782 and 1790.

These advances encouraged foes of slavery to hope that the institution would soon disappear. But slavery died only where it was not economically important. Except for owners whose slaves were "carried off" by the British, only a few owners in Massachusetts, where the state supreme court ruled slavery unconstitutional in 1783, were deprived of existing slaves against their will.

Despite the continuing subordination of blacks, the Revolution changed the tone of American society. Most people paid at least lip service to the idea of equality in the way they dressed, their manner of speech, and in how they dealt with one another in public places. After the publication of *Common Sense* and the Declaration of Independence, it became fashionable to denounce "aristocrats" and any privilege based on birth. In 1783 a group of army officers founded a fraternal organization, the Society of Cincinnati. Although the revered George Washington was its president, many citizens found the mere existence of a club restricted to officers alarming; the fact that membership was to be hereditary, passing on death to the deceased's oldest son, caused a furor.

Nevertheless, little of the social and economic upheaval usually associated with revolutions occurred. At least some of the urban violence of the

The Continental Army brought together men from all over the colonies and from a wide range of backgrounds. Their variety is suggested in this watercolor by a French officer who served in America during the Revolution. From left to right are a black infantryman with a light rifle, a musketman, a soldier carrying a heavy rifle, and an artilleryman.

period had no social objective. America had its share of criminals and people unable to resist the temptation to break the law when it could be done without much risk of punishment.

The property of Tories was frequently seized by the state governments, but almost never with the idea of redistributing wealth or providing the poor with land. The war disrupted many traditional business relationships. Some merchants were unable to cope with the changes. Others adapted well and grew rich. But the changes occurred without regard for the political beliefs or social values of either those who profited or those who lost.

That the new governments were liberal but moderate reflected the spirit of the times, a spirit typified by a man like Thomas Jefferson, who had great faith in the democratic process yet owned a large estate and many slaves and had never suggested a drastic social revolution. More individuals of middling wealth were elected to the legislatures because the Revolution stimulated popular interest in politics. But high property qualifications for office holding remained the general rule. Few "ordinary" people wanted radical changes.

During the war, conflicts erupted over economic issues yet no single class or interest triumphed in all the states or in the national government. In Pennsylvania, where the western radical element was strong, the constitution was extremely democratic; in Maryland and South Carolina the conservatives maintained control handily. Throughout the country, many great landowners were ardent Patriots, but others became Tories—and so did many small farmers.

In some instances the state legislatures wrote the new constitutions. In others the legislatures ordered special elections to choose delegates to conventions empowered to draft the charters. The convention method was an additional illustration of the idea that constitutions are contracts between the people and their leaders.

All the new governments became more responsive to public opinion, principally because the experience of participating in a revolution had made people conscious of their rights in a republic and of their power to enforce those rights. Conservatives swiftly discovered that state constitutions designed to insulate legislators and officials from popular pressures were ineffective when the populace felt strongly about any issue.

The Effects of the Revolution on Women

In the late 18th century there was a trend in the Western world toward increasing the legal rights of married women. For example, it became somewhat easier for women to obtain divorces. In Massachusetts, before the 1770s no woman is known to have obtained a divorce on the ground of her husband's adultery. In 1791 a South Carolina judge went so far as to say that the law protecting "the absolute dominion" of husbands was "the offspring of a rude and barbarous age." The "progress of civilization," he continued, "has tended to ameliorate the condition of women, and to allow even to wives, something like personal identity." As the tone of this "liberal" opinion indicates, the change in male attitudes that took place was small. Some state courts refused to take action against Tory women whose husbands were Tories on the ground that it was the duty of women to obey their husbands, and when John Adams's wife Abigail warned him in 1776 that if he and his fellow rebels did not "Remember the Ladies" when reforming society, the women would "foment a Rebellion" of their own, he treated her remarks as a joke. He insisted that voting was "not the Province of the ladies."

However, the war effort did increase the influence of women. With so many men in uniform, women took over the management of countless farms, shops, and businesses. Their experiences made both them and, in many cases, their male relatives more aware of their ability to take on chores previously considered exclusively masculine in character. Furthermore, the rhetoric of the Revolution, with its stress on liberty and equality, affected women in the same way that it caused many whites of both sexes to question the morality of slavery.

Attitudes toward the education of women also changed. At least half the white women in America could not read or write as late as the 1780s. But as the historian Linda K. Kerber writes, "the

In asking her husband John to "remember the ladies" when reforming society, Abigail Adams was not advocating political rights for women. Rather, she wanted fairer treatment for women within the family. "Do not put such unlimited power into the hands of the husbands," she wrote him. "Remember all men would be tyrants if they could."

republican experiment demanded a well-educated citizenry." In a land of opportunity like the United States, women seemed particularly important, not only because they themselves were citizens, but also because of their role in training the next generation. "You distribute mental nourishment along with physical," one orator told the women of America in 1795. Therefore, the idea of female education began to catch on. Schools for girls were founded and the level of female literacy gradually rose.

Growth of a National Spirit

American independence and control of a wide and rich domain were the most obvious results of the Revolution. Changes in the structure of society, as we have seen, were relatively minor. Economic developments, such as the growth of new trade connections and the expansion of manufacturing in an effort to replace British goods, were of only modest significance. By far the most important social and economic changes involved the Tories and were thus by-products of the political revolution rather than a determined reorganization of a people's way of life.

There was another important result of the Revolution: the growth of American nationalism. Most modern revolutions have been *caused* by nationalism and have *resulted* in independence. In the case of the American Revolution the desire to be free antedated any very intense national feeling. The colonies entered into a political union not because they felt an overwhelming desire to bring all Americans under one rule, but because unity offered the only hope of winning a war against Great Britain. That they remained united after throwing off British rule reflects the degree to which nationalism had developed during the conflict.

By the middle of the 18th century, the colonists had begun to think of themselves as a separate society distinct from Europe and even from Britain. To cite one small example, in 1750 a Boston newspaper urged its readers to drink "American" beer in order to free themselves from being "beholden to Foreigners" for their alcoholic beverages. But little political nationalism existed before the Revolution, in part because most people knew little about life outside their own colony. When a delegate to the First Continental Congress mentioned "Colonel Washington" to John Adams, Adams had to ask him who this "Colonel Washington" was. He had never heard the name before. Local ties remained predominant. People who really put America first were rare indeed before the final break with Great Britain.

The new nationalism rose from a number of sources and expressed itself in different ways. Common sacrifices in war certainly played a part; the soldiers of the Continental Army fought in the summer heat of the Carolinas for the same cause that had led them to brave the ice floes of the Delaware in order to surprise the Hessians. Such men lost interest in state boundary lines; they became Americans.

John Marshall of Fauquier County, Virginia, for example, was a 20-year-old militiaman in 1775. The next year he joined the Continental Army. He served in Pennsylvania, New Jersey, and New York and endured the winter of 1777–1778 at Valley Forge. "I found myself associated with brave men from different states who were risking life and everything valuable in a common cause," he later wrote. "I was confirmed in the habit of considering America as my country and Congress as my government."

Andrew Jackson, child of the Carolina frontier, was only nine when the Revolution broke out. One brother was killed in battle, another died as a result of untreated wounds. Young Andrew took up arms and was captured by the Redcoats. A British officer ordered Jackson to black his boots and, when the boy refused, struck him across the face with the flat of his sword. Jackson bore the scar to his grave—and became an ardent nationalist on the spot. He and Marshall had very different ideas and came to be bitter enemies in later life. Nevertheless, they were both American nationalists, and for the same reason.

With its 13 stars and 13 stripes representing the states, the American flag symbolized national unity and reflected the common feeling that such a symbol was necessary. Yet the flag had separate stars and stripes; local loyalties remained strong and they could be divisive when conflicts of interest arose.

Certain practical problems that demanded common solutions also drew the states together. No one seriously considered having 13 postal systems or 13 sets of diplomatic representatives abroad. Every new diplomatic appointment, every treaty of friendship or commerce signed, committed all to a common policy and thus bound them more closely together. And economic developments had a unifying effect. Cutting off English goods encouraged local manufacturing, making America more nearly self-sufficient and stimulating both interstate trade and national pride.

The Great Land Ordinances

The western lands, which had divided the states in the beginning, became a force for unity once they had been ceded to the national government. Everyone realized what a priceless national asset they were, and although many greedily sought to possess them by fair means or foul, all now understood that no one state could determine the future of the west.

The politicians argued hotly about how these lands should be developed. Some advocated selling the land in township units in the traditional New England manner to groups or companies; others favored letting individual pioneers stake out farms in the helter-skelter manner common in the colonial south. The decision was a compromise. The Land Ordinance of 1785 provided for surveying western territories into six-mile-square townships before sale. Every other township was to be further subdivided into 36 sections of 640 acres (one square mile) each. The land was sold at auction at a minimum price of one dollar an acre. The law favored speculative land development companies, for even the 640-acre units were far too large and expensive for the typical frontier family. But the fact that the land was to be surveyed and sold by the central government was a nationalizing force. It ensured orderly development of the west and simplified the task of defending the frontier in the event of Indian attack. Congress set aside one section of every township for the maintenance of schools, another farsighted decision.

Still more significant was the Northwest Ordinance of 1787, which established governments for the west. As early as 1775 settlers on the frontier were petitioning Congress to allow them to enter the union as independent states, and in 1780 Congress had resolved that all lands ceded to the nation by the existing states should be "formed into distinct republican States" with "the same rights of sovereignty, freedom and independence" as the original 13. In 1784 a committee headed by Jefferson worked out a plan for doing this, and in 1787 it was enacted into law. The area bounded by the Ohio, the Mississippi, and the Great Lakes was to be carved into not less than three or more than five territories. Until the adult male population of each reached 5,000, it was to be ruled by a governor and three judges, all appointed by Congress. Acting together, these officials would make and enforce the necessary laws. When 5,000 men of voting age had settled in the territory, the ordinance authorized them to elect a legislature, which could send a nonvoting delegate to Congress. Finally, when 60,000 persons had settled in any one of the political subdivisions, it was to become a state. It could draft a constitution and operate in any way it wished, save that the government had to be "republican" and that slavery was prohibited.

Seldom has a legislative body acted more wisely. That the western districts must become states everyone conceded from the start. The people had had their fill of colonialism under British rule. On the other hand, it would have been unfair to turn the territories over to the first comers, who would have been unable to manage such large domains and who would surely have taken advantage of their priority to dictate to later arrivals. A period of tutelage was necessary, a period when the "mother country" must guide and nourish its offspring.

Thus the intermediate territorial governments corresponded almost exactly to the governments of British royal colonies. The appointed governors could veto acts of the assemblies and could "convene, prorogue, and dissolve" them at their discretion. The territorial delegates to Congress were not unlike colonial agents. Yet it was vital that this intermediate stage end and that its end be determined in advance so that no argument could develop over when the territory was ready for statehood. The system worked well and was applied to nearly all the regions absorbed by the nation as it advanced westward.

National Heroes

The Revolution further fostered nationalism by giving the people their first commonly revered heroes. Benjamin Franklin was widely known before the break with Great Britain through his experiments with electricity, his immensely successful *Poor Richard's Almanack,* and his invention of the Franklin stove. His staunch support of the Patriot cause, his work in the Continental Congress, and his diplomatic successes in France, where he was extravagantly admired, added to his fame. Franklin demonstrated, to Europeans and to Americans themselves, that all Americans need not be ignorant rustics.

Washington, however, was "the chief human symbol of a common Americanism." Stern, cold, a man of few words, the great Virginian did not seem a likely candidate for hero worship. "My countenance never yet revealed my feelings," he himself admitted. Yet he had qualities that made people name babies after him and call him "the Father of his Country" long before the war was won: His personal sacrifices in the cause of independence, his unyielding integrity, and above all, his obvious desire to retire to his Mount Vernon estate (for many Americans feared any powerful leader and worried lest Washington seek to become a dictator).

"The chief human symbol of a common Americanism," George Washington attained heroic status perhaps as much for his modesty as for his devotion to the new nation.

People of all sections, from every walk of life, looked upon Washington as the embodiment of American virtues: a man of deeds rather than words; a man of substance accustomed to luxury, yet capable of enduring great hardships stoically and as much at home in the wilderness as an Indian; and a bold Patriot, quick to take arms against British tyranny, yet eminently respectable. The Revolution might have been won without Washington, but it is unlikely that the free United States would have become so easily a true nation had he not been at its call.

A National Culture

Breaking away from Great Britain accentuated certain trends toward social and intellectual independence and strengthened the national desire to create an *American* culture. The Anglican Church in America had to form a new organization once the connection with the Crown was severed; in 1786 it became the Protestant Episcopal church.

The Dutch and German reformed churches also became independent of their European connections. Roman Catholics in America had been under the administration of the vicar apostolic of England; after the Revolution Father John Carroll of Baltimore assumed these duties, and in 1789 he became the first American Roman Catholic bishop.

The impact of post-Revolutionary nationalism on American education was best reflected in the immense success of the textbooks of Noah Webster, later famous for his American dictionary. The first of these, the *Spelling Book,* which appeared in 1783, emphasized American forms and usage and contained a patriotic preface urging Americans to pay proper respect to their own literature. Webster's *Reader,* published shortly thereafter, included selections from the speeches of Revolutionary leaders who, according to Webster, were the equals of Cicero and Demosthenes as orators. Some 15 million copies of the *Speller* were sold in the next five decades, several times that number by 1900. The *Reader* was also a continuing best seller.

Nationalism affected the arts and sciences in the years after the Revolution. Jedidiah Morse's popular *American Geography* (1789) was a paean in praise of the "astonishing" progress of the country, all the result of the "natural genius of Americans." The American Academy of Arts and Sciences, founded at Boston during the Revolution, was created "to advance the interest, honor, dignity and happiness of a free, independent and virtuous people."

American painters and writers of the period usually employed patriotic themes. Joel Barlow intended his *Vision of Columbus,* to prove that America was "the noblest and most elevated part of the earth." The poems of Philip Freneau dealt with the horrors of British prison camps and the naval triumphs of John Paul Jones and predicted a great future for the United States.

The United States in the 1780s was far from being the powerful centralized nation it has since become. Probably most citizens still gave their first loyalty to their own states. In certain important respects the Confederation was pitifully ineffectual. However, people were increasingly aware of their common interests and increasingly proud of their common heritage. The motto of the new nation, *"E pluribus unum*—from many, one,"* perfectly describes a process that was gradually gathering strength in the years after Yorktown.

Milestones

1774	Thomas Jefferson, *A Summary View of the Rights of British America*	**1777**	Battle of Princeton
	General Thomas Gage, commander-in-chief of British army in America, named governor of Massachusetts		Battle of Saratoga, leading to alliance with France
			Battle of Germanown; British occupy Philadelphia
1775	Battles of Lexington and Concord	**1777–1778**	Continental Army winters at Valley Forge
	Second Continental Congress names George Washington commander-in-chief of the Continental Army	**1778**	British capture Savannah
			British capture Charleston
	Battle of Bunker Hill; Gage replaced as British commander by General Sir William Howe	**1781**	Articles of Confederation ratified
			General Cornwallis surrenders at Yorktown
1776	Tom Paine, *Common Sense*	**1783**	Peace of Paris; Great Britain recognizes the independence of the United States
	Washington's troops occupy Boston		
	Declaration of Independence		
	Battle of Long Island		
	Washington evacuates New York City	**1785**	Land Ordinance of 1785
	Battle of Trenton	**1787**	Northwest Ordinance

Supplementary Reading

The best brief surveys of the Revolutionary years are E. S. Morgan, **The Birth of the Republic*** (1977), and Edward Countryman, **The American Revolution** (1985). See also Robert Middlekauf, **The Glorious Cause** (1982), and Eric Foner, **Tom Paine and Revolutionary America*** (1976). Don Higgenbotham, **The War of American Independence*** (1971), treats the military aspects of the Revolution, and Charles Royster, **A Revolutionary People at War** (1979), describes the attitudes of soldiers and civilians toward the army.

On the Continental Congress and the Articles of Confederation, see Merrill Jensen, **The Articles of Confederation*** (1940) and **The New Nation*** (1950). The early history of the state governments is covered in Elisha P. Douglass, **Rebels and Democrats*** (1955). Political and social ideas during the Revolutionary era are described and analyzed in G. S. Wood, **The Creation of the American Republic*** (1969), and **The Radicalism of the American Revolution** (1992). The financial problems of this period are covered in E. J. Ferguson, **The Power of the Purse*** (1968).

For social history, see J. T. Main, **The Social Structure of Revolutionary America*** (1965). On the fate of the Tories, see M. B. Norton, **The British-Americans** (1972), and R. M. Calhoun, **The Loyalists in Revolutionary America** (1973). The effects of the Revolution on slavery are treated in W. D. Jordan, **White Over Black*** (1968). See also Ira Berlin and Ronald Holfman (eds.), **Slavery and Freedom in the Age of the American Revolution** (1983). On women during the Revolution, see L. K. Kerber, **Women of the Republic** (1980), and M. B. Norton, **Liberty's Daughters** (1980).

On the diplomacy of the American Revolution, see S. F. Bemis, **The Diplomacy of the American Revolution*** (1935), on the peace treaty, R. B. Morris, **The Peacemakers*** (1965). On the emerging national culture, consult R. B. Nye, **The Cultural Life of the New Nation** (1960). A fine biography of Washington that shows his influence on public attitudes is Marcus Cunliffe, **George Washington: Man and Monument*** (1958). P. S. Onuf, **Statehood and Union** (1987), deals with the Northwest Ordinance.

*Availabie in paperback.

CHAPTER 5

The Federalist Era: Nationalism Triumphant

Border Problems

Foreign Trade

The Specter of Inflation

Daniel Shays's "Little Rebellion"

The Road to Philadelphia

The Great Convention

The Settlement

Ratifying the Constitution

Washington as President

Congress Under Way

Hamilton and Financial Reform

The Ohio Country: A Dark and Bloody Ground

The New Revolution: France

Federalists and Republicans: The Rise of Political Parties

1794: Crisis and Resolution

Jay's Treaty

1795: All's Well That Ends Well

Washington's Farewell

The Election of 1796

The XYZ Affair

The Alien and Sedition Acts

The Kentucky and Virginia Resolves

*A*t first, few citizens resented the constraints imposed by the Articles of Confederation on the power of the central government. But once the war was over, the need for unity seemed less pressing and interstate conflicts reasserted them-selves. Research has modified, but not contra-dicted the thesis, advanced by John Fiske in *The Critical Period of American History* (1888), that the national government was demoralized and inade-quate. If, as Washington said, it moved "on crutches . . . tottering at every step," nevertheless it did move. The negotiation of peace ending the Revolutionary War, the humane and farsighted federal land policies, and even the establishment of a rudimentary federal bureaucracy to manage routine affairs were remarkable achievements, all carried out under the Articles. Yet the country's evolution placed demands on the national govern-ment that its creators had not anticipated.

Border Problems

The government had to struggle to win actual con-trol over the territory granted the United States in the treaty ending the Revolution. Both Great Britain and Spain stood in the way of this objec-tive. The British had promised to withdraw all their troops from American soil promptly, and so they did—within the settled portions of the 13 states. Beyond the frontier, however, they had es-tablished a string of military posts. These, despite the Treaty of Paris, they refused to surrender. Pressing against America's exposed frontier like hot coals, the posts seared national pride. They threatened to set off another Indian war, for the British intrigued constantly to stir up the tribes. The prize was the rich fur trade of the region, which the British now controlled but which might be drained off through Albany and other Ameri-can centers if British military was removed.

The British justified holding on to these posi-tions by citing the failure of the Americans to live up to some terms of the peace treaty. The United States had agreed not to impede British creditors seeking to collect prewar debts in America and to "earnestly recommend" that the states restore Tory property confiscated during the revolt. The national government complied with these require-ments (which called for nothing more than words on Congress's part), but the separate states did not cooperate. Many passed laws making it impos-sible for British creditors to collect debts, and in general the property of Tory *émigrés* was not re-turned. Yet those violations of the peace terms had little to do with the continued presence of the British on American soil. They would not have evacuated the posts at this time even if every farthing of the debt had been paid and every acre of confiscated land restored.

Then there was the question of the Spanish in the Southwest. In the peace negotiations Spain had won back Florida and the Gulf Coast region east of New Orleans. Far more serious, in 1784 the Spaniards had closed the lower Mississippi River to American commerce. Because of the prohibitive cost of moving bulky farm produce over the mountains, settlers beyond the Appalachians depended on the Mississippi and its network of tributaries to get their corn, tobacco, and other products to eastern and European markets. The Spanish governor of Louisiana, Esteban Miró, soon opened the river to American produce, subject only to a modest tariff, but if Spain even denied them the right to "deposit" goods at New Orleans while awaiting oceangoing transportation, westerners could not sell their surpluses.

A stronger central government might have dealt with these foreign problems more effectively, but it could not have eliminated them. United or decentralized, America was too weak in the 1780s to challenge a major European nation. Until the country grew more powerful, or until the Europeans began to fight among themselves, the United States was bound to suffer at their hands.

Foreign Trade

The fact that the Revolution freed American trade from the restrictions of British mercantilism proved a mixed blessing in the short run. Americans could now trade directly with the continental powers, and commercial treaties were negotiated with a number of them. Beginning in 1784, a valuable Far Eastern trade sprang up where none had existed before. At the same time, exclusion from Britain's imperial trade union brought losses of a much larger magnitude.

Immediately after the Revolution a controversy broke out in Great Britain over fitting the former colonies into the mercantilistic system. Some people, influenced by Adam Smith's brilliant exposition of the subject in *The Wealth of Na-*

tions, published in 1776, argued that placing restrictions on the buying and selling of goods was wasteful. Others, while remaining mercantilists, realized how important the American trade was for British prosperity and argued that special treatment should be afforded the former colonists. Unfortunately, a proud empire recently humbled in war could hardly be expected to exercise such forbearance. Persuaded in part by the reasoning of Sheffield, who claimed that Britain could get all the American commerce it wished without making concessions, Parliament voted to try building up exports to America while holding imports to a minimum, all according to the best tenets of mercantilism.

The British attitude hurt American interests severely. In the southern states the termination of royal bounties hit North Carolina producers of naval stores and South Carolina indigo planters hard. In addition, a new British duty on rice drastically reduced the export of that product by almost 50 percent.

In 1783 British Orders in Council barring American cured meat, fish, and dairy products from the British West Indies and permitting other American products to enter the islands only in British ships struck at the northern states. Fishermen lost the lucrative West Indian market, merchants a host of profitable opportunities. Trade with the West Indies fell off, idling many American ships. More than a thousand American sailors lost their jobs. Shipbuilding slumped because of these facts and because British merchants stopped ordering American-made vessels.

At the same time, British merchants, eager to regain markets closed to them during the Revolution, poured low-priced manufactured goods of all kinds into the United States. Americans, long deprived of British products, rushed to take advantage of the bargains. Soon imports of British goods were approaching the levels of the early 1770s, whereas exports to the empire reached no more than half their earlier volume.

America had always had an unfavorable balance of trade. The economy was essentially colonial; the people produced bulky, relatively cheap raw materials and voraciously consumed expensive manufactures. The influx of British goods after the Revolution aggravated the imbalance just when the economy was suffering a certain dislocation as a result of the ending of the war. From 1784 to 1786 the country went through a period of bad times. The inability of Congress to find money to pay the nation's debts undermined public confidence. Veterans who had not yet been paid, private individuals, and foreign governments that had lent the United States money were clamoring for their due. In some regions crop failures compounded the difficulties. The depression made the states stingier than ever about supplying the requisitions of Congress; at the same time many of them levied heavy property taxes in order to pay off their own war debts.

The depression of the mid-1780s was not by any stretch of the imagination a major economic collapse. By 1786 all signs pointed to a revival of good times. Nevertheless, dislike of British trade policy remained widespread. The obvious tactic would have been to place tariffs on British goods in order to limit imports or force the British to open the West Indies to American products, but the Confederation lacked the authority to do this. When individual states erected tariff barriers, British merchants easily got around them by bringing their goods in through states that did not. That the central government lacked the power to control commerce disturbed merchants, other businessmen, and the ever-increasing number of national-minded citizens in every walk of life.

Thus a movement developed to give the Confederation the power to tax imports. Although several attempts by Congress to do so failed, the attempts indicated that a large percentage of the states were ready to increase the power of the national government, and they pointed up the need for revising the Articles of Confederation. Although many individuals in every region were worried about creating a centralized monster that might gobble up the sovereignty of the states, the practical needs of the times convinced many others that this risk must be taken.

The Specter of Inflation

The depression and the unfavorable balance of trade led to increased pressures in the states for the printing of paper money and the passage of laws designed to make life easier for debtors. In response to wartime needs, both the Continental Congress and the states issued large amounts of paper money during the Revolution, with inflationary results (the Continental dollar became utterly worthless by 1781, and Virginia eventually called in its paper at 1,000 to 1).

After the war some states set out to restore their credit by imposing heavy taxes and severely restricting new issues of money. Combined with the postwar depression and the increase in imports, this policy had a powerful deflationary effect on prices and wages. Soon debtors, especially farmers, were crying for relief, both in the form of stay laws designed to make it difficult to collect debts (these laws were popular because of the anti-British feeling of the times) and through the printing of more paper money.

More than half the states yielded to this pressure in 1785 and 1786. The most disastrous experience was that of Rhode Island, where the government attempted to legislate public confidence in £100,000 of paper. Landowners could borrow a share of this money from the state for 14 years, using their property as security. Creditors feared that the loans would never be repaid and had no confidence in the money, but the legislature passed a law fining persons who refused to accept it. When creditors fled the state to avoid being confronted, the legislature authorized debtors to discharge their obligations by turning the necessary currency over to a judge. Of course, these measures further weakened public confidence. The Rhode Island Supreme Court, in *Trevett* v. *Weeden* (1786) declared that it was unconstitutional to fine a creditor for refusing it, and soon there was a reaction. The element of compulsion was withdrawn, and then the paper depreciated rapidly.

Daniel Shays's "Little Rebellion"

Although the Rhode Island case was atypical, it alarmed conservatives. Then, close on its heels, came a disturbing outbreak of violence in Massachusetts. The Massachusetts legislature had been almost fanatical in its determination to pay off the state debt and maintain a sound currency. Taxes amounting to almost £1.9 million were levied between 1780 and 1786, the burden falling most heavily on farmers and others of moderate income. Bad times and deflation led to many foreclosures, and the prisons were crowded with honest men unable to pay their debts. "Our Property is torn from us," one town complained, "our Gaols filled and still our Debts are not discharged."

In the summer of 1786, mobs in the western communities began to stop foreclosures by forcibly preventing the courts from holding their sessions. Under the leadership of Daniel Shays, the "rebels" marched on Springfield and prevented the state supreme court from meeting. When the state sent troops against them, the rebels attacked the Springfield arsenal. They were routed, and the uprising then collapsed. Shays fled to Vermont.

Organized under the direction of former Continental Army Captain Daniel Shays, hundreds of Massachusetts farmers took up arms to protest high taxes and aggressive eastern creditors. The uprising was known as Shays's Rebellion.

As Thomas Jefferson observed at a safe distance from the trouble in Paris, where he was serving as minister to France, Shays's uprising was only "a *little* rebellion" and as such "a medicine necessary for the sound health of government." But Shays and his followers were genuinely exasperated by the refusal of the government even to try to provide relief for their troubles. By taking up arms they forced the authorities to heed them.

Yet the episode had an impact far beyond the borders of Massachusetts. Unlike Jefferson, most responsible Americans considered the uprising "Liberty run mad." During the crisis, private persons had had to subscribe funds to put the rebels down, and when Massachusetts had appealed to Congress for help, there was little Congress could legally do. The lessons seemed plain: Liberty must not become an excuse for license; and therefore greater authority must be vested in the central government.

The Road to Philadelphia

If most people wanted to increase the power of Congress, they were also afraid to shift the balance too far lest they destroy the sovereignty of the states and the rights of individuals. The first fumbling step toward reform was taken in March 1785, when representatives of Virginia and Maryland suggested a conference of all the states to discuss common problems of commerce. In January 1786 the Virginia legislature sent out a formal call for such a gathering, to be held in September at Annapolis. However, the Annapolis convention disappointed advocates of reform; delegates from only five states appeared. Being so few the group did not feel it worthwhile to propose changes.

Among the delegates was a young New York lawyer named Alexander Hamilton, a brilliant, imaginative, and daring man who was convinced that only drastic centralization would save the nation from disintegration. Hamiltgon described himself as a "nationalist." He liked to contrast the virtues of a "Federal Republic" with the existing system of "petty states with the appearance only of union, jarring, jealous, and perverse." Instead of giving up, he proposed calling another convention to meet at Philadelphia to deal generally with constitutional reform. Delegates to the new convention should be empowered to work out a broad plan for correcting "such defects as may be discovered to exist" in the Articles of Confederation.

The Annapolis group approved Hamilton's suggestion, and Congress reluctantly endorsed it. This time all the states but Rhode Island sent delegates. On May 25, 1787, the convention opened its proceedings at the State House in Philadelphia and unanimously elected George Washington its president. When it adjourned four months later, it had drafted the Constitution.

The Great Convention

The Founding Fathers were remarkable men. Though he later had reason to quarrel with certain aspects of their handiwork, Jefferson, who was in Europe and could not attend the convention, called them "demigods." Collectively they

James Madison was a key figure at the Great Convention of 1787. He not only influenced the shaping of the Constitution, but also kept the most complete record of proceedings. "Every person," wrote one delegate, "seems to acknowledge his greatness."

possessed a rare combination of talents. Most of them had had considerable experience in politics, and the many lawyers among them were skilled in logic and debate.

Fortunately, they were nearly all of one mind on basic questions. That there should be a federal system, with both independent state governments and a national government with limited powers to handle matters of common interest, was accepted by all but one or two of them. Republican government, drawing its authority from the people and remaining responsible to them, was a universal assumption. A measure of democracy followed inevitably from this principle, for even the most aristocratic delegates agreed that ordinary citizens should share in the process of selecting those who were to make and execute the laws.

All agreed, however, that no group within society, no matter how numerous, should have unrestricted authority. They looked upon political power much as we today view nuclear energy: a force with tremendous potential value for mankind, but one easily misused and therefore dangerous to unleash. People meant well and had limitless possibilities, the constitution makers believed, but they were selfish by nature and could not be counted on to respect the interests of others. The ordinary people—farmers, artisans, any taxpayer—should have a say in government in order to be able to protect themselves against those who would exploit their weakness, and the majority must somehow be prevented from plundering the rich, for property must be secure or no government could be stable. No single state or section must be allowed to predominate, nor should the legislature be supreme over the executive or the courts. Power, in short, must be divided, and the segments must be balanced one against the other.

Although the level of education among them was high and a number might fairly be described as learned, the delegates' approach was pragmatic rather than theoretical. This was perhaps their most useful asset, for their task called for reconciling clashing interests. It could never have been accomplished without compromise and an acute sense of what was possible as distinct from what was ideally best.

At the outset the delegates decided to keep the proceedings secret. That way no one was tempted to play to the gallery. Next they agreed to go beyond their instructions to revise the Articles of Confederation and draft an entirely new frame of government. This was a bold, perhaps illegal act, but it was not irresponsible because nothing the convention might recommend was binding on anyone and because under the Articles, a single state could have prevented the adoption of any change. Alexander Hamilton, eager to scrap the Confederation, captured the mood of the gathering when he said: "We can only propose and recommend—the power of ratifying or rejecting is still in the States. . . . We ought not to sacrifice the public Good to narrow Scruples."

The Settlement

The delegates voted on May 30 that "a *national* Government ought to be established" and then set to work hammering out a specific plan. Furthermore, the delegates believed that the government should have separate executive and judicial branches as well as a legislature. But two big questions had to be answered. The first, "What powers should this national government be granted?" occasioned relatively little discussion. The right to levy taxes and to regulate interstate and foreign commerce was assigned to the central government almost without debate. So was the power to raise and maintain an army and a navy and to summon the militia of the states to enforce national laws and suppress insurrections. With equal absence of argument, the states were deprived of their rights to issue money (coin or paper), to make treaties, and to tax either imports or exports without the permission of Congress. Thus, in summary fashion, they brought about the shift of power made necessary by the problems of the day and made practicable by the new nationalism of the 1780s.

The second major question, "Who shall control the national government?"proved more difficult to answer in a manner satisfactory to all. Led by Virginia, the larger states pushed for representation in the national legislature based on population. The smaller states wished to maintain the existing system of equal representation for each state regardless of population. The large states rallied behind the Virginia Plan, drafted by James

Madison and presented to the convention by Edmund Randolph, governor of the state. The small states supported the New Jersey Plan, prepared by William Paterson, a former attorney general of that state.

The question was important; equal state representation would have been undemocratic, but a proportional system would have effectively destroyed the influence of all the states *as states*. But the delegates saw it in terms of combinations of large or small states, and this old-fashioned view was unrealistic: When the states combined they did so on geographic, economic, or social grounds that seldom had anything to do with size. Nevertheless, the debate was long and heated, and for a time it threatened to disrupt the convention. Finally, in mid-July, the delegates agreed to what is called the Great Compromise. In the lower branch of the new legislature—the House of Representatives—places were to be assigned according to population and filled by popular vote. In the upper house—the Senate—each state was to have two members, elected by the state legislature.

Then a complicated struggle took place between northern and southern delegates, occasioned by the institution of slavery. About one American in seven in the 1780s was a slave. Northerners contended that slaves should be counted in deciding each state's share of direct federal taxes. Southerners, of course, wanted to exclude slaves from the count. Yet they wished to include slaves in determining each district's representation in the House of Representatives, though they had no intention of permitting the slaves to vote. In the Three-fifths Compromise it was agreed that "three-fifths of all other Persons" should be counted for both purposes. (As it turned out, the compromise was a victory for the southerners, for direct taxes were only rarely levied by Congress before the Civil War.) Settlement of the knotty issue of the African slave trade was postponed by a clause making it illegal for Congress to outlaw the trade before 1808.

Many other differences of opinion were resolved by the give-and-take of practical compromise. As the historian David M. Potter once said, the Constitution was "an exchange of promises." The final document, signed on September 17, established a legislature of two houses, an executive consisting of a president with wide powers and a vice president whose only function was to preside over the Senate, and a national judiciary consisting of a supreme court and such "inferior courts" as Congress might decide to create.

The establishment of a powerful president was the most drastic departure from past experience, and it is doubtful that the Founding Fathers would have gone so far had not everyone counted on General Washington, a man universally esteemed for character, wisdom, and impartiality, to be the first to occupy the office. Besides giving him general responsibility for executing the laws, the Constitution made the president commander in chief of the armed forces of the nation and general supervisor of its foreign relations. He was to appoint federal judges and other officials, and he might veto any law of Congress, although his veto could be overridden by a two-thirds majority of both houses.

Looking beyond Washington, whose choice was sure to come about under any system, the Constitution established a cumbersome method of electing presidents. Each state was to choose "electors" equal in number to its representation in Congress. The electors, meeting separately in their own states, were to vote for two persons for president. Supposedly the procedure would prevent anyone less universally admired than Washington from getting a majority in the "electoral college," in which case the House of Representatives would choose the president from among the leading candidates, each state having but one vote. However, the swift rise of national political parties prevented the expected fragmentation of the electors' votes, and only two elections have ever gone to the House for settlement.

That the Constitution reflected the commonly held beliefs of its framers is everywhere evident in the document. It greatly expanded the powers of the central government yet did not seriously threaten the independence of the states. Foes of centralization, at the time and ever since, have predicted the imminent disappearance of the states as sovereign bodies. But despite a steady trend toward centralization, probably inevitable as American society has grown ever more complex, the states remain powerful political organizations that are sovereign in many areas of government.

The Founders believed that since the new powers of government might easily be misused,

each should be held within safe limits by some countervailing force. The Constitution is full of ingenious devices ("checks and balances") whereby one power controls and limits another without reducing it to impotence. "Let Congress Legislate, let others execute, let others judge," John Jay suggested. This separation of legislative, executive, and judicial functions is the fundamental example of the principle. Other examples are the president's veto; Congress's power of impeachment, cleverly divided between House and Senate; the Senate's power over treaties and appointments; and the balance between Congress's right to declare war and the president's control of the armed forces.

Ratifying the Constitution

Influenced by the widespread approval of Massachusetts's decision to submit its state constitution of 1780 to the voters for ratification, the framers of the Constitution provided (in Article 7) that their handiwork be ratified by special state conventions. This procedure gave the Constitution what Madison called "the highest source of authority"—the endorsement of the people, expressed through representatives chosen specifically to pass upon it.

Such a complex and controversial document as the Constitution naturally excited argument throughout the country. Those who favored it called themselves Federalists, thereby avoiding the more accurate but politically unattractive label of Centralizers. Their opponents thus became the Antifederalists. It is difficult to generalize about the members of these groups. The Federalists tended to be substantial individuals, members of the professions, well-to-do, active in commercial affairs, and somewhat alarmed by the changes wrought by the Revolution. They were more interested, perhaps, in orderly and efficient government than in safeguarding the maximum freedom of individual choice.

The Antifederalists were more often small farmers, debtors, and people to whom free choice was more important than power and who resented those who sought power. Power seekers, one Antifederalist warned, want to "swallow up all us little folks . . . just as the whale swallowed up Jonah."

But many rich and worldly citizens opposed the Constitution, and many poor and obscure persons were for it.

Whether the Antifederalists were more democratic than the Federalists is an interesting question. Those who were loud for local autonomy did not necessarily believe in equal rights for all the locals. Many Antifederalist leaders, including Richard Henry Lee, the man who introduced the resolution that resulted in the Declaration of Independence, had reservations about democracy. Yet, even Hamilton, no admirer of democracy, believed that ordinary citizens should have some say about their government. In general, practice still stood well ahead of theory when it came to popular participation in politics.

Various Antifederalists criticized many of the specific grants of authority in the new Constitution. But the chief force behind the opposition was a vague fear that the new system would destroy the independence of the states. It is important to keep in mind that the country was large and sparsely settled, that communication was primitive, and that the central government did not influence the lives of most people to any great degree. Many persons, including some who had been in the forefront of the struggle for independence, believed that a centralized republican system would not work in a country so large and with so many varied interests as the United States. That Congress could pass all laws "necessary and proper" to carry out the functions assigned it and legislate for the "general welfare" of the country seemed alarmingly all-inclusive. The Constitution "squints toward monarchy," Patrick Henry complained. The first sentence of the Constitution, beginning "We the *people* of the United States" rather than "We the states," convinced many that the document represented centralization run wild. Another old revolutionary who expressed doubts was Samuel Adams, who remarked: "As I enter the Building I stumble at the Threshold."

Many delegates to the Philadelphia convention were well-to-do and stood to profit from the establishment of a sound and conservative government that would honor its obligations, foster economic development, and preserve a stable society. Since the Constitution was designed to do all these things, it has been suggested that the Founders were not true patriots but selfish men out to protect their own interests. Charles A.

Beard advanced this thesis in *An Economic Interpretation of the Constitution* (1913). Certainly the Founders wanted to advance their own interests, as every normal human being does. Beard provided a necessary corrective to the 19th-century tendency to deify them. But there is abundant evidence that the closest thing to a general spirit at Philadelphia was a public spirit.

Most people were ready to give the new government a chance if they could be convinced that it would not destroy the states. When backers agreed to add amendments guaranteeing the civil liberties of the people against challenge by the national government and reserving all unmentioned power to the states, much of the opposition disappeared. Sam Adams ended up voting for the Constitution in the Massachusetts convention after the additions had been promised.

The Constitution met with remarkably little opposition in most of the state ratifying conventions, considering the importance of the changes it instituted. Delaware acted first, ratifying unanimously on December 7, 1787. Pennsylvania followed a few days later, voting for the document by a 2-to-1 majority. New Jersey approved unanimously on December 18; so did Georgia on January 2, 1788. A week later Connecticut fell in line, 128 to 40.

The Massachusetts convention provided the first close contest. Early in February, after extensive debate, the Constitution was ratified by a vote of 187 to 168. In April, Maryland accepted it by nearly 6 to 1, and in May, South Carolina approved, 149 to 73. New Hampshire came along on June 21, voting 57 to 47 for the Constitution. This was the ninth state, making the Constitution legally operative. Before the news from New Hampshire had spread throughout the country, the Virginia convention ratified, 89 to 79.

Aside from Rhode Island, this left only New York and North Carolina outside the Union. The Antifederalists, well organized and competently led in New York, won 46 of the 65 seats at the ratifying convention. But the New York Federalists had one great asset in the fact that so many states had already ratified and another in the person of Alexander Hamilton. Although contemptuous of the weakness of the Constitution, Hamilton supported it with all his energies as being incomparably stronger than the old government. Working with Madison and John Jay, he produced the *Fed-*

eralist Papers, a brilliant series of essays explaining and defending the new system. These were published in the local press and later in book form. Although generations of judges and lawyers have treated them almost as parts of the Constitution, their impact on contemporary public opinion was probably slight. Open-minded members of the convention were undoubtedly influenced, but few delegates were open-minded.

Hamilton became virtually a one-man army in defense of the Constitution, plying hesitating delegates with dinners and drinks, facing obstinate ones with the threat that New York City would secede from the state if the Constitution were rejected. In the end, by promising to support a call for a second national convention to consider amendments, the Federalists carried the day, 30 to 27. With New York in the fold, the new government was free to get under way.

Washington as President

Elections took place during January and February 1789, and by early April enough congressmen had gathered in New York, the temporary national capital, to commence operation. The ballots of the presidential electors were officially counted

His hand on the Bible, Washington takes the presidential oath administered by Robert Livingston on the portico of New York's Federal Hall. Engraving by Amos Doolittle, after a drawing by Peter Lacour.

in the Senate on April 6, Washington being the unanimous choice. John Adams, with 34 electoral votes, won the vice presidency. On April 30, Washington took the oath of office at Federal Hall.

Washington made a firm, dignified, conscientious, but cautious president. His acute sense of responsibility led him to face the job "with feelings not unlike those of a culprit who is going to the place of his execution." He meticulously avoided treading on the toes of Congress, for he took seriously the principle of the separation of powers. Never would he speak for or against a candidate for Congress, nor did he think that the president should push or even propose legislation. When he knew a controversial question was to be discussed in Congress, he avoided the subject in his annual message. The veto, he believed, should be employed only when the president considered a bill unconstitutional.

Although the Constitution said nothing about a presidential cabinet, Washington established the practice of calling his department heads together for general advice. In selecting them, he favored no particular faction. He insisted only that appointees be competent and "of known attachment to the government we have chosen." He picked Hamilton for secretary of the treasury, Jefferson for secretary of state, General Henry Knox of Massachusetts for secretary of war, and Edmund Randolph for attorney general. He called on them for advice according to the logic of his particular needs and frequently without regard for their own specialties. Thus he sometimes consulted Jefferson about financial matters and Hamilton about foreign affairs. But despite his respect for the opinions of others, Washington was a strong chief executive. As Hamilton put it, he "consulted much, pondered much, resolved slowly, resolved surely."

Congress Under Way

The first Congress had the task of constructing the machinery of government. By September 1789 it had created the State, Treasury, and War Departments and passed a Judiciary Act establishing 13 federal district courts and three circuit courts of appeal. The number of Supreme Court justices was set at six, and Washington named John Jay chief justice.

True to Federalist promises—for a large majority of both houses were friendly to the Constitution—Congress prepared a list of a dozen amendments (ten were ratified) guaranteeing what Representative James Madison, who drafted the amendments, called the "great rights of mankind." These amendments, known as the Bill of Rights, provided that Congress should make no law infringing freedom of speech, the press, or religion. The right of trial by jury was reaffirmed, the right to bear arms guaranteed. No one was to be subject to "unreasonable" searches or seizures or compelled to testify against himself in a criminal case. No one was to "be deprived of life, liberty, or property, without due process of law." The Tenth Amendment, not, strictly speaking, a part of the Bill of Rights, was designed to mollify those who feared that the states would be destroyed by the new government. It provided that powers not delegated to the United States or denied specifically to the states by the Constitution were to reside either in the states or in the people.

As experts pointed out, the amendments were not logically necessary because the federal government had no authority to act in such matters to begin with. But many had wanted to be reassured. Experience has proved repeatedly that whatever the logic of the situation, the protection afforded individuals by the Bill of Rights has been anything but unnecessary.

The Bill of Rights did much to convince doubters that the new government would not become too powerful. More complex was the task of proving that it was powerful enough to deal with those national problems that the Confederation had not been able to solve: the threat to the West posed by the British, Spaniards, and Indians; the disruption of the pattern of American foreign commerce resulting from independence; the collapse of the financial structure of the country.

Hamilton and Financial Reform

One of the first acts of Congress in 1789 was to employ its new power to tax. Congress levied a 5 percent duty on all foreign products entering the United States, applying higher rates to certain products, such as hemp, glass, and nails, as a measure of protection for American producers. The Tariff Act of 1789 also placed heavy tonnage du-

ties on all foreign shipping, a mercantilistic measure designed to stimulate the American merchant marine.

Raising money for current expenses was a small and relatively simple aspect of the financial problem faced by Washington's administration. The nation's debt was large, its credit shaky, its economic future uncertain. In October 1789, Congress deposited upon the slender shoulders of Secretary of the Treasury Hamilton the task of straightening out the fiscal mess and stimulating the country's economic development.

At 34, Hamilton had already proved himself a remarkable man. Born in the British West Indies, the illegitimate son of a shiftless Scot who was little better than a beachcomber, and raised by his mother's family, he went to New York in 1773 to attend King's College. When the Revolution broke out, he joined the army. At 22 he was a staff colonel, aide-de-camp to Washington. Later, at Yorktown, he led a line regiment, displaying a bravery approaching foolhardiness. He married the daughter of Philip Schuyler, a wealthy and influential New Yorker, and after the Revolution he practiced law in that state.

"To confess my weakness," Hamilton wrote when he was only 14, "my ambition is prevalent." This pastel drawing by James Sharples was made about 1796.

Hamilton was a bundle of contradictions. Witty, charming, possessed of a mind like a sharp knife, he was sometimes the soul of practicality, sometimes an incurable romantic. No more hard-headed realist ever lived, yet he was quick to resent any slight to his honor, even—tragically—ready to fight a duel though he abhorred the custom of dueling. A self-made man, he admired aristocracy and disparaged the abilities of the common run of mankind who, he said, "seldom judge or determine right." Although granting that Americans must be allowed to govern themselves, he was as apprehensive of the "turbulence" of the masses as a small boy passing a graveyard in the dark.

The country, Hamilton insisted, needed strong national government. "I acknowledge," he wrote in one of the *Federalist Papers*, "my aversion to every project that is calculated to disarm the government of a single weapon, which . . . might be usefully employed for the general defense and security." He wished to reduce the states to mere administrative units, like English counties.

As secretary of the treasury, Hamilton proved to be a farsighted economic planner. The United States, a "Hercules in the cradle," needed capital to develop its untapped material and human resources. To persuade investors to commit their funds in America, the country would have to convince them that it would meet every obligation in full. His *Report on the Public Credit* outlined the means for accomplishing this objective. The United States owed more than $11 million to foreigners and over $40 million to its own citizens. Hamilton suggested that this debt be funded at par, which meant calling in all outstanding securities and issuing new bonds to the same face value in their stead, and establishing an untouchable sinking fund to assure payment of interest and principal. Further, the remaining state debts, over $21 million, should be assumed (taken over) by the United States on the same terms.

Although most members of Congress agreed that the debt should be funded at par, many believed that at least part of the new issue should go to the original holders of the old securities: the soldiers, farmers, and merchants who had been forced to accept them in lieu of cash for goods and services rendered the Confederation during the Revolution. Many of these people had sold their securities for a fraction of their face value to spec-

ulators; under Hamilton's proposal, the speculators would make a killing. To the argument for divided payment, Hamilton answered coldly: "[The speculator] paid what the commodity was worth in the market, and took the risks. . . . He . . . ought to reap the benefit of his hazard."

Hamilton was essentially correct, and in the end Congress had to go along. What infuriated his contemporaries and still attracts the scorn of many historians was Hamilton's motive. He deliberately intended his plan to give a special advantage to the rich. The government would be strong, he thought, only if well-to-do Americans enthusiastically supported it. What better way to win them over than to make it worth their while financially to do so?

In part, opposition to the funding plan was sectional, for citizens of the northern states held more than four-fifths of the national debt. The scheme for assuming the state debts aggravated the controversy, since most of the southern states had already paid off much of their Revolutionary War obligations. For months, Congress was deadlocked. Finally, in July 1790, Hamilton worked out an arrangement with Representative James Madison of Virginia and Secretary of State Jefferson. The two Virginians swung a few southern votes, and Hamilton induced some of his followers to support the southern plan for locating the permanent capital of the Union on the Potomac River. The entire funding plan was a great success. Soon the United States had the highest possible credit rating in the world's financial centers. Foreign capital poured into the country.

Hamilton next proposed that Congress charter a national bank. Such an institution would provide safe storage for government funds and serve as an agent for the government in the collection, movement, and expenditure of tax money. Most important, it would issue bank notes, thereby providing a vitally needed medium of exchange for the specie-starved economy. This Bank of the United States was to be partly owned by the government, but 80 percent of the $10 million stock issue was to be sold to private individuals.

The country had much to gain from such a bank, but again—Hamilton's devilish cleverness was never more in evidence—the well-to-do commercial classes would gain still more. Government balances in the bank belonging to all the people would earn dividends for a handful of rich investors. Manufacturers and other capitalists would profit from the bank's credit facilities. Public funds would be invested in the bank, but control would remain in private hands, since the government would appoint only 5 of the 25 directors. Nevertheless, the bill creating the bank passed both houses of Congress with relative ease in February 1791.

President Washington, however, hesitated to sign it, for the bill's constitutionality had been questioned during the debate in Congress. Nowhere did the Constitution specifically authorize Congress to charter corporations or engage in the banking business. As was his wont when in doubt, Washington called on Jefferson and Hamilton for advice.

Hamilton defended the legality of the bank by enunciating the doctrine of "implied powers." If a logical connection existed between the purpose of the bill and powers clearly stated in the Constitution, he wrote, the bill was constitutional. Jefferson disagreed. Congress could only do what the Constitution specifically authorized, he said. The "elastic clause" granting it the right to pass "all Laws which shall be necessary and proper" to carry out the specified powers must be interpreted literally or Congress would "take possession of a boundless field of power, no longer susceptible to any definition." Because a bank was obviously not necessary, it was not authorized.

Although not entirely convinced, Washington accepted Hamilton's reasoning and signed the bill. He could just as easily have followed Jefferson, for the Constitution is not clear. If one stresses *proper* in the "necessary and proper" clause, one ends up a Hamiltonian; if one stresses *necessary,* then Jefferson's view is correct. Historically (and this is the important point), politicians have nearly always adopted the "loose" Hamiltonian "implied powers" interpretation when they favored a measure and the "strict" Jeffersonian one when they did not. Jefferson disliked the bank; therefore he claimed it was unconstitutional. Had he approved, he doubtless would have taken a different tack. In 1819 the Supreme Court officially sanctioned Hamilton's construction of the "necessary and proper" clause, and in general that interpretation has prevailed. Because the majority tends naturally toward an argument that increases its freedom of action, the pressure for this view has been continual and formidable.

The Bank of the United States succeeded from the start. People eagerly accepted its bank notes at face value. Business ventures of all kinds found it easier to raise new capital. Soon state-chartered banks entered the field. There were only 3 state banks in 1791; by 1801 the number was 32.

Hamilton had not finished. In December 1791 he submitted his *Report on Manufactures,* a bold call for economic planning. The pre-Revolutionary nonimportation agreements and wartime shortages had stimulated interest in manufacturing. In his *Report* he called for government tariffs, subsidies, and awards to encourage American manufacturing. He hoped to change an essentially agricultural nation into one with a complex, self-sufficient economy.

Once again, business and commercial interests in particular would benefit. They would be protected against foreign competition and otherwise subsidized, whereas the general taxpayer, particularly the farmer, would pay the bill in the form of higher taxes and higher prices on manufactured goods. Hamilton argued that in the long run every interest would profit, and he was undoubtedly sincere, being too much the nationalist to favor one section at the expense of another. A majority of the Congress, however, balked at such a broadly gauged scheme. Hamilton's *Report* was pigeonholed, though many of the specific tariffs he recommended were enacted into law in 1792.

The Ohio Country: A Dark and Bloody Ground

The western issues and those related to international trade proved more difficult because other nations were involved. The British showed no disposition to evacuate their posts on American soil simply because the American people had decided to strengthen their central government, nor did the western Indians suddenly agree to abandon their hunting grounds to the white invaders.

Trouble came swiftly when white settlers moved onto the land north of the Ohio River in large numbers. The Indians, determined to hold this country at all costs, struck hard at the invaders. In 1790 the Miami chief Little Turtle, a gifted strategist, inflicted a double defeat on militia units commanded by General Josiah Harmar.

The next year, Little Turtle and his men defeated the forces of General Arthur St. Clair still more convincingly. Both Harmar and St. Clair resigned from the army, their careers ruined, but the defeats led Congress to authorize raising a regular army of 5,000 men.

By early 1792 the Indians had driven the whites into "beachheads" at Marietta and Cincinnati on the Ohio. Resentment of the federal government in the western counties of every state from New York to the Carolinas mounted. The people were convinced that the British were inciting the Indians to attack them, yet the supposedly powerful national government seemed unable to force Great Britain to surrender its forts in the West.

Still worse, the westerners believed, was the way the government was taxing them. In 1791, as part of his plan to take over the debts of the states, Hamilton had persuaded Congress to adopt an excise tax of eight cents a gallon on American-made whiskey. Excise taxes were particularly disliked by most Americans. A duty on imported products could be avoided by purchasing a domestic alternative. Moreover, the collection of excise taxes required hordes of tax collectors, armed with the power to snoop into one's affairs. Westerners, who were heavy drinkers and who turned much of their grain into whiskey in order to cope with the high cost of transportation, were especially angered by the tax on whiskey.

Hamilton knew that the tax would be unpopular, but he was determined to enforce the law. To western complaints, he coolly suggested that farmers drank too much to begin with. Of course this did nothing to reduce western opposition to the tax. Resistance was especially intense in western Pennsylvania. When treasury agents tried to collect the tax there, they were forcibly prevented from doing so.

The New Revolution: France

Events in Europe also affected the situation. In 1789 the French Revolution erupted, and four years later war broke out between France and Great Britain and most of the rest of Europe.

With France fighting Great Britain and Spain, there arose the question of America's obligations under the Alliance of 1778. That treaty required the United States to defend the French West Indies "forever against all other powers." Suppose the British attacked Martinique; must America then go to war? Morally the United States was so obligated, but no responsible American statesman urged such a policy. With British and Spanish troops on its borders, the nation would be in serious danger if it entered the war. Instead, in April 1793, Washington issued a proclamation of neutrality commiting the United States to be "friendly and impartial" to both sides in the war.

Meanwhile, the French had sent a special representative, Edmond Charles Genet, to the United States to seek support. The French Revolution had excited much enthusiasm in the United States, for it seemed to indicate that American democratic ideas were already engulfing the world. Genet, a charming, ebullient young man, quickly concluded that the proclamation of neutrality was "a harmless little pleasantry designed to throw dust in the eyes of the British." He began, in plain violation of American law, to license American vessels to operate as privateers against British shipping and to grant French military commissions to a number of Americans in order to mount expeditions against Spanish and British possessions in North America.

Washington received Genet coolly, then demanded that he stop his illegal activities. Genet, whose capacity for self-deception was monumental, appealed to public opinion over the president's head and continued to commission privateers. Washington then requested his recall.

The Genet affair was incidental to a far graver problem. Although the European war increased the foreign demand for American products, it also led to attacks on American shipping by both France and Great Britain. Each power captured American vessels headed for the other's ports whenever it could. In 1793 and 1794 about 600 United States ships were seized. The British attacks caused far more damage because the British fleet was much larger than France's. The merchant marine, one American diplomat declared angrily, was being "kicked, cuffed, and plundered all over the Ocean." The attacks roused a storm in America, reviving hatreds that had been smoldering since the Revolution. Washington sent Chief Justice John Jay to London as minister plenipotentiary to seek a settlement with the British.

Federalists and Republicans: The Rise of Political Parties

The furor over the violations of neutral rights focused attention on a new development, the formation of political parties. Why parties emerged after the ratification of the Constitution has long intrigued historians. Probably the main reason was the obvious one: by creating a strong central government, the Constitution produced national issues. Furthermore, by failing to create machinery for nominating candidates for federal offices, the Constitution left a vacuum, which informal party organizations filled. Washington's principal advisers, Hamilton and Jefferson, were in sharp disagreement, and they soon became the leaders around which parties coalesced.

In the spring of 1791, Jefferson and James Madison began to sound out other politicians about forming an informal political organization. Jefferson also appointed the poet Philip Freneau to a minor state department post and Freneau then began publishing a newspaper, the *National Gazette*, to disseminate the views of what became known as the Republican Party. The *Gazette* was soon flailing away editorially at Hamilton's policies. Hamilton hit back promptly, organizing his own followers in the Federalist Party, the organ of which was John Fenno's *Gazette of the United States*.

The personal nature of early American political controversies goes far toward explaining why the party battles of the era were so bitter. So does the continuing anxiety that plagued partisans of both persuasions about the supposed frailty of a republican government. The United States was still very much an experiment; leaders who sincerely proclaimed their own devotion to its welfare suspected that their opponents wanted to undermine its institutions.

The conflict came to a head slowly. At the start, Hamilton had the ear of the president, and his allies controlled a majority in Congress. Jefferson went along with Hamilton's funding plan and traded the assumption of state debts for a capital on the Potomac. However, when Hamilton proposed the Bank of the United States, he dug in his heels. It seemed designed to benefit the northeastern commercial classes at the expense of southern and western farmers.

The growing controversy over the French Revolution and the resulting war between France and Great Britain widened the split. After the radicals in France executed Louis XVI and began the Reign of Terror, American conservatives were horrified. The Jeffersonians, however, continued to defend the Revolution. Slaveowners could be heard singing the praises of *liberté, egalité, fraternité,* and extolling "the glorious successes of our Gallic brethren." In the same way the Federalists began to idealize the British, whom they considered the embodiment of the forces that were resisting French radicalism.

This created an explosive situation. Hamilton came to believe that Jefferson was so prejudiced in favor of France as to be unable to conduct foreign affairs rationally, and Jefferson could say contemptuously: "Hamilton is panick struck, if we refuse our breech to every kick which Great Britain may choose to give it."

In fact, Jefferson never lost his sense of perspective. When the Anglo-French war erupted, he recommended neutrality. He considered Genet "hot-headed, all imagination, no judgment, passionate, disrespectful and even indecent," and cordially approved Washington's decision to send him packing. Hamilton perhaps went a little too far in his friendliness to Great Britain, but the real danger was that some of Hamilton's and Jefferson's excitable followers might become so committed as to forget the true interests of the United States.

1794: Crisis and Resolution

During the summer of 1794, several superficially unrelated events brought the partisan conflicts of the period to a peak. The government had not been able to collect Hamilton's whiskey tax in the west. Mobs had burned the homes of revenue agents. Late in July, 1794, 7,000 "rebels" converged on Pittsburgh, threatening to burn the town to the ground. They were turned away by the sight of federal artillery and the liberal dispensation of whiskey by the frightened inhabitants, but as the historian Thomas P. Slaughter has pointed out, this was "the largest example of armed resistance to a law between the ratification of the Constitution and the Civil War."

Early in August, President Washington mustered an enormous army of nearly 13,000 militiamen and marched westward. But when the troops arrived, rebels were nowhere to be seen; the expected Whiskey Rebellion simply did not happen. Good sense had triumphed. Moderates in the region (not everyone, after all, was a distiller) agreed that even unpopular laws should be obeyed.

More important, perhaps, than President Washington's army in pacifying the frontier was the Battle of Fallen Timbers in Ohio near present-day Toledo, where in August 1794 Major General "Mad Anthony" Wayne won a decisive victory over the Indians. Wayne's victory opened the way for the settlement of the region. Some 2,000 of the Whiskey rebels simply pulled up stakes after the effort to avoid the excise collapsed and headed for Ohio.

Jay's Treaty

Still more significant was the outcome of President Washington's decision to send John Jay to England to seek a treaty settling the conflicts that vexed the relations of the two nations. The British genuinely wanted to reach an accommodation with the United States—as one minister quipped, the Americans "are so much in debt to this country that we scarcely dare to quarrel with them." They also feared that the two new republics, France and the United States, would draw together in a battle against Europe's monarchies. But they were riding the crest of a wave of important victories in the war in Europe and were not disposed to make concessions to the Americans simply to avoid trouble.

Jay spent months in England in 1794, discussing various issues. The treaty he brought home contained one major concession: The British agreed to evacuate the posts in the West. They also promised to compensate American shipowners for seizures in the West Indies and to open up their colonies in Asia to American ships. The British conceded nothing, however, to American demands that the rights of neutrals on the high seas be respected; in effect, Jay submitted to the "Rule of 1756," a British regulation stating that neutrals could not trade in wartime with ports normally closed to them by mercantilistic restrictions in time of peace.

Jay also assented to an arrangement that prevented the United States from imposing discriminatory duties on British goods, an idea that a number of congressmen had proposed as a means of forcing Great Britain to treat American commerce more gently. He committed the United States government to paying pre-Revolutionary debts still owed British merchants, a slap in the face to states whose courts had been impeding their collection. Yet nothing was said about the British paying for the slaves they had "abducted" during the fighting in the south.

Although Jay could perhaps have driven a harder bargain, this was a valuable treaty for the United States. But it was also a humiliating one because most of what the United States gained already legally belonged to it, and the treaty sacrificed principles of tremendous importance to a nation dependent on foreign trade. It seemed certain to be rejected. But Washington, swallowing his disappointment, submitted the treaty to the Senate.

1795: All's Well That Ends Well

Washington's decision was one of the wisest and luckiest of his career and after long debate the Senate ratified the treaty in June 1795. The treaty marked an important step toward regularizing Anglo-American relations, which was essential for both the economic and political security of the nation. And the evacuation of the British forts was an enormous advantage.

Still another benefit was unplanned. The Jay Treaty enabled the United States to solve its problems on its southeastern frontier. During the early 1790s, Spain had made alliances with Indian tribes hostile to the Americans and built forts on territory ceded to the United States by Great Britain in the Treaty of Paris. In 1795, however, Spain intended to withdraw from the European war against France. Fearing a joint Anglo-American attack on Louisiana and its other American possessions, it decided to improve relations with the United States. The king's chief minister suddenly offered the American envoy Thomas Pinckney a

The United States, 1787–1802

treaty granting the United States the free navigation of the Mississippi River and the right of deposit at New Orleans that western Americans so urgently needed. This Treaty of San Lorenzo, popularly known as Pinckney's Treaty, also accepted the American version of the boundary between Spanish Florida and the United States.

The Senate ratified the Jay Treaty in June 1795. Pinckney signed the Treaty of San Lorenzo in October. That August, after their defeat in the Battle of Fallen Timbers, 12 western tribes signed the Treaty of Greenville, surrending huge sections of their lands to the United States. After these events, settlers poured into the West as water bursts through a broken dike. Kentucky had

become a state in 1792. In 1796, Tennessee was admitted to the Union and by 1800 Mississippi and Indiana territories had been organized.

Washington's Farewell

However, settlement of western problems did not put an end to partisan strife. Even the sainted Washington was neither immune to attack nor entirely above the battle. On questions of finance and foreign policy he usually sided with Hamilton and thus increasingly incurred the anger of the Jeffersonians. But he was, after all, a Virginian. Only the most rabid partisan could think him a tool of northern commercial interests. He remained a symbol of national unity. But he was determined to put away the cares of office. In September 1796 he announced his retirement in a "Farewell Address" to the nation.

Washington found the acrimonious rivalry between Federalists and Republicans most disturbing. Hamilton advocated national unity, yet he seemed prepared to smash any individual or faction that disagreed with his vision of the country's future. Jefferson had risked his neck for independence, but he opposed the economic development needed to make America strong enough to defend that independence. Washington was less brilliant than either Hamilton or Jefferson but wiser. He appreciated how important it was that the new nation remain at peace and he deplored the "baneful effects of the spirit of party" that led honest people to use unscrupulous means to win a mean advantage over fellow Americans. He tried to show how the North benefited from the prosperity of the South, the South from that of the North, and the East and West also, in reciprocal fashion. In his farewell he urged the people to avoid both "inveterate antipathies" and "passionate attachments" to any foreign nation. Nothing had alarmed him more than the sight of Americans dividing into "French" and "English" factions. America should develop its foreign trade but steer clear of foreign political connections as far as possible. "Permanent alliances" should be avoided, although "temporary alliances for extraordinary purposes" might sometimes be useful.

The Election of 1796

Washington's Farewell Address was destined to have a long and important influence on American thinking, but its immediate impact was small. He had intended it to cool political passions. Instead, in the words of one Federalist congressman, people took it as "a signal, like dropping a hat, for the party racers to start." By the time the 1796 presidential campaign had ended, many Federalists and Republicans were refusing to speak to one another.

Jefferson was the only Republican candidate seriously considered in 1796. The logical Federalist was Hamilton, but, as was to happen so often in

American history with powerful leaders, he was not considered "available" because his controversial policies had made him many enemies. Gathering in caucus, the Federalists in Congress nominated Vice President John Adams for the top office and Thomas Pinckney of South Carolina, negotiator of the popular Spanish treaty, for vice president. In the election the Federalists were victorious.

Hamilton, hoping to run the new administration from the wings, preferred Pinckney, a relatively weak character, to the tough-minded Adams. He arranged for some of the Federalist electors from South Carolina to vote only for Pinckney. Catching wind of this, a number of New England electors retaliated by cutting Pinckney. As a result, Adams won in the electoral college, 71 to 68, over Jefferson, who had the solid support of the Republican electors. Pinckney got only 59 electoral votes.

The unexpected result seemed to presage a decline in partisanship. Adams actually preferred the Virginian to Pinckney for the vice presidency, and Jefferson said that if Adams would "reliquish his bias to an English constitution," he might make a fine chief executive. The two had in common a distaste for Hamilton—a powerful bond.

However, the closeness of the election indicated a trend toward the Republicans. Without Washington to lead them, the Federalist politicians were already quarreling among themselves; honest, able, hardworking John Adams was too caustic and too scathingly frank to unite them. Everything seemed to indicate a Republican victory at the next election.

The XYZ Affair

At this point one of the most remarkable reversals of public feeling in American history occurred. French attacks on American shipping, begun out of irritation at the Jay Treaty and in order to influence the election, continued after Adams took office. Hoping to stop them, Adams appointed three commissioners to negotiate a settlement. Their mission was a fiasco. Talleyrand, the French foreign minister, sent three agents (later spoken of as X, Y, and Z) to demand a huge bribe as the price of making a deal. The Americans refused, the talks broke up, and in April 1798 President Adams released the commissioners' reports.

They caused a sensation. Americans' sense of national honor, perhaps overly tender because the country was so young and insecure, was outraged. Adams, never a man with mass appeal, suddenly found himself a national hero. Federalist hotheads burned for a fight. Congress unilaterally abrogated the French Alliance, created a Navy Department, and appropriated enough money to build 40-odd warships and triple the size of the army. On the seas, American privateers began to attack French shipping.

Adams did not much like the French and he could be extremely stubborn. A declaration of war would have been immensely popular. But perhaps—it is not an entirely illogical surmise about John Adams—the president did not want to be popular. Instead of calling for war, he contented himself with approving the buildup of the armed forces.

The Republicans, committed to friendship with France, were thrown into consternation. Although angered by the XYZ Affair, they hoped to avoid war and tried, as one angry Federalist said, "to clog the wheels of government" by opposing the military appropriations. Their newspapers spewed abuse on Adams and his administration. Benjamin Bache, editor of the Philadelphia *Aurora*, referred to the president as "blind, bald, toothless, querulous," which was three-quarters true but irrelevant.

Many Federalists expected the Republicans to side with France if war broke out. Hysterical and near panic, they persuaded themselves that the danger of subversion was acute. The French Revolution and the resulting war were churning European society to the depths, stirring the hopes of liberals, and striking fear in the hearts of conservatives. Refugees of both persuasions were flocking to the United States. Suddenly the presence of these foreigners seemed threatening to "native" Americans.

The Alien and Sedition Acts

Conservative Federalists saw in this situation a chance to smash the opposition. In June and July 1798 they pushed through Congress a series of repressive measures known as the Alien and Sedition Acts. The least offensive of these laws, the Naturalization Act, increased the period a foreigner had to reside in the United States before being eligible for citizenship from 5 to 14 years. The Alien Enemies Act gave the president the power to arrest or expel aliens in time of "declared war," but since the quasi-war with France was never declared, this measure had no practical importance. The Alien Act authorized the president to expel all aliens whom he thought "dangerous to the peace and safety of the United States." (Adams never invoked this law, but a number of aliens left the country out of fear that he might.)

Finally, there was the Sedition Act. Its first section, making it a crime "to impede the operation of any law" or to attempt to instigate a riot or insurrection, was reasonable enough; but the act also made it illegal to publish, or even to utter, any "false, scandalous and malicious" criticism of high government officials. Although milder than British sedition laws, this proviso rested, as James Madison said, on "the exploded doctrine" that government officials "are the masters and not the servants of the people."

As the election of 1800 approached, the Federalists made a systematic attempt to silence the leading Republican newspapers. Twenty-five persons were prosecuted and ten convicted, all in patently unfair trials. In a typical case, the editor Thomas Cooper, an English-born radical, later president of the University of South Carolina, was sentenced to six months in jail and fined $400.

The Kentucky and Virginia Resolves

Although Thomas Jefferson did not object to state sedition laws, he believed that the Alien and Sedition Acts violated the First Amendment's guarantees of freedom of speech and the press and were an invasion of the rights of the states. He and Madison decided to draw up resolutions arguing that the laws were unconstitutional. Madison's draft was presented to the Virginia legislature and Jefferson's to the legislature of Kentucky. Jefferson argued that since the Constitution was a compact made by sovereign states, each state had "an equal right to judge for itself" when the compact had been violated. Thus a state could declare a law of Congress unconstitutional. Madison's Virginia Resolves took an only slightly less forthright position.

Neither Kentucky nor Virginia tried to implement these resolves or to prevent the enforcement of the Alien and Sedition Acts. Jefferson and Madison were protesting Federalist high-handedness and firing the opening salvo of Jefferson's campaign for the presidency, not advancing a new constitutional theory of extreme states' rights. "Keep away all show of force," Jefferson advised his supporters.

This was sound advice, for events were again playing into the hands of the Republicans. Talleyrand had never wanted war with the United States. When he discovered how vehemently the Americans had reacted to his little attempt to replenish his personal fortune, he let Adams know that new negotiators would be properly received.

President Adams quickly grasped the importance of the French change of heart. Other leading Federalists, however, had lost their heads. By shouting about the French danger, they had roused the country against radicalism, and they did not intend to surrender this advantage tamely. Hamilton in particular wanted war at almost any price—if not against France, then against Spain. He saw himself at the head of the new American army sweeping first across Louisiana and the Floridas, then on to the South. "We ought to squint at South America," he suggested. "Tempting objects will be without our grasp."

But the Puritan John Adams specialized in resisting temptation. At this critical point his intelligence, his moderate political philosophy, and his integrity stood him in good stead. He would neither go to war merely to destroy the political opposition in America nor follow "the fools who were intriguing to plunge us into . . . wild expeditions to South America." Instead he submitted to the Senate the name of a new minister plenipotentiary to France, and when the Federalists tried to block the appointment, he threatened to resign. That would have made Jefferson president! The furious

Milestones

1781	States fail to approve Congress's "impost" (tariff)		First ten amendments (the Bill of Rights) ratified
1783	British Order in Council bans trade with West Indies		Republican and Federalist political parties organized
1786	Rhode Island Supreme Court upholds state legal tender act (*Trevett* v. *Weeden*)		Philip Freneau's *National Gazette* and John Fenno's *Gazette of the United States* founded
	Shays's Rebellion in Massachusetts	**1793**	King Louis XVI of France executed
	Annapolis Convention		
1787	Philadelphia Constitutional Convention		Washington's Declaration of Neutrality
1787–1788	All states but North Carolina and Rhode Island ratify the Constitution	**1794**	Battle of Fallen Timbers
			Whiskey Rebellion in Pennsylvania
1789	Washington inaugurated as President	**1795**	Jay's Treaty ratified
	Storming of Paris Bastille begins French Revolution	**1796**	Washington's Farewell Address
		1798	XYZ Affair
1790	Hamilton's *Report on Public Credit*		Congress passes the Alien and Sedition Acts
			Madison's Virginia Resolutions
1791	Hamilton's *Report on Manufactures*	**1798–1799**	Jefferson's Kentucky Resolutions

Federalists had to give in, though they forced Adams to send three men instead of one.

Napoleon had taken over France by the time the Americans arrived, and he drove a harder bargain than Talleyrand would have. But in the end he signed an agreement (the Convention of 1800) abrogating the Franco-American treaties of 1778. Nothing was said about the damage done to American shipping by the French, but the war scare was over.

Supplementary Reading

On the "critical period," the drafting of the Constitution, and the early history of the new nation, see R. B. Morris, **The Forging of the Union** * (1987), and J. T. Main, **Political Parties before the Constitution** (1973). On economic development, see E. J. Ferguson, **The Power of the Purse** * (1968), and C. P. Nettels, **The Emergence of a National Economy** * (1962). D. P. Szatmary, **Shays's Rebellion** (1980), is the most recent study.

The political thinking of the period is discussed lucidly in Forrest McDonald, **Novus Ordo Seculorum: The Intellectual Origins of the Constitution** (1985). A good general account of the convention is Clinton Rossiter, **1787: The Grand Convention** * (1966). The best treatment of Alexander Hamilton's connection with the Constitution and of his political views generally is Clinton Rossiter, **Alexander Hamilton and the Constitution** (1964). Madison's role is discussed in D. R. McCoy, **The Last of the Fathers** (1989).

C. A. Beard, **An Economic Interpretation of the Constitution** * (1913), caused a veritable revolution in the thinking of historians about the motives of the Founding Fathers, but later works have caused a major reaction away from the Beardian interpretation; see especially R. E. Brown, **Charles Beard and the Constitution** * (1956), and a more detailed critique, Forrest McDonald, **We the People** * (1958). R. A. Rutland, **The Ordeal of the Constitution** (1966), and J. T. Main, **The Antifederalists** * (1961), are helpful in understanding the opposition to the Constitution, and the **Federalist Papers** * of Hamilton, Madison, and Jay, available in many editions, are essential for the arguments of the supporters of the new government. For the Bill of Rights, consult Bernard Schwartz, **The Great Rights of Mankind** (1977).

On the organization of the federal government and the history of the Washington administration, see L. D. White, **The Federalists** (1948), an administrative history and J. C. Miller, **The Federalist Era** * (1960), a more general history of the period. Washington's presidency is treated in detail in the latter volumes of D. S. Freeman, **George Washington** (1948–1957). Joseph Charles, **Origins of the American Party System** * (1961), is thought provoking, and the early chapters of W. N. Chambers, **Political Parties in a New Nation** * (1963), are also useful. For the Whiskey Rebellion see T. P. Slaughter, **The Whiskey Rebellion (1986)**.

Good biographies of Hamilton include Broadus Mitchell, **Alexander Hamilton** * (1976), and J. E. Cooke, **Alexander Hamilton** (1982). For foreign affairs, see Alexander De Conde, **Entangling Alliance: Politics and Diplomacy under George Washington** (1958) and William Stinchcombe, **The XYZ Affair** (1980).

On the Adams administration consult S. G. Kurtz, **The Presidency of John Adams** (1957). For the Alien and Sedition Acts, see J. M. Smith, **Freedom's Fetters** * (1956) and L. W. Levy, **Freedom of Speech and Press in Early American History** * (1963).

*Available in paperback.

CHAPTER 6

Jeffersonian Democracy

The Election of 1800
The Federalist Contribution
Thomas Jefferson: Political Theorist
Jefferson as President
Attack on the Judiciary
The Barbary Pirates
The Louisiana Purchase
Federalism Discredited
Lewis and Clark
Jeffersonian Democracy
Flies in the President's Ointment
The Burr Conspiracy
Napoleon and the British
The Impressment Controversy
The Embargo Act

The Election of 1800

*O*nce the furor over war and subversion subsided, public attention focused on the presidential contest between Adams and Jefferson. Because of his stand for peace, Adams personally escaped the brunt of popular indignation against the Federalist party. His solid qualities had a strong appeal to conservatives, and fear that the Republicans would introduce radical "French" social reforms did not disappear. Many nationalist minded voters worried lest the strong government established by the Federalists be weakened by the Republicans in the name of states' rights. The economic progress stimulated by Hamilton's

financial reforms also seemed threatened. But when the electors' votes were counted in February 1801, the Republicans were discovered to have won narrowly, 73 to 65.

But *which* Republican? The Constitution did not distinguish between presidential and vice presidential candidates; it provided only that each elector should vote for two candidates, the one with the most votes becoming president and the runner-up vice president. The development of national political parties made this system impractical. The vice presidential candidate of the Republicans was Aaron Burr of New York, a former senator and a rival of Hamilton in law and politics. But Republican party solidarity had been perfect: Jefferson and Burr received 73 votes each. Because of the tie, the Constitution required that the House of Representatives (voting by states) had to choose between them.

The Revolution of 1800

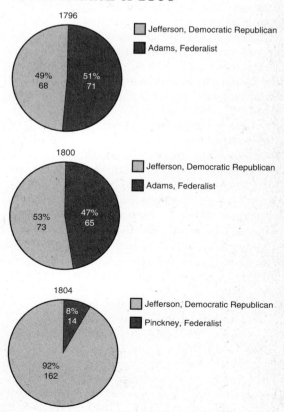

1796

49% 68 — Jefferson, Democratic Republican
51% 71 — Adams, Federalist

1800

53% 73 — Jefferson, Democratic Republican
47% 65 — Adams, Federalist

1804

8% 14 — Pinckney, Federalist
92% 162 — Jefferson, Democratic Republican

In the House, the Republicans could control only 8 of the 16 state delegations. On the first ballot, Jefferson got these 8 votes, one short of election; 6 states voted for Burr. Two state delegations, being evenly split, lost their votes. Through 35 ballots the deadlock persisted; the Federalist congressmen, fearful of Jefferson's supposed radicalism, voted solidly for Burr. Finally Hamilton, who detested Burr, threw his weight to Jefferson. The Federalists yielded, and Jefferson was elected. Burr became vice president.

To make sure that this deadlock would never be repeated, the Twelfth Amendment was drafted, providing for separate balloting in the electoral college for president and vice president. This change was ratified in 1804, shortly before the next election.

The Federalist Contribution

On March 4, 1801, in the raw new national capital on the Potomac River named in honor of the father of his country, Thomas Jefferson took the presidential oath and delivered his inaugural address. The new president believed that a revolution as important as that heralded by his immortal Declaration of Independence had occurred, and for once most of his political enemies agreed with him.

Certainly an era had ended. In the years between the Peace of Paris and Jay's Treaty, the Federalists had practically monopolized the political good sense of the nation. In the perspective of history, they were "right" in strengthening the federal government, in establishing a sound fiscal system, in trying to diversify the economy, in seeking an accommodation with Great Britain, and in refusing to be carried away with enthusiasm for France despite the bright dreams inspired by the French Revolution. The Constitution is their monument, with its wise compromises, its balance of forces, its restraint, and its practical concessions to local prejudices.

But the Federalists were unable to face up to defeat. When they saw the Republicans gathering strength by developing clever new techniques of party organization and propaganda, they panicked. Abandoning the sober wisdom of their great period, they fought to save themselves at any cost. The effort turned defeat into rout. The Republican victory, fairly close in the electoral college, approached landslide proportions in the congressional elections, where popular feeling expressed itself directly.

Jefferson erred, however, in calling this triumph a revolution. The real upheaval had been attempted in 1798; it was Federalist-inspired, and it had failed. In 1800 the voters expressed a preference for the old over the new, that is, for individual freedom and limited national power. And Jefferson, despite Federalist fears that he would destroy the Constitution and establish a radical social order, presided instead over a regime that confirmed the great achievements of the Federalist era.

What was most significant about the election of 1800 was that it was *not* a revolution. After a bitter contest, the Jeffersonians took power and proceeded to change the policy of the government. They did so peacefully. Thus American republican government passed a crucial test: Control of its machinery had changed hands in a democratic and orderly way. And only slightly less significant, the informal party system had demonstrated its usefulness. The Jeffersonians had organized popular dissatisfaction with Federalist policies, formulated a platform of reform, chosen leaders to put their plans into effect, and elected those leaders to office.

Thomas Jefferson: Political Theorist

Jefferson hardly seemed cut out for politics. Although in some ways a typical, pleasure-loving southern planter, he had in him something of the Spartan. He grew tobacco but did not smoke. Unlike most planters he never hunted or gambled, though he was a fine horseman and enjoyed dancing, music, and other social diversions. His practical interests ranged enormously—from architecture and geology to natural history and scientific farming—yet he displayed little interest in managing men. Controversy dismayed him, and he tended to avoid it by assigning to some thicker-skinned associate the task of attacking his enemies.

Like Hamilton, Jefferson thought human beings basically selfish. "Lions and tigers are mere lambs compared with men," he once said. Al-

THE PROVIDENTIAL DETECTION

This anti-Jefferson cartoon shows the newly selected president kneeling before the altar to Gallic Despotism, whereon he is burning the writings of prominent Enlightenment philosophers. The American eagle appears to be wrestling the Constitution from Jefferson's grasp.

though he claimed to have some doubts about the subject, he suspected that blacks were "inferior to whites in the endowments both of body and mind." (Hamilton, who also owned slaves, stated flatly of blacks: "Their natural faculties are as good as ours.")

Yet like a good child of the Enlightenment, Jefferson believed that "no definite limits can be assigned to the improvability of the human race" and that unless people were free to follow the dictates of reason, the march of civilization would grind quickly to a halt. Democracy seemed to him not so much an ideal as a practical necessity. If people could not govern themselves, how could they be expected to govern their fellows? He had no patience with Hamilton's fondness for magnifying the virtues of the rich and the well-born. He believed that "genius" was a rare quality but one "which nature has shown as liberally among poor as rich." When a very old man, he wrote: "The

mass of mankind has not been born with saddles on their backs, nor a favored few booted and spurred, ready to ride them legitimately, by the grace of God."

Jefferson believed *all* government a necessary evil at best, for by its nature it restricted the freedom of the individual. For this reason, he wanted the United States to remain a society of small independent farmers. Such a nation did not need much political organization.

Jefferson's main objection to Hamilton was that Hamilton wanted to commercialize and centralize the country. This Jefferson feared, for it would mean the growth of cities, which would complicate society and hence require more regulation. Like Hamilton, he believed that city workers were easy prey for demagogues. "I consider the class of artificers as the panders of vice, and the instruments by which the liberties of a country are usually overturned," he said. "Those who labor in the earth," he also said, "are the chosen people of God, if ever He had a chosen people."

Jefferson objected to what he considered Hamilton's pro-British orientation. Despite his support of the Revolution, Hamilton admired English society and the orderliness of the British government, and he modeled much of his financial program on the British example. To the author of the Declaration of Independence, these attitudes passed all understanding. Jefferson thought English society immoral and decadent, the British system of government fundamentally corrupt.

Jefferson as President

The novelty of the new administration lay in its style and its moderation. Both were apparent in Jefferson's inaugural address. The new president's opening remarks showed that he was neither a demagogue nor a firebrand. "The task is above my talents," he said modestly, "and . . . I approach it with . . . anxious and awful presentiments." The people had spoken, and their voice must be heeded, but the rights of dissenters must be respected. "All . . . will bear in mind this sacred principle," he said, "that though the will of the majority is in all cases to prevail, that will to be rightful must be reasonable; that the minority possess their equal rights, which equal law must protect, and to violate would be oppression."

Jefferson spoke at some length about specific policies. He declared himself against "entangling alliances" and for economy in government, and he promised to pay off the national debt, preserve the government's credit, and stimulate both agriculture and its "handmaid," commerce. His main stress was on the cooling of partisan passions. "Every difference of opinion is not a difference of principle. We have called by different names brethren of the same principle. We are all Republicans—we are all Federalists." And he promised the country "a wise and frugal Government, which shall restrain men from injuring one another . . . [and] leave them otherwise free to regulate their own pursuits."

Jefferson quickly demonstrated the sincerity of his remarks. He saw to it that the Whiskey Tax and other Federalist excises were repealed, and he made sharp cuts in military and naval expenditures to keep the budget in balance. The national debt was reduced from $83 million to $57 million during his eight years in office. The Naturalization Act of 1798 was repealed and the old five years' requirement for citizenship restored. The Sedition Act and the Alien Act expired of their own accord in 1801 and 1802.

The changes were not drastic. Jefferson made no effort to tear down the fiscal structure that Hamilton had erected. "We can pay off his debt," the new president confessed, "but we cannot get rid of his financial system." Nor did the author of the Kentucky Resolves try to alter the balance of federal-state power.

Yet there was a different tone to the new regime. In the White House, Jefferson often wore a frayed coat and carpet slippers, even to receive the representatives of foreign powers when they arrived, resplendent with silk ribbons and a sense of their own importance, to present their credentials. During business hours, congressmen, friends, foreign officials, and plain citizens coming to call took their turn in the order of their arrival. "The principle of society with us," Jefferson explained, "is the equal rights of all. . . . Nobody shall be above you, nor you above anybody, *pell-mell* is our law."

"Pell-mell" was also good politics, and Jefferson turned out to be a superb politician. He gave dozens of small stag dinner parties for congress-men, serving the food personally from a dumbwaiter connected with the White House kitchen. These were ostensibly social occasions—shoptalk was avoided—yet they paid large political dividends. "You see, we are alone and *our walls have no ears*," he would say, and while the wine flowed and the guests sampled delicacies prepared by Jefferson's French chef, the president manufactured political capital. "You drink as you please and converse at your ease," one senator-guest reported.

Jefferson made effective use of his close supporters in Congress, and of Cabinet members as well, in persuading Congress to go along with his proposals. His state papers were models of sweet reason, minimizing conflicts, stressing areas where all honest citizens must agree. After all, as he indicated in his inaugural address, nearly all Americans did believe in having both a federal government and a republican system. No great principle divided them into irreconcilable camps. Jefferson set out to bring them all into *his* camp and succeeded so well in four years that when he ran for reelection against Charles Pinckney, he got 162 of the 176 electoral votes cast.

Attack on the Judiciary

Although notably open-minded and tolerant, Jefferson had a few stubborn prejudices. One was against kings, another against the British system of government. A third was against judges, or rather, against entrenched judicial power. While recognizing that judges must have a degree of independence, he feared what he called their "habit of going out of the question before them, to throw an anchor ahead, and grapple further hold for future advances of power." The biased behavior of Federalist judges during the trials under the Sedition Act had enormously increased this distrust. It burst all bounds when the Federalist majority of the dying Congress rammed through the Judiciary Act of 1801.

The Judiciary Act created 6 new circuit courts, presided over by 16 new federal judges, and a small army of attorneys, marshals, and clerks. The expanding country needed the judges, but with the enthusiastic cooperation of President Adams the Federalists made shameless use of the opportunity to fill all the new positions with conservative members of their own party. The appointees were dubbed "midnight justices" because Adams had stayed up till midnight on March 3, his last day as president, feverishly signing their commissions.

The Republicans retaliated as soon as the new Congress met by repealing the Judiciary Act of 1801, but on taking office Jefferson had discovered that in the confusion of Adams's last hours the commissions of a number of justices of the peace for the new District of Columbia had not been distributed. Although these were small fry indeed, Jefferson was so angry that he ordered the commissions held up even though they had been signed by Adams. One of Adams's appointees, William Marbury, then petitioned the Supreme Court for a writ of *mandamus* (Latin for "we order") directing the new secretary of state, James Madison, to give him his commission.

The case of *Marbury* v. *Madison* (1803) placed one of Adams's "midnight" appointments, Chief Justice Marshall, in an embarrassing position. Marbury had a strong claim. If Marshall refused to issue a *mandamus,* everyone would say he dared not stand up to Jefferson, and the prestige of the Court would suffer. If he issued the writ, however, he would place the Court in direct conflict with the executive. Madison would probably ignore the order, and in the prevailing state of public opinion nothing would be done to make him act. This would be a still more staggering blow to the judiciary. What should the chief justice do?

Marshall had studied law only briefly and had no previous judicial experience, but in this crisis he first displayed the genius that was to mark him as a great judge. By right Marbury should have his commission, he announced. However, the Court could not require Madison to give it to him. Marbury's request for a *mandamus* had been based on an ambiguous clause in the Judiciary Act of 1789. That clause was unconstitutional, Marshall declared, and therefore void. Congress could not legally give the Supreme Court the right to issue writs of mandamus in such circumstances.

With the skill and foresight of a chess grand master, Marshall turned what had looked like a trap into a triumph. By sacrificing the pawn, Marbury, he established the power of the Supreme Court to invalidate federal laws that conflicted with the Constitution. Jefferson could not check him because instead of throwing an anchor ahead, as Jefferson had feared, Marshall had *refused*

power. Yet he had certainly grappled a "further hold for future advances of power," and the president could do nothing to stop him.

The Marbury case made Jefferson more determined to strike at the Federalist-dominated courts. He decided to press for the impeachment of some of the more partisan judges. First he had the House of Representatives bring charges against District Judge John Pickering. Pickering was clearly insane—he had frequently delivered profane and drunken harangues from the bench—and the Senate quickly voted to remove him. Then Jefferson went after a much larger fish, Samuel Chase, associate justice of the Supreme Court, whose handling of cases under the Sedition Act had been outrageously high-handed. But the trial demonstrated that Chase's actions had not constituted the "high crimes and misdemeanors" required by the Constitution to remove a judge. Even Jefferson became disenchanted with the efforts of some of his more extreme followers and accepted Chase's acquittal with equanimity.

The Barbary Pirates

Aside from these perhaps salutary setbacks, Jefferson's first term was a parade of triumphs. Although he cut back the army and navy sharply in order to save money, he temporarily escaped the consequences of leaving the country undefended because of the lull in the European war signalized by the Treaty of Amiens between Great Britain and France in March 1802. Despite the fact that he had only seven frigates in commission, he even managed to fight a small naval war with the Barbary pirates without damage to American interests or prestige.

The North African Arab states of Morocco, Algiers, Tunis, and Tripoli had for decades made a business of piracy, seizing vessels and their cargoes and holding passengers and crews for ransom. The European powers found it simpler to pay them annual protection money than to crush them. Under Washington and Adams, the United States joined in the payment of this tribute. Such pusillanimity ran against Jefferson's grain, and, when the pasha of Tripoli tried to raise the charges, he balked. Tripoli then declared war in May 1801, and Jefferson dispatched a squadron to the Mediterranean.

The pirates were not overwhelmed, but America, though far removed from the pirate bases, was the only maritime nation that tried to resist their shameful blackmail. In 1815 the tribute was ended and the pasha agreed to a new treaty more favorable to the United States.

The Louisiana Purchase

The major achievements of Jefferson's first term had to do with the American West, and of them the greatest by far was the acquisition of the huge area between the Mississippi River and the Rocky Mountains, called Louisiana.

Along with every other American who had even a superficial interest in the West, Jefferson understood that the United States must have access to the mouth of the Mississippi and the city of New Orleans or eventually lose everything beyond the Appalachians. Thus, when he learned shortly after his inauguration that Spain had given Louisiana back to France, he was immediately on his guard. Control of Louisiana by Spain, a "feeble" country with "pacific dispositions," could be tolerated; control by a resurgent France dominated by Napoleon, the greatest military genius of the age, was entirely different. Did Napoleon have designs on Canada? Did he perhaps mean to resume the old Spanish and British game of encouraging the Indians to harry the American frontier? And what now would be the status of Pinckney's precious treaty? Deeply worried, the president instructed his newly appointed minister to France, Robert R. Livingston, to seek assurances that American rights in New Orleans would be respected and to negotiate the purchase of West Florida in case that region had also been turned over to France.

Jefferson's concern was well founded; France was indeed planning new imperial ventures in North America. The secret Treaty of San Idefonso with Spain (1800) returned Louisiana to France. Napoleon hoped to use this region as a breadbasket for the French West Indian sugar plantations, just as colonies like Pennsylvania and Massachusetts had fed the British sugar islands before the Revolution.

However, the most important French island, Saint Domingue, or Haiti, had slipped from French control. At the time of the French Revolution the slaves of the island had revolted. In 1793 they were granted personal freedom, but they fought on under the leadership of the "Black Napoleon," a self-taught genius named Toussaint L'Ouverture, and by 1801 the island was entirely in their hands. The original Napoleon, taking advantage of the slackening of war in Europe, dispatched an army of 20,000 men under General Charles Leclerc to reconquer it.

When Jefferson learned of the Leclerc expedition, he had no trouble divining its relationship to Louisiana. His uneasiness became outright alarm. In April 1802 he again urged Minister Livingston to attempt the purchase of New Orleans and Florida. If the right of deposit could not be preserved through negotiation, it must be purchased with gunpowder, even if that meant acting in conjunction with the despised British. "The day that France takes possession of New Orleans," he warned, "we must marry ourselves to the British fleet and nation."

In October 1802 the Spanish, who had not yet actually turned Louisiana over to France, heightened the tension by suddenly revoking the right of deposit at New Orleans. With the West clamoring for relief, Jefferson appointed his friend and disciple James Monroe minister plenipotentiary and sent him to Paris with instructions to offer up to $10 million for New Orleans and Florida. If France refused, he and Livingston should open negotiations for a "closer connection" with the British.

Before Monroe reached France, the tension was broken. General Leclerc's expedition to Saint Domingue ended in disaster. Although Toussaint surrendered, Haitian resistance continued. Yellow fever raged through the French army; Leclerc himself fell before the fever, which wiped out practically his entire force.

Napoleon then began to have second thoughts about reviving French imperialism in the New World. Without Saint Domingue, the wilderness of Louisiana seemed of little value. On April 10 he ordered Foreign Minister Talleyrand to offer not merely New Orleans but all of Louisiana to the Americans. Talleyrand summoned Livingston to his office on the rue du Bac and dropped this bombshell. Livingston was almost struck speechless but quickly recovered his composure. When Talleyrand asked what the

United States would give for the province, he suggested the French equivalent of about $5 million. Talleyrand pronounced the sum "too low" and urged Livingston to think about the subject for a day or two.

Livingston faced a situation that could never confront a modern diplomat. His instructions said nothing about buying an area almost as large as the entire United States, and there was no time to write home for new instructions. The offer staggered the imagination. Luckily, Monroe arrived the next day to share the responsibility. The two Americans agreed—they could scarcely have done otherwise—to accept the proposal. Early in

May they signed a treaty. For 60 million francs—about $15 million—the United States was to have all Louisiana. Never, as the historian Henry Adams wrote, "did the United States government get so much for so little."

Napoleon's unexpected concession caused consternation in America. Jefferson did not believe that the government had the power under the Constitution to add new territory or to grant American citizenship to the 50,000 residents of Louisiana by executive act, as the treaty required. But his advisers convinced him that it would be dangerous to delay approval of the treaty until an amendment could be acted on by three-fourths of

Exploring the Louisiana Purchase

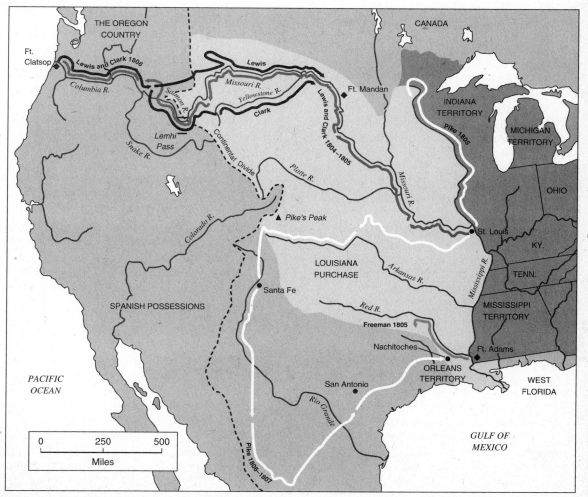

the states. Since what he called "the good sense of our country" clearly wanted Louisiana, he decided to "acquiesce with satisfaction" while Congress overlooked the "metaphysical subtleties" of the problem and ratified the treaty.

Some Federalists who had been eager to fight Spain for New Orleans now attacked Jefferson for undermining the Constitution. One critic described Louisiana contemptuously as a "Gallo-Hispano-Indian" collection of "savages and adventurers." But there was never real doubt that the treaty would be ratified, and it was.

Federalism Discredited

The West and the South were solid for Jefferson, and the North was rapidly succumbing to his charm. The addition of new western states would soon further reduce New England's power in national affairs. So complete did the Republican triumph seem that certain die-hard Federalists in New England began to think of secession. Led by former Secretary of State Timothy Pickering, a sour, implacable conservative, a group known as the Essex Junto organized in 1804 a scheme to break away from the Union and establish a "Northern Confederacy."

Even within the dwindling Federalist ranks, the Junto had little support. Nevertheless, Pickering and his friends pushed ahead, drafting a plan whereby, having captured political control of New York, they would take the entire Northeast out of the Union. Since they could not begin to win New York for anyone in their own ranks, they supported Vice President Aaron Burr, who was running against the "regular" Republican candidate for governor of New York. Although Burr did not promise to bring New York into their confederacy if elected, he encouraged them enough to win their backing. The foolishness of the plot was revealed in the April elections: Burr was overwhelmed by the regular Republican. The Junto's scheme collapsed.

The incident, however, had a tragic aftermath. Hamilton had campaigned against Burr, whom he considered "an embryo Caesar," in his most vitriolic style. When he continued after the election to cast aspersions on Burr's character

(not a very difficult assignment, since Burr frequently violated both the political and sexual mores of the day), Burr challenged him to a duel. The two met with pistols on July 11, 1804, at Weehawken, New Jersey, across the Hudson from New York City. Hamilton made no effort to hit the challenger, but Burr took careful aim. Hamilton fell, mortally wounded. Thus a great, if enigmatic, man was cut off in his prime. His work, in a sense, had been completed, and his philosophy of government was being everywhere rejected, yet the nation's loss was large.

Lewis and Clark

While the disgruntled Federalists dreamed of secession, Jefferson was planning the exploration of Louisiana and the region beyond. Early in 1803 he got $2,500 from Congress and obtained the permission of the French to send his exploring party across Louisiana. To command the expedition he appointed his private secretary, Meriwether Lewis, a young Virginian who had served with the army in the West and accumulated what Jefferson described as a "mass of accurate information on all the subjects of nature." Lewis chose as his companion officer William Clark, a veteran of the Battle of Fallen Timbers, who had much experience in negotiating with Indians.

Lewis and Clark gathered a group of 48 men near St. Louis during the winter of 1803–1804. In the spring they made their way slowly up the Missouri River in a 55-foot keelboat and two dugout canoes called pirogues. By late fall they had reached what is now North Dakota, where they built a small station, Fort Mandan, and spent the winter. In April 1805, having shipped back to the president more than 30 boxes of plants, minerals, animal skins and skeletons, and Indian artifacts, they struck out again toward the mountains, accompanied by a Shoshone squaw, Sacagawea, and her French-Canadian husband, who acted as interpreters and guides. They passed the Great Falls of the Missouri and then clambered over the Continental Divide at Lemhi Pass in southwestern Montana. Soon thereafter the going became easier, and they descended to the Pacific by way of the Cleanwater and Columbia rivers, reaching their destination in November. They had hoped to return by ship, but during the long, damp winter not a single vessel appeared. In the spring of 1806 they headed back by land, reaching St. Louis on September 23.

The country greeted the news of their return with delight. Besides locating several passes across the Rockies, Lewis and Clark had established friendly relations with a great many Indian tribes and brought back a wealth of data about the country and its resources. The journals kept by members of the group were published and, along with their accurate maps, became major sources for scientists, students, and future explorers. To Jefferson's personal satisfaction, Lewis provided him with many specimens of the local wildlife, including two grizzly bear cubs, which he kept for a time in a stone pit in the White House lawn.

Jeffersonian Democracy

With the purchase of Louisiana, Jefferson completed the construction of the political institution known as the Republican Party and the philosophy of government known as Jeffersonian Democracy. From what sort of materials had he built his juggernaut? In part his success was a matter of personality; in the march of American democracy he stood halfway, temperamentally, between George Washington and Andrew Jackson, perfectly in tune with the thinking of his times. The colonial American had practiced democracy without really believing in it; hence, for example, the maintenance of property qualifications for voting in regions where nearly everyone owned property. Stimulated by the libertarian ideas of the Revolution, Americans were rapidly adjusting their beliefs to conform with their practices. However, it took a Jefferson, a man of large estates, possessed of the general prejudice in favor of the old-fashioned citizen rooted in the soil, yet deeply committed to majority rule, to oversee the transition.

Jefferson prepared the country for democracy by proving that a democrat could establish and maintain a stable regime. The Federalist tyranny of 1798 was compounded of selfishness and stupidity, but it was also based in part on honest fears that an egalitarian regime would not protect the fabric of society from hotheads and crackpots. The impact of the French Revolution on conservative thinking in the middle 1790s can scarcely be overestimated. America had fought a seven-year revolution without executing a single Tory, yet during the months that the Reign of Terror ravaged France, nearly 17,000 persons were officially put to death for political "crimes," and many thousands more were killed in civil disturbances. Worse, in the opinion of many, the French extremists had attempted to destroy Christianity, substituting for it a "cult of reason." They confiscated property, imposed price controls, abolished slavery in the French colonies. Little wonder that many Americans feared that the Jeffersonians, lovers of France and of *liberté, égalité, fraternité,* would try to remodel American society in a similar way.

Jefferson calmed these fears. "Pell-mell" might scandalize the British and Spanish ministers and a few other mossbacks, but it was scarcely revolutionary. The most partisan Federalist was hard put to see a Robespierre in the amiable president scratching out state papers at his desk or chatting with a Kentucky congressman at a "republican" dinner party. Furthermore, Jefferson accepted Federalist ideas on public finance, even learning to live with Hamilton's bank. As a good democrat, he drew a nice distinction between his own opinions and the wishes of the majority, which he felt must always take priority.

During his term the country grew and prospered, the commercial classes sharing in the bounty along with the farmers so close to Jefferson's heart. Blithely he set out to win the support of all who could vote. "It is material to the safety of Republicanism," he wrote in 1803, "to detach the mercantile interests from its enemies and incorporate them into the body of its friends."

Thus Jefferson undermined the Federalists all along the line. They had said that the country must pay a stiff price for prosperity and orderly government, and they demanded prompt payment in full, both in cash (taxes) and in the form of limitations on human liberty. Under Jefferson these much-desired goals had been achieved cheaply and without sacrificing freedom. Order without discipline, security without a large military establishment, prosperity without regulatory legislation, freedom without license—truly the Sage of

This engraving by J. Stoner, *American Stage Wagon,* depicts the common mode of transportation along federal roads during the Jefferson administration.

Monticello appeared to have led his fellow Americans into a golden age.

Flies in the President's Ointment

Republican virtue seemed to have triumphed, both at home and abroad. "With nations as with individuals," Jefferson proclaimed as he took the oath of office at the start of his second term, "our interests soundly calculated, will ever be found inseparable from our moral duties." And he added more complacently still: "Fellow citizens, you best know whether we have done well or ill." Such smugness and complacency are luxuries that politicians can seldom afford. Jefferson soon found himself in trouble both at home and abroad.

His domestic troubles were not of critical importance, but they were vexing. To a considerable extent they resulted from the same characteristics that explain his success: his facility in adjusting his principles to practical conditions and his readiness to take over the best of Federalism. Some of his disciples were less ready than he to surrender principle to expediency.

The most prominent of the Republican critics was John Randolph of Roanoke, congressman from Virginia. Randolph was unique. Although he had wit, charm, and imagination, he was a vitriolic and unyielding obstructionist when he thought some principle was at stake. Randolph made a fetish of preserving states' rights against invasion by the central government. "Asking one of the States to surrender part of her sovereignty is like asking a lady to surrender part of her chastity," he remarked in one of his typical epigrams.

Randolph first clashed with Jefferson in 1804 over an attempted settlement of the so-called Yazoo land frauds. In 1795 the Georgia legislature had sold a huge area to four land companies for less than two cents an acre. When it was revealed that many of the legislators had been corrupted, the next legislature canceled the grants, but not before the original grantees had unloaded large tracts on various third parties. These innocents turned to the federal government for relief when the grants were canceled. Jefferson favored a bill giving 5 million acres to these interests, but Randolph would have none of this. Rising in righteous wrath, he denounced in his shrill soprano all those who would countenance fraud. The compromise bill was defeated. The controversy then entered the courts, and in 1810 Chief Justice Marshall held in *Fletcher* v. *Peck* that in rescinding the grant Georgia had committed an unconstitutional breach of contract. Before Marshall's ruling, however, the federal grant was finally approved by Congress. Had it not been, *Fletcher* v. *Peck* would have provided the "victims" of the Yazoo frauds with an area considerably larger than the state of Mississippi!

The Burr Conspiracy

Another Republican who caused trouble for Jefferson was Aaron Burr, and again the president was partially to blame for the difficulty. After their contest for the presidency in 1801, Jefferson pursued Burr vindictively and replaced him as the 1804 Republican vice presidential candidate with Governor George Clinton, Burr's chief rival in the state.

While still vice president, Burr began to flirt with treason. He approached Anthony Merry, the British minister in Washington, and offered to "effect a separation of the Western part of the United States." His price was £110,000 and the support of a British fleet off the mouth of the Mississippi. The British did not fall in with his scheme, but he went ahead nonetheless. He joined forces with General James Wilkinson, whom Jefferson had appointed governor of Louisiana Territory, and who, it will be recalled, had been involved in secessionist movements in the West and who was secretly in the pay of Spain.

In 1806 Burr and Wilkinson raised a small force at a place called Blennerhassett Island, on the Ohio River. Some six dozen men began to move downriver toward New Orleans under Burr's command. Whether the objective was New Orleans or some part of Mexico, the scheme was clearly illegal. For some reason, however—possibly because he was incapable of loyalty to anyone—Wilkinson betrayed Burr to Jefferson at the last moment. Burr tried to escape to Spanish Florida but was captured in February 1807, taken to Richmond, Virginia, under guard, and charged with high treason.

Any president will deal summarily with traitors, but Jefferson's attitude during Burr's trial reveals the depth of his hatred. He "made himself a party to the prosecution," personally sending evidence to the United States attorney who was handling the case and offering blanket pardons to associates of Burr who would agree to turn state's

evidence. On the other hand Chief Justice Marshall, presiding at the trial, repeatedly showed favoritism to the prisoner.

In this contest between two great men at their worst, Jefferson as a vindictive executive and Marshall as a prejudiced judge, the victory went to the judge. In his charge to the jury, Marshall made a verdict of not guilty almost mandatory. To "advise or procure treason" was not in itself treason, he said. In light of this charge, the jury, deliberating only 25 minutes, found Burr not guilty.

The Burr affair was a blow to Jefferson's prestige; it left him more embittered against Marshall and the federal judiciary, and it added nothing to his reputation as a statesman.

Napoleon and the British

Jefferson's difficulties with Burr may be traced at least in part to the purchase of Louisiana, which empty and unknown, excited the cupidity of men like Burr and Wilkinson. But problems infinitely more serious were also related to that territory.

Napoleon had jettisoned Louisiana to clear the decks before resuming the battle for control of Europe. This war had the effect of stimulating the American economy, for the warring powers needed American goods and American vessels. Shipbuilding boomed; foreign trade, which had quintupled since 1793, nearly doubled again between 1803 and 1805. By the summer of 1807, however, the situation had changed: A most unusual stalemate had developed in the war. In October 1805 Britain's Horatio Nelson demolished the combined Spanish and French fleets in the Battle of Trafalgar off the coast of Spain. On land, however, Napoleon quickly redressed the balance, smashing army after army thrown against him by Great Britain's continental allies. By 1807 he was master of Europe, while the British controlled the seas around the Continent. Neither nation could strike directly at the other.

They therefore resorted to commercial warfare, striving to disrupt each other's economy. Napoleon set up a paper blockade of the British Isles which made "all commerce and correspondence" with Great Britain illegal. The British retaliated by blockading most continental ports and barring from them all foreign vessels unless they first stopped at a British port and paid customs duties. Napoleon then issued his Milan Decree (December 1807), declaring any vessel that submitted to the British rules "to have become English property" and thus subject to seizure.

The blockades seemed designed to stop commerce completely, yet this was not the case. Napoleon's "Continental System" was supposed to make Europe self-sufficient and isolate Great Britain. But he was willing to sell European products to the Brirish (if the price were right); his chief objective was to deprive them of their continental markets. The British were ready to sell anything on the Continent, and to allow others to do so too, provided they first paid a toll.

When war first broke out between Britain and France in 1792, the colonial trade of both sides had fallen largely into American hands because the danger of capture drove many belligerent merchant vessels from the seas. This commerce had engaged Americans in some devious practices. Under the Rule of War of 1756, it will be recalled, the British denied to neutrals the right to engage in trade during time of war from which they were barred by mercantilistic regulations in time of peace. If an American ship carried sugar from the French colony of Martinique to France, for example, the British claimed the right to capture it because such traffic was normally confined to French bottoms by French law. To avoid this risk, American merchants brought the sugar first to the United States, a legal peacetime voyage under French mercantilism. Then they reshipped it to France as American sugar.

This underhanded commerce irritated the British. In 1806 a British judge, Sir William Grant, decreed that American ships could no longer rely on "mere voluntary *ceremonies*" to circumvent the Rule of 1756. Thus, just when Britain and France were cracking down on direct trade by neutrals, Britain determined to halt the American reexport trade, thereby gravely threatening American prosperity.

The Impressment Controversy

More dismaying were the cruel indignities being visited upon American seamen by the British practice of impressment. Under British law, any able-bodied subject could be drafted for service in the Royal Navy in an emergency. Normally, when the commander of a warship found himself shorthanded, he put into a British port and sent a "press gang" ashore to round up the necessary men in harborside pubs. When far from home waters, he might hail any passing British merchant ship and commandeer the necessary men, though this practice was understandably unpopular in British maritime circles. He might also stop a *neutral* merchantman on the high seas and remove any British subject. Since the United States owned by far the largest merchant fleet among the neutrals, its vessels bore the brunt of this practice.

Impressment had been a cause of Anglo-American conflict for many years. American pride suffered every time a vessel carrying the flag was forced to back topsails and heave to at the command of a British man-of-war, and British officers made little effort to be sure they were impressing British subjects; any likely looking lad might be taken when the need was great. Furthermore, there were legal questions in dispute. When did an English immigrant become an American? When he was naturalized, the United States claimed. Never, the British retorted; "Once an Englishman, always an Englishman."

Because working conditions in the American merchant marine were superior to those of the British, at least 10,000 British-born tars were serving on American ships. Some became American citizens legally; others obtained false papers; some admitted to being British subjects; some were deserters from the Royal Navy. From the British point of view, all were liable to impressment.

The Jefferson administration conceded the right of the British to impress their own subjects from American merchant ships. When naturalized Americans were impressed, however, the administration was irritated, and when native-born Americans were taken, it became incensed. Between 1803 and 1812 at least 5,000 sailors were snatched from the decks of United States vessels and forced to serve in the Royal Navy. Most of them—estimates run as high as three out of every four—were Americans.

The combination of impressment, British interference with the reexport trade, and the general harassment of neutral commerce instituted by both Great Britain and France would have perplexed the most informed and hardheaded of leaders, and in dealing with these problems Jefferson was neither informed nor hardheaded. Fundamentally, he was an isolationist, ready "to let every treaty we have drop off without renewal." He believed it much wiser to stand up for one's rights than to compromise, yet he hated the very thought of war. Perhaps, being from the South, he was less sensitive than he might have been to the interests of New England commercial interests. He kept only a skeleton navy on active service, despite the fact that the great powers were fighting a worldwide, no-holds-barred war. Instead of building a navy that other nations would have to respect, he relied on a tiny fleet of frigates and a swarm of gunboats that were useless against the Royal Navy—"a macabre monument," in the words of one historian, "to his hasty, ill-digested ideas" about defense.*

The Embargo Act

The frailty of Jefferson's policy became obvious once the warring powers began to attack neutral shipping in earnest. Between 1803 and 1807 the British seized over 500 American ships, Napoleon over 200 more. The United States could do nothing.

The ultimate in frustration came on June 22, 1807, off Norfolk, Virginia. The 46-gun American frigate *Chesapeake* had just left port. Among its crew were a British sailor who had deserted from HMS *Halifax* and three Americans who had been illegally impressed by the captain of HMS *Melampus* and had later escaped. The USS *Chesapeake* was barely out of sight of land when HMS *Leopard* (56 guns) signaled it to heave to. Thinking that *Leopard* wanted to make some routine communication, Captain James Barron did so. A British officer came aboard and demanded that the four "deserters" be handed over. Barron refused, whereupon as soon as the officer was back on board, *Leopard* opened fire on the unsuspect-

ing American ship, killing three sailors. Barron had to surrender. The "deserters" were seized and then the crippled *Chesapeake* was allowed to limp back to port.

The American press clamored for war, but the country had nothing to fight with. Jefferson contented himself with ordering British warships out of American territorial waters. However, he was determined to put a stop to the indignities being heaped on the flag by Great Britain and France. The result was the Embargo Act of 1807.

The Embargo Act prohibited all exports. American vessels could not clear for any foreign port, and foreign vessels could do so only if empty. Importing was not forbidden, but few foreign ships would come to the United States if they had to return without a cargo. Although the law was sure to injure the American economy, Jefferson hoped that it would work in two ways to benefit the nation. By keeping United States merchant ships off the seas it would end all chance of injury to them and to the national honor. By denying American goods and markets to Britain and France, great economic pressure would be put on them to moderate their policies toward American shipping. The fact that boycotts had repeatedly wrested concessions from the British during the crises preceding the Revolution was certainly in Jefferson's mind when he devised the embargo.

But the embargo demanded of the maritime interests far greater sacrifices than they could reasonably be expected to make. Massachusetts-owned ships alone were earning over $15 million a year in freight charges by 1807, and Bay State merchants were making far larger gains from the buying and selling of goods. Losses through seizure were exasperating, but they could be insured against. Impressment excited universal indignation, but it hit chiefly at the defenseless, the disreputable, and the obscure and never caused a labor shortage in the merchant marine. The profits of commerce were still tremendous. A Massachusetts senator estimated that if only one vessel in three escaped the blockade, the owner came out ahead. As John Randolph remarked in another typical sally, the administration was trying "to cure the corns by cutting off the toes."

The Embargo Act had catastrophic effects. Exports fell from $108 million in 1807 to $22 million in 1808, imports from $138 million to less than $57 mil-

---

*The gunboats had performed effectively against the Barbary pirates, but Jefferson was enamored of them mainly because they were cheap. A gunboat cost about $10,000 to build, a frigate well over $300,000.

lion. Prices of farm products and manufactured goods reacted violently; seamen were thrown out of work; merchants found their businesses disrupted.

How many Americans violated the law is difficult to determine, but they were ingenious at discovering ways to do so. The most obvious way was to smuggle goods back and forth across the Canadian border. As for ocean commerce, American ships made hastily for blue water before the machinery of enforcement could be put into operation, not to return until the law was repealed. Lawbreakers were difficult to punish. In the seaport towns, juries were no more willing to convict men of violating the Embargo Act than their fathers had been to convict those charged with violating the Townshend Acts. A mob at Gloucester, Massachusetts, destroyed a revenue cutter in the same spirit that Rhode Islanders exhibited in 1772 when they burned the *Gaspee*.

Surely the embargo was a mistake. The United States ought either to have suffered the indignities heaped on its vessels for the sake of profits or, by constructing a powerful navy, made it dangerous for the belligerents to treat its merchantmen so roughly. Jefferson was too proud to choose the former alternative, too parsimonious to choose the latter. Instead he applied harsher and harsher regulations in a futile effort to accomplish his purpose. Militiamen patrolled the Canadian border; revenuers searched out smuggled goods without proper warrants. The illegal trade continued, and in his last months as president Jefferson simply gave up. Even then he would not admit that the embargo was a fiasco and urge its repeal. Only in Jefferson's last week in office did a leaderless Congress finally abolish it, substituting the Non-Intercourse Act, which forbade trade only with Great Britain and France and authorized the president to end the boycott against either power by proclamation when and if it stopped violating the rights of Americans.

Milestones

1800	Jefferson elected president	**1804**	Alexander Hamilton killed by Aaron Burr in a duel
1801	Judiciary Act allows Adams to appoint many Federalist judges before leaving office	**1804–1806**	Lewis and Clark expedition
1801–1805	War with the Barbary pirates	**1806**	Burr Conspiracy
1803	Supreme Court declares part of Judiciary Act of 1789 unconstitutional	**1806–1807**	Napoleon's Berlin and Milan decrees
	Louisiana Territory purchased from France	**1807**	HMS *Leopard* attacks USS *Chesapeake*
			Embargo Act

Supplementary Reading

A useful compilation of Jefferson's writings is Adrienne Koch and William Peden, **The Life and Selected Writings of Thomas Jefferson** (1944). See also M. D. Peterson, **Thomas Jefferson and the New Nation*** (1970), Lance Banning, **The Jeffersonian Persuasion** (1978), and Joyce Appleby, **Capitalism and a New Social Order** (1984).

On the Federalist and Democratic-Republican parties, see M. J. Dauer, **The Adams Federalists*** (1953), N. E. Cunningham, Jr., **The Jeffersonian Republicans*** (1958), Linda Kerber, **Federalists in Dissent** (1970), and W. N. Chambers, **Political Parties in a New Nation*** (1963).

On Jefferson's presidency, consult Marshall Smelser, **The Democratic Republic*** (1968). On the parties of the era, see N. E. Cunningham, Jr., **The Jeffersonian Republicans in Power*** (1963), and D. H. Fischer, **The Revolution of American Conservatism: The Federalist Party in the Era of Jeffersonian Democracy***

(1965). J. S. Young, **The Washington Community*** (1966), is a fascinating account of political life during the Jefferson administration.

On the Louisiana Purchase, see George Dangerfield, **Chancellor Robert R. Livingston of New York** (1960). For the Lewis and Clark expedition, see P. R. Cutright, **Lewis and Clark: Pioneering Naturalists** (1976), and D. F. Hawke, **Those Tremendous Mountains** (1980). On Jefferson and the Supreme Court, T. P. Abernethy, **The Burr Conspiracy** (1954), is important, as is R. E. Ellis, **The Jeffersonian Crisis** (1971). The best account of the neutral rights question is Bradford Perkins, **Prologue to War** (1961).

*Available in paperback.

CHAPTER 7

National Growing Pains

Madison in Power

Tecumseh and the Prophet

Depression and Land Hunger

Resistance to War

The War of 1812

Britain Assumes the Offensive

The Treaty of Ghent

The Hartford Convention

The Battle of New Orleans

Fruits of "Victory"

Anglo-American Rapprochement

The Transcontinental Treaty

The Monroe Doctrine

The Era of Good Feelings

New Sectional Issues

Northern Leaders

Southern Leaders

Western Leaders

The Missouri Compromise

The Election of 1824

J.Q. Adams as President

Calhoun's Exposition and Protest

The Meaning of Sectionalism

*I*t is a measure of Jefferson's popularity and of the political ineptitude of the Federalists that the Republicans won the election of 1808 handily despite the embargo. James Madison got 122 of the 173 electoral votes for the presidency, and the party carried both houses of Congress, although by reduced majorities.

Madison in Power

Madison was a small, rather precise person, narrower in his interests than Jefferson but in many ways a deeper thinker. He was more conscientious in the performance of his duties and more consistent in adhering to his principles. But he had no better solution to offer for the problem of the hour than had Jefferson. The Non-Intercourse Act proved difficult to enforce—once an American ship left port, there was no way to prevent the skipper from steering for England or France—and it exerted little economic pressure on the British, who continued to seize American vessels. In May 1810 a measure known as Macon's Bill No. 2 removed all restrictions on commerce with France and Britain, though French and British warships were still barred from American waters. It authorized the president to reapply the principle of nonintercourse to either of the major powers if they "cease to violate the neutral commerce of the United States."

The volume of United States commerce with the British Isles swiftly zoomed to pre-embargo levels. Trade with France remained much more limited because of the British fleet. Napoleon therefore announced that his restrictions would be revoked in November on the understanding that Great Britain would abandon its own restrictive policies. Treating this ambiguous proposal as a statement of French policy, and hoping to obtain concessions from the British, Madison reapplied the nonintercourse policy to Great Britain. Napoleon, having thus tricked Madison into closing American ports to British ships and goods, continued to seize American ships and cargoes whenever it suited him to do so.

The British grimly refused to modify the blockade unless it could be shown that the French had actually lifted theirs, and this despite mounting complaints from their own businessmen that the new American nonimportation policy was cutting off a major market for their manufactures. Madison, on the other hand, could not afford either to admit that Napoleon had deceived him or to reverse American policy still another time. Reluctantly he came to the conclusion that unless

Britain ended its restrictions, the United States must declare war.

Tecumseh and the Prophet

There were other reasons for fighting besides British violations of neutral rights. The Indians were again making trouble, and western farmers believed that the British in Canada were egging them on.

American political leaders tended to believe that Indians should be encouraged to become farmers and to copy the "civilized" ways of whites. However, no government had been able to control the white settlers, who by bribery, trickery, and force were driving the tribes back year after year from the rich lands of the Ohio Valley. General William Henry Harrison, governor of Indiana Ter-

The Prophet lent religious fervor to his brother Tecumseh's antiwhite doctrine.

ritory, a tough, relentless soldier, kept a constant pressure on them. He wrested land from one tribe by promising it aid against a traditional enemy, from another as a penalty for having murdered a white man, from others by corrupting a few chiefs. As early as 1805, it was clear that unless something drastic was done, Harrison's aggressiveness, together with the corroding effects of the 40,000 whites who were seizing their lands, infecting them with European diseases, and burning their villages, would soon obliterate the tribes.

At this point the Shawnee chief Tecumseh made a bold and imaginative effort to reverse the trend. He was able to unite nearly all the tribes east of the Mississippi into a great confederation. "Let the white race perish," Tecumseh declared. "They seize your land; they corrupt your women. . . . Back whence they came, upon a trail of blood, they must be driven!"

To Tecumseh's political movement his brother Tenskwatawa, known as the Prophet, added the force of a moral crusade. Instead of aping white customs, said the Prophet, Indians must give up white ways, white clothes, and white liquor and reinvigorate their own culture. Ceding lands to the whites must stop because the Great Spirit intended that the land be used in common by all.

The Prophet was a visionary who claimed to be able to control the movement of heavenly bodies. Tecumseh, however, possessed true genius. A powerful orator and a great organizer, he had deep insight into the needs of his people. General Harrison himself said of Trecumseh: "He is one of those uncommon geniuses which spring up occasionally to produce revolutions and overturn the established order of things." The two brothers made a formidable team. By 1811 thousands of Indians were organizing to drive the whites off their lands. Alarm swept through the West.

With about 1,000 soldiers, General Harrison marched boldly against the brothers' camp at Prophetstown, where Tippecanoe Creek joins the Wabash, in Indiana. Tecumseh was away recruiting men, and the Prophet recklessly ordered an assault on Harrison's camp outside the village on November 7, 1811. When the white soldiers held their ground despite the Prophet's magic, the Indians lost confidence and fell back. Harrison then destroyed Prophetstown. Although the Battle of

Tippecanoe was pretty much a draw, it disillusioned the Indians and shattered their confederation. Frontier warfare continued, but in the disorganized manner of former times. Like all such fighting, it was brutal and bloody. Unwilling as usual to admit that their own excesses were the chief cause of the trouble, the settlers directed their resentment at the British in Canada. "This combination headed by the Shawanese prophet is a British scheme," a resolution adopted by the citizens of Vincennes, Indiana, proclaimed. As a result, the cry for war with Great Britain rang along the frontier.

Depression and Land Hunger

Some westerners pressed for war because they were suffering an agricultural depression. The prices they received for their wheat, tobacco, and other products in the markets of New Orleans were falling, and they attributed the decline to the loss of foreign markets and the depredations of the British. American commercial restrictions had more to do with the western depression than the British, and in any case the slow and cumbersome transportation and distribution system that western farmers were saddled with was the major cause of their difficulties. But the farmers were no more inclined to accept these explanations than they were to absolve the British from responsibility for the Indian difficulties. If only the seas were free, they reasoned, costs would go down, prices would rise, and prosperity would return.

Western expansionism also heightened the war fever. Canada would surely fall to American arms in the event of war, the frontiersmen believed. So, apparently, would Florida, for Spain was now Britain's ally. But Canada was the real prize. Madison saw attacking Canada as a way to force the British to respect neutral rights, since if Canadian food products could be cut off from the British West Indies, their sugar plantations would be devastated.

But westerners and easterners alike were more patriots than imperialists in 1811 and 1812. When the "War Hawks" (the young western leaders in Congress) called for war against Great Britain, they did so because they saw no other way to defend the national honor. The choice seemed to lie between war and surrender of true independence. As Madison put it, to accept British policy would be to "recolonize" American foreign commerce.

Resistance to War

There were, however, people who thought that a war against Great Britain would be a national calamity. Some Federalists would have resisted anything the administration proposed. Congressman Josiah Quincy of Massachusetts declared that he "could not be kicked' into a war that he believed to be designed primarily to insure the reelection of Madison. No shipowner could view with equanimity the idea of taking on the largest navy in the world. Self-interest led them to urge patience and fortitude.

Such a policy would have been wise, for Great Britain did not represent a real threat to the United States. Language, culture, and economic ties bound the two countries. Napoleon, on the other hand, represented a tremendous potential danger. He had offhandedly turned over Louisiana, but even Jefferson, the chief beneficiary of his largess, hated everything he stood for. Jefferson called Napoleon "an unprincipled tyrant who is deluging the continent of Europe with blood." Yet by going to war with Britain, the United States was aiding the French leader.

The War of 1812

The illogic of the War Hawks in pressing for a fight was exceeded only by their ineffectiveness in planning and managing the struggle. By what possible strategy could the ostensible objective of the war be achieved? To construct a navy capable of challenging the British fleet would have been the work of many years and a more expensive proposition than the War Hawks were willing to consider. So hopeless was that prospect that Congress failed to undertake *any* new construction in the first year of the conflict. Several hundred merchant ships lashed a few cannon to their decks and sailed off as privateers to attack British commerce. The navy's seven modern frigates, built during the war scare after the XYZ affair, put to sea. But these forces could make no pretense of disputing Britain's mastery of the Atlantic.

For a brief moment the American frigates held center stage, for they were faster, tougher, larger, and more powerfully armed than their British counterparts. Barely two months after the declaration of war, Captain Isaac Hull in USS *Constitution* chanced upon HMS *Guerrière* in mid-Atlantic, outmaneuvered her brilliantly, brought down her mizzenmast with his first volley, and then gunned her into submission, a hopeless wreck. In October USS *United States,* captained by Stephen Decatur, a hero of the war against the Barbary pirates, caught HMS *Macedonian* off the Madeiras, pounded her unmercifully at long range, and forced her to surrender. *Macedonian* was taken into New London as a prize; more than a third of the 300-man crew were casualties, whereas American losses were but a dozen. Then, in December, the *Constitution,* now under Captain William Bainbridge, took on the British frigate *Java* off Brazil. "Old Ironsides" shot away *Java's* mainmast and reduced it to a hulk too battered for salvage.

These victories had little influence on the outcome of the war. The Royal Navy had 34 frigates, 7 still more powerful ships of the line, and dozens of smaller vessels. As soon as these forces could concentrate against them, the American frigates were immobilized, forced to spend the war gathering barnacles at their moorings while powerful British squadrons ranged offshore.

Great Britain's one weak spot seemed to be Canada. The colony had but half a million inhabitants to oppose 7.5 million Americans. According to the War Hawk Congressman Henry Clay of Kentucky, the West was one solid horde of ferocious frontiersmen, armed to the teeth and thirsting for Canadian blood. Yet such talk was mostly bluster; when Congress authorized increasing the army by 25,000 men, Kentucky produced only 400 enlistments.

American military leadership proved extremely disappointing. Instead of a concentrated strike against Canada's St. Lawrence River lifeline, which would have isolated Upper Canada, the generals planned a complicated three-pronged attack. It was a total failure. In July 1812, General William Hull marched forth with 2,200 men against the Canadian positions facing Detroit. Hoping that the Canadian militia would desert, he delayed his assault, only to find his communications threatened by hostile Indians, led by Tecumseh. Hastily he retreated to Detroit, and when the Canadians, under General Isaac Brock, pursued him, he surrendered the fort without firing a shot! In October another force attempted to invade Canada from Fort Niagara; it was crushed by superior numbers, while a large contingent of New York militiamen watched from the east bank of the Niagara River, unwilling to fight outside their own state. The third arm of the American "attack" was equally unsuccessful.

Meanwhile, the British had captured Fort Michilimackinac in northern Michigan, and the Indians had taken Fort Dearborn (now Chicago), massacring 85 captives. Instead of sweeping triumphantly through Canada, the Americans found themselves desperately trying to keep the Canadians out of Ohio.

Stirred by these disasters, westerners rallied somewhat in 1813. General Harrison, the victor of Tippecanoe, headed an army of Kentuckians in a series of inconclusive battles against British troops and Indians led by Tecumseh. He found it impossible to recapture Detroit because a British squadron controlling Lake Erie threatened his communications. President Madison, therefore, assigned Captain Oliver Hazard Perry to the task of building a fleet to challenge this force. In September 1813, at Put-in-Bay near the western end of the lake, Perry destroyed the British vessels in a bloody battle in which 85 of the 103 men on Perry's flagship were casualties. "We have met the enemy and they are ours," he reported modestly.

With the Americans in control of Lake Erie, Detroit became untenable for the British, but American attempts to win control of Lake Ontario and to invade Canada in the Niagara region were again thrown back. Late in 1813 the British captured Fort Niagara and burned the town of Buffalo. The conquest of Canada was as far from accomplishment as ever.

The British fleet had intensified its blockade of American ports, extending its operations to New England waters previously spared to encourage the antiwar sentiments of local maritime interests. All along the coast patrolling cruisers, contemptuous of Jefferson's puny gunboats, captured small craft, raided shore points to commandeer provisions, and collected ransom from port towns by threatening to bombard them. One captain even sent a detail ashore to dig potatoes for his ship's mess.

Britain Assumes the Offensive

By the spring of 1814 British strategists had devised a master plan for crushing the United States. One army, 11,000 strong, was to march from Montreal, tracing the route that General Burgoyne had followed to disaster in the Revolution. A smaller amphibious force was to make a feint at the Chesapeake Bay area, destroying coastal towns and threatening Washington and Baltimore. A third army was to assemble at Jamaica and sail to attack New Orleans and bottle up the West.

It is necessary, in considering the War of 1812, to remind oneself repeatedly that in the course of the conflict many brave young men lost their lives. Without this sobering reflection it would be easy to dismiss the conflict as a great farce compounded of stupidity, incompetence, and brag. While the main British army was assembling in Canada, 4,000 veterans under General Robert Ross sailed from Bermuda for the Chesapeake and landed in Maryland at the mouth of the Patuxent River, southeast of Washington. A squadron of gunboats "protecting" the capital promptly withdrew upstream, and when the British pursued, their commander ordered them blown up to keep them from being captured. The British troops marched rapidly toward Washington, swarmed into the capital, and put most of the public buildings to the torch.

This was the sum of the British success. When they attempted to take Baltimore, they were stopped by a formidable line of defenses, General Ross falling in the attack. The fleet then moved up the Patapsco River and pounded Fort

McHenry with its cannon, raining 1,800 shells on it in a 25-hour bombardment on September 13 and 14. While this attack was in progress, an American civilian, Francis Scott Key, who had been temporarily detained on one of the British ships, watched anxiously through the night. Key had boarded the vessel before the attack in an effort to obtain the release of an American doctor who had been taken into custody by the British. As twilight faded he had seen the Stars and Stripes flying proudly over the battered fort. During the night the glare of rockets and bursting of bombs gave proof that the defenders were holding out. Then, by the first light of the new day, Key saw again the flag, still waving over Fort McHenry. Drawing an old letter from his pocket, he dashed off the words to "The Star Spangled Banner," which, when set to music, was to become the national anthem of the United States.

Francis Scott Key spies Old Glory flying above Fort Mchenry, thus inspiring him to compose the lyrics for the national anthem, "The Star Spangled Banner."

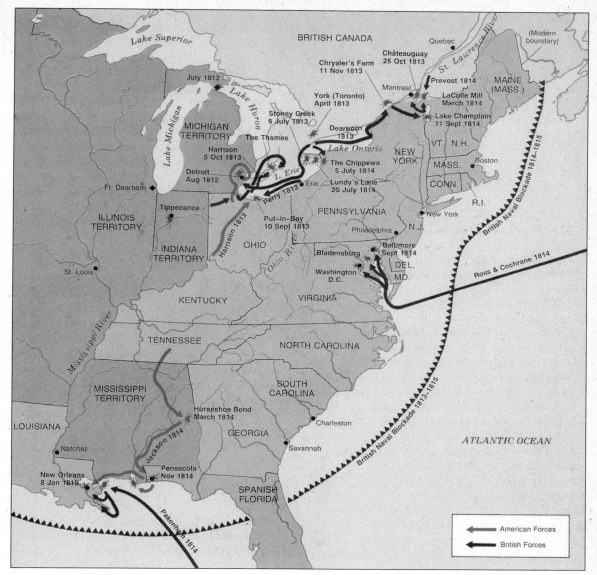

The War of 1812

To Key that dawn seemed a turning point in the war. He was roughly correct, for in those last weeks of the summer of 1814 the confrontation began to move toward resolution. Unable to crack the defenses of Baltimore, the British withdrew. The destruction of Washington had been a profound shock. Thousands came forward to enlist in the army. The new determination and spirit were strengthened by news from the northern front,

where General Sir George Prevost had been leading the main British invasion force south from Montreal. At Plattsburg, on the western shore of Lake Champlain, his 11,000 Redcoats came up against a well-designed defense line manned by 3,300 Americans under General Alexander Macomb. Prevost called up his supporting fleet of four ships and a dozen gunboats. An American fleet of roughly similar strength under Captain

Thomas Macdonough destroyed the British ships and drove off the gunboats. With the Americans now threatening his flank, Prevost lost heart. Despite his overwhelming numerical superiority, he retreated to Canada.

The Treaty of Ghent

The war might as well have ended with the battles of Plattsburg, Washington, and Baltimore, for later military developments had no effect on the outcome. Earlier in 1814, both sides had agreed to discuss peace terms. Commissioners were appointed and negotiations begun during the summer at Ghent, in Belgium. The talks were long, drawn out, and frustrating. The British were in no hurry to sign a treaty, believing that their three-pronged offensive in 1814 would swing the balance in their favor.

News of the defeat at Plattsburg modified their ambitions, and when the Duke of Wellington advised that from a military point of view they had no case for territorial concessions so long as the United States controlled the Great Lakes, they agreed to settle for *status quo ante bellum,* which is what the Americans sought. The other issues, everyone suddenly realized, had simply evaporated. The mighty war triggered by the French Revolution seemed finally over. The seas were free to all ships, and the Royal Navy no longer had need to snatch sailors from the vessels of the United States or of any other power. On Christmas Eve 1814, the treaty, which merely ended the state of hostilities, was signed. Although, like other members of his family, he was not noted for tact, John Quincy Adams rose to the spirit of the occasion. "I hope," he said, "it will be the last treaty of peace between Great Britain and the United States." And so it was.

The Hartford Convention

Before news of the treaty could cross the Atlantic, two events took place that had important effects but that would not have occurred had the news reached America more rapidly. The first was the Hartford Convention, a meeting of New England Federalists held in December 1814 and January 1815 to protest the war and to plan for a convention of the states to revise the Constitution.

Sentiment in New England had opposed the war from the beginning, and the Federalist party had been quick to employ the discontent to revive its fortunes. Federalist-controlled state administrations refused to provide militia to aid in the fight and discouraged individuals and banks from lending money to the hard-pressed national government. Trade with the enemy flourished as long as the British fleet did not crack down on New England ports, and goods flowed across the Canadian line in as great or greater volume as during Jefferson's embargo.

Their attitude toward the war made the Federalists even more unpopular with the rest of the country, and this in turn encouraged extremists to talk of seceding from the Union. After Massachusetts summoned the meeting of the Hartford Convention, the fear was widespread that the delegates would propose a New England confederacy, thereby striking at the Union in a moment of great trial.

Luckily for the country, moderate Federalists controlled the convention. They approved a statement that was similar to the concept expressed in the Kentucky and Virginia resolves by the Republicans when they were in the minority, and it was accompanied by a list of proposed constitutional amendments designed to make the national government conform more closely to New England interests. Nothing formally proposed at Hartford was treasonable, but the proceedings were kept secret, and rumors of impending secession were rife. In this atmosphere came the news from Ghent of an honorable peace. The Federalists had been denouncing the war and predicting a British triumph; now they were discredited.

The Battle of New Orleans

Still more discrediting to Federalists was the second event that would not have happened had communications been more rapid: the Battle of New Orleans. During the fall of 1814, the British had gathered an army of about 7,500 veterans, commanded by Major General Sir Edward Pakenham, at Negril Bay in Jamaica. Late in November an armada of more than 60 ships set out for New Orleans with 11,000 soldiers. Instead of sailing directly up from the mouth of the Mississippi as the Americans expected, this force approached the city by way of Lake Borgne, to the east. Proceeding through a maze of swamps and bayous, it advanced close to the city's gates before being detected. Early on the afternoon of December 23, mud-spattered local planters burst into the headquarters of General Andrew Jackson, commanding the defenses of New Orleans, with the news.

For once in this war of error and incompetence the United States had the right man in the right place at the right time. After his Revolutionary War experiences, Jackson had studied law, then moved west, settling in Nashville, Tennessee. When the war broke out, he was named major general of volunteers. Almost alone among nonprofessional troops during the conflict, his men won impressive victories, crushing the Creek Indians in a series of battles in Alabama. Discipline, based on fear and respect, and their awareness of his concern for their well-being, made his individualistic frontier militiamen into an army. His men called Jackson Old Hickory; the Indians called him Sharp Knife.

Although he had misjudged the Redcoats' destination, he was ready when the news of their arrival reached him. "By the Eternal," he vowed, "they shall not sleep on our soil." While the British rested and waited reinforcements, planning to take the city the next morning, Jackson rushed up men and guns. At 7:30 P.M. on December 23 he struck hard, taking the British by surprise. But General Pakenham's veterans rallied quickly, and the battle was inconclusive. With Redcoats pouring in from the fleet, Jackson prudently fell back to a point 5 miles below New Orleans and dug in.

For two weeks Pakenham probed the American line. Jackson strengthened his defenses daily. Finally, on January 8, 1815, through the lowland mists, 5,300 Redcoats moved forward with fixed bayonets. The Americans did not run. Perhaps they feared the wrath of their commander more than enemy bayonets. Artillery raked the advancing British, and when the range closed to about 150 yards, the riflemen opened up. Nothing could stand against this rain of lead. General Pakenham was wounded twice, then killed by a shell fragment while calling up his last reserves. During the battle a single brave British officer reached the American line. When retreat was finally sounded, the British had suffered almost 2,100 casualties. Thirteen Americans lost their lives, and 58 more were wounded or missing.

Fruits of "Victory"

Word of Jackson's magnificent triumph reached Washington almost simultaneously with the good news from Ghent. People found it easy to confuse the chronology and consider the war a victory won on the battlefield below New Orleans instead of the standoff the war had been. Jackson became the "Hero of New Orleans"; proud Americans rated his military abilities superior to those of the Duke of Wellington, the conqueror of Napoleon. The entire nation rejoiced. The Senate ratified the peace treaty unanimously, and the frustrations and failures of the past few years were forgotten. Moreover, American success in holding off Great Britain despite internal frictions went a long way toward convincing European nations that both the United States and its republican form of government were here to stay. The powers might accept these truths with less pleasure than the Americans, but accept them they did.

The war completed the destruction of the Federalist Party. Federalists had not supported the war effort; they had argued that the British could not be defeated; they had dealt clandestinely with the enemy; they had even threatened to break up the Union. So long as the issue remained in doubt, these policies won considerable support, but New Orleans made the party an object of ridicule and scorn. It soon disappeared even in New England, swamped beneath a wave of confidence and patriotism that flooded the land.

The chief reason for the happy results of the war had little to do with American events. After

1815 Europe settled down to what was to be a century of relative peace. With peace came an end to serious foreign threats to America and a revival of commerce. European emigration to the United States, long held back by the troubled times, spurted ahead, providing the expanding country with its most valuable asset—strong, willing hands to do the work of developing the land. The mood of Jefferson's first term, when democracy had reigned amid peace and plenty, returned with a rush. And the nation, having had its fill of international complications, turned in on itself as Jefferson had wished. The politicians had learned what seemed a valuable lesson: Foreign affairs could cause domestic conflicts, and this was another reason why America should avoid involvement in European affairs.

Anglo-American Rapprochement

There remained a few matters to straighten out with Great Britain, Spain, and Europe generally. Since no territory had changed hands at Ghent, neither signatory had reason to harbor a grudge. In this atmosphere the two countries worked out peaceful solutions to a number of old problems. In July 1815 they signed a commercial convention ending discriminatory duties and making other adjustments favorable to trade. Boundary difficulties also moved toward resolution.

Immediately after the war the British sent fresh troops to Canada and began to rebuild their shattered Great Lakes fleet. The United States took similar steps. When the United States suggested demilitarizing the lakes, however, the British agreed. The Rush-Bagot Agreement of 1817 limited each country to one 100-ton vessel armed with a single 18-pounder on Lake Champlain and another on Lake Ontario. They were to have two each for all the other Great Lakes. Gradually, as an outgrowth of this decision, the entire border was demilitarized, a remarkable achievement. In the Convention of 1818 the two countries agreed to the 49th parallel as the northern boundary of Louisiana Territory between Lake of the Woods and the Rockies, and to the joint control of the Oregon country for ten years. The question of the rights of Americans in the Labrador and New-

foundland fisheries, which had been much disputed during the Ghent negotiations, was settled amicably.

The Transcontinental Treaty

The acquisition of Spanish Florida and the settlement of the western boundary of Louisiana were also accomplished as an aftermath of the War of 1812, but in a far different spirit. Spain's control of the Floridas was feeble. West Florida had passed into American hands by 1813, and frontiersmen in Georgia were eyeing East Florida greedily. Indians struck frequently into American territory from Florida, then fled to sanctuary across the line. American slaves who escaped across the border could not be recovered. In 1818 James Monroe, who had been elected president in 1816, ordered General Andrew Jackson to clear raiding Seminole Indians from American soil and to pursue them into Florida if necessary. Seizing on these instructions, Jackson marched into Florida and easily captured two Spanish forts.

Although Jackson eventually withdrew from Florida, the impotence of the Spanish government made it obvious even in Madrid that if nothing were done, the United States would soon fill the power vacuum by seizing the territory. The Spanish also feared for the future of their tottering Latin American empire, especially the northern provinces of Mexico, which stood in the path of American westward expansion. Spain and the United States had never determined where Louisiana Territory ended and Spanish Mexico began. In return for American acceptance of a boundary as far east of the Rio Grande as possible, Spain was ready to surrender Florida.

For these reasons, the Spanish minister in Washington, Luis de Onís, undertook in December 1817 to negotiate a treaty with John Quincy Adams, Monroe's secretary of state. Adams pressed the minister mercilessly on the question of the western boundary, demanding a line running through present-day Texas. Onís professed to be shocked. Justice, not power, should determine the settlement, he said. "Truth is of all times, and reason and justice are founded upon immutable principles." To this Adams replied: "That truth is of all times and that reason and justice are founded upon immutable principles has never been contested by the United States, but neither, truth, reason, nor justice consists in stubbornness of assertion, nor in the multiplied repetition of error."

In the end Onís could only yield. He saved Texas for his monarch but accepted a boundary to Louisiana Territory that followed the Sabine, Red, and Arkansas rivers to the Continental Divide and the 42nd parallel to the Pacific, thus abandoning Spain's claim to a huge area beyond the Rockies that had no connection at all with the Louisiana Purchase. The United States obtained Florida in return for a mere $5 million, and that paid not to Spain but to Americans who held claims against the Spanish government.

This "Transcontinental Treaty" was signed in 1819, though ratification was delayed until 1821. Most Americans at the time thought the acquisition of Florida the most important part of the treaty, but Adams, whose vision of America's future was truly continental, knew better. "The acquisition of a definite line of boundary to the [Pacific] forms a great epoch in our history," he recorded in his diary.

The Monroe Doctrine

Concern with defining the boundaries of the United States did not reflect a desire to limit expansion, rather the feeling that there should be no more quibbling and quarreling with foreign powers that might distract the people from the great task of national development. The classic enunciation of this point of view, the completion of America's withdrawal from Europe, was the Monroe Doctrine.

Two separate strands met in this pronouncement. The first led from Moscow to Alaska and down the Pacific Coast to the Oregon country. Beginning with the explorations of Vitus Bering in 1741, the Russians had maintained an interest in fishing and fur trading along the northwest coast of North America. In 1821 the czar extended his claim south to the 51st parallel and forbade the ships of other powers to enter coastal waters north of that point. This announcement was disturbing.

The second strand ran from the courts of the European monarchs to Latin America. Between 1817 and 1822 practically all of the region from the Rio Grande to the Strait of Magellan had won its independence. Spain, former master of all the area except Brazil, was too weak to win it back by force, but Austria, Prussia, France, and Russia decided at the Congress of Verona in 1822 to try to regain the area for Spain in the interests of "legitimacy." There was talk of sending a French army to South America. This possibility also caused grave concern in Washington.

To the Russian threat, President Monroe and Secretary of State Adams responded with a terse warning: "The American continents are no longer subjects for any new European colonial establishments." This statement did not impress the Russians, since they had no intention of colonizing the region. In 1824 they signed a treaty with the United States abandoning all claims below the present southern limit of Alaska (54 degrees 40 minutes north latitude) and removing their restrictions on foreign shipping.

The Latin American problem was more complex. The United States was not alone in its alarm at the prospect of a revival of French or Spanish power in that region. Great Britain, having profited greatly from the breakup of the mercantilistic Spanish empire by developing a thriving commerce with the new republics, had no intention of permitting a restoration of the old order. But the British monarchy preferred not to recognize the new revolutionary South American republics. Therefore, in 1823 the British foreign minister, George Canning, suggested to the American minister in London that the United States and Britain issue a joint statement opposing any French interference in South America, pledging that they themselves would never annex any part of Spain's old empire, and saying nothing about recognition of the new republics.

This proposal of joint action with the British was flattering to the United States but scarcely in its best interests. The United States had already recognized the new republics and had no desire to help Great Britain retain its South American trade. As Secretary Adams pointed out, to agree to the proposal would be to abandon the possibility of someday adding Cuba or any other part of Latin America to the United States. America should act independently, Adams urged. "It would be more candid, as well as more dignified, to avow our

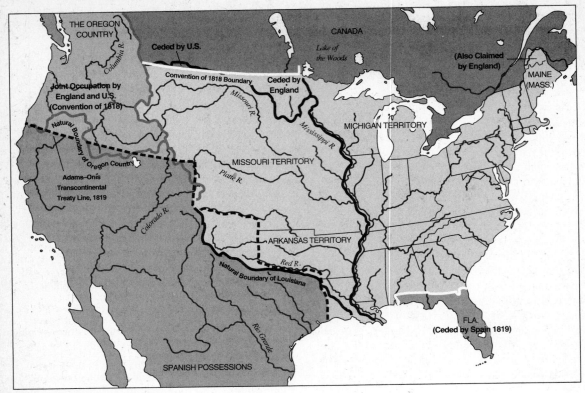

The United States, 1819

principles explicitly . . . than to come in as a cock-boat in the wake of the British man-of-war."

Monroe heartily endorsed Adams's argument and decided to include a statement of American policy in his annual message to Congress in December 1823. "The American continents," he wrote, "by the free and independent condition which they have assumed and maintain, are henceforth not to be considered as subjects for future colonization by any European powers." Europe's political system was "essentially different" from that developing in the New World, and the two should not be mixed. The United States would not interfere with existing European colonies in North or South America and would avoid involvement in strictly European affairs, but any attempt to extend European control to countries in the hemisphere that had already won their independence would be considered, Monroe warned, "the manifestation of an unfriendly disposition toward the United States" and consequently a threat to the nation's "peace and safety."

This policy statement—it was not dignified with the title Monroe Doctrine until decades later—attracted little notice in Europe or Latin America and not much more at home. European statesmen dismissed Monroe's message as "arrogant" and "blustering," worthy only of "the most profound contempt." Latin Americans, although appreciating the intent behind it, knew better than to count on American aid in case of attack. Nevertheless, the principles laid down by President Monroe so perfectly expressed the wishes of the people of the United States that when the country grew powerful enough to enforce them, there was little need to alter or embellish his pronouncement.

The Monroe Doctrine may be seen as the final stage in the evolution of American independence. The famous Declaration of 1776 merely be-

The Monroe Doctrine, drafted by Secretary of State John Quincy Adams and endorsed and proclaimed by President James Monroe, stated that the United States opposed any further European colonization of the Americas and pledged that the United States would not interfere in the internal affairs of any European power.

gan a process of separation and self-determination. The peace treaty ending the Revolutionary War was a further step, and Washington's neutrality proclamation of 1793 was another, demonstrating as it did the capacity of the United States to determine its own best interests despite the treaty of alliance with France. The removal of British troops from the northwest forts, achieved by the Jay Treaty, marked the next stage. Then the Louisiana Purchase made a further advance toward true independence by assuring that the Mississippi River could not be closed to the commerce so vital to the development of the western territories. The standoff War of 1812 ended any lingering British hope of regaining control of America, the Latin American revolutions further weakened colonialism in the Western Hemisphere, and the Transcontinental Treaty pushed the last European power from the path of westward expansion. Monroe's "doctrine" was a kind of public announcement that the sovereign United States had completed its independence and wanted nothing better than to be left alone to con-

centrate on its own development. Better yet if Europe could be made to allow the entire hemisphere to follow its own path.

The Era of Good Feelings

The person who gave his name to the so-called doctrine was an unusually lucky man. James Monroe lived a long life in good health and saw close up most of the great events in the history of the young republic. At the age of 18 he shed his blood for liberty at the glorious Battle of Trenton. He was twice governor of Virginia, a United States senator, and a Cabinet member. He was at various times the nation's representative in Paris, Madrid, and London.

Elected president in 1816, his good fortune continued. The world was finally at peace, the country united and prosperous. A person of good feeling who would keep a steady hand on the helm and hold to the present course seemed called for. Monroe possessed exactly the qualities that the times required. He originated few policies. The Monroe Doctrine, by far the most significant achievement of his administration, was as much the work of Secretary of State Adams as his own.

No one ever claimed that Monroe was much better than second-rate, yet when his first term ended, he was reelected without organized opposition. He seemed to epitomize the resolution of the conflicts that had divided the country between the end of the Revolution and the Peace of Ghent. "The existence of parties is not necessary to free government," he had told Andrew Jackson in 1816. All the issues of earlier days had vanished. Monroe dramatized their disappearance by beginning his first term with a goodwill tour of New England, heartland of the opposition. The tour was a triumph. Everywhere the president was greeted with tremendous enthusiasm. After he visited Boston, once the headquarters and now the graveyard of Federalism, a Federalist newspaper, the *Columbian Centinel,* gave the age its name. Pointing out that the celebrations attending Monroe's visit had brought together in friendly intercourse many persons "whom party politics had long severed," it dubbed the times the "Era of Good Feelings."

It has often been said that the harmony of Monroe's administrations was superficial, that beneath the calm lay potentially disruptive issues that had not yet begun to influence national politics. The dramatic change from the unanimity of Monroe's second election to the fragmentation four years later, when four candidates divided the vote and the House of Representatives had to choose the president, supports the point.

Nevertheless, the people of the period had good reasons for thinking it extraordinarily harmonious. Peace, prosperity, liberty, and progress—all flourished in 1817 in the United States. The heirs of Jefferson had accepted, with a mixture of resignation and enthusiasm, most of the economic policies advocated by the Hamiltonians. In 1816 Madison put his signature to a bill creating a new national bank almost exactly in the image of Hamilton's, which had expired before the War of 1812, and to a protective tariff which, if less comprehensive than the kind Hamilton had wanted, marked an important concession to the rising manufacturing interests. Monroe accepted the principle of federal aid for transportation projects, approving a bill authorizing Congress to invest $300,000 in the Chesapeake and Delaware Canal Company.

The Jeffersonian balance between individual liberty and responsible government, having survived both bad management and war, had justified itself to the opposition. When political divisions appeared again, as they soon did, it was not because the old balance had been shaky. Few of the new controversies challenged Republican principles or revived old issues. Instead, these controversies were children of the present and the future, products of the continuing growth of the country. National unity speeded national expansion, yet expansion, paradoxically, endangered national unity. For as the country grew, new differences appeared within its sections even as the ties binding the parts became stronger and more numerous. The area of the United States doubled, but very little of the Louisiana Purchase had been settled by 1820. More significant, the population of the nation had more than doubled, from 4 million to 9.6 million. The pace of the westward movement had also quickened; by 1820 the moving edge of the frontier ran in a long, irregular curve from Michigan to Arkansas.

New Sectional Issues

The War of 1812 and the depression that struck the country in 1819 shaped many of the controversies that agitated political life during the Era of Good Feelings. The tariff question was affected by both. Before the War of 1812 the level of duties averaged about 12.5 percent of the value of dutiable products, but to meet the added expenses occasioned by that conflict, Congress doubled all tariffs. In 1816, when the revenue was no longer needed, a new act kept duties close to wartime levels.

There was backing for high duties in every section. Except for New England, where the shipping interests favored free trade and where the booming mills of the Boston Associates were not seriously injured by foreign competition, the North favored protection. A few southerners hoped that textile mills would spring up in their region; more supported protection on the ground that national self-sufficiency was necessary in case of war. In the West, small manufacturers in the towns added their support, and so did farmers, who were counting on workers in the new eastern factories to consume much of their wheat and corn and hogs. But with the passage of time, the South rejected protection almost completely. Industry failed to develop, and since they exported most of their cotton and tobacco, southerners soon concluded that besides increasing the cost of nearly everything they bought, high duties on imports would limit the foreign market for southern staples by inhibiting international exchange.

National banking policy was another important political issue affected by the war and the depression. Presidents Jefferson and Madison had managed to live with the Bank of the United States despite its supposed constitutionality, but its charter was not renewed when it expired in 1811. Aside from the constitutional question, the major opposition to recharter came from state banks eager to take over the business of the Bank for themselves.

Many more state banks were created after 1811, and most extended credit recklessly. When the British raid on Washington and Baltimore in 1814 sent panicky depositors scurrying to convert their deposits into gold or silver, the overextended financiers could not oblige them. All banks outside New England suspended specie payments; that is, they stopped exchanging their bank notes for hard money on demand. Paper money immediately fell in value; a paper dollar was soon worth only 85 cents in coin in Philadelphia, still less in Baltimore. Government business also suffered from the absence of a national bank. In October 1814, Secretary of the Treasury Alexander J. Dallas submitted a plan for a second Bank of the United States, and after considerable wrangling over its precise form, the institution was authorized in April 1816.

The new bank was much larger than its predecessor, being capitalized at $35 million. However, unlike the earlier bank, it was badly managed at the start. When depression struck the country in 1819, it was as hard pressed as many of the state banks. But it pursued a policy of stern curtailment, and it regained a sound position, though at the expense of hardship to borrowers. "The Bank was saved," the contemporary economist William Gouge wrote somewhat hyperbolically, "and the people were ruined." Indeed, it reached a low point in public favor. Irresponsible state banks resented it, and so did the advocates of hard money.

Regional lines were less sharply drawn on the Bank issue than on the tariff. Northern congressmen voted against the Bank 53 to 44 in 1816—many of them because they objected to the particular proposal, not because they were against *any* national bank. Those from other sections favored it, 58 to 30. The collapse occasioned by the Panic of 1819 produced further opposition to the institution in the West.

Land policy also caused sectional controversy. By 1814 sales had reached an all-time high and were increasing rapidly. In 1818 the government sold nearly 3.5 million acres. Thereafter, continuing expansion and the rapid shrinkage of the foreign market as European farmers resumed production after the Napoleonic wars led to disaster. Prices fell, the panic struck, and western debtors were forced to the wall by the hundreds.

Sectional attitudes toward the public lands were fairly straightforward. The West wanted cheap land; the North and South tended to regard the national domain as an asset that should be converted into as much cash as possible. Northern manufacturers feared that cheap land in the West would drain off surplus labor and force wages up and southern planters were concerned about the competition that would develop when the virgin lands of the Southwest were put to the plough to make cotton. The West, however, was ready to fight to the last line of defense over land policy, whereas the other regions would usually compromise on the issue to gain support for their own vital interests. Sectional alignments on the question of internal improvements were similar to those on land policy, but this issue, soon to become very important, had not agitated national affairs before 1820.

The most divisive sectional issue was slavery. After the compromises affecting the "peculiar institution" made at the Constitutional Convention, it caused remarkably little conflict in national politics before 1819. As the nation expanded, free and slave states were added to the Union in equal numbers, Ohio, Indiana, and Illinois being balanced by Louisiana, Mississippi, and Alabama. In

The cotton boom in the early 19th century led southerners to support slavery more vehemently. This period painting depicting the "peculiar institution" is titled *After the Sale: Slaves Going Home from Richmond.*

1819 there were 22 states, 11 slave and 11 free. To the extent that slavery was a national question, the North opposed it and the South defended it ardently. The West leaned toward the southern point of view, for in addition to the southwestern slave states, the Northwest was sympathetic, partly because much of its produce was sold on southern plantations and partly because at least half of the early settlers of that area came from Virginia, Kentucky, and other slave states.

Northern Leaders

By 1824 the giants of the Revolutionary generation had completed their work. In every section new leaders had come forward, men shaped by the past but chiefly concerned with the present. Quite suddenly, between the war and the panic, they had inherited power. They would shape the future of the United States.

John Quincy Adams was the best known political leader of the North in the early 1820s. Just completing his brilliant work as secretary of state under Monroe, he had behind him a record of public service dating to the Confederation period. After graduating from Harvard in 1787, he practiced law for some years, served as American minister to the Netherlands and to Prussia. Next he

was a Federalist United States senator from Massachusetts. As time passed, he gradually switched to the Republican point of view, supporting the Louisiana Purchase and even the Embargo Act. Madison sent him back to Europe as minister to Russia in 1809.

Adams was farsighted, imaginative, hardworking, and extremely intelligent, but inept in personal relations. He had all the virtues and most of the defects of the Puritan, being suspicious both of others and of himself. He suffered in two ways from being his father's child: As the son of a president, he was under severe pressure to live up to the Adams name, and his father expected a great deal of him. His training made John Quincy an indefatigable worker. Even in winter he normally rose at 5 A.M., and he could never convince himself that most of his associates were not lazy dolts. He set a standard no one could meet and consequently was continually dissatisfied with himself.

Like his father, John Quincy Adams was a strong nationalist. He supported the second Bank of the United States and, unlike most easterners, he believed that the federal government should spend freely on roads and canals in the West. To slavery he was, like most New Englanders, personally opposed. As Monroe's second term drew toward its close, Adams seemed one of the most likely candidates to succeed him. (He said he would like to be president because it would please his father.)

Daniel Webster was recognized as one of the coming leaders of New England. Born in New Hampshire in 1782, he graduated from Dartmouth College in 1801, and by the time of the War of 1812 he had made a local reputation as a lawyer and orator. After serving two terms in Congress during the conflict, he moved to Boston to concentrate on his legal practice. He soon became one of the leading constitutional lawyers of the country. In 1823 he was again elected to Congress.

Webster owed much of his reputation to his formidable presence and his oratorical skill. Dark, broad-chested, craggy of brow, with deep-set, brooding eyes and a firm mouth, he projected a remarkable appearance of heroic power and moral strength. His thunderous voice, his resourceful vocabulary, his manner—all backed by the mastery of every oratorical trick—made him unique.

Webster had a first-rate mind. His faults were largely those of temperament. He was too fond of money, good food and fine broadcloth, of alcohol and adulation. He borrowed large sums from his well-to-do admirers, but rarely paid them back. Webster opposed the high tariff of 1816 because the merchants favored free trade, and he voted against establishing the Bank chiefly on partisan grounds. (His view changed when the Bank hired him as its lawyer.) He was against cheap land and federal construction of internal improvements, but basically he was a nationalist.

New York's man of the future was a little sandy-haired politico named Martin Van Buren. The Red Fox, as he was called, was one of the most talented politicians ever to play a part in American affairs. He was clever and hardworking, but his mind and his energy were always devoted to some political purpose. From 1812 to 1820 he served in the state legislature; in 1820 he was elected United States senator.

Van Buren had great charm and immense tact. By nature affable, he never allowed partisanship to mar his personal relationships with other leaders. The members of his political machine, known as the Albany Regency, were almost fanatically loyal to him, and even his enemies could seldom dislike him as a person.

Somehow Van Buren could reconcile deviousness with honesty. He "rowed to his objective with muffed oars," as Randolph of Roanoke said, yet he was neither crooked nor venal. Politics for him was like a game or a complex puzzle: The object was victory, but one must play by the rules or lose all sense of achievement. Only a fool will cheat at solitaire, and despite his gregariousness Van Buren was at heart a solitary operator.

His positions on the issues of the 1820s are hard to determine because he never took a position if he could avoid doing so. No one could say with assurance what he thought about the tariff, and since slavery did not arouse much interest in New York, it is safe to suppose that at this time he had no opinion at all about the institution.

Southern Leaders

The most prominent southern leader was William H. Crawford, Monroe's secretary of the treasury. Crawford was direct and friendly, a marvelous storyteller, and one of the few persons in Washington who could teach the fledgling senator Martin Van Buren anything about politics. Van Buren supported him enthusiastically in the contest for the 1824 presidential nomination.

Crawford had something interesting to say on most of the important issues of the times. Although predisposed toward the states' rights position, he was willing to go along with a moderately protective tariff. During the depression that began in 1819 he devised an excellent relief plan for farmers who were unable to meet installment payments due on land purchased from the government. He suggested a highly original scheme for a flexible paper currency not convertible into hard money.

Crawford was controversial. Many of his contemporaries considered him no more than a cynical spoilsman, though his administration of the treasury was first-rate. Yet he had many friends. His ambition was vast, his power great. Fate, however, was about to strike Crawford a crippling blow.

John C. Calhoun, the other outstanding southern leader, was born in South Carolina in 1782 and graduated from Yale in 1804. Returning to South Carolina, Calhoun served in the state legislature; in 1811 he went to Washington as a congressman. A prominent War Hawk, he took a strong nationalist position on all the issues of the day. In 1817 Monroe made him secretary of war.

Although, being a well-to-do planter, he was devoted to the South and its institutions, Calhoun took the broadest possible view of political affairs. "Our true system is to look to the country," he said in 1820, "and to support such measures and such men, without regard to sections, as are best calculated to advance the general interest."

Calhoun was intelligent, bookish, and given to the study of abstractions. Legend has it that he once tried to write a poem but after putting down the word "Whereas" gave it up as beyond his powers. Some obscure failing made it impossible for him to grasp the essence of the human condition. An English observer once said that Calhoun had "an imperfect acquaintance with human nature." Few contemporaries could maintain themselves in debate against his powerful intelligence, yet that mind—so sharp, so penetrating—was the blind bondsman of his ambition.

Western Leaders

The outstanding western leader of the 1820s was Henry Clay of Kentucky, one of the most charming and colorful of American statesmen. Clay was the kind of person who made men cheer and women swoon. On the platform he ranked with Webster; behind the political scenes he was the peer of Van Buren. In every environment he was warm and open—what a modern political scientist might call a charismatic personality. He was a reasonable man, skilled at arranging political compromises, but he possessed a reckless streak: Like so many westerners, his sense of honor was exaggerated. Twice in his career he challenged men to duels for having insulted him. Fortunately, all concerned were poor shots.

Clay was elected to Congress in 1810. He led the War Hawks in 1811 and 1812 and was Speaker of the House from 1811 to 1820 and from 1823 to 1825. Although intellectually the inferior of Adams, Calhoun, and Webster, Clay had a perfect temperament for politics. He loved power and understood that in the United States it had to be shared to be exercised. His great gift was in seeing national needs from a broad perspective and

fashioning a program that could inspire ordinary citizens with something of his vision.

In the early 1820s he was just developing his "American System." In return for eastern support of federal aid in the construction of roads and canals, the West would back the protective tariff. He justified this deal on the widest national grounds. By stimulating manufacturing, it would increase the demand for western raw materials, while western prosperity would lead to greater consumption of eastern manufactured goods. Although himself a slaveowner, he called slavery the "greatest of human evils." He favored freeing the slaves and "colonizing" them in Africa, which could, he said, be accomplished gradually and at relatively minor cost.

Another western leader was General William Henry Harrison. Although he sat in the Ohio legislature and in both houses of Congress between 1816 and 1828, Harrison was primarily a soldier. He did not identify himself closely with any policy other than the extermination of Indians. He had little to do with the newly developing political alignments of the 1820s.

Much like Harrison was Andrew Jackson, the "Hero of New Orleans," whose popularity greatly exceeded Harrison's. He had many friends, shrewd in the ways of politics, who were working devotedly, if not entirely unselfishly, to make him president. No one knew his views on most questions, but few cared. His military reputation and his forceful personality were his chief assets, but both, and especially the latter, were likely to get him into political hot water.

The Missouri Compromise

The sectional concerns of the 1820s repeatedly influenced politics. One of the first and most critical concerned the admission of Missouri as a slave state. When Louisiana entered the Union in 1812, the rest of the Louisiana Purchase was organized as Missouri Territory. Building on a nucleus of Spanish and French inhabitants, the region west and north of St. Louis grew rapidly, and in 1817 the Missourians petitioned for statehood. A large percentage of the settlers were southerners who had moved into the valleys of the Arkansas and

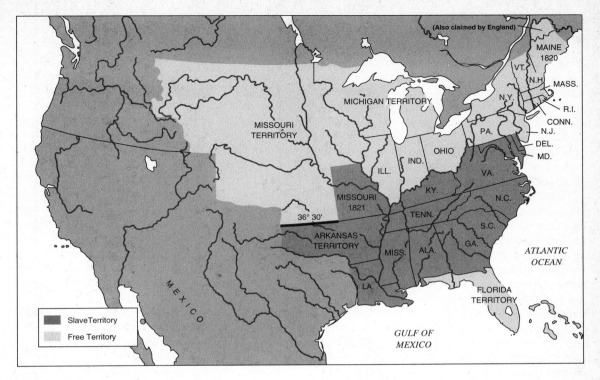

(Also claimed by England)

MAINE
1820

MICHIGAN TERRITORY

MISSOURI
TERRITORY

VT.
N.H
MASS.
N.Y.
R.I.
CONN.
PA.
N.J.
DEL.
OHIO
MD.
IND.
ILL.
VA.
MISSOURI
1821
KY.
N.C.
36° 30'
TENN.
S.C.
ARKANSAS
TERRITORY
MISS.   ALA.   GA.

ATLANTIC
OCEAN

LA.
FLORIDA
TERRITORY

MEXICO

GULF OF
MEXICO

SlaveTerritory

Free Territory

The Missouri Compromise, 1820–1821

Missouri rivers. Since many of them owned slaves, Missouri would become a slave state.

The admission of new states had always been a routine matter, in keeping with the admirable pattern established by the Northwest Ordinance. But during the debate on the Missouri Enabling Act in February 1819, Congressman James Tallmadge of New York introduced an amendment prohibiting "the further introduction of slavery" and providing that all slaves born in Missouri after the territory became a state should be freed at age 25.

Although Tallmadge was merely seeking to apply in the territory the pattern of race relations that had developed in the states immediately east of Missouri, his amendment represented, at least in spirit, something of a revolution. The Northwest Ordinance had prohibited slavery in the land beween the Mississippi and the Ohio, but that area had only a handful of slaveowners in 1787 and little prospect of attracting more. Elsewhere no effort to restrict the movement of slaves into new territory had been attempted. If one assumed

(as whites always had) that the slaves themselves should have no say in the matter, it appeared democratic to let the settlers of Missouri decide the slavery question for themselves. Nevertheless, the Tallmadge amendment passed the House, the vote following sectional lines closely. The Senate, however, resoundingly rejected it. The less populous southern part of Missouri was then organized separately as Arkansas Territory, and an attempt to bar slavery there was stifled. The Missouri Enabling Act failed to pass before Congress adjourned.

When the next Congress met in December 1819, the Missouri issue came up at once. The debate did not turn on the morality of slavery or the rights of blacks. Northerners objected to adding new slave states because under the Three-fifths Compromise these states would be overrepresented in Congress (60 percent of their slaves would be counted in determining the size of the states' delegations in the House of Representatives) and because they did not relish competing with slave labor. Since the question was political influence rather than the rights and wrongs of slavery, a compromise was worked out in 1820. Missouri entered the Union as a slave state, and Maine, having been separated from Massachusetts, was admitted as a free state to preserve the balance in the Senate.

To prevent further conflict, Congress adopted a proposal of Senator Jesse B. Thomas of Illinois, which "forever prohibited" slavery in all other parts of the Louisiana Purchase north of 36 degrees 30 minutes north latitude, the westward extension of Missouri's southern boundary.

The Missouri Compromise did not end the crisis. When Missouri submitted its constitution for approval by Congress (the final step in the admission process), the document, besides authorizing slavery and prohibiting the emancipation of any slave without the consent of the owner, *required* the state legislature to pass a law barring free blacks from entering the state "under any pretext whatever." This provision plainly violated Article IV, Section 2 of the United States Constitution: "The Citizens of each State shall be entitled to all Privileges and Immunities of Citizens in the several States." Once more the debate raged. Again, since few northerners cared to defend the rights of blacks, the issue was compromised. In March 1821 Henry Clay found a face-saving formula: Out of respect for the "supreme law of the land," Congress accepted the Missouri constitution with the demurrer that no law passed in conformity to it should be construed as contravening Article IV, Section 2.

Every thinking person recognized the political dynamite inherent in the Missouri controversy. The sectional lineup had been terrifyingly compact. What meant the Union if so trivial a matter as one new state could so divide the people? Moreover, despite the timidity and hypocrisy of the North, everyone realized that slavery lay at the heart of the conflict. "We have the wolf by the ears, and we can neither safely hold him, nor safely let him go," Jefferson wrote a month after Missouri became a state. The dispute, he said, "like a fire bell in the night, awakened and filled me with terror." Jefferson knew that the compromise had not quenched the flames ignited by the Missouri debates. "This is a reprieve only," he

said. John Quincy Adams called it the "title page to a great tragic volume."

The Election of 1824

Other controversies that aroused strong feelings did not seem to divide the country so deeply. The question of federal internal improvements caused endless debate that split the country on geographical lines, but no one threatened the Union on this issue. The tariff continued to divide the country. When a new, still higher tariff was enacted in 1824, the slave states voted almost unanimously against it, the North and Northwest in favor, and New England remained of two minds. Webster (after conducting a poll of business leaders before deciding how to vote), made a powerful speech against the act, but the measure passed without creating a major storm.

The divisions on these questions were not severely disruptive, in part because the major politicians, competing for the presidency, did not dare risk alienating any section by taking too extreme a position. Another reason was that the old party system had broken down; the Federalists had disappeared as a national party and the Jeffersonians, lacking an organized opposition, had become less aggressive and more troubled by many factional disputes.

The presidential fight was therefore waged on personal grounds. The candidates were Calhoun, Jackson, Crawford, Adams, and Clay. The maneuvering among them was complex, the infighting savage. In March 1824, Calhoun, who was young enough to wait for the White House, withdrew and declared for the vice presidency, which he won easily. Crawford suffered a series of paralytic strokes that ruined his chances.

Despite the bitterness of the contest, it attracted relatively little public interest; barely a quarter of those eligible took the trouble to vote. In the electoral college Jackson led with 99; Adams had 84, Crawford 41, and Clay 37. Since no one had a majority, the contest was thrown into the House of Representatives, which, under the Constitution, had to choose from among the three leaders, each state delegation having one vote. By employing his great influence in the House, Clay swung the balance to Adams, who was thereupon elected.

J. Q. Adams as President

Adams, who took a Hamiltonian view of the future of the country, hoped to use the national authority to foster all sorts of useful projects: internal improvements, aid to manufacturing and agriculture, scientific and educational projects (including a national university), and many administrative reforms. For a nationalist of unchallengeable Jeffersonian origins like Clay or Calhoun to have pressed for so extensive a program would have been politically risky. For the son of John Adams to do so was disastrous; every doubter remembered his Federalist background and decided that he was trying to overturn the glorious "Revolution of 1800."

Adams was his own worst enemy, as inept a politician as ever lived. He hoped to build a national astronomical observatory, but, knowing that many citizens considered things like observatories impractical extravagances, he urged Congress not to be "palsied by the will of our constituents." There was wide support in the country for a federal bankruptcy law, but instead of describing himself in plain language as a friend of poor debtors, Adams called for the "amelioration" of the "often oppressive codes relating to insolvency" and buried the recommendation at the tail end of a dull state paper.

One of Adams's worst political failings was his refusal to use his power of appointment to win support. "I will not dismiss . . . able and faithful political opponents to provide for my own partisans," he said. Nevertheless, by appointing Henry Clay secretary of state, he laid himself open to the charge that he had won the presidency by a "corrupt bargain."

Calhoun's *Exposition and Protest*

The tariff question added to the president's troubles. High duties, increasingly more repulsive to the export-conscious South, attracted more and more favor in the North and West. Besides eastern manufacturers, lead miners in Missouri, hemp raisers in Kentucky, woolgrowers in New York, and many other interest groups demanded protection against foreign competition. In 1828 a new tariff was hammered into shape by the House Committee on Manufactures. Northern and western agricultural interests were in command; they wrote into the bill extremely high duties on raw wool, hemp, flax, fur, and liquor. New England manufacturers protested vociferously, for although their products were protected, the proposed law would increase the cost of their raw materials. This gave southerners, now hopelessly in the minority on the tariff question, a chance to block the bill. When the New Englanders proposed amendments lowering the duties on raw materials, the southerners voted nay, hoping to force them to reject the measure on the final vote. This desperate strategy failed. New England had by this time committed its future to manufacturing, a change signalized by the somersault of Webster, who, ever responsive to local pressures, now voted for protection. After winning some minor concessions in the Senate, largely through the intervention of Van Buren, enough New Englanders accepted the so-called Tariff of Abominations to assure its passage.

Vice President Calhoun, who had watched the debate from the vantage point of his post as president of the Senate, now came to a great turning point in his career. He had thrown in his lot with Jackson, whose running mate he was to be in the coming election, and had been assured that the Jacksonians would oppose the bill. Yet northern Jacksonians had been responsible for drafting and passing it. The new tariff would impoverish the South, he believed. He warned Jackson that relief must soon be provided or the Union would be shaken to its foundations. Then he returned to his South Carolina plantation and wrote an essay, the *South Carolina Exposition and Protest,* repudiating the nationalist philosophy he had previously championed.

The South Carolina legislature released this document to the country in December 1828, along with eight resolutions denouncing the protective tariff as unfair and unconstitutional. The theorist

Calhoun, however, was not content with outlining the case against the tariff. His *Exposition* provided an ingenious defense of the right of the people of a state to reject a law of Congress. Starting with John Locke's revered concept of government as a contractual relationship, he argued that since the states had created the Union, logic dictated that they be the final arbiters of the meaning of the Constitution which was its framework. If a special state convention, representing the sovereignty of the people, decided that an act of Congress violated the Constitution, it could interpose its authority and "nullify" the law within its boundaries.

Calhoun did not seek to implement this theory in 1828, for he hoped that the next administration would lower the tariff and make nullification unnecessary.

The Meaning of Sectionalism

The sectional issues that occupied the energies of politicians and strained the ties between the people of the different regions were produced by powerful forces that actually bound the sections together. Growth caused differences that sometimes led to conflict, but growth itself was the product of prosperity. People were drawn to the West by the expectation that life would be better there. Henry Clay based his "American System" on the idea that western farmers would profit by selling their crops to eastern city dwellers and that spending public money on building roads and other internal improvments would make transportation and communication less expensive and thus benefit everyone.

Another force unifying the nation was patriotism: The increasing size and prosperity of the nation made people proud to be part of a growing, dynamic society. Still others were the uniqueness of the American system of government and the people's knowledge that their immediate ancestors had created it. John Adams and Thomas Jefferson died on the same day, July 4, 1826, the 50th anniversary of the signing of the Declaration of Independence. People took this remarkable coincidence as a sign from the heavens, an indication that God looked with favor upon the American experiment.

Milestones

Year	Event	Year	Event
1808	James Madison elected president		Hartford Convention
1809	Non-Intercourse Act		Treaty of Ghent officially ends War of 1812
1810	Macon's Bill Number 2	1815	Battle of New Orleans
1811	Battle of Tippecanoe	1817	Rush-Bagot Agreement with Great Britain
1812	Congress declares war on Great Britain		
	Naval victories of USS *Constitution* and *United States*	1819	Transcontinental Treaty with Spain
		1820–1850	Rapid increase in European immigration
1813	Battle of Lake Erie		
	Battle of the Thames, death of Tecumseh		Rapid growth of cities and of manufacturing
1814	British burn Washington, D.C.	1823	Monroe Doctrine
	Francis Scott Key writes "The Star Spangled Banner" during the British bombardment of Fort McHenry		

Supplementary Reading

On the economic issues of this period, see G. R. Taylor, **The Transportation Revolution** (1958), P. W. Gates, **The Farmer's Age** (1960), and Stuart Bruchey, **The Growth of the American Economy** (1975). See also Bray Hammond, **Banks and Politics in America from the Revolution to the Civil War** (1957).

M. D. Peterson, **The Great Triumvirate** (1987), deals with the careers of Clay, Webster, and Calhoun. Other biographies of the statesmen of the era are S. F. Bemis, **John Quincy Adams** (1949, 1956), I. H. Bartlett, **Daniel Webster** (1978), John Niven, **Martin Van Buren** (1983), R. N. Current, **John C. Calhoun** (1963), and R. V. Remini, **Henry Clay** (1991). R. V. Remini, **Andrew Jackson and the Course of American Empire** (1977) and **Andrew Jackson and the Course of American Freedom** (1981) also deal with this period. See also W. W. Freehling, **The Road to Disunion** (1990).

Madison's administration can be followed in D. R. McCoy, **The Last of the Fathers*** (1991), and Ralph Ketcham, **James Madison** (1971).

For the war itself, see H. L. Coles, **The War of 1812*** (1965), a good brief account. Jackson's part in the conflict is described vividly in R. V. Remini, **Andrew Jackson and the Course of American Empire** (1977). On the Treaty of Ghent, see Bradford Perkins, **Castlereagh and Adams** (1964). S. F. Bemis, **John Quincy Adams and the Foundations of American Foreign Policy*** (1949), and George Dangerfield, **The Era of Good Feelings*** (1952), also discuss the settlement intelligently. On Monroe, see Harry Ammon, **James Monroe: The Quest for National Identity** (1971).

*Available in paperback.

CHAPTER 8

Toward a National Economy

America's Industrial Revolution
Birth of the Factory
An Industrial Proletariat?
Francis Cabot Lowell's Waltham System
Strangers at the Door
The Persistence of the Household System
Corporations
Cotton Revolutionizes the South
Revival of Slavery
Roads to Market
Transportation and the Government
"Organs of Communication"
The Canal Boom
The Emporium of the Western World
Government Aid to Business
The Marshall Court

*P*oliticians might attribute the growth of the country to their own patriotism and ingenuity, but without the economic and technological developments of the period, that growth would not have occurred. The country was still overwhelmingly agricultural in 1820, but was on the brink of a major economic readjustment. Certain obscure seeds planted in the early years of the republic had taken root. The industrial revolution was coming to America with a rush.

America's Industrial Revolution

Between 1790 and 1803 a series of events took place that were basic to the industrialization of the United States and the evolution of a truly national economy. In 1790 a young English-born genius named Samuel Slater, employed by the Rhode Island merchant firm of Almy & Brown, began to spin cotton thread by machine in the first factory in the United States. In 1800 a youthful graduate of Yale College, Eli Whitney, having contracted to make 10,000 rifles for the government, succeeded in manufacturing them by such precise methods that the parts were interchangeable, a major step toward the perfection of the assembly-line system of production. Three years later Oliver Evans, a Philadelphia inventor, had come close to achieving automation in flour milling. A worker poured wheat down a chute at one end of the plant and a second headed the barrels of superfine flour that emerged at the other end. The intervening steps of weighing, cleaning, grinding, and packing were all performed by machines.

Other important technological advances included John Fitch's construction and operation of the world's first regularly scheduled steamboat in 1790 and Eli Whitney's invention of the cotton gin in 1793. The steamboat and the gin affected American history almost as much as the factory system and mass production. The former, when employed on western waters, cut the cost of transportation dramatically and brought the West into the national economy. The latter made possible the widespread cultivation of cotton, which transformed the South and fed the cotton factories of the world for decades.

Innovations in the way businesses were organized and financed accompanied technological developments. The establishment of the first Bank of the United States was of key importance because it provided a source of credit for private business. Its success led to the founding of 29 state-charted banks by 1800.

Birth of the Factory

Slater's factory did not signal the disappearance of the family spinning wheel or the spread of the factory system to other forms of manufacturing.

Methods of distributing goods, keeping records, and accounting remained primitive. Interchangeable firing pins for rifles did not lead at once even to matching pairs of shoes. More than 15 years were to pass after the invention of Fitch's steamboat before it was widely accepted.

By the 1770s British manufacturers, especially those in textiles, had made astonishing progress in mechanizing their operations, bringing workers together in buildings called factories where waterpower, and later steam, supplied the force to run new spinning and weaving devices that increased productivity and reduced labor costs.

Since machine-spun cotton was cheaper and of better quality than that spun by hand, producers in other countries were eager to adopt British methods. Americans had depended on Great Britain for such products until the Revolution cut off supplies; then the new spirit of nationalism gave impetus to the development of local industry. A number of state legislatures offered bounties to anyone who would introduce the new machinery. The British, however, guarded their secrets vigilantly. It was illegal to export any of the new machines or to send their plans abroad. Workers skilled in their construction and use were forbidden to leave the country.

These restrictions were effective for a time. The principles on which the new machines were based were simple enough, but to construct workable models without plans was another matter. Although a number of persons tried to do so, it was not until Samuel Slater installed his machines in Pawtucket, Rhode Island, that a successful factory was constructed.

Slater was more than a skillful mechanic. Attracted by stories of the rewards offered in the United States, he slipped out of England in 1789. Not daring to carry any plans, he depended on his memory and his mechanical sense for all the complicated specifications of the necessary machines. When Moses Brown took him to Rhode Island, he insisted on scrapping the crude machinery Almy & Brown had assembled. Then, working in secrecy with a carpenter who was "under bond not to steal the patterns nor disclose the nature of the work," he built and installed his machinery. In December 1790 the first American factory began production.

It was a humble beginning indeed. Slater's machines made only cotton thread, which Almy & Brown sold in its Providence store and "put out" to individual artisans, who, working for wages, wove it into cloth in their homes. The machines were tended by a labor force of nine children, for the work was simple and the pace slow. The young operatives' pay ranged from 33 cents to 67 cents per week, about what a youngster could earn in other occupations. This labor pattern persisted for decades.

The factory was profitable from the start. Slater soon branched out on his own, and others trained by him opened their own establishments. By 1800 seven mills possessing 2,000 spindles were in operation; by 1815, after production had been stimulated by the War of 1812, there were 130,000 spindles turning in 213 factories.

Before long the Boston Associates, a group of merchants headed by Francis Cabot Lowell, added a new dimension to factory production. Beginning at Waltham, Massachusetts, where the Charles River provided the necessary waterpower, between 1813 and 1850 they revolutionized textile production. Lowell, after an extensive study of British mills, smuggled the plans for an efficient power loom into America. His Boston Manufacturing Company at Waltham, capitalized at $300,000, combined machine production, large-scale operation, efficient management, as well as centralized marketing procedures. It concentrated on the mass production of a standardized product.

Lowell's cloth was durable and cheap, though plain and rather coarse. His profits averaged almost 20 percent a year during the Era of Good Feelings. In 1823 the Boston Associates began to harness the power of the Merrimack River, setting up a new $600,000 corporation at the sleepy village of East Chelmsford, Massachusetts (population 300), where there was a fall of 32 feet in the river. Within three years the town, appropriately renamed Lowell, had 2,000 inhabitants.

An Industrial Proletariat?

As the importance of skilled labor declined, so did the ability of workers to influence working conditions. If skilled, they either became employers and developed entrepreneurial and managerial skills, or they descended into the mass of wage earners. Simultaneously, the changing structure of production widened the gap between owners and workers and blurred the distinction between skilled and unskilled labor.

These trends generated some hostility between workers and employers. There were strikes throughout the 1830s and again in the 1850s. But well into the 1850s Americans displayed few signs of the class solidarity common among European workers.

Why America did not produce a self-conscious working class is a question that has long intrigued historians. Some argue that the existence of the frontier siphoned off displaced and dissatisfied workers. Other historians believe that ethnic and racial differences kept workers from seeing themselves as a distinct class with common needs and common enemies. The influx of needy immigrants willing to accept almost any wage was certainly resented by native-born workers. The growing number of free blacks in northern cities—between 1800 and 1830 the number tripled in Philadelphia and quadrupled in New York— also inhibited the development of a self-conscious working class. Black city dwellers got only the lowliest jobs and were often forced by poverty and white pressure to live in dreadful slums. Notwithstanding the bad conditions in the early shops, the new factories still represented an improvement for most of the people who worked in them. This was the case with nearly all European immigrants, though less so for urban free blacks, since in the South many found work in the skilled trades.

Most workers in the early textile factories were drawn from outside the regular labor market. Relatively few artisan spinners and weavers became factory workers, nor did immigrants. Instead, the mill owners relied chiefly on women and children. They did so because machines lessened the need for skill and strength and because the labor shortage made it necessary to tap unexploited sources. By the early 1820s about half the cotton textile workers in the factories were under 16 years of age.

Most people of that generation considered this a good thing. They reasoned that the work was easy and provided families with extra income. Roxanna Foote, whose daughter Harriet Beecher Stowe wrote *Uncle Tom's Cabin,* came from a solid middle-class family. Nevertheless, she worked full-time before her marriage in her grandfather's small spinning mill. Roxanna explained her daily regimen as a mill girl matter-of-factly: "I generally rise with the sun, and, after breakfast, take my wheel, which is my daily companion, and the evening is generally devoted to reading, writing, and knitting."

This seems a somewhat idealized picture, or perhaps working for one's grandfather made a difference. Another young girl, Emily Chubbock, had less pleasant memories. "My principal recollections . . . are of noise and filth, bleeding hands and aching feet, and a very sad heart." But people accustomed to seeing the children of farmers working full-time in the fields were not shocked by the sight of children working all day in mills. In factories where laborers were hired in family units, no member earned very much, but with a couple of adolescent daughters and perhaps a 9- or 10-year-old son helping out, a family could take home enough to live decently.

Francis Cabot Lowell's Waltham System

Instead of hiring children, the Boston Associates developed the so-called Waltham System of employing young, unmarried women in their mills. The thriving factory towns of Lowell, Chicopee, and Manchester provided the background for a remarkable industrial idyll. Young women came from farms all over New England to work for a year or two in the mills. They were lodged in company boardinghouses, which, like college dormitories, became centers of social life. They were strictly supervised; the regulations laid down by one company, for example, required that all employees "show that they are penetrated by a laudable love of temperance and virtue." "Ardent spirits" were banished from company property, "games of hazard and cards" prohibited. A 10 P.M. curfew was strictly enforced.

Most of these young women did not have to support themselves. They worked to save for a trousseau, to help educate a younger brother, or simply for the experience. "The feeling that at this new work, the few hours they had of everyday leisure was entirely their own was a satisfaction to them," one Lowell worker recalled. Anything but an industrial proletariat, they filled the windows of the factories with flowering plants, edited their own literary periodicals, and attended lectures on edifying subjects. The English novelist Charles Dickens, though scarcely enchanted by most American ways, was impressed by his visit to Lowell, which he compared most favorably to "those great haunts of misery," the English manufacturing towns.

However, life in the mills was not as harmonious as it seemed. Though they made up 85 percent of the work force, women were kept out of supervisory positions. In 1834 workers in several mills "turned out" to protest cuts in their wages and a hike in what they paid for board. When a drop in prices in the 1840s led the owners to introduce new rules designed to increase production, however, workers lacked the organizational strength to block them. By then young women of the kind that had flocked to the mills in the 1820s and 1830s were beginning to find work as schoolteachers and clerks. Mill owners turned increasingly to Irish immigrants to operate their machines.

Strangers at the Door

Between 1790 and 1820 the population of the United States had more than doubled to 9.6 million. The most remarkable feature of this growth was that it resulted almost entirely from natural increase: The birthrate in the early 19th century exceeded 50 per 1,000 population. Fewer than 250,000 immigrants entered the United States between 1790 and 1820.

But soon after the final defeat of Napoleon in 1815, immigration began to pick up. In the 1820s, some 150,000 European immigrants arrived; in the 1830s, 600,000; and in the 1840s, 1.7 million. The 1850 census, the first to make the distinction, estimated that of the nation's population of 23 million, more than 10 percent were foreign born. In the Northeast the proportion exceeded 15 percent.

Most of this human tide came from Germany and Ireland, but substantial numbers also came from Great Britain and the Scandinavian countries. As with earlier immigrants, most were drawn to America by what are called "pull" factors—the prospect of abundant land, good wages, and economic opportunity generally, or by the promise of political and religious freedom. Conversely, many others came because of "push" factors—to stay where they were meant to face starvation. This was particularly true of those from Ireland, where a potato blight triggered the flight of tens of thousands.

Once ashore in New York, Boston, or Philadelphia, the more prosperous immigrants tended to head directly westward. Others found work in the new factory towns. But most of the Irish immigrants, "the poorest and most wretched population that can be found in the world," one of their priests called them, lacked the means to go west. Like it or not, they had to settle in the eastern cities.

Viewed in historical perspective, this massive wave of immigration stimulated the American economy. In the short run, the influx depressed living standards and strained the social fabric. For the first time the nation had acquired a culturally distinctive, citybound, and propertyless class. The poor Irish immigrants had to accept whatever wages employers offered them. By doing so they caused resentment among native workers, resentment exacerbated by their Roman Catholic faith, which the Protestant majority associated with European authoritarianism and corruption.

The Persistence of the Household System

The efficiency of the "Lowell System" was obvious, yet it caused no immediate transformation of American manufacturing. Although the embargo and the war with Great Britain aided the new factories by limiting foreign competition, they also stimulated nonfactory production. In President Monroe's time the "household-handicraft-mill complex" was still dominant nearly everywhere. Except in the manufacture of textiles, factories employing as many as 50 workers did not exist. Traveling artisans and town craftsmen produced goods ranging from hats, shoes, and other articles of clothing to barrels, clocks, pianos, ship's supplies, cigars, lead pencils, and pottery. Ironworks, brickyards, flour mills, distilleries, and lumberyards could be found even in the most rural parts of the country.

Nearly all these "manufacturers" produced only to supply local needs, but in some instances large industries grew up without advancing to the factory stage. In the neighborhood of Danbury, Connecticut, hundreds of small shops turned out hats by handicraft methods. The hats were sold in all sections of the country, the trade being organized by wholesalers. The shoe industry followed a related pattern, with centers of production in Pennsylvania, New Jersey, and especially eastern Massachusetts.

Some strange combinations of production techniques appeared, none more peculiar than in the manufacture of stockings. Frequently the feet and legs were knit by machine in separate factories and then "put out" to handworkers who sewed the parts together in their homes.

Since technology affected American industry unevenly, contemporaries found the changes difficult to evaluate. Few persons in the 1820s appreciated how profound the impact of the factory system would be. The city of Lowell seemed remarkable and important but not necessarily a herald of future trends. Yet in nearly every field apparently minor changes were being made. Beginning around 1815, small improvements in the design of water wheels made possible larger and more efficient machinery in mills and factories. Improvements were made soon after the War of 1812 in the manufacture of paper, glass, and pottery. The commercial canning of sterilized foods in airtight containers also began about 1820.

Corporations

Mechanization required substantial capital investment, and capital was chronically in short supply. The modern method of organizing large enterprises, the corporation, was slow to develop. Between 1781 and 1801 only 326 corporations were chartered by the states, and only a few of them were engaged in manufacturing.

The general opinion was that only quasi-public projects, such as roads and waterworks, were entitled to the privilege of incorporation. Anyone interested in organizing a corporation had to obtain a special act of a state legislature. And even among businessmen there was a tendency to associate corporations with monopoly, corruption, and the undermining of individual enterprise. In 1820 the economist Daniel Raymond wrote: "The very object . . . of the act of incorporation is to produce inequality, either in rights, or in the division

of property. Prima facie, therefore all money corporations are detrimental to national wealth. They are always created for the benefit of the rich." Such feelings help to explain why as late as the 1860s most manufacturing was being done by unincorporated companies.

The growth of industry reshaped American society. For a time it lessened the importance of foreign commerce by reducing the need for European manufactured goods. Furthermore, as the country moved closer to self-sufficiency, nationalistic and isolationist sentiments were subtly augmented. The rise of manufacturing also affected farmers, because as cities grew in size and number, the need to feed the populace caused commercial agriculture to flourish. Dairy farming, truck gardening, and fruit growing flourished around the new manufacturing centers.

Cotton Revolutionizes the South

By far the most important indirect effect of industrialization occurred in the South, which soon began to produce cotton to supply the new textile factories of Great Britain and New England. The possibility of growing large amounts of this crop in America had not been seriously considered in colonial times, but by the 1780s the demand for raw cotton to feed the voracious British mills was so great that many American farmers were eager to experiment with the crop. Most of the world's cotton at this time came from Egypt, India, and the East Indies. The plant was considered tropical, most varieties being unable to survive the slightest frost.

Beginning in 1786, "sea island" cotton was grown successfully in the mild, humid lowlands and offshore islands along the coasts of Georgia and South Carolina. This was a high-quality cotton, silky and long-fibered like the Egyptian. But its susceptibility to frost severely limited the area of its cultivation. Elsewhere in the South, "green-seed," or upland, cotton flourished, but this plant had little commercial value because the seeds could not be easily separated from the lint. When sea island cotton was passed between two rollers, its shiny black seeds simply popped out; with upland cotton the seeds were pulled through with the lint and crushed, the oils and broken bits destroying the value of the fiber. To remove the seeds by hand was laborious; a slave working all day could clean scarcely a pound of the white fluff. This made it an uneconomical crop.

However, the planters of South Carolina and Georgia, suffering from hard times after the Revolution, needed a new cash crop. Rice production was not expanding, and indigo, the other staple of the area, had ceased to be profitable when it was no longer possible to claim the British bounty. Cotton seemed an obvious answer. Farmers were experimenting hopefully with different varieties of the plant and mulling the problem of how upland cotton could be more easily deseeded.

This was the situation in the spring of 1793, when Eli Whitney was a guest at Mulberry Grove, a plantation some dozen miles from Savannah belonging to Catherine Greene, widow of General Nathanael Greene. Whitney, who had never seen a cotton plant before, met a number of the local landowners. To his father he wrote:

> I heard much of the extreme difficulty of ginning Cotton, that is, separating it from its seed. There were a number of very respectable Gentlemen at Mrs. Greene's who all agreed that if a machine could be invented that would clean the Cotton with expedition, it would be a great thing both to the Country and to the inventor.

Within ten days Whitney had solved the problem that had baffled the planters. His gin (engine) consisted of a cylinder covered with rows of wire teeth rotating in a box filled with cotton. As the cylinder turned, the teeth passed through narrow slits in a metal grating. Cotton fibers were caught by the teeth and pulled through the slits. The seeds, too thick to pass through the openings, were left behind. A second cylinder, with brushes rotating in the opposite direction to sweep the cotton from the wires, prevented matting and clogging.

This "absurdly simple contrivance" almost instantly transformed southern agriculture. With a gin a slave could clean 50 times as much cotton as by hand; soon larger models driven by mules and horses were available. Cotton production figures tell the story: In 1790 about 3,000 bales (the average bale weighed 500 pounds) were produced in the United States. In 1793, 10,000 bales were produced; two years later, 17,000; by 1801, 100,000. The embargo and the War of 1812 temporarily checked expansion, but in 1816 output spurted ahead by more than 25 percent, and in the early 1820s annual production averaged well over 400,000 bales.

Despite this avalanche, the price of cotton remained high. Profits of $50 an acre were not unusual, and the South boomed. The crop engulfed

Eli Whitney's cotton gin drastically reduced the costs involved in cleaning the "green seed" variety of cotton and contributed to the rapid expansion of the cotton industry in the United States.

Cotton Production and Slave Population, 1800–1860

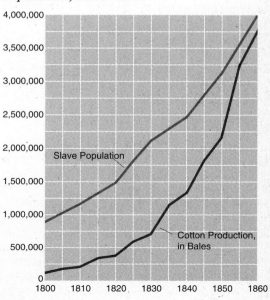

Georgia and South Carolina and spread north into parts of Virginia. After Andrew Jackson smashed the southwestern Indians during the War of 1812, the rich "Black Belt" area of central Alabama and northern Mississippi and the delta region along the lower Mississippi River were rapidly taken over by the fluffy white staple. In 1821 Alabama alone raised 40,000 bales. Central Tennessee also became important cotton country.

Cotton stimulated the economy of the rest of the nation as well. Most of it was exported, the sale paying for much-needed European products. The transportation, insurance, and final disposition of the crop fell largely into the hands of northern merchants, who profited accordingly. And the surplus corn and hogs of western farmers helped feed the slaves of the new cotton plantations. As Douglass North explained in *The Economic Growth of the United States: 1815–1860,* cotton was "the major expansive force" in the American economy for a generation beginning about 1815.

Revival of Slavery

Amid the national rejoicing over this prosperity, one aspect both sad and ominous was easily overlooked. Slavery, a declining or at worst stagnant institution in the decade of the Revolution, was revitalized in the following years.

Libertarian beliefs inspired by the Revolution ran into the roadblock of race prejudice as soon as some of the practical aspects of freedom for blacks became apparent. As disciples of John Locke, the Revolutionary generation had a deep respect for property rights; in the last analysis most white Americans placed these rights ahead of the personal liberty of black Americans in their constellation of values. Forced abolition of slavery therefore attracted few recruits.

In the 1780s many opponents of slavery began to think of solving the "Negro problem" by colonizing freed slaves in some distant region—in the western districts or perhaps in Africa. The colonization movement had two aspects. One, a manifestation of an embryonic black nationalism, reflected the disgust of black Americans with local racial attitudes and their interest in African civilization. Paul Cuffe, a Massachusetts Quaker, managed to finance the emigration of 38 of his fellow blacks to Sierra Leone in 1815. But few others

followed. Most influential northern blacks, such as Bishop Richard Allen of the African Methodist Church, opposed the idea vigorously.

The other colonization movement, led by whites, was paternalistic. Some white colonizationists genuinely abhorred slavery. Others could not stomach living with free blacks; to them *colonization* was a polite word for deportation. Most white colonizationists were conservatives who considered themselves realists: They were sure that American conditions gave blacks no chance to better their lot and that both races would profit from separation.

The colonization idea became popular in Virginia in the 1790s, but nothing was achieved until after the founding of the American Colonization Society in 1817. The society purchased African land and established the Republic of Liberia. However, despite the cooperation of a handful of black nationalists and the patronage of many important white southerners, including presidents Madison and Monroe and Chief Justice Marshall, it accomplished little and declined rapidly after about 1830. As late as 1850, the black American population of Liberia was only 6,000.

The cotton boom of the early 19th century acted as a brake on the colonization movement. As cotton production expanded, the need for labor in the South grew apace. The price of slaves doubled between 1795 and 1804. As it rose, the inclination of even the most kindhearted masters to free their slaves began to falter.

Prices for Cotton and for Slaves, 1802–1860

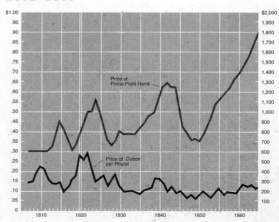

An increase in the interstate slave trade also resulted from the cotton boom. Although it had always been legal for owners to transport their own slaves to a new state if they were settling there, many states forbade, or at least severely restricted, interstate commercial transactions in human flesh. Once cotton became important, these laws were either repealed or systematically evaded. There was a surplus of slaves in one part of the United States and an acute shortage in another. A migration from the Upper South to the cotton lands quickly sprang up. Soon the slave trade became an organized business, cruel and shameful, frowned on by the "best" people of the South, managed by the depraved and the greedy, yet patronized by nearly anyone who needed labor. "The native land of Washington, Jefferson, and Madison," one disgusted Virginian told a French visitor, had "become the Guinea of the United States."

The lot of blacks in the northern states was almost as bad as that of southern free blacks. Except in New England, where there were few of them to begin with, most were denied the vote, either directly or by extralegal pressures. They could not testify in court, intermarry with whites, obtain decent jobs or housing, or get even a rudimentary education. Most states segregated them in theaters, hospitals, and churches and on public transportation facilities. As a rule, they were barred from hotels and restaurants patronized by whites.

Northern blacks could at least protest and try to convince the white majority of the injustice of their treatment. These rights were denied their southern brethren. They could and did publish newspapers and pamphlets, organize for political action, petition legislatures and the Congress for redress of grievances—in short, they applied methods of peaceful persuasion in an effort to improve their position in society.

Roads to Market

Inventions and technological improvements were extremely important in the settlement of the West. On superficial examination, this may not seem to have been the case, for the hordes of settlers who struggled across the mountains immediately after the War of 1812 were no better equipped than their ancestors who had pushed up the eastern slopes in previous generations. Many plodded on foot over hundreds of miles, dragging crude carts laden with their meager possessions. More fortunate pioneers traveled on horseback or in heavy, cumbersome wagons.

In many cases the pioneers followed trails and roads no better than those of colonial days—quagmires in wet weather, rutted and pitted with potholes a good part of the year. When they settled down, their way of life was no more advanced than that of the Pilgrim Fathers. At first they were creatures of the forest, feeding upon its abundance, building their homes and simple furniture with its wood, and clothing themselves in the furs of forest animals. They usually planted the first crop in a natural glade; thereafter, year by year, they pushed back the trees with ax and saw and fire until the land was cleared. Any source of power more complicated than an ox was beyond their ken. Until the population of the territory had grown large enough to support town life, settlers were as dependent on crude household manufactures as any earlier pioneer.

The spread of settlement into the Mississippi Valley created challenges that required technological advances if they were to be met. Most were related to transportation, the major problem for westerners. Without economical means of getting their produce to market, they were condemned to lives of crude self-sufficiency. Everyone recognized that an efficient transportation network would increase land values, stimulate domestic and foreign trade, and strengthen the economy.

The Mississippi River and its tributaries provided a natural highway for western commerce and communication, but it had grave disadvantages. Farm products could be floated down to New Orleans on rafts and flatboats, but the descent from Pittsburgh took at least a month. Transportation upstream was out of the question for anything but the lightest and most valuable products, and even for them it was extremely expensive. In any case the natural flow of trade was between East and West. That is why, from early in the westward movement, much attention was given to building roads linking the Mississippi Valley to the eastern seaboard. The first such road, connecting Philadelphia and Lancaster, Pennsylvania, was opened to traffic in 1794.

In heavily populated sections the volume of traffic made good roads worth their cost, which

Much of the east-west traffic in the growing United States passed through St. Louis, a vital port on the Mississippi River and the terminus of several western trails. The city looked like this in the 1830s.

ran to as much as $13,000 a mile where the terrain was difficult. In some cases good roads ran out into fairly remote areas. In New York, always a leading state in the movement for improved transportation, an excellent road had been built all the way from Albany to Lake Erie by the time of the War of 1812, and by 1821 the state had some 4,000 miles of good roads.

Transportation and the Government

Most of the improved highways and many bridges were built as business ventures by private interests. Promoters charged tolls, the rates being set by the states. Tolls were collected at gates along the way; hinged poles suspended across the road were turned back by a guard after receipt of the toll. Hence these thoroughfares were known as turnpikes, or simply pikes.

The profits earned by a few early turnpikes, such as the one between Philadelphia and Lancaster, caused the boom in private road building, but even the most fortunate of the turnpike companies did not make much money. Some states bought stock to bolster weak companies, and others built and operated turnpikes as public enterprises. Local governments everywhere provided considerable support, for every town was eager to develop efficient communication with its neighbors.

Despite much talk about individual self-reliance and free enterprise, local, state, and national governments contributed heavily to what in the jargon of the day were called "internal improvements." The federal government poured money in an erratic and unending stream into turnpike companies and other organizations created to improve transportation. Logically, the major highways, especially those over the mountains, should have been built by the national government. Strategic military requirements alone would have justified such a program. One major artery, the Old National Road, running from Cumberland, Maryland, to Wheeling, in western Virginia, was constructed by the United States between 1811 and 1818. In time it was extended as far west as Vandalia, Illinois. However, further federal road building was hampered by squabbles in Congress, usually phrased in constitutional terms but in fact based on sectional rivalries and other economic conflicts.

Although the National Road, the New York Pike, and other, rougher trails such as the Wilderness Road into the Kentucky country were adequate for the movement of settlers, they did not begin to answer the West's need for cheap and efficient transportation. Wagon freight rates varied considerably but averaged at least 30 cents a ton-mile around 1815. At such rates, to transport a ton of oats from Buffalo to New York would have cost 12 times the value of the oats!

Turnpikes made it possible to transport goods such as clothing, hardware, coffee, and books across the Appalachians, but the expense was considerable. It cost more to ship a ton of freight 300 miles over the mountains from Philadelphia to Pittsburgh than from Pittsburgh to Philadelphia by way of New Orleans, more than ten times as far. Until the coming of the railroad, which was just being introduced in England in 1825, shipping bulky goods by land over the great distances common in America was uneconomical. Businessmen and inventors concentrated instead on improving water transport, first by designing better boats and then by developing artificial waterways.

"Organs of Communication"

After John Fitch's work in around 1790, a number of others made important contributions to the development of steam navigation. One early enthusiast was John Stevens, a wealthy New Jerseyite, who designed an improved steam boiler for which he received one of the first patents issued by the United States. Stevens got his brother-in-law, Robert R. Livingston, interested in the problem, and the latter used his political influence to obtain an exclusive charter to operate steamboats on New York waters. In 1802, while in France trying to buy New Orleans from Napoleon, Livingston got to know Robert Fulton, a young American artist and engineer who was experimenting with steam navigation, and agreed to finance his work. In 1807, after returning to New York, Fulton constructed the *North River Steam Boat,* famous to history as the *Clermont.* Nothing about the *Clermont* was radically new, but Fulton brought the various essentials—engine, boiler, paddle wheels, and hull—into proper balance and thereby produced an efficient vessel.

No one could patent a steamboat; soon the new vessels were plying the waters of every navigable river from the Mississippi east. The day of the steamboat had dawned, and although the following generation would experience its high noon, even in the 1820s its major effects were clear. The great Mississippi Valley, in the full tide of its development, was immensely enriched. Produce poured down to New Orleans, which soon ranked with New York and Liverpool among the world's great ports. Only 80,000 tons of freight reached New Orleans from the interior in 1816–1817, more than 542,000 tons in 1840–1841. Upriver traffic was affected even more spectacularly. Freight charges plummeted, in some cases to a tenth of what they had been after the War of 1812. The Northwest emerged from self-sufficiency with a rush and became part of the national market.

The Canal Boom

While the steamboat was conquering western rivers, canals were being constructed that further improved the transportation network. Since the midwestern rivers all emptied into the Gulf of Mexico, they did not provide a direct link with the eastern seaboard. If an artificial waterway could be cut between the great central valley and some navigable stream flowing into the Atlantic, all sections would profit immensely.

Although canals were as old as Egypt, only about 100 miles of them existed in the United States as late as 1816. Construction costs aside, in a rough and mountainous country canals presented formidable engineering problems. To link

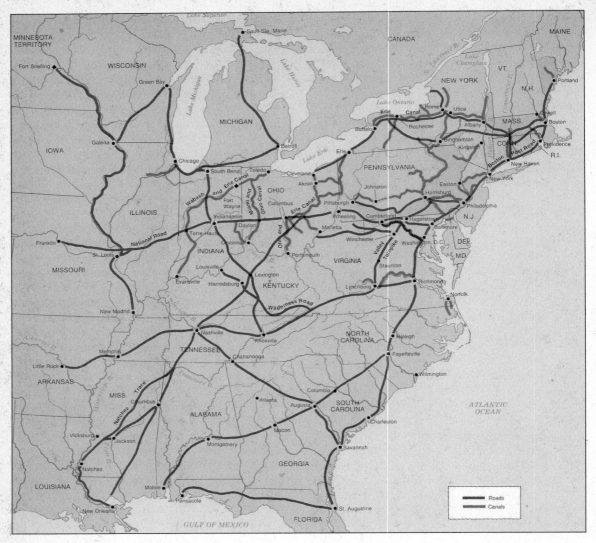

Canals and Roads, 1820–1850

the Mississippi Valley and the Atlantic meant somehow circumventing the Appalachian Mountains. Most persons thought this impossible.

Mayor De Witt Clinton of New York believed that such a project was feasible in New York State. In 1810, while serving as canal commissioner, he traveled across central New York and convinced himself that it would be practicable to dig a canal from Buffalo, on Lake Erie, to the Hudson River; at no point along the route to Buffalo does the land rise more than 570 feet above the level of the Hudson. Marshaling a mass of technical, financial,

and commercial information (and using his political influence cannily), Clinton placed his proposal before the New York legislature. The legislators were convinced, and in 1817 the state began construction along a route 363 miles long, most of it across densely forested wilderness. At the time, the longest canal in the United States ran less than 28 miles!

The Erie, completed in 1825, was an immediate financial success. Together with the companion Champlain Canal, which linked Lake Champlain and the Hudson, it brought in over half a million dollars in tolls in its first year. Soon its entire $7 million cost had been recovered, and it was earning profits of about $3 million a year. The effect of this prosperity on New York State was enormous. Buffalo, Rochester, Syracuse, and half a dozen lesser towns along the canal flourished.

The Emporium of the Western World

New York had already become the largest city in the nation, thanks chiefly to its merchants, who had established a reputation for their rapid and orderly way of doing business. In 1818 the Black Ball Line opened the first regularly scheduled freight and passenger service between New York and England. Previously, shipments might languish in port for weeks while a skipper waited for additional cargo. Now merchants on both sides of the Atlantic could count on the Black Ball packets to move their goods between Liverpool and New York on schedule whether or not the transporting vessel had a full cargo.

This improvement brought much new business to the port. In the same year New York enacted an auction law requiring that imported goods having been placed on the block could not be withdrawn if a bid satisfactory to the seller was not forthcoming. This, too, was a boon to businessmen, who could be assured that if they outbid the competition, the goods would be theirs.

Now the canal cemented New York's position as the national metropolis. Most European manufactured goods destined for the Mississippi Valley entered the country at New York and passed on to the West over the canal. The success of the Erie also sparked a nationwide canal-building boom. Most canals were constructed either by the states, as in the case of the Erie, or as "mixed enterprises" that combined public and private resources.

No state profited as much from this construction as New York, for none possessed New York's geographical advantages. In New England the terrain was so rugged as to discourage all but fanatics. The Delaware and Hudson Canal, running from northeastern Pennsylvania across northern New Jersey and lower New York to the Hudson, was completed by private interests in 1828. It man-

aged to earn respectable dividends by barging coal to the eastern seaboard, but it made no attempt to compete with the Erie for the western trade. Pennsylvania, desperate to keep up with New York, engaged in an orgy of construction. In 1834 it completed a complicated system, part canal and part railroad, over the mountains to Pittsburgh. This Mainline Canal was slow and expensive to operate and never competed effectively with the Erie. Efforts of Maryland to link Baltimore with the west by water failed utterly.

Beyond the mountains there was even greater zeal for canal construction in the 1820s and still more in the 1830s. Once the Erie opened the way across New York, farmers in the Ohio country demanded that links be built between the Ohio River and the Great Lakes so that they could ship their produce by water directly to the East. Even before the completion of the Erie, Ohio had begun construction of the Ohio and Erie Canal running from the Ohio River to Cleveland. Another, from Toledo to Cincinnati, was begun in 1832. Meanwhile, Indiana had undertaken the 450-mile Wabash and Erie Canal. These canals were well conceived, but the western states overextended themselves building dozens of feeder lines, trying, it sometimes seemed, to supply all farmers west of the Appalachians with water connections from their barns to the New York docks.

The result was frequently financial disaster. There was not enough traffic to pay for all the waterways that were dug. By 1844, $60 million in state "improvement" bonds were in default. Nevertheless, the canals benefited both western farmers and the national economy.

Government Aid to Business

Throughout this period both the United States and the individual states were active in areas that directly affected the economy. Federal banking, tariff, and land legislation influenced economic expansion. While prejudice against corporations in the manufacturing field continued, the device was such a useful means of bringing together the substantial amounts of capital needed for building roads and canals and for organizing banks and insurance companies that a steadily increasing number of promoters applied for charters. In 1811

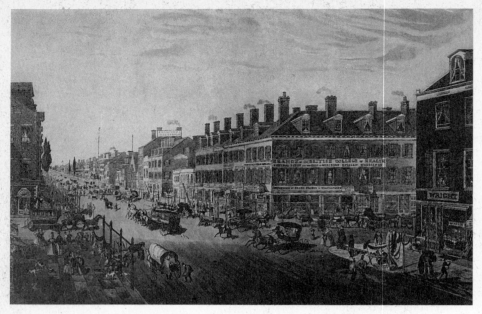

A view of New York's Broadway in 1835. The broad avenue was home to many of the large, modern stores that helped make New York City the commercial center of the nation.

New York enacted the first general incorporation law, permitting the issuance of charters without specific legislative action in each case.

Manufacturers in some states received valuable tax benefits, and all could make use of the United States Patent Office, created in 1790. The attitude of most courts and juries toward labor unions and strikes in this period also favored employers. Before the end of the 1820s, craft unions had become numerous and active, yet judges tended to consider strikes unlawful conspiracies and to find against unions that tried to establish the closed shop. Though the public's attitude toward organized labor was beginning to change, the legal right of unions to exist was not fully established until the 1840s.

The Marshall Court

The most important legal advantages bestowed upon businessmen in the period were the gifts of Chief Justice John Marshall. Historians have tended to forget he had six colleagues on the Supreme Court, and that is easy to understand. Marshall's particular combination of charm, logic, and forcefulness made the Court during his long reign, if not a rubber stamp, remarkably submissive to his view of the Constitution.

Marshall's belief in a powerful central government explains his tendency to hand down decisions favorable to the manufacturing and business interests. He also thought that "the business community was the agent of order and progress" and tended to interpret the Constitution in a way that would advance its interests.

Many important cases came before the Court between 1819 and 1824, and in each one Marshall's decision was applauded by most of the business community. The cases involved two major principles: the "sanctity" of contracts and the supremacy of federal legislation over the laws of the states.

Marshall shared the conviction of the Revolutionary generation that property had to be protected against arbitrary seizure if liberty was to be

The artist Chester Harding painted John Marshall in 1828, during the Chief Justice's 27th year on the Supreme Court. "The unpretentious dignity [and] the sober factualism" of Harding's style (as art historian Oliver Larkin describes it) was well suited to capturing Marshall's character.

preserved. He therefore gave the widest possible application to the constitutional provision that no state could pass any law "impairing the Obligation of Contracts."

Two controversies settled in February 1819 illustrate Marshall's views on the subject of contracts. In *Sturges* v. *Crowninshield* he found a New York bankruptcy law unconstitutional. States could pass such laws, he conceded, but they could not make them applicable to debts incurred before the laws were passed, for debts were contracts.

In *Dartmouth College* v. *Woodward* he held that a charter granted by a state was a contract and might

not be canceled or altered without the consent of both parties. Contracts could scarcely be more sacred than Marshall made them in the Dartmouth College case, which involved an attempt by New Hampshire to alter the charter granted to Dartmouth by King George III in 1769. The state had sought not to destroy the college but to change it from a private to a public insti-tution, yet Marshall held that to do so would vi-olate the contract clause. In the light of this de-cision, corporations licensed by the states seemed immune against later attempts to regulate their activities.

Marshall's decisions concerning the division of power between the federal government and the states were even more important. The question of the constitutionality of a national bank, first debated by Hamilton and Jefferson, had not been submitted to the courts during the life of the first Bank of the United States. By the time of the second Bank there were many state banks, and some of them believed that their interests were threatened by the national institution. Responding to pressure from local banks, the Maryland legislature placed an annual tax of $15,000 on "foreign" banks. The Maryland branch of the Bank of the United States refused to pay, whereupon the state brought suit against its cashier, John W. McCulloch.

McCulloch v. *Maryland* was crucial to the Bank, for five other states had levied taxes on its branches, and others would surely follow suit if the Maryland law were upheld. Marshall extinguished the threat. The Bank was constitutional, its legality was implied in many of the powers specifically granted to Congress. Since the Bank was legal, the Maryland tax was unconstitutional. According to Marshall, "The power to tax involves the power to destroy . . . the power to destroy may defeat and render useless the power to create." The long-range significance of the decision lay in its strengthening of the implied powers of Congress and its confirmation of the Hamiltonian or "loose" interpretation of the Constitution. By establishing the legality of the Bank, it also aided the growth of the economy.

In 1824 Marshall handed down an important decision involving the regulation of interstate commerce. This was the "steamboat case," *Gibbons* v. *Ogden*. In 1815 Aaron Ogden, former United States senator and governor of New Jersey, had purchased the right to operate a ferry between Elizabeth Point, New Jersey, and New York City from Fulton's backer, Robert R. Livingston, who held a New York monopoly of steamboat navigation on the Hudson. When Thomas Gibbons, who held a federal coasting license, set up a competing line, Ogden sued him. Ogden argued in effect that Gibbons could operate his boat (whose captain was Cornelius Vanderbilt, later a famous railroad magnate) on the New Jersey side of the Hudson but had no right to cross into New York waters. After complicated litigation in the lower courts, the case reached the Supreme Court on appeal.

Marshall decided in favor of Gibbons, effectively destroying the New York monopoly. He ruled that a state can regulate commerce which begins and ends in its own territory but not when the transaction involves crossing a state line; then the national authority takes precedence. "The act of Congress," he said, "is supreme; and the law of the state . . . must yield to it."

This decision threw open the interstate steamboat business to all comers. More important in the long run was the fact that in order to include the ferry business within the federal government's power to regulate interstate commerce, Marshall had given the word the widest possible meaning. "Commerce, undoubtedly, is traffic, but it is something more—it is intercourse." By construing the commerce clause so broadly, he made it easy for future generations of judges to extend its coverage to include the control of interstate electric power lines and even radio and television transmission.

Many of Marshall's decisions aided the economic development of the country in specific ways, but his chief contribution lay in his broadly national view of economic affairs. His nationalism enabled him to add form and substance to Hamilton's vision of the economic future of the United States. Marshall and his colleagues firmly established the principle of judicial limitation on the power of legislatures and made the Supreme Court a vital part of the American system of government. In an age plagued by narrow sectional jealousies, Marshall's contribution was of immense influence and significance, and on it rests his claim to greatness.

John Marshall died in 1835. Two years later, in the Charles River Bridge case, the Court, speaking

Milestones

1790	Samuel Slater sets up the first American factory	1819–1822	Depression of 1819
1793	Eli Whitney invents the cotton gin	1820–1821	Missouri Compromise
		1824	Steamboat Case (*Gibbons* v. *Ogden*)
1807	Robert Fulton constructs *North River Steam Boat*	1825	John Quincy Adams's presumed "corrupt bargain" with Henry Clay
1813	Boston Manufacturing Company opens in Waltham, Massachusetts		Erie Canal completed
1816	Second Bank of the United States	1837	*Charles River Bridge* v. *Warren Bridge*
1817	Founding of American Colonization Society		
1817–1825	Administration of James Monroe		
1819	Dartmouth College Case (*Dartmouth College* v. *Woodward*)		
	Bank Case (*McCulloch* v. *Maryland*)		

through Roger Taney, the new Chief Justice, decided that a state government could favor "the comfort and convenience" of the whole community over the property rights of a private company. How Marshall would have voted in this case, which would have forced him to choose between his Dartmouth College and steamboat case arguments, can never be known. But like most of Marshall's decisions, the Charles River Bridge case advanced the interests of those favoring economic development.

Supplementary Reading

On the forces changing the American economy and stimulating the development of industry, see D. C. North, **The Economic Growth of the United States*** (1961). G. R. Taylor, **The Transportation Revolution*** (1951), also discusses this subject intelligently.

On the Industrial Revolution, see A. D. Chandler, Jr., **The Visible Hand** (1977), and B. M. Tucker, **Samuel Slater and the Origins of the American Textile Industry** (1984).

Richard C. Wade, **The Urban Frontier*** (1957), and Howard Chudacoff, **The Evolution of American Urban Society*** (1981), cover urban changes. On immigration and ethnicity, see P. T. Knoble, **Paddy and the Republic** (1986), and J. P. Dolan, **Immigrant Church: New York's Irish and German Catholics*** (1982).

On changes in the nature of work in America, consult A.F.C. Wallace, **Rockdale*** (1978), Alan Dawley, **Class and Community** (1976), Thomas Dublin, **Women at Work** (1979), and Sean Wilencz, **Chants Democratic** (1984).

On the spread of cotton cultivation in the south, see C. McL. Green, **Eli Whitney and the Birth of American Technology*** (1956). W. D. Jordan, **White Over Black*** (1968), and L. F. Litwack, **North of Slavery: The Negro in the Free States*** (1961), discuss the fate of blacks. See also P. J. Staudenraus, **The African Colonization Movement** (1961).

Taylor's **Transportation Revolution** is the best introduction to the changes in transportation that took place. George Dangerfield, **Chancellor Robert R. Livingston of New York** (1960), contains an excellent account of the planning and operation of the *Clermont*, and no student should miss Mark Twain, **Life on the Mississippi*** (1883).

R. E. Shaw, **Canals for a Nation** (1990), describes the development of the canal network. On the Erie Canal, see Nathan Miller, **The Enterprise of a Free People** (1962), and Shaw's **Erie Water West** (1966). Carter Goodrich ed., **Canals and American Economic Development** (1961), authoritatively describes the role of government aid in canal construction. The most important of the decisions of the Marshall court in this period are discussed in J. A. Garraty, ed., **Quarrels That Have Shaped the Constitution*** (1987), and R. K. Newmyer, **The Supreme Court under Marshall and Taney*** (1968). F. N. Stites, **John Marshall: Defender of the Constitution** (1981), is a useful biography.

*Available in paperback.

CHAPTER 9

Jacksonian Democracy

The "Coronation" of King Mob
"Democratizing" Politics
1828: The New Party System in Embryo
The Jacksonian Appeal
The Spoils System
President of all the People
Sectional Tensions Revived
"The Bank . . . I Will Kill It!"
Jackson's Bank Veto
Jackson Versus Calhoun
Indian Removals
The Nullification Crisis
Boom and Bust
The Jacksonians
Rise of the Whigs
Martin Van Buren: Jacksonianism Without Jackson
The Log Cabin Campaign

At 11 A.M. on March 4, 1828, a bright, sunny day, Andrew Jackson, hatless and dressed severely in black, walked up Pennsylvania Avenue to the Capitol. A few minutes after noon, before a throng of more than 15,000 people, he delivered an almost inaudible and thoroughly commonplace inaugural address. He then shouldered his way through the crush, mounted a splendid white horse, and rode off to the White House. A reception had been announced, to which "the officially and socially eligible as defined by precedent" had been invited.

The "Coronation" of King Mob

As Jackson rode down Pennsylvania Avenue, the crowds that had turned out to see the Hero of New Orleans followed—on horseback, in rickety wagons, and on foot. Nothing could keep them out of the executive mansion, and the result was chaos. Long tables laden with cakes, ice cream, and orange punch had been set up in the East Room, but they scarcely deflected the well-wishers. Jackson was pressed back helplessly as men tracked mud across valuable rugs and clambered up on delicate chairs to catch a glimpse of him. The White House shook with their shouts. Glassware splintered; furniture was overturned; women fainted.

Jackson was a thin old man despite his toughness, and soon he was in real danger. Fortunately, friends formed a cordon and managed to extricate him through a rear door. Only a generation earlier Jefferson had felt obliged to introduce pell-mell to encourage informality in the White House. Now a man whom John Quincy Adams called "a barbarian" held Jefferson's office, and, as one Supreme Court justice complained, "The reign of King 'Mob' seemed triumphant."

"Democratizing" Politics

Jackson's inauguration symbolized the triumph of "democracy." Having been taught by Jefferson that all men are created equal, the Americans of Jackson's day (ignoring males with black skin, to say nothing of women, regardless of color), found it easy to believe that every person was as competent and politically important as his neighbor.

The difference between Jeffersonian Democracy and the Jackson variety was more one of attitude than of practice. Jefferson had believed that ordinary citizens could be educated to determine right. Jackson insisted that they knew what was right by instinct. Jefferson's pell mell encouraged the average citizen to hold up his head; by the time of Jackson, the "common man" had become so proud of himself that he gloried in his ordinariness and made mediocrity a virtue. The slightest hint of distinctiveness or servility became suspect. The word *servant* itself fell out of fashion, being replaced by the egalitarian *help*.

The Founding Fathers had not foreseen all the implications of political democracy for a society like the one that existed in the United States. They believed that the ordinary man should have political power in order to protect himself against the superior man, but they assumed that the latter would always lead. The people would naturally choose the best men to manage public affairs. In Washington's day and even in Jefferson's, this was generally the case, but the inexorable logic of democracy gradually produced a change. The new western states, unfettered by systems created in a less democratic age, drew up constitutions that eliminated property qualifications for voting and holding office; the eastern states revised their own frames of government to accomplish the same purpose. Many more public offices were made elective rather than appointive.

Even the presidency, designed to be removed from direct public control by the electoral college, felt the impact of the new thinking. By Jackson's time only Delaware and South Carolina still provided for the choice of presidential electors by the legislature; elsewhere they were elected by popular vote. The system of permitting the congressional caucus to name the candidates for the presidency came to an end before 1828. Jackson and Adams were put forward by state legislatures, and soon thereafter the still more democratic system of nomination by national party conventions was adopted.

Certain social changes reflected a new way of looking at political affairs. The final disestablishment of churches revealed a dislike of special privilege. The beginnings of the free-school movement, the earliest glimmerings of interest in adult education, and the slow spread of secondary education all bespoke a concern for improving the knowledge and judgment of ordinary citizens.

These changes emphasized the idea that every citizen was equally important and the conviction that all should participate actively in government. Officeholders began to stress the fact that they were *representatives* as well as leaders and to appeal more frankly and much more intensively for votes. The public responded with a surge of interest. At each succeeding presidential election, a larger percentage of the population went to the polls. Roughly 300,000 ballots were cast in 1824, 2.4 million in 1840.

As voting became more important, so did competition between the candidates. This led to changes in party politics. It took money, people, and organized effort to run campaigns and get out the vote. Party managers, often holders of relatively minor offices, held rallies, dreamed up slogans, published newspapers, and printed ballots containing the names of the party's nominees for distribution to their supporters. This development took place at different times and in different states. The 1828 election stimulated party formation because instead of several sectional candidates, it pitted two nationally known men against each other. This compelled local leaders to make a choice and then convince local voters to accept their judgment. This was especially true in states where neither Adams nor Jackson had a preponderance of backers. Thus the new system established itself much faster in New York and Pennsylvania than in New England, where Adams was strong, or Tennessee, where the "native son" Jackson had overwhelming support.

Like most institutions, the new parties created bureaucracies to keep them running smoothly. Devoted party workers were rewarded with political office when their efforts were successful. "To the victors belong the spoils," said the New York politician William L. Marcy, and the image, drawn from war and piracy, was appropriate. Although the vigorous wooing of voters constituted a recognition of their importance and a commitment to keeping them informed, campaigning—another military term—frequently degenerated into demagoguery. The most effective way to attract the average voter, politicians soon decided, was by flattery.

Andrew Jackson was the first product of this system to become president. He was chosen because he was popular, not because he was experienced in government. No one knew for sure where he stood on such subjects as the tariff and internal improvements because he did not really know himself, having never been much concerned with them. But he was valiant, honest, patriotic, and eager to do his duty—qualities the presidency has always required.

1828: The New Party System in Embryo

The new system could scarcely have been imagined in 1825 when John Quincy Adams was president. Adams was ill-equipped to lead King Mob. Indeed, it was the battle to succeed him that caused the system to develop. The campaign began almost on the day he was selected by the House of Representatives. Jackson felt that he had been cheated of the presidency by the "corrupt bargain" Adams had made with Henry Clay and he sought vindication.

Relying on his military reputation and Adams's talent for making enemies, he avoided taking a stand on issues that might displease one or another faction. The political situation thus became monumentally confused, one side unable to marshal support for its policies, the other unwilling to adopt policies for fear of losing support.

The campaign was disgraced by character assassination and lies of the worst sort on both sides. Administration supporters denounced Jackson as a bloodthirsty military tyrant, a drunkard, and a gambler. Furious, the Jacksonians (now calling themselves Democrats) replied in kind. They charged that Adams, while serving as American minister to Russia, had supplied a beautiful American virgin for the delectation of the czar. Additionally, discovering that the president had purchased a chess set and a billiard table for the White House, they accused him of squandering public money on gambling devices. The great questions of the day were largely ignored.

All this was inexcusable, and both sides must share the blame. But when the votes were counted, it was discovered that *each* candidate had received many more votes than all four candidates had received in the 1824 election.

When inauguration day arrived, Adams refused to attend the ceremonies because Jackson had failed to pay the traditional preinaugural courtesy call on him at the White House. The Old Puritan may have been equally, if unconsciously, motivated by shame at tactics he had countenanced during the campaign. In any case, deep personal feelings were uppermost in everyone's mind at the formal changing of the guard. The real issues, however, remained. Andrew Jackson would now have to deal with them.

The Jacksonian Appeal

Some historians claim that despite his supposed fondness for "the common man," Andrew Jackson was not a democrat at all and anything but a consistent friend of the weak and underprivileged. They point out that he was a wealthy land speculator, owner of a fine Tennessee plantation, the Hermitage, and of many slaves. Although his supporters liked to cast him as the political heir of Jefferson, he was in many ways like the conservative Washington: a soldier first, an inveterate speculator in western lands, a man with few intellectual interests, and only sketchily educated.

It is of small importance to anyone interested in Jacksonian Democracy to know exactly how "democratic" Jackson was or how sincere his interest in the welfare of the "common man" might have been. Whatever his personal convictions, he stood as the symbol for a movement supported by a new, democratically oriented generation that had grown up under the spell of the American and French revolutions. That he was both a great hero and in many ways a most extraordinary person helps explain his mass appeal. Perhaps he was rich, perhaps conservative, but he was a man of the people, born in a frontier cabin, familiar with the problems of the average citizen.

Jackson epitomized many American ideals. He was patriotic, generous to a fault, and natural and democratic in manner (at home alike in the forest and in the ballroom of a fine mansion). He admired good horseflesh and beautiful women, yet no sterner moralist ever lived; he was a fighter, a relentless foe, but a gentleman in the best American sense. That some special providence watched over him (as over the United States) appeared beyond argument to those who had followed his career. He seemed, in short, both an average and an ideal American, one the people could identify with and still revere. For these reasons Jackson drew support from every section and every social class: western farmers and southern planters, urban workers, bankers, and merchants.

The Spoils System

Jackson took office with the firm intention of punishing the "vile wretches" who had attacked him

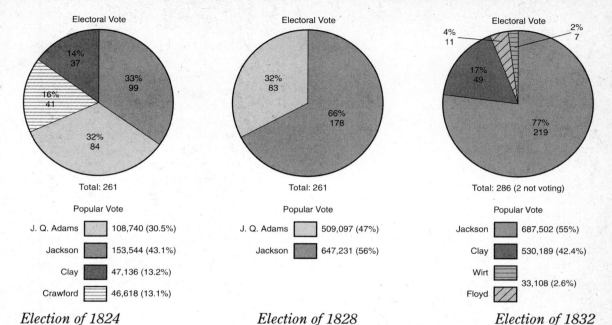

Election of 1824
Election of 1828
Election of 1832

so viciously during the campaign. The new concept of office as a reward for electoral success seemed to justify a housecleaning in the federal bureaucracy. Eager for "the spoils," an army of politicians invaded Washington. "I am ashamed of myself," one such character confessed when he met a friend on the street. "I feel as if every man I meet knew what I came for." "Don't distress yourself," his friend replied, "for every man you meet is on the same business."

There was nothing especially innovative about this invasion, for the principle of filling offices with one's partisans was almost as old as the republic. However, the long lapse of time since the last real political shift, and the recent untypical example of John Quincy Adams, who rarely removed anyone for political reasons, made Jackson's policy appear revolutionary. His removals were not entirely unjustified, for many government workers had grown senile and others corrupt. Even Adams admitted that some of those Jackson dismissed deserved their fate.

Aside from going along with the spoils system and eliminating crooks and incompetents, Jackson advanced another reason for turning experienced government employees out of their jobs—the principle of rotation. "No man has any more intrinsic right to official station than an-

other," he said. Those who hold government jobs for a long time "are apt to acquire a habit of looking with indifference upon the public interests and of tolerating conduct from which an unpracticed man would revolt."

"Rotating" jobholders periodically meant that more citizens could participate in running the government, an obvious advantage in a democracy. The problem was that the constant replacing of trained workers by novices was not likely to increase the efficiency of the government. Jackson's response to this argument was typical: "The duties of all public officers are . . . so plain and simple that men of intelligence may readily qualify themselves for their performance." Contempt for expert knowledge and the belief that ordinary Americans can do anything they set their minds to became fundamental tenets of Jacksonian Democracy. Actually, a solid majority of Jackson's appointments came from the same social and intellectual elite as those they replaced.

President of All the People

Jackson was not cynical about the spoils system. More than any earlier president, he believed that as the direct representative of all the people he was the embodiment of national power. From Washington to John Quincy Adams, his predecessors together had vetoed only 9 bills, always on the ground that they considered the measures unconstitutional. Jackson vetoed 12, some simply because he thought the proposed legislation inexpedient. Yet he had no ambition to expand the scope of federal authority at the expense of the states. Furthermore, he was a poor administrator, given to penny-pinching and lacking in imagination. His strong prejudices and his contempt for expert advice, even in fields like banking where his ignorance was almost total, did him no credit and the country considerable harm.

Jackson's great success (not merely his popularity) was primarily the result of his personality. A shrewd French observer, Michel Chevalier, after commenting on "his chivalric character, his lofty integrity, and his ardent patriotism," pointed out what was probably the central element in Jackson's appeal. "His tactics in politics, as well as in war," Chevalier wrote in 1824, "is to throw himself forward with the cry of *Comrades, follow me!*"

Sectional Tensions Revived

In office, Jackson had to say something about western lands, the tariff, and other issues. He tried to steer a moderate course, urging a slight reduction of the tariff and "constitutional" internal improvements. He suggested that once the rapidly disappearing federal debt had been paid off, the surplus revenues of the government might be "distributed" among the states.

Even these cautious proposals caused conflict, so complex were the interrelations of sectional disputes. If the federal government turned its expected surplus over to the states, it could not afford to reduce the price of public land without going into the red. This disturbed some westerners, notably Senator Thomas Hart Benton of Missouri. Western anxiety in turn suggested to southern opponents of the protective tariff an alliance of South and West. The southerners argued that a tariff levied only to raise revenue would increase foreign imports, bring more money into the treasury, and thus make it possible to reduce the price of public land.

The question came up in the Senate in December 1829, when Senator Samuel A. Foot of Connecticut suggested restricting the sale of government land. Benton promptly denounced the proposal as a plot concocted by eastern manufacturers to check the westward migration of their workers. On January 19, 1830, Senator Robert Y. Hayne of South Carolina, a spokesman for Vice President Calhoun, supported Benton vigorously, suggesting an alliance of South and West based on cheap land and low tariffs.

Daniel Webster then rose to the defense of northeastern interests, cleverly goading Hayne by accusing South Carolina of advocating disunionist policies. Responding to this attack, the South Carolinian launched into an impassioned exposition of the states' rights doctrine. Webster then took the floor again and for two days, before galleries packed with the elite of Washington society, he cut Hayne's argument to shreds. The Constitution was a compact of the American people, not merely of the states, he insisted, the Union perpetual and indissoluble. Webster made the states' rights position appear close to treason; his "second reply to Hayne" effectively prevented the formation of a West–South alliance and made Webster a national figure and a perennial presidential candidate.

"The Bank . . . I Will Kill It!"

In the fall of 1832 Jackson was reelected president, handily defeating Henry Clay. The main issue in the election, aside from Jackson's personal popularity, was the president's determination to destroy the second Bank of the United States. In the "Bank War" Jackson won a complete victory, yet the effects of his triumph were anything but beneficial to the country.

After *McCulloch* v. *Maryland* had presumably established its legality, the Bank of the United States had flourished. Its president, Nicholas Biddle, managed it brilliantly. Almost alone in the United States, Biddle realized that his institution could act as a rudimentary central bank, regulating the availability of credit throughout the nation by controlling the lending policies of the state banks.

Small banks possessing limited amounts of gold and silver sometimes overextended themselves in making large amounts of bank notes available to borrowers in order to earn interest. All this paper money was legally convertible into hard cash on demand, but in the ordinary run of business people seldom bothered to convert their notes so long as they thought the issuing bank was sound. Bank notes passed freely from hand to hand and from bank to bank in every section of the country.

Eventually much of the paper money of the local banks came across the counter of one or another of the 22 branches of the Bank of the United States. By collecting these notes and presenting them for conversion into specie, Biddle could compel the local banks to maintain adequate reserves of gold and silver—in other words, make them hold their lending policies within bounds.

Biddle's policies in the 1820s were good for his own institution, which earned substantial profits, for the state banks, and probably for the country. By making liberal loans to produce merchants, for example, rural bankers indirectly stimulated farmers to expand their output beyond current demand, which eventually led to a decline in prices and an agricultural depression. In every field of economic activity, reckless lending caused inflation and greatly exaggerated the ups and downs of the business cycle. It can be argued, however, that by restricting the lending of state banks, Biddle was slowing the rate of economic growth and that in a predominantly agricultural society an occasional slump was not a large price to pay for rapid economic development.

Biddle's policies acted to stabilize the economy. Many state bankers supported them. But they roused a great deal of opposition too. In part, the opposition originated in pure ignorance: The distrust of paper money did not disappear, and those who disliked *all* paper saw the Bank as merely the largest (and thus the worst) of many bad institutions. At the other extreme, some bankers chafed under Biddle's restraints because by discouraging them from lending freely, he was limiting their profits. New York City bankers resented the fact that a Philadelphia institution could wield so much power over their affairs. New York was the nation's largest importing center; huge amounts of tariff revenue were collected there. Yet, since this money was deposited in the Bank of the United States, Biddle controlled it from Philadelphia. Finally, some people objected to the Bank because it had a monopoly of public funds but was managed by a private citizen and controlled by a handful of rich men.

Jackson's Bank Veto

This formidable opposition to the Bank was diffuse and unorganized until Andrew Jackson brought it together. When he did, the Bank was quickly destroyed. Jackson belonged among the ignorant enemies of the institution; he was a hard-money man suspicious of all commercial banking. His attitude dismayed Biddle who, almost against his will, found himself gravitating toward Clay and the National Republicans, offering advantageous loans and retainers to politicians and newspaper editors in order to build up a following. Thereafter events moved inevitably toward a showdown, for the president's combative instincts were easily aroused. "The Bank," he told Van Buren, "is trying to kill me, *but I will kill it!*"

Henry Clay, Daniel Webster, and other prominent National Republicans hoped to use the Bank controversy against Jackson. They reasoned that the institution was so important to the country that Jackson's opposition to it would undermine his popularity. They therefore urged Biddle to ask Congress to renew the Bank's charter. The charter would not expire until 1836, but by pressing the issue before the 1832 presidential election they could force Jackson either to approve the recharter bill or to veto it (which would give candidate Clay a lively issue in the campaign). The banker yielded to this strategy reluctantly, for he would have preferred to postpone the showdown, and a recharter bill passed Congress early in July 1832. Jackson promptly vetoed it.

Jackson's message explaining why he had rejected the bill adds nothing to his reputation as a statesman. Being a good Jeffersonian—and no friend of John Marshall—he insisted that the Bank was unconstitutional. (*McCulloch* v. *Maryland* he brushed aside, saying that as president he had sworn to uphold the Constitution as *he* understood it.) The Bank was also inexpedient, he argued. Being a dangerous private monopoly that allowed a handful of rich men to accumulate "many millions" of dollars, the bank was making "the rich richer and the potent more powerful."

The most unfortunate aspect of Jackson's veto was that he could have reformed the Bank instead of destroying it. The central banking function was too important to be left in private hands. Biddle once boasted that he could put nearly any bank in the United States out of business simply by forcing it to exchange specie for its bank notes. He thought he was demonstrating his forbearance, but in fact he was revealing a dangerous flaw in the system. When the Jacksonians called him "Czar Nicholas," they were not far from the mark. Moreover, private bankers *were* making profits that in justice belonged to the people, for the government received no interest from the large sums it kept on deposit in the Bank. Jackson would not consider reforms. He set out to smash the Bank of the United States without any real idea of what might be put in its place—a foolhardy act.

Biddle considered Jackson's veto "a manifesto of anarchy," its tone like "the fury of a chained panther biting the bars of his cage." Voters, however, approved of Jackson's hard-hitting attack.

Buttressed by his election triumph, Jackson acted swiftly. "Until I can strangle this hydra of corruption, the Bank, I will not shrink from my duty," he said. Shortly after the start of his second term, he decided to withdraw the government funds deposited in its vaults. Under the law only the secretary of the treasury could remove the deposits. After two secretaries of the treasury had refused to do so, he appointed to the post Roger B. Taney, who had been advising him closely on Bank affairs. Taney carried out the order by depositing new federal receipts in seven state banks in eastern cities while continuing to meet government expenses with drafts on the Bank of the United States.

The situation was extremely confused and slightly unethical. Set on winning the "Bank War," Jackson lost sight of his fear of unsound paper money. Taney, however, knew exactly what he was doing. One of the state banks receiving federal funds was the Union Bank of Baltimore. Taney owned stock in this institution, and its president was his close friend. Little wonder that Jackson's enemies were soon calling the favored state banks "pet" banks. This charge was not entirely fair because Taney took pains to see that the deposits were placed in financially sound institutions. By 1836 the government's funds had been spread out in about 90 banks. But neither was the charge entirely unfair; the administration certainly favored institutions whose directors were politically sympathetic to it.

When Taney began to remove the deposits, the government had more than $9.8 million to its credit in the Bank of the United States; within three months the figure fell to about $4 million. Faced with the withdrawal of so much cash, Biddle had to contract his operations. He decided to exaggerate the contraction, pressing the state banks hard by presenting all their notes and checks that came across his counter for conversion into specie and drastically limiting his own bank's business loans. He hoped that the resulting shortage of credit would be blamed on Jackson and that it would force the president to return the deposits.

For a time the strategy appeared to be working. Paper money became scarce, specie almost unobtainable. A serious panic threatened. Jackson would not budge. He swore he would sooner cut off his right arm and "undergo the torture of ten Spanish inquisitions" than restore the deposits. When delegations came to him, he roared: "Go to Nicholas Biddle. . . . Biddle has all the money!" And in the end—because he was right—business leaders began to take the old general's advice. Pressure on Biddle mounted swiftly, and in July 1834 he reversed his policy and began to lend money freely. The artificial crisis ended.

Jackson Versus Calhoun

The Webster-Hayne debate had revived discussion of John C. Calhoun's argument about nullification. Although southern-born, Jackson had devoted too much of his life to fighting for the entire United States to countenance disunion. Therefore, in April 1830, when the states' rights faction invited him to a dinner to celebrate the anniversary of Jefferson's birth, he came prepared. The evening reverberated with speeches and toasts of a states' rights tenor, but when the president was called on to volunteer a toast, he raised his glass, fixed his eyes on John C. Calhoun, and said: "Our *Federal* Union: It must be preserved!" Calhoun took up the challenge. "The Union," he retorted, "next to our liberty, most dear!"

Jackson and Calhoun were not far apart ideologically except on the ultimate issue of the right of a state to overrule federal authority. Jackson was a strong president, but he did not believe that the area of national power was large or that it should be expanded. His interests in government economy, in the distribution of federal surpluses to the states, and in interpreting the powers of Congress narrowly were all similar to Calhoun's.

Like most westerners, he favored internal improvements, but he preferred that local projects be left to the states. In 1830 he vetoed a bill providing aid for the construction of the Maysville Road because the route was wholly within Kentucky. There were political reasons for this veto, which was a slap at Kentucky's hero, Henry Clay, but it could not fail to please Calhoun.

Indian Removals

The president also took a states' rights position in the controversy that arose between the Cherokee Indians and Georgia. Although he shared many of the typical westerner's feelings about Indians, Jackson insisted that he did not hate them. He subscribed to the theory, advanced by Jefferson, that Indians were "savage" because they roamed wild in a trackless wilderness. The "original inhabitants of our forests" were "incapable of self-government," Jackson claimed, ignoring the fact that the Cherokee lived settled lives and had governed themselves without trouble before the whites arrived.

The Cherokee inhabited a region coveted by whites because it was suitable for growing cotton. Since most Indians preferred to maintain their tribal ways, Jackson pursued a policy of "removing" them from the path of white settlement. This policy seems heartless to modern critics, but most whites considered removal the only humane solution if the nation was to continue to expand.

Many tribes resigned themselves to removal. Between 1831 and 1833, at least 15,000 Choctaw migrated from Mississippi to the region west of Arkansas territory. In *Democracy in America* the Frenchman Alexis de Tocqueville described "the frightful sufferings that attended these forced migrations." He penned a vivid account of a group of Choctaw crossing the Mississippi in the dead of winter.

> *The cold was unusually severe; the snow had frozen hard upon the ground, and the river was drifting huge masses of ice. The Indians . . . possessed neither tents nor wagons, but only their arms and some provisions. I saw them embark to pass the mighty river, and never will that solemn spectacle fade from my remembrance.*

A few tribes, such as Black Hawk's Sac and Fox in Illinois and Osceola's Seminoles in Florida, resisted being "removed" and were subdued by troops. The Cherokee instead sought to hold on to their lands by adjusting to white ways. They took up farming and cattle raising, developed a written language, drafted a constitution, and tried to establish a state within a state in northwestern Georgia. Several treaties with the United States seemed to establish the legality of their government. Georgia, however, would not recognize the Cherokee Nation. It passed a law in 1828 declaring all Cherokee laws void and the region a part of Georgia.

The Indians challenged this law in the Supreme Court. In *Cherokee Nation* v. *Georgia* (1831) Chief Justice Marshall had ruled that the Cherokee were "not a foreign state" and therefore could not sue in a United States court. However, in *Worcester* v. *Georgia* (1832), a case involving two missionaries to the Cherokee who had not procured licenses required by Georgia law, he ruled that the state could not control the Cherokee or their territory. Later, when a Cherokee named Corn Tassel, convicted in a Georgia court of the murder of another Indian, appealed on the ground that the crime had taken place in Cherokee territory, Marshall declared the Georgia action unconstitutional on the same ground.

Jackson backed Georgia's position. No independent nation could exist within the United States, he insisted. Georgia thereupon hanged Corn Tassel. In 1838 the United States forced 15,000 Cherokees to leave Georgia for Oklahoma. At least 4,000 of them died on the way; the route has been aptly named "The Trail of Tears."

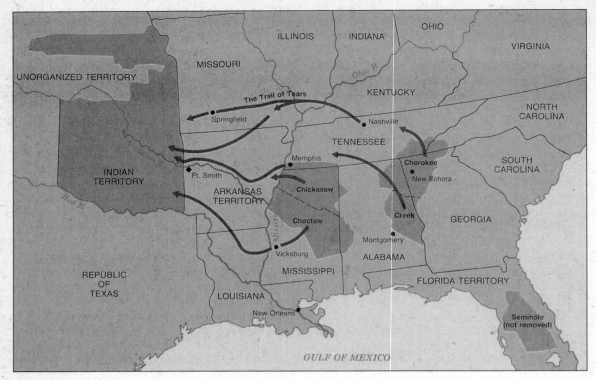

Indian Removals

Jackson's willingness to allow Georgia to ignore decisions of the Supreme Court persuaded extreme southern states' righters that he would not oppose the doctrine of nullification should it be formally applied to a law of Congress. They deceived themselves egregiously. Jackson did not challenge Georgia because he approved of the state's position. He was not the type to worry about being inconsistent. When South Carolina revived the talk of nullification in 1832, he acted in quite a different manner.

The Nullification Crisis

The proposed alliance of South and West to reduce the tariff and the price of land had not materialized. When a new tariff law was passed in 1832, it lowered duties much less than southerners desired. At once talk of nullifying it began to be heard in South Carolina.

In addition to the economic woes of the upcountry cotton planters, the great planter-aristo-crats of the rice-growing tidewater region, though relatively prosperous, were troubled by northern criticisms of slavery. In the rice-growing region, blacks outnumbered whites by two to one. Thousands of these slaves were African-born—brought in during the burst of importations before Congress outlawed the trade in 1808.

In 1822 the exposure in Charleston of a planned revolt organized by Denmark Vesey, who had bought his freedom with money won in a lottery, had alarmed many whites. News of a far more serious uprising in Virginia led by the slave Nat Turner in 1831 added to popular concern. Radical South Carolinians saw protective tariffs and agitation against slavery as the two sides of one coin; against both, nullification seemed the logical defense. Yield on the tariff, editor Henry L. Pinckney of the influential Charleston *Mercury* warned, and "abolition will become the order of the day."

Endless discussions of Calhoun's doctrine after the publication of his *Exposition and Protest* in 1828 had produced much interesting theorizing without clarifying the issue. Admirers of Calhoun

This Robert Lindneux painting of the Cherokee "Trail of Tears" captures the essence of the Indian removals during the period. As many as 4,000 died of starvation and exposure during the 1,200-mile walk.

praised his "power of analysis & profound philosophical reasonings," but his idea was ingenious rather than profound. Plausible at first glance, the argument was based on several false assumptions: that the Constitution was subject to definitive interpretation; that one party could be permitted to interpret a compact unilaterally without destroying it; that a minority of the nation could reassume its sovereign independence but that a minority of a state could not.

President Jackson was in this respect Calhoun's exact opposite. He brushed aside the South Carolinian's mental gymnastics, because intuitively he realized the central reality: If a state could nullify a law of Congress, the Union could not exist. "Tell . . . the Nullifiers from me that they can talk and write resolutions and print threats to their hearts' content," he warned a South Carolina representative when Congress adjourned in July 1832. "But if one drop of blood be shed there in defiance of the laws of the United States, I will

hang the first man of them I can get my hands on to the first tree I can find."

The warning was not taken seriously in South Carolina. In October the state legislature provided for the election of a special convention, which, when it met, contained a solid majority of nullifiers. On November 24, 1832, the convention passed an Ordinance of Nullification, prohibiting the collection of tariff duties in the state after February 1, 1833. The legislature then authorized the raising of an army and appropriated money to supply it with weapons.

Jackson quickly began military preparations of his own. He also made a statesmanlike effort to end the crisis peaceably. First he suggested to Congress that it lower the tariff further. On December 10, he addressed a "Proclamation to the People of South Carolina." Nullification could only lead to the destruction of the Union, he said. "Disunion by armed force is *treason*. Are you really ready to incur its guilt?" Jackson's reasoning shocked even opponents of nullification. His threat to use force would mean civil war if South Carolina did not back down and possibly the destruction of the Union the president claimed to be defending.

Calhoun sought desperately to control the crisis. By pre-arrangement with Senator Hayne, he resigned as vice president and was appointed to replace Hayne in the Senate, where he led the search for a peaceful solution. Clay was a willing ally. In addition, large numbers of people who admired Jackson, feared that his threat to use force would mean a civil war if South Carolina did not back down.

Jackson was perfectly willing to see the tariff reduced, but he insisted that the law must be enforced. His determination sobered the South Carolina radicals. Their appeal for the support of other southern states fell on deaf ears; all rejected the idea of nullification. Calhoun, though a brave man, was alarmed for his own safety; Jackson had threatened to "hang him as high as Haman" if nullification were attempted. Suddenly eager to avoid a showdown, he joined forces with Henry Clay to push a compromise tariff through Congress. Ten days before the deadline, South Carolina postponed nullification pending the outcome of the tariff debate. Its passage early in March 1833 reflected the willingness of the North and West to make concessions in the interest of national harmony.

And so the Union weathered the storm. Having teetered on the brink of civil war, the nation had drawn hastily back. The South Carolina legislature professed to be satisfied with the new tariff (in fact, it made few immediate reductions, providing for a gradual lowering of rates over a ten- year period) and repealed the Nullification Ordinance.

However, the radical South Carolina planters were becoming convinced that only secession would protect slavery. The nullification fiasco had proved that they could not succeed without the support of other slave states. Thereafter they devoted themselves ceaselessly to obtaining it.

Boom and Bust

During 1833 and 1834, Secretary of the Treasury Taney insisted that the pet banks maintain large reserves. But other state banks began to offer credit on easy terms. Bank notes in circulation jumped from $82 million in January 1835 to $120 million in December 1836. Bank deposits rose even more rapidly.

Much of the new money flowed into speculation in land; a mania to invest in property swept the country. Chicago at this time had only 2,000 to 3,000 inhabitants, yet most of the land for 25 miles around had been sold and resold in small lots by speculators anticipating the growth of the area. Throughout the West, farmers borrowed money from local banks by mortgaging their land, used the money to buy more land from the government, and then borrowed still more money from the banks on the strength of their new deeds.

As long as prices continued to rise, the process could be repeated endlessly. In 1832, when the Bank of the United States still regulated the money supply, federal income from the sale of land was $2.6 million. In 1834, it was $4.9 million; in 1835, $14.8 million; in 1836, it peaked at $24.9 million, and the government found itself totally free of debt and with a surplus of $20 million!

Finally Jackson became alarmed by the speculative mania. In the summer of 1836, he issued the Specie Circular, which provided that purchasers must henceforth pay for public land in gold or silver. The rush to buy land ground to a halt. When demand slackened, prices sagged. Hordes of depositors sought to withdraw their money in the form of specie, and soon the banks exhausted their supplies. Panic swept through the land in the spring of 1837 as every bank in the nation had to suspend specie payments. The boom was over.

Major swings of the business cycle can never be attributed to the actions of a single person, but there is no doubt that Jackson's war against the Bank exaggerated the swings of the economic pendulum if only by its impact on popular thinking. His Specie Circular did not *prevent* speculators from buying land—at most it caused purchasers to pay a premium for gold and silver. But it convinced potential buyers that the boom was going to end and led them to do things that in fact ended it. Old Hickory's combination of impetuousness, combativeness, arrogance, and ignorance rendered the nation he loved so dearly a serious disservice. He lacked, as Glyndon Van Deusen wrote in *The Jacksonian*

Era, "the capacity for that slow and often painful balancing of opposite viewpoints . . . which is the characteristic of a man of culture." This was his greatest failing, both as a president and as a human being.

The Jacksonians

Jackson's personality had a large impact on the shape and tone of the second party system. He had ridden to power at the head of a diverse political army, but he left behind him an organization with a fairly cohesive, if not necessarily consistent, body of ideas. The newly formed Democratic Party contained rich citizens and poor, easterners and westerners, abolitionists and slaveholders. It was not yet a close-knit national organization, but most Jacksonians agreed on certain underlying principles. These included suspicion of special privilege and large business corporations, both typified by the Bank of the United States; freedom of economic opportunity, unfettered by private or governmental restrictions; absolute political freedom, at least for white males; and the conviction that any ordinary man is capable of performing the duties of most public offices.

Jackson's ability to reconcile his belief in the supremacy of the Union with his conviction that the area of national authority should be held within narrow limits tended to make the Democratic Party attractive to those who believed that the powers of the states should not be diminished. Alexis de Toqueville caught this aspect of Jackson's philosophy perfectly: "Far from wishing to extend Federal power, the president belongs to the party that wishes to limit that power."

Nearly all Jacksonians, like their leader, favored giving the small man his chance—by supporting public education, for example, and by refusing to place much weight on a person's origin, dress, or manners. "One individual is as good as another" (again we must insert the adjective *white*) was axiomatic with them. This attitude helps explain why immigrants, Catholics, and other minority groups usually voted Democratic. However, the Jacksonians showed no tendency either to penalize the wealthy or to intervene in economic affairs to aid the underprivileged. The motto "That government is best which governs least" graced the masthead of the chief Jackson-ian newspaper, the Washington *Globe,* throughout the era.

Rise of the Whigs

The opposition to Jackson was far less cohesive. Henry Clay's National Republican Party provided a nucleus, but Clay never dominated that party as Jackson dominated the Democrats. Its orientation was basically anti-Jackson. It was as though the American people were a great block of granite from which some sculptor had fashioned a statue of Jackson, the chips from the sculptor's chisel, scattered about the floor of his studio, representing the opposition.

While Jackson was president, the impact of his personality delayed the formation of a true two-party system, but as soon as he surrendered power, the opposition, taking heart, began to coalesce. By 1834 dissident groups were calling themselves Whigs. The name (harking back to the Revolution) implied distaste for too-powerful executives, expressed specifically as patriotic resistance to the tyranny of "King Andrew."

This coalition possessed great resources of wealth and talent. Anyone who understood banking was almost obliged to become a Whig. Those spiritual descendants of Hamilton who rejected the administration's refusal to approach economic problems from a broadly national perspective also joined in large numbers. People who found the coarseness and "pushiness" of the Jacksonians offensive made up another element. The anti-intellectual bias of the administration drove many lawyers, ministers, and other well-educated people into the Whig fold. But Whig arguments also appealed to ordinary voters who were predisposed to favor strong governments that would check the "excesses" of unrestricted individualism.

The Whigs were slow to develop an effective party organization. They had too many generals and not enough troops. It was hard for them to agree on any issue more complicated than opposition to Jackson. Furthermore, they stood in conflict with the major trend of their age: the glorification of the common man.

Lacking a dominant leader in 1836, the Whigs relied on "favorite sons," hoping to throw the presidential election into the House of Representatives. This sorry strategy failed. Jackson's hand-

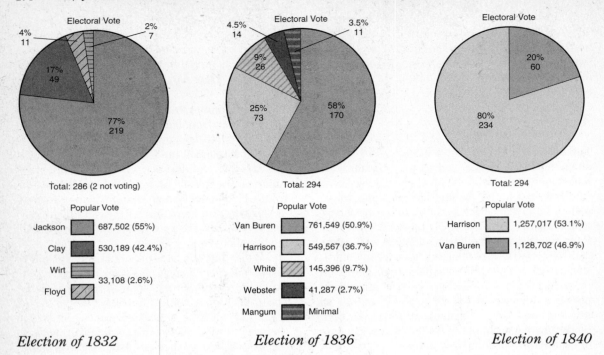

Electoral Vote

4% 11
2% 7
17% 49
77% 219

Total: 286 (2 not voting)

Popular Vote

Jackson		687,502 (55%)
Clay		530,189 (42.4%)
Wirt		33,108 (2.6%)
Floyd		

Election of 1832

Electoral Vote

4.5% 14
3.5% 11
9% 26
25% 73
58% 170

Total: 294

Popular Vote

Van Buren		761,549 (50.9%)
Harrison		549,567 (36.7%)
White		145,396 (9.7%)
Webster		41,287 (2.7%)
Mangum		Minimal

Election of 1836

Electoral Vote

20% 60
80% 234

Total: 294

Popular Vote

Harrison		1,257,017 (53.1%)
Van Buren		1,128,702 (46.9%)

Election of 1840

picked candidate, Martin Van Buren, won a majority of both the popular and the electoral votes.

Martin Van Buren: Jacksonianism Without Jackson

Van Buren's brilliance as a political manipulator has tended to obscure his statesmanlike qualities. He made a powerful argument, for example, that political parties were a force for unity, not for partisan bickering. In addition, high office sobered him and improved his judgment. He fought the Bank of the United States as a monopoly, but he also opposed irresponsible state banks. New York's "Safety Fund System"—requiring all banks to contribute to a fund, supervised by the state, to be used to redeem the notes of any member bank that failed—was established largely through his efforts. Van Buren believed in public construction of internal improvements, but he favored state rather than national programs, and he urged a rational approach: Each project must be a useful and profitable public utility. He approached most questions rationally and pragmatically. In 1832 he was

elected vice president and thereafter was conceded to be the "heir apparent." In 1835 the Democratic National Convention nominated him for president unanimously.

Van Buren took office just as the Panic of 1837 struck the country. Its effects were frightening but short-lived. Late in 1838 the banks resumed specie payments. But in 1839 a bumper crop caused a sharp decline in the price of cotton. Then a number of state governments that had overextended themselves in road- and canal-building projects were forced to default on their debts. This discouraged investors, particularly foreigners. An economic depression ensued that lasted until 1843.

Van Buren was not responsible for the panic or the depression. But his manner of dealing with economic issues was scarcely helpful. He saw his role as being concerned only with problems plaguing the government, ignoring the economy as a whole. "The less government interferes with private pursuits the better for the general prosperity," he pontificated. As Daniel Webster scornfully pointed out, Van Buren was following a policy of "leaving the people to shift for themselves," one which many Whigs rejected.

Van Buren's main goal was to find a substitute for the state banks as a place to keep federal funds. He soon settled on the idea of "divorcing" the government from all banking activities. His Independent Treasury Bill called for the construction of government-owned vaults where federal revenues could be stored until needed. To insure absolute safety, all payments to the government were to be made in hard cash. After a battle that lasted until the summer of 1840, the Independent Treasury Act passed both the House and the Senate.

Opposition to the Independent Treasury system had been bitter, and not all of it was partisan. Bankers and businessmen objected to the government's withholding so much specie from the banks, which needed all the hard money they could get to support loans that were the lifeblood of economic growth. It seemed irresponsible for the federal government to turn its back on the banks, when they so obviously performed a semipublic function.

These criticisms made good sense, but through a combination of circumstances the system worked reasonably well for many years. By creating suspicion in the public mind, officially stated distrust of banks acted as a damper on their tendency to overexpand. No acute shortage of specie developed because heavy agricultural exports and the investment of much European capital in American railroads beginning in the mid-1840s brought in large amounts of new gold and silver. After 1849 the discovery of gold in California added another source of specie.

The supply of money and bank credit kept pace roughly with the growth of the economy, but through no fault of the government. "Wildcat" banks proliferated, fraud and counterfeiting were common, and the operation of everyday business affairs was inconvenienced in countless ways. The disordered state of the currency remained a grave problem until corrected by Civil War banking legislation.

The Log Cabin Campaign

It was not his financial policy that led to Van Buren's defeat in 1840. The depression hurt the Democrats, and the Whigs were far better organized than in 1836. The Whigs also adopted a different strategy. The Jacksonians had come to power on the coattails of a popular general whose views on public questions they concealed or ignored. They had maintained themselves by shouting the praises of the common man. Now the Whigs seized on these techniques and carried them to their logical—or illogical—conclusion. Not even bothering to draft a program, and passing over Clay and Webster, whose views were known and therefore controversial, they nominated General Harrison for president. To "balance" the ticket, the Whigs chose a former Democrat, John Tyler of Virginia, an ardent supporter of states' rights, as their vice presidential candidate.

The Whig argument was specious but effective: General Harrison is a plain man of the people who lives in a log cabin (where the latchstring is always out). Contrast him with the suave Van Buren, luxuriating amid "the Regal Splendor of the President's Palace." Harrison drinks ordinary hard cider and eats hog meat and grits, while Van Buren drinks expensive foreign wines and fattens on fancy concoctions prepared by a French chef.

Harrison came from a distinguished family, being the son of Benjamin Harrison, a signer of the Declaration of Independence and a former governor of Virginia. He was well educated and in at least comfortable financial circumstances, and he certainly did not live in a log cabin. The Whigs ignored these facts. The log cabin and the cider barrel became their symbols, which every political meeting saw reproduced in a dozen forms.

The Democrats used the same methods as the Whigs and were equally well organized, but they had little heart for the fight. Van Buren tried to focus public attention on issues, but his voice could not be heard above the huzzas of the Whigs. A huge turnout (four-fifths of the eligible voters, more than 2.4 million as against 1.5 million four years earlier) carried Harrison to victory by a margin of almost 150,000. The electoral vote was 234 to 60.

The Whigs continued to repeat history by rushing to gather the spoils of victory. Washington was again flooded by office seekers; the political confusion was monumental. Harrison had no ambition to be an aggressive leader. He be-

The 1840 presidential campaign was the first to use circus hoopla and the techniques of mass appeal that came to characterize political contests in the United States. This financial drawing adorned the sheet music for "General Harrison's Log Cabin March."

lieved that Jackson had misused the veto and professed to put as much emphasis as had Washington on the principle of the separation of legislative and executive powers. This delighted the Whig leaders in Congress, who had had their fill of the "executive usurpation" of Jackson. Either Clay or Webster seemed destined to be the real ruler of the new administration, and soon the two were squabbling over their old general like sparrows over a crust.

At the height of their squabble, less than a month after his inauguration, Harrison died. John Tyler of Virginia, honest, conscientious, but doctrinaire, became president of the United States. The political climate of the country changed drastically. Events began to march in a new direction, one that led ultimately to Bull Run, to Gettysburg, and to Appomattox.

Milestones

1828	Tariff of Abominations		Force Bill
	John C. Calhoun, *Exposition and Protest*		Jackson vetoes the Bank Recharter Bill
1829	Andrew Jackson's "Kitchen Cabinet"	**1833**	Removal of Treasury funds from the Bank of the United States
1830	Daniel Webster's, "Second Reply to Hayne"		Compromise Tariff
	Jackson vetoes the Maysville Road Bill	**1836**	Specie Circular
1831–1838	Removal of southern Indians to Oklahoma	**1837–1838**	Panic of 1837
		1840	Independent Treasury Act
1832	South Carolina Ordinance of Nullification		"Log Cabin" Campaign

Supplementary Reading

On Jackson's presidency, see G. G. Van Deusen, **The Jacksonian Era*** (1959), and R. V. Remini, **Andrew Jackson and the Course of American Freedom** (1981). See also A. M. Schlesinger, Jr., **The Age of Jackson*** (1945), Edward Pessen, **Riches, Class and Power Before the Civil War** (1973) and **Jacksonian America** (1979).

On the development of parties, see R. P. McCormick, **The Second American Party System*** (1966), and Richard Hofstadter, **The Idea of a Party System** (1970). The struggle with the Bank is discussed in Bray Hammond, **Banks and Politics in America from the Revolution to the Civil War*** (1957), but see also Peter Temin, **The Jacksonian Economy*** (1969), which minimizes the effects of Jackson's policies on economic conditions. T. P. Govan, **Nicholas Biddle** (1959), explains Biddle's view of banking.

For Indian policy, consult R. N. Satz, **American Indian Policy in the Jacksonian Era** (1975), and and two books by Angie Debo, **And Still the Waters Run** (1973) and **The Road to Disappearance** (1991). The best treatment of the nullification controversy is W. W. Freehing, **The Road to Disunion** (1990), which stresses the relation between nullification and the slavery question.

The political and economic ideas of Whigs and Democrats are discussed in Lee Benson, **The Concept of Jacksonian Democracy*** (1961), and D. W. Howe, **The Political Culture of the American Whigs** (1980). For the Van Buren administration, see John Niven, **Martin Van Buren** (1983), and M. L. Wilson, **The Presidency of Martin Van Buren** (1984).

*Available in paperback.

Tocqueville and Beaumont in America
Tocqueville in Judgment
A Restless People
Off to Work
The Family Recast
The Second Great Awakening
The Era of Associations
Backwoods Utopias
The Age of Reform
"Demon Rum"
The Abolitionist Crusade
Women's Rights

CHAPTER 10

The Making of Middle-Class America

*O*n May 12, 1831, two French aristocrats, Alexis de Tocqueville and Gustave de Beaumont, arrived in New York City from Le Havre. They came, as Tocqueville explained, "to see what a great republic is like."

Tocqueville and Beaumont were perhaps the most insightful of dozens of Europeans who visited the United States in the early 19th century to study the "natives." Their visit, for example, overlapped with that of Frances Trollope, whose *Domestic Manners of Americans* (1834) advised English readers that Americans were just as uncouth as they had imagined. A decade later Charles Dickens made what by then had become for foreigners an almost obligatory pass through this crude outpost of civilization, before publishing his

Tocqueville and Beaumont in America

Unlike Trollope and Dickens, Tocqueville and Beaumont believed that Europe was passing from its aristocratic past into a democratic future. How better to prepare for the change, they believed, than by studying the United States, where democracy was already the "enduring and normal state" of the land. They traveled from New York to Boston, then back through New York in order to inspect the state prison at Auburn, then on to Ohio. They examined conditions on the frontier in Michigan Territory, then sailed down the Mississippi River to New Orleans, where they heard an opera good enough to make them imagine they were back in France. From New Orleans they went on to "semi-barbarous" Alabama before turning north to Washington. They sailed for France from New York on February 20, 1832. All told, they had met and interviewed some 250 individuals, ranking from President Jackson—Beaumont insisted on referring to Old Hickory as "Monsieur"—to a number of Chippewa Indians.

It had indeed been a "useful" trip for the two Frenchmen. Above all else, the visit provided the material for Tocqueville's classic *De la Démocratie en Amérique,* published in France in 1835 and a year later in an English translation. *Democracy in America* has been the starting point for virtually all subsequent writers who have tried to describe what Tocqueville called "the creative elements" of American institutions.

Tocqueville in Judgment

The gist of *Democracy in America* is contained in the book's first sentence: "No novelty in the United States struck me more vividly during my stay there than the equality of conditions." Tocqueville meant not that Americans lived in a state of total equality, but that the inequalities that did exist among white Americans were not enforced by institutions or supported by public opinion. Moreover, the inequalities paled when compared with those of Europe. "In America," he concluded, "men are nearer equality than in any other country in the world." The circumstances of one's birth meant little, one's education less, and one's intelligence scarcely anything. Economic differences, although real and certainly "paraded" by those who enjoyed "a pre-eminence of wealth," were transitory. "Such wealth," Tocqueville assured his readers, "is within reach of all."

These sweeping generalizations were simplifications. Few modern students of Jacksonian America would accept them without qualification. In the 1830s and 1840s, a wide and growing gap existed between the rich and poor in the eastern cities. The wealthiest 4 percent of the population of New York controlled about half the city's wealth in 1828, about two-thirds in 1845. A similar concentration of wealth was occurring in Philadelphia and Boston.

Moreover, there was substantial poverty in Jacksonian America. Particularly in the cities, bad times forced many unskilled laborers and their families into dire poverty. Tocqueville took little notice of such inequalities. He also had little interest in how industrialization and urbanization were affecting society. When he did take notice of working conditions, he remarked that wages were higher in America than in Europe and the cost of living was lower.

Despite his blind spots, Tocqueville realized that America was undergoing some fundamental social changes. These changes, he wrote, were being made by "an innumerable crowd who are . . . not exactly rich nor yet quite poor [and who] have enough property to want order and not enough to excite envy." In his notes he put it even more succinctly: "The whole society seems to have turned into one middle class."

A Restless People

"In America, men never stay still," Tocqueville noted; "Something is almost always provisional about their lives." Frances Trollope thought their "incessant bustling" of a piece with their eating too fast and spitting too often. It stemmed from their "universal pursuit of money," she claimed.

One reason Americans seemed continually on the move was that every year there were more of them. The first federal census in 1790 recorded that there were 3.9 million people in the country. In the early 1850s there were six times as many. The population was doubling every 22 years, just about what Franklin had predicted in 1751!

Yet by European standards, even the settled parts of the United States were sparsely populated in the 1830s and 1840s. But for people accustomed to the wide open spaces, the presence of more than a handful of neighbors was reason enough for moving on. Abraham Lincoln's father Thomas (1778–1851) was typical. He grew up in Kentucky, pioneered in Indiana, and died in Illinois.

The urge to move had an urban dimension as well. For every "young man" who followed the advice of the New York newspaperman Horace Greeley to "go west," several young men and women went instead to town. By the tens of thousands they exchanged the rigors of farming for the uncertain risks and rewards of city life. Boston had 40,000 residents in 1820, nearly 140,000 in 1850. Philadelphia grew even more rapidly, from just under 100,000 in 1820 to almost 400,000 in 1850. New York, which had forged ahead of Philadelphia around 1810, grew from 125,000 in 1820 to more than 500,000 in 1850.

In 1820 the Northeast contained 5 cities with populations above 25,000 and 13 with populations above 10,000. Thirty years later, 26 cities had more than 25,000 residents and 62 had more than 10,000. While the Old Northwest remained primarily agricultural, its towns grew as fast as its farms. Pittsburgh, St. Louis, Cincinnati, Louisville, and Lexington attracted settlers in such numbers that by 1850 all but Lexington had populations of over 35,000.

The trek to town that was transforming the Northeast did not occur in the South. There were four cities of respectable size in the region—Mobile, Savannah, Charleston, and Baltimore—and one large city, New Orleans, which had a population of 120,000 in 1850. Neither Virginia nor North Carolina had an urban center of even modest dimensions. Charleston, the oldest and most typically southern city, scarcely grew at all after 1830.

Off to Work

"It is as if all America were but one gigantic workshop," the Austrian Francis Grund remarked in 1838. However enlightening to European readers, the fact that practically all Americans worked for their living must have struck Americans as a blinding glimpse of the obvious. Ever since John Smith's assurances to the Jamestown settlers that if they did not work they would not eat, they had always done the one to assure themselves of the other. What was changing in the 1830s was that they worked outside their homes.

In 1820, despite the growth of cities, three out of every four Americans were still engaged in agriculture. An efficient farming family used the labor of all its members, with chores assigned according to age, strength, and experience. Parents, children, and sometimes grandparents lived in the same house, or in adjoining houses. Except on large southern plantations run by overseers, farming remained a family enterprise.

By 1850, however, fewer than two out of three workers were farmers, in Massachusetts one of three. Outside the South, the way people earned a

Rural Versus Urban Population, 1820–1860

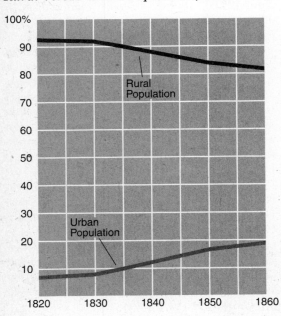

living had been transformed. Until the 1820s and 1830s, the household was also the focus of most nonagricultural pursuits. The typical urban worker was a self-employed artisan who had been apprenticed to a master while still a lad. After five to seven years of training, he became a journeyman and began to earn wages. Eventually, if he was reasonably talented, frugal, and industrious, he could open a shop of his own.

Since an apprentice lived and worked under the same roof as his master and his family, it was natural for the master to have familial as well as occupational authority over him. So intertwined did the life of an apprentice and his master become that the words *employee* and *employer* do not describe the relationship accurately. Apprentices were sometimes exploited and even physically abused, but just as often strong, personal bonds developed.

Forced reliance on domestically manufactured goods during the embargo and the War of 1812 and the improvements in transportation that were taking place steadily in the 1820s and 1830s, prompted many master craftsmen and artisans to expand production. They took on more workers, in some cases as apprentices, more often as relatively unskilled wage earners. Work was broken down into separate simple tasks that the unskilled help could learn easily. As a business grew bigger and the division of labor became more complex, the master-turned-businessman spent less time working with his employees and more marketing the product. Elaborate rules evolved regulating the hours of labor and the on-the-job behavior of workers. Drinking on the job, which in an earlier day had been considered normal and even desirable, was by 1850 almost universally forbidden.

Larger operations required more work space, and the need to locate near suppliers, customers, or a source of waterpower meant that the owner's home could no longer serve as a workplace. During the second quarter of the 19th century, Boston, New York, Philadelphia, and other cities sorted themselves into commercial and residential districts. By the 1830s the shoe manufacturers of Lynn, Massachusetts, had shifted from making finely finished shoes for individual customers to mass-producing the rough brogans worn by slaves and other farmers. Custom-fitted shoes required the attention of a skilled craftsman, but brogans were made by several unskilled laborers.

The Family Recast

The factory system and the growth of cities undermined the importance of home and family as the unit of economic production. This happened first in the cities of the Northeast, then in the West, and eventually wherever nonagricultural jobs occupied a substantial percentage of the work force. More and more people did their work in shops, in offices, or on factory floors. Whether a job was skilled or unskilled, it took the family breadwinner out of the house during working hours six days a week. The labor of the father and any children with jobs came home in the form of cash, thus at least initially in the custody of the individual earners. The social consequences of this change were enormous.

Because he was away so much, the husband had to surrender to his wife some of the power in the family that he had formerly possessed, if for no other reason than that she was always there. This explains why Tocqueville concluded that "a sort of equality reigns around the domestic hearth" in America. It also explains why American men began to place women on a pedestal, presuming them to be by nature selflessly devoted to the care of others.

The new power and prestige that wives and mothers enjoyed was not obtained without cost. Since they were exercising day-to-day control over household affairs, they were expected to tend only to those affairs. Anything that might take them away from the family hearth was frowned on. Where the typical wife had formerly been a partner in a family enterprise, she now left earning a living entirely to her husband. Time spent away from home or devoted to matters unrelated to the care of husband and family was, according to the new doctrine of "separate spheres," time misappropriated.

This trend widened the gap between the middle and lower classes. For a middle-class wife and mother to take a job or, still worse, to devote herself to any "frivolous" activity outside the home was considered a dereliction of duty.

Some women objected to the discrimination implicit in what the historian Barbara Welter has called "the cult of true womanhood." Others escaped its more suffocating aspects by forming close friendships with other women. But most women, including such forceful proponents of women's rights as the educator Catharine Beecher and Sarah Hale, the editor of *Godey's Ladies Book*, subscribed in their writing to the view that a woman's place was in the home. "The formation of the moral and intellectual character of the young is committed mainly to the female hand," Beecher wrote in *A Treatise on Domestic Economy for the Use of Young Ladies* (1841). "The mother forms the character of the future man."

Another reason for the switch in power and influence from husbands to wives was that women began to have fewer children. People married later, probably because prospective marriage partners were becoming more choosy. On average, women began having their children two or three years later than their mothers had, and they stopped two or three years sooner.

Having fewer children led parents to value children more highly, or so it would seem from the additional time and affection they lavished on them. Here again, the mother provided most of both. Child rearing fell within her "sphere" and occupied the time that earlier generations of mothers had devoted to such tasks as weaving, sewing, and farm chores.

As families became smaller, relations within them became more caring. Parents ceased to think of their children mostly as future workers. The earlier tendency even among loving parents to keep their children at arm's length, yet within reach of the strap, gave way to more intimate relationships. Gone was the Puritan notion that children possessed "a love of what's forbid," and with it the belief that parents were responsible for crushing all juvenile resistance to their authority. In its place arose the view described by Lydia Maria Child in *The Mother's Book* (1831) that children "come to us from heaven, with their little souls full of innocence and peace." Bronson Alcott, another proponent of gentle child-rearing practices, banished "the rod and all its appendages" from his household, and urged other parents to follow his example.

Family structure changed as a result of the industrial revolution. Not only did couples have fewer children, but husbands were also expected to earn the family's living and concern themselves with worldly business while their wives assumed all domestic duties.

The Second Great Awakening

Belief in the innate goodness of children was of course in direct conflict with the Calvinist doctrine of infant damnation, to which most American Protestant churches subscribed. The inclination to set aside other Calvinist tenets, such as predestination, became more pronounced as a new wave of revivalism took shape in the 1790s. This Second Great Awakening began as a counteroffensive to the deistic thinking that New England Congregationalists and southern Methodists alike identified with the French Revolution. Prominent New England ministers, who considered themselves traditionalists but also revivalists, men such as Yale's president, Timothy Dwight, and Dwight's student, the Reverend Lyman Beecher, placed less stress in their sermons on God's arbitrary power over mortals, and more on the salvation of sinners because of God's mercy and "disinterested benevolence."

Calvinism came under more direct assault from Charles Grandison Finney. In 1821 Finney abandoned a promising career as a lawyer and became an itinerant preacher. His most spectacular successes occurred during a series of revivals conducted in towns along the Erie Canal, a region Finney called "the burned-over district" because it

had been the site of so many revivals before his own.

Finney exhorted his listeners to take their salvation into their own hands. He insisted that people could control their own fate. He dismissed Calvinism as a "theological fiction." But the day of judgment was just around the corner; there was little time to waste. During and after Finney's efforts in Utica, New York, conversions increased sharply. In Rochester, church membership doubled in six months. Elsewhere in the country, churches were packed.

The success of the evangelists of the Second Great Awakening stemmed from the timeliness of their assault on Calvinist doctrines and even more from their methods. Finney, for example, consciously set out to be entertaining as well as edifying. The singing of hymns and the solicitation of personal testimonies provided his meetings with emotional release and human interest. Prominent among his innovations was the "anxious bench," where leading members of the community awaited the final prompting from within before coming forward to declare themselves saved.

But the impact of economic changes on family life had as important effects on the Second Awakening as the evangelists. The growth of industry and commerce that followed the completion of the Erie Canal in 1825 led hundreds of young men to leave family farms to seek their fortunes in towns along the canal. There, uprooted, buffeted between ambition, hope, and anxiety, they found it hard to resist the comfort promised by the revivalists.

But middle-class women were, as Mary P. Ryan writes in *Cradle of the Middle Class* (1981), the people "most receptive to the admonitions of the evangelical clergy." Aside from concern for their own salvation, they felt particularly responsible for the Christian education of their children, which fell within their separate sphere.

Paradoxically, this caused many of them to venture out of that sphere and in doing so they moved further out of the shadow of their husbands. They did most of the organizing and a good deal of the financing of the climactic years of the Second Awakening. The Female Missionary Society of Oneida County, New York, raised more than $1,000 a year (no small sum at that time) to support the revival in the burned over district. "These women," Professor Ryan explains, "devised a sphere for women that had not been anticipated."

The Era of Associations

A third pillar of the emerging American middle class was the voluntary association. Unlike the other two, it had neither colonial precedents nor contemporary European equivalents. The leaders of these associations tended to be ministers, lawyers, or merchants, but the rank and file consisted of tradesmen, foremen, clerks, and their wives. Some of these associations were formed around a local cause that some townspeople wished to advance, such as the provision of religious instruction for orphaned children. Others were affiliated with associations elsewhere for the purposes of combating some national evil, such as drunkenness. Some, such as the American Board of Commissioners of Foreign Missions, founded in Boston in 1810, quickly became large and complex enterprises. Others lasted only as long as it took to accomplish a specific good work, such as the construction of a school or a library.

In a sense, the associations were assuming functions previously performed in the family, such as caring for old people and providing moral guidance to the young, but without the paternalistic discipline of the old way. They constituted a "benevolent empire," eager to make society over into their members' idea of how God wanted it to be.

Backwoods Utopias

Americans frequently belonged to several associations at the same time and more than a few made reform their life's work. The most adventuresome tested their reform theories by establishing experimental communities. The "communitarian" point of view aimed at "commencing a wholesale social reorganization by first establishing and demonstrating its principles completely on a small scale." The first communitarians were religious reformers. In a sense the Pilgrims also fall into this category, along with a number of other groups in colonial times. But only in the 19th century did the idea flourish.

One of the earliest significant groups was founded by George Rapp, who brought some 600 Germans to western Pennsylvania in 1804. Rappites renounced marriage and sex and took every word in the Bible literally. They believed that people must have their affairs constantly in order so as to be ready to meet their Maker on short notice. Industrious, pious, and isolated from other Americans by their language and beliefs, the Rappites prospered but had little influence on their neighbors.

More influential were the Shaker communities founded by an Englishwoman, Ann Lee, who came to America in 1774. With a handful of followers she founded a community near Albany, New York. The group grew rapidly, and by the 1830s her followers had established about 20 successful communities.

Like the Rappites, the Shakers practiced celibacy; believing that the millennium was imminent, they saw no reason for perpetuating the human race. Each group lived in a large Family House, the sexes strictly segregated. Property was held in common. Much stress was placed on equality of labor and reward and on voluntary acceptance of the rules.

The Shaker religion, joyful and fervent, was marked by much group singing and dancing, which provided the members with emotional release from their tightly controlled regimen. An industrious, skillful people, they made a virtue of simplicity; their designs for buildings and, especially, furniture achieved a classic beauty seldom equaled among untutored artisans.

There were many other religious colonies, such as the Amana Community, which flourished in New York and Iowa in the 1840s and 1850s, and John Humphrey Noyes's Oneida Community, where the members practiced "complex" marriage—a form of promiscuity based on the principle that every man in the group was married to every woman. They prospered by developing a number of manufacturing skills.

The most important of the religious communitarians were the Mormons. A young farmer, Joseph Smith, founded the religion in western New York in the 1820s. Smith saw visions; he claimed to have discovered and translated an ancient text, the Book of Mormon, written in hieroglyphics on plates of gold, which described the adventures of a tribe of Israelites that had populated America from biblical times.

Persecution forced the Mormons to move from New York to Ohio to Missouri, before settling for a time in Nauvoo, Illinois. In 1830, Mormon leaders were tarred and feathered, as this print shows. Fourteen years later, founder Joseph Smith and his brother Hyrum were arrested by local authorities and murdered in their jail cell by a hostile mob.

With his small group of followers, Smith established a community in Ohio in 1831. The Mormons' dedication and economic efficiency attracted numbers of converts, but their unorthodox religious views and their exclusivism, product of their sense of being a chosen people, caused resentment among unbelievers. The Mormons were forced to move first to Missouri and then back to Illinois, where in 1839 they founded the town of Nauvoo.

Nauvoo flourished—by 1844 it was the largest city in the state—but once again the Mormons ran into trouble. They quarreled among themselves, especially after Smith secretly authorized polygamy (he called it "celestial marriage") and a number of other unusual rites for the top leaders of the church.* Smith announced that he was a candidate for president of the United States, and created a paramilitary organization, the Nauvoo Legion.

Rumors circulated that the Mormons intended to take over the entire Northwest for their "empire." Local "gentiles" rose against them. Smith was arrested, then murdered by a mob.

Under a new leader, Brigham Young, the Mormons sought a haven beyond the frontier. In 1847 they marched westward, pressing through the mountains until they reached the desolate wilderness on the shores of the Great Salt Lake. There, at last, they established their Zion and began to make a significant impact on American history. Irrigation made the desert flourish, precious water wisely being treated as a community asset. Hard, cooperative, intelligently directed effort spelled growth and prosperity; more than 11,000 people were living in the area when it became part of Utah Territory in 1850. In time the communal Mormon settlement broke down, but the Mormon church is still by far the most powerful single influence in Utah and is a thriving organization in many other parts of the United States and in Europe.

Despite many common characteristics, the religious communities varied enormously. Their sexual practices, for example, ranged from the "complex marriage" of the Oneidans through

* The justification of polygamy, paradoxically, was that marriage was a sacred, eternal state. If a man remarried after his wife's death, eventually he would have two wives in heaven. Therefore why not on earth?

Mormon polygamy and ordinary monogamy to the reluctant acceptance of sexual intercourse by the Amana Community and the celibacy of the Rappites and Shakers. The communities are more significant as reflections of the urgent reform spirit of the age than they are for their accomplishments.

The communities did influence reformers who wished to experiment with social organization. When Robert Owen, a British utopian socialist who believed in economic as well as political equality and who considered competition debasing, decided to create an ideal community in America, he purchased the Rappite settlement at New Harmony, Indiana. But Owen's advocacy of free love and "enlightened atheism" did not add to the stability of his group or to its popularity among outsiders. The colony was a costly failure.

The American followers of Charles Fourier, a French utopian socialist who proposed that society should be organized in cooperative units called phalanxes, fared better. Fourierism did not seek to tamper with sexual and religious mores. Its advocates included important journalists, such as Horace Greeley of the *New York Tribune* and Parke Godwin of the *New York Evening Post*.

In the 1840s several dozen Fourierist colonies were established in the northern and western states. Members worked at whatever tasks they wished and only as much as they wished. Wages were paid according to the "repulsiveness" of the tasks performed; the person who "chose" to clean out a cesspool would receive more than someone hoeing corn or mending a fence or engaging in some task requiring complex skills. As might be expected, none of the communities lasted very long.

The Age of Reform

The communitarians were the most colorful of the reformers. More effective, however, were the many individuals who took upon themselves responsibility for caring for the physically and mentally disabled and for the rehabilitation of criminals. The work of Thomas Gallaudet in educating deaf people reflects the spirit of the times. Gallaudet's school in Hartford, Connecticut, opened its doors in 1817; by 1851 similar schools for the deaf had been established in 14 states.

Dr. Samuel Gridley Howe did similar work with the blind, devising means for making books with raised letters and operating a school for the blind in Boston, the pioneering Perkins Institution, which opened in 1832. Howe's success in educating 12-year-old Laura Bridgman, who was deaf, mute, and blind, attracted wide attention. "Every creature in human shape should command our respect," Howe insisted. "The strong should help the weak, so that the whole should advance as a band of brethren."

One of the most striking aspects of the reform movement was the emphasis reformers placed on establishing special institutions for dealing with social problems. In the colonial period, orphans, indigent persons, the insane, and the feebleminded were usually cared for by members of their own families or boarded in a neighboring household. They remained part of the community. Criminals were commonly punished by whipping, being placed in stocks in the town square, or (for serious crimes) by execution. But once persuaded that people were primarily shaped by their surroundings, reformers demanded that deviant and dependent members of the community be placed in institutions where they could be trained or rehabilitated. The result, according to the historian David J. Rothman, was "the discovery of the asylum." Almshouses, orphanages, prisons, and lunatic asylums sprang up throughout the United States like mushrooms in a forest after a summer rain.

The rationale for this movement was scientific, the motivating spirit of the founders humane (though many of the institutions seem anything but humane to the modern eye). The highly regarded Philadelphia prison system was based on strict solitary confinement, which was supposed to lead culprits to reflect on their sins and then reform their ways. The prison was literally a penitentiary, a place to repent.

In fact, the system drove some inmates mad, and soon a rival Auburn system was introduced in New York, which allowed for some social contact among prisoners and for work in shops and stone quarries. Absolute silence was required at all times. The prisoners were herded about in lock step and punished by flogging for the slightest infraction of the rules. Regular "moral and religious instruction" was provided, which the authorities believed would lead inmates to reform their lives. Tocqueville and Beaumont, in their report on American prisons, concluded that the Philadelphia system produced "the deepest impression on the soul of the convict," whereas the Auburn system made the convict "more conformable to the habits of man in society."

The hospitals for mental patients were intended to cure inmates, not merely to confine them. The emphasis was on isolating them from the pressures of society; on control but not on punishment. The unfortunates were seen as *deranged*; the task was to *arrange* their lives in a rational manner. In practice, shortages of trained personnel, niggardly legislative appropriations, and the inherent difficulty of managing violent and irrational patients often produced deplorable conditions in the asylums.

This situation led Dorothea Dix, a woman of almost saintlike selflessness, to devote 30 years of her life to a campaign to improve the care of the insane. She traveled to every state in the Union and as far afield as Turkey and Japan, inspecting asylums and poorhouses. Insane persons in Massachusetts, she wrote, were being kept in cages and closets, *chained, naked, beaten with rods, and lashed into obedience!*" Her reports led to some improvement in conditions in Massachusetts and other states, but in the long run the bright hopes of the reformers were never realized. Institutions founded to uplift the deviant and dependent soon became places where "misfits" might safely be kept out of sight.

"Demon Rum"

Reformers must of necessity interfere with the affairs of others; thus there is often something of the busybody about them. How they are regarded usually turns on the observer's own attitude toward their objectives. Consider the temperance movement, the most widely supported and successful reform of the age of reform.

Americans in the 1820s consumed prodigious amounts of alcohol. Because neither political nor religious leaders considered drinking dangerous, there was no alcohol "problem." Most doctors recommended the regular consumption of alcohol as healthy. John Adams, certainly the soul of propriety, drank a tankard of hard cider every day for breakfast.

However, alcohol consumption increased markedly in the early years of the new republic, thanks primarily to the availability of cheap corn and rye whiskey distilled in the new states of Kentucky and Tennessee. Many women drank, if mostly at home, and reports of carousing among 14-year-old college freshmen show that youngsters did too. But the bulk of the heavy drinking occurred when men got together, at taverns or grogshops and at work.

Artisans and common laborers regarded their twice-daily "dram" of whiskey as part of their wages. In 1829 Secretary of War John Eaton estimated that three-quarters of the nation's laborers drank at least 4 ounces of hard liquor a day. Many prominent politicians, including Clay and Webster, were heavy consumers. Webster is said to have kept several thousand bottles of wine, whiskey, and other alcoholic beverages in his cellar.

The foundation of the American Temperance Union in 1826 signaled the start of a national crusade against drunkenness. Employing lectures, pamphlets, rallies, essay contests, and other techniques, the union set out to persuade people to "sign the pledge" not to drink liquor. Primitive sociological studies of the effects of drunkenness (reformers were able to show a high statistical correlation between alcohol consumption and crime) added to the effectiveness of the campaign.

In 1840 an organization of reformed drunkards, the Washingtonians, set out to reclaim alcoholics. One of the most effective Washingtonians was John B. Gough, rescued by the organization after seven years in the gutter. "Crawl from the slimy ooze, ye drowned drunkards," Gough would shout, "and with suffocation's blue and livid lips speak out against the drink!"

Revivalist ministers like Charles Grandison Finney argued that alcohol was one of the great barriers to conversion. Employers announced that their businesses henceforward to be "cold-water" enterprises. Soon the temperance movement claimed 1 million members.

The temperance people aroused bitter opposition, particularly after they moved beyond calls for restraint to demands for the prohibition of all alcoholic beverages. German and Irish immigrants, for the most part Catholics, and members of Protestant sects where wine was used in religious services, objected to being told by reformers that their drinking would have to stop. By the early 1840s, however, the reformers had secured legislation in many states that imposed strict licensing systems and heavy liquor taxes. In 1851 Maine passed the first effective law prohibiting the manufacture and sale of alcoholic beverages, and by 1855 a dozen other states had passed laws based on the Maine statute.

The Abolitionist Crusade

No reform movement of this era was more significant, more ambiguous, or more provocative of later historical investigation than the drive to abolish slavery. That slavery should have been a cause of indignation to reform-minded Americans was inevitable. Humanitarians were outraged by the master's whip and by the practice of disrupting families. Democrats protested the denial of political and civil rights to slaves. However, well into the 1820s, the abolitionist cause attracted few followers because there seemed to be no way of getting rid of slavery short of revolution. Most people believed that under the Constitution the institution was not subject to federal control.

Particularly in the wake of the Missouri Compromise, antislavery northerners neatly compartmentalized their thinking. Slavery was wrong; they would not tolerate it in their own communities. But since the Constitution obliged them to tolerate it in states where it existed, they felt no responsibility to fight it. People who advocated any kind of forced abolition in states where it was legal were judged irresponsible in the extreme. In 1820 presidential hopeful John Quincy Adams called slavery "the great and foul stain upon the North American Union." "If the Union must be dissolved," he added, "slavery is precisely the question upon which it ought to break." But Adams expressed these opinions in the privacy of his diary, not in a public speech. Most critics of slavery therefore confined themselves to urging "colonization" or persuading slave owners to treat their property humanely.

One of the few Americans in the 1820s to go further was Benjamin Lundy, editor of a Baltimore newspaper, *The Genius of Universal Emancipation.* Lundy was no fanatic; he urged the use of persuasion rather than interference by the federal government. But he refused to mince words, and consequently he was subject to frequent harassment.

Even more provocative and less accommodating to local sensibilities was Lundy's youthful assistant, William Lloyd Garrison of Massachusetts. Garrison pronounced himself for "immediate" abolition. When his extreme position made continued residence in Baltimore impossible, he returned to Boston, where in 1831 he established his own newspaper, *The Liberator.* "I am in earnest," he announced in the first issue. "I will not equivocate—I will not excuse—I will not retreat a single inch—and I will be heard."

Garrison's position, and that espoused by the New England Anti-Slavery Society, which he organized in 1831, was absolutely unyielding: Slaves must be freed immediately and treated as equals; compensated emancipation was unacceptable, colonization unthinkable. Because the United States government countenanced slavery, Garrison refused to engage in political activity to achieve his ends. Burning a copy of the Constitution—that "agreement with hell"—became a regular feature at Society-sponsored public lectures.

Few white Americans found Garrison's line of argument convincing, and many were outraged by his confrontational tactics. Whenever he spoke in public, he risked being mobbed. In 1835 an angry crowd dragged him through the streets of Boston. In 1837 Elijah Lovejoy, a Garrisonian newspaper editor in Alton, Illinois, first saw his press destroyed by fire and then was himself murdered by a mob. The historian Leonard L. Richard has documented more than 100 attacks on abolitionists in the North between 1833 and 1838.

In the wake of this violence some of Garrison's backers had second thoughts about his strategy of immediatism. The wealthy New York businessmen Arthur and Lewis Tappan, who had subsidized *The Liberator,* turned instead to Theodore Dwight Weld, a young revivalist minister. Weld and his followers spoke of "immediate" emancipation "gradually" achieved, and they were willing to engage in political activity to achieve that goal.

In 1840 the Tappans and Weld broke with Garrison over the issue of involvement in politics and the participation of female abolitionists as public lecturers. Garrison, ever the radical, supported the women; Weld thought they would needlessly antagonize would-be supporters. The Tappans then organized the Liberty Party, which nominated as its presidential candidate James G. Birney, a Kentucky slaveholder who had been converted to evangelical Christianity and abolitionism by Weld. Running on a platform of universal emancipation to be gradually brought about through legislation, Birney received only 7,000 votes.

Many blacks were abolitionists long before the white movement began to attract attention. In 1830 some 50 black antislavery societies existed, and thereafter these groups grew in size and importance, being generally associated with the Garrisonian wing. White abolitionists eagerly sought out black speakers, especially runaway slaves, whose heartrending accounts of their experiences aroused sympathies and who, merely by speaking clearly and with conviction, stood as living proof that blacks were neither animals nor fools.

Frederick Douglass, a former slave who had escaped from Maryland, was one of the most remarkable Americans of his generation. While a bondsman he had received a full portion of beatings and other indignities; but he had been allowed to learn to read and write and to master a trade, opportunities denied the vast majority of slaves. Settling in Boston, he became an agent of the Massachusetts Anti-Slavery Society and a featured speaker at its public meetings.

Douglass was a tall, majestically handsome man who radiated determination and indignation. Slavery, he told white audiences, "brands your republicanism as a sham, your humanity as a base pretense, your Christianity as a lie." In 1845 he published his *Narrative of the Life of Frederick Douglass,* one of the most gripping autobiographical accounts of a slave's life ever written.

Douglass insisted that freedom for blacks required not merely emancipation but full equality, social and economic as well as political. Not many white northerners accepted his reasoning, but few who heard him or read his works could afterward

Former slave Frederick Douglass was one of the most effective spokesmen of the Massachusetts Anti-Slavery Society in the 1840s.

maintain the illusion that all blacks were dull-witted or resigned to inferior status.

At first Douglass was, in his own words, "a faithful disciple" of Garrison, prepared to tear up the Constitution and destroy the Union to gain his ends. In the late 1840s, however, he changed his mind, deciding that the Constitution, created to "establish Justice . . . and secure the Blessings of Liberty," as its preamble states, "could not well have been designed at the same time to maintain and perpetuate a system of rapine and murder like slavery." Thereafter he fought slavery and race prejudice from within the system, something Garrison was never willing to do.

Garrison's importance cannot be measured by the number of his followers, which was never large. Unlike more moderately inclined enemies of slavery, he recognized that abolitionism was a revolutionary movement. He also understood that achieving racial equality, not merely "freeing" the slaves, was the only way to reach the abolitionists' professed objective: full justice for blacks. And he saw clearly that few whites, even among abolitionists, believed that blacks were their equals.

At the same time, Garrison seemed utterly indifferent to what effect the "immediate" freeing of the slaves would have on the South. He said he would rather be governed by "the inmates of our penitentiaries" than by southern congressmen, whom he characterized as "desperadoes." The life of the slave-owner, he wrote, is "one of unbridled lust, of filthy amalgamation, of swaggering braggadocio, of haughty domination, of cowardly ruffianism, of boundless dissipation, of matchless insolence, of infinite self-conceit, of unequaled oppression, of more than savage cruelty."

Both Garrison's insights into the limits of northern racial egalitarianism and his blind contempt for southern whites led him to the conclusion that American society was rotten to the core. He was hated in the North as much for his explicit denial of the idea that a constitution that supported slavery merited respect as for his implicit denial of the idea that a professed Christian who tolerated slavery for even an instant could hope for salvation. He was, in short, a perfectionist, a trafficker in moral absolutes who wanted his Kingdom of Heaven in the here and now. By contrast, most American reformers were willing to settle for perfection on the installment plan.

Women's Rights

The question of slavery was related to the crusade for women's rights. The relationship was personal and ideological, direct and indirect, simple and profound. Superficially, the connection can be explained in this way: Women were as likely as men to find slavery offensive and to protest against it. When they did so, they ran into even more adamant resistance, the prejudices of those who objected to abolitionists being reinforced by their feelings that women should not speak in public or participate in political affairs. Thus female abolitionists, driven by the urgencies of conscience, were almost forced to become advocates of women's rights. "We have good cause to be grateful to the slave," the feminist Abby Kelley wrote. "In striving to strike his irons off, we found most surely, that we were manacled ourselves."

At a more profound level, the reference that abolitionists made to the Declaration of Independence to justify their attack on slavery radicalized women with regard to their own place in society. Were only all *men* created equal? For many women the question was a consciousness-raising experience; they began to believe that, like blacks, they were imprisoned from birth in a caste system, legally subordinated and assigned menial social and economic roles that prevented them from developing their full potentialities. Such women considered themselves in a sense worse off than blacks, who had at least the psychological advantage of confronting an openly hostile and repressive society rather than one concealed behind the cloying rhetoric of romantic love.

Nearly all the leading advocates of equal rights for women began their public careers in the abolitionist movement. Among the first were Sarah and Angelina Grimké, South Carolinians who abandoned their native state and the domestic sphere to devote themselves to speaking out against slavery. (In 1841 Angelina married Theodore Dwight Weld.) Male objections to the Grimkés' activities soon made them advocates of women's rights. Similarly, the refusal of delegates to the World Anti-Slavery Convention held in London in 1840 to let women participate in their debates precipitated the decision of two American abolitionists, Lucretia Mott and Elizabeth Cady Stanton, to turn their attention to the women's rights movement.

Slavery aside, there were other aspects of feminist consciousness-raising. Some women rejected the idea that they should confine themselves to a "sphere" consisting of child rearing and housekeeping. As the historian Nancy Cott has shown, the very effort to enforce this kind of specialization made women aware of their second-class citizenship and thus more likely to be dissatisfied. They lacked not merely the right to vote, of which they did not make a major issue, but if married, the right to own property or to make a will. Lydia Maria Child, a popular novelist, claimed that this last restriction excited her "towering indignation." "I was indignant for womankind made chattels personal from the beginning of time."

When women sought to involve themselves in reform, they became aware of perhaps the most serious handicap that society imposed on them—the conflict between their roles as wives and mothers and their urge to participate in the affairs of the larger world. Elizabeth Cady Stanton has left a striking description of this dilemma. When, stimulated by her interest in abolition and women's rights, she sought to become active in the movements, her family responsibilities made it almost impossible even to read about them.

"I now fully understood the practical difficulties most women had to contend with," she recalled in her autobiography, *Eighty Years and More* (1898). "The general discontent I felt with woman's portion as wife, mother, housekeeper, physician, and spiritual guide, the chaotic condition into which everything fell without her constant supervision, and the wearied, anxious look of the majority of women, impressed me with the strong feeling that some active measures should be taken." Together with Lucretia Mott and a few others of like mind, she organized a meeting, the Seneca Falls Convention (July 1848), and drafted a Declaration of Sentiments patterned on the Declaration of Independence. "We hold these truths to be self-evident: that all men and women are created equal," it stated, and it went on to list the "injuries and usurpations" of men, just as Jefferson had outlined those of George III.

From this seed the movement grew. During the 1850s a series of national conventions was held, and more and more reformers, including William Lloyd Garrison, joined the cause. Of the recruits, Susan B. Anthony was the most influential, for she was the first to see the need for thorough organization if effective pressure was to be brought to bear on male-dominated society. The feminists achieved very few practical results during the age of reform. Their leaders, however, were persevering types, most of them extraordinarily long-lived. Their major efforts lay in the future.

Despite the aggressiveness of many reformers and the extremity of some of their proposals, little social conflict blighted these years. Most citizens readily accepted the need for improving society and showed a healthy tolerance for even the most harebrained schemes. When Sylvester Graham, inventor of the graham cracker, traveled up and down the land praising the virtues of hard mattresses, cold showers, and homemade bread, he was mobbed by professional bakers, but otherwise he was free to speak his mind.

Americans argued about everything from prison reform to vegetarianism, but they seldom came to blows. Even the abolitionist movement might not have caused serious social strife if the territorial expansion of the late 1840s had not dragged the slavery issue back into politics. When that happened, politics again assumed center stage, public discourse grew embittered, and the first great age of reform came to an end.

Milestones

1774	Ann Lee founds first Shaker community	**1837**	Murder of the abolitionist Elijah Lovejoy
1817	Founding of Thomas Gallaudet's school for the deaf	**1843**	Dorothea Dix, *Memorial to the Legislature of Massachusetts*
1826	Founding of American Temperance Union	**1844**	Lynching of Joseph Smith
1830	Joseph Smith, *The Book of Mormon*	**1845**	Frederick Douglass, *Narrative of the Life of Frederick Douglass*
1830s	Second Great Awakening	**1847**	Mormon migration to the Great Salt Lake
1830–1850	Utopian communities flourish	**1848**	Seneca Falls Convention Declaration of Principles
1831–1832	Alexis de Tocqueville and Gustave de Beaumont tour America	**1851**	Maine bans alcoholic beverages
1831	William Lloyd Garrison founds *The Liberator*		
1832	Founding of Perkins Institution for the Blind		

Supplementary Reading

On Tocqueville and his view of American society, see Alexis de Tocqueville, **Democracy in America**,* J. P. Mayer, ed. (1966 edition). Edward Pessen, **Riches, Class, and Power Before the Civil War*** (1973), and Rowland Berthoff, **An Unsettled People*** (1971), offer views different from Tocqueville's.

On changes in the nature of work, consult A. F. C. Wallace, **Rockdale*** (1978), Alan Dawley, **Class and Community** (1976), Thomas Dublin, **Women at Work** (1979), and Sean Wilencz, **Chants Democratic** (1984).

On the changing place of the family and the changes within it, see Mary P. Ryan, **Cradle of the Middle Class** (1981), Nancy Cott, **The Bonds of Womanhood*** (1977), and Philip Greven, **The Protestant Temperament: Patterns of Child-Rearing, Religious Experience, and the Self in Early America** (1980). On demographic developments, see Walter Nugent, **Structures in American Social History** (1981).

The Second Great Awakening is described in William McLoughlin, **Modern Revivalism** (1959) and **Revivals, Awakenings, and Reform** (1978), P. Ryan, **Cradle of the Middle Class**, and Paul E. Johnson, **A Shopkeeper's Millennium** (1978).

On utopianism generally, see R. G. Walters, **American Reformers** (1978), and D.B. Davis, ed., **Ante-Bellum Reform** (1967). On the social-control implications of reform, see Clifford S. Griffin, **Their Brothers' Keepers*** (1960), and David J. Rothman, **Age of the Asylum: Social Order and Disorder in the New Republic*** (1971). Accounts of the temperance movement include Ian Tyrrell, **Sobering Up: From Temperance to Prohibition in Ante-Bellum America** (1979), and W. J. Rorabaugh, **The Alcoholic Republic*** (1979). For the Mormons, consult N. G. Bringhurst, **Brigham Young and the Expanding American Frontier** (1985).

For sharply contrasting views of the abolitionist movement, see Stanley Elkins, **Slavery*** (1975), and Aileen Kraditor, **Means and Ends in American Abolitionism*** (1967) and Lewis Perry and Michael Fellman, eds., **Anti-Slavery Reconsidered*** (1979). On anti-abolitionists, see Leonard L. Richards, **"Gentlemen of Property and Standing"*** (1970).

Interpretive accounts of the history of women and women's rights are Carl Degler, **At Odds: Women and Family in America from the Revolution to the Present*** (1980), and Nancy Woloch, **Women and the American Experience*** (1984). Elizabeth Griffith, **In Her Own Rights: The Life of Elizabeth Cady Stanton** (1984), and Kathryn K. Sklar, **Catharine Beecher** (1973), are solid biographies of important women in the Jacksonian era.

*Available in paperback.

CHAPTER 11

A Democratic Culture

In Search of Native Grounds

The Romantic View of Life

Emerson and Thoreau

Edgar Allan Poe

Nathaniel Hawthorne

Herman Melville

Walt Whitman

The Wider Literary Renaissance

Domestic Tastes

Education for Democracy

Engines of Culture

The State of the Colleges

Civic Cultures

Scientific Stirrings

American Humor

*A*s the United States grew larger, richer, and more centralized, it began to evolve a more distinctive culture. Still the child of Europe, by mid-century it was more clearly the offspring rather than an imitation of the parent society. Jefferson had drawn most of his ideas from classical authors and 17th-century English thinkers. He gave to these doctrines an American cast, as when he stressed the separation of church and state or the pursuit of happiness instead of property in describing the "unalienable rights" of men. But Ralph Waldo Emerson, whose views were roughly similar to Jefferson's and served later generations of liberals in much the way that Jefferson's did,

was an American philosopher despite the fact that he was influenced by European thinkers.

In Search of Native Grounds

Early-19th-century literary groups such as Boston's Anthology Club and the Friendly Club in New York consciously set out to "foster American genius" and to encourage the production of a distinctively American literature. According to the historian Russel B. Nye, in the period between the Revolution and 1830 "every author of note made at least one effort to use American history in a major literary work." Yet in nearly every case "nothing of consequence appeared." Of the novelists before 1830, only James Fenimore Cooper made successful use of the national heritage. Beginning with *The Spy* (1821), *The Pioneers* (1823), and *The Last of the Mohicans* (1826), he wrote a long series of tales of Indians and settlers that presented a vivid, if romanticized, picture of frontier life. (Cooper's Indians, Mark Twain quipped, belonged to "an extinct tribe that never existed.")

Most novelists of the period slavishly imitated British writers. Most popular were historical romances done in the manner of the Waverley novels of Sir Walter Scott. None approached the level of the best British writers, and as a result American novelists were badly outdistanced in their own country by the British, both in prestige and popularity. Since foreign copyrights were not recognized in the United States, British books were shamelessly pirated and sold cheaply. Half a million volumes of Scott were sold in America before 1823.

New York City was the literary capital of the country. Its leading light was Washington Irving, whose comical *Diedrich Knickerbocker's History of New York* (1809) made its young author famous on both sides of the Atlantic. Outside New York there was much less literary activity. New England was only on the verge of its great literary flowering.

American painting in this period reached a level comparable to that of contemporary European work. Benjamin West, the first and in his day the most highly regarded, went to Europe before the Revolution and never returned; he can scarcely be considered an American. John Singleton Copley, whose stern, straightforward portraits display a more distinctly American character than the work of any of his contemporaries, was a Bostonian. No one so well captured the vigor and integrity of the Revolutionary generation. Charles Willson Peale, after studying under West in London, settled in Philadelphia, where he helped found the Pennsylvania Academy of the Fine Arts. Not the least of his achievements was the production of a large brood of artistic children to whom he gave such names as Rembrandt, Titian, and Rubens. The most talented of Peale's children was (appropriately) Rembrandt, whose portrait of Jefferson, executed in 1800, is one of the finest likenesses of the Sage of Monticello.

Another outstanding artist of this generation was Gilbert Stuart, who is best known for his many studies of George Washington. He was probably the most technically accomplished of the early American portrait painters. He was fond of painting his subjects with ruddy complexions (produced by means of a judicious mixture of vermilion, purple, and white pigment), which made many of his elderly sitters appear positively cherubic.

In general, the painting of the period was less obviously imitative of European models than the national literature. Wealthy merchants, manufacturers, and planters wished their likenesses preserved, and the demand for portraits of the nation's Revolutionary heroes seemed insatiable. Since paintings could not be reproduced as books could be, American artists did a flourishing business. And they remained unmistakably in the European tradition.

Exceptions to this generalization can be found in the work of a number of self-trained artists like Jonathan Fisher, Charles Octavius Cole, and J. William Jennys. These primitive painters supplied rural and middle-class patrons in the same way that Copley and Stuart catered to the tastes of the rich and prominent. Cole specialized in New England sea captains, whom he often painted holding brassbound spyglasses. Some of these primitive canvases have great charm and distinction.

The Romantic View of Life

In the Western world the romantic movement was a revolt against the bloodless logic of the Age of Reason. "Romantics" believed that change and growth were the essence of life. They valued feeling and intuition over pure thought and they stressed the differences between individuals and societies. Ardent love of country characterized the movement; individualism, optimism, ingenuousness, emotion were its bywords.

Romanticism perfectly fitted the mood of 19th-century America. Interest in raw nature and in primitive peoples, worship of the individual, praise of folk culture, the subordination of intellect to feeling—were these primarily romantic ideas or American ideas? Jacksonian democracy with its self-confidence, careless prodigality, contempt for learning, glorification of the ordinary—was it a product of the American experience or a reflection of a wider world view?

The romantic way of thinking found its fullest American expression in the transcendentalist movement. Transcendentalism, a New England creation, is difficult to describe because it emphasized the indefinable and the unknowable. It was a mystical, intuitive way of looking at life that subordinated facts to feelings. Human beings were truly divine because they were part of nature, itself the essence of divinity. Their intellectual capacities did not define their capabilities, for they could "transcend" reason by having faith in themselves and in the fundamental benevolence of the universe. Transcendentalists were complete individualists, seeing the social whole as no more than the sum of its parts. Organized religion, indeed all institutions, were unimportant; what mattered was the single person and people's inborn desire to stretch *beyond* their known capabilities. Failure, according to that philosophy, resulted only from lack of effort.

Emerson and Thoreau

The leading transcendentalist thinker was Ralph Waldo Emerson. Emerson's philosophy was at once buoyantly optimistic and rigorously intellectual, self-confident and conscientious. He favored change and believed in progress. It was America's destiny, he said, to fulfill "the postponed expectations of the world." Temperamentally, however, he was too serene to fight for the causes other reformers espoused, and he was too idealistic to accept the compromises that most reformers make to achieve their ends. Because he put so much emphasis on self-reliance, Emerson disliked powerful governments. "The less government we have the better," he said. In a sense he was the prototype of some modern alienated intellectuals, so repelled by the world as it was that he would not actively try to change it.

Closely identified with Emerson was his Concord neighbor Henry David Thoreau, a strange man, gentle, a dreamer, content to absorb the beauties of nature almost intuitively, yet stubborn and individualistic to the point of selfishness. The hectic scramble for wealth that he saw all about him he found disgusting—and alarming, for he believed it was destroying both the natural and the human resources of the country.

Like Emerson, Thoreau objected to many of society's restrictions on the individual. "That government is best which governs not at all," he said. He was perfectly prepared to see himself as a majority of one. "When were the good and the brave ever in a majority?" he asked. "If a man does not keep pace with his companions," he wrote on another occasion, "perhaps it is because he hears a different drummer."

In 1845 Thoreau decided to put to the test his theory that a person need not depend on society for a satisfying existence. He built a cabin at Walden Pond on some property owned by Emerson and lived there alone for two years. He did not try to be entirely self-sufficient: He was not above returning to his family or to Emerson's for a square meal on occasion, and he generally purchased the building materials and other manufactured articles that he needed. In his experiment he set out to prove that if *necessary* an individual could get along without the products of civilization. He used manufactured plaster in building his Walden cabin, but he also gathered a bushel of clamshells and made a small quantity of lime himself, to prove that it could be done.

At Walden, Thoreau spent much time observing the quiet world around the pond, thinking, and writing in his journal. The best fruit of this period was that extraordinary book, *Walden* (1854). Superficially *Walden* is the story of Thoreau's experiment, but it is also an acid indictment of the social behavior of the average American, an attack on unthinking conformity, the subordinating of one's personal judgment to that of the herd.

The most graphic illustration of Thoreau's confidence in his own values occurred while he was living at Walden. At that time the Mexican War was raging. Thoreau considered the war immoral because it advanced the cause of slavery. To protest he refused to pay his Massachusetts poll tax. For this he was arrested and lodged in jail, although only for one night because an aunt promptly paid the tax for him. His essay "Civil Disobedience," explaining his view of the proper relation between the individual and the state, resulted from this experience. Like Emerson, however, Thoreau refused to participate in practical reform movements.

Edgar Allan Poe

The work of all the imaginative writers of the period reveals romantic influences. Edgar Allan Poe, for example, was almost a caricature of the romantic image of the tortured genius. Few persons as neurotic as he have been able to produce first-rate work. In college he ran up debts of $2,500 in less than a year and had to withdraw. He won an appointment to West Point but was discharged after a few months for disobedience and "gross neglect of duty." He was a lifelong alcoholic and an occasional taker of drugs. As his most recent biographer, Kenneth Silverman, points out, he was obsessed with thoughts of death. Yet he was an excellent magazine editor, a penetrating critic, a poet of unique if somewhat narrow talents, and a fine short story writer. Although he died at 40, he turned out a large volume of serious, highly original work.

Poe responded strongly to the lure of romanticism. His works abound with examples of wild imagination and fascination with mystery, fright, and the occult. If he did not invent the detective story, he perfected it; his tales "The Murders in the Rue Morgue" and "The Purloined Letter" stressed the thought processes of a clever detective in solving a mystery by reasoning from evidence. Poe was also one of the earliest writers to deal with what are today called science fiction themes, and "The Pit and the Pendulum" and "The Cask of Amontillado" show that he was a master of the horror tale. His famous poem "The Raven" won instantaneous popularity when it was published in 1845. Had he been a little more stable, he might have made a good living with his pen—but in that case he might not have written as he did.

Edgar Allan Poe, widely appreciated in his lifetime, inspired generations of later writers with his detective stories and horror tales.

Nathaniel Hawthorne

Another product of the prevailing romanticism was Nathaniel Hawthorne of Salem, Massachusetts, a lonely, introspective person, bookish and imaginative. Wandering about New England by himself in summertime, he soaked up local lore, which he drew on in writing short stories. Hawthorne disliked the egoism of the transcendental point of view and rejected its bland optimism outright. He called Emerson a "rejector of all that is." Yet in his fiction he scorned "minute fidelity" to the real world, seeking "a severer truth . . . the truth of the human heart."

Hawthorne's early stories made excellent use of New England history for background but were concerned chiefly with the struggles of individuals with sin, guilt, and pride. His greatest works were two novels written after the Whigs turned him out of his government job in 1849. *The Scarlet Letter* (1850), a grim yet sympathetic analysis of adultery, condemned not the woman, Hester Prynne, but the people who presumed to judge her. *The House of the Seven Gables* (1851) was a gripping account of the decay of an old New England family.

Despite Hawthorne's acute perception of the tragic element in life, there was a certain gruffness in him too. He had no patience with the second-rate. And despite his success in creating word pictures of a somber, mysterious world, he considered America too prosaic a country to inspire good literature. "There is no shadow, no antiquity, no mystery, no picturesque and gloomy wrong, nor anything but a commonplace prosperity," he complained.

Herman Melville

While writing *The House of the Seven Gables,* Hawthorne's publisher introduced him to another writer who was in the midst of a novel. The writer was Herman Melville, the book *Moby Dick.* The two became good friends at once. Melville had left school at 15, worked briefly as a bank clerk, and in 1837 went to sea. For 18 months, during 1841 and 1842, he was crewman on the whaler *Acushnet.* Then he jumped ship in the South Seas. For a time he lived among a tribe of cannibals in the Marquesas; later he made his way to Tahiti, where he idled away nearly a year. After his return to the United States in 1844, he wrote *Typee* (1846), an account of his life in the Marquesas. The book was a great success. "The man who had lived among the cannibals" became suddenly a well-known figure. Success inspired him to write a sequel, *Omoo* (1847); other books followed quickly.

As he wrote, Melville became conscious of deeper powers. Like Hawthorne, he could not accept the prevailing optimism of his generation. He considered Emerson's vague talk about striving and the inherent goodness of mankind complacent nonsense. Yet Melville was no cynic; in his writing he expressed deep sympathy for the Indians and for immigrants crowded like animals into the holds of transatlantic vessels. His essay "The Tartarus of Maids," a moving if somewhat overdrawn description of young women working in a paper factory, protested the subordination of human beings to machines.

Hawthorne encouraged Melville to press ahead with *Moby Dick* (1851). Against the background of a whaling voyage (no better account of whaling has ever been written), he dealt subtly and symbolically with the problems of good and evil, of courage and cowardice, of faith, stubbornness, and pride. In Captain Ahab, driven relentlessly to hunt down the huge white whale, Moby Dick, which had destroyed his leg, Melville created one of the great figures of literature; in the book as a whole, he produced one of the finest novels written by an American, comparable to the best in any language.

Walt Whitman

Walt Whitman, whose *Leaves of Grass* (1855) was the last of the great literary works of this brief outpouring of genius, was by far the most distinctly American writer of his age. Although genuinely a "common man," thoroughly at home among tradesmen and laborers, he was surely not an ordinary man. During the early 1850s, while employed as a carpenter and composing the poems that made up *Leaves of Grass,* he regularly carried a book of Emerson's writings in his lunch box. "I was simmering, simmering, simmering," he later recalled. "Emerson brought me to a boil." The transcendental idea that inspiration and aspiration are at the heart of all achievement captivated him. A poet could best express himself, he believed, by relying uncritically on his natural inclinations without regard for rigid metrical forms.

Leaves of Grass consisted of a preface, in which Whitman made the extraordinary statement that Americans had "probably the fullest poetical nature" of any people in history, and 12 strange poems in free verse: rambling, uneven, appearing to most readers shocking both in the commonplace nature of the subject matter and the coarseness of the language. Emerson, Thoreau, and a few others saw a fresh talent in these poems, but most readers and reviewers found them offensive. Indeed, the work was so undisciplined and so much of it had no obvious meaning that it was easy to miss its many passages of great beauty and originality.

Part of Whitman's difficulty arose because there was much of the charlatan in his makeup. In reality a sensitive, effeminate person, he tried to pose as a great, rough character. He displayed a love of show and bombast, but his egoism—he titled one of his finest poems "Song of Myself"—

Criticized as undisciplined and pretentious, Walt Whitman expressed a fresh viewpoint on commonplace subjects.

was tempered by his belief that he was typical of all humanity.

> I celebrate myself, and sing myself,
> And what I assume you shall assume,
> For every atom belonging to me as good
>   belongs to you.

He had a remarkable ear for rendering common speech poetically, for employing slang, for catching the breezy informality of Americans and their faith in themselves.

> Earth! you seem to look for something at my
>   hands,
> Say, old top-knot, what do you want?

The Wider Literary Renaissance

Emerson, Thoreau, Poe, Hawthorne, Melville, and Whitman were the great figures of American literature before the Civil War. Others, if they lacked genius, were leading literary lights in their own day and are still worth reading. One was Henry Wadsworth Longfellow. In 1835, while still in his twenties, Longfellow became professor of modern languages at Harvard, but his fame came from his poems: "The Village Blacksmith," "Paul Revere's Ride," "The Courtship of Miles Standish," a sentimental tale of Pilgrim days; and "The Song of Hiawatha," the romantic retelling of an Indian legend.

Longfellow was the most talented of a group of New England writers who collectively gave that region great intellectual vitality. John Greenleaf Whittier, a poet nearly as popular as Longfellow, believed ardently in the abolition of slavery. A few of his poems can still be read with pleasure, among them "The Barefoot Boy," dealing with his rural childhood. Somewhat more weighty was the achievement of James Russell Lowell, the first editor of the *Atlantic Monthly,* founded in Boston in 1857. Lowell's humorous stories written in the New England dialect made an original and influential contribution to the national literature. Dr. Oliver Wendell Holmes, professor of medicine at Harvard, was widely known as a poet and essayist. A few of his poems, such as "The Chambered Nautilus" and "Old Ironsides," are interesting examples of American romantic verse.

The important historians of the period were all New Englanders. George Bancroft, one of the first Americans to study in Germany, published a ten-volume *History of the United States,* based on thorough research. William Hickling Prescott, though nearly blind, wrote extensively on the history of Spain and Spain's American empire. John Lothrop Motley, another German-trained historian, published his *Rise of the Dutch Republic* in 1856, and Francis Parkman began his great account of the struggle between France and Great Britain for the control of North America with *Conspiracy of Pontiac* in 1851.

The public read these histories avidly. They suited the taste of the times, they were written with a mass audience in mind, and they were thoroughly in the romantic tradition. As David Levin said in his important study *History as Romantic Art,* "they all shared an 'enthusiastic' attitude toward the Past, an affection for grand heroes, an affection for Nature and the 'natural.'"

Southern literature was even more markedly romantic. John Pendleton Kennedy wrote several novels with regional historical themes. Kennedy was also a Whig politician of some importance who served several terms in Congress. The more versatile and influential William Gilmore Simms of South Carolina wrote nearly two dozen novels, several volumes of poetry, and a number of biographies. Simms's writing seems too melodramatic for modern tastes. His portraits of the planter class are too bloodless and reverential to be convincing and his female characters are nearly all pallid and fragile. But when he wrote of frontier life and its people, his work possessed considerable power.

Domestic Tastes

Architecture flourished in the northern cities chiefly as a result of the work of Charles Bulfinch and some of his disciples. Bulfinch was influenced by British architects, but he developed a manner all his own. His "Federal" style, gave parts of Boston a dignity and charm equal to the finest sections of London. The State House, numerous other public buildings, and, best of all, many of Bulfinch's private houses—austere yet elegant, solid yet airy and graceful—gave the town a distinction it had lacked before the Revolution.

In the 1830s and 1840s, new techniques made it possible to weave colored patterns into cloth by machine and to produce rugs and hangings that looked like tapestries. Combined with the use of machine methods in the furniture business, these inventions had a powerful impact on public taste. As Russell Lynes writes in his entertaining study *The Tastemakers,* "styles ran riot. . . . The new chairs and sofas, bedecked with fruit, flowers, and beasties and standing on twisted spindles, crowded into living rooms and parlors."

Wood-turning machinery added to the popularity of the elaborately decorated "Gothic" style of architecture. The irregularity and uniqueness of Gothic buildings suited the prevailing romanticism, their aspiring towers, steeples, and arches and their flexibility (a new wing or extension could always be added without spoiling the effect) made them especially attractive to a people enamored of progress. The huge pile of pink masonry of the Smithsonian Institution in Washington, with its nine distinct types of towers, represents American Gothic at its most giddy and lugubrious

The Smithsonian Institution Building, made of red sandstone, is popularly known as "The Castle" because of its eight crenelated towers. Its architect, James Renwick, Jr., also designed New York's Grace Church and St. Patrick's cathedral in the popular Gothic Revival style.

stage. The building, which has confounded generations of architects, has aptly been called "the nation's attic."

Increasingly, Americans of the period were purchasing native art. George Catlin, who painted hundreds of pictures of Indians and their surroundings, displayed his work before admiring crowds in many cities. Genre painters (artists whose canvases told stories, usually drawn from everyday life) were wildly popular. The best were William Sidney Mount of New York and George Caleb Bingham of Missouri.

The more academic artists of the period were popular as well. The "luminists" and members of the romantic Hudson River school specialized in grandiose pictures of wild landscapes. In the 1840s Thomas Doughty regularly collected $500 each for his paintings. The works of Asher B. Durand, John Kensett, and Thomas Cole were in demand. The collector Luman Reed commissioned five large Cole canvases for an allegorical series, *The Course of Empire,* and crowds flocked to see another of Cole's series, *The Voyage of Life,* when it was exhibited in New York.

In 1839 the American Art-Union was formed in New York to encourage native art. The Art-Union hit on the ingenious device of selling what were in effect lottery tickets and using the proceeds to purchase paintings, which became the prizes in the lottery. Annual "memberships" sold for $5; 814 people subscribed in 1839, nearly 19,000 ten years later. The organization had to disband after a New York court outlawed the lottery in 1851, but in 1854 a new Cosmopolitan Art-Union was established in Ohio. In the years before the Civil War it boomed, reaching a peak of 38,000 members and paying as much as $6,000 for an individual work—the sculptor Hiram Powers's boneless female nude, *The Greek Slave.*

Beginning in the late 1850s, the prints of the firm of Currier and Ives brought a crude but charming kind of art to a still wider audience. Currier and Ives lithographs portrayed horse racing, trains, rural landscapes, and "every tender domestic moment, every sign of national progress, every regional oddity, every private or public disaster from a cut finger to a forest fire." They were issued in very large editions and sold for as little as 15 cents.

Education for Democracy

Except on the edge of the frontier and in the South, most youngsters between the ages of 5 and 10 attended a school for at least a couple of months of the year. These schools, however, were privately run and charged fees. Attendance was not required and fell off sharply once children learned to read and do their sums. The teachers were usually young men waiting for something better to turn up.

All this changed with the rise of the common school movement, which resulted from the belief that a democratic government must provide the means, as Jefferson put it, to "diffuse knowledge throughout the mass of the people." This meant free tax-supported schools for all and thus an educational system administered on a statewide basis.

The typical one-room schoolhouse could hold up to 80 students. The schoolyard was a clearing nearby, as artist Henry Inman shows in *Dismissal of School on an October Afternoon.* Inspired by Horace Mann, the great educational awakening of the mid-1800s led to such improvements as the first normal schools to train teachers.

It also made teaching a profession that required formal training.

The most effective leaders of the common school movement were Henry Barnard and Horace Mann. They shared an unquenchable faith in the improvability of the human race through education. Barnard served in educational posts in Connecticut, Rhode Island, and New York in the 1840s and 1850s. Mann drafted the 1837 Massachusetts law creating a state school board, and then became its first secretary.

Over the next decade Mann's annual reports carried the case for common schools to every corner of the land. Seldom given to understatement, Mann called common schools "the greatest discovery ever made by man." In his reports he criticized wealthy parents who sent their children to private academies rather than bring them into contact with their poorer neighbors in the local school. He encouraged young women to become teachers while commending them to school boards by claiming that they could get along on lower salaries than men.

By the 1850s every state outside the South provided free elementary schools and supported institutions for training teachers. Many extended public education to include high schools, and Michigan and Iowa even established publicly supported colleges.

Historians differ in explaining the success of the common school movement. Some stress the arguments Mann used to win support from employers by appealing to their need for trained and well-disciplined workers. Others see the schools as designed to "Americanize" the increasing numbers of non-English and non-Protestant immigrants who were flooding into the country. Still others argue that middle class reformers favored public elementary school on the theory that they would instill the values of hard work, punctuality, and submissiveness to authority in children of the laboring classes.

All these reasons played a part in advancing the cause of the common schools. Yet the most compelling argument for common schools was cultural; more effectively than any other institution, they brought Americans of different economic circumstances and ethnic backgrounds into early and mutually beneficial contact with one another. They were, as Mann said, "the great equalizer."

Engines of Culture

As the population grew and became more concentrated, popular concern for "culture" increased. Industrialization made it easier to satisfy this new demand for culture. Improved printing techniques reduced the cost of books, magazines, and newspapers. The first penny newspaper was the *New York Sun* (1833), but James Gordon Bennett's *New York Herald,* founded in 1835, brought the cheap new journalism to perfection. The penny newspapers depended on sensation, crime stories, and society gossip to attract readers, but they covered important national and international news too.

In the 1850s the moralistic and sentimental "domestic" novel entered its prime. The most successful writers in this genre were women, which prompted Hawthorne to complain bitterly that "a d————d mob of scribbling women" was taking over American literature. Typical were Susan Warner's book *The Wide, Wide World* (1850), a sad tale about a pious, submissive girl who cried "more readily and more steadily than any other tormented child in a novel at the time," and Maria Cummins's book *The Lamplighter* (1854), the story of little Gerty, an orphan rescued by a kindly lamplighter, appropriately named Trueman Flint. The historian Ann Douglas claims in *The Feminization of American Culture,* that such novels provided readers (most of whom were women)

with the consumer pleasures that today are provided by television soaps.

Besides reading countless volumes of sentimental nonsense, Americans consumed reams of religious literature. In 1840 the American Tract Society distributed 3 million copies of its publications; in 1855, more than 12 million. These publications played down denominational differences in favor of a generalized brand of evangelical Christianity. Americans also devoured books on self-improvement, some aimed at uplifting the reader's character, others, which would today be called "how-to-do-it" books, aimed at teaching everything from raising chickens to carving tombstones.

Philanthropists contributed large sums to charity and other good causes; Stephen Girard left $6 million for "educating poor white orphan boys" in his adopted Philadelphia; John Jacob Astor of New York and George Peabody of Massachusetts endowed libraries; John Lowell, son of the pioneer cotton manufacturer, left $500,000 to establish the Lowell Institute in Boston to sponsor free public lectures. Mechanics' libraries sprang up in every industrial center and attracted many readers. In 1848 Massachusetts led the way by authorizing the use of public money to back the Boston Public Library, and soon several states were encouraging local communities to found tax-supported libraries.

The desire for knowledge and culture in America is well illustrated by the success of the mutual improvement societies known as lyceums. The first was organized by Josiah Holbrook in 1826. Lyceums conducted discussions, established libraries, and lobbied for better schools. Soon they began to sponsor lecture series on topics of every sort. Many of the nation's political and intellectual leaders, such as Webster, Emerson, Melville, and Lowell, regularly graced their platforms.

The State of the Colleges

Private colleges had at best a precarious place in Jacksonian America. For one thing, there were too many of them. Any town with pretensions of becoming a regional center felt it had to have a college. Ohio had 25 in the 1850s, Tennessee 16.

The problem of supply was compounded by a demand problem—too few students. Enrollment at the largest, Yale never topped 400 until the mid–1840s. On the eve of the Civil War the largest state university, North Carolina, had fewer than 500 students. Higher education was beyond the means of the average family. So desperate was the shortage that colleges accepted applicants as young as 11 and 12 and as old as 30.

Once enrolled, students had little worry about making the grade, not least because grades were not given. Classwork was relatively unimportant, discipline lax. Official authority was frequently challenged, and rioting was known to break out over such weighty matters as the quality of meals. The typical college curriculum, dominated by the study of Latin and Greek, had almost no practical relevance except for future clergymen. Professors spent most of their time in and out of the classroom trying to maintain a semblance of order, "to the exclusion of any great literary undertakings to which their choice might lead them," one explained. "Professors," a Bostonian informed a foreign visitor in the 1830s, "are too poorly paid to induce first rate men to devote themselves to the business of lecturing. . . . We consider professors as secondary men."

Fortunately some college officials recognized the need for a drastic overhaul of their institutions. President Francis Wayland of Brown University called for a thorough revamping of the curriculum to make it responsive to the economic realities of American society. This meant more courses in science, economics (where Wayland's own *Elements of Political Economy* might be used), modern history, and applied mathematics; fewer in Hebrew, biblical studies, Greek, and ancient history.

Yale established a separate school of science in 1847, which it hoped would attract serious minded students and research-minded professors. At Harvard, which also opened a scientific school, students were allowed to choose some of their courses and were compelled to earn grades. Colleges in the West and the South began to offer mechanical and agricultural subjects relevant to their regional economies. Oberlin enrolled four female students in 1837, and the first women's college, the Georgia Female College, opened its doors in 1839.

These reforms slowed the downward spiral of colleges; they did not restore them to the honored place they had enjoyed in the Revolutionary era. Of the first six presidents of the United States, only Washington did not graduate from college. Beginning in 1829, seven of the next eleven did not: Jackson, Van Buren, Harrison, Taylor, Fillmore, Lincoln, and Johnson. In this the presidents were like 98 of every 100 white males, all blacks and Indians, and all but a handful of white women in mid-19th-century America. Going to college had yet, in Wayland's words, to "commend itself to the good sense and patriotism of the American people."

Civic Cultures

Unlike the capitals of Europe, Washington was a cultural backwater, and the politicians seemed content to keep it that way. Whether the United States had *any* cultural center, and if so, where it was, is another matter. Boston, Philadelphia, and New York vied for primacy, but many smaller cities, such as Lexington, Kentucky, the self-proclaimed "Athens of the West," set the tone for the surrounding hinterland.

Emerson only half mockingly called Boston "the hub of the universe," but this was a case when local pride triumphed over good judgment. Boston was indeed the home of the country's leading literary magazine, the *North American Review,* founded in 1815, but Philadelphia had *Graham's,* the country's first illustrated magazine, and *Godey's Ladies Book,* which reached 150,000 subscribers in the 1850s, an enormous number for that date. By 1825 New York's House of Harper, organized in 1817, was the largest book publisher in the nation. Boston was the home of the nation's leading historians, and Philadelphia, with the Pennsylvania Academy of Fine Arts (1815) and the Philadelphia Academy of Music (1857), was conceded by all but blind Bostonians and tin-eared New Yorkers to predominate in artistic and musical matters.

In the West, Cincinnati could point to its seven weekly and two daily newspapers, a literary monthly, a medical journal, and a magazine for teenagers. The first Beethoven symphony ever heard in America was performed in Cincinnati in 1817. Even cities like Portland, Providence, Hartford, Albany, and Pittsburgh had literary and natural history societies and were regular stops on the lyceum circuit. All in all, American cities had a vitality and diversity that foreign visitors both celebrated and decried.

Scientific Stirrings

Despite Jefferson's assurances in the 1780s that the United States would soon "produce her full quota of genius," a half century had gone by without a single American scientist even approaching the international recognition accorded Benjamin Franklin. Now there was some progress. State-sponsored geological surveys provided at least temporary livings for would-be scientists. Additional jobs opened up with the expansion of the United States Coastal Survey, directed by Benjamin Franklin's great-grandson, Alexander Dallas Bache, in 1843. The opening in 1846 of the Smithsonian Institution in Washington, to which the physicist Joseph Henry was appointed first secretary, helped too. Henry's research ventures in electromagnetism in the 1830s led to Samuel F. B. Morse's invention of the telegraph.

Yet few Americans pursued science except on a part-time basis. The star sightings and tidal measurements that went into Nathaniel Bowditch's internationally recognized manual, *The New American Practical Navigator,* had to be made in his spare time. He made his living as an actuary in an insurance company. Maria Mitchell, America's best-known 19th-century woman scientist, won international celebrity and a gold medal from the king of Denmark for calculating the position of a new comet in 1847. She was employed as a librarian.

For all the practical obstacles in the way of doing serious science in Jacksonian America, its near-wilderness circumstances sometimes provided those on the lookout with unexpected targets of opportunity. An almost literal case in point is that of Dr. William Beaumont. In 1822, while serving as an army surgeon in upstate New York, Beaumont was called to attend to Alexis St. Martin, a 19-year-old Canadian woodsman who had been shot by accident. The shell, fired from no more than 3 feet away, had blasted a hole in his

chest the size of a grapefruit. "What at first view I could not believe possible," Beaumont recorded in his diary, "on closer observation, I found to be actually the stomach with a puncture in the protruding portion large enough to receive my forefinger." The young man survived, exposed stomach and all. Eventually a flap formed over the opening in the stomach, but it could be pushed back, exposing the inner workings of the organ.

Over the next decade Beaumont performed hundreds of experiments testing the relative digestibility of foods and analyzing the chemical properties of gastric juices. These won him a reputation among European physiologists as the world's leading expert on the human gastric system.

American Humor

The clash between the desire of a few for a "high" culture and the simpler tastes of the majority led James Fenimore Cooper to conclude that Americans would be forever "wanting in most of the high tastes, and consequently in the high enjoyments." But other writers were not so sure, and some, rather than despair over the cultural incongruities, found in them a rich source of humor.

They were hardly the first to do so. The comic potential in juxtaposing high ideals and low reality had been exploited by the Greek playwright Aristophanes; by Rabelais, the creator of *Gargantua*; and by Cervantes in *The Adventures of Don Quixote*—all, incidentally, works available in mid-century America. In colonial times William Byrd and Benjamin Franklin had both used the differences between the pretensions of colonial sophisticates and the ways of common folk to good comic effect. But the possibilities of this kind of humor were greatly enlarged in the Jacksonian era.

One of the first writers to exploit the comic aspects of Jacksonian Democracy was Seba Smith, a newspaperman from Portland, Maine. Smith's fictional creation, Major Jack Downing, was a Jackson man from a part of the country suspicious of both the general's politics and his intelligence. Smith had Major Downing accompany the president on his 1833 tour of New England, which included, among other adventures, an appearance at Harvard to receive an honorary degree. In the presence of so many learned gentlemen with political views contrary to his own, Downing advised the president "jest to say nothing, but look as knowing as any of them." Which was exactly what Jackson did, even when faced by snickering "sassy students."

A writer who turned the possibilities of "Down East" humor to more telling satirical effect was James Russell Lowell, author of the *Biglow Papers,* which began appearing in 1847. Lowell juxtaposed Hosea Biglow, a Yankee farmer of "homely common-sense heated up by conscience," and Birdofredum Sawin, a scoundrel hoping to turn a profit on his patriotism. When approached by a recruiting officer, Hosea Biglow set his opposition to the Mexican War (actually Lowell's) to verse:

> They may talk o' Freedom's airy
> Till they're pupple in the face,—

> It's a grand gret cemetary
> For the barthrights of our race. . . .

The Old Southwest provided another locale for juxtaposing the genteel and the vulgar. Life in the region provided chroniclers with more than enough violence to capture the attention of their "gentle readers." Johnson J. Hooper's creation Simon Suggs was the ultimate frontier rogue as confidence man. Whether engaged in horse swapping or faking a conversion experience at a camp meeting in order to steal the collection basket, Suggs lived by the maxim "It is good to be shifty in a new country." He was not alone in this opinion. In a new country, it made sense not to take oneself too seriously. Although the outcome of the nation's experiment in combining democracy and cultural aspiration remained in doubt, most Americans took their laughs where they could find them.

Milestones

1827–1838	John Audubon, *Birds of America*	**1845–1846**	Henry David Thoreau lives at Walden Pond
1834	George Bancroft, *History of the United States*	**1845**	Edgar Allan Poe, "The Raven"
1835	James Gordon Bennett founds *New York Herald*	**1846**	Opening of Smithsonian Institution
1836	John Lowell endows Lowell Institute public lectures	**1847**	James Russell Lowell, *Bigelow Papers*
1837	Ralph Waldo Emerson, "TheAmerican Scholar"	**1848**	Founding of American Association for the Advancement of Science
	Oberlin College enrolls the first women students	**1850**	Nathaniel Hawthorne, *The Scarlet Letter*
1837–1848	Horace Mann serves as secretary of the Massachusetts Board of Education	**1851**	Herman Melville, *Moby Dick*
			Francis Parkman, *The Conspiracy of Pontiac*
1839	Establishment of the American Art-Union	**1854**	Henry David Thoreau, *Walden*
1842–1843	Herman Melville lives in Tahiti and other South Pacific islands	**1855–1892**	Walt Whitman, *Leaves of Grass* (various editions)
		1857	*Atlantic Monthly* first published
1843	Hiram Powers sculpts *The Greek Slave*	**1859**	Peter Cooper founds Cooper Institute

Supplementary Reading

Useful surveys of cultural and intellectual currents in this period are D. J. Boorstin, **The Americans: The National Experience** (1967), R. B. Nye, **Society and Culture in America*** (1974), and Rush Welter, **The Mind of America** (1975).

On transcendentalism, see Perry Miller, ed., **The American Transcendentalists** (1957), and Joel Porte, **Representative Man: Ralph Waldo Emerson in His Time*** (1979). On literature, Van Wyck Brooks, **The Flowering of New England*** (1936), and Alfred Kazin, **On Native Grounds** (1942), are still useful surveys. Biographies of the novelists include Kenneth Silverman, **Edgar A. Poe** (1991), J. R. Mellow, **Nathaniel Hawthorne and His Times** (1980), and Justin Kaplan, **Walt Whitman** (1980).

Popular culture is discussed in Carl Bode, **The Anatomy of American Popular Culture** (1959), and Russell Lynes, **The Tastemakers*** (1954). Neil Harris, **The Artist in American Society*** (1966), puts art in its social setting. See also Ann Douglas, **The Feminization of American Culture** (1977).

On education, see L. A. Cremin, **American Education: The National Experience** (1980), and C. F. Kaestle, **Pillars of the Republic** (1983). See also Jonathan Messerli, **Horace Mann** (1972). For higher education, consult Fred Rudolph, **The American College and University** (1961), David Allmendinger, **Paupers and Scholars** (1975), and Colin Burke, **American Collegiate Populations** (1982).

Scientific developments are discussed in G. H. Daniels, **American Science in the Age of Jackson** (1968), and A. H. Dupree, **Science in the Federal Government** (1957).

*Available in paperback.

CHAPTER 12

Expansion and Slavery

Tyler's Troubles

The Webster-Ashburton Treaty

The Texas Question

Manifest Destiny

Life on the Trail

California and Oregon

The Election of 1844

Polk as President

War with Mexico

To the Halls of Montezuma

The Treaty of Guadalupe Hidalgo

Fruits of Victory

Slavery: The Fire Bell in the Night Rings Again

The Election of 1848

The Gold Rush

The Compromise of 1850

*P*resident John Tyler, the new president, was a thin, rather delicate-appearing man with pale blue eyes and a long nose. Courteous, tactful, soft-spoken, he gave the impression of being weak. This was a false impression; John Tyler was stubborn and proud, and these characteristics combined with an almost total lack of imagination to make him worship consistency, as so many second-raters do. He had turned away from Jackson because of the aggressive way the president had used his powers of appointment and the veto, but he also disagreed with Senator Henry Clay and the northern Whigs about the Bank, protection, and federal internal improvements. Being a states' rights southerner, Tyler considered such measures to be unconstitutional. Nevertheless, he was prepared to cooperate with Clay as the leader of what he called the "more immediate representatives" of the people, the members of Congress. But he was not prepared to be Clay's puppet. He asked all of Harrison's Cabinet to remain in office.

Tyler's Troubles

Tyler and Clay did not get along and for this Clay was chiefly to blame. He behaved in an overbearing manner that was out of keeping with his nature, probably because he resented having been passed over by the Whigs in 1840. He considered himself the real head of the Whig Party and intended to exercise his leadership.

In Congress Clay announced a comprehensive "program" that ignored Tyler's states' rights view of the Constitution. Most important was his plan to set up a new Bank of the United States. A bill to repeal the Independent Treasury Act caused no difficulty, but when Congress passed a new Bank bill, Tyler vetoed it. The entire Cabinet except Secretary of State Webster thereupon resigned in protest.

Abandoned by the Whigs, Tyler attempted to build a party of his own. He failed to do so and for the remainder of his term the political squabbling in Washington continued. Clay wanted to distribute the proceeds from land sales to the states, presumably to bolster their sagging finances but actually to reduce federal revenues in order to justify raising the tariff. To win western votes for distribution, he agreed to support the Preemption Act of 1841 legalizing the right of squatters to occupy unsurveyed land and to buy it later at $1.25 an acre without bidding for it at auction. However, the southerners insisted on an amendment pledging that distribution would be stopped if the tariff were raised above the 20 percent level, and when the Whigs blithely tried to push a high tariff through Congress without repealing the Distribution Act, Tyler vetoed the bill. Finally, the Distribution Act was repealed and Tyler signed the new Tariff Act of 1842, raising duties to about the levels of 1832.

The Webster-Ashburton Treaty

Webster's decision to remain in the Cabinet was motivated in part by his desire to settle the boundary between Maine and New Brunswick. The intent of the peace treaty of 1783 had been to award the United States all land in the area drained by rivers flowing into the Atlantic rather than the St. Lawrence, but the wording was obscure and the old maps conflicting. In 1842 the British sent a new minister, Lord Ashburton, to the United States to try to settle all outstanding disputes. Webster and Ashburton easily worked out a compromise boundary. The British needed only a small part of the territory to build a military road connecting Halifax and Quebec. Webster, who thought any settlement desirable simply to eliminate a possible cause of war, willingly agreed.

Nevertheless, Webster's generosity made excellent sense. Lord Ashburton, gratified by having obtained the strategic territory, made concessions elsewhere along the Canadian-American border. British dependence on foreign foodstuffs was increasing; America's need for British capital was rising. War, or even unsettled affairs, would have injured vital business relations and produced no compensating gains.

The Texas Question

The settlement with Great Britain won support in every section of the United States, but the same could not be said for Tyler's attempt to annex the Republic of Texas, for this involved the question of slavery. In the Transcontinental Treaty of 1819 with Spain, the boundary of the United States had been drawn in such a way as to exclude Texas. This seemed unimportant at the time, yet within months of the ratification of the treaty in February 1821, Americans led by Stephen F. Austin had begun to settle in the area. Almost simultaneously Mexico threw off the last vestiges of Spanish rule. Cotton flourished on the fertile Texas plains, and, and for a time, the new Mexican authorities offered free land and something approaching local autonomy to groups of settlers from the United States. By 1830 there were some 20,000 white Americans in Texas, together with about 2,000 slaves, while only a few thousand Mexicans lived there.

President John Quincy Adams had offered Mexico $1 million for Texas, and Jackson was willing to pay $5 million, but Mexico would not sell. Nevertheless, by the late 1820s the flood of American settlers was giving the Mexican authorities second thoughts. The immigrants apparently felt no loyalty to Mexico. Most were Protestants, though Mexican law required that all immigrants be Catholics. Few attempted to learn more than a few words of Spanish. When Mexico outlawed slavery in 1829, they evaded the law by "freeing" their slaves and then signing them to lifetime contracts as indentured servants. In 1830 Mexico prohibited further immigration of Americans into Texas, though again the law proved impossible to enforce.

As soon as the Mexican government began to restrict them, the Texans began to seek independence. In 1835 a series of skirmishes escalated into a full-scale rebellion, as Texans were receiving much military and financial aid from American "volunteers." The Mexican president, Antonio Lopez de Santa Anna, marched north with 6,000 soldiers to subdue the rebels. Late in February 1836 he reached San Antonio.

A force of 187 men under Colonel William B. Travis held the city. They took refuge behind the stout walls of a former mission called the Alamo. For ten days they beat off Santa Anna's assaults, inflicting terrible casualties on the attackers. Finally, on March 6, the Mexicans carried the walls. Once inside, they killed everyone, even the wounded, then soaked the corpses in oil and burned them. Among the dead were the legendary Davy Crockett and Jim Bowie, who is especially remembered for his characteristic Bowie knife.

After the carnage in the Alamo, the Texans declared their independence. Sam Houston, a former congressman and governor of Tennessee and an experienced Indian fighter, was placed in charge of the rebel army. On April 21, 1836, at San Jacinta shouting "Forward! Charge! Remember the Alamo!" he ordered the attack. His troops routed the Mexican army, which soon retreated across the Rio Grande. In October Houston was elected president of the Republic of Texas and a month later a plebiscite revealed that an overwhelming majority favored annexation by the United States.

President Jackson hesitated. To take Texas might lead to war with Mexico. Certainly it would stir up the slavery controversy. On his last day in office he recognized the republic, but he made no move to accept it into the Union, nor did his successor, Van Buren. Texas thereupon went its own way, which involved developing friendly ties with Great Britain. An independent Texas suited British tastes perfectly, for it could provide an alternative supply of cotton and a market for manufactures unfettered by tariffs.

These events caused alarm in the United States, especially among southerners, who dreaded the possibility that a Texas dominated by Great Britain might abolish slavery. As a southerner, Tyler shared these feelings; he saw in annexation a chance to revive his fortunes. In the West and even the Northeast the patriotic urge to add such a magnificent new territory to the national domain was great. Counting noses, Abel P. Upshur, Tyler's secretary of state, convinced himself that the Senate would approve annexation by the necessary two-thirds majority. He negotiated a treaty in February 1844, but before he could sign it, he was killed by the accidental explosion of a cannon on USS *Princeton* during a weapons demonstration.

To ensure the accession of Texas, Tyler appointed John C. Calhoun secretary of state. This was a blunder; by then Calhoun was so closely associated with the South and with slavery that his appointment alienated thousands of northerners who might otherwise have welcomed annexation. Suddenly Texas became a hot political issue. Clay and Van Buren, who seemed assured of the 1844 Whig and Democratic presidential nominations, promptly announced that they opposed annexation, chiefly on the ground that it would probably lead to war with Mexico. With a national election in the offing, northern and western senators refused to vote for annexation, and in June the Senate rejected the treaty, 35 to 16.

Manifest Destiny

The Senate, Clay, and Van Buren had all misinterpreted public opinion. For two centuries Americans had been gradually conquering a continent. The westward march from the 17th century to the 1840s had seemed fraught with peril, the prize golden but attainable only through patient labor and fearful hardships. Wild animals and wild men, mighty forests and mighty foreign powers beset the path. John Adams wrote of "conquering" the West "from the trees and rocks and wild beasts." He was "enflamed" by the possibilities of "that vast scene which is opening in the West," but to win it the nation would have to "march *intrepidly* on."

Quite rapidly (as historians measure time) the atmosphere changed. Each year of national growth increased the power and confidence of the people, and every forward step revealed a wider horizon. Now the West seemed a ripe apple, to be picked almost casually. Where pioneers had once stood in awe before the majesty of the Blue Ridge, then hesitated to venture from the protective shadows of the forest into the open prairies of Illinois, they now shrugged their shoulders at great deserts and began to talk of the Rocky Mountains as "mere molehills" along the road to the Pacific. After 200 years of westward expansion had brought them as far as Missouri and Iowa, Americans suddenly perceived their destined goal. *The whole continent was to be theirs!* Theirs to exploit, theirs to make into one mighty nation, a land of opportunity, a showcase to display the virtues of democratic institutions, living proof that Americans were indeed God's chosen people. A New York journalist, John L. O'Sullivan, captured the new mood in a sentence. Nothing must interfere, he wrote in 1845, with "the fulfilment of our *manifest destiny* to overspread the continent allotted by Providence for the free development of our yearly multiplying millions."

The politicians did not sense the new mood in 1844. In fact, the expansion, stimulated by the natural growth of the population and by a revived flood of immigration, was going on in every section and with little regard for political boundaries. New settlers rolled westward in hordes. Between 1830 and 1835, 10,000 entered "foreign" Texas, and this was a trickle compared to what the early 1840s were to bring. By 1840 many Americans had also settled far to the west in California, which was unmistakably Mexican territory, and in the Oregon country, jointly claimed by the United States and Great Britain.

Life on the Trail

The romantic myths attached to this mighty human tide have obscured the adjustments forced on the pioneers and focused attention on the least significant of the dangers they faced and the hardships they endured. Pioneers were more likely to complain that the Indians they encountered were dirty, lazy, and thieving than to worry about the danger of Indian attack. Far more dangerous was the possibility of accidents, particularly to children, and also unsanitary conditions.

"Going west" had always been laborious, but in the 1840s the distances covered were longer by far. Moving west disrupted the new pattern of family life; there were few, if any, "separate spheres" on the trail. According to the historian Julie Roy Jeffries, "the pioneer family had to become self-sufficient. Much of the model of appropriate female behavior had to be disregarded." Women learned to load wagons, pitch tents, and chase stray cattle. Men, for their part, had to keep an eye on children and help with tasks like cooking and washing.

Travel on the plains west of the Mississippi was especially taxing for women. Guidebooks did not prepare them for having to collect dried buffalo dung for fuel, for the heat and choking dust of summer, for enduring a week of steady rain, for the monotony, the dirt, and the cramped quarters. Caring for an infant or a 2-year-old in a wagon could be torture week after week on the trail, for there were limits to what the average husband could or would do on the way west. Pioneer women mostly complained of being bone weary and about the difficulties of day-to-day existence. "It is impossible to keep anything clean," one recorded, and it is not hard to envisage the difficulty of doing so while living for weeks on end on the trail. "Oh dear," another wrote in her journal, "I do so want to get there."

California and Oregon

By 1840 many Americans had settled in California, which was Mexican territory, and in the Oregon country, jointly claimed by the United States and Great Britain, and they went to these distant regions in increasing numbers as the decade progressed. California was inhabited by some 7,000 Spanish-speaking ranchers, a handful of "Anglo" settlers from the United States, and many thousands of Indians. Until the 1830s, when their estates were broken up by the anticlerical Mexican government, 21 Catholic missions controlled more than 30,000 Indian converts, who were little better off than slaves.

Richard Henry Dana, a Harvard College student, sailed around South America to California as an ordinary seaman in 1834. His book, *Two Years Before the Mast* (1840), describes what life was like in California: "There is no working class (the Indians being practically serfs and doing all the hard work) and every rich man looks like a grandee, and every poor scamp like a broken-down gentleman."

Oregon, a vaguely defined area between California and Russian Alaska, proved still more allur-

"Oregon Fever" swept the country in the mid-1840s, setting thousands of emigrants on the Oregon Trail. People full of hope assembled in wagon trains at jumping-off places along the Missouri River. Their optimism often turned to despair as they faced the hardships of the journey, from fording rivers to hauling wagons by ropes, chains, and pulleys over steep rocky ridges.

ing to Americans. In 1811 John Jacob Astor's Pacific Fur Company had established trading posts on the Columbia River. Some two decades later Methodist, Presbyterian, and Catholic missionaries began to find their way into the Willamette Valley, a green land of rich soil, mild climate, and tall forests teeming with game. Gradually a small number of settlers followed, until by the year 1840 there were about 500 Americans in the Willamette area.

In the early 1840s, fired by the spirit of manifest destiny, the country suddenly burned with "Oregon fever." Land hunger (stimulated by the glowing reports of those on the scene) drew the new migrants most powerfully, but the patriotic concept of manifest destiny gave the trek across the 2,000 miles of wilderness separating Oregon from the western edge of American settlement in Missouri the character of a crusade. In 1843 nearly 1,000 pioneers made this long trip.

The Oregon Trail began at the western border of Missouri and followed the Kansas River and the Platte River past Fort Laramie to the Rockies. It crossed the Continental Divide by the relatively easy South Pass then ran through the valley of the Columbia to Fort Vancouver, a British post guarding the entrance to the Willamette Valley.

Over this tortuous path wound the canvas-covered caravans with their scouts and their accompanying herds. Each group became a self-governing community on the march, with regulations democratically agreed on "for the purpose of keeping good order and promoting civil and military discipline." Most wagon trains consisted of young families of middling wealth; the trip for a family of four cost about $600, a considerable sum. For large groups, the Indians posed no great threat, though constant vigilance was necessary. Naturally, the five-month trip was full of labor, discomfort, and uncertainty, an "unending, weatherscoured, nerve-rasping plod on and on and on and on, foot by aching foot." At the end lay the regular tasks of pioneering. The spirit of the trailblazers is caught in an entry from the diary of James Nesmith:

Friday, October 27.—Arrived at Oregon City at the falls of the Willamette.
Saturday, October 28.—Went to work.

Behind the dreams of the Far West as an American Eden lay the commercial importance of the three major West Coast harbors: San Diego, San Francisco, and the Strait of Juan de Fuca leading into Puget Sound. Eastern merchants considered these harbors the keys to the trade of the Orient. That San Diego and San Francisco were Mexican and the Puget Sound district was claimed by Great Britain only heightened their desire to possess them.

The Election of 1844

In the spring of 1844 expansion did not seem likely to affect the presidential election. The Whigs nominated Clay unanimously and ignored Texas in their party platform. When the Democrats gathered in convention at Baltimore in May, Van Buren appeared to have the nomination in his pocket. He too, wanted to keep Texas out of the campaign. This, however, John C. Calhoun was determined to prevent. The result, in the words of the historian William Freehling, was a "climactic battle between Van Buren and Calhoun for the soul of the Jackson [Democratic] party." With the aid of a few northern expansionists, southern delegates forced through a rule requiring that the choice be by a two-thirds majority. This Van Buren could not muster. After a brief deadlock, a "dark horse," James K. Polk of Tennessee, swept the convention.

Polk was a good Jacksonian; his supporters called him "Young Hickory." He opposed high tariffs and was dead set against establishing another national bank. But he believed in taking Texas, and he favored expansion generally. To mollify the Van Burenites, the convention nominated Senator Silas Wright of New York for vice president, but Wright was Van Buren's friend and equally opposed to annexation. When the word was flashed to him in Washington over the new "magnetic telegraph" which Samuel F. B. Morse had just installed between the convention hall in Baltimore and the Capitol, he refused to run. The delegates then picked an annexationist, George M. Dallas of Pennsylvania. The Democratic platform demanded that Texas be "reannexed" (implying that it had been part of the Louisiana Purchase) and

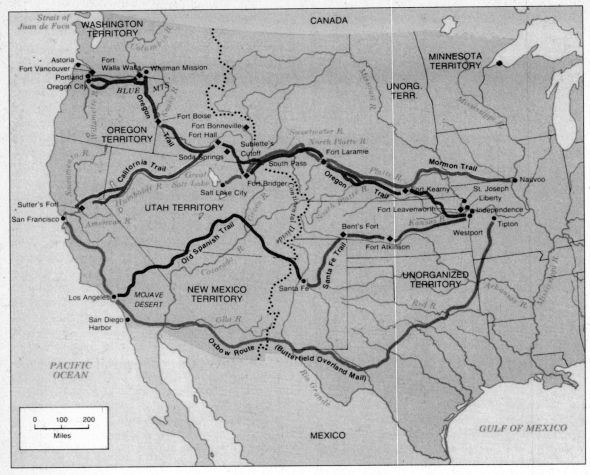

Trails West

that all of Oregon be "reoccupied" (suggesting that the joint occupation of the region with Great Britain, which had been agreed to in the Convenrion of 1818, be abrogated).

When Clay sensed the new expansionist sentiment of the voters, he tried to hedge on his opposition to annexation, but by doing so he probably lost as many votes as he gained. The election was extremely close. Polk carried the country by only 38,000 of 2.7 million votes. In the electoral college the vote was 170 to 105.

The decisive factor was the Liberty Party, an antislavery splinter group organized in 1840. Only 62,000 voters supported candidate James G. Birney, a "reformed" Kentucky slaveholder, but nearly 16,000 of them lived in New York, most in the western part of the state, a Whig stronghold. Since Polk carried New York by barely 5,000, the votes for Birney probably cost Clay the state. Had he won New York's 36 electoral votes, he would have been elected, 141 to 134.

Polk's victory was nevertheless taken as a mandate for expansion. Tyler promptly called on Congress to take Texas by joint resolution, which would avoid the necessity of obtaining a two-thirds majority in the Senate. This was done a few days before Tyler left the White House. Under the resolution if the new state agreed, as many as four new states might be carved from its territory, but only with its approval. Polk accepted this arrangement, and in December 1845 Texas was admitted to the Union.

Polk as President

Polk's mind was not of the first order, for he was too tense and calculating to allow his intellect free rein. He was an efficient, hard worker with a strong will and a tough skin, qualities that stood him in good stead in the White House, and he made politics his whole life. It was typical of the man that he developed a special technique of handshaking in order better to cope with the interminable reception lines that every leader has to endure. "When I observed a strong man approaching," he once explained, "I generally took advantage of him by . . . seizing him by the tip of his fingers, giving him a hearty shake, and thus preventing him from getting a full grip upon me." In four years in office he was away from his desk in Washington for a total of only six weeks.

Polk was uncommonly successful in doing what he set out to do as president. He persuaded Congress to lower the tariff of 1842 and to restore the independent treasury. He opposed federal internal improvements and managed to have his way. He made himself the spokesman of American expansion by committing himself to obtaining, in addition to Texas, both Oregon and the great Southwest. Here again, he succeeded.

Oregon was the first order of business. In his inaugural address Polk stated the American claim to the entire region in the plainest terms, but he informed the British minister in Washington, Richard Pakenham, that he would accept a boundary following the 49th parallel to the Pacific. Pakenham rejected this proposal without submitting it to London, and Polk thereupon decided to insist again on the whole area. When Congress met in December 1845, he asked for authority to give the necessary one year's notice for abrogating the 1818 treaty of joint occupation. "The only way to treat John Bull," he told one congressman, "was to look him straight in the eye." Following considerable discussion, Congress complied, and in May 1846 Polk notified Great Britain that he intended to terminate the joint occupation.

The British then decided to compromise. Officials of the Hudson's Bay Company had become alarmed by the rapid growth of the American settlement in the Willamette Valley. By 1845 some 5,000 persons lived there, whereas the country north of the Columbia contained no more than 750 British subjects. A clash between the groups could have but one result; the company decided to shift its base from the Columbia to Vancouver Island. And British experts outside the company reported that the Oregon country could not possibly be defended in case of war. Thus, when Polk accompanied the one-year notice with a hint that he would again consider a compromise, the British foreign secretary, Lord Aberdeen, suggested dividing the Oregon territory along the 49th parallel. Polk, abandoning his belligerent attitude, agreed. The treaty followed that line from the Rockies to Puget Sound, but Vancouver Island, which extended below the line, was left entirely to the British, so both nations retained free use of the Strait of Juan de Fuca. Although some northern Democrats accused Polk of treachery because he had failed to fight for all of Oregon, the treaty so obviously accorded with the national interest that the Senate approved it by a large majority in June 1846. Polk was then free to tackle the Texas question in earnest.

War with Mexico

One reason for the popularity of the Oregon compromise was that the country was already at war with Mexico and wanted no trouble with Great Britain. The expansionist spirit and the confidence born of its overwhelming advantages of size and wealth had encouraged the United States to bully Mexico. In addition, Mexico had defaulted on debts owed the United States, which caused some people to suggest using force to obtain the money. But from the Mexican perspective, national pride was at stake. Texas had been independent for the better part of a decade. Although Mexico had made no serious effort to reconquer it, the Mexican government never recognized Texas's independence and broke off diplomatic relations as soon as the United States annexed the republic in 1845.

Polk then ordered General Zachary Taylor into Texas to defend the border. However, the location of that border was in dispute. Texas claimed the Rio Grande; Mexico insisted that the boundary was the Nueces River, which emptied into the Gulf about 150 miles to the north. Taylor reached the Nueces in July 1845 with about 1,500

*Gen.ª Wool & Staff
Calle Real to South.*

This 1846 daguerreotype is the earliest known American war photograph. U.S. General John E. Wool poses with his staff in Saltillo, Mexico.

troops and crossed into the disputed territory. He stopped on the southern bank at Corpus Christi, not wishing to provoke the Mexicans by marching to the Rio Grande.

In November Polk sent an envoy, John Slidell, on a secret mission to Mexico to try to obtain the disputed territory by negotiation. Polk authorized Slidell to cancel the Mexican debt in return for recognition of the annexation of Texas and acceptance of the Rio Grande boundary. The president also empowered Slidell to offer as much as $30 million if Mexico would sell to the United States all or part of New Mexico and California.

It would probably have been to Mexico's advantage, at least in the short run, to have made a deal with Slidell. The area Polk wanted, lying in the path of American expansion, was likely to be engulfed as Texas had been, without regard for the actions of the American or Mexican governments. But the Mexican government refused to receive Slidell. Amid a wave of anti-American feeling, a military coup occurred and General Mariano Paredes, the new head of state, promptly reaffirmed his country's claim to all of Texas. Slidell returned to Washington convinced that the Mexi-

cans would not give an inch until they had been "chastised."

Polk had already ordered Taylor to advance to the Rio Grande. By late March 1846 the army, swelled to about 4,000, had taken up positions near the Mexican town of Matamoros. The Mexicans crossed the river on April 25 and attacked an American mounted patrol. They were driven back easily, but when news of the fighting reached Washington, Polk asked Congress to declare war. He treated the matter as a *fait accompli*: "War exists," he stated flatly. Without declaring war, Congress voted to raise and supply an additional 50,000 troops. For the first time (but not the last) a president had led the nation into war without the formal declaration required by the Constitution.

From the first battles, the outcome of the Mexican War was never in doubt. At Palo Alto, north of the Rio Grande, 2,300 Americans scattered a Mexican force more than twice their number. Then, hotly pursuing, 1,700 Americans routed 7,500 Mexicans at Resaca de la Palma. Within a week of the declaration of war the Mexicans had been driven across the Rio Grande and

General Taylor had his troops firmly established on the southern bank.

The Mexican army was poorly equipped and, despite a surfeit of high-ranking officers, poorly led. The well-supplied American forces had a hard core of youthful West Pointers eager to make their reputations and regulars trained in Indian warfare to provide the leadership needed to turn volunteer soldiers into first-rate fighting men. Yet Mexico was a large, rugged country with few decent roads; conquering it proved to be a formidable task.

To the Halls of Montezuma

President Polk insisted not only on directing grand strategy but on supervising hundreds of petty details, down to the purchase of mules and the promotion of enlisted men. But he allowed politics to influence his choice of generals. This partisanship caused unnecessary turmoil in army ranks. Try as he might, he could not find a good Democratic general. Both Zachary Taylor and Winfield Scott, the commanding general in Washington, were Whigs. Polk, who suspected the motives of people who disagreed with him, feared that one or the other would make political capital of his popularity as a military leader.

Polk's concern was heightened because domestic opposition to the war was growing. Many northerners feared that the war would lead to the expansion of slavery. Others (including an obscure Illinois congressman named Abraham Lincoln) felt that Polk had misled Congress about the outbreak of fighting and that the United States was the aggressor. The farther from the Rio Grande one went in the United States, the less popular "Mr. Polk's War" became; in New England opposition was almost as widespread as it had been to "Mr. Madison's War" in 1812.

Polk's design for prosecuting the war consisted of three parts. First, he would clear the Mexicans from Texas and occupy the northern provinces of Mexico. Second, he would take possession of California and New Mexico. Finally, he would march on Mexico City. Proceeding west from the Rio Grande, Taylor swiftly overran the northern provinces. In June 1846 American settlers in the Sacramento Valley seized Sonoma and raised the "Bear Flag" of the Republic of California. Another group, headed by Captain John C.

Frémont, clashed with the Mexican authorities around Monterey, California, and then joined with the Sonoma rebels. A naval squadron under Commodore John D. Sloat captured Monterey and San Francisco in July 1846 and a squadron of cavalry commanded by General Stephen Watts Kearny joined the other American units in mopping-up operations around San Diego and Los Angeles. By February 1847 the United States had won control of nearly all of Mexico north of the capital city.

The campaign against Mexico City was the most difficult of the war. Polk put Winfield Scott in charge of the offensive. Scott was nearly six and a half feet tall; in uniform his presence was commanding. He was intelligent and cultivated, though somewhat pompous, as his nickname, Old Fuss and Feathers, indicated. After a sound but not spectacular record in the War of 1812, he had added to his reputation by helping to modernize military administration and to strengthen the professional training of officers.

Scott landed his army south of Veracruz, Mexico, on March 9, 1847, laid siege to the city, and obtained its surrender in less than three weeks with the loss of only a handful of his 10,000 men. Marching westward through hostile country, he maintained effective discipline, avoiding atrocities that might have inflamed the countryside against him. At Cerro Gordo, where the national road rose steeply toward the central highlands, Scott outflanked the Mexican position and then carried it by storm, capturing more than 3,000 prisoners and much equipment. By mid-May he had advanced to Puebla, only 80 miles southeast of Mexico City. After delaying until August for the arrival of reinforcements, he pressed on, won two hard-fought victories at the outskirts of the capital, and on September 14 hammered his way into the city.

The Treaty of Guadalupe Hidalgo

The Mexicans were thoroughly beaten, but they refused to accept the situation. As soon as the news of the capture of Veracruz reached Washington, Polk sent Nicholas P. Trist, chief clerk of the State Department, to accompany Scott's army and to act as peace commissioner after the fall of Mexico City. Because of the confused state of affairs after the fall of

Mexico City, Trist was unable to open negotiations with Mexican peace commissioners until January 1848. Polk, unable to understand the delay, became impatient. He had authorized Trist to pay $30 million for New Mexico, Upper and Lower California, and the right of transit across Mexico's narrow Isthmus of Tehuantepec. Now, observing the disorganized state of Mexican affairs, he began to consider demanding more territory and paying less for it. He summoned Trist home.

Trist, with Scott's backing, ignored the order. He realized that unless a treaty was arranged soon, the Mexican government might disintegrate, leaving no one in authority to sign a treaty. He wrote a long letter to Polk, in effect refusing to be recalled, and proceeded to negotiate. Early in February the Treaty of Guadalupe Hidalgo was completed. By its terms Mexico accepted the Rio Grande as the boundary of Texas and ceded New Mexico and Upper California to the United States. In return the United States agreed to pay Mexico $15 million and to take on the claims of American citizens against Mexico, which by that time amounted to another $3.25 million.

When he learned that Trist had ignored his orders, the president seethed. Trist was "contemptibly base," he said, an "impudent and unqualified scoundrel." He ordered him placed under arrest and fired him from his State Department job.* Yet Polk had no choice but to submit the treaty to the Senate, for to have insisted on more territory would have meant more fighting, and the war had become increasingly unpopular. The relatively easy military victory made some people ashamed that their country was crushing a small neighbor. Abolitionists called it an "invasion . . . waged solely for the detestable and horrible purpose of extending and perpetuating American slavery." The Senate, subject to the same pressures as the president, ratified the agreement by a vote of 38 to 14.

Fruits of Victory

The Mexican War, won quickly and at relatively small cost in lives and money, brought huge terri-

*Trist was retired to private life without being paid for his time in Mexico. In 1870, when he was on his deathbed, Congress finally awarded him $14,299.20.

torial gains. The Pacific Coast from south of San Diego to the 49th parallel and all the land between the coast and the Continental Divide had become the property of the American people. Immense amounts of labor and capital would have to be invested before this new territory could be made to yield its bounty, but the country clearly had the capacity to accomplish the job.

In this atmosphere came what seemed a sign from the heavens. In January 1848, while Scott's veterans rested after their victorious campaign in Mexico City, a mechanic named James W. Marshall was building a sawmill on the American River in the Sacramento Valley east of San Francisco. One day, while supervising the deepening of the millrace, he noticed a few flecks of yellow in the bed of the stream. These he gathered up and tested. They were pure gold.

Other strikes had been made in California and been treated skeptically or as matters of local curiosity; since the days of Jamestown, too many pioneers had run fruitlessly in search of El Dorado, too much fool's gold had been passed off as the real thing. Yet this discovery produced an international sensation. The gold was real and plentiful, but equally important was the fact that everyone was ready to believe the news. The gold rush reflected the heady confidence inspired by the Treaty of Guadalupe Hidalgo; it seemed the ultimate justification of manifest destiny. Surely an era of continental prosperity and harmony had dawned.

Slavery: The Fire Bell in the Night Rings Again

Prosperity came in full measure but not harmony, for once again expansion brought the nation face to face with the divisive question of slavery. This giant chunk of North America, most of it vacant, its future soon to be determined—should it be slave or free? The question, in one sense, seems hardly worth the national crisis it provoked. Slavery appeared to have little future in New Mexico and California, none in Oregon. Why did the South fight so hard for the right to bring slaves into a region that seemed so poorly suited to their exploitation?

Narrow partisanship provides part of the explanation. In districts where slavery was entrenched, a congressman who watched over the institution with the eyes of an eagle, ever ready to defend it against the most trivial slight, usually found himself a popular hero. In the northern states representatives who were vigilant in what they might describe as "freedom's cause" seldom regretted it on election day. But slavery raised a moral question that most Americans tried to avoid confronting. As patriots, they assumed that any sectional issue could be solved by compromise. Although the majority of whites had little respect for blacks, slave or free, few persons, northern or southern, could look on the ownership of one human being by another as simply an alternative form of economic organization and argue its merits as they would those of the protective tariff or a national bank. Twist the facts as they might, slavery was either right or it was wrong; being on the whole honest and moral, they could not, having faced that truth, stand by unconcerned while the question was debated.

The question could come up in Congress only indirectly because the Constitution did not give the federal government any control over slavery in the states. But Congress could decide the fate of slavery in the territories. For foes of slavery, the fact that the institution had no future in the Mexican Cession was an advantage. By attacking it where it could probably never exist, they could conceal from the slaveholders—and perhaps even from themselves—their hope ultimately to extinguish the institution everywhere.

Slavery had complicated the Texas problem from the start, and it beclouded the future of the Southwest even before the Mexican flag had been stripped from the staffs at Santa Fe and Los Angeles. On August 8, 1846, during the debate on a bill appropriating money for the conduct of the war, Democratic Congressman David Wilmot of Pennsylvania introduced an amendment that provided "as an express and fundamental condition to the acquisition of any territory from the Republic of Mexico" that "neither slavery nor involuntary servitude shall ever exist in any part of said territory, except for crime, whereof the party shall first be duly convicted."

Free and Slave Areas, 1850

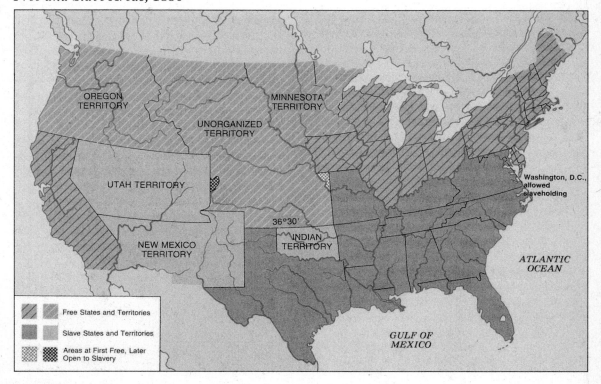

Southerners found the Wilmot Proviso particularly insulting. Nevertheless, it passed the House but met defeat in the Senate, where southerners held the balance of power. To counter it, Calhoun, again senator from South Carolina, introduced resolutions in February 1846 that argued that Congress had no right to bar slavery from any territory; since territories belonged to all the states, slave and free, all should have equal rights in them. From this position it was only a step (soon taken) to demanding that Congress guarantee the right of slaveowners to bring slaves into the territories and establish federal slave codes in the territories. Most northerners considered this proposal as repulsive as southerners found the Wilmot Proviso.

Calhoun's resolutions could never pass the northern-dominated House of Representatives, and Wilmot's Proviso had no chance in the Senate. Yet their existence threatened the Union. They were like the blades of a scissors—ineffective separately, an efficient cutting tool taken together.

To resolve the territorial problem, two compromises were offered. One, backed by President Polk, would extend the Missouri Compromise line to the Pacific. The majority of southerners were willing to go along with this scheme, but most northerners would no longer agree to the reservation of *any* new territory for slavery. The other possibility, advocated by Senator Lewis Cass of Michigan, called for organizing new territories without mention of slavery, thereby leaving it to local territorial legislatures to determine their own institutions. Cass's "popular sovereignty," known more vulgarly as "squatter sovereignty," had the superficial merit of appearing to be democratic. Its virtue for the members of Congress, however, was that it allowed them to escape the responsibility of deciding the question themselves.

The Election of 1848

Plainly the time had come, in a democracy, to go to the people. The coming presidential election seemed to provide an ideal opportunity. The opportunity was missed. The politicians of both parties hedged, fearful of losing votes in one section or another. With the issues blurred, the electorate had no real choice. The Whigs nominated Zachary Taylor for president. They chose the general despite his total lack of political sophistication and after he had flatly refused to state his opinion on any current subject. The party offered no platform.

The Democratic Party had little better to offer. The nominee was Lewis Cass, the father of popular sovereignty, but the party did not endorse that or any other solution to the territorial question. Cass was at least an experienced politician, having been governor of Michigan Territory, secretary of war, minister to France, and senator. Nevertheless, he was vain, aloof, and extremely conservative.

The Van Buren wing of the Democratic Party was now known as the "Barnburners" to call attention to their radicalism—supposedly they would burn down the barn to get rid of the rats. The Barnburners could not stomach Cass, in part because he was willing to countenance the extension of slavery into new territories and in part because he had led the swing to Polk in the 1844 Democratic Convention. Combining with the proslavery Liberty Party, they formed the Free Soil Party and nominated Van Buren.

Van Buren knew he could not be elected, but he believed the time had come to take a stand. The Free Soil Party polled nearly 300,000 votes, about 10 percent of the total. Offered a choice between the honest ignorance of Taylor and the cynical opportunism of Cass, the voters—by a narrow margin—chose the former. Taylor received 1.36 million votes against Cass's 1.22 million. Taylor carried 8 of the 15 slave states and 7 of the 15 free states, proof that the sectional issue had been avoided.

The Gold Rush

It was now clear that the question of slavery in the territories had to be faced. The discovery of gold had brought an army of prospectors into California. Armed with pickaxes and shovels, with washing pans, even with knives and spoons, they hacked and dug and sifted, each accumulating a hoard of gleaming yellow metal, some of them great, some small. During 1849, 25,000 Americans made their way to California from the East by ship; more than 55,000 others crossed the continent by overland routes. About 8,000 Mexicans,

5,000 South Americans, and uncounted Europeans joined the rush.

The rough limits of the gold country had been quickly marked out. For 150 miles and more along the western slope of the Sierra stretched the great mother lode. Along any stream or canyon or gravel bed might be a treasure in nuggets, flakes, or dust.

The impact on the region was enormous. Between 1849 and 1860 about 200,000 people, nearly all males, flocked to California. Almost overnight the Spanish-American population was reduced to the status of a minority. Disregarding justice and reason alike, the newcomers from the East referred to everyone of Latin American origin as a "greaser" and sought by law and by violence to keep them from mining for gold. Even the local Californians (now American citizens) were discriminated against. The blacks who came to California in search of gold were treated no better. As for the 150,000 Indians in California in 1849, they were almost exterminated. Only 35,000 remained in 1860.

The ethnic conflict was only part of the problem. Rough, hard men, separated from women, lusting for gold in a strange wild country where fortunes could be made in a day, gambled away in an hour, or stolen in an instant—such a lawless situation demanded the establishment of a territorial government. President Taylor, after weighing matters, in his gruff, simple-hearted way, suggested an uncomplicated answer: admit California directly as a state, letting the Californians decide for themselves about slavery. The rest of the Mexican Cession could be formed into another state.

The Californians reacted favorably to Taylor's proposal. They opposed slavery, though not for humanitarian reasons. They regarded blacks as poorly as they did Mexicans and feared that if slavery were permitted, white gold seekers would be disadvantaged. By October 1849 California had drawn up a constitution that outlawed slavery, and by December the new state government was functioning.

At this the South stood aghast. Taylor was the owner of a large plantation and more than 100 slaves. But being a military man, he was above all a nationalist; he disliked the divisiveness that partisan discussion of the issue was producing. Southerners were horrified by the president's reasoning. To admit California would destroy the balance between free and slave states in the Senate; to allow all the new land to become free would doom the South to wither in a corner of the country, surrounded by hostile free states. Should that happen, how long could slavery sustain itself even in South Carolina?

The Compromise of 1850

This was no longer a squabble over territorial governments. With the Union itself at stake, Senator Henry Clay rose to save the day. He had been as angry and frustrated when the Whigs nominated Taylor as he was when they passed him over for Harrison. Now, well beyond 70 and in ill health, he put away his ambition and his resentment and for the last time concentrated his remarkable vision on a great, multifaceted national problem. California must be free and soon admitted to the Union, but the South must have some compensation. For that matter, why not seize the opportunity to settle every outstanding sectional conflict related to slavery? Clay pondered long and hard, drew up a plan, then consulted his old Whig rival Webster and obtained his general approval. On January 29, 1850, he laid his proposal, "founded upon mutual forbearance," before the Senate. A few days later he defended it on the floor of the Senate in the last great speech of his life.

California should be brought directly into the Union as a free state, he argued. The rest of the Southwest should be organized as a territory without mention of slavery: The southerners would retain the right to bring slaves there, while in fact none would do so. The empty lands in dispute along the Texas border should be assigned to New Mexico Territory, Clay continued, but in exchange the United States should take over Texas' preannexation debts. The slave trade should be abolished in the District of Columbia (but not slavery itself), and a more effective federal fugitive slave law should be enacted and strictly enforced in the North.

Clay's proposals occasioned one of the most magnificent debates in the history of the Senate. Every important member had his say; every possible viewpoint was presented, argued, rebutted, and rehashed. The majority clearly favored some compromise. But nothing could have been accom-

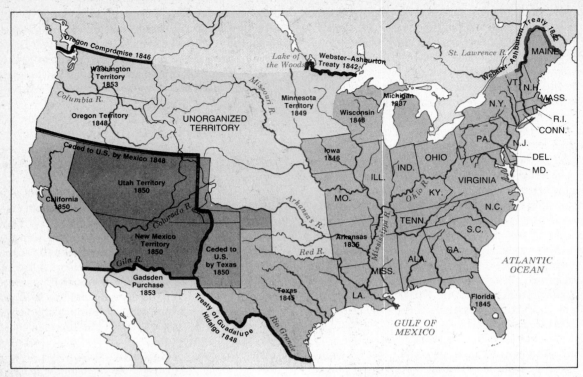

The United States at Mid-Century

plished without the death of President Taylor on July 9. Obstinate, probably resentful because few people paid him half the heed they paid Clay and other prominent members of Congress, he had insisted on his own plan to bring both California and New Mexico directly into the Union. When Vice President Millard Fillmore, who was a politician, not an ideologue, succeeded him, the deadlock between the White House and Capitol Hill was broken. Even so, each part of the compromise had to be voted on separately, for too many stubborn congressmen were willing to overturn the whole plan because they objected to specific parts of it.

The final congressional maneuvering was managed by a relative newcomer, Senator Stephen A. Douglas of Illinois, who took over when Washington's summer heat prostrated the exhausted Clay. Partisanship and economic interests complicated Douglas's problem. According to rumor, Clay had persuaded an important Virginia newspaper editor to back the compromise by

promising him a $100,000 government printing contract. This inflamed many southerners. New York merchants, fearful of the disruption of their southern business, submitted a petition bearing 25,000 names in favor of compromise, a document that had a favorable effect in the South. The prospect of the federal government's paying the debt of Texas made ardent compromisers of a horde of speculators. Between February and September, Texas bonds rose erratically from 29 to over 60, while men like W. W. Corcoran, whose Washington bank held more than $400,000 of these securities, entertained legislators and supplied lobbyists with large amounts of cash.

In the Senate and then in the House, tangled combinations pushed through the separate measures, one by one. California became the thirty-first state. The rest of the Mexican Cession was divided into two territories, New Mexico and Utah, each to be admitted to the Union when qualified, "with or without slavery as [its] constitution may prescribe." Texas received $10 million to pay off its debt in return for accepting a narrower western boundary. The slave trade in the District of Columbia was abolished as of January 1, 1851. The Fugitive Slave Act of 1793 was amended to provide for the appointment of federal commissioners with authority to issue warrants, summon posses, and compel citizens under pain of fine or imprisonment to assist in the capture of fugitives. Commissioners who decided that an accused person was a runaway received a larger fee than if they decided the black was legally free. The accused could not testify in their own defense. They were to be returned to the South without jury trial merely on the submission of an affidavit by their "owner."

Only four senators and 28 representatives voted for all these bills. The two sides did not meet somewhere in the middle, as is usual with compromises. A large number of congressmen absented themselves when parts of the settlement unpopular in their home districts came to a vote; 21 senators and 36 representatives failed to commit themselves on the new fugitive slave bill. Sen-

ator Jefferson Davis of Mississippi voted for the fugitive slave measure and the bill creating Utah Territory, remained silent on the New Mexico bill, and opposed the other measures. Senator Salmon P. Chase of Ohio, an abolitionist, supported only the admission of California and the abolition of the slave trade.

In this piecemeal fashion the Union was preserved. The credit belongs mostly to Clay, whose original conceptualization of the compromise enabled lesser minds to understand what they must do.

Everywhere sober and conservative citizens sighed with relief. When Congress met again in December, it seemed that party asperities had been buried forever. "I have determined never to make another speech on the slavery question," Senator Douglas told his colleagues. "Let us cease agitating, stop the debate, and drop the subject." If this were done, he predicted, the compromise would be accepted as a "final settlement." With this bit of wishful thinking, the year 1850 passed into history.

Milestones

1835	Fall of the Alamo		1845	Annexation of Texas
1836	Battle of San Jacinto			John L. O'Sullivan coins the expression *manifest destiny*
1837	United States recognizes the Republic of Texas		1846	Settlement of Oregon boundary dispute
1840	Richard Henry Dana, *Two Years Before the Mast*			War with Mexico
1841	Vice President John Tyler becomes president			House of Representatives adopts the Wilmot Proviso
	Preemption Act grants "squatters' rights"		1847	General Winfield Scott captures Mexico City
1842	Webster-Ashburton Treaty determines Maine boundary		1848	Discovery of gold at Sutter's Mill, California
1843	Opening of Oregon Trail			Treaty of Guadalupe Hidalgo
			1850	Compromise of 1850

Supplementary Reading

G. G. Van Deusen, **The Jacksonian Era*** (1959), provides a convenient summary of the period. On the Tyler administration, see R. J. Morgan, **A Whig Embattled** (1954). On diplomatic affairs, see P. A. Varg, **United States Foreign Rela-** **tions:** 1820–1860 (1979), and D. M. Pletcher, **The Diplomacy of Annexation** (1973). Expansionism is discussed in A. K. Weinberg, **Manifest Destiny*** (1935), and in Frederick Merk, **Manifest Destiny and Mission in American History*** (1963). Western development is treated in R. A. Billington and Martin Ridge, **The Far Western**

Frontier* (1982). J. R. Jeffrey, **Frontier Women** (1979), and J. M. Faragher, **Women and Men on the Overland Trail** (1979), describe the life of pioneers on the way west.

W. W. Freehling, **The Road to Disunion** (1990), covers political developments in this period, stressing sectional differences. For the election of 1844, see J. C. N. Paul, **Rift in the Democracy*** (1961). The best biography of Polk is C. G. Sellers, **James K. Polk** (1957–1966). N. A. Graebner, **Empire on the Paciflc** (1955), describes the factors influencing the Oregon boundary compromise.

Good accounts of the Mexican War include R. W. Johannsen, **To the Halls of Montezuma** (1987), K. J. Bauer, **The Mexican War** (1974), and J. H. Schroeder, **Mr. Polk's War**, stressing American opposition to the conflict. Marshall De Bruhl, **Sword of San Jacinto** (1993), is a biography of Sam Houston. On the discovery of gold in California, see R. W. Paul, **Mining Frontiers of the Far West** (1963), but see also R. F. Heizer and A. J. Almquist, **The Other Californians*** (1971), and R. M. Lapp, **Blacks in Gold Rush California** (1977). The fullest study of the Compromise of 1850 is Holman Hamilton, **Prologue to Conflict*** (1964), but see also R. W. Johannsen, **Stephen A. Douglas** (1973).

*Available in paperback.

CHAPTER 13

The Sections Go Their Ways

The South
The Economics of Slavery
Antebellum Plantation Life
The Sociology of Slavery
Psychological Effects of Slavery
Manufacturing in the South
The Northern Industrial Juggernaut
Self-Generated Expansion
A Nation of Immigrants
How Wage Earners Lived
Progress and Poverty
Foreign Commerce
Steam Conquers the Atlantic
Canals and Railroads
Financing the Railroads
Railroads and the Economy
Railroads and the Sectional Conflict
The Economy on the Eve of Civil War

A nation growing as rapidly as the United States in the middle decades of the 19th century changed continually in hundreds of ways. The country was developing a national economy marked by the dependence of each area on all the others, the production of goods in one region for sale in all, the increased specialization of agricultural and industrial producers, and the growth in size of the average unit of production.

The South

The South was less affected than the other sections by urbanization, by European immigration, by the transportation revolution, and by industrialization. The region remained chiefly agricultural; cotton was still king, slavery the most distinctive southern institution. But important changes were occurring. Cotton continued to march westward until, by 1859, 1.3 million of the 4.3 million bales grown in the United States came from beyond the Mississippi. In the Upper South, Virginia held its place as the leading tobacco producer, but states beyond the Appalachians were raising more than half the crop. The older sections of Maryland, Virginia, and North Carolina shifted to the kind of diversified farming usually associated with the Northeast. By 1849 the wheat crop of Virginia was worth twice as much as the tobacco crop.

Edmund Ruffin introduced the use of marl, an earth rich in calcium, to counteract the acidity of worn-out tobacco fields. Ruffin discovered that dressings of marl, combined with the use of fertilizers and with proper drainage and plowing methods, doubled and even tripled the yield of corn and wheat. In the 1840s some southerners began to import Peruvian guano, a high-nitrogen fertilizer of bird droppings, which also increased yields. Others experimented with contour plowing to control erosion, with improved breeds of livestock, and with new types of plows and other agricultural machinery.

The Economics of Slavery

The increased importance of cotton in the South strengthened the hold of slavery on the region. The price of slaves rose until by the 1850s a prime field hand was worth as much as $1,800, roughly three times the cost in the 1820s. In the cotton fields of the Deep South slaves brought several hundred dollars per head more than in the older regions; thus the tendency to sell them "down the river" continued. Mississippi took in some 10,000 slaves a year throughout the period; by 1830 the black population of the state exceeded the white. Slave trading became a big business. There were about 50 dealers in Charleston in the 1850s, and 200 in New Orleans.

As blacks became more expensive, the ownership of slaves became more concentrated. In 1860 only about 46,000 of the 8 million white residents of the slave states had as many as 20. When one calculates the cost of 20 slaves and the land to keep them profitably occupied, it is easy to understand why this figure is so small. On the eve of the Civil War only one family in four owned any slaves at all.

There were few genuine economies of scale in southern agriculture. Small farmers grew the staple crops, and many of them owned a few slaves, often working beside them in the fields. These yeomen farmers were hardworking, self-reliant, and moderately prosperous, quite unlike the "poor white trash" of the pine barrens and the remote valleys of the Appalachians who scratched a meager subsistence from substandard soils and lived in ignorance and squalor.

Well-managed plantations yielded annual profits of 10 percent and more, and in general, money invested in southern agriculture earned at least a modest return. Considering the way the work force was exploited by the masters, this is not surprising. However, the South failed to develop locally owned marketing and transportation facilities, and for this slavery was at least partly responsible. New York capitalists gradually came to control much of the South's cotton from the moment it was picked, and a large percentage of the crop found its way into New York warehouses before being sold to manufacturers. The same middlemen supplied most of the foreign goods that the planters purchased with their cotton earnings.

Southerners complained about this state of affairs but did little to correct it. Capital tied up in the ownership of labor could not be invested in anything else, and social pressures in the South militated against investment in trade and commerce. Ownership of land and slaves yielded a kind of psychic income not available to any middleman. As one British visitor pointed out, the southern blacks were "a nonconsuming class." Still more depressing, under slavery the reservoir of intelligence and skill that the blacks represented was almost entirely wasted.

Antebellum Plantation Life

A medium-to-large plantation employing 20 or more slaves was more like a small village than a northern-type agricultural unit, but at the same time it resembled more a self-sufficient colonial farm than a 19th century commercial operation. In addition to the master's house with its complement of barns and stables, there would usually be a kitchen, a smoke house, a wash house, a home for the overseer should one be employed, perhaps a schoolhouse, a gristmill, a forge, and of course the slave quarters.

Slaveholding families were also quite different from northern families of similar status because of their "peculiar institution." Husbands and wives did not function in *separate* spheres to nearly the same extent, though their individual functions were different and gender related.

Although planter families purchased their clothing, furniture, and china, as well as products such as sewing machines, books, and musical instruments, plantations were busy centers of household manufacture, turning out most of the clothing of slaves except for shoes, and the everyday clothing of their own children, along with bedding and other textiles. Spinning, weaving, and sewing were women's work, both for whites and blacks. Nearly all the food consumed was raised on the land; only tea and coffee and a few other food items were commonly purchased.

The master was in general charge and his word was law, but his wife nearly always had immense responsibilities. Running the household meant supervising the servants (and punishing them when necessary), nursing the sick, planning meals, and seeing to the education of her own children and the training of young slaves. It could also involve running the entire plantation on the frequent occasions when her husband was away on business. At the same time, her role entailed being refined, graceful, and supposedly untroubled by worldly affairs. Most slaveholding women had to learn all these things by doing; in general, unmarried "young ladies" had few responsibilities beyond caring for their own rooms and persons and perhaps such "ladylike" tasks as arranging flowers.

The majority of the slaves of both sexes labored on the land from dawn to dusk. Household servants and artisans might also be called on for such labor when needed. Slave women were expected to cook for their own families and do other chores after working in the fields.

Children, free and slave, were cared for by slaves, the former by household servants, the latter usually by an elderly woman. Infants were

Profits from cash crops allowed successful planters to build graceful homes like this one on the Mississippi River. The "Big House" in which the master and his family lived, might be a splendid mansion that offered imported luxuries, or a much simpler, plain wooden dwelling.

brought to their mothers in the fields for nursing several times a day, for after a month or two at most, slave mothers were required to go back to work. Until they were 6 or 7, slave children were given only small tasks such as feeding the chickens or minding a smaller child. Black and white youngsters played together and were often cared for by the same nursemaid.

Slave cabins were simple and crude; most consisted of a single room, dark, with a fireplace for cooking and heat. Usually the flooring was raised above ground level. Though certainly Spartan, these quarters compared favorably with those of European peasants of the time and the poorest white American farmers. And as Elizabeth Fox-Genovese explains in *Within the Plantation Household* (1988), they were "primarily places to sleep, take shelter, and eat the last meal of the day," and "did not harbor the real life of slave families, much less the slave community."

The Sociology of Slavery

It is difficult to generalize about the peculiar institution because so much depended on the individual master's behavior. The plantation environment forced the two races to live in close proximity. From this circumstance could rise the most paradoxical human relationships. One planter, using the appropriate pseudonym Clod Thumper, might write: "Africans are nothing but brutes, and they will love you better for whipping, whether they deserve it or not." Another, describing a slave named Bug, might say: "No one knows but myself what feeling I have for him. Black as he is we were raised together." Such diametrically conflicting sentiments often existed within the same person. Certainly almost all white southerners had no difficulty exploiting the labor of slaves for whom they felt genuine affection.

The United States was the only nation in the Western Hemisphere where the slave population grew by natural increase. After the ending of the slave trade in 1808, the black population increased at nearly the same rate as the white. Put differently, during the entire period from the founding of Jamestown to the Civil War only a little more than half a million slaves were imported. Yet in 1860 there were about 4 million blacks in the country. Surely this proves that American slaves were not driven to extinction. Most owners provided adequate clothing, housing, and food for their slaves, for only a fool or a sadist would fail to take care of such valuable property. But the slave diet (chiefly corn and hog fat) was deficient in protein, and this could make slaves disease-prone. Infant mortality among slaves was twice the white rate, life expectancy at least five years less.

Slaves were without rights; they developed a distinctive way of life by attempting to resist oppression and injustice while adjusting to the system. Their marriages had no legal status, but their partnerships seem to have been as loving and stable as those of their masters and they were acutely conscious of family relationships and responsibilities. Slave religion, a form of Christianity tinctured with African survivals, seemed to most slaveowners a useful instrument for teaching meekness and resignation and for providing harmless emotional release, which it sometimes was and did. However, religious meetings provided slaves with the opportunity to organize, which sometimes led to riotous ways of resisting white domination. Religion also sustained the slaves' sense of their own worth as beings made in the image of God, and it taught them, therefore, that while human beings can be enslaved in body, their spirits cannot be enslaved without their consent.

Nearly every white observer claimed that slaves were congenitally lazy; George Washington, for example, wrote that "when an overlooker's back is turned, the most of them will slight their work, or be idle altogether." Sarah Gayle convinced herself that her "indulgence" made her slaves "idle and full of complaints," a charge that her description of what they actually did totally disproves. If the typical slave was indeed lazy, it can be explained as a rational response to forced, uncompensated labor. "Laziness" was also a reflection of a peasantlike view of the world, one that was a product of their surroundings, not of their servile status. The historian Eugene D. Genovese says that owners might have liked their slaves to behave like clock-punching factory workers, but plantations were not factories, and no one, least of all the masters, punched a clock. "Do as I say, not as I do," is not an effective way of teaching anything. Moreover, it must be remembered that under slavery the "overlooker's back" was rarely turned. Slaves worked long and hard.

Most whites persuaded themselves that the blacks accepted the system without resentment and indeed preferred slavery to the uncertainties

of freedom. There was much talk about "loyal and faithful servants."

As slaves rose in price and as northern opposition to the institution grew more vocal, the system hardened perceptibly. Southerners made much of the danger of insurrection. When a plot was uncovered or a revolt took place, instant and savage reprisals resulted. In 1822, after the conspiracy of Denmark Vesey was exposed by informers, 37 slaves were executed and another 30-odd deported, although no overt act of rebellion had occurred. After a rising in Louisiana, 16 blacks were decapitated, their heads left to rot on poles along the Mississippi as a grim warning.

The Nat Turner revolt in Virginia in 1831 was the most sensational of the slave uprisings; 57 whites lost their lives before it was suppressed. Southerners treated runaways almost as brutally as rebels, though they posed no real threat to whites. The authorities tracked down fugitives with bloodhounds and subjected captives to merciless lashings.

After Nat Turner's uprising, interest in doing away with slavery simply vanished in the white South. The southern states made it increasingly difficult for masters to free their slaves. During 1859 only about 3,000 in a slave population of nearly 4 million were given their freedom.

Slavery goes a long way toward explaining why the South was so rural and why it had so little industry. Blacks were much harder to control in cities, and, as the historian Barbara Jeanne Fields has shown, there was a "profound basis for antagonism between slavery and urban development."

Psychological Effects of Slavery

The injustice of slavery needs no proof; less obvious is the fact that it had a corrosive effect on the personalities of southerners, slave and free alike. The system bore heavily on all slaves' sense of their own worth. Some found the condition absolutely unbearable. These individuals became the habitual runaways who collected whip scars like medals; the "loyal" servants who struck out in rage against a master, knowing that the result would be quick and certain death; the leaders of slave revolts.

Denmark Vesey of South Carolina, even after buying his freedom, could not stomach the subservience demanded of slaves by the system. For years he preached resistance to his fellows, drawing his texts from the Declaration of Independence and the Bible and promising help from black Haiti. He planned his uprising for five years, patiently working out the details, only to see it aborted at the last moment when a few of his recruits lost their nerve and betrayed him. For Denmark Vesey death was probably preferable to living with such rage as his soul contained.

Yet Veseys were rare. Most slaves appeared, if not contented, at least resigned to their fate. Many seemed even to accept the whites' evaluation of their inherent abilities and place in society. Of course in most instances it is impossible to know whether or not this apparent subservience was feigned in order to avoid trouble.

Slaves had strong family and group attachments and a complex culture, maintained, so to speak, under the noses of their masters. By a mixture of subterfuge, accommodation, and passive resistance, they erected subtle defenses against exploitation, achieving a sense of community that helped sustain the psychic integrity of individuals. But slavery discouraged independence of judgment and self-reliance. These qualities are difficult enough to develop in human beings under the best circumstances; when every element in white society encouraged slaves to let others do their thinking for them, to avoid questioning the status quo, to lead a simple, animal existence, many did so willingly enough. Was this not slavery's greatest shame?

Slavery also warped the whites. Professor Fox-Genovese has shown how southern whites developed contradictory stereotypes of slave nature. Black males were typecast either as "Sambos" (lazy and subservient) or "Bucks" (superpotent and aggressive), females as "Mammies" (nurturing and faithful) or "Jezebels" (wanton and seductive). If "Sambo" was lazy there was nothing wrong in whipping him to make him work, but by picturing black men as sexual threats to white women, slaveowners avoided facing the fact that they could and often did take advantage of their power to avail themselves of black women. The harm done to the slaves by such mental distortions is obvious. More obscure is the effect on the masters: self-indulgence is perhaps only contemptible; self-delusion is pitiable and ultimately destructive.

Probably the large majority of owners respected the most fundamental personal rights of their slaves. For those of exceptional character the responsibilties of ownership could be enobling, and as far as sexual behavior is concerned, there are countless known cases of lasting relationships based on love and mutual respect between owners and what law and the community defined as their "property." But for hotheads, alcoholics, and others with psychological problems, the power could be brutalizing. Slavery provided the weak, the shiftless, and the unsuccessful with a scapegoat that made their own miserable state easier to bear but harder to escape. Even those whites who abhorred slavery sometimes let it corrupt their thinking: "I consider the labor of a breeding woman as no object, and that a child raised every 2 years is of more profit than the crop of the best laboring man." This cold calculation came from the pen of the author of the Declaration of Independence.

Manufacturing in the South

Although the temper of southern society discouraged business and commercial activity, considerable manufacturing developed. Small flour and lumber mills flourished. Iron and coal were mined in Virginia, Kentucky, and Tennessee. The availability of the raw material and the abundance of waterpower along the southern Appalachian slopes made it possible to manufacture textiles profitably. By 1825 a thriving factory was functioning at Fayetteville, North Carolina, and soon others sprang up elsewhere in North Carolina and in adjoining states.

William Gregg's factory at Graniteville, South Carolina established in 1846, was a consistent moneymaker. An able propagandist as well as a good businessman, Gregg saw the textile business not only as a source of profit, but also as a device for improving the lot of the South's poor whites. He worked hard to weaken the southern prejudice against manufacturing and made his plant a model of benevolent paternalism similar to that of the early mills of Lowell. As with every other industry, however, southern textile manufacturing amounted to very little when compared with that of the North. Gregg employed only about 300 textile workers in 1850, the whole state of South Carolina fewer than 900. Lowell, Massachusetts, had more spindles turning in 1860 than did the entire South. Less than 15 percent of all the goods manufactured in the United States in 1860 came from the South; the region did not really develop an industrial society. Its textile manufacturers depended on the North for machinery, for skilled workers, for financing, and for insurance.

The Northern Industrial Juggernaut

The most obvious change in the North in the decades before the Civil War was the rapid growth of industry. The best estimates suggest that immediately after the War of 1812 the United States was manufacturing annually less than $200 million worth of goods. In 1859 the northeastern states alone produced $1.27 billion of the national total of almost $2 billion.

Manufacturing expanded in so many directions that it is difficult to summarize its evolution. The factory system made great strides. The development of rich anthracite coalfields in Pennsylvania was particularly important in this connection. The coal could be floated cheaply on canals to convenient sites and used to produce both heat for smelting and metalworking and steam power to drive machinery. Steam permitted greater flexibility in locating factories and in organizing work within them, and since waterpower was already being used to capacity, steam was essential for the expansion of output.

American industry displayed a remarkable receptivity to technological change. A society in flux put a premium on resourcefulness; an environment that offered so much freedom to the individual encouraged experimentation. The expanding market inspired businessmen to use new techniques. With skilled labor always in short supply, the pressure to substitute machines for trained hands was great.

In the 1820s a foreign visitor noted: "Everything new is quickly introduced here, and all the latest inventions. . . . The moment an American hears the word 'invention' he pricks up his ears." Twenty years later a Frenchman wrote: "If they continue to work with the same ardor . . . all the mountains will be flattened, the valleys filled, all matter rendered productive." By 1850 the United States led the world in the manufacture of goods that required the use of precision instruments; American clocks, pistols, rifles, and locks were outstanding.

The American exhibits at the London Crystal Palace Exhibition of 1851 so impressed the British that they sent two special commissions to the United States to study manufacturing practices. The British visitors were amazed by the lock and clock factories of New England and by the plants where screws, files, and similar metal objects were turned out in volume by automatic machinery.

Invention alone does not account for the industrial advance. Every year new natural resources were discovered and made available by the westward march of settlement, and the expansion of agriculture produced an ever larger supply of raw materials for the mills and factories. Of the ten leading industries in 1860, eight (flour milling, cotton textiles, lumber, shoes, men's clothing, leather, woolen goods, and liquor) relied on farm products for their raw materials.

In the 1850s the earlier prejudice against corporations began to break down; by the end of the decade the northern and northwestern states had all passed general incorporation laws. Of course the corporate device made possible larger accumulations of capital.

Industrial growth caused an increase in the demand for labor. The effects, however, were mixed. Skilled artisans, technicians, and toolmakers earned good wages and found it relatively easy to set themselves up first as independent craftsmen, later as small manufacturers. The expanding frontier drained off much agricultural labor that might otherwise have been attracted to industry, and the thriving new towns of the West absorbed large numbers of eastern artisans of every kind. At the same time, the pay of an unskilled worker was never enough to support a family decently, and the new machines weakened the bargaining power of artisans by making skill less important.

Many other forces acted as stimulants to manufacturing. Immigration increased rapidly. An

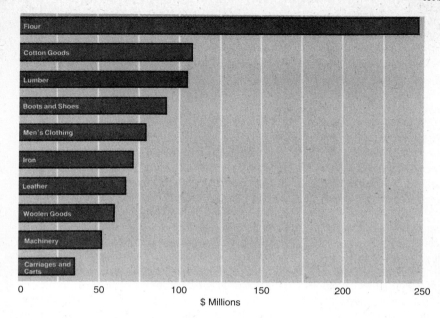

Flour
Cotton Goods
Lumber
Boots and Shoes
Men's Clothing
Iron
Leather
Woolen Goods
Machinery
Carriages and Carts

0   50   100   150   200   250

$ Millions

Ten Leading Manufactured Products, 1860

avalanche of strong backs and willing hands and thousands of keen minds descended on the country from Europe. European investors poured large sums into the booming American economy, and the savings of millions of Americans and the hoard of new California gold added to the supply of capital. Improvements in transportation, the growth of the population, the absence of internal tariff barriers, and the relatively high per capita wealth of the people all meant an ever-expanding market for manufactured goods.

Self-Generated Expansion

The pace of the advance is best explained by the many interactions that industrial activity produced. The cotton textile business was clearly the most important example. Samuel Slater built his first machines in his own little plant, but soon the industry spawned dozens of companies devoted to the manufacture of looms, spinning frames, and other machines. They in turn stimulated the growth of machine-tool production, metalworking companies, and eventually the mining and refining of iron.

Examples abound. The invention of the sewing machine in 1846 by Elias Howe (who got his early training in a Lowell cotton-machine factory) resulted in the rapid growth of the ready-made clothing industry. The sewing machine also revolutionized the shoe industry, speeding the trend toward factory production and triggering the same kind of secondary growth that characterized textile manufacturing. The new agricultural machinery business, besides stimulating other industries, made possible a huge expansion of farm production, which stimulated economic growth still more.

A Nation of Immigrants

Rapid industrialization influenced American life in countless ways, none more significant than its effect on the character of the work force and consequently on the structure of society. The jobs created by industrial expansion attracted European immigrants by the tens of thousands. It is a truism that America is a nation of immigrants—even the ancestors of the Indians came to the New World from Asia. But only with the establishment of the independent United States did the word *immigrant*, meaning a foreign-born resident, come into existence.

The flow of newcomers was slow for several decades, first because of European wars and then because of bad times following the defeat of Napoleon. Fewer than 300,000 people entered the United States between 1775 and 1820. As late as

1840 less than 8 percent of the population was foreign born or the children of immigrants. Then 1.5 million people came to the United States in the 1840s and 2.6 million in the 1850s. In proportion to the population, this was the heaviest immigration in American history.

Most of this human tide came from two countries, Ireland and Germany. This was especially true between 1847 and 1854, when the Irish potato blight and a series of crop failures in Germany drove thousands to try their luck in America. Many thousands of substantial Germans and Scandinavians pushed on directly into the western regions.

But the poorer immigrants could not afford to do this; farming required capital that the majority did not have. The Irish in particular tended to settle in the large eastern seaports. For the first time the nation had a culturally distinctive working class with its own habits and values. Irish immigrants were so desperately poor that they would accept whatever wage employers offered them. They thus roused resentment among native workers, resentment exacerbated by the unfamiliarity of the Irish with city ways and by their Roman Catholic faith, which the Protestant majority associated with Old World authoritarianism and corruption.

The Irish, in turn, developed prejudices against blacks, with whom they often competed for work. And of course blacks responded with equal bitterness. "Every hour sees us elbowed out of some employment to make room for some newly arrived emigrant from the Emerald Isle, whose hunger and color entitle him to special favor," one of them complained. Antiblack prejudice was less noticeable among other immigrant groups but by no means absent.

Social and racial rivalries aside, unskilled immigrants caused serious disruptions of economic patterns wherever they appeared. Their absorption into the factories of New England speeded the disintegration of the system of hiring young women. Already competition and technical advances in the textile industry were increasing the pace of the machines and reducing the number of skilled workers needed to run them. Fewer young farm women were willing to work under these conditions. Recent immigrants, who required less "coddling" and who seemed to provide the mills

with a "permanent" working force, replaced the women. By 1860 Irish immigrants alone made up more than 50 percent of the labor force in the New England mills.

How Wage Earners Lived

The influx of immigrants does not entirely explain the low standard of living of industrial workers during this period. Low wages and the crowding that resulted from the swift expansion of city populations produced slums that would make the most noisome modern ghetto seem a paradise. A Boston investigation in the late 1840s described one district as "a perfect hive of human beings . . . huddled together like brutes." In New York tens of thousands of the poor lived in dark, rank cellars, those in the waterfront districts often invaded by high tides. Tenement houses like great gloomy prisons rose back to back, each with many windowless rooms and often without heat or even running water.

Out of doors, city life for the poor was almost equally squalid. Slum streets were littered with garbage and trash. Recreational facilities were almost nonexistent; work on Central Park in New York City, the country's first important urban park, did not begin until the mid-1850s. Police and fire protection were pitifully inadequate. "Urban problems" were less critical than a century later only because they affected a smaller part of the population; for those who experienced them they were, all too often, crushing. There were child beggars in New York City who had to scavenge for food and who took shelter at night in coal bins and empty barrels.

In 1851 the New York *Tribune* published a minimum weekly budget for a family of five. The budget, which allowed nothing for recreation, savings, medical bills, or other amenities—it did include 12 cents a week for newspapers—came to $10.37. Since the weekly pay of a factory hand seldom reached $5, the wives and children of most workers labored in the factories merely to survive. And child labor in the 1850s differed fundamentally from child labor in the 1820s. The pace of the machines had become much faster by then, the working environment more depressing.

Nevertheless, skilled workers improved their lot somewhat in the 1840s and 1850s. The working day declined from about 12.5 hours to 10 or 11 hours. Most states enacted effective mechanic's lien laws, giving workers first call on the assets of bankrupt and defaulting employers, and the Massachusetts court's decision in the case of *Commonwealth* v. *Hunt* (1842), establishing the legality of labor unions, became a judicial landmark when other state courts followed the precedent.

Progress and Poverty

Any investigation of American society before the Civil War reveals a paradox that is obvious but difficult to resolve. The United States was a land of opportunity, a democratic society with a prosperous, expanding economy and few class distinctions. Its people had a high standard of living in comparison with the citizens of European countries. Yet within this rich, confident nation there existed a class of miserably underpaid and depressed unskilled workers, mostly immigrants, who were worse off materially than nearly any southern slave.

The middle-class majority seemed indifferent to or at best unaware of these conditions. Some skilled workers protected their own interests by organizing trade unions, but did not consider themselves perment members of any wage-earning class. To many, working for wages seemed almost un-American, a rejection of the republican values of freedom asnd independence that had triumphed in the Revolution.

There were reformers who conducted investigations, published exposés, and labored to help the victims of urbanization and industrialization. They achieved very little. Great fires burned in these decades to release the incredible energies of America. The poor were the ashes, sifting down silent and unnoticed beneath the dazzle and the smoke. Although the industrial revolution was making the United States the richest nation in the world, it was also creating, as the historian Robert H. Bremner has said, "a poverty problem, novel in kind and alarming in size." Industrialization produced poverty (in Marxian terminology, a proletarian class) and an aristocracy of capitalists. Ten-

ements sprang up cheek by jowl with the urban palaces of the new rich and the tree-lined streets of the prosperous middle class.

Economic opportunities were great, taxation minimal. Little wonder that as the generations passed, the rich got richer. Industrialization accelerated the process and, by stimulating the immigration of masses of poor workers, skewed the social balance still further. Society became more stratified, differences in wealth and status among citizens greater. But the ideology of egalitarian democracy held its own. This situation endured for the rest of the century, and in some respects it still endures.

Foreign Commerce

Changes in the pattern of foreign commerce were less noticeable than those in manufacturing but nevertheless significant. After increasing erratically during the 1820s and 1830s, both imports and exports leaped forward in the next 20 years. The nation remained primarily an exporter of raw materials and an importer of manufactured goods, and in most years it imported more than it exported. Cotton continued to be the most valuable export, in 1860 accounting for a record $191 million of total exports of $333 million. Despite America's own thriving industry, textiles still held the lead among imports, with iron products second. As in earlier days, Great Britain was both the best customer of the United States and its leading supplier.

The success of sailing packets, those "square-riggers on schedule," greatly facilitated the movement of passengers and freight. Fifty-two packets were operating between New York and Europe by 1845, and many more plied between New York and other American ports. The packets accelerated the growing tendency for trade to concentrate in New York and to a lesser extent in Philadelphia, Baltimore, and New Orleans. The commerce of Boston and many smaller towns, which had flourished in earlier days, now languished.

The increase in the volume and value of trade and its concentration at larger ports had a marked effect on the construction of ships. By the 1850s the average vessel was three times the size of those built 30 years earlier. Startling improvements in design, culminating in the long, sleek, white-winged clipper ships, made possible speeds previously undreamed of. Appearing just in time to supply the need for fast transportation to the California gold fields, the clippers cut sailing time around the Horn to San Francisco from five or six months to three, the record of 89 days being held jointly by the *Andrew Jackson* and by Donald McKay's famous *Flying Cloud.* Another McKay-designed clipper, aptly named *Champion of the Seas,* once logged 465 nautical miles in 24 hours. To achieve such speeds, cargo capacity had to be sacrificed, making clippers uneconomical for carrying bulky produce. But for specialty goods, in their brief heydey the clippers were unsurpassed.

Steam Conquers the Atlantic

The reign of the clipper ship was short. Like so many other things, ocean commerce was being mechanized. Steamships conquered the high seas more slowly than the rivers because early models were unsafe in rough waters and uneconomical. However, by the late 1840s steamships were cap-

turing most of the passenger traffic, mail contracts, and first-class freight. By 1860 the Atlantic had been crossed in less than ten days.

The steamship, and especially the iron ship, which had greater cargo-carrying capacity and was stronger and less costly to maintain, took away the advantages that American shipbuilders had held since colonial times. American lumber was cheap, but the British excelled in iron technology. Although the United States invested about $14.5 million in subsidies for the shipping industry, the funds were not employed intelligently and did little good. In 1858 government aid to shipping was ended.

The combination of competition, government subsidy, and technological advance drove down shipping rates. Between the mid-twenties and the mid-fifties the cost of moving a pound of cotton from New York to Liverpool fell from one cent to about one-third of a cent. Transatlantic passengers could obtain the best accommodations on the fastest ships for under $200 and good accommodations on slower packets for as little as $75.

Rates were especially low for European emigrants willing to travel to America on cargo vessels. Conditions on these ships were crowded and foul. Frequently epidemics took a fearful toll among steerage passengers. Yet without this

Commerce on the lower Mississippi depended heavily on steamboats because railroads were far less extensive in the South than in the North.

cheap means of transportation, thousands of poor immigrants would simply have remained at home. Bargain freight rates also help explain the clamor of American manufacturers for high tariffs, for transportation costs added relatively little to the price of European goods.

Canals and Railroads

Another dramatic change was the shift in the direction of the nation's internal commerce and its immense increase. From the time of the first settlers in the Mississippi Valley, the Great River had controlled the flow of goods from farm to market. The completion of the Erie Canal in 1825 heralded a shift, speeded by the feverish canal construction of the following decade. In the late 1830s the bulk of the trade of the valley still flowed down to New Orleans, but each year saw more western produce moving to market through the canals. The volume of western commerce over the Erie in 1851 amounted to more than 20 times what it had been in 1836, whereas the value of western goods reaching New Orleans in this period increased only two and a half times.

The expanding traffic and New York's enormous share of it caused businessmen in other eastern cities whose canal projects had been unsuccessful to respond promptly when a new means of transport, the railroad, became available. The first railroads were built in England in the 1820s. In 1830 the first American line, the ambitiously named Baltimore and Ohio Railroad, carried in its first year 80,000 passengers over a 13-mile stretch of track. By 1833 Charleston, South Carolina, had a line reaching 136 miles to Hamburg, on the Savannah River. Two years later the cars began rolling on the Boston and Worcester Railroad. The Panic of 1837 slowed construction, but by 1840 the United States had 3,328 miles of track, equal to the canal mileage and nearly double the railroad mileage of all Europe.

The first railroads did not compete with the canals for intersectional traffic. The through connections needed to move goods economically over great distances materialized slowly. Of the 6,000 miles of track operating in 1848, nearly all

lay east of the Appalachians, and little of it had been coordinated into railroad systems.

Engineering problems held back growth. Steep grades and sharp curves—unavoidable in many parts of the country if the cost of the roads were not to be prohibitive—required more powerful and flexible engines than yet existed. Sparks from wood-burning locomotives caused fires. Wooden rails topped with strap iron wore out quickly and broke loose under the weight and vibration of heavy cars. In time the iron T-rail and the use of crossties set in loose gravel to reduce vibration increased the durability of the tracks and made possible heavier, more efficient equipment. Modifications in the design of locomotives enabled the trains to negotiate sharp curves. Engines that could burn hard coal appeared, thereby eliminating the danger of starting fires along the tracks and reducing fuel costs.

Between 1848 and 1852 railroad mileage nearly doubled. Three years later it had doubled again, and by 1860 the nation had 30,636 miles of track. During this extraordinary burst of activity, four companies drove lines of gleaming iron from the Atlantic seaboard to the great interior valley. In 1851 the Erie, longest road in the world with 537 miles of track, linked the Hudson River north of New York City with Dunkirk on Lake Erie. Late the next year the Baltimore and Ohio reached the Ohio River at Wheeling, and in 1853 a banker named Erastus Corning consolidated eight short lines connecting Albany and Buffalo to form the New York Central. Finally, in 1858 the Pennsylvania Railroad completed a line across the mountains from Philadelphia to Pittsburgh. By 1855 passengers could travel from Chicago or St. Louis to the East Coast at a cost ranging from about $20 to $30, the trip taking, with luck, less than 48 hours. A generation earlier such a trip required two to three weeks.

Financing the Railroads

Railroad building required immense amounts of labor and capital at a time when many other demands for these resources existed. Immigrants or (in the South) slaves did most of the heavy work.

Raising the necessary money proved a more complex task.

Private investors supplied about three-quarters of the money invested in railroads before 1860. Much of this capital came from local merchants and businessmen and from farmers along the proposed routes. Funds were easy to raise because subscribers seldom had to lay out the full price of their stock at one time; instead they were subject to periodic "calls" for a percentage of their commitment as construction progressed. If the railroad made money, much of the additional mileage could be paid for out of earnings from the first sections built. The Utica and Schenectady Railroad, one of the lines that became part of the New York Central, was capitalized in 1833 at $2 million (20,000 shares at $100). Only $75 per share was ever called; in 1844 the track had been completed, shares were selling at $129, and shareholders were receiving handsome cash dividends.

The Utica and Schenectady was a short railroad in a rich territory; for less favorably situated lines, stocks were hard to sell. Of the lines connecting the seaboard with the Middle West, the New York Central alone needed no public aid, chiefly because it ran through prosperous, well-populated country and across level terrain. The others were all "mixed enterprises," drawing about half their capital from state and local governments, the rest from bonds sold to American and foreign investors.

Public aid took many forms. Towns, counties, and the states themselves lent money to railroads and invested in their stock. Special privileges, such as exemption from taxation and the right to condemn property, were often granted, and in a few cases states built and operated railroads as public corporations.

As with earlier internal improvement proposals, federal financial aid to railroads was usually blocked in Congress by a combination of eastern and southern votes. But in 1850 a scheme for granting federal lands to the states to build a line from Lake Michigan to the Gulf of Mexico passed both houses. The main beneficiary was the Illinois Central Railroad, which received a 200-foot right of way and alternate strips of land along the track one mile wide and six miles deep, a total of almost 2.6 million acres. By mortgaging this land and by selling portions of it to farmers, the Illinois Cen-

A pre–Civil War lithograph of Chicago viewed from the lakefront shows its importance as the railroad center for the Midwest.

tral raised nearly all the $23.4 million it spent on construction. The success of this operation led to additional grants of almost 20 million acres in the 1850s, benefiting more than 40 railroads. Far larger federal grants were made after the Civil War, when the transcontinental lines were built.

Frequently the capitalists who promoted railroads were more concerned with making money out of the construction of the lines than with operating them. The banker Erastus Corning was a good railroad executive; his lines were well maintained and efficiently run. Yet he was also Mayor of Albany, an important figure in New York and national politics, and a manufacturer of iron. He accepted no salary as president of the Utica and Schenectady, "asking only that he have the privilege of supplying all the rails, running gear, tools and other iron and steel articles used." When he could not himself produce rails of the proper quality, he purchased them in England, charging the railroad a commission for his services.

Corning's actions led to stockholder complaints, and a committee was appointed to investigate. He managed to control this group easily enough, but it did report that "the practice of buying articles for the use of the Railroad Company from its own officers might in time come to lead to abuses of great magnitude." The prediction proved all too accurate in the generation following the Civil War.

Corning was basically honest; others in the railroad business were not. Some issued stock to themselves without paying for it and sold it to gullible investors. Others used inside information to make killings in the stock market, still others set up special construction companies and awarded themselves contracts at inflated prices. At the same time that the country was developing a truly national economy it was also producing its first really big time crooks.

Railroads and the Economy

The effects of so much railroad construction were profound. While the main reason that farmers put more land under the plow was an increase in the price of agricultural products, the railroad helped determine just what land was utilized and how profitably it could be farmed.

Much of the fertile prairie through which the Illinois Central ran had been available for settlement for many years before 1850, but development had been slow because it was remote from navigable waters and had no timber. In 1840 the three counties immediately northeast of Springfield had a population of about 8,500. They produced about 59,000 bushels of wheat and 690,000 bushels of corn. In the next decade the region grew slowly by the standards of that day: The three counties had about 14,000 inhabitants in 1850 and produced 71,000 bushels of wheat and 2.2 million bushels of corn. Then came the railroad and with it an agricultural revolution. By 1860 the population of the three counties had soared to over 38,000, wheat production had topped 550,000 bushels, and corn 5.7 million bushels. "Land-grant" railroads such as the Illinois Central stimulated agricultural expansion by advertising their lands widely and selling farm sites at low rates on liberal terms.

Access to world markets gave the farmers of the upper Mississippi Valley an incentive to increase output. Land was plentiful and cheap, but wages rose sharply, especially after 1850. New tools and machines appeared in time to ease the labor shortage. First came the steel plowshare, invented by John Deere, a Vermont-born blacksmith who had settled in Illinois in 1854. The prairie sod was tough and sticky, but Deere's smooth metal plows cut through it easily. By 1857 he was selling 10,000 plows a year.

Still more important was the perfection of the mechanical reaper. The major figure in the development of the reaper was Cyrus Hall McCormick. McCormick's horsedrawn reaper bent a swath of grain against the cutting knife and then deposited it neatly on a platform, whence it could easily be raked into windrows. With this machine, two workers could cut 14 times as much wheat as with scythes. By 1860 nearly 80,000 reapers had been sold; their efficiency helps explain why wheat output rose by nearly 75 percent in the 1850s.

The railroad had an equally powerful impact on American cities. The eastern seaports benefited, and so did countless intermediate centers such as Buffalo and Cincinnati. By 1855 Chicago was terminal for 2,200 miles of track and controlled the commerce of an imperial domain.

The railroads, like the textile industry, stimulated other kinds of economic activity. They transformed agriculture, as we have seen; both real estate values and buying and selling of land increased whenever the iron horse puffed into a new district. The railroads spurred regional concentration of industry and an increase in the size of business units. Their insatiable need for capital stimulated the growth of investment banking. The complexity of their operations made them, as the historian Alfred D. Chandler, Jr., writes, "the first modern business enterprises," the first to employ large numbers of salaried managers and to develop "a large internal organizational structure with carefully defined lines of responsibility."

Although they apparently did not have much effect on general manufacturing before the Civil War, railroad construction consumed nearly half the nation's output of bar and sheet iron in 1860. Probably more labor and more capital were occupied in economic activities resulting from the development of railroads than in the railway business itself—another way of saying that the railroads were immensely valuable internal improvements.

The proliferation of trunk lines and the competition of the canal system (for many products the slowness of canal transportation was not a serious handicap) led to a sharp decline in freight and passenger rates. Periodically, railroads engaged in "wars" to capture business. At times a person

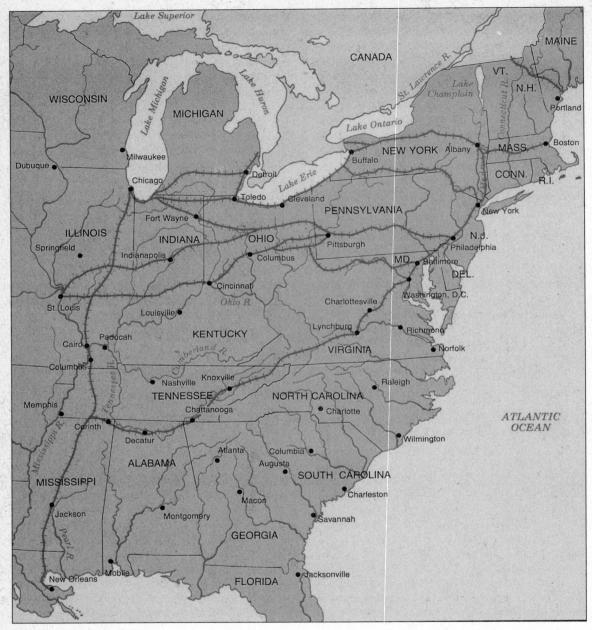

Primary Railroads, 1860

could travel from New York to Buffalo for as little as $4; anthracite was being shipped from the Pennsylvania mines to the coast for $1.50 a ton.

Cheap transportation had a revolurionary effect on western agriculture. Farmers in Iowa could now raise grain to feed the factory workers of Lowell and even of Manchester, England. Two-thirds of the meat consumed in New York City was soon arriving by rail from beyond the Appalachians. Success bred success for farmers and for the railroads. Profits earned carrying wheat enabled the railroads to build feeder lines that opened up still wider areas to commercial agriculture and made it easy to bring in lumber, farm machinery, household furnishings, and the settlers themselves at a low cost.

Railroads and the Sectional Conflict

Increased production and cheap transportation boosted the western farmer's income and standard of living. The days of isolation and self-sufficiency, even for the family on the edge of the frontier, rapidly disappeared. Pioneers quickly became businessmen and, to a far greater extent than their forebears, consumers, buying all sorts of manufactured articles that their ancestors had made for themselves or done without. This development had its costs. Like southern planters, western farmers became dependent on middlemen and lost some of their feeling of self-reliance. Overproduction became a problem. It began to take more capital to buy a farm, for as profits increased, so did the price of land. Machinery was an additional expense. The proportion of farm laborers and tenants increased.

The linking of East and West had fateful effects on politics. The increased ease of movement from section to section and the ever more complex social and economic integration of East and West stimulated nationalism and thus became a force for the preservation of the Union. Without the railroads and canals, Illinois and Iowa would scarcely have dared to side against the South in 1861. When the Mississippi ceased to be essential to them, citizens of the upper valley could afford to be more hostile to slavery and especially to its westward extension. Economic ties with the Northeast reinforced cultural connections.

The South might have preserved its influence in the Northwest if it had pressed forward its own railroad-building program. It failed to do so because of the scattered population of the South, the paucity of passenger traffic, the seasonal nature of much of the freight business, and the absence of large cities. Southerners placed too much reliance on the Mississippi: The fact that traffic on the river continued heavy throughout the 1850s blinded them to the precipitous rate at which their relative share of the nation's trade was declining. But the fundamental cause of the South's backwardness in railroad construction was the attitude of its leaders. Southeners of means were no more interested in commerce than in industry; their capital found other outlets.

Milestones			
1808	Congress bans further importation of slaves	**1842**	*Commonwealth* v. *Hunt* establishes legality of unions
1822	"Conspiracy" of Denmark Vesey	**1846**	Elias Howe invents the sewing machine
1825	Completion of Erie Canal	**1850**	Congress grants land to aid construction of the Illinois Central Railroad
1830	Baltimore and Ohio Railroad begins operation		
1831	Nat Turner's slave uprising	**1854**	Clipper ship *Flying Cloud* sails from New York to San Francisco in 89 days
	Cyrus Hall McCormick invents the reaper		
1839	John Deere begins manufacturing steel plows	**1857**	Brief economic depression (Panic of 1857)
1840–1857	Boom in manufacturing, railroad construction, and foreign commerce		

The Economy on the Eve of Civil War

Between the mid-forties and the mid-fifties, the United States experienced one of the most remarkable periods of growth in the history of the world. Every economic indicator surged forward: manufacturing, grain and cotton production, population, railroad mileage, gold production, sales of public land. The building of the railroads stimulated business, and by making transportation cheaper the completed lines energized the nation's economy. The "American System" that Henry Clay had dreamed of arrived with a rush just as Clay was passing from the scene.

Inevitably this growth caused dislocations, which were aggravated by the boom psychology that once again infected the popular mind. In 1857 there was a serious collapse. People called this abrupt downturn the Panic of 1857. Yet the vigor of the economy was such that the bad times did not last long. The South, somewhat out of the hectic rush to begin with, was affected very little by the collapse of 1857, for cotton prices continued high. This gave planters the false impression that their economy was immune to violent downturns. Some began to argue that the South would be better off out of the Union.

Before the revival of the national economy was complete, however, the sectional crisis between North and South shook people's confidence in the future. Then the war came, and with it a new set of forces shaped economic development.

Supplemental Reading

G. R. Taylor, **The Transportation Revolution** (1958), P. W. Gates, **The Farmer's Age** (1960), and Stuart Bruchey, **The Growth of the American Economy** (1965), works already mentioned in Chapter 8 continue to be useful for this period. See also D. C. North, **The Economic Growth of the United States** (1961), and J. L. Hutson, **The Panic of 1857 and the Coming of the Civil War** (1987).

An excellent survey of the antebellum South is Clement Eaton, **The Growth of Southern Civilization*** (1961). For the economy of the South, consult Gavin Wright, **The Political Economy of the Cotton South** (1978). On slavery, see E. D. Genovese, **Roll, Jordan, Roll*** (1975), Catharine Clinton, **Plantation Mistress** (1984), Elizabeth Fox-Genovese, **Within the Plantation Household** (1988), J. W. Blassingame, **The Slave Community** (1972), L. W. Levine, **Black Culture and Black Consciousness** (1977), K. S. Greenberg, **Masters and Statesmen** (1985), M. L. Dillon, **Slavery Attacked** (1990), and Catharine Clinton, **Plantation Mistress** (1984). R. C. Wade, **Slavery in the Cities***, (1964) and Ira Berlin, **Slaves Without Masters** (1975), contain much interesting material, as does W. K. Scarborough, **The Overseer: Plantation Management in the Old South** (1966).

On various aspects of industrial and urban development see Nathan Rosenberg, **Technology and American Economic Growth** (1972), Thomas Dublin, **Women at Work** (1977), C. E. Rosenberg, **The Care of Strangers** (1987), R. H. Bremner, **From the Depths** (1956), and R. A. Mohl, **Poverty in New York** (1977). Immigration is dealt with in M. A. Jones, **American Immigration** (1960), and Leonard Dinnerstein and D. M. Reimers, **Ethnic Americans** (1975).

On the development of the railroad network see J. F. Stover, **Iron Road to the West** (1978), and Albert Fishlow, **American Railroads and the Transformation of the Ante-Bellum Economy** (1965).

*Available in paperback.

CHAPTER 14

The Coming of the Civil War

The Slave Power Comes North
Uncle Tom's Cabin
"Young America"
The Little Giant
The Kansas-Nebraska Act
Know-Nothings and Republicans
"Bleeding Kansas"
Making a Senator a Martyr
Buchanan Tries His Hand
The Court's Turn
The Lecompton Constitution
The Emergence of Lincoln
The Lincoln-Douglas Debates
John Brown's Raid
The Election of 1860
The Secession Crisis

*T*he political settlement between North and South designed by Henry Clay in 1850 lasted only four years. The issues it was supposed to resolve neither died nor faded away. Americans continued to migrate westward, and as long as slaveholders could carry their human property into federally controlled territories, northern resentment would smolder. Slaves continued to seek freedom in the North, and the Fugitive Slave Act did not guarantee their capture and return.

The Slave Power Comes North

The new fugitive slave law caused a sharp increase in the efforts of southerners to recover escaped slaves. Something approaching panic reigned in the black communities of northern cities after its passage. Thousands of blacks, not all of them former slaves, fled to Canada, but many remained, and northerners frequently refused to stand aside when such people were dragged off in chains.

Shortly after the passage of the act, James Hamlet, was seized in New York City, convicted, and returned to slavery in Maryland without being allowed to communicate with his wife and children. The New York black community was outraged, and with help from white neighbors it swiftly raised $800 to buy his freedom. In 1851 Euphemia Williams, who had lived for years as a free woman in Pennsylvania, was seized, her presumed owner claiming also her six children, all Pennsylvania-born. A federal judge released the Williamses, but the case created more alarm in the North.

Abolitionists often interfered with the enforcement of the law. When two Georgians went to Boston to reclaim William and Ellen Craft, admitted fugitives, a "Vigilance Committee" hounded them through the streets shouting "slave hunters, slave hunters," and forced them to return home empty-handed.

Such incidents exacerbated sectional feelings. Southerners accused the North of reneging on one of the main promises made in the Compromise of 1850, while the sight of harmless human beings being hustled off to a life of slavery disturbed many northerners who were not abolitionists. However, most white northerners were not prepared to interfere with the enforcement of the Fugitive Slave Act themselves. Of the 332 blacks put on trial under the law, about 300 were returned to slavery, most without incident. Nevertheless, enforcing the law in the northern states became steadily more difficult.

Uncle Tom's Cabin

Tremendously important in increasing sectional tensions and bringing home the evils of slavery to still more people in the North was Harriet

Beecher Stowe's novel *Uncle Tom's Cabin* (1852). Stowe was neither a professional writer nor an abolitionist and she had almost no firsthand knowledge of slavery. Her conscience was roused by the Fugitive Slave Act, which she called a "nightmare abomination." She dashed her book off quickly; as she later recalled, it seemed to write itself. It was an enormous success: 10,000 copies were sold in a week, 300,000 in a year. Soon it was being translated into dozens of languages. Dramatized versions were staged in countries throughout the world.

Uncle Tom's Cabin avoided the self-righteous, accusatory tone of most abolitionist tracts and did not try to make readers believe in racial equality. Many of the southern characters were fine, sensitive people and the cruel Simon Legree was a transplanted Connecticut Yankee. There were many heartrending scenes of pain, self-sacrifice, and heroism. The story proved especially effective on the stage: The slave Eliza crossing the frozen Ohio River to freedom, the death of Little Eva, Eva and Tom ascending to heaven—these scenes left audiences in tears.

Southern critics pointed out, correctly enough, that Stowe's picture of plantation life was distorted, the black characters atypical. They called her a "coarse, ugly, long-tongued woman" and accused her of trying to "awaken rancorous hatred and malignant jealousies" that would undermine national unity.

Most northerners, having little basis on which to judge the accuracy of the book, tended to discount southern criticism as biased. In any case, *Uncle Tom's Cabin* raised questions that transcended the issue of its accuracy. Did it matter if every slave was not as kindly as Uncle Tom, or as determined as George Harris? What if only one white master was as evil as Simon Legree? No earlier white American writer had looked at slaves as people. Countless readers asked themselves as they put the book down: Is slavery just?

A poster advertising *Uncle Tom's Cabin* in 1852, the year of its publication. The following year, Harriet Beecher Stowe published *A Key to Uncle Tom's Cabin,* intended to provide documentary evidence in support of disputed details of her indictment of slavery.

"Young America"

Clearly a distraction was needed to help keep the lid on sectional troubles in both North and South. Some people hoped to find one in foreign affairs. The spirit of manifest destiny explains this in large part; once the United States had reached the Pacific, expansionists began to think of transmitting the dynamic, democratic spirit of the United States to other countries by aiding local revolutionaries, opening up new markets, perhaps even annexing foreign lands.

To an extent this "Young America" spirit was purely emotional, a mindless confidence that democracy would triumph everywhere. At the time of the European revolutions of 1848, Americans talked freely about helping the liberals in their struggles against autocratic governments. However, the same democratic-expansionist sentiment led to dreams of conquests in the Caribbean area.

In 1855 a freebooter named William Walker, backed by an American company engaged in transporting migrants to California across Central America, seized control of Nicaragua and elected himself president. He was ousted two years later but made repeated attempts to regain control until, in 1860, he died before a Honduran firing squad. Although many northerners suspected them of engaging in dastardly plots to obtain more territory for slavery, men like Walker were primarily adventurers using the prevailing mood of buoyant expansionism for selfish ends.

The aggressive talk of the period was not all mere bombast. In 1850 Secretary of State John M. Clayton and the British minister to the United States, Henry Lytton Bulwer, negotiated a treaty providing for the demilitarization and joint Anglo-American control of any future canal across Central America. As this area assumed strategic importance to the United States, the desire to obtain Cuba grew stronger.

In 1854 President Franklin Pierce instructed his minister to Spain, Pierre Soulé of Louisiana, to offer $130 million for the island. The administration arranged for him first to confer in Belgium with the American ministers to Great Britain and France. Out of this meeting came the Ostend Manifesto, a confidential dispatch to the State Department suggesting that if Spain refused to sell Cuba, "the great law of self-preservation" might justify "wresting" it from Spain by force.

News of the manifesto leaked out, and it had to be published. Northern opinion was outraged by this "slaveholders' plot," and any hope of obtaining Cuba or any other territory in the Caribbean vanished.

The expansionist mood of the moment also explains President Fillmore's dispatching an expedition under Commodore Matthew C. Perry to try for commercial concessions in the isolated kingdom of Japan in 1852. Perry's expedition was a great success. The Japanese, impressed by American naval power, agreed to establish diplomatic relations. In 1858 an American envoy, Townsend Harris, negotiated a commercial treaty that opened six Japanese ports heretofore closed to foreigners to American ships. President Pierce's negotiation of a Canadian reciprocity treaty with Great Britain in 1854 and his unsuccessful attempt to annex the Hawaiian Islands are further illustrations of the assertive foreign policy of the period.

The Little Giant

The most prominent spokesman of the Young America movement was Senator Stephen A. Douglas of Illinois. Douglas was the Henry Clay of his generation. Like Clay at his best, Douglas was able to see the needs of the nation in the broadest perspective. He was born in Vermont in 1813 and moved to Illinois when barely 20. He studied law and was soon deep in Democratic politics, holding a succession of state offices before being elected to Congress in 1842. After two terms in the House, he was chosen United States senator.

Politics suited Douglas to perfection. Although very short, his appearance was so imposing that men called him the Little Giant. "I live with my constituents," he once boasted, "drink with them, lodge with them, pray with them, laugh, hunt, dance, and work with them. I eat their corn dodgers and fried bacon and sleep two in a bed with them." Yet he was no mere backslapper. He read widely, wrote poetry, financed a number of young American artists, served as a regent of the Smithsonian Institution, and was interested in scientific farming.

The foundations of Douglas's politics were expansion and popular sovereignty. He had been willing to fight for all of Oregon in 1846, and he supported the Mexican War to the hilt, in sharp contrast to his Illinois colleague in Congress, Abraham Lincoln. That local settlers should determine their own institutions was, to his way of thinking, axiomatic.

Arguments over the future of slavery in the territories he believed a foolish waste of energy and time since he was convinced that natural conditions would keep the institution out of the West. He believed slavery "a curse beyond computation" for both blacks and whites, but he refused to admit that any moral issue was involved. He cared not, he boasted, whether slavery was voted up or voted down. This was not really true, but the slavery question was interfering with the rapid exploitation of the continent. Let the nation build railroads, acquire new territory, expand its trade, Douglas urged.

Douglas's success in steering the Compromise of 1850 through Congress added to his already considerable reputation. In 1851, although only 38, he set out to win the Democratic presidential nomination. He reasoned that since he was the brightest, most imaginative, and hardest-working Democrat around, he had every right to press his claim. This brash aggressiveness proved his undoing, for his rivals combined against him, and he had no chance.

The 1852 Democratic convention, however, was deadlocked between Lewis Cass, inventor of popular sovereignty, and James Buchanan of Pennsylvania, who had a long record as congressman and diplomat. The delegates therefore settled on a dark horse, Franklin Pierce of New Hampshire. The Whigs, rejecting the colorless Fillmore, nominated General Winfield Scott. In the campaign both sides supported the Compromise of 1850. The Democrats won an easy victory, 254 electoral votes to 42.

So handsome a triumph seemed to insure stability, but in fact it was a prelude to political chaos. The Whig Party was crumbling fast. The "Cotton Whigs" of the South, alienated by the antislavery sentiments of their northern brethren, were flocking into the Democratic fold. In the North, the radical "Conscience" Whigs and the "Silver Gray" faction that was undisturbed by slavery found themselves more and more at odds with each other. Congress fell overwhelmingly into the hands of proslavery southern Democrats, a development profoundly disturbing to northern Democrats as well as to Whigs.

The Kansas-Nebraska Act

Franklin Pierce was generally well liked by politicians. His career had included service in both houses of Congress. Drinking had become a problem for him and in 1842 he had resigned from the Senate. But he overcame his alcoholism and restored his reputation by serving as a brigadier general during the Mexican War. Though his nomination for president came as a surprise, once made, it had appeared perfectly reasonable. Great things were expected of his administration, especially after he surrounded himself with men of all factions: To balance his appointment of a radical states' rights Mississippian, Jefferson Davis, as secretary of war, for example, he named a conservative northerner, William L. Marcy of New York, as secretary of state.

Only a strong leader, however, can manage a ministry of all talents, and that President Pierce was not. He could not control the extremists. The ship of state was soon drifting; Pierce seemed incapable of holding firm the helm.

This was the situation in January 1854 when Senator Douglas, chairman of the Committee on Territories, introduced what looked like a routine bill organizing the land west of Missouri and Iowa as Nebraska Territory. Since settlers were beginning to trickle into the area, the time had arrived to set up a civil administration. But besides his expansionist motives, Douglas also acted because a territorial government was essential to railroad development. As a director of the Illinois Central line and as a land speculator, he hoped to make Chicago the terminus of a transcontinental railroad. Construction could not begin, however, until the route was cleared of Indians and brought under some kind of civil control.

The powerful southern faction in Congress would not go along with Douglas's proposal as it stood. The railroad question aside, Nebraska would presumably become a free state, for it lay north of latitude 36 degrees 30 minutes in a district from which slavery had been excluded by the Missouri Compromise. Under pressure from the southerners, Douglas agreed first to divide the region into two territories, Kansas and Nebraska, and then—a fateful concession—to repeal the part of the Missouri Compromise that excluded slavery from land north of 36 degrees 30 minutes. Whether the new territories should become slave or free, he argued, should be left to the decision of the settlers in accordance with the democratic principle of popular sovereignty. The fact that he might advance his presidential ambitions by making concessions to the South must have influenced Douglas too, as must the local political situation in Missouri, where slaveholders feared being "surrounded" on three sides by free states.

Douglas's miscalculation of northern sentiment was monumental. It was one thing to apply popular sovereignty to new territories in the Southwest, quite another to apply it to a region that had been part of the United States for half a century and free soil for 34 years. The news caused an indignant outcry in the North; many moderate opponents of slavery were radicalized. The unanimity and force of the reaction was like nothing in America since the days of the Stamp Act and the Intolerable Acts.

But protests could not defeat the bill. Southerners in both houses backed it regardless of party. Douglas pushed it with all his power. President Pierce added whatever force the administration could muster. As a result, the northern Democrats split and the bill became law late in May 1854. In this manner the nation took the greatest single step in its blind march toward the abyss of secession and civil war.

The repeal of the Missouri Compromise struck the North like a slap in the face—at once shameful and challenging. Presumably the question of slavery in the territories had been settled forever; now, it seemed without justification, it had been reopened.

After passage of the Kansas-Nebraska Act, nearly everyone opposed the return of fugitive slaves. When one fugitive, Anthony Burns, was captured in Boston, Massachusetts abolitionists organized a protest meeting at which they enflamed the crowd into attacking the courthouse where Burns was being held. Federal marshals drove the attackers off and two companies of milita were rushed to Boston. It took these soldiers and a thousand policemen to hold back protesters while Burns was being taken back to slavery. A few months later, northern sympathizers bought Burns his freedom—for a few hundred dollars.

Know Nothings and Republicans

The Democratic Party lost heavily in the North as a result of the Kansas-Nebraska Act. With the Whig Party already moribund, dissidents flocked to two new parties: One was the American, or "Know-Nothing," Party, so called because it grew out of a secret society whose members used the password "I don't know." Immigration was soaring in the early 1850s, and the influx of poor foreigners was causing genuine social problems. In addition, the fact that a large percentage of the immigrants were Irish and German Catholics also troubled the Know-Nothings because these immigrants favored public financing of parochial schools and opposed the prohibition of alcoholic beverages. Since these were divisive issues, the established political parties tried to avoid them; hence the development of the new party.

Northern Know-Nothings won a string of local victories in 1854 and elected more than 40 congressmen. But the party was also important in the South. Most southern Know-Nothings adopted the dominant view of slavery there.

Far more significant in the long run was the formation of the Republican Party, which was made up of former Free Soilers, Conscience Whigs, and "Anti-Nebraska" Democrats. The Republican Party was purely sectional. It sprang up spontaneously throughout the Old Northwest and caught on with a rush in New England. Republicans were not abolitionists, but they insisted that slavery be kept out of the territories. If America was to remain a land of opportunity, they argued, free white labor must have exclusive access to the West. Thus the party could appeal both to voters opposed to slavery and to those who wished to keep blacks—free or slave—out of their states. In 1854 the Republicans won over 100 seats in the House of Representatives and control of many state governments.

The Whig Party had almost disappeared in the northern states and the Democratic Party had been gravely weakened. The Know-Nothing Party had a nationwide organization, but where slavery was concerned, this was anything but advantageous. And many northerners were troubled by the harsh Know-Nothing policies toward immigrants and Catholics. If the Know-Nothings were in control, said former Whig congressman Abraham Lincoln in 1855, the Declaration of Independence would read "all men are created equal, except negroes, and foreigners, and catholics."

"Bleeding Kansas"

The furor might have died down if settlement of the new territories had proceeded in an orderly manner. But both North and South were determined to have Kansas. They made of the territory first a testing ground and then a battlefield, thus exposing the fatal flaw in the Kansas-Nebraska Act and the idea of popular sovereignty. The law said that the people of Kansas were "perfectly free" to decide the slavery question. But the citizens of territories were not entirely free because territories were not sovereign political units. The act had created a political vacuum, which its vague statement that the settlers must establish their domestic institutions "subject . . . to the Constitution" did not begin to fill. When should the institutions be established? Was it democratic to let a handful of early arrivals make decisions that would affect the lives of the thousands soon to follow?

More serious was the fact that outsiders, North and South, refused to allow Kansans to work out their own destiny. In the North, a New England Emigrant Aid Society was formed, with grandiose plans for transporting antislavery settlers to the area. It sent only a handful of New Englanders to Kansas, but it helped many Midwesterners to make the move.

In doing so, the society stirred southerners to action. In November 1854 an election was held in Kansas to pick a territorial delegate to Congress. A large band of Missourians crossed over specifically to vote for a proslavery man and elected him easily. In March 1855 some 5,000 "Border Ruffians" again descended upon Kansas and elected a territorial legislature. A census had recorded 2,905 eligible voters, but 6,307 ballots were cast.

The legislature promptly enacted a slave code and laws prohibiting abolitionist agitation. Antislavery settlers refused to recognize this regime and held elections of their own. By January 1856 two governments existed in Kansas, one based on fraud, the other extralegal.

The proslavery settlers assumed the offensive. In May, 800 of them sacked the antislavery town of Lawrence. An extremist named John Brown then took the law into his own hands in retaliation. In May 1856, together with six companions (four of them his sons) Brown stole into a settlement on Pottawatomie Creek in the dead of night. They dragged five unsuspecting men from their rude cabins, and murdered them. The killers escaped and were never indicted for their crime.

This slaughter brought men on both sides to arms by the hundreds. Irregular fighting broke out, and by the end of 1856 some 200 persons had lost their lives. Exaggerated accounts of "Bleeding Kansas" filled the pages of northern newspapers.

Unquestionably, both northern agitators and unscrupulous Missourians were in the wrong. However, the main responsibility for the Kansas tragedy must be borne by the Pierce administration. Under popular sovereignty the national government was supposed to see that elections were orderly and honest. Instead, the president acted as a partisan. When the first governor of the territory objected to the manner in which the proslav-

ery legislature had been elected, Pierce replaced him with a man who backed the southern group without question.

Making a Senator a Martyr

As counterpoint to the fighting in Kansas there rose an almost continuous cacophony in the halls of Congress. Red-faced legislators traded insults and threats. Epithets like "liar" were freely tossed about. Prominent in these angry outbursts was a new senator, Charles Sumner of Massachusetts. Sumner possessed great magnetism and was, according to the tastes of the day, an accomplished orator, but he suffered inner torments of a complex nature that warped his personality. He was egotistical and humorless. Reform movements evidently provided him a kind of emotional release; he became combative and totally lacking in objectivity when espousing a cause.

In the Kansas debates Sumner displayed an icy disdain for his foes. In the spring of 1856 he loosed a dreadful blast entitled "the crime against Kansas." Characterizing administration policy as tyrannical, imbecilic, absurd, and infamous, he demanded that Kansas be admitted to the Union at once as a free state. Then he began a long and intemperate personal attack on both Douglas and the elderly Senator Andrew P. Butler of South Carolina, who was not present to defend himself.

Sumner described Butler as a "Don Quixote" who had taken "the harlot slavery" as his mistress. Douglas shrugged off such language as part of the game, but since Butler was absent from Washington, Congressman Preston S. Brooks, his nephew, who was probably as mentally unbalanced as Sumner, assumed the responsibility of defending his kinsman's honor. Two days after the speech, Brooks walked up to Sumner in the Senate and rained blows on his head with a guttapercha cane until he fell, unconscious and bloody, on the floor.

Both sides made much of this disgraceful incident. When the House censured him, Brooks resigned, returned to his home district, and was triumphantly reelected. A number of well-wishers even sent him souvenir canes. Northerners viewed the affair as illustrating the brutalizing effect of slavery on southern whites and made a hero of Sumner.

Buchanan Tries His Hand

Such was the atmosphere surrounding the 1856 presidential election. The Republican Party now dominated much of the North, where it stood not for abolition but for restricting slavery to areas where it already existed. It nominated John C. Frémont, "the Pathfinder," one of the heroes of the conquest of California during the Mexican War. Frémont fitted the Whig tradition of presidential candidates: a popular military man with almost no political experience. Republicans expressed their objectives in one simple slogan: "Free soil, free speech, and Frémont."

The Democrats cast aside the ineffectual Pierce and nominated James Buchanan, chiefly because he had been out of the country serving as minister to Great Britain during the long debate over Kansas! The American Party nominated ex-president Fillmore, a choice the remnants of the Whigs ratified. On election day Buchanan won only a minority of the popular vote, but he had strength in every section. He got 174 electoral votes to Frémont's 114 and Fillmore's 8.

Buchanan was a bundle of contradictions. Dignified in bearing and by nature cautious, he could consume enormous amounts of liquor without showing the slightest sign of inebriation. A big, heavy man, he was nonetheless remarkably graceful and light on his tiny feet, of which he was inordinately proud. Over the years many strong men in politics had held him in contempt. Yet he was patriotic, conscientious, and anything but radical. Republican extremists called him a "Doughface"—they believed he lacked the force of character to stand up against southern extremists—but many voters in 1856 thought he could steer the nation to calmer waters.

The Court's Turn

Before Buchanan could fairly take the Kansas problem in hand, an event occurred that drove another wedge between North and South. Back in 1834 Dr. John Emerson of St. Louis had joined the army as a surgeon and was assigned to duty at Rock Island, Illinois. Later he was transferred to Fort Snelling, in Wisconsin Territory. In 1838 he returned to Missouri. Accompanying him on these travels was his body servant, Dred Scott, a slave.

In 1846, after Emerson's death, Scott and his wife, Harriet, whom he had married while in Wisconsin, brought suit in the Missouri courts for their liberty with the help of a friendly lawyer. They claimed that residence in Illinois, where slavery was barred under the Northwest Ordinance, and in Wisconsin Territory, where the Missouri Compromise outlawed it, had made them free.

After many years of litigation, the case reached the Supreme Court. On March 6, 1857, two days after Buchanan's inauguration, the high tribunal ruled. Free or slave, the Court declared, blacks were not citizens. Therefore Scott could not sue in a federal court. Further, since the plaintiff had returned to Missouri, the laws of Illinois no longer applied to him. His residence in Wisconsin Territory—this was the most controversial part of the decision—did not make him free because the Missouri Compromise was unconstitutional. According to the Bill of Rights (the Fifth

Dred Scott. In the Dred Scott decision, the Supreme Court ruled that slaves were "beings of an inferior order [with] no rights which white men were bound to respect."

Amendment), the federal government could not deprive any person of life, liberty, or property without due process of law. Therefore, Chief Justice Roger B. Taney reasoned, "an Act of Congress which deprives a person [in this case, Emerson] . . . of his liberty or property merely because he came himself or brought his property into a particular Territory . . . could hardly be dignified with the name of due process of law."

The Dred Scott decision has been widely criticized on legal grounds. Some critics have made much of the fact that a majority of the justices were southerners and proslavery northerners. It would be going too far, however, to accuse the Court of plotting to extend slavery. The judges were trying to settle the vexing question of slavery in the territories once and for all.

In addition to invalidating the Missouri Compromise, which had already been repealed, the decision threatened Douglas's principle of popular sovereignty. If Congress could not exclude slaves from a territory, how could a mere territorial legislature do so? Until statehood was granted, slavery seemed as inviolate as freedom of religion or speech or any other civil liberty guaranteed by the Constitution. Where formerly freedom (as guaranteed in the Bill of Rights) was a national institution and slavery a local one, now, according to the Court, slavery was nationwide, excluded only where states had specifically abolished it.

The irony of employing the Bill of Rights to keep blacks in chains did not escape northern critics. If this "greatest crime in the judicial annals of the Republic" was allowed to stand, northerners argued, the Republican Party would have no reason to exist: Its program had been declared unconstitutional! The Dred Scott decision convinced thousands that the South was engaged in an aggressive attempt to extend the "peculiar institution" so far that it could no longer be considered peculiar.

The Lecompton Constitution

Kansas soon provided a test for northern suspicions. Initially, Buchanan handled the problem of Kansas well by appointing Robert J. Walker governor. Although he was from Mississippi, Walker had no desire to foist slavery on the territory

against the will of its inhabitants. The proslavery leaders in Kansas had managed to convene a constitutional convention at Lecompton, but the Free Soil forces had refused to participate in the election of delegates. When this rump body drafted a proslavery constitution and then refused to submit it to a fair vote of all the settlers, Walker denounced its work. He hurried back to Washington to explain the situation to Buchanan.

The president refused to face reality. His prosouthern advisers were clamoring for him to "save" Kansas. Instead of rejecting the Lecompton constitution, he asked Congress to admit Kansas to the Union with this document as its frame of government.

Buchanan's decision brought him head-on against Stephen A. Douglas, and the repercussions of their clash shattered the Democratic Party. Principle and self-interest (an irresistible combination) forced Douglas to oppose the leader of his party. If he stood aside while Congress admitted Kansas, he would not only be abandoning popular sovereignty, he would be committing political suicide. He was up for reelection to the Senate in 1858. Fifty-five of the 56 newspapers in Illinois had declared editorially against the Lecompton constitution; if he supported it, defeat was certain. He openly joined the Republicans in the fight. Congress rejected the bill.

Meanwhile, the extent of the fraud perpetrated at Lecompton became clear. In October 1857 a new legislature had been chosen in Kansas, the antislavery voters participating in the balloting. It ordered a referendum on the Lecompton constitution in January 1858. The constitution was overwhelmingly rejected.

The Emergence of Lincoln

These were dark days. Dissolution threatened the Union. To many Americans Stephen A. Douglas seemed to offer the best hope of preserving it. For this reason unusual attention was focused on his campaign for reelection to the Senate in 1858.

The importance of the contest and Douglas's national prestige put great pressure on the Republicans of Illinois to nominate someone who would make a good showing against him. The man they chose was Abraham Lincoln.

After a towering figure has passed from the stage, it is always difficult to reconstruct what he was like before his rise to prominence. This is especially true of Lincoln, who changed greatly when power and responsibility and fame came to him. Lincoln was not unknown in 1858, but his public career had not been distinguished. When barely 25, he won a seat in the Illinois legislature as a Whig. He studied law and was admitted to the bar in 1836. However, he prospered only moderately. He remained in the legislature until 1842, displaying a perfect willingness to adopt the Whig position on all issues, and in 1846 was elected to a single term in Congress marked by his partisan opposition to Polk's Mexican policy. After that term his political career had petered out. He seemed fated to pass his remaining years as a typical small-town lawyer.

Even during this period Lincoln's personality was extraordinarily complex. His bawdy sense of humor and his endless fund of stories and tall tales made him a legend first in Illinois and then in Washington. Yet he was subject to periods of melancholy so profound as to appear almost psychopathic. In a society where most men drank heavily, he never touched liquor. In a region swept by repeated waves of religious revivalism, Lincoln managed to be at once a man of calm spirituality and a skeptic without appearing offensive to conventional believers. He was a party wheelhorse, a corporation lawyer, even a railroad lobbyist. Yet his reputation for integrity was stainless.

The revival of the slavery controversy in 1854 stirred Lincoln deeply. He was not an abolitionist and had always tried to take a "realistic" view of the problem. However, the Kansas-Nebraska bill led him to see the moral issue more clearly. "If slavery is not wrong, nothing is wrong," he stated with the clarity and simplicity of expression for which he later became famous. Yet unlike most northern Free Soilers, he did not blame the southerners for slavery. "They are just what we would be in their situation," he said.

The fairness and moderation of his position combined with its moral force won Lincoln many admirers in the great body of citizens who were trying to reconcile their low opinion of blacks and their patriotic desire to avoid an issue that threatened the Union with their growing conviction that slavery was sinful. Anything that aided slavery was wrong, Lincoln argued. But before casting the first stone, northerners should look into their own hearts: "If there be a man amongst us who is so impatient of [slavery] as a wrong as to disregard its actual presence among us and the difficulty of getting rid of it suddenly in a satisfactory way . . . that man is misplaced if he is on our platform." And Lincoln confessed:

> If all earthly power were given to me, I should not know what to do as to the existing institution. But . . . [this] furnishes no more excuse for permitting slavery to go into our free territory than it would for reviving the African slave trade.

Without minimizing the difficulties or urging a hasty and ill-considered solution, Lincoln demanded that the people look toward a day, however remote, when not only Kansas but the entire country would be free.

The Lincoln-Douglas Debates

In July Lincoln challenged Douglas to a series of seven debates. The senator accepted. The debates were well attended, closely argued, and widely reported, for the idea of a direct confrontation between candidates for an important office captured the popular imagination.

The candidates had completely different political styles, each calculated to project a particular image. Douglas epitomized efficiency and success. He dressed in the latest fashion, favoring flashy vests and the finest broadcloth. He was a glad-hander and a heavy drinker. Ordinarily he arrived in town in a private railroad car, to be met by a brass band, then to ride at the head of a parade to the appointed place.

Lincoln appeared before the voters as a man of the people. He wore ill-fitting black suits and a stovepipe hat—repository for letters, bills, scribbled notes, and other scraps—that exaggerated his great height. He presented a worn and rumpled appearance, partly because he traveled from place to place on day coaches, accompanied by only a few advisers. When local supporters came to meet him at the station, he preferred to walk

How Lincoln aged during his term of office is evident when one compares Alexander Hesler's portrait, taken on June 3, 1860, with one by an unnamed photographer, taken on April 10, 1865.

with them through the streets to the scene of the debate.

Lincoln and Douglas maintained a high intellectual level in their speeches, but these were *political* debates. They were seeking not to influence future historians (who have nonetheless pondered their words endlessly) but to win votes. Both tailored their arguments to appeal to local audiences—more antislavery in the northern counties, more proslavery in the southern. They also tended to exaggerate their differences, which were not in fact large. Neither wanted to see slavery established in the territories or thought it economically efficient, and neither sought to abolish it by political action or force. Both believed blacks congenitally inferior to whites.

Douglas's strategy was to make Lincoln look like an abolitionist. He accused the Republicans of favoring racial equality and refusing to abide by the decision of the Supreme Court in the Dred Scott case. Lincoln tried to picture Douglas as proslavery and a defender of the Dred Scott decision. "Slavery is an unqualified evil to the negro,

to the white man, to the soil, and to the State," he said. "Judge Douglas," he also said, "is blowing out the moral lights around us, when he contends that whoever wants slaves has a right to hold them."

However, he often weakened the impact of his arguments, being perhaps too eager to demonstrate his conservatism. The historian David M. Potter drew a nice distinction in Lincoln's position between "what he would do for the slave" and "what he would do for the Negro." "All men are created equal," he would say, on the authority of the Declaration of Independence, only to add: "I am not, nor ever have been, in favor of bringing about in any way the social and political equality of the white and black races." He opposed allowing blacks to vote, to sit on juries, to marry whites, even to be citizens. He took a fence-sitting position on the question of abolition in the District of Columbia and stated flatly that he did not favor repeal of the Fugitive Slave Act.

In the debate at Freeport, a town northwest of Chicago near the Wisconsin line, Lincoln cleverly asked Douglas if, considering the Dred Scott decision, the people of a territory could exclude slavery before the territory became a state. Unhesitatingly Douglas replied that they could, simply by not passing the local laws essential for holding blacks in bondage. "The people have the lawful means to introduce or exclude it as they please, for the reason that slavery cannot exist . . . unless it is supported by local police regulations."

This argument saved Douglas in Illinois. The Democrats carried the legislature by a narrow margin, whereas it is almost certain that if Douglas had accepted the Dred Scott decision outright, the balance would have swung to the Republicans. But the "Freeport Doctrine" cost him heavily two years later when he made his bid for the Democratic presidential nomination. Southern extremists would not accept a man who suggested that the Dred Scott decision could be circumvented.

However, defeat did Lincoln no harm politically. He had more than held his own against one of the most formidable debaters in politics, and his distinctive personality and point of view had impressed themselves on thousands of minds. Indeed, the defeat revitalized his political career.

Elsewhere the elections in the North went heavily to the Republicans. In early 1859 even many moderate southerners were uneasy about the future. The radicals, made panicky by Republican victories and their own failure to win in Kansas, spoke openly of secession if a Republican was elected president in 1860. They demanded a federal slave code for the territories and talked of annexing Cuba and reviving the African slave trade.

John Brown's Raid

In October 1859 John Brown, the scourge of Kansas, made his second contribution to the unfolding sectional drama. Gathering a group of 18 followers, white and black, he staged an attack on Harpers Ferry, Virginia, a town on the Potomac river upstream from Washington. The attack was a fiasco. Federal troops, sent quickly from Washington, trapped Brown's men in an engine house of the Baltimore and Ohio Railroad. After a two-

day siege in which the attackers picked off ten of his men, Brown was captured.

No incident so well illustrates the role of emotion and irrationality in the sectional crisis as John Brown's raid. After his ghastly Pottawatomie murders it should have been obvious to anyone that he was both a fanatic and mentally unstable: Some of the victims were hacked to bits. Yet numbers of high-minded northerners, including Emerson and Thoreau, had supported him and his antislavery "work" after 1856. Some contributed directly and knowingly to his Harpers Ferry enterprise. After Brown's capture, Emerson, in an essay on "Courage," called him a martyr who would "make the gallows as glorious as the cross." Many southerners reacted to Harpers Ferry with equal irrationality, some with a rage similar to Brown's. Dozens of hapless northerners in the southern states were arrested, beaten, or driven off.

Brown's fate lay in the hands of the Virginia authorities. Ignoring his obvious derangement, they charged him with treason, conspiracy, and murder. He was speedily convicted and hanged. And so a megalomaniac became to the North a hero and to the South a symbol of northern ruthlessness.

The Election of 1860

By 1860 the nation was teetering on the brink of disunion. Extremism was more evident in the South, and to any casual observer that section must have seemed the aggressor in the crisis. Yet even in demanding the reopening of the African slave trade, southern radicals believed they were defending themselves against attack. They felt surrounded by hostility. The North was growing at a much faster rate; if nothing were done, they feared, a flood of new free states would soon be able to amend the Constitution and emancipate the slaves. John Brown's raid, with its threat of an insurrection like Nat Turner's, reduced them to a state of panic.

When legislatures in state after state in the South cracked down on freedom of expression, made the manumission of slaves illegal, banished free blacks, and took other steps that northerners considered blatantly provocative, the advocates of these policies believed that they were only defending the status quo. Secession provided an emotional release—a way of dissipating tension by striking back at criticism.

Stephen A. Douglas was probably the last hope of avoiding a rupture between North and South, but when the Democrats met at Charleston, South Carolina, in April 1860 to choose their presidential candidate, the southern delegates would not accept him. Most of the delegates from the Deep South walked out. Without them Douglas could not obtain the required two-thirds majority, and the convention adjourned without naming a candidate.

In June the Democrats reconvened at Baltimore. Again they failed to reach agreement. The two wings then met separately, the northerners nominating Douglas, the southerners John C. Breckinridge of Kentucky, Buchanan's vice president.

Meanwhile, the Republicans had met in Chicago and drafted a platform attractive to all classes and all sections of the northern and western states. For manufacturers they proposed a high tariff, for farmers a homestead law providing free land for settlers. Internal improvements "of a National character," notably a railroad to the Pacific, should receive federal aid. No restrictions should be placed on immigration. As to slavery in the territories, the Republicans did not equivocate: "The normal condition of all the territory of the United States is that of freedom." Neither Congress nor a local legislature could "give legal existence to Slavery in any Territory."

In choosing a presidential candidate the Republicans displayed equally shrewd political judgment by selecting Abraham Lincoln. His thoughtful and moderate views on the main issue of the times and his formidable debating skills attracted many, and so did his political personality. "Honest Abe," the "Railsplitter," a man of humble origins (born in a log cabin), self-educated, self-made, a common man but by no means an ordinary man—the combination seemed unbeatable.

A few days earlier the remnants of the American and Whig parties had formed the Constitutional Union Party and nominated John Bell of Tennessee for president. "It is both the part of patriotism and of duty," they resolved, "to recognize no political principle other than the Constitution of the country, the union of the states, and the enforcement of the laws." Ostrichlike, the Constitutional Unionists ignored the conflicts rending the nation. Only in the border states, where the consequences of disunion were sure to be most tragic, did they have any following.

With four candidates in the field, no one could win a popular majority, but it soon became clear that Lincoln was going to be elected. Breckinridge had most of the slave states in his pocket and Bell would run strong in the border regions, but the populous northern and western states had a large majority of the electoral vote, and there the choice lay between the Republicans and the Douglas Democrats. In such a contest the Republicans, with their attractive economic program and their strong stand against slavery in the territories, were sure to come out on top.

When the votes were counted, Lincoln had 1,866,000, almost a million fewer than the combined total of his three opponents, but he swept the North and West, which gave him 180 electoral votes and the presidency. Lincoln was therefore a minority president, but his title to the office was unquestionable. Even if his opponents could have combined their popular votes in each state, Lincoln would have won.

The Secession Crisis

Only days after Lincoln's victory, the South Carolina legislature ordered an election of delegates to a convention to decide the state's future course. On December 20 the convention voted unanimously to secede. By February 1, 1861, the other six states of the Lower South had followed suit. A week later, at Montgomery, Alabama, a provisional government of the Confederate States of America was established.

Why were southerners willing to wreck the Union their grandfathers had put together with so much love and labor? No simple explanation is possible. The danger that the expanding North would overwhelm them was for neither today nor tomorrow. Lincoln had assured them that he would respect slavery where it existed. The Democrats had retained control of Congress in the election; the Supreme Court was firmly in their hands as well. If the North *did* try to destroy slav-

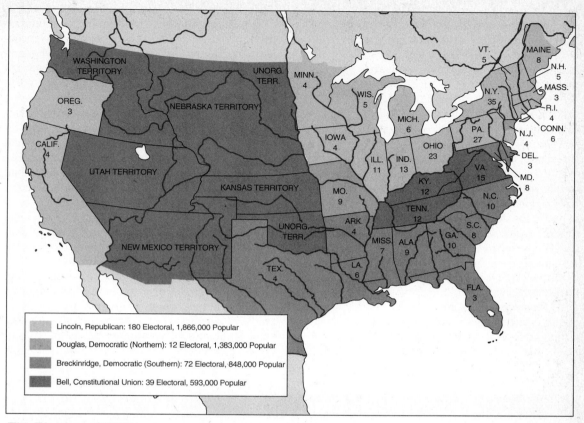

The Election of 1860

ery, *then* secession was perhaps a logical tactic, but why not wait until the threat materialized?

One reason why the South rejected this line of thinking was the tremendous economic energy generated in the North, which seemed to threaten the South's independence. As one southerner complained at a commercial convention in 1855:

From the rattle with which the nurse tickles the ear of the child born in the South to the shroud which covers the cold form of the dead, everything comes from the North. We rise from between sheets made in Northern looms, and pillows of Northern feathers, to wash in basins made in the North. . . . We eat from Northern plates and dishes; our rooms are swept with Northern brooms, our gardens dug with North-

ern spades . . . and the very wood which feeds our fires is cut with Northern axes, helved with hickory brought from Connecticut and New York.

Secession, southerners argued, would "liberate" the South and produce the kind of balanced economy that was proving so successful in the North.

The years of sectional conflict, the growing northern criticism of slavery, perhaps even an unconscious awareness that this criticism was well founded, had undermined and in many cases destroyed the patriotic feelings of southerners. In addition, a Republican president might appoint abolitionists or even blacks to federal posts in the South. Fear approaching panic swept the region.

Although states' rights provided the rationale for leaving the Union, and southerners expounded the strict-constructionist interpretation of the Constitution with great fervor and ingenuity, the economic and emotional factors were far more basic. The Lower South decided to go ahead with secession regardless of the cost.

In the North there was a foolish but understandable reluctance to believe the South really intended to break away permanently. In the South there was an equally unrealistic expectation that the North would not resist secession forcibly. President-elect Lincoln was inclined to write off secession as a bluff designed to win concessions he was determined not to make. He also showed a lamentable political caution in refusing to announce his plans or to cooperate with the outgoing Democratic administration before taking over on March 4. As for President Buchanan, he claimed to be powerless. Secession, he said, was illegal, but the federal government had no legal way to prevent it.

Appeasers, well-meaning believers in compromise, and those prepared to fight to preserve the Union were alike incapable of effective action. A group of moderates headed by Senator John J. Crittenden of Kentucky proposed a constitutional amendment in which slavery would be "recognized as existing" in all territories south of latitude 36 degrees 30 minutes. Crittenden had a special reason for seeking to avoid a conflict. His oldest son was about to become a Confederate general, another son a Union general. The amendment also promised that no future amendment would tamper with the institution in the slave states and offered other guarantees to the South. But Lincoln refused to consider any arrangement that would open new territory to slavery. "On the territorial question," he wrote, "I am inflexible."

The Crittenden Compromise got nowhere. The new southern Confederacy set to work drafting a constitution, choosing Jefferson Davis as provisional president, seizing arsenals and other federal property within its boundaries, and preparing to dispatch diplomatic representatives to enlist the support of foreign powers. Buchanan bumbled helplessly in Washington. And out in Illinois, Abraham Lincoln juggled Cabinet posts and grew a beard.

Milestones

1850	Compromise of 1850	**1856**	Pottawatomie Massacre
	Clayton-Bulwer Treaty with Great Britain		Caning of Senator Charles Sumner in the Senate
1851–1860	Northern resistance to enforcement of Fugitive Slave Act	**1857**	Dred Scott Case (*Dred Scott* v. *Sandford*)
			Panic of 1857
1852	Harriet Beecher Stowe, *Uncle Tom's Cabin*	**1858**	Lincoln-Douglas debates
		1859	John Brown's raid on Harper Ferry
1853	Commodore Matthew Perry opens Japan to U.S. trade Gadsden Purchase	**1860**	South Carolina secedes from the Union
1854	Ostend Manifesto	**1861**	Establishment of Confederate States of America\
	Kansas-Nebraska Act (repeals Missouri Compromise)		Lincoln rejects Crittenden Compromise
1855	William Walker seizes power in Nicaragua		
1856–1858	Unrest in Kansas Territory ("Bleeding Kansas")		

Supplementary Reading

An excellent analysis of the events leading to the Civil War is D. M. Potter, **The Impending Crisis*** (1976). See also the interpretations of W. J. Cooper, Jr., **Liberty and Slavery** (1983), and Michael Holt, **The Political Crisis of the 1850s** (1978). W. E. Gienapp, **The Origins of the Republican Party** (1987), is a fine study. Eric Foner, **Free Soil, Free Labor, Free Men*** (1970), analyzes Republican ideas and policies.

On the enforcement of the Fugitive Slave Act, see S. W. Campbell, **The Slave Catchers** (1970), and T. D. Morris, **Free Men All** (1974). V. J. Voegeli, **Free but Not Equal** (1967), deals with the treatment of blacks in the North.

On foreign policy, see C. H. Brown, **Agents of Manifest Destiny** (1980), P. B. Wiley and Korogi Ichiro, **Yankees in the Land of the Gods** (1990), dealing with the Perry expedition, and R. E. May, **The Southern Dream of a Caribbean Empire** (1974).

On Stephen A. Douglas, see R. W. Johannsen, **Stephen A. Douglas** (1973); on John Brown, S. B. Oates, **To Purge This Land with Blood** (1970). On the Kansas controversy, see J. A. Rawley, **Race and Politics: "Bleeding Kansas"** (1969). Senator Sumner's role in the deepening crisis is discussed in David Donald, **Charles Sumner and the Coming of the Civil War** (1960). On the Dred Scott case, see Don Fehrenbacher, **The Dred Scott Case*** (1978).

Of the many biographies of Lincoln, consult David Donald, **Lincoln** (1995), and B. P. Thomas, **Abraham Lincoln** (1952). On the Lincoln-Douglas debates, see H. V. Jaffa, **Crisis of the House Divided*** (1959). K. M. Stampp, **America in 1857** (1990), focuses on the blunders of President Buchanan. For the secession crisis and the outbreak of the Civil War, consult William Barney, **The Road to Secession** (1972), and S. A. Channing, **Crisis of Fear*** (1970).

*Available in paperback.

CHAPTER 15

The War to Save the Union

Fort Sumter: The First Shot
The Blue and the Gray
The Test of Battle: Bull Run
Paying for the War
Politics as Usual
Behind Confederate Lines
War in the West: Shiloh
McClellan: The Reluctant Warrior
Lee Counterattacks: Antietam
The Emancipation Proclamation
Negrophobia and the Draft Riots
The Emancipated People
Antietam to Gettysburg
Lincoln Finds His General: Grant Wins Vicksburg
Economic and Social Effects, North and South
Women in Wartime
Grant in the Wilderness
Sherman in Georgia
To Appomattox Court House
Costs and Prospects

*T*he nomination of Lincoln had succeeded brilliantly for the Republicans, but had his election been a good thing for the country? As the inauguration approached, everyone waited tensely to see whether he would oppose secession with force. His inaugural address was conciliatory but firm. Southern institutions were in no danger from his administration. Secession, however, was illegal. "A husband and wife may be divorced," Lincoln said, employing one of his homely and, by

the Victorian standards of the day, slightly risqué metaphors, "but the different parts of our country cannot." His concluding words catch the spirit of the inaugural perfectly:

> *I am loath to close. We are not enemies, but friends. We must not be enemies. Though passion may have strained, it must not break, our bonds of affection. The mystic chords of memory . . . will yet swell the chorus of the Union when again touched, as surely they will be, by the better angels of our nature.*

Border-state moderates found the speech encouraging. So did the fiery Charles Sumner. The Confederates, however, read Lincoln's denial of the right of secession as justifying their decision to secede.

Fort Sumter: The First Shot

While denying the legality of secession, Lincoln had in fact temporized. The Confederates had seized most federal property in the Deep South. Lincoln admitted frankly that he would not attempt to reclaim this property. However, two strongholds, Fort Sumter, on an island in Charleston harbor, and Fort Pickens, at Pensacola, Florida, were still in loyal hands. Most Republicans, Lincoln included, did not want to surrender them without a show of resistance. To do so, one wrote, would be to turn the American eagle into a "debilitated chicken."

Yet to reinforce the forts might mean bloodshed that would make reconciliation impossible. After weeks of indecision, Lincoln took the moderate step of sending a naval expedition to supply the Sumter garrison with food.

Unwilling to permit this, the Confederates opened fire on the fort on April 12, 1861. After holding out against the bombardment of shore batteries for 34 hours, Major Robert Anderson and his men surrendered.

The attack precipitated an outburst of patriotic indignation in the North. Lincoln promptly issued a call for 75,000 volunteers. This caused Virginia, North Carolina, Arkansas, and Tennessee to secede. After years of crises and compromises, the nation chose to settle the quarrel between the parties by force of arms.

Southerners considered Lincoln's call for troops an act of naked aggression. They were seeking what a later generation would call the right of self-determination. How could the North square its professed belief in democratic free choice with its refusal to permit the southern states to leave the Union when a majority of their citizens wished to do so?

Lincoln took the position that secession was a rejection of democracy. If the South could refuse to abide by the result of an election in which it had freely participated, then everything that monarchists and other conservatives had said about the instability of republican governments would be proved true. This was the proper ground for Lincoln to take, both morally and politically. A majority of northerners would not have supported a war against slavery. Slavery was the root cause of secession, but the North's determination to resist secession resulted from the people's commitment to the Union.

The Blue and the Gray

In any test between the United States and the 11 states of the Confederacy, the former possessed tremendous advantages. There were 20.7 million people in the northern states (excluding Kentucky and Missouri, where opinion was divided), only 9 million in the South, of which about 3.5 million were slaves, whom the whites hesitated to trust with arms. The North's economic capacity to wage war was even more preponderant. It was manufacturing nine times as much as the Confederacy and had a far larger and more efficient railroad system. Northern control of the merchant marine and the navy made possible a blockade of the Confederacy, a particularly potent threat to a region so dependent on foreign markets.

The Confederates discounted these advantages. Many doubted that public opinion in the North would sustain Lincoln if he attempted to meet secession with force. Northern manufacturers needed southern markets, and merchants depended heavily on southern business. Many western farmers were still sending their produce down the Mississippi. Should the North try to cut Europe off from southern cotton, the powers, particularly Great Britain, would force open southern ports, and provide the Confederacy with the means of defending itself forever.

The Confederacy also counted on certain military advantages. The new nation, it was assumed, need only fight a defensive war, less costly in men and material and of great importance in maintaining morale and winning outside sympathy. Southerners would be defending not only their social institutions but their homes and families.

Luck played a part; the Confederacy quickly found a great commander, whereas many northern generals in the early stages of the war proved either bungling or indecisive. Since there was little to choose between northern and southern common soldiers, superior generalship made some difference.

Both sides faced massive difficulties in organizing for war. The Union mustered its military, economic, and administrative resources slowly because it had had little experience with war, none with civil war. After southern defections, the regular army consisted of only 13,000 officers and men, far too few to absorb the 186,000 volunteers who had joined the colors by early summer, much less the additional 450,000 men who had volunteered by the end of the year. The hastily composed high command, headed by the elderly Winfield Scott, debated grand strategy endlessly while regimental commanders even lacked decent maps of Virginia.

The Whig prejudice against powerful presidents was part of Lincoln's political heritage; consequently he did not display the firmness of a Jackson or a Polk in his dealings with Congress. Fortunately, in the early stages of the war, Congress proved to be cooperative. But he proved capable of handling heavy responsibilities. His strength lay in his ability to think problems through, to accept their implications, and then to act unflinchingly. Anything but a tyrant by nature, he boldly exceeded the conventional limits of presidential power in the emergency, expanding the army without congressional authorization and even suspending the writ of *habeas corpus* when he thought military necessity demanded that action.

Lincoln displayed a remarkable patience and depth of character: He would willingly accept snubs and insults from lesser men in order to advance the cause. He kept a close check on every aspect of the war effort, yet he found time for thought too. His secretary John Nicolay reported seeing him sit sometimes for a whole hour like "a petrified image," lost in contemplation.

The Confederacy faced far greater problems than the North, for it had to create an entire administration under pressure of war, with the additional handicap of the states' rights philosophy to which it was committed. The Confederate Constitution explicitly recognized the sovereignty of the states and contained no broad authorization for laws designed to advance the general welfare. State governments repeatedly defied the central administration, located at Richmond after Virginia seceded, even with regard to military affairs.

Of course the Confederacy made heavy use of the precedents and administrative machinery taken over from the United States. The government quickly decided that all federal laws would remain in force until specifically repealed, and many former federal officials continued to perform their duties under the new auspices. The call to arms produced a turnout even more impressive than that in the North; by July 1861 about 112,000 men were under arms.

President Jefferson Davis represented the best type of slaveowner. A graduate of West Point,

he was a fine soldier and a planter noted for his humane treatment of his slaves. He was courageous, industrious, and intelligent, but rather too reserved and opinionated to make either a good politician or a popular leader. He devoted too much time to details, failed to delegate authority, and was impatient with dull-witted people, a type politicians often have to deal with. He fancied himself a military expert because of his West Point training and his Mexican War service, but unfortunately for the South, he was a mediocre military thinker. Unlike Lincoln, he quarreled frequently with his subordinates, held grudges, and allowed personal feelings to distort his judgment.

The Test of Battle: Bull Run

As summer approached, the two nations prepared for battle, full of pride, enthusiasm, and ignorance. The tragic confrontation was beginning. "Forward to Richmond!" "On to Washington!" Such shouts propelled the armies into battle long before either was properly trained. On July 21, at Manassas Junction, Virginia, 20 miles below Washington, on a stream called Bull Run, 30,000 men under General Irvin McDowell attacked a roughly equal force of Confederates commanded by the "Napoleon of the South," Pierre G. T. Beauregard. McDowell swept back the Confederate left flank. Victory seemed sure. But then the southerners counterattacked, driving the Union soldiers back. As often happens with green troops, retreat quickly turned to rout. Panic engulfed Washington and Richmond exulted, both sides expecting the northern capital to fall within hours.

The inexperienced southern troops were too disorganized to follow up their victory. Casualties on both sides were light, and the battle had little direct effect on anything but morale. Southern confidence soared, while the North began to realize how immense the task of subduing the Confederacy would be.

After Bull Run, Lincoln devised a broader, more systematic strategy for winning the war. The navy would clamp a tight blockade on southern ports as part of General Scott's "Anaconda Plan" to starve the South into submission. In the West, operations designed to gain control of the Mississippi would be undertaken. Most important, a new army would be mustered at Washing-

Jefferson Davis sat for this portrait in 1863 in his mansion in Richmond. It is the only wartime portrait from the life of the Confederate president.

ton to invade Virginia. To lead this army and to command all the Union forces, Lincoln appointed a 34-year-old major general, George B. McClellan.

McClellan possessed a fine military bearing, a flair for the dramatic, the ability to inspire troops, remarkable talent as an administrator, and a sublime faith in his own destiny. He dreamed of striking swiftly at the heart of the Confederacy to capture Richmond, Nashville, even New Orleans. Yet he was sensible enough to insist on massive logistical support, thorough training for the troops, iron discipline, and meticulous staff work before making a move.

Paying for the War

By the fall of 1861 a real army was taking shape along the Potomac: disciplined, confident, and adequately supplied. Northern shops and factories were producing guns, ammunition, wagons, uniforms, and the countless other supplies needed to fight a war.

At the beginning of the war Secretary of the Treasury Salmon P. Chase failed to ask Congress for enough money to fight the war properly. In August 1861 Congress passed an income tax law (3 percent on incomes over $800, which effectively exempted ordinary wage earners) and assessed a direct tax on the states. Loans amounting to $140 million were authorized. As the war dragged on and expenses mounted, new excise taxes on every imaginable product and service were passed, and still further borrowing was necessary. In 1863 the banking system was overhauled.

During the war the federal goverment borrowed a total of $2.2 billion and collected $667 million in taxes, about twenty percent of its total expenditures. These unprecedentedly large sums proved inadequate. Some obligations were met by printing paper money unredeemdable in coin. About $431 million in "greenbacks"—the term distinguished this *fiat* money from the redeemable yellowback bills—were issued during the conflict. Public confidence in paper money vacillated with each change in the fortunes of the Union armies, but by the end of the war the cost of living in the North had doubled.

The heavy emphasis on borrowing and currency inflation was expensive but not irresponsible. In a country still chiefly agricultural, people had relatively low cash incomes and therefore could not easily bear a heavy tax load.

Politics as Usual

Partisan politics was altered by the war but not suspended. The secession of the southern states left the Republicans with large majorities in Congress. Most Democrats supported measures necessary for the conduct of the war but objected to the way the Lincoln administration was conducting it. When slavery and race relations were under discussion, the Democrats adopting a conservative stance and the Republicans dividing into Moderate and Radical wings.

As the war progressed, the Radical faction became increasingly powerful. In 1861 the most prominent Radical senator was Charles Sumner, brimful of hatred for slaveholders. In the House, Thaddeus Stevens of Pennsylvania was the rising power. Sumner and Stevens were uncompromising. They demanded not merely abolition but the granting of full political and civil rights to blacks. Moderate Republicans objected to treating blacks as equals and opposed making abolition a war aim.

Even many of the so-called Radicals disagreed with Sumner and Stevens on race relations. Senator Benjamin Wade of Ohio, for example, was a lifelong opponent of slavery, yet he had convinced himself that blacks (he habitually called them "niggers") had a distinctive and unpleasant smell. He considered the common white prejudice against blacks perfectly understandable. But prejudice, he maintained, gave no one the right "to do injustice to anybody." He insisted that blacks were as intelligent as whites and were entitled not merely to freedom but to political equality.

At the other end of the political spectrum stood the so-called Peace Democrats. These "Copperheads" (apparently the reference was not to the poisonous snake but to an earlier time when some hard-money Democrats wore copper pennies around their necks) opposed all measures in support of the war. Few were actually disloyal, but their activities at a time when thousands of men were risking their lives in battle infuriated many northerners.

Lincoln treated dissenters with a curious mixture of repression and tolerance. He suspended the writ of *habeas corpus* in critical areas and applied martial law freely, arguing that the government dared not stand on ceremony in a national emergency. His object, he explained, was not to punish but to prevent. Elections were held in complete freedom throughout the war. After the war, in *Ex parte Milligan* (1866), the Supreme Court declared illegal the military trials of civilians in areas where the regular courts were functioning, but by that time the question was of only academic interest.

The most notorious domestic foe of the administration was the Peace Democrat Congressman Clement L. Vallandigham of Ohio. Vallandigham was a zealot. "Perish life itself," he once said, "but do the thing that is right." In 1863, after he had made a speech urging that the war be ended by negotiation, Vallandigham was jailed by the military. Of course his followers protested indignantly. Lincoln ordered him released and banished to the Confederacy. Once at liberty Vallandigham moved to Canada, from which refuge he ran unsuccessfully for governor of Ohio. In 1864 he returned to Ohio. Although he campaigned against Lincoln in the presidential election, he was not molested.

Behind Confederate Lines

The South also revised its strategy after Bull Run. President Davis relied primarily on a strong defense to wear down the Union's will to fight. Although the Confederacy did not develop a two-party system, there was plenty of internal political strife. Davis made enemies easily, and the southern devotion to states' rights and individual liberty (for white men) caused endless trouble.

Finance was the Confederacy's most vexing problem. The blockade made it impossible to raise much money through tariffs. The Confederate Congress passed an income tax together with many excise taxes, but these taxes raised only two percent of the government's needs. The most effective levy was a tax-in-kind, amounting to one-tenth of each farmer's production. The South borrowed as much as it could ($712 million), even mortgaging cotton undeliverable because of the blockade in order to gain European credits. But it relied mainly on printing paper currency; over $1.5 billion poured from the presses during the war. When the military fortunes of the Confederacy began to decline, the bottom fell out, and by early 1865 a Confederate dollar was worth less than two cents in gold.

Because of the shortage of manufacturing facilities, the task of outfitting the army strained southern resources to the limit. Large supplies of small arms (some 600,000 weapons during the entire war) came from Europe, but as the blockade became more effective, it was increasingly difficult to obtain European goods.

The Confederates did manage to build a number of munitions plants, and they captured huge amounts of northern arms. No battle was lost because of a lack of guns or other military equipment, though shortages of shoes and uniforms handicapped the Confederate forces on some occasions.

Foreign policy loomed large in Confederate thinking, for the "cotton is king" theory presupposed that the Europeans would break any northern blockade to get cotton for their textile mills. Southern expectations were not realized, however. The attitude of Great Britain was decisive. The cutting off of cotton did not hit the British as hard as the South had hoped, and British crop failures necessitated the importation of large amounts of northern wheat. The fact that the mass of ordinary people in Great Britain favored the North was also important in determining British policy.

Nevertheless, the British government gave serious thought to recognizing the Confederacy. In November 1861 the American warship *San Jacinto* stopped a British vessel, the *Trent,* on the high seas and forcibly arrested two Confederate envoys, James M. Mason and John Slidell, who were en route to London. This violation of international law would probably have led to war had not Lincoln decided to turn the southerners loose. In 1862 two powerful cruisers, the *Florida* and the *Alabama,* were built for the Confederates in English shipyards under the most transparent of subterfuges. Despite Unionist protests, they were permitted to put to sea.

But when two ironclad "rams" were also built in Britain for the Confederates, the United States made it clear that it would declare war if they were delivered. The British government then confiscated the vessels, avoiding a showdown. In the last analysis the military situation determined British policy; once the North obtained a clear superiority on the battlefield, the possibility of British intervention vanished.

War in the West: Shiloh

Northern superiority was achieved slowly and at enormous cost. After Bull Run, no heavy fighting took place until early 1862. Then, while McClellan continued his deliberate preparations to attack Richmond, important fighting occurred far to the west. In March 1862, a Texas army advancing beyond Santa Fe clashed with a Union force in the Battle of Glorieta Pass. The battle was indecisive, but a Union unit destroyed the Confederates' supply train. They then retreated to the Rio Grande, ending the Confederate threat to the Far West.

Meanwhile, far larger Union forces led by a shabby, cigar-smoking West Pointer named Ulysses S. Grant invaded Tennessee from a base at Cairo, Illinois. Grant captured Forts Henry and Donelson, strongpoints on the Tennessee and Cumberland rivers. Next he marched toward Corinth, Mississippi, an important railroad junction.

To check Grant's invasion, the Confederates massed 40,000 men under Albert Sidney Johnston. On April 6 Johnston struck suddenly at Shiloh, 20 miles north of Corinth. Grant's men stood their ground, and in the course of the second day of battle the tide turned. The Confederates fell back toward Corinth, exhausted and demoralized.

Grant, shaken by the unexpected attack and appalled by his losses, allowed the enemy to escape. For this blunder he was relieved of his command and his battle-tested army was broken up, its strength dissipated in a series of uncoordinated campaigns. A great opportunity had been lost.

Shiloh had other results. The staggering casualties shook the confidence of both belligerents. More Americans fell there in two days than in all the battles of the Revolution, the War of 1812, and the Mexican War combined. Union losses exceeded 13,000 out of 63,000 engaged; the Confederates lost 10,699, including General Johnston.

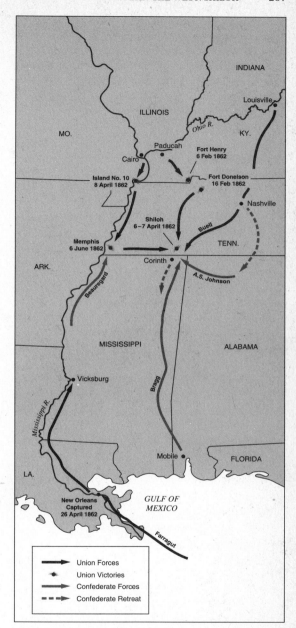

War in the West, 1862

More accurate guns and more powerful artillery were responsible for the carnage. The generals began to reconsider their tactics and to experiment with field fortifications and other defensive measures. And the people, North and

South, stopped thinking of the war as a romantic test of courage and military guile.

McClellan: The Reluctant Warrior

In Virginia, General McClellan was finally moving against Richmond. Instead of trying to advance across the difficult terrain of northern Virginia, he transported his army by water to the tip of the peninsula formed by the York and James rivers in order to attack Richmond from the southeast.

McClellan's plan alarmed many congressmen because it seemed to leave Washington relatively unprotected. But it simplified the task of supplying the army in hostile country. However, McClellan now displayed the weaknesses that eventually ruined his career. His problems were intellectual and psychological. He saw the Civil War not as a mighty struggle over fundamental beliefs but as a complex game (like chess with its castles and knights) that gentlemanly commanders played at a leisurely pace and for limited stakes. He believed it more important to capture Richmond than to destroy the army protecting it. The idea of crushing the South seemed to him wrongheaded and uncivilized.

Beyond this, McClellan was temperamentally unsuited for a position of so much responsibility. Beneath the swagger and the charm he was a profoundly insecure man. He talked like Napoleon, but he did not like to fight. He knew how to get ready, but he was never ready in his own mind.

Proceeding deliberately, he floated an army of 112,000 men down the Potomac and by May 14 had established a base less than 25 miles from Richmond. A swift thrust might have ended the war quickly, but McClellan delayed, despite the fact that he had 80,000 men in striking position and large reserves. As he advanced slowly, the Confederates caught part of his force separated from the rest by the Chickahominy River and attacked it. The Battle of Seven Pines was indecisive yet resulted in more than 10,000 casualties.

At Seven Pines the Confederate commander, General Joseph E. Johnston, was severely wounded; leadership of the Army of Northern Virginia then fell to Robert E. Lee. Although a most reluctant supporter of secession, Lee was a superb soldier. He was McClellan's antithesis: gentle, courtly, and entirely without McClellan's swagger and vainglorious belief that he was a man of destiny. McClellan seemed almost deliberately to avoid understanding his foes, acting as though every southern general was an Alexander. Lee, a master psychologist on the battlefield, cleverly took the measure of each Union general and devised his tactics accordingly. Where McClellan was complex, egotistical, perhaps even unbalanced, Lee was tactful, unassuming, and level headed. Yet on the battlefield Lee's boldness sometimes skirted the edge of foolhardiness.

To relieve the pressure on Richmond, Lee sent General Thomas J. "Stonewall" Jackson on a diversionary raid in the Shenandoah Valley, west of Richmond and Washington. In response, Lincoln dispatched 20,000 reserves to the Shenandoah to check Jackson—to the dismay of McClellan, who wanted the troops to attack Richmond from the north. But after Seven Pines, Lee ordered Jackson back to Richmond. While Union armies streamed toward the valley, Jackson slipped stealthily between them.

Jackson's troops gave Lee a numerical advantage. On June 26 he launched a massive surprise attack. For seven days the battle raged. McClellan, who excelled in defense, fell back, his lines intact, exacting a fearful toll. Under difficult conditions he transferred his troops to a new base on the James River. Again the losses were terrible: northern casualties totaled 15,800, those of the South nearly 20,000.

Lee Counterattacks: Antietam

McClellan was still within striking distance of Richmond, in an impregnable position with secure supply lines and 86,000 soldiers ready to resume the battle. Yet Lincoln, exasperated with McClellan for having surrendered the initiative, reduced his authority by placing him under General Henry W. Halleck, who ordered him to move his army to the Potomac, near Washington. A great opportunity had been squandered, but as James McPherson suggests in *Battle Cry of Freedom*, if Richmond had fallen, the war would probably have ended and the Union restored without the abolition of slavery. Ironically, as McPherson puts it,

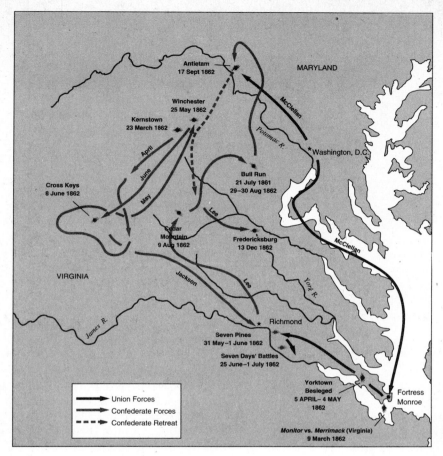

War in the East, 1861–1862

"by defeating McClellan, Lee assured the prolongation of the war until it destroyed slavery." Of course no one expressed this idea at the time.

Putting such might-have-beens aside, to allow Halleck to pull back the troops was a bad mistake. Had the Union army made any aggressive thrust, Lee would not have dared to move from the defenses of Richmond. When it withdrew, Lee, with typical decisiveness and daring, marched north. Late in August, after some complex maneuvering, the Confederates drove confused troops commanded by General John Pope from the field. It was the same ground, Bull Run, where the first major engagement of the war had been fought.

Thirteen months had passed since the first failure at Bull Run, and despite the expenditure of thousands of lives and millions of dollars the Union army stood as far from Richmond as ever.

Dismayed by Pope's incompetence, Lincoln turned in desperation back to McClellan, who regrouped the shaken army.

Despite his successful defense of Richmond, Lee believed that unless some dramatic blow, delivered on northern soil, persuaded the people of the United States that military victory was impossible, the South would be crushed in the long run by the weight of superior resources. He therefore marched rapidly northwestward around the defenses of Washington.

Acting with his usual boldness, Lee divided his army of 60,000 into a number of units. One, under Stonewall Jackson, descended upon weakly defended Harpers Ferry, capturing more than 11,000 prisoners. Another pressed as far north as Hagerstown, Maryland, nearly to the Pennsylvania line. McClellan pursued with his usual deliberation until a captured dispatch revealed to him

Lee in 1863, by Julian Vannerson. "So great is my confidence in General Lee," Stonewall Jackson remarked, "that I am willing to follow him blindfolded."

Lee's dispositions. Then he moved a bit more swiftly, forcing Lee to stand and fight on September 17, 1862 at Sharpsburg, Maryland, between the Potomac and Antietam Creek.*

On a field that offered Lee no room to maneuver, 70,000 Union soldiers clashed with 40,000 Confederates. When darkness fell, more than 22,000 lay dead or wounded on the bloody field. Although casualties were evenly divided and the Confederate lines intact, Lee's position was perilous. McClellan, however, did nothing. For an entire day, while Lee scanned the field in futile search of some weakness in the Union lines, he held his fire. That night the Confederates slipped back across the Potomac into Virginia.

The invasion had failed, Lee's army had been badly mauled, the gravest threat to the Union in the war had been checked. But McClellan had let victory slip through his fingers. Soon Lee was

*Southerners tended to identify battles by nearby towns, northerners by bodies of water. Thus Manassas and Bull Run, Sharpsburg and Antietam, and so forth.

back behind the defenses of Richmond, rebuilding his army. Once again, this time finally, Lincoln dismissed McClellan from his command.

The Emancipation Proclamation

Antietam gave Lincoln the excuse he needed to take a step that changed the character of the war. As we have seen, when the fighting started, only a few radicals wanted to free the slaves by force. However, pressures to act against the South's "peculiar institution" mounted steadily. Slavery had divided the nation; now it was driving northerners to war within themselves. Love of country led them to fight to save the Union, but fighting roused hatreds and caused many to desire to smash the enemy. Sacrifice, pain, and grief made abolitionists of many who had no love for blacks—they sought to free the slave only to injure the master. To make abolition an object of the war might encourage the slaves to revolt. Lincoln disclaimed this objective; nevertheless the possibility existed.

Lincoln would have preferred to see slavery done away with by state law, with compensation for slaveowners and federal aid for all freed slaves willing to leave the United States. He tried repeatedly to persuade the loyal slave states to adopt this policy, but without success. He moved cautiously. By the summer of 1862 he was convinced that for military reasons and to win the support of liberal opinion in Europe, the government should make abolition a war aim. He delayed temporarily, fearing that a statement in the face of military reverses would be taken as a sign of weakness. The "victory" at Antietam gave him his opportunity, and on September 22 he made public the Emancipation Proclamation. After January 1, 1863, it said, all slaves in areas in rebellion against the United States "shall be then, thenceforward, and forever free."

No single slave was freed directly by Lincoln's announcement, which did not apply to the border states or to those sections of the Confederacy, like New Orleans and Norfolk, Virginia, already controlled by federal troops. But henceforth every Union victory would speed the destruction of slavery.

Some of the president's advisers thought the proclamation inexpedient and others considered it illegal. Lincoln justified it as a way to weaken the enemy. Southerners considered the proclamation an incitement to slave rebellion—an "infamous attempt to incite flight, murder, and rapine . . . and convert the quiet, ignorant, dependent black son of toil into a savage." Most antislavery groups approved but thought it did not go far enough. Foreign opinion was mixed: Liberals tended to applaud, conservatives to react with alarm or contempt.

As Lincoln anticipated, the proclamation had a subtle but continuing impact in America. Its immediate effect was to aggravate racial prejudices. Millions of white Americans disapproved of slavery yet abhorred the idea of equality for blacks. In 1857 the people of Iowa rejected Negro suffrage by a vote of 49,000 to 8,000. To some people, emancipation threatened an invasion of the North by blacks who would compete with them for jobs, drive down wages, commit crimes and spread diseases, and—eventually—destroy the "purity" of the white race.

The Democrats tried to make political capital of these fears and prejudices. So strong was the antiblack feeling that most of the Republican politicians who defended emancipation did so with racist arguments. Far from encouraging southern blacks to move north, they claimed, the ending of slavery would lead to a mass migration of northern blacks to the South. When the Emancipation Proclamation began actually to free slaves, the government pursued a policy of "containment," that is, of keeping the freedmen in the South. Panicky fears of an inundation of blacks then subsided.

Negrophobia and the Draft Riots

In March 1863, volunteering having fallen off, Congress passed a conscription act drafting men between 20 and 45. However, the law allowed draftees to hire substitutes or even to obtain exemptions for $300, which was obviously unfair to the poor. In addition, conscription represented an enormous expansion of governmental authority over the citizenry, and it was bitterly resented.

Widespread rioting broke out, the most serious occurring in New York City in July 1863. Most of the New York rioters were poor Irish laborers who resented both the local blacks who competed with them for work and the middle-class whites who seemed sympathic to the blacks. Public buildings, shops, and private residences were put to the torch. Blacks were hunted down and killed without reason. They in turn fought back with equal ferocity. By the time order was restored more than a hundred people had lost their lives.

Northern hostility to emancipation rose from fear of change more than from hatred of blacks. Liberal disavowals of any intention to treat blacks as equals were in large measure designed to quiet this fear. To a degree the racial backlash reflected the public's awareness that a change, frightening but irreversible, *had occurred*.

Most white northerners did not surrender their comforting belief in black inferiority, and Lincoln was no exception. Yet Lincoln was evolving. He talked about deporting ex-slaves to the tropics, but he did not send any there. And he began to receive black leaders in the White House and to allow black groups to hold meetings on the grounds.

The Emancipated People

To blacks, both slave and free, the Emancipation Proclamation served as a beacon. Even if it failed immediately to liberate one slave or to lift the burdens imposed by white prejudice from one black back, it stood as a promise of future improvement. "I took the proclamation for a little more than it purported," Frederick Douglass recalled in his autobiography.

After January 1, 1863, whenever the "Army of Freedom" approached, slaves laid down their plows and hoes and flocked to the Union lines. "We-all knows about it," one black confided to a northern clergyman. "Only we darsen't let on. We *pretends* not to know." Such behavior came as a shock to slaveowners. "[The slaves] who loved us best—as we thought—were the first to leave us," one planter mourned. Talk of slave "ingratitude" increased.

A revolutionary shift occurred in white thinking about using black men as soldiers. Although they had fought in the Revolution and in the Battle of New Orleans during the War of 1812, a law of 1792 barred blacks from the army. During the early stages of the rebellion, despite the eagerness of thousands of free African Americans to enlist, the prohibition remained in force. By 1862, however, the need for manpower was creating pressure for change. After the Emancipation Proclamation specifically authorized the enlistment of blacks, the governor of Massachusetts organized a black regiment, the famous Massachusetts 54th. Swiftly thereafter, other states began to recruit black soldiers, and by the end of the war one soldier in eight in the Union army was black. This changed the war from a struggle to save the Union to a kind of revolution. "Let the black man . . . get an eagle on his button and a musket on his shoulder," wrote Frederick Douglass, "and there is no power on earth which can deny that he has won the right to citizenship."

Black soldiers were segregated and commanded by white officers. But they soon proved themselves in battle; of the 180,000 who served in the Union army, 37,000 were killed, a rate of loss about 40 percent higher than that among white troops. Their bravery—21 were awarded the Congressional Medal of Honor—convinced thousands of northern white soldiers that blacks were not by nature childish or cowardly.

Southerners were another matter. Black soldiers were cruelly mistreated in Confederate prison camps. Still worse, many black captives were killed on the spot. Lincoln was tempted to order reprisals, but he and his advisers realized that this would have been both morally wrong (two wrongs never make a right) and likely to lead to still more atrocities. "Blood can not restore blood," Lincoln said in his usual direct way.

Antietam to Gettysburg

To replace McClellan, Lincoln chose General Ambrose E. Burnside, known to history for his magnificent side-whiskers, ever after called burnsides. Unlike McClellan, Burnside was aggressive—too aggressive. He planned to ford the Rappahannock River at Fredericksburg. Lee concentrated his army in impregnable positions behind the town.

Burnside should have called off the attack when he saw Lee's advantage; instead he he sent his troops across the river over pontoon bridges and occupied Fredericksburg. Then, in wave after wave, they charged the Confederate defense line while Lee's artillery riddled them from nearby Marye's Heights. They were stopped with frightful losses.

On December 14, the day following this futile assault, Burnside, tears streaming down his cheeks, ordered the evacuation of Fredericksburg. Shortly thereafter General Joseph Hooker replaced him.

Hooker proved no better than his predecessor, but his failings were more like McClellan's than Burnside's. By the spring of 1863 he had 125,000 men ready for action. Late in April he forded the Rappahannock and concentrated at Chancellorsville, about ten miles west of Fredericksburg. His army outnumbered the Confederates by more than two to one; he should have forced a battle at once. Instead he delayed, and when he did, Lee sent Stonewall Jackson's corps (28,000 men) across tangled countryside to a position directly athwart Hooker's unsuspecting flank. At 6 P.M. on May 2, Jackson attacked.

Completely surprised, the Union army crumbled. If the battle had begun earlier in the day, the Confederates might have won a decisive victory; as it happened, nightfall brought a lull, and the next day the Union troops rallied and held their ground. Heavy fighting continued until May 5, when Hooker retreated in good order behind the Rappahannock.

Chancellorsville cost the Confederates dearly, for their losses, in excess of 12,000, were almost as heavy as the North's and harder to replace. They also lost Stonewall Jackson, struck by the bullet of one of his own men while returning from a reconnaissance. Nevertheless, the Union army had suffered another fearful blow to its morale.

Lee now took the offensive. With 75,000 soldiers he crossed the Potomac again, a larger Union force dogging his right flank. By late June his army was in southern Pennsylvania, 50 miles *northwest* of Baltimore, within 10 miles of Harrisburg, the capital of the state.

On July 1 a Confederate division looking for shoes in the town of Gettysburg clashed with two brigades of Union cavalry northwest of the town.

Both sides sent out calls for reinforcements. Like iron filings drawn to a magnet, the army of Northern Virginia and the Army of the Potomac converged.

The Confederates won control of the town, but the Union army, now commanded by General George G. Meade, took a strong position on Cemetery Ridge, just to the south. Lee's men occupied Seminary Ridge, a parallel position. On this field the fate of the Union was probably decided.

For two days the Confederates attacked Cemetery Ridge. During General George E. Pickett's famous charge, a handful of his men actually carried the Union lines, but reserves drove them back. By nightfall on July 3 the Confederate army was spent and bleeding, the Union lines unbroken. For the first time Lee had been clearly bested on the field of battle.

Lincoln Finds His General: Grant Wins Vicksburg

On Independence Day, far to the west, Union soldiers won another great victory. When General Halleck was called east in July 1862, Ulysses S. Grant reassumed command of Union troops in the area. Grant was by then one of the most controversial officers in the army. At West Point he had compiled an indifferent record, ranking 21st in a class of 39. During the Mexican War he served well, but when he was later assigned to a lonely post in Oregon, he took to drink and was forced to resign his commission.

The war gave him a second chance. His reputation as a ne'er-do-well and his unmilitary bearing worked against him, as did the heavy casualties suffered by his troops at Shiloh. Yet the fact that he knew how to manage a large army and win battles did not escape Lincoln.

Grant's major aim was to capture Vicksburg, a city of tremendous strategic importance. Vicksburg sits on a high bluff overlooking a sharp bend in the Mississippi River. So long as it remained in southern hands, the trans-Mississippi region could send men and supplies to the rest of the Confederacy.

When Vicksburg proved unapproachable from either west or north, Grant crossed to the

In outward appearance, Ulyssses S. Grant was an unlikely leader. Despite his neatness in the formal portrait, Grant usually wore a sloppy, tobacco-stained uniform, and he had a reputation as a drunkard. During the war, critics pressed Lincoln to replace Grant, but the president replied, "I can't spare this man. He fights!"

west bank of the Mississippi and slipped quickly southward. Recrossing the river below Vicksburg, he abandoned his supply lines and in a series of engagements his troops captured Jackson, Mississippi, cutting off the army of General John C. Pemberton, defending Vicksburg from other Confederate units. Turning next on Pemberton, Grant won two decisive battles and drove him inside the Vicksburg fortifications. By mid-May the city was under siege. Grant applied relentless pressure, and on July 4 Pemberton surrendered. With Vicksburg in Union hands, federal gunboats could range the entire length of the Mississippi. Texas and Arkansas were isolated, for all practical purposes lost to the Confederacy.

Grant's victory had another result: Lincoln gave him command of all federal troops west of the Appalachians. Grant promptly took charge of the fighting in south-central Tennessee. Shifting corps commanders and bringing up fresh units, he won another decisive victory at Chattanooga. This cleared the way for an invasion of Georgia. Suddenly this unkempt, stubby little man, who looked more like a tramp than a general, emerged as the military leader the North had been so desperately seeking. In March 1864 Lincoln summoned him to Washington, named him lieutenant general, and gave him supreme command of the armies of the United States.

Economic and Social Effects, North and South

Though much blood would yet be spilled, by the end of 1863 the Confederacy was on the road to defeat. Northern military pressure, gradually increasing, was eroding the South's most precious resource, manpower. An ever-tightening naval blockade was reducing its economic strength. Shortages developed that, combined with the flood of currency pouring from the presses, led to a drastic inflation. By 1864 an officer's coat cost $2,000 in Confederate money, cigars sold for $10 each, butter was $25 a pound, and flour $275 a barrel. Wages rose not nearly so rapidly. The southern railroad network was gradually wearing out, the major lines maintaining operations only by cannibalizing less vital roads. Imported products such as coffee disappeared; even salt became scarce. Efforts to increase manufacturing were only moderately successful because of the shortage of labor, capital, and technical knowledge.

In the North, after a brief depression in 1861 caused by the uncertainties of the situation and the loss of southern business, the economy flourished. Government purchases greatly stimulated certain lines of manufacturing; the railroads operated at close to capacity and with increasing efficiency; the farm machinery business boomed because so many farmers left their fields to serve in the army; a series of bad harvests in Europe boosted agricultural prices.

Congress passed a number of economic measures long desired but held up in the past by southern opposition: (1) the Homestead Act (1862) gave 160 acres to any settler who would farm the land for five years; (2) the Morrill Land Grant Act of the same year provided the states with land at the rate of 30,000 acres for each member of Congress to support state agricultural colleges; (3) various tariff acts raised the duties on manufactured goods to an average rate of 47 percent in order to protect domestic manufacturers from foreign competition; (4) the Pacific Railway Act (1862) authorized subsidies in land and money for the construction of a transcontinental railroad; (5) the National Banking Act of 1863 gave the country, at last, a uniform currency. Under this last act, banks could obtain federal charters by investing at least one-third of their capital in United States bonds. They might then issue currency up to 90 percent of the value of those bonds.

All these laws stimulated the economy and added to public confidence. Whether the overall economic effect of the Civil War on the Union was beneficial is less clear. Although the economy expanded, it did so more slowly during the 1860s than in the decades preceding and following. Prices soared beginning in 1862, averaging about 80 percent over the 1860 level by the end of the war. As in the South, wages did not keep pace. This condition did not make for a healthy economy—nor did the fact that there were chronic shortages of labor in many fields, shortages aggravated by a sharp drop in the number of immigrants entering the country. The war undoubtedly hastened industrialization. It posed problems of organization and planning, both military and civilian, that challenged the talents of creative persons and thus led to a more complex and efficient economy. The mechanization of production, the growth of large corporations, the creation of a better banking system, and the emergence of business leaders attuned to these conditions would surely have occurred in any case, for industrialization was under way long before the South seceded. Nevertheless, the war greatly speeded all these changes.

Civilian participation in the war effort was far greater than in earlier conflicts. In North and South, church leaders took the lead in recruitment drives and in charitable activities supporting the armed forces. They raised the money and coordinated the personnel needed to provide soldiers with Bibles, religious tracts, and other books, along with fruit, coffee, and spare clothing.

Women in Wartime

Many southern women took over the management of farms and small plantations when their menfolk went off to war. Others became volunteer nurses, and some served in the Confederate medical corps. Quite a few southern women worked as clerks in newly organized government departments. On the other side, large numbers of northern women also contributed their share to the war effort. Farm women went out into fields to plant and harvest crops, aided in many instances by new farm machinery. Many others took jobs in textile factories, in establishments making shoes, uniforms, and other supplies for the army, and in government agencies.

Besides working in factories and shops and on farms, northern women, again like their southern counterparts, aided the war effort more directly. Elizabeth Blackwell, the first American woman doctor of medicine, helped set up what became the United States Sanitary Commission, an organization of women dedicated to improving sanitary conditions at army camps, supplying hospitals with volunteer nurses, and raising money for medical supplies. Additionally, over 3,000 northern women served as army nurses during the conflict. The "proper sphere" of American women was expanding, another illustration of the modernizing effect of the war.

Grant in the Wilderness

Grant's strategy as supreme commander was simple and ruthless. He would attack Lee and try to capture Richmond. General William Tecumseh Sherman would drive from Chattanooga toward Atlanta, Georgia. Like a lobster's claw, the two armies could then close to crush all resistance. Early in May 1864 Grant and Sherman commenced operations, each with more than 100,000 men.

Grant marched the Army of the Potomac into the tangled wilderness south of the Rappahannock, where Hooker had been routed a year earlier. Lee, having only 60,000 men, forced the battle in the roughest possible country, where Grant found it difficult to maneuver his larger force. For two days (May 5–6) the Battle of the Wilderness raged. When it was over, the North had sustained 18,000 casualties, far more than the Confederates.

But unlike his predecessors, Grant did not fall back after being checked. Instead he shifted his troops to the southeast, attempting to outflank the Confederates. Lee rushed his divisions southeastward and disposed them behind hastily thrown up earthworks around Spotsylvania Court House.

Grant attacked. After five more days, which cost the Union army another 12,000 men, the Confederate lines were still intact.

Grant remained undaunted. He was certain that the war could be won only by grinding the South down beneath the weight of numbers. He could replace his losses, Lee could not. When critics complained of the cost, he replied doggedly that he intended to fight on in the same manner if it took all summer. Once more he pressed southeastward in an effort to outflank the enemy. At Cold Harbor, nine miles from Richmond, he found the Confederates once more in strong defenses. At dawn on June 3 he attacked and was thrown back with frightful losses.

Sixty thousand casualties in less than a month! The news sent a wave of dismay through the North. There were demands that "Butcher" Grant be removed from command. Lincoln, however, stood firm. Although the price was high, Grant was gaining his objective. At Cold Harbor, Lee had not a single regiment in general reserve while Grant's army was larger than at the start of the offensive. When Grant next swung round his flank, striking toward Petersburg, Lee had to rush his troops to that city to hold him.

Grant put Petersburg under siege. Soon both armies had constructed breastworks and trenches running for miles in a great arc south of Petersburg. Methodically the Union forces extended their lines, seeking to weaken the Confederates and cut the rail connections supplying Lee's troops and the city of Richmond. By late June, Lee was pinned to earth. Moving again would mean abandoning Richmond—tantamount, in southern eyes, to surrender.

Sherman in Georgia

The summer of 1864 saw the North submerged in pessimism. The Army of the Potomac held Lee at bay but appeared powerless to defeat him. In Georgia, General Sherman inched forward against the wily Joseph E. Johnston, but when he tried a direct assault at Kennesaw Mountain on June 27, he was thrown back with heavy casualties. Huge losses and the absence of decisive victory were taxing the northern will to continue the fight.

In June Lincoln had been renominated on a National Union ticket, with the staunch Tennessee Unionist Andrew Johnson, a former Democrat, as his running mate. He was under attack not only from the Democrats, who nominated George B. McClellan and came out for a policy that might almost be characterized as peace at any price, but from the Radical Republicans, many of whom had wished to dump him in favor of Secretary of the Treasury Chase.

Then, almost overnight, the atmosphere changed. On September 2 General Sherman's army fought its way into Atlanta. When the Confederates countered with an offensive northward toward Tennessee, Sherman did not follow. Instead he abandoned his communications with Chattanooga and marched unopposed through Georgia, "from Atlanta to the sea."

Sherman, like Grant, was a West Pointer who resigned his commission only to fare poorly in civilian occupations. Back in the army in 1861, he suffered a brief nervous breakdown. After recovering he fought under Grant at Shiloh and the two became close friends. "He stood by me when I was crazy," Sherman later recalled, "and I stood by him when he was drunk."

Far more completely than most military men of his generation, Sherman believed in total war— in appropriating or destroying everything that might help the enemy continue the fight. "We have devoured the land," he wrote his wife. "All the people retire before us and desolation is behind."

Another object of Sherman's march was psychological. "If the North can march an army right through the South," Sherman told General Grant, southerners will take it "as proof positive that the North can prevail." This was certainly true of Georgia's blacks, who flocked to the invaders by the thousands, cheering as the soldiers put their former masters' homes to the torch.

Sherman's victories staggered the Confederacy and the anti-Lincoln forces in the North. In November the president was easily reelected, 212 electoral votes to 21. The country was determined to carry on the struggle.

At last the South's will to resist began to crack. Sherman entered Savannah on December 22, having denuded a strip of Georgia 60 miles wide. Early in January 1865 he marched northward. In February his troops captured Columbia, South Carolina. Soon thereafter they were in North Carolina, advancing relentlessly. In Virginia Grant's vise grew daily tighter, the Confederate lines thinner and more ragged.

To Appomattox Court House

On March 4 Lincoln took the presidential oath and delivered his second inaugural address. With victory sure, he spoke for tolerance, mercy, and reconstruction. "Let us judge not," he said after stating again his personal dislike of slavery, "that we be not judged." He urged all Americans to turn without malice to the task of mending the damage and to make a just and lasting peace between the sections.

Now the Confederate troops around Petersburg could no longer withstand the federal pressure. Desperately Lee tried to pull his forces back to the Richmond and Danville Railroad, but the swift wings of Grant's army enveloped him. Richmond fell on April 3. With fewer than 30,000 effectives to oppose Grant's 115,000, Lee recognized the futility of further resistance. On April 9 he and Grant met by prearrangement at Appomattox Court House.

It was a scene at once pathetic and inspiring. Lee was noble in defeat, Grant, despite his rough-hewn exterior, sensitive and magnanimous in victory. Acting on Lincoln's instructions, with which he was in full accord, Grant outlined his terms. All that would be required was that the Confederate soldiers lay down their arms. They could return to their homes in peace. When Lee hinted that his men would profit greatly if allowed to retain possession of their horses, Grant agreed to let them do so.

Costs and Prospects

And so the war ended. It cost the nation more than 600,000 lives, nearly as many as in all other American wars combined. The story of one of the lost thousands must stand for all, Union and Confederate. Jones Budbury, a 19-year-old Pennsylvania textile worker, enlisted at once when the war broke out. He saw action at Bull Run, in McClel-

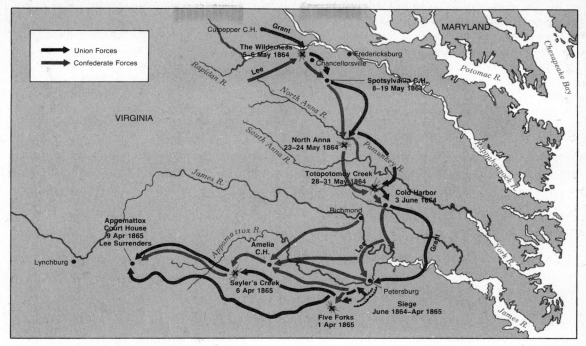

War Ends in Virginia, 1864–1865

lans's Peninsula campaign, at Second Bull Run, at Chancellorsville, and at Gettysburg. A few months after Gettysburg he was wounded in the foot and spent some time in an army hospital. By the spring of 1864 he was a first sergeant, and his hair had turned gray.

In June he was captured and sent to Andersonville military prison, but he fell ill and the Confederates released him. In March 1865 he was back with his regiment. On April 6, three days before Lee's surrender, Jones Budbury was killed while pursuing Confederate units near Sailor's Creek, Virginia.

The war also caused enormous property losses, especially in the Confederacy. All the human and material destruction explains the hatred and resentment that the war implanted in millions of hearts.

What had been obtained at this price? Slavery was dead. Paradoxically, although the war had been fought to save the Union, after 1865 the United States was less a union of separate states than a *nation*. Secession had become inconceivable. In a strictly political sense, as Lincoln had predicted from the start, the northern victory heartened friends of republican government and

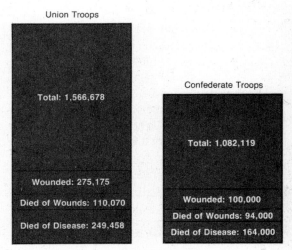

Casualties of the Civil War

democracy throughout the world. A better integrated society and a more technically advanced and productive economic system also resulted from the war.

The Americans of 1865 estimated the balance between cost and profit according to their individual fortunes and prejudices. Only the wisest realized that no final accounting could be made until the people had decided what to do with the fruits of victory. That the physical damage would be repaired no one could reasonably doubt; that even the loss of human resources would be restored in short order was equally apparent. But would the nation make good use of the opportunities the war had made available? What would the ex-slaves do with freedom? How would whites, northern and southern, react to emancipation? To what end would the new technology and social efficiency be directed? Would the people be able to forget the recent past and fulfill the hopes for which so many brave soldiers had given, as Lincoln put it at Gettysburg, their "last full measure of devotion"?

Milestones

1861	Confederates attack Fort Sumter; Lincoln calls for 75,000 volunteers	**1863**	Congress passes Conscription and National Banking Acts
	First Battle of Bull Run		Draft Riots in New York City
	Lincoln appoints George B. McClellan commander of the Union army		Battle of Chancellorsville
			Battle of Gettysburg
	Ex parte Merryman		Siege and capture of Vicksburg
	Trent Affair	**1864**	Battle of the Wilderness
1862	Confederate Congress passes Conscription Act		Battle of Spotsylvania Court House
	Battle of Glorieta Pass		Battle of Cold Harbor
	Battle of Shiloh		Capture of Atlanta
	Robert E. Lee named commander of Army of Northern Virginia		Sherman's March through Georgia; Capture of Savannah
	Seven Day's Battle for Richmond	**1864–1865**	Siege of Petersburg
	Second Battle of Bull Run	**1865**	Capture of Columbia
	Battle of Antietam; McClellan relieved of his command		Lee surrenders to Grant at Appomattox Court House
	Lincoln issues Emancipation Proclamation		
	Congress passes Homestead, Morrill Land Grant, and Pacific Railway Acts		
	Battle of Fredericksburg		

Supplementary Reading

The best recent survey of the Civil War is J. M. McPherson, **Battle Cry of Freedom** (1988), but Allan Nevins, **The Ordeal of the Union** (1947–1971), is the fullest and most judicious interpretation of the period. Constitutional issues are covered in H. M. Hyman, **A More Perfect Union** (1973). On Lincoln's dealings with Radicals, see H. L. Trefousse, **The Radical Republicans*** (1969), and A. G. Bogue, **The Earnest Men: Republicans in the Civil War Senate** (1981); on the northern Democrats, see J. H. Silbey, **A Respectable Minority: The Democratic Party in the Civil War Era*** (1977).

For the movement to make abolition a war aim and the reaction to it, see J. M. McPherson, **The Struggle for Equality: Abolitionists and** the Negro in the Civil War and Reconstruction* (1964), and G. M. Frederickson, **The Inner Civil War: Northern Intellectuals and the Crisis of the Union*** (1965). The activities and attitudes of blacks during the war are summarized in L. F. Litwak, **Been in the Storm So Long** (1979), C. L. Mohr, **On the Threshold of Freedom** (1986), and B. J. Fields, **Slavery and Freedom on the Middle Ground** (1985). The New York draft riots are described in Adrian Cook, **The Armies of the Streets** (1974),

For economic and social history, see P. S. Paludan, **"A People's Contest"** (1988). More specialized studies include P. W. Gates, **Agriculture and the Civil War** (1965), R. P. Sharkey, **Money, Class, and Party*** (1959), and M. E. Massey, **Bonnet Brigades: American Women and the Civil War** (1966).

E. M. Thomas, **The Confederate Nation** (1979), is a brief account of the South during the war. On the military history of the Civil War, T. H. Williams, **Lincoln and His Generals*** (1952), and Bruce Catton, **The Centennial History of the Civil War** (1961–1965), are vivid and detailed. B. I. Wiley, **The Life of Billy Yank*** (1952), discusses the role of Union soldiers.

Among the better biographies of Civil War generals are W. S. McFeely, **Grant** (1981), S. W. Sears, **George B. McClellan** (1988), Lloyd Lewis, **Sherman, Fighting Prophet** (1932), D. S. Freeman, **R. E. Lee** (1934–1935), and Frank Vandiver, **Mighty Stonewall** (1957).

The diplomacy of the Civil War period is covered in D. P. Cook, **The North, the South, and the Powers** (1974), and M. B. Duberman, **Charles Francis Adams*** (1961).

*Available in paperback

CHAPTER 16

Reconstruction and the South

Presidential Reconstruction
Republican Radicals
The Fourteenth Amendment
The Reconstruction Acts
Congress Takes Charge
The Fifteenth Amendment
"Black Republican" Reconstruction: Scalawags and Carpetbaggers
The Ravaged Land
Sharecropping and the Crop Lien System
The White Backlash
Grant as President
The Disputed Election of 1876
The Compromise of 1877

O n April 5, 1865, Abraham Lincoln visited Richmond. The fallen capital lay in ruins, sections blackened by fire, but the president was able to walk the streets unmolested. Black people crowded around him, hailing him as a messiah. A few days later, in Washington, Lincoln delivered an important speech on reconstruction, urging compassion and open-mindedness. Then, on April 14, while he was watching a play at Ford's Theater, a half-mad actor, John Wilkes Booth, slipped into his box and shot him in the head with a small pistol. The next morning, without having regained consciousness, Lincoln died. With him perished the South's best hope for a mild peace. The awesome drama was still unfolding; retribution and a final humbling of the South were inevitable.

Presidential Reconstruction

Despite its bloodiness, the Civil War had caused less intersectional hatred than might have been expected. Although civilian property was often seized or destroyed, the invading armies treated the southern population with remarkable forbearance, both during the war and after Appomattox. Jefferson Davis and a few other Confederate officials spent short periods behind bars, but the only southerner executed for war crimes was Major Henry Wirz, the commandant of Andersonville military prison.

The legal questions related to bringing the defeated states back into the Union were extremely complex. Since Southerners believed that secession was legal, logic should have compelled them to argue that they were out of the Union and would thus have to be formally readmitted. Northerners should have taken the contrary position, for they had fought to prove that secession was illegal. Yet the people of both sections did just the opposite. Senator Charles Sumner and Congressman Thaddeus Stevens, in 1861 uncompromising expounders of the theory that the Union was indissoluble, now insisted that the Confederate states had "committed suicide" and should be treated like "conquered provinces." Lincoln believed the issue a "pernicious abstraction" and tried to ignore it.

The process of readmission began in 1862, when Lincoln appointed provisional governors for those parts of the South that had been occupied by federal troops. On December 8, 1863, he issued a proclamation setting forth a general policy. With the exception of high Confederate officials and a few other special groups, Southerners could reinstate themselves by taking a simple loyalty oath. When, in any state, a number equal to ten percent of those voting in the 1860 election had taken this oath, they could set up a state government. Such governments must recognize the "permanent freedom" of the slaves, and provide for black education. The plan, however, did not require that blacks be given the right to vote.

The "10 Percent Plan" reflected Lincoln's lack of vindictiveness but also his political shrewdness. By basing the plan on the presidential power to grant pardons, he was avoiding the touchy problem of obtaining congressional approval. The regimes established under this plan in Tennessee,

Louisiana, and Arkansas bore, in his mind, the same relation to finally reconstructed states that an egg bears to a chicken. "We shall sooner have the fowl by hatching it than by smashing it," he remarked. Eventually representatives of the southern states would again be sitting in Congress, and he wished to lay the groundwork for a strong Republican Party in the section. Yet he realized that Congress had no intention of seating representatives from the "10 percent" states at once.

The Radicals in Congress disliked the 10 Percent Plan, partly because of its moderation and partly because it enabled Lincoln to determine policy toward the recaptured regions. In July 1864 they passed the Wade-Davis Bill, which provided for readmission only after a *majority* of the voters in a southern state had taken a loyalty oath. Besides prohibiting slavery, the new state constitutions would have to repudiate Confederate debts. Lincoln disposed of the Wade-Davis Bill with a pocket veto and there matters stood when Andrew Johnson became president following the assassination.

From origins even more lowly than Lincoln's, Johnson had risen to be governor of Tennessee and United States senator. He was able, but fundamentally unsure of himself, as could be seen in his boastfulness and stubbornness. His political strength came from the poor whites and yeomen farmers of eastern Tennessee, and he was fond of attacking "stuck-up aristocrats." Free homesteads, public education, absolute social equality—such were his objectives. The father of communism, Karl Marx, wrote approvingly of Johnson's "deadly hatred of the oligarchy."

Johnson was a Democrat, but because of his record and his reassuring penchant for excoriating southern aristocrats, the Republicans in Congress were ready to cooperate with him. But like Randolph of Roanoke, his antithesis intellectually and socially, opposition was Johnson's specialty; he soon alienated every powerful Republican in Washington.

Radical Republicans listened to Johnson's diatribes against secessionists and the great planters and assumed that he was anti-southern. Nothing could have been further from the truth. He believed in states rights and shared most of his poor white Tennessee constituents' contempt for blacks. "Damn the negroes, I am fighting these traitorous aristocrats, their masters," he told a friend during the war. "I wish to God," he said on another occasion, "every head of a family in the United States had one slave to take the drudgery and menial service off his family."

The new president did not want to injure or humiliate all southerners. He issued an amnesty proclamation only slightly more rigorous than Lincoln's. By the time Congress convened in December, all the southern states had organized governments, ratified the Thirteenth Amendment abolishing slavery, and elected senators and representatives. Johnson promptly recommended these new governments to Congress.

Republican Radicals

Peace found the Republicans in Congress no more united than they had been during the war. A small group of "ultra" Radicals were demanding immediate civil and political equality for blacks as well as a plot of land and access to a decent education. Senator Sumner led this faction. A second group of Radicals agreed with the ultras' objectives but were prepared to accept half a loaf if necessary to win the support of less radical colleagues. Nearly all Radicals, however, drew the line at social equality.

The moderate Republicans wanted to protect ex-slaves from exploitation and guarantee their basic rights but were unprepared to push for full political equality. A handful of Republicans sided with the Democrats in support of Johnson's approach, but all the rest insisted at least on the minimum demands of the moderates.

Johnson's proposal had no chance in Congress for reasons having little to do with black rights. The Thirteenth Amendment had the effect of increasing the representation of the southern states in Congress because it made the Three-fifths Compromise meaningless. Henceforth those who had been slaves would be counted as whole persons in apportioning seats in the House of Representatives. If Congress seated the southerners, the balance of power might swing to the Democrats.

Furthermore, southern voters had provoked northern resentment by their choice of congressmen. Several dozen men who had served in the Confederate Congress had been elected to either the House or the Senate, together with four generals and many other high officials. Georgia elected Alexander H. Stephens, vice president of the Confederacy, to the Senate, though he was still in a federal prison awaiting trial for treason! Understandably, these choices would sit poorly with northerners.

Finally, the so-called Black Codes enacted by the new southern governments to control former slaves alarmed the North. Although the codes were a considerable improvement over slavery, they placed formidable limitations on freedom. Blacks could not be employed in occupations other than farming and domestic service, or leave their jobs without forfeiting back pay. The Louisiana code required them to sign labor contracts for the year during the first ten days of January. In Mississippi drunkards, vagrants, beggars, "common night-walkers," and even persons who "misspend what they earn" and who could not pay the stiff fines assessed, were to be "hired out . . . at public outcry" to the white person who would take them for the shortest period in return for paying their fines. Such laws, apparently designed to get around the Thirteenth Amendment, outraged northerners.

For all these reasons the Republicans in Congress rejected Johnsonian Reconstruction. Quickly they created a joint committee on Reconstruction, headed by Senator William P. Fessenden of Maine, a moderate, to study the question of readmitting the southern states. The committee held hearings that produced much evidence of the mistreatment of blacks. The hearings strengthened the Radicals, who had been claiming all along that the South was perpetuating slavery under another name.

President Johnson's attitude speeded the swing toward the Radical position. While the hearings were in progress, Congress passed a bill expanding the Freedmen's Bureau, which had been established in March 1865 to care for refugees. The bureau was already exercising considerable coercive and supervisory power in the South. Now Congress added to its authority in order to protect the black population. Although the bill had wide support, Johnson vetoed it.

Congress then passed a Civil Rights Act that, besides declaring that blacks were citizens of the United States, denied the states the power to restrict their rights to testify in court, make contracts, and hold property. In other words, it put teeth in the Thirteenth Amendment.

Once again the president refused to go along though his veto was sure to drive more moderates into the arms of the Radicals. On April 9, 1866, Congress repassed the Civil Rights Act by a two-thirds majority, the first time in American history that a major piece of legislation became law over the veto of a president. This event marked a revolution in the history of Reconstruction. Thereafter Congress, not President Johnson, had the upper hand.

But the Radicals encountered grave problems in fighting for their program. Northerners might object to the Black Codes and to seating "rebels" in Congress, but few believed in racial equality. Between 1865 and 1868, Wisconsin, Minnesota, Connecticut, Nebraska, New Jersey, Ohio, Michigan, and Pennsylvania, all rejected bills granting blacks the vote.

The Radicals were in effect demanding not merely equal rights for freedmen but extra rights: not merely the vote but special protection of that right against the pressure that southern whites would surely apply to undermine it. This idea flew in the face of conventional American beliefs in equality before the law and individual self-reliance. Events were to show that the Radicals were correct—that what amounted to a political revolution in state–federal relations was essential if blacks were to achieve real equality. But in the climate of that day their proposals encountered bitter resistance, and not only from southerners.

Thus, while the Radicals sought partisan advantage in their battle with Johnson and sometimes played on war-bred passions, they were taking large political risks in defense of genuinely held principles. One historian has aptly called them the "moral trustees" of the Civil War.

The Fourteenth Amendment

In June 1866 Congress submitted to the states another constitutional amendment. This Fourteenth Amendment was a truly radical measure. Never before had newly freed slaves been granted significant political rights. It was also a milestone along the road to the centralization of political power in the United States, for it significantly reduced the power of *all* the individual states. In this sense it confirmed the great change wrought by the Civil War: the growth of a more complex, more closely integrated social and economic structure requiring closer national supervision. Few persons understood this aspect of the amendment at the time.

First the amendment supplied a broad definition of American citizenship: "All persons born or naturalized in the United States, and subject to the jurisdiction thereof, are citizens of the United States and of the State wherein they reside." Obviously this included blacks. Then it struck at discriminatory legislation like the Black Codes: "No State shall make or enforce any law which shall abridge the privileges or immunities of citizens of the United States; nor shall any State deprive any person of life, liberty, or property, without due process of law."

The next section attempted to force the southern states to permit blacks to vote. If a state denied the vote to any class of its adult male citizens, its representation was to be reduced proportionately. Under another clause, former federal officials who had served the Confederacy were barred from holding either state or federal office unless specifically pardoned by a two-thirds vote of Congress. Finally, the Confederate debt was repudiated.

The amendment did not specifically outlaw segregation or prevent a state from disfranchising blacks. Nevertheless the southern states would have none of it, and without them the necessary three-fourths majority of the states could not be obtained.

President Johnson vowed to make the choice between the Fourteenth Amendment and his own policy the main issue of the 1866 congressional elections. He embarked on "a swing around the circle" to persuade voters to defeat congressmen who opposed his policy. He failed dismally. Voters have nearly always been offended when a president attempts to influence local elections, and this time was no exception. Northern women objected to the implication that black men were more fitted to vote than white women, but most northern voters were determined that blacks must have at least formal legal equality. The Republicans won better than two-thirds of the seats in both houses, thus insuring that they could override any presi-

dential veto. The party also won control of all the northern state governments. Johnson emerged from the campaign discredited, the Radicals stronger and determined to have their way.

The Reconstruction Acts

Had the southern states been willing to accept the Fourteenth Amendment, coercive measures might have been avoided. Their refusal and continuing indications that local authorities were persecuting blacks finally led to the passage, in March 1867, of the First Reconstruction Act. This law divided the former Confederacy—exclusive of Tennessee, which had ratified the Fourteenth Amendment—into five military districts, each controlled by a major general. It gave these officers almost dictatorial power to protect the civil rights of "all persons," maintain order, and supervise the administration of justice. To rid themselves of military rule, the former states were required to adopt constitutions guaranteeing blacks the right to vote and disfranchising broad classes of ex-Confederates. If these new constitutions proved satisfactory to Congress, and if the new governments ratified the Fourteenth Amendment, their representatives would be admitted to Congress and military rule ended. Johnson's veto of the act was easily overridden.

Although drastic, the Reconstruction Act was so vague that it proved unworkable. In deference to moderate Republican views, it did not spell out the process by which the new constitutions were to be drawn up. Southern whites preferred the status quo, even under army control, to enfranchising blacks and retiring their own respected leaders. They made no effort to follow the steps laid down in the law. Congress therefore passed a second act, requiring the military authorities to register voters and supervise the election of delegates to constitutional conventions. A third act further clarified procedures.

Still white southerners resisted. The laws required that the constitutions be approved by a majority of the registered voters. Simply by staying away from the polls, whites prevented ratification in state after state. At last, in March 1868, a full year after the First Reconstruction Act was passed, Congress changed the rules again. The constitutions were to be ratified by a majority of the actual *voters*. In June 1868 Arkansas, having fulfilled the requirements, was readmitted to the Union, and by July a sufficient number of states had ratified the Fourteenth Amendment to make it part of the Constitution. But it was not until July 1870 that the last southern state, Georgia, qualified to the satisfaction of Congress.

Congress Takes Charge

To carry out this program in the face of determined southern resistance required a degree of single-mindedness over a long period seldom demonstrated by an American legislature. The persistence resulted in part from the suffering and frustrations of the war years and the refusal of the South to accept the spirit of even the mild Reconstruction designed by Johnson. President Johnson's stubbornness also influenced the Republicans. They became obsessed with the need to defeat him. The unsettled times and the large Republican majorities, always threatened by the possibility of a Democratic resurgence if "unreconstructed" southern congressmen were readmitted, sustained their determination.

These considerations led Republicans to attempt a revision of the federal government that almost destroyed the balance between judicial, executive, and legislative power established in 1789. Measures passed between 1866 and 1868 increased the authority of Congress over the army, over the process of amending the Constitution, and over Cabinet members and lesser appointive officers. Finally, in a showdown caused by emotion more than by practical considerations, the Republicans attempted to remove President Johnson from office.

Johnson was a poor president and out of touch with public opinion, but he had done nothing to merit ejection from office. Although he had a low opinion of blacks, his opinion was so widely shared by whites that it is unhistorical to condemn him as a reactionary on this ground. Johnson believed that he was fighting to preserve constitutional government. He was honest and devoted to duty, and his record easily withstood the most searching examination. When Congress passed laws taking away powers granted him by the Constitution, he refused to submit.

The chief issue was the Tenure of Office Act of 1867, which prohibited the president from removing officials who had been appointed with the consent of the Senate without first obtaining Senate approval. In February 1868 Johnson "violated" this act by dismissing Secretary of War Edwin M. Stanton, who had been openly in sympathy with the Radicals for some time. The House, acting under the procedure set up in the Constitution for removing the president, promptly impeached him before the bar of the Senate, Chief Justice Salmon P. Chase presiding.

The trial was conducted in a partisan and vindictive manner. Johnson's lawyers easily established that he had removed Stanton only in an effort to prove the Tenure of Office Act unconstitutional. Nevertheless the Radicals pressed the charges (11 separate articles) relentlessly. Tremendous pressure was applied to the handful of Republican senators who were unwilling to disregard the evidence. Seven of them resisted to the end, and the Senate failed by a single vote to convict Johnson. This was probably fortunate. The trial weakened the presidency, but if Johnson had he been forced from office on such flimsy grounds, the independence of the executive might have been permanently undermined. Then the legislative branch would have become supreme.

The Fifteenth Amendment   1870

The failure of the impeachment did not affect the course of Reconstruction. The president was acquitted on May 16, 1868. A few days later the Republican National Convention nominated General Ulysses S. Grant for the presidency. At the Democratic convention Johnson had considerable support, but the delegates nominated Horatio Seymour, a former governor of New York.

In November Grant won an easy victory in the electoral college, 214 to 80, but the popular vote total was close: 3 million, to 2.7 million. Grant's margin was supplied by southern blacks enfranchised under the Reconstruction Acts, about 450,000 of whom supported him. A majority of white voters probably preferred Seymour. Since many citizens undoubtedly voted Republican because they admired General Grant, the

"The First Vote," the cover illustration from the November 16, 1867 issue of *Harper's Weekly,* shows blacks exercising their right to vote guaranteed to them by the Fifteenth Amendment to the Constitution.

"Black Republican" Reconstruction: Scalawags and Carpetbaggers

The Radicals had at last succeeded in imposing their will on the South. Throughout the region former slaves voted, held office, and exercised the "privileges" and enjoyed the "immunities" guaranteed them by the Fourteenth Amendment. Almost to a man they voted Republican.

The spectacle of blacks not five years removed from slavery in positions of power and responsibility attracted much attention at the time and has since been examined exhaustively by historians. The subject is controversial, but certain facts are beyond argument.

Black officeholders were neither numerous nor inordinately influential. None was ever elected governor of a state; fewer than a dozen and a half during the entire period served in Congress. Blacks held many minor offices and were influential in southern legislatures, though (except in South Carolina) they never made up the majority.

The real rulers of the "black Republican" governments were white: the "scalawags"—southerners willing to cooperate with the Republicans even to the extent of appealing for the support of black voters—and the "carpetbaggers"—northerners who went South as idealists eager to help the freedmen, as employees of the federal government, or more commonly as settlers hoping to improve themselves.

A few scalawags were pre-war politicans or well-to-do planters, but most were ordinary people who had supported the Whig Party before secession. The carpetbaggers were a particularly varied lot. Most had mixed motives and personal gain was among them. But so were opposition to slavery and belief that blacks deserved to be treated decently. Many northern blacks became carpetbaggers: ex-soldiers, ministers, teachers, and lawyers. Some of these blacks became southern office holders, but their influence was limited.

That blacks should fail to dominate southern governments is certainly understandable. They lacked experience in politics and were mostly poor and uneducated. They were nearly everywhere a minority. Those blacks who held office during Reconstruction tended to be better edu-

election statistics suggest that a substantial white majority opposed the policies of the Radicals.

The Reconstruction Acts and the ratification of the Fourteenth Amendment achieved the purpose of enabling black Southerners to vote. The Radicals, however, were not satisfied; they wished to guarantee the right of blacks to vote in every state. Another amendment seemed the only way to accomplish this objective. The 1868 presidential election, which demonstrated how important the black vote could be, strengthened their determination. After considerable bickering over details, the Fifteenth Amendment was sent to the states for ratification in February 1869. It forbade all the states to deny the vote to anyone "on account of race, color, or previous condition of servitude." Once again nothing was said about denial of the vote on the basis of sex.

Most southern states, still under federal pressure, ratified the amendment swiftly. The same was true in most of New England and in some western states. Bitter battles were waged in Connecticut, New York, Pennsylvania, and the states immediately north of the Ohio River, but by March 1870 most of them had ratified the amendment and it became part of the Constitution.

cated and more prosperous. In his interesting analysis of South Carolina black politicians, Thomas Holt shows that a disproportionate number of them had been free before the war. Of the rest, a large percentage had been house servants or artisans, not field hands. Mulatto politicians were also disproportionately numerous and (as a group) more conservative and economically better off than other black leaders.

In South Carolina and elsewhere, blacks proved in the main able and conscientious public servants: able because the best tended to rise to the top in such a fluid situation and conscientious because most of those who achieved importance sought eagerly to demonstrate the capacity of their race for self-government.

It is true that not every black legislator and administrator was a paragon of virtue. In *The Prostrate South* (1874), James S. Pike, a northern journalist, called the government of South Carolina "a huge system of brigandage." This was a gross exaggeration, but waste and corruption were common enough. Some legislators paid themselves large salaries and surrounded themselves with armies of incompetent clerks. An Arkansas black took $9,000 from the state for repairing a bridge that had cost only $500 to build. A South Carolina legislator was voted an additional $1,000 in salary after he lost that sum on a horse race.

However, the corruption must be seen in perspective. The big thieves were nearly always white; blacks got mostly crumbs. Furthermore, graft and callous disregard of the public interest characterized government in every section and at every level during the decade after Appomattox. Big-city bosses in the North embezzled sums that dwarfed the most brazen southern frauds. The New York City Tweed Ring probably made off with more money than all the southern thieves, black and white, combined. The unique features of reconstruction politics—black suffrage, military supervision, carpetbagger and scalawag influence—do not explain all of the southern political corruption.

Southerners who complained about the ignorance and irresponsibility of blacks conveniently forgot that the tendency of 19th-century American democracy was away from educational, financial, or any other restrictions on the franchise. Thousands of white southerners were as illiterate and uncultured as the freedmen, yet no one suggested depriving them of the ballot.

In fact, the Radical southern governments accomplished a great deal. They spent money freely but not entirely wastefully. Tax rates zoomed, but the money financed the repair and expansion of the South's dilapidated railroad network, rebuilt crumbling levees, and expanded social services. Before the Civil War, as Eric Foner points out in *Reconstruction: America's Unfinished Revolution,* planters possessed a disproportionate share of political as well as economic power, and they spent relatively little public money on education and other public services. During Reconstruction an enormous gap had to be filled, and it took money to fill it. The Freedmen's Bureau made a major contribution, establishing more than 4,000 schools, attended by about 250,000 ex-slaves. Northern religious and philanthropic organizations also did important work. Eventually, however, the state governments established and supported hospitals, asylums, and school systems that, although segregated, greatly benefited everyone, whites as well as blacks.

The former slaves grasped eagerly at the opportunity to learn. Nearly all appreciated the immense importance of knowing how to read and write; the sight of elderly men and women poring laboriously over elementary texts beside their grandchildren was common everywhere. Schools and other institutions were supported chiefly by property taxes, and these, of course, hit well-to-do planters hard. Hence much of the complaining about the "extravagance" of Reconstruction governments concealed traditional selfish objections to paying for necessary public projects.

The Ravaged Land

The South's grave economic problems complicated the rebuilding of its political system. The section had never been as prosperous as the North, and wartime destruction left it desperately poor by any standard. The war also disorganized the southern economy. In the long run the abolition of slavery released immeasurable quantities of human energy previously stifled, but the immediate effect was to create confusion. Freedom to travel without a pass, to "see the world," was one

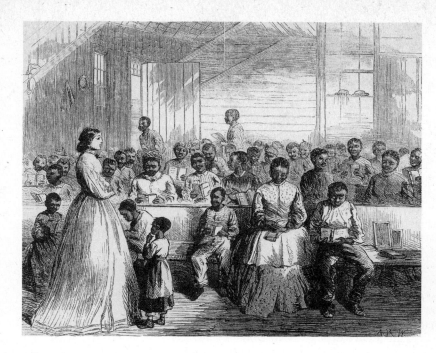

The Freeman's Bureau established 4,329 schools, attended by some 250,000 ex-slaves, in the postwar South. *Harper's Weekly* artist Alfred Waud sketched a Freedmen's Bureau school in Vicksburg, Mississippi, in 1866. Many of the teachers were white women from the North.

of the ex-slaves' most cherished rights. Understandably, many at first equated legal freedom with freedom from having to earn a living, a tendency reinforced for a time by the willingness of the Freedmen's Bureau to provide rations and other forms of relief in war devastated areas.

Most, however, soon realized they would have to earn a living; a small plot of land, they hoped would complete their independence. This objective was forcefully supported by the relentless Congressman Thaddeus Stevens, whose hatred of the planter class was pathological. "The property of the chief rebels should be seized," he stated. If the lands of the richest "70,000 proud, bloated and defiant rebels" were confiscated, the federal government would obtain 394 million acres. Every adult male ex-slave could easily be supplied with 40 acres. The beauty of his scheme, Stevens insisted, was that "nine-tenths of the [southern] people would remain untouched." Dispossessing the great planters would make the South "a safe republic," its lands cultivated by "the free labor of intelligent citizens." If the plan drove the planters into exile, "all the better."

Although Stevens's figures were faulty, many Radicals agreed with him. "We must see that the freedmen are established on the soil," Senator Sumner declared. "The great plantations, which have been so many nurseries of the rebellion, must be broken up, and the freedmen must have the pieces." But the extremists' view was simplistic. Land without tools, seed, and other necessities would have done the freedmen little good. Congress did throw open 46 million acres of poor-quality federal land in the South to blacks under the Homestead Act, but few settled on it. Establishing former slaves on small farms with adequate financial aid would have been of incalculable benefit to them. This would have been practicable, but extremely expensive. It was not done.

The former slaves therefore had either to agree to work for their former owners or strike out on their own. White planters expected the ex-slaves to be incapable of self-directed effort. If allowed to become independent farmers, they would either starve to death or descend into barbarism. Of course the blacks did neither. True, southern agriculture output declined precipitously after slavery was abolished. On the average, free blacks produced much less than slaves had produced. However, the decline in productivity was not caused by the inability of free blacks to work independently. It was simply that being free, they chose no longer to work like slaves. They let their children play instead of forcing them into the fields. Mothers devoted more time to child care and housework, less to farm labor. Elderly blacks worked less. In any case, emancipated blacks were far better off materially than under slavery, when all they got from their masters was mere subsistence.

White southerners misunderstood the reasonable desire of blacks to devote more time to leisure and family activities; they took it as evidence that blacks were lazy. Even General O. O. Howard, head of the Freedmen's Bureau, used the phrase "wholesome compulsion" in describing the policy of forcing blacks to sign labor contracts. A leading southern magazine complained in 1866 that black women now expected their husbands "to support them in idleness." It would never have made such a comment about white wives who devoted themselves to housework and child care.

The family life of ex-slaves was changed in other ways. Male authority increased when husbands became true heads of families. When blacks became citizens, the men acquired rights and powers denied to all women, such as the right to hold public office and serve on juries. Similarly, black women became more like white women, devoting themselves to separate "spheres" where their lives revolved around housekeeping and child rearing.

Sharecropping and the Crop Lien System

Immediately after the war, blacks usually labored for wages, but the wage system did not work well for two reasons. Money was scarce, and banking capital, never adequate even before the collapse of the Confederacy, accumulated slowly. This situation made it difficult for landowners to pay workers in cash. More important, blacks did not like working for wages because it kept them under the direction of whites and thus reminded them of slavery.

Since the voluntary withdrawal of so much black labor from the work force had produced a shortage, they had their way. Quite swiftly, a new agricultural system known as sharecropping emerged. Instead of cultivating the land by gang labor as in antebellum times, planters broke up their estates into small units and established on

each a black family. The planter provided housing, agricultural implements, draft animals, seed, and other supplies, and the family provided labor. The crop was divided between them, usually on a fifty-fifty basis. If the landlord supplied only land and housing, the laborer got a larger share. This was called share tenancy.

Sharecropping gave blacks the day-to-day independence they craved and the hope of earning enough to buy a small farm. In *The Promise of the New South*, Edward L. Ayers described how the family of Daniel Trotter, a Louisiana black, managed to obtain a farm of their own. Trotter started out as a farm laborer. Then he spent six years as a sharecropper. Next he rented land from a series of white farmers. While renting, his wife raised chickens, whose eggs she sold "one or two dozen at a time." The Trotters also raised a few pigs for the market, and Daniel made some "cash money" repairing farm machinery, clocks, and guns. After 14 years the Trotters had saved $175 in greenbacks and $33 in silver, enough to buy what Trotter proudly described as a "plantation." But relatively few blacks possessed the Trotters' energy, determination, and good luck. As late as 1880 blacks owned less than 10 percent of the agricultural land in the South, though they made up more than half of the region's farm population.

Many white farmers were also trapped by the sharecropping system. New fencing laws kept them from grazing livestock on undeveloped land, a practice common before the Civil War. But the main cause of southern rural poverty for whites as well as blacks was the lack of enough capital to finance the sharecropping system. Like their colonial ancestors, the landowners had to borrow against October's harvest to pay for April's seed. Thus the crop-lien system developed, and to protect their investments, lenders insisted that growers concentrate on readily marketable cash crops: tobacco, sugar, and especially cotton.

The system injured everyone. Diversified farming would have reduced the farmers' need for cash, preserved the fertility of the soil, and, by placing a premium on imagination and shrewdness, aided the best of them to rise in the world. Under the crop-lien system, both landowner and sharecropper depended on credit supplied by local bankers, merchants, and storekeepers for everything from seed, tools, and fertilizer to overalls, coffee, and salt. Small southern merchants

After the Civil War, most blacks worked as share-croppers on land owned by whites. In this photograph, black sharecroppers pick cotton, a major cash crop of the South. Because the price for cotton remained low, sharecroppers often fell into debt and were tied to the land almost as tightly as under slavery.

were almost equally victimized by the system, for they also lacked capital, bought goods on credit, and had to pay high interest rates.

Seen in broad perspective, the situation is not difficult to understand. The South, drained of every resource by the war, was competing for funds with the North and West, both vigorous and expanding and therefore voracious consumers of capital. Reconstruction, in the literal sense of the word, was accomplished chiefly at the expense of the standard of living of the producing classes. The crop-lien system and the small storekeeper were only agents of an economic process dictated by national, perhaps even worldwide, conditions.

This does not mean that recovery and growth did not take place. But compared with the rest of the country, progress was slow. Just before the Civil War, cotton harvests averaged about 4 million bales. During the conflict, output fell to about half a million, and the former Confederate states did not enjoy a 4-million bale year again until 1870. Only after 1874 did the crop begin to top that figure consistently.

In manufacturing the South made important gains after the war. The tobacco industry, stimu-lated by the sudden popularity of the cigarette, expanded rapidly. The exploitation of the coal and iron deposits of northeastern Alabama in the early 1870s made a boom town of Birmingham. The manufacture of cotton cloth also increased, productive capacity nearly doubling between 1865 and 1880. Yet the mills of Massachusetts alone had eight times the capacity of the entire South in 1880. Despite the increases, the South's share of the national output of manufactured goods declined sharply during the Reconstruction era.

The White Backlash

Radical southern governments could sustain themselves only so long as they had the support of a significant proportion of the white population, for except in South Carolina and Louisiana, the blacks were not numerous enough to win elections alone. The key to Radical survival lay in the hands of the wealthy merchants and planters, mostly former Whigs. People of this sort did not fear black economic competition. Taking a broad view, they could see that improving the lot of former slaves would benefit all classes.

Southern Republicans had to attract white voters to remain in power. This meant chiefly well-to-do merchants and planters who had formerly been Whigs, people who did not have to fear the competition of blacks. These Republicans used the Union League of America, a patriotic club founded during the war, to control the black vote. Powerless to check the League by open methods, dissident southerners established a number of secret terrorist societies, bearing such names as the Ku Klux Klan, the Knights of the White Camelia, and the Pale Faces.

The most notorious of these organizations was the Klan, which originated in Tennessee in 1866. At first it was purely a social club, but by 1868 it had been taken over by vigilante types dedicated to driving blacks out of politics, and it was spreading rapidly across the South. Sheet-clad nightriders roamed the countryside, frightening the impressionable and chastising the defiant:

Niggers and Leaguers, get out of the way,
We're born of the night and we vanish by day.
No rations have we, but the flesh of man—
And love niggers best—the Ku Klux Klan;

We catch'em alive and roast'em whole,
Then hand'em around with a sharpened pole.
Whole Leagues have been eaten, not leaving a
*   man,*
And went away hungry—the Ku Klux Klan. . .

When intimidation failed, the Klansmen resorted to force, in hundreds of cases murdering their victims, often in the most gruesome manner.

Congress struck at the Klan with three Force Acts, which placed elections under federal jurisdiction and imposed fines and prison sentences on persons convicted of interfering with any citizen's exercise of the franchise. Troops were dispatched, and by 1872 the federal authorities had arrested enough Klansmen to break up the organization.

Nevertheless the Klan contributed substantially to the destruction of Radical regimes in the South. Even respectable white southerners came to the conclusion that terrorism was the most effective way of controlling the black population and escaping northern domination.

Gradually it became respectable to intimidate black voters. Beginning in Mississippi in 1874, terrorism spread through the South. Instead of hiding behind masks and operating in the dark, these terrorists donned red shirts, organized into military companies, and paraded openly. The Mississippi red-shirts seized militant blacks and whipped them publicly. When blacks dared to fight back, heavily armed whites easily put them to rout. In other states similar results followed.

Terrorism fed on fear, fear on terrorism. White violence led to fear of black retaliation and thus to even more brutal attacks. The slightest sign of resistance came to be seen as the beginning of race war, and when the blacks suffered indignities and persecutions in silence, the awareness of how much they must resent the mistreatment made them appear more dangerous still. Thus self-hatred was displaced, guilt suppressed, aggression justified as self-defense, individual conscience submerged in the animality of the mob. Before long the blacks learned to stay home on election day. "Conservative" parties—Democratic in national affairs—took over southern state governments.

The North had subjected the South to control from Washington while preserving state sovereignty in the North itself. In the long run this discrimination proved unworkable. The war was fading into the past and with it the anger it had generated. Northern voters could still be stirred by references to the sacrifices Republicans had made to save the Union and by reminders that the Democratic Party was the organization of rebels, Copperheads, and the Ku Klux Klan. Yet emotional appeals could not convince northerners that it was still necessary to maintain a large army in the South. In 1869 the occupying forces were down to 11,000 men.

Nationalism was reasserting itself. Had not Washington and Jefferson been Virginians? Was not Andrew Jackson Carolina-born? Since most northerners had little real love or respect for blacks, their interest in racial equality flagged once they felt reasonably certain that blacks would not be reenslaved if left to their own devices in the South.

Still another, subtler, force was at work. Before the war, Republicans had stressed the common interest of workers, industrialists, and farmers in a free society in which self-reliant citizens worked together harmoniously. Southern whites had argued that labor must be strictly controlled in the interest of efficiency. As industry became more important in the 1870s, northern manufacturers saw less virtue in "free labor" because of increasing conflicts with their work force. They became more sympathetic to the southern point of view, and therefore more willing to let southern whites reassert control over the blacks.

Grant as President

Other matters occupied the attention of northern voters. The expansion of industry and the rapid development of the West, stimulated by a new wave of railroad building, loomed more important to many than the fortunes of ex-slaves. Heated controversies arose over tariff policy, with western agricultural interests seeking to force reductions from the high levels established during the war, and over the handling of the wartime greenback paper money. Debtor groups and many manufacturers favored further expansion of the supply of dollars, and conservative merchants and bankers argued for retiring the greenbacks in order to return to a "sound" currency.

More damaging to the Republicans was the failure of Ulysses S. Grant to live up to expectations as president. Qualities that had made Grant a fine military leader for a democracy—his dislike of political maneuvering and his simple belief that the popular will could best be observed in the actions of Congress—made him a poor chief executive. When Congress failed to act on his suggestion that the quality of the civil service needed improvement, he announced meekly that if Congress did nothing he would assume the country did not want anything done. Grant was honest, but his honesty was of the naive type that made him the dupe of unscrupulous friends and schemers.

Grant did nothing to prevent the scandals that disgraced his administration and, out of a misplaced belief in the sanctity of friendship, he protected some of the worst culprits and allowed calculating tricksters to use his good name and the prestige of his office to advance their own interests at the country's expense.

The worst of the scandals—such as the Whiskey Ring affair, which implicated Grant's private secretary, Orville E. Babcock, and cost the government millions in tax revenue, and the defalcations of Secretary of War William W. Belknap in the management of Indian affairs—did not become public knowledge during Grant's first term. However, in 1872 Republican reformers, alarmed by rumors of corruption and disappointed by Grant's failure to press for civil service reform, organized the Liberal Republican Party and nominated Horace Greeley, the able but eccentric editor of the *New York Tribune,* for president.

The Liberal Republicans were well-educated, socially prominent types—editors, college presidents, economists, along with a sprinkling of businessmen and politicians. Their liberalism was of the laissez-faire variety; they were for low tariffs and sound money, and against measures benefiting particular groups, whether labor unions or railroad companies or farm organizations. They disparaged universal suffrage, which, one of them said, "can only mean in plain English the government of ignorance and vice."

The Democrats also nominated Greeley, though he had devoted his political life to flailing the Democratic Party in the *Tribune.* That surrender to expediency, together with Greeley's temperamental unsuitability for the presidency, made the campaign a fiasco for the reformers. Grant triumphed easily, with a popular majority of nearly 800,000.

Nevertheless the defection of the Liberal Republicans hurt the Republican Party in Congress. So, of course did the depression that followed the Panic of 1873. In the 1874 elections, no longer hampered as in the presidential contest by Greeley's notoriety and Grant's fame, the Democrats carried the House of Representatives. It was clear that the days of military rule in the South were ending. By the end of 1875 only three southern states, South Carolina, Florida, and Louisiana, were still under Republican control.

The Disputed Election of 1876

Against this background the presidential election of 1876 took place. Since corruption in government was the most widely discussed issue, the Republicans nominated Governor Rutherford B. Hayes of Ohio, a former general with an unsmirched reputation. The Democrats picked Governor Samuel J. Tilden of New York, a wealthy lawyer who had attracted national attention for his part in breaking up the Tweed Ring in New York City.

In November early returns indicated that Tilden had carried New York, New Jersey, Connecticut, Indiana and the entire South, including Louisiana, Florida, and South Carolina, where the Republican Party was still in control. This seemed to give him 203 electoral votes to Hayes's 165.

However, Republican leaders had anticipated the possible loss of Florida, South Carolina, and Louisiana and were prepared to use their control of the election machinery in those states to throw out sufficient Democratic ballots to alter the results if doing so would change the national outcome. Realizing that the electoral votes of those states were exactly enough to elect their man, they telegraphed their henchmen on the scene and ordered them to go into action. The local Republicans then invalidated Democratic ballots in wholesale lots and filed returns showing Hayes the winner. Naturally the local Democrats protested vigorously and filed their own returns.

Congress created an electoral commission to decide the disputed cases. The commission consisted of five senators (three Republicans and two Democrats), five representatives (three Democrats and two Republicans), and five justices of the Supreme Court (two Democrats, two Republicans, and one "independent" judge, David Davis). Since it was a foregone conclusion that the others would vote for their party no matter what the evidence, Davis would presumably swing the balance in the interest of fairness.

However, before the commission met, the Illinois legislature elected Davis senator! He had to resign from the Court and the commission. Since, in those partisan times, independents were rare even on the Supreme Court, no neutral was available to replace him. The vacancy went to Associate Justice Joseph P. Bradley of New Jersey, a Republican.

Evidence presented before the commission revealed a disgraceful picture of election shenanigans. On the one hand, in all three disputed states

Democrats had clearly cast a majority of the votes; on the other, it was unquestionable that many blacks had been forcibly prevented from voting.

In truth, both sides were shamefully corrupt. Lew Wallace, a northern politician later famous as the author of the novel *Ben Hur,* visited Louisiana and Florida shortly after the election. "It is terrible to see the extent to which all classes go in their determination to win," he wrote his wife from Florida. "Money and intimidation can obtain the oath of white men as well as black to any required statement. . . . If we win, our methods are subject to impeachment for possible fraud. If the enemy win, it is the same thing."

Most modern authorities take the view that in a fair election the Republicans would have carried South Carolina and Louisiana but that Florida would have gone to Tilden, giving him the election, 188 electoral votes to 181. In the last analysis, this opinion has been arrived at simply by counting white and black noses: Blacks were in the majority in South Carolina and Louisiana. Amid the tension and confusion of early 1877, however,

The Compromise of 1877

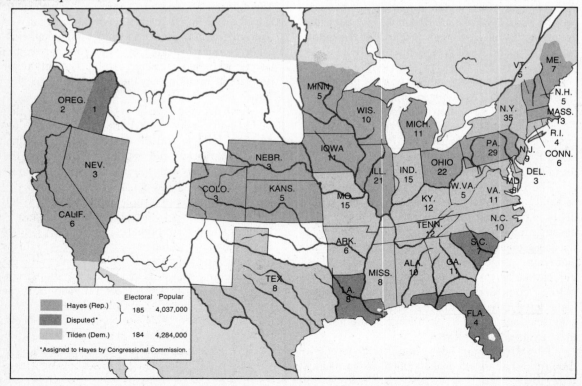

	Electoral	Popular
Hayes (Rep.)	185	4,037,000
Disputed*		
Tilden (Dem.)	184	4,284,000

*Assigned to Hayes by Congressional Commission.

even a Solomon would have been hard pressed to judge rightly amid the rumors, lies, and contradictory statements, and the electoral commission was not composed of Solomons. The Democrats had some hopes that Justice Bradley would be sympathetic to their case, for he was known to be opposed to harsh Reconstruction policies. On the eve of the commission's decision in the Florida controversy, he was apparently ready to vote in favor of Tilden. But the Republicans subjected him to tremendous political pressure. When he read his opinion on February 8, it was for Hayes. Thus, by a vote of 8 to 7, the commission awarded Florida's electoral votes to the Republicans.

Vote after vote, both on details and in the final decisions in the other cases, went exactly according to party lines. The atmosphere of judicial inquiry and deliberation was a facade. The commission assigned all the disputed electoral votes to Hayes.

To such a level had the republic of Jefferson and John Adams descended. Democratic institutions, shaken by the South's refusal to go along with the majority in 1860 and by the suppression of civil rights during the rebellion, and further weakened by military intervention and the intimidation of blacks in the South during Reconstruction, seemed now a farce. Democrats talked of not being bound by so obviously partisan a judgment. Tempers flared in Congress, where some spoke ominously of a filibuster that would prevent the recording of the electoral vote and leave the country, on March 4, with no president at all.

The Compromise of 1877

Fortunately, forces for compromise had been at work behind the scenes in Washington for some time. Although northern Democrats threatened to fight to the last ditch, many southern Democrats were willing to accept Hayes if he would promise to remove the troops and allow the southern states to

Milestones

1863	Lincoln announces "10 Percent Plan" for Reconstruction		Fourth Reconstruction Act
1865	Establishment of the Freedmen's Bureau		Senate acquits Johnson
	General Lee surrenders at Appomattox Court House		Ratification of Fourteenth Amendment
	Assassination of Abraham Lincoln; Andrew Johnson becomes president		Ulysses S. Grant is elected president
	Johnson's Amnesty Plan	1868–1872	Ku Klux Klan in action
	Ratification of Thirteenth Amendment	1870	Ratification of Fifteenth Amendment
1865–1866	Enactment of Black Codes by Southern states	1870–1871	Force (Ku Klux Klan) Act destroys Klan
1866	Civil Rights Act passes over Johnson's veto	1872	Liberal Republican Party nominates Horace Greeley for president
	Johnson campaigns for his Reconstruction policy		Grant is reelected president
1867	First Reconstruction Act	1876	Disputed presidential election
	Tenure of Office Act	1877	Electoral commission awards disputed votes to Rutherford B. Hayes
1868	House of Representatives impeaches Johnson		Hayes agrees to Compromise of 1877

manage their internal affairs by themselves. Ex-Whig planters and merchants who had reluctantly abandoned the carpetbag governments and who sympathized with Republican economic politices hoped that by supporting Hayes they might contribute to the restoration of the two party system. With the tacit support of many Democrats, the electoral vote was counted by the president of the Senate on March 2, and Hayes was declared elected, 185 votes to 184.

Like all compromises, this agreement was not entirely satisfactory; like most, it was not honored in every detail. Hayes recalled the last troops from South Carolina and Louisiana in April. He appointed a former Confederate general, David M. Key of Tennessee, postmaster general and delegated to him the congenial task of finding southerners willing to serve their country as officials of a Republican administration. The new alliance of ex-Whigs and northern Republicans did not flourish, however, and the South remained solidly Democratic. The hoped-for federal aid for the Texas and Pacific did not materialize. The major significance of the compromise, one of the great intersectional political accommodations of American history, has been well summarized by C. Vann Woodward:

> The Compromise of 1877 marked the abandonment of principles and force and a return to the traditional ways of expediency and concession. . . . It wrote an end to Reconstruction and recognized a new regime in the South. More profoundly than Constitutional amendments and wordy statutes it shaped the future of four million freedmen and their progeny for generations to come.

For most of the former slaves, this future was to be bleak. Forgotten in the North, manipulated and then callously rejected by the South, rebuffed by the Supreme Court, voiceless in national affairs—they and their descendants were condemned in the interests of sectional harmony to lives of poverty, indignity, and little hope. Meanwhile, the rest of the United States continued its golden march toward wealth and power.

Supplementary Reading

Eric Foner, **Reconstruction: America's Unfinished Revolution** (1988), is an excellent survey or the period; see also, Foner, **Nothing but Freedom** (1983). W. E. B. Du Bois's classic **Black Reconstruction in America*** (1935), is militantly problack.

On Andrew Johnson, J. E. Sefton, **Andrew Johnson and the Uses of Constitutional Power*** (1980), is a good brief biography. See also E. L. McKitrick, **Andrew Johnson and Reconstruction*** (1960), H. L. Trefousse, **The Radical Republicans** (1969), and M. L. Benedict, **The Impeachment and Trial of Andrew Johnson** (1973). J. M. McPherson, **The Struggle for Equality: Abolitionists and the Negro in the Civil War and Reconstruction*** (1964), is also important. On the Fourteenth Amendment, see Joseph James, **The Framing of the Fourteenth Amendment*** (1956); on the Fifteenth, William Gillette, **The Right to Vote: Politics and the Passage of the Fifteenth Amendment*** (1965).

Conditions in the South during Reconstruction are discussed in R. H. Abbott, **The Republican Party and the South** (1986), Joel Williamson, **The Crucible of Race: Black-White Relations in the South** (1984), Michael Perman, **Reunion Without Compromise** (1973), H. N. Rabinowitz, **Race Relations in the Urban South** (1978), and J. L. Roark, **Masters Without Slaves** (1977).

Useful state studies include Thomas Holt, **Black over White: Negro Political Leadership in South Carolina** (1977), and Joel Wiliamson, **After Slavery: The Negro in South Carolina during Reconrtruction*** (1965).

On the Ku Klux Klan, see G. C. Rable, **But There Was No Peace** (1984), and A. W. Trelease, **White Terror: the Ku Klux Klan Conspiracy** (1971). On southern agriculture during Reconstruction see E. L. Ayers, **The Promise of the New South** (1992), and G. D. Jaynes, **Branches Without Roots** (1986).

The best treatment of Grant's presidency is W. S. McFeely, **Grant** (1981). See also J. G. Sproat, **"The Best Men": Liberal Reformers in the Gilded Age*** (1968). For the disputed election of 1876 and the compromise following it, consult C. V. Woodward, **Reunion and Reaction*** (1951). William Gillette, **Retreat from Reconstruction** (1980), is also useful.

---

*Available in paperback.

CHAPTER 17

In the Wake of War

The American Commonwealth
"Root, Hog, or Die"
The Shape of Politics
Issues of the Gilded Age
Blacks After Reconstruction
Booker T. Washington and the Atlanta
 Compromise
The West After the Civil War
The Plains Indians
Indian Wars
The Destruction of Tribal Life
Exploiting Mineral Wealth in the West
The Land Bonanza
Western Railroad Building
The Cattle Kingdom
Open-Range Ranching
Barbed-Wire Warfare

When Americans turned from fighting and making weapons to more constructive occupations, they transformed their agriculture, trade, manufacturing, mining, and means of communication. Immigration increased rapidly. Cities grew in size and number, exerting on every aspect of life an influence at least as pervasive as that exercised on earlier generations by the frontier. Farm production rose to new heights, invigorated by new marketing methods and the increased use of machinery. Railroad construction stimulated and unified the economy, helping to make possible still larger and more efficient industrial and agricultural enterprises. The flow of gold and silver from western mines excited people's imagina-

tions and their avarice. More than a mere change of scale, these developments altered the structure of the economy and the society.

The American Commonwealth

Most students of the subject have concluded that the political history of the United States in the last quarter of the 19th century was singularly divorced from the meaningful issues of that day. When controversial measures were debated, they excited far less argument than they merited. A graduated income tax was enacted during the Civil War, repealed after that conflict, reenacted in 1894, and then declared unconstitutional in 1895 without causing much more than a ripple in the world of partisan politics. This was typical; as the English observer James Bryce noted in *The American Commonwealth* (1888), his brilliant analysis of the American political system, the politicians were "neglecting to discover and work out new principles capable of solving the problems which now perplex the country."

"Root, Hog, or Die"

After Appomattox, the immense resources of the United States, combined with the high value most Americans assigned to work and achievement, made the people strongly materialistic. From colonial times they had assumed that prosperity was the natural state of things, and they had shown an inordinate respect for wealth. The Civil War further encouraged the glorification of money and the things it could buy. The North's capacity to produce the tools of war had helped preserve the Union; the role of businessmen and manufacturers in winning the struggle was clear to every soldier from General Grant to the lowliest private.

After the failures of Reconstruction, Americans seemed even more enamored of material values. They were tired of sacrifice, eager to act for themselves. committed more strongly to a government policy of noninterference, or laissez-faire. Imbued with the entrepreneurial spirit and never especially noted for their sophistication, taste, or interest in preserving the resources of the country, the people now tolerated the grossest kind of waste and seemed to care little about corruption in high places, so long as no one interfered with their personal pursuit of profit. Mark Twain, raised in an earlier era, called this a Gilded Age, dazzling on the surface, base metal below.

Certain intellectual currents encouraged the exploitative drives of the people. By the seventies Charles Darwin's theory of evolution was beginning to influence opinion in the United States. That nature had ordained a kind of inevitable progress, governed by the natural selection of those individual organisms best adapted to survive in a particular environment, seemed eminently reasonable to most Americans, for it fitted well with their own experiences. All-out competition, unhampered by government regulations or other restrictions, would mean that only the most efficient would "survive" in every field of human endeavor.

Yale professor William Graham Sumner sometimes used the survival-of-the-fittest analogy in teaching undergraduates. "Professor," one student asked Sumner, "don't you believe in any government aid to industries?" "No!" Sumner replied, "it's root, hog, or die." The student persisted: "Suppose some professor of political science came along and took your job away from you. Wouldn't

Charles Darwin's theory of evolution and natural selection challenged traditional thinking in America and across Europe. Many fundamentalists felt that his views were a blatant rejection of biblical teachings.

you be sore?" "Any other professor is welcome to try," Sumner answered promptly. "If he gets my job, it is my fault. My business is to teach the subject so well that no one can take the job away from me." Sumner's argument came to be called *Social Darwinism,* the idea that economic and social relations were controlled by Darwin's concept, "the survival of the fittest."

Few businessmen were directly influenced by Darwin's ideas. Most accepted any aid they could get from the government. Nevertheless, most were sincere individualists. They believed in competition, being convinced that the nation would best prosper if all people were free to seek their personal fortunes by their own methods.

The Shape of Politics

A succession of weak presidents presided over the White House, and Congress dominated the government. Within Congress, the Senate generally overshadowed the House of Representatives. Critics called the Senate a "rich man's club," and it did contain many millionaires. However, the true sources of the Senate's influence lay in the long tenure of many of its members and in its long-established reputation for wisdom, intelligence, and statesmanship.

The House of Representatives, on the other hand, was one of the most disorderly and inefficient legislative bodies in the world. An infernal din rose from the crowded chamber. Desks slammed; members held private conversations, hailed pages, shuffled from place to place, clamored for the attention of the Speaker—and all the while some poor orator tried to discuss the question of the moment. Speaking in the House, one writer said, was like trying to address the crowd on a passing Broadway bus from the curb in front of the Astor House in New York City.

The major political parties seldom took clearly opposing positions on the questions of the day. Democrats were separated from Republicans more by accidents of geography, religious affiliation, and ethnic background than by economic issues.

The fundamental division between Democrats and Republicans was sectional, a result of the Civil War. The South, after the political rights of blacks had been drastically circumscribed, became heavily Democratic. Most of New England was solidly Republican. Elsewhere the two parties stood in fair balance, though the Republicans tended to have the advantage. A preponderance of the well-to-do were Republicans. Immigrants, Catholics, and—except for blacks—other minority groups tended to vote Democratic. But there were many exceptions.

The personalities of political leaders often dictated the voting patterns of individuals and groups. In 1892, when Grover Cleveland defeated Benjamin Harrison for president, a prominent steel manufacturer wrote to his even more prominent competitor, Andrew Carnegie: "I am very sorry for President Harrison, but I cannot see that our interests are going to be affected one way or the other." And Carnegie replied: "We have nothing to fear. . . . Cleveland is [a] pretty good fellow. Off for Venice tomorrow."

Most voters—farmers, laborers, shopkeepers, white-collar workers—usually distributed their ballots fairly evenly between the two parties; the balance of political power after 1876 was almost perfect. Majorities in both the Senate and the House fluctuated continually. Between 1876 and 1896, the "dominant" Republican Party controlled both houses of Congress and the presidency at the same time for only one two-year period.

Issues of the Gilded Age

Four questions obsessed politicians in these years. One was the "bloody shirt." The term, which became part of the language after a Massachusetts congressman dramatically displayed the bloodstained shirt of an Ohio carpetbagger who had been flogged by terrorists in Mississippi, referred to the tactic of reminding northern voters that the men who had taken the South out of the Union had been Democrats and that they and their descendants were still Democrats. "Every man that endeavored to tear down the old flag," a Republican orator proclaimed in 1876, "was a Democrat. . . . The man that assassinated Abraham Lincoln was a Democrat. . . . Soldiers, every scar you have on your heroic bodies was given you by a Democrat." Republicans waved the bloody shirt in order to divert the attention of voters from their

party's shortcomings. Nothing, of course, so effectively obscured the real issues of the day.

Waving the bloody shirt was related intimately to the issue of the rights of blacks. Throughout this period Republicans vacillated between trying to build up their organization in the South by appealing to black voters—which required them to make sure that blacks in the South could vote—and trying to win conservative white support by stressing economic issues such as the tariff. When the former strategy seemed wise, they waved the bloody shirt with vigor; in the latter case, they piously announced that the blacks' future was "as safe in the hands of one party as it is in the other."

The question of veterans' pensions also bore a close relationship to the bloody shirt. Republican politicians played on the emotions of the ex-soldiers by waving the bloody shirt, but the tough-minded leaders of the veterans demanded that they prove their sincerity by treating in open-handed fashion the warriors whose blood had stained the shirt.

The tariff was another perennial issue in post–Civil War politics. Despite considerable loose talk about free trade, almost no one in the United States believed in eliminating duties on imports. Manufacturers desired protective tariffs to keep out competing products, and a majority of their workers were convinced that wage levels would fall if goods produced by cheap foreign labor entered the United States untaxed. Many farmers supported protection, though almost no competing agricultural products were being imported. Congressman William McKinley of Ohio, who reputedly could make reciting a tariff schedule sound like poetry, stated the majority opinion in the clearest terms: High tariffs foster the growth of industry and thus create jobs. "Reduce the tariff and labor is the first to suffer," he said.

The tariff could have been a real political issue because American technology was advancing so rapidly that many industries no longer required protection from foreign competitors. A powerful argument could have been made for scientific rate-making that would adjust duties to actual conditions and avoid overprotection. The Democrats professed to believe in moderation, yet whenever party leaders tried to revise the tariff downward, Democratic congressmen from industrial states like Pennsylvania and New York sided with the Republicans. Every new tariff bill became an occasion for logrolling, lobbying, and outrageous politicking rather than for sane discussion and careful evaluation of the public interest.

A third political question in this period was currency reform. During the Civil War, it will be recalled, the government, faced with obligations it could not meet by taxing or borrowing, suspended specie payments and issued about $450 million in paper money. The greenbacks did not command the full confidence of a people accustomed to money readily convertible into gold or silver. Greenbacks seemed to threaten inflation, for how could one trust the government not to issue them in wholesale lots to avoid passing unpopular tax laws? Thus, when the war ended, strong sentiment developed for withdrawing the greenbacks from circulation and returning to a bullion standard.

In fact, beginning during Reconstruction prices declined sharply. The deflation increased the real income of bondholders and other creditors but injured debtors. Farmers were particularly hard hit, for many of them had borrowed heavily during the wartime boom to finance expansion.

Here was a question of real significance. Many groups supported some kind of currency inflation. A National Greenback Party nominated Peter Cooper, an iron manufacturer, for president in 1876. Cooper received only 81,000 votes, but a new Greenback Labor Party polled over a million in 1878, electing 14 congressmen. However, the major parties refused to confront each other over the currency question. While Republicans in general professed to be the party of sound money, most western Republicans favored expansion of the currency. And while one wing of the Democrats flirted with the Greenbackers, the conservative, or "Bourbon" Democrats favored deflation as much as Republicans did.

In 1874 a bill to increase the supply of greenbacks was defeated in a Republican-dominated Congress only by the veto of President Grant. The next year Congress voted to resume specie payments, but in order to avoid a party split on the question, the Republicans agreed to allow $300 million in greenbacks to remain in circulation and to postpone actual resumption of specie payments until 1879. Spurred on by the silver miners and by

those advocating any measure that would increase the volume of money in circulation, numbers of congressmen introduced proposals to coin large amounts of silver. Neither party took a clear-cut stand on silver.

The final major political issue of these years was civil service reform. That the federal bureaucracy needed overhauling nearly everyone agreed. As American society grew larger and more complex, the government necessarily took on more functions. The need for professional administration increased. The number of federal employees rose from 53,000 in 1871 to 256,000 at the end of the century. Corruption flourished; waste and inefficiency were the normal state of affairs.

Every honest observer could see the need for reform, but the politicians refused to surrender the power of dispensing government jobs to their lieutenants without regard for their qualifications. They argued that patronage was the lifeblood of politics, that parties could not function without armies of loyal political workers, and that the workers expected and deserved the rewards of office when their efforts were crowned with victory at the polls. Typical was the attitude of the New York assemblyman who, according to Theodore Roosevelt, had "the same idea about Public Life and the Civil Service that a vulture has of a dead sheep." When reformers suggested establishing the most modest kind of professional, nonpartisan civil service, politicians of both parties subjected them to every kind of insult and ridicule.

Blacks After Reconstruction

Minorities were treated with callousness and contempt in the postwar decades. That the South would deal harshly with the former slaves once federal control was relaxed probably should have been expected. President Hayes had urged blacks to trust southern whites. A new Era of Good Feelings had dawned, he announced after making a good-will tour of the South shortly after his inauguration. By December 1877 he had been sadly disillusioned. However, he did nothing to remedy the situation. Frederick Douglass called Hayes's policy "sickly conciliation."

Hayes's successors in the 1880s did no better. "Time is the only cure," President Garfield said, thereby confessing that he had no policy at all. President Arthur gave federal patronage to antiblack groups in an effort to split the Democratic South. In President Cleveland's day blacks had scarcely a friend in high places, North or South. Hayes, Garfield, and Arthur were Republicans, Cleveland a Democrat; party made little difference. Both parties subscribed to hypocritical statements about equality and constitutional rights. Neither did anything to implement them.

For a time blacks were not totally disfranchised in the South, but in the nineties the southern states, led by Mississippi, began to deprive blacks of the vote despite the Fifteenth Amendment. Poll taxes raised a formidable economic barrier, one that also disfranchised many poor whites. Literacy tests completed the work; a number of states provided a loophole for illiterate whites by including an "understanding" clause whereby an illiterate person could qualify by demonstrating an ability to explain the meaning of a section of the state constitution when an election official read it to him. Blacks who attempted to take the test were uniformly declared to have failed it.

In Louisiana 130,000 blacks voted in the election of 1896. Then the law was changed. In 1900 only 5,000 votes were cast by blacks. With unctuous hypocrisy, white southerners insisted that they loved "their" blacks dearly and wished only to protect them from "the machinations of those who would use them only to further their own base ends." "We take away the Negroes' votes," a Louisiana politician explained, "to protect them just as we would protect a little child and prevent it from injuring itself with sharp-edged tools."

Practically every Supreme Court decision after 1877 that affected blacks somehow "nullified or curtailed" their rights. The *Civil Rights Cases* (1883) declared the Civil Rights Act of 1875 unconstitutional. Blacks who were refused equal accommodations or privileges by hotels, theaters, and other privately owned facilities had no recourse at law, the Court announced. The Fourteenth Amendment guaranteed their civil rights against invasion by the states, not by individuals.

In *Plessy* v. *Ferguson* (1896) the Court ruled that even in places of public accommodation, such as railroads and, by implication, schools, segregation was legal so long as facilities of equal quality were provided. "If one race be inferior to the other socially, the Constitution of the United States cannot put them upon the same plane." In a noble dissent in the *Plessy* case, Justice John Marshall Harlan protested this line of argument. "Our Constitution is color-blind," he said. "The destinies of the two races . . . are indissolubly linked together, and the interests of both require that the common government of all shall not permit the seeds of race hate to be planted under the sanction of law." Alas, more than half a century was to pass before the Court came around to Harlan's reasoning and reversed the *Plessy* decision. Meanwhile, total segregation was imposed throughout the South. Separate schools, prisons, hospitals, recreational facilities, and even cemeteries were provided for blacks, and these were almost never equal to those available to whites.

Most northerners supported the government and the Court. Nearly all the newspapers commented favorably on the decision in the *Civil Rights Cases*. In news stories papers presented a stereotyped, derogatory picture of blacks, no matter what the circumstances. "The Negro's day is over," the tough-minded William Graham Sumner explained.

Booker T. Washington and the Atlanta Compromise

Since nearly all biologists, physicians, and other supposed experts on race were convinced that blacks were inferior beings, educated northerners could hardly avoid accepting black inferiority as fact. James Bryce saw many Americans of this type and often absorbed their point of view. Negroes, Bryce wrote, were docile, pliable, submissive, lustful, childish, impressionable, emotional, heedless, and "unthrifty." They had "no capacity for abstract thinking, for scientific inquiry, or for any kind of invention."

Like Bryce, most Americans did not especially wish blacks ill; they simply refused to consider them quite human and consigned them complacently to oblivion, along with the Indians. A vicious circle was established: By denying blacks decent educational opportunities and good jobs, the dominant race could use the blacks' resultant ignorance and poverty to justify the inferior facilities offered them.

Southern blacks reacted to this deplorable situation in a variety of ways. Some sought redress in racial pride and what would later be called black nationalism. A few became so disaffected with American life that they tried to revive the African colonization movement. "Africa is our home," insisted Bishop Henry M. Turner, a huge, plain-spoken man who had served as an army chaplain during the war and as a member of the Georgia legislature during Reconstruction. "Every man that has the sense of an animal must see there is no future in this country for the Negro." Another militant, T. Thomas Fortune, editor of the *New York Age* and founder of the Afro-American League (1887), called on blacks to demand full civil rights, better schools, and fair wages and to fight against discrimination of every sort. "Let us stand up like men in our own organization," he urged. "If others use . . . violence to combat our peaceful arguments, it is not for us to run away from violence."

Militancy and black separatism won few adherents among southern blacks. Life was better than it had been under slavery. But the forces of repression were extremely powerful and blacks fumed with resentment. "The things Southern whites and blacks said about each other at the turn of the century," writes the historian Edward L. Ayers, were "filled with bitterness, hatred and confusion." The late 19th century saw more lynchings in the South than any other period of American history.

This helps explain the tactics of Booker T. Washington, one of the most extraordinary Americans of that generation. Washington had been born a slave in Virginia in 1856. Laboriously he obtained an education, supporting himself while a student by working as a janitor. In 1881, with the financial help of northern philanthropists, he founded Tuskegee Institute in Alabama, which specialized in vocational training. His experiences convinced him that blacks must lift themselves by their own bootstraps but that they must also accommodate themselves to white prejudices.

In 1895 Washington made a now-famous speech to a mixed audience in Atlanta. To the blacks he said: "Cast down your bucket where you are," by which he meant stop fighting segregation and second-class citizenship and concentrate on learning useful skills. Progress up the social and economic ladder would come not from "artificial

Booker T. Washington's famous Atlanta address in 1895 received mixed reactions in the black community. His most fervent challenge came from W.E.B. DuBois, a professor at Atlanta University, who rejected Washington's call for patience and accommodation as a means to end racial segregation.

forcing" but from self-improvement. He asked the whites of what he called "our beloved South" to lend blacks a hand in their efforts to advance themselves. If you will do so, he promised, you will be "surrounded by the most patient, faithful, lawabiding, and unresentful people that the world has seen."

This "Atlanta Compromise" delighted white southerners, but blacks responded to it with mixed feelings. Accepting Washington's approach might relieve them of many burdens and dangers. Being obsequious might, like discretion, be the better part of valor. But Washington was asking them to give up specific rights in return for vague promises of future help. The cost was high in surrendered personal dignity and lost hopes of obtaining real justice.

Washington's career illustrates the terrible dilemma that American blacks have always faced: the choice between confrontation and accommodation. This choice was particularly difficult in the late 19th century.

Washington chose accommodation. It is easy to condemn him as a toady but difficult to see how, at that time, a more aggressive policy could have succeeded. One can even interpret the Atlanta Compromise as a subtle form of black nationalism; in a way, Washington was not urging blacks to accept inferiority and racial slurs but to ignore them. His own behavior lends force to this view, for his method of operating was indeed subtle, even devious. In his public speeches he minimized the importance of civil and political rights and accepted separate but equal facilities—if they were truly equal. Behind the scenes he lobbied against restrictive measures, marshaled large sums of money to fight test cases in the courts, and worked hard in northern states to organize the black vote and make sure that black political leaders got a share of the spoils of office. He may not have been an admirable man, but he was a useful one. His defects point up more the unlovely aspects of the age than those of his own character.

The West After the Civil War

The West displayed these aspects of the age, and a number of others, in heightened form. Nearly a third of all Californians were foreign born, as were more than 40 percent of Nevadans and over half the residents of Idaho and Arizona. There were, of course, large populations of Spanish speaking Americans of Mexican origin all over the Southwest. Chinese and Irish laborers were pouring into California by the thousands, and there were substantial numbers of Germans, Scandinavians, and other Europeans on the high plains east of the Rockies.

Although the image of the West as the land of great open spaces is accurate enough, the region contained several bustling cities. San Francisco, with a population approaching 250,000 in the late 1870s, had long outgrown its role as a rickety boom town. Denver, San Antonio, and Salt Lake City were far smaller, but growing rapidly and equally "urban."

There was, in short, no one West, no typical westerner. If the economy was predominantly agricultural and extractive, it was also commercial and entering the early stages of industrial devel-

opment. The seeds of such large enterprises as Wells Fargo, Levi Strauss, and half a dozen important department store empires were sown in the immediate postwar decades.

Above all, however, the West epitomized the "every man for himself" psychology of post-Reconstruction American society. In 1879 several thousand southern blacks suddenly migrated to western Kansas. When asked why the move, one of their leaders replied: "The white people [in the South] treat our people so bad . . . that it is impossible for them to stand it." But their treatment in Kansas was not much better. California had been a free state from the moment of its entry in the Union, but it treated its black citizens poorly, even refusing to ratify the Fifteenth Amendment.

Beginning in the mid-1850s a steady flow of Chinese immigrated to the West Coast region. About four or five thousand a year came until the negotiation of the Burlingame Treaty of 1868, the purpose of which was to provide cheap labor for railroad construction crews. Thereafter the annual influx more than doubled. When the railroads were completed and the Chinese began to compete with native workers, riots broke out in San Francisco. Chinese workers were called "groveling worms," "more slavish and brutish than the beasts that roam the fields." The California constitution of 1879 denied the right to vote to any "native of China" along with idiots, the insane, and persons convicted of "any infamous crime."

When Chinese immigration suddenly increased in 1882 to nearly 40,000, Congress passed a law prohibiting all Chinese immigration for ten years. Later legislation extended the ban indefinitely.

The Plains Indians

"Whites," the historian Rodman Paul wrote, "did not shed their old attitudes when they crossed into a new country." Paul's generalization applies with special force to the way western whites dealt with the Indians. For 250 years the Indians had been driven back steadily, yet on the eve of the Civil War they still inhabited roughly half the United States. By the time of Hayes's inauguration, however, the Indians had been shattered as an independent people, and in another decade the survivors were penned up on reservations.

In 1860 in the deserts of the Great Basin between the Sierras and the Rockies, in the mountains themselves, and on the semiarid, grass-covered plains between the Rockies and the edge of white civilization in eastern Kansas and Nebraska—nearly a quarter of a million Indians dominated the land. By far the most important lived on the High Plains. These tribes possessed a generally uniform culture. Although they seemed the epitome of freedom, pride, and self-reliance, they had already begun to fall under the sway of white power, They eagerly adopted the products of the more technically advanced culture—cloth, metal tools, weapons, cheap decorations. However, the most important thing the whites gave them had nothing to do with technology—it was the horse.

Cortés brought the first modern horses to America in the 16th century. Multiplying rapidly thereafter, the animals soon roamed wild from Texas to the Argentine. By the 18th century the Indians of the plains had made them a vital part of their culture. Mounted Indians could run down buffalo instead of stalking them on foot. They could move more easily over the country and fight more effectively too. The Indians also adopted modern weapons: the cavalry sword and the rifle. Both added to their effectiveness as hunters and fighters. However, like the whites' liquor and diseases, horses and guns caused problems too. The buffalo herds began to diminish, and warfare became bloodier and more frequent.

In a familiar tragic pattern, the majority of the western tribes greeted the first whites to enter their domains in a friendly fashion. As late as the 1830s, white hunters and trappers ranged freely over most of the West, trading with the Indians and often marrying Indian women.

After the start of the gold rush, the whites began to undermine the Indian empire in the West. Deliberately the government in Washington prepared the way. In 1851 Thomas Fitzpatrick, an Indian agent, summoned a great "council" of the tribes at Horse Creek, 37 miles east of Fort Laramie, in what is now Wyoming. The Indians respected Fitzpatrick, who had recently married a woman who was half Indian. At Horse Creek he persuaded each tribe to accept definite limits to its hunting grounds. For example, the Sioux nations were to keep north of the Platte River, and the Cheyenne and Arapaho were to confine themselves to the Colorado foothills. In return the Indians were promised gifts and annual payments. This policy, known as "concentration," was designed to cut down on intertribal warfare and—far more important—to enable the government to negotiate separately with each tribe. It was the classic strategy of divide and conquer.

Although it made a mockery of diplomacy to treat with Indian tribes as though they were European powers, the United States maintained that each tribe was a sovereign nation, to be dealt with as an equal in solemn treaties. Both sides knew that this was not the case. When Indians agreed to meet in council, they were tacitly admitting defeat. They seldom drove hard bargains or broke off negotiations. Moreover, tribal chiefs had only limited power; young braves frequently refused to respect agreements made by their elders.

Indian Wars

No sooner had the Kansas–Nebraska Bill become law, than the Kansa, Omaha, Pawnee, and Yankton Sioux tribes began to feel pressure for further concessions of territory. By 1860 most of Kansas and Nebraska had been cleared; the Indians had lost all but 1.5 million of their 19-odd million acres. A gold rush into Colorado in 1859 sent thousands of greedy prospectors across the plains to drive the Cheyenne and Arapaho from land guaranteed them in 1851. Thus it happened that in 1862, after federal troops had been pulled out of the West for service against the Confederacy, most of the plains Indians rose up against the whites. For five years intermittent but bloody clashes kept the entire area in a state of alarm.

This was guerrilla warfare, with all its horror and treachery. In 1864 a party of Colorado militia fell upon an unsuspecting Cheyenne community at Sand Creek and killed an estimated 450. "Kill and scalp all, big and little," Colonel J. M. Chivington, a minister in private life, told his men. "Nits make lice." Another Indian fighter, General Nelson A. Miles called this "Chivington Massacre" the "foulest and most unjustifiable crime in the annals of America," but it was no worse than many incidents in earlier conflicts with Indians, and not very different from what was later to occur in guerrilla wars involving American troops in the Philippines (which General Miles also found disturbing) and, more recently, in Vietnam. In turn, the Indians slaughtered dozens of isolated white families, ambushed small parties, and fought many successful skirmishes against troops and militia. They achieved their most notable triumph in December 1866, when the Oglala Sioux, under their great chief Red Cloud, wiped out a party of 82 soldiers under Captain W. J. Fetterman.

In 1867 the government tried a new strategy. All the plains Indians would be confined to two small reservations, one in the Black Hills of Dakota Territory, the other in Oklahoma, and be forced to become farmers. At two great conclaves held in 1867 and 1868 at Medicine Lodge Creek and Fort Laramie, the principal chiefs yielded to the government's demands.

Many Indians refused to abide by these agreements. With their way of life at stake, they swept across the plains like a prairie fire—and were almost as destructive.

That a relative handful of "savages," without central leadership or plan, could hold off the cream of the army, battle hardened in the Civil War, can be explained by the character of the vast, trackless country and the ineptness of many American commanders. Few Indian chiefs were capable of organizing a campaign. But Indians made superb guerrillas. Every observer called them the best cavalry soldiers in the world. Armed with stubby, powerful bows capable of driving an arrow clear through a bull buffalo, they were a fair match for troops equipped with carbines and Colt revolvers. They could sometimes be rounded up, as when General Philip Sheridan herded the tribes of the Southwest into Indian Territory in 1869, but once the troops withdrew, braves began to melt away into the emptiness of the surrounding grasslands. The distinction between "treaty" Indians, who had agreed to live on the new reservations, and the "nontreaty" variety shifted almost from day to day. Trouble flared here one week, next week somewhere else, perhaps 500 miles away. No less an authority than General William Tecumseh Sherman testified that a mere 50 Indians could often "checkmate" 3,000 soldiers.

If one concedes that no one could reverse the direction of history or stop the invasion of Indian lands, then some version of the "small reservation" policy would probably have been the best solution for the Indians. Had they been guaranteed a reasonable amount of land and adequate subsidies and allowed to maintain their way of life, they might have accepted the situation and ceased to harry the whites.

Whatever chance that policy had was weakened by the government's maladministration of

Preparing to surrender to General Crook, Geronimo (mounted left) and Natiche stand with their respective sons and Geronimo's grandson; the sons wear ceremonial paint. This photograph was taken in the Sierra Madre mountains of Mexico in 1886, just before the surrender.

Indian affairs. An "Indian Ring" in the Department of the Interior systematically stole funds and supplies intended for the reservation Indians. General Sherman, in overall command of the Indian country, claimed in 1875: "We could settle Indian troubles in an hour, but Congress wants the patronage of the Indian bureau, and the bureau wants the appropriations without any of the trouble of the Indians themselves." General Sheridan, no lover of Indians, said: "We took away their country and their means of support . . . and it was for this that they made war. Could anyone expect less?"

President Grant wished to place the reservations under army control, but the Indians opposed this. They fared no better around army camps than on the reservations. In 1869 Congress created a nonpolitical Board of Indian Commissioners to oversee Indian affairs, but bureaucrats in Washington stymied the commissioners at every turn.

In 1874 gold was discovered in the Black Hills Indian reservation. By the next winter thousands of miners had invaded the reserved area. Already alarmed by the approach of crews building the Northern Pacific Railroad, the Sioux once again went on the warpath. Joining with nontreaty tribes to the west, they concentrated in the region of the Bighorn River, in southern Montana Territory.

The summer of 1876 saw three columns of troops in the field against them. The commander of one column, General Alfred H. Terry, sent ahead a small detachment of the Seventh Cavalry under Colonel George A. Custer with orders to locate the Indians' camp and then block their escape route into the inaccessible Bighorn Mountains.

Custer was vain and rash, and vanity and rashness were grave handicaps when fighting Indians. Grossly underestimating the number of Indians, he decided to attack directly with his tiny force of 264 men. At the Little Bighorn late in June he found himself surrounded by 2,500 Sioux under Rain-in-the-Face and Crazy Horse. He and all his men died on the field.

Because it was so one-sided, "Custer's Last Stand" was not a typical battle, though it may be taken as symbolic of the Indian warfare of the period in the sense that it was characterized by bravery, foolhardiness, and a tragic waste of life. The battle greatly heartened the Indians, but it did not gain them their cause. That autumn, short of rations and hard pressed by overwhelming numbers of soldiers, they surrendered and returned to the reservation.

The Destruction of Tribal Life

Thereafter the fighting slackened. For this the building of the transcontinental railroads and the destruction of the buffalo were chiefly responsible. An estimated 13 to 15 million buffalo, or bison, had roamed the plains in the mid-sixties. Then the slaughter began. Thousands were butchered to feed the gangs of laborers engaged in building the Union Pacific Railroad. Thousands more fell before the guns of sportsmen. Railroads made it possible to move supplies and troops swiftly to trouble spots during conflicts with the Indians. The railroads also ran excursion trains for hunters. The discovery in 1871 of a way to make commercial use of buffalo hides completed the tragedy. In the next three years about 9 million head were killed; after another decade the animals were almost extinct.

By the 1880s, the advance of whites into the plains had become irresistible and large numbers of disinterested whites believed that the only way to solve the "Indian problem" was to persuade the Indians to abandon their tribal cultures and live on family farms. The "wild" Indian must become a "civilized" member of "American" society.

To accomplish this goal, Congress passed the Dawes Severalty Act of 1887. Tribal lands were to be split into individual allotments. To keep speculators from wresting the allotments from the Indians while they were adjusting to the new way of life, the land could not be disposed of for 25 years. Funds were to be appropriated for educating and training the Indians, and those who accepted allotments and "adopted the habits of civilized life" were to be granted United States citizenship.

The sponsors of the Severalty Act thought they were effecting a fine humanitarian reform. "We must throw some protection over the Indian," Senator Henry L. Dawes declared. "We must hold up his hand." But despite the good intentions of the sponsors, the Dawes Act had disastrous results in the long run. It assumed that Indians could be transformed into small agricultural capitalists by an act of Congress. It shattered what was left of the Indians' culture without enabling them to adapt to white ways. Moreover, unscrupulous white men tricked many Indians into leasing their allotments for a pittance, and local authorities often taxed Indian lands at excessive rates. In 1934, after about 86 million of the 138 million acres assigned under the Dawes Act had passed into white hands, the government returned to a policy of encouraging tribal ownership of Indian lands, but irreparable damage had already been done.

Exploiting Mineral Wealth in the West

The natural resources of the nation were exploited in these decades even more ruthlessly and thoughtlessly than were its human resources. Americans had long regarded the West as a limitless treasure to be grasped as rapidly as possible, and after 1865 they engrossed its riches still faster and in a wider variety of ways. From the mid-fifties to the mid-seventies thousands of prospectors fanned out through the Rockies, panning every stream and hacking furiously at every outcropping from the Fraser River country of British Columbia to Tucson in southern Arizona, from the eastern slopes of the Sierras to the Great Plains.

Gold and silver were scattered throughout the area, though usually too thinly to make mining profitable. Whenever anyone made a strike, prospectors, driven by what a critic called an "unhealthy desire" for sudden wealth, flocked to the site, drawn by rumors of stream beds gleaming with gold-rich gravel and of nuggets the size of a man's fists. For a few months the site teemed with activity. Towns of 5,000 or more sprang up overnight; improvised roads were crowded with men and supply wagons. Claims were staked out along every stream and gully. Then, usually, expectations faded in the light of reality: high prices, low yields, hardships, violence, and deception. The boom collapsed and the towns died as quickly as they had risen. A few would have found wealth, the rest only backbreaking labor and disappointment—until tales of another strike sent them dashing feverishly across the land on another golden chase.

In a sense the Denvers, Aurarias, Virginia Cities, Orofinos, and Gold Creeks of the West during the war years were harbingers of the attitudes that flourished in the East in the age of President Grant and his immediate successors. The miners enthusiastically adopted the get-rich-quick philosophy, willingly enduring privations and laboring hard, always with the objective of striking it rich. The idea of reserving any part of the West for future generations never entered their heads.

The sudden prosperity of the mining towns attracted every kind of shady character—according to one Forty-Niner, "rascals from Oregon, pickpockets from New York, accomplished gentlemen from Europe, interlopers from Lima and Chile, Mexican thieves, gamblers from no particular spot, and assassins manufactured in Hell." Gambling dens, dance halls, saloons, and brothels mushroomed wherever precious metal was found.

Law enforcement was a constant problem. Much of the difficulty lay in the antisocial attitudes of the miners themselves. Gold and silver dominated people's thoughts and dreams. Ostentation characterized the successful, braggadocio those who failed. During the administration of President Grant, Virginia City, Nevada, was at the peak of its vulgar prosperity, producing an average of $12 million a year in ore. Built atop the richness of the Comstock Lode ($306 million in gold and silver was extracted from the Comstock in 20 years), it had 25 saloons before it had 4,000 people. By the seventies its mountainside site was disfigured by ugly, ornate mansions where successful mine operators ate from fine china and swilled champagne as though it were water.

In 1873, after the discovery of the Big Bonanza, a seam of ore more than 50 feet thick, the future of Virginia City seemed boundless. Other discoveries shortly thereafter indicated to optimists that the mining boom in the West would continue indefinitely. The finds in the Black Hills district in 1875 and 1876, heralding deposits yielding eventually $100 million, led to the mushroom growth of Deadwood, home of Wild Bill Hickok, Deadwood Dick, Calamity Jane, and such lesser-known characters as California Jack and Poker Alice. New strikes in Colorado in 1876 and 1877 caused the town of Leadville to boom; in 1880 there were 30,000 people in the area. However, this was the last important flurry to ruffle the mining frontier. The West continued to yield much gold and silver, especially silver, but big corporations produced nearly all of it. The mines around Deadwood were soon controlled by one large company, Homestake Mining.

This is the culminatig irony of the mining frontier: shoestring prospectors, independent and enterprising, made the key discoveries, established local institutions, and supplied the West with much of its color and folklore. But the stockholders of large corporations, many of whom had never seen a mine, made off with the lion's share of the wealth. To operate profitably, large capital investments, heavy machinery, railroads, and hundreds of hired hands were required. Typical of the successful mine owner was George Hearst, senator from California and father of the newspaper tycoon William Randolph Hearst, who, by shrewd speculation, obtained large blocks of stock in mining properties scattered from Montana to Mexico.

Though marked by violence, fraud, greed, and lost hopes, the gold rushes caused a great increase of interest in the West. A valuable literature appeared, part imaginative, part reportorial, describing the mining camps and the life of the prospectors. These works fascinated contemporaries (as they have continued to fascinate succeeding generations when adapted to the motion picture and to television). Mark Twain's *Roughing It* (1872), based in part on his experiences in the Nevada mining country, is the most famous example of this literature.

Each new strike and rush, no matter how ephemeral, brought permanent settlers along with the prospectors: farmers, cattlemen, storekeepers, teamsters, lawyers, and ministers. In every mining town—along with the saloons and brothels—schools, churches, and newspaper offices sprang up.

The mines also speeded the political organization of the West. Colorado and Nevada became territories in 1861, Arizona and Idaho in 1863, Montana in 1864. Although Nevada was admitted before it had 60,000 residents in 1864 to ratify the Thirteenth Amendment and help reelect Lincoln, most of these territories did not become states for

decades. But because of the miners, the framework for future development was early established.

The Land Bonanza

While the miners were engrossing the mineral wealth of the West, other interests were snapping up the region's choice farmland. Presumably the Homestead Act of 1862 had ended the reign of the speculator and the large landholder. The West, land reformers had assumed, would soon be dotted with 160-acre family farms.

They were doomed to disappointment. Most landless Americans were too poor to become farmers, even when they could obtain land without cost. The expense of moving a family to the ever-receding frontier exceeded the means of many, and the costs of hoes and scythes, harvesting machines, draft animals, fencing, a well, and housing, might come to $1,000, a formidable barrier. As for the industrial workers for whom the free land was supposed to provide a "safety valve," they had neither the skills nor the inclination to become farmers. And despite the intent of the law, speculators often managed to obtain large tracts. They hired men to stake out claims, falsely swear that they had fulfilled the conditions laid down in the law for obtaining legal title, and then deed the land over to their employers.

Furthermore, 160 acres was not enough for raising livestock or for the kind of commercial agriculture that was developing west of the Mississippi. Congress made a feeble attempt to make larger holdings available to homesteaders by passing the Timber Culture Act of 1873, which permitted individuals to claim an additional 160 acres if they would agree to plant a quarter of it in trees within ten years. This law proved helpful to some farmers in Kansas, Nebraska, and the Dakotas. Nevertheless, fewer than 25 percent of the 245,000 who took up land under it obtained final title to the property. Raising large numbers of seedling trees on the plains was a difficult task.

While futilely attempting to make a forest of parts of the treeless plains, the government permitted private interests to gobble up and destroy many of the great forests that clothed the slopes of the Rockies and the Sierras. The Timber and Stone Act of 1878 allowed anyone to acquire a quarter section of forest land for $2.50 an acre if it was "unfit for civilization." This laxly drawn measure enabled lumber companies to obtain thousands of acres by hiring dummy entrymen, whom they marched in gangs to the land offices, paying them a few dollars for their time after they had signed over their claims.

Had the land laws been better drafted and more honestly enforced, it is still unlikely that the policy of granting free land to small homesteaders would have succeeded. Aside from the built-in difficulties faced by small-scale agriculturalists in the West, too many people in every section were eager to exploit the nation's land for their own profit.

However they attained their acres, frontier farmers of the 1870s and 1880s grappled with novel problems as they pushed across the plains with their families. The soil was rich, but the climate, especially in the semiarid regions beyond the 98th meridian of longitude, made agriculture frequently difficult and often impossible. Blizzards, floods, grasshopper plagues, and prairie fires caused repeated heartaches, but periodic drought and searing summer heat were the worst hazards, destroying the hopes and fortunes of thousands.

At the same time the flat immensity of the land, combined with newly available farm machinery and the development of rail connections with the East, encouraged the growth of enormous corporation-controlled "bonanza" farms. Bonanza farmers could buy supplies wholesale and obtain concessions from railroads and processors, which added to their profits.

Even the biggest organizations could not cope with prolonged drought, however, and most of the bonanza outfits failed in the dry years of the late eighties. Those wise farmers who diversified their crops and cultivated their land intensively fared better in the long run, though even they could not hope to earn a profit in really dry years.

Despite the hazards of plains agriculture, the region became the breadbasket of America in the decades following the Civil War. By 1889 Minnesota topped the nation in wheat production, and ten years later four of the five leading wheat states lay west of the Mississippi. The plains also accounted for heavy percentages of the nation's other cereal crops, together with immense quantities of beef, pork, and mutton.

Like other exploiters of the nation's resources, farmers took whatever they could from the soil with little heed for preserving its fertility and preventing erosion. The consequent national loss was less apparent because it was diffuse and slow to assume drastic proportions, but it was nonetheless real.

Western Railroad Building

Further exploitation of land resources by private interests resulted from the government's policy of subsidizing western railroads. Here was a clear illustration of the conflict between the idea of the West as a national heritage to be disposed of to deserving citizens and the concept of the region as a cornucopia pouring forth riches to be carted off by anyone powerful and determined enough to take them. On the one hand, when it came to a choice between giving a particular tract to railroads or to homesteaders, the homesteaders nearly always lost out; on the other hand, the swift development of western railroads was essential if farmers, miners, and cattle ranchers were to prosper.

Federal land grants to railroads began in 1850 with those allotted the Illinois Central, but the most lavish gifts of the public domain were those made directly to builders of intersectional trunk lines. These roads received more than 155 million acres, although about 25 million acres reverted to the government because some companies failed to lay the required miles of track. Unless the government had been willing to build the transcontinental lines itself—and this was unthinkable in an age dominated by belief in individual exploitation and wary of any activity that entrusted the spending of large sums by politicians—some system of subsidy was essential. Private investors would not hazard the huge sums needed to lay tracks across hundreds of miles of rugged, empty country when traffic over the road could not possibly produce profits for many years. Grants of land seemed a sensible way of financing construction.

The method avoided direct outlays of public funds, for the companies could pledge the land as security for bond issues or sell it directly for cash. Moreover, land and railroad values were intimately linked in contemporary thinking. In many cases the value of the land granted might be recovered by the government when it sold other lands in the vicinity, for such properties would certainly be worth more after transportation facilities to eastern markets had been constructed.

The Pacific Railway Act of 1862 established the pattern for these grants. It gave the builders of the Union Pacific and Central Pacific railroads five square miles of public land on each side of their right of way for each mile of track laid. The land was allotted in alternate sections, forming a pattern like a checkerboard, the squares of one color representing railroad property, the other government property. Presumably this arrangement benefited the entire nation, since half the land close to the railroad remained in public hands. However, whenever grants were made to railroads, the adjacent government lands were not opened to homesteaders—on the theory that free land in the immediate vicinity of a line would prevent the road from disposing of its properties at good prices.

Historians have argued at length about the fairness of the land-grant system. No railroad corporation waxed fat directly from the sale of its lands, which were sold at prices averaging between $2 and $5 an acre. Collectively the roads have taken in between $400 million and $500 million from this source, but only over the course of a century. Land-grant lines encouraged the growth of the West by advertising their property widely and by providing cheap transportation for settlers and shipping services for farmers. They were required by law to carry troops and handle government business free or at reduced rates, which saved the government many millions over the years. At the same time the system imposed no effective restraints on how the railroads used the funds raised with federal aid. Being able to lay track with money obtained from land grants, the operators tended to be extravagant and often downright corrupt.

The Union Pacific was built by a construction company, the Crédit Mobilier, which was owned by the promoters. These men awarded themselves contracts at prices that assured the Crédit Mobilier fat profits. When Congress threatened to investigate the Union Pacific in 1868, Oakes Ames, a stockholder in both companies who was also a member of Congress, sold key congressmen and government officials over 300 shares of Crédit Mobilier stock at a price far below its real value. When these transactions were exposed, the House of Representatives censured Ames, but such was the temper of the times that neither he nor most of his associates believed he had done anything wrong.

The construction of the Central Pacific in the 1860s illustrates how the system encouraged extravagance. In addition to land grants, the Central Pacific and the Union Pacific were given loans in the form of government bonds—from $16,000 to $48,000 for each mile of track laid, depending on the difficulty of the terrain. The two competed with each other for the subsidies, the Central Pacific building eastward from Sacramento, the Union Pacific westward from Nebraska. They put huge crews to work grading and laying track, bringing up supplies over the already completed road. The Union Pacific employed Civil War veterans and Irish immigrants, the Central Pacific Chinese immigrants.

This plan favored the Union Pacific. While the Central Pacific was inching upward through the gorges and granite of the mighty Sierras, the Union Pacific, was racing across the level plains. To prevent the Union Pacific from making off with most of the government aid, the Central Pacific wasted huge sums by working through the winter in the High Sierras. Often the men labored in tunnels dug through 40-foot snowdrifts to get at the frozen ground. In 1866, over the most difficult terrain, they laid 28 miles of track—at a cost of more than $280,000 a mile. Experts later estimated that 70 percent of this sum could have been saved had speed not been a factor.

But these Herculean efforts paid off. The mountains were conquered, and then the crews raced across the Great Basin to Salt Lake City and beyond. The final meeting of the rails—the occasion of a national celebration—took place at Promontory, north of Ogden, Utah, on May 10, 1869. The Union Pacific had built 1,086 miles of track, the Central 689 miles.

In the long run, the wasteful way in which the Central Pacific was built hurt the railroad severely. It was ill constructed, over grades too steep and around curves too sharp, and burdened with debts that were too heavy. Such was the fate of nearly all the railroads constructed with the help of government subsidies. The only transcontinental built without land grants was the Great Northern, running from St. Paul, Minnesota, to the Pacific. Spending private capital, its guiding genius, James J. Hill, was compelled to build economically and to plan carefully. As a result, his was the only transcontinental line to weather the depression of the 1890s without going into bankruptcy.

The Cattle Kingdom

While miners were digging out the mineral wealth of the West and railroaders were taking possession of much of its land, another group was exploiting endless acres of its grass.

Columbus brought the first cattle to the New World in 1493, on his second voyage, and later *conquistadores* took them to every corner of Spain's American empire. Mexico proved to be so well suited to cattle raising that many were allowed to roam loose. They multiplied rapidly, and by the late 18th century what is now southern Texas harbored enormous herds. The beasts interbred with nondescript "English" cattle, brought into the area by settlers from the United States to produce the Texas Longhorn. Hardy, wiry, ill-tempered, and fleet, with horns often attaining a spread of six feet, these animals were far from ideal as beef cattle and almost as hard to capture as wild horses, but they existed in southern Texas by the million, most of them unowned.

The lack of markets and transportation explains why Texas cattle were so lightly regarded. But conditions were changing. Industrial growth in the East was causing an increase in the urban population and a consequent rise in the demand for food. At the same time, the expansion of the railroad network made it possible to move cattle cheaply over long distances.

As the iron rails inched across the plains, astute cattlemen began to do some elementary figuring. Longhorns could be had locally for $3 or $4 a

head. In the northern cities they would bring at least ten times that much. Why not herd them northward to the railroads, allowing them to feed along the way on the abundant grasses of the plains? The land was owned by the federal government. Anyone could drive cattle across it without paying a fee. The grass the cattle ate on the way swiftly renewed itself.

In 1866 a number of Texans drove large herds northward toward Sedalia, Missouri, railhead of the Missouri Pacific. This route took the herds through wooded and settled country and across Indian reservations, which provoked many difficulties. At the same time Charles Goodnight and Oliver Loving drove 2,000 head through New Mexicxo Territory to Colorado.

The next year the drovers, inspired by an Illinois cattle dealer named Joseph G. McCoy and other entrepreneurs, led their herds north across unsettled grasslands, to the Kansas Pacific line at Abilene, Kansas, which McCoy described as "a very small, dead place." They earned excellent profits, and during the next five years about 1.5 million head made the "long drive" over the Chisholm Trail to Abilene, where they were sold to ranchers, feedlot operators, and eastern meat packers. Other shipping points sprang up as the railroads pushed westward.

The technique of the long drive, which involved guiding herds of 2,000 to 3,000 cattle slowly across as much as a thousand miles of country, produced the American cowboy, renowned in song, story, and on film. Half a dozen of these men could control several thousand heads. Mounted on wiry ponies, they would range alongside the herd, keeping the animals on the move but preventing stampedes, allowing them time to rest yet steadily pressing them toward the yards of Abilene.

Cattle towns such as Abilene had their full share of saloons, gambling dens, and "dance houses" patronized by cowboys and by other transients bent on having a good time. Most were young, male, and single. Violence punctuated their activities, but not nearly as frequently as legend suggests. Tales of individual desperadoes and gangs of outlaws "shooting up" cattle towns and terrorizing honest citizens are fictitious. Police forces were well organized. Indeed, "respectable"

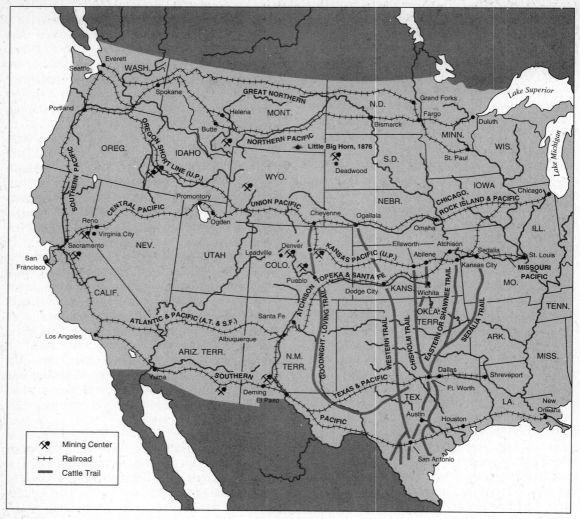

The West: Cattle, Railroads, and Mining, 1850–1893

town residents tended to urge leniency for law-breakers because of the money they and their fellows brought to the towns.

Open-Range Ranching

Soon cattlemen discovered that the hardy Texas stock could survive the winters of the northern plains. Attracted by the apparently limitless forage, they began to bring up herds to stock the vast regions where the buffalo had so recently roamed. By 1880 some 4.5 million head had spread across the sea of grass that ran from Kansas to Montana and west to the Rockies.

The prairie grasses offered cattlemen a bonanza almost as valuable as the gold mines. Open-range ranching required actual ownership of no more than a few acres along some watercourse. In this semiarid region control of water enabled a rancher to dominate all the surrounding area back to the divide separating his range from the next stream without investing a cent in the purchase of land. His cattle, wandering freely on the public domain, fattened on grass owned by all the people, to be turned into profit for the rancher.

Generally a group of ranchers acted together, obtaining legal title to the lands along the bank of a stream and grazing their cattle over the area drained by it. The herds became thoroughly intermixed, each owner's being identified by an individual brand mark. Every spring and fall the ranchers staged a great roundup, driving in all the cattle to a central place, separating them by brand marks, culling steers for shipment to market, and branding new calves.

With the demand for meat rising and transportation cheap, princely fortunes could be made in a few years. Capitalists from the East and from Europe began to pour funds into the business. Eastern "dudes" like Theodore Roosevelt, a young New York assemblyman who sank over $50,000 into his Elkhorn Ranch in Dakota Territory in 1883, bought up cattle as a sort of profitable hobby. (Roosevelt, clad in buckskin and bearing a small arsenal of rifles and six-shooters, made quite a splash in Dakota Territory, but not as a rancher.) Soon large outfits such as the Nebraska Land and Cattle Company dominated the business, just as large companies had taken over most of the important gold and silver mines.

Barbed-Wire Warfare

The leading ranchers banded together in cattlemen's associations to deal with overcrowding and with such problems as quarantine regulations, water rights, and thievery, functions that would better have been performed by the government.

To keep other ranchers' cattle from those sections of the public domain they considered their own, the associations, and many individuals, began to fence huge areas. This was possible only because of the invention in 1874 of barbed wire by Joseph F. Glidden. By the 1880s thousands of miles of the new fencing had been strung across the plains, often across roads and in a few cases around entire communities. "Barbed-wire wars" resulted, fought by rancher against rancher, cattleman against sheepman, herder against farmer.

By stringing so much wire the cattlemen were unwittingly destroying their own way of do-

ing business. On a truly open range, cattle could fend for themselves, instinctively finding water during droughts, drifting safely downwind before blizzards. Barbed wire prevented their free movement. During winter storms these slender strands became as lethal as high-tension wires: The drifting cattle piled up against them and died by the thousands. "The advent of barbed wire," Walter Prescott Webb wrote in his classic study *The Great Plains* (1931), "brought about the disappearance of the open, free range and converted the range country into the big-pasture country."

The boom times were ending. Overproduction was driving down the price of beef; expenses were on the rise; many sections of the range were overgrazed. The dry summer of 1886 left the stock in poor condition. Winter that year arrived early and with unparalleled fury. Blizzards raged and temperatures plummeted far below zero. Cattle crowded into low places only to be engulfed in giant snowdrifts; barbed wire took a fearful toll. When spring finally came, between 80 and 90 percent of all cattle on the range were dead. "We have had a perfect smashup all through the cattle country," Theodore Roosevelt wrote sadly in April 1887 from Elkhorn Ranch.

That cruel winter finished open-range cattle raising. The large companies were bankrupt; many independent operators, Roosevelt among them, became discouraged and sold out. When the industry revived, it was on a smaller, more efficiently organized scale. The fencing movement continued, but now each stockman enclosed land he actually owned. It then became possible to bring in pedigreed bulls to improve the breed. Cattle raising, like mining before it, ceased to be an adventure in rollicking individualism and became a business.

By the late eighties the bonanza days of the West were over. No previous frontier had caught the imagination of Americans so completely as the Great West, with its heroic size, its awesome emptiness, its massive, sculptured beauty. Now the frontier was no more. Big companies were taking over all the West's resources. The nation was becoming more powerful, richer, larger, and its economic structure more complex and diversified as the West yielded its treasures. But the East, and especially eastern industrialists and financiers, were increasingly dominating the economy of the entire nation.

Milestones

1859	Charles Darwin, *Origin of Species*	**1881**	Tuskeegee Institute founded
	Discovery of the Comstock Lode	**1883**	*Civil Rights Cases*
1864	Chivington massacre	**1886–1887**	Blizzards put an end to open-range ranching
1869	Union Pacific Railroad completed		
	Board of Indian Commissioners established	**1887**	Dawes Severalty Act
1873	Timber Culture Act	**1888**	James Bryce, *The American Commonwealth*
1875	Civil Rights Act	**1890–1900**	Blacks deprived of the vote in the South
1876	Battle of the Little Bighorn		
1877	Desert Land Act	**1895**	Booker T. Washington's Atlanta Compromise Speech
1878	Timber and Stone Act		
1879	Major Powell, *Report on the Lands of the Arid Region*	**1896**	*Plessy* v. *Ferguson*
	Specie payments resumed		

Supplementary Reading

James Bryce, **The American Commonwealth** (1888), is a fascinating contemporary analysis of the American political system. The economic and political ideas current in this period are covered in Sidney Fine, **Laissez Faire and the General Welfare State*** (1956). Morton Keller, **Affairs of State** (1977), describes the public life of the era. For the views of businessmen, see E. C. Kirkland, **Dream and Thought in the Business Community*** (1956), and T. C. Cochran, **Railroad Leaders** (1953).

National political issues are covered in P. S. Hirshson, **Farewell to the Bloody Shirt** (1962), Allen Weinstein, **Prelude to Populism** (1970), Irwin Unger, **The Greenback Era** (1964), and W. T. K. Nugent, **Money and American Society** (1968).

R. A. Billington and Martin Ridge, **Westward Expansion** (1982), is an excellent survey. R. W. Paul, **The Far West and the Great Plains** (1988), and P. N. Limerick, **The Legacy of Conquest** (1987), put more emphasis on social developments. J. R. Jeffrey, **Frontier Women** (1979), covers the immediate post–Civil War era.

On western Indians, see R. W. Mardock, **The Reformers and the American Indian** (1971), Robert Wooster, **The Military and U. S. Indian Policy** (1988), and F. P. Prucha, **The Great Father: The U. S. Government and the Indians** (1984). On other minority groups, consult R. W. Logan, **The Negro in American Life and Thought** (1954), Joel Williamson, **The Crucible of Race** (1984), L. R. Harlan, **Booker T. Washington** (1972), and Gunther Barth, **Bitter Strength: A History of the Chinese in the United States** (1964).

The mining frontier is described in R. W. Paul, **Mining Frontiers of the Far West** (1963), D. A. Smith, **Rocky Mountain Mining Camps** (1967), and Paula Petric, **No Step Backward: Women and Family on the Rocky Mountain Frontier** (1987). F. A. Shannon describes **The Farmer's Last Frontier** (1945); bonanza farming is described in H. M. Drache, **The Day of the Bonanza** (1964).

For western railroad development see O. O. Winther, **The Transportation Frontier** (1964), Albro Martin, **James J. Hill** (1976), and R. G. Athearn, **Union Pacific Country** (1971). The cattle kingdom is described in Lewis Atherton, **The Cattle Kings** (1961), R. R. Dykstra, **The Cattle Towns** (1968), and Don Worcester, **The Chisholm Trail** (1980).

*Available in paperback.

CHAPTER 18

An Industrial Giant

Industrial Growth: An Overview

Railroads: The First Big Business

Iron, Oil, and Electricity

Competition and Monopoly: The Railroads

Competition and Monopoly: Steel

Competition and Monopoly: Oil

Competition and Monopoly: Retailing and Utilities

Americans React to Big Business

Reformers: George, Bellamy, Lloyd

Reformers: The Marxists

The Government Reacts to Big Business: Railroad Regulation

The Government Reacts to Big Business: The Sherman Antitrust Act

The Union Movement

The American Federation of Labor

Labor Militancy Rebuffed

Whither America, Whither Democracy?

W hen the Civil War began, the country's industrial output, while increasing, did not approach that of major European powers. By the end of the century it had become far and away the colossus among world manufacturers, dwarfing the production of Great Britain and Germany. The world had never seen such rapid economic growth. The output of goods and services in the country (the gross national product, or GNP) increased by 44 percent between 1874 and 1883 and continued to expand in succeeding years.

Industrial Growth: An Overview

American manufacturing flourished after the Civil War for many reasons. New natural resources were discovered and exploited steadily, thereby increasing opportunities. These opportunities, in turn, attracted the brightest and most energetic of a vigorous and expanding population. The growth of the country added constantly to the size of the national market, and high tariffs shielded that market from foreign competition. The dominant spirit of the time encouraged businessmen to maximum effort by emphasizing progress, glorifying material wealth, and justifying aggressiveness. Yet industrial growth also produced a generation of Robber Barons. Aggressiveness led to corrupt business practices such as stock manipulation, and ultimately to "combinations in restraint of trade," an American euphemism for monopoly.

European immigrants provided the additional labor needed by expanding industry; 2.5 million arrived in the seventies, twice that number in the eighties. These immigrants saw America as a land of opportunity, and for many it was. But for others life in the United States meant a constant struggle for survival and grinding poverty.

It was a period of rapid advance in basic science, and technicians created a bountiful harvest of new machines, processes, and power sources that increased productivity and created new industries. In agriculture there were better harvesters, binding machines, and combines that could thresh and bag 450 pounds of grain a minute. An 1886 report of the Illinois Bureau of Labor Statistics claimed that "new machinery has displaced fully 50 percent of the muscular labor formerly required to do a given amount of work in the manufacture of agricultural implements." Of course that also meant that many farm families were also "displaced" from their homes and livelihoods.

As a result of improvements in the milling of grain, packaged cereals appeared on the American breakfast table. The commercial canning of food expanded rapidly. The Bonsack cigarette-rolling machine created a new industry that changed the habits of millions. The perfection of the typewriter by the Remington company in the 1880s revolutionized the way office work was performed. But even some of these inventions were mixed blessings. The harm done by the popularity of cigarettes, for example, needs no explanation.

Railroads: The First Big Business

The railroads were probably the most significant element in American economic development. Railroads were important first as an industry in themselves. Less than 35,000 miles of track existed when Lee laid down his sword at Appomattox. By 1900 the nation had 193,000 miles of track.

The emphasis in railroad construction after 1865 was on organizing integrated systems. The lines had high fixed costs: taxes, interest on their bonds, maintenance of track and rolling stock, salaries of office personnel. A short train with half-empty cars required almost as many workers and as much fuel to operate as a long one jammed with freight or passengers. In order to earn profits, the railroads had to carry as much traffic as possible. They therefore spread out feeder lines to draw business to their main lines the way the root network of a tree draws water into its trunk.

Before the Civil War, as we have seen, passengers and freight could travel by rail from beyond Chicago and St. Louis to the Atlantic Coast, but only after the war did true trunk lines appear. In 1861, for example, the New York Central ran from Albany to Buffalo. In 1867 the Central passed into the hands of "Commodore" Cornelius Vanderbilt, who had made a large fortune in the shipping business. In the mid–1870s he added the Michigan Cerntral and the Lake Shore and Michigan Southern to his empire. At his death in 1877 the Central operated a network of more than 4,500 miles of track between New York City and most of the principal cities of the Middle West.

While Vanderbilt was putting together the New York Central complex, Thomas A. Scott was fusing railroads to Cincinnati, Indianapolis, St. Louis, and Chicago to his Pennsylvania Railroad, which linked Pittsburgh and Philadelphia. He also obtained access to New York, Baltimore and Washington. During this period the Erie Railroad and the Baltimore and Ohio also put together similar systems.

The transcontinentals were trunk (interregional) lines from the start; the emptiness of the

western country would have made short lines unprofitable, and builders quickly grasped the need for direct connections to eastern markets and thorough integration of feeder lines.

The dominant system builder of the Southwest was Jay Gould. With millions acquired in shady railroad and stock market ventures, Gould invaded the West in the 1870s, buying 370,000 shares of Union Pacific stock. He took over the Kansas Pacific, running from Denver to Kansas City, which he consolidated with the Union Pacific, and the Missouri Pacific, a line from Kansas City to St. Louis, which he expanded through mergers and purchases into a 5,300-mile system.

In the Northwest, Henry Villard, a German-born ex-newspaperman, constructed another great complex based on his control of the Northern Pacific. James J. Hill controlled the Great Northern system, still another western network.

The trunk lines interconnected and thus had to standardize many of their activities. The present system of time zones was developed in 1883 by the roads. The standard track gauge (4 feet $8\frac{1}{2}$ inches) was established in 1886. Standardized signal systems, even standard methods of accounting were essential to the effective functioning of the network.

The lines sought to work out fixed rates for carrying different types of freight, charging more for valuable manufactured goods than for bulky products like coal or wheat, and they agreed to permit rate concessions to shippers when necessary to avoid hauling empty cars. To enforce cooperation they founded regional organizations such as the Eastern Trunk Line Association and the Western Traffic Association.

The railroads stimulated the economy indirectly. Like foreign commerce and the textile industry in earlier times, they were a "multiplier" speeding development. In 1869 they bought $41.6 million worth of cars and locomotives, in 1889 $90.8 million. The railroads purchases created thousands of jobs and led to countless technological advances.

Because of their voracious appetite for traffic, railroads in sparsely settled regions and in areas with undeveloped resources devoted much money and effort to stimulating local economic growth. To speed the settlement of new regions, the land-grant railroads sold land cheaply and on

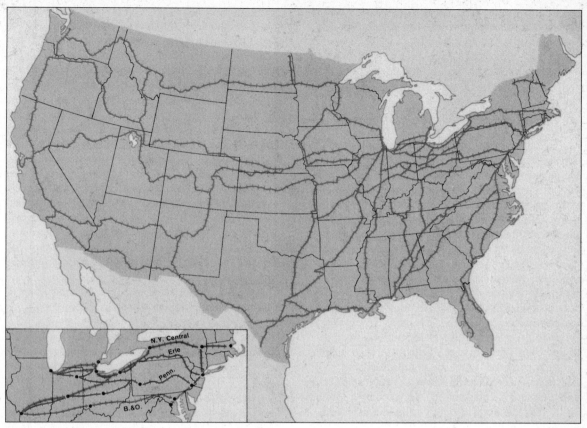

Primary Railroads, 1890

easy terms, for sales meant future business as well as current income. They offered reduced rates to travelers interested in buying farms, and distributed elaborate brochures describing the wonders of the new country. Their agents greeted immigrants at the great eastern ports and tried to steer them to railroad property.

Technological advances in railroading accelerated economic development in complex ways. In 1869 George Westinghouse invented the air brake. By enabling an engineer to apply the brakes to all cars simultaneously (formerly each car had to be braked separately by its own conductor or brakeman), this invention made possible revolutionary increases in the size of trains and the speed at which they could safely operate. The sleeping car, invented in 1864 by George Pullman, now came into its own.

To pull the heavier trains, more powerful locomotives were needed. They in turn produced a call for stronger and more durable rails to bear the additional weight. Steel, itself reduced in cost because of technological developments, supplied the answer, for steel rails outlasted iron many times despite the use of much heavier equipment.

Iron, Oil, and Electricity

The transformation of iron manufacturing affected the nation almost as much as railroad development. Output rose from 920,000 tons in 1860 to 10.3 million tons in 1900, but the big change came in the development of ways to mass produce steel. Steel was expensive to manufacture until the invention in the 1850s of the Bessemer process, perfected independently by Henry Bessemer, an Englishman, and William Kelly of Kentucky. The Bessemer process and the open-hearth method, a slower but more precise technique that enabled producers to sample the molten mass and thus control quality closely, were introduced commercially in the United States in the sixties. In 1870, 77,000 tons of steel were manufactured and by 1900 nearly 11.4 million.

Such growth would have been impossible but for the huge supplies of iron ore in the United States and the coal necessary to fire the furnaces that refined it. In the 1870s the great iron fields rimming Lake Superior began to yield their treasures. The enormous iron concentrations of the Mesabi region made a compass needle spin like a top. Mesabi ores could literally be mined with steam shovels, almost like gravel. Pittsburgh, surrounded by vast coal deposits, became the iron and steel capital of the country, the Minnesota ores reaching it by way of steamers on the Great Lakes and rail lines from Cleveland.

The petroleum industry expanded even more swiftly than iron and steel. Edwin L. Drake drilled the first successful well in Pennsylvania in 1859. During the Civil War, production ranged between 2 million and 3 million barrels a year. By 1890 the figure had leaped to about 50 million barrels.

Before the invention of the gasoline engine and the automobile, the most important petroleum product was kerosene, which was burned in lamps. It accounted for well over two-thirds of all oil production in the early 1870s. Technological advances came rapidly. By the early 1870s, refiners had learned how to "crack" petroleum by applying high temperatures to the crude in order to increase the percentage of kerosene yielded. By-products such as naphtha, rhigolene (a local anesthetic), cymogene (a coolant for refrigerating machines), and many lubricants and waxes began to appear on the market. At the same time a great increase in the supply of crude oil—especially after the German-born chemist Herman Frasch perfected a method for removing sulfur from low-quality petroleum—drove prices down. These circumstances put a premium on refining efficiency. Larger plants utilizing expensive machinery and employing skilled technicians became more important.

Two other important new industries were the telephone and electric light businesses. Both were typical of the period, being products of technical advances and intimately related to the growth of a high-speed, urban civilization that put great stress on communication. The telephone was invented in 1876 by Alexander Graham Bell, who had been led to the study of acoustics through his interest in the education of the deaf. By 1900 there were almost 800,000 phones in the country, twice the total for all Europe. The American Telephone and Telegraph Company, a consolidation of over 100 local systems, dominated the business.

When Western Union realized the importance of the telephone, it tried for a time to compete with Bell by developing a machine of its own. The man it commissioned to devise this machine was Thomas A. Edison, but Bell's patents proved unassailable. Edison had already made a number of contributions toward solving what he called the "mysteries of electrical force," including a multiplex telegraph capable of sending four messages

Alexander Graham Bell making the first telephone call between New York and Chicago. Bell's invention revolutionized communications in America, liberating people from traditional face-to-face exchanges and written correspondence.

over a single wire at the same time. At Menlo Park, New Jersey, he built the prototype of the modern research laboratory, where specific problems could be attacked on a mass scale by a team of specialists.

Edison's most significant achievement was unquestionably his perfection of the incandescent lamp, or electric light bulb. Others before Edison had experimented with the idea of producing light by passing electricity through a filament in a vacuum. Always, however, the filaments quickly burned out. Edison tried hundreds of fibers before producing, in 1879, a carbonized filament that would glow brightly in a vacuum tube for as long as 170 hours without crumbling.

In 1882 his Edison Illuminating Company opened a power station in New York and began to supply current for lighting to 85 consumers. Soon central stations were springing up everywhere until, by 1898, there were about 3,000 in the country.

Electricity was soon used to produce power as well as light. The substitution of electricity for steam power in factories was as liberating as that of steam for waterpower before the Civil War. Small, safe electric motors replaced dangerous and cumbersome mazes of belts and wheels.

Competition and Monopoly: The Railroads

During the post–Civil War era, expansion in industry went hand in hand with concentration. The principal cause of this trend, aside from the obvious economies resulting from large-scale production, was the downward trend of prices after 1873. The deflation, which was caused by the failure of the money supply to keep pace with the rapid increase in the volume of goods produced, lasted until 1896 or 1897.

Falling prices kept a steady pressure on profit margins, and this led to intense competition for markets. According to contemporary economists, competition advanced the public interest by keeping prices low and assuring the most efficient producer the largest profit. Up to a point it accomplished these purposes in the years after 1865, but it also fathered side effects that injured both the economy and society as a whole. Railroad managers, for instance, found it impossible to enforce "official" rate schedules once competi-

tive pressures mounted. In 1865 it had cost from 96 cents to $2.15 per hundred pounds, depending on the class of freight, to ship goods from New York to Chicago. In 1888 rates ranged from 35 cents to 75 cents.

Competition cut deeply into railroad profits, causing the lines to seek desperately to increase volume. They did so chiefly by reducing rates still more, on a selective basis. They gave rebates (secret reductions below the published rates) to large shippers in order to capture their business. In the 1870s the New York Central regularly reduced the rates charged important shippers by 50 to 80 percent.

Railroad officials disliked rebating but found no way to avoid the practice. In extreme cases the railroads even gave large shippers drawbacks, which were rebates on the business of the shippers' competitors!

To make up for losses forced on them by competitive pressures, railroads charged higher rates at way points along their tracks where no competition existed. Frequently it cost more to ship a product a short distance than a longer one. Rochester, New York, was served only by the New York Central. In the 1870s it cost 30 cents to transport a barrel of flour from Rochester to New York City, a distance of 350 miles. At the same time flour could be shipped from Minneapolis to New York, a distance of well over 1,000 miles, for only 20 cents a barrel.

Although cheap transportation stimulated the economy, few persons benefited from cutthroat competition. Small shippers—and all businesses in cities and towns with limited rail outlets—suffered heavily; railroad discrimination speeded the concentration of industry in large corporations located in major centers. The instability of rates even troubled interests like the midwestern flour millers who benefited from the competitive situation, because it hampered planning. Nor could manufacturers who received rebates be entirely happy, since few could be sure that some other producer was not getting a larger reduction.

Probably the worst sufferers were the railroads themselves. The loss of revenue resulting from rate cutting, combined with inflated debts, put most of them in grave difficulty when faced with a downturn in the business cycle. In 1876 two-fifths of all railroad bonds were in default; three years later 65 lines were bankrupt. Since the public would not countenance bankrupt railroads going out of business, these companies were placed in the hands of court-appointed receivers. Wits called Samuel J. Tilden, the 1876 Democratic presidential candidate, "the Great Forecloser" because of his work reorganizing bankrupt railroads at this time.

During the 1880s the major roads responded to these pressures by creating interregional systems. These were the first giant corporations, capitalized in the hundreds of millions of dollars. Their enormous cost led to another wave of bankruptcies when a depression struck in the 1890s. The consequent reorganizations brought most of the big systems under the control of financiers, notably J. Pierpont Morgan, and such other private companies as Kuhn, Loeb of New York and Lee, Higginson of Boston.

Critics called the reorganizations "Morganizations." Representatives of the bankers sat on the board of every line they saved and their influence was predominant. They consistently opposed rate wars, rebating, and other competitive practices. In effect, control of the railroad network became centralized, even though the companies maintained their separate existences and operated in a seemingly independent manner. When Morgan died in 1913, "Morgan men" dominated the boards of the New York Central, the Erie, the New York, New Haven and Hartford, the Southern, the Pere Marquette, the Atchison, Topeka and Santa Fe, and many other lines.

Competition and Monopoly: Steel

The iron and steel industry was also intensely competitive. Despite the trend toward higher production, demand varied erratically from year to year, even from month to month. In good times producers built new facilities, only to suffer heavy losses when demand declined. The forward rush of technology put a tremendous emphasis on efficiency; expensive plants quickly became obsolete. Improved transportation facilities allowed manufacturers in widely separated places to compete with one another.

The kingpin of the industry was Andrew Carnegie. Carnegie was born in Scotland and came to the United States in 1848 at the age of 12. His first job as a bobbin boy in a cotton mill brought him $1.20 a week, but his talents perfectly fitted the times, and he rose rapidly: to Western Union messenger boy, to telegrapher, to private secretary, to railroad manager. He saved his money, made some shrewd investments, and by 1868 had an income of $50,000 a year.

At about this time he decided to specialize in the iron business, saying, in an oft-quoted remark, that he believed in putting all his eggs in one basket and then watching the basket. Carnegie possessed great talent as a salesman, boundless faith in the future of the country, an uncanny knack of choosing top-flight subordinates, and enough ruthlessness to survive in the iron and steel jungle. Where other steelmen built new plants in good times, he preferred to expand in bad times, when it cost far less to do so. During the 1870s, he later recalled, "many of my friends needed money. . . . I . . . bought out five or six of them. That is what gave me my leading interest in this steel business."

Andrew Carnegie in later life. His phenomenal rags-to-riches career was one of the real-life models for Horatio Alger's dime novels on the theme "poor boy makes good."

Carnegie grasped the importance of technological improvements. He was also a merciless competitor. When a plant manager announced: "We broke all records for making steel last week," Carnegie replied: "Congratulations! *Why not do it every week?*" By 1890 the Carnegie Steel Company dominated the industry, and its output increased nearly tenfold during the next decade. Profits soared.

Alarmed by his increasing control of the industry, the makers of finished steel products such as barbed wire and tubing began to combine and to consider entering the primary field. Carnegie, his competitive temper aroused, threatened to turn to finished products himself. A colossal steel war seemed imminent.

However, Carnegie longed to retire in order to devote himself to philanthropic work. He believed that wealth entailed social responsibilities and that it was a disgrace to die rich. When J. P. Morgan approached him through an intermediary with an offer to buy him out, he assented readily. In 1901 Morgan put together United States Steel, the "world's first billion-dollar corporation." This combination included all the Carnegie properties, the Federal Steel Company (Carnegie's largest competitor), and such important fabricators of finished products as the American Steel and Wire Company, the American Tin Plate Company, and the National Tube Company. Vast reserves of Minnesota iron ore and a fleet of Great Lakes ore steamers were also included. U. S. Steel was capitalized at $1.4 billion, about twice the value of its component properties but not necessarily an overestimation of its profit-earning capacity. The owners of Carnegie Steel received $492 million, of which $250 million went to Carnegie himself.

Competition and Monopoly: Oil

The pattern of fierce competition leading to combination and monopoly is well illustrated by the history of the petroleum industry. Irresistible pressures pushed the refiners into a brutal struggle to dominate the business. Production of crude oil, subject to the uncertainties of prospecting and drilling, fluctuated constantly and without regard for need. In general, output surged far ahead of demand.

By the 1870s the largest oil-refining center was Cleveland, chiefly because the New York Central and Erie railroads competed fiercely for its oil trade and the Erie Canal offered an alternative route. The Standard Oil Company of Cleveland, founded in 1870 by a 31-year-old merchant named John D. Rockefeller, emerged as the giant among the refiners. Rockefeller exploited every possible technical advance and employed fair means and foul to persuade competitors either to sell out or to join forces. By 1879 he controlled 90 percent of the nation's oil refining capacity, along with a network of oil pipelines and large reserves of petroleum in the ground.

Standard Oil emerged victorious in the competitive wars because Rockefeller and his associates were the toughest and most imaginative fighters as well as the most efficient refiners in the business. In addition to obtaining from the railroads a 10 percent rebate and drawbacks on its competitors' shipments, Standard Oil cut prices locally to force small independents to sell out or face ruin. Bribery was also a Standard practice; the reformer Henry Demarest Lloyd quipped that the company had done everything to the Pennsylvania legislature except refine it.

Although a bold planner and a daring taker of necessary risks, Rockefeller was far too orderly and astute to enjoy the free-swinging battles that plagued his industry. He sought efficiency, order, and stability. His forte was meticulous attention to detail: Stories are told of his ordering the number of drops of solder used to seal oil cans reduced from 40 to 39, and of his insisting that the manager of one of his refineries account for 750 missing barrel bungs. Not miserliness but a profound grasp of the economies of large-scale production explain this behavior. He competed ruthlessly not primarily to crush other refiners but to persuade them to join with him, to share the business peaceably and rationally so that all could profit.

Having achieved his monopoly, Rockefeller stabilized and structured it by creating a new type of business organization, the trust. Standard Oil was an Ohio corporation, prohibited by local law from owning plants in other states or holding stock in out-of-state corporations. As Rockefeller and his associates took over dozens of companies with facilities scattered across the country, serious legal and managerial difficulties arose. How

John D. Rockefeller as monarch of the railroads and the Standard Oil monopoly; a cartoon from *Puck*.

How could these many organizations be integrated with Standard Oil of Ohio?

A rotund, genial little Pennsylvania lawyer named Samuel C. T. Dodd came up with an answer to this question in 1879. The stock of Standard of Ohio and of all the other companies that the Rockefeller interests had swallowed up was turned over to nine trustees, who were empowered to "exercise general supervision" over all the properties. Stockholders received in exchange trust certificates, on which dividends were paid. This seemingly simple device brought order to

the petroleum business. Competition almost disappeared; prices steadied; profits skyrocketed.

From the company's point of view, monopoly was not the purpose of the trust—that had been achieved before the device was invented. Centralization of the management of diverse and far-flung operations in the interest of efficiency was its chief function. Standard Oil headquarters in New York became the brain of a complex network where information from salaried managers in the field was collected and digested, where top managerial decisions were made, and whence orders went out to armies of drillers, refiners, scientists, and salesmen.

Competition and Monopoly: Retailing and Utilities

The pattern of competition leading to dominance by a few great companies was repeated in many other businesses. The period saw the growth of huge department stores by merchants such as Alexander T. Stewart in New York, John Wanamaker in Philadelphia, and Marshall Field in Chicago. In life insurance, an immense expansion took place. High-pressure salesmanship prevailed; agents gave rebates to customers by shaving their own commissions; companies stole crack agents from their rivals and raided new territories. By 1900, three giants dominated the industry, Equitable, New York Life, and Mutual Life, each with approximately $1 billion of insurance in force.

The telephone and electric lighting industries were also plagued by competition. Bell and Edison had to fight mighty court battles to protect their patents. Western Union hired Edison himself in a futile effort to get around Bell's telephone patents. In 1892 Edison merged with his most powerful competitor to form General Electric. It and the Westinghouse Company thereafter dominated in business.

Americans React to Big Business

The expansion of industry and its concentration in fewer and fewer hands changed the way many people felt about the role of government in economic and social affairs. The fact that Americans disliked powerful governments in general and strict regulation of the economy in particular had never meant that they objected to all government activity in the economic sphere. Banking laws, tariffs, and the granting of public land to railroads are only the most obvious of the economic regulations enforced in the 19th century by both the federal government and the states. Americans saw no contradiction between government activities of this type and the free enterprise philosophy, for such laws were intended to release human energy and thus increase the area in which freedom could operate. Tariffs stimulated industry and created new jobs, railroad grants opened up new regions for development, and so on.

The growth of huge industrial and financial organizations and the increasing complexity of economic relations frightened people yet made them at the same time greedy for more of the goods and services the new society was turning out. To many, the great new corporations and trusts resembled Frankenstein's monster—marvelous and powerful but a grave threat to society. "Modern civilization," the astute James Bryce wrote in *The American Commonwealth* (1888):

> discerns more benefits which the organized power of government can secure, and grows more anxious to attain them. . . . The power of groups of men organized by incorporation as joint-stock companies, or of small knots of rich men acting in combination, has developed with unexpected strength in unexpected ways, overshadowing individuals and even communities, and showing that the very freedom of association which men sought to secure by law . . . may, under the shelter of the law, ripen into a new form of tyranny.

To some extent public fear of the industrial giants reflected concern about monopoly. If Standard Oil dominated oil refining, it might raise prices inordinately at vast cost to consumers. Although in isolated cases monopolists did raise prices unreasonably, generally they did not. On the contrary, prices tended to fall until by the 1890s a veritable "consumer's millennium" had arrived.

Far more important in causing resentment was the fear that the monopolists were destroying economic opportunity and threatening democratic institutions. It was not the wealth of tycoons like Carnegie and Rockefeller and Morgan so much as their influence that worried people. In the face of the growing disparity between rich and poor, could republican institutions survive?

Some observers believed either autocracy or a form of revolutionary socialism to be almost inevitable. In 1890 former president Hayes pondered "the wrong and evils of the money-piling tendency of our country, which is changing laws, government, and morals and giving all power to the rich" and decided that he was going to become a "nihilist." John Boyle O'Reilly, a liberal Catholic journalist, wrote in 1886: "There is something worse than Anarchy, bad as that is; and it is irresponsible power in the hands of mere wealth." William Cook, a New York lawyer, warned in *The Corporation Problem* (1891) that "colossal aggregations of capital" were "dangerous to the republic."

As criticism mounted, business leaders rose to their own defense. Rockefeller described in graphic terms the chaotic conditions that plagued the oil industry before the rise of Standard Oil: "It seemed absolutely necessary to extend the market for oil . . . and also greatly improve the process of refining so that oil could be made and sold cheaply, yet with a profit. We proceeded to buy the largest and best refining concerns and centralized the administration of them with a view to securing greater economy and efficiency." Carnegie, in an essay published in 1889, insisted that the concentration of wealth was necessary if humanity was to progress, softening this "Gospel of Wealth" by insisting that the rich must use their money "in the manner which . . . is best calculated to produce the most beneficial results for the community."

Reformers: George, Bellamy, Lloyd

The voices of the critics were louder if not necessarily more influential. In 1879 Henry George published *Progress and Poverty,* a forthright attack on the maldistribution of wealth in the United States. George argued that labor was the true and only source of capital. Observing the speculative fever of the West, which enabled landowners to reap profits merely by holding property while population increased, George proposed a property tax that would confiscate this "unearned increment." The value of land depended on society and should belong to society. This "Single Tax," as others called it, would bring in so much money that no other taxes would be necessary, and the government would have plenty of funds to establish new schools, museums, theaters, and other badly needed social and cultural services.

While the Single Tax was never adopted, George's ideas attracted enthusiastic attention. Single Tax clubs sprang up throughout the nation, and *Progress and Poverty* became a best seller.

Even more spectacular was the reception afforded *Looking Backward, 2000–1887,* a utopian novel written in 1888 by Edward Bellamy. This book, which sold over a million copies in its first few years, described a future America that was completely socialized, all economic activity carefully planned. Bellamy suggested that the ideal socialist state, in which all citizens shared equally, would arrive without revolution or violence. The trend toward consolidation would continue, he predicted, until one monster trust controlled all economic activity. At this point everyone would realize that nationalization was essential.

A third influential attack on monopoly was that of Henry Demarest Lloyd, whose *Wealth Against Commonwealth* (1894) denounced the Standard Oil Company. Lloyd's forceful, uncomplicated arguments and his copious references to official documents made *Wealth Against Commonwealth* utterly convincing to thousands.

The popularity of these books indicates that the trend toward monopoly in the United States worried many people. But despite the drastic changes suggested in their pages, none of these writers questioned the underlying values of the middle-class majority. They insisted that reform could be accomplished without serious inconvenience to any individual or class.

Nor did most of their millions of readers seriously consider trying to apply the reformers' ideas. The national discontent was apparently not as profound as the popularity of these works might suggest. If John D. Rockefeller became the bogeyman of American industry because of

Lloyd's attack, no one prevented him from also becoming the richest man in the United States.

Reformers: The Marxists

By the 1870s the ideas of Marxist socialists were beginning to penetrate the United States and in 1877 a Marxist Socialist Labor Party was founded. The first serious attempt to explain Marx's ideas to Americans was Laurence Gronlund's *The Cooperative Commonwealth*, which was published in 1884.

Capitalism, Gronlund claimed, contained the seeds of its own destruction. The state ought to own all the means of production, middlemen were "parasites," speculators "vampires." "Capital and Labor," he wrote in one of the rare humorous lines in his book, "are just as harmonious as roast beef and a hungry stomach." Gronlund expected the millenium to arrive in an orderly manner.

The leading voice of the Socialist Labor Party, Daniel De Leon, was a different type. He was born in the West Indies, and emigrated to the United States in the 1870s, where he was progressively attracted by the ideas of Henry George, then Edward Bellamy, and finally Marx. While personally mild-mannered and kindly, when he put pen to paper De Leon became a doctrinaire revolutionary. He insisted that industrial workers could only improve their lot by adopting socialism and joining the Socialist Labor Party. He paid scant attention, however, to the practical needs or even to the opinions of rank-and-file working people. The labor historian Philip Taft aptly characterized him as a "verbal revolutionary."

The Government Reacts to Big Business: Railroad Regulation

Political action to check big business came first on the state level and dealt chiefly with the regulation of railroads. Although a number of New England states established railroad commissions before the Civil War, strict regulation was largely the result of agitation by farm groups, principally the National Grange of the Patrons of Husbandry.

The Grange, founded in 1867 by Oliver H. Kelley, was created to provide social and cultural benefits for isolated rural communities. As it spread and grew in influence, the movement became political too. "Granger" candidates won control of a number of state legislatures in the West and South. Railroad regulation invariably followed.

The Illinois Granger laws were typical. The revised state constitution of 1870 declared railroads to be public highways and authorized the legislature to "pass laws establishing reasonable maximum rates" and to "prevent unjust discrimination." The legislature did so and set up a commission to enforce the laws and punish violators. The railroads protested, insisting that they were being deprived of property without due process of law.

In *Munn* v. *Illinois* (1877), a case that involved the owner of a grain elevator who refused to comply with a state warehouse act, the Supreme Court upheld the constitutionality of this kind of act. Any business that served a public interest, such as a railroad or a grain warehouse, was subject to state control, the justices ruled. Legislatures might fix maximum charges; if the charges seemed unreasonable, the parties concerned should direct their complaints to the legislatures or to the voters, not to the courts.

Regulation of the railroad network by the individual states was inefficient, and in some cases the commissions were incompetent and even corrupt. When the Supreme Court, in the *Wabash* case (1886), declared unconstitutional an Illinois regulation outlawing the long-and-short-haul evil, federal action became necessary. The Wabash, St. Louis and Pacific Railroad had charged 25 cents a hundred pounds for shipping goods from Gilman, Illinois, to New York City and only 15 cents from Peoria, which was 86 miles farther from New York. Illinois judges had held this to be illegal, but the Supreme Court decided that Illinois could not regulate interstate shipments.

Congress filled the gap created by the Wabash decision in 1887 by passing the Interstate Commerce Act. All charges made by railroads "shall be reasonable and just," the act stated. Rebates, drawbacks, and other competitive practices were declared unlawful, and so were their monopolistic counterparts: pools and traffic-sharing agreements. Railroads were required to publish schedules of rates and forbidden to change them without due public notice. Most important, the law established the Interstate Commerce Commission (ICC), the first federal regulatory board, to supervise the affairs of railroads, investigate complaints, and issue "cease and desist" orders when the roads acted illegally.

The Interstate Commerce Act broke new ground, yet it was neither a radical nor a particularly effective measure. Its terms contradicted one another, some being designed to stimulate, others to penalize competition. The chairman of the commission soon characterized the law as an "anomaly." It sought, he said, to "enforce competition" at the same time that it outlawed "the acts and inducements by which competition is ordinarily effected." The new commission had less power than the law seemed to give it. It could not fix rates, only take the roads to court when it considered rates unreasonably high. Such cases could be extremely complicated; applying the law "was like cutting a path through a jungle." With the truth so hard to determine and the burden of proof on the commission, the courts in nearly every instance decided in favor of the railroads.

Not effective [margin note]

Nevertheless, by describing so clearly the right of Congress to regulate private corporations engaged in interstate commerce, the Interstate Commerce Act challenged the philosophy of laissez-faire. Later legislation made the commission more effective. The commission also served as the prototype of a host of similar federal administrative authorities, such as the Federal Communications Commission (1934).

The Government Reacts to Big Business: The Sherman Antitrust Act

As with railroad legislation, the first antitrust laws originated in the states, but they were southern and western states with relatively little industry, and most of the statutes were vaguely worded and ill enforced. Federal action came in 1890 with the passage of the Sherman Antitrust Act. Any combination "in the form of trust or otherwise" that was "in restraint of trade or commerce among the several states, or with foreign nations," was declared illegal. Persons forming such combinations were subject to fines of $5,000 and a year in jail. Individuals and businesses suffering losses because of actions that violated the law were authorized to sue in the federal courts for triple damages.

Where the Interstate Commerce Act sought to outlaw the excesses of competition, the Sherman Act was supposed to restore competition. If businessmen joined together to "restrain" (monopolize) trade in a particular field, they should be punished and their deeds undone. But the Sherman Act was rather loosely worded. Thurman Arnold, a modern authority, once said that it made it "a crime to violate a vaguely stated economic policy." Critics have argued that the congressmen were more interested in quieting the public clamor for action against the trusts than in actually breaking up any of the new combinations. Quieting the clamor was certainly one of their objectives. However, they were trying to solve a new problem and were not sure how to proceed. A law with teeth too sharp might do more harm than good. Most Americans assumed that the courts would deal with the details, as they always had in common-law matters.

In fact, the Supreme Court quickly emasculated the Sherman Act. In *United States* v. *E. C. Knight Company* (1895) it held that the American Sugar Refining Company had not violated the law by taking over a number of important competitors. Although the Sugar Trust now controlled about 98 percent of all sugar refining in the United States, it was not restraining trade. "Doubtless the power to control the manufacture of a given thing involves in a certain sense the control of its disposition," the Court said in one of the greatest feats of judicial understatement of all time. "Although the exercise of that power may result in bringing the operation of commerce into play, it does not control it, and affects it only incidentally and indirectly."

If the creation of the Sugar Trust did not violate the Sherman Act, it seemed unlikely that any other combination of manufacturers could be convicted under the law. But in several cases in 1898 and 1899 the Supreme Court ruled that agreements to fix prices or divide markets did violate the act. These decisions precipitated a wave of outright mergers in which a handful of large corporations swallowed up hundreds of smaller ones. Presumably mergers were not illegal. When, some years after his retirement, Andrew Carnegie

was asked by a committee of the House of Representatives to explain how he had dared participate in the formation of the U.S. Steel Corporation, he replied: "Nobody ever mentioned the Sherman Act to me, that I remember."

The Union Movement

At the time of the Civil War most union members were artisans such as cigarmakers, printers, and carpenters. Aside from ironworkers, railroad workers, and miners, few industrial laborers were organized. Nevertheless the union was the workers' response to the big corporation: a combination designed to eliminate competition for jobs and to provide efficient organization for labor.

After 1865 the growth of national craft unions, which had been stimulated by labor dissatisfaction during the Civil War, quickened perceptibly. In 1866 a federation of these organizations, the National Labor Union, was founded, but most of its leaders were out of touch with the practical needs and aspirations of workers. They opposed the wage system, strikes, and anything that increased the laborers' sense of being members of the working class.

Far more remarkable was the Knights of Labor, founded in 1869 by Philadelphia garment workers. Its head, Uriah S. Stephens, was a reformer of wide interests. He and his successor, Terence V. Powderly, supported political objectives that had no direct connection with working conditions, such as currency reform and the curbing of land speculation. They rejected the idea that workers must resign themselves to remaining wage earners. "There is no good reason," Powderly wrote in his autobiography, "why labor cannot, through cooperation, own and operate mines, factories, and railroads." The leading Knights saw no contradiction between their denunciation of "soulless" monopolies and "drones" like bankers and lawyers and their talk of "combining all branches of trade in one common brotherhood." Such muddled thinking led the Knights to attack the wage system and to frown on strikes as "acts of private warfare."

But if the Knights had one foot in the past, they also had one foot in the future. They rejected the traditional grouping of workers by crafts and developed a concept closely resembling modern industrial unionism. They welcomed blacks (though mostly in segregated locals), women, and immigrants, and they accepted unskilled workers as well as artisans. The eight-hour day was one of their basic demands.

The growth of the union, however, had little to do with ideology. As late as 1879, it had fewer than 10,000 members. But between 1882 and 1886 successful strikes by local "assemblies," including one against Jay Gould's Missouri Pacific Railroad, brought recruits by the thousands. The membership passed 110,000 in 1885 and in 1886 it soared beyond the 700,000 mark. Alas, sudden prosperity was too much for the Knights. Its national leadership was unable to control local groups. A number of poorly planned strikes failed dismally, and the public was alienated by sporadic acts of violence and intimidation. Disillusioned recruits began to drift away.

Largely fortuitous circumstances caused the collapse of the organization. By 1886 the movement for the eight-hour day had gained wide support among workers. In Chicago, a center of the eight-hour movement, about 80,000 workers were involved, and a small group of anarchists was trying to take advantage of the excitement to win support. When a striker was killed in a fracas at the McCormick Harvesting Machine Company, the anarchists called a protest meeting on May 4, at Haymarket Square. Police intervened to break up the meeting, and someone—his identity was never established—hurled a bomb into their ranks. Seven policemen were killed and many others injured.

The American Federation of Labor

Organized labor, especially the Knights, suffered heavily as a result of the Haymarket bombing. No tie with the Knights could be established, but the union had been closely connected with the eight-hour agitation, and the public tended to associate that with violence and radicalism. Its membership declined and soon it ceased to exist.

The Knights' place was taken by the American Federation of Labor (AFL), a combination of national craft unions established in 1886. Its principal leaders, Adolph Strasser and Samuel Gompers of the Cigarmakers Union, concentrated on organizing skilled workers and fighting for "bread-and-butter" issues such as higher wages and shorter hours. "Our organization does not consist of idealists," Strasser explained to a congressional committee. "We do not control the production of the world. That is controlled by the employers. . . . I look first to cigars."

The AFL accepted the fact that most workers would remain wage earners all their lives and tried to develop in them a sense of common purpose and pride in their skills and station. Rank-and-file AFL members were naturally eager to win wage increases and other benefits, but most also valued their unions for the companionship they provided, the sense of belonging to a group. In other words, despite statements such as Strasser's, unions, in and out of the AFL, were a kind of club as well as a means of defending and advancing their members' material interests.

The chief weapon of the federation was the strike. "I have my own philosophy and my own dreams," Gompers once told a left-wing French politician, "but first and foremost I want to increase the workingman's welfare year by year. . . . The French workers waste their economic force by their political divisions."

Gompers's approach to labor problems produced solid, if unspectacular, growth for the AFL. Unions with a total of about 150,000 members formed the federation in 1886. By 1892 the membership had reached 250,000, and in 1901 it passed the million mark.

Labor Militancy Rebuffed

The stress of the AFL on the strike weapon reflected the increasing militancy of labor. Workers felt themselves threatened by the growing size and power of their corporate employers, the substitution of machines for human skills, and the invasion of foreign workers willing to accept substandard wages.

The average employer behaved like a tyrant when dealing with workers. He discharged any who tried to organize unions; he hired scabs to replace strikers; he frequently failed to provide the most rudimentary protections against injury on

Steelmen insisted

the job. Most employers would not bargain with labor collectively.

The industrialists of the period were not all ogres; they were as alarmed by the rapid changes of the times as their workers, and since they had more at stake materially, they were probably more frightened by the uncertainties. Deflation, technological change, and intense competition kept even the most successful under constant pressure. Their thinking was remarkably confused. They considered workers who joined unions "disloyal," and at the same time they treated labor as a commodity to be purchased as cheaply as possible. When labor was scarce, employers resisted demands for higher wages by arguing that the price of labor was controlled by its productivity; when it was plentiful, they justified reducing wages by referring to the law of supply and demand.

Thus capital and labor were often spoiling for a fight. In 1877 a great railroad strike convulsed much of the nation. It began on the Baltimore and Ohio system in response to a wage cut and spread until about two-thirds of the railroad mileage of the country had been shut down. Violence broke out, rail yards were put to the torch. Frightened businessmen formed militia companies to patrol the streets of Chicago and other cities. Eventually President Hayes sent federal troops to restore order, and the strike collapsed.

The disturbances of 1877 were a response to a business slump, those of the next decade a response to good times. Twice as many strikes occurred in 1886 as in any previous year. The situation was so disturbing that President Grover Cleveland, in the first presidential message devoted to labor problems, urged Congress to create a voluntary arbitration board to aid in settling labor disputes—a remarkable suggestion for a man of Cleveland's conservative, *laissez-faire* approach to economic issues.

In 1892 a violent strike broke out among silver miners at Coeur d'Alene, Idaho, and a far more important clash shook Andrew Carnegie's Homestead steel plant near Pittsburgh when strikers attacked 300 private guards brought in to protect strikebreakers. The Homestead affair was part of a struggle between capital and labor in the steel industry. The steelmen insisted that the workers were holding back progress by resisting technological advances, whereas the workers believed that the company was refusing to share the fruits of more efficient operation fairly. The defeat of the 24,000-member Amalgamated Association of Iron and Steel Workers destroyed unionism as an effective force in the steel industry and set back the progress of organized labor all over the country.

As in the case of the Haymarket bombing, the activities of radicals on the fringe of the dispute turned the public against the steelworkers. The boss of Homestead was Henry Clay Frick, a tough-minded foe of unions. Frick made the decision to bring in strikebreakers and to employ Pinkerton detectives to protect them. During the course of the strike, Alexander Berkman, an anarchist unconnected with the union, burst into Frick's office and shot him. Frick was only slightly wounded, but the attack brought him much sympathy and unjustly discredited the strikers.

The most important strike of the period took place in 1894. It began when the workers at George Pullman's Palace Car factory outside Chicago walked out in protest against wage cuts. Some Pullman workers belonged to the American Railway Union, headed by Eugene V. Debs and the union voted to refuse to handle trains with Pullman cars. The resulting railroad strike tied up trunk lines running in and out of Chicago. The railroad owners appealed to President Cleveland to send troops to preserve order. On the pretext that the soldiers were needed to ensure the movement of the mails, Cleveland agreed. When Debs defied a federal injunction to end the walkout, he was jailed for contempt and the strike was broken.

Whither America, Whither Democracy?

Each year more of the nation's wealth and power seemed to fall into fewer hands. As with the railroads, other industries were coming to be influenced, if not completely dominated, by bankers. The firm of J. P. Morgan and Company controlled many railroads; the largest steel, electrical, agricultural machinery, rubber, and shipping companies; two life insurance companies; and a number of banks. By 1913 Morgan and the Rockefeller National City Bank group between them could name 341 directors to 112 corporations worth over $22.2 billion. The "Money Trust," a loose but potent fraternity of financiers, seemed fated to become the ultimate monopoly.

Centralization increased efficiency in industries that used a great deal of expensive machinery to turn out goods for the mass market, and in those where close coordination of output, distribution, and sales was important. The public benefited immensely from the productive efficiency of the new empires. Living standards rose. But the trend toward giantism raised doubts. With ownership falling into fewer hands, what would be the ultimate effect of big business on American democracy? What did it mean for ordinary people when a few tycoons possessed huge fortunes and commanded such influence even on the Congress and the courts?

The crushing of the Pullman strike demonstrated the power of the courts to break strikes by issuing injunctions. And the courts seemed only concerned with protecting the interests of the rich and powerful. Particularly ominous for organized labor was the fact that the federal government based its request for the injunction that broke the strike on the Sherman Antitrust Act, arguing that the American Railway Union was a combination in restraint of trade.

While serving his sentence for contempt, Eugene Debs was visited by a number of prominent socialists who sought to convert him to their cause. One gave him a copy of Karl Marx's *Capital,* which he found too dull to finish, but he did read *Looking Backward* and *Wealth Against Commonwealth.* In 1897 he became a socialist.

Milestones

1859	First oil well drilled in Pennsylvania		**1886**	Haymarket bombing American Federation of Labor founded
1868	Carnegie Steel Company formed			Interstate Commerce Act
1869	George Westinghouse invents air brake		**1888**	Edward Bellamy, *Looking Backward, 2000–1887*
	Knights of Labor founded		**1889**	Andrew Carnegie's "Gospel of Wealth"
1870	Standard Oil Company formed		**1890**	Sherman Antitrust Act
1870–1890	Completion of railroad trunk lines		**1892**	Homestead strike
				General Electric Company formed
1876	Alexander Graham Bell invents the telephone		**1894**	Pullman strike
1877	Great Railroad Strike			Henry Demarest Lloyd, *Wealth Against Commonwealth*
	Munn v. *Illinois* upholds state regulatory laws		**1895**	*U.S.* v. *E. C. Knight Company* weakens Sherman Act
1879	Thomas Edison invents the electric light		**1901**	U.S. Steel Corporation formed
1884	Henry George, *Progress and Poverty*			
	Laurence Gronlund, *The Cooperative Commonwealth*			

Supplementary Reading

Of works dealing with industrial growth, E. C. Kirkland, **Industry Comes of Age*** (1961), is the best general introduction. Matthew Josephson, **The Robber Barons*** (1934), is highly critical but provocative. A. D. Chandler, Jr., **The Visible Hand** (1977), covers the way businesses were organized and managed.

For the railroad industry, consult A. D. Chandler, Jr., **Railroads: The Nation's First Big Business** (1965), J. F. Stover, **American Railroads*** (1961), and Julius Grodinsky, **Transcontinental Railway Strategy** (1962).

The iron and steel business is discussed in detail in J. F. Wall, **Andrew Carnegie** (1970), and Peter Temin, **Iron and Steel in Nineteenth-Century America** (1964), an economic analysis. For the oil industry, see Carl Solberg, **Oil Power*** (1976), a good survey, and for more detail, H. F. Williamson and A. R. Daum, **The American Petroleum Industry: Age of Illumination** (1959). The electrical industry is discussed in Matthew Josephson, **Edison*** (1959). On the telephone, see John Brooks, **Telephone** 1976), and R. V. Bruce, **Alexander Graham Bell** (1973).

Many of these volumes deal with the problems of competition and monopoly. See also, Gabriel Kolko, **Railroads and Regulation*** (1965), which is critical of both railroad leaders and government policy. H. D. Lloyd, **Wealth Against Commonwealth** (1894), attacks the oil trust mercilessly.

For the radical critics, see J. L. Thomas, **Alternative Americas: Henry George, Edward Bellamy, Henry Demarest Lloyd** (1983), and also the radicals' own writings. On the growth of unions, see David Montgomery, **Beyond Equality** (1967), Harold Livesay, **Samuel Gompers and Organized Labor in America** (1978), and Nick Salvatore, **Eugene V. Debs** (1982). The important strikes and labor violence of the period are covered in R. V. Bruce, **1877: Year of Violence** (1959), Paul Arvich, **The Haymarket Tragedy** (1984), Leon Wolff, **Lockout** (1965), and Almont Lindsey, **The Pullman Strike** (1942).

The background of government regulation of industry is treated in Sidney Fine, **Laissez Faire and the General-Welfare State*** (1956), and J. A. Garraty, **The New Commonwealth*** (1968). Other useful volumes include Ari and Olive Hoogenboom, **A History of the ICC*** (1976), and G. W. Miller, **Railroads and the Granger Laws** (1971).

*Available in paperback.

CHAPTER 19

American Society in the Industrial Age

Middle-Class Life
Wage Earners
Working Women
Farmers
Working-Class Family Life
Working-Class Attitudes
Mobility: Social, Economic, and Educational
The "New" Immigration
The Old Immigrants and the New
The Expanding City and Its Problems
The Urban "Infrastructure"
The Cities Modernize
Leisure Activities: More Fun and Games
The Churches Respond to Industrial Society
The Settlement Houses
Civilization and Its Discontents

The industrialization that followed the Civil War profoundly affected every aspect of American life. New machines, improvements in transportation and communication, the appearance of the great corporation with its uncertain implications for the future—all made deep impressions on the economy and on the social and cultural development of the nation. Indeed, the history of the period may be treated, the historian Samuel P. Hays suggests, as a "response to industrialism," the "story of the impact of industrialism on every phase of human life."

Middle-Class Life

It is hard to generalize about how people lived and worked in so large and diverse a country as the United States. Some people, as we have just seen, became fabulously wealthy in the new industrial society, in no small part because neither the federal government nor the states taxed their incomes.

Members of the professions and the shopkeepers, small manufacturers, skilled craftsmen, and established farmers that made up the middle class lived in varying degrees of comfort. A family with an annual income of $1,000 in the 1880s would have no need to skimp on food, clothing, or shelter. When Professor Woodrow Wilson moved with his family to Wesleyan University in 1888, he was able to rent a large house and employ two full-time servants on his salary of $2,500 a year.

In such families husbands and wives continued to maintain their separate spheres, the men going off to their shops and offices, the women devoting their main energies to caring for (or at least supervising the care of) children and household. Middle-class women maintained the trend toward having fewer children. The children in these families, although much treasured, were carefully supervised. Much stress was placed on their being "little ladies and gentlemen," meaning having good manners and doing what their elders told them to do. This was the height of Victorian prudery, so in most families "teen-agers" (the term itself had not yet been invented) were closely chaperoned when in the company of "members of the opposite sex."

Wage Earners

Wage earners felt the full force of the tide, being affected in countless ways—some beneficial, others unfortunate. As manufacturing and mining became more important, the number of workers in these fields multiplied rapidly: from 885,000 in 1860 to more than 3.2 million in 1890. More efficient methods of production enabled them to increase their output, making possible a rise in their standard of living. The working day was shortening perceptibly. In 1860 the average had been 11 hours, but by 1880 only one worker in four labored more than 10 hours and radicals were beginning to talk about 8 hours as a fair day's work.

Skilled industrial workers—such types as railroad engineers and conductors, machinists, and iron molders—were quite well off. But unskilled laborers could still not earn enough to maintain a family decently by their own efforts alone.

James H. Ducker's *Men of the Steel Rails* throws much light on working conditions and workers' attitudes. Laborers were paid from $1 to $1.25 a day, whereas engineers received three times that amount or more. In addition, many of the better-paid workers picked up additional sums by renting spare rooms to other workers.

Railroad management tried to discipline the labor force by establishing rules, but it had difficulty enforcing them. Drunkenness on the job was a constant problem. Many conductors were said to be "color blind," the term referring not to any physical defect or to their lack of racial prejudice but to their inability to tell the difference between the railroad's money and their own. Transient workers, called "boomers," had "a deserved reputation as rowdies," Ducker reports. Many other workers, of course, were law-abiding, hardworking family men.

Industrialization created other problems. By and large, skilled workers, always better off than the unskilled, improved their positions relatively, despite the increased use of machinery. Furthermore, when machines took the place of human skills, jobs became monotonous. Mechanization undermined both the artisans' pride and their bargaining power vis-à-vis their employers. Machines more than workers controlled the pace of work and its duration. The time clock regulated the labor force more rigidly than the most exacting foreman. The pace of work and the danger involved in working around heavy, high-speed machinery increased.

As businesses grew larger, personal contact between employer and hired hand tended to disappear. Relations between them became more businesslike and ruthless. But large enterprises usually employed a higher percentage of managerial and clerical workers than smaller companies, thus providing opportunities for more blue-collar workers to rise in the industrial hierarchy.

Another problem for workers was that industrialization tended to accentuate swings of the

business cycle. On the upswing something approaching full employment existed, but in periods of depression unemployment affected workers without regard for their individual abilities. It is significant that the word unemployment (though not, of course, the condition itself) was a late-19th-century invention.

Working Women

Women continued to supply a significant part of the industrial working force, but now many more of them were working outside their homes. At least half of all working women were domestic servants, and textile mills and "the sewing trades" absorbed a large percentage of the rest. In all fields, women were paid substantially lower wages than men.

Women found many new types of work in these years, a fact commented on by the *New York Times* as early as 1869. They made up the overwhelming majority of salespersons and cashiers in the big new department stores. Managers considered women more polite, easier to control, and more honest than male workers, all qualities especially valuable in the huge emporiums. Over half of the more than 1,700 employees in A. T. Stewart's New York store were women.

Educated, middle class women also dominated the new profession of nursing. To nearly all doctors, to most men, and indeed to many women of that day, nursing seemed the perfect female profession, since it required the same characteristics that women were thought to have by nature: selflessness, cleanliness, kindliness, tact, sensitivity, and submissiveness to male control. "Since God could not care for all the sick, he made women to nurse," one (male) "authority" pontificated. Why it had not occurred to the Lord to make more women physicians or, for that matter, members of other prestigious professions like law and the clergy, this man did not explain, probably because it had not occurred to him either.

Middle-class women did replace men as teachers in most of the nation's grade schools, as clerks and secretaries, and as operators of the new typewriters in goverment departments and in

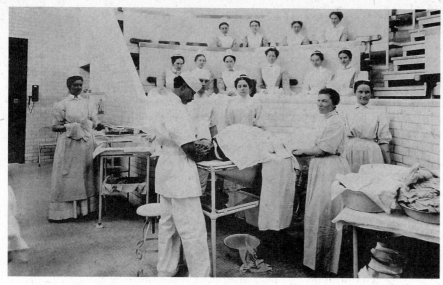

In a society that still believed that the sexes should maintain "separate spheres," the new profession of nursing was viewed as particularly suited for women. Doctoring was reserved for men.

business offices. Most men with the knowledge of spelling and grammar that these positions required had better opportunities and were uninterested in office work, so women high school graduates, of whom there was an increasing number, filled the gap.

Both department store clerks and "typewriters" (as they were called) earned more money than unskilled factory workers. According to one advertisement of the period, "no invention has opened for women so broad and easy an avenue to profitable and suitable employment." However, managerial posts in these fields remained almost exclusively in the hands of men.

Farmers

Long the backbone of American society, independent farmers and the agricultural way of life were rapidly being left behind in the race for wealth and status. The number of farmers and the volume of agricultural production continued to rise, but agriculture's relative place in the national economy was declining. Industry was expanding far faster, and the urban population, quadrupling in the period, would soon overtake and pass that of the countryside.

Along with declining income, farmers suffered a decline in status. Compared to middle-class city dwellers, they seemed provincial and behind the times. People in the cities began to refer to farmers as "rubes," "hicks," and "hayseeds" and to view them with amused tolerance or even contempt.

This combination of circumstances angered and frustrated farmers. Waves of radicalism swept the agricultural regions, giving rise to demands for social and economic experiments that played a major role in breaking down rural laissez-faire prejudices.

Farmers were not all affected by economic developments in the same way. Because of the steady decline of the price level, those in newly settled regions were usually worse off than those in older areas, since they had to borrow money to get started and were therefore burdened with fixed interest charges that became harder to meet each year. In the 1870s farmers in Illinois and Iowa suffered most—which accounts for the strength of the Granger movement in that region.

By the late 1880s, farmers in the old Middle West had also become better established. Even when prices dipped and a general depression gripped the country, they were able to weather the bad times nicely by taking advantage of lower transportation costs, better farm machinery, and new fertilizers and insecticides to increase output, and by shifting from wheat to the production of corn, oats, hogs, and cattle, which had not declined so drastically in price.

On the agricultural frontier from Texas to the Dakotas, and through the states of the old Confederacy, farmers were less fortunate. The burdens of the crop-lien system kept thousands of southern farmers in penury, while on the plains life was a succession of hardships. The first settlers in western Kansas, Nebraska, and the Dakotas took up land along the rivers and creeks where they found enough timber for home building, fuel, and fencing. Later arrivals who settled on the plains had to build houses of the tough prairie sod and depend on hay, sunflower stalks, and buffalo dung for fuel.

Frontier farm families had always had to work hard and endure the hazards of storm, drought, and insect plagues, along with isolation and loneliness. But all these burdens were magnified on the prairies and the high plains. Life was particularly hard for farm women, who in addition to child care and housework, performed endless farm chores—milking cows, feeding livestock, raising vegetables, and so on. "I . . . am set and running every morning at half-past four o'clock, and run all day, often until half-past eleven P.M.," one farm woman explained. "Is it any wonder I have become slightly demoralized?"

On the plains, women also had to endure drab, cheerless surroundings without the companionship of neighbors or the respites and stimulations of social life. After the writer Hamlin Garland's mother read the grim discussions of women's lot in his book, *Main-Travelled Roads,* she wrote him: "You might have said more, but I'm glad you didn't. Farmers' wives have enough to bear as it is."

Working-Class Family Life

Social workers who visited the homes of industrial laborers in this period reported enormous differences in the standard of living of people engaged

in the same line of work, differences related to such variables as health, intelligence, the wife's ability as a homemaker, and pure luck. Some families spent most of their income on food; others saved substantial sums even when earning no more than $400 or $500 a year.

Consider the cases of two Illinois coal miners, hard-working union men with large families, each earning $1.50 a day in 1883. One was out of work nearly half the year; his income in 1883 was only $250. He, his wife, and their five children existed almost exclusively on a diet of bread and salt meat. Nevertheless, as an investigator reported, their two-room tenement home was neat and clean, and three of the children were attending school.

The other miner, father of four children, worked full time and brought home $420 in 1883. He owned a six-room house and an acre of land, where the family raised vegetables. Their food bill for the year was more than ten times that of the family just described. Two admirable families, probably similar in social attitudes and perhaps in political loyalties, but possessed of very different standards of living.

The cases of two families headed by railroad brakemen provide a different kind of variation. One man brought home only $360 to house and feed a wife and eight children. Here is the report of a state official who interviewed the family: "Clothes ragged, children half-dressed and dirty. They all sleep in one room regardless of sex. . . . The entire concern is as wretched as could be imagined. Father is shiftless. . . . Wife is without ambition or industry."

The other brakeman and his wife had only two children, and he earned $484 in 1883. They owned a well-furnished house, kept a cow, and raised vegetables for home consumption. Although they were far from rich, they managed to put aside enough money for insurance, reading matter, and a few small luxuries.

Working-Class Attitudes

Social workers and government officials made many efforts in the 1880s and 1890s to find out how working people felt about all sorts of matters connected with their jobs. Their reports reveal a wide spectrum of opinion. To the question, asked of two Wisconsin carpenters, "What new laws, in your opinion, ought to be enacted?" one replied: "Keep down strikes and rioters. Let every man attend to his own business." But the other answered: "Complete nationalization of land and all ways of transportation. Burn all government bonds. A graduated income tax. . . . Abolish child labor and [pass] any other act that capitalists say is wrong."

Every variation of opinion between these extremes was expressed by working people. In 1881 a woman textile worker in Lawrence, Massachusetts, said to an interviewer: "If you will stand by the mill, and see the people coming out, you will be surprised to see the happy, contented look they all have."

Despite such remarks and the general improvement in living standards, it is clear from the many bitter strikes of the period that there was a great deal of dissatisfaction among industrial workers. Writing in 1885, the labor leader Terence V. Powderly reported that "a deep-rooted feeling of discontent pervades the masses." A few years later, a Connecticut official conducted an informal survey of labor opinion in the state and found a "feeling of bitterness" and "distrust of employers" endemic.

The discontent had many causes. For some, poverty was still the chief problem, but for others, rising aspirations triggered discontent. Workers were confused. They wanted to believe their bosses and the politicians when those worthies voiced the old slogans about a classless society and the community of interest of capital and labor. "Our men," William Vanderbilt of the New York Central said in 1877, "feel that, although I . . . may have my millions and they the rewards of their daily toil, still we are about equal in the end. If they suffer, I suffer, and if I suffer, they cannot escape." "The poor," another conservative spokesman said a decade later, "are not poor because the rich are rich." Instead "the service of capital" softened their lot and gave them many benefits.

Statements such as these, though self-serving, were essentially correct. The rich were growing richer and more people were growing rich, but ordinary workers were better off too. However, the gap between the very rich and the ordinary citizen was widening.

Mobility: Social, Economic, and Educational

To study mobility in a large industrial country is extraordinarily difficult. Census records show that there was considerable geographical mobility in urban areas throughout the last half of the 19th century and into the 20th. In most cities this mobility was accompanied by some economic and social improvement. On the average about a quarter of the manual laborers traced rose to middle-class status during their lifetimes, and the sons of manual laborers were still more likely to improve their place in society. Progress from rags to real riches was another question.

Progress was primarily the result of the economic growth the nation was experiencing and of the energy and ambition of the people, native born and immigrant alike, who were pouring into the cities in such numbers. The public education system gave an additional boost to the upwardly mobile.

The history of American education after about 1870 reflects the impact of social and economic change. While Horace Mann, Henry Barnard, and others had laid the foundations for state-supported school systems, most of these systems became compulsory only after the Civil War, when the growth of cities provided the concentration of population and financial resources necessary for economical mass education.

In the 1860s about half the children in the country were getting some formal education, but this did not mean that half the children were attending school at any one time. Sessions were short, especially in rural areas. President Calvin Coolidge noted in his autobiography that the one-room school he attended in rural Vermont in the 1880s was open only when the 20-odd students were not needed in the fields.

After the Civil War, steady growth and improvement took place. Attendance in the public schools increased from 6.8 million in 1870 to 15.5 million in 1900. A typical elementary school graduate, at least in the cities, could count on having studied, besides the traditional "Three *R*s," history, geography, a bit of science, drawing, and physical training. But fewer than half a million of these graduates went on to high school; secondary education was still assumed to be only for those with special abilities and youths whose families were well off.

Industrialization created many demands for vocational and technical training; both employers and unskilled workers quickly grasped the possibilities. In 1880 Calvin M. Woodward opened a Manual Training School in St. Louis, and soon a number of similar schools were offering courses in carpentry, metalwork, sewing, and other crafts. By 1890, 36 cities had established vocational public high schools.

Because manual training attracted the backing of industrialists, organized labor was at first suspicious of the new trend. One union leader called trade schools "breeding schools for scabs and rats." Fortunately, the usefulness of such training soon became evident to the unions; by 1910 the American Federation of Labor (AFL) was lobbying side by side with the National Association of Manufacturers for more trade schools.

The unrealistic expectations inspired by the rags-to-riches myth more than the absence of real opportunity probably explains why so many workers, even when expressing dissatisfaction with life as it was, continued to subscribe to such middle-class values as hard work and thrift—that is, they continued to hope.

The "New" Immigration

Industrial expansion increased the need for labor, and this in turn powerfully stimulated immigration. Between 1866 and 1915, about 25 million foreigners entered the United States. Industrial growth alone does not explain the influx. The launching of the 19,000-ton English steamship *Great Eastern* in 1858 opened a new era in transatlantic travel, and competition soon made the crossing cheap as well as safe and rapid. Improved transportation produced unexpected and disruptive changes in the economies of many European countries. Cheap wheat from the United States, Russia, and other parts of the world poured

into Europe, bringing disaster to farmers from England and the Scandinavian countries to Italy and Greece. The spreading industrial revolution and the increased use of farm machinery led to the collapse of the peasant economy of central and southern Europe. Political and religious persecutions pushed still others into the migrating stream, but the main reason for emigrating remained the desire for economic betterment.

While immigrants continued to people the farms of America, industry absorbed an ever-increasing number of them. In 1870 one industrial worker in three was foreign born. When congressional investigators examined 21 major industries early in the new century, they discovered that well over half of the labor force had not been born in the United States.

Before 1882, when—in addition to the Chinese—criminals, idiots, lunatics, and persons liable to become public charges were excluded, entry into the United States was almost unrestricted. Indeed, until 1891 the Atlantic Coast states, not the federal government, exercised whatever controls were imposed on newcomers. On average, only one immigrant in fifty was rejected.

Private agencies, philanthropic and commercial, served as a link between the new arrivals and employers looking for labor. Numerous nationality groups assisted (and sometimes exploited) their compatriots by organizing "immigrant banks" that recruited labor in the old country, arranged transportation, and then housed the newcomers in boarding houses in the United States while finding them jobs. The *padrone* system of the Italians and Greeks was typical. The *padrone,* a sort of contractor who agreed to supply gangs of unskilled workers to companies for a lump sum, usually signed on immigrants unfamiliar with American wage levels at rates that assured him a healthy profit.

Beginning in the 1880s, the spreading effects of industrialization in Europe caused a shift in the sources of immigration from northern and western to southern and eastern sections of the Continent. In 1882, 789,000 immigrants entered the United States; more than 350,000 came from Great Britain and Germany, only 32,000 from Italy, and less than 17,000 from Russia. In 1907—the all-time peak year, with 1,285,000 immigrants—Great Britain and Germany supplied fewer than half the number they had 25 years earlier, while Russia and Italy were supplying 11 times as many as then.

The Old Immigrants and the New

The "new" immigrants, like the "old" Irish of the 1840s and 1850s, were mostly peasants. They seemed more than ordinarily clannish; southern Italians typically called all people outside their families *forestieri,* foreigners. Old-stock Americans thought them harder to assimilate, and in fact many were. Some Italian immigrants, for example, had come to the United States only to earn enough money to buy a farm back home. Such people made hard and willing workers but were not much concerned with rising in an American community.

The "birds of passage" were a substantial minority but the immigrants who saved in order to bring wives and children or younger brothers and sisters to America were more typical. They were almost desperately eager to become Americans, though of course they retained and nurtured much of their traditional culture.

Cultural differences among immigrants were often large and had important effects on their relations with native-born Americans and with other immigrant groups. Italians who settled in the city of Buffalo, the historian Virginia Yans-McLaughlin has shown, adjusted relatively smoothly to urban industrial life because of their close family and kinship ties. Polish immigrants in Buffalo, having different traditions, found adjustment more difficult.

German American and Irish American Catholics had different attitudes that caused them to clash over such matters as the policies of the Catholic University in Washington. Controversies, for example, erupted between Catholic and Protestant German Americans, among Greek American groups supporting various political factions in their homeland, and various other ethnic factions.

Confused by such differences and conflicts, many "older" Americans concluded, wrongly but understandabJy, that the new immigrants were incapable of becoming good citizens and should be kept out. The first to show concern were reformers, who were worried by the social problems that arose when so many poor immigrants flocked into cities already bursting at the seams. The directors of charitable organizations that bore the burden of aiding the most unfortunate of the immigrants were soon complaining that their resources were being exhausted by the needs of the human flood.

Social Darwinists and people obsessed with pseudoscientific ideas about "racial purity" also found the new immigration alarming. Misunderstanding the findings of the new science of genetics, they attributed the social problems associated with mass immigration to supposed physiological characteristics of the newcomers. Forgetting that earlier Americans had accused pre–Civil War Irish and German immigrants of similar deficiencies, they decided that the peoples of southern and eastern Europe were racially (and therefore permanently) inferior to "Nordic" and "Anglo-Saxon" types and ought to be kept out.

Workers, fearing the competition of people with low living standards and no bargaining power, spoke out against the "enticing of penniless and unapprised immigrants . . . to undermine our wages and social welfare." Some corporations, especially in fields like mining, which employed large numbers of unskilled workers, made use of immigrants as strikebreakers, and this particularly angered union members.

Conversely, employers were not at all disturbed by the influx of people with strong backs willing to work hard for low wages. Nevertheless, by the late 1880s many of them were alarmed about the supposed radicalism of the immigrants. The Haymarket bombing focused attention on the handful of foreign-born extremists in the country and loosed a flood of unjustified charges that "anarchists and communists" were dominating the labor movement. Nativism, which had waxed in the 1850s under the Know-Nothing banner and waned during the Civil War, now flared up again. Denunciations of "long-haired, wild-eyed, bad-smelling, atheistic, reckless foreign wretches," of "Europe's human and inhuman rubbish," of the "cutthroats of Beelzebub from the Rhine, the Danube, the Vistula and the Elbe" crowded the pages of the nation's press.

The nativists denounced Catholics and other minority groups more than immigrants as such.

The largest nativist organization of the period, the American Protective Association, founded in 1887, existed primarily to resist what its members called "the Catholic menace." But nowhere in America did prejudice lead to interference with religious freedom in the narrow sense. The Protestant majority treated "new" immigrants as underlings, tried to keep them out of the best jobs, and discouraged their efforts to climb the social ladder. This prejudice functioned only at the social and economic level. And neither labor leaders nor important industrialists, despite their misgivings about immigration, took a broadly antiforeign position.

After the Exclusion Act of 1882 and an almost meaningless 1885 ban on importing contract labor, no further restrictions were imposed on immigration until the 20th century. Strong support for a literacy test for admission developed in the 1890s, pushed by a new organization, the Immigration Restriction League. Since there was much more illiteracy in the southeastern quarter of Europe than in the northwestern, such a test would discriminate without seeming to do so on national or racial grounds. A literacy-test bill passed both houses of Congress in 1897, but President Cleveland vetoed it.

The Expanding City and Its Problems

Americans who favored restricting immigration made much of the fact that so many of the newcomers crowded into the cities, aggravating problems of housing, public health, crime, and immorality. Immigrants concentrated in the cities because the jobs created by expanding industry were located there. So, of course, did native Americans; the proportion of urban dwellers had been steadily increasing since about 1820. By 1890 one person in three lived in a city.

After 1890 the immigrant concentration became even more dense. The "new" migrants from eastern and southern Europe lacked the resources to travel to the agriculturally developing regions, to say nothing of the sums necessary to acquire land and farm equipment. As the concentration progressed it fed on itself, for all the eastern cities developed many ethnic neighborhoods, in each of

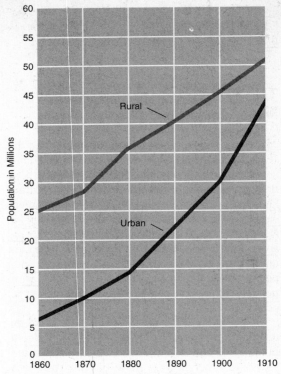

Rural and Urban Population, 1860–1910

which immigrants of one particular nationality congregated. Lonely, confused, often unable to speak English, the Italians, the Greeks, the Polish and Russian Jews, and other immigrants tended to settle where their predecessors had settled.

Most of the newsomers intended to become United States citizens, to be absorbed in the famous American melting pot. But they also wanted to maintain their traditional culture, they supported "national" churches, schools, newspapers, and clubs. Each great American city became a Europe in microcosm. New York, the great entrepôt, had a Little Italy, Polish, Greek, Jewish, and Bohemian quarters—even a Chinatown.

Although "ethnic" neighborhoods were crowded, unhealthy, and crime ridden, and many of the residents were desperately poor, they were also places where hopes and ambitions were fulfilled, where people worked hard and endured hardships in order to improve their own and their children's lot.

An alley known as "Bandit's Roost," on New York's Lower East Side, photographed for the *New York Sun* in 1887 by police reporter Jacob Riis, himself an immigrant. "What sort of an answer, think you, would come from these tenements to the question 'Is Life worth living?'" Riis asked in his book *How the Other Half Lives.*

Observing the immigrants' attachment to "foreign" values and institutions, numbers of "natives" accused the newcomers of resisting Americanization and blamed them for urban problems. The immigrants were involved in these problems, but the rapidity of urban expansion explains the troubles associated with city life far better than the high percentage of foreigners.

The Urban "Infrastructure"

The cities were suffering from growing pains. Sewer and water facilities frequently could not keep pace with skyrocketing needs; fire protection became increasingly inadequate; garbage piled up in the streets faster than it could be carted away; and the streets themselves crumbled beneath the pounding of heavy traffic. Urban growth proceeded with such speed that new streets were laid out more rapidly than they could be paved. Chicago, for example, had more than 1,400 miles of dirt streets in 1890.

People poured into the great cities faster than housing could be built to accommodate them. The influx into areas already densely packed in the 1840s became unbearable as rising property values and the absence of zoning laws conspired to make builders utilize every possible foot of space, squeezing out light and air ruthlessly in order to wedge in a few additional family units.

Substandard living quarters aggravated other evils such as disease and the disintegration of family life with its attendant mental anguish, crime, and juvenile delinquency. The bloody New York City riots of 1863, though sparked by dislike of the Civil War draft and of blacks, reflected the bitterness and frustration of thousands jammed together amid filth and threatened by disease. A citizens' committee seeking to discover the causes of the riots expressed its amazement after visiting the slums "that so much misery, disease, and wretchedness can be huddled together and hidden . . . unvisited and unthought of, so near our own abodes."

New York City created a Metropolitan Health Board in 1866, and a state tenement house law the following year made a feeble beginning at regulating city housing. Another law in 1879 placed a limit on the percentage of lot space that could be covered by new construction and established minimal standards of plumbing and ventilation.

Despite these efforts at reform, in 1890 more than 1.4 million persons were living on Manhattan Island, and in some sections the population density exceeded 900 persons per acre. Jacob Riis, a reporter, captured the horror of these crowded warrens in his classic study of life in the slums, *How the Other Half Lives* (1890):

Be a little careful, please! The hall is dark and you might stumble. . . . Here where the hall turns and dives into utter darkness is . . . a flight of stairs. You can feel your way, if you cannot see it. Close? Yes! What would you have? All the fresh air that enters these stairs comes from the hall-door that is forever slamming. . . . The sinks are in the hallway, that all the tenants may have access—and all be poisoned alike by their summer stenches. . . . Here is a door. Listen! That short, hacking cough, that tiny, helpless wail—what do they mean? . . . The child is dying of measles. With half a chance it might have lived; but it had none. That dark bedroom killed it.

The unhealthiness of the tenements was notorious. No one knows exactly, but as late as 1900 about three-quarters of the residents of New York City's Lower East Side lacked indoor toilets and had to use backyard outhouses to relieve themselves. In 1900 three out of five babies born in one poor district of Chicago died before their first birthday. Equally frightening was the impact of overcrowding on the morals of tenement dwellers. The number of prison inmates in the United States increased by 50 percent in the eighties and the homicide rate nearly tripled, most of the rise occurring in cities. Driven into the streets by the squalor of their homes, slum youths formed gangs bearing names like Alley Gang, Rock Gang, and Hell's Kitchen Gang. From petty thievery and shoplifting they graduated to housebreaking, bank robbery, and murder.

Slums bred criminals—the wonder was that they bred so few. They also drove well-to-do residents to exclusive sections and to the suburbs. From Boston's Beacon Hill and Back Bay to San Francisco's Nob Hill, the rich retired into great cluttered mansions and ignored conditions in the poorer parts of town.

The Cities Modernize

As American cities grew larger and more crowded, thereby aggravating a host of social problems, practical forces operated to bring about improvements. Once the relationship between polluted water and disease was fully understood, everyone saw the need for decent water and sewage systems. Whereas some businessmen profited from corrupt dealings with the city machines, more of them wanted efficient and honest government in order to reduce their tax bills. City dwellers of all classes resented dirt, noise, and ugliness, and in many communities public-spirited groups formed societies to plant trees, clean up littered areas, and develop recreational facilities. When one city undertook improvements, others tended to follow suit, spurred on by local pride and the booster spirit.

Gradually the basic facilities of urban living were improved. Streets were paved, first with cob-

blestones and wood blocks and then with smoother, quieter asphalt. Gaslight, then electric arc lights, and finally Edison's incandescent lamps brightened the cities after dark, making law enforcement easier, stimulating night life, and permitting factories and shops to operate after sunset.

Urban transportation underwent tremendous changes. Until the 1880s, horse-drawn cars were the main means of urban transportation. But horsecars had drawbacks. Enormous numbers of horses were needed and feeding and stabling the animals was costly. Their droppings (ten pounds per day per horse) became a major source of urban pollution. That is why the invention of the electric trolley car in the 1880s put an end to horsecar transportation. Trolleys were cheaper and less unsightly than horsecars asnd quieter than steam-powered trains. By 1895 some 850 lines were busily hauling city dwellers over 10,000 miles of track, and mileage more than tripled in the following decade. As with other new enterprises, control of street railways quickly became centralized until a few big operators controlled the trolleys of more than 100 eastern cities and towns.

Streetcars changed the character of big-city life. Before their introduction, urban communities were limited by the distances people could conveniently walk to work. The "walking city" could not

However noisy and unsightly their overhead rails, the electric trolleys represented a tremendous improvement in the urban environment over their waste-discharging horsecar predecessors when introduced in the 1880s.

easily extend more than two and a half miles from its center. Streetcars increased this radius to six miles or more, which meant that the area of the city expanded enormously. Dramatic population shifts resulted as the better-off moved from the center in search of air and space, abandoning the crumbling, jam-packed older neighborhoods to the poor. Thus economic segregation speeded the growth of ghettos. Older peripheral towns that had maintained some of the self-contained qualities of village life were swallowed up, becoming metropolitan centers. The village of Medford, Massachusetts, had 11,000 residents in 1890 when the first trolley line from Boston reached it. In 1905 its population was 23,000.

As time passed, each new area, originally peopled by rising economic groups, tended to become crowded and then to deteriorate. The middle class pushed steadily outward—which helps to explain why this group abandoned its interest in city government. By extending their tracks beyond the developed areas, the streetcar companies further speeded suburban growth because they assured developers and home buyers of efficient transport to town. By keeping fares low, the lines also enabled poor people to "escape" to the countryside on holidays. As Kenneth T. Jackson explains in *Crabgrass Frontier*, "First, streetcar lines were built out to existing villages. . . . These areas subsequently developed into large communities. Second, the tracks actually created residential neighborhoods where none existed before." In Los Angeles, Henry E. Huntington built his Pacific Electric Railway primarily to aid in selling home sites on land he had bought for a song before the tracks were laid.

"For the first time in the history of the world," Jackson writes, the combined activities of builders, trolley operators, and real estate developers made it possible for middle-class families "to buy a detached home on an accessible lot in a safe and sanitary environment."

Advances in bridge design, notably the perfection of the steel-cable suspension bridge by John A. Roebling, aided the ebb and flow of metropolitan populations. The Brooklyn Bridge, described by a poet as "a weird metallic Apparition . . . the cables, like divine messages from above . . . cutting and dividing into innumerable musical spaces the nude immensity of the sky," was Roebling's triumph. Completed in 1883 at a cost of $15

million, it was soon carrying more than 33 million passengers a year over the East River between Manhattan and Brooklyn.

Even the high cost of urban real estate, which fathered the tenement, produced some beneficial results in the long run. Instead of crowding squat structures cheek by jowl on 25-foot lots, architects began to build upward. Stone and brick apartment houses, sometimes elegantly known as "French Flats," replaced many dumbbell tenements. The introduction of the iron-skeleton type of construction, which freed the walls from bearing the immense weight of a tall building, was the work of a group of Chicago architects including William Le Baron Jenney, John A. Holabird, Martin Roche, John W. Root, and Louis H. Sullivan. Jenney's Home Insurance Building, completed in 1885, was the first metal-frame edifice. Height alone, however, did not satisfy these innovators; they sought a form that would reflect the structure and purpose of their buildings.

Their leader was Louis Sullivan. Builders must discard "books, rules, precedents, or any such educational impedimenta" and design functional buildings, he argued. Sullivan's Wainwright Building in St. Louis and his Prudential Building in Buffalo, both completed in the early nineties, combined beauty, modest construction costs, and efficient use of space in path-breaking ways. Soon a "race to the skies" was on in the cities, and the words *skyscraper* and *skyline* entered the language.

The remarkable "White City" built for the Chicago World's Fair of 1893 by Daniel H. Burnham, with its broad vistas and acres of open space, led to a "City Beautiful" movement, the most lasting result of which was the development of many public parks. But efforts to relieve congestion in slum districts made little headway.

Leisure Activities: More Fun and Games

By bringing together large numbers of people, cities made possible many kinds of social activity difficult or impossible to maintain in rural areas. Cities remained unsurpassed as centers of artistic and intellectual life. New York saw the founding of the American Museum of Natural History and the Metropolitan Museum of Art in 1870, and the Metropolitan Opera in 1883. Boston's Museum of Fine

Arts was founded in 1870 and the Boston Symphony in 1881. Other cities were equally hospitable to such endeavors, and less sophisticated forms of recreation also flourished in urban environments.

There often seemed to be a saloon on nearly every street corner. Saloons were strictly male working-class institutions, usually decorated with pictures and other mementoes of sports heroes, the bar perhaps under the charge of a retired pugilist.

For workingmen the saloon was a kind of club, a place to meet friends, exchange news and gossip, gamble, and eat, as well as to drink. The gradual reduction of the work day left men with more free time, which may explain why both saloons and burlesque shows, the latter described by one straight-laced critic as a "disgraceful spectacle of padded legs juggling and tight-laced wriggling," also proliferated.

Opposition to sports as a frivolous waste of valuable time was steadily evaporating, replaced among the upper- and middle-classes by the realization that games like golf and tennis were "healthy occupation[s] for mind and body." Bicycling became a fad, both as a means of getting from place to place and as a form of exercise and recreation.

Many of the new streetcar companies built picnic grounds and amusement parks at their outer limits. Thousands seeking to relax flocked to these "trolley parks" to enjoy a fresh-air meal or to patronize the shooting galleries, merry-go-rounds, and "freak shows."

The postwar era also saw the development of spectator sports, again because cities provided the concentrations of population necessary to support them. Curious relationships developed between upper- and working-class interests and between competitive sports as pure enjoyment for players and spectators and sports as something to bet on. Horse racing, had strictly upper-class origins, but racetracks attracted huge crowds of ordinary people more intent on picking a winner than on improving the breed.

Professional boxing was in a sense a hobby of the rich, who sponsored favorite gladiators, offered prizes, and often wagered large sums on the matches. But the audiences were made up overwhelmingly of young working-class males. The gambling and also the brutality of the bloody, bare-knuckle character of the fights caused many communities to outlaw boxing.

The first widely popular pugilist was the legendary "Boston Strong Boy," John L. Sullivan, who became heavyweight champion in 1882. Sullivan's idea of fighting, according to his biographer, "was simply to hammer his opponent into unconsciousness." He became an international celebrity and made and lost large sums during this period. Yet boxing remained a raffish, clandestine occupation. One of Sullivan's important fights took place in France, on the estate of Baron Rothchild, yet when it ended both he and his opponent were arrested.

Three major team games, baseball, football, and basketball, developed in something approaching their modern form during the last quarter of the century. Organized baseball teams, in most cases made up of upper-class amateurs, had emerged in the 1840s, but the game only became truly popular during the Civil War, when it was a major form of camp recreation for the troops.

The first professional team, the Cincinnati Red Stockings, paid players between $800 and $1,400 for the season. In 1876 teams in eight cities formed the National League. The American League followed in 1901. After a brief period of rivalry, the two leagues made peace in 1903, the year of the first World Series.

Organized play led to codification of the rules and improvements in technique and strategy, for example, the development of "minor" leagues; impartial umpires calling balls and strikes and ruling on close plays; the use of catcher's masks and of padded gloves; the invention of various kinds of curves and other erratic pitches. As early as the 1870s, baseball was being called "the national game." Despite its urban origins, its broad green fields and dusty basepaths gave the game a rural character that only recently has begun to fade away.

Nobody "invented" baseball, but both football and basketball owe their present form to individuals. In 1891, while a student at a YMCA school, James Naismith attached peach baskets to the edge of an elevated running track in the gymnasium and drew up what are still the basic rules of basketball. The game was popular from the start, but being played indoors it was not an important spectator sport until much later.

Football evolved out of English rugby. For many decades it remained almost entirely a college sport (and thus played almost entirely by up- and middle-class types). The first intercollege football game occurred when Princeton defeated Rutgers in 1869 and by the 1880s college football had become extremely popular.

Much of the game's modern character was the work of Walter Camp, the athletic director and football coach of Yale. Camp cut the size of teams from 15 to 11, and he invented the scrimmage line, the four-down system, and the key position of quarterback. Camp's prestige was such that when he named his first All America team after the 1889 season, no one challenged his judgment.

Camp claimed that amateur sports like football taught the value of hard work, cooperation, and fair play, but he recruited players who could not meet Yale's academic standards and found means of putting money in his players' pockets. All the problems that emphasis on athletic achievement poses for modern institutions of higher education existed in microcosm well before 1900.

Spectator sports had little appeal to women at this time and indeed for decades thereafter. And few women participated in organized athletics. Sports were "manly" activities; a women might ride a bicycle, play croquet and perhaps a little tennis, but to display any concentrated interest in excelling in a sport was considered unfeminine.

The Churches Respond to Industrial Society

The modernization of the great cities was not solving most of the social problems of the slums. As this fact became clear, a number of urban religious leaders began to take a hard look at the situation. Traditionally, American churchmen had insisted that where sin was concerned, there were no extenuating circumstances. To the well-to-do they preached the virtues of thrift and hard work; to the poor they extended the possibility of a better existence in the next world; to all they stressed ones responsibility for one's own behavior—and thus for one's own salvation.

Such a point of view brought meager comfort to residents of slums. Consequently the churches lost influence in the poorer sections. Furthermore, as better-off citizens followed the streetcar lines out from the city centers, their church leaders followed them.

An increasing proportion of the residents of the blighted districts were Catholics, and the Catholic Church devoted much effort to distributing alms, maintaining homes for orphans and old people, and other forms of social welfare. But Church leaders seemed unconcerned with the social causes of the blight; they were deeply committed to the idea that sin and vice were personal, poverty an act of God. They deplored the rising tide of crime, disease, and destitution among their coreligionists, yet failed to see the connection between these evils and the squalor of the slums.

The Catholic hierarchy tended to be at best neutral toward organized labor. Cardinal James Gibbons spoke favorably of the Knights of Labor when it was under attack in 1886 after the Haymarket bombing, but he took a dim view of strikes. The clergy's attitude changed somewhat after Pope Leo XIII issued his encyclical *Rerum novarum* (1891), which criticized the excesses of capitalism, defended the right of labor to form unions, and stressed the duty of government to care for the poor. Workers were entitled to wages that would guarantee their families a reasonable and frugal comfort, Leo declared. Concrete action by American Catholic leaders, however, was slow in coming.

The conservatism of most Protestant and Catholic clergymen did not prevent some earnest preachers from working directly to improve the lot of the city poor. Some followed the path blazed by Dwight L. Moody, a lay evangelist who conducted a vigorous campaign in the 1870s to persuade the denizens of the slums to cast aside their sinful ways. He went among them full of enthusiasm and God's love and made an impact no less powerful than that of George Whitefield during the Great Awakening of the 18th century or Charles Grandison Finney in the first part of the 19th century. The evangelists founded mission schools in the slums and were prominent in the establishment of the Young Men's Christian Association (1851) and the Salvation Army (1880).

However, the evangelists paid little heed to the causes of urban poverty and vice. But a number of Protestant clergymen who had become familiar with the terrible problems of the slums began to preach a "Social Gospel" that focused on improving living conditions rather than on saving souls. If people were to lead pure lives, they must have enough to eat, decent homes, and opportunities to develop their talents. Social Gospelers advocated child labor legislation, the regulation of big corporations, and heavy taxes on incomes and inheritances.

The most influential preacher of the Social Gospel was probably Washington Gladden. At first Gladden, who was raised on a Massachusetts farm, had opposed all government interference in social and economic affairs, but his experiences as a minister in Springfield, Massachusetts, and Columbus, Ohio, exposed him to the realities of life in industrial cities, and his views changed. In *Applied Christianity* (1886) he defended labor's right to organize and strike and denounced the idea that supply and demand should control wage rates. He favored factory inspection laws, strict regulation of public utilities, and other reforms.

Gladden never questioned the basic values of capitalism. By the nineties a number of ministers had gone all the way to socialism. The Reverend William D. P. Bliss of Boston, for example, believed in the kind of welfare state envisioned by Edward Bellamy in *Looking Backward*. In addition to nationalizing industry, Bliss and other Christian Socialists advocated government unemployment relief programs, public housing and slum-clearance projects, and other measures designed to aid the city poor.

The Settlement Houses

A number of earnest souls began to grapple with slum problems by organizing what were known as settlement houses. These were community centers located in poor districts which provided guidance and services to all who would use them. The settlement workers, most of them idealistic, well-to-do young people, lived in the houses and were active in neighborhood affairs.

The prototype of the settlement house was London's Toynbee Hall, founded in the early eighties; by the turn of the century, 100 such houses had been established in America, the most famous being Jane Addams's Hull House in Chicago (1889), Robert A. Woods's South End House in Boston (1892), and Lillian Wald's Henry Street Settlement in New York (1893).

Although men were also active in the movement, the most important settlement house workers were women fresh from college—the first generation of young women to experience the shock of having developed their abilities only to find that society offered few opportunities to use them. The settlements provided an outlet for their hopes and energies. A reformer who visited Hull House around the turn of the century described the residents as "strong-minded energetic women, bustling about their various enterprises" and "mild-mannered men who slide from room to room apologetically."

Settlement workers explained American ways to the immigrants. Unlike most charity workers, who acted out of a sense of upper-class responsibility toward the unfortunate, they expected to benefit themselves by experiencing a way of life different from their own. Lillian Wald, a nurse by training, explained the concept succinctly in *The House on Henry Street* (1915): "We were to live in the neighborhood . . . identify ourselves with it socially, and, in brief, contribute to it our citizenship."

Settlement workers soon discovered that practical problems absorbed most of their energies. They agitated for tenement-house laws, the regulation of the labor of women and children, and better schools. They established playgrounds in the slums, along with libraries, classes in arts and crafts, social clubs, and day nurseries. In Chicago Jane Addams developed classes in music and art and an excellent "little theater" group. Hull House soon boasted a gymnasium, a day nursery, and several social clubs. Addams also campaigned tirelessly for improved public services and for social legislation of all kinds.

A few critics considered the settlement houses mere devices to socialize the unruly poor, but almost everyone appreciated their virtues. By the end of the century, even the Catholics, laggard in entering the arena of practical social reform, were joining the movement, partly because they were losing many communicants to socially minded Protestant churches.

With all their accomplishments, the settlement houses seemed to be fighting a losing battle. "Private beneficence," Jane Addams wrote of Hull House, "is totally inadequate to deal with the vast numbers of the city's disinherited." The slums, fed by an annual influx of hundreds of thousands, blighted new areas more rapidly than settlement-house workers could clean up old ones. It became increasingly apparent that the wealth and authority of the state must be brought to bear in order to keep abreast of the problem.

Civilization and Its Discontents

As the 19th century died, the majority of the American people, especially those comfortably well off, the residents of small towns, the shopkeepers, many farmers, and some skilled workers, remained confirmed optimists and uncritical admirers of their civilization. However, blacks, immigrants, and others who failed to share equitably in the good things of life, along with a growing number of humanitarian reformers, found much to lament in their increasingly industrialized society. Giant monopolies flourished despite federal restrictions. The gap between rich and poor appeared to be widening, while the slum spread its poison and the materially successful made a god of their success. Human values seemed in grave danger of being crushed by impersonal forces typified by the great corporations.

In 1871 Walt Whitman, usually so full of extravagant praise for everything American, had called his fellow countrymen the "most materialistic and money-making people ever known":

I say we had best look our times and lands searchingly in the face, like a physician diagnosing some deep disease. Never was there, perhaps, more hollowness of heart than at present. . . .

By the late eighties a well-known journalist could write to a friend: "The wheel of progress is to be run over the whole human race and smash us all." Others noted an alarming jump in the national divorce rate and an increasing taste for all kinds of luxury. "People are made slaves by a desperate struggle to keep up appearances," a Massachusetts commentator declared, and the economist David A. Wells expressed concern over statistics showing that heart disease and mental illness were on the rise. These "diseases of civilization," Wells explained, were "one result of the continuous mental and nervous activity which modern high-tension methods of business have necessitated."

Intellectuals tend to be critical of the world they live in; Thoreau, for example, denounced materialism and the worship of progress in the 1840s as vigorously as any late-19th-century prophet of gloom. But the voices of the dissatisfied were rising. Despite the many benefits that industrialization had made possible, it was by no means clear around 1900 that the American people were really better off under the new dispensation.

Milestones

1858	English liner *Great Eastern* launched	1888	First urban electric streetcar system
1876	National Baseball League founded	1889	Jane Addams founds Hull House
1880	Salvation Army founded		Walter Camp's first All-American football team
1880s	"New" immigration begins		
1882	John L. Sullivan wins heavyweight boxing championship	1890	Jacob Riis, *How the Other Half Lives*
	Chinese Exclusion Act		Calvin Woodward opens his Manual Training School
1883	Brooklyn Bridge completed	1891	Pope Leo XIII issues *Rerum novarum* encyclical
1885	Foran Contract Labor Act		
1887	American Protective Association founded	1896	Charles M. Sheldon, *In His Steps*

Supplementary Reading

An enormous number of books deals with the social history of late-19th century America. J. A. Garraty, **The New Commonwealth*** (1968), treats most of the subjects covered in this chapter; A. M. Schlesinger's classic study, **The Rise of the City** (1933), provides a wealth of information about social trends. See also the appropriate sections of Steven Mintz and Susan Kellogg, **Domestic Revolutions: A Social History of the American Family** (1988), and C. N. Degler, **At Odds: Women and the Family in America** (1980).

Henry Adams, **The Education of Henry Adams*** (1918), is a fascinating if highly personal view of the period and James Bryce, **The American Commonwealth*** (1888), although primarily a political analysis, contains a great deal of information about social conditions, as does D. A. Wells, **Recent Economic Changes** (1889).

On industrial workers, see David Montgomery, **Beyond Equality*** (1967), J. E. Drucker, **Men of the Steel Rails** (1983), Walter Licht, **Working on the Railroad** (1984), and H. G. Gutman, **Work, Culture, and Society in Industrializing America*** (1977). J. A. Garraty, ed., **Labor and Capital in the Gilded Age*** (1968), provides a convenient selection of testimony from the great 1883 Senate investigation of that subject, whereas David Brody, **Steelworkers in America*** (1960), and Stephan Thernstrom, **Poverty and Progress: Social Mobility in a Nineteenth-Century City** (1964), throw much light on the lives of workingmen. S. M. Rothman, **Woman's Proper Place** (1978), discusses the new job opportunities for women. Stephan Thernstrom's **The Other Bostonians** (1973), is a brilliant analysis of social and geographical mobility and an excellent summary of work on these important topics.

Businessmen's attitudes are covered in T. C. Cochran, **Railroad Leaders** (1953), and E. C. Kirkland, **Dream and Thought in the Business Community** (1956).

On immigration, see M. A. Jones, **American Immigration*** (1960), and John Higham, **Send These to Me*** (1975). Oscar Handlin, **The Uprooted*** (1951), describes the life of the new immigrants somewhat romantically but with sensitivity, while John Higham, **Strangers in the Land*** (1955), stresses the reactions of native Americans to successive waves of immigration. Moses Rischin, **The Promised City: New York's Jews*** (1962), Thomas Kessner, **The Golden Door: Italian and Jewish Immigrant Mobility** (1977), Humbert Nelli, **The Italians of Chicago*** (1970), Virginia Yans-McLaughlin, **Family and Community: Italian Immigrants in Buffalo** (1977), and T. N. Brown, **Irish-American Nationalism** (1966), are important monographs.

A brief interpretive history of urban development is C. N. Glaab and A. T. Brown, **A History of Urban America*** (1967). K. T. Jackson, **Crabgrass Frontier** (1985), is a pioneering history of suburban development, and J. C. Teaford, **The Unheralded Triumph** (1984), gives weight to the accomplishments of the cities as well as their inadequacies. For the growing pains of American cities, consult R. H. Bremner, **From the Depths*** (1956), Jacob Riis, **How the Other Half Lives*** (1890), and Roy Lubove, **The Progressives and the Slums** (1962). Urban architecture is discussed in J. E. Burchard and Albert Bush-Brown, **The Architecture of America*** (1961). S. B. Warner, Jr., **Streetcar Suburbs** (1962), is an interesting study of Boston's development that is full of suggestive ideas about late-19th-century growth.

On the early development of intercollegiate sports see R. A. Smith, **Sports and Freedom: The Rise of Big-Time College Athletics** (1988). The response of religion to industrialism is discussed in H. F. May, **Protestant Churches and Industrial America*** (1949), A. I. Abell, **American Catholicism and Social Action** (1960), and Arthur Mann, **Yankee Reformers in the Urban Age*** (1954). For the settlement house movement, see A. F. Davis, **Spearheads for Reform** (1967), Davis's **American Heroine** (1973), a life of Jane Addams, and two classic personal accounts, Jane Addams, **Twenty Years at Hull House*** (1910), and Lillian Wald, **The House on Henry Street** (1915).

*Available in paperback.

CHAPTER 20

Intellectual and Cultural Trends

The Pursuit of Knowledge

Magazine Journalism

Colleges and Universities

Scientific Advances

The New Social Sciences

Progressive Education

Law and History

Realism in Literature

Mark Twain

William Dean Howells

Henry James

Realism in Art

The Pragmatic Approach

*I*ndustrialization altered the way Americans thought at the same time that it transformed their ways of making a living. Technological advances revolutionized the communication of ideas more drastically than they did the transportation of goods or the manufacture of steel. The materialism that permeated American attitudes toward business affected contemporary education and literature. Charles Darwin's theory of evolution influenced American philosophers, lawyers, and historians. New ideas about how children should be educated and what they should be taught emerged along with new methods of communicating information to adults. As the society became more complex, higher education became more important and Americans began to make significant contributions both in the "hard" sciences, such as chemistry and physics, and in relatively new "soft" social sciences, such as psychology, political science, and sociology. A new literary flowering comparable to the "renaissance" of the 1840s and 1850s occurred in the 1870s and 1880s. By the end of the century, America had finally emerged intellectually from the shadow of Europe.

The Pursuit of Knowledge

Improvements in public education and the needs of an increasingly complex society for every type of intellectual skill caused a veritable revolution in how knowledge was discovered, disseminated, and put to use. Observing the effects of formal education on their children, many older people were eager to experience some of its benefits. Nothing so well illustrates the desire for new information as the rise of the Chautauqua movement, founded by John H. Vincent, a Methodist minister, and Lewis Miller, an Ohio manufacturer of farm machinery. In 1874 they organized a two-week summer course for Sunday-school teachers on the shores of Lake Chautauqua in New York. Besides instruction, they offered good meals, evening song fests around the campfire, and a relaxing atmosphere—all for $6 for the two weeks. The idea caught on, and soon the leafy shore of Lake Chautauqua became a city of tents each summer as thousands poured into the region from all over the country. The founders expanded their offerings to include instruction in literature, science, government, and economics. Eventually, Chautauqua even offered correspondence courses leading over a four-year period to a diploma.

By 1900 there were about 200 Chautauqua-type organizations. Intellectual standards in these programs varied; in general they were low, for they reflected the prevailing tastes of the American people—diverse, enthusiastic, uncritical, and shallow. Nevertheless the movement provided opportunities for thousands seeking stimulation and intellectual improvement.

Newspapers were an even more important means for disseminating information and educating the masses. Here new technology supplied the major incentive for change. The development by Richard Hoe and Stephen Tucker of the web press (1871), which printed simultaneously on both sides of paper fed into it from large rolls, and

Ottmar Mergenthaler's linotype machine (1886), which cast rows of type as needed directly from molten metal, cut printing costs dramatically. By 1895 machines were printing, cutting, and folding 24,000 32-page newspapers an hour.

The telegraph and transoceanic cables wrought a similar transformation in the gathering of news. Press associations, led by the New York Associated Press, flourished; the syndicated article appeared; and a few publishers—Edward W. Scripps was the first—began to acquire chains of newspapers.

Population growth and better education created an ever larger demand for printed matter. At the same time, the integration of the economy enabled manufacturers to sell their goods all over the country. Advertising became important, and sellers soon learned that newspapers and magazines were excellent means of placing their products before millions of eyes. Rich men such as the railroad magnate Jay Gould and the mining tycoon George Hearst invested heavily in newspapers in the postwar decades.

Publishers tended to be conservative, but reaching the masses meant lowering intellectual and cultural standards, appealing to emotions, and adopting popular, sometimes radical, causes. The first to reach a truly massive audience was Joseph Pulitzer, a Hungarian-born immigrant who made a first-rate paper of the St. Louis *Post-Dispatch*. In 1883 Pulitzer bought the New York *World,* a sheet with a circulation of perhaps 20,000. Within a year he was selling 100,000 copies daily, and by the late nineties the *World's* circulation regularly exceeded 1 million.

Pulitzer achieved this brilliant success by casting a wide net. To the masses he offered bold black headlines devoted to crime (ANOTHER MURDERER TO HANG), scandal (VICE ADMIRAL'S SON IN JAIL), catastrophe (TWENTY-FOUR MINERS KILLED), society and the theater (LILY LANGTRY'S NEW ADMIRER), together with feature stories, political cartoons, sports pages, comics, and pictures. For the educated and affluent he provided better political and financial coverage than the most respectable New York journals. Pulitzer made the *World* a crusader for civic improvement by attacking political corruption, monopoly, and slum problems. "The *World* is the people's newspaper," he boasted, and in the sense that it interested men and women of every sort, he was correct.

John Singer Sargent's 1905 portrait of Joseph Pulitzer. Following his death six years later, Pulitzer's will provided for the endowment of the Columbia School of Journalism and the establishment of Pulitzer Prizes for journalism, letters, and other categories.

Pulitzer's methods were quickly copied by competitors, especially George Hearst's son, William Randolph Hearst, who purchased the New York *Journal* in 1895 and soon outdid the *World* in sensationalism. But no other newspaperman of the era approached Pulitzer in originality, boldness, and the knack of reaching the masses without abandoning seriousness of purpose and basic integrity.

Magazine Journalism

Growth and ferment also characterized the magazine world. In 1865 there were about 700 magazines in the country, by the turn of the century more than 5,000. Until the mid-eighties, few of the new magazines were in any way unusual. A handful of serious periodicals, such as the *Atlantic Monthly, Harper's,* and the *Century*, dominated the field. They were staid in tone and conservative in political taste. Articles on current affairs, a good deal of fiction and poetry, historical and biographical studies, and similar material filled their pages. But none approached a mass circulation because of the limited size of the upper-middle-class audience at which they aimed.

After about 1885 vast changes began to take place. New magazines such as the *Forum* (1886) and the *Arena* (1889) emphasized hard-hitting articles on controversial subjects by leading experts. In 1889 Edward W. Bok became editor of the *Ladies' Home Journal.* Besides advice columns ("Ruth Ashmore's Side Talks with Girls"), he offered articles on child care, gardening, and interior decorating, published fine contemporary novelists, and commissioned public figures to discuss important questions. He printed colored reproductions of art masterpieces—the invention of cheap photoengraving was of enormous significance in the success of mass-circulation magazines—and crusaded for women's suffrage, conservation, and other reforms. Bok did more than cater to public tastes, he created new tastes. He even refused to accept patent medicine advertising, a major source of revenue for many popular magazines.

Bok and his many competitors reached millions of readers. Like Pulitzer in the newspaper field, they found ways of interesting rich and poor, the cultivated and the ignorant. Under Bok, the *Journal* reached a circulation of 2 million.

Colleges and Universities

The same forces that were affecting the dissemination of information were also altering higher education and professional training. Less than 2 percent of the college-age population attended college, but the aspirations of young people were rising, and more and more parents had the financial means necessary for fulfilling them.

More significant than the expansion of the colleges were the alterations in their curricula and in the atmosphere permeating the average campus. State universities proliferated; the federal government's land-grant program in support of training in "agriculture and the mechanic arts," established under the Morrill Act of 1862, came into its own; wealthy philanthropists poured fortunes into old institutions and founded new ones; educators introduced new courses and adopted new teaching methods; professional schools of law, medicine, education, business, journalism, and other specialties increased in number.

In the forefront of reform was Harvard, the oldest and most prestigious college in the country. In the 1860s it possessed an excellent faculty, but teaching methods were antiquated, and the curriculum had remained almost unchanged since the colonial period. In 1869, however, a dynamic president, the chemist Charles W. Eliot, undertook a transformation of the college. Eliot introduced the elective system, gradually eliminating required courses and expanding offerings in such areas as modern languages, economics, and the laboratory sciences. He encouraged the faculty to experiment with new teaching methods. The standards of the medical school were raised, and the case method was introduced in the law school. For the first time, students were allowed to borrow books from the library! In some respects Eliot went too far—the elective system encouraged superficiality and laxness in many students—but on balance he transformed Harvard from a college, "a place to which a young man is sent," to a university, a place "to which he goes."

An even more important development in higher education was the founding of Johns Hopkins in 1876. This university was one of many established in the period by wealthy industrialists; its benefactor, the Baltimore merchant Johns Hopkins, had made his fortune in the Baltimore and Ohio Railroad. Its distinctiveness, however, was due to the vision of Daniel Coit Gilman, its first president. Gilman modeled Johns Hopkins on the German universities, where meticulous research and freedom of inquiry were the guiding principles. In staffing the institution, he sought scholars of the highest reputation, scouring Europe as well as America in his search for talent. Gilman promised his teachers good students and ample opportunity to pursue their own research (which explains why Hopkins professors repeatedly turned down attractive offers from other universities).

Johns Hopkins specialized in graduate education. In the generation after its founding, it turned out a remarkable percentage of the most important scholars in the nation, including Woodrow

Wilson in political science, John Dewey in philosophy, Frederick Jackson Turner in history, and John R. Commons in economics. The seminar conducted by Herbert Baxter Adams was particularly productive: The Adams-edited *Johns Hopkins Studies in Historical and Political Science,* consisting of the doctoral dissertations of his students, was both voluminous and "the mother of similar studies in every part of the United States."

The example of Johns Hopkins encouraged other wealthy individuals to endow universities offering advanced work. Of these, the most important was John D. Rockefeller's creation, the University of Chicago (1892). The president of the University, William Rainey Harper, was a brilliant Biblical scholar—he received his Ph.D. from Yale at the age of 18—and an imaginative administrator. The new university, he told Rockefeller, should be designed "with the example of Johns Hopkins before our eyes."

Like Daniel Coit Gilman, Harper sought topflight scholars for his faculty. He offered such high salaries that he was besieged with over 1,000 applications. Chicago offered first-class graduate and undergraduate education. During its first year there were 120 instructors for fewer than 600 students, and despite fears that the mighty tycoon Rockefeller would enforce his social and economic views on the institution, academic freedom was the rule.

State and federal aid to higher education expanded rapidly. The Morrill Act, granting land to each state at a rate of 30,000 acres for each senator and representative, provided the endowments that gave many important modern universities, such as Illinois, Michigan State, and Ohio State, their start. The federal assistance was earmarked for specific subjects, but the land-grant colleges offered a full range of courses, and all received additional state funds.

The land-grant universities adopted new ideas quickly. They were coeducational from the start, and most developed professional schools and experimented with extension work and summer programs. Typical of the better state institutions was the University of Michigan, which reached the top rank among the nation's universities during the presidency of James B. Angell (1871–1909).

Important advances were made in women's higher education. Beginning with Vassar College, which opened its doors to 300 women students in 1865, the opportunity for young women to pursue serious academic work gradually expanded. Wellesley and Smith, both founded in 1875, completed the so-called Big Three women's colleges. Together with the already established Mount Holyoke, and with Bryn Mawr (1885), Barnard (1889), and Radcliffe (1893), they became known as the Seven Sisters.

Opportunities for women graduates were severely limited. The only professional careers easily available to them were teaching, nursing, and the new area called social work. Nevertheless, the women that these institutions trained were conscious of their uniqueness and determined to demonstrate their capabilities. But they provided most of the leaders of the early-20th-century drive for equal rights for women.

Not all the changes in higher education were beneficial. The elective system led to superficiality; students gained a smattering of knowledge of many subjects and mastered none. Intensive graduate work often produced narrowness of outlook and research monographs on trivial subjects. The gifts of rich industrialists sometimes came with strings, and college boards of trustees tended to be dominated by businessmen who sometimes attempted to impose their own social and economic beliefs on faculty members. Although few professors lost their positions because their views offended trustees, at many institutions trustees exerted constant nagging pressures that limited academic freedom and scholarly objectivity. At state colleges politicians often interfered in academic affairs, even treating professorships as part of the patronage system.

When universities grew bigger, their administration became more complicated and the prestige of administrators rose inordinately. At many institutions professors came to be regarded as mere employees of the governing boards. And as the number of college graduates increased and colleges ceased being primarily training institutions for clergymen, the influence of alumni on educational policies began to make itself felt, not always happily. Campus social activities became more important. Fraternities proliferated. Interest in organized sports first appeared as a laudable outgrowth of the general expansion of the curriculum, but soon athletic contests were playing a role all out of proportion to their significance. By the early nineties, important games were attracting huge crowds (over 50,000 attended the Yale-Princeton football game in 1893). Football became a source of revenue that many colleges dared not neglect. Since students, alumni, and the public demanded winning teams, college administrators stooped to subsidizing student athletes, in extreme cases employing players who were not students at all.

Higher education reflected American values, with all their strengths and weaknesses. A complex society required a more professional and specialized education for its youth; the coarseness and the rampant materialism and competitiveness of the era inevitably found expression in the colleges and universities.

Scientific Advances

Much has been made of the crassness of late-19th-century American life, yet the period produced intellectual achievements of the highest quality. If the business mentality dominated society, and if the great barons of industry, exalting practicality over theory, tended to look down on the life of the mind, intellectuals, quietly pondering the problems of their generation, nonetheless created works that affected the country as profoundly as the achievements of industrial organizers like Rockefeller and Carnegie and technicians like Edison and Bell.

In pure science America produced a number of outstanding figures in these years. The giant among them, whose contributions some experts rank with those of Newton, Darwin, and Einstein, was Josiah Willard Gibbs, professor of mathematical physics at Yale from 1871 to 1903. Gibbs created an entirely new science, physical chemistry, and made possible the study of how complex substances respond to changes in temperature and pressure. Purely theoretical at the time, Gibbs's ideas led to vital advances in metallurgy and in the manufacture of plastics, drugs, and other products.

Of lesser but still major significance was the work of Albert A. Michelson of the University of Chicago, who made the first accurate measure-

ments of the speed of light. Michelson's researches in the 1870s and 1880s helped prepare the way for Einstein's theory of relativity; in 1907 he became the first American scientist to win a Nobel Prize.

The New Social Sciences

In the social sciences a close connection existed between the practical issues of the age and the achievements of the leading thinkers. The application of the theory of evolution to every aspect of human relations, the impact of industrialization on society, the development of institutions and their interactions—such topics were of intense concern to American social scientists. Controversies over trusts, slum conditions, and other problems drew scholars out of their towers and into practical affairs.

Among the economists something approaching a revolution took place in the 1880s. The classical school, which maintained that immutable natural laws governed all human behavior, and which used the insights of Darwin only to justify unrestrained competition and laissez-faire, was challenged by a group of young economists who argued that as times changed, economic theories and laws must be modified in order to remain relevant. Richard T. Ely, another of the scholars who made Johns Hopkins a font of new ideas in the eighties, summarized the thinking of this group in 1885. "The state" Ely proclaimed, is "an educational and ethical agency whose positive aid is an indispensable condition of human progress." Laissez-faire was outmoded and dangerous. Economic problems were basically moral problems; their solution required "the united efforts of Church, state and science." The proper way to study these problems was by analyzing actual conditions, not by applying abstract laws or principles. This approach produced the so-called institutionalist school of economics, whose members made detailed, on-the-spot investigations of labor unions, sweatshops, factories, and mines.

A similar revolution struck sociology in the mid-eighties. Prevailing opinion up to that time rejected the idea of government interference with the organization of society. The influence of the

English social Darwinist Herbert Spencer, who objected even to public schools and the postal system, was immense. Spencer twisted the ideas of Darwin to mean that society could be changed only by the force of evolution, which moved with cosmic slowness.

Such a point of view made little sense in America, where society was changing rapidly and the range of government social and economic activity was expanding. It was first challenged by an obscure scholar employed by the U.S. Geological Survey, Lester Frank Ward, whose *Dynamic Sociology* was published in 1883. Ward assailed the Spencerians for ignoring the possibility of "the improvement of society by cold calculation." In *The Psychic Factors of Civilization* (1893) he blasted the "law of competition." Human progress, he argued, consisted of "triumphing little by little over this law,"—for example, by interfering with biological processes through the use of medicines to kill harmful bacteria. Society must indeed evolve, but it would evolve through careful social planning.

Ward had little direct influence because his writings were highly technical. However, his arguments laid the theoretical basis for the modern welfare state.

The new political scientists were also evolutionists and institutionalists. The Founding Fathers had conceived of the political system as an impersonal set of institutions and principles—a government of laws rather than of men. Nineteenth-century thinkers (John C. Calhoun is the best example) concerned themselves with abstractions, such as states' rights, and ignored the extralegal aspects of politics, such as parties and pressure groups. In the 1880s political scientists began to employ a different approach. In his doctoral dissertation at Johns Hopkins, *Congressional Government* (1885), Woodrow Wilson analyzed the American political system. He concluded that the real locus of authority lay in the committees of Congress, which had no constitutional basis at all. Wilson viewed politics as a dynamic process and offered no theoretical objection to the expansion of state power. In *The State* (1889) he distinguished between essential functions of government, such as the punishment of crime, and "ministrant" functions, such as education, the regulation of corporations, and social welfare legislation. The desirability of any particular state action of the latter type was simply a matter of expediency.

Progressive Education

Traditionally, American teachers had emphasized the three *R*s and relied on strict discipline and rote learning. But the ideas of early-19th-century German educators, notably Johann Friedrich Herbart, were attracting attention in the United States. According to Herbart, teachers could best arouse the interest of their students by relating new information to what they already knew; good teaching called for professional training, psychological insight, enthusiasm, and imagination, not merely facts and a birch rod. At the same time, evolutionists were pressing for a kind of education that would help children to "survive" by adapting to the demands of their environment.

Forward-looking educators seized upon these ideas because social changes were making the old system increasingly inadequate. Settlement-house workers discovered that slum children needed training in handicrafts, good citizenship, and personal hygiene as much as in reading and writing. Gradually they came to regard educational reform as central to the problem of improving society. "We are impatient with the schools which lay all stress on reading and writing," Jane Addams declared. This type of education "fails to give the child any clew to the life about him."

The philosopher who summarized and gave direction to these forces was John Dewey, a professor at the University of Chicago. Essentially Dewey's approach was ethical. Was the nation's youth being properly prepared for the tasks it faced in the modern world?

"Education," Dewey insisted, was "the fundamental method of social progress and reform." Moreover, in an industrial society the family no longer performed many of the educational functions it had carried out in an agrarian society. Farm children learn about nature, about work, about human character in countless ways denied to children in cities. At the same time, education should center on the child, and new information should be related to what the child already knows. Children's imagination, energy, and curiosity are tools for broadening their outlook and increasing their store of information. Finally, the school should become an instrument for social reform, "saturating [the child] with the spirit of service" and helping to produce a "society which is worthy, lovely, and harmonious."

Although the gains made in public education before 1900 were more quantitative than qualitative and the philosophy dominant in most schools was not very different at the end of the century from that prevailing in Horace Mann's day, change was in the air. The best educators of the period were full of optimism, convinced that the future was theirs.

Law and History

Even jurisprudence, by its nature conservative and rooted in tradition, felt the pressure of evolu-

Appointed to the Supreme Court in 1902 by his friend Theodore Roosevelt, Oliver Wendell Holmes, Jr., remained there for 29 years and seven presidents.

tionary thought and the new emphasis on studying institutions as they actually are. In 1881 Oliver Wendell Holmes, Jr., published *The Common Law*. Rejecting the ideas that judges should limit themselves to the mechanical explication of statutes and that law consisted only of what was written in lawbooks, Holmes argued that "the felt necessities of the time" rather than precedent should determine the rules by which people are governed. "The life of the law has not been logic; it has been experience," he wrote. "It is revolting," he added on another occasion, "to have no better reason for a rule of law than that so it was laid down in the time of Henry IV."

Holmes went on to a long and brilliant judicial career, during which he repeatedly stressed the right of the people, through their elected representatives, to deal with contemporary problems in any reasonable way, unfettered by outmoded ideas of the proper limits of government authority.

The new approach to knowledge did not always advance the cause of liberal reform. Historians in the graduate schools became intensely interested in studying the origins and evolution of political institutions. They concluded, after much "scientific" study of old charters and law codes, that the roots of democracy were to be found in the customs of the ancient tribes of northern Europe. This theory of the "Teutonic origins" of democracy, which has since been thoroughly discredited, fitted well with the prejudices of people of British stock, and it provided ammunition for those who favored restricting immigration and for those who argued that blacks were inferior beings.

Out of this work, however, came an essentially democratic concept, the frontier thesis of Frederick Jackson Turner, still another scholar trained at Johns Hopkins. Turner's essay "The Significance of the Frontier in American History" (1893) argued that the frontier experience, through which every section of the country had passed, had affected the thinking of the people and the shape of American institutions. The isolation of the frontier and the need during each successive westward advance to create civilization anew Turner wrote, accounted for the individualism of Americans and the democratic character of their society. Nearly everything unique in our culture, he claimed, could be traced to the existence of the frontier.

Turner, and still more his many disciples, made too much of his basic insights. Life on the frontier was not as democratic as Turner believed, and it certainly does not "explain" American development as completely as he said it did. Nevertheless, his work showed how important it was to investigate the evolution of institutions, and it encouraged historians to study social and economic, as well as purely political, subjects.

Realism in Literature

When what Mark Twain called the Gilded Age began, American literature was dominated by the romantic mood. Romanticism, however, had lost its creative force; most writing in the decade after 1865 was sentimental trash pandering to the preconceptions of middle-class readers. The unreality, even dishonesty, of contemporary fiction eventually caused a reaction, but the most important forces giving rise to the Age of Realism were those that were transforming every other aspect of American life: industrialism, with its associated complexities and social problems; the theory of evolution, which made people more aware of the force of the environment and the basic conflicts of existence; and the new science, which taught dispassionate, empirical observation.

Novelists examined social problems such as slum life, the conflict between capital and labor, and political corruption. They created multidimensional characters, depicted persons of every social class, used dialect and slang to capture the flavor of particular types, and fashioned painstaking descriptions of the surroundings into which they placed their subjects. By 1880 realism was rapidly becoming the approach of the finest literary talents in the country.

Mark Twain

Although it was easy to romanticize the West, that region lent itself better to the realistic approach. Almost of necessity, novelists writing about the West described coarse characters from the lower levels of society, and dealt with crime and violence. It would have been difficult indeed to write a genteel romance about a mining camp. The outstanding figure of western literature, the first great American realist, was Mark Twain.

Twain, whose real name was Samuel L. Clemens, was born in 1835. He grew up in Hannibal, Missouri, on the banks of the Mississippi. After having mastered the printer's trade and worked as a riverboat pilot, he went west to Nevada in 1861. Soon he was publishing humorous stories about the local life under the *nom de plume* Mark Twain. In 1865, while working in California, he wrote "The Celebrated Jumping Frog of Calaveras County," a story that brought him national recognition. A tour of Europe and the Holy Land in 1867–1868 led to the writing of *The Innocents Abroad* (1869), which made him famous.

Twain's greatness stemmed from his keen reportorial eye and ear, his eagerness to live life to the full, his marvelous sense of humor, his ability to be at once "in" society and outside it, to love humanity yet be repelled by human vanity and perversity. He wrote tirelessly and endlessly about America and Europe, his own times and the feudal past, about tourists, slaves, tycoons, cracker-barrel philosophers—and human destiny.

Twain surpassed every contemporary in the portrayal of character. In his biting satire *The Gilded Age* (1873), he created that magnificent mountebank Colonel Beriah Sellers, purveyor of eyewash ("the Infallible Imperial Oriental Optic Liniment") and false hopes, ridiculous, unscrupulous, but lovable. In *Huckleberry Finn* (1884), his masterpiece, his portrait of the slave Jim, loyal, patient, naive, yet withal a man, is unforgettable. When Huck takes advantage of Jim's credulity merely for his own amusement, the slave turns from him coldly and says: "Dat truck dah is *trash*; en trash is what people is dat puts dirt on de head er dey fren's en makes 'em ashamed." And there is Huck Finn himself, full of deviltry, romantic, amoral—up to a point—and at bottom the complete realist.

Twain always put much of his own experience and feeling into his work. "The truth is," he wrote in 1886, "my books are mainly autobiographies." He could not rise above the sentimentality and prudery of his generation entirely, for these qualities were part of his nature. Often—even in *Huckleberry Finn*—he contrived to end his tales on absurdly optimistic notes that ring false after so

Mark Twain was both a satirist of American optimism in his writings and its victim in misguided business ventures that brought him to the brink of bankruptcy. This photograph was taken five years before his death in 1910.

many brilliant pages portraying life as it is. On balance, Twain's achievement was magnificent. Rough and uneven like the man himself, his works catch more of the spirit of the age he named than those of any other writer.

William Dean Howells

Mark Twain's realism was far less self-conscious than that of his long-time friend William Dean Howells. Like Twain, Howells had little formal education. He learned the printer's trade from his father and became a reporter. After the Civil War he worked briefly for the *Nation* in New York and

then moved to Boston, where he became editor of the *Atlantic Monthly.* In 1886 he returned to New York as editor of *Harper's.*

A long series of novels and much literary criticism poured from Howells's pen over the next 34 years. Although he insisted on treating his material honestly, he was not at first a critic of society, being content to write about what he called "the smiling aspects" of life.

Howells had a real social conscience. Gradually he became aware of the problems that industrialization had created. In 1885, in *The Rise of Silas Lapham,* he dealt with some of the ethical conflicts faced by businessmen in a competitive society. The harsh public reaction to the Haymarket bombing in 1886 stirred him, and he threw himself into a futile campaign to prevent the execution of the anarchist suspects. Thereafter he moved rapidly toward the left; soon he was calling himself a socialist.

But Howells was more than a reformer. In *A Hazard of New Fortunes* (1890), he attempted to portray the entire range of metropolitan life, its plot weaving the destinies of a dozen interesting personalities from diverse sections and social classes. The book represents a triumph of realism in its careful descriptions of various sections of New York and the ways of life of rich and poor, in the intricacy of its characters, and in its rejection of sentimentality and romantic love. "A man knows that he can love and wholly cease to love, not once merely, but several times," the narrator says, "but in regard to women he cherishes the superstition of the romances that love is once for all, and forever."

Aside from his own works, which were widely read, Howells was the most influential critic of his time. He helped bring the best contemporary foreign writers, including Tolstoy, Dostoyevsky, Ibsen, and Zola, to the attention of readers in the United States, and he encouraged many important young American novelists, among them Stephen Crane, Theodore Dreiser, Frank Norris, and Hamlin Garland.

Some of these writers went far beyond Howells's realism to what they called naturalism. They believed that the human being was essentially an animal, a helpless creature whose fate was determined by environment. Their world was Darwin's world—mindless, without mercy or justice. They wrote chiefly about the most primitive emotions—lust, hate, greed. In *Maggie, A Girl of the Streets* (1893) Stephen Crane described the seduction, degradation, and eventual suicide of a young woman, all set against the background of a sordid slum; in *The Red Badge of Courage* (1895) he captured the pain and humor of war. In *McTeague* (1899) Frank Norris told the story of a brutal, dull-witted dentist who murdered his greed-crazed wife with his bare fists.

Such stuff was too strong for Howells, yet he recognized its importance and befriended the younger writers in many ways. Even Theodore Dreiser, who was contemptuous of Howells's writings and considered him hopelessly middle class in point of view, appreciated his aid and praised his influence on American literature. Dreiser's first novel, *Sister Carrie* (1900), treated sex so forthrightly that it was withdrawn after publication.

Henry James

Henry James was very different in spirit and background from the tempestuous naturalists. Born to wealth, he spent most of his mature life in Europe, writing novels, short stories, plays, and volumes of criticism. Although far removed from the world of practical affairs, he was preeminently a realist, determined, as he once said, "to leave a multitude of pictures of my time" for the future to contemplate. "All life belongs to you," he told his fellow novelists. "There is no impression of life, no manner of seeing it and feeling it, to which the plan of the novelist may not offer a place."

James's major theme was the clash of American and European cultures, his primary interest the close-up examination of wealthy, sensitive, yet often corrupt persons in a cultivated but far from polite society. He dealt with social issues such as feminism and the difficulties faced by artists in the modern world, but he subordinated them to his interest in his subjects as individuals. *The American* (1877) told the story of the love of a wealthy American in Paris for a French noblewoman who rejected him because her family disapproved of his "commercial" background. *The Portrait of a Lady* (1881) described the disillusionment of an intelligent woman married to a charming but morally bankrupt man and her eventual decision to remain with him nonetheless. *The Bostonians* (1886) was a complicated and psychologically sensitive study of the varieties of female behavior in a seemingly uniform social situation.

Realism In Art

American painters responded to the times as writers did, but with this difference: Despite the new concern for realism, the romantic tradition retained its vitality. Preeminent among the realists was Thomas Eakins. The scientific spirit of the age suited Eakins perfectly. He mastered human anatomy; some of his finest paintings, such as *The Gross Clinic* (1875), are graphic illustrations of surgical operations. He was an early experimenter with motion pictures, using the camera to capture exactly the attitudes of human beings and animals in action. Like his friend Walt Whitman, whose portrait is one of his greatest achievements, Eakins gloried in the ordinary. But he had none of Whitman's weaknesses for sham and self-delusion.

Winslow Homer, a master of the watercolor medium, was also influenced by realist ideas. Aesthetics seemed not to concern him at all; he liked to shock people by referring to his profession as "the picture line." His concern for accuracy was so intense that in preparation for painting *The Life Line* (1884) he made a trip to Atlantic City to observe the handling of a breeches buoy. There are romantic elements in his work. His *Gulf Stream* (1899), showing a sailor on a small, broken boat menaced by an approaching waterspout and a school of sharks, and his *Fox Hunt* (1893), in which huge, ominous crows hover over a fox at bay, express his interest in the violence and drama of raw nature, a distinctly romantic theme. However, his approach, even in these works, was utterly prosaic. When some silly women complained about the fate of the black sailor in *Gulf Stream,* Homer wrote his dealer sarcastically: "Tell these ladies that the unfortunate Negro . . . will be rescued and returned to his friends and home, and live happily ever after."

The careers of Eakins and Homer show that the late-19th-century American environment was not uncongenial to first-rate artists. Nevertheless, at least two major American painters abandoned native shores for Europe. One was James A. McNeill Whistler, whose portrait of his mother, which he called *Arrangement in Grey and Black,* is probably the most famous canvas ever painted by an American. Whistler made a profession of eccentricity, but he was a remarkably talented and versatile artist. Some of his portraits are triumphs of realism, while his misty studies of the London waterfront, which he described as visual expressions of poetry, are thoroughly romantic in conception. Paintings such as "Whistler's Mother" represent still another expression of his talent. Spare and muted in tone, they are more interesting as precise arrangements of color and space than as images of particular objects; they had a tremendous influence on the course of modern art.

The second important expatriate artist was Mary Cassatt, daughter of a wealthy Pittsburgh banker and sister of Alexander J. Cassatt, who was president of the Pennsylvania Railroad around the turn of the century. She went to Paris as a tourist and dabbled in art like many conventional young socialites, then was caught up in the impressionist movement and decided to become a serious painter. Her work is more French than American and was little appreciated in the United States before the First World War. When once she returned to America for a visit, the Philadelphia *Public Ledger* reported: "Mary Cassatt, sister of Mr. Cassatt, president of the Pennsylvania Railroad, returned from Europe yesterday. She has been studying painting in Paris, and owns the smallest Pekinese dog in the world."

If Mary Cassatt was unappreciated and if Whistler had reasons for considering Americans uncultured, it remains true that interest in art was considerable. Museums and art schools increased in number. Settlement-house workers put on ex-hibitions that attracted enthusiastic crowds. Wealthy patrons gave commissions to portrait painters and poured fortunes into collecting. Martin A. Ryerson, with a fortune made in lumber, bought the works of the French impressionists when few Americans understood their importance. Charles L. Freer of the American Car and Foundry Company, a friend and admirer of Whistler, was a specialist in oriental art.

Now widely recognized as one of America's finest impressionist painters, Mary Cassatt found her talent ignored in this country during her lifetime. She portrayed mothers and children with a grace and tenderness that (some would say) only a woman artist could convey.

The Pragmatic Approach

It would have been remarkable indeed if the intellectual ferment of the late 19th century had not affected contemporary ideas about the meaning of life, the truth of revealed religion, moral values, and similar fundamental problems. In particular, the theory of evolution—so important in altering contemporary views of science, history, and social relations—produced significant changes in American thinking about religious and philosophical questions.

Evolution posed an immediate challenge to religion: If Darwin was correct, the Biblical account of the creation was obviously untrue and the idea that man had been formed in God's image was highly unlikely. A bitter controversy erupted. While millions continued to believe in the literal truth of the Bible, among intellectuals, lay and clerical, victory went to the evolutionists because in addition to the arguments of the geologists and the biologists, scholars were throwing light on the historical origins of the Bible, showing it to be of human rather than divine inspiration.

Evolution did not undermine the faith of any large percentage of the population. If the account of the creation in *Genesis* could not be taken literally, the Bible remained a repository of wisdom and inspiration. As the liberal preacher Washington Gladden put it, evolution was "a most impressive demonstration of the presence of God in the world."

The effects of Darwinism on philosophy were less dramatic but in the end far more significant. Fixed systems and eternal verities were difficult to justify in a world that was constantly evolving. By the early 1870s, a few philosophers had begun to reason that ideas and theories mattered little except when applied to specifics. In "How to Make Our Ideas Clear" (1878), Charles S. Peirce argued that concepts could be fairly understood only in terms of their practical effects. Once the mind accepted the truth of evolution, Peirce believed, logic required that it accept the impermanence even of scientific laws. There was, he wrote, "an element of indeterminacy, spontaneity, or absolute chance in nature."

This startling philosophy, which Peirce called pragmatism, was presented in more understandable language by William James, brother of the novelist. James, one of the most remarkable Americans of his generation, was professor at Harvard successively of comparative anatomy, psychology, and finally philosophy. His *Principles of Psychology* (1890) may be said to have established that discipline as a modern science. His *Varieties of Religious Experience* (1902), which treated the subject from both psychological and philosophical points of view, helped thousands of readers to reconcile their religious faith with their increasing knowledge of psychology and the physical universe.

Although less rigorous a logician than Peirce, James's wide range and his verve and imagination as a writer made him by far the most influential philosopher of his times. He re-

jected the deterministic interpretation of Darwinism and all other one-idea explanations of existence. Belief in free will was one of his axioms; environment might influence survival, but so did the *desire* to survive, which existed independently of surrounding circumstances. Even truth was relative; it did not exist in the abstract; it *happened* under particular circumstances. What a person thought helped to make what he thought occur, or come true. The mind, James wrote in a typically vivid phrase, has "a vote" in determining truth. Religion was true, for example, because people were religious.

The pragmatic approach inspired much of the reform spirit of the late 19th century and even more of that of the early 20th. James's hammer blows shattered the laissez-faire extremism of Herbert Spencer. In "Great Men and Their Environment" (1880) he argued that social changes were brought about by the actions of geniuses whom society had selected and raised to positions of power, rather than by the impersonal force of the environment. Such reasoning fitted the preconceptions of rugged individualists yet encouraged those dissatisfied with society to work for change. Educational experts like John Dewey, the institutionalist school of economists, settlement-house workers, and other reformers adopted pragmatism eagerly.

Yet pragmatism brought Americans face to face with somber problems. Although relativism made them optimistic, it bred insecurity, for there could be no certainty, no comforting reliance on any eternal value in the absence of absolute truth. Pragmatism also seemed to suggest that the end justified the means, that what worked was more important than what ought to be. By emphasizing practice at the expense of theory, the new philosophy encouraged materialism, anti-intellectualism, and other unlovely aspects of the American character. And what place had conventional morality in such a system? Perhaps pragmatism placed too much reliance on the free will of human beings, ignoring their capacity for selfishness and self-delusion.

The people of the new century found pragmatism a heady wine. They would quaff it freely and enthusiastically—down to the bitter dregs.

Milestones

1865	Vassar College founded	1886	Ottmar Mergenthaler invents the linotype machine
1869	Charles W. Eliot becomes president of Harvard		William Dean Howells becomes editor of *Harper's*
1874	Chautauqua movement begins	1889	Edward W. Bok becomes editor of the *Ladies' Home Journal*
1876	Johns Hopkins University founded		
1881	Oliver Wendell Holmes, Jr., *The Common Law*	1890	William James, *Principles of Psychology*
1883	Joseph Pulitzer purchases the *New York World*	1893	Frederick Jackson Turner, "Significance of the Frontier in American History"
		1899	John Dewey, *The School and Society*

Supplementary Reading

H. S. Commager, **The American Mind*** (1950), and P. A. Carter, **The Spiritual Crisis of the Gilded Age** (1971), discuss the intellectual history of this period. On education, see L. A. Cremin, **The Transformation of the School: Progressivism in American Education*** (1961). The best treatment of the Chautauqua movement is Victoria and R. O. Case, **We Called It Culture** (1948). Trends in the history of journalism are discussed in B. A. Weisberger, **The American Newspaperman** (1961). Also useful are George Juergens, **Joseph Pulitzer** (1966), and W. A.Swanberg, **Citizen Hearst** (1961).

On higher education, see L. R. Veysey, **The Emergence of the American University** (1965), two books by Hugh Hawkins, **Pioneer** (1960), on Johns Hopkins University, and **Be-tween Harvard and America** (1972), on Charles W. Eliot, and E. A. Green, **Mary Lyon and Mount Holyoke** (1979). For developments in American science, see the essay by P. F. Boller, Jr., in H. W. Morgan, ed., **The Gilded Age*** (1970). A good introduction to the work of the social scientists is Sidney Fine, **Laissez-Faire and the General-Welfare State*** (1957).

The literary figures of the age are discussed in Everett Carter, **Howells and the Age of Realism** (1954), E. H. Cady, **The Realist at War** (1958), Justin Kaplan, **Mr. Clemens and Mark Twain*** (1966), and Leon Edel, **Henry James*** (1953–1962). Art is discussed in Barbara Novak, **American Painting of the Nineteenth Century** (1969), and Russell Lynes, **The Lively Audience** (1985). On pragmatism, see Bruce Kuklick, **The Rise of American Philosophy** (1977).

*Available in paperback.

CHAPTER 21

Politics: Local, State, and National

Political Strategy and Tactics
Political Decision Making: Ethnic and Religious Issues
City Government
Republicans and Democrats
The Men in the White House
Congressional Leaders
Agricultural Discontent
The Populist Movement
Showdown on Silver
The Election of 1896
The Meaning of the Election

Political Strategy and Tactics

The major American political parties have nearly always avoided clear-cut stands on controversial questions in order to appeal to as wide a segment of the electorate as possible, but in the last quarter of the 19th century, their equivocations assumed abnormal proportions. This was due in part to the precarious balance of power between them. Neither dared declare itself too clearly on any question lest it drive away more voters than it attracted.

The rapid pace of social and economic change also militated against political decisiveness. No one in or out of politics had as yet devised effective solutions for many current problems. When party leaders tried to deal with the money question, they discovered that the bankers and the professional economists were as confused as the public at large. How could mere politicians act rationally or consistently in such circumstances?

The parties stumbled badly when they confronted the tariff problem because tariffs in a complex industrial economy are not susceptible to determination by counting noses. Reformers could thunder self-righteously against the spoils system, but how could political parties exist without it? Young economists like Richard T. Ely were insisting that laissez-faire was outmoded, but no one had yet devised the techniques and instruments that would have to be used if the economy was to be measured and managed effectively by a central authority. If the politicians steered clear of the "real" issues, they did so as much out of a healthy respect for their own ignorance as out of any desire to avoid controversy.

Politicial Decision Making: Ethnic and Religious Issues

The major parties met in national conventions every four years to select their presidential candidates and draft "platforms," but they remained essentially separate state organizations. Professionals spent far more time dealing with local people and local issues than they did thinking about matters of broad national concern. That meant entering a veritable maze of diverse and often conflicting interests. People's ethnic backgrounds, their religious affiliations, whether they lived in cities or on farms, and how

Detail from an engraving by Compton & Dry, "1888 Democratic National Convention, St. Louis."

they felt about the Civil War had no apparent relationship to national political issues, but affected whether they voted Republican or Democratic.

The politicians were not shy about explaining why people voted the way they did. Senator George Frisbie Hoar of Massachusetts, for example, offered such an analysis in an 1889 magazine article. The Republicans, he wrote, were

> *the men who do the work of piety and charity in our churches . . . who administer our school systems . . . who own and till their own farms . . . who perform skilled labor . . . who went to the war . . . who paid the debt, and kept the currency sound, and saved the nation's honor. . . . [The Democrats were] the old slave-owner and slave-driver, the saloon-keeper, the ballot-box-stuffer, the Kuklux, the criminal class of the great cities, and men who cannot read or write.*

Despite the partisan character of Hoar's analysis, it contained an element of truth; at least in the North most of "the best people" were Republicans. But if Hoar had been correct, the Republicans would have swept the northern states at every election, which they assuredly did not. In any case, it was even more difficult to discover *why* people voted one way or the other. People of Irish descent tended to vote Democratic, but whether they did so because they lived in cities or because they were Roman Catholics or because they believed that most Americans of British descent voted Republican, was not always clear.

Plausible generalizations disintegrate when examined closely. Northerners were Republicans, southerners Democrats; Catholics were Democrats, Protestants Republicans; German Americans voted Democratic, Americans of Scandinavian descent Republican. All these statements are subject to a multitude of exceptions. They offer little guidance for predicting how, for example, a German Lutheran living in Tennessee would vote.

Local and state issues also interacted with religious and ethnic backgrounds to affect political attitudes. Prohibition, public education, and other matters subject to state and local control that seemed to have little or no relation to religion were in fact questions on which voters split along religious and ethnic lines. All these tangles influenced the way political leaders devised their strategies and chose candidates for office. And how voters felt about local issues almost invariably affected how they voted in national elections.

City Government

City governments were influenced by the religious and ethnic character of the inhabitants and further complicated by the special problems of late–19th century urban life: rapid, helter-skelter growth; the influx of European immigrants; crime; corruption; the need to develop costly transportation, and public utility systems.

The movement to the suburbs of middle-class city people who might have been expected to supply the political leadership needed to deal with these problems created a vacuum that was filled by political bosses, with their informal but powerful "machines."

The immigrants who flocked into American cities in the 1880s and early 1890s had come from societies unacquainted with the blessings of democracy; they had no experience with representative government. The tendency of urban workers to move frequently in search of better jobs further lessened the likelihood that they would develop political influence independently.

Furthermore, the difficulties of life in the slums bewildered newcomers, both native and foreign born. They could hardly be expected to take a broad view of social problems when so beset by personal ones. This enabled shrewd urban politicians, most of them in this period of Irish origin, to take command of the city masses and march them in obedient phalanxes to the polls.

Most city machines were loose-knit neighborhood organizations headed by ward bosses, not bureaucracies ruled by a single leader. "Big Tim" Sullivan of New York's Lower East Side was typical of the breed. People like Sullivan performed many useful services for what they liked to think of as their constituents. They found jobs for new arrivals and distributed food and other help to all in bad times. Sullivan provided turkey dinners for 5,000 or more homeless people each Christmas, distributed new shoes to the poor children of his district on his birthday, and arranged summer boat rides and picnics for young and old alike. Informally, probably without consciously intending to do so, the bosses educated the immigrants in the complexities of American civilization.

The price of such aid—the bosses were not altruists—was unquestioning political support, which the bosses converted into cash. In New York, Sullivan levied tribute on gambling, had a hand in the liquor business, and controlled the issuance of peddlers' licenses. When he died in 1913, he was reputedly worth $1 million. Yet 25,000 grieving constituents followed Big Tim's coffin on its way to the grave.

The more visible and better-known city bosses played less socially justifiable roles than the ward bosses. Their principal technique for extracting money from the public till was the kickback. To get city contracts, suppliers were made to pad their bills and turn over the excess to the politicians. Similarly, operators of streetcar lines, gas and electricity companies, and other public utilities were compelled to pay huge bribes to obtain favorable franchises.

The most notorious of the 19th-century city bosses was William Marcy Tweed, whose "Tweed Ring" extracted tens of millions of dollars from New York City during the brief period 1869 to 1871. Tweed was swiftly jailed. More typical was Richard Croker, who ruled New York's Tammany Hall organization from the mid-1880s to the end of the century. Croker's power rested on his position as chairman of the Tammany Hall finance committee. He accumulated a large fortune and owned a $200,000 mansion and a stable of racehorses, one of which was good enough to win the English Derby.

Despite their welfare work and their popularity, most bosses were essentially thieves. Efforts to romanticize them as the Robin Hoods of industrial society grossly distort the facts. However, the system developed and survived because too many middle-class city dwellers were indifferent to the fate of the poor.

Honest citizens who had no selfish stake in the system and who were repelled by the sordidness of city government were seldom sufficiently concerned to do anything about it. When young Theodore Roosevelt decided to seek a political career in 1880, his New York socialite friends laughed in his face. They told him, Roosevelt wrote in his autobiography, "that politics were 'low'; that the organizations were not controlled by 'gentlemen'; that I would find them run by saloon-keepers, horse-car conductors, and the like." A British visitor in Chicago struck at the root of the urban problem of the era. "Everybody is fighting to be rich," he said, "and nobody can attend to making the city fit to live in."

Republicans and Democrats

As for national politics, with the Democrats invincible in the South and the Republicans predominant in New England and most of the states beyond the Mississippi, the outcome of presidential elections was usually determined in a handful of populous states: New York (together with its satellites, New Jersey and Connecticut), Ohio, Indiana, and Illinois. The fact that opinion in these states on important questions such as the tariff and monetary policy was divided and that every imaginable religious and ethnic interest was represented in the electorate goes far to explain why the parties hesitated to commit themselves on issues. In every presidential election, Democrats and Republicans concentrated their heaviest guns on these states. Between 1868 and 1900, only three presidental candidates were not from New York, Ohio, Indiana, or Illinois, and all three lost.

Partisanship was intense in these states. Campaigns were conducted in a carnival atmosphere, entertainment being substituted for serious debate. Large sums were spent on brass bands, barbecues, uniforms, and banners. Speakers of national reputation were imported to attract crowds, and spellbinders noted for their leather lungs—this was before the day of the loudspeaker—and their ability to rouse popular emotions were brought in to address mass meetings.

With so much depending on so few, the level of political morality was abysmal. Mudslinging, character assassination, and plain lying were standard practice, bribery was routine. Drifters and other dissolute citizens were paid in cash—or more often in free drinks—to vote the party ticket. The names of persons long dead were solemnly inscribed in voting registers, their suffrages exercised by impostors. During the 1880 campaign the Democratic national chairman, hearing that the Republicans were planning to transport Kentuckians into Indiana to vote illegally in that crucial state, urged Indiana Democrats to "check this outrageous fraud." Then, perhaps seeking an easier solution to the problem, he added: "If necessary . . . keep even with them." Yet presidents were sometimes made and unmade in this sordid fashion.

The Men in the White House

The leading statesmen of the period showed as little interest in important contemporary questions as the party hacks who made up the rank and file of their organizations. Consider the presidents. Rutherford B. Hayes, president from 1877 to 1881, came to office with a distinguished record. Although he had a family to support, he volunteered for service within weeks after the first shell fell on Fort Sumter. He was wounded at South Mountain, on the eve of Antietam, and later served under Sheridan in the Shenandoah Valley campaign of 1864. Entering the army as a major, he emerged a major general. In 1864 he was elected to Congress; four years later he became governor of Ohio, serving three terms altogether. The Republicans nominated him for president in 1876 because of his reputation for honesty and moderation, and his election, made possible by the Compromise of 1877, seemed to presage an era of sectional harmony and political probity.

Hayes was a president in the Whig tradition. He saw himself more as a caretaker than a leader and believed that Congress should assume the main responsibility for solving national problems. According to a recent biographer, "he had no intention of . . . trying to be a President in the heroic mold," and another historian writes that he showed "no capacity for such large-minded leadership as might have tamed the political hordes and aroused the enthusiasm, or at least the interest, of the public."

Hayes hated having to make decisions on controversial questions. He complained about the South's failure to treat blacks decently after the withdrawal of federal troops, but he took no action. He worked for civil service reform yet failed to achieve the "thorough, rapid and complete" change he had promised. In this as in most other matters, he was content to "let the record show

that he had made the requests." In the eyes of contemporaries he was a failure. Neither he nor they seriously considered him for a second term.

James A. Garfield, who succeeded Hayes, was cut down by an assassin's bullet four months after his inauguration. Even in that short time, however, his ineffectiveness had been demonstrated. His great weakness was indecisiveness, and political patronage proved to be his undoing: The Republican Party in 1880 was split into two factions, the "Stalwarts" and the "Half-Breeds." The Stalwarts, led by the New York politico Senator Roscoe Conkling, believed in the blatant pursuit of the spoils of office. The Half-Breeds did not disagree but behaved more circumspectly, hoping to attract the support of independents. Competition for office was the main reason for their rivalry.

Garfield had been a compromise choice at the 1880 Republican Convention. His election precipitated a great battle over patronage, the new president standing in a sort of no man's land between the factions. He did stand up to the most grasping politicians, resisting in particular the demands of Senator Conkling. By backing the investigation of a post office scandal, and by appointing a Half-Breed collector of the Port of New York, he infuriated the Stalwarts. In July 1881 an unbalanced Stalwart lawyer named Charles J. Guiteau, who had been haunting Washington offices in search of a consulship or some other minor post, shot Garfield in the Washington railroad station. After lingering for weeks, the president died on September 19.

The assassination of Garfield elevated Chester A. Arthur to the presidency. Arthur was an early convert to the Republican Party and rose rapidly in its local councils. In 1871 Grant gave him the juiciest political plum in the country, the collectorship of the Port of New York, which he held until removed by Hayes in 1878 for refusing to keep his hands out of party politics. The only elective position he ever held was the vice presidency.

The tragic circumstances of his elevation to the presidency sobered Arthur considerably. He did not cut his ties with the Stalwart faction, but he handled patronage matters with restraint. He continued the investigation of the post office scandals over the objections of important Republican politicians who were involved in them, and he gave at least nominal support to the movement for civil service reform, which had been strengthened by the public indignation following the assassination of Garfield. In 1883 Congress passed the Pendleton Act, "classifying" about 10 percent of all government jobs and creating a bipartisan Civil Service Commission to administer competitive examinations for these positions. The law made it illegal to force officeholders to make political contributions and empowered the president to expand the list of classified positions at his discretion.

Although many politicians resented the new system—one senator denounced it as "un-American"—the Pendleton Act opened a new era in government administration. The results have been summed up by the historian Ari Hoogenboom: "An unprofessional civil service became more professionalized. Better educated civil servants were recruited and society accorded them a higher place. . . . Local political considerations gave way in civil servants' minds to the national concerns of a federal office. Business influence and ideals replaced those of the politician."

Arthur urged the appointment of a nonpartisan commission to study tariff rates and to suggest rational reductions. When such a commission was created, he urged Congress to adopt its recommendations. He came out for federal regulation of railroads several years before the passage of the Interstate Commerce Act. As an administrator he was systematic, thoughtful, businesslike, and at the same time cheerful and considerate. Just the same, he too was a political failure. He made relatively little effort to push his program through Congress. In any case, the Stalwarts would not forgive his "desertion," and the reform element could not forget his past. He did not seek a second term in 1884.

The election of 1884 brought the Democrat Grover Cleveland to the White House. Elected governor of New York in 1882, his no-nonsense attitude toward public administration endeared him to civil service reformers at the same time that his basic conservatism pleased businessmen. When he vetoed a popular bill to force a reduction of the fares charged by the New York City elevated railway on the ground that it was an unconstitutional violation of the company's franchise, his stock soared, and the Democrats nominated him for president in 1884.

The election revolved around personal issues, for the platforms of the parties were almost identical. The Republican candidate, the dynamic James G. Blaine, had an immense following, but his reputation had been soiled by the publication of the "Mulligan letters," which connected him with the corrupt granting of congressional favors to the Little Rock and Fort Smith Railroad. On the other hand, it came out during the campaign that Cleveland, a bachelor, had fathered an illegitimate child.

Blaine lost more heavily in the mudslinging than Cleveland, whose quiet courage in saying "Tell the truth" when his past was brought to light contrasted favorably with Blaine's glib and unconvincing denials. A significant group of eastern Republicans, known as Mugwumps, campaigned for the Democrats.* However, Blaine ran a strong race against a general pro-Democratic trend; Cleveland won the election by fewer than 25,000 votes. The change of 600 ballots in New York would have given that state, and the presidency, to his opponent.

As a Democrat, Cleveland had no stomach for refighting the Civil War. He did not overly favor the South when in office, thereby quieting Republican fears that a Democratic administration would fill Washington with unreconstructed rebels. Civil service reformers overestimated his commitment to their cause, for he believed in rotation in office, being as convinced as Andrew Jackson that anyone of "reasonable intelligence" could handle most government jobs. He did, however, insist on honesty and efficiency regardless of party. As a result, he made few poor appointments.

Cleveland had little imagination and too narrow a conception of his powers and duties to be a successful president. He could defend a position against heavy odds, yet he lacked flexibility. He took a fairly broad view of the powers of the federal government, but he thought it unseemly to put pressure on Congress, believing in "the entire independence of the executive and legislative branches."

---

*The Mugwumps considered themselves reformers, but on social and economic questions nearly all of them were very conservative. They were sound-money proponents and advocates of laissez-faire. Reform to them consisted almost entirely of doing away with corruption and making the government more efficient.

Toward the end of his term, Cleveland bestirred himself and tried to provide constructive leadership on the tariff question. The government was embarrassed by a large surplus revenue, which Cleveland hoped to reduce by cutting the duties on necessities and on raw materials used in manufacturing. He devoted his entire annual message of December 1887 to the tariff, thereby focusing public attention on the subject.

The House of Representatives, dominated by southern Democrats, passed a bill reducing many duties, but the measure, known as the Mills Bill, was flagrantly partisan: It slashed the rates on iron products, glass, wool, and other items made in the North and left those on southern goods almost untouched. The Republican-controlled Senate rejected the Mills Bill, and the issue was left to be settled by the voters at the 1888 election. However, in a fashion typical of the period, it did not work out this way. Other issues attracted attention, and corruption was flagrant. Cleveland obtained a plurality of the popular vote, but his opponent, Benjamin Harrison, grandson of President William Henry Harrison, carried most of the key northeastern industrial states by narrow margins, thereby obtaining a comfortable majority in the electoral college, 233 to 168.

The new president was intelligent and able, but he was too reserved to make a good politician. He did not suffer fools gladly and kept even his most important advisers at arm's length. One observer called him a "human iceberg." He believed ardently in the principle of protection, stating firmly if somewhat illogically that he was against "cheaper coats" because cheaper coats seemed "necessarily to involve a cheaper man and woman under the coat." No more flamboyant waver of the bloody shirt existed. "I would a thousand times rather march under the bloody shirt, stained with the lifeblood of a Union soldier," he said in 1883, "than to march under the black flag of treason or the white flag of cowardly compromise."

Harrison professed to favor civil service reform. He appointed the vigorous young reformer Theodore Roosevelt to the Civil Service Commission and then proceeded to undercut him systematically. Before long the frustrated Roosevelt was calling the president a "cold blooded, narrow minded, prejudiced, obstinate, timid old psalm singing Indianapolis politician."

Under Harrison, Congress distinguished itself by expending, for the first time in a period of peace, more than $1 billion in a single session. It raised the tariff to an all-time high. The Sherman Antitrust Act was passed; so was a Silver Purchase Act authorizing the government to coin large amounts of that metal, a measure much desired by mining interests and those favoring inflation. A Federal Elections, or "Force" Bill, providing for federal control of elections as a means of protecting the right of southern blacks to vote—a right increasingly under attack—passed the House only to be filibustered to death in the Senate.

Harrison had little to do with these measures. By and large he failed, as one historian has said, to give the people "magnetic and responsive leadership." The Republicans lost control of Congress in 1890, and two years later Grover Cleveland swept back into power, defeating Harrison by more than 350,000 votes.

Congressional Leaders

Among the lesser politicians of the period, the most outstanding was unquestionably James G. Blaine of Maine, who served in Congress from 1863 to 1881, first in the House and then in the Senate. Blaine had many of the qualities that mark a great leader: personal dynamism, imagination, political intuition, oratorical ability, and a broad view of the national interest. He was essentially a reasonable man. He favored sound money without opposing inflexibly every suggestion for increasing the volume of the currency; he supported the protective system yet advocated reciprocity agreements to increase trade; and he adopted a tolerant attitude toward the South. Almost alone among the politicians of his generation, he was deeply interested in foreign affairs. His personal warmth captivated thousands.

That Blaine, though perennially an aspirant, never became president was in part a reflection of his very abilities and his participation in so many controversial affairs. Naturally, he aroused jealousies and made many enemies. But some inexplicable flaw marred his character. He had a streak of recklessness entirely out of keeping with his reasonable position on most issues. The scandal of the Mulligan letters made a dark blot on his record, and there is reason to doubt his general honesty, for, as one historian has pointed out, he "became wealthy without visible means of support." Blaine moved through history amid cheers and won a host of spectacular if petty triumphs, yet his career was barren, essentially tragic.

Roscoe Conkling's was another remarkable but empty career. Conkling served in Congress almost continually from 1859 to 1881 and was a great power, yet no measure of importance was attached to his name. He squandered his energies in acrimonious personal quarrels, caring only for partisan advantage. Although he wanted very much to be president, he had no conception of what a president must be, and in the end even his own hack followers deserted him.

Dozens of other figures might be mentioned; the following are representative types. Congressman William McKinley of Ohio was the most personally attractive. He was a man of simple honesty, showed nobility of character and quiet warmth—and was a politician to the core. The tariff was McKinley's special competence, the principle of protection his guiding star. The peak of his career still lay in the future in the early 1890s.

Another Ohioan, John Sherman, brother of the famous Civil War general, accomplished the remarkable feat of holding national office continuously for nearly half a century, from 1855 to 1898. However, he was colorless and stiff—he was called the Ohio Icicle—and altogether too willing to compromise his beliefs for political advantage. Sherman gave his name (and not much else) to the Antitrust Act of 1890 and to other important legislation, but in retrospect he left little mark on the history of the country despite his long service.

Another prominent figure of the age was Thomas B. Reed, Republican congressman from Maine. In 1890 Reed was elected Speaker of the House and quickly won the nickname "Czar" because of his autocratic way of expediting business. His control became so absolute that Washington jokesters said that representatives dared not breathe without his permission. Reed had large ambitions and the courage of his convictions, but his vindictiveness kept him from exercising a constructive influence on his times.

More colorful yet utterly sterile was the career of Benjamin F. Butler of Massachusetts. Butler was a political chameleon. A states' rights Democrat before the Civil War, he supported Jefferson Davis for the Democratic presidential nomination in 1860. During the conflict he served as a Union general, during Reconstruction as a Radical Republican congressman. In 1878 he came out for currency inflation and won a seat in Congress as a Greenbacker. In 1882 he was elected governor of Massachusetts, this time as a Democrat! Butler had a sharp wit, a vivid imagination, a real feeling for the interests of industrial workers. He detested sham and pretense. He was also a brutal, corrupt demagogue, almost universally hated by persons of culture and public spirit. By no means a typical politician, Butler typified many aspects of the age—its shaky morality, its extremism, its intense interest in meaningless political controversy.

Agricultural Discontent

The vacuity of American politics may well have stemmed from the complacency of the middle-class majority. The country was growing; no foreign enemy threatened it; the poor were mostly recent immigrants, blacks, and others with little influence, who were easily ignored by those in comfortable circumstances. However, one important group in society suffered increasingly as the years rolled by: the farmers. Out of their travail came the force that finally, in the 1890s, brought American politics face to face with the problems of the age.

Immediately after the Civil War, wheat sold at nearly $1.50 a bushel, and in the early 1870s it was still worth well over a dollar. By the mid-1890s the average price stood in the neighborhood of 60 cents. Cotton, the great southern staple, which sold for more than 30 cents a pound in 1866 and 15 cents in the early 1870s, at times in the 1890s fell below 6 cents.

The tariff on manufactured goods appeared to aggravate the farmers' predicament, and so did the domestic marketing system, which enabled a multitude of middlemen to gobble up a large share of the profits of agriculture. The shortage of credit, particularly in the South, was an additional burden. Furthermore, the improvements in transportation that made it practicable for farmers in Australia, Canada, Russia, and Argentina to sell their produce in western European markets increased the competition faced by Americans seeking to dispose of surplus produce abroad.

Throughout the mid-1880s farmers on the plains had experienced boom conditions. Adequate rainfall produced bountiful harvests, credit was available, and property values rose rapidly. In the 1880s the population of Kansas increased by 43 percent, that of Nebraska by 134 percent, that of the Dakotas by 278 percent. This agricultural expansion contributed to the destruction of open-range cattle raising and changed the economy of cattle towns like Dodge City, which came to depend more on farmers than on cowboys and ranchers for business.

Speculative booms occurred periodically in every frontier district; like all others, this one collapsed when settlers and investors took a more realistic look at the prospects of the region. In this case special circumstances turned the slump into a catastrophe. A succession of dry years shattered the hopes of the farmers. The downward swing of the business cycle in the early 1890s completed the devastation. Settlers who had paid more for their lands than they were worth and borrowed money at high interest rates to do so found themselves squeezed relentlessly. Thousands lost their farms and returned eastward, penniless and dispirited. The population of Nebraska increased by fewer than 4,000 persons in the entire decade of the 1890s.

The Populist Movement

The agricultural depression triggered a new outburst of farm radicalism, the Alliance movement. Alliances were organizations of farmers' clubs, most of which had sprung up during the bad times of the late seventies. The first "Knights of Reliance" was founded in 1877 in Lampasas County, Texas. Under the name The Farmers Alliance this organization expanded in northeastern Texas, and after 1885 it spread rapidly throughout the cotton states. Alliance leaders stressed cooperation. Their co-ops bought fertilizer and other supplies in bulk and sold them at fair prices to members. They sought to market their crops cooperatively but could not raise the necessary capital from banks—with the result that some of them

began to question the workings of the American financial and monetary system. They became economic and social radicals in the process. In the northern regions a similar though less influential alliance movement developed.

The alliances adopted somewhat differing policies, but all agreed that agricultural prices were too low, that transportation costs were too high, and that something was radically wrong with the nation's financial system. All agreed, too, on the need for political action if the lot of the agriculturalist was to be improved.

Although the state alliances of the Dakotas and Kansas joined the Southern Alliance in 1889, for a time local prejudices and conflicting interests prevented the formation of a single national organization. Northern farmers mostly voted Republican, southerners Democratic, and resentments created during the Civil War lingered in all sections. Cotton-producing southerners opposed the protective tariff; most northerners, fearing the competition of foreign grain producers, favored it. Railroad regulation and federal land policy seemed vital questions to northerners, financial reform loomed most important in southern eyes. Northerners were receptive to the idea of forming a third party, whereas southerners, wedded to the one-party system, preferred working to capture local Democratic machines.

The farm groups entered local politics in the 1890 elections. Convinced of the righteousness of their cause, they campaigned with tremendous fervor. The results were encouraging. In the South, Alliance-sponsored gubernatorial candidates won in Georgia, Tennessee, South Carolina, and Texas; 8 southern legislatures fell under Alliance control, 44 congressmen and 3 senators committed to Alliance objectives were sent to Washington. In the West, Alliance candidates swept Kansas and captured a majority in the Nebraska legislature. In Minnesota and South Dakota they won enough offices to hold the balance of power between the major parties.

Such success, coupled with the reluctance of the Republicans and Democrats to make concessions to their demands, encouraged Alliance leaders to create a new national party. By uniting southern and western farmers, they broke the sectional barrier erected by the Civil War. If they could recruit industrial workers, perhaps a real

DONNELLY

political revolution could be accomplished. In February 1892 farm leaders, representatives of the Knights of Labor, and various professional reformers organized the People's, or Populist Party, and issued a call for a national convention to meet at Omaha in July.

That convention nominated General James B. Weaver of Iowa for president and drafted a platform that called for a graduated income tax and national ownership of railroads and the telegraph and telephone systems. A "subtreasury" plan that would permit farmers to hold nonperishable crops off the market when prices were low was also advocated. To further combat deflation, the platform demanded the unlimited coinage of silver and an increase in the money supply "to no less than $50 per capita."

To make the government more responsive to public opinion, the Populists urged the adoption of the initiative and referendum procedures and the election of United States senators by popular vote. To win the support of industrial workers the platform denounced the use of Pinkerton detectives in labor disputes and backed the eight-hour day and the restriction of "undesirable" immigration.

The Populists created what the historian Lawrence Goodwyn has called "a multi-sectional institution of reform." They were not, however, revolutionaries. They saw themselves not as a persecuted minority but as a victimized majority betrayed by what would now be called the establishment. They were ambivalent about the free-enterprise system, and they tended to attribute social and economic injustices not to built-in inequities in the system but to nefarious conspiracies organized by selfish interests in order to subvert the system.

The appearance of the new party was the most exciting and significant aspect of the presidential campaign of 1892, which saw Harrison and Cleveland refighting the election of 1888. The Populists put forth a host of colorful spellbinders: Tom Watson, a hot-tempered Georgia congressman; William A. Peffer, a senator from Kansas whose long beard and grave demeanor gave him the look of a Hebrew prophet; "Sockless Jerry" Simpson of Kansas, unlettered but full of grassroots shrewdness and wit; Ignatius Donnelly, who claimed to be an authority on science, Shakespeare, and economics, and who had just published a widely read novel, *Caesar's Column* (1891), which pictured an America of the future wherein a handful of plutocrats tyrannized masses of downtrodden workers and serfs.

In the one-party South, Populist strategists sought to wean black farmers away from the ruling Democratic organization. Their competition forced the "subsidies" paid for black votes up to as much as a dollar—two days' wages. Southern black farmers had their own Colored Alliance, and even before 1892 their leaders had worked closely with the white alliances. Of course the blacks would be useless if they could not vote; therefore white Populist leaders opposed the southern trend toward disfranchising blacks and called for full civil rights for all. In the Northwest the Populists assailed the "bankers' conspiracy" in unbridled terms. Ignatius Donnelly, running for governor of Minnesota, made 150 speeches, vowing to make the campaign "the liveliest ever seen" in the state.

The results proved disappointing. Tom Watson lost his seat in Congress, and Donnelly ran a poor third in the Minnesota gubernatorial race. The Populists did sweep Kansas. They elected local officials in other western states and cast over a million votes for General Weaver. But the effort to unite white and black farmers in the South failed miserably. Conservative Democrats, while continuing with considerable success to attract black voters, played on racial fears cruelly, insisting that the Populists sought to undermine white supremacy. Since most white Populists saw the alliance with blacks as at most a marriage of convenience, this argument had a deadly effect. Elsewhere, the party made no significant impression. Urban workers remained aloof.

By standing firmly for conservative financial policies, Cleveland attracted considerable Republican support and won a solid victory over Harrison in the electoral college, 277 to 145. Weaver's electoral vote was 22.

Showdown on Silver

One conclusion that politicians reached after analyzing the 1892 returns was that the money question was of paramount interest to the voters. By the early 1890s, discussion of federal monetary policy revolved around the coinage of silver. Traditionally the United States had been on a bimetallic standard. Both gold and silver were coined, the number of grains of each in the dollar being adjusted periodically to reflect the commercial value of the two metals. An act of 1792 established a 15:1 ratio—371.25 grains of silver and 24.75 grains of gold were each worth one dollar at the Mint. In 1834 the ratio was changed to 16:1, and in 1853 to 14.8:1, the latter reduction in the value of gold reflecting the new discoveries in California. This ratio slightly undervalued silver. In 1861, for example, the amount of silver bullion in a dollar was worth $1.03 in the open market, so no one took silver to the Mint for coinage. However, an avalanche of silver from the mines of Nevada and Colorado gradually depressed the price until, around 1874, it again became profitable for miners to coin their bullion. Alas, when they tried to do so, they discovered that the Coinage Act of 1873, taking account of the fact that no silver had been presented to the Mint in years, had demonetized the metal.

The silver miners denounced this "Crime of 1873," and inflationists, who wanted more money put into circulation regardless of its base, joined them in demanding a return to bimetallism. Conservatives, still fighting the battle against greenback paper money, resisted strongly. The result was a series of compromises. In 1878 the Bland-Allison Act authorized the purchase of $2 to $4 million of silver a month at the market price, but this had little inflationary effect because the government consistently purchased only the minimum amount. In 1890 the Sherman Silver Purchase Act required the government to buy 4.5 million *ounces* of silver monthly, but in the face of increasing supplies the price of silver fell still further. The ratio reached 26:1 in 1893 and 32:1 in 1894.

The compromises satisfied no one. Silver miners grumbled because their bullion brought in only half what it had in the early seventies. Debtors noted angrily that because of the general decline of prices, the dollars they used to meet their obligations were worth more than twice as much as in 1865. Advocates of the gold standard feared that unlimited silver coinage would be au-

thorized, "destroying the value of the dollar." When a financial panic brought on by the collapse of the London banking house of Baring Brothers ushered in a severe industrial depression, the confidence of both silverites and "gold bugs" was further eroded.

President Cleveland believed that the controversy over silver had caused the depression by shaking the confidence of the business community. He summoned a special session of Congress, and by exerting immense political pressure, he obtained the repeal of the Sherman Silver Purchase Act in October 1893. All that this accomplished was to split the Democratic Party, its southern and western wings deserting him almost to a man.

During 1894 and 1895, while the nation floundered in the worst depression it had ever experienced, a series of events further undermined public confidence. In the spring of 1894, several "armies" of the unemployed, the most imposing led by Jacob S. Coxey, an eccentric Ohio businessman, marched on Washington to demand relief. Coxey wanted the government to undertake a program of federal public works and to authorize local communities to exchange noninterest-bearing bonds with the Treasury for $500 million in paper money, the funds to be used to hire unemployed workers to build roads. The scheme, Coxey claimed, would pump money into the economy, provide work for the jobless, and benefit the entire nation by improving transportation facilities.

When Coxey's group of demonstrators, perhaps 500 in all, reached Washington, he and two other leaders were arrested for trespassing on the grounds of the Capitol. Their followers were dispersed by club-wielding policemen. This callous treatment convinced many Americans that the government had little interest in the suffering of the people, an opinion strengthened when Cleveland, in July 1894, used federal troops to crush the Pullman strike.

The next year the Supreme Court handed down several reactionary decisions. In *United States* v. *E. C. Knight Company* it refused to employ the Sherman Antitrust Act to break up the Sugar Trust. In *Pollock* v. *Farmers' Loan and Trust Company* it invalidated a federal income tax law. Finally, the Court denied a writ of *habeas corpus* to

Eugene V. Debs of the American Railway Union, who was languishing in prison for disobeying a federal injunction during the Pullman strike.

On top of these indications of official conservatism came a desperate financial crisis. Throughout 1894 the Treasury's supply of gold dwindled as worried citizens exchanged greenbacks (now convertible into gold) for hard money and foreign investors cashed in large amounts of American securities. Early in 1895 the gold reserve touched a low point of $41 million.

At this juncture a syndicate of bankers headed by J. P. Morgan turned the tide by underwriting a $62 million bond issue, guaranteeing that half the gold would come from Europe. This caused a great public outcry; the spectacle of the nation being saved from bankruptcy by a private banker shocked millions.

As the presidential election of 1896 approached, with the Populists demanding unlimited coinage of silver at a ratio of 16:1, the major parties found it impossible to continue straddling the money question. The Populist vote had increased by 42 percent in the 1894 congressional elections. After a generation of political equivocation, the major parties had to face an important issue squarely.

The Republicans, meeting to choose a candidate at St. Louis in June 1896, announced for the gold standard and nominated Ohio's William McKinley for president. The Democratic Convention met in July at Chicago. The pro-gold Cleveland element made a hard fight, but the silverites swept them aside. The high point came when a youthful Nebraskan named William Jennings Bryan spoke for silver against gold, for western farmers against the industrial East. His every sentence provoked ear-shattering applause. "Burn down your cities and leave our farms," he said, "and your cities will spring up again as if by magic; but destroy our farms and the grass will grow in the streets of every city in the country." He ended with a marvelous figure of speech that set the tone for the coming campaign. "You shall not press down upon the brow of labor this crown of thorns," he warned, bringing his hands down suggestively to his temples. "You shall not crucify mankind upon a cross of gold!" Dramatically, he extended his arms to the side, the very figure of the crucified Christ.

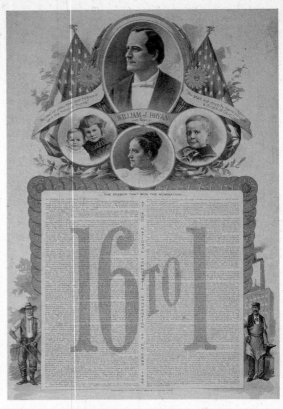

Portraits of William Jennings Bryan with his wife and children, along with the text of the "cross of gold" speech, appeared on this typically colorful campaign poster for the 1896 election.

The convention promptly adopted a platform calling for "the free and unlimited coinage of both silver and gold at the present legal ratio of 16 to 1" and went on to nominate Bryan, who was barely 36, for president. This action put tremendous pressure on the Populists. If they supported Bryan, they risked losing their party identity; if they nominated another candidate, they would insure McKinley's election.

Those more concerned with immediate political advantage, especially holders of and seekers after office, took the former position. Those (mostly old Alliance members raised in the cooperative movement) who considered free silver a minor issue and a poor substitute for the subtreasury plan as an approach to the deflation problem, rejected "fusion" with the Democrats. It was a difficult decision for all. In the end, in part because the delegates could not find a Populist of stature willing to become a candidate against him, the convention nominated Bryan, seeking to preserve the party identity by substituting Tom Watson for the Democratic vice presidential nominee, Arthur Sewall of Maine.

The Election of 1896

Never did a presidential campaign raise such intense emotions. The Republicans from the silvermining states swung solidly behind Bryan. The gold Democrats refused to accept the decision of the Chicago convention and nominated a candidate of their own, 79-year-old Senator John M. Palmer of Illinois. Palmer ran only to injure Bryan. "Fellow Democrats," he announced, "I will not consider it any great fault if you decide to cast your vote for William McKinley."

At the start the Republicans seemed to have everything in their favor. Bryan's youth and relative lack of political experience—two terms in the House—contrasted unfavorably with McKinley's long service in Congress and as governor of Ohio and with his reputation for honesty and good judgment. The severe depression operated in favor of the party out of power. Furthermore, the newspapers came out almost unanimously for the Republicans. The Democrats had very little money and few well-known speakers to fight the campaign.

But Bryan proved to be a formidable opponent. Casting aside tradition, he took to the stump personally, traveling 18,000 miles and making over 600 speeches. He was one of the greatest of orators: He projected an image of absolute sincerity without appearing fanatical or argumentative. At every major stop on his tour, huge crowds assembled. Everywhere he hammered away at the money question. Yet he did not totally neglect other issues. He was defending, he said, "all the people who suffer from the operations of trusts, syndicates, and combines."

McKinley's campaign was managed by a new type of politician, Marcus Alonzo Hanna, an Ohio businessman. In a sense, Hanna was a product of the Pendleton Civil Service Act. When deprived of the contributions of officeholders, the parties turned to business for funds.

Hanna spent about $100,000 of his own money on the preconvention campaign. Before most Republicans realized how effective Bryan was on the stump, Hanna perceived the danger and sprang into action. Since the late 1880s the character of political organization had been changing. The Civil Service Act was also cutting down on the number of jobs available to reward campaign workers. At the same time, the new mass-circulation newspapers and the nationwide press associations were increasing the pressure on candidates to speak openly and often on national issues.

This trend put a premium on party organization and consistency—the political trick of speaking out of one side of the mouth to one audience, out the other to another, no longer worked very well. The old military metaphors of political discourse, the terms *campaign* and *spoils* and *standard bearer,* remained. But others more businesslike became popular: *boss, machine, lobbyist.*

As the federal government became more involved in economic issues, business interests found more reason to be concerned about national elections and were more willing to spend money on behalf of candidates whose views they approved. In the campaign of 1888 the Republicans had set up a businessmen's "advisory board" to raise money and stir up enthusiasm for Benjamin Harrison.

Hanna understood what was happening to politics. Certain that money was the key to political power, he raised an enormous campaign fund. When businessmen hesitated to contribute, he pried open their purses by a combination of persuasiveness and intimidation. Banks and insurance companies were "assessed" a percentage of their assets, big corporations a share of their receipts, until some $3.5 million had been collected.

Hanna disbursed these funds with efficiency and imagination. He sent 1,500 speakers into the doubtful districts and blanketed the land with 250 million pieces of campaign literature, printed in a dozen languages. "He has advertised McKinley as if he were a patent medicine," Theodore Roosevelt exclaimed.

McKinley conducted a "front-porch campaign." Superficially the proceedings were delightfully informal. From every corner of the land, groups representing various regions, occupations, and interests descended on McKinley's unpretentious frame house in Canton, Ohio. Gathering on the lawn—the grass was soon reduced to mud, the fence stripped of pickets by souvenir hunters—the visitors paid their compliments to the candidate and heard him deliver a brief speech, while beside him on the porch his aged mother and adoring invalid wife listened with rapt attention. Then there was a small reception, during which the delegates were given an opportunity to shake their host's hand.

Despite the air of informality, these performances were carefully staged. The delegations arrived on a tightly coordinated schedule worked out by McKinley's staff and the railroads, which operated cut-rate excursion trains to Canton from all over the nation. McKinley was fully briefed on the special interests and attitudes of each group and on occasion even wrote the visitors' speeches himself. Naturally, his own talks were carefully prepared, each calculated to make a particular point. All were reported fully in the newspapers. Thus, without moving from his doorstep, McKinley met thousands of people from every section.

These tactics worked admirably. On election day McKinley carried the East, the Middle West, including even Iowa, Minnesota, and North Dakota, and the Pacific Coast states of Oregon and California. Bryan won in the South, the plains states, and the Rocky Mountain region. McKinley collected 271 electoral votes to Bryan's 176, the popular vote being 7,036,000 to 6,468,000.

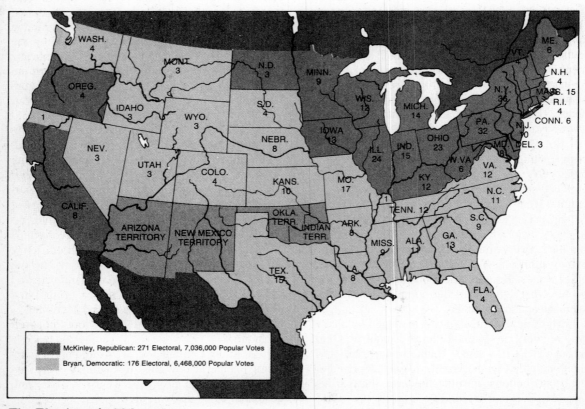

The Election of 1896

The Meaning of the Election

The sharp sectional division marked the failure of the Populist effort to unite northern and southern farmers and also the triumph of the industrial part of the country over the agricultural. Business and financial interests voted solidly for the Republicans, but other groups were far from being united. Many thousands of farmers voted for McKinley, and a preponderance of the labor vote went to him. The Republicans carried nearly all the large cities, and in closely contested states like Illlinois and Ohio this made the difference between victory and defeat.

During the campaign, some frightened Republicans had laid plans for fleeing the country if Bryan were elected, and belligerent ones, such as Theodore Roosevelt, then police commissioner of New York City, readied themselves to meet the "social revolutionaries" on the battlefield. Victory sent such people into transports of joy. Most conservatives concluded happily that the way of life they so fervently admired had been saved for all time.

However heartfelt, such sentiments were not founded on fact. With workers standing beside capitalists and with the farm vote split, it cannot be said that the election divided the nation class against class or that McKinley's victory saved the country from revolution.

Far from representing a triumph for the status quo, the election marked the coming of age of modern America. The battle between gold and silver, which everyone had considered so vital, had little real significance. The inflationists seemed to have been beaten, but new gold discoveries in Alaska and South Africa and improved methods of extracting gold from low-grade ores soon led to a great expansion of the money supply. Within two decades the system of basing the volume of currency on bullion had been abandoned.

Bryan and the "political" Populists who supported him, supposedly the advance agents of revolution, were oriented more toward the past than the future. Their ideal was the rural America of Jefferson and Jackson. McKinley, for all his innate conservatism, was capable of looking ahead toward the new century. His approach was national where Bryan's was basically parochial. Although never daring and seldom imaginative, he was able to deal pragmatically with current problems. Before long, as the United States became increasingly an exporter of manufactures, he would even modify his position on the tariff. And no one better reflected the spirit of the age than Mark Hanna, the outstanding political realist of his generation. Far from preventing change, the outcome of the election of 1896 made possible still greater changes as the United States moved into the 20th century.

Milestones

Year	Event		Year	Event
1873	Congress suspends the coining of silver (the "Crime of '73")		1892	Founding of the People's (Populist) Party
1877	Beginning of Farmers Alliance movement		1893	Panic of 1893
1878	Bland-Allison Act		1894	Coxey's Army marches to Washington to demand relief
1879	Greenback paper money made convertible into gold		1895	Supreme Court declares federal income tax unconstitutional (Pollock v. Farmers' Loan and Trust Company)
1881	President Garfield is assassinated			
1883	Pendleton Civil Service Act			J. P. Morgan raises $62 million in gold for the Treasury
1884	Mugwump movement			
1887	Interstate Commerce Act		1896	William Jennings Bryan's "Cross of Gold" speech
1890	Sherman Silver Purchase Act Cleveland's tariff message			

Supplementary Reading

The political history of this period is covered in H. W. Morgan, **From Hayes to McKinley** (1969). H. U. Faulkner, **Politics, Reform, and Expansion*** (1959), treats the politics of the 1890s in some detail, while J. A. Garraty, **The New Commonwealth*** (1968), attempts to trace the changing character of the political system after 1877 and D. J. Rothman, **Politics and Power: The United States Senate*** (1966), analyzes the shifting structure of the upper House.

J. C. Teaford, **The Unheralded Triumph: City Government** (1984), B. C. Campbell, **Representative Democracy** (1980), R. J. Jensen, **The Winning of the Midwest** (1971), and Paul Kleppner, **The Cross of Culture** (1977), are important studies of the character of state and local politics.

Among biographies of political leaders, the following are especially worth consulting: Ari Hoogenboom, **The Presidency of Rutherford B. Hayes** (1988), Allan Peskin, **Garfield** (1978), F. C. Reeves, **Gentleman President: Chester A. Arthur** (1978), J. D. Doenecke, **The Presidency of James A. Garfield and Chester A. Arthur** (1981), Allan Nevins, **Grover Cleveland** (1932), H. E. Socolovsky and A. B. Spetter, **The Presidency of Benjamin Harrison** (1987), and H. W. Morgan, **William McKinley and His America** (1963).

For the farmers' problems, see F. A. Shannon, **The Farmer's Last Frontier*** (1945), J. D. Hicks, **The Populist Revolt*** (1931), and Theodore Saloutos, **Farmer Movements in the South*** (1960). Populism has been the subject of intensive study. Richard Hofstadter, **The Age of Reform*** (1955), takes a dim view of Populism as a reform movement, whereas Lawrence Goodwyn, **Democratic Promise: The Populist Movement in America** (1976), calls it "a people's movement of mass democratic aspiration." R. W. Cherny, **Populism, Progressivism, and the Transformation of Nebraska Politics** (1981), and Sheldon Hackney, **Populism to Progressivism in Alabama** (1969), are more than local studies. See also Steven Hahn, **The Roots of Southern Populism** (1983).

On the depression of the 1890s, consult Charles Hoffman, **The Depression of the Nineties** (1970), Carlos Schwantes, **Coxey's Army** (1985), Stanley Buder, **Pullman** (1967), and Nick Salvatore, **Eugene V. Debs** (1982). On Bryan and the election of 1896, see P. E. Glad, **The Trumpet Soundeth** (1960), R. W. Cherny, **William Jennings Bryan** (1985), and S. L. Jones, **The Presidential Election of 1896** (1964).

*Available in paperback.

CHAPTER 22

The Age of Reform

Roots of Progressivism
The Muckrakers
The Progressive Mind
"Radical" Progressives: The Wave of the Future
Political Reform: Cities First
Political Reform: The States
State Social Legislation
Political Reform in Washington
Theodore Roosevelt: Cowboy in the White House
Roosevelt and Big Business
Square Dealing
TR: In His Own Right
Tilting Left
William Howard Taft: The Listless Progressive
Breakup of the Republican Party
The Election of 1912
Wilson: The New Freedom
The Progressives and Minority Rights
Black Militancy

*T*he first two decades of the 20th century are usually called the Progressive Era. Like all such generalizations about complex subjects, this title involves a great simplification. Whether *progressive* is taken to mean "tending toward change," or "improvement," or is merely used to suggest an attitude of mind, it was neither a unique nor a universal characteristic of those years. Progressive elements existed in the 1880s and 1890s and did not disappear in the 1920s. Nevertheless, the word provides a useful description of this exciting and significant period of American history.

Roots of Progressivism

The progressives were never a single group seeking a single objective. The movement sprang from many sources. One of them was the fight against corruption and inefficiency in government, which began with the Liberal Republicans of the Grant era and was continued by the mugwumps of the 1880s. The continuing power of corrupt big-city political machines and the growing influence of large corporations outraged thousands of citizens and led them to seek ways of purifying politics and making the machinery of government at all levels responsive to the majority rather than to special-interest groups.

Progressivism also had roots in the effort to regulate and control big business, which characterized the Granger and Populist agitation of the 1870s and 1890s. The failure of the Interstate Commerce Act to end railroad abuses and of the Sherman Antitrust Act to check the growth of monopolies became increasingly apparent after 1900. Between 1897 and 1904, the trend toward concentration in industry accelerated. Such new giants as U.S. Steel (1901) and International Harvester (1902) attracted most of the attention, but in a single year (1899) over 1,200 firms were absorbed in mergers, the resulting combinations being capitalized at $2.2 billion. By 1904 there were 318 industrial combinations with an aggregate capital of $7.5 billion in the country. Those who considered bigness inherently evil demanded that the huge new "trusts" be broken up or at least strictly controlled.

Settlement-house workers and other late-19th-century reformers concerned about the welfare of the urban poor made up a third battalion in the progressive army. This was the area in which women were most involved in the movement. The working and living conditions of slum dwellers remained abominable and the child labor problem was particularly acute; in 1900 about 1.7 million children under the age of 16 were working full time—more than the membership of the American Federation of Labor. In addition, laws regulating the hours and working conditions of women in industry were far from adequate, and almost nothing had been done to enforce safety rules or to provide some kind of compensation or insurance for workers injured on the job. As the number of professionally competent social workers grew, the movement for social-welfare legislation gained momentum.

All these tendencies may be summed up in Robert H. Wiebe's phrase, "the search for order." America was becoming more urban, more industrial, more mechanized, more centralized—in short, more complex. This trend put a premium on efficiency and cooperation. It seemed obvious to the progressives that people must become more socially minded, the economy more carefully organized.

By attracting additional thousands of sympathizers to the general cause of reform, the return of prosperity after 1896 produced the progressive movement. Good times made the average person more tolerant and generous. Middle-class Americans became conscience-stricken when they compared their own comfortable circumstances with those of the "huddled masses" of immigrants and native poor.

Giant corporations threatened not so much the economic well-being as the ambitions and sense of importance of the middle class. What owner of a small mill or shop could now hope to rise to the heights attained by Andrew Carnegie or by merchants like John Wanamaker and Marshall Field? The growth of large labor organizations worried such types; individual relationships between employer and worker no longer counted for much. In general, human character and moral values seemed less influential; organizations—cold, impersonal, heartless—were coming to control business, politics, and too many other aspects of life.

The historian Richard Hofstadter suggested still another explanation of the progressive movement: the status revolution. Numbers of moderately prosperous businessmen, together with members of the professions and other educated persons, felt threatened by the increasing power and status of the new tycoons, many of them coarse, domineering, and fond of vulgar display. The antics of machine politicians, who made a mockery of the traditions of duty, service, and patriotism associated with statesmanship, also troubled them.

Protestant pastors, accustomed to the respect and deference of their flocks, found their moral leadership challenged by materialistic vestrymen who did not even pay them decent salaries. College professors worried about their institutions falling under the sway of wealthy trustees who had little interest in or respect for learning. Lawyers, once "the aristocracy of the United States," had become merely tools of industrial and financial enterprise.

Such people could support reform measures without feeling that they were being very radical because they were resisting change and because the intellectual currents of the time harmonized with their ideas of social improvement and the welfare state. The new doctrines of the social scientists, the Social Gospel religious leaders, and the philosophers of pragmatism provided a salubrious climate for progressivism. Many of the thinkers who formulated these doctrines in the eighties and nineties turned to the task of putting them into practice in the new century.

The Muckrakers

As the diffuse and unorganized progressive army gradually formed its battalions, a new journalistic fad suddenly brought the movement into focus. For many years, magazines had been publishing articles discussing current political, social, and economic problems. The tempo and forcefulness of this type of literature steadily increased. Then, in the fall of 1902, *McClure's* began publishing two particularly hard-hitting series of articles, one on Standard Oil by Ida Tarbell, the other on big-city political machines by Lincoln Steffens. These articles caused much comment. When editor S. S. McClure decided to include in the January 1903 issue an attack on labor gangsterism in the coal fields along with installments of the Tarbell and Steffens series, he called attention to the circumstance in a striking editorial.

Something was radically wrong with the "American character," McClure wrote. These articles showed that large numbers of American employers, workers, and politicians were fundamentally immoral. Lawyers were becoming tools of big business, judges were permitting evildoers to escape justice, the churches were materialistic, the colleges were incapable of understanding what was happening. "There is no one left; none but all of us," McClure concluded. "We have to pay in the end." This editorial loosed a chain reaction. Thousands of readers found their own vague apprehensions brought into focus, some becoming active in progressive movements, more lending passive support.

Other editors jumped to adopt the McClure formula. A small army of professional writers was soon flooding the periodical press with denunciations of the insurance business, drug business, college athletics, prostitution, sweatshop labor, political corruption, and dozens of other muckraking subjects.

Theodore Roosevelt, with his gift for vivid language, compared these journalists to "the Man with the Muck-Rake" in John Bunyan's *Pilgrim's Progress,* whose attention was so fixed on the filth at his feet that he could not notice the "celestial crown" that was offered him in exchange. Roosevelt's characterization misrepresented the literature of exposure, but the label *muckraking* was thereafter affixed to the type. Despite the connotations, *muckraker* became a term of honor.

The Progressive Mind

Progressives were essentially middle-class moralists seeking to arouse the conscience of "the people" in order to purify American life. They were convinced that human beings were by nature decent, well intentioned, and kind. More deeply than earlier reformers they believed that the source of society's evils lay in the structure of its institutions, not in the weaknesses or sinfulness of individuals.

Therefore the solution to social problems lay in changing faulty institutions. Local, state, and national government must be made more responsive to the will of citizens who stood for the traditional virtues. In the South, many progressives even argued that measures designed to disfranchise blacks were reforms because they discouraged a class of people they considered unthinking and shiftless from voting. When government had been thus reformed, then it must act. Whatever its virtues, laissez-faire was obsolete. Businessmen, especially big businessmen, must be compelled to behave fairly, their acquisitive drives curbed in the interests of justice and equal opportunity for all. The weaker elements in society—women, children, the poor, the infirm—must be protected against unscrupulous power. The people, by

which (whether they realized it or not) most progressives meant the middle class, must assume new responsibilities toward the unfortunate.

Despite its fervor and democratic rhetoric, progressivism was paternalistic, moderate, and often soft-headed. Typical reformers of the period oversimplified complicated issues and treated their personal values as absolute standards of truth and morality. Many progressives who genuinely wanted to improve the living standards of industrial workers rejected the proposition that workers could best help themselves by organizing powerful national unions. Union leaders favored government action to outlaw child labor and restrict immigration but adopted a laissez-faire attitude toward wages-and-hours legislation; they preferred to win these objectives through collective bargaining, thereby justifying their own existence. Progressives stressed individual freedom yet gave strong backing to the drive to deprive the public of its right to drink alcoholic beverages.

It must be emphasized that the progressives never challenged the fundamental principles of capitalism, nor did they attempt a basic reorganization of society. They would have little to do with the socialist brand of reform, they were anti-immigrant, and only a handful had anything to offer blacks, surely the most exploited group in American society.

Neither the confusions nor the limitations of the progressives should, however, obscure their accomplishments. They elevated the tone of politics, raised the aspirations of the American people, and fashioned many valuable practical reforms.

A good example of the limited radicalism of most progressives is offered by the experiences of progressive artists. Early in the century, a number of painters turned to city streets and the people of the slums for their models. These "ashcan school" artists supported political and social reform and were caught up in the progressive movement. Most saw themselves as rebels. But artistically the ashcan painters were not very advanced. They were uninfluenced by the outburst of postimpressionist activity then taking place in Europe. To their dismay, when they included canvases by European painters like Matisse and Picasso in a show of their own works they put on at the 69th Regiment Armory in New York City in 1913, the Europeans got all the attention.

"Radical" Progressives: The Wave of the Future

There were, of course, some Americans whose views were more fundamentally radical. In 1900 the labor leader Eugene V. Debs ran for president on the Socialist ticket. He polled fewer than 100,000 votes. When he ran again in1904, he got more than 400,000, in later elections still more. Labor leaders hoping to organize unskilled workers in heavy industry were frustrated by the craft orientation of the American Federation of Labor, and some saw in socialism a way to win rank-and-file backing.

In 1905 Debs, William "Big Bill" Haywood of the Western Federation of Miners, Mary Harris "Mother" Jones, a former organizer for the United Mine Workers, and a few others organized a new union, the Industrial Workers of the World. The IWW was openly anticapitalist. The preamble to its constitution began: "The working class and the employing class have nothing in common."

Other "advanced" European ideas affected the thinking and behavior of some important progressive intellectuals. Sigmund Freud's psychoanalytical theories attracted numbers of Americans, especially after Freud lectured at Clark University in 1909. Not many progressives actually read any of Freud's works, none of which was translated into English before 1909, but many picked up enough of the vocabulary of psychoanalysis to discourse impressively about the significance of slips of the tongue, sublimation, and infant sexuality.

Some saw in Freud's ideas reason to effect a "revolution of manners and morals" that would have shocked (or at least embarrassed) Freud, who was personally quite conventional. They advocated easy divorce, trial marriage, the legalization of contraception, and doing away with the double standard in all matters relating to sex.

Most large cities boasted groups of these "bohemian" thinkers, by far the most famous being the one centered in New York City's Greenwich Village. The dancer Isadora Duncan, the photographer Alfred Stieglitz, several of the ashcan artists, and the playwright Eugene O'Neill rubbed shoulders with Big Bill Haywood of the IWW, the anarchist Emma Goldman, and the militant feminist advocate of birth control Margaret Sanger.

The impact of *The Silent War,* a 1906 novel by J. Ames Mitchell that dealt with the growing class struggle in America, was enhanced by William Balfour-Ker's graphic illustration *From the Depths.*

The typical Greenwich Village intellectual displayed what their historian Leslie Fishbein calls "a highly personalistic concern" for their own interests, but Goldman, Haywood, Sanger, and a few others were genuine radicals who sought basic changes in bourgeois society.

The creative writers of the era, applying the spirit of progressivism to the realism they had inherited from Howells and the naturalists, tended to adopt an optimistic tone. Ezra Pound talked grandly of an American Renaissance and fashioned a new kind of poetry called imagism, which, while not appearing to be realistic, abjured all abstract generalizations and concentrated on concrete word pictures to convey meaning. The poet Carl Sandburg, the best-known representative of the "Chicago school," denounced the local plutocrats but sang the praises of the city they had made: "Hog Butcher for the World . . . City of the Big Shoulders."

Most progressive writers took Freud's teachings to mean that they should cast off the restrictions of Victorian prudery; they ignored his essentially dark view of human nature. Theirs was an "innocent rebellion," exuberant and rather muddleheaded.

Political Reform: Cities First

To ordinary progressives, political corruption and inefficiency lay at the root of the evils plaguing American cities. Despite the efforts of the 19th-century urban reformers, corruption and inefficiency persisted into the Progressive Era. As the cities grew, their boss-ridden administrations became more and more disgraceful. In San Francisco, for example, Abe Ruef, a shrewd lawyer, ruled one of the most powerful and dissolute political machines in the nation. When the gas company sought a rate increase, Ruef, who was already collecting a $1,000-a-month "retainer" from the company, demanded and got a bribe of $20,000 for granting it. Prostitution flourished, with the Ruef machine sharing in the profits. There was a brisk illegal trade in liquor licenses and other favors.

Similar conditions existed in dozens of communities. For his famous muckraking series for *McClure's,* Lincoln Steffens visited St. Louis, Minneapolis, Pittsburgh, New York, Chicago, and Philadelphia and found them all riddled with corruption.

Beginning in the late nineties, progressives mounted a massive assault on dishonest and inefficient urban governments. In San Francisco a group headed by the newspaperman Fremont Older and a wealthy sugar manufacturer, Rudolph Spreckels, broke the Ruef machine and eventually lodged Ruef in jail. In Toledo, Ohio, Samuel M. "Golden Rule" Jones won election as mayor in 1897 and succeeded in arousing the local citizenry against the corruptionists. Other important progressive mayors included Tom L. Johnson of Cleveland—whose administration Lincoln Steffens called the best in the United States—Seth Low, and later John P. Mitchell of New York and Hazen S. Pingree of Detroit.

City reformers could seldom destroy the machines without changing urban political institutions. Some cities obtained "home rule" charters that gave them greater freedom from state control in dealing with local matters. Many created research bureaus that investigated government problems in a scientific and nonpartisan manner. A number of middle-sized communities (Galveston, Texas, provided the prototype) experimented with a system that integrated executive and legislative powers in the hands of a small elected commission, thereby concentrating responsibility and making it easier to coordinate complex activities. Out of this experiment came the city manager system under which the commissioners appointed a professional manager to administer city affairs on a nonpartisan basis.

Political Reform: The States

To carry out this kind of change required the support of state legislatures, since all municipal government depended on the authority of a sovereign state. Such approval was often difficult to obtain—local bosses were usually entrenched in powerful state machines and most legislatures were controlled by rural majorities insensitive to urban needs. The progressives, therefore, had to strike at inefficiency and corruption at the state level too.

During the first decade of the new century, Wisconsin, the progressive state par excellence, was transformed by Robert M. La Follette, one of the most remarkable figures of the age. La Follette had served three terms as a Republican congressman (1885–1891) and developed a reputation as an uncompromising foe of corruption before being elected governor in 1900. That the people would always do the right thing if properly informed and inspired was the fundamental article of his political faith.

While governor, La Follette overhauled the political structure of the state. Over the opposition of railroad and lumbering interests, he obtained a direct primary system for nominating candidates, a corrupt practices act, and laws limiting campaign expenditures and lobbying activities. In power he became something of a boss himself. He made ruthless use of patronage, demanded absolute loyalty of his subordinates, and often stretched, or at least oversimplified, the truth in presenting complex issues to the voters.

La Follette was a consummate showman, and he never rose entirely above rural prejudices, being prone to scent a nefarious "conspiracy" organized by what he called "the interests" behind even the mildest opposition to his proposals. But he was devoted to the cause of honest government. Realizing that some state functions called for specialized technical knowledge, he used commissions and agencies to handle such matters as railroad regulation, tax assessment, conservation, and highway construction.

The success of these policies, which became known as the Wisconsin Idea led other states to adopt similar programs. Reform administrations swept into office in Iowa and Arkansas (1901), Oregon (1902), Minnesota, Kansas, and Mississippi (1904), New York and Georgia (1906), Nebraska (1909), and New Jersey and Colorado (1910). In some cases the reformers were Republicans, in others Democrats, but in all these states and in many others, the example of Wisconsin was influential.

State Social Legislation

The first state laws aimed at social problems long antedated the Progressive Era. In 1874 Massachusetts restricted the working hours of women to ten per day, and by the 1890s, many other states, mostly in the East and Middle West, had followed suit. Illinois passed an eight-hour law for women workers in 1893. A New York law of 1882 struck at the sweatshops of the slums by prohibiting the manufacture of cigars on premises "occupied as a house or residence."

As part of this trend, some states established special rules for workers in hazardous industries. In the 1890s several states limited the hours of railroad workers on the ground that fatigue sometimes caused railroad accidents. New York set a ten-hour-per-day limit for bakers (1897). Utah restricted miners to eight hours in 1896. Before 1900, the impact of these laws was not impressive. Powerful manufacturers and landlords often suc-

ceeded in defeating the bills or rendering them innocuous.

The federal system further complicated the task of obtaining effective legislation. The Fourteenth Amendment to the Constitution, although enacted to protect the civil rights of blacks, imposed a revolutionary restriction on the states by forbidding them to "deprive any person of life, liberty, or property without due process of law." Since much state social legislation represented new uses of police power that conservative judges considered dangerous and unwise, the Fourteenth Amendment gave them an excuse to overturn the laws on the ground that they deprived someone of liberty or property.

As stricter and more far-reaching laws were enacted, many judges, sensing what they took to be a trend toward socialism and regimentation, adopted an increasingly narrow interpretation of state police power. The United States Supreme Court upheld the Utah mining law of 1896 (*Holden* v. *Hardy,* 1898), but in 1905 it declared in the case of *Lochner* v. *New York* that New York's ten-hour act for bakers deprived the bakers of the liberty of working as long as they wished and thus violated the Fourteenth Amendment.

Nevertheless, the progressives continued to battle for legislation based on police power. Women played a particularly important part in these struggles. Sparked by the National Child Labor Committee, organized in 1904, reformers over the next ten years obtained laws in nearly every state banning the employment of young children. Many states also limited the hours of older children to eight or ten per day, and outlawed night work and labor in dangerous occupations by minors. These laws fixed no uniform standards and many were poorly enforced, yet when Congress passed a federal child labor law in 1916, the Supreme Court, in *Hammer* v. *Dagenhart* (1918), declared it unconstitutional.[*]

By 1917 nearly all the states had placed limitations on the hours of women industrial workers, and about ten states had set minimum wage standards for women. But once again federal action

---

[*]A second child labor law, passed in 1919, was also thrown out by the Court, and a child labor amendment, submitted in 1924, failed to achieve ratification by the necessary three-quarters of the states.

Child labor in the early 1900s was especially evident in the coal mines. Here, in Pittsburgh, Pennsylvania, boys pick through slate in an anthracite mine. Ironically the seating arrangement of these young workers bears a resemblance to students sitting in a schoolhouse.

sincerely in most instances, that no government had the power to deprive either workers or employers of the right to negotiate any kind of labor contract they wished. But when an Oregon law limiting women laundry workers to ten hours a day was challenged in *Muller* v. *Oregon* (1908), Florence Kelley and Josephine Goldmark of the Consumers' League persuaded Louis D. Brandeis to defend the statute before the Court.

The Consumer's League, whose slogan was "investigate, agitate, legislate," was probably the most effective of the many women's reform organizations of the period. With the aid of League researchers, Brandeis prepared a remarkable brief stuffed with economic and sociological evidence indicating that long hours damaged both the health of individual women and the health of society.

This nonlegal evidence impressed the justices. After 1908 the right of states to protect the weaker members of society by special legislation was widely accepted. The use of the "Brandeis brief" technique to demonstrate the need for legislation became standard practice.

Progressives also launched a massive if ill-coordinated attack on problems related to monopoly. When the evils of the boss system could be connected to the threat posed by big business, the public reaction was formidable. The variety of regulatory legislation passed by the states between 1900 and 1917 was almost infinite. Wisconsin created a powerful railroad commission staffed with nonpartisan experts; they enacted a graduated income tax and strengthened the state tax commission, which then proceeded to force corporations to bear a larger share of the cost of government; it overhauled the laws regulating insurance companies and set up a small state-owned life insurance company to serve as a yardstick for evaluating the rates of private companies. In 1911, besides creating an industrial commission to enforce the state's labor and factory legislation, Wisconsin progressives established a conservation commission, headed by Charles R. Van Hise, president of the University of Wisconsin.

A similar spate of legislation characterized the brief reign of Woodrow Wilson as governor of New Jersey (1911–1913). Economic reforms in other states were less spectacular but impressive in the mass. In New York an investigation of the

that would have extended such regulation to the entire country did not materialize.

Laws protecting workers against on-the-job accidents were enacted by many states. Disasters like the 1911 fire in New York City, in which nearly 150 women perished because the Triangle shirtwaist factory had no fire escapes, led to the passage of stricter municipal building codes and to factory inspection acts. By 1910 most states had modified the common-law principle that a worker accepted the risk of accident as a condition of employment and was not entitled to compensation if injured unless it could be proved that the employer had been negligent. Gradually the states adopted accident insurance plans, and some began to grant pensions to widows with small children. Most manufacturers favored these measures, if for no other reason than that they regularized procedures and avoided costly lawsuits. Women played key roles in most of these struggles.

The passage of so much state social legislation sent conservatives scurrying to the Supreme Court for redress. Such persons believed, quite big life insurance companies led to comprehensive changes in the insurance laws. In Iowa stiff laws regulating railroads were passed in 1906. In Nebraska the legislature created a system of bank deposit insurance in 1909. Minnesota levied an inheritance tax and built a harvesting machine factory to compete with the harvester trust at about this time. Georgia raised the taxes on corporations. However, piecemeal state regulation failed to solve the problems of an ever-more-complex economy. The most significant battles for economic reform were fought in Congress.

Political Reform in Washington

On the national level, the Progressive Era saw the culmination of the struggle for women's suffrage. The shock occasioned by the failure of the Thirteenth and Fourteenth Amendments to give women the vote continued to embitter most leaders of the movement. But it resulted in a split among feminists. One group, the American Women's Suffrage Association, focused on the vote question alone. The more radical National Women's Suffrage Association (NWSA), led by Elizabeth Cady Stanton and Susan B. Anthony, concerned itself with many issues of importance to women as well as the suffrage. The NWSA put the immediate interests of women ahead of everything else. It was deeply involved in efforts to unionize women workers, yet it urged women to be strikebreakers if they could get better jobs by doing so.

Aside from their lack of unity, the feminists were handicapped by Victorian sexual inhibitions, which most of their leaders shared. Dislike of male-dominated society is hard enough to separate from dislike of men under the best of circumstances. At a time when sexual feelings were often deeply repressed, some of the advocates of women's rights probably did not understand their own feelings. Most feminists, for example, opposed contraception, insisting that birth control by any means other than continence would encourage what they called masculine lust. The Victorian idealization of female "purity" and the popular image of women as the revered guardians of home and family further confused many reformers.

These ideas and prejudices enticed feminists into a logical trap. If women were morally superior

A banner in a 1911 women's suffrage parade carries one of the longest-standing arguments in favor of women getting the vote.

to men—a tempting conclusion—giving women the suffrage would improve the character of the electorate. Politics would become less corrupt, war would become a thing of the past. "City housekeeping has failed," said Jane Addams of Hull House in arguing for the reform of municipal government, "partly because women, the traditional housekeepers, have not been consulted."

The trouble with this argument (aside from the fact that opponents could easily demonstrate that in states where women did vote, governments were no better or worse than elsewhere) was that it surrendered the principle of equality. In the long run, this was to have serious consequences for the women's movement, though the immediate effect of the "purity" argument probably was to advance the suffragists' cause.

In 1890 the two major women's groups combined as the National American Women's Suffrage Association (NAWSA). New leaders were emerging, the most notable being Carrie Chapman Catt, a woman who combined superb organizing abilities and political skills with commitment to broad social reform. The NAWSA made winning the right to vote its main objective and concentrated on a state-by-state approach. Wyoming gave women the vote in 1869 and Utah, Colorado, and Idaho had been won over to women's suffrage by 1896. The burgeoning of the progressive movement helped, as middle-class recruits of both sexes adopted the cause. California voted for women's suffrage in 1911, and then several other states fell in line. Large numbers of working-class women began to agitate for the vote.

The suffragists then shifted the campaign back to the national level, the lead taken by a new organization, the Congressional Union, headed by Alice Paul and the wealthy reformer Alva Belmont. When President Wilson refused to support a constitutional amendment granting women the vote, militant women picketed the White House. A number of them, including the daughter of Thomas Bayard, a former senator and secretary of state, were arrested and sentenced to 60 days in the workhouse. This roused a storm and Wilson quickly pardoned the picketers. After some hesitation the NAWSA stopped concentrating on the state-by-state approach and began to campaign for a constitutional amendment. Pressure on Congress mounted steadily. Later Vice President Thomas R. Marshall complained of the "everlasting clatter of the militant suffragettes" that (he said) was keeping Congress from transacting other business. This was an overstatement, but, in any case, by 1920 the necessary three-quarters of the states had approved the Nineteenth Amendment; the long fight was over.

The progressive reform drive also found expression in the Sixteenth Amendment to the Constitution, authorizing federal income taxes, and the Seventeenth, which required the popular election of senators, both ratified in 1913. A group of "insurgent" congressmen also managed to reform the House of Representatives by limiting the power of the Speaker. Thereafter, appointments to committees were determined by the whole membership, acting through party caucuses. The spirit of this change was thoroughly progressive. "We want the House to be representative of the people and each individual member to have his ideas presented and passed on," explained George W. Norris, who had led the insurgents.

Theodore Roosevelt: Cowboy in the White House

In September 1901 an anarchist named Leon Czolgosz assassinated President McKinley, and Theodore Roosevelt became president of the United States. His ascension to the presidency marked the beginning of a new era in national politics.

Although only 42, by far the youngest president in the nation's history up to that time, Roosevelt brought solid qualifications to the office. In addition to political experience that included three terms in the New York Assembly, six years on the United States Civil Service Commission, two years as police commissioner of New York City, another as assistant secretary of the navy, and a term as governor of New York, he had been a rancher in Dakota Territory and a soldier in the Spanish-American War. Politically, he had always been a loyal Republican. He rejected the mugwump heresy in 1884, despite his distaste for Blaine, and during the tempestuous nineties he vigorously denounced Populism, Bryanism, and "labor agitators."

Nevertheless Roosevelt's elevation to the presidency alarmed many conservatives, and not without reason. He did not fit their conception, based on a composite image of the chief executives from Hayes to McKinley, of what a president should be like. He seemed too undignified, too energetic, too outspoken, too unconventional. It was one thing to have operated a cattle ranch, another to have captured a gang of rustlers at gunpoint; one thing to have run a metropolitan police force, another to have roamed New York slums in the small hours in order to catch patrolmen fraternizing with thieves and prostitutes; one thing to have commanded a regiment, another to have killed a Spaniard personally.

Roosevelt had been a sickly child, plagued by asthma and poor eyesight, and he seems to have spent much of his adult life compensating for the sense of inadequacy that these troubles bred in him. He worshiped aggressiveness and was extremely sensitive to any threat to his honor as a gentleman. When another young man showed some slight interest in Roosevelt's fiancée, he sent off for a set of French dueling pistols. His teachers found him an interesting student, for he was intelligent and imaginative if rather annoyingly argumentative. "Now look here, Roosevelt," one Harvard professor finally said to him, "let me talk. I'm running this course."

Few individuals have rationalized or sublimated their feelings of inferiority as effectively as Roosevelt and to such good purpose. And few have been more genuinely warmhearted, more full of spontaneity, more committed to the ideals of public service and national greatness. As a political leader he was energetic and hard-driving. Conservatives and timid souls, sensing his aggressiveness even when he held it in check, distrusted Roosevelt's judgment, fearing he might go off half-cocked in some crisis. In fact, his judgment was nearly always sound; responsibility usually tempered his aggressiveness.

Above all Roosevelt believed in action. It would have been unthinkable for him to preside over a mere caretaker administration devoted to maintaining the status quo. However, the reigning Republican politicos, basking in the sunshine of the prosperity that had contributed so much to their victory in 1900, distrusted anything suggestive of change.

Had Roosevelt been the impetuous hothead that conservatives feared, he would have plunged ahead without regard for their feelings and influence. Instead he moved slowly and often got what he wanted by using his executive power rather than by persuading Congress to pass new laws. His domestic program included some measure of control of big corporations, more power for the Interstate Commerce Commission (ICC), and the conservation of natural resources. By consulting congressional leaders and following their advice not to bring up controversial matters like the tariff and currency reform, he obtained a modest budget of new laws.

The Newlands Act (1902) funneled the proceeds from land sales in the West into federal irrigation projects. The Expedition Act (1903) speeded the handling of antitrust suits in the courts. Another 1903 law created a Department of Commerce and Labor, which was to include a Bureau of Corporations with authority to investigate industrial combines and issue reports. The Elkins Railroad Act of 1903 strengthened the lCC's hand against the railroads by making the receiving as well as the granting of rebates illegal and by forbidding the roads to deviate in any way from their published rates.

Roosevelt and Big Business

Roosevelt soon became known as a trustbuster, and in the sense that he considered the monopoly problem the most pressing issue of the times, the term has some meaning. But he did not believe in breaking up big corporations indiscriminately. "Much of the legislation . . . enacted against trusts," he said in 1900 while governor of New York, "is not one whit more intelligent than the mediaeval bull against the comet, and has not been one particle more effective." Regulation seemed the best way to deal with large corporations.

With Congress unwilling to pass a stiff regulatory law, Roosevelt resorted to the Sherman Act to get at the problem. Although the Supreme Court decision in the Sugar Trust case seemed to have emasculated that law, in 1902 he ordered the Justice Department to bring suit against the Northern Securities Company.

The Northern Securities Company controlled the Great Northern, the Northern Pacific, and the Chicago, Burlington, and Quincy railroads. It had been created in 1901 after a titanic battle on the New York Stock Exchange between the forces of J. P. Morgan and James J. Hill and those of E. H. Harriman, who was associated with the Rockefeller interests. Neither side could win a clear-cut victory, so they decided to put the stock of all three railroads in a holding company owned by the two groups. Since Harriman already controlled the Union Pacific and the Southern Pacific, a virtual monopoly of western railroads was effected.

The announcement of the suit caused consternation in the business world. Attorney General Philander C. Knox pressed the case vigorously, and in 1904 the Court ordered the dissolution of the Northern Securities Company—a decision that served notice on the great corporations that they could no longer ignore the Sherman Act. Roosevelt ordered suits against the meat packers, the Standard Oil Trust, and the American Tobacco Company. His stock among progressives rose, yet he had not embarrassed the conservatives in Congress by demanding new antitrust legislation.

The president went out of his way to assure cooperative corporation magnates that he was not against size per se. "In our industrial and social system," he explained, "the interests of all men are so closely intertwined that in the immense majority of cases a straight-dealing man who by his efficiency, by his ingenuity and industry, benefits himself must also benefit others." At a White House conference in 1905, Roosevelt and Elbert H. Gary, chairman of the board of U.S. Steel, reached a "gentlemen's agreement" whereby Gary promised "to co-operate with the Government in every possible way." The Bureau of Corporations would conduct an investigation of U.S. Steel, Gary allowing it full access to company records. Roosevelt in turn promised that if the investigation revealed any corporate malpractices, he would allow Gary to set matters right voluntarily, thereby avoiding an antitrust suit. He reached a similar agreement with the International Harvester Company two years later.

There were limits to the effectiveness of such arrangements; Standard Oil, for example, agreed to a similar détente and then reneged, refusing to turn over vital records to the bureau. The Justice Department therefore brought suit against the company under the Sherman Act, and eventually it was broken up at the order of the Supreme Court. Roosevelt would have preferred a more binding kind of regulation, but when he asked for laws giving the government supervisory authority over big combinations, Congress refused to act. Given this situation, gentlemen's agreements seemed the best alternative.

Square Dealing

Roosevelt made remarkable use of his executive power during the anthracite coal strike of 1902. In June the United Mine Workers, led by John Mitchell, laid down their picks and demanded higher wages, an eight-hour day, and recognition of the union. The coal companies were dead set against concessions; when the men walked out, they shut down their properties and prepared to starve the strikers into submission.

The strike dragged on through the summer and early fall. The miners conducted themselves with great restraint, avoiding violence and offering to submit their claims to arbitration. As the price of anthracite soared with the approach of winter, sentiment in their behalf mounted. The fact that railroad corporations controlled most of the mines and that the operators refused even to negotiate with the union predisposed the most people in the workers' favor.

Roosevelt shared the public's sympathy for the miners, and the threat of a coal shortage naturally alarmed him. Early in October he summoned both sides to a conference in Washington and urged them to sacrifice "personal consideration[s]" for the "general good." His action enraged the coal operators, for they believed he was trying to force them to recognize the union. Mitchell, aware of the immense prestige that Roosevelt had conferred on the union by calling the conference, cooperated fully with the president.

Encouraged by this state of affairs, Roosevelt took a bold step: He announced that unless a settlement was reached promptly, he would order federal troops into the anthracite regions, not to break the strike but to seize and operate the mines. The threat of government intervention brought the owners to terms. The miners went back to the pits, and all issues between them and the coal companies were submitted for settlement to a commission appointed by Roosevelt. In March 1903 the commission granted the miners a 10 percent wage increase and a nine-hour day.

To the public the incident seemed a perfect illustration of the progressive spirit—in Roosevelt's words, everyone had received a "square deal." In fact, the results were by no means so clear-cut. The miners gained relatively little, and the companies lost still less; for they were not required to recognize the union. And when the commission recommended a 10 percent increase in the price of coal, the mining companies obtained ample compensation for their increased wage costs. The president was the main winner. The public acclaimed him as a fearless, imaginative, public-spirited leader. Construing the powers of his office broadly, he had interjected the federal government into a labor dispute, forced both sides to accept his leadership, and established an extralegal committee of neutrals representing the national interest to arbitrate the questions at issue.

TR: In His Own Right

By reviving the Sherman Act, settling the coal strike, and pushing moderate reforms through Congress, Roosevelt insured that he would be reelected president in 1904. Progressives were pleased by his performance if not yet captivated. Conservative Republicans offered no serious objection. Sensing that Roosevelt had won over the liberals, the Democrats nominated a conservative, Judge Alton B. Parker of

New York, and bid for the support of eastern industrialists. This strategy failed, for businessmen continued to eye the party of Bryan with intense suspicion. Roosevelt swept the country, piling up a majority of more than 2.5 million votes.

Encouraged by this landslide and by the increasing militancy of progressives, Roosevelt began to press for more reform legislation. The Elkins Railroad Act had proved a disappointment, for the courts continued to favor the railroads in most cases. Rebating remained a serious problem. With progressive state governors demanding federal action and with farmers and manufacturers, especially in the Middle West, clamoring for relief against discriminatory rates, Roosevelt was ready by 1905 to make railroad legislation his major objective. The ICC should be empowered to fix rates, not merely to challenge unreasonable ones. It should have the right to inspect the private records of the railroads, since fair rates could not be determined unless the true financial condition of the roads was known.

Because these proposals struck at rights that businessmen considered sacrosanct, many congressmen balked. But Roosevelt applied presidential pressure, and in June 1906 the Hepburn Bill became law. It gave the commission the power to inspect the books of railroad companies, to set maximum rates (once a complaint had been filed by a shipper), and to control sleeping-car companies, owners of oil pipelines, and other firms engaged in transportation. Railroads could no longer issue passes freely, an important check on their political influence.

The Hepburn Act made the ICC a more powerful and more active body. Although it did not outlaw judicial review of lCC decisions, thereafter those decisions were seldom overturned by the courts. The staff of the commission grew from fewer than 200 in 1905 to more than 500 in 1909. The number of complaints filed by shippers jumped from 65 to 1,097 in the same period.

Congress also passed meat inspection and pure food and drug legislation in 1906. The publication in that year of Upton Sinclair's novel *The Jungle,* a devastating exposé of the filthy conditions in the Chicago slaughterhouses, focused attention on the issue. Sinclair was more interested in writing a socialist tract than in meat inspection, but his book, a best-seller, raised a storm against

the packers. After Roosevelt read *The Jungle,* he sent two officials to Chicago to investigate. Their report was so shocking, he said, that its publication would "be well-nigh ruinous to our export trade in meat." He threatened to release the report, however, unless Congress acted. After a hot fight, the meat inspection bill passed. A Pure Food and Drug Act, forbidding the manufacture and sale of adulterated and fraudulently labeled products, rode through Congress on the coattails of this measure.

To liberals Roosevelt's achievements seemed limited when placed beside his professed objectives and his smug evaluations of what he had done. How could he be a reformer and a defender of established interests at the same time? Roosevelt found no difficulty in holding such a position. As one historian has said, "he stood close to the center and bared his teeth at the conservatives of the right and the liberals of the extreme left."

Tilting Left

As the progressive movement advanced, Roosevelt advanced with it. He never accepted all the ideas of what he called its "lunatic fringe," but he took steadily more liberal positions. He always insisted that he was not hostile to business interests, but when these interests sought to exploit the national domain, they had no more implacable foe.

Conservation of natural resources was probably Roosevelt's most significant achievement as president. He placed some 150 million acres of forest lands in federal reserves, and he strictly enforced the laws governing grazing, mining, and lumbering. In 1908 he organized a National Conservation Conference, attended by 44 governors and 500 other persons, to discuss conservation matters. As a result of this meeting, most of the states created conservation commissions.

As Roosevelt became more liberal, conservative Republicans began to balk at following his lead. The sudden panic that struck the financial world in October 1907 speeded the trend considerably. Government policies had no direct bearing on the panic, which began with a run on several important New York trust companies and spread to the Stock Exchange when speculators found themselves unable to borrow money to meet their obligations. In this emergency, Roosevelt authorized the deposit of large amounts of government cash in New York banks. He informally agreed to the acquisition of the Tennessee Coal and Iron Company by U.S. Steel when the bankers told him that the purchase was necessary to end the panic. In spite of his efforts, conservatives referred to the financial collapse as "Roosevelt's Panic" and blamed the president for the depression that followed on its heels.

Roosevelt, however, turned left rather than right. In 1908 he came out for federal income and inheritance taxes, for stricter regulation of interstate corporations, and for reforms designed to help industrial workers. He denounced "the speculative folly and the flagrant dishonesty" of "malefactors of great wealth," further alienating conservative, or Old Guard Republicans, who resented the attacks on their integrity implicit in many of Roosevelt's statements. When the president began criticizing the courts, the last bastion of conservatism, he lost all chance of obtaining further reform legislation.

William Howard Taft: The Listless Progressive

Roosevelt remained popular and politically powerful; before his term ended, he chose William Howard Taft, his secretary of war, to succeed him and easily obtained the nomination. William Jennings Bryan was again the Democratic candidate. Campaigning on Roosevelt's record, Taft carried the country by well over a million votes, defeating Bryan 321 to 162 in the electoral college.

Taft was intelligent, experienced, and public spirited; he seemed ideally suited to carry out Roosevelt's policies. He supported the "Square Deal" loyally. This, together with his mentor's ardent endorsement, won him the backing of most progressive Republicans. Yet the conservatives liked him too; although outgoing, he had none of Roosevelt's impetuosity and aggressiveness. His genial personality and his obvious desire to avoid conflict appealed to moderates.

However, Taft lacked the physical and mental stamina required of a modern chief executive. Although he was not really lazy, he weighed over 300 pounds and needed to rest this vast bulk more than the job allowed. Campaigning bored him, speechmaking seemed a needless chore, He was too reasonable to control a coalition and not ambitious enough to impose his will on others. He found extremists irritating and persistent people (such as his wife) difficult to resist. He supported many progressive measures, but he never absorbed the progressive spirit.

Taft honestly desired to carry out most of Roosevelt's policies. He enforced the Sherman Act vigorously and continued to expand the national forest reserves. He signed the Mann-Elkins Act of 1910 which empowered the Interstate Commerce Commission to suspend rate increases without waiting for a shipper to complain and established a Commerce Court to speed the settlement of railroad rate cases. An eight-hour day for all persons engaged in work on government contracts, mine-safety legislation, and several other reform measures received his approval. He even summoned Congress into special session specifically to reduce tariff duties—something Roosevelt had not dared to attempt.

But Taft had been disturbed by Roosevelt's sweeping use of executive power. Where Roosevelt had excelled at finding ways to accomplish his objectives without waiting for Congress to act, Taft adamantly refused to use such tactics. His restraint was in many ways admirable, but it reduced his effectiveness.

In case after case, Taft's lack of vigor and his political ineptness led to trouble. He had an uncanny ability to alienate politicians with views substantially like his own. In the matter of the tariff, he favored downward revision. When the special session met in 1909, the House promptly passed a bill that was roughly in line with his desires. But Senate protectionists restored the high rates of the Act of 1897 on most items. A group of "insurgent" senators fought these changes. They were fighting the president's battle, yet Taft did little to help them. He signed the final Payne-Aldrich measure and called it "the best [tariff] bill that the Republican party ever passed." He had some small justification for this faint praise, since the act did make important reductions in the duties on cotton goods, hides, shoes, and iron ore. But his attitude dumbfounded the progressives.

In 1910 Taft got into difficulty with the conservationists. The issue concerned the integrity of his secretary of the interior, Richard A. Ballinger. A less than ardent conservationist, Ballinger returned to the public domain certain waterpower sites that the Roosevelt administration had withdrawn. Ballinger's action alarmed Chief Forester Gifford Pinchot, the darling of the conservationists. When Pinchot learned that Ballinger intended to validate the shaky claim of powerful mining interests to a large tract of coal-rich land in Alaska, he launched an intemperate attack on the secretary.

In the Ballinger-Pinchot controversy, Taft felt obliged to support his own man. When Pinchot persisted in criticizing Ballinger, Taft dismissed him, bringing down on himself the wrath of the conservationists.

Breakup of the Republican Party

One ominous aspect of the Ballinger-Pinchot affair was that Pinchot was a close friend of Theodore Roosevelt. After Taft's inauguration, Roosevelt had gone off to hunt big game in Africa. When he emerged from the wilderness in March 1910, bearing more than 3,000 trophies, including 9 lions, 5 elephants, and 13 rhinos, he was caught up in the squabble between the progressive members of his party and its titular head. Roosevelt hoped to steer a middle course, but the progressives' complaints impressed him. No immediate break took place, but Taft sensed the former president's coolness and was offended by it.

Perhaps the resulting rupture was inevitable. The Republican Party was dividing into two factions, the progressives and the Old Guard. Forced to choose between them, Taft threw in his lot with the Old Guard. Roosevelt in turn backed the progressives. Speaking at Osawatomie, Kansas, in August 1910, he came out for a comprehensive program of social legislation. Besides attacking "special privilege" and the "unfair money-getting" practices of "lawbreakers of great wealth," he called for a broad expansion of federal power.

The final break came in October 1911, when the president ordered an antitrust suit against U.S. Steel. Roosevelt, of course, opposed breaking up large corporations. "The effort at prohibiting all combinations has substantially failed," he said. What angered Roosevelt, however, was Taft's emphasis in the steel suit on U.S. Steel's absorption of the Tennessee Coal and Iron Company, which Roosevelt had unofficially authorized during the panic of 1907. He began to criticize Taft publicly, and early in 1912 he declared himself a candidate for the Republican presidential nomination.

This dramatic split between the nation's two leading Republicans intensified the conflict within the party. In January 1911 the liberal faction had organized a National Progressive Republican League, which was pushing Senator La Follette for the Republican nomination. Roosevelt's entry into the race encouraged the progressives to strike more boldly against the administration.

Roosevelt plunged into the preconvention campaign with typical energy. He was almost uniformly victorious in the states that held presidential primaries, carrying even Ohio, Taft's home state. However, the president controlled the party machinery and at the national convention won easily on the first ballot.

If Roosevelt had swallowed his resentment and bided his time, Taft would almost certainly have been defeated in the election and the 1916 Republican nomination would have been Roosevelt's for the asking. But when his leading supporters urged him to organize a third party, he agreed to make the race. In August, amid scenes of hysterical enthusiasm, the first convention of the Progressive Party met at Chicago and nominated him for president. Announcing that he felt "as strong as a bull moose," Roosevelt delivered a stirring "confession of faith," calling for strict regulation of corporations, a tariff commission, national presidential primaries, minimum-wage and workmen's compensation laws, the elimination of child labor, and many other reforms.

The Election of 1912

The Democrats made the most of the Republican schism. They nominated Woodrow Wilson, who had achieved a remarkable liberal record as governor of New Jersey. Wilson called his program the New Freedom. The federal government could best advance the cause of social justice, he reasoned, by eradicating the special privileges that had enabled the "interests" to flourish. Where Roosevelt had lost faith in competition as a way of protecting the public against monopolies, Wilson insisted that competition could be restored. "If America is not to have free enterprise, then she can have freedom of no sort whatever," he said. Although rather vague, this argument appealed to thousands of voters who found the growing power of corporations disturbing, but who hesitated to make the thoroughgoing commitment to government control of business that Roosevelt was advocating.

Roosevelt's reasoning was perhaps theoretically more sound. He called for a New Nationalism. Laissez-faire made less sense than it had in earlier times. As Herbert Croly pointed out in *The Promise of American Life* (1909), the time had come to employ Hamiltonian means to achieve Jeffersonian ends.

Roosevelt dismissed Wilson's New Freedom as "rural toryism," but being less drastic and more in line with American experience than the New Nationalism, it had much to recommend it. The danger that selfish individuals would use the power of the state for their own ends had certainly not disappeared, despite the efforts of progressives to make government more responsive to popular opinion. Any considerable expansion of national power would increase the danger and probably create new difficulties. Managing so complicated an enterprise as an industrialized nation was sure to be a formidable task. Furthermore, individual freedom of opportunity merited the toleration of a certain amount of inefficiency.

To choose between the New Nationalism and the New Freedom, between the dynamic Roosevelt and the idealistic Wilson, was indeed difficult. Thousands grappled with this problem before going to the polls, but partisan politics determined the outcome of the election. Taft got the hard-core Republican vote and lost the progressive wing of the GOP to Roosevelt. Wilson had the solid support of both conservative and liberal Democrats. As a result, Wilson won an easy victory in the electoral college, receiving 435 votes to Roosevelt's 88 and Taft's 8. The popular vote was Wilson, 6,286,000; Roosevelt, 4,126,000; and Taft, 3,484,000. But if partisan politics had determined the winner, the election was nonetheless an overwhelming endorsement of progressivism. Wilson was a minority president, but he took office with a clear mandate to press forward with further reforms.

Wilson: The New Freedom

No man ever rose more suddenly and spectacularly in American politics than Woodrow Wilson. In the spring of 1910, he was president of Princeton University; in the fall of 1912, he was president-elect of the United States. Yet if his rise was meteoric, in a sense he had devoted his life to preparing for it. While still in college he dreamed of representing his state in the Senate. He studied law solely because he thought it the best avenue to public office, and when he discovered that he did not like legal work, he took a doctorate at Johns Hopkins in political science. He wrote several influential books, among them *Congressional Government* (1885) and *The State* (1889), and achieved an outstanding reputation as a teacher and lecturer. In 1902 he was chosen president of Princeton and soon won a place among the nation's leading educators.

Wilson was an immediate success as president. Since Roosevelt's last year, Congress had been almost continually at war with the executive branch and with itself. Legislative achievements had been few. Now a small avalanche of important measures received the approval of the lawmakers. In October 1913 came the Underwood Tariff, the first significant reduction of duties since before the Civil War. To compensate for the expected loss of revenue, the act provided for a graduated tax on personal incomes.

Two months later the Federal Reserve Act was passed, giving the country a central banking system for the first time since Jackson destroyed the Bank of the United States. The measure divided the nation into 12 banking districts, each under the supervision of a Federal Reserve Bank, a sort of bank for bankers. All national banks in each district and those state banks that wished to participate had to invest 6 percent of their capital and surplus in the Reserve Bank, which was empowered to exchange (the technical term is rediscount) paper money, called Federal Reserve notes, for the commercial and agricultural paper that member banks took in as security from borrowers. The volume of currency was no longer at the mercy of the supply of gold or any other particular commodity.

The crown and nerve center of the system was a Federal Reserve Board in Washington, which appointed a majority of the directors of the Federal Reserve Banks and had some control over rediscount rates (the commission charged by the Reserve Banks for performing the rediscounting function). The board exercised some public control over the banks, but the power of the great New York banks remained great. Nevertheless, a true central banking system was created. When inflation threatened, the Reserve Banks could raise the rediscount rate, discouraging borrowing and thus reducing the amount of money in circulation. In bad times it could lower the rate, making it easier to borrow and injecting new dollars into the economy. The nation finally had a flexible yet safe currency.

In 1914 Congress passed two important laws affecting corporations. One created a Federal Trade Commission (FTC) to replace Roosevelt's Bureau of Corporations. In addition to investigating corporations and publishing reports, this nonpartisan board could issue "cease and desist" orders against "unfair" trade practices brought to light through its researches. The law did not define "unfair," and the commission's rulings could be taken on appeal to the federal courts, but the FTC was nonetheless a powerful instrument for protecting the public against the trusts.

The second measure, the Clayton Antitrust Act, made certain specific business practices illegal, including price discrimination that tended to foster monopoly, "tying" agreements—which forbade retailers from handling the products of a firm's competitors—and the creation of interlocking directorates as a means of controlling competing companies. The act exempted labor unions and agricultural organizations from the antitrust laws, and curtailed the use of injunctions in labor disputes. Furthermore, the officers of corporations could be held individually responsible when their companies violated the antitrust laws.

Although Wilson was not in sympathy with all the terms of these laws, they reflected his desires and his imaginative and aggressive use of presidential power was decisive. He called the legislators into special session in April 1913 to lay out his program. He followed the course of administration bills closely. When lobbyists tried to frustrate his plans for tariff reform by bringing pressure to bear on key senators, he made a dramatic appeal to the people. "The public ought to know the ex-

traordinary exertions being made by the lobby in Washington," he told reporters. "Only public opinion can check and destroy it." The voters responded so strongly that the Senate passed the tariff bill substantially as Wilson desired it.

Despite his lack of political experience, Wilson proved to be a masterful politician and an inspiring leader. He explained his success by saying, only half humorously, that running the government was child's play for anyone who had managed the faculty of a university. Despite his career as a political theorist, he was not doctrinaire. In practice, the differences between his New Freedom and Roosevelt's New Nationalism tended to disappear. The Underwood Tariff and the Clayton Antitrust Act fitted the philosophy Wilson had expounded during the campaign, but the Federal Trade Commission represented a step toward the kind of regulated economy that Roosevelt advocated. So did the Federal Reserve system.

There were limits to Wilson's progressivism, limits imposed partly by his temperament and partly by his philosophy. He objected as strenuously to laws granting special favors to farmers and workers as to those benefiting the tycoons. When a bill was introduced in 1914 making low-interest loans available to farmers, he refused to support it. He considered the provision exempting unions from the antitrust laws equally unsound. Nor would he push for a federal law prohibiting child labor. He also refused to back the constitutional amendment giving the vote to women. Perhaps he thought it improper for women to mix in politics, but he argued publicly that it was wrong to deprive the states of their control of the suffrage.

By the end of 1914, the Wilsonian record, on balance, was positive but distinctly limited. The president believed that the major progressive goals had been achieved; he had no plans for further reform. Many other progressives thought that a great deal more remained to be done.

The Progressives and Minority Rights

On one important issue, race relations, Wilson was distinctly reactionary. With a handful of exceptions, the progressives exhibited strong prejudices against nonwhite people, and against certain categories of whites as well. Many were as unsympathetic to immigrants from Asia and eastern and southern Europe as any of the "conservative" opponents of immigration in the 1880s and 1890s. American Indians were also affected by the progressive's racial attitudes. Where sponsors of the Dawes Act had assumed that Indians were capable of adopting the ways of "civilized" people, progressives tended to write Indians off as fundamentally inferior, second-class citizens at best. Theodore Roosevelt knew from personal experience that some Indians were as energetic and capable as whites, but he considered these "exceptional" types. It would be many generations before most Indians could "move forward" enough to become "ordinary citizens," Roosevelt believed.

To say that blacks did not fare well at the hands of progressives would be a gross understatement. In the South, segregation became more rigid, white opposition to black voting more monolithic. Elsewhere, many progressive women, eager to attract southern support for their campaign for the vote, adopted racist arguments. They contrasted the supposed corruption and incompetence of black voters with their own "purity" and intelligence. Southern progressives of both sexes argued that disfranchising blacks would reduce corruption by removing from unscrupulous white politicians the temptation to purchase black votes!

The typical southern attitude toward the education of blacks was summed up in the folk proverb: "When you educate a Negro, you spoil a good field hand." In 1910, only about 8,000 black children in the entire South were attending high schools. In connection with the almost total suppression of black rights, lynchings continued to occur.

Booker T. Washington was shaken by this trend, but he could find no way to combat it. The times were passing him by. He appealed to his white southern "friends" for help but got nowhere. By the turn of the century a number of young, well-educated blacks, most of them northerners, were beginning to break away from his accommodationist leadership.

Black Militancy

William E. B. Du Bois was the most prominent of the militants. Du Bois was born in Great Barring-

Outside the windows of the NAACP headquarters in New York City, a banner announces that another lynching has taken place somewhere in the United States.

ton, Massachusetts in 1868. He showed such brilliance in school that his future education was assured by scholarships: to Fisk University, then to Harvard, then to the University of Berlin. In 1895 he became the first American black to earn a Ph.D. from Harvard; his dissertation, *The Suppression of the African Slave Trade* (1896), remains a standard reference.

Personal success and "acceptance" by whites did not make Du Bois complacent. Outraged by white racism and by the willingness of many blacks to settle for second-class citizenship, he set out to make American blacks proud of their color—"beauty is black," he said—and of their African origins and culture. American blacks must organize themselves, Du Bois argued. They must establish their own businesses, run their own newspapers and colleges, write their own literature; they must preserve their identity rather than seek to amalgamate themselves into a society that offered them only crumbs and contempt.

Du Bois rejected Washington's limited goals and his accommodating approach to white prejudices. Washington "apologizes for injustice," Du Bois charged. "He belittles the emasculating effects of caste distinctions, and opposes the higher training and ambitions of our brightest minds." This was totally wrong in Du Bois's opinion. "The way for a people to gain their reasonable rights is not by voluntarily throwing them away," he said.

Du Bois was not an uncritical admirer of the ordinary American black. He believed that "immorality, crime, and laziness" were common vices. Quite properly he blamed the weaknesses of blacks on the treatment afforded them by whites, but his approach to the solution of racial problems was frankly elitist. "The Negro race," he wrote, "is going to be saved by its exceptional men," what he called the "talented tenth" of the black population.

Du Bois exposed both the weaknesses of Washington's strategy and the callousness of white American attitudes. "Accommodation" was not working. Washington was praised, even lionized by prominent southern whites, yet when Theodore Roosevelt invited him to a meal at the White House they exploded with indignation, and

Roosevelt, though not personally prejudiced, meekly backtracked, never repeating his "mistake." He defended his record by saying, "I have stood as valiantly for the rights of the negro as any president since Lincoln." That, sad to relate, was true enough.

Not mere impatience but despair led Du Bois and a few like-minded blacks to meet at Niagara Falls in July 1905 and to issue a list of demands: the unrestricted right to vote; an end to every kind of segregation; equality of economic opportunity; higher education for the talented; equal justice in the courts; an end to trade union discrimination. This Niagara Movement did not attract mass support, but it did stir the consciences of some whites, many of them the descendants of abolitionists, who were also becoming disenchanted by the failure of accommodation to provide blacks with real opportunity.

Milestones

1890	Natinal American Women's Suffrage Association is founded
1900	Robert La Follette elected governor of Wisconsin
1901	President McKinley is assassinated
1902	National coal strike
	Oregon adopts initiative system for proposing legislation
1904	Northern Securities case revives the Sherman Antitrust Act
	The National Child Labor Committee is established
1905	Industrial Workers of the World (IWW) is founded
1906	Hepburn Act strengthens Interstate Commerce Commission
	Upton Sinclair, *The Jungle*
1907	U.S. Steel absorbs the Tennessee Coal and Iron Company
1908	Theodore Roosevelt convenes National Conservation Conference
	Muller v. *Oregon* upholds law limiting the hours of women
1909	Herbert Croly, *The Promise of American Life*
	NAACP is founded
1910	Ballinger-Pinchot affair
1911	Roosevelt's New Nationalism speech
1912	Roosevelt runs for president on the Progressive Party ticket
1913	Sixteenth Amendment authorizes federal income taxes
	Seventeenth Amendment provides for direct election of United States senators
	Underwood Tariff and Federal Reserve Act passed
1914	Federal Trade Commission and Clayton Antitrust acts passed
1920	Nineteenth Amendment guarantees women the right to vote

In 1909, the centennial of the birth of Abraham Lincoln, a group of these liberals founded the National Association for the Advancement of Colored People (NAACP). The organization was dedicated to the eradication of racial discrimination. Its leadership was predominantly white in the early years, but Du Bois became a national officer and the editor of its journal, *The Crisis.*

A great turning point had been reached: After 1909 virtually every important leader of the blacks, white and black alike, rejected the Washington approach. More and more, blacks turned to the study of their past in an effort to stimulate pride in their heritage. In 1915 Carter G. Woodson founded the Association for the Study of Negro Life and History; the following year he began editing the *Journal of Negro History,* which became the major organ for the publishing of scholarly studies of the subject.

This militancy produced few results in the Progressive Era. Theodore Roosevelt behaved no differently than earlier Republican presidents: He courted blacks when he thought it advantageous, turned his back when he did not. The southern-born Wilson was actively antipathetic to blacks. During the 1912 campaign he appealed to them for support and promised to "assist in advancing the interest of their race." Once elected, he refused even to appoint a privately financed commission to study the race problem.

Southerners dominated his administration and the Congress; as a result, blacks were still further degraded. In Washington, D.C., employees in many government offices were rigidly segregated, those who objected being summarily discharged. These actions roused such a storm that Wilson backtracked a little, but he never abandoned his belief that segregation was in the best interest of both races.

Du Bois, who had supported Wilson in 1912, attacked administration policy in *The Crisis.* In November 1914 the militant editor of the Boston *Guardian,* William Monroe Trotter, led a delegation to the White House to protest the segregation policy of the government. When Wilson accused him of blackmail, Trotter lost his temper and an ugly confrontation resulted. The mood of black leaders had changed completely.

By this time the Great War had broken out in Europe. Soon its effects would be felt by every American, by blacks perhaps more than by any other group. In November 1915, a year almost to the day after Trotter's clash with Wilson, Booker T. Washington died. One era had ended; a new one was beginning.

Supplementary Reading

The political history of the Progressive Era is surveyed in G. E. Mowry, **The Era of Theodore Roosevelt*** (1958). Other influential interpretations of progressivism include Richard Hofstadter's, **The Age of Reform*** (1955), which stresses the idea of the status revolution, and Gabriel Kolko's, **The Triumph of Conservatism*** (1963), which sees the period as dominated by the efforts of big business to attain its objectives with the aid of the government. See also J. M. Cooper, Jr., **The Warrior and the Priest: Theodore Roosevelt and Woodrow Wilson** (1983), and D. W. Grantham, **Southern Progressivism** (1983).

On muckraking, consult D. M. Chalmers, **The Social and Political Ideas of the Muckrakers** (1964). The radicals of the period are discussed in Leslie Fishbein, **Rebels in Bohemia** (1982), Thomas Bender, **New York Intellectuals** (1987), and N. G. Hale, **Freud and the Americans** (1971).

State and local progressivism are considered in R. S. Maxwell, **La Follette and the Rise of Progressivism in Wisconsin** (1956), Sheldon Hackney, **Populism to Progressivism in Alabama** (1969), G. B. Tindall, **The Emergence of the New South** (1967), and J. D. Buenker, **Urban Liberalism and Progressive Reform** (1973).

The movement for women's suffrage is described in A. S. Kraditor, **The Ideas of the Woman Suffrage Movement** (1981). Books treating other progressive reforms include A. F. Davis, **Spearheads for Reform: The Social Settlements and the Progressive Movement*** (1967), Melvin Dubofsky, **When Workers Organize** (1868), J. H. Timberlake, **Prohibition and the Progressive Movement*** (1963), James Weinstein, **The Corporate Ideal and the Liberal State** (1981), Ruth Rosen, **The Lost Sisterhood** (1982), and Albro Martin, **Enterprise Denied:**

Origins and Decline of American Railroads (1971). On blacks in this period, see E. M. Rudwick, **W. E. B. Du Bois*** (1960), J. R. Kirby, **Darkness at the Dawning** (1972), and August Meier, **Negro Thought in America: 1880–1915*** (1963). F. E. Hoxie, **A Final Promise** (1984), deals with the treatment of Indians.

W. H. Harbaugh, **Power and Responsibility: The Life and Times of Theodore Roo-**sevelt* (1961), is the soundest scholarly treatment of Roosevelt's career. On Taft, see D. F. Anderson, **William Howard Taft** (1973). The standard biography of Wilson, A. S. Link **Wilson** (1947–), is still incomplete; a good one-volume biography is August Heckscher, **Woodrow Wilson** (1991).

*Available in paperback.

CHAPTER 23

From Isolation to Empire

America's Divided View of the World
Origins of the Large Policy
The Course of Empire in the Pacific
The Course of Empire in Latin America
The Cuban Revolution
The "Splendid Little" Spanish-American War
Developing a Colonial Policy
The Anti-Imperialists
The Philippine Insurrection
Cuba and the United States
The United States in the Caribbean
The Open Door Policy
The Isthmian Canal
"Noncolonial Imperial Expansion"

*A*mericans have always been somewhat ambivalent in their attitudes toward other nations. At no time was this more clearly the case than in the decades following the Civil War. Occupied with the task of exploiting the West and building their great industrial machine, they gave little thought to foreign affairs.

America's Divided View of the World

Late-19th-century Americans never ignored world affairs entirely. They had little direct concern for what went on in Europe, but their interest in Latin America was great and growing, in the Far East only somewhat less so. Economic developments, especially certain shifts in foreign commerce resulting from industrialization, were strengthening this interest with every passing year.

The disdain of the people of the United States for Europe was based on faith in the unique character of American civilization—and the converse of that belief, suspicion of Europe's supposedly aristocratic and decadent society. When occasional conflicts with one or another of the Great Powers erupted, the United States pressed its claims hard. It insisted, for example, that Great Britain pay for the loss of some 100,000 tons of American shipping sunk by Confederate cruisers that had been built in British yards during the rebellion. In 1871 the two nations signed the Treaty of Washington, agreeing to arbitrate these so-called *Alabama* claims. The next year the judges awarded the United States $15.5 million for the ships and cargoes that had been destroyed.

In the 1880s a squabble developed with Germany, France, and a number of other countries over their banning of American pork products, ostensibly because some uninspected American pork was discovered to be diseased. The affair produced a great deal of windy oratory denouncing European autocracy and led to threats of economic retaliation. Congress eventually provided for the inspection of meat destined for export, and in 1891 the European nations lifted the ban. Similarly, there were repeated alarms and outbursts of anti-British feeling in the United States in connection with Great Britain's treatment of Ireland—all motivated chiefly by the desire of politicians to appeal to Irish American voters. None of the incidents amounted to much.

Origins of the Large Policy

The nation's interests elsewhere in the world gradually increased. During the Civil War France had established a protectorate over Mexico, installing the Archduke Maximilian of Austria as emperor. In 1866 Secretary of State William H. Seward demanded that the French withdraw, and the government moved 50,000 soldiers to the Rio Grande. Although fear of American intervention was only one of many reasons for their action, the French did pull their troops out of Mexico during the winter of 1866–1867. In 1867, at the instigation of Seward, the United States purchased Alaska from Russia for $7.2 million, thereby ridding the continent of another foreign power.

In 1867 the aggressive Seward acquired the Midway Islands in the western Pacific, which had been discovered in 1859 by an American naval officer, N. C. Brooks. Seward also made overtures toward annexing the Hawaiian Islands and he looked longingly at Cuba. But the nation was unready for such grandiose schemes; Seward had to admit that there was no significant support in the country for his expansionist plans.

The internal growth that preoccupied Americans eventually led them to look outward. In the late 1880s, the country was exporting a steadily increasing share of its agricultural and industrial output. The character of foreign trade was also changing: Manufactures loomed ever more important among exports until in 1898 the country shipped abroad more manufactured goods than it imported. When American industrialists became conscious of their ability to compete with Europeans in far-off markets, they took more interest in world affairs, particularly during periods of depression, when domestic consumption fell.

The shifting intellectual currents of the times further altered the attitudes of Americans. Darwin's theories, applicable by analogy to international relations, gave the concept of manifest destiny a new plausibility. Darwinists like the historian John Fiske argued that the American democratic system of government was so clearly the world's "fittest" that it was destined to spread peacefully over "every land on the earth's surface." In *Our Country* (1885), Josiah Strong found racist and religious justifications for American expansionism, again based on the theory of evolution.

The completion of the conquest of the American West encouraged Americans to consider expansion beyond the seas. "For nearly 300 years the dominant fact in American life has been expansion," declared Frederick Jackson Turner, propounder of the frontier thesis. "That these energies of expansion will no longer operate would be a rash prediction."

Finally, military and strategic arguments were advanced to justify adopting a "large" policy. Although no foreign power menaced the country, top army commanders became much concerned with developing and maintaining a professional officer corps, and the decrepit state of the navy vexed many of its officers. Captain Alfred Thayer Mahan developed a startling theory about the importance of sea power, which he explained to the public in *The Influence of Sea Power upon History* (1890) and *The Influence of Sea Power upon the French Revolution and Empire* (1892). History proved, according to Mahan, that a nation with a powerful navy and the overseas bases necessary to maintain it would be invulnerable in war and prosperous in time of peace.

Applied to the current American situation, this meant that in addition to building a modern fleet, the United States should obtain a string of coaling stations and bases in the Caribbean, annex the Hawaiian Islands, and cut a canal across Central America. Writing at a time when the imperialist-minded European nations were showing signs of extending their influence in South America and the Pacific islands, Mahan attracted many influential disciples who helped persuade Congress to increase naval appropriations.

The Course of Empire in the Pacific

The interest of the United States in the Pacific and the Far East began in the late 18th century, when the first American merchant ship dropped anchor in Canton harbor. The Hawaiian Islands were an important way station on the route to China, and by 1820 merchants and missionaries were making contacts there. As early as 1854, a movement to annex the islands existed, though this foundered because Hawaii insisted on being admitted to the Union as a state. Commodore Perry's expedition to Japan led to the signing of a commercial treaty (1858) that opened several Japanese ports to American traders.

The United States pursued a policy of cooperating with the European powers in expanding commercial opportunities in the Far East. This policy did not change radically after the Civil War. Despite Chinese protests over the exclusion of their nationals from the United States after 1882, American commercial privileges in China were not disturbed. American influence in Hawaii increased; the descendants of missionary families, most of them engaged in raising sugar, dominated the Hawaiian monarchy. Although they made no overt effort to make the islands an American colony, all the expansionist ideas of the era—manifest destiny, Darwinism, Josiah Strong's racist and religious assumptions, and the relentless force of American commercial interests—pointed them in that direction. In 1875 a reciprocity treaty admitted Hawaiian sugar to the United States free of duty in return for a promise to yield no territory to a foreign power. When this treaty was renewed in 1887, the United States obtained the right to establish a naval base at Pearl Harbor. In addition to occupying Midway, America obtained a foothold in the Samoan Islands in the South Pacific.

During the 1890s American interest in the Pacific area steadily intensified. Conditions in Hawaii had much to do with this. The McKinley Tariff Act of 1890, discontinuing the duty on raw sugar and compensating American producers of cane and beet sugar by granting them a bounty of two cents a pound, struck Hawaiian sugar growers hard, for it destroyed the advantage they had gained in the reciprocity treaty. The following year the death of the complaisant King Kalakaua brought Queen Liliuokalani, a determined nationalist, to the throne. Placing herself at the head of a "Hawaii for the Hawaiians" movement, she abolished the existing constitution under which the white minority had pretty much controlled the islands and attempted to rule as an absolute monarch.

The resident Americans then staged a coup. In January 1893, with the connivance of the United States minister, John L. Stevens, who ordered 150 marines from the cruiser *Boston* into Honolulu, they deposed Queen Liliuokalani and set up a provisional government. Stevens recognized their regime at once, and the new government promptly sent a delegation to Washington to seek a treaty of annexation.

In the closing days of the Harrison administration such a treaty was negotiated and sent to the Senate, but when Cleveland took office in March, he withdrew it, dismissed Stevens, and attempted to restore Queen Liliuokalani. Since the provisional government was by that time firmly entrenched, this could not be accomplished peacefully, and Cleveland was unwilling to use force against the Americans in the islands, however much he objected to their actions. The revolutionary government of Hawaii remained in power, independent yet eager to be annexed.

The Hawaiian debate continued sporadically over the next four years. It provided a thorough airing of the question of overseas expansion. Fears that another power—Great Britain or perhaps Japan—might step into the void created by Cleveland's refusal to act alarmed those who favored annexation. When the Republicans returned to power in 1897, a new annexation treaty was negotiated, but domestic sugar producers now threw their weight against it, and the McKinley administration could not obtain the necessary two-thirds majority in the Senate. Finally, in July 1898, after the outbreak of the Spanish-American War, Congress annexed the islands by joint resolution, a procedure requiring only a simple majority vote.

The Course of Empire in Latin America

Most of the arguments for extending American influence in the Pacific applied more strongly to Central and South America, where the United States had much larger economic interests and where the strategic importance of the region was clear. Furthermore, the Monroe Doctrine had long conditioned the American people to the idea of acting to protect national interests in the Western Hemisphere.

As early as 1869, president Grant had come out for an American-owned canal across the Isthmus of Panama, in spite of the fact that the United States had agreed in the Clayton-Bulwer Treaty with Great Britain (1850) that neither nation would "obtain or maintain for itself any exclusive control" over an interoceanic canal. In 1880, when the French engineer Ferdinand de Lesseps organized a company to build a canal across the isthmus, President Hayes announced that the United States would not permit a European power to control such a waterway. "The policy of the country is a canal under American control," he announced, another blithe disregard of the Clayton-Bulwer agreement.

Aside from minor incidents, no trouble developed in Latin America until 1895. Then, quite suddenly, the United States found itself on the verge of war as a result of a crisis in Venezuela. Before this issue was settled, Cleveland had proclaimed the most powerful statement of American hegemony in the hemisphere ever uttered.

The tangled borderland between Venezuela and British Guiana had long been in dispute, Venezuela demanding more of the region than it was entitled to and Great Britain submitting exaggerated claims and imperiously refusing to submit the question to arbitration. What made a crisis of the controversy was the political situation in the United States. With his party rapidly deserting him because of his stand on the silver question, and with the election of 1896 approaching, the president desperately needed a popular issue.

There was considerable latent anti-British feeling in the United States. By taking the Venezuelan side in the boundary dispute, Cleveland would be defending a weak neighbor against a great power, a position certain to evoke a popular response.

Cleveland did not resist the temptation to intervene. In July 1895 he ordered Secretary of State Richard Olney to send a near-ultimatum to the British. By occupying the disputed territory, Olney insisted, Great Britain was invading Venezuela and violating the Monroe Doctrine. Quite gratuitously, he went on to boast: "To-day the United States is practically sovereign on this continent, and its fiat is law upon the subjects to which it confines its interposition." Unless Great Britain responded promptly by agreeing to arbitration, the president would call the question to the attention of Congress.

The note threatened war, but the British ignored it for months. They did not take the United States seriously as a world power. When Lord Salisbury, the prime minister and foreign secretary, finally replied, he rejected outright the argument that the Monroe Doctrine had any status under international law and refused to arbitrate what he called the "exaggerated pretentions" of the Venezuelans.

If Olney's note had been belligerent, this reply was supercilious and sharp to the point of asperity. Cleveland was furious. On December 17, 1895, he asked Congress for authority to appoint an American commission to determine the correct line between British Guiana and Venezuela. When that had been done, he added, the United States should "resist by every means in its power" the appropriation by Great Britain of any territory "we have determined of right belongs to Venezuela." Congress responded at once, and unanimously, appropriating $100,000 for the boundary commission. Popular approval was almost universal.

In Great Britain government and people suddenly awoke to the seriousness of the situation. No one wanted a war with the United States over a remote patch of tropical real estate. Canada would be terribly vulnerable to American attack. The immense potential strength of the United States could no longer be ignored. Why make an enemy of a nation of 70 million, already the richest industrial power in the world? To fight with the United States, the British now realized, "would be an absurdity as well as a crime."

Great Britain agreed to arbitrate the boundary. The war scare subsided. When the arbitrators awarded nearly all the disputed region to Great Britain, whatever ill feeling the surrender may have occasioned in that country faded away. Instead of leading to war, the affair marked the beginning of an era of Anglo-American friendship. It had the unfortunate effect, however, of adding to the long-held American conviction that the nation could get what it wanted in international affairs by threat and bluster—a dangerous illusion.

The Cuban Revolution

On February 10, 1896, scarcely a week after Venezuela and Great Britain signed the treaty ending their dispute, General Valeriano Weyler arrived in Havana from Spain to take up his duties as governor of Cuba. His assignment to this post was occasioned by the guerrilla warfare that Cuban nationalist rebels had been waging for almost a year. Weyler began herding the rural population into wretched "reconcentration" camps in order to deprive the rebels of food and recruits. Resistance in Cuba hardened.

Public sympathy went to the Cubans, who seemed to be fighting for liberty and democracy against an autocratic Old World power. Most American newspapers supported the rebels; labor unions, veterans' organizations, many Protestant clergymen, a great majority of American blacks, and important politicians in both major parties demanded that the United States aid their cause. Rapidly increasing American investments in

Cuban sugar plantations, now approaching $50 million, were endangered by the fighting and by the social chaos sweeping across the island. Cuban propagandists in the United States played on American sentiments cleverly. When reports, often exaggerated, of the cruelty of "Butcher" Weyler and the horrors of his reconcentration camps began to filter into America, the cry for action intensified.

In April 1896 Congress adopted a resolution suggesting that the revolutionaries be granted the rights of belligerents. Since it would have been akin to formal recognition, Cleveland would not go that far, but he did exert diplomatic pressure on Spain to remove the causes of the rebels' complaints, and he offered the services of his government as mediator. The Spanish rejected the suggestion.

For a time the issue subsided. The election of 1896 deflected American attention from Cuba, and then McKinley refused to take any action that might disturb Spanish-American relations. Business interests—except those with holdings in Cuba—backed McKinley because they were afraid that a crisis would upset the economy, which was just beginning to pick up after the depression. In Cuba General Weyler made some progress toward stifling rebel resistance.

American expansionists, however, continued to demand intervention, and the press, especially Joseph Pulitzer's New York *World* and William Randolph Hearst's New York *Journal,* competing fiercely to increase circulation, kept resentment alive with tales of Spanish atrocities. McKinley remained adamant. In a message to Congress in December 1897, he urged that Spain be given "a reasonable chance to realize her expectations" in the island.

Spain, however, failed to "realize her expectations." The fighting in Cuba continued. When riots broke out in Havana in January 1898, McKinley ordered the battleship *Maine* to Havana harbor to protect American citizens. Shortly thereafter Hearst's *Journal* printed a letter written to a

Instability in Latin America led to speculation that the United States would play an increasingly dominant role in the region. In Louis Dalrymple's 1895 cartoon, Uncle Sam wins the affections of the damsel Cuba as Spanish misrule and native insurgency lay waste to each other.

friend in Cuba by the Spanish minister in Washington, Depuy de Lôme. The letter had been stolen by a spy. De Lôme, an experienced but arrogant diplomat, failed to appreciate McKinley's efforts to avoid intervening in Cuba. In the letter he characterized the president as a *politicastro,* or "small-time politician," which was a gross error, and a "bidder for the admiration of the crowd," which was equally insulting, though somewhat closer to the truth. Americans were outraged, and De Lôme's hasty resignation did little to soothe their feelings.

Then, on February 15, USS *Maine* exploded and sank in Havana harbor, 260 of her crew perishing in the disaster. Interventionists in the United States accused Spain of having destroyed the ship and clamored for war. The willingness of Americans to blame Spain indicates the extent of anti-Spanish opinion in the United States by 1898. No one has ever discovered what actually happened. A naval court of inquiry decided that the vessel had indeed been sunk by a submarine mine, but it now seems more likely that an internal explosion destroyed the *Maine.* The Spanish government could hardly have been so foolish as to commit an act so likely to bring American troops into Cuba.

With admirable courage, McKinley refused to panic; but he could not resist the wishes of millions of citizens that something be done to stop the fighting and allow the Cubans to determine their own fate. The president faced a dilemma. Most of the business interests of the country, to which he was particularly sensitive, opposed intervention. His personal feelings were equally firm. "I have been through one war," he told a friend. "I have seen the dead piled up, and I do not want to see another." Congress, however, seemed determined to act, and should Congress declare war on its own, the administration would be discredited. In April the president drafted a message asking for authority to use the armed forces "to secure a full and final termination of hostilities" in Cuba.

The "Splendid Little" Spanish-American War

On April 20 Congress, by joint resolution, recognized the independence of Cuba and authorized the use of the armed forces to drive out the Spanish. An amendment proposed by Senator Henry

M. Teller disclaiming any intention of adding Cuban territory to the United States passed without opposition. Four days later Spain declared war on the United States.

The Spanish-American War was fought to free Cuba, but the first action took place on the other side of the globe, in the Philippine Islands. Weeks earlier, Assistant Secretary of the Navy Theodore Roosevelt had alerted Commodore George Dewey, who was in command of the United States Asiatic Squadron located at Hong Kong, to move against the Spanish base at Manila if war came. When word of the declaration of war reached Dewey, he steamed from Hong Kong across the South China Sea with four cruisers and two gunboats. On the night of April 30, he entered Manila Bay, and at daybreak his warships opened fire on the Spanish fleet at 5,000 yards. All ten of Admiral Montojo's ships were destroyed. Not a single American was killed in the engagement.

The American people received the news of Dewey's victory joyfully, although many had never heard of the Philippines before the bold headlines announced his triumph. McKinley took the fateful step of dispatching some 11,000 soldiers and additional naval support. On August 13 these forces, assisted by Filipino irregulars under the nationalist leader Emilio Aguinaldo, captured Manila.

Meanwhile, in the main theater of operations, the United States had won a swift and total victory. Since a Spanish fleet under Admiral Pascual Cervera was known to be in Caribbean waters, no invading army could safely embark until the fleet could be located. On May 29, American ships found Cervera at Santiago harbor, on the eastern end of Cuba, and established a blockade. In June a 17,000-man expeditionary force commanded by General William Shafter landed at Daiquiri, east of Santiago, and pressed quickly toward the city, handicapped more by its own poor staff work than by the enemy, though the Spanish troops resisted bravely. On July 1 they broke through undermanned Spanish defenses and stormed San Juan Hill; the intrepid Theodore Roosevelt, who had resigned as assistant secretary of the navy to raise the "Rough Riders" regiment, in the vanguard.

With Santiago harbor in range of American artillery, Admiral Cervera had to run the blockade. On July 3 his black-hulled ships, flags proudly flying, steamed forth from the harbor and fled westward along the coast. Like hounds after rabbits, five American battleships and two cruisers, commanded by Rear Admiral William T. Sampson and Commodore Winfield Scott Schley, ran them down. In four hours the entire Spanish force was destroyed by a hail of eight-inch and thirteen-inch projectiles. Damage to the American ships was superficial; only one seaman lost his life in the engagement.

The end then came abruptly. Santiago surrendered on July 17. A few days later, other United States troops completed the occupation of Puerto Rico. On August 12, one day before the fall of Manila, Spain agreed to get out of Cuba and to cede Puerto Rico and an island in the Marianas (Guam) to the United States. The future of the Philippines was to be settled at a formal peace conference, convening in Paris on October 1.

Developing a Colonial Policy

Although the Spanish resisted surrendering the Philippines at Paris, they had been so thoroughly defeated that they had no choice. The decision hung rather on the outcome of a conflict over policy within the United States. The war, won at so little cost militarily, produced problems far larger than those it solved. The nation had become a great power in the world's eyes. European leaders had been impressed by the forcefulness of Cleveland's diplomacy in the Venezuela boundary dispute and by the efficiency displayed by the navy in the war. The annexation of Hawaii and other overseas bases intensified their conviction that the United States was determined to become a major force in international affairs.

But were the American people going to exercise that force? The debate over taking the Philippine Islands throws much light on their attitudes. The imagination of Americans had been captured by the trappings of empire, not by its essence. It was titillating to think of a world map liberally sprinkled with American flags and of the economic benefits that colonies might bring, but most citizens were not prepared to join in a worldwide struggle for power and influence. They entered blithely on adventures in far-off regions without facing the implications of their decision.

Since Congress (in the Teller Amendment) had foresworn any claim to Cuba, logic dictated that a similar policy be applied to the Philippines.

But now expansionists were eager to annex the entire archipelago. President McKinley adopted a more cautious stance, but he too favored "the general principle of holding on to what we can get." A speaking tour of the Middle West in October 1898, during which he experimented with varying degrees of commitment to expansionism, convinced him that the public wanted the islands. Business opinion had shifted dramatically during the war. Business leaders were now calling the Philippines the gateway to the markets of the Far East.

The Anti-Imperialists

An important minority objected strongly to the United States' acquiring overseas possessions. These anti-imperialists insisted that since no one would even consider the possibility of future statehood for the Philippines, it would be unconstitutional to annex them. It was a violation of the spirit of the Declaration of Independence to govern a foreign territory without the consent of its inhabitants. Senator Hoar of Massachusetts argued: by taking over "vassal states" in "barbarous archipelagoes" the United States was "trampling . . . on our own great Charter, which recognizes alike the liberty and the dignity of individual manhood."

McKinley was sensitive to this appeal to idealism and tradition, which was the heart of the anti-imperialist argument, but he rejected it for several reasons. Many people who opposed Philippine annexation were neither idealists nor constitutional purists. Partisanship led numbers of Democrats to object. Other anti-imperialists were governed by racial and ethnic prejudices, as Senator Hoar's statement indicates. They opposed not expansion as such but expansion that brought under the American flag people whom they believed unfit for American citizenship. Labor leaders particularly feared the competition of "the Chinese, the Negritos, and the Malays" who presumably would flood into the United States if the Philippines were taken over.

More compelling to McKinley was the absence of any practical alternative to annexation. Public opinion would not sanction restoring Spanish authority in the Philippines or allowing some other power to have them. That the Filipinos were sufficiently advanced and united socially to form a stable government if granted independence seemed unlikely. Senator Hoar believed that "for years and for generations, and perhaps for centuries, there would have been turbulence, disorder and revolution" in the islands if they were left to their own devices.

Strangely—for he was a kind and gentle man—Hoar faced this possibility with equanimity. McKinley was unable to do so. The president searched the depths of his soul and could find no solution but annexation. Of course, the state of public feeling made the decision easier. And he probably found the idea of presiding over an empire appealing. Certainly the commercial possibilities did not escape him. In the end it was with a heavy sense of responsibility that he ordered the American peace commissioners to insist on acquiring the Philippines. To salve the feelings of the Spanish, the United States agreed to pay $20 million for the archipelago, but it was a forced sale, accepted by Spain under duress.

The peace treaty faced a hard battle in the United States Senate, where a combination of partisan politics and anticolonialism made it difficult to amass the two-thirds majority necessary for ratification. McKinley had shrewdly appointed three senators, including one Democrat, to the peace commission. This predisposed many members of the upper house to approve the treaty, but the vote was close. William Jennings Bryan, titular head of the Democratic Party, could probably have prevented ratification. Although he was personally opposed to taking the Philippines, he did not do so. To reject the treaty would leave the United States technically at war with Spain and the fate of the Philippines undetermined; better to accept the islands and then grant them independence. The question should be decided, Bryan said, in the forthcoming presidential election. Perplexed by Bryan's stand, a number of Democrats allowed themselves to be persuaded by the expansionists' arguments and by McKinley's judicious use of patronage; the treaty was ratified in February 1899 by a vote of 57 to 27.

The Philippine Insurrection

The national referendum that Bryan had hoped for never materialized. Bryan himself confused the issue in 1900 by making free silver a major plank in his platform, thereby driving conservative anti-imperialists into McKinley's arms. Moreover, early in 1899, the Filipino nationalists under Aguinaldo, furious because the United States would not withdraw, took up arms. A savage guerrilla war resulted, one that cost far more in lives and money than the Spanish-American conflict.

Like in all such conflicts waged in tangled country chiefly by small, isolated units surrounded by a hostile civilian population, neither side displayed much regard for the "rules" of war. Horrifying tales of rape, arson, and murder by United States troops began to filter into the country, providing ammunition for the anti-imperialists. A commission that had been sent to the Philippines by McKinley in 1899 attributed the insurrection to the ambitions of the nationalist leaders and recommended that the Philippines be granted independence at some indefinite future date. In 1900 McKinley sent a federal judge, William Howard Taft, to establish a government. Taft's policy of encouraging Filipinos to participate in a territorial government attracted many converts.

Actually, the reelection of McKinley in 1900 settled the Philippine question, so far as most Americans were concerned. Anti-imperialists still claimed that it was unconstitutional to take over territories without the consent of the local population. Their reasoning, although certainly not specious, was unhistorical. No American government had seriously considered the wishes of the American Indians, the French and Spanish settlers in Louisiana, the Inuit Indians of Alaska, or the people of Hawaii when it had seemed in the national interest to annex new lands.

Cuba and the United States

Nevertheless, grave constitutional questions arose as a result of the acquisitions that followed the Spanish-American War. McKinley had acted with remarkable independence in handling the problems involved in expansion. He set up military governments, for example, in Cuba, Puerto Rico, and the Philippines without specific congressional authority. But eventually both Congress and the Supreme Court took a hand in shaping colonial policy. In 1900 Congress passed the Foraker Act, establishing a civil government for Puerto Rico. It did not give the Puerto Ricans either American citizenship or full local self-government, and it placed tariffs on Puerto Rican products imported into the United States.

The tariff provision was promptly challenged in the courts on the ground that Puerto Rico was part of the United States, but in *Downes* v. *Bidwell* (1901) the Supreme Court upheld the legality of the duties. In this and other "insular cases" the reasoning of the judges was more than ordinarily difficult to follow. The effect, however, was clear: the Constitution did not follow the flag; Congress could act toward the colonies almost as it pleased. A colony, as one dissenting justice put it, could be kept "like a disembodied shade, in an indeterminate state of ambiguous existence for an indefinite period."

While the most heated arguments raged over Philippine policy, the most difficult colonial problems concerned the relationship between the United States and Cuba, for there idealism and self-interest clashed painfully. Despite the desire of most Americans to free Cuba, an independent government could not easily be created. The insurgent government was feeble, corrupt, and oligarchic, the Cuban economy in a state of collapse, life chaotic. The first Americans entering Havana found the streets littered with garbage and the corpses of horses and dogs. All public services were at a standstill; it seemed essential for the United States, as McKinley said, to give "aid and direction" until "tranquillity" could be restored.

As soon as American troops landed in Cuba, trouble broke out between them and the populace. Most American soldiers viewed the ragged, half-starved insurgents as "thieving dagoes" and displayed an unfortunate race prejudice against their dark-skinned allies. General Shafter did not help matters. He believed the Cubans "no more fit for self-government than gun-powder is for hell," and he used the insurgents chiefly as labor troops. After the fall of Santiago, he refused to let rebel leaders participate in the formal surrender of the city. This infuriated the proud and idealistic Cuban commander, General Calixto García.

When McKinley established a military government for Cuba late in 1898, it was soon embroiled with local leaders. Then an eager horde of American promoters descended on Cuba in search of profitable franchises and concessions.

The problems were indeed knotty, for no strong local leader capable of uniting Cuba appeared. European observers expected that the United States would eventually annex Cuba, and many Americans, including General Leonard Wood, who became military governor in December 1899, considered this the best solution. The desperate state of the people, the heavy economic stake of Americans in the region, and its strategic importance militated against withdrawal.

In the end the United States did withdraw, after doing a great deal to modernize sugar production, improve sanitary conditions, establish schools, and restore orderly administration. In November 1900 a Cuban constitutional convention met at Havana and proceeded without substantial American interference or direction to draft a frame of government. The chief restrictions imposed on Cuba's freedom concerned foreign relations; it authorized American intervention whenever necessary "for the preservation of Cuban independence" and "the maintenance of a government adequate for the protection of life, property, and individual liberty." Cuba had to grant naval bases on its soil to the United States.

This arrangement, known as the Platt Amendment, was accepted, after some grumbling, by the Cubans. It also had the support of most American opponents of imperialism. In May 1902 the United States turned over the reins of government to the new republic. The next year the two countries signed a reciprocity treaty tightening the economic bonds between them.

True friendship did not result. Although American troops occupied Cuba only once more, in 1906, and then at the specific request of Cuban authorities, the United States repeatedly used the threat of intervention to coerce the Cuban government. American economic penetration proceeded rapidly and without regard for the well-being of the Cuban peasants, many of whom lived in a state of peonage on great sugar plantations. Nor did their good intentions make up for the tendency of Americans to consider themselves innately superior to the Cubans and to overlook the fact that Cubans did not always wish to adopt American customs and culture.

The United States in the Caribbean

If the purpose of the Spanish-American War had been to bring peace and order to Cuba, the Platt Amendment was a logical step. The same purpose soon necessitated a further extension of the principle, for once the United States accepted the role of protector and stabilizer in part of the Caribbean, it seemed desirable, for the same economic, strategic, and humanitarian reasons, to supervise the entire region.

The Caribbean countries were economically underdeveloped, socially backward, politically unstable, and desperately poor. Everywhere a few families owned most of the land and dominated social and political life. The mass of the people were uneducated peasants, many of them little better off than slaves. Rival cliques of wealthy families struggled for power, force being the usual method of effecting a change in government. Most of the meager income of the average Caribbean state was swallowed up by the military or diverted into the pockets of the current rulers.

Cynicism and fraud poisoned the relations of most of these nations with the Great Powers. European merchants and bankers systematically cheated their Latin American customers, who in turn frequently refused to honor their obligations. Foreign bankers floated Caribbean bond issues on outrageous terms, while revolutionary Caribbean governments annulled concessions and repudiated debts with equal disdain for honest business dealing. Because these countries were weak, the European powers tended to intervene whenever their nationals were cheated or when chaotic conditions endangered the lives and property of foreigners. This roused the concern of the United States government.

In 1902, shortly after the United States had pulled out of Cuba, trouble erupted in Venezuela, where a dictator, Cipriano Castro, was refusing to honor debts owed the citizens of European nations. To force him to pay up, Germany and Great Britain established a blockade of Venezuelan ports and destroyed a number of Venezuelan gunboats and harbor defenses. Under American pressure the Europeans agreed to arbitrate the dispute. For the first time, European powers had accepted the broad implications of the Monroe Doctrine.

By this time Theodore Roosevelt had become president of the United States, and he quickly capitalized on the new European attitude. In 1903 the Dominican Republic defaulted on bonds totaling some $40 million. When European investors urged their governments to intervene, Roosevelt announced that under the Monroe Doctrine the United States could not permit foreign nations to intervene in Latin America. But, he added, Latin American nations should not be allowed to escape their obligations.

The president therefore arranged for the United States to take charge of the Dominican customs service—the one reliable source of revenue in that poverty-stricken country. Fifty-five percent of the customs duties would be devoted to debt payment, the remainder turned over to the Dominican government to care for its internal needs. Roosevelt defined his policy, known as the Roosevelt Corollary to the Monroe Doctrine, in a message to Congress in December 1904. "Chronic wrongdoing" in Latin America, he stated with his typical disregard for the subtleties of complex affairs, might require outside intervention. Since, under the Monroe Doctrine, no other nation could step in, the United States must "exercise . . . an international police power."

In the short run, this policy worked admirably. Dominican customs were honestly collected for the first time and the country's finances put in order. The presence of American warships in the area provided a needed measure of political stability. In the long run, however, the Roosevelt Corollary caused resentment in Latin America, for it added to nationalist fears that the United States wished to exploit the region for its own benefit.

The Open Door Policy

The insular cases, the Platt Amendment, and the Roosevelt Corollary established the framework for American policy both in Latin America and in the Far East. Coincidental with the Cuban rebellion of the nineties, a far greater upheaval had convulsed the ancient empire of China. In 1894–1895 Japan had easily defeated China in a war over Ko-

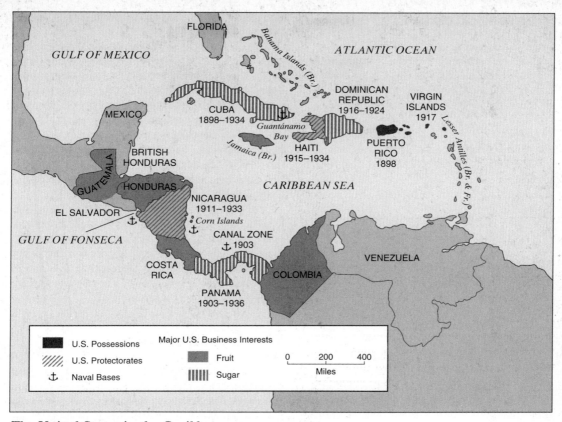

The United States in the Caribbean

rea. Alarmed by Japan's aggressiveness, the European powers hastened to carve out for themselves new spheres of influence along China's coast. After the annexation of the Philippines, McKinley's secretary of state, John Hay, urged on by businessmen fearful of losing out in the scramble to exploit the Chinese market, tried to prevent the further absorption of China by the Great Powers. For the United States to join in the dismemberment of China was politically impossible because of anti-imperialist feeling, so Hay sought to protect American interests by clever diplomacy. In "Open Door" notes to the Powers in 1899, he asked them to agree to respect the trading rights of all countries and to impose no discriminatory duties within their spheres of influence.

The replies to the Open Door notes were at best noncommittal, yet Hay blandly announced in March 1900 that the powers had "accepted" his suggestions! Thus he could claim to have pre-

vented the breakup of the empire and protected the right of Americans to do business freely in its territories. In reality nothing had been accomplished; the imperialist nations did not extend their political control of China only because they feared that by doing so they might precipitate a major war among themselves. Nevertheless, Hay's action marked a bold advance into the complicated and dangerous world of international power politics.

Within a few months of Hay's announcement, the Open Door policy was put to the test. Chinese nationalists launched the so-called Boxer Rebellion. They swarmed into Peking and drove foreigners within the walls of their legations, which were placed under siege. For weeks, until an international rescue expedition broke through to free them, the fate of the foreigners was unknown. Fearing that the Europeans would use the rebellion as a pretext for further expropriations, Hay sent off another round of Open Door notes announcing that the United States believed in the preservation of "Chinese territorial and administrative entity" and in "the principle of equal and impartial trade with all parts of the Chinese Empire." This broadened the Open Door policy to include all China, not merely the European spheres of influence.

Hay's diplomacy was superficially successful. While the United States maintained no important military force in the Far East, American business and commercial interests there were free to develop and to compete with Europeans. But once again European jealousies and fears rather than American cleverness were responsible for Hay's success. The United States was being caught up in the power struggle in the Far East without having faced the implications of its actions.

Eventually the country would pay a heavy price for this unrealistic attitude, but in the decade following 1900 its policy of diplomatic meddling unbacked by bayonets worked fairly well. Japan attacked Russia in a quarrel over Manchuria, smashing the Russian fleet in 1905 and winning a series of battles on the mainland. Eager to preserve the nice balance in the Far East, which enabled the United States to exert influence without any significant commitment of force, Roosevelt invited the belligerents to a conference at Portsmouth, New Hampshire. At the conference the Japanese won title to Russia's sphere around Port Arthur, a free hand in Korea, and part of Sakhalin Island, but the Japanese people had expected more and blamed Roosevelt for forcing a compromise. Ill feeling against Americans increased in 1906 when the San Francisco school board, responding to opposition to the influx of cheap labor from Japan, instituted a policy of segregating Oriental children in a special school. Japan protested, and President Roosevelt persuaded the San Franciscans to abandon segregation in exchange for his pledge to cut off further Japanese immigration. He accomplished this through a "Gentlemen's Agreement" (1907) in which the Japanese promised not to issue passports to laborers seeking to come to America. Discriminatory legislation based specifically on race was thus avoided. However, the atmosphere between the two countries remained charged. Japanese resentment at American race prejudice

was great; many Americans talked fearfully of the "yellow peril."

Theodore Roosevelt was preeminently a realist in foreign relations. "Don't bluster," he once said. "Don't flourish a revolver, and never draw unless you intend to shoot." In the Far East, however, he failed to follow his own advice. He considered the situation in that part of the world fraught with peril. The Philippines, he said, were "our heel of Achilles," indefensible in case of a Japanese attack. Although he did not increase appreciably American naval and military strength in the Orient, neither did he stop trying to influence the course of events in the area. "The 'Open Door' policy," he advised his successor, "completely disappears as soon as a powerful nation determines to disregard it." Nevertheless, he allowed the belief to persist in the United States that the nation could influence the course of Far Eastern history without risk or real involvement.

The Isthmian Canal

In the Caribbean region American policy centered on building an interoceanic canal across Central America. The first step was to get rid of the old Clayton-Bulwer Treaty with Great Britain, which barred the United States from building a canal on its own. In 1901 Lord Pauncefote, the British ambassador, and Secretary of State John Hay negotiated an agreement abrogating the Clayton-Bulwer Pact and giving America the right to build, and by implication fortify, a trans-isthmian waterway. The United States agreed in turn to maintain any such canal "free and open to the vessels of commerce and of war of all nations."

One possible canal route lay across the Colombian province of Panama, where the French-controlled New Panama Canal Company had taken over the franchise of the old De Lesseps company. Only 50 miles separated the oceans in Panama, but the terrain was rugged and unhealthy: Although the French company had sunk much money into the project, it had little to show for its efforts aside from some rough excavations. A second possible route ran across Nicaragua. This route was about 200 miles long but was relatively easy. Much of it traversed Lake Nicaragua and other natural waterways.

President McKinley appointed a commission to study the alternatives. It reported that the Panamanian route was technically superior but recommended building in Nicaragua because the New Panama Canal Company was asking $109 million for its assets, which the commission valued at only $40 million. Lacking another purchaser, the French company quickly lowered its price to $40 million, and President Roosevelt settled on the Panamanian route.

In January 1903 Secretary of State Hay negotiated a treaty with Colombia. In return for a 99-year lease on a zone across Panama six miles wide, the United States agreed to pay Colombia $10 million and an annual rent of $250,000. The Colombian senate, however, unanimously rejected this treaty, demanding $15 million directly from the United States, plus $10 million of the company's share.

A little more patience might have produced a mutually satisfactory settlement, but Roosevelt looked on the Colombians as highwaymen who were "mad to get hold of the $40,000,000 of the Frenchmen." When Panamanians, egged on by the French company, staged a revolution in November 1903, he ordered the cruiser *Nashville* to Panama. Colombian government forces found themselves looking down the barrels of the guns of the *Nashville* and shortly thereafter eight other American warships. The revolution succeeded. Roosevelt instantly recognized the new Republic of Panama and negotiated a treaty granting the United States a zone ten miles wide in perpetuity, on the same terms as those rejected by Colombia.*

Historians have condemned Roosevelt for his actions in this shabby affair, and with good reason. It was not that he fomented the revolution, for he did not. Nor was it that he prevented Colombia from suppressing the revolution. He sinned, rather, in his disregard of Latin American sensibilities. He referred to the Colombians as "dagoes" and insisted smugly that he was defending "the interests of collective civilization" when he overrode their opposition to his plans. "Have I defended myself?" Roosevelt asked Secretary of

War Elihu Root. "You certainly have, Mr. President," Root retorted. "You were accused of seduction and you have conclusively proved that you were guilty of rape." Throughout Latin America, especially as nationalist sentiments grew stronger, Roosevelt's intolerance and aggressiveness in the canal incident bred resentment and fear.

The canal was built—the first vessels passed through its locks in 1914—and American hegemony in the Caribbean expanded. Yet even in that strategically vital area there was more show than substance to American strength. The navy ruled Caribbean waters largely by default.

The tendency was to try to influence outlying areas without actually controlling them. Roosevelt's successor, William Howard Taft, called this policy "dollar diplomacy," his reasoning being that economic penetration would bring stability to underdeveloped areas and power and profit to the United States without having to commit American troops or spend public funds.

Under Taft the State Department won a place for American bankers in an international syndicate engaged in financing railroads in Manchuria. When Nicaragua defaulted on its foreign debt in 1911, the

The Panama Canal under construction. Cutting the path between the seas consumed more than 61 million pounds of dynamite and the lives of hundreds of workers, most of whom were black laborers from Barbados and Jamaica.

---

*Panama was independent only in name because of American control of the canal. In 1978 the United States and Panama agreed to a treaty turning the entire Canal Zone over to Panama in the year 2000.

department arranged for American bankers to reorganize Nicaraguan finances and manage the customs service. Although the government truthfully insisted that it did not "covet an inch of territory south of the Rio Grande," dollar diplomacy provoked further apprehension in Latin America.

Economic penetration proceeded briskly. American investments in Cuba reached $500 million by 1920, and smaller but significant investments were made in the Dominican Republic and in Haiti. In Central America the United Fruit Company accumulated large holdings in banana plantations, railroads, and other ventures. Other firms plunged heavily in Mexico's rich mineral resources.

"Noncolonial Imperial Expansion"

The United States deserves fair marks for effort in its foreign relations following the Spanish-American War, barely passable marks for performance, and failing marks for results. If one defines imperialism narrowly as a policy of occupying and governing foreign lands, American imperialism lasted for an extremely short time. With trivial exceptions, all the American colonies—Hawaii, the Philippines, Guam, Puerto Rico, the Guantanamo base, and the Canal Zone—were obtained between 1898 and 1903. In retrospect it seems clear that the urge to own colonies was only fleeting; the questions raised by anti-imperialists and the headaches connected with the management of overseas possessions soon produced a change of policy.

Hay's Open Door notes (which anti-imperialists praised) marked the beginning of the retreat from imperialism as thus defined, and the Roosevelt Corollary and dollar diplomacy signaled the consolidation of a new policy. Elihu Root summarized this policy toward underdeveloped countries in 1905: "We do not want to take them for ourselves. We do not want any foreign nations to take them for themselves. We want to help them."

Yet imperialism can be given a broader definition. The historian William Appleman Williams, a sharp critic, described 20th-century American foreign policy as one of "non-colonial imperial expansion." Its object was to obtain profitable American economic penetration of underdeveloped areas without the trouble of owning and controlling them. Its subsidiary aim was to encourage these countries to "modernize," that is, to remake themselves in the image of the United States.

Williams criticizes American policy not because it failed to work or because it led to trouble with the powers, but because of its harmful effects on underdeveloped countries. Its creators were not evil but only of limited vision. They did not recognize the contradictions in their ideas and values. They saw American expansion as beneficial to all concerned—and not exclusively in materialistic terms. They genuinely believed that they were exporting democracy along with capitalism and industrialization.

Williams probably goes too far in arguing that American statesmen consciously planned their foreign policy in these terms. Yet he is correct in pointing out that western economic penetration has had many unfortunate results for the nonindustrial nations. It is also true that Americans were particularly, though not uniquely, unimpressed by the different social and cultural patterns of people in far-off lands and insensitive to the wishes of such people to develop in their own way.

Dollar diplomacy had as its primary objectives the avoidance of violence and the economic development of Latin America; it paid small heed to how peace was maintained and how the fruits of development were distributed. The policy, therefore, was self-defeating because, in the long run, stability depended on the support of the people, which was seldom forthcoming.

By the eve of World War I, the United States had become a world power and had assumed what it saw as a duty to guide the development of many countries with traditions far different from its own. The American people, however, did not really understand what these changes involved. While they stood ready to extend their influence into distant lands, they did so with little awareness of the implications of their behavior for themselves or for other peoples. The national psychology, if such a term has any meaning, remained fundamentally isolationist. Americans understood that their wealth and numbers made their nation strong and that geography made it practically invulnerable. They proceeded, then, to do what they wanted to do in foreign affairs, limited more by their humanly flexible consciences than by any rational analysis of the probable consequences. This seemed safe enough—in 1914.

Milestones

1850	Clayton-Bulwer Treaty		Spanish-American War breaks out
1858	Commercial treaty with Japan		Battle of Manila Bay
1867	Alaska purchased from Russia		Battle of San Juan Hill
1871	Treaty of Washington, settling the *Alabama* claims		Annexation of Hawaii
		1899	Open Door notes
1875	Hawaiian reciprocity treaty	**1900**	Platt Amendment to the Cuban constitution
1885	Josiah Strong, *Our Country*		
1889	First pan-American conference	**1901**	Hay-Pauncefote Treaty
1890	A. T. Mahan, *The Influence of Sea Power Upon History*		Supreme Court decides insular cases on control of colonies
1891	*Baltimore* crisis with Chile	**1902**	Venezuela bond dispute
1893	Overthrow of Queen Liliuokalani of Hawaii	**1904**	Roosevelt Corollary to the Monroe Doctrine
1895	Venezuela boundary dispute	**1907**	"Gentlemen's Agreement" with Japan
1898	*Maine* explodes in Havana harbor		

Supplementary Reading

For the foreign relations of the era, Walter LaFeber, **The New Empire** (1963), presents a forceful but somewhat overstated argument on the extent of expansionist sentiment, especially on the part of American businessmen. See also Milton Plesur, **America's Outward Thrust*** (1971), and C. S. Campbell, Jr., **Transformation of American Foreign Relations** (1976).

On the Spanish-American War, consult D. F. Trask, **The War with Spain in 1898** (1981), Frank Freidel, **The Splendid Little War** (1958), H. W. Morgan, **America's Road to Empire*** (1965), and E. R. May, **Imperial Democracy** (1961). American imperialism is discussed in D. F. Healy, **U.S. Expansionism** (1970), Healy's **Drive to Hegemony** (1988), and W. A. Williams, **The Tragedy of American Diplomacy*** (1962), the last a critical assessment of what the author calls "non-colonial imperial expansion."

R. L. Beisner, **Twelve Against Empire: The Anti-imperialists** (1968), contains lively and thoughtful sketches of leading foes of expansion. See also E. B. Thompkins, **Anti-Imperialism in the United States** (1970). For colonial problems, see D. F. Healy, **The United States in Cuba: 1898–1902** (1963), R. E. Welch, **Response to Imperialism: The United States and the Philippine-American War** (1979), D. G. Munro, **Intervention and Dollar Diplomacy in the Caribbean: 1900–1921** (1964), and David McCullough, **The Path Between the Seas*** (1977). R. E. Osgood, **Ideals and Self-Interest in America's Foreign Relations*** (1953), and G. F. Kennan, **American Diplomacy: 1900–1950*** (1951) are important interpretations of early-20th-century United States policy.

*Available in paperback.

CHAPTER 24

Woodrow Wilson and the Great War

Missionary Diplomacy

Outbreak of the Great War

Freedom of the Seas

The Election of 1916

The Road to War

Mobilizing the Economy

Workers in Wartime

Paying for the War

Propaganda and Civil Liberties

Wartime Reforms

Women and Blacks in Wartime

"Over There"

Preparing for Peace

The Paris Peace Conference

The Senate and the League of Nations

Demobilization

The Red Scare

The Election of 1920

Woodrow Wilson's approach to foreign relations was well intentioned and idealistic but somewhat confused. He wanted to help other countries, especially the republics of Latin America. At the same time he felt obliged to sustain and protect American interests abroad. The maintenance of the Open Door in China and the completion of the Panama Canal were as important to him as they had been to Theodore Roosevelt. His attitude resembled that of 19th-century Christian missionaries: He wanted to spread the gospel of American democracy, to lift and enlighten the unfortunate and the ignorant—but in his own way.

Missionary Diplomacy

Wilson set out to raise the moral tone of American foreign policy by denouncing dollar diplomacy. Encouraging bankers to lend money to countries like China, he said, implied the possibility of "forcible interference" if the loans were not repaid, and that would be "obnoxious to the principles upon which the government of our people rests." To seek special economic concessions in Latin America was "unfair" and "degrading." The United States would deal with Latin American nations "upon terms of equality and honor."

In certain small matters Wilson succeeded in conducting American diplomacy on this idealistic basis. He withdrew the government's support of the international consortium that was arranging a loan to develop Chinese railroads, and the American bankers pulled out. When the Japanese attempted, in the notorious Twenty-one Demands (1915), to reduce China almost to the status of a Japanese protectorate, he persuaded them to modify their conditions slightly. He also permitted Secretary of State William Jennings Bryan to negotiate conciliation treaties with 21 nations. The distinctive feature of these agreements was the provision for a "cooling-off" period of one year, during which signatories agreed, in the event of a dispute, not to engage in hostilities.

Where more vital interests of the United States were concerned, Wilson sometimes failed to live up to his promises. Because of the strategic importance of the Panama Canal, he was unwilling to tolerate "unrest" anywhere in the Caribbean. Soon after his inauguration he was pursuing the same tactics that circumstances had forced on Roosevelt and Taft. The Bryan-Chamorro Treaty of 1914, which gave the United States an option to build a canal across Nicaragua, made that country virtually an American protectorate and served to maintain in power an unpopular dictator, Adolfo Diaz.

A much more serious example of missionary diplomacy occurred in Mexico. In 1911 a liberal coalition overthrew the dictator Porfirio Díaz, who had been exploiting the resources and people of Mexico for the benefit of a small class of wealthy landowners, clerics, and military men since the 1870s. Francisco Madero became president.

Madero, though a wealthy landowner, was committed to economic reform and to the drafting of a democratic constitution, but he was both weak-willed and a terrible administrator. Conditions in Mexico deteriorated rapidly, and less than a month before Wilson's inauguration, one of Madero's generals, Victoriano Huerta, seized power and had Madero murdered. Since he seemed capable of maintaining the stability that foreign investors desired, most of the European powers promptly recognized Huerta's government.

The American ambassador, together with important American financial and business interests, urged Wilson to do so too, but he refused. "I will not recognize a government of butchers," he said. This was unconventional, since nations do not ordinarily consider the means by which a foreign regime has come to power before deciding to establish diplomatic relations.

Wilson brought enormous pressure to bear against Huerta. He dragooned the British into withdrawing recognition. He dickered with other Mexican factions. He demanded that Huerta hold free elections. Huerta would not yield an inch.

In this contest of wills, Wilson subordinated his wish to let the Mexicans solve their own problems to his desire to destroy Huerta. The situation exploded in April 1914, when a small party of American sailors was arrested in the port of Tampico, Mexico. Wilson fastened on the affair as an excuse for sending troops into Mexico. When, he learned that a German merchantman laden with munitions was expected at Veracruz, Wilson ordered the city occupied to prevent the weapons from reaching the Huertistas. The Mexicans resisted tenaciously, suffering 400 casualties before falling back. This bloodshed caused dismay throughout Latin America and failed to unseat Huerta. At this point Argentina, Brazil, and Chile offered to mediate the dispute. Wilson accepted, Huerta also agreed, and the conferees met at Niagara Falls, Ontario, in May. Although no settlement was reached, Huerta, hard pressed by Mexican opponents, finally abdicated. On August 20, 1914, General Venustiano Carranza entered Mexico City in triumph.

Carranza favored representative government, but he proved scarcely more successful than the tyrant Huerta in controlling the country. One of his own generals, Francisco "Pancho" Villa, rose against him and seized control of Mexico City.

Wilson now made a monumental blunder. Villa professed to be willing to cooperate with the United States, and Wilson, taking him at his word, gave him his support. However, Villa was little more than an ambitious bandit. Carranza, although no radical, was committed to social reform. Fighting back, he drove the Villistas into the northern provinces.

Wilson finally realized the extent of Carranza's influence in Mexico, and in October 1915 he recognized his government. Still, his Mexican troubles were not over. Early in 1916, Villa, seeking to undermine Carranza by forcing the United States to intervene, stopped a train in northern Mexico and killed 16 American passengers in cold blood. Then he crossed into New Mexico and burned the town of Columbus, killing 19. Having learned his lesson, Wilson would have preferred to bear even this assault in silence, but public opinion forced him to send American troops under General John J. Pershing across the border in pursuit of Villa.

Villa proved impossible to catch. Cleverly he drew Pershing deeper and deeper into Mexico, which caused Carranza to insist that the Americans withdraw. Several clashes occurred between Pershing's men and Mexican regulars, and for a brief period in June 1916 war seemed imminent. Wilson now acted bravely and wisely. Early in 1917 he recalled Pershing's force, leaving the Mexicans to work out their own destiny.

Missionary diplomacy in Mexico had produced mixed, but in the long run, beneficial results. By opposing Huerta, Wilson had surrendered to his prejudices, yet he had also helped the real revolutionaries even though they opposed his acts. His bungling bred anti-Americanism in Mexico, but by his later restraint in the face of stinging provocations, he permitted the constitutionalists to consolidate their power.

Outbreak of the Great War

On June 28, 1914, in the Austro-Hungarian provincial capital of Sarajevo, Gavrilo Princip, a young student, assassinated the Archduke Franz Ferdinand, heir to the imperial throne. This rash act precipitated a general European war. Within little more than a month, following a complex series of diplomatic challenges and responses, the Central Powers (chiefly Germany and Austria Hungary) and the Allied Powers (chiefly Great Britain, France, and Russia) were locked in a brutal struggle that brought one era in world history to a close and inaugurated another.

The outbreak of the Great War caught Americans psychologically unprepared. Few understood the significance of what had happened. President Wilson promptly issued a proclamation of neutrality, and the almost unanimous reaction of Americans, aside from dismay, was that the conflict did not concern them. They were wrong, for this was a World War and Americans were sure to be affected by its outcome.

There were good reasons why the United States sought to remain neutral. More than a third of its 92 million inhabitants were either European-born or the children of Europeans. Sentimental ties bound them to the lands of their ancestors. American involvement would create new internal stresses in a society already strained by the task of assimilating so many diverse groups. War was also an affront to the prevailing progressive spirit, which assumed that human beings were reasonable, high-minded, and capable of settling disputes peaceably. Along with the traditional American fear of entanglement in European affairs, these were ample reasons for remaining aloof.

Although most Americans hoped to keep out of the war, nearly everyone was partial to one side or the other. People of German or Austrian descent, about 8 million in number, and the nation's 4.5 million Irish Americans, motivated chiefly by hatred of the British, sympathized with the Central Powers. The majority of the people, however, influenced by bonds of language and culture, preferred an Allied victory, and when the Germans launched a mighty assault across neutral Belgium in an effort to outflank the French armies, this unprovoked attack on a tiny nation whose neutrality the Germans had previously agreed to respect caused a great deal of anti-German feeling.

As the war progressed, the Allies cleverly exploited American prejudices, and the Germans also conducted an extensive propaganda campaign. But propaganda did not basically alter American attitudes; far more important were questions rising out of trade and commerce.

Freedom of the Seas

All the warring nations wanted to draw on American resources. Under international law neutrals could trade freely with any belligerent. Americans were prepared to do so, but because the British fleet dominated the North Atlantic, they could not. The British declared nearly all commodities, even foodstuffs, to be contraband of war. They set limits on exports to neutral nations such as Denmark and the Netherlands so that these countries could not transship supplies to Germany. They forced neutral merchantmen into Allied ports in order to search them for goods headed for the enemy. Many cargoes were confiscated, often without payment.

Had the United States insisted that Great Britain abandon these "illegal" practices, as the Germans demanded, no doubt it could have had its way. It is ironic that an embargo, which failed so ignominiously in Jefferson's day, would have been almost instantly effective if applied at any time after 1914, for American supplies were absolutely vital to the Allies. Though British tactics frequently exasperated Wilson, they did not cause the loss of innocent lives; he never considered taking such a drastic step. He faced a dilemma. To allow the British to make the rules meant siding against the Central Powers. Yet to insist on the old rules meant siding against the Allies, because that would have deprived them of much of the value of their naval superiority. *Nothing* the United States might do would be truly impartial.

In any event, the immense expansion of American trade with the Allies made an embargo unthinkable. While commerce with the Central Powers fell to a trickle, that with the Allies soared from $825 million in 1914 to over $3.2 billion in 1916. An attempt to limit this commerce would have raised a storm; to have eliminated it would have caused a catastrophe.

The Allies soon exhausted their ready cash and had to borrow in order to continue their purchases. Wilson first refused to let American bankers lend them money but soon reversed himself. By early 1917, Britain and France had borrowed well over $2 billion. Although these loans violated no principle of international law, they fastened the United States still more closely to the Allies' cause.

During the first months of the Great War, the Germans were not especially concerned about neutral trade or American goods because they expected to crush the Allied armies quickly. When their first swift thrust into France was blunted along the Marne River and the war became a bloody stalemate, they began to challenge the Allies' control of the seas. Unwilling to risk their battleships and cruisers against the much larger British fleet, they resorted to a new weapon, the submarine, commonly known as the U-boat (*das Unterseeboot*).

German submarines played a role in World War I not unlike that of American privateers in the Revolution and the War of 1812: They ranged the seas stealthily in search of merchantmen. However, submarines could not operate under the ordinary rules of war, which required that a raider stop its prey, examine its papers and cargo, and give the crew and passengers time to get off in lifeboats before sending it to the bottom. When surfaced, U-boats were vulnerable to the deck guns that many merchant ships carried; therefore they commonly launched their torpedoes from below the surface without warning. The result was often a heavy loss of lives on the torpedoed ships.

In February 1915 the Germans declared the waters surrounding the British Isles a zone of war and announced that they would sink, without warning, all enemy merchant ships encountered in the area. Since Allied vessels sometimes flew neutral flags to disguise their identity, neutral ships entering the zone would do so at their own risk. Wilson, perhaps too hurriedly considering the importance of the question, warned the Germans that he would hold them to "strict accountability" for any loss of American life or property resulting from violations of "acknowledged [neutral] rights on the high seas." "Strict accountability" ultimately meant war unless the Germans backed down. Yet Wilson was not prepared to fight; he refused even to ask Congress for increased military appropriations, saying that he did not want to "turn America into a military camp."

Wise or unwise, Wilson's position accurately reflected the attitude of most Americans. It seemed barbaric to them that defenseless civilians should be killed without warning, and they refused to surrender their "rights" as neutrals to cross the North Atlantic on any ship they wished.

The depth of their feeling was demonstrated when, on May 7, 1915, the submarine U-20 sank the British liner *Lusitania* off the Irish coast. Nearly 1,200 persons, including 128 Americans, lost their lives in this catastrophe.

The torpedoing of the *Lusitania* caused as profound and emotional a reaction in the United States as that following the destruction of the *Maine* in Havana harbor. Wilson, like McKinley in 1898, was shocked, but he kept his head. He demanded that Germany disavow the sinking, indemnify the victims, and promise to stop attacking passenger vessels. When the Germans quibbled about these points, he responded with further diplomatic correspondence rather than with an ultimatum.

It would have been difficult politically for the German government to have backed down before an American ultimatum; however, after dragging the controversy out for nearly a year, it did apologize and agree to pay an indemnity. Finally, after the torpedoing of the French Channel steamer *Sussex* in March 1916 had produced another stiff American protest, the Germans at last promised— the *Sussex* pledge—to stop sinking merchant ships without warning.

The Election of 1916

Part of Wilson's confusion in 1916 resulted from the political difficulties he faced in his fight for reelection. He had won the presidency in 1912 only because the Republican Party had split in two. Now Theodore Roosevelt, the chief defector, had become so incensed by Wilson's refusal to commit the United States to the Allied cause that he was ready to support almost any Republican in order to guarantee the president's defeat. At the same time, many progressives were complaining about Wilson's unwillingness to work for further domestic reforms. Unless he could find additional support, he seemed likely to be defeated.

He attacked the problem by wooing the progressives. In January 1916 he appointed Louis D. Brandeis to the Supreme Court. In addition to being an advanced progressive, Brandeis was Jewish, the first American of that religion ever appointed to the Court. Wilson's action won him many friends among people who favored fair treatment of minority groups. In July he bid for the farm vote by signing the Farm Loan Act to provide low-cost loans based on agricultural credit. Shortly hereafter he approved the Keating-Owen Child Labor Act, barring goods manufactured by the labor of children under 16 from interstate commerce, and a workmen's compensation act for federal employees. He persuaded Congress to pass the Adamson Act, establishing an eight-hour day for railroad workers, and he modified his position on the tariff by approving the creation of a tariff commission and accepting "antidumping" legislation designed to protect American industry from cutthroat foreign competition after the war.

Each of these actions represented a sharp reversal. They paid spectacular political dividends when Roosevelt refused to run as a Progressive and came out for the Republican nominee, Associate Justice Charles Evans Hughes. The Progressive Convention then endorsed Hughes, who had compiled a fine liberal record as governor of New York, but many of Roosevelt's 1912 supporters felt he had betrayed them and voted for Wilson in 1916.

The key issue in the campaign was American policy toward the warring powers. Wilson intended to stress preparedness, which he was now wholeheartedly supporting. However, during the Democratic Convention the delegates shook the hall with cheers whenever orators referred to the president's success in keeping the country out of the war. One spellbinder, referring to the *Sussex* pledge, announced that the president had "wrung from the most militant spirit that ever brooded above a battlefield an acknowledgement of American rights and an agreement to American demands," and the convention erupted in a demonstration that lasted more than 20 minutes. Thus "He Kept Us Out of War" became the Democratic slogan.

The combination of progressivism and the peace issue placed the Democrats on substantially equal terms with the Republicans; thereafter personal factors probably tipped the balance. Hughes proved a poor campaigner: He was very stiff (Theodore Roosevelt called him a bearded Woodrow Wilson) and an ineffective speaker; he offended a number of important politicians, especially in crucial California, where he inadvertently snubbed the popular progressive governor, Hiram Johnson; and he equivocated on a number of issues. On election night he appeared to have won, having carried nearly all the East and Middle West. Late returns gave Wilson California, however, and with it victory by the narrow margin of 277 to 254 in the electoral college. He led Hughes in the popular vote, 9.1 million to 8.5 million.

The Road to War

Encouraged by his triumph, appalled by the continuing slaughter on the battlefields, and fearful that the United States would be dragged into the holocaust, Wilson made one last effort to end the war by negotiation. In 1915 he had sent his friend Colonel Edward M. House on a secret mission to London, Paris, and Berlin to try to mediate among the belligerents. House had been received cordially, but he made little progress and his negotiations were disrupted by the *Lusitania* crisis. A second House mission (January–February 1916) had proved equally fruitless. Now, after another long season of bloodshed, perhaps the powers would listen to reason.

Wilson's own feelings were more genuinely neutral than at any other time during the war, for the Germans had stopped sinking merchantmen without warning and the British had irritated him repeatedly by their arbitrary restrictions on neutral trade. He drafted a note to the belligerents asking them to state the terms on which they would agree to lay down their arms. When neither side responded encouragingly, Wilson, on January 22, 1917, delivered a moving, prophetic speech aimed, as he admitted, at "the people of the countries now at war" more than at their governments. Any settlement imposed by a victor, he declared, would breed hatred and more wars. There must be a "peace without victory" based on the principles that all nations were equal and that every nationality group should determine its own form of government. He suggested the creation of some kind of international organization to preserve world peace.

This noble appeal met a tragic fate. The Germans had already decided to renounce the *Sussex* pledge and unleash their submarines against all vessels headed for Allied ports. After February 1, any ship in the war zone would be attacked without warning. Possessed now of more than 100 U-boats, the German military leaders had convinced themselves that they could starve the British people into submission and reduce the Allied armies to impotence by cutting off American supplies. The United States would probably declare war, but the Germans believed they could overwhelm the Allies before the Americans could get to the battlefields in force.

After the Germans had made their decision, events moved relentlessly, almost uninfluenced by the actors who presumably controlled the fate of the world:

February 3: Housatonic *torpedoed. Wilson announces to Congress that he has severed diplomatic relations with Germany. Secretary of State Lansing hands the German ambassador, Count von Bernstorff, his passport. February 24: Walter Hines Page, United States ambassador to Great Britain, transmits to the State Department an intercepted German dispatch (the "Zimmermann Telegram") revealing that Germany has proposed a secret alliance with Mexico, Mexico to receive, in the event of war with the United States, "the lost territory in Texas, New Mexico, and Arizona." February 25: Cunard liner* Laconia *torpedoed, two American women perish. February 26: Wilson asks Congress for authority to arm American merchant ships. March 1: Zimmermann Telegram released to the press. March 4: President Wilson takes oath of office, beginning his second term. Congress adjourns without passing the Armed Ship Bill, the measure having been filibustered to death by antiwar senators. Wilson characterizes the filibusters, led by Senator Robert M. La Follette, as "a little group of willful men, representing no opinion but their own." March 9: Wilson, acting under his executive powers, orders the arming of American merchantmen. March 12: Revolutionary provisional government established in Russia.* Algonquin *torpedoed. March 15: Czar Nicholas II of Russia abdicates. March 16: City of Memphis, Illinois,* Vigilancia *torpedoed. March 21: New York* World, *a leading Democratic newspaper, calls for declaration of war on Germany. Wilson summons Congress to convene in special session on April 2. March 25: Wilson calls up the National Guard. April 2: Wilson asks Congress to declare war. Germany is guilty of*

"throwing to the winds all scruples of humanity," he says. America must fight, not to conquer, but for "peace and justice. . . . The world must be made safe for democracy." April 4, 6: Congress declares war—the vote, 82:6 in the Senate, 373:50 in the House.

The bare record conceals Wilson's agonizing search for an honorable alternative to war. To admit that Germany posed a threat to the United States meant confessing that interventionists had been right all along. To go to war meant, besides sending innocent Americans to their death, unleashing the forces of hatred and intolerance in the United States and allowing "the spirit of ruthless brutality [to] enter into the very fibre of our national life."

The president's Presbyterian conscience tortured him relentlessly. He lost sleep, appeared gray and drawn. When someone asked him which side he hoped would win, he answered petulantly, "Neither." In the end, he could satisfy himself only by giving intervention an idealistic purpose. The war had become a threat to humanity. Unless the United States threw its weight into the balance, Western civilization itself might be destroyed. Out of the long bloodbath must come a new and better world. The war must be fought to end, for all time, war itself. Thus in the name not of vengeance and victory but of justice and humanity, he sent his people into battle.

Mobilizing the Economy

America's entry into the World War determined its outcome. The Allies were rapidly running out of money and supplies; their troops, decimated by nearly three years in the trenches, were disheartened and rebellious. After the outbreak of the Russian Revolution in March 1917, the Russian armies collapsed. By December 1917, Russia was out of the war and the Germans were moving masses of men and equipment from the eastern front to France. Without the aid of the United States, it is likely that the war would have ended in 1918 on terms dictated from Berlin. Instead, American men and supplies helped contain the Germans' last drives and then push them back to final defeat.

It was a close thing, for the United States entered the war little better prepared to fight than it had been in 1898. The conversion of American industry to war production had to be organized and carried out without prearrangement. Confusion and waste resulted. The hurriedly designed shipbuilding program was a fiasco. Heavy traffic caused a monumental railroad tie-up in December and January 1917–1918. Wilson finally appointed Secretary of the Treasury William G. McAdoo director general of the railroads, with power to run the roads as a single system.

Airplane, tank, and artillery construction programs, all too large to begin with, developed too slowly to affect the war. "The American doughboy," writes David M. Kennedy in *Over Here,* was "transported in a British ship, wore a steel helmet modeled on the British Tommy's, and fought with French ordnance." American pilots, such as the great "ace" Captain Eddie Rickenbacker, flew British Sopwiths and De Havillands or French Spads and Nieuports.

The problem of mobilization was complicated. It took Congress six weeks of hot debate merely to decide on conscription. Only in September 1917, nearly six months after the declaration of war, did the first draftees reach the training camps, and it is hard to see how Wilson could have speeded this process appreciably.

Wilson was a forceful and inspiring war leader once he grasped what needed to be done. Waste there was, and inefficiency, but no one in the country worked harder or displayed such patience in the face of frustration and criticism. Raising an army was only a small part of the job. The Allies had to be supplied with food and munitions, and immense amounts of money had to be collected.

After a series of experiments, Wilson created (July 1917) the War Industries Board (WIB) to oversee all aspects of industrial production and distribution. The head of the WIB, Bernard M. Baruch, a Wall Street speculator by trade, was given almost dictatorial power to allocate scarce materials, standardize production, fix prices, and coordinate American and Allied purchasing.

Evaluating the mobilization effort raises interesting historical questions. The antitrust laws were suspended and producers were encouraged, even compelled, to cooperate with one another. Wilson accepted the kind of government–industry agreements developed under Theodore Roosevelt that he had denounced in 1912. Prices were set by the WIB at levels that allowed large profits—U.S.

Steel, for example, despite high taxes, cleared over half a billion dollars in two years. Baruch justified these returns with what seemed to him irrefutable logic: "You could be forgiven if you paid too much to get the stuff, but you could never be forgiven if you did not get it, and lost the war." It is at least arguable that producers would have turned out just as much even though compelled to charge lower prices.

At the start of the war, army procurement was decentralized and inefficient. One official bought 1,200 typewriters, stacked them in the basement of a government building, and announced proudly: "There is going to be the greatest competition for typewriters around here, and I have them all."

Mobilization required close cooperation between business and the military. However the army resisted cooperating with civilian agencies. Wilson finally compelled the War Department to place officers on WIB committees, and when the army discovered that its interests were not injured by the system, the foundation for what was later to be known as the industrial-military complex was laid, the alliance between business and military leaders that was to cause so much controversy after World War II.

The problem of mobilizing agricultural resources was solved more quickly, and this was fortunate because in April 1917 the British had on hand only a six-weeks' supply of food. Wilson named Herbert Hoover, a mining engineer who had headed the Belgian Relief Commission earlier in the war, food administrator. Acting under powers granted by the Lever Act of August 1917, Hoover set the price of wheat at $2.20 a bushel in order to encourage production. He established a government corporation to purchase the entire American and Cuban sugar crop, which he then doled out to American and British refiners.

To avoid rationing, Hoover organized a campaign to persuade consumers to conserve food voluntarily. One slogan ran: "If U fast U beat U boats," another "Serve beans by all means." "Wheatless Mondays" and "Meatless Tuesdays" were the rule, and although no law compelled their observance, the public responded patriotically. Boy Scouts dug up back yards and vacant lots to plant vegetable gardens, chefs devised new recipes to save on scarce items, restaurants added horsemeat, rabbit, and whale steak to their menus and doled out butter and sugar to diners in minuscule portions. Mothers pressured their children to "Hooverize" their plates. Without subjecting its own citizens to serious inconvenience, the United States increased food exports from 12.3 million tons to 18.6 million tons. Farmers, of course, profited: Their real income went up nearly 30 percent between 1915 and 1918.

Workers in Wartime

With the army siphoning so many men from the labor market and with immigration reduced to a trickle, unemployment disappeared and wages rose. Although the cost of living soared, the boom produced unprecedented opportunities. Americans, always a mobile people, pulled up stakes in unprecedented numbers. Disadvantaged groups, especially blacks, were particularly attracted by jobs in big-city factories.

The movement of blacks from the former slave states began with emancipation, but the mass exodus that many people had expected did not materialize. Between 1870 and 1890, only about 80,000 moved to the North. Around the turn of the century the northward movement quickened—about 200,000 migrated between 1890 and 1910. Then, after 1914, the war boom drew blacks north in a flood, half a million in five years.

Early in the conflict, the government began regulating the wages and hours of workers building army camps and manufacturing uniforms. In April 1918 Wilson created a National War Labor Board to settle labor disputes. The board considered more than 1,200 cases and prevented many strikes. A War Labor Policies Board (WLPB) set wages-and-hours standards for each major war industry. Since these were determined in consultation with employers and representatives of labor, they speeded the unionization of workers by compelling management, even in antiunion industries like steel, to deal with labor leaders. Union membership rose by 2.3 million during the war.

Paying for the War

Wilson managed the task of financing the war effectively. The struggle cost the United States

In order to win public approval, the Wilson administration set in motion a widespread advertising campaign to sell Americans on the European war. Liberty bond posters, such as this one, were useful public relations tools to win support for the war effort.

about $33.5 billion, not counting pensions and other postwar expenses. About $7 billion of this was lent to the Allies, but since this money was largely spent in America, it contributed to the national prosperity. Over two-thirds of the cost of the war was met by borrowing. Five Liberty and Victory Loan drives, spurred by advertising, parades, and other appeals to patriotism, persuaded the people to open their purses.

In addition to borrowing, the government collected about $10.5 billion in taxes during the war. A steeply graduated income tax took more than 75 percent of the incomes of the wealthiest citizens. A 65 percent excess-profits tax and a 25 percent inheritance tax were also enacted. Thus, although many individuals made fortunes out of the war, its cost was distributed far more equitably than was that of the Civil War.

Propaganda and Civil Liberties

Wilson was preeminently a teacher and preacher, a specialist in the transmission of ideas and ideals. He excelled at mobilizing public opinion and inspiring Americans to work for the better world he hoped would emerge from the war. In April 1917 he created a Committee on Public Information (CPI), headed by the journalist George Creel. Soon 75,000 speakers and writers were deluging the country with propaganda: picturing the war as a crusade for freedom and democracy, the Germans as a bestial people bent on world domination.

Most people supported the war enthusiastically, but thousands of persons—for example, German Americans and Irish Americans, people of pacifist leanings such as Jane Addams of Hull House, and some who thought both sides in the war wrong—still opposed American involvement. Creel's committee, and a number of unofficial "patriotic" groups, allowed their enthusiasm for the conversion of the hesitant to become suppression of dissent. Persons who refused to buy war bonds were often exposed to public ridicule and even to assault. People with German names were persecuted without regard for their views; some school boards outlawed the teaching of the German language; sauerkraut was renamed "liberty cabbage." Opponents of the war of unquestionable patriotism were subjected to coarse abuse.

Wilson, "a friend of free speech in theory," David M. Kennedy has written, "was its foe in fact." He signed the Espionage Act of 1917, which imposed fines of up to $10,000 and jail sentences ranging to 20 years on persons convicted of aiding the enemy or obstructing recruiting, and he authorized the postmaster general to ban from the mails any material that seemed treasonable or seditious.

In May 1918, again with Wilson's approval, Congress passed the Sedition Act, which made "saying anything" to discourage the purchase of war bonds a crime. The law also made it illegal to "utter, print, write, or publish any disloyal, profane, scurrilous, or abusive language" about the government, the Constitution, or the uniform of the army or navy. Socialist periodicals were suppressed, and Eugene V. Debs was sentenced to

ten years in prison for making an antiwar speech. Ricardo Flores Magon, an anarchist, was sentenced to 20 years in jail for publishing a statement criticizing Wilson's Mexican policy, an issue that had nothing to do with the war.

These laws went far beyond what was necessary to protect the national interest. Citizens were jailed for suggesting that the draft law was unconstitutional and for criticizing private organizations like the Red Cross and the YMCA. One woman was sent to prison for writing: "I am for the people, and the government is for the profiteers."

The wartime hysteria far exceeded anything that happened in Great Britain and France. In 1916 the French novelist Henri Barbusse published *Le Feu (Under Fire),* a graphic account of the horrors and purposelessness of trench warfare. In one chapter, Barbusse described a pilot flying over the trenches on a Sunday, observing French and German soldiers at Mass in the open fields, each worshiping the same God. Yet *Le Feu* circulated freely in France, even winning the coveted Prix Goncourt.

Wartime Reforms

The American mobilization experience was part and product of the Progressive Era. The work of the progressives at the national and state levels in expanding government functions in order to deal with social and economic problems provided precedents and conditioned the people for the all-out effort of 1917–1918. Social and economic planning and the management of huge business operations by public boards and committees got their first practical tests. College professors, technicians, and others with complex skills entered government service en masse. The federal government for the first time entered actively such fields as housing and labor relations.

Many progressives believed that the war was creating a sense of common purpose that would stimulate the people to act unselfishly to benefit the poor and to eradicate social evils. As one reformer said, "enthusiasm for social service is epidemic." Patriotism and public service seemed at last united. Men and women worked for a dozen causes only remotely related to the war effort. The women's suffrage movement was brought to fruition, as was the campaign against alcohol. Reformers began to talk about health insurance and to press older drives for workmen's compensation laws. A national campaign against prostitution and venereal disease gained strength, supported both by persons worried about inexperienced local girls being seduced by soldiers and by those concerned lest prostitutes lead innocent soldiers astray.

Women and Blacks in Wartime

Although a number of prominent feminists were pacifists, most supported the war. Opposition would lessen their chances of gaining the vote, and they expected that the war would open up many kinds of high-paying jobs to women. To some extent it did; about a million women replaced men in uniform, but the number actually engaged in war industries was small, and the gains fleeting. When the war ended, most women industrial workers either left their jobs voluntarily or were fired to make room for returning veterans. Some women served overseas as nurses, and a few were ambulance drivers and YMCA workers.

Most unions were unsympathetic to the idea of enrolling women, and the government did little to encourage women to do more for the war effort than prepare bandages, knit warm clothing for soldiers, participate in food conservation programs, and encourage people to buy war bonds. There was a Women in Industry Service and a Woman's Committee of the Council of National Defense, but both served primarily as window dressing. The *Final Report* of another wartime agency admitted that few women war workers had been paid as much as men and that women had been promoted more slowly than men, were not accepted by unions, and were discharged promptly when the war ended.

The wartime "great migration" of southern blacks to northern cities where jobs were available brought them important economic benefits. Between 1870 and 1890, only about 80,000 blacks had moved to northern cities. Compared with the influx from Europe and from northern farms, this was a trivial number. The black proportion of the population of New York City, for example, fell from over 10 percent in 1800 to under 2 percent in 1900.

Around the turn of the century, as southern repression increased, the northward movement quickened—about 200,000 blacks migrated be-

tween 1890 and 1910. Then, after 1914, the war boom drew blacks north in a flood. "Leave the benighted land," the *Chicago Defender*, a newspaper with a considerable circulation in southern states, urged. "Get out of the South." Half a million made the move between 1914 and 1919.

Life for the newcomers was difficult; workers feared them as potential strikebreakers yet refused to admit them into their unions. In East St. Louis, Illinois, a bloody riot erupted during the summer of 1917 in which nine whites and a undetermined number of blacks were killed. As in peacetime, the Wilson administration was at worst antagonistic and at best indifferent to blacks' needs and aspirations.

Nevertheless, the blacks who moved north during the war were infinitely better off, materially and psychologically, than those they left behind. They earned good wages and were accorded at least some human rights. They could vote, send their children to decent schools, and within reasonable limits do and say what they pleased without fear of humiliation or physical attack.

There were two black regiments in the regular army and a number of black national guard units when the war began. At first no blacks were conscripted; southerners in particular found the thought of giving large numbers of blacks guns and teaching them how to use them most disturbing. Blacks were, however, soon drafted, and once they were, a larger proportion of them than whites were taken. After a riot in Texas in which black soldiers killed 17 white civilians, black recruits were dispersed among many camps for training to lessen the possibility of trouble.

In the service, all blacks were placed in segregated units. Only a handful were commissioned officers. Most, even those sent overseas, were assigned to labor battalions, working as stevedores and common laborers. But many fought and died for the country. Altogether about 200,000 served overseas. There were black Red Cross nurses in France, and some blacks held relatively high posts in government agencies in Washington, the most important being Emmett J. Scott, who was special assistant for Negro affairs in the War Department.

W. E. B. Du Bois supported the war wholeheartedly. He praised Wilson for making, at last, a strong statement against lynching, which had increased to a shocking extent during the previous decade. He even went along with the fact that black officer candidates were trained in a segregated camp. "Let us," he wrote in *The Crisis,* "while the war lasts, forget our special grievances and close ranks shoulder to shoulder with our fellow citizens and the allied nations that are fighting for democracy."

Many blacks condemned Du Bois's accommodationism (which he promptly abandoned when the war ended), but most saw the war as an opportunity to demonstrate their patriotism and prove their worth to whites. For the moment the prevailing mood was one of optimism. If winning the war would make the world safe for democracy, surely blacks in the United States would be better off when it was won.

"Over There"

All activity on the home front had one ultimate objective: defeating the Central Powers on the battlefield. This was accomplished. The navy performed with special distinction. In April 1917 German submarines sank more than 870,000 tons of Allied shipping; after April 1918, monthly losses never reached 300,000 tons. American destroyers helped control the U-boats. The decision to send merchantmen across the Atlantic in convoys screened by warships made the reduction possible. Checking the U-boats was essential because of the need to transport American troops to Europe. More than 2 million made the voyage safely.

The first units of the American Expeditionary Force (AEF), elements of the regular army commanded by General John J. Pershing, reached Paris on Independence Day 1917. They took up positions on the front near Verdun in October. Not until the spring of 1918, however, did the "doughboys" play a significant role in the fighting, though their presence boosted French and British morale.

In March 1918 the Germans launched a great spring offensive, their armies strengthened by thousands of veterans from the Russian front. By late May, they had reached a point on the Marne River near the town of Château-Thierry, only 50 miles from Paris. Early in June the AEF fought its first major engagements, driving the Germans back from Château-Thierry and Belleau Wood.

In this fighting only about 27,500 Americans saw action, and thery suffered appalling losses. By mid-July 85,000 Americans were in the lines, and by late August the American First Army, 500,000 strong, was poised before the Saint-Mihiel salient, a deep extension of the German lines southeast of Verdun. On September 12 this army, buttressed by French troops, struck and in two days wiped out the salient.

Late in September began the greatest American engagement of the war. No fewer than 1.2 million doughboys drove forward west of Verdun into the Argonne Forest. For over a month of indescribable horror, they inched ahead through the tangle of the Argonne and the formidable defenses of the Hindenburg Line, while to the west French and British armies staged similar drives. In this one offensive the AEF suffered 120,000 casualties. Finally, on November 1, they broke the German center and raced toward the vital Sedan-Mézières railroad. On November 11, with Allied armies advancing on all fronts, the Germans signed the armistice, ending the fighting.*

Preparing for Peace

The fighting ended on November 11, 1918, but the shape of the postwar world remained to be determined. Confusion reigned. People wanted peace yet burned for revenge. Millions faced starvation. Other millions were disillusioned by the seemingly purposeless sacrifices of four years of horrible war. Communism—to some an idealistic promise of human betterment, to others a commitment to rational economic and social planning, to still others a danger to individual freedom, toleration, and democracy—having conquered Russia, threatened to envelop Germany and much of the defunct Austro-Hungarian empire, perhaps

---

*American losses in the war amounted to 112,432 dead and 230,074 wounded. More than half of the deaths, however, resulted from disease. Although severe, these casualties were trivial compared with those of the other belligerents. British Commonwealth deaths amounted to 947,000, French to 1.38 million, Russian to 1.7 million, Italian to 460,000. Among the Central Powers, Germany lost 1.8 million men, Austria-Hungary 1.2 million, Turkey 325,000. In addition, about 20 million European soldiers were wounded.

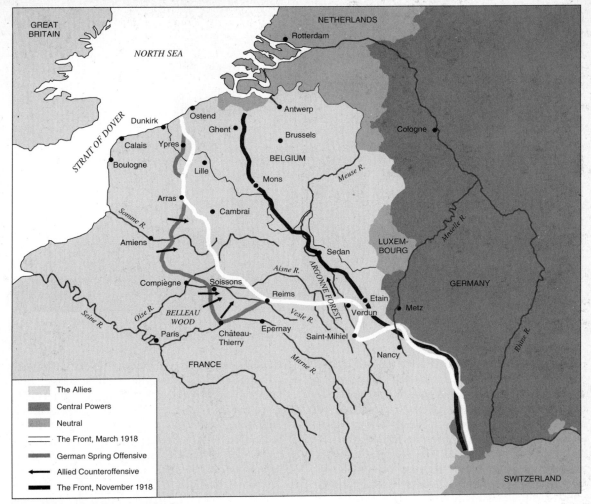

The Western Front, 1918

even the victorious Allies. How could stability be restored? How could victory be made worth its enormous cost?

Woodrow Wilson had grasped the significance of the war while most statesmen still thought that triumph on the battlefield would settle everything automatically. He faced the future on November 11 with determination and sober confidence. As early as January 1917, he had realized that victory would be wasted if the winners permitted themselves the luxury of vengeance. Such a policy would disrupt the balance of power and lead to economic and social chaos. American participation in the struggle had not blurred his vi-

sion. The victors must build a better society, he insisted, not punish those they believed had destroyed the old.

Long before the war ended, in a speech to Congress on January 8, 1918, Wilson outlined a plan, known as the Fourteen Points, designed to make the world "fit and safe to live in." The peace treaty should be negotiated in full view of world opinion, not in secret. It should guarantee the freedom of the seas to all nations, in war as in peacetime. It should tear down barriers to international trade, provide for a drastic reduction of armaments, and establish a colonial system that would take proper account of the interests of the

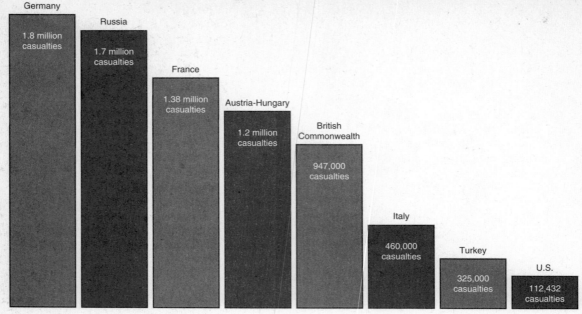

Germany
1.8 million casualties

Russia
1.7 million casualties

France
1.38 million casualties

Austria-Hungary
1.2 million casualties

British Commonwealth
947,000 casualties

Italy
460,000 casualties

Turkey
325,000 casualties

U.S.
112,432 casualties

Casualties of the Great War

native peoples concerned. European boundaries should be redrawn so that no substantial group would have to live under a government not of its own choosing. More specifically, captured Russian territory should be restored, Belgium evacuated, Alsace-Lorraine returned to France, the heterogeneous nationalities of Austria-Hungary accorded autonomy. Italy's frontiers should be adjusted "along clearly recognizable lines of nationality," the Balkans made free, Turkey divested of its subject peoples, an independent Polish state (with access to the Baltic Sea) created. To oversee the new system, Wilson insisted, "a general association of nations must be formed under specific covenants for the purpose of affording mutual guarantees of political independence and territorial integrity to great and small states alike."

Wilson's Fourteen Points for a fair peace lifted the hopes of people everywhere. After the guns fell silent, however, the vagueness and inconsistencies in the Points became apparent. Complete national self-determination was impossible in polyglot Europe; there were too many regions of mixed population for every group to be satisfied. Furthermore, the Allies had made certain territor-

ial commitments to one another in secret treaties that ran counter to the principle of self-determination, and they were not ready to give up all claim to Germany's colonies. In every Allied country, millions rejected the idea of a peace without indemnities. They expected to make the enemy pay for the war, as Sir Eric Geddes, the first lord of the Admiralty said, to squeeze Germany "as a lemon is squeezed—until the pips squeak."

Wilson assumed that the practical advantages of his program would compel opponents to fall in line. He had the immense advantage of seeking nothing for his own country and the additional strength of being leader of the one important nation to emerge from the war richer and more powerful than it had been in 1914. Yet this combination of altruism, idealism, and power was his undoing; it intensified his tendency to be overbearing and undermined his judgment. Believing that the fate of humanity hung on his actions, he became in his own mind a prophet, almost, one fears, a kind of god.

In the last weeks of the war Wilson proved to be a brilliant diplomat, first dangling the Fourteen Points before the German people to encourage them to overthrow Kaiser Wilhelm II and sue for an armistice, then sending Colonel House to Paris to persuade Allied leaders to accept the Fourteen Points as the basis for the peace. When the Allies raised objections, House made certain small concessions, but by hinting that the United States might make a separate peace with Germany, he forced them to agree. Under the armistice, Germany had to withdraw behind the Rhine River and surrender its submarines, together with quantities of munitions and other materials. In return it received the assurance of the Allies that the Wilsonian principles would prevail at the peace conference.

Wilson then came to a daring decision: He would personally attend the conference, which convened on January 12, 1919, at Paris, as a member of the United States Peace Commission. This was a precedent-shattering step, for no previous president had left American territory while in office.

Wilson probably erred in going to Paris, but not because of the novelty or possible illegality of the act. In leaving the country, he was turning his back on certain obvious domestic problems. Western farmers believed they had been discriminated against during the war, since wheat prices had been controlled while the price of southern cotton had been allowed to rise from 7 cents a pound in 1914 to 35 cents in 1919.

The administration's drastic tax program had angered businessmen. Labor, despite its gains, was restive in the face of reconversion to peacetime conditions. Most important, Wilson intended to break with the isolationist tradition and take the United States into a League of Nations. Such a revolutionary change required explanation; he should have undertaken a major campaign to convince the people of the wisdom of this step.

Wilson also erred in his choice of the other commissioners. He selected Colonel House, Secretary of State Lansing, General Tasker H. Bliss, and Henry White, a career diplomat. These men were all thoroughly competent, but House had never held a government office, Lansing did not sympathize with Wilson's proposals, and White, the only Republican, had no stature as a politician. Since the peace treaty would have to be ratified by the Senate, Wilson should have given that body some representation on the commission, and since the Republicans would have a majority in the new Senate, a Republican senator or someone who had the full confidence of the Republican leadership should have been appointed. (The wily McKinley named three senators to the American delegation to the peace conference after the Spanish-American War.)

The Paris Peace Conference

Wilson arrived in Europe a world hero. He toured England, France, and Italy briefly and was greeted ecstatically almost everywhere. The reception tended to increase his sense of mission and to convince him, in the fashion of a typical progressive, that whatever the European politicians might say about it, "the people" were behind his program.

When the conference settled down to its work, control quickly fell into the hands of the so-called Big Four: Wilson, Prime Minister David Lloyd George of Great Britain, Premier Georges Clemenceau of France, and Prime Minister Vittorio Orlando of Italy. Wilson stood out in this group but did not dominate it.

The 78-year-old Clemenceau cared only for one thing: French security. He viewed Wilson most cynically, saying that since mankind had been unable to keep God's Ten Commandments, it was unlikely to do better with Wilson's Fourteen Points. Lloyd George's approach was pragmatic and almost cavalier. He sympathized with much that Wilson was trying to accomplish but found the president's frequent sermonettes about "right being more important than might, and justice being more eternal than force" incomprehensible. Orlando was not the equal of his three colleagues in influence. He left the conference in a huff when they failed to meet all his demands.

The conference labored from January to May 1919 and finally brought forth the Versailles Treaty. American liberals whose hopes had soared at the thought of a peace based on the Fourteen Points found the document abysmally disappointing. The peace settlement failed to carry out the principle of self-determination completely. It gave Italy a large section of the Austrian Tyrol, though the area contained 200,000 persons who considered themselves Austrians. Other German-speaking groups were incorporated into the new states of Poland and Czechoslovakia. Japan was allowed to take over the Chinese province of Shantung, and one or another of the Allies swallowed up all the German colonies in Africa and the Far East.

The victors forced Germany to accept responsibility for having caused the war—an act of senseless vindictiveness as well as a gross oversimplification—and to sign a "blank check," agreeing to pay for all damage to civilian properties and even future pensions and other indirect war costs. Instead of attacking imperialism, the treaty attacked German imperialism; instead of seeking a new international social order based on liberty and democracy, it created a Great Power entente designed to crush Germany and to exclude Bolshevist Russia from the family of nations. It said nothing about freedom of the seas, the reduction of tariffs, or disarmament.

The complaints of the critics were individually reasonable, yet their conclusions were not entirely fair. The new map of Europe left fewer people on "foreign" soil than in any earlier period of history. Although the Allies seized the German colonies, they were required, under the mandate system, to render the League of Nations annual accounts of their stewardship and to prepare the inhabitants for eventual independence. Above all, Wilson persuaded the powers to incorporate the League of Nations in the treaty.

Wilson expected the League of Nations to make up for all the inadequacies of the Versailles Treaty. Once the League had begun to function, problems like freedom of the seas and disarmament would solve themselves, he argued, and the relaxation of trade barriers would surely follow. The League would arbitrate international disputes, act as a central body for registering treaties, and employ military and economic sanctions against aggressor nations.

Liberal critics of the League were correct in saying that Wilson was seeking to prop up the existing social and economic system. He was gravely concerned lest communism or even democratic socialism gain the upper hand in Central Europe. He hoped, unrealistically as it turned out, to see Europe develop a capitalist-worker consensus like that which existed in the United States.

By any standard, Wilson had achieved a remarkably moderate peace, one full of hope for the future. Except for the war-guilt clause and the heavy reparations imposed on Germany, he could be justly proud of his work.

The Senate and the League of Nations

When Wilson returned from France, he finally directed his attention to the task of winning public approval of his handiwork. A large majority of the people probably favored the League of Nations in principle, though few understood all its implications or were entirely happy with every detail. Wilson had persuaded the Allies to accept certain changes in the original draft to mollify American opposition. One provided that no nation could be forced to accept a colonial mandate, another that "domestic questions" such as tariffs and the control of immigration did not fall within the competence of the League.

Many senators found the modifications insufficient. Even before the peace conference ended, 37 Republican senators signed a manifesto, devised by Henry Cabot Lodge of Massachusetts, opposing Wilson's League and demanding that the question of an international organization be put off until "the urgent business of negotiating peace terms with Germany" had been completed. Wilson rejected this suggestion icily. Thus the stage was set for a monumental test of strength between the president and the Republican majority in the Senate.

Partisanship, principle, and prejudice clashed mightily in this contest. A presidential election loomed. Should the League prove a success, the Republicans wanted to be able to claim a share of the credit, but Wilson had refused to allow them to participate in drafting the document. This predisposed all of them to favor changes. Politics aside, genuine alarm at the possible sacrifice of American sovereignty to an international authority led many Republicans to urge modification of the League Covenant, or constitution. Personal dislike of Wilson and his high-handed methods motivated others. Yet the noble purpose of the League made many reluctant to reject it entirely.

The "Big Four" at the Hotel Crillon in Paris. First row, from the left: Orlando of Italy, Lloyd George of Great Britain, Clemenceau of France, and Wilson of the United States.

Wilson could count on the Democratic senators almost to a man, but he had to win over many Republicans to obtain the two-thirds majority necessary for ratification. Republican opinion divided roughly into three segments. At one extreme were some dozen "irreconcilables" led by William E. Borah of Idaho. At the other extreme stood another dozen "mild" reservationists who were in favor of the League but who hoped to alter it in minor ways, chiefly for political purposes. In the middle were the "strong" reservationists, senators willing to go along with the League only if American sovereignty were fully protected and it were made clear that their party had played a major role in fashioning the final document.

Senator Lodge, the leader of the Republican opposition, was chairman of the Senate Foreign Relations Committee. Although not an isolationist, he had little faith in the League. He also had a profound distrust of Democrats, especially Wilson, whom he considered a hypocrite and a coward. The president's pious idealism left him cold.

While perfectly ready to see the country participate actively in world affairs, Lodge insisted that its right to determine its own best interests in every situation be preserved. He had been a senator since 1893 and an admirer of senatorial independence since early manhood; when a Democratic president tried to ram the Versailles Treaty through the Upper House, he fought him with every weapon he could muster.

Lodge belonged to the strong reservationist faction. His own proposals, known as the Lodge Reservations, limited the United States' obligations to the League and stated in unmistakable terms the right of Congress to decide when to honor these obligations. Some of the reservations were mere quibbles. Others, such as the provision that the United States would not endorse Japan's seizure of Chinese territory, were included mainly to embarrass Wilson by pointing up compromises he had made at Versailles. The most important reservation applied to Article X of the League Covenant, which committed signatories to protect the political independence and territorial integrity of all member nations. Wilson had rightly called Article X "the heart of the Covenant." Lodge's reservation made it inoperable so far as the

United States was concerned "unless in any particular case the Congress . . . shall by act or joint resolution so provide."

Lodge performed brilliantly if somewhat unscrupulously in uniting the three Republican factions behind the reservations. He got the irreconcilables to agree to them by conceding their right to vote against the final version in any event, and he held the mild reservationists in line by modifying some of his demands and stressing the importance of party unity. Since Lodge's proposals (whatever his personal motivation) dealt forthrightly with the problem of reconciling traditional concepts of national sovereignty with the new idea of world cooperation, supporters of the League could accept them without sacrifice of principle. Wilson, however, refused to budge.

This foolish intransigence seems almost incomprehensible in a man of Wilson's intelligence and political experience. In part his hatred of Lodge accounts for it, in part his faith in his League. His physical condition in 1919 also played a role. At Paris he had suffered a violent attack of indigestion that was probably a symptom of a minor stroke. Thereafter many observers noted small changes in his personality, particularly an increased stubbornness and a loss of good judgment.

Instead of making concessions, the president set out early in September on a nationwide speaking tour to rally support for the League. Although some of his speeches were brilliant, they had little effect on senatorial opinion, and the effort drained his last physical reserves. On September 25, after an address in Pueblo, Colorado, he collapsed. The rest of the trip had to be canceled. A few days later, in Washington, he suffered a stroke that partially paralyzed his left side.

For nearly two months, the president was almost totally cut off from affairs of state, leaving supporters of the League leaderless while Lodge maneuvered the reservations through the Senate. Gradually, popular attitudes toward the League shifted. Organized groups of Italian, Irish, and German Americans, angered by what they considered unfair treatment of their native lands in the Versailles Treaty, clamored for outright rejection. The arguments of the irreconcilables persuaded many citizens that Wilson had made too sharp a break with America's isolationist past and that the Lodge Reservations were therefore necessary. Other issues connected with the reconversion of society to a peacetime basis increasingly occupied the public mind.

A coalition of Democratic and moderate Republican senators could easily have carried the treaty. However, Wilson, bitter and emotionally distraught, urged the Democrats to vote for rejection, Thus the amended treaty failed, 35 to 55, the irreconcilables and the Democrats voting against it. Lodge then allowed the original draft without his reservations to come to a vote. Again the result was defeat, 38 to 53. Only one Republican cast a ballot for ratification.

Dismayed but not yet crushed, friends of the League in both parties forced reconsideration of the treaty early in 1920. Neither Lodge nor Wilson would yield an inch. Lodge, who had little confidence in the effectiveness of any league of nations, was under no compulsion to compromise. That Wilson, whose entire being was tied up in the Covenant, would not do so is further evidence of his physical and mental decline. Probably he was incompetent to perform the duties of his office. When the Senate balloted again in March, half the Democrats voted for the treaty with the Lodge Reservations. The others, mostly southern party regulars, joined the irreconcilables. Together they mustered 35 votes, 7 more than the one-third that meant defeat.

Demobilization

To win the war, the nation had accepted drastic regulation of the economy. When it ended, the Wilson administration blithely assumed that the economy could readjust itself without direction. The army was demobilized, pouring millions of veterans into the job market without plan. Nearly all controls established by the War Industries Board and other agencies were dropped overnight. Billions of dollars' worth of war contracts were canceled.

Business boomed in 1919 as consumers spent wartime savings on automobiles, homes, and other goods that had been in short supply during the conflict. But temporary shortages caused inflation; by 1920 the cost of living stood at more than twice the level of 1913.

Inflation in turn produced labor trouble. The unions, grown strong during the war, struck for wage increases. More than 4 million workers, one out of five in the labor force, were on strike at some time during 1919. Then came one of the most precipitous economic declines in American history. Between July 1920 and March 1922, prices, especially agricultural prices, plummeted. Unemployment soared.

The Red Scare

Far more serious than the economic losses were the social effects of these difficulties. Most Americans found strikes frustrating and drew invidious comparisons between the lot of the unemployed soldier who had risked his life for a dollar a day and that of the striker who had drawn fat wages during the war in perfect safety.

The activities of radicals in the labor movement led millions of citizens to associate unionism and strikes with the new threat of communist world revolution. Although there were only a relative handful of communists in the United States, Russia's experience persuaded many people that a tiny minority of ruthless revolutionaries could take over a nation of millions if conditions were right. When strikes broke out, some accompanied by violence, many people interpreted them as communist-inspired preludes to revolution. Louis Wiley, an experienced *New York Times* reporter, told a friend at this time that anarchists, socialists, and radical labor leaders were "joining together with the object of overthrowing the American Government through a bloody revolution."

Organized labor in America had seldom been truly radical, but some labor leaders had been attracted to socialism, and many Americans failed to distinguish between the common ends sought by communists and socialists and the entirely different methods by which they proposed to achieve those ends. A general strike paralyzed Seattle in February 1919. In September 1919 a total of 343,000 steelworkers walked off their jobs, and in the same month the Boston police struck. Violence marked the steel strike, and the suspension of police protection in Boston led to looting and fighting that ended only when Governor Calvin Coolidge called out the National Guard.

During the same period, a handful of terrorists attempted to murder various prominent persons, including John D. Rockefeller, Justice Oliver Wendell Holmes, Jr., and Attorney General A. Mitchell Palmer. What particularly aroused the public was the fact that most radicals were not American citizens. Wartime fear of alien saboteurs easily transformed itself into peacetime terror of foreign radicals. In this muddled way, radicalism, unionism, and questions of racial and national origins combined to make many Americans believe that their way of life was in imminent danger. Thus the "Red Scare" was born.

Attorney General Palmer was the key figure in the resulting purge. Pressure from Congress and his growing conviction that the communists really were a menace led him to join the "red hunt." Soon he was saying of the radicals: "Out of the sly and crafty eyes of many of them leap cupidity, cruelty, insanity, and crime; from their lopsided faces, sloping brows, and misshapen features may be recognized the unmistakable criminal type."

In August 1919, Palmer established within the Department of Justice the General Intelligence Division, headed by J. Edgar Hoover, to collect information about clandestine radical activities. In November, Justice Department agents swooped down on the meeting places of an anarchist organization known as the Union of Russian Workers in a dozen cities. More than 650 persons were arrested but in only 43 cases could evidence be found to justify deportation.

Nevertheless, the public reacted so favorably that Palmer planned an immense roundup of communists. On January 2, 1920, his agents, reinforced by local police and self-appointed vigilantes, struck simultaneously in 33 cities.

About 6,000 persons were taken into custody, many of them citizens and therefore not subject to the deportation laws, many others unconnected with any radical cause. In a number of cases, individuals who went to visit prisoners were themselves thrown behind bars on the theory that they too must be communists. Hundreds of suspects were jammed into filthy "bullpens," beaten, and forced to sign "confessions."

The public tolerated these wholesale violations of civil liberties because of the supposed menace of communism. Gradually, however, protests began to be heard. No revolutionary outbreak had taken place. Of 6,000 seized in the Palmer raids, only 556 proved liable to deportation.

Palmer, attempting to maintain the crusade, announced that the radicals planned a gigantic terrorist demonstration for May Day 1920. In New York and other cities, thousands of police were placed on round-the-clock duty; federal troops stood by anxiously. But the day passed without even a rowdy meeting. Suddenly Palmer appeared ridiculous. The Red Scare swiftly subsided.

The Election of 1920

Wilson still hoped for vindication at the polls in the presidential election, which he sought to make a "great and solemn referendum" on the League. He would have liked to run again himself, but in his enfeebled condition, he attracted no support. The Democrats nominated James M. Cox of Ohio. Cox favored joining the League, but the election did not produce the referendum on the organization that Wilson desired. The Republicans, whose candidate was another Ohioan, Senator Warren G. Harding, equivocated shamelessly on the issue. The election turned on other matters, largely emotional.

Disillusioned by the results of the war, many Americans had had their fill of idealism. They wanted, apparently, to end the long period of moral uplift and reform agitation that had begun under Theodore Roosevelt and return to what Harding called "normalcy." To the extent that the voters were expressing opinions on Wilson's League, they responded overwhelmingly in the negative. Harding had been a strong reservationist, yet he swept the country, winning over 16.1 million votes to Cox's 9.1 million. In July 1921 Congress formally ended the war with the Central Powers by passing a joint resolution.

Milestones

Year	Event	Year	Event
1914	United States invades Veracruz, Mexico		Herbert Hoover named food administrator
	War breaks out in Europe		Bernard Baruch named head of War Industries Board
1915	U-boat torpedoes *Lusitania*		Ex-President Taft heads War Labor Board
	United States recognizes the Carranza government in Mexico		
1916	Louis D. Brandeis named to Supreme Court	1918	Sedition Act
	Adamson Act gives railroad workers the eight-hour day		Republicans gain control of both houses of Congress
	"Pancho" Villa burns Columbus, New Mexico		Armistice ends the Great War
1917	Wilson's "peace without victory" speech	1919	Steel Strike
	Germany resumes unrestricted submarine warfare		Red Scare, climaxing in the Palmer raids
	United States declares war on Central Powers		Paris Peace Conference
			Senate rejects Versailles Treaty
		1920	Senate again rejects Versailles Treaty

Supplementary Reading

R. H. Ferrell, **Woodrow Wilson and World War I** (1985), surveys the war years. Wilson's handling of foreign relations is discussed in Volumes 2 and 3 of A. S. Link's **Wilson** and in his **Wilson the Diplomatist*** (1957). See also F. S. Calhoun, **Power and Principle: Armed Intervention in Wilsonian Foreign Policy** (1986), N. G. Levin, Jr., **Woodrow Wilson and World Politics** (1968), and E. H. Buehrig, **Woodrow Wilson and World Power** (1955).

The war on the home front is covered in D. M. Kennedy, **Over Here: The First World War and American Society*** (1980), N. A. Wynn, **From Progressivism to Prosperity** (1986), R. D. Cuff, **The War Industries Board** (1973), M. W. Greewald, **Women, War, and Work** (1980), S. L. Vaughn, **Holding Fast the Inner Lines** (1980), and E. M. Coffman, **The War to End All Wars** (1968). Laurence Stallings, **The Doughboys*** (1963), is a good popular account of the American army in France. A. E. Barbeau and F. H. Florette describe the role of blacks in the army in **The Unknown Soldiers** (1974).

On the peace settlement, in addition to the biographies of Wilson, consult A. J. Mayer, **Politics and Diplomacy of Peacemaking** (1967), Ralph Stone, **The Irreconcilables*** (1970), W. C. Widenor, **Henry Cabot Lodge and the Search for an American Foreign Policy** (1980), and J. A. Garraty, **Henry Cabot Lodge** (1953). On the election of 1920, see Wesley Bagby, **The Road to Normalcy*** (1962), and R. K. Murray, **The Harding Era** (1969).

*Available in paperback.

CHAPTER 25

Postwar Society and Culture: Change and Adjustment

Closing the Gates

New Urban Social Patterns

The Younger Generation

The "New" Woman

Popular Culture: Movies and Radio

The Golden Age of Sports

Urban–Rural Conflicts: Fundamentalism

Urban–Rural Conflicts: Prohibtion

The Ku Klux Klan

Sacco and Vanzetti

Literary Trends

The "New Negro"

The "New Era"

The Age of the Consumer

Henry Ford

The Airplane

*T*he Great War seemed to many of those who lived through it a turning point in history, the real division separating the 19th from the new 20th century. Actually most of what seemed characteristically new to the people of the 1920s had begun to appear before well before 1917 and the changes they noticed were still going on. They were in the midst of adjusting to new social, cultural, and economic forces, forces that were to shape their lives and those of their children and grandchildren.

Closing the Gates

The ending of the Red Scare did not herald the disappearance of xenophobia. It was perhaps inevitable and possibly wise that some limitation be placed on the entry of immigrants into the United States after the war. An immense backlog of prospective migrants had piled up during the conflict, and the desperate postwar economic condition of Europe led hundreds of thousands to seek better circumstances in the United States.

Congress, reflecting a widespread prejudice against eastern and southern Europeans, passed an emergency act establishing a quota system. Each year 3 percent of the number of foreign-born residents of the United States in 1910 (about 350,000 persons) might enter the country. Each country's quota was based on the number of its nationals in the United States in 1910. This meant that only a relative handful of the total would be from southern and eastern Europe. In 1929 Congress further reduced the total admitted to 150,000 immigrants a year. In fact, far fewer than 150,000 people entered because the favored European nations failed to fulfill their quotas. British immigration between 1931 and 1939, for example, amounted to only 23,000 even though the annual British quota was over 65,000.

The system ignored America's long history of constantly changing ethnic heterogeneity. The motto *e pluribus unum*, conceived to represent the unity of the original 13 states, applied even more appropriately to the blending of different cultures into one nationality. The new law sought to freeze the mix, turn the American melting pot into a kind of gigantic ice cube. Instead of an open, cosmopolitan society eager to accept, in Emma Lazarus's stirring line, the "huddled masses yearning to breathe free," the United States had closed the gates.

New Urban Social Patterns

The census of 1920 revealed that for the first time a majority of Americans lived in "urban" rather than "rural" places. This statement is somewhat misleading because the census classified anyone in a community of 2,500 or more as urban. Of the 54 million "urban" residents in 1920, over 16 million lived in villages and small towns; a large majority of them held ideas and values like those of rural citizens. But the one person in four who lived in a city of 100,000 or more—and particularly the nearly 16.4 million who lived in metropolises of at least half a million—were increasing steadily in number and influence.

Being a city dweller affected family structure, educational opportunities, and dozens of other aspects of human existence. Indeed, since most of the changes in the relations of husbands, wives, and children that had occurred in the 19th century were related to the fact that people were leaving farms to work in towns and cities, these trends intensified in the early 20th. In addition, couples continued to marry more because of love and physical attraction and each decade people married slightly later in life and had fewer children.

Earlier differences between working-class and middle-class family structures persisted. In 1920 about one-quarter of the American women who were working were married, but middle-class married women who worked were nearly all either childless or highly paid professionals who were able to employ servants. Most male skilled workers now earned enough to support a family in modest comfort so long as they could work steadily, but an unskilled laborer still could not. Wives in most such families had to work.

However, there were important variations in the roles of wives of different ethnic backgrounds. Those who could not speak English well had difficulty obtaining work. Italian immigrant women rarely worked outside the home. Irish American wives, on the other hand, often found jobs as domestics or if better educated, as nurses or telephone operators or clerks. Out of necessity a far larger proportion of black women, married or single, worked than white women.

By the 1920s the idea of intra-family democracy had emerged. In such families husbands and wives would deal with each other as equals, which downplayed male authority, and stressed mutual satisfaction in sexual and other matters. Procreation did not have to be the main purpose of matrimony, but if there were children, they should be left as free as possible; rigid discipline was limiting and therefore wrong. On the other hand, divorce should be made easier for couples that did not get along, provided they did not have children.

Much attention was given to "scientific" child raising. One school stressed rigid training: children could be "spoiled" by indulgence; toilet training should begin early; too much kissing could turn male youngsters into "mama's boys." "Children are made not born," John B. Watson explained in *The Psychological Care of Infant and Child* (1928). "Never hug and kiss them, never let them sit in your lap. If you must, kiss them once on the forehead when they say good night."

The other school favored a more permissive approach. Toilet training could wait, parents should pay attention to their children's expressed needs, not impose a generalized set of rules on them. In *The Companionate Marriage* (1927), Benjamin B. Lindsey, a juvenile court judge, suggested a kind of trial marriage, a period during which a young couple could get used to one another before undertaking to raise a family.

Lindsey was one among many "experts" who advocated more freedom for young people and open discussion of all questions related to sex. He was most concerned about the welfare of children, whose natural sexuality, he insisted, was being stupidly repressed by Victorian prudes. Others put more emphasis on married women's rights and the injustice of the double standard. Still others were interested in breaking down 19th-century sexual taboos for all people, married or single.

The Younger Generation

All of these matters were of particular concern to the generation born that had grown up before and during the Great War. That war had raised, and its outcome dashed, their hopes for the future. Now the narrowness and prudery of so many of their elders and the stuffy conservatism of nearly all politicians seemed not merely old-fashioned but ludicrous. Their models and indeed some of their leaders were the prewar Greenwich Village Bohemians.

The 1920s have been described as the "Jazz Age," the era of "flaming youth," when young people danced to syncopated "African" rhythms, careened about the countryside in automobiles in search of pleasure and forgetfulness, and made gods of movie stars and professional athletes.

This view of the period bears a superficial resemblance to reality. But the resemblance is only superficial; if people appreciated having a good time and, like any generation moving from adolescence to maturity, they were eager to understand the world and make their way in it. They were unconventional because they were adjusting to more rapid changes in their world than their grandparents could have imagined.

Trends that were barely perceptible during the Progressive Era now reached avalanche proportions. This was particularly noticeable in relationships between the sexes. In the late 19th century, a typical young man "paid a call" on a female friend. The couple remained at home, the parents nearby if not actually participating in what was essentially a social (one might say, public) event held in a private place.

By the 1920s, paying calls was being replaced by *dating;* the young man called only to "pick up" his "date," the two to go off, free of parental supervision, for whatever diversion they wished. Unlike a call, Professor Beth Bailey has pointed out, a date was "a private act in the public world."

There is no question that for the young people of the 1920s, relations between the sexes were becoming more relaxed and uninhibited. Respectable young women smoked cigarettes, something previously done in public only by prostitutes and bohemian types. They cast off their heavy corsets, wore lipstick, and shortened both their hair and their skirts.

Freudian psychology and the more accessible ideas of the British "sexologist" Havelock Ellis, reached steadily deeper into the popular psyche. Since sex was "the central function of life," Ellis argued, it must be "simple and natural and pure and good." Bombarded by these exciting ideas, to say nothing of their own inclinations, young people found casting off their inhibitions more and more tempting.

Conservatives bemoaned what they described as the breakdown of moral standards, the fragmentation of the family, and the decline of parental authority—all with some reason. Nevertheless, society was not collapsing. Much of the rebelliousness of the young was faddish in nature, a kind of youthful conformity. This was particularly true of college students, where every aspect of their extracurricular life was governed by elaborate rituals. In *The Damned and the Beautiful,* Paul S. Fass has shown how such matters as fraternity and sorority initiations, styles of dress, and college slang, seemingly aspects of independence and free choice, were nearly everywhere shaped and controlled by peer pressure.

But young people's new ways of relating to one another were not mere fads, and were not confined to people under 30. This can be seen most clearly in the birth control movement, the drive to legalize the use of contraceptives.

The "New" Woman

The young people of the 1920s were more open about sex but this does not mean that most of them engaged in sexual intercourse before marriage. Single young people might "believe in" birth control, but relatively few (at least by modern standards) had occasion to practice it. Contraception was a concern of married people, and particularly of married women.

The leading American proponent of birth control in the 1920s was Margaret Sanger, one of the less self-centered Greenwich Village Bohemians. Before the war she was a political radical. Gradually, however, her attention focused on the plight of the poor women she encountered while working as a nurse; many of these women were burdened by large numbers of children yet knew nothing about contraception. Sanger began to write articles and pamphlets designed to enlighten them and when she did she was frequently in trouble with the law. But she was persistent to the edge of fanaticism. In 1921 she founded the American Birth Control League and two years later a research center.

The medical profession gave some support to the birth control movement as did the eugenicists, who claimed that unless the fecundity of "unfit" types (people others might describe simply as poor) was curbed, "race suicide" would result. By the end of the decade, Sanger was no longer on the cutting edge of the movement or even a very radical feminist. But by that time resistance to the use of contraception was crumbling.

Other sex-based restrictions of particular importance to women also seemed to be breaking down. The divorce laws had been modified in most states. More women were taking jobs; more than 10.6 million women were working by the end of the decade in contrast with 8.4 million in 1920. The Department of Labor's Women's Bureau was founded in 1920 and was soon conducting investigations of the working conditions women faced in different industries and how various laws affected them.

But most of these gains were illusory. Relaxation of the strict standards of sexual morality did not eliminate the double standard. More women worked, but most of the jobs they held were still ones that few men wanted: domestic service, elementary school teaching, clerical work, or selling behind a counter.

Where they competed for jobs with men, women usually received much lower wages. Yet when the head of the Women's Bureau, Mary Anderson, tried to get employers to raise women's wages, most of them claimed that the men had families to support. When she reminded them that many female employees also had family responsibilities, they told her that there was a "tacit understanding" that women were to make less than men. Efforts to get the American Federation of Labor to take up the issue met with failure; few of the unions in the federation admitted women.

The number of women college graduates continued to expand, but the colleges placed more emphasis on subjects like home economics that seemed designed to make them better housewives rather than professional nutritionists or business executives. As one Vassar College administrator (a woman!) said, colleges should provide "education for women along the lines of their chief interests and responsibilities, motherhood and the home."

The twenties proved disillusioning to feminists, who now paid a price for their single-minded pursuit of the right to vote in the Progressive Era. After the ratification of the Nineteenth Amendment, Carrie Chapman Catt was exultant, "We are no longer petitioners," she announced, "but free and equal citizens." Many activists, assuming the battle won, lost interest in agitating for change. They believed that the suffrage amendment had given them the one weapon needed to achieve whatever women still lacked. In fact, it soon became apparent that women did not vote as a bloc. Many, perhaps most, married women voted for the candidates their husbands supported.

When radical feminists discovered that voting did not automatically bring true equality, they founded the Women's Party and began campaigning for an equal rights amendment. Their leader, Alice Paul, a dynamic if somewhat single-issue person, disdained specific goals such as disarmament, ending child labor, and liberalized birth control. Total equality for women was the one objective. The party considered protective legislation governing the hours and working conditions of women discriminatory. This caused the so-called social feminists, who believed that children and working women needed the protection provided by such laws, to break away.

The Women's Party never attracted a wide following, but only partly because of the split with the social feminists. Many of the younger radical women, like the bohemians of the Progressive Era, were primarily concerned with their personal freedom to behave as they wished; politics did not interest them. But a more important reason was that nearly all the radicals failed to see that questions of gender—the *attitudes* that men and women *were taught* to take toward each other, not immutable *physical* or *psychological differences*—stood in the way of sexual equality. Many more women joined the more moderate League of Women Voters, which attempted to mobilize support for a broad spectrum of reforms, some of which had no specific connection with the interests of women as such. The entire women's movement lost momentum. The battle for the equal rights amendment persisted through the 1930s, but it was lost. By the end of that decade the movement was moribund.

Popular Culture: Movies and Radio

The postwar decade saw immense changes in popular culture. Unlike the literary flowering of the era, these changes seemed in tune with the times, not a reaction against them. This was true in part because they were products as much of technology as of human imagination.

The first motion pictures were made around 1900, but the medium only came into its own after the Great War. The early films, such as the eight-minute epic *The Great Train Robbery* (1903), were brief, action-packed, and unpretentious. Professional actors and most educated people viewed them with contempt. But their success was instantaneous. By 1912 there were more than 13,000 movie houses in the United States. Many were mere store fronts, called nickelodeons because the admissions charge was five cents.

Success led to rapid technical and artistic improvements. David W. Griffith's 12-reel *Birth of a Nation* (1915) was a particularly important breakthrough in both areas, though Griffith's sympathetic treatment of the Ku Klux Klan of Reconstruction days angered blacks and white liberals.

By the mid-twenties, the industry, centered in Hollywood, California, was the fourth largest in the nation in capital investment. Movie "palaces" seating several thousand people sprang up in the major cities, and they counted their yearly audiences in the tens of millions. With the introduction of talking movies, beginning with *The Jazz Singer* (1927), and color films a few years later, the motion picture reached technological maturity. Costs and profits mounted: By the thirties, million-dollar productions were common.

Many movies were tasteless trash catering to the prejudices of the multitude. Popular actors and actresses tended to be either handsome, talentless sticks or so-called character actors who were typecast over and over again as heroes, villains, and comedians. The stars were paid thousands of dollars a week. Critics charged that the movies were destroying the legitimate stage, corrupting the morals of youths, and glorifying the materialistic aspects of life.

Nevertheless the motion picture made positive contributions to American culture. Beginning with the work of Griffith, filmmakers created an entirely new theatrical art, using close-ups to portray character and heighten tension, broad panoramic shots to transcend the limits of the stage. They employed with remarkable results special lighting effects, the fade-out, and other techniques impossible in the live theater. Movies enabled dozens of established actors to reach wider audiences and developed many first-rate new ones. In Charlie Chaplin, whose characterization of the sad little tramp with his toothbrush moustache and his cane, tight frock coat, and baggy trousers became famous throughout the world, the new form found perhaps the supreme comic artist of all time. The animated cartoon, perfected by Walt Disney in the 1930s, was a lesser but significant achievement that gave endless delight to millions of children. And as the medium matured, it produced many dramatic works of high quality. At its best, the motion picture offered a breadth and power of impact superior to anything on the traditional stage.

Even more pervasive than movies in its effects on the American people was radio. Wireless transmission of sound was developed in the late 19th century by many scientists in Europe and the United States. In 1920 the first commercial station (KDKA in Pittsburgh) began broadcasting, and by the end of 1922 over 500 stations were in operation.

The immediacy of radio explained its tremendous impact. As a means of communicating the latest news, it had no peer; beginning with the broadcast of the 1924 presidential nominating conventions, all major public events were covered "live." Advertisers seized on radio too; it proved to be as useful for selling soap as for transmitting news.

Advertising had mixed effects on broadcasting. The sums paid by business for air time made possible elaborate entertainments performed by the finest actors and musicians, all without cost to listeners. However, advertisers hungered for mass markets. They preferred to sponsor programs of little intellectual content, aimed at the lowest tastes and utterly uncontroversial. And good and bad alike, programs were constantly interrupted by irritating pronouncements extolling the supposed virtues of one commercial product or another.

In 1927 Congress limited the number of stations and parceled out wave lengths to prevent interference. Further legislation in 1934 established the Federal Communications Commission (FCC) with power to revoke the licenses of stations that failed to operate in the public interest. But the FCC placed no effective controls on programming or on advertising practices.

The Golden Age of Sports

The extraordinary popularity of sports in the post-war period can be explained in a number of ways. People had more money to spend and more free time to fill. Radio was bringing suspenseful, play-by-play accounts of sports contests into millions of homes thus encouraging tens of thousands to want to see similar events with their own eyes.

There had been great athletes before, such as Jim Thorpe, a Sac and Fox Indian, who won both the pentathalon and the decathalon at the 1912 Olympic Games, made Walter Camp's All-America football team in 1912 and 1913, then played major league baseball for several years before becoming a pioneer founder and player in the National Football League. But what truly made the 1920s a Golden Age was the emergence of a remarkable collection of what today would be called "superstars."

In football there was the University of Illinois's Harold "Red" Grange, who averaged over ten yards a carry during his college career and who in one incredible quarter during the 1924 game between Illinois and Michigan carried the ball four times and scored a touchdown each time, gaining in the process 263 yards. In prize fighting, heavyweight champion Jack Dempsey, the "Manassa Mauler," knocked out a succession of challengers in bloody battles.

During the same years, William "Big Bill" Tilden dominated tennis, winning the national singles title every year from 1920 to 1925 along with nearly every other tournament he entered. Beginning in 1923, Robert T. "Bobby" Jones ruled over the world of golf with equal authority, his climactic achievement being his capturing of the amateur and open championships of both the United States and Great Britain in 1930.

A few women athletes dominated their sports during this Golden Age in similar fashion. In tennis Helen Wills was three times United States singles champion and the winner of the women's singles at Wimbledon eight times in the late 1920s

and early 1930s. The swimmer Gertrude Ederle, holder of 18 world's records by the time she was 17, swam the English Channel on her second attempt in 1926. She was not only the first woman to do so, but she did it faster than any of the four men who had previously made it across.

However, the sports star among stars was "the Sultan of Swat," baseball's Babe Ruth. Ruth changed baseball from a game ruled by pitchers and low scores to one where hitting was more greatly admired. Originally himself a brilliant pitcher, his incredible hitting ability made him more valuable in the outfield, where he could play every day. Ruth hit 54 home runs in 1920, his first year with the New York Yankees, and 60 in 1927. By 1923 he was so feared that he was given a base on balls more than half the times he appeared at the plate.

Football was the preeminent school sport. At many colleges football afternoons came to resemble religious rites—a national magazine entitled a 1928 article "The Great God Football," and the editor of a college newspaper denounced "disloyal" students who took seats in the grandstand where they could see what was happening rather than doing their bit in the student cheering section in the end zone.

Gertrude Ederle being greased before the start of her 1926 swim across the English Channel. She not only made it, but also did it faster than any of the four men who had preceded her.

Tens of thousands of men and women took up tennis, golf, swimming, and calisthenics. Social dancing became more energetic. The turkey trot, a popular prewar dance, led in the next decade to the Charleston and what one historian called "an imitative swarm of hops, wriggles, squirms, glides and gallops named after all the animals in the menagerie."

Urban–Rural Conflicts: Fundamentalism

These were buoyant times for "modern" people, most of whom lived in big cities. However, the tensions and hostilities of the 1920s exaggerated an older rift in American society—the conflict between the urban and the rural ways of life. To many among the scattered millions who tilled the soil and among the millions who lived in towns and small cities, the new city-oriented culture seemed sinful, overly materialistic, and unhealthy. Change was something to be resisted.

Yet there was no denying the appeal of the city, which radio and the movies made farmers and townspeople aware of. They coveted the excitement of city life at the same time that they condemned its vices. Rural society proclaimed the superiority of its ways at least in part to protect itself from temptation as to denounce urban life. Change, omnipresent in the postwar world, must be resisted even at the cost of individualism and freedom.

One expression of this resistance was a resurgence of religious fundamentalism. Fundamentalism was a conservative attitude of mind rather than a religious idea. Fundamentalists rejected the theory of evolution, indeed, all knowledge about the origins of the universe and the human race that had been discovered during the 19th century. Urban sophisticates tended to dismiss fundamentalists as boors and hayseed fanatics, yet the persistence of old-fashioned ideas was understandable. In rural areas where educational standards were low and culture relatively static, old ideas remained unchallenged. The power of reason, so obvious in a technologically advanced society, seemed much less obvious to rural people. Farmers, living in close contact with the capricious, elemental power of nature, tended to have more respect for the force of divine providence than city folk. Beyond this, the majesty and beauty of the King James translation of the Bible, the only book in countless rural homes, made it extraordinarily difficult for many persons to abandon their belief in its literal truth.

What made crusaders of the fundamentalists, however, was their resentment of modern urban culture. The teaching of evolution must be prohibited, they insisted. Throughout the early twenties they campaigned vigorously for laws banning discussion of Darwin's theory in textbooks and classrooms. Their greatest asset in this unfortunate crusade was William Jennings Bryan. Age had not improved the "Peerless Leader." After leaving Wilson's Cabinet in 1915 he devoted much time to religious and moral issues but without applying himself conscientiously to the study of these difficult questions. He went about the country charging that "they"—meaning the mass of educated Americans—had "taken the Lord away from the schools." He denounced the use of public money to undermine Christian principles, and he offered $100 to anyone who would admit to being descended from an ape. His immense popularity in rural areas assured him a wide audience, and no one came forward to take his money.

The fundamentalists won a minor victory in 1925, when Tennessee passed a law forbidding instructors in the state's schools and colleges to teach "any theory that denies the story of the Divine Creation of man as taught in the Bible." In response to the passage of this act, the American Civil Liberties Union announced that it would finance a test case challenging its constitutionality if a Tennessee teacher would deliberately violate the statute. Urged on by friends, John T. Scopes, a young biology teacher in Dayton, reluctantly agreed to do so. He was arrested. A battery of nationally known lawyers came forward to defend him, while the state obtained the services of Bryan himself. The Dayton "Monkey Trial" became an overnight sensation.

Clarence Darrow, chief counsel for the defendant, stated the issue clearly. "Scopes isn't on trial," he said, "civilization is on trial." The comic aspects of the trial obscured this issue. Big-city reporters like H. L. Mencken of the Baltimore *Evening Sun* flocked to Dayton to make sport of the fundamentalists. Scopes's conviction was a foregone conclusion; after the jury rendered its verdict, the judge fined him $100.

Nevertheless, the trial exposed both the stupidity and the danger of the fundamentalist position. The highpoint came when Bryan agreed to testify as an expert witness on the Bible. In a sweltering courtroom, both men in shirt sleeves, the lanky, rough-hewn Darrow cross-examined the aging champion of fundamentalism, exposing his childlike faith and his scientific ignorance. Bryan admitted to believing that Eve had been created from Adam's rib, and that a whale had swallowed Jonah.

The Monkey Trial ended in frustration for nearly everyone concerned. Scopes moved away from Dayton, the judge, John Raulston, was defeated when he sought reelection. Bryan died in his sleep a few days after the trial. But fundamentalism continued to flourish. In retrospect, the heroes of the Scopes trial—science and freedom of thought—seem somewhat less stainless than they did to liberals at the time. The account of evolution in the textbook used by Scopes was far from satisfactory, and it contained statements that to the modern mind seem at least as bigoted as anything that Bryan said at Dayton. A section on "the Races of Man" for example, described Caucasians as "the highest type of all . . . represented by the civilized white inhabitants of Europe and America."

Urban–Rural Conflicts: Prohibition

The conflict between the countryside and the city was fought on many fronts, and in one sector the rural forces achieved a quick victory. This was the prohibition of the manufacture, transportation, and sale of alcoholic beverages by the Eighteenth Amendment, ratified in 1919. Although there were some big-city advocates of prohibition, the Eighteenth Amendment, in the words of the historian Andrew Sinclair, marked a triumph of the "Corn Belt over the conveyor belt."

The temperance movement had been important since the age of Jackson; it was an issue in many states during the Gilded Age and by the Progressive Era powerful organizations like the Anti-Saloon League and the Women's Christian Temperance Union were seeking to have drinking outlawed entirely. Indeed, prohibition was a typical progressive reform, moralistic, backed by the middle class, and aimed at frustrating "the interests"—in this case the distillers.

World War I aided the prohibitionists by increasing the need for food. The Lever Act of 1917 outlawed the use of grain in the manufacture of alcoholic beverages, primarily as a conservation measure. The prevailing dislike of foreigners helped the dry cause still more: Beer drinking was associated with Germans. State and local laws had made a large part of the country dry by 1917. National prohibition became official in January 1920.

This "experiment noble in purpose," as Herbert Hoover called it, achieved a number of socially desirable results. It reduced the national consumption of alcohol. Arrests for drunkenness fell off sharply, as did deaths from alcoholism. Fewer workers squandered their wages on drink. If the drys had been willing to legalize beer and wine, the experiment might have worked. Instead, by insisting on total abstinence, they drove moderates to violate the law. Strict enforcement became impossible, especially in the cities.

In areas where popular opinion favored prohibition strongly, liquor was difficult to find. Elsewhere smuggling became a major business, bootlegger a household word. Private individuals busied themselves learning how to manufacture "bathtub gin." Fraudulent druggists' prescriptions for alcohol were issued freely. The saloon disappeared, replaced by the speakeasy, a supposedly secret bar or club operating usually under the benevolent eye of the local police.

That the law was often violated does not mean that it was ineffective any more than violations of laws against theft and murder mean that those laws are ineffective. While gangsters such as Alphonse "Scarface Al" Capone of Chicago were in the 1920s engaged in the liquor traffic, their "organizations" had existed before the ratification of the Eighteenth Amendment. But prohibition almost destroyed the Democratic Party as a national organization; Democratic immigrants in the cities hated it, but southern Democrats sang its praises, often while continuing to drink.

The hypocrisy of prohibition had a deleterious effect on politicians, a class seldom famous for candor. Congressmen catered to the demands of the Anti-Saloon League yet failed to grant adequate funds to the Prohibition Bureau. Democratic and Republican leaders, from Wilson and La Follette to Hoover and Franklin D. Roosevelt, equivocated shamelessly on the liquor question. By the end of the decade almost every competent observer recognized that prohibition at least needed to be overhauled, but the well-organized and powerful dry forces rejected all proposals for modifying it.

The Ku Klux Klan

The most horrible manifestation of the social malaise of the 1920s was the revival of the Ku Klux Klan. This new Klan, founded in 1915 by William J. Simmons, a preacher, admitted only native-born, white Protestants. The distrust of foreigners, blacks, Catholics, and Jews implicit in this regulation explains why it flourished in the social climate that spawned religious fundamentalism, immigration restriction, and prohibition. By 1923 it claimed the astonishing total of 5 million members.

The Klan had relatively little appeal in the Northeast or in metropolitan centers in other parts of the country, but it found many members in middle-sized cities and in the small towns and villages of midwestern and western states like Indiana, Ohio, and Oregon. The scapegoats in such regions were immigrants, Jews, and especially Catholics. The rationale was an urge to return to an older, supposedly finer America and to stamp out all varieties of nonconformity. They persecuted gamblers, "loose" women, violators of the prohibition laws, and anyone who happened to differ from them on religious questions or who belonged to a "foreign race."

The very success of the Klan led to its undoing. Factionalism sprang up and rival leaders squabbled over the large sums that had been collected from the membership. The cruel and outrageous behavior of the organization roused both liberals and conservatives in every part of the country. When the powerful leader of the Indiana Klan, a middle-aged reprobate named David C. Stephenson, was convicted of assaulting and causing the death of a young woman, the rank and file abandoned the organization in droves. It remained influential for a number of years, con-

tributing to the defeat of the Catholic Alfred E. Smith in the 1928 presidential election, but it ceased to be a dynamic force after 1924. By 1930 it had only some 9,000 members.

Sacco and Vanzetti

The excesses of the fundamentalists, the xenophobes, the Klan, the red-baiters, and the prohibitionists disturbed American intellectuals profoundly. More and more they became alienated, yet their alienation came at a time when society was growing more dependent on brains and sophistication. This compounded the confusion and disillusionment characteristic of the period.

Nothing demonstrates this fact so clearly as the Sacco-Vanzetti case. In April 1920 two men in South Braintree, Massachusetts, killed a paymaster and a guard in a daring daylight robbery of a shoe factory. Shortly thereafter Nicola Sacco and Bartolomeo Vanzetti were charged with the crime, and in 1921 they were convicted of murder. Sacco and Vanzetti were anarchists and Italian immigrants. Their trial was a travesty of justice. The presiding judge, Webster Thayer, conducted the proceedings like a prosecuting attorney; privately he referred to the defendants as "those anarchist bastards."

The case became a cause célèbre. Prominent persons throughout the world protested. Vanzetti's quiet dignity and courage in the face of death wrung the hearts of millions. When the two were at last electrocuted, the disillusionment of American intellectuals with current values was profound.

Literary Trends

The literature of the twenties reflects the disillusionment of the intellectuals. The prewar period had been a time of hopeful experimentation in the world of letters. But writers, along with most other intellectuals, were beginning to abandon this view by about 1912. The wasteful horrors of the World War and then the antics of the fundamentalists and the cruelty of the red-baiters turned them into critics of society. Soon hundreds of young men and women were referring to themselves with a self-pity almost maudlin as the "lost generation." The poet Ezra Pound gave up anticipating an American Renaissance and wrote instead of "a botched civilization."

The symbol of the lost generation, in his own mind as well as to his contemporaries and to later critics, was F. Scott Fitzgerald, who rose to sudden fame in 1920 when he published *This Side of Paradise,* a somewhat sophomoric novel that appealed powerfully to college students and captured the fears and confusions of the lost generation. In *The Great Gatsby* (1925), a more mature work, Fitzgerald dissected a modern millionaire—coarse, unscrupulous, jaded, in love with another man's wife. Gatsby's tragedy lay in his dedication to a woman who, Fitzgerald made clear, did not merit his passion.

The tragedy of *The Great Gatsby* was related to Fitzgerald's own. Pleasure-loving and extravagant, he squandered the money earned by *This Side of Paradise.* When *The Great Gatsby* failed to sell as well, he turned to writing potboilers. He descended into the despair of alcoholism and ended his days as a Hollywood scriptwriter.

Many young American writers and artists became expatriates in the twenties. They flocked to Rome, Berlin, and especially Paris, where they could live cheaply and escape what seemed to them the "conspiracy against the individual" prevalent in their own country. Ernest Hemingway, the most talented of this group, settled in Paris in 1922 to write. His first novel, *The Sun Also Rises* (1926), portrayed the café world of the expatriate and the rootless desperation, amorality, and sense of outrage at life's meaninglessness that obsessed so many in those years. In *A Farewell to Arms* (1929) he described the confusion and horror of war.

Hemingway's books were best-sellers and he became a legend in his own time, but his style rather than his ideas explains his towering reputation. Few novelists have been such self-conscious craftsmen or so capable of suggesting powerful emotions and action in so few words.

> *I went out the door and down the hall to the room where Catherine was to be after the baby came. I sat in a chair there and looked at the room. I had the paper in my coat that I had bought when I went out for lunch and I read it. . . . After a while I stopped reading and turned off the light and watched it get dark outside.*
>
> *A Farewell to Arms*

Contrasting images of two literary stars of the "lost generation": F. Scott Fitzgerald (top) as the thoughtful, introspective artist, and Ernest Hemingway (bottom), sportsman and man of action.

This kind of writing, evoking rather than describing emotion, fascinated readers and inspired hundreds of imitators; it has made a permanent mark on world literature. What

Hemingway had to say was of less universal interest—he was an unabashed, rather muddled romantic, an adolescent emotionally. He wrote about bullfights, hunting and fishing, violence. Although he did so with masterful penetration, these themes placed limits on his work that he never transcended.

Although neither was the equal of Hemingway or Fitzgerald, two other writers of the twenties deserve mention: H. L. Mencken and Sinclair Lewis. Mencken, a Baltimore newspaperman and founder of one of the great magazines of the era, *American Mercury,* was a thoroughgoing cynic. He coined the word *booboisie* to define the complacent, middle-class majority, and he fired superbly witty broadsides at fundamentalists, prohibitionists, and "Puritans." "Puritanism," Mencken once said, "is the haunting fear that someone, somewhere, may be happy."

But Mencken was never indifferent to the many aspects of American life that roused his contempt. Politics at once fascinated and repelled him, and he assailed the statesmen of his generation with magnificent impartiality:

BRYAN: If the fellow was sincere, then so was P. T. Barnum. . . . He was, in fact, a charlatan, a mountebank, a zany without sense or dignity.

WILSON: The bogus Liberal. . . . A pedagogue thrown up to 1,000 diameters by a magic lantern.

HARDING: The numskull, Gamaliel . . . the Marion stonehead. . . . The operations of his medulla oblongata . . . resemble the rattlings of a colossal linotype charged with rubber stamps.

COOLIDGE: A cheap and trashy fellow, deficient in sense and almost devoid of any notion of honor—in brief, a dreadful little cad.

HOOVER: Lord Hoover is no more than a pious old woman, a fat Coolidge. . . . He would have made a good bishop.

While amusing, Mencken's diatribes were not profound. In retrospect he seemed more a professional iconoclast than a constructive critic; like both Fitzgerald and Hemingway, he was something of a perennial adolescent. However, he consistently supported freedom of expression of every sort.

Sinclair Lewis was probably the most popular American novelist of the twenties. Like Fitzgerald, his first major work brought him instant fame and notoriety—and for the same reason. *Main Street* (1920) portrayed the smug ignorance and bigotry of the American small town so accurately that even Lewis's victims recognized themselves; its title became a symbol for provinciality and middle-class meanness of spirit. In *Babbitt* (1922) he created a businessman of the twenties, a "booster," blindly orthodox in his political and social opinions, a slave to every cliché, and full of loud self-confidence, but under the surface a bumbling, rather timid fellow.

Lewis went on to dissect the medical profession in *Arrowsmith* (1925), religion in *Elmer Gantry* (1927), fascism in *It Can't Happen Here* (1935).

Lewis was preeminently a product of the twenties. When times changed, he could no longer portray society with such striking verisimilitude; none of his later novels approached the level of *Main Street* and *Babbitt*. When critics noticed this, Lewis became bewildered, almost disoriented. He died in 1951 a desperately unhappy man.

The "New Negro"

Even more than for white liberals, the postwar reaction had brought despair for blacks. Aside from the barbarities of the Klan, they suffered from the postwar middle-class hostility to labor (and from the persistent reluctance of organized labor to admit black workers to its ranks). The increasing presence of southern blacks in northern cities also caused conflict. Some 393,000 settled in New York, Pennsylvania, and Illinois in the twenties, most of them in New York City, Philadelphia, and Chicago.

This influx speeded the development of urban ghettos. Harlem, a white, middle-class residential section of New York City as late as 1910, had 50,000 blacks in 1914 and nearly 165,000 in 1930. The restrictions of ghetto life produced a vicious circle of degradation. Population growth and segregation caused a desperate housing shortage;

rents in Harlem doubled between 1919 and 1927. Since the average black worker was unskilled and ill paid, tenants were forced to take in boarders. Landlords converted private homes into rooming houses and allowed their properties to fall into disrepair. These conditions caused disease and crime rates to rise sharply.

Even in small northern cities where they made up only a tiny proportion of the population, blacks were badly treated. When Robert S. and Helen M. Lynd made their classic sociological analysis of *Middletown* (Muncie, Indiana), they discovered that although black and white children attended the same schools, the churches, the larger movie houses, and other places of public accommodation were segregated.

Coming after the hopes inspired by wartime gains, the disappointments of the 1920s produced a new militancy among many blacks. In 1919 W. E. B. Du Bois wrote in *The Crisis*: "We are cowards and jackasses if . . . we do not marshal every ounce of our brain and brawn to fight . . . against the forces of hell in our own land." He increased his commitment to black nationalism, organizing a series of Pan African Conferences in an effort—futile as it turned out—to create an international black movement.

Du Bois never made up his mind whether to work for integration or black separatism. Marcus Garvey, a West Indian whose Universal Negro Improvement Association attracted hundreds of thousands of followers in the early twenties, had nothing but contempt for whites, for light-skinned Negroes like Du Bois, and for organizations such as the NAACP that sought to bring whites and blacks together to fight segregation and other forms of prejudice. "Back to Africa" was his slogan; the black man must "work out his salvation in his motherland."

Garvey's message was naive, but it served to build racial pride among the masses of poor and unschooled blacks. Both God and Christ were black, he insisted. He organized black businesses of many sorts, including a company that manufactured black dolls. He established a corps of Black Cross nurses and a Black Star Line Steamship Company to transport blacks to Africa.

More sophisticated blacks, including Du Bois, considered Garvey a charlatan. His motives were unclear, and part of his trouble was that he was a terrible businessman. In 1923 his steamship line went into bankruptcy. He was convicted of defrauding the thousands of his supporters who had invested in its stock and was sent to prison. Nevertheless, his message, if not his methods, helped to create the "New Negro," proud of being black and prepared to resist both white mistreatment and white ideas: "Up, you mighty race, you can accomplish what you will!"

The ghettos produced compensating advantages for blacks. One effect, not fully utilized until later, was to increase their political power by enabling them to elect representatives to state legislatures and to Congress and to exert great influence on the parties in closely contested elections. More immediately, city life stimulated self-confidence; despite their horrors, the ghettos offered economic opportunity, political rights, and freedom from the everyday debasements of life in the South.

Black writers, musicians, and artists found in the ghettos both an audience and the "spiritual emancipation" that unleashed their capacities. Jazz, the great popular music of the age, was largely the creation of black musicians working in New Orleans before the turn of the century. By the 1920s it had spread throughout the country and to most of the rest of the world. White musicians and white audiences took it up—in a way, it became a force for racial tolerance and understanding.

Jazz meant improvisation, and both players and audiences experienced in it a kind of liberation. Jazz was the music of the 1920s in part because it expressed the desire of so many people to break with tradition and throw off conventional restraints. Surely this helps to explain why it was so important to blacks.

Harlem, the largest black city in the world, became in the 1920s a cultural capital, center of the "Harlem Renaissance." Black newspapers and magazines flourished along with theatrical companies and libraries. Du Bois opened *The Crisis* to young writers and artists, and a dozen "little" magazines sprang up. Langston Hughes, one of the best poets of the era, described the exhilaration of his first arrival in this city within a city, a "magnet" for every black intellectual and artist. "Harlem! I . . . dropped my bags, took a deep breath, and felt happy again."

With some exceptions, black writers like Hughes did not share in the disillusionment that afflicted so many white intellectuals. The persistence of prejudice angered them and made them militant. But to be militant, one must be at some level hopeful, and this they were. Sociologists and psychologists (for whom the ghettos were indispensable social laboratories) were demonstrating that environment rather than heredity was preventing black economic progress. Together with the achievements of creative blacks, which for the first time were being appreciated by large numbers of white intellectuals, these discoveries seemed to herald the eventual disappearance of race prejudice. The black, wrote Alain Locke in *The New Negro* (1925), "lays aside the status of beneficiary and ward for that of a collaborator and participant in American civilization." Alas, as Locke and other black intellectuals were soon to discover, this prediction, like so many made in the 1920s, did not come to pass.

The "New Era"

Despite the turmoil of the times and the dissatisfactions expressed by some of the nation's best minds, the 1920s were an exceptionally prosperous decade. Business boomed, real wages rose, and unemployment declined. The United States was as rich as all Europe; perhaps 40 percent of the world's total wealth lay in American hands. Little wonder that business leaders and other conservatives described the period as a "New Era."

The prosperity rested on many bases, one of which was the friendly, hands-off attitude of the federal government, which bolstered the confidence of the business community. The Federal Reserve Board kept interest rates low, a further stimulus to economic growth. Pent-up wartime demand helped to power the boom; the construction business in particular profited from a series of extremely busy years. The continuing mechanization and rationalization of industry provided a more fundamental stimulus to the economy. Greater use of power, especially of electricity, also encouraged expansion—by 1929 the United States was producing more electricity than the rest of the world combined.

Most important, American manufacturing was experiencing a remarkable improvement in efficiency. The method of breaking down the complex processes of production into many simple operations and the use of interchangeable parts were 19th-century innovations; in the 1920s they were adopted on an almost universal scale. The moving assembly line, which carried the product to the worker, first devised by Henry Ford in his automobile plant in the decade before World War I, speeded production and reduced costs. In ten years the hourly output of Ford workers quadrupled.

The Age of the Consumer

The growing ability of manufacturers to produce goods meant that great effort had to be made to create new consumer demands. Advertising and salesmanship were raised almost to the status of fine arts. Bruce Barton, one of the advertising "geniuses" of the era, wrote a best-selling book, *The Man Nobody Knows* (1925), in which he described Jesus as the "founder of modern business," the man who "picked up twelve men from the bottom ranks . . . and forged them into an organization that conquered the world." In 1930 Eleanor Roosevelt, wife of the governor of New York, gave a testimonial for a breakfast cereal. It had, she said, "undoubtedly played its part" in building the "robust physique" of her teen-age son John.

Producers concentrated on making their goods more attractive and on changing models frequently to entice buyers into the market. The practice of selling goods on the installment plan helped bring expensive items within the reach of the masses. Inventions and technological advances created new or improved products: radios, automobiles, electric appliances such as vacuum cleaners and refrigerators, gadgets like cigarette lighters, and new forms of entertainment like motion pictures.

Undoubtedly the automobile had the single most important impact on the nation's economy in the twenties. Although well over a million cars a year were being regularly produced by 1916, the real expansion of the industry came after 1921. Output reached 3.6 million in 1923 and fell below that figure only twice during the remainder of the decade. By 1929, 23 million private cars clogged the highways, an average of nearly one per family.

The auto industry created industries that manufactured tires and spark plugs and other products. It consumed immense quantities of rubber, paint, glass, nickel, and petroleum products. It triggered a gigantic road-building program. Thousands found employment in filling stations, roadside stands, and other businesses catering to the motoring public. The tourist industry profited, and the shift of population from the cities to the suburbs was accelerated.

The automobile made life more mobile yet also more encapsulated. It created a generation of amateur mechanics and explorers. It gave Americans a freedom never before imagined. The owner of the most rickety jalopy could travel farther, faster, and far more comfortably than a monarch of old with his blooded steeds and gilded coaches.

These benefits were real and priceless. But cars came to have an equally important symbolic significance; they gave their owners a feeling of power and status similar to that which owning a horse gave to a medieval knight.

In time there were undesirable, even dangerous results of the automotive revolution: roadside scenery disfigured by billboards and gas stations; traffic jams; soaring accident rates; air pollution; the neglect of public transportation, which was an important cause of the deterioration of inner cities. All these disadvantages were noticed during the 1920s, but they were discounted. The automobile seemed an unalloyed blessing—part toy, part tool, part symbol of American freedom, prosperity, and individualism.

Henry Ford

The person most responsible for the growth of the automobile industry was Henry Ford, a self-taught mechanic from Greenfield, Michigan. In 1908 he designed the Model T Ford, a simple, tough box on wheels. In a year he sold 11,000 Model Ts. Thereafter, relentlessly cutting costs and increasing efficiency by installing the assembly-line system, he expanded production at an unbelievable rate. By 1925 he was turning out more than 9,000 cars a day, one approximately every ten seconds, and the price of the Model T had been reduced to below $300.

Ford's profits soared along with sales; since he owned the entire company, he became a billionaire. He also became an authentic folk hero: His homespun style, his dislike of bankers and sophisticated society, and his intense individualism endeared him to millions. He stood as a symbol of the wonders of the American system—he had given the nation a marvelous convenience at a low price, at the same time enriching himself and raising the living standards of his thousands of employees.

Unfortunately, Ford had the defects of his virtues in full measure. He paid high wages but refused to deal with any union. When he discovered a worker driving any car but a Ford, he had him dismissed.

Success made Ford stubborn. The Model T remained essentially unchanged for nearly 20 years. Other companies, notably General Motors, were soon turning out better vehicles for very little more money. Customers, increasingly affluent and style-conscious, began to shift to Chevrolets and Chryslers. Although his company continued to make a great deal of money, Ford never regained the dominant position he had held for so long.

Ford was enormously uninformed, yet—because of his success and the praise the world heaped on him—he did not hesitate to speak out on subjects far outside his area of competence, from the evils of drink and tobacco to medicine and international affairs. He developed political ambitions and published virulent anti-Semitic propaganda. He said he would not give five cents for all the art in the world.

While praising his talents as a manufacturer, historians have not dealt kindly with Ford the man, in part, no doubt, because he once said: "History is more or less the bunk."

The Airplane

Henry Ford also manufactured airplanes, and although the airplane industry was not economically important in the 1920s, its development led to changes in lifestyles and attitudes at least as important as those produced by automobiles. The internal combustion gasoline engine with its high ratio of power to weight made the airplane possible, which explains why the first "flying machines" and "gas buggies" were built at about the same time. Wilbur and Orville Wright made their famous flight at Kitty Hawk, North Carolina, in 1903, five years before Ford produced his Model T. Another pair of brothers, Malcolm and Haimes Lockheed, built one of the earliest commercial planes (they used it to take passengers up at five dollars a ride) in 1913.

World War I speeded the advance of airplane technology, but practical commercial flight was long delayed. Aerial acrobats, parachute jumpers, wing walkers, and other "daredevils" who put on shows at county fairs and similar places where crowds gathered were the principal aviators of the 1920s. They "barnstormed" from town to town, living the same kind of inbred, encapsulated lives that circus people did.

The great event of the decade for aviation, still an achievement that must strike awe in the hearts of reflective persons, was Charles A. Lindbergh's nonstop flight from New York to Paris in May 1927. It took more than 33 hours for Lindbergh's single-engine *Spirit of St. Louis* to cross the Atlantic, a formidable physical achievement for the pilot as well as an example of skill and courage. When the public learned that the intrepid "Lucky Lindy" was handsome, modest, uninterested in converting his new fame into cash, and a model of propriety (he neither drank nor smoked), his role as American hero was assured. It was a role Lindbergh detested—one biographer has described him as "by nature solitary"—but could not avoid.

Charles Lindbergh with his famed plane, *Spirit of St. Louis.* His 1927 flight from New York to Paris made him an instant American hero.

Lindbergh's flight enormously increased public interest in flying, but it was a landmark in aviation technology as well. The day of routine passenger flights was at last about to dawn. Two

Milestones

1908	Henry Ford begins production of his Model T automobile	**1925**	Scopes trial in Dayton, Tennessee
1914	Ford establishes the $5 day for autoworkers	**1926**	Gertrude Ederle swims the English Channel
1919	Eighteenth Amendment outlaws alcoholic beverages		Ernest Hemingway, *The Sun Also Rises*
	Nineteenth Amendment gives women the vote	**1927**	Charles A. Lindbergh flies solo from New York to Paris
	Sinclair Lewis, *Main Street*		Sacco and Vanzetti executed
1920	First commercial radio station, KDKA, begins broadcasting		*The Jazz Singer* is the first motion picture with sound
	F. Scott Fitzgerald, *This Side of Paradise*		Jack Dempsey loses heavyweight boxing title to Gene Tunney
1921	Margaret Sanger founds the American Birth Control League		Babe Ruth hits 60 home runs
1923	Supreme Court overturns the law limiting hours of work for women	**1930**	Bobby Jones wins the United States and British amateur and open golf championships

months after the *Spirit of St. Louis* touched down in France, William E. Boeing of Boeing Air Transport began flying passengers and mail between San Francisco and Chicago, using a plane of his own design and manufacture. Early in 1928 he changed the company name to United Aircraft and Transport, ancestor of the modern giant, United Airlines. Two years later Boeing produced the first all-metal, low-wing plane, and in 1933 the twin-engine 247, called by historian John B. Rae "the first genuinely modern transport plane."

In retrospect the postwar era seems even more a period of transition than it appeared at the time. Rarely had change come so swiftly, and rarely had old and new existed side by side in such profusion. Creativity and reaction, hope and dispair, freedom and repression—the modern world in all its unfathomable complexity was emerging.

Supplementary Reading

A comprehensive survey of the twenties is J. D. Hicks, **Republican Ascendancy*** (1960), but see also Geoffrey Perrett, **America in the Twenties** (1982), and P. A. Carter, **Another Part of the Twenties** (1977). F. L. Allen, **Only Yesterday*** (1931), is still useful.

For nativism and immigration restriction, see John Higham, **Strangers in the Land** (1955). On changes in the family see Steven Mintz and Susan Kellogg, **Domestic Revolutions** (1988). Other social trends are discussed in N. G. Hale, **Freud and the Americans**; Paula Fass, **The Damned and the Beautiful** (1977); and John D'Emilio and Estelle Freedman, **Intimate Matters** (1988). Women's issues are treated in D. M. Brown, **Setting a Course: American Women in the 1920s** (1987); William Chafe, **The American Woman** (1972); and W. D. Wandersee, **Women's Work and Family Values** (1981).

On popular culture, see Russell Lynes, **The Lively Audience** (1985), Robert Sklar, **Moviemade America** (1976), and S. J. Douglas, **Inventing American Broadcasting** (1987).

Fundamentalism is treated in N. F. Furniss, **The Fundamentalist Controversy** (1954), and Lawrence Levine, **Defender of the Faith** (1965). On prohibition, see Andrew Sincair, **Prohibition: The Era of Excess** (1962), and N. H. Clark, **Deliver Us from Evil** (1976). For the Ku Klux Klan, see D. M. Chalmers, **Hooded Americanism** (1965), and K. T. Jackson, **The Ku Klux Klan in the City** (1967).

The history of blacks is covered in Gilbert Osofsky, **Harlem: The Making of a Ghetto** (1965), E. D. Cronon, **Black Moses: The Story of Marcus Garvey** (1955), and N. I. Huggins, **Harlem Renaissance** (1971).

Literature during the period is discussed in Alfred Kazin, **On Native Grounds** (1942), and F. J. Hoffman, **The Twenties** (1955). Biographies of novelists include Arthur Mizener, **The Far Side of Paradise** (1951), on Fitzgerald; Mark Shorer, **Sinclair Lewis** (1961); and C. H. Baker, **Hemingway** (1956).

On the New Era, see E. W. Hawley, **The Great War and the Search for a Modern Order** (1979); on consumerism in the 1920s, see Daniel Horowitz, **The Morality of Spending** (1985), and Roland Marchand, **Advertising the American Dream** (1985). On the influence of Henry Ford and the automobile, see Keith Sward, **The Legend of Henry Ford** (1948), J. B. Rae, **The American Automobile Industry** (1984), and J. J. Flink, **The Car Culture** (1975).

*Available in paperback.

CHAPTER 26

The New Era: 1921–1933

"Normalcy"
"Regulating" Business
The Harding Scandals
Coolidge Prosperity
Peace Without a Sword
The Peace Movement
The Good Neighbor Policy
The Totalitarian Challenge
War Debts and Reparations
The Election of 1928
Economic Problems
The Crash of 1929
Hoover and the Depression
The Economy Hits Bottom
The Depression and Its Victims
The Election of 1932

*T*he men who presided over the government of the United States from 1921 to 1933 were Warren G. Harding, Calvin Coolidge, and Herbert Hoover. Harding was a newspaperman by trade, publisher of the Marion *Star,* with previous political experience as a legislator and lieutenant governor in his home state, Ohio, and as a United States senator. No president, before or since, looked more like a statesman; few were less suited for running the country. Coolidge, was a taciturn, conservative New Englander with a long record in Massachusetts politics climaxed by his inept but much-admired suppression of the Boston police strike while governor. Harding referred to him as

"that little fellow from Massachusetts." Coolidge preferred to follow public opinion and hope for the best. Hoover was best known for his wartime service as food administrator and for his many speeches and writings about what he called "progressive individualism."

"Normalcy"

Harding won the 1920 Republican nomination because his genial nature and lack of strong convictions made him attractive to many of the politicos after eight years of the headstrong Wilson. During the campaign he exasperated sophisticates by his ignorance and imprecision. "Why does he not get a private secretary who can clothe . . . his 'ideas' in the language customarily used by educated men?" one Boston gentleman demanded of Senator Lodge, who was strongly supporting Harding. Lodge, ordinarily a stickler for linguistic exactitude, replied acidly that he found Harding a paragon by comparison with Wilson, "a man who wrote English very well without ever saying anything." A large majority of the voters, untroubled by the candidate's lack of erudition, shared Lodge's confidence that he would be a vast improvement over Wilson.

Harding has often been characterized as lazy and incompetent. In fact he was hardworking and politically shrewd; his major weaknesses were indecisiveness and an unwillingness to offend. He turned the most important government departments over to efficient administrators of impeccable reputation: Charles Evans Hughes as secretary of state, Herbert Hoover in Commerce, Andrew Mellon in the Treasury, and Henry C. Wallace in Agriculture. He kept track of what these men did but seldom initiated policy in their areas. However, Harding gave many lesser offices, and a few of major importance, to the unsavory "Ohio Gang" headed by Harry M. Daugherty whom he made attorney general.

The president was too too unambitious to be dishonest. He appointed corruptionists like Daugherty, out of a sense of personal obligation or because they were old friends who shared his taste for poker and liquor. Before 1921 he had enjoyed officeholding; he was adept at mouthing platitudes, a loyal party man who seldom questioned the decisions of his superiors. In the lonely eminence of the White House, whence, as President Harry Truman later said, the buck cannot be passed, he found only misery.

"Regulating" Business

In domestic affairs, Secretary of the Treasury Mellon, multimillionaire banker and master of the aluminum industry, dominated administration domestic policy. Mellon set out to lower the taxes of the rich, reverse the low-tariff policies of the Wilson period, return to the laissez-faire philosophy of McKinley, and reduce the national debt by cutting expenses and administrating the government more efficiently.

In principle his program had considerable merit, but he carried his policies to unreasonable extremes. He proposed eliminating inheritance taxes and reducing the tax on high incomes by two-thirds in order to stimulate investment, but he opposed lower rates for taxpayers earning less than $66,000 a year, apparently not realizing that economic expansion required greater mass consumption as well. Freeing the rich from "oppressive" taxation, he argued, would enable them to invest more in potentially productive enterprises, the success of which would create jobs for ordinary people.

Although the Republicans had large majorities in both houses of Congress, Mellon's proposals were too reactionary to win unqualified approval. His tax and tariff program ran into stiff opposition from middle-western Republicans and southern Democrats, who combined to form the so-called Farm Bloc. The revival of European agriculture after the World War cut the demand for American farm produce just when the increased use of fertilizers and machinery was boosting output. As in the era after the Civil War, farmers found themselves burdened with heavy debts while their income dwindled. In the decade after 1919, their share of the national income fell by nearly 50 percent.

Mellon epitomized everything the Farm Bloc disliked. Rejecting his more extreme suggestions, it pushed through the Revenue Act of 1921, which abolished the excess-profits tax and cut the top income tax rate from 73 to 50 percent but raised the tax on corporate profits slightly and left inheritance taxes untouched. Three years later, Congress cut the maximum income tax to 40 percent, reduced taxes on lower incomes significantly, and raised inheritance levies.

Congress also overhauled Mellon's tariff proposals. It placed heavy duties on agricultural products in 1921. The Fordney-McCumber Tariff of 1922 granted more than adequate protection to the "infant industries" (rayon, china, toys, and chemicals), yet held to the Wilsonian principle of moderate protection for most industrial products. Agricultural machinery and other items used by farmers remained on the free list.

Mellon nevertheless succeeded in balancing the budget and reducing the national debt by an average of over $500 million a year. So committed were the Republican leaders to retrenchment that they even resisted the demands of veterans, organized in the politically potent American Legion, for an "adjusted compensation" bonus. Arguing not entirely without reason that they had served for a pittance while war workers had been drawing down high wages, the veterans sought grants equal to a dollar a day for their period in uniform ($1.25 for time overseas). Congress responded sympathetically, but Harding and Coolidge both vetoed bonus bills in the name of economy. Finally, in 1924, a compromise bill granting the veterans paid-up life insurance policies was passed over Coolidge's veto.

That the business community heartily approved the policies of Harding and Coolidge is not surprising. Both presidents were uncritical advocates of the business point of view. "We want less government in business and more business in government," Harding pontificated, to which Coolidge added: "The business of the United States is business." Harding and Coolidge used the power of appointment to convert regulatory bodies like the Interstate Commerce Commission and the Federal Reserve Board into pro-business agencies that ceased almost entirely to restrict the activities of the industries they were supposed to be controlling.

The Harding Scandals

At least Mellon was honest. The "Ohio Gang," however, used its power in the most corrupt way imaginable. Jesse Smith, a crony of Attorney General Daugherty, was what today would be called an "influence peddler." When he was exposed in 1923, he committed suicide. Charles R. Forbes of the Veterans Bureau siphoned millions of dollars appropriated for the construction of hospitals into his own pocket. When he was found out, he was sentenced to two years in prison. His assistant, Charles F. Cramer, committed suicide. Daugherty himself was implicated in the fraudulent return of German assets seized by the alien property custodian to their original owners. He escaped imprisonment only by refusing to testify on the ground that he might incriminate himself.

The worst scandal involved Secretary of the Interior Albert B. Fall, a former senator. In 1921 Fall arranged with the complaisant Secretary of the Navy Edwin Denby for the transfer to the Interior Department of government oil reserves being held for the future use of the navy. He then leased these properties to private oil companies. Edward L. Doheny's Pan-American Petroleum Company got the Elk Hills reserve in California; the Teapot Dome reserve in Wyoming was turned over to Harry F. Sinclair's Mammoth Oil Company. In 1923 the Senate ordered a full-scale investigation, conducted by Senator Thomas J. Walsh of Montana. It soon came out that Doheny had "lent" Fall $100,000 in hard cash, handed over secretly in a "little black bag." Sinclair had given Fall over $300,000 in cash and negotiable securities.

Although the three culprits escaped conviction on the charge of conspiring to defraud the government, Sinclair was sentenced to nine months in jail for contempt of the Senate and for tampering with a jury, and Fall was fined $100,000 and given a year in prison for accepting a bribe. In 1927 the Supreme Court revoked the leases and the two reserves were returned to the government.

The public still knew little of the scandals when in June 1923 Harding, on a western speaking tour, came down with what his physician, an incompetent crony whom he had made surgeon general of the United States, diagnosed as ptomaine poisoning resulting from his having eaten a tainted Japanese crab. In fact the president had suffered a heart attack. He died in San Francisco on August 2.

Few presidents have been more deeply mourned by the people at the moment of their passing. Soon, however, as the scandals came to light, sadness turned to scorn and contempt. The poet e. e. cummings came closer to catching the final judgment of Harding's contemporaries than has any historian:

> the first president to be loved by his
> "bitterest enemies" is dead
> the only man woman or child who wrote
> a simple declarative sentence with seven
>   grammatical
> errors "is dead"
> beautiful Warren Gamaliel Harding
> "is" dead
> he's
> "dead"
> if he wouldn't have eaten them Yapanese
>   Craps
> somebody might hardly never not have been
> unsorry, perhaps

Coolidge Prosperty

Had he lived, Harding might well have been defeated in 1924 because of the scandals. Vice President Coolidge, unconnected with the troubles and not the type to surround himself with cronies of any kind, seemed the ideal person to clean out the corruptionists. He soon became the darling of the conservatives. His admiration for businessmen and his devotion to laissez-faire knew no limit. "The man who builds a factory builds a temple," he said in all seriousness. Andrew Mellon, whom he kept on as secretary of the treasury, became his mentor in economic affairs.

Coolidge won the 1924 Republican nomination easily. The Democrats, badly split, required 103 ballots to choose a candidate. The southern wing, dry, anti-immigrant, pro-Klan, had fixed on William G. McAdoo, Wilson's secretary of the treasury. The eastern, urban, wet element supported Governor Alfred E. Smith of New York, child of the slums, a Catholic who had compiled a distinguished record in the field of social-welfare legislation. After days of futile politicking, the party compromised on John W. Davis, a conservative corporation lawyer closely allied with the Morgan banking interests.

Dismayed by the conservatism of Coolidge and Davis, the aging Robert M. La Follette, backed by the Farm Bloc, the Socialist Party, the American Federation of Labor, and numbers of intellectuals, entered the race as the candidate of a new Progressive Party. The Progressives adopted a neopopulist platform calling for the nationalization of railroads, the direct election of the president, the protection of labor's right to bargain collectively, and other reforms.

The situation was almost exactly the opposite of 1912, when one conservative had run against two liberals and had been swamped. Coolidge received 15.7 million votes, Davis 8.4 million, La Follette only 4.8 million. In the electoral college, La Follette won only his native state Wisconsin; Coolidge defeated Davis, 382 to 136. Conservatism was clearly the dominant mood of the country.

Peace Without a Sword

Presidents Harding and Coolidge handled foreign relations in much the same way they managed domestic affairs. Harding deferred to senatorial prejudice against executive domination in the area and let his secretary of state, Charles Evans Hughes, make policy. Coolidge adopted a similar course.

In directing foreign relations, they faced the obstacle of a resurgent isolationism. The same forces of war-bred hatred, postwar disillusion, and fear of communist subversion that produced the Red Scare at home led Americans to back away from close involvement in world affairs. The bloodiness and apparent senselessness of the Great War convinced millions that the only way to be sure it would not happen again was to "steer clear" of "entanglements." That these famous words had been used by Washington and Jefferson in vastly different contexts did not deter the isolationists of the 1920s from attributing to them the same authority they gave to Scripture. But the need for both raw materials for industry and foreign markets for America's agricultural and manufactured goods made involvement in developments all over the world unavoidable.

The Open Door concept remained predominant; the State Department worked to obtain opportunities in underdeveloped countries for exporters and investors, hoping both to stimulate the American economy and to bring stability to "backward" nations. This policy sometimes roused local resentments because it often bene-

fited entrenched elites while the mass of peasants and city workers lived in poverty.

The first important diplomatic event of the period revealed a great deal about American foreign policy after the World War. During the war, Japan had greatly increased its influence in the Far East. To maintain the Open Door in China, it would be necessary to check Japanese expansion. In addition, Japan, the United States, and Great Britain were engaged in expensive naval-building programs, a competition none wanted.

In November 1921, hoping to reach a general agreement, that would keep China open to the commerce of all and slow the armaments race, Secretary of State Hughes convened a conference in Washington. By the following February, the Washington Conference had drafted three major treaties and a number of lesser agreements.

In the Five-Power Treaty, the United States, Great Britain, France, Japan, and Italy agreed to stop building battleships for ten years and to reduce their fleets of capital ships to a fixed ratio, with Great Britain and the United States limited to 525,000 tons, Japan to 315,000 tons, and France and Italy to 175,000 tons. The new ratio was expected to produce a balance of forces in the Pacific.

The Four-Power Treaty, signed by the United States, Great Britain, Japan, and France, committed these nations to respect one another's interests in the islands of the Pacific and to confer in the event that any other country launched an attack in the area.

All the conferees signed the Nine-Power Treaty, agreeing to respect China's independence and to maintain the Open Door. On the surface, this seemed to mean that Japan had given up its territorial ambitions on the Asian mainland and that both the Japanese and the Europeans had formally endorsed the Open Door concept.

By taking the lead in drafting these agreements, the United States regained some of the moral influence it had lost by not joining the League of Nations. The treaties, however, were uniformly toothless. The signers of the Four-Power Pact agreed only to consult in case of aggression in the Pacific; they made no promise to restrict their own freedom of action.

The naval disarmament treaty said nothing about the number of other warships that the powers might build, about the far more important

Leaders of the Women's International League for Peace and Freedom assembled at the end of the Great War to argue in favor of United States participation in a worldwide peace organization, such as the League of Nations. Jane Addams is in front, fourth from the left; at her left is Mrs. Robert La Follette, wife of the Wisconsin senator.

question of land and air forces, or about the underlying industrial and financial structures that controlled the ability of the nations to make war. In addition, the 5:5:3 ratio actually enabled the Japanese to dominate the western Pacific. It made the Philippine Islands undefendable and exposed Hawaii to possible attack. In a sense these American bases became hostages of Japan. Yet Congress was so unconcerned about Japanese sensibilities that it refused to grant any immigration quota to Japan under the National Origins Act of 1924, even though the formula applied to other nations would have allowed only 100 Japanese a year to enter the country. The law, Secretary Hughes warned, produced in Japan "a sense of injury and antagonism instead of friendship and cooperation."

Resentment of "white imperialism" played into the hands of the military party in Japan, where many army and navy officers considered war with the United States inevitable. "The emotional resentment against America," Akira Iriye writes in *Across the Pacific,* "was reinforced by a more sophisticated view of future Japanese-American conflict that was advocated by some army strategists."

As for the key Nine-Power Treaty, Japan did not abandon its territorial ambitions in China and China remained so riven by conflict among the warlords and so resentful of the "imperialists" that the economic advantages of the Open Door turned out to be small indeed.

The United States entered into all these agreements without realizing their full implications and not really prepared to play an active part in far eastern affairs. The Japanese soon realized that the United States would not do much to defend its interests in China. The result, in Professor

Iriye's words, was "a new image of America, as a country that delighted in moralism . . . but that was not likely to challenge Japan with force."

The Peace Movement

The Americans of the twenties wanted peace but would neither surrender their prejudices and dislikes nor build the defenses necessary to make it safe to indulge these passions. "The people have had all the war, all the taxation, and all the military service that they want," President Coolidge announced in 1925.

Peace societies flourished, among them the Carnegie Endowment for International Peace, designed "to hasten the abolition of war, the foulest blot upon our civilization," and the Woodrow Wilson Foundation, aimed at helping "the liberal forces of mankind throughout the world . . . who intend to promote peace by the means of justice." In 1923 Edward W. Bok, retired editor of the *Ladies' Home Journal,* offered a prize of $100,000 for the best workable plan for preserving international peace. He was flooded with suggestions. Former Assistant Secretary of the Navy Franklin D. Roosevelt drafted one while recovering from an attack of infantile paralysis. Such was the temper of the times that he felt constrained to include in the preamble this statement:

> We seek not to become involved as a nation in the purely regional affairs of groups of other nations, nor to give to the representatives of other peoples the right to compel us to enter upon undertakings calling for a leading up to the use of armed force without our full and free consent, given through our constitutional procedure.

So great was the opposition to international cooperation that the United States refused to accept membership on the World Court, although this tribunal could settle disputes only when the nations involved agreed. Probably a majority of the American people favored joining the Court, but its advocates were never able to persuade two-thirds of the Senate to ratify the necessary treaty. Too many peace lovers believed that their goal could be attained simply by pointing out the moral and practical disadvantages of war.

The culmination of this illusory faith in preventing war by criticizing it came with the signing of the Kellogg-Briand Pact in 1928. The treaty was born in the fertile brain of French Foreign Minister Aristide Briand, who was eager to collect allies against possible attack by a resurgent Germany. In 1927 Briand proposed to Secretary of State Frank B. Kellogg that their countries agree never to go to war with each other. Kellogg found the idea as repugnant as any conventional alliance, but American isolationists and pacifists found the suggestion fascinating. They plagued Kellogg with demands that he negotiate such a treaty.

To extricate himself from this situation, Kellogg suggested that the pact be broadened to include all nations. Now Briand was angry. Like Kellogg, he saw how meaningless such a treaty would be, especially when Kellogg insisted that it be hedged with a proviso that "every nation is free at all times . . . to defend its territory from attack and it alone is competent to decide when circumstances require war in self-defense." Nevertheless, Briand too found public pressures irresistible. In August 1928, at Paris, diplomats from 15 nations bestowed upon one another an "international kiss," condemning "recourse to war for the solution of international controversies" and renouncing war "as an instrument of national policy." Seldom has so unrealistic a promise been made by so many intelligent people. Yet most Americans considered the Kellogg-Briand Pact a milestone in the history of civilization: The Senate, habitually so suspicious of international commitments, ratified it 85 to 1.

The Good Neighbor Policy

The conflict between the desire to avoid foreign "entanglements" and the desire to advance American economic interests is well illustrated by events in Latin America. "Yankeephobia" had long been a chronic condition south of the Rio Grande. The continued presence of marines in Central America fed this ill feeling. Basic was the objection to being controlled by foreigners. The immense wealth and power of the "Colossus of the

North" and the feeling of most Latin Americans that the wielders of this strength had little respect for the needs and values of their southern neighbors were further causes of distrust. However, the evident desire of the United States to limit its international involvements had a gradually mollifying effect on Latin American opinion.

In dealing with this part of the world, Harding and Coolidge performed neither better nor worse than Wilson had. In the face of continued radicalism and instability in Mexico, which caused Americans with interests in land and oil rights to suffer heavy losses, President Coolidge acted with forbearance. His appointment of Dwight W. Morrow, a patient, sympathetic ambassador, resulted in an improvement in Mexican-American relations. The Mexicans were able to complete their social and economic revolution in the twenties without significant interference by the United States.

Under Coolidge's successor, Herbert Hoover, the United States began at last to treat Latin American nations as equals. Hoover reversed Wilson's policy of trying to teach them "to elect good men." The Clark Memorandum (1930), written by Undersecretary of State J. Reuben Clark, disassociated the right of intervention in Latin America from the Roosevelt Corollary. The corollary had been an improper extension of the Monroe Doctrine, Clark declared. The right of the United States to intervene depended rather on "the doctrine of self-preservation."

The distinction seemed slight to Latin Americans, but since it seemed unlikely that the existence of the United States could be threatened in the area, it was important. By 1934 the marines who had been occupying Nicaragua, Haiti, and the Dominican Republic had all been withdrawn, and the United States had renounced the right to intervene in Cuban affairs. Unfortunately, the United States did little to try to improve social and economic conditions in the Caribbean region, so the underlying envy and resentment of "rich Uncle Sam" did not disappear.

The Totalitarian Challenge

The futility and danger of isolationism were exposed in September 1931 when the Japanese, long dominant in Chinese Manchuria, marched in an army and converted it into a puppet state named Manchukuo. This violated both the Kellogg-Briand and Nine-Power pacts. China, now controlled by General Chiang Kai-shek, appealed to the League of Nations and to the United States for help. Neither would intervene. When League officials asked about the possibility of American cooperation in some kind of police action, President Hoover refused to consider either economic or military reprisals. The United States was not a world policeman, he said. The Nine-Power and Kellogg-Briand treaties were "solely moral instruments."

The League sent a commission to Manchuria to investigate. Henry L. Stimson, Hoover's secretary of state, announced (the Stimson Doctrine) that the United States would never recognize the legality of seizures made in violation of American treaty rights. This served only to irritate the Japanese.

In January 1932 Japan attacked Shanghai, the bloody battle marked by the indiscriminate bombing of residential districts. When the League at last officially condemned their aggressions, the Japanese withdrew from the organization and extended their control of northern China. The lesson of Manchuria was not lost on Adolf Hitler, who became chancellor of Germany on January 30, 1933.

It is easy, in surveying the diplomatic events of 1920 to 1933, to condemn the United States and the European democracies for their unwillingness to stand up for principles, their refusal to resist when Japan and later Germany and Italy embarked on the aggressions that led to World War II. It is also proper to place some of the blame for the troubles of the era on the same powers: They controlled much of the world's resources and were primarily interested in holding on to what they had.

War Debts and Reparations

The democracies did not take a strong stand against Japan in part because they were quarreling about other matters. Particularly divisive was the controversy over war debts—those of Germany to the Allies and those of the Allies to the United States. The United States had lent more than $10 billion to its comrades in arms. Since most of this money had been spent on weapons and other supplies in the United States, it might well have been considered part of America's contribution to the war effort. The public, however, demanded full repayment—with interest. "These were loans, not contributions," Secretary of the Treasury Mellon firmly declared. Even when the Foreign Debt Commission scaled down the interest rate from 5 percent to about 2 percent, the total, to be repaid over a period of 62 years, amounted to more than $22 billion.

The Allies tried to load their obligations to the United States, along with the other costs of the war, on the backs of the Germans. They demanded reparations amounting to $33 billion. If this sum were collected, they declared, they could rebuild their economies and obtain the international exchange needed to pay their debts to the United States. But Germany was reluctant even to try to pay such huge reparations, and when Germany defaulted, so did the Allies.

Everyone was bitterly resentful: the Germans because they felt they were being bled white; the Americans, as Senator Hiram Johnson of California would have it, because the wily Europeans were treating the United States as "an international sucker"; the Allies because, as the French said, *l'oncle Shylock* (a play on the names Uncle Sam and Shylock, the moneylender in Shakespeare's *Merchant of Venice*) was demanding his pound of flesh with interest.

Everyone shared the blame: the Germans because they resorted to a runaway inflation that reduced the mark to less than one trillionth of its prewar value, at least in part in hopes of avoiding their international obligations; the Americans because they refused to recognize the connection between the tariff and the debt question; the Allies because they made little effort to pay even a reasonable proportion of their obligations.

In 1924 an international agreement, the Dawes Plan, provided Germany with a $200 million loan designed to stabilize its currency. Germany agreed to pay about $250 million a year in reparations. In 1929 the Young Plan further scaled down the reparations bill. In practice, the Allies paid the United States about what they collected from Germany. Since Germany got the money largely from private American loans, the United States would have served itself and the rest of the world far better had it written off the war debts at the start. In any case, in the late 1920s Americans stopped lending money to Germany, the Great Depression struck, Germany defaulted on its reparations payments, and the Allies then gave up all pretense of meeting their obligations to the United States. The last token payments were made in 1933. All that remained was a heritage of mistrust and hostility.

The Election of 1928

Meanwhile, dramatic changes had occurred in the United States. The climax of Coolidge prosperity came in 1928. The president—somewhat cryptically, as was his wont—decided not to run again, and Secretary of Commerce Hoover, whom he detested, easily won the Republican nomination. Hoover was the intellectual leader, almost the philosopher, of the New Era. American capitalists, he believed, had learned to curb their selfish instincts.

The Democrats, having had their fill of factionalism in 1924, could no longer deny the nomination to Governor Al Smith. Superficially, Smith was Hoover's antithesis. He was a Catholic, Hoover a Quaker; a wet where Hoover supported prohibition; he dealt easily with people of every race and nationality, while Hoover had little interest in and less knowledge of blacks and immigrants. But like Hoover, Smith managed to combine a basic conservatism with humanitarian concern for the underprivileged.

Unwilling to challenge the public's complacent view of Coolidge prosperity, the Democrats adopted a conservative platform. Smith appointed John J. Raskob, a wealthy automobile executive, to manage his campaign. Franklin D. Roosevelt, who ran for governor of New York at Smith's urging in 1928, charged that Hoover's expansion of the functions of the Department of Commerce had been at least mildly socialistic. This strategy failed miserably. Nothing Smith could do or say was capable of convincing many businessmen that he was a better choice than Hoover. His Catholicism, his brashness, his criticism of prohibition, his machine connections, and his urban background hurt him in rural areas, especially in the normally Democratic South. In the election Hoover won a smashing triumph, 444 to 87 in the electoral college, 21.4 million to 15 million in the popular vote.

After this defeat, the Democratic Party appeared on the verge of extinction. Nothing could have been further from the truth. The religious question and his big-city roots had hurt Smith, but the chief reason he lost was the prosperity—and the good times were soon to end. Hoover's overwhelming victory also concealed a political realignment that was taking place. Working-class voters in the cities, largely Catholic and unimpressed by Coolidge prosperity, had swung heavily to the Democrats. In 1924 the 12 largest cities had been solidly Republican; in 1928 all went Democratic. In agricultural states like Iowa, Smith ran far better than Davis had in 1924, for Coolidge's vetoes of the bills designed to raise farm prices had caused considerable resentment. A new coalition of urban workers and dissatisfied farmers was in the making.

Economic Problems

The American economic system of the twenties had grave flaws. Certain industries, coal for example, and textiles, did not share in the good times. The movement toward consolidation in industry, somewhat checked during the latter part of the Progressive Era, resumed. By 1929, 200 corporations controlled nearly half the nation's corporate assets. General Motors, Ford, and Chrysler turned out nearly 90 percent of all American cars and trucks. Four tobacco companies produced over 90 percent of the cigarettes. Even retail merchandising, traditionally the domain of the small shopkeeper, reflected the trend. The A&P food chain expanded from 400 stores in 1912 to 17,500 in 1928. The Woolworth chain of five and ten cent stores experienced similar growth.

Consolidation did not necessarily lead to monopoly. "Regulated" competition was the order of the day, oligopoly the typical situation. The trade association movement flourished; producers formed voluntary organizations to exchange information, discuss policies toward government and the public, and "administer" prices in their industry. Usually the largest corporation, such as U.S. Steel in the iron and steel business, became the "price leader," its competitors, some themselves giants, following slavishly.

The success of the trade associations depended in part on the attitude of the federal government, for such organizations might well have been attacked under the antitrust laws. Their defenders argued that the associations made business more efficient and prevented violent gyrations of prices and production. President Harding accepted this line of reasoning. Secretary of Commerce Hoover put the facilities of his department at the disposal of the associations. After Coolidge became president, the Antitrust Division of the Justice Department itself encouraged policies that had previously been considered violations of the Sherman Act.

Even more important to the trade associations were the good times. With profits high and markets expanding, the most powerful producers could afford to share the bounty with smaller, less efficient competitors.

The weakest element in the economy was agriculture. In addition to the slump in farm prices, farmers' costs mounted. Besides having to purchase expensive machinery in order to compete, farmers were confronted by high foreign tariffs and in some cases quotas on the importation of foodstuffs.

Despite the efforts of the Farm Bloc, the government did little to improve the situation. President Harding opposed direct aid to agriculture as a matter of principle. "Every farmer is a captain of industry," he declared. "The elimination of competition among them would be impossible without sacrificing that fine individualism that still keeps the farm the real reservoir from which the nation draws so many of the finest elements of its citizenship." During his administration, Congress strengthened the laws regulating railroad rates and grain exchanges and made it easier for farmers to borrow money, but it did nothing to increase agricultural income. Nor did the high tariffs on agricultural produce have much effect. Being forced to sell their surpluses abroad, farmers found that world prices depressed domestic prices despite the tariff wall.

In 1921 George N. Peek, a plow manufacturer, advanced a scheme to "make the tariff effective for agriculture." The federal government, Peek suggested in "Equality for Agriculture," should buy up the surplus American production of wheat.* This additional demand would cause domestic prices to rise. Then the government could sell the wheat abroad at the lower world price. It

---

*He soon extended his plan to cover cotton and other staples.

could recover its losses by assessing an "equalization fee" on the wheat farmers.

Peek's plan had flaws. If the price of staples rose, farmers would tend to increase output. Yet this problem might have been solved by imposing production controls. It was certainly a promising idea; hundreds of organizations in the farm belt endorsed it. Farm Bloc congressmen took it up and in 1927 the McNary-Haugen Bill was passed, only to be vetoed by President Coolidge. Congress passed a similar bill in 1928, and again Coolidge rejected it.

Thus, while most economic indicators reflected an unprecedented prosperity, the boom times rested on unstable foundations. The problem was mainly one of maldistribution of resources. Productive capacity raced ahead of buying power. Too large a share of the profits went into too few pockets. The 27,000 families with the highest annual incomes in 1929 received as much money as the 11 million with annual incomes of under $1,500, which was the minimum sum required at that time to maintain a family decently. High earnings and low taxes permitted huge sums to pile up in the hands of individuals who did not invest the money productively. A good deal of it went into stock market speculation, which led to the "big bull market" and eventually to the Great Depression.

The Crash of 1929

In the spring of 1928, prices on the New York Stock Exchange, already at a historic high, began to surge ahead. As the presidential campaign gathered momentum, the market increased its upward pace. Through the first half of 1929, the market climbed still higher. A mania for speculation swept the country, thousands of small investors pouring their savings into common stocks.

In September the market wavered. Amid volatile fluctuations, stock averages eased downward. Most analysts contended that the Exchange was "digesting" previous gains. A Harvard economist expressed the prevailing view when he said that stock prices would soon resume their advance. On October 24 a wave of selling sent prices spinning. Nearly 13 million shares changed hands—a record. Bankers and politicians rallied to check the decline, as they had during the Panic of 1907. President Hoover assured the people that "the business of the country . . . is on a sound and prosperous basis." But on Tuesday, October 29, the bottom seemed to drop out. More than 16 million shares were sold, prices plummeting. The boom was over.

Hoover and the Depression

The collapse of the stock market did not cause the depression; stocks rallied late in the year and business activity did not begin to decline significantly until the spring of 1930. The Great Depression was a worldwide phenomenon caused chiefly by economic imbalances resulting from the chaos of World War I. In the United States too much wealth had fallen into too few hands, with the result that consumers were unable to buy all the goods produced. The trouble came to a head mainly because of the easy-credit policies of the Federal Reserve Board and the Mellon tax structure, which favored the rich. Its effects were so profound and prolonged because the politicians

James N. Rosenberg, an attorney and amateur artist, sketched this grim view of the Wall Street financial district. October 29, 1929 ("Black Tuesday"), as a Day of Judgment.

did not fully understand what was happening or what to do about it.

The chronic problem of underconsumption operated to speed the downward spiral. Unable to rid themselves of mounting inventories, manufacturers closed plants and laid off workers, thereby causing demand to shrink further. Automobile output fell from 4.5 million units in 1929 to 1.1 million in 1932. When Ford closed his Detroit plants in 1931, some 75,000 workers lost their jobs, and the decline in auto production affected a host of suppliers and middlemen as well.

The financial system cracked under the strain. More than 1,300 banks closed their doors in 1930, 3,700 more during the next two years. Each failure deprived thousands of persons of funds that might have been used to buy goods. And of course the industrial depression worsened the depression in agriculture by further reducing the demand for American foodstuffs. Every economic indicator reflected the collapse. New investments declined and the national income fell. Unemployment, under 1 million at the height of the boom, rose to at least 13 million.

President Hoover was an intelligent man, experienced in business matters and knowledgeable in economics. Secretary of the Treasury Mellon believed that the economy should be allowed to slide unchecked until the cycle had found its bottom. Hoover realized that such a policy would cause unbearable hardship for millions.

Hoover's program for ending the depression evolved gradually. At first it called on business to maintain prices and wages. The government should cut taxes in order to increase consumers' spendable income, institute public works programs to stimulate production and create jobs for the unemployed, lower interest rates to make it easier for businesses to borrow in order to expand, and make loans to banks and industrial corporations threatened with collapse and to homeowners unable to meet mortgage payments. The president also proposed measures making it easier for farmers to borrow money, and he suggested that cooperative farm marketing schemes designed to solve the problem of overproduction be supported by the government. He also suggested expanding state and local relief programs and he urged all who could afford it to give more to charity. Above all he tried to restore public confidence. The economy was basically healthy. The

depression was only a minor downturn. Prosperity was "just around the corner."

In other words, Hoover rejected classical economics. Indeed, many laissez-faire theorists attacked his handling of the depression. Numbers of "liberal" economists, on the other hand, praised the Hoover program.

Although Hoover's plans were theoretically sound, they failed to check the economic slide, in part because he placed far too much reliance on his powers of persuasion and the willingness of citizens to act in the public interest without legal compulsion. He urged manufacturers to maintain wages and keep their factories in operation, but the manufacturers, under the harsh pressure of economic realities, soon slashed wages and curtailed output sharply. He permitted the Federal Farm Board (created under the Agricultural Marketing Act of 1929) to establish semipublic stabilization corporations with authority to buy surplus wheat and cotton, but he refused to countenance crop or acreage controls. The stabilization corporations poured out hundreds of millions of dollars without checking falling agricultural prices because farmers increased production faster than the corporations could buy up the excess for disposal abroad.

Hoover resisted proposals to shift responsibility from state and local agencies to the federal government, despite the fact—soon obvious—that they lacked the resources to cope with the emergency. More serious was his refusal, on constitutional grounds, to allow federal funds to be used for the relief of individuals. State and municipal agencies and private charities must take care of the needy.

Unfortunately the depression was drying up the sources of funds of private charities just as the demands on these organizations were expanding. State and municipal agencies were swamped at a time when their capacities to tax and borrow were shrinking. By 1932, 40,600 Boston families were on relief (compared with 7,400 families in 1929); in Chicago 700,000 persons—40 percent of the work force—were unemployed. Only the national government possessed the power and the credit to deal adequately with the crisis. Yet Hoover would not act. For the federal government to take over relief would "lead to the super-state where every man becomes the servant of the state and real liberty is lost."

Federal loans to business were constitutional, he believed, because the money could be put to productive use and eventually repaid. When drought destroyed the crops of farmers in the South and Southwest in 1930, the government lent them money to buy seed and even food for their livestock, but Hoover would permit no direct relief for the farmers themselves. In 1932 he approved the creation of the Reconstruction Finance Corporation to lend money to banks, railroads, and insurance companies. Its loans were commercial transactions, not gifts; the agency did almost nothing for individuals in need of relief. The same could be said of the Glass-Steagall Banking Act of 1932, which eased the tight credit situation by permitting Federal Reserve banks to accept a wider variety of commercial paper as security for loans. The public grew increasingly resentful of the president's doctrinaire adherence to principle while breadlines lengthened and millions of willing workers searched fruitlessly for jobs.

As the depression worsened, Hoover put more stress on balancing the federal budget, reasoning that since citizens had to live within their limited means in hard times, the government should set a good example. This policy was counterproductive; by reducing its expenditures the government made things worse. The policy was also impossible to carry out because the government's income fell precipitously. By June 1931 the budget was nearly $500 million in the red.

Hoover understood the importance of pumping money into the economy. The difficulty lay in the fact that nearly all "informed" people believed that a balanced budget was essential to recovery. When Hoover said, "Prosperity cannot be restored by raids on the public Treasury," he was mistaken; but it would be equally wrong to criticize him for failing to understand what almost no one understood in the 1930s.

Hoover can, however, be faulted for allowing his anti-European prejudices to interfere with the implementation of his program. In 1930 Congress passed the Hawley-Smoot Tariff Act, which raised duties on most manufactured products to prohibitive levels. This measure made it impossible for European nations to earn the dollars they needed to continue making payments on their World War I debts to the United States, and it helped bring on a financial collapse in Europe in 1931. When that happened, Hoover wisely proposed a one-year

"moratorium" on all international obligations. But the efforts of Great Britain and many other countries to save their own skins by devaluing their currencies in order to encourage foreigners to buy their goods led him to blame them for the depression itself.

Much of the contemporary criticism of Hoover and a good deal of that heaped on him by later historians was unfair. Yet his record as president shows that he was too rigidly wedded to a particular theory of government to cope effectively with the problems of the day. He was his own worst enemy, being too uncompromising to get on well with the politicians and too aloof to win the confidence and affection of ordinary people. As the historian Joan Hoff-Wilson wrote, he refused "to backslap, fraternize with local supporters, kiss babies." When he failed to achieve the results he anticipated, he attracted, despite his devotion to duty and his concern for the welfare of the country, not sympathy but scorn.

The Economy Hits Bottom

During the spring of 1932, as the economy sounded the depths, thousands of Americans faced starvation. In Philadelphia during an 11-day period when no relief funds were available, hundreds of families existed on stale bread, thin soup, and garbage. In the nation as a whole, only about one-quarter of the unemployed were receiving any public aid. Many people who had been evicted from their homes gathered in ramshackle communities constructed of packing boxes, rusty sheet metal, and similar refuse on swamps, garbage dumps, and other wasteland. People began to call these places "Hoovervilles."

Thousands of unemployed, homeless people roamed the countryside begging for food. At the same time, food prices fell so low that farmers burned corn for fuel. The world seemed to have been turned upside down. Professor Felix Frankfurter of the Harvard Law School remarked only half humorously that henceforth the terms *B.C.* and *A.D.* would mean "Before Crash" and "After Depression."

The national mood ranged from apathy to resentment. In 1931 federal immigration agents and local groups in the Southwest began rounding up

Mexican-Americans and deporting them. Unemployed Mexicans were ejected because they might become public charges, those with jobs because presumably they were taking bread from the mouths of citizens.

In June and July 1932, 20,000 veterans marched on Washington to demand immediate payment of their "adjusted compensation" bonuses. When Congress rejected their appeal, some 2,000 refused to leave, settling in a jerry-built camp of shacks and tents at Anacostia Flats, a swamp bordering the Potomac. President Hoover, alarmed, charged incorrectly that the "Bonus Army" was largely composed of criminals and radicals and sent troops into the Flats to disperse it with bayonets, tear gas, and tanks. The task was accomplished amid much confusion; fortunately no one was killed. The protest had been aimless and not entirely justified, yet the spectacle of the United States government chasing unarmed veterans with tanks appalled the nation.

The unprecedented severity of the depression led some persons to favor radical economic and political changes. The disparity between the lots of the rich and the poor, always a challenge to democracy, became more striking and engendered considerable bitterness. The Communist Party gained few converts among farmers and industrial workers, but a considerable number of intellectuals, alienated by the trends of the twenties, responded positively to the communists' emphasis on economic planning and the total mobilization of the state to achieve social goals. Even the popular cracker-barrel humorist Will Rogers was impressed by reports of the absence of serious unemployment in Russia. "All roads in our day lead to Moscow," the former muckraker Lincoln Steffens wrote.

The Depression and Its Victims

Depression is a word used by economists but also by psychologists, and the depression of the 1930s had profound psychological effects on its victims. Almost without exception, people who lost their jobs first searched energetically for new ones, but when they remained unemployed for more than a few months they sank gradually into apathy. E. Wight Bakke, a Yale sociologist who interviewed

hundreds of unemployed men in the United States and England during the Depression, described the final stage of decline as "permanent readjustment," by which he meant that the long-term jobless simply gave up.

People who had worked all their adult lives often became ashamed of themselves when they could not find a job. A purely physiological factor was often involved as well. When money ran low, people had to cut down on relatively expensive foods like fruit, meat, and dairy products. In New York City, for example, milk consumption fell by a million quarts a day. In nutritional terms they consumed more carbohydrates and less food rich in energy-building vitamins and proteins. Listlessness (another word for apathy) often resulted.

This psychological depression helps explain why the unemployed were not, in general, very radical. There were meetings and protest marches and also strikes, but the former were usually organized by people who were not themselves unemployed and strikers, almost by definition, are people who are refusing to work, not those who have no job to quit.

The depression caused a dramatic drop in the birth rate, from 27.7 per thousand population in 1920 to 18.4 per thousand in the early 1930s, the lowest in American history. Sometimes it strengthened family ties. Some unemployed men spent more time with their children and helped their wives with cooking and housework. Others, however, refused to help around the house, sulked, or took to drink.

The influence of wives in families struck by unemployment tended to increase, and in this respect women suffered less psychologically from the depression. They were usually too busy trying to make ends meet to become apathetic. Some were sympathetic, others scornful when the "breadwinner" came home with empty hands.

Children often caused strains. Parental authority declined when there was less money available to supply children's needs. Some youngsters became angry when denied something they particularly wanted. Some adolescents found part-time jobs to help out. Others refused to go to school. If there is any generalization about the effects of the Depression on family relations it is probably an obvious one—where relationships were close and loving, they became stronger,

A breadline in Chicago. The Great Depression, an English observer said, "outraged and baffled" the nation that took it as an "article of faith . . . that America, somehow, was different from the rest of the world."

where they were not, the results could be disastrous.

The Election of 1932

As the end of his term approached, President Hoover seemed to grow daily more petulant and pessimistic. The depression, coming after 12 years of Republican rule, probably insured a Democratic victory in any case, but his attitude as the election neared alienated many voters and turned defeat into rout.

Confident of victory, the Democrats chose Governor Franklin Delano Roosevelt of New York as their presidential candidate. Roosevelt owed his nomination chiefly to his success as governor. Under his administration, New York had led the nation in providing relief for the needy and had enacted an impressive program of old-age pensions, unemployment insurance, and conservation and public power projects. The governor also had the advantage of the Roosevelt name (he was a distant cousin of the inimitable TR), and his sunny, magnetic personality contrasted favorably with that of the glum and colorless Hoover.

Roosevelt was far from being a radical. During the twenties he had not seriously challenged the basic tenets of Coolidge prosperity. He never had much difficulty adjusting his views to prevailing attitudes. For a time he even served as head of the American Construction Council, a trade association. Indeed, his life before the depression gave little indication that he understood the aspirations of ordinary people or had any deep commitment to social reform.

Roosevelt was born to wealth and social status. He was educated at the exclusive Groton School and then at Harvard, where he proceeded, as his biographer Frank Freidel wrote, "from one extracurricular triumph to another." Ambition as much as the desire to render public service motivated his career in politics; even after an attack of polio in 1921 left him badly crippled in both legs, he refused to abandon his hopes for high office.

To some observers Roosevelt seemed rather a lightweight intellectually. Many critics judged him too irresolute, too amiable, too eager to please all factions to be a forceful leader. Herbert Hoover thought he was "ignorant but well-meaning," and the political analyst Walter Lippmann, in a now-famous observation, called him "a pleasant man who, without any important qualifications for the job, would very much like to be President."

Despite his physical handicap, Roosevelt was a marvelous campaigner. He traveled back and forth across the country, radiating confidence and good humor even when directing his sharpest barbs at the Republicans. He soaked up information and ideas from a thousand sources—from professors like Raymond Moley and Rexford Tugwell of Columbia, from politicians like the Texan vice presidential candidate John N. Garner, from social workers, businessmen, and lawyers.

To those seeking specific answers to the questions of the day, Roosevelt was seldom satisfying. On such vital matters as farm policy, the tariff, and government spending, he equivocated, contradicted himself, or remained silent. Aided by hindsight, historians have discovered portents of much of his later program in his campaign speeches. These pronouncements, buried among dozens of conflicting generalities, often passed unnoticed at the time. He said, for example, "if starvation and dire need on the part of any of our citizens make necessary the appropriation of additional funds which would keep the budget out of balance, I shall not hesitate to . . . ask the people to authorize the expenditure of that additional amount." In the same speech, however, he called for steep cuts in federal spending and a balanced budget, and he castigated Hoover for presiding over "the greatest spending administration in peace time in our history."

Nevertheless Roosevelt's basic position was unmistakable. There must be a "re-appraisal of values," a "New Deal." Instead of adhering to conventional limits on the extent of federal power, the government should do whatever was necessary to protect the unfortunate and advance the public good. Lacking concrete answers, Roosevelt advocated a point of view rather than a plan: "The country needs bold, persistent experimentation. It is common sense to take a method and try it. If it fails, admit it frankly and try another. But above all, try something."

Milestones

1921	Budget and Accounting Act	**1929**	New York Stock Exchange crash ends big bull market
	Washington Disarmament Conference		Young Plan further reduces German reparations
1922	Fordney-McCumber Tariff protecting "infant industries"	**1930**	Clark Memorandum renounces Roosevelt Corollary to Monroe Doctrine
1923	President Harding dies		Hawley-Smoot Tariff raises duties on foreign manufactures
	Teapot Dome and other Harding scandals exposed	**1931**	Japanese invasion of Manchuria
1924	Dawes Plan restructures German reparations payments		Hoover moratorium on war debts
	National Origins Act establishes immigration quotas	**1932**	Bonus marchers in Washington dispersed by troops
1927	McNary-Haugen farm relief bill vetoed by President Coolidge		Reconstruction Finance Corporation created
1928	Kellogg-Briand Treaty "outlaws" war as "an instrument of national policy"		Franklin D. Roosevelt elected president

The popularity of this approach was demonstrated in November. Hoover, who had lost only eight states in 1928, won only six, all in the Northeast, in 1932. Roosevelt amassed 22.8 million votes to Hoover's 15.8 million and carried the electoral college, 472 to 59.

During the interval between the election and Roosevelt's inauguration in March 1933, the Great Depression reached its nadir. The holdover "lame duck" Congress, last of its kind, proved incapable of effective action.[†]

The nation, curiously apathetic in the face of so much suffering, drifted aimlessly, like a sailboat in a flat calm.

Supplementary Reading

The political history of the twenties is surveyed in R. K. Murray, **The Politics of Normalcy*** (1973), and E. W. Hawley, **The Great War and the Search for a Modern Order*** (1979). On the labor history of the postwar decade see R. H. Zieger, **Republicans and Labor** (1969). The best brief biography of Harding is Andrew Sinclair, **The Available Man*** (1965). D. R. McCoy, **Calvin Coolidge: The Quiet President** (1967), is the best biography of Coolidge. On Hoover, see M. L. Fausold, **The Presidency of Herbert Hoover** (1985), and Joan Hoff Wilson, **Herbert Hoover: Forgotten Progressive*** (1975).

[†]The Twentieth Amendment (1933) provided for convening new Congresses in January instead of the following December. It also advanced the date of the president's inauguration from March 4 to January 20.

David Burner, **The Politics of Provincialism** (1968), deals with the Democratic Party in the 1920s. On the trade association movement, see R. F. Himmelberg, **The Origins of the National Recovery Act** (1976).

Diplomatic developments are summarized in Selig Adler, **The Uncertain Giant*** (1965), and Akira Iriye, **After Imperialism** (1965) and **Across the Pacific** (1967), T. H. Buckley, **The United States and the Washington Conference** (1970), Charles De Benedetti, **Origins of the Modern Peace Movement** (1978), and J. H. Wilson, **American Business and Foreign Policy*** (1971).

On farm problems, see J. D. Hicks, **Twentieth-Century Populism** (1951), and G. C. Fite, **George N. Peek and the Fight for Farm Parity** (1954). On the election of 1928, see Oscar Handlin, **Al Smith and His America** (1958).

On isolationism, see R. A. Divine, **The Reluctant Belligerent** (1965) and **The Illusion of Neutrality** (1962). On Latin American relations, see I. F. Gellman, **Good Neighbor Diplomacy** (1979).

For the stock market crash, see Robert Sobel, **The Great Bull Market*** (1968), and J. K. Galbraith, **The Great Crash*** (1961). L. V. Chandler, **America's Greatest Depression*** (1970), is a good introduction to the economic problems of the period, but see also M. A. Bernstein, **The Great Depression** (1987), and J. A. Garraty, **The Great Depression*** (1986), which puts American developments in world perspective.

*Available in paperback.

CHAPTER 27

The New Deal: 1933–1941

The Hundred Days

The National Recovery Administration (NRA)

The Agricultural Adjustment Act (AAA)

The Tennessee Valley Authority (TVA)

The New Deal Spirit

The Unemployed

Literature in the Depression

The Extremists

The Second New Deal

The Election of 1936

Roosevelt and the "Nine Old Men"

The New Deal Winds Down

Significance of the New Deal

Women as New Dealers: The Network

Blacks During the New Deal

A New Deal for Indians

The Role of Roosevelt

The Triumph of Isolationism

War Again in Europe

A Third Term for FDR

The Undeclared War

*A*s the date of Franklin Roosevelt's inauguration approached, the banking system disintegrated—no word less strong portrays the extent of the collapse. Starting in the rural West and spreading to major cities like Detroit and Baltimore, a financial panic swept the land. Hundreds of banks collapsed. By inauguration day, four-fifths of the states had suspended all banking operations.

The Hundred Days

Something drastic had to be done. The most conservative business leaders were as ready for government intervention as the most advanced radicals. Partisanship, though not disappearing, was for once subordinated to broad national needs. Even before Roosevelt took office, Congress submitted to the states the Twenty-first Amendment, putting an end to prohibition, to the states. By the end of the year it had been ratified by the necessary three-quarters and the prohibition era was over.

But it was undoubtedly Franklin D. Roosevelt who provided the spark that re-energized the American people. His inaugural address reassured the country and at the same time stirred it to action: "The only thing we have to fear is fear itself. . . . This Nation asks for action, and action now. . . . I assume unhesitatingly the leadership of this great army of our people. . . ." Many such lines punctuated the brief address, which concluded with a stern pledge:

> *In the event that Congress shall fail . . . I shall not evade the clear course of duty that will then confront me. I shall ask the Congress for the one remaining instrument to meet the crisis— broad Executive power to wage a war against the emergency.*

The inaugural address captured the heart of the country. When Roosevelt summoned Congress into special session on March 9, the legislators outdid one another to enact his proposals into law. "I had as soon start a mutiny in the face of a foreign foe as . . . against the program of the President," one representative declared. In the following "Hundred Days," opposition, in the sense of an organized group committed to resisting the administration, simply did not exist.

Roosevelt had the power and the will to act but no comprehensive plan of action. He and his eager congressional collaborators proceeded in a dozen directions at once, sometimes wisely, sometimes not, often at cross-purposes with themselves and one another. As a result, one of the first administration measures was the Economy Act, which reduced the salaries of federal employees and cut veterans' benefits. Such belt-tightening could only make the depression worse. But most New Deal programs were designed to stimulate the economy. All in all, an impressive body of new legislation was placed on the statute books.

On March 5 Roosevelt declared a nationwide bank holiday and placed an embargo on the exportation of gold. To explain the complexities of the banking problem to the public, Roosevelt delivered the first of his "fireside chats" over a national radio network. "I want to talk for a few minutes with the people of the United States about banking," he explained. His warmth and steadiness reassured millions of listeners. A plan for reopening the banks under Treasury Department licenses was devised, and soon most of them were functioning again, public confidence in their solvency restored. This solved the problem but it also determined that the banks would remain private institutions. Reform, not radical change, had been decided on at the very start of Roosevelt's presidency.

In April Roosevelt took the country off the gold standard, hoping thereby to cause prices to rise. Before the session ended, Congress established the Federal Deposit Insurance Corporation (FDIC) to guarantee bank deposits. It also forced the separation of investment banking and commercial banking concerns while extending the

Well-wishers greet the president at Warm Springs, Georgia, in 1933. The Roosevelt "magic," unfeigned and inexhaustible, amazed his associates. "I have never had contact with a man who was loved as he is," reported Secretary of the Interior.

power of the Federal Reserve Board over both types of institutions, and it created the Home Owners Loan Corporation (HOLC) to refinance mortgages and prevent foreclosures. It passed a Federal Securities Act requiring promoters to make public full financial information about new stock issues and giving the Federal Trade Commission the right to regulate such transactions.*

The National Recovery Administration (NRA)

Problems of unemployment and industrial stagnation had high priority during the Hundred Days. Congress appropriated $500 million for relief of the needy and created the Civilian Conservation Corps to provide jobs for men between the ages of 18 and 25 in reforestation and other conservation projects. To stimulate industry, Congress passed one of its most controversial measures, the National Industrial Recovery Act (NIRA).

Besides establishing the Public Works Administration, with authority to spend $3.3 billion, this law permitted manufacturers to draw up industrywide codes of "fair business practices." Under the law, producers could agree to raise prices and limit production, without violating the antitrust laws. The law gave workers the protection of minimum-wage and maximum-hours regulations and guaranteed them the right "to organize and bargain collectively through representatives of their own choosing," an immense stimulus to the union movement.

The act created a government agency, the National Recovery Administration (NRA) headed by General Hugh Johnson, to supervise the drafting and operation of the business codes. Drafting posed difficult problems, first because each industry insisted on tailoring the agreements to its special needs and second because most manufacturers were unwilling to accept all the provisions of Section 7a of the law dealing with the rights of labor. While thousands of employers agreed to the pledge "We Do Our Part" in order to receive the

*In 1934 this task was transferred to the new Securities and Exchange Commission, which was given broad authority over the activities of stock exchanges.

Blue Eagle symbol of NRA, many were more interested in the monopolistic aspects of the act than in boosting wages and encouraging unionization. In practice, the codes were drawn up by the largest manufacturers in each industry.

The effects of NIRA were both more and less than the designers of the system had intended. It did not end the depression. There was a brief upturn in the spring of 1933, but the expected revival of industry did not take place; in nearly every case the dominant producers in each industry used their power to raise prices and limit production rather than to hire more workers and increase output.

Beginning with the cotton textile code, the agreements succeeded in doing away with the centuries-old problem of child labor in industry. They established the principle of federal regulation of wages and hours and led to the organization of thousands of workers, even in industries where unions had seldom been significant. Within a year John L. Lewis's United Mine Workers expanded from 150,000 members to half a million. About 100,000 automobile workers joined unions, as did a comparable number of steelworkers.

Labor leaders used the NIRA to persuade workers that Roosevelt wanted them to join unions—which was something of an overstatement. In 1935, because the craft-oriented AFL had displayed little enthusiasm for enrolling unskilled workers on an industrywide basis, John L. Lewis, together with officials of the garment trade unions, formed the Committee for Industrial Organization (CIO) and set out to rally workers in each of the mass-production industries into one union without regard for craft lines. Since a union containing all the workers in a factory was easier to organize and direct than separate craft unions, this was a far more effective way of unionizing factory labor. The AFL expelled these unions, however, and in 1938 the CIO became the Congress of Industrial organizations. Soon it rivaled the AFL in size and importance.

The Agricultural Adjustment Act (AAA)

Roosevelt was more concerned about the plight of the farmers than that of any other group because he believed that the nation was overcommitted to industry. The New Deal farm program, incorporated in the Agricultural Adjustment Act of May 1933, combined compulsory restrictions on production with government subsidies to growers of wheat, cotton, tobacco, pork, and a few other crops. The money for these payments was raised by taxing middlemen such as flour millers. The object was to lift agricultural prices to "parity" with industrial prices. In return for withdrawing part of their land from cultivation, farmers received "rental" payments from the Agricultural Adjustment Administration (AAA).

Since the 1933 crops were growing when the law was passed, Secretary of Agriculture Henry A. Wallace decided to pay farmers to destroy the crops in the field. Cotton planters plowed up 10 million acres of growing crops, receiving $100 million in return. Six million baby pigs and 200,000 pregnant sows were slaughtered. Such ruthlessness appalled observers, particularly when they thought of the millions of hungry Americans who could have eaten all that pork.

Thereafter, limitation of acreage proved sufficient to raise some agricultural prices considerably. Tobacco growers benefited and so did those who raised corn and hogs. The price of wheat also rose, though more because of bad harvests than the AAA program. But dairy farmers and cattlemen were hurt, as were the railroads (which had less freight to haul) and, of course, consumers. A far more serious weakness of the program was its effect on tenant farmers and sharecroppers, many of whom lost their livelihoods when owners took land out of production to obtain AAA payments. Yet in 1933 even farmers with large holdings were in desperate trouble, and they at least were helped. Acreage restrictions and mortgage relief saved thousands.

The Tennessee Valley Authority (TVA)

Another achievement of the Hundred Days was the creation of the Tennessee Valley Authority (TVA). During World War I the government had constructed a hydroelectric plant at Muscle Shoals, Alabama, to provide power for factories manufacturing synthetic nitrate explosives. After

1920 farm groups and public power enthusiasts had blocked administration plans to turn these facilities over to private capitalists. Their efforts to have the site operated by the government had been defeated by presidential vetoes.

Roosevelt wanted to make the Tennessee Valley area a broad experiment in social planning. Besides expanding the hydroelectric plants and developing nitrate manufacturing in order to produce cheap fertilizers, he envisioned a coordinated program of soil conservation, reforestation, and industrialization. Since the Tennessee River flowed through seven states, national control of the project was essential.

Over the objections of private power companies, led by Wendell L. Willkie of the Commonwealth and Southern Corporation, Congress passed the TVA Act in May 1933. This law created a board authorized to build dams, power plants, and transmission lines and sell fertilizers and electricity to individuals and local communities. The board could undertake flood control, soil conservation, and reforestation projects. TVA greatly improved the standard of living of millions of inhabitants of the valley. In addition to producing electricity and fertilizers and providing a "yardstick" whereby the efficiency, and thus the rates, of private power companies could be tested, it took on other functions, ranging from the eradication of malaria to the development of recreational facilities.

The New Deal Spirit

By the end of the Hundred Days, the country had made up its mind about Roosevelt's New Deal, and despite the vicissitudes of the next decade, it never changed it. A large majority labeled the New Deal a solid success. Considerable recovery had taken place, but more basic was the fact that Roosevelt, recruiting an army of officials to staff the new government agencies, had infused his administration with a spirit of bustle and optimism.

Although Roosevelt was not much of an intellectual, he was eager to draw on the ideas and energies of experts of all sorts. New Deal agencies soon teemed with college professors and young lawyers without political experience. However, the New Deal lacked any consistent ideological

base. It drew on the old populist tradition, as seen in its antipathy to bankers and its willingness to adopt schemes for inflating the currency; on the New Nationalism of Theodore Roosevelt in its dislike of competition and its de-emphasis of the antitrust laws; and on the ideas of social workers trained in the Progressive Era. Techniques developed by the Wilsonians also found a place in the system: Louis D. Brandeis had considerable influence on Roosevelt's financial reforms, and New Deal labor policy was an outgrowth of the experience of the War Labor Board of 1917–1918.

Within the administrative maze that Roosevelt created, rival bureaucrats battled to enforce their views. The "spenders," led by Columbia economist Rexford G. Tugwell, clashed with those favoring strict economy, who gathered around Lewis Douglas, director of the budget. Roosevelt mediated between the factions, deciding this time in favor of one, next in favor of the other. Washington became a battleground for dozens of special-interest groups, such as the Farm Bureau Federation, the unions, the trade associations, and the silver miners. William E. Leuchtenburg has described New Deal policy as "interest-group democracy." Although, as Leuchtenburg says, the system was superior to that of Roosevelt's predecessors, who had allowed one interest, big business, to predominate, it slighted the unorganized majority. NRA aimed frankly at raising the prices paid by consumers of manufactured goods; the AAA processing tax came ultimately from the pocketbooks of ordinary citizens. Yet the public assumed that Roosevelt's objective was to improve the lot of all classes of society and that he was laboring imaginatively in pursuit of this goal.

The Unemployed

At least 9 million persons were still without work in 1934, and hundreds of thousands of them were in real need. Malcolm Little, later the black radical Malcolm X, remembered growing up in the depression this way:

> *1934 . . . was about the worst depression year, and no one we knew had enough to eat. . . . There were times when there wasn't even a nickle and we would be so hungry we were*

dizzy. My mother would boil a big pot of dande-
lion greens and we would eat that.

Yet the Democrats confounded the political experts, including their own, by increasing their already large majorities in both houses of Congress
in the 1934 elections. All the evidence indicates
that most of the jobless continued to support the
administration. Their loyalty can best be explained by Roosevelt's unemployment policies.

In May 1933 Congress had established the
Federal Emergency Relief Administration (FERA)
and given it $500 million to be dispensed through
state relief organizations. Roosevelt appointed
Harry L. Hopkins, a social worker, to direct FERA.
Hopkins insisted that the unemployed needed
jobs, not handouts. In November he persuaded
Roosevelt to create a Civil Works Administration
(CWA) and swiftly put 4 million persons to work
building and repairing roads and public buildings,
teaching, decorating the walls of post offices with
murals, and using their special skills in dozens of
other ways.

The cost of this program frightened Roosevelt—Hopkins spent about $1 billion in less
than five months—and he soon abolished the
CWA. But an extensive public works program was
continued throughout 1934 under FERA. Even
those who did not benefit took the program as an
indication of Roosevelt's determination to attack
the unemployment problem on a broad front.

In May 1935 Roosevelt put Hopkins in charge
of a new agency, the Works Progress Administration (WPA). By the time this agency was disbanded in 1943, it had spent $11 billion and found
employment for 8.5 million persons. Besides
building public works, the WPA made important
cultural contributions. It developed the Federal
Theatre Project, which put thousands of actors, directors, and stagehands to work; the Federal Writers' Project, which turned out valuable guidebooks, collected local lore, and published about a
thousand books and pamphlets; and the Federal
Art Project, which employed painters and sculp-
tors. In addition, the National Youth Administration created part-time jobs for more than 2 million
high school and college students and a larger
number of other youths.

WPA did not reach all the unemployed. At no
time in the thirties did unemployment fall below
10 percent of the work force. Like so many New

Deal programs, WPA did not go far enough,
chiefly because Roosevelt could not escape his
fear of unbalancing the federal budget drastically.
Halfway measures did not provide the stimulus
the economy needed. The president also hesitated to pay adequate wages to WPA workers and
to undertake projects that might compete with private enterprises. Yet his caution did him no good
politically; the business interests he sought to pla-
cate were becoming increasingly hostile to the
New Deal.

Literature in the Depression

Some American novelists found Soviet communism attractive and wrote "proletarian" novels in
which ordinary workers were the heroes. Most of
these were of little artistic merit. The best of the
depression writers avoided the party line, though
they were critical of many aspects of American
life. One was John Dos Passos, author of the trilogy *U. S. A.* (1930–1936). This massive work, rich
in detail and intricately constructed, advanced a
fundamentally anticapitalist and deeply pessimistic point of view. It portrayed American society between 1900 and 1930 in broad perspective,
interweaving the stories of five major characters
and a galaxy of lesser figures. Throughout the
narrative Dos Passos scattered capsule sketches
of famous people, ranging from Andrew Carnegie
and William Jennings Bryan to the movie idol
Rudolph Valentino and the architect Frank Lloyd
Wright. He included "newsreel" sections recounting events of the period and "camera eye" sections
in which he revealed his personal reactions to the
passing parade. Dos Passos's method was relentless, cold, methodical—utterly realistic. He displayed immense craftsmanship but no sympathy
for his characters or their world.

James T. Farrell was less talented than Dos
Passos, a clumsy novelist in the naturalist tradition established by Theodore Dreiser, around the
turn of the century. He also wrote a trilogy in the
thirties, the saga of *Studs Lonigan* (1932–1935). It
described the squalid life of Chicago's Irish
slums. Farrell's overly literal realism was full of
anger and conviction, and was therefore powerful.

The novel that best portrayed the desperate
plight of the millions impoverished by the depression was John Steinbeck's *The Grapes of Wrath*

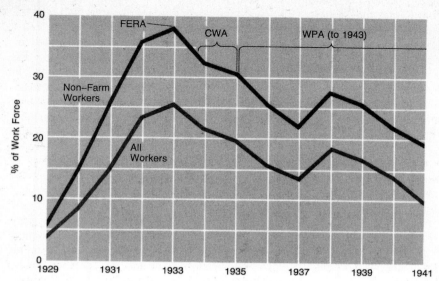

40

FERA

CWA

WPA (to 1943)

Unemployment of Non-Farm Workers

30

Non–Farm Workers

20

All Workers

10

0

% of Work Force

1929   1931   1933   1935   1937   1939   1941

(1939), which described the fate of the Joads, an Oklahoma farm family driven by drought and bad times to abandon the land and become migratory laborers in California. Steinbeck captured the patient bewilderment of the downtrodden, the callous brutality bred of fear that characterized their exploiters, and the ultimate indignation of a people repeatedly degraded. "In the eyes of the hungry there is a growing wrath. In the souls of the people the grapes of wrath are filling and growing heavy, growing heavy for the vintage."

Like so many other writers of the thirties, Steinbeck was an angry man. "There is a crime here that goes beyond denunciation," he wrote. He had the compassion that Dos Passos and Farrell lacked, and this quality raised *The Grapes of Wrath* to the level of great tragedy. In other works Steinbeck described the life of California cannery workers and ranchers with moving warmth without becoming overly sentimental.

William Faulkner, perhaps the finest of modern American novelists, responded to the era in still another way. Born in 1897, within a year of Fitzgerald and Hemingway, he attained literary maturity only in the thirties. Between 1929 and 1932 he burst into prominence with four major novels: *The Sound and the Fury, As I Lay Dying, Sanctuary,* and *Light in August.*

Faulkner created a local world, Yoknapatawpha County, and peopled it with some of the most

remarkable characters in American fiction—the Sartoris family, typical of the old southern aristocracy worn down at the heels, the Snopes clan, shrewd, unscrupulous, boorish representatives of the new day, and many others. He pictured vividly the South's poverty and its pride, its dreadful racial problem, the guilt and obscure passions plaguing white and black alike. He also dealt effectively with the clash of urban and rural values. Yet Faulkner was far more than a local colorist. No contemporary excelled him as a commentator on the multiple dilemmas of modern life. His characters are possessed, driven to pursue high ideals yet weighted down with their awareness of their inadequacies and their sinfulness. They are imprisoned in their surroundings however they may strive to escape them. As the French novelist Simone de Beauvoir once wrote, Faulkner "offered us a glimpse of . . . those secret, shameful fires that rage in the bellies of men and women alike."

Unlike so many other novelists of the period, Faulkner maintained a high level in his later years. He was awarded the 1949 Nobel Prize for Literature.

The Extremists

Roosevelt's moderation roused extremists both on the Left and on the Right. The most formidable was Louisiana's Senator Huey Long, the "King-fish." Long was a controversial figure in his day and so he has remained. In many ways he was a typical southern conservative, and he was certainly a demagogue. Yet the plight of all poor people concerned him deeply. More important, he tried to do something about it. His record in Louisiana is a mixture of egotism, sordid politicking, and genuine efforts to improve the lot of the poor, black as well as white.

Long did not question segregation or white supremacy. He used the word *nigger* with total lack of self-consciousness, even when addressing northern black leaders. But he treated black-baiters with scathing contempt. When Hiram W. Evans, Imperial Wizard of the Ku Klux Klan, announced that he intended to campaign against him in Louisiana, Long told reporters: "Quote me as saying that that Imperial bastard will never set foot in Louisiana, and that when I call him a sonofabitch I am not using profanity, but am referring to the circumstances of his birth."

As a reformer, Long stood in the populist tradition; he hated bankers and "the interests." He believed that poor people, regardless of color, should have a chance to earn a decent living and get an education. His arguments were simplistic, patronizing, possibly insincere, but effective. "Don't say I'm working for niggers," he told a northern black journalist. "I'm for the poor man—all poor men. Black and white, they all gotta have a chance. . . . 'Every Man a King'—that's my slogan."

Raffish, totally unrestrained, yet shrewd, Long had supported the New Deal at the start, but partly because he thought Roosevelt too conservative and partly because of his own ambition, he soon broke with the administration. By 1935 his "Share-Our-Wealth" movement had a membership of over 4.6 million. His program called for the confiscation of family fortunes of more than $5 million and a tax of 100 percent on incomes of over $1 million a year. The money collected would be enough to buy every family a "homestead" (a house, a car, and other necessities) and provide an annual family income of $2,000 to $3,000 plus old-age pensions, educational benefits, and veterans' pensions.

Long planned to organize a third party to split the liberal vote in the 1936 election. He assumed that the Republicans would win the election and

so botch the job of fighting the depression that he could sweep the country in 1940.

Less powerful than Long but more widely influential was Father Charles E. Coughlin, the "Radio Priest." Coughlin began his public career in 1926, broadcasting a weekly religious message over station WJR in Detroit. His mellifluous voice and orotund rhetoric won him a huge national audience, and the depression gave him a secular cause. In 1933 he had been an eager New Dealer, but his need for ever more sensational ideas to hold his radio audience from week to week led him to turn against the New Deal. By 1935 he was calling Roosevelt a "great betrayer and liar."

Although Coughlin's National Union for Social Justice was especially appealing to Catholics, it attracted people of every faith, particularly in the lower-middle-class districts of the big cities. Coughlin attacked bankers, New Deal planners, Roosevelt's farm program, and the alleged sympathy of the administration for communists and Jews, both types Coughlin detested. His program resembled fascism more than any leftist philosophy, but he posed a threat, especially in combination with Long, to the continuation of Democratic rule.

Another rapidly growing movement alarmed the Democrats in 1934–1935: Dr. Francis E. Townsend's campaign for "Old-Age Revolving Pensions." Townsend was colorless and low-keyed, but he had an oversimplified and thus appealing "solution" to the nation's troubles: paying every person 60 and over a pension of $200 a month, the only conditions being that the pensioners must not hold jobs and must spend the entire sum within 30 days. A stiff transactions tax, collected whenever any commodity changed hands, would pay for the program.

Economists quickly pointed out that with about 10 million persons eligible for the Townsend pensions, the cost would amount to $24 billion a year, roughly half the national income. But among the elderly the scheme proved extremely popular. Although most Townsendites were anything but radical politically, their plan, like Long's Share-Our-Wealth scheme, would have revolutionized the distribution of wealth in the country. On the one hand, the movement reflected a reactionary spirit like that of religious fundamentalists, on the other hand, the emergence of a new force in American society. With

Californian Francis E. Townsend embarked on a national campaign for pensions for the elderly. A determined Townsend spoke to his adherents at the opening of the National Convention in Chicago, proposing a $200 per month pension for those over 60 years of age.

medical advances lengthening the average life span, the percentage of old people in the population was rising. Townsend's program focused the attention of the country on a new problem—one it has not yet resolved.

With the possible exception of Long, the extremists had little understanding of practical affairs. (It could be said that Townsend knew what to do with money but not how to get it and Coughlin knew how to get money but not what to do with it.) Collectively they represented a threat to Roosevelt; their success helped to make him see that he must move boldly to restore good times or face serious political trouble in 1936.

Political imperatives had much to do with his decision, and the influence of Justice Brandeis and his disciples, notably Felix Frankfurter, was great. They urged Roosevelt to abandon his pro-business programs, especially NRA, and stress restoring competition and taxing corporations more heavily. The fact that most businessmen were turning from him encouraged the president to accept this advice; so did the Supreme Court's decision in *Schechter* v. *United States* (May 1935), which declared the National Industrial Recovery Act unconstitutional.

The Second New Deal

Existing laws had failed to end the depression; extremists were luring away some of Roosevelt's supporters and conservatives had failed to appreciate his moderation. Thousands of ordinary people were clamoring for further reforms. At the same time, the Supreme Court was declaring many New Deal laws unconstitutional. For these many reasons, Roosevelt, in June 1935, launched the "Second New Deal."

The Second Hundred Days was one of the most productive periods in the history of American legislation. The National Labor Relations Act—commonly known as the Wagner Act—restored the labor guarantees wiped out by the Schechter decision. It gave workers the right to bargain collectively and prohibited employers from interfering with union organizational activities in their factories. A National Labor Relations Board (NLRB) was established to supervise plant elections and designate successful unions as official bargaining agents when a majority of the workers approved. The NLRB forced antiunion corporations to bargain "in good faith" as the law required and to rehire workers discharged for union activities. The law also gave union leaders great control over the rank and file, and although in the long run this produced serious problems, its immediate effect was to make labor more powerful.

The Social Security Act of August 1935 set up a system of old-age insurance, financed partly by a tax on wages (paid by workers) and partly by a tax on payrolls (paid by employers). It created a state–federal system of unemployment insurance, similarly financed. Liberal critics considered this

Social Security system inadequate because it did not cover agricultural workers, domestics, self employed persons, and some other groups particularly in need of its benefits. Health insurance was not included, and because the size of pensions depended on the amount earned, the lowest-paid workers could not count on much support after reaching 65. Yet the law was of major significance. Over the years, the pension payments were increased and the classes of workers covered expanded.

Among other important laws enacted at this time was a Public Utility Holding Company Act, which outlawed the pyramiding of control of gas and electricity companies through the use of holding companies and gave various federal commissions the power to regulate strictly the rates and financial practices of these companies. The Rural Electrification Administration (REA), created by executive order, also began to function during this remarkable period. REA lent money at low interest rates to utility companies and to farmer cooperatives interested in supplying electricity to rural areas. When REA went into operation, only one farm in ten had electricity; by 1950 only one in ten did not.

Another important measure was the Wealth Tax Act of August 1935, which, while not the "soak the rich" measure both its supporters and opponents claimed, raised taxes on large incomes considerably. Estate and gift taxes were increased.

Herbert Hoover epitomized the attitude of conservatives when he called the New Deal "the most stupendous invasion of the whole spirit of Liberty that the nation has witnessed." Undoubtedly many opponents of the New Deal sincerely believed that it was undermining the foundations of American freedom. The cost of the New Deal also alarmed them. By 1936 some members of the administration had fallen under the influence of the British economist John Maynard Keynes, who argued that the world depression could be conquered if governments would unbalance their budgets by reducing interest rates and taxes and increasing expenditures in order to stimulate consumption and investment.

Roosevelt never accepted Keynes's theories, but the imperatives of the depression forced him to spend more than the government was collecting in taxes. Conservative businessmen considered him financially irresponsible, and the fact that deficit spending seemed to be good politics made them seethe with rage.

The Election of 1936

The election of 1936 loomed as a showdown. "America is in peril," the Republican platform declared. The GOP candidate, Governor Alfred M. Landon of Kansas, was reasonably liberal, but he was handicapped by the reactionary views of many of his backers. Against the charm and political astuteness of Roosevelt, Landon's arguments—chiefly that he could administer the government more efficiently than the president—made little impression.

The radical fringe put a third candidate in the field—Congressman William Lemke of North Dakota, who ran on the Union Party ticket. Father Coughlin rallied his National Union for Social Justice behind Lemke; Dr. Townsend also supported him. However, the extremists were losing ground by 1936. Huey Long had fallen victim of an assassin in September 1935, and his organization was taken over by a blatantly demagogic rightist, Gerald L. K. Smith. The Townsendites fell under a cloud because of rumors that some of their leaders had their fingers in the organization's treasury. Father Coughlin's slanderous assaults on Roosevelt caused a backlash; a number of American Catholic prelates denounced him, and the Vatican issued an unofficial but influential rebuke. Lemke made little impression on the country, polling only 892,000 votes.

On election day the country gave the president a tremendous vote of confidence. He carried every state but Maine and Vermont. Both Roosevelt's personality and his program had captivated the land. The Democrats also made large gains in local elections. Roosevelt seemed irresistible, the most powerfully entrenched president in the history of the United States.

Roosevelt did not win in 1936 because of the inadequacies of his foes. Having abandoned his efforts to hold the businessmen, whom he now denounced as "economic royalists," he appealed for the votes of workers and the underprivileged. The new labor unions gratefully poured thousands of dollars into the campaign to reelect him. Black voters switched to the Democrats in record numbers. In 1932 they had maintained their traditional loyalty to the Republican Party. "Who but Hoover?" had been their slogan. In 1936 more than three-quarters of northern black voters supported Roosevelt.

Farmers liked Roosevelt because of his evident concern for their welfare: When the Supreme Court declared the Agricultural Adjustment Act unconstitutional (*United States* v. *Butler,* 1936), he immediately rushed through a new law, the Soil Conservation and Domestic Allotment Act, which accomplished the same objective by paying farmers to divert land from commercial crops to soil-building plants like clover and soybeans. Countless elderly persons backed him out of gratitude for the Social Security Act. Homeowners were grateful for his program guaranteeing mortgages. A modest upturn, which raised industrial output to the levels of 1930, played into Roosevelt's hands. For the first time since 1931 U.S. Steel was showing a profit.

Roosevelt and the "Nine Old Men"

On January 20, in his second inaugural, Roosevelt spoke feelingly of the plight of millions of citizens. A third of the nation, he said without exaggeration, was "ill-housed, ill-clad, ill-nourished." He interpreted his landslide victory as a mandate for further reforms, and with his prestige and his immense congressional majorities, nothing appeared to stand in his way. Nothing, that is, except the Supreme Court.

Throughout Roosevelt's first term the Court had stood almost immovable against increasing the scope of federal authority and broadening the general power of government, state as well as national, to cope with the exigencies of the depression. Four of the nine justices, James C. McReynolds, Willis Van Devanter, Pierce Butler, and George Sutherland, were intransigent reactionaries. Chief Justice Charles Evans Hughes and Justice Owen J. Roberts, although more open-minded, tended to side with the reactionaries on many questions.

Much of the early New Deal legislation had been drafted without proper regard for the Consti-

tution. Even the liberal justices considered the National Industrial Recovery Act unconstitutional (the Schechter decision was a unanimous one).

The Court had voided the federal Guffey-Snyder Act, establishing minimum wages in the coal industry, and a New York minimum-wage law, thereby creating, as Roosevelt remarked, a "no man's land" where neither national nor state government could act. Worse, the reactionaries on the Court seemed governed by no consistent constitutional philosophy; they tended to limit the police power of the states when wages-and-hours laws came before them and to interpret it broadly when state laws restricting civil liberties were under consideration. In 1937 all the major measures of the Second Hundred Days appeared doomed.

Faced with this situation, Roosevelt decided to ask Congress to shift the balance on the Court by increasing the number of justices, thinly disguising the purpose of his plan by making it part of a general reorganization of the judiciary. A member of the Court reaching the age of 70 would have the option of retiring at full pay. Should such a justice choose not to retire, the president was to appoint an additional justice, up to a maximum of six, in order to ease the burden of work for the aged jurists who remained on the bench.

Roosevelt knew that this measure would run into strenuous resistance, but he expected Congress to pass it. No astute politician had erred so badly in estimating the effects of an action since Stephen A. Douglas introduced the Kansas-Nebraska Bill in 1854. To the expected denunciations of conservatives were added the complaints of liberals fearful that the principle of Court packing might in the future be used to subvert civil liberties. Opposition in Congress was immediate and intense; many who had cheerfully supported every New Deal Bill came out against the plan. The press denounced it, and so did most local bar associations. Chief Justice Hughes released a devastating critique; even the liberal Brandeis—the oldest judge on the court—rejected the bill out of hand.

For months Roosevelt stubbornly refused to concede defeat, thus tying up the rest of his legislative program while Congress wrangled over the court reform bill. Finally, in July 1937, he had to yield. Minor administrative reforms of the judiciary were enacted, but the size of the Court remained unchanged.

The struggle did result in saving the legislation of the Second New Deal. Alarmed by the threat to the Court, Justices Hughes and Roberts, never entirely committed to the conservative position, beat a strategic retreat on a series of specific issues. While the debate was raging in Congress, they sided with the liberals in upholding first a minimum-wage law of the state of Washington that was little different from the New York act the Court had recently rejected, then the Wagner Act, and then the Social Security Act. In May Justice Van Devanter retired, and Roosevelt replaced him with Senator Hugo Black of Alabama, an advanced New Dealer. The conservative justices thereupon gave up the fight, and soon Roosevelt was able to appoint enough new judges to give the Court a large pro–New Deal majority. No further measure of significance was declared unconstitutional during his presidency.

The Court fight hurt Roosevelt severely. His prestige never fully recovered. Conservative Democrats who had feared to oppose him because of his supposedly invulnerable popularity took heart and began to join with the Republicans on key issues. When the president summoned a special session of Congress in November 1937 and submitted a program of "must" legislation, not one of his bills was passed.

The New Deal Winds Down

The Court fight marked the beginning of the end of the New Deal. Social and economic developments contributed to its decline, and the final blow originated in the area of foreign affairs. With unemployment high, wages low, and workers relatively powerless against their employers, most Americans had liked New Deal labor legislation and sympathized with the industrial unions whose growth it stimulated. NRA, the Wagner Act, and the CIO's organizing of industries like steel and automobiles changed the power structure within the economy. Aside from higher wages, shorter hours, and similar benefits, unionization had meant fair methods of settling labor–management disputes and job security based on seniority for thousands. The CIO had also increased the influence of labor in politics, and brought many blacks and other minorities into the labor movement.

In 1937 a series of "sit-down strikes" broke out, beginning at General Motors' Flint, Michigan, plant. Striking workers barricaded themselves inside the factories; when police and strikebreakers tried to dislodge them, they fought with barrages of soda bottles, tools, spare parts, and crockery. The tolerant attitude of the Roosevelt administration insured the strikers against government intervention. Fearful that all-out efforts to clear their plants would result in the destruction of expensive machinery, most employers capitulated to the workers' demands.

The major steel companies, led by U.S. Steel, recognized the CIO and granted higher wages and a 40-hour week. The auto and steel unions alone boasted more than 725,000 members by late 1937; other CIO units conquered the rubber industry, the electrical industry, the textile industry, and many more. These gains gave many members of the middle class second thoughts concerning the justice of labor's demands. The enthusiasm of such people for all reform cooled rapidly.

While the sit-down strikes and the Court fight were going on, the New Deal suffered another heavy blow. Business conditions had been gradually improving since 1933. Heartened by the trend, Roosevelt, who had never fully grasped the importance of government spending in stimulating recovery, cut back sharply on the relief program in June 1937—with disastrous results. Between August and October, the economy slipped downward like sand through a chute. Stock prices plummeted. Unemployment rose by 2 million, industrial production slumped. This "Roosevelt recession" further damaged the president's reputation.

In April 1938 Roosevelt finally committed himself to heavy deficit spending. At his urging Congress passed a $3.75 billion public works bill. Two major pieces of legislation were also enacted at about this time. A new AAA program (February 1938) set marketing quotas and acreage limitations for growers of staples like wheat, cotton, and tobacco and authorized the Commodity Credit Corporation to lend money to farmers on their surplus crops. The surpluses were to be stored by the government. When prices rose, farmers could repay the loans, reclaim their produce, and sell it on the open market, thereby maintaining an "ever-normal granary."

The second measure, the Fair Labor Standards Act, abolished child labor and established a national minimum wage of 40 cents an hour and a maximum work week of 40 hours, with time-and-a-half for overtime. Although the law failed to cover many of the poorest-paid types of labor, its passage meant wage increases for 750,000 workers. In later years, many more workers were brought within its protection and the minimum wage was repeatedly increased.

These measures further alienated conservatives without dramatically improving economic conditions. The resistance of many Democratic congressmen to additional economic and social "experiments" hardened. As the 1938 elections approached, Roosevelt decided to go to the voters in an effort to strengthen party discipline and reenergize the New Deal. He singled out a number of conservative Democratic senators and tried to "purge" them by backing other Democrats in the primaries.

The purge failed. Voters liked Roosevelt but resented his interference in local politics. The senators were easily renominated and then reelected in November. In the nation at large, the Republicans made important gains for the first time since Roosevelt had taken office.

Significance of the New Deal

By 1939 Roosevelt was ready to abandon further efforts at reform. The mounting danger of war in Europe as a result of the aggressions of the German dictator Adolf Hitler dominated his thinking. After war broke out in 1939, the Great Depression was swept away on a wave of orders from the beleaguered European democracies. For this prosperity Roosevelt received much undeserved credit. His New Deal had not returned the country to full employment.

The perspective of time reveals other inadequacies of the New Deal. Despite the aid given the jobless, the generation of workers born be-

tween 1900 and 1910 who entered the 1930s as unskilled laborers had their careers permanently stunted by the depression. Roosevelt's willingness to experiment with different means of combating the Depression made sense because no one really knew what to do; however, his uncertainty about the ultimate objectives of the New Deal was counterproductive. He vacillated between seeking to stimulate the economy by deficit spending and trying to balance the budget; between a narrow "America First" economic nationalism and a broad-gauged international approach; between regulating monopolies and trust-busting; and between helping the underprivileged and bolstering those already strong. He could never really make up his mind whether to try to rally liberals to his cause without regard for party or to run the government as a partisan leader, conciliating the conservative Democrats.

Roosevelt's fondness for establishing new agencies to deal with specific problems vastly increased the federal bureaucracy. His cavalier attitude toward constitutional limitations on executive power, which he justified as being necessary in a national emergency, set in motion trends that so increased the prestige and authority of the presidency that the balance between the executive, legislative, and judicial branches was threatened.

Yet these criticisms ignore what one historian has called the "sense of urgency and haste" that made the New Deal "a mixture of accomplishment, frustration, and misdirected effort." On balance, the New Deal had an immense constructive impact. By 1939 the country was committed to the idea that the federal government should accept responsibility for the national welfare and act to meet specific problems in every necessary way. What was most significant was not the proliferation of new agencies or the expansion of federal power. The importance of the "Roosevelt revolution" was that it removed the issue from politics. "Never again," the Republican presidential candidate was to say in 1952, "shall we allow a depression in the United States."

Because of New Deal decisions, many formerly unregulated areas of American life became subject to federal authority: the stock exchange, agricultural prices and production, labor relations, old-age pensions, relief of the needy. If the New Deal failed to end the Depression, it effected changes that have—so far, at least—prevented later economic declines from becoming catastrophes. By encouraging the growth of unions, the New Deal probably helped workers obtain a larger share of the profits of industry. By putting a floor under the income of many farmers, it checked the decline of agricultural living standards, though not that of the agricultural population. The Social Security program, with all its inadequacies, lessened the impact of bad times on an increasingly large proportion of the population and provided immense psychological benefits to all.

Among other important social changes, the TVA and the New Deal rural electrification program made farm life literally more civilized. Urban public housing, although never undertaken on a massive scale, helped rehabilitate some of the nation's worst slums. Exploitation of the natural resources of the West was checked. The NIRA and later labor legislation forced businessmen to reexamine their role in American life and to become more socially conscious. The WPA art and theater programs widened the horizons of millions. All in all, the spirit of the New Deal heightened the people's sense of community, revitalized national energies, and stimulated the imagination and creative instincts of countless citizens.

Women as New Dealers: The Network

Largely because of the influence of Eleanor Roosevelt and Molly Dewson, head of the Women's Division of the Democratic National Committee, the Roosevelt administration employed far more women in positions of importance than any earlier one. Secretary of Labor Frances Perkins, the first woman appointed to a Cabinet post, had been active in labor relations for more than 20 years, as secretary of the Consumers' League, as a factory inspector, and as chair of the New York State Industrial Commission. As secretary of labor she helped draft New Deal labor legislation and kept Roosevelt informed on various labor problems outside the government.

In addition to Perkins, there were dozens of other women New Dealers; Dewson and Eleanor Roosevelt headed an informal but effective "network"—women in key posts who were always seeking to place reform-minded women in government jobs. (According to the historian William Chafe, "Washington seemed like a perpetual convention of social workers as women . . . [took] on government assignments.")

As for Eleanor Roosevelt, through her newspaper column, "My Day," and as a speaker on public issues, she became a major political force—in the words of historian Tamara Hareven, "an ombudsman with the increasingly bureaucratized and impersonal [federal] government." Her influence was large, especially in the area of civil rights, where the administration needed constant prodding.

She was particularly identified with efforts to obtain better treatment for blacks, in and out of government. Her best-known action occurred in 1939 after the Daughters of the American Revolution (DAR) refused to permit the use of their Washington auditorium for a concert by the black contralto, Marian Anderson. Eleanor Roosevelt resigned from the DAR in protest, and, after the president arranged for Anderson to sing at the Lincoln Memorial, she persuaded a small army of dignitaries to sponsor the concert. An interracial crowd of 75,000 people attended the performance. The Chicago *Defender,* noted that the First Lady "stood like the Rock of Gibraltar against pernicious encroachments on the rights of minorities." (A disgruntled southerner made the same point differently: "She goes around telling the Negroes they are as good as anyone else.")

Blacks During the New Deal

The shift of black voters from the Republican to the Democratic Party during the New Deal years was one of the most significant political turnarounds in American history. In 1932 when things were at their worst, fewer blacks defected from the Republican Party than the members of any other traditionally Republican group. Four years later, however, blacks voted for Roosevelt in overwhelming numbers.

Blacks supported the New Deal for the same reasons that whites did, but how the New Deal affected blacks in general and racial attitudes specifically are more complicated questions. Many of the early New Deal programs treated blacks as second-class citizens. They were often paid at lower rates than whites under NIRA codes (and so joked that NRA stood for "Negro Run Around" and "Negroes Ruined Again"). The early farm programs shortchanged black tenants and sharecroppers. Blacks in the Civilian Conservation Corps were assigned to all-black camps. TVA developments were rigidly segregated too. New Deal urban housing projects effectively increased the concentration of blacks in particular neighborhoods. The Social Security Act excluded agricultural laborers and domestic servants from coverage and thus did nothing for hundreds of thousands of poor black workers or for Mexican American farmhands. In 1939 unemployment was twice as high among blacks as among whites, and whites' wages were double the level of blacks' wages.

The fact that members of racial minorities got less than they deserved did not keep most of them from becoming New Dealers. Aside from the direct benefits, blacks profited in other ways. Secretary of the Interior Harold L. Ickes appointed Charles Forman as a special assistant assigned "to keep the government honest when it came to race." Mary McLeod Bethune, founder of Bethune-Cookman College, was appointed head of the Division of Negro Affairs in the National Youth Administration (NYA). She developed training programs for disadvantaged black youngsters and lobbied throughout the Washington bureaucracy on behalf of better opportunities for blacks.

In the labor movement the new CIO unions brought blacks members, and this was particularly significant because these unions were organizing industries—steel, automobiles, and mining among others—that employed large numbers of blacks. Thus, although black Americans suffered horribly during the Depression, New Deal efforts to counteract its effects brought them some relief and a measure of hope.

A New Deal for Indians

New Deal policy toward American Indians built on early trends but carried them further. During the Harding and Coolidge adminstrations, more Indian land had passed into the hands of whites and agents of the Bureau of Indian Affairs had tried to suppress elements of Indian culture that they considered "pagan" or "lascivious." In 1924 Congress finally granted citizenship to all Indians, but it was still generally agreed by whites that Indians should be treated as wards of the state. Assimilation had failed. Indian languages and religious practices, patterns of family life, as well as Indian arts and crafts had all resisted generations of efforts to "civilize" the tribes.

Government policy took a new direction in 1933 when President Roosevelt named John Collier commissioner of Indian affairs. Collier had studied the Indians of the Southwest and was appalled by what he learned. He became executive secretary of the American Indian Defense Association and, in 1925, editor of a reform-oriented magazine, *American Indian Life.* By the time he was appointed commissioner, the depression had reduced perhaps one-third of the 320,000 Indians living on reservations to penury.

Collier tried to revive the spirits of these people. He favored a pluralistic approach, seeking to help the Indians preserve their ancient cultures but also (somewhat contradictorily) to help them earn more money and make use of modern medical advances and modern techniques of soil conservation. He was particularly eager to encourage the revival of tribal governments that could represent the Indians in dealings with the U.S. government and function as community service centers.

In part because of Collier's urging, Congress passed the Indian Reorganization Act of 1934. This law did away with the Dawes Act allotment system and enabled Indians to establish tribal governments with powers like those of cities, and it encouraged Indians to return individually owned lands to tribal control. About 4 million of the 90 million acres of Indian land lost under the allotment system were returned to the tribes. In addition, Harry Hopkins made special efforts to see that needy Indians who were not living on reservations got relief aid. There was also a special Indian division of the Civilian Conservation Corps which organized work for Indians right on their reservations.

New Deal Indian policy was controversial—among Indians as well as among white groups. Some critics charged Collier with trying to turn back the clock. Others attacked him as a segregationist and claimed that he was trying to restore "pagan" religious practices and convert the Indians to communism.

In truth the problem was more complicated than Collier had imagined. Indians who owned profitable allotments, such as those in Oklahoma who held valuable oil and mineral rights, did not relish turning their land over to tribal control. In New Mexico, the Navajos, whose lands had relatively little commercial value, nonetheless voted decisively against going back to the communal system. All told, 77 of 269 tribes voted against communal holdings. Nevertheless, like so many of its programs, the New Deal's Indian policy was a bold effort to deal constructively with a long-standing national problem.

The Role of Roosevelt

How much of the credit for New Deal policies belongs personally to Franklin D. Roosevelt is debatable. He had little to do with many of the details and some of the broad principles behind the New Deal. His knowledge of economics was skimpy, his understanding of many social problems superficial, his political philosophy distressingly vague. The British leader Anthony Eden described him as "a conjurer, skillfully juggling with balls of dynamite, whose nature he failed to understand," and the historian David Brody writes shrewdly of Roosevelt's "unreflective acceptance" of the basic structure of American society.

Nevertheless, every aspect of the New Deal bears the brand of Roosevelt's remarkable personality. Rexford Tugwell has left one of the best-balanced judgments of the president. "Roosevelt was not really very much at home with ideas," Tugwell explained. But he was always open to new facts, and something within him "forbade inaction when there was something to be done." Roosevelt constructed the coalition that made the program possible; his humanitarianism made it a reform movement of major significance. Although considered by many a terrible administrator because he encouraged rivalry among his subordinates, assigned different agencies overlapping responsibilities, failed to discharge many incompetents, and frequently put off making difficult decisions, he was in fact one of the most effective chief executives in the nation's history. His seemingly haphazard practice of dividing authority among competing administrators unleashed the energies and sparked the imaginations of his aides.

Like Andrew Jackson, Roosevelt maximized his role as leader of all the people. His informal biweekly press conferences kept the public in touch with developments and himself in tune with popular thinking. His "fireside chats" convinced millions that he was personally interested in each citizen's life and welfare, as in a way he was. At a time when the size and complexity of the government made it impossible for any one person to direct the nation's destiny, Roosevelt managed the minor miracle of personifying that government to 130 million people. Under Hoover, a single clerk was able to handle the routine mail that flowed into the office of the president from ordinary citizens. Under Roosevelt, the task required a staff of 50.

While the New Deal was still evolving, contemporaries recognized Roosevelt's right to a place beside Washington, Jefferson, and Lincoln among the great presidents. The years have not altered their judgment. Yet as his second term drew toward its close, some of his most important work still lay in the future.

The Triumph of Isolationism

Franklin Roosevelt was at heart an internationalist, but he placed revival of his own country's limping economy ahead of general world recovery. In April 1933 he took the United States off the gold standard, hoping that devaluing the dollar would make it easier to sell American goods abroad. His decision increased international ill feeling.

Against this background, vital changes in American foreign policy took place. Unable to persuade the country to take positive action against aggressors, internationalists like Secretary of State Stimson had begun in 1931 to work for a discretionary arms embargo law, to be applied by the president in time of war against whichever side had broken the peace. By early 1933 Stimson had obtained President Hoover's backing for an embargo bill, as well as the support of president-elect Roosevelt. First the munitions manufacturers and then the isolationists pounced on it, and in the resulting debate it was amended to make the embargo apply to *all* belligerents. Stimson's policy would have permitted arms shipments to China but not to Japan. As amended, the embargo would have automatically applied to both sides, thus removing the United States as an influence in the conflict. Roosevelt accepted the change, but the internationalists in Congress did not. When they withdrew their support, the measure died.

The attitude of the munitions makers, who opposed both forms of the embargo, led to a series of studies of the industry. The most important was a Senate investigation (1934–1936) headed by Gerald P. Nye of North Dakota. Nye was convinced that "the interests" had conspired to drag America into World War I; his investigation was more an inquisition than an honest effort to discover what American bankers and munitions makers had been doing between 1914 and 1918. The committee's staff, ferreting into subpoenaed records, uncovered sensational facts about the lobbying activities and profits of various concerns. The Du Pont company's earnings, for example, had soared from $5 million in 1914 to $82 million in 1916. The Nye Report convinced millions of citizens that the bankers who had lent the Allies money and the "merchants of death" who had sold them arms had tricked the country into war and that the "mistake" of 1917 must never be repeated.

These developments led in 1935 to what the historian Robert A. Divine has called "the triumph of isolation." The danger of another World War mounted steadily as Germany, Italy, and Japan repeatedly resorted to force to achieve their expansionist aims. In March 1935 Hitler instituted universal military training. In May Mussolini massed troops in Italian Somaliland, using a trivial border clash as pretext for threatening the ancient kingdom of Ethiopia.

Congress responded by passing the Neutrality Act of 1935, which forbade the sale of munitions to all belligerents whenever the president should proclaim that a state of war existed. Americans who took passage on belligerent ships after such a proclamation had been issued would do so at their own risk. Roosevelt would have preferred a discretionary embargo or no new legislation at all, but he dared not rouse the ire of the isolationists by vetoing the bill.

The next summer, civil war broke out in Spain. The rebels, led by General Francisco Franco and strongly backed by Italy and Germany, sought to overthrow the somewhat leftist Spanish Republic. Here, clearly, was a clash between democracy and fascism, and the neutrality laws did not apply to civil wars. However, Roosevelt now became more fearful of involvement than some isolationists. He was afraid that American interference might cause the conflict in Spain to become a global war, and he was wary of antagonizing the substantial number of American Catholics who were sympathetic to the Franco regime. At his urging Congress passed another neutrality act broadening the arms embargo to cover civil wars.

Isolationism now reached its peak. A public opinion poll revealed in March 1937 that 94 percent of the people thought American policy should be directed at keeping out of all foreign wars rather than trying to prevent wars from breaking out. In April Congress passed still another neutrality law. It continued the embargo on munitions and loans, forbade Americans to travel on belligerent ships, and gave the president discretionary authority to place the sale of other goods to belligerents on a cash-and-carry basis. In theory this would preserve the nation's profitable foreign trade without the risk of war; in fact it played into the hands of the aggressors. While German planes and cannons were turning the tide in Spain, the United States was denying the hard-pressed Spanish loyalists even a case of cartridges. The New York *Herald Tribune* pointed out that the neutrality legislation was literally reactionary—designed to keep the United States out of the war of 1914–1918, not the conflict looming on the horizon. The American people, like wild creatures before a forest fire, were rushing in blind panic from the conflagration.

War Again in Europe

There were limits beyond which Americans would not go. In July 1937 Japan again attacked China, pressing ahead on a broad front. Roosevelt believed that invoking the neutrality law would only help the well-armed Japanese. Taking advantage of the fact that neither side had formally declared war, he allowed the shipment of arms and supplies to both sides.

Then, in October, he proposed a "quarantine" of nations that were "creating a state of international anarchy." But his "quarantine speech" produced a windy burst of isolationist rhetoric that forced him to back down. "It's a terrible thing," he said, "to look over your shoulder when you are trying to lead—and to find no one there."

Roosevelt came gradually to the conclusion that resisting aggression was more important than keeping out of war, but when he did, the need to keep the country united led him at times to be less than candid in his public statements. Hitler's annexation of Austria in March 1938 caused him deep concern. The Nazis' vicious anti-Semitism had caused many of Germany's 500,000 Jewish citizens to seek refuge abroad. Now 190,000 Austrian Jews were under Nazi control. When Roosevelt learned that the Germans were burning synagogues, expelling Jewish children from schools, and otherwise mistreating innocent people, he said that he "could scarcely believe that such things could occur." But public opinion opposed changing the immigration law so that more refugees could be admitted, and the president did nothing.

In September 1938 Hitler forced Czechoslovakia to cede the German-speaking Sudetenland region to the Reich. Roosevelt failed again to speak out, but when the Nazis seized the rest of Czechoslovakia in March 1939, Roosevelt called for "methods short of war" to demonstrate America's determination to check the fascists.

In August 1939 Germany and Russia signed a nonaggression pact, prelude to their joint assault on Poland, which began on September 1. This at last provoked Great Britain and France to declare war on Germany. Roosevelt immediately summoned Congress into special session and again asked for repeal of the arms embargo. In November, in a vote that followed party lines closely, the Democratic majority pushed through a law permitting the sale of arms and other contraband on a cash-and-carry basis. American vessels were forbidden to carry any products to the belligerents. Since the Allies controlled the seas, cash-and-carry gave them a tremendous advantage.

The German attack on Poland effected a basic change in American public opinion. Keeping out of the war remained an almost universal hope, but preventing a Nazi victory became the ultimate, if not always conscious, objective. In Roosevelt's case it was perfectly conscious. But he moved slowly, responding to rather than directing the course of events.

Cash-and-carry did not stop the Nazis. Poland fell in less than a month; then, after a winter lull that cynics called the "phony war," between April 9 and June 22, 1940, the Germans taught the world the awful meaning of *Blitzkrieg*—lightning war. Denmark, Norway, the Netherlands, Bel-

gium, and France were successively overwhelmed. The British army, pinned against the sea at Dunkirk, saved itself from annihilation only by fleeing across the English Channel. After the French submitted to his harsh terms on June 22, Hitler controlled nearly all of Western Europe.

Roosevelt responded to these disasters in a number of ways. In the fall of 1939, reacting to warnings from Albert Einstein and other scientists that the Germans were trying to develop atomic weapons, he committed federal funds to a top-secret program to build an atom bomb. Without legal authority, he authorized the sale of surplus government arms to Britain and France. When Italy entered the war and invaded France, the president called the attack a stab in the back. To strengthen national unity, he named Henry L. Stimson secretary of war* and another Republican, Frank Knox, secretary of the navy.

After the fall of France, Hitler attempted to bomb and starve the British into submission. The epic air battles over England during the summer of 1940 ended in a decisive defeat for the Nazis, but the Royal Navy, which had only about 100 destroyers, could not control German submarine attacks on shipping. Far more destroyers were needed. In this desperate hour, Prime Minister Winston Churchill, who had replaced Chamberlain in May 1940, asked Roosevelt for 50 old American destroyers to fill the gap.

The navy had 240 destroyers in commission and more than 50 under construction. But direct loan or sale of the vessels would have violated both international and American laws. Roosevelt therefore arranged to "trade" the destroyers for six British naval bases in the Caribbean. In addition, Great Britain leased bases in Bermuda and Newfoundland to the United States.

The destroyers-for-bases deal was a masterful achievement. It helped Great Britain, and at the same time it circumvented isolationist prejudices, since the president could present it as a shrewd bargain that bolstered America's defenses. A string of island bastions in the Atlantic was more valuable than 50 old destroyers.

Lines were hardening throughout the world. In September 1940, Congress enacted the first

---

*Stimson had held this post from 1911 to 1913 in the Taft Cabinet.

peacetime draft in American history. Some 1.2 million draftees were summoned for one year of service, and 800,000 reservists were called to active duty. That same month Japan signed a mutual-assistance pact with Germany and Italy, thus turning the struggle into a global war.

A Third Term for FDR

In the midst of these events, the 1940 presidential election took place. Why Roosevelt decided to run for a third term is a much-debated question. Partisanship had something to do with it, for no other Democrat seemed so likely to carry the country. In addition the president was probably tempted to hold on to power, especially in such critical times. But his conviction that no one else could keep a rein on the isolationists was probably decisive. Vice President Garner, who had become disenchanted with Roosevelt and the New Deal, did not seek a third term; at Roosevelt's dictation, the Democratic convention nominated Secretary of Agriculture Henry A. Wallace to replace him.

By using concern about the European war to justify running just when they thought they would be rid of him, Roosevelt brought down on his head the hatred of conservative Republicans and isolationists of both major parties. The leading Republican presidential candidates were Senator Robert A. Taft of Ohio, son of the former president, and District Attorney Thomas E. Dewey of New York, who had won fame as a "racket buster." But Taft was extremely conservative and lacking in political glamour, and Dewey, barely 38, seemed too young and inexperienced. Instead the Republicans nominated the darkest of dark horses, Wendell L. Willkie of Indiana, the utility magnate who had led the fight against the TVA in 1933.

Despite his political inexperience, Willkie made an appealing candidate. He was energetic and openhearted, and his rough-hewn rural manner (one Democrat called him "a simple, barefoot Wall Street lawyer") won him wide support in farm districts. Willkie had difficulty, however, finding issues on which to oppose Roosevelt. Good times were at last returning. The New Deal reforms were too popular and too much in line with his own thinking to invite attack. He believed

as strongly as the president that America could no longer ignore the Nazi threat.

Although rejecting the isolationist position, Willkie paradoxically accused Roosevelt of dragging the United States into the war. Roosevelt retorted (disingenuously, since he knew he was not an entirely free agent in the situation), "I have said this before, but I shall say it again and again and again: Your boys are not going to be sent into any foreign wars." In November Roosevelt carried the country handily. The popular vote was 27 million to 22 million, the electoral count 449 to 82.

The Undeclared War

The election encouraged Roosevelt to act more boldly. When Prime Minster Churchill informed him that Great Britain was rapidly exhausting its financial resources, he decided at once to provide the British with whatever they needed. Lending them money was certain to rouse memories of the vexatious war debt controversies, so he devised the "lend-lease" program, one of his most ingenious and imaginative creations.

First he delivered a "fireside chat" that stressed the dangers that a German victory would create for America. Aiding Britain should be looked at as a form of self-defense. "As planes and ships and guns and shells are produced," he said, American defense experts would decide "how much shall be sent abroad and how much shall remain at home." Then, in January 1941, he asked Congress for $7 billion for war materials that the president could sell, lend, lease, exchange, or transfer to any country whose defense he deemed vital to that of the United States. After two months of debate, Congress gave him what he had asked for.

Roosevelt did not minimize the dangers involved. Yet his mastery of practical politics was never more in evidence. To counter Irish American prejudices against the English, he pointed out that Ireland would surely fall under Nazi domination if Hitler won the war. He coupled his demand for heavy military expenditures with his enunciation of the idealistic "Four Freedoms"—freedom of speech, freedom of religion, freedom from want, and freedom from fear—for which, he said, the war was being fought.

After the enactment of lend-lease, the American navy began to patrol the North Atlantic, shadowing German submarines and radioing their locations to British warships and planes. In May the president declared a state of unlimited national emergency. After Hitler invaded the Soviet Union in June, Roosevelt moved slowly, for anti-Soviet feeling in the United States was intense, but in November $1 billion in lend-lease aid was put at the disposal of the Russians.

Meanwhile, the draft law was extended in August—by the margin of a single vote in the House of Representatives. In September the German submarine *U-652* fired a torpedo at the destroyer *Greer* in the North Atlantic. The *Greer,* which had provoked the attack by tracking *U-652* and flashing its position to a British plane, avoided the torpedo and dropped 19 depth charges in an effort to sink the submarine.

Roosevelt (nothing he ever did provided more ammunition for his critics) announced that the *Greer* had been innocently "carrying mail to Iceland." He called the U-boats "the rattlesnakes of the Atlantic" and ordered the navy to "shoot on sight" any German craft in the waters south and west of Iceland. After the sinking of the destroyer *Reuben James* by a submarine on October 30, Congress voted to allow the arming of American merchant ships and to permit them to carry cargoes to Allied ports. For all practical purposes, though not yet officially, the United States had gone to war.

Milestones

1933	Civilian Conservation Corps (CCC)	**1934**	Securities and Exchange Commission (SEC)
	Federal Emergency Relief Administration (FERA)		Federal Communications Commission (FCC)
	Agricultural Adjustment Administration (AA)		Federal Housing Administration (FHA)
	Tennessee Valley Authority (TVA)	**1935**	Works Progress Administration (WPA)
	Home Owners Loan Corporation (HOLC)		Resettlement Administration (RA)
	National Recovery Administration (NRA)		Rural Electrification Administration (REA)
	Federal Deposit Insurance Corporation (FDIC)		National Youth Administration (NYA)
	Public Works Administration (PWA)		National Labor Relations Board (NLRB)
	Civil Works Administration (CWA)		

Supplementary Reading

The Great Depression and the New Deal are covered in J. D. Hicks, **Republican Ascendancy** (1960), and W. E. Leuchtenburg, **Franklin Roosevelt and the New Deal** (1963). Broadus Mitchell, **Depression Decade** (1947), is a good economic history. R. H. Pells, **Radical Visions and American Dreams** (1973), covers intellectual currents.

For the stock market crash, consult J. K. Galbraith, **The Great Crash** (1955). The Hoover administration is discussed in A. U. Romasco, **The Poverty of Abundance** (1965), but see also Joan Hoff-Wilson, **Herbert Hoover: Forgotten Progressive** (1975). On literature, see Alfred Kazin, **On Native Grounds** (1942) and **Contemporaries** (1962).

Of the many biographies of Roosevelt, see especially J. M. Burns, **Roosevelt: The Lion and** the Fox* (1956). Richard Hofstadter has interesting essays on Hoover and Roosevelt in **The American Political Tradition*** (1948).

Useful special studies of the New Deal include Theodore Saloutos, **American Farmers and the New Deal** (1982), D. E. Conrad, **The Forgotten Farmers: The Story of Sharecroppers in the New Deal** (1965), Donald Wooster, **Dust Bowl** (1979), Richard Lowitt, **The New Deal in the West** (1984), E. W. Hawley, **The New Deal and the Problem of Monopoly*** (1966), J. D. Matthews, **The Federal Theatre** (1967), Barbara Blumberg, **The New Deal and the Unemployed** (1979), Harvard Sitkoff, **A New Deal for Blacks*** (1978), N. J. Weiss, **Farewell to the Party of Lincoln** (1983), and Raymond Wolters, **Negroes and the Great Depression*** (1970). Irving Bernstein, **Turbulent Years***

(1969), deals with industrial workers and their problems. On constitutional developments, see P. L. Murphy, **The Constitution in Crisis Times*** (1972); on blacks in the thirties, Raymond Wolters, **Negroes and the Great Depression*** (1970); on women, see W. H. Chafe, **The American Woman*** (1972), and Susan Ware, **Beyond Suffrage: Women in the New Deal** (1981); on Indians, see K. R. Philip, **John Collier's Crusade for Indian Reform** (1977).

For the activities of the "radical fringe," consult D. H. Bennett, **Demagogues in the Depression: American Radicalism and the Union Party** (1969), Alan Brinkley, **Voices of Protest** (1982), and T. H. Williams, **Huey Long: A Biography** (1969).

*Available in paperback.

CHAPTER 28

War and Peace

The Road to Pearl Harbor

Mobilizing the Home Front

The War Economy

War and Social Change

Minorities in Time of War: Blacks, Hispanics, and Indians

The Treatment of German, Italian, and Japanese Americans

Women's Contribution to the War Effort

Allied Strategy: Europe First

Germany Overwhelmed

The Naval War in the Pacific

Island Hopping

"The Shatterer of the Worlds"

Wartime Diplomacy

Mounting Suspicions

Yalta and Potsdam

*B*y December 1941 the United States was in fact at war, but it is hard to see how a formal declaration could have come about, had it not been for Japan. Japanese–American relations had worsened steadily after Japan resumed its war on China in 1937. In July 1940, with Japanese troops threatening French Indochina, Congress placed exports of aviation gasoline and certain types of scrap iron to Japan under a licensing system; in September all sales of scrap were banned and loans to China increased. After the Japanese signed a treaty of alliance with Germany and Italy in September 1940, Roosevelt extended the embargo to include machine tools and other items.

The Japanese, determined to create what they euphemistically called a Greater East Asia Co-Prosperity Sphere, pushed ahead relentlessly despite the economic pressures.

The Road to Pearl Harbor

Neither the United States nor Japan wanted war. In the spring of 1941, Secretary of State Hull conferred in Washington with the Japanese Ambassador Kichisaburo Nomura in an effort to resolve their differences. Hull demanded that Japan withdraw from China and promise not to attack the Dutch and French colonies in Southeast Asia. How he expected to get Japan to give up its conquests without either making concessions or going to war is not clear.

Japan might well have accepted limited annexations in the area in return for the removal of American trade restrictions, but Hull seemed bent on converting the Japanese to pacifism by exhortation. He insisted on total withdrawal, to which even the moderates in Japan would not agree. When Hitler invaded the Soviet Union, thereby removing the threat of Russian intervention in the Far East, Japan decided to occupy Indochina even at the risk of war with the United States. Roosevelt retaliated (July 1941) by freezing Japanese assets in the United States and clamping an embargo on oil.

Now the war party in Japan assumed control. Nomura was instructed to tell Hull that his country would refrain from further expansion if the United States and Great Britain would cut off all aid to China and lift the economic blockade. When the United States rejected these demands, the Japanese prepared to assault the Dutch East Indies, British Malaya, and the Philippines. To immobilize the United States Pacific Fleet, they planned a surprise aerial raid on the Hawaiian naval base at Pearl Harbor.

An American cryptanalyst, Colonel William F. Friedman, had "cracked" the Japanese diplomatic code; the government therefore had good reason to believe that war was imminent. But in the hectic rush of events, both military and civilian authorities failed to make effective use of the information collected. They expected the blow to fall somewhere in Southeast Asia, possibly in the Philippines.

The garrison at Pearl Harbor was alerted against "a surprise aggressive move in any direction." The commanders there, Admiral Husband E. Kimmel and General Walter C. Short, believing an attack impossible, took precautions only against Japanese sabotage. Thus when planes from Japanese aircraft carriers swooped down on Pearl Harbor on the morning of December 7, they found easy targets. In less than two hours, they reduced the Pacific Fleet to a smoking ruin.

Never had American arms suffered a more devastating or shameful defeat. On December 8 Congress declared war on Japan. Formal war with Germany and Italy was still not inevitable—isolationists were far more ready to resist the "yellow peril" in Asia than to fight in Europe. The Axis Powers, however, honored their treaty obligations to Japan and on December 11 declared war on the United States. America was now fully engaged in the great world conflict.

Mobilizing the Home Front

War placed immense strains on the American economy and produced immense results. About 15 million men and women entered the armed ser-

vices; they, and in part the millions more in Allied uniforms, had to be fed, clothed, housed, and supplied with equipment ranging from typewriters and paper clips to rifles and grenades, tanks and airplanes. Congress granted wide emergency powers to the president. It refrained from excessive meddling in administrative problems and in military strategy.

Roosevelt was an inspiring war leader but not a very good administrator. Any honest account of the war on the home front must reveal glaring examples of confusion, inefficiency, and pointless bickering. The squabbling and waste characteristic of the early New Deal period made relatively little difference—what mattered then was raising the nation's spirits and keeping people occupied; efficiency was less than essential, however desirable. In wartime the nation's fate, perhaps that of the entire free world, depended on delivering weapons and supplies to the battlefronts.

The confusion attending economic mobilization can easily be overstressed. Nearly all Roosevelt's basic decisions were sensible and humane: to pay a large part of the cost of the war by collecting taxes rather than by borrowing and to base taxation on ability to pay; to ration scarce raw materials and consumer goods; to regulate prices

Japan's surprise attack on Pearl Harbor on December 7, 1941, killed more than 2,400 American servicemen and launched the United States into World War II.

and wages. If these decisions were not always translated into action with perfect effectiveness, they always operated in the direction of efficiency and the public good.

Roosevelt's greatest accomplishment was his inspiring of businessmen, workers, and farmers with a sense of national purpose. In this respect, his function duplicated his earlier role in fighting the depression, and he performed it with even greater success.

A sense of the tremendous economic expansion caused by the demands of war can most easily be captured by reference to official statistics of production. In 1939 the United States was still mired in the Great Depression. The gross national product amounted to about $91.3 billion. In 1945, after allowing for changes in the price level, it was $166.6 billion. More specifically, manufacturing output nearly doubled and agricultural output rose 22 percent. In 1939 the United States turned out fewer than 6,000 airplanes, in 1944 more than 96,000.

Wartime experience proved that the Keynesian economists were correct in predicting that government spending would spark economic growth. About 8 million persons were unemployed in June 1940. After Pearl Harbor, unemployment practically disappeared and by 1945 the civilian work force had increased by nearly 7 million. Military mobilization had begun well before December 1941, by which time 1.6 million men were already under arms. Economic mobilization proceeded much more slowly, mainly because the president refused to centralize authority. For months after Pearl Harbor, various civilian agencies squabbled with the military over everything from the allocation of scarce raw materials to the technical specifications of weapons. Roosevelt refused to settle these conflicts as only he could have.

The War Economy

Yet by early 1943 the nation's economic machinery had been converted to a wartime footing and was functioning smoothly. Supreme Court Justice James F. Byrnes resigned from the Court to become a sort of "economic czar." His Office of War Mobilization had complete control over the issuance of priorities and over prices. Rents, food prices, and wages were strictly regulated, and

items in short supply were rationed to consumers. Wages and prices had soared during 1942, but after April 1943 they leveled off. Thereafter the cost of living scarcely changed until controls were lifted after the war.

Expanded industrial production together with conscription caused a labor shortage that increased the bargaining power of workers. At the same time, the national emergency required some limitation on the workers' right to take advantage of this power. After Pearl Harbor, Roosevelt created a National War Labor Board to arbitrate disputes and "stabilize" wage rates. All changes in wages had to have the board's approval.

Prosperity and stiffer government controls added significantly to the strength of organized labor; indeed, the war had more to do with institutionalizing industrywide collective bargaining than the New Deal period. As workers recognized the benefits of union membership, they flocked into the organizations. Generally speaking, wages and prices remained in fair balance. Overtime work fattened paychecks, and a new stress in labor contracts on paid vacations, premium pay for night work, and various forms of employer-subsidized health insurance were added benefits. The war effort had almost no adverse effect on the standard of living of the average citizen, a vivid demonstration of the productivity of the American economy. The manufacture of automobiles ceased and pleasure driving became next to impossible because of gasoline rationing, but most civilian activities went on much as they had before Pearl Harbor. Plastics replaced metals in toys, containers, and other products. Although items such as meat, sugar, and shoes were rationed, they were doled out in amounts adequate for the needs of most persons. Americans had both guns *and* butter; belt-tightening of the type experienced by the other belligerents was unheard of.

The federal government spent twice as much money between 1941 and 1945 as in its entire previous history. This made heavy borrowing necessary. The national debt, which stood at less than $49 billion in 1941, increased by more than that amount each year between 1942 and 1945. However, more than 40 percent of the total was met by taxation, a far larger proportion than in any earlier war.

This policy helped to check inflation by siphoning off money that would otherwise have competed for scarce consumer goods. High taxes on incomes (up to 94 percent) and on excess profits (95 percent), together with a limit of $25,000 a year after taxes on salaries, convinced the people that no one was profiting inordinately from the war effort.

The income tax, which had never before touched the mass of white-collar and industrial workers, was extended downward until nearly everyone had to pay it. To collect efficiently the relatively small sums paid by most persons, Congress adopted the payroll-deduction system proposed by Beardsley Ruml, chairman of the Federal Reserve Bank of New York. Employers withheld the taxes owed by workers from their paychecks and turned the money over to the government.

The steeply graduated tax rates combined with a general increase in the income of workers and farmers effected a substantial shift in the distribution of wealth in the United States. The poor became richer, while the rich, if not actually poorer, collected a smaller proportion of the national income. The wealthiest 1 percent of the population had received 13.4 percent of the national income in 1935 and 11.5 percent in 1941. In 1944 this group received 6.7 percent.

War and Social Change

Enormous social effects stemmed from this shift, but World War II altered the patterns of American life in so many ways that it would be wrong to ascribe the transformations to any single source. Never was the population more fluid. The millions who put on uniforms found themselves transported first to training camps in every section of the country and then to battlefields scattered from Europe and Africa to the far reaches of the Pacific. Burgeoning new defense plants drew other millions to places like Hanford, Washington, and Oak Ridge, Tennessee, where great atomic energy installations were constructed, and to the aircraft factories of California and other states. The population of California increased by more than 50 percent in the forties, that of other far western states almost as much.

During the war, marriage and birth rates rose steeply because many people had been forced to put off marrying and having children for financial reasons during the Great Depression. Now wartime prosperity put an end to that problem at the same time that young couples were feeling the need to put down roots when the husbands were going off to risk death in distant lands. The population of the United States had increased by only 3 million during the Depression decade of the thirties; during the next *five* years it rose by 6.5 million.

Minorities in Time of War: Blacks, Hispanics, and Indians

The war affected black Americans in many ways. Several factors operated to improve their lot. One was their own growing tendency to demand fair treatment. Another was the reaction of Americans to Hitler's barbaric treatment of millions of Jews, which compelled millions of white citizens to reexamine their views about race. If the nation expected blacks to risk their lives for the common good, how could it continue to treat them as second-class citizens? Black leaders pointed out the inconsistency between fighting for democracy abroad and ignoring it at home. "We want democracy in Alabama," the NAACP announced, and this argument too had some effect on white thinking.

Blacks in the armed forces were treated more fairly than they had been in World War I. They were enlisted for the first time in the air force and the marines, and they were given more responsible positions in the army and navy. The army commissioned its first black general. Some 600 black pilots won their wings. Altogether about a million served, about half of them overseas.

However, segregation in the armed services was maintained. The navy continued to confine black and Hispanic sailors to demeaning non-combat tasks and and black soldiers were mistreated in and around army camps, especially those in the South. In some cases, German prisoners of war were seated in front of black American soldiers at camp movies. In 1943 Willian Hastie, a former New Dealer who was serving as an adviser on racial matters, resigned in protest because of the "reactionary policies and discriminatory practices of the Army and Air Forces in matters affecting Negroes."

However, economic realities operated significantly to the advantage of black civilians. More of them had been unemployed in proportion to their numbers than any other group; now the labor shortage brought employment for all. More than 5 million blacks moved from rural areas to cities between 1940 and 1945 in search of work. At least a million found defense jobs in the North and on the West Coast and many of these involved developing valuable skills difficult for blacks to acquire before the war because of the policies of trade unions and many employers. The black population of a dozen important cities more than doubled in that brief period. The migrants were mostly forced to live in dreadful urban ghettoes, but their very concentration made them important politically.

These gains failed to satisfy black leaders. The NAACP, which increased its membership tenfold during the war, adopted a more militant stance than in World War I. Discrimination in defense plants seemed far less tolerable than it had in 1917–1918. A. Philip Randolph, president of the Brotherhood of Sleeping Car Porters, organized a march of blacks on Washington in 1941 to demand equal opportunity for black workers. Fearing possible violence and the wrath of southern congressmen, Roosevelt tried to persuade Randolph to call off the march. "It would make the country look bad," he claimed. But Randolph persisted and Roosevelt finally agreed to issue an order prohibiting discrimination in plants with defense contracts. He also set up a Fair Employment Practices Committee to see that the order was carried out. Executive Order 8802 was poorly enforced, but it opened up better jobs to some workers.

Prejudice and mistreatment did not cease. In areas around defense plants, white resentment of the black "invasion" mounted. By 1943 50,000 new blacks had crowded into Detroit. A wave of strikes disrupted production at plants where white workers were protesting the hiring of blacks. In June a race riot marked by looting and bloody fighting went on for three days. By the time federal troops restored order, 25 blacks and 9 whites had been killed. Rioting also erupted in New York and many other cities.

In Los Angeles the attacks were on Hispanic "zoot suiters," gangs whose "uniforms" were broad-brimmed fedoras, long coats, and pegged trousers. Wartime employment needs resulted in a reversal of the depression policy of forcing Mexicans out of the Southwest and many thousands flocked north. Most had to accept menial jobs but work was plentiful and well paid compared to Mexican rates.

A larger proportion of young Mexican American men served in the armed forces than the national average, but some civilian young Hispanics formed gangs. They had money in their pockets and their behavior was not always as circumspect as local residents would have preferred. A grand jury undertook an investigation, and the Los Angeles City Council even debated banning the wearing of zoot suits. In 1943 rioting broke out when sailors on shore leave began roaming the area attacking anyone they could find wearing a zoot suit.

There were at least understandable reasons why white city dwellers resented the black and Hispanic newcomers, but the willingness of white leaders to tolerate such behavior at a time when national unity was so necessary was particularly frustrating. For example, blood plasma from blacks and whites was kept separately even though the two "varieties" were indistinguishable and the process of storing plasma had been devised by a black doctor, Charles Drew.

Blacks became increasingly embittered. Roy Wilkins, head of the NAACP, put it this way in 1942: "No Negro leader with a constituency can face his members today and ask full support for the war in the light of the atmosphere the government has created." Many black newspaper editors were so critical of the administration that conservatives demanded they be indicted for sedition.

Roosevelt would have none of that, but he thought the militants should hold their demands in abeyance until the war had been won. Apparently he failed to realize the depth of black anger, and in this he was no different from the majority of whites. A revolution was in the making, yet in 1942 a poll revealed that a solid majority of whites still believed that black Americans were "satisfied" with their place in society.

Concern about national unity did lead to a reaction against the New Deal policy of encouraging Indians to develop self-governing communities. There was even talk of trying to "assimilate" Indians into the larger society. John Collier resigned as commissioner of Indian affairs in disgust in 1945.

The war encouraged assimilation in several ways. More than 24,000 Indians served in the armed forces, an experience that brought them in contact with new people, new places, and new ideas. Many thousands more left the reservations to work in defense industries in cities all over the country.

The Treatment of German, Italian, and Japanese Americans

World War II affected the American people far more drastically than World War I had, but it produced much less intolerance and fewer examples of the repression of individual freedom of opinion. People seemed able to distinguish between Italian fascism and Italian Americans, and between the government of Nazi Germany and Americans of German descent in a way that had escaped their parents. The fact that few Italian Americans admired Mussolini and that nearly all German Americans were anti-Nazi helps explain this. So does the fact that both groups were prepared to use their considerable political power to protect themselves against abuse.

But the underlying public attitude was more important. Americans went to war in 1941 without illusions and without enthusiasm, determined to win but expecting only to preserve what they had. They therefore found it easier to tolerate dissent and to concentrate on the real foreign enemy without venting their feelings on domestic scapegoats.

The one flagrant example of intolerance was the relocation of the West Coast Japanese in internment camps in Wyoming, Arizona, and other interior states. About 110,000 Americans of Japanese ancestry, the majority of them native-born citizens, were rounded up and sent off against their will. Not one was accused of sabotage or being an enemy agent.

The Japanese Americans were properly indignant but also baffled, in some cases hurt more than angry. "We didn't feel Japanese. We felt American," one woman, the mother of three small children, recalled many years later. A fisherman remembered that besides his nets and all his other equipment, he had to leave behind a "brand-new 1941 Plymouth." "We hadn't done anything wrong. We obeyed the laws," he told an interviewer. "I lost everything." Then he added, almost plaintively, "But I don't blame anyone. It was a war."

The government's excuse was fear that some of the Japanese *might* be disloyal. Nevertheless, racial prejudice (the "yellow peril") and frustration at not being able to strike a quick blow at Japan in retaliation had much to do with the callous decision to force people into camps. The Supreme Court upheld the relocation order in *Korematsu* v. *United States* (1944), but in *Ex Parte Endo* it forbade the internment of loyal Japanese American citizens. Unfortunately the latter decision was not handed down until December 1944.

Women's Contribution to the War Effort

With economic activity on the rise and millions of men going off to war, a sudden need for women workers developed. By 1944, 6.5 million additional women had entered the work force and at the peak of war production in 1945, more than 19 million women were employed. Thousands more were serving in the armed forces

At first there was considerable resistance to what was happening. About one husband in three objected in principle to his wife taking a job. Many employers in fields traditionally dominated by men doubted that women could handle such tasks.

Unions frequently made the same point. A Seattle official of the International Brotherhood of Boilermakers and Iron Shipbuilders said of women job applicants: "If one of these girls pressed the trigger on the yard rivet guns, she'd be going one way and the rivet the other." Actually, many women were soon doing "men's work" in the shipyards. The Seattle taxicab union objected to women drivers on the ground that "drivers are forced to do things and go places that would be embarrassing for a woman to do."

These male attitudes lost force in the face of the escalating demand for labor. That employers usually did not have to pay women as much as men made them attractive, as did the fact that they were not subject to the draft. Soon women were working not only as riveters and cab drivers, but as welders, machine tool operators, and in dozens of other occupations formerly the exclusive domain of men.

Women took wartime jobs for many reasons other than the obvious economic ones. Patriotism was important, but so were the desire for independence, and even loneliness. "It's thrilling work, and exciting, and something women have never done before," one women reported. She was talking about driving a taxi.

Black women workers had a particularly difficult time, employers often hesitating to hire them because they were black, black men looking down on them because they were women. But the need for willing hands was infinite. Sybil Lewis of Sapula, Oklahoma, went to Los Angeles and found a job as a waitress. Then she entered a training program at Lockheed Aircraft and became a riveter making airplane gas tanks. When an unfriendly foreman gave her a less attractive assignment she moved on to Douglas Aircraft. By 1943 she was working as a welder in a shipyard.

Few wartime jobs were easy and for women there were special burdens, not the least of which was the prejudice of many of the men they worked with. For married women there was housework to do after a long day. One War Manpower Commission bureaucrat figured out that Detroit defense plants were losing 100,000 woman-hours a month because of employees taking a day off to do the family laundry. Although the government made some effort to provide day care facilities, there were never nearly enough; this was one reason why relatively few women with small children entered the labor market during the war.

The war also affected the lives of women who did not take jobs. Families by the tens and hundreds of thousands pulled up stakes and moved to the centers of war production, such as Detroit and southern California. Housing was always in short supply and while the men went off to the familiar surroundings of yard and factory, their wives had to cope with cramped quarters, ration books, the absence of friends and relatives, the problems encountered by their children in strange schools and playgrounds.

Newlywed wives of soldiers and sailors (known generally as "war brides") often followed their husbands to training camps, where life was often as difficult as it was around defense plants. Whatever their own behavior, war brides quickly learned that society applied a double standard to infidelity, especially when it involved a man presumably risking his life in some far off land.

There was a general relaxation of sexual inhibitions, part of a decades-long trend, but accelerated by the war. So many hasty marriages, followed by long periods of separation, also brought a rise in divorces.

Of course "ordinary" housewives also had to deal with shortages, ration books, and other inconveniences during the war. In addition, most took on other duties and bore other burdens, such as tending "victory gardens" and preserving their harvests, using crowded public transportation when there was no gas for the family car, mending and patching old clothes, participating in salvage drives, and doing volunteer work for hospitals, the Red Cross, or various civil defense and servicemen's centers.

Allied Strategy: Europe First

Only days after Pearl Harbor, Prime Minister Churchill and his military chiefs met in Washington with Roosevelt and his advisers. In every quarter of the globe disaster threatened. The Japanese were gobbling up the Far East. Hitler's armies were preparing for a massive attack in the direction of Stalingrad, on the Volga River. German divisions under General Erwin Rommel, were beginning a drive across North Africa toward the Suez Canal. U-boats were taking a heavy toll in the North Atlantic.

The decision of the strategists was to concentrate first against the Germans. Japan's conquests were in remote and, from the Allied point of view, relatively unimportant regions. If Russia surrendered, Hitler might well be able to invade Great Britain, thus making his position in Europe impregnable.

During the summer of 1942, Allied planes began to bomb German cities. Although air attacks did not destroy the German armies' capacity to fight, they hampered war production, tangled communications, and brought the war home to the German people in awesome fashion.

In November 1942 an Allied army commanded by General Dwight D. Eisenhower struck at French North Africa. After the fall of France, the Nazis had set up a puppet regime in those parts of France not occupied by their troops, with headquarters at Vichy in central France. This collaborationist Vichy government controlled French

North Africa. But the North African commandant, Admiral Jean Darlan, promptly switched sides when Eisenhower's forces landed. After a brief show of resistance, the French surrendered.

Eisenhower then pressed forward quickly against the Germans. In February 1943 at Kasserine Pass in the desert south of Tunis, American tanks met Rommel's *Afrika Korps*. The battle ended in a standoff, but with British troops closing in from Egyptian bases to the east, the Germans were soon trapped and crushed. In May, after Rommel had been recalled to Germany, his army surrendered.

In July 1943, while air attacks on Germany continued and the Russians slowly pushed the Germans back from the gates of Stalingrad, the Allies invaded Sicily from Africa. In September they advanced to the Italian mainland. Mussolini had already fallen from power, and his successor, Marshal Pietro Badoglio, surrendered. However, the German troops in Italy threw up an almost impregnable defense across the rugged Italian peninsula. The Anglo-American army inched forward, paying heavily for every advance. Rome did not fall until June 1944, and months of hard fighting remained before the country was cleared of Germans.

Germany Overwhelmed

By the time the Allies had taken Rome, the mighty army needed to invade France had been collected in England under Eisenhower's command. On D-Day, June 6, 1944, the assault forces stormed ashore along the coast of Normandy supported by a great armada and thousands of planes and paratroops. Against fierce but ill-coordinated German resistance, they established a beachhead: Within a few weeks a million troops were on French soil.

Thereafter victory was assured, though nearly a year of fighting still lay ahead. In August the American Third Army under General George S. Patton erupted southward into Brittany and then veered east toward Paris. Another Allied army invaded France from the Mediterranean in mid-August and advanced rapidly north. Free French troops were given the honor of liberating Paris on August 25, and by mid-September the Allies were fighting on the edge of Germany itself.

While Eisenhower was regrouping, the Germans on December 16 launched a counterattack, planned by Hitler himself, against the Allied center in the Ardennes Forest. The Germans hoped to break through to the Belgian port of Antwerp, thereby splitting the Allied armies in two. The plan was foolhardy and therefore unexpected, and it almost succeeded. But once the element of surprise had been overcome, their chance of breaking through to the sea was lost. Eisenhower concentrated first on preventing them from broadening the break in his lines and then on blunting the point of their advance. By late January 1945, the old line had been reestablished. The "Battle of the Bulge" cost the United States 77,000 casualties and delayed Eisenhower's offensive, but it exhausted the Germans' last reserves.

The Allies then pressed forward to the Rhine, winning a bridgehead on the far bank of the river on March 7. Thereafter another German city fell almost daily. With the Russians racing westward against crumbling resistance, the end could not be long delayed.

As the Americans drove swiftly forward, they began to overrun Nazi concentration camps where millions of Jews had been murdered. Word of this holocaust in which no less than 6 million people were slaughtered had reached the United States much earlier. At first the news had been dismissed as propaganda. Hitler was known to hate Jews and to have persecuted them, but that he could order the murder of millions of innocent people, even children, seemed beyond belief. By 1943, however, the truth could not be denied.

Little could be done about those already in the camps, but there were thousands of refugees in occupied Europe who might have been spirited to safety. President Roosevelt declined to make the effort; he even refused to bomb the death camps on the ground that the destruction of German soldiers and military equipment took precedence over any other objective. Thus, when American journalists entered the camps with the advancing troops, saw the heaps of still-unburied corpses, and talked with the emaciated survivors, their reports caused a storm of protest.

Why Roosevelt acted as he did has never been satisfactorily explained. In April American and Russian forces made contact at the Elbe River. A few days later, with Russian shells reducing his capital to rubble, Hitler, by then probably

World War II, European Theater

insane, took his own life in his Berlin air raid shelter. On May 8 Germany surrendered.

The Naval War in the Pacific

While armies were being trained and matériel accumulated for the attack on Germany, much of the available American strength was diverted to the task of preventing further Japanese expansion. The navy's aircraft carriers had escaped destruction at Pearl Harbor, a stroke of immense good fortune because without most tacticians realizing it, the airplane had revolutionized naval warfare. Commanders discovered that carrier-based planes were far more effective against warships than the heaviest naval artillery because of their greater range and more concentrated firepower.

Once into Germany, the Third Army advanced so quickly in the spring of 1945 that it came upon military installations almost without warning. The photograph here is of General Dwight D. Eisenhower inspecting the condition of the concentration camp at Gotha, Germany, where slain inmates had been left unburied by their fleeing captors.

This truth was demonstrated in May 1942 in the Battle of the Coral Sea, northeast of Australia and south of New Guinea and the Solomon Islands. Mastery of these waters would cut Australia off from Hawaii and thus from American aid. Japanese Admiral Isoroku Yamamoto had dispatched a large fleet of troop ships, screened by many warships to attack Port Moresby, on the southern New Guinea coast. On May 7 and 8, planes from the American carriers *Lexington* and *Yorktown* struck the convoy's screen, sinking a small carrier and damaging a large one. Superficially, the battle seemed a victory for the Japanese, for their planes mortally wounded the *Lexington* and sank two other ships, but the troop transports had been forced to turn back—Port Moresby was saved. Although large numbers of cruisers and destroyers took part in the action, all the destruction was wrought by carrier aircraft.

Encouraged by the Coral Sea "victory," Yamamoto decided to attack Midway Island, west of Hawaii. Between June 4 and 7 control of the Central Pacific was decided, entirely by air power. American dive bombers sent four large carriers to the bottom. About 300 Japanese planes were destroyed. The United States lost only the *Yorktown* and a destroyer, retaining the bulk of its planes. Thereafter the initiative in the Pacific War shifted to the Americans.

American land forces were under the command of Douglas MacArthur, a brilliant but egocentric general whose judgment was sometimes distorted by his intense concern for his own reputation. MacArthur was in command of American

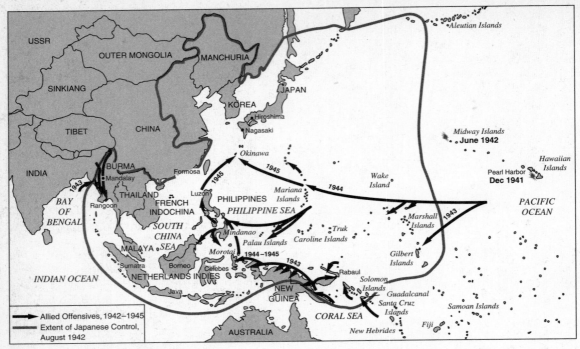

World War II, Pacific Theater

troops in the Philippine Islands when the Japanese struck in December 1941. President Roosevelt had him evacuated by PT boat to escape capture.

Thereafter MacArthur was obsessed with the idea of personally leading an American army back to the Philippines, and he convinced the Joint Chiefs of Staff, who determined strategy. They organized two separate drives, one from New Guinea toward the Philippines under MacArthur, the other through the Central Pacific toward Tokyo under Admiral Chester W. Nimitz.

Island Hopping

Before commencing this two-pronged advance, the Americans had to eject the Japanese from the Solomon Islands. Beginning in August 1942, a series of land, sea, and air battles raged around Guadalcanal Island in this archipelago. Once again American air power was decisive, and by February of 1943 Guadalcanal had been secured.

In the autumn of 1943, the American drives toward Japan and the Philippines got under way at last. In the Central Pacific campaign the Guadalcanal action was repeated on a smaller scale from Tarawa in the Gilbert Islands to Kwajalein and Eniwetok in the Marshalls. The Japanese soldiers on these islands fought like the Spartans at Thermopylae for every foot of ground. They had to be blasted and burned from tunnels and concrete pillboxes with hand grenades, flame throwers, and dynamite. They almost never surrendered. But Admiral Nimitz's forces were in every case victorious. By midsummer of 1944, this arm of the American advance had taken Saipan and Guam in the Marianas. Now land-based bombers were within range of Tokyo.

Meanwhile, MacArthur was leapfrogging along the New Guinea coast toward the Philippines. In October 1944 he made good his promise to return to the islands, landing on Leyte, south of Luzon. Two great naval clashes in Philippine waters, the Battle of the Philippine Sea (June 1944) and the Battle for Leyte Gulf (October 1944), completed the destruction of Japan's sea power and reduced its air force to a band of fanatical suicide pilots called *kamikazes,* who tried to crash bomb-laden planes against American warships and airstrips. The *kamikazes* caused much damage but could not turn the tide. In February 1945 MacArthur liberated Manila.

The end was now inevitable. B–29 Superfortress bombers from the Marianas rained high explosives and firebombs on Japan. The islands of Iwo Jima and Okinawa, only a few hundred miles from Tokyo, fell to the Americans in March and June 1945. But it seemed possible that it would take another year of fighting and a million more American casualties to subdue the main Japanese islands.

"The Shatterer of Worlds"

At this point came the most controversial decision of the entire war, and it was made by a newcomer on the world scene. In November 1944 Roosevelt had been elected to a fourth term, easily defeating Thomas E. Dewey. Instead of renominating Henry A. Wallace for vice president, the Democrats had picked Senator Harry S. Truman of Missouri. Then, in April 1945, President Roosevelt died of a cerebral hemorrhage. Thus it was Truman who had to decide what to do when, in July 1945, American scientists placed in his hands a new and awful weapon, the atomic bomb.

After Roosevelt had responded to Albert Einstein's warning in 1939, government-sponsored atomic research had proceeded rapidly. The manufacture of the artificial element plutonium at Hanford, Washington, and uranium 235 at Oak Ridge, Tennessee, continued along with the design and construction of a transportable atomic bomb at Los Alamos, New Mexico. A successful bomb was exploded in the New Mexican desert on July 16, 1945.

Should a bomb with the destructive force of 20,000 tons of TNT be employed against Japan? By striking a major city, its dreadful power could be demonstrated convincingly, yet doing so would bring death to tens of thousands of Japanese civilians. Truman was torn between his awareness that

the bomb was "the most terrible thing ever discovered" and his hope that using it "would bring the war to an end," thus saving thousands of lives. On a less humane level, Truman hoped the bomb might end the war before the Soviet Union could intervene effectively and thus claim a role in the peacemaking, the president chose to go ahead.

The moral soundness of Truman's decision has been debated ever since. Hatred of the Japanese must have had something to do with the decision. But it is also likely that more Japanese civilians would have died, far more than the American soldiers who would have perished, if Japan had had to be invaded.

In any case, on August 6 the Superfortress *Enola Gay* dropped an atomic bomb on Hiroshima, killing about 78,000 persons and injuring nearly 100,000 more out of a population of 344,000. Three days later, while the stunned Japanese still hesitated, a second bomb, the only other one so far assembled, hit Nagasaki. This second drop was far less defensible morally, but it had the desired result. On August 15 Japan surrendered.

Thus ended the greatest war in history. Its cost was beyond calculation. No accurate count could be made even of the dead; we know only that it was in the neighborhood of 20 million. No one could call the war a benefit to mankind, but in the late summer of 1945 the future looked bright. Fascism was dead. Many believed that the Russian communists were ready to cooperate in rebuilding Europe. In the United States isolationism had disappeared.

Out of the death and destruction had come new technology that seemed to herald a better world as well as a peaceful one. Advances in airplane design and the development of radar were about to revolutionize travel and the transportation of goods. Improvements in surgery and other medical practices gave promise of saving millions of lives. The development of penicillin and other antibiotics, which had greatly reduced the death rate among troops, would perhaps banish all infectious disease. Above all, there was the power of the atom, which could be harnessed to serve peaceful needs.

The period of reconstruction would be prolonged, but with all the great powers adhering to the new United Nations charter, drafted at San Francisco in June 1945, international cooperation could be counted on to ease the burdens of the victims of war and help the poor and underdeveloped parts of the world toward economic and political independence. Such at least was the hope of millions in the victorious summer of 1945.

Wartime Diplomacy

That hope was not realized, chiefly because of a conflict that developed between the Soviet Union and the Western Allies. During the course of World War II, every instrument of mass persuasion in the country had been directed at convincing the people that the Russians were fighting America's battle as well as their own. Even before Pearl Harbor, former Ambassador Joseph E. Davies wrote in his best-selling *Mission to Moscow* (1941) that the communist leaders were "a group of able, strong men" with "honest convictions and integrity of purposes" who were "devoted to the cause of peace for both ideological and practical reasons." Communism was based "on the same principle of the 'brotherhood of man' which Jesus preached."

During the war Americans with as different points of view as General Douglas MacArthur and Vice President Henry A. Wallace took strongly pro-Soviet positions. In 1943 *Time* named Stalin its Man of the Year. A number of motion pictures also contributed to revising the attitude of the average American toward the USSR. In *One World* (1943) Wendell Willkie wrote glowingly of the Russian people, their "effective society," and their simple, warmhearted leader. When he suggested jokingly to Stalin that if he continued to make progress in improving the education of his people he might educate himself out of a job, the dictator "threw his head back and laughed and laughed," Willkie recorded. "Mr. Willkie, you know I grew up a Georgian peasant. I am unschooled in pretty talk. All I can say is I like you very much."

These views were naive, to say the least, but the identity of interest of the United States and the Soviet Union was very real during the war. Russian military leaders conferred regularly with their British and American counterparts and fulfilled their obligations scrupulously.

The Soviets repeatedly expressed a willingness to cooperate with the Allies in dealing with postwar problems. Russia was one of the 26 signers of the Declaration of the United Nations (January 1942), in which the Allies promised to eschew territorial aggrandizement after the war, to respect the right of all peoples to determine their own form of government, to work for freer trade and international economic cooperation, and to force the disarmament of the aggressor nations.

In October 1943, during a conference in Moscow with Secretary of State Hull and British Foreign Minister Anthony Eden, Soviet Foreign Minister V. M. Molotov joined in setting up a European Advisory Commission to divide Germany into occupation zones after the war. That December, at a conference in Teheran, Iran, Roosevelt, Churchill, and Stalin discussed plans for a new league of nations. When Roosevelt described the kind of world organization he envisaged, the Russian dictator offered a number of constructive suggestions.

At another conference, held in February 1945 at Yalta in the Soviet Union, the three leaders joined in a call for a meeting in San Francisco to draft a charter for the United Nations. At the San Francisco gathering, it was decided that each member of the 50-nation UN should have a seat in the General Assembly. The locus of authority, however, was placed in the Security Council, which was to consist of five permanent members (the United States, the Soviet Union, Great Britain, France, and China) and six others elected for two-year terms. Thus any great power could veto any UN action it did not like. The charter paid lip service to the Wilsonian ideal of an international police force, but it limited that force by incorporating the limitations Henry Cabot Lodge had proposed in his 1919 reservations to the League of Nations Covenant.

Mounting Suspicions

Long before the war in Europe ended, however, the Allies had clashed over important policy matters. Since later world tensions developed from decisions made at this time, an understanding of the disagreements is essential for evaluating several decades of history. Unfortunately, complete understanding is not yet possible, which explains why the subject remains controversial.

Much depends on one's view of the postwar Soviet system. If the Soviet government under Stalin was bent on world domination, events fall readily into one pattern of interpretation. If, having at enormous cost endured an unprovoked assault by the Nazis, it was seeking only to protect itself against the possibility of another invasion, these events are best explained differently.

Because the United States has opened nearly all its diplomatic records, we know a great deal about how American foreign policy was formulated and about the mixed motives and mistaken judgments of American leaders. This helps explain why many scholars have been critical of American policy and the "cold warriors" who made and directed it. The Soviet Union, on the other hand, has excluded historians from its archives, and consequently we know little about the motivations and inner workings of Soviet policy.

The Soviets resented the British-American delay in opening up a second front. They were fighting for survival against the full power of the German armies; any invasion, even an unsuccessful one, would relieve some of the pressure. Roosevelt and Churchill would not move until they were ready, and Stalin had to accept their decision. At the same time, Stalin never concealed his determination to protect his country against future attack by extending their western boundary after the war. He warned the Allies repeatedly that he would not tolerate any anti-Soviet government along Russia's western boundary.

Most Allied leaders, including Roosevelt, admitted privately during the war that the Soviet Union would annex territory and possess preponderant power in Eastern Europe after the defeat of Germany, but they never said this publicly. They believed that free governments could somehow be created in countries like Poland and Bulgaria and that the Soviets would trust them enough to leave them to their own devices.

The Polish question was a terribly difficult one. The war, after all, had been triggered by the German attack on Poland; the British in particular felt a moral obligation to restore that nation to its prewar independence. Public opinion in Poland (and indeed in all the states along Russia's western frontier) was strongly anti-Soviet. Yet Russia's legitimate interests (to say nothing of its power in the area) could not be ignored.

Yalta and Potsdam

At the Yalta Conference, Roosevelt and Churchill agreed to Soviet annexation of part of Poland. In return they demanded that free elections be held in Poland itself. Stalin apparently could not understand why his allies were so concerned about the fate of a small country so remote from their strategic spheres; he could see no difference between the Soviet Union's dominating Poland and maintaining a government there that did not reflect the wishes of a majority of the Polish people, and the United States' dominating many Latin American nations and supporting unpopular regimes within them. Roosevelt, however, feared that Polish-Americans of Eastern European extraction would be furious if the communists took over their homeland.

Churchill, Roosevelt, and Stalin photographed at the week-long Yalta conference in February 1945. By April 1945, Roosevelt was dead.

The free elections were never held; Poland was run by a pro-Russian puppet regime. Thus the West "lost" Poland. How it might have "won" the country when it was already occupied by the Red Army has never been explained, but had Roosevelt described the difficulties to the American people more frankly, their reaction might have been less angry. Part of the problem was that Roosevelt believed he could charm Stalin into modifying his demands. "I think I can personally handle Stalin better than either your Foreign Office or my State Department," he told Prime Minister Churchill in 1942.

President Truman, being at first somewhat unsure of himself in foreign affairs, had no such illusion and perhaps for that reason took a much tougher stand. In July 1945, following the surrender of Germany, he, Stalin, and Churchill met at Potsdam, outside Ber1in.*

They agreed to try the Nazi leaders as war criminals, made plans for exacting reparations from Germany, and confirmed the division of the country into four zones to be occupied separately by American, Soviet, British, and French troops. Berlin, deep in the Soviet zone, had been split into four sectors too. Stalin rejected all arguments that he loosen his hold on Eastern Europe, and Truman (who received news of the successful testing of the atom bomb while at Potsdam) made no concessions. On both sides suspicions were mounting, positions hardening.

Yet all the advantages seemed to be with the United States. Besides its army, navy, and air force and its immense industrial potential, alone among the nations it possessed the atomic bomb. When Stalin's actions made it clear that he intended to control Eastern Europe and to exert influence elsewhere in the world, most Americans first reacted somewhat in the manner of a mastiff being worried by a yapping terrier: Their resentment was tempered by amazement. The war had caused a fundamental change in international politics. The United States might be the strongest country in the world, but the Western European nations, victor and vanquished alike, were reduced to their own and America's suprise to the status of second-class powers. The Soviet Union, by way of contrast, had gained more influence than it had under the czars and regained the territory it had lost as a result of World War I and the Communist Revolution.

* Clement R. Attlee replaced Churchill during the conference after his Labour Party won the British elections.

Milestones

1941 Roosevelt creates Fair Employment Practices Committee (FEPC)	**1944** Allied invasion of Normandy, France
Japanese attack on Pearl Harbor	Liberation of Paris
	Battle of the Bulge
1942 West Coast Japanese ordered to relocation camps	**1945** Yalta Conference
Fall of the Philippines	San Francisco Conference to draft UN Charter
Battle of the Coral Sea	Germany surrenders (V-E Day)
Battle of Midway	Capture of Okinawa
American troops invade North Africa	Atom bomb tested at Alamogordo, New Mexico
1943 Manhattan Project to make atomic bomb	Potsdam Conference
Race riots in Detroit and Los Angeles	Atom bombs dropped on Hiroshima and Nagasaki, Japan
Invasion of Italy	Japan surrenders (V-J Day)
Teheran Conference	

Supplementary Reading

Selig Adler, **The Uncertain Giant: American Foreign Policy Between the Wars*** (1965), summarizes diplomatic developments. Robert Dallek, **Franklin D. Roosevelt and American Foreign Policy*** (1979), is judicious and up-to-date. On isolationism and the events leading to Pearl Harbor, see R. A. Divine, **The Reluctant Belligerent*** (1965); brief but comprehensive, W. S. Cole, **Roosevelt and the Isolationists** (1983); and W. F. Kimball, **The Most Unsordid Act** (1969), on lend-lease. L. C. Gardner, **Economic Aspects of New Deal Diplomacy*** (1971), is critical but based on solid research. Akira Iriye, **Power and Culture: The Japanese-American War** (1981), is good on Japanese actions and motives.

A. R. Buchanan, **The United States in World War II*** (1964), briefly treats American mobilization and also provides an excellent overall survey of the military side of the conflict. Social trends are covered in Richard Polenberg, **War and Society*** (1972). The effect of the war on blacks is discussed in N. A. Wynn, **The Afro-American and the Second World War** (1976).

*Available in paperback.

CHAPTER 29

The American Century

The Postwar Economy
Postwar Society: The Baby Boomers
The Containment Policy
The Marshall Plan
Dealing with Japan and China
The Election of 1948
Containing Communism Abroad
Hot War in Korea
The Communist Issue at Home
"McCarthyism"
Dwight D. Eisenhower
The Eisenhower-Dulles Foreign Policy
McCarthy Self-destructs
Asian Policy After Korea
The Middle East Cauldron
Eisenhower and the Soviet Union
Latin America Aroused
The Politics of Civil Rights
The Election of 1960

*I*n late 1945 most Americans were probably more concerned with what was happening at home than with foreign developments, and no one was more aware of this than Harry Truman. When he received the news of Roosevelt's death, he claimed that he felt as though "the moon, the stars, and all the planets" had suddenly fallen upon him. Although he could not have been quite as surprised as he indicated (Roosevelt was known to be in extremely poor health), he was acutely conscious of his own limitations.

Truman was born in Missouri in 1884. After service with a World War I artillery unit, he became a minor cog in the Missouri political machine of boss Tom Pendergast. In 1934 he was elected to the United States Senate, where he proved to be a loyal but obscure New Dealer. The 1944 vice presidential nomination marked for him the height of achievement.

As president, Truman sought to carry on in the Roosevelt tradition. Curiously, he was both humble and cocky, idealistic and cold-bloodedly political. He adopted liberal objectives only to pursue them sometimes by rash, even repressive means. Too often he insulted opponents instead of convincing or conciliating them. Complications tended to confuse him, in which case he either dug in his heels or struck out blindly, usually with unfortunate results. On balance, however, he was a strong and in many ways a successful chief executive.

The Postwar Economy

Nearly all the postwar leaders were worried by the possibility of a serious postwar depression and nearly all accepted the necessity of employing federal authority to stabilize the economy and speed national development. The Great Depression and the huge government expenditures made necessary by the war had proved the theories of John Maynard Keynes and convinced Democrats and Republicans alike that it was possible to prevent sharp swings in the business cycle and therefore to do away with serious unemployment by monetary and fiscal manipulation. "The agents of government must . . . put a brake at certain points where boom forces develop . . . and support purchasing power when it becomes unduly depressed," the newly created Council of Economic Advisers reported.

When World War II ended, nearly everyone wanted to demobilize the armed forces, remove wartime controls, and reduce taxes. Yet everyone also hoped to prevent any sudden economic dislocation, check inflation, and make sure that goods in short supply were fairly distributed. Neither the politicians nor the public were able to reconcile these conflicting objectives. Labor wanted price controls retained but wage controls lifted; industrialists wished to raise prices and to keep the lid on wages. Farmers wanted subsidies but opposed price controls and the extension of Social Security benefits to agricultural workers.

President Truman failed to win either the confidence of the people or the support of Congress. On the one hand, he proposed a comprehensive program of new legislation that included a public housing scheme, aid to education, medical insurance, civil rights guarantees, a higher minimum wage, broader Social Security coverage, additional conservation and public power projects patterned after TVA, increased aid to agriculture, and the retention of anti-inflationary controls. On the other hand, he ended rationing and other controls and signed a bill cutting taxes by some $6 billion. Whenever opposition to his plans developed, he vacillated between compromise and inflexibility.

Yet the country weathered the reconversion period with remarkable ease. The pent-up demand for homes, automobiles, clothing, washing machines, and countless other products, backed by the war-enforced savings of millions, kept factories operating at capacity. Economists had feared that the flood of millions of veterans into the job market would cause serious unemployment. But when the veterans returned few were unoccupied for long. The demand for labor was large and growing. In addition, the government made an unprecedented educational opportunity available to veterans. Instead of a general bonus, in 1944 Congress passed the GI Bill of Rights, which subsidized veterans who wished to continue their education, learn new trades, or start small businesses. About 8 million veterans took advantage of these grants.

Cutting taxes and removing price controls did cause a period of rapid inflation. Food prices rose more than 25 percent between 1945 and 1947, which led to demands for higher wages and a wave of strikes—nearly 5,000 in 1946 alone. Inflation and labor unrest helped the Republicans to win control of both houses of Congress in 1946 for the first time since the 1920s.

High on the Republican agenda was the passage of a new labor relations act. Labor leaders tended to support the Democrats, for they remembered gratefully the Wagner Act and other help given them by the Roosevelt administration during the labor–management struggles of the 1930s. In 1943 the CIO had created a Political Action Committee to mobilize the labor vote. But the strikes of 1946 had alienated many citizens because they delayed the satisfaction of the demand for consumer goods. They even led President Truman, normally sympathetic to organized labor, to seize the coal mines, threaten to draft railroad workers, and ask Congress for other special powers to prevent national tie-ups.

This was the climate when in June 1947 the new Congress passed the Taft-Hartley Act over the veto of President Truman. The measure outlawed the closed shop (a provision written into many labor contracts requiring new workers to join the union before they could be employed) and declared illegal secondary boycotts and strikes called as a result of disputes between unions over the right to represent workers. Most important, it authorized the president to seek court injunctions to prevent strikes that in his opinion endangered the national interest. The injunctions would hold for 80 days—a "cooling off" period during which a presidential fact-finding board could investigate and make recommendations.

The Taft-Hartley Act made the task of unionizing unorganized industries more difficult, but it did not seriously hamper existing unions. While it outlawed the closed shop, it permitted union-shop contracts, which forced new workers to join the union after accepting employment.

Postwar Society: The Baby Boomers

The trend toward early marriage and larger families begun during the war accelerated when the conflict ended. In one year, 1946, more than 10 percent of all the single females over the age of fourteen in the country got married. The birthrate soared.

Most servicemen had idealized the joys of domesticity while abroad and they and their wives and sweethearts were eager to concentrate on "making a home and raising a family" now that the war had ended. People faced the future hopefully, being encouraged by the booming economy and the sudden profusion of consumer goods. At the same time, perhaps because of the confusion produced by rapid change, people tended to be conformists, looking over their shoulders, so to speak, rather than tackling life head on.

The period was marked by "a reaffirmation of domesticity," Elaine Tyler May writes in *Homeward Bound: American Families in the Cold War Era.* "Nearly everyone believed that family togetherness, focused on children, was the mark of a successful and wholesome personal life." In 1955 a University of Michigan psychologist completed a study conducted over two decades of 300 middle-class couples. Many of the women queried were college graduates who had gone to college primarily to find a mate with a good future, but others had cheerfully sacrificed plans for a professional career when "the right man" had come along. Encouraged by magazines like the *Ladies' Home Journal* and *Women's Home Companion,* and by films that described the trials and triumphs of family life, the majority of college-educated women made a "career" of home management and child development.

The men of this generation also professed to have found fulfillment in family life. They stressed such things as the satisfactions gained by taking on the responsibilties that marriage and fatherhood entailed, and "the incentive to succeed" produced by such responsibilties. For many men, however, these responsibilities provided a refuge from the competitive corporate world where they earned their livings. The need to subordinate one's personal interests to the requirements of "the organization," described in William Whyte's *Organization Man* (1956) and in novels like Sloan Wilson's *The Man in the Grey Flannel Suit* (1955), caused strains that could best be relieved in the warmth and security of one's family. Blue collar workers and clerical employees were not as subject to these pressures, but most had similar attitudes toward marriage and child rearing.

Goverment policies buttressed the inclinations of the people. Income tax deductions to purchase houses by obtaining low-cost mortgages from the Federal Housing Administration and to buy appliances and furniture on the installment plan. One result was an explosion of house building on the fringes of cities. New suburbs appeared almost like mushrooms after a spring rain. All this activity led to the construction of shopping malls in suburban areas.

Having a large family became a kind of national objective. If suburban life was family-centered, family life was certainly child-centered. Doctor Benjamin Spock's *Baby and Child Care*

Returning veterans and their growing families needed homes. Wartime earnings and veterans' mortgages made possible their financing; developers were ready to build them. One result was the construction of hundreds of thousands of single-family homes laid out in massive tracts.

(1946), which sold well over 20 million copies in 20-odd years, was not as "permissive" as has often been suggested. But Spock emphasized the importance of loving care. "Children raised in loving families want to learn, want to conform, want to grow up," he explained.

The Containment Policy

While ordinary people seemed to concentrate almost compulsively on their personal affairs, foreign policy issues continued to vex the Truman presidency. Stalin seemed intent on extending his power deep into war-devasted Central Europe. The Soviet Union also controlled Outer Mongolia, parts of Manchuria, and northern Korea, and it was fomenting trouble in Iran. By January 1946, Truman had decided to stop "babying" the Russians. "Only one language do they understand," he noted in a memorandum. "How many divisions have you?"

American and Russian attitudes stood in sharp confrontation when the control of atomic energy came up for discussion in the UN. Every-one recognized the threat to human survival posed by the atomic bomb. In November 1945 the United States suggested allowing the UN to su-pervise all nuclear energy production, and the General Assembly promptly created an Atomic Energy Commission to study the question. In June 1946 Commissioner Bernard Baruch offered a plan for the eventual outlawing of atomic weapons. A system would be set up under which UN inspectors could operate without restriction anywhere in the world to make sure that no coun-try was making bombs clandestinely. When, at an unspecified date, the system had been estab-lished, the United States would destroy its stock-pile of bombs.

Most Americans thought the Baruch Plan magnanimous and some considered it positively foolhardy, but the Soviets rejected it. They would neither permit UN inspectors in the Soviet Union nor surrender their veto power over Security Council actions dealing with atomic energy. They demanded that the United States destroy its bombs at once.

"What struck most observers," the historian John Lewis Gaddis wrote, "was the utter impervi-ousness of Stalin's regime to the gestures of re-straint and goodwill that eminated from the West." Unwilling under the circumstances either to trust the Russians or to surrender what they considered their "winning weapon," the American leaders refused to agree. The resulting stalemate increased international tension.

Postwar cooperation had failed. By early 1946 a new policy was emerging. Many minds con-tributed to its development, but the key ideas were provided by George F. Kennan, a scholarly Foreign Service officer. Kennan, a close student of Soviet history, believed that the Soviet leaders saw the world as divided into socialist and capital-ist camps separated by irreconcilable differences. Nothing the United States might do would reduce Soviet hostility, Kennan claimed. Therefore the nation should accept this hostility as a fact of life and wait for time to bring about some change in Soviet policy.

Kennan made this arument in an anonymous article in the July 1947 issue of *Foreign Affairs,* "The Sources of Soviet Conduct." A policy of "long-term, patient but firm and vigilant contain-ment" based on the "application of counter-force"

was the best means of dealing with Soviet pres-sures. The Cold War could be won if America maintained its own strength and convinced the communists that it would resist aggression firmly in any quarter of the globe.

The idea of "getting tough with Russia" found wide popular support. According to polls, a major-ity considered American policy "too soft." During 1946 the Truman administration gradually adopted a tougher stance. The decisive policy shift came early in 1947 as a result of a crisis in Greece, where communists were receiving aid from com-munist Yugoslavia and Bulgaria. Great Britain was assisting the monarchists, but could not long af-ford this drain on its resources. In February 1947 the British informed President Truman that they would have to cut off further aid to Greece.

The news shocked American policymakers because it made them realize that their European allies had not been able to rebuild their war-weak-ened economies. Russia's "Iron Curtain" (a phrase coined by Winston Churchill) seemed about to ring down on another nation.

If Greece or Turkey fell to the communists, he said, all the Middle East might be lost. To pre-vent this "unspeakable tragedy," he asked for $400 million for military and economic aid for Greece and Turkey. "It must be the policy of the United States to support free peoples who are re-sisting attempted subjugation by armed minori-ties or by outside pressures," he said.

By exaggerating the consequences of inac-tion, Truman attained his objective. But once offi-cial sanction was given to the communism-versus-democracy approach to foreign relations, foreign policy began to dominate domestic policy and to become more rigid.

The communist threat loomed large. With Western Europe, in the words of Winston Churchill (the great phrase maker of the era) "a rubble-heap, a charnel house, a breeding-ground of pestilence and hate," the entire continent seemed in danger of falling into communist hands.

The Marshall Plan

George Kennan disagreed with the psychology of the Truman Doctrine, which seemed to him es-sentially defensive as well as vulnerable to criti-cism by anti-imperialists. He proposed a broad program to finance European economic recovery. The Europeans themselves should work out the details, America providing the money, materials, and technical advice.

George C. Marshall, army chief of staff during World War II and now secretary of state, formally suggested this program, which became known as the Marshall Plan, in a commencement speech at Harvard in June 1947. The objective, he said, was to restore "the confidence of the European people in the economic future of their own countries. . . . The program should be a joint one, agreed to by a number, if not all European nations."

The European powers seized eagerly on Marshall's suggestion. Within six weeks, 16 nations were setting up a Committee for European Economic Cooperation, which soon submitted plans calling for up to $22.4 billion in American aid. After protracted debate, much influenced by a communist coup in Czechoslovakia in February 1948, which drew still another country behind the Iron Curtain, Congress appropriated over $13 billion for the program. Results exceeded all expectations. By 1951 Western Europe was booming.

Containment and the Marshall Plan were America's response to the power vacuum created in Europe by the debilitating effects of the war. Just as the Soviet Union extended its influence over the eastern half of the continent, the United States extended its influence in the western. Both powers were driven by worry that the other was seeking world domination. It was no mere coincidence that in 1947 Congress converted the wartime Office of Strategic Services into the Central Intelligence Agency (CIA), charged it with the gathering of foreign intelligence, and authorized it to engage in covert operations overseas. The result was what we call the Cold War.

The Marshall Plan formed the basis for a Western European economic recovery and political cooperation. In March 1948 Great Britain, France, Belgium, the Netherlands, and Luxembourg signed an alliance aimed at social, cultural, and economic collaboration. The western nations soon abandoned their understandable but self-defeating policy of crushing Germany economically. They instituted currency reforms in their zones and announced plans for creating a single West German republic with a large degree of autonomy.

In June 1948 the Soviets retaliated by closing off surface access to Berlin from the west. For a time it seemed that the Allies must either fight their way into the city or abandon it to the communists. Unwilling to adopt either alternative, Truman decided to fly supplies through the air corridors leading to the capital from Frankfurt, Hanover, and Hamburg. American C-47 and C-54 transports shuttled back and forth in weather fair and foul, carrying enough food, fuel, and other goods necessary to maintain more than 2 million West Berliners. The "Berlin Airlift" put the Soviets in an uncomfortable position: If they were really determined to keep supplies from West Berlin, they would have to begin the fighting. They were not prepared to do so. In May 1949 they lifted the blockade.

Containment, some of its advocates argued, required the development of a powerful military force. In May 1948 Republican Senator Arthur H. Vandenberg of Michigan, a prewar leader of the isolationists who had been converted to internationalism largely by President Roosevelt's solicitous attention to his views, introduced a resolution stating the "determination" of the United States "to exercise the right of individual or collective self defense . . . should any armed attack occur affecting its national security." The Senate approved this resolution by a vote of 64 to 4, proof that isolationism had ceased to be an important force in American politics.

Dealing with Japan and China

Containment worked well in Europe, at least in the short run; in the Far East, where the United States lacked powerful allies, it was both more expensive and less effective. V-J Day found the Far East a shambles. Much of Japan was a smoking ruin. In China chaos reigned: Nationalists under Chiang Kai-shek dominated the south, communists under Mao Tse-tung controlled the northern countryside, and Japanese troops still held most northern cities.

President Truman acted decisively and effectively with regard to Japan, unsurely and with unfortunate results where China was concerned. Even before the Japanese surrendered, he had decided not to allow the Soviet Union any significant role in the occupation of Japan. A four-power Allied Control Council was established, but American troops commanded by General MacArthur governed the country.

The Japanese, revealing the same remarkable adaptability that had made possible their swift westernization in the latter half of the 19th century, accepted political and social changes that involved universal suffrage and parliamentary government, the encouragement of labor unions, the breakup of some large estates and big industrial combines, and the deemphasis of the importance of the emperor. Japan lost its far-flung island empire and all claim to Korea and the Chinese mainland. Japan emerged economically strong, politically stable, and firmly allied with the United States.

The difficulties in China were probably insurmountable. Few Americans appreciated the latent power of the Chinese communists. When the war ended, Truman tried to bring Chiang's nationalists and Mao's communists together. He sent General Marshall to China to seek a settlement, but neither Chiang nor Mao would make significant concessions. Mao was convinced—correctly, as time soon proved—that he could win all China by force, whereas Chiang, presiding over a corrupt and incompetent regime, exaggerated his popularity among the Chinese people. In January 1947 Truman recalled Marshall and named him secretary of state. Soon thereafter civil war erupted in China.

The Election of 1948

In the spring of 1948 President Truman's fortunes were at low ebb. Public opinion polls suggested that a majority of the people considered him incompetent or worse. The Republicans seemed sure to win the 1948 presidential election, especially if Truman was the Democratic candidate. Governor Dewey, who again won the Republican nomination, ran confidently, even complacently, certain that he would carry the country with ease.

Truman's position seemed hopeless because he had alienated both southern conservatives and northern liberals. The southerners were particularly distressed because in 1946 the president had established a Committee on Civil Rights, which had recommended anti-lynching and anti–poll tax legislation and the creation of a permanent Fair Employment Practices Commission. When the

Democratic Convention adopted a strong civil rights plank, the southern delegates walked out. Southern conservatives then founded the States' Rights ("Dixiecrat") Party and nominated J. Strom Thurmond of South Carolina for president.

As for the liberals, in 1947 a group of them had founded Americans for Democratic Action (ADA) and sought an alternative candidate for the 1948 election. A faction led by former Vice President Henry A. Wallace, which believed Truman's containment policy a threat to world peace, organized a new Progressive Party and nominated Wallace. Most members of ADA, however, thought Wallace too pro-Soviet; in the end the organization supported Truman. Yet with two minor candidates sure to cut into the Democratic vote, the president's chances seemed minuscule.

Truman launched an aggressive campaign, making hundreds of informal but hard-hitting speeches. He excoriated the "do-nothing" Republican Congress, which had rejected his program and passed the Taft-Hartley Act, and he warned labor, farmers, and consumers that if Dewey won, Republican "gluttons of privilege" would do away with all the gains of the New Deal years.

Millions were moved by his arguments and by his courageous fight against great odds. The success of the Berlin Airlift during the presidential campaign helped him considerably. The Progressive Party fell increasingly into the hands of communist sympathizers, driving away many liberals who might otherwise have supported Wallace. Dewey's smug, lackluster campaign failed to attract independents. The president, therefore, was able to reinvigorate the New Deal coalition, and he won an amazing upset victory on election day. He collected 24.1 million votes to Dewey's 21.9 million, the two minor candidates being held to about 2.3 million. In the electoral college his margin was a thumping 303 to 189.

Truman's victory gave the ADA considerable influence over what the president called his Fair Deal program. ADA leaders took a middle-of-the-road approach, well described in Arthur M. Schlesinger, Jr.'s *The Vital Center* (1949), which left room for both individualism and social welfare, government regulation of the economy and the encouragement of private enterprise. The approach fitted well with Cold War conditions, which favored both massive military output and continued expansion of the supply of civilian

In 1948 the strongly Republican *Chicago Daily Tribune* guessed its postelection editions before all the returns were in. For Truman, it was the perfect climax to his hard-won victory.

goods. Economic growth would solve all problems, social as well as material. Through growth the poor could be helped without taking from the rich. The way to check inflation, for example, was not by freezing prices, profits, or wages but by expanding production.

However, relatively little of Truman's Fair Deal was enacted into law. Congress approved a federal housing program and measures increasing the minimum wage and Social Security benefits, but these were merely extensions of New Deal legislation.

Containing Communism Abroad

During Truman's second term, the confrontation between the United States and the Soviet Union, and more broadly between what was seen as "democracy" and "communism," dominated the headlines and occupied a major part of the attention of the president and most other government officials. To strengthen ties with the European democracies, in April 1949 the North Atlantic Treaty was signed in Washington. Under this pact the North Atlantic Treaty Organization (NATO) was established. Further disturbed by the news,

released in September 1949, that the Soviet Union had produced an atomic bomb, Congress appropriated $1.5 billion to arm NATO, and in 1951 General Eisenhower was recalled to active duty and placed in command of all NATO forces.

The success of containment was heartening but not without price; every move evoked a Russian response. The Marshall Plan led to the seizure of Czechoslovakia, the buildup of Germany to the Berlin blockade, the creation of NATO to the multilateral military alliance known as the Warsaw Pact. George Kennan, the "father" of containment, now downplayed the Soviet military threat. He called the rearmament of Europe a "regrettable diversion" from the task of economic reconstruction. In any case, both sides contributed by their actions and their continuing suspicions to the heightening of Cold War tensions.

In Asia the effort to contain communism exploded into war. By the end of 1949, Mao Tsetung's communist armies had administered a crushing defeat to the nationalists. The remnants of Chiang Kai-shek's forces fled to the island of Formosa, now called Taiwan. The "loss" of China to communism strengthened right-wing opponents of internationalism in the Republican Party. They and other critics charged that Truman had not backed the nationalists strongly enough and that he had stupidly underestimated Mao's dedication to the cause of world revolution.

Despite a superficial plausibility, neither charge made much sense. American opinion would not have supported military intervention, but that any American action could have changed the outcome in China is unlikely.

Hot War in Korea

The attacks of his American critics roused Truman's combativeness and led him into serious miscalculations elsewhere in Asia. After the war, the province of Korea was taken from Japan and divided Korea at 38° north latitude into the Democratic People's Republic, backed by the Soviet Union, and the Republic of Korea, backed by the United States and the UN. Both the powers withdrew their troops from the peninsula, the Russians leaving behind a well-armed local force while the Republic of Korea's army was weak and ill trained.

American strategists sought to "contain" communism in the Far East, but they decided that the Asiatic mainland was too difficult to defend. In January 1950, Dean Acheson, who had succeeded Marshall as secretary of state, deliberately excluded Korea from the "defensive perimeter" of the United States in Asia. It was up to the South Koreans, backed by the UN, to protect themselves. This they were unable to do when a North Korean army struck suddenly across the 38th parallel in June 1950.

At this point President Truman exhibited his finest qualities: decisiveness and courage. With the backing of the UN Security Council (but without asking Congress to declare war), he sent American planes into battle.* Ground troops soon followed.

Nominally, the Korean War was a struggle between the invaders and the United Nations. General MacArthur, placed in command, flew the blue UN flag over his headquarters, and no less than 16 nations supplied troops for his army. However, more than 90 percent of the forces employed were American. At first the North Koreans pushed them back rapidly to the southern tip of Korea. Then MacArthur executed a brilliant amphibious flanking maneuver, striking at the westcoast city of Inchon, about 50 miles south of the 38th parallel. Outflanked, the North Koreans retreated in disorder. By October the battlefront had moved north of the 1945 boundary.

General MacArthur now proposed the conquest of North Korea, the bombing of "privileged sanctuaries" on the Chinese side of the Korean border, and the redeployment of Chinese Nationalist troops on the mainland. Most of Truman's civilian advisers, led by George Kennan, opposed any advance beyond the 38th parallel, fearing intervention not only by the Red Chinese, but by the Russians.

Faced with conflicting advice, Truman authorized MacArthur to advance as far as the Yalu River, the boundary between North Korea and China, but to avoid war with China or the Soviet Union at all cost. It was a momentous and unfortunate decision, an example of how power, once unleashed, so often gets out of hand. As the advance progressed, ominous rumblings came from the Chinese that they would not "supinely tolerate seeing their neighbors being savagely invaded by imperialists." Chinese "volunteers" began to turn up among the captives taken by UN units. Alarmed, Truman flew to Wake Island in the Pacific to confer with MacArthur, but the general assured him that the Chinese would not dare to intervene. If they did, MacArthur added, his army would crush them easily; the war would be over by Christmas.

Seldom has a general miscalculated so badly. Ignoring intelligence reports and dividing his advancing units recklessly, he drove toward the Yalu. Suddenly, on November 26, 33 Chinese divisions smashed through the center of MacArthur's line. Overnight a triumphant advance became a disorganized retreat. MacArthur now justified his earlier confidence by claiming, not without reason, that he was fighting "an entirely new war."

The UN army rallied south of the 38th parallel, and by the spring of 1951 the front had been stabilized. MacArthur then urged that he be permitted to bomb Chinese installations north of the Yalu. He also suggested a naval blockade of the coast of China and the use of Chinese nationalist troops in Korea. When Truman rejected these proposals on the ground that they would lead to a third world war, MacArthur attempted to rouse Congress and the public against the president by criticizing administration policy openly. Truman ordered him to be silent, and when the general persisted, he removed him from command.

At first the Korean "police action" had been popular in the United States, but as the months passed and the casualties mounted, many citizens became disillusioned and angry. To Americans accustomed to triumph and fond of oversimplifying complex questions, containment seemed, as its costs in blood and dollars mounted, a monumentally frustrating policy.

But in time the fundamental correctness of Truman's policy and his decision to remove MacArthur became apparent. Military men backed the president almost unanimously. General Omar N. Bradley, chairman of the Joint Chiefs of Staff, declared that a showdown with the Chinese "would involve us in the wrong war, at the wrong place, at the wrong time and with the wrong enemy." In June 1951 the communists

---

*Russia, which could have vetoed this action, was at the moment boycotting the Security Council because the UN had refused to give the Mao Tse-tung regime China's seat on that body.

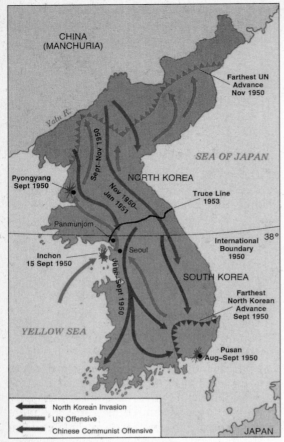

CHINA
(MANCHURIA)

Yalu R.

Farthest UN
Advance
Nov 1950

Sept–Nov 1950

SEA OF JAPAN

Pyongyang
Sept 1950

NORTH KOREA

Nov 1950–
Jan 1951

Truce Line
1953

Panmunjom

Inchon
15 Sept 1950

Seoul

International
Boundary
1950

38°

June–Sept 1950

SOUTH KOREA

Farthest
North Korean
Advance
Sept 1950

YELLOW SEA

Pusan
Aug–Sept 1950

North Korean Invasion

UN Offensive

Chinese Communist Offensive

JAPAN

The Korean War, 1950–1953

agreed to discuss an armistice in Korea, although the negotiations dragged on interminably. Finally, in late July 1953, an armistice was signed, but not before thousands more had died along the static battlefront.

The Communist Issue at Home

The frustrating Korean War highlighted the paradox that, at the pinnacle of its power, the influence of the United States in world affairs was declining. Its monopoly of nuclear weapons had been lost. China had passed into the communist orbit. Elsewhere in Asia and throughout Africa, new nations, formerly colonial possessions of the Western Powers, were adopting a "neutralist" position in the Cold War. Despite the billions poured into ar-

maments and foreign aid, the safety and even the survival of the country seemed far from assured.

Internal as well as external dangers loomed. Alarming examples of communist espionage in Canada, Great Britain, and in America itself convinced many citizens that clever conspirators were everywhere at work undermining American security. Both the Republicans and Democratic critics were charging that Truman was "soft" on communists.

There were relatively few communists in the United States and party membership plummeted after the start of the Cold War. However, the possibility that a handful of spies could do enormous damage fueled a kind of panic that could be used for partisan purposes. In 1947, hoping to defuse the communists-in-government issue by being more zealous in pursuit of spies than his critics, Truman established a Loyalty Review Board. Even sympathy for a long list of vaguely defined "totalitarian" or "subversive" organizations was made grounds for dismissal. During the following 10 years, about 2,700 government workers were discharged, hardly any for legitimate reasons. A much larger number resigned.

In 1948 Whittaker Chambers, an editor of *Time* who had formerly been a communist, charged that Alger Hiss, president of the Carnegie Endowment for International Peace and a former State Department official, had been a communist in the thirties. Hiss denied the charge and sued Chambers for libel. Chambers then produced microfilms purporting to show that Hiss had copied classified documents for dispatch to Moscow. Hiss could not be indicted for espionage because of the statute of limitations; instead he was charged with perjury. His first trial resulted in a hung jury, his second, ending in January 1950, in conviction and a five-year jail term.

The Hiss case fed the fears of those who believed in the existence of a powerful communist underground in the United States. The disclosure in February 1950 that a respected British scientist Klaus Fuchs had betrayed atomic secrets to the Russians heightened these fears, as did the arrest and conviction of his American associate Harry Gold and two other Americans, Julius and Ethel Rosenberg, on the same charge.

Although the information the Rosenbergs revealed was not very important, they were executed, to the consternation of many liberals. However, information gathered by other spies had speeded the Soviet development of nuclear weapons. This fact encouraged some Republicans to press the communists-in-government issue hard.

"McCarthyism"

In February 1950, an obscure senator, Joseph R. McCarthy of Wisconsin, casually introduced this theme in a speech before the Women's Republican Club of Wheeling, West Virginia. The State Department, he said, was "infested" with communists. He had no shred of evidence to back up this statement, as a Senate committee headed by the conservative Democrat Millard Tydings of Maryland soon demonstrated. He never exposed a single spy or even a secret American communist. One reporter quipped that McCarthy could not tell Karl Marx from Groucho. But thousands of people were too eager to believe him to listen to reason. Within a few weeks, he was the most talked-of person in Congress. Inhibited neither by scruples nor by logic, he lashed out in every direction, attacking international experts like Professor Owen Lattimore of Johns Hopkins and diplomats such as John S. Service and John Carter Vincent, who were already under attack for having pointed out the deficiencies of the Chiang Kai-shek regime during the Chinese civil war.

When McCarthy's victims indignantly denied his charges, he distracted the public by striking out with still more sensational accusations directed at other innocents. The "big lie" was McCarthy's most effective weapon: The enormity of his charges and the status of his targets convinced thousands that there must be *some* truth to what he was saying. Faint-hearted congressmen dared not incur his wrath, and large numbers of Republicans hastened to take advantage of his voter appeal.

Dwight D. Eisenhower

As the 1952 presidential election approached, Truman's popularity was again at a low ebb. Senator McCarthy attacked him relentlessly for his han-

dling of the Korean conflict and his "mistreatment" of General MacArthur. In choosing their candidate, the Republicans passed over the twice-defeated Dewey and their most prominent leader, Senator Robert A. Taft of Ohio, an outspoken conservative, and nominated General Dwight D. Eisenhower.

Eisenhower's popularity did not grow merely out of his achievements in World War II. After the bristly, combative Truman, his genial tolerance and evident desire to avoid controversy proved widely appealing. His reluctance to seek political office reminded the country of Washington, while his seeming ignorance of current political issues was no more a handicap to his campaign than the similar ignorance of Jackson and Grant in their times. People "liked Ike" because of his personality—he radiated warmth and sincerity—and because his management of the Allied armies promised that he would be equally competent as head of the complex federal government. His promise to go to Korea if elected to try to bring the war to an end was a master political stroke.

The Democrats nominated Governor Adlai E. Stevenson of Illinois, whose grandfather had been vice president under Cleveland. Stevenson's unpretentiousness and his witty, urbane speeches captivated intellectuals. In retrospect, however, it is clear that he had not the remotest chance of defeating the popular Eisenhower. Disillusionment with the Korean War and a widespread belief that the Democrats had been too long in power were added handicaps. His foes turned his strongest assets against him, denouncing his humor as frivolity, characterizing his appreciation of the complexities of life as self-doubt, and tagging his intellectual followers "eggheads," an appellation that effectively caricatured the balding, slope-shouldered, somewhat endomorphic candidate. "The eggheads are for Stevenson," one Republican pointed out, "but how many eggheads are there?" There were far too few to carry the country, as the election revealed. The result was a Republican landslide: Eisenhower received almost 34 million votes to Stevenson's 27 million, and in the electoral college his margin was 442 to 89.

On the surface, Eisenhower seemed the antithesis of Truman. The Republicans had charged the Democratic administration with being wasteful and extravagant. Eisenhower planned to run his administration on sound business principles and to eschew increases in the activities of the federal government. He spoke scornfully of "creeping socialism," called for more local control of government affairs, and promised to reduce federal spending in order to balance the budget and cut taxes. He believed that by battling with congressmen and pressure groups over the details of legislation, his immediate predecessors had sacrificed part of their status as chief representative of the American people. Like Washington, he tried to avoid being caught up in narrow partisan conflicts. Like Washington, he was not always able to do so.

Having successfully managed the complexities of military administration, Eisenhower used the same kind of staff system as president. He gave his Cabinet officers more responsibility than many modern presidents because he did not like to devote time and energy to administrative routine. This did not mean that he was lazy or politically naive. He knew that if he left too many small decisions to others, they would soon be controlling, if not actually making, the large decisions as well.

Some economists claimed that he reacted too slowly in dealing with business recessions and that he showed insufficient concern for speeding the rate of national economic growth. Yet he adopted a Rooseveltian, almost a Keynesian, approach to economic problems, that is, he tried to check downturns in the business cycle by stimulating the economy. In his memoir *Mandate for Change* (1963) he wrote of resorting to "preventative action to arrest the downturn [of 1954] before it might become severe" and of being ready to use "any and all weapons in the federal arsenal, including changes in monetary and credit policy, modification of the tax structure, and a speed-up in the construction of . . . public works" to accomplish this end. He approved the extension of Social Security to an additional 10 million persons, created the Department of Health, Education, and Welfare, and in 1955 came out for federal support of school and highway construction.

Eisenhower's somewhat doctrinaire belief in decentralization and private enterprise reduced the effectiveness of his social-welfare measures, but on balance, he proved to be a first-rate politician. He knew how to be flexible without compromising his basic values. His "conservatism" became first "dynamic conservatism" and then "progressive moderation." He summarized his attitude by saying that he was liberal in dealing with individuals but conservative "when talking about . . . the individual's pocketbook."

The Eisenhower-Dulles Foreign Policy

After the 1952 election, Eisenhower kept his pledge to go to Korea. His trip produced no immediate result, but the truce talks, suspended before the election, were resumed. In July 1953, perhaps influenced by a hint that the United States might use small "tactical" atomic bombs in Korea, the communists agreed to an armistice. Korea remained divided, its people far worse off than when the fighting began. The United States had suffered more than 135,000 casualties, including 33,000 dead. Yet aggression had been confronted and fought to a standstill.

The American people, troubled and uncertain, were counting on Eisenhower to find a way to employ the nation's immense strength constructively. The new president shared the general feeling that a drastic change of tactics in foreign affairs was needed. He counted on Congress and his secretary of state to solve the practical problems.

Given this attitude, his choice of John Foster Dulles as secretary of state seemed inspired. Dulles's experience in diplomacy dated to 1907; he had served as secretary to the Chinese delegation at the Second Hague Conference and as an adviser to Wilson at Versailles. More recently he had been an adviser to the American delegation to the San Francisco Conference and a representative of the United States in the UN General Assembly.

Dulles combined strong moral convictions with amazing energy. Only "the force of Christianity," he said, could solve "the great perplexing international problems" of the day. His objectives were magnificent, his strategy grandiose. Instead of waiting for the communist powers to make a move and then "containing" them, the United States should put more emphasis on nuclear bombs and less on conventional weapons. Such a "New Look" would prevent the United States from becoming involved in "local" conflicts like the Korean War and save money too. Potential enemies would know that "massive retaliation," would be the fate of aggressors. With the communists immobilized by this threat, positive measures aimed at "liberating" Eastern Europe and "unleashing" Chiang Kai-shek against the Chinese mainland would follow. Dulles professed great faith in NATO, but he believed that if America's allies lacked the courage to follow its lead, the nation would have to undertake an "agonizing reappraisal" of its commitments to them.

Despite his determination, energy, and high ideals, Dulles failed to make the United States a more effective force in world affairs. Massive retaliation made little sense when the Soviet Union possessed nuclear weapons as powerful as those of the United States. In November 1952 America had won the race to make a hydrogen bomb, but the Russians duplicated this feat the following August. Thereafter the only threat behind massive retaliation was the threat of human extinction.

To his credit, Dulles eventually recognized this. In January 1956 he said: "There is throughout the world a . . . not unreasonable fear that nuclear weapons . . . endanger human life on this planet." It might be best, he suggested, to turn over control of them to the UN Security Council. Willy nilly, nuclear power had established itself as a formidable force for world peace.

McCarthy Self-destructs

Dulles's saber-rattling tactics were badly timed. While he was planning to avert future Koreas, the Soviet Union was shifting its approach. Stalin died in March 1953, and after a period of internal conflict within the Kremlin, Nikita Khrushchev emerged as the new master of Russia. Khrushchev set out to obtain his objectives by indirection. He appealed to the anti-Western prejudices of countries just emerging from the yoke of colonialism, offering them economic aid and pointing to Soviet achievements in science and technology, such as the launching of *Sputnik*, the first satellite (1957), as proof that communism would soon "bury" the capitalist system without troubling to destroy it by force. The Soviet Union was the friend of all peace-loving nations, he insisted.

Khrushchev was a master hypocrite, yet he was a realist too. Whereas Dulles, product of a system that made a virtue of compromise and tolerance, insisted that the world must choose between American good and Russian evil, Khrushchev, trained to believe in the incompatibility of communism and capitalism, began to talk of "peaceful coexistence."

Dulles failed to win the confidence of America's allies or even that of the State Department. Senator McCarthy moderated his attacks on the department not a jot when it came under the control of his own party. In 1953 its overseas information program received his special attention. He denounced Voice of America broadcasters for quoting the works of "controversial" authors and sent Roy M. Cohn, youthful special counsel of his Committee on Governmental Operations, on a mission to Europe to ferret out subversives in the United States Information Service.

Dulles did not come to the defense of his people. Instead he seemed determined to out-McCarthy McCarthy in his zeal to get rid of "undesirables" of all sorts. He sanctioned the discharge of nearly 500 State Department employees, not one of whom was proved to have engaged in subversive activities. By making "concessions" to McCarthy, Dulles hoped to end attacks on the administration's foreign policy. The tactic failed; its only result was to undermine the morale of Foreign Service officers.

But McCarthy finally overreached himself. Early in 1954 he turned his guns on the army. After a series of charges and countercharges, he accused army officials of trying to blackmail his committee and announced a broad investigation. The resulting Army–McCarthy hearings, televised before the country, proved the senator's undoing. For weeks his dark scowl, his blind combativeness and disregard for every human value stood exposed for millions to see. After the hearings ended, the Senate, with President Eisenhower quietly applying pressure behind the scene, at last moved to censure him in December 1954. This reproof completed the destruction of his influence. Although he continued to issue statements and wild charges, the country no longer listened. In 1957 he died, victim of cirrhosis of the liver.

Asian Policy After Korea

Shortly after an armistice was finally arranged in Korea in July 1953, new trouble erupted far to the south in the former French colony of Vietnam, which had been divided into pro- and anti-communist sectors. An election was scheduled to settle the future of Vietnam in 1956, but it did not take place. Since December 1946, nationalist rebels led by the communist Ho Chi Minh had been harassing the French in Vietnam. When Communist China recognized the rebels and supplied them with arms, Truman, applying the containment policy, countered with economic and military assistance to the French. When Eisenhower succeeded to the presidency, he continued and expanded this assistance.

Early in 1954 Ho Chi Minh's troops trapped and besieged a French army in the remote stronghold of Dien Bien Phu. Faced with the loss of 20,000 soldiers, France asked the United States to commit its air force to the battle. Eisenhower, after long deliberation, refused. Since the communists were "secreted all around in the jungle," he said, "how are we, in a few air strikes, to defeat them?"

In May the garrison at Dien Bien Phu surrendered, and in July, while the United States watched from the sidelines, France, Great Britain, Russia, and China signed an agreement at Geneva dividing Vietnam along the 17th parallel. France withdrew from the area. The northern sector became the Democratic Republic of Vietnam, controlled by Ho Chi Minh; the southern remained in the hands of the emperor, Bao Dai. In 1955 Bao Dai was overthrown by Ngo Dinh Diem, who established an authoritarian but pro-Western republic. An election to settle the future of all Vietnam was scheduled for 1956.

When it seemed likely that the communists would win that election, Bao Dai was overthrown by Ngo Dinh Diem. The United States supplied the new South Vietnamese government liberally with aid. The planned election was never held. Vietnam remained divided.

Dulles responded to this diplomatic setback by establishing the Southeast Asia Treaty organization (September 1954), but only three Asian nations—the Philippine Republic, Thailand, and Pakistan—joined this alliance.*

*The other signatories were Great Britain, France, the United States, Australia, and New Zealand.

The Middle East Cauldron

Within a year, trouble erupted in the Middle East. American policy in that region, aside from the ubiquitous problem of restraining Russian expansion, was influenced by the huge oil resources—about 60 percent of the world's known reserves—and by the conflict between the new Jewish state of Israel (formerly the British mandate of Palestine) and its Arab neighbors. Although he tried to woo the Arabs, President Truman had consistently placed support for Israel before other considerations in the Middle East.

Angered by the creation of Israel, the surrounding Arab nations tried to destroy the country, but the Israelis drove them off with relative ease. With them departed nearly a million Palestinian Arabs thereby creating a desperate refugee problem in nearby countries. Truman's support of Israel and the millions of dollars contributed to the new state by American Jews produced much Arab resentment of the United States.

Dulles and Eisenhower tried to redress the balance by de-emphasizing American support of Israel. In 1952 a revolution in Egypt had overthrown the dissolute King Farouk. Colonel Gamal Abdel Nasser emerged as the strongman of Egypt. The United States promptly offered Nasser economic aid and tried to entice him into a broad Middle East security pact. But it would not sell Egypt arms; the communists would. For this reason, Nasser drifted steadily toward the communist orbit.

When Eisenhower withdrew his offer of American financial support for the giant Aswan Dam project, the key element in an Egyptian irrigation and electric power program designed to expand and modernize the country, Nasser responded by nationalizing the Suez Canal. This move galvanized the British and French; without consulting the United States, they decided to take back the canal by force. The Israelis, alarmed by repeated Arab hit-and-run raids along their borders, also decided to attack Egypt.

Events moved swiftly. Israeli armored columns crushed the Egyptian army in the Sinai Peninsula in a matter of days. France and Britain occupied Port Said, at the northern end of the canal. Nasser blocked the canal by sinking ships in the channel. In the UN, the Soviet Union and the United States introduced resolutions calling for a cease-fire. Both were vetoed by Britain and France.

Then Khrushchev threatened to send "volunteers" to Egypt and launch atomic missiles against France and Great Britain if they did not withdraw. President Eisenhower also demanded that the invaders pull out of Egypt. On November 6, only nine days after the first attack, British Prime Minister Eden announced a cease-fire. Israel withdrew its troops. The crisis subsided as rapidly as it had arisen.

The United States had won a measure of respect in the Arab countries, but at what cost! Its major allies had been humiliated. The ill-timed attack had enabled Russia to recover much of the prestige lost as a result of its brutal suppression of a Hungarian revolt which had broken out a week before the Suez fiasco. Britain and France believed that Dulles's futile attempt to win Arab friendship without abandoning Israel had placed them in a dilemma and that the secretary had behaved dishonorably or at least disingenuously in handling the Egyptian problem.

The bad feeling within the Western Alliance soon passed. When Russia seemed likely to profit from its "defense" of Egypt in the crisis, the president announced the "Eisenhower Doctrine" (January 1957), which stated that the United States was "prepared to use armed force" anywhere in the Middle East against "aggression from any country controlled by international communism."

Eisenhower and the Soviet Union

In Europe the Eisenhower and Dulles policies differed little from those of Truman. When Eisenhower announced his plan to rely more heavily on nuclear deterrents, the Europeans drew back in alarm, believing that in any atomic showdown they were sure to be destroyed. Khrushchev's talk of peaceful coexistence found many receptive ears, especially in France.

The president therefore yielded to European pressures for a diplomatic "summit" conference with the Russians (July 1955) to discuss disarmament and the reunification of West and East Germany. The meeting produced no specific agreement, but with the Russians talking of peaceful coexistence and with Eisenhower pouring martinis and projecting his famous charm, observers noted a softening of tensions that was dubbed "the spirit of Geneva." In 1956 Eisenhower was reelected, defeating Adlai Stevenson even more decisively than he had in 1952. Despite their evident satisfaction with their leader, however, the mood of the American people was sober. Hopes of pushing back the Soviet Union with clever stratagems and moral fervor were fading. America's first successful earth satellite, launched in January 1958, brought cold comfort, for it was much smaller than the earth-circling Russian *Sputnik*.

In 1957 Dulles underwent surgery for an abdominal cancer, and in April 1959 he had to resign. Only a month later he died. Eisenhower then took over much of the task of conducting foreign relations himself. Amid the tension that followed the Suez crisis, the belief persisted in many quarters that the "spirit of Geneva" could be revived if only a new summit meeting could be arranged. World opinion was insistent that the Great Powers stop making and testing nuclear weapons, for every test explosion was contaminating the atmosphere with radioactive debris that threatened the future of all life. Unresolved controversies, especially the argument over divided Germany, might erupt at any moment into a globe-shattering war.

Neither the United States nor the Soviet Union dared ignore these dangers; each, therefore, adopted a more accommodating attitude. In the summer of 1959, Vice President Richard M. Nixon visited the Soviet Union and in September Khrushchev came to America. At the end of his stay, he and President Eisenhower agreed to convene a new four-power summit conference.

The meeting never took place. On May 1, 1960, high over Sverdlovsk, an industrial center deep in the Soviet Union, an American U-2 reconnaissance plane was shot down by anti-aircraft fire. The pilot of the plane survived the crash and confessed to being a spy. When Eisenhower assumed full responsibility for the mission,

Khrushchev accused the United States of "piratical" and "cowardly" acts of aggression. The summit was cancelled.

Latin America Aroused

Events in Latin America compounded Eisenhower's difficulties. During World War II the United States, needing Latin American raw materials, had supplied its southern neighbors liberally with economic aid. In the period following victory, an era of amity and prosperity seemed assured. A hemispheric mutual-defense pact was signed at Rio de Janeiro in September 1947, and the following year the Organization of American States (OAS) came into being. In the OAS, decisions were reached by a two-thirds vote; the United States had neither a veto nor any special position.

The United States tended to neglect Latin America during the Cold War years. Economic problems plagued the region, and in most nations reactionary governments reigned. Radical Latin Americans accused the United States of supporting cliques of wealthy tyrants, and indeed, checking communism continued to receive first priority.

Eisenhower, eager to improve relations, stepped-up economic assistance. Nevertheless, he continued to support conservative regimes kept in power by bayonets.

That there was no easy solution to Latin American problems was demonstrated by events in Cuba. In 1959 a revolutionary movement headed by Dr. Fidel Castro overthrew Fulgencio Batista, one of the most noxious of the Latin American dictators. Eisenhower recognized the Castro government, but the Cuban leader soon began to criticize the United States in highly colored speeches and to seize American property in Cuba without adequate compensation. Castro entered into close relations with the Soviet Union. After he negotiated a trade agreement with the Soviet Union in February 1960, which enabled the Russians to obtain Cuban sugar at bargain rates, the United States retaliated by prohibiting the importation of Cuban sugar into America.

Khrushchev then announced that if the United States intervened in Cuba, he would defend the country with atomic weapons. "The Monroe Doctrine has outlived its time," he warned. Shortly before he left office, Eisenhower broke off diplomatic relations with Cuba.

The Politics of Civil Rights

During Eisenhower's presidency a major change occurred in the legal status of American blacks. Eisenhower had relatively little to do with this change, which was part of a broad shift in attitudes toward the rights of minorities in democracies. After 1945 the question of racial equality took on special importance because of the ideological competition with communism. Evidence of color prejudice in the United States damaged the nation's image, particularly in Asia and Africa, where the United States and the Soviet Union were competing for influence. An awareness of foreign criticism of American racial attitudes, along with resentment that almost a century after the Emancipation Proclamation they were still second-class citizens, produced a growing militancy among American blacks. At the same time, fears of communist subversion in the United States led to the repression of the rights of many whites, culminating in the excesses of McCarthyism. Both these aspects of the civil rights question divided Americans along liberal and conservative lines.

As we have seen, the World War II record of the federal government on civil rights was mixed. As early as 1940, in the Smith Act, Congress made it illegal to advocate or teach the overthrow of the government by force or to belong to an organization with this objective. The law was used in the Truman era to jail the leaders of the American Communist Party.

In 1950 Congress passed the McCarran Internal Security Act, which made it unlawful "to combine, conspire or agree with any other person to perform any act that would substantially contribute to the establishment . . . of a totalitarian dictatorship." The law required every "Communist-front organization" to register with the attorney general. Members of "front" organizations were barred from defense work and from traveling abroad. Aliens who had ever been members of any "totalitarian party" were denied admission to the United States, a foolish provision that prevented many anticommunists behind the Iron Curtain from fleeing to America; even a person who had belonged to a communist youth organization was kept out by this provision.

As for blacks, besides setting up the Committee on Civil Rights and beginning to desegregate the armed forces, Truman sought to establish a permanent Fair Employment Practices Commission. Congress, however, did not pass the necessary legislation.

Under Eisenhower, while the McCarthy hysteria reached its peak and declined, the government compiled a spotty record on civil rights. The search for subversive federal employees continued. Eisenhower did complete the formal integration of blacks in the armed forces and appointed a Civil Rights Commission, but he was temperamentally incapable of a frontal assault on the racial problem. This was done by the Supreme Court, which interjected itself into the civil rights controversy in dramatic fashion in 1954.

For some years, the Court had been gradually undermining the "separate but equal" principle laid down in *Plessy* v. *Ferguson* in 1896. First it ruled that in graduate education segregated facilities must be truly equal. In 1938 it ordered a black student admitted to the University of Missouri law school because no law school for blacks existed in the state. This decision gradually forced some southern states to admit blacks to advanced programs. In 1950, when Texas actually attempted to fit out a separate law school for a single black applicant, the Court ruled that truly equal education could not be provided under such circumstances.

In 1953 President Eisenhower appointed California's Governor Earl Warren chief justice of the United States. Convinced that the Court must take the offensive in the cause of civil rights, Warren succeeded in welding his associates into a unit on the question. In 1954 an NAACP-sponsored case, *Brown* v. *Board of Education of Topeka,* came up for decision. This case challenged the "separate but equal" doctrine at the elementary school level. Speaking for a unanimous Court, Warren reversed the *Plessy* decision. "In the field of public education, the doctrine of 'separate but equal' has no place," he declared. "Separate educational facilities are inherently unequal." The next year the Court ordered the states to proceed "with all deliberate speed" in integrating their schools.

Despite these decisions, few districts in the southern and border states tried to integrate their schools. White citizens councils dedicated to all-out opposition sprang up throughout the South. In Virginia the governor announced a plan for "massive resistance" to integration that denied state aid to local school systems that wished to desegregate. When the University of Alabama admitted a single black woman in 1956, riots broke out. University officials forced the student to withdraw and then expelled her when she complained more forcefully than they deemed proper.

President Eisenhower thought equality for blacks could not be obtained by government edict. "The fellow who tries to tell me you can do these things by force is just plain nuts," he said. But in 1957 events compelled him to act. When the school board of Little Rock, Arkansas, opened Central High School to a handful of black children, the governor called out the National Guard to prevent them from attending. Unruly crowds taunted the children and their parents.

Eisenhower could not ignore the direct flouting of federal authority. After the mayor of Little Rock informed him that his police could not control the situation he dispatched 1,000 paratroopers to Little Rock and called 10,000 National Guardsmen to federal duty. The black children then began to attend classes. A token force of soldiers was stationed at Central High for the entire school year to protect them.

Extremist resistance strengthened the determination of blacks and many northern whites to make the South comply with the desegregation decision. Besides pressing cases in the federal courts, leaders of the movement organized a voter registration drive among southern blacks. As a result, the administration introduced what became the Civil Rights Act of 1957.

Angry jeers from whites rain down on Elizabeth Eckford, one of the first black students to arrive for registration at Little Rock's Central High School in 1957. State troops turned black students away from the school until President Eisenhower overruled the state decision and called in the National Guard to enforce integration.

It authorized the attorney general to obtain injunctions to stop election officials from interfering with blacks seeking to register and vote. The law also established a Civil Rights Commission with broad investigatory powers and a Civil Rights Division in the Department of Justice. Enforcing this Civil Rights Act was another matter. A later study of a typical county in Alabama revealed that between 1957 and 1960 more than 700 blacks with high school diplomas were rejected as unqualified by white election officials when they sought to register.

The Supreme Court under Chief Justice Warren did not limit itself to protecting the rights of black people. It reinstated the "clear and present danger" principle that had been undermined in a case upholding the Smith Act ban on merely "advocating" the overthrow of the government by force. The rights of persons accused of crimes were enlarged in cases providing free legal counsel for indigent defendants, requiring the police to inform accused persons of their right to remain silent, and giving accused persons the right to have a lawyer present while being questioned by the authorities.

In *Baker* v. *Carr* (1962), *Lucas* v. *Colorado* (1964), and other decisions, the Court declared unequal representation in state and local legislative bodies unconstitutional, thus establishing the

principle known as "one man, one vote." In a different area, the Court in *Griswold* v. *Connecticut* (1965) struck down a Connecticut statute banning the use of contraceptives on the ground that it violated individuals' right of privacy.

The Election of 1960

As the end of his second term approached, Eisenhower somewhat reluctantly endorsed Vice President Nixon as the Republican candidate to succeed him. Richard Nixon had skyrocketed to national prominence by exploiting the public fear of communist subversion. "Traitors in the high councils of our government," he charged in 1950, "have made sure that the deck is stacked on the Soviet side of the diplomatic tables." In 1947 he was an obscure young congressman from California; in 1950 he won a seat in the Senate; two years later, Eisenhower chose him as his running mate.

Whether Nixon believed what he was saying at this period of his career is not easily discovered; with his "instinct for omnidirectional placation," he seemed wedded to the theory that politicians should slavishly represent their constituents' opinions rather than hold to their own views. Frequently he appeared to count noses before deciding what he thought. He projected an image of almost frantic earnestness, yet he pursued a flexible course more suggestive of calculation than sincerity.

Reporters generally had a low opinion of Nixon, and relatively few independent voters found him attractive. He was always controversial, distrusted by liberals even when he supported liberal measures. But his defense of traditional American values made him popular with concervatives.

The Democrats nominated Senator John F. Kennedy of Massachusetts, with his chief rival at the convention, Lyndon B. Johnson of Texas, the Senate majority leader, as his running mate. Kennedy was the son of a wealthy businessman and promoter who had served as ambassador to Great Britain under Franklin Roosevelt. As a PT boat commander in World War II, he was severely injured in action. In 1946 he was elected to Congress. Besides wealth, intelligence, good looks, and charm, Kennedy had the advantage of his war record and his Irish-Catholic ancestry,

the latter a particularly valuable asset in heavily Catholic Massachusetts. After three terms in the House, he moved on to the Senate in 1952 by defeating Henry Cabot Lodge, Jr.

After his landslide reelection in 1958, only Kennedy's religion seemed to limit his political future. No Catholic had ever been elected president, and the defeat of Alfred E. Smith in 1928 had convinced most students of politics (including Smith) that none ever would be elected. Nevertheless, influenced by his victories in the Wisconsin and West Virginia primaries—the latter establishing him as an effective campaigner in a predominantly Protestant region—the Democratic Convention nominated him.

Kennedy had not been a particularly liberal congressman. He was friendly with Richard Nixon and admitted frankly that he liked Senator Joseph McCarthy and thought that "he may have something" in his campaign against supposed communists in government. However, as a presidential candidate, he sought to appear more forward looking. He promised to open a "New Frontier," and accused the Republicans of

Milestones

1944	GI Bill of Rights	**1950**	North Korea invades South Korea
1945	Franklin Roosevelt dies; Harry Truman becomes president		Alger Hiss convicted of perjury
1946	Benjamin Spock, *Baby and Child Care*		Senator McCarthy charges that the State Department is riddled with communists
	Baruch plan for control of atomic energy		UN counterattack in Korea driven back by Red Chinese army
1947	Taft-Hartley Act	**1953**	John Foster Dulles institutes "New Look" foreign policy
	Truman Doctrine		Korean War armistice agreement
	"X" (Goerge Kennan), "Sources of Soviet Conduct"	**1954**	Army–McCarthy hearings
	Marshall Plan proposed		Siege of Dien Bien Phu; French withdraw from Vietnam
	Loyalty Review Board	**1956**	Suez crisis
1948–1949	Berlin airlift	**1960**	U-2 affair
1949	North Atlantic Treaty Organization (NATO) established		United States breaks diplomatic relations with Cuba

neglecting national defense and losing the Cold War. Nixon ran on the Eisenhower record, which he promised to extend in liberal directions.

A series of television debates between the candidates, observed by some 70 million viewers, helped Kennedy by enabling him to demonstrate his warmth, maturity, and mastery of the issues. Where Nixon appeared to lecture the unseen audience like an ill-at-ease schoolmaster, Kennedy seemed relaxed, thoughtful, and confident of his powers. Although both candidates laudably avoided it, the religious issue was important. His Catholicism helped Kennedy in eastern urban areas but injured him in many farm districts and throughout the West. On balance, it probably hurt him more than it helped. Nevertheless, he won. His margin of victory, 303 to 219 in the electoral college, was paper thin in the popular vote, 34,227,000 to 34,109,000. Kennedy carried Illinois by fewer than 9,000 votes out of nearly 4.8 million, and it is possible that the Democratic machine of Mayor Richard J. Daley of Chicago supplied that margin by unlawful means.

Although Kennedy was rich, white, and a member of the upper crust by any definition, his was a victory of minority groups (Jews, blacks, and blue-collar "ethnics" as well as Catholics gave him overwhelming support) over the "traditional" white Protestant majority, which went as heavily for Nixon as it had four years earlier for Eisenhower.

Supplementary Reading

A good summary of the Cold War is T. G. Paterson, **On Every Front: The Making of the Cold War*** (1979), which makes an effort to explain Soviet motives and tactics objectively. See also two books by J. L. Gaddis, **Strategies of Containment** (1982) and **The Long Peace** (1987), and, more critical of American policy, Walter La Feber, **America, Russia and the Cold War*** (1968), and Daniel Yergin, **Shattered Peace** (1977). Harry Truman's **Memoirs*** (1955–1956) contain much useful information.

Postwar domestic politics is treated in W. L. O'Neill, **Riding High*** (1986), and A. L. Hamby, **The Imperial Years** (1976) and **Beyond the New Deal: Harry S. Truman** and **American Liberalism*** (1973). Interpretive works useful for understanding the period include A. M. Schlesinger Jr., **The Vital Center*** (1949), R. E. Neustadt, **Presidential Power*** (1960), and J. M. Burns, **The Deadlock of Democracy*** (1963).

Biographical material on postwar political leaders is voluminous. On Truman, see D. R. McCoy, **The Presidency of Harry S. Truman** (1984), and R. J. Donovan, **Conflict and Crisis** (1977). S. E. Ambrose's two-volume biography, **Eisenhower** (1983, 1984), is the fullest scholarly treatment of Dwight Eisenhower.

Among many analyses and evaluations of American foreign policy, G. F. Kennan's writings stand out, both as primary sources and as interpretations. See his **Memoirs*** (1969, 1972), **Realities of American Foreign Policy*** (1954), and **Russia and the West under Lenin and Stalin*** (1961).

On Truman's foreign policy, see Donovan, **Conflict and Crisis**, and M. J. Hogan, **The Marshall Plan** (1987). W. P. Davison, **The Berlin Blockade** (1958), is also useful. On the Korean War, consult Clay Blair, **Forgotten War: America in Korea** (1988).

McCarthyism and the Hiss case are covered in David Caute, **The Great Fear** (1978), Allen Weinstein, **Purgery: The Hiss-Chambers Case** (1978), and Robert Griffith, **The Politics of Fear*** (1970).

Economic trends are considered in Herbert Stein, **The Fiscal Revolution in America*** (1969). On labor, consult Philip Taft, **Organized Labor in American History** (1964), E. L. Dayton, **Walter Reuther** (1958), and R. H. Zieger, **John L. Lewis** (1988). On agriculture, see A. J. Matusow, **Farm Policies & Politics in the Truman Years*** (1970).

Eisenhower's own view of his terms can be found in D. D. Eisenhower, **Mandate for Change*** (1963), and **Waging Peace** (1965). Herbert Parmet, **Eisenhower and the American Crusades** (1972), is a balanced account of his two administrations. See also C. C. Alexander, **Holding the Line: The Eisenhower Era** (1975).

John Foster Dulles's views are discussed in M. A. Gun, **John Foster Dulles** (1972). The diplomacy of the Eisenhower era is also discussed in R. A. Divine, **Eisenhower and the Cold War*** (1981).

For postwar constitutional issues, see P. L. Murphy, **The Constitution in Crisis Times*** (1972). Richard Kluger, **Simple Justice*** (1976), is an excellent account of the Brown case.

On Kennedy, consult H. S. Parmet, **Jack: The Struggles of John F. Kennedy** (1980), and **JFK: The Presidency of John F. Kennedy** (1983), together a fair-minded account. A. M. Schlesinger, Jr., **A Thousand Days*** (1965), and Theodore Sorensen, **Kennedy*** (1965), are rich in eyewitness detail but extremely pro-Kennedy.

*Available in paperback

CHAPTER 30

The Best of Times, the Worst of Times

John Fitzgerald Kennedy

The Cuban Crises

Kennedy's Domestic Program

Tragedy in Dallas

"We Shall Overcome"

The Great Society

War in Vietnam

Hawks and Doves

The Election of 1968

Nixon as President: "Vietnamizing" the War

The Cambodian "Incursion"

Détente

Nixon in Triumph

The Economy Under Nixon

The Watergate Break-in

More Troubles

The Oil Crisis

The Judgment: Expletive Deleted

The Meaning of Watergate

John Fitzgerald Kennedy

Right from the start of his administration, the new president projected an image of originality and imaginativeness. (He flouted convention by making his younger brother Robert F. Kennedy attorney general and when critics objected to this appointment, he responded with a quip, saying that he had "always thought it was a good thing for a young attorney to get some government experience before going out into private practice.") He had a genuinely inquiring mind. He kept up with dozens of magazines and newspapers and consumed books of all sorts voraciously. He invited leading scientists, artists, writers, and musicians to the White House; Jefferson had sought to teach Americans to value the individual regardless of status; Kennedy seemed intent on teaching the country to respect its most talented minds.

The Cuban Crises

Kennedy hoped to reverse the Truman-Eisenhower policy of backing reactionary regimes merely because they were anti-Communist. Recognizing that American economic aid could accomplish little in Latin America unless accompanied by internal reforms, he organized the Alliance for Progress, which aimed at committing the Latin Americans to land reform and economic development projects backed by the assistance of the United States. At the first sign of pro-Soviet activity in any Latin American country, however, he tended to overreact.

His most serious blunder involved Cuba. Anti-Castro exiles were eager to organize an invasion of their homeland, reasoning that the Cuban masses would rise up against Castro as soon as "democratic" forces provided a standard they could rally to. Under Eisenhower the Central Intelligence Agency had begun training some 2,000 of these men in Central America.

Kennedy was of two minds about this plan, but in the end, he authorized the attack. The exiles were given American weapons, but no planes or warships were committed to the operation. The invaders struck in April 1961, landing at the Bay of Pigs, on Cuba's southern coast. Contrary to expectations, the Cuban people failed to flock to their lines, and they were soon pinned down and forced to surrender. Since America's involvement could not be disguised, the affair exposed the country to all the criticisms that a straightforward assault would have produced without accomplishing the overthrow of Castro. Worse, it made Kennedy appear impulsive as well as unprincipled. Castro soon acknowledged that he was a Marxist and tightened his connections with the Soviet Union. For his part, Kennedy imposed an economic blockade on Cuba and he authorized a CIA attempt to assassinate Castro.

In June Kennedy met with Premier Khrushchev in Vienna. During their discussions he evidently failed to convince the Russian that he would resist pressure with determination. In August Khrushchev abruptly closed the border between East and West Berlin and erected an ugly wall of concrete blocks and barbed wire across the city to check the exodus of dissident East Germans. Resuming the testing of nuclear weapons, Khrushchev exploded a series of gigantic hydrogen bombs, one with a power 3,000 times that of the bomb that had devastated Hiroshima.

When the Soviets resumed nuclear testing, Kennedy followed suit. He expanded the American space program,* vowing that an American would land on the moon within ten years. He also called on Congress for a large increase in military spending. At the same time, he pressed forward along more constructive lines by establishing the Agency for International Development to administer American economic aid throughout the world, and the Peace Corps, an organization that mobilized American idealism and technical skills to help developing nations.

These actions had no observable effect on Soviet policy. In 1962 Khrushchev devised the boldest and most reckless challenge of the Cold War—he moved military equipment and thousands of Soviet technicians into Cuba. U-2 reconnaissance planes photographed these sites and by mid-October Kennedy had proof the sites were approaching completion.

The president faced a dreadful decision. When he confronted Soviet Foreign Minister Andrey Gromyko, the Russian insisted that only "defensive" (anti-aircraft) missiles were being installed.

Kennedy decided that he must take a strong action stand. On October 22 he went before the nation on television. The Soviet buildup was "a deliberately provocative and unjustified change in the status quo," he said. The navy would stop and search all vessels headed for Cuba and turn back any containing "offensive" weapons. Kennedy

*Russian superiority in space was gradually reduced. In April 1961 the "cosmonaut" Yuri Gagarin orbited the earth; in August another Russian circled the globe 17 times. The first American to orbit the earth, John Glenn, made his voyage in February 1962. In 1965 the United States kept a two-man Gemini craft in orbit two weeks, effecting a rendezvous between it and a second Gemini.

called on Khrushchev to dismantle the missile bases and remove from the island all weapons capable of striking the United States. Any Cuban-based nuclear attack would result, he warned, in "a full retaliatory response upon the Soviet Union."

For days, while the world held its breath, work on the missile bases continued. Then Khrushchev backed down. He withdrew the missiles and cut back his military establishment in Cuba to modest proportions. Kennedy then lifted the blockade.

Critics have argued that Kennedy overreacted to the Cuban missiles. There was no evidence that the Soviets were planning an attack and they already had missiles in Siberia capable of striking American targets. The Cuban missiles might be seen as a deterrent against a possible attack on the Soviet Union by United States missiles in Europe. By demanding their withdrawal, Kennedy risked triggering a nuclear holocaust as much as Khrushchev had. Yet he probably felt that he had no choice once the existence of the sites was known to the public. (In some respects this is the most frightening aspect of the crisis.)

Whatever Kennedy's reasoning, the missile crisis led to a lessening of Soviet-American tensions. Khrushchev agreed to the installation of a "hot line" telephone between the White House and the Kremlin so that in any future crisis leaders of the two nations could be in instant communication. The arms race continued, but in July 1963 all the powers except France and China signed a treaty banning the testing of nuclear weapons in the atmosphere.

Kennedy's Domestic Program

Kennedy had large plans for domestic reform. In the presidential campaign he had promised to "get the country moving again." The relatively slow growth of the economy in the Eisenhower years had troubled some economists. Three recessions occurred between 1953 and 1961, each marked by increases in unemployment.

During these recessions, the Eisenhower administration reacted by cutting taxes, easing credit, and expanding public works programs. However, liberal economists argued that it was not employing this economic medicine in large enough doses. In January 1963 the economist

Walter Heller convinced Kennedy that if personal and corporate income taxes were lowered, consumers would have more money to spend and corporations would invest in new facilities for producing things for them to buy. The resulting increase in economic activity would raise private and corporate incomes so much that tax revenues would rise even as the tax rate was falling.

Kennedy, however, was no Woodrow Wilson or Franklin Roosevelt when it came to bending Congress to his will. Perhaps he was too amiable, too diffident and conciliatory in his approach. A coalition of Republicans and conservative southern Democrats resisted his tax-cutting scheme and also blocked his plans for federal aid to education, for urban renewal, for a higher minimum wage, and for medical care for the aged.

The president reacted mildly, almost ruefully, when opponents in Congress blocked these proposals. He seemed to doubt at times that the cumbersome machinery of the federal government could be made to work. Pundits talked of a "deadlock of democracy" in which party discipline had crumbled and positive legislative action had become next to impossible.

Tragedy in Dallas

Although his domestic policies were making little progress, Kennedy retained his hold on public opinion. Most observers believed he would easily win a second term. Then, while visiting Dallas, Texas, on November 22, 1963, he was shot in the head by an assassin, Lee Harvey Oswald, and died almost instantly.

This senseless murder precipitated an extraordinary series of events. Oswald had fired on the president with a rifle from an upper story of a warehouse. No one saw him pull the trigger, but a mass of evidence connected him with the crime. Before he could be brought to trial, however, he was himself murdered in full view of television cameras by the owner of a Dallas nightclub, while being transferred from one place of detention to another.

This amazing incident, together with the fact that Oswald had defected to the Soviet Union in 1959 and then returned to the United States, convinced many people that some nefarious conspiracy lay at the root of the tragedy. Oswald, the argument ran, was a pawn, his murder designed to keep him from exposing the masterminds who had engineered the assassination. An investigation by a special commission headed by Chief Justice Earl Warren came to the conclusion that Oswald acted alone, yet doubts persisted in many minds.

Kennedy's election had seemed the start of a new era in American history. Instead, his assassination marked the end of an old one. The three postwar presidents had achieved, at minimum, the respect of nearly everyone. There were those

Jacqueline Kennedy and Robert F. Kennedy returning from the Arlington Cemetery on November 26, 1963, following the burial of President John F. Kennedy. Not since Lincoln's funeral had there been such an intense display of grief over the loss of a political leader.

who felt that the job was too big for Truman, others who considered Eisenhower a political amateur and Kennedy a compulsive, even reckless womanizer, and too much a showman. But their honesty and patriotism seemed beyond question. This was not to be said of all their successors.

John F. Kennedy's death made Lyndon B. Johnson president. From 1949 until his election as vice president, Johnson had been a senator and, for most of that time, Senate Democratic leader. Early on he had displayed what one adviser called an extraordinary "capacity for manipulation and seduction." He could be both heavy-handed and subtle, and also devious, domineering, peristent, and obliging. Above all, he knew what to do with political power. "Some men," he said, "want power so they can strut around to 'Hail to the Chief'. . . . I wanted it to use it."

Johnson benefited from the sympathy of the world and from the shame felt by many who had opposed Kennedy's proposals for political or selfish reasons. Sensing the public mood, he pushed Kennedy's programs with great skill and energy. Bills that had been buried in committee sailed through Congress. Early in 1964, Kennedy's tax cut was passed, and the resulting economic stimulus caused a boom of major dimensions. A few months later an expanded version of another Kennedy measure, the Civil Rights Act of 1964, became law.

"We Shall Overcome"

Kennedy's original approach to the race question had been exceedingly cautious. His lack of full commitment dismayed many who were concerned about the persistence of racial discrimination in the country. But during and after the war, like a glacier, slowly but with massive force, a demand for change had developed in the South. Its roots lay in southern industrialization; in the vast wartime expenditures of the federal government on aircraft factories and army bases in the region; in the impact of the GI Bill on southern colleges and universities; in the gradual development of a southern black middle class.

The change first came to national attention in the tightly segregated city of Montgomery, Alabama. On the evening of Friday, December 1, 1955, Rosa Parks boarded a bus on her way home from her job as a seamstress at the Montgomery Fair department store. She dutifully took a seat toward the rear as law and custom required. After white workers and shoppers had filled the forward section, the driver ordered her to give up her place. Parks, who was also secretary of the Montgomery NAACP chapter, refused. She had decided, she later recalled, "that I would have to know once and for all what rights I had."

Rosa Parks was arrested. The blacks of Montgomery then organized a boycott. The boycott was a success. The black people of Montgomery, writes Taylor Branch in his stirring account, *Parting the Waters,* "were turning the City Bus Lines into a ghost fleet."

Most Montgomery blacks could not afford to miss even one day's wages, and getting to work was difficult. Black-owned taxis reduced their rates and when the city declared this illegal, car pools were organized. But few blacks owned cars; there were never more than 350 available to carry about 10,000 people back and forth to their jobs. Nevertheless, the boycott went on.

A young clergyman, Martin Luther King, Jr., a gifted speaker who was emerging as a leader of the boycott, became an national celebrity; money poured in from all over the country. Finally, after more than a year, the Supreme Court ruled that the Montgomery segregation law was unconstitutional. Montgomery had to desegregate its transportation system.

This success had encouraged blacks elsewhere in the South to band together against the caste system. A new organization, the Southern Christian Leadership Conference (SCLC), headed by King, moved to the forefront of the civil rights movement. Other organizations joined the struggle, notably the Congress of Racial Equality (CORE), which had been founded in 1942.

In February 1960 four black students in Greensboro, North Carolina, sat down at a lunch counter in a Woolworth five-and-ten and refused to leave when they were denied service. Their "sit-in" sparked a national movement; students in dozens of other southern towns and cities copied the Greensboro blacks' example.

Then in May 1961 black and white foes of segregation organized a "freedom ride" to test the effectiveness of federal regulations prohibiting

On August 28, 1963, Dr. Martin Luther King, Jr., told the crowd of demonstrators gathered in front of the Lincoln Memorial in Washington, D.C., of his dream of an end to racial discrimination and inequality.

discrimination in interstate transportation. Boarding buses in Washington, they traveled across the South, heading for New Orleans. In Alabama they ran into bad trouble: At Anniston racists set fire to their bus; in Birmingham they were assaulted by a mob. But violence could not stop the freedom riders. Other groups descended on the South, many deliberately seeking arrest in order to test local segregation ordinances in the courts. Repeatedly these actions resulted in the breaking down of legal racial barriers.

Integrationists like Martin Luther King attracted an enormous following, but some blacks, proud of their race and contemptuous of white prejudices, were urging their fellows to reject "American" society and all it stood for. Black nationalism became a potent force. The followers of Elijah Muhammad, leader of the Black Muslim movement, disliked whites so intensely that they demanded that a part of the United States be set aside for the exclusive use of blacks. The Muslims called Christianity "a white man's religion." They urged their followers to be industrious, thrifty, and abstemious—and to view all whites with suspicion and hatred.

"This white government has ruled us and given us plenty of hell," Elijah Muhammad said.

Another important Black Muslim, Malcolm X, put it this way: "For the white man to ask the black man if he hates him is just like the rapist asking the raped, or the wolf asking the sheep, 'Do you hate me?'"

Pushed by all these developments, President Kennedy reluctantly began to change his policy. Although his administration gave lip service to desegregation, when confrontations arose the president hesitated, arguing that it was up to state officials to enforce the law. Ordinary black southerners (even schoolchildren) became increasingly impatient. In the face of brutal repression by local police, many adopted Martin Luther King's tactic of nonviolent protest. After leading a series of demonstrations in Birmingham, Alabama, in 1963, King was thrown in jail. When local white clergymen urged black leaders to cease their "untimely" protests, which (the clergymen claimed) "incite hatred and violence," King wrote his now-famous "Letter from Birmingham Jail."

When you have seen hate-filled policemen curse, kick, brutalize and even kill your black brothers and sisters with impunity; . . . when you take a cross-country drive and find it necessary to sleep night after night in the uncomfortable corners of your automobile because no motel will accept you; when you are humiliated day in and day out by nagging signs reading "white" and "colored": . . . then you will understand why we find it so difficult to wait.

The brutal repression of the Birmingham demonstrations brought a flood of recruits and money to the protesters' cause. Finally Kennedy gave his support to a comprehensive new civil rights bill that made racial discrimination in hotels, restaurants, and other places of public accommodation illegal.

When this bill ran into stiff opposition in Congress, blacks organized a demonstration in Washington, attended by 200,000 people. At this gathering King delivered his "I have a dream" address, looking forward to a time when racial prejudice no longer existed and people of all religions and colors could join hands and say, "Free at last! Free at last!" Kennedy had sympathized with the purpose of the Washington gathering, but he feared it would make passage of the Civil Rights Bill more difficult rather than easier. As in other areas, he was not a forceful advocate of his own proposals.

The Great Society

As finally passed, the new Civil Rights Act outlawed discrimination against blacks, and also against women. It broke down the last legal barriers to black voting in the southern states and banned formal racial segregation of all sorts. Johnson's success in steering this and other Kennedy measures through Congress convinced him that he could be a reformer in the tradition of Franklin Roosevelt. He declared war on poverty and set out to create a "Great Society" in which poverty no longer existed.

During the New Deal, Franklin Roosevelt was accused of exaggeration when he said that one-third of the nation was "ill-housed, ill-clad, ill-nourished." In fact, Roosevelt had underestimated the extent of poverty when he made that statement in 1937. Wartime economic growth reduced the percentage of poor people in the country substantially, but in 1960 between 20 and 25 percent of all American families—about 40 million persons— were living below the poverty line, a government standard of minimum subsistence based on income and family size.

That so many millions could be poor in an "affluent" society was deplorable but not difficult to explain. There were in the United States entire regions, the best known being the Appalachian area, that had been by-passed by economic development. More specific to the postwar situation was the fact that technological advances, while raising living standards, also raised job requirements. A strong back and a willingness to work no longer guaranteed that the possessor could earn a decent living. Educated workers with special skills could easily find well-paid jobs. Persons who had no special skills or who were poorly educated could often find nothing.

Certain less obvious influences were at work too. Poverty tends to be more prevalent among the old and the young than among those in the prime of life; in the postwar decades these two groups were growing more rapidly than any other. Social Security payments amounted to less than the elderly needed to maintain themselves decently, and some of the poorest workers, such as agricultural laborers, were not covered by the system at all. Unemployment was twice as high among youths in their late teens as in the nation as a whole and far higher among young blacks than young whites.

Poverty exacted a heavy price, both from its victims and from society. Statistics reflected the relationship between low income and bad health. Only about 4 percent of people from middle-income families were chronically ill, whereas more than 16 percent of those with less than $2,000 were so afflicted. Mental illness varied inversely with income, as did alcoholism, drug addiction, and crime.

Johnson's war on poverty had two objectives: to give poor people a chance to improve themselves, and to provide them with direct assistance. The first took the form of the Economic Opportunity Act of 1964. This law created a mélange of programs, among them a Job Corps similar to the New Deal Civilian Conservation Corps; a community action program to finance local efforts; an educational program for small children; a work-study program for college students; and a system for training the unskilled unemployed and for lending money to small businessmen in poor areas. The Economic Opportunity Act combined the progressive concept of the welfare state with the conservative idea of individual responsibility. The government would support the weak and disadvantaged by giving them a fair chance to make it on their own.

Buttressed by this and other legislative triumphs, Johnson sought election as president in his own right in 1964. He achieved this ambition in unparalleled fashion. His championing of civil rights won him the almost unanimous support of blacks; his tax policy attracted the well-to-do and the business interests; his war on poverty held the allegiance of labor and other elements traditionally Democratic. His southern antecedents counterbalanced his liberalism on the race question in the eyes of many white southerners.

The Republicans played into his hands by nominating a conservative, Senator Barry M. Goldwater of Arizona. A large majority of the voters found Goldwater out of date on economic questions and dangerously aggressive on foreign affairs. During the campaign, Democrats told a joke that went something like this:

Goldwater is president. An aide rushes into his office.

AIDE: Mr. President, the Russians have just launched an all-out nuclear attack on us. Their missiles will strike in 15 minutes. What shall we do?

GOLDWATER: Have all the wagons form a circle.

In November Johnson won a sweeping victory, collecting over 61 percent of the popular vote and carrying all the country except Goldwater's Arizona and five states in the Deep South. Quickly he pressed ahead with his Great Society program. In January 1965 he proposed a compulsory hospital insurance system for persons over the age of 65. As amended by Congress, this system, known as Medicare, combined hospital insurance for retired people (funded by Social Security taxes) with a voluntary plan to cover doctors' bills (paid for in part by the government). The law also provided for grants to the states to help pay the medical expenses of poor people below the retirement age of 65. This part of the system was called Medicaid.

Next Congress passed the Elementary and Secondary Education Act. This measure supplied funds to improve the education of poor children, the theory being that children from city slums and impoverished rural areas tended to be "educationally deprived" and thus in need of extra help. Related to the Education Act was a program for poor preschool children known as Head Start. Besides preparing young children for elementary school, this program contributed incidentally to improving their health by providing medical examinations and good meals.

Other laws passed at Johnson's urging in 1965 and 1966 dealt with support for the arts and for scientific research, highway safety, crime control, slum clearance, clean air, and the preservation of historic sites. Of special siginicance was the Immigration Act of 1965, which did away with the national origins system of admitting newcomers. Instead, priorities were based on such things as skill and the need for political asylum.

The Great Society program was one of the most remarkable outpourings of legislation in American history. The results, however, were mixed. Head Start and a related program to help students in secondary schools prepare for college were unqualified successes; the 1965 Education Act proved a disappointment; and although Medicare and Medicaid provided good medical treatment for millions of people, patients no longer paid most of the bills, and doctors, hospitals, and drug companies were therefore able to raise fees and prices without fear of losing business. The Job Corps, which was designed to help poor people get better-paying jobs by providing them with vocational training, had no measurable effect on the unemployment rate. On balance, the achievements of the Great Society were far below what President Johnson had promised and his supporters had expected.

The same, of course, can be said of most ambitious reform programs—of Reconstruction, of the Progressive movement, and certainly of the New Deal. Johnson tried to accomplish too many things too quickly. He relied too heavily on his mastery of the techniques of political manipulation. Perhaps he was carried away by his good fortune—that he would ever become president had seemed most unlikely after he failed to win the nomination in 1960. He seized his unexpected opportunity to make history too avidly. Without the crisis atmosphere that had appeared to justify hasty experimentation during the New Deal years, the public judged the results of the Great Society and the president who had shaped it skeptically.

War in Vietnam

In the fall of 1967, the limitations of the Great Society were not yet obvious. Johnson seemed to have every intention of running for a second full term. Whether he would be reelected was not clear, but that any Democrat could prevent this shrewd and powerful politician from being nominated seemed out of the question. Nevertheless, within a few months opposition to him had become so bitter that he withdrew as a candidate for renomination. The cause of this opposition was his handling of a conflict on the other side of the world—a war in the former French colony of Vietnam.

The conflict in Vietnam first came to American attention in 1954 when rebels led by the communist Ho Chi Minh trapped and beseiged a French army in the remote stronghold of Dien Bien Phu. Faced with the loss of 20,000 soldiers, France asked the United States to commit its air force to the battle. President Eisenhower refused, and in May the French garrison at Dien Bien Phu surrendered. Then France, Great Britain, the Soviet Union, and China signed an agreement dividing Vietnam in two. France withdrew from the entire area. The northern sector became the Democratic Republic of Vietnam, controlled by Ho Chi Minh. Ngo Dinh Diem, a conservative anti-Communist, became president of South Vietnam.

President Eisenhower sent a handful of American military "advisers" to South Vietnam to train a South Vietnamese army. As time passed, more American aid and "advice" were dispatched in a futile effort to establish a stable government. Pro-Communist forces called Vietcong soon controlled large sections of the country, some almost within sight of the capital city of Saigon.

Gradually the Vietcong, drawing supplies from North Vietnam and indirectly from China and the Soviet Union, increased in strength. In response, more American money and more military advisers were sent to bolster Ngo Dinh Diem's regime. By the end of 1961, there were 3,200 American military men in the country; by late 1963, the American military presence had risen to more than 16,000. Although no so-called combat troops were involved, 120 American soldiers had been killed.

Kennedy said he intended to cut back on the size of the American military in Vietnam. Whether he would have done so had he lived is a matter of debate among historians. In any case, shortly before he was killed, a group of South Vietnamese generals assassinated Diem and took over the government. The new regime, however, proved equally unable to defeat the Vietcong.

President Johnson continued the increasing involvement of American forces in Vietnam. In the summer of 1964, after claiming that North Vietnamese gunboats had fired on American destroyers in the Gulf of Tonkin, he demanded, and in an air of crisis obtained, an authorization from Congress to "repel any armed attack against the forces of the United States and to prevent further aggression."

With this blank check, and buttressed by his sweeping defeat of Goldwater in the 1964 presidential election, Johnson sent *combat* troops to South Vietnam and ordered air attacks against targets in both South and North Vietnam.

At first the American ground troops were supposed to be merely teachers and advisers of the South Vietnamese army. Then they were said to be there to defend air bases, with the understanding that they would return fire if they were attacked. Next came word that the troops were being used to assist South Vietnamese units when they came under enemy fire. In fact, the Americans were soon attacking the enemy directly, mounting "search and destroy missions" aimed at clearing the foe from villages and entire sections of the country.

At the end of 1965, 184,000 Americans were in the field; a year later, 385,000; after another year, 485,000. By the middle of 1968, the number exceeded 538,000. Each increase was met by corresponding increases from the other side. The United States was engaged in a full-scale war, one that Congress never declared.

Hawks and Doves

From the beginning the war divided the American people sharply. Defenders of the president's policy, who were called hawks, emphasized the nation's moral responsibility to resist aggression and what President Eisenhower had called the "domino" theory, which predicted that if the communists were allowed to "take over" one country, they would soon take its neighbors, then their neighbors, and so on until the entire world had been conquered. The United States was not an aggressor in Vietnam, the hawks insisted.

American opponents of the war, called doves, argued that the struggle between the South Vietnamese government and the Vietcong was a civil war in which Americans should not meddle. They stressed the repressive, undemocratic character

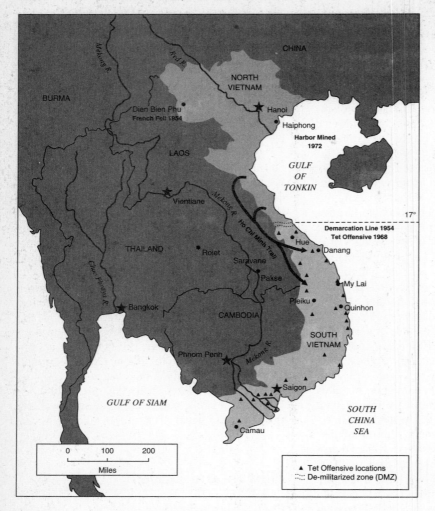

CHINA

NORTH
VIETNAM

BURMA

Mekong R.

Red R.

Dien Bien Phu
French Fell 1954

★ Hanoi

● Haiphong

Harbor Mined
1972

LAOS

*GULF
OF
TONKIN*

★ Vientiane

Mekong R.

Ho Chi Minh Trail

17°

Demarcation Line 1954
Tet Offensive 1968

THAILAND

● Roiet

Saravane

Pakse

Hue ●
▲ ● Danang

● My Lai

Chao Phraya R.

★ Bangkok

CAMBODIA

Pleiku ●

● Quinhon

SOUTH
VIETNAM

★ Phnom Penh

Mekong R.

▲ ● Saigon

GULF OF SIAM

*SOUTH
CHINA
SEA*

● Camau

| 0 | 100 | 200 |
Miles

▲ Tet Offensive locations
⋮⋮⋮⋮ De-militarized zone (DMZ)

*Southeast Asia,
1954–1975*

of the Diem regime and of those that followed as proof that the war was not a contest between democracy and communism. They objected to the massive aerial bombings (more explosives were dropped on Vietnam between 1964 and 1968 than on Germany and Japan combined in World War II), to the use of napalm and other chemical weapons such as the defoliants that were sprayed on forests and crops and which wreaked havoc among noncombatants, and to the killing of civilians by American troops. And they deplored the heavy loss of American life—over 40,000 dead by 1970—and the enormous cost in money.

Because so many people objected to the war, Johnson refused to ask Congress to raise taxes to pay for it. The resulting deficits forced the gov-

ernment to borrow huge sums, which caused interest rates to soar, adding to the upward pressure on prices.

Although Johnson's financial policies were shortsighted if not outrightly irresponsible, and although his statements about the war were often lacking in candor, he and his advisers believed they were defending freedom and democracy. "If I got out of Vietnam," the President said, "I'd be doing exactly what [Neville] Chamberlain did in World War II. I'd be giving a big fat reward for aggression."

What became increasingly clear as time passed was that military victory was impossible. Yet American leaders were extraordinarily slow to grasp this fact. Repeatedly they advised the president that one more escalation would break the enemy's will to resist. The smug arrogance bred by America's brief postwar monopoly of nuclear weapons persisted in some quarters long after the monopoly had been lost. This "superpower mentality," the belief that the United States was destined to be a kind of world policeman, was the cause of much future trouble.

Kennedy's authorization of the Bay of Pigs fiasco was an example of this, but as late as 1965, McGeorge Bundy, President Johnson's special assistant for national security affairs, apparently told an interviewer that "the United States was the locomotive at the head of mankind, and the rest of the world the caboose." And like the proverbial donkey plodding after the carrot on the stick, Johnson repeatedly followed the advice of hawks like Bundy.

The Election of 1968

Gradually the doves increased in number. Then, in November 1967, Senator Eugene McCarthy of Minnesota announced that he was a candidate for the 1968 Democratic presidential nomination. Opposition to the war was his issue.

Preventing Johnson from getting the Democratic nomination in 1968 seemed on the surface impossible. Aside from the difficulty of defeating a "reigning" president, there were the solid domestic achievements of Johnson's Great Society program: Medicare, expanded federal funding of primary and secondary education and public housing, and the Civil Rights Act of 1965. McCarthy took his chances of being nominated so lightly that he did not trouble to set up a real organization. He entered the campaign only because he believed that someone must step forward to put the Vietnam question before the voters.

Suddenly, early in 1968, North Vietnam and Vietcong forces launched a general offensive to correspond with their Lunar New Year (Tet). Striking 39 of the 44 provincial capitals, many other towns and cities, and every American base, they caused chaos throughout South Vietnam. They held Hue, the old capital of the country, for weeks. To root them out of Saigon, the Americans had to level large sections of the city. Elsewhere the destruction was total, an irony highlighted by the remark of an American officer after the recapture of the village of Ben Tre: "It became necessary to destroy the town to save it."

Tet cost North Vietnam and the Vietcong heavily, but the psychological impact of the offensive in South Vietnam and in the United States made it a clear victory for the communists. When the American commander in Vietnam, General William C. Westmoreland, described Tet as a communist defeat and when it came out that the administration was considering sending an additional 206,000 troops to South Vietnam, McCarthy, who was campaigning in the New Hampshire primary, became a formidable figure. Thousands of students and other volunteers flocked to the state to ring doorbells in his behalf. On election day he polled 42 percent of the Democratic vote.

The political situation was monumentally confused. Many New Hampshire voters had supported McCarthy because they believed that Johnson was not prosecuting the war vigorously enough and saw voting for another person as a way to rebuke him. After the primary, former attorney general Robert F. Kennedy, brother of the slain president, entered the race. Had Kennedy done so earlier, McCarthy might have withdrawn. After New Hampshire, McCarthy understandably decided to remain in the contest.

Confronting this confusion, President Johnson withdrew from the race. Vice President Hubert H. Humphrey then announced his candidacy, though not until it was too late for him to run in the primaries. Kennedy carried the primaries in Indiana and Nebraska. McCarthy won in Wisconsin and Oregon. In the climactic contest in California, Kennedy won by a small margin. However, immediately after his victory speech in a Los Angeles hotel, he was assassinated by Sirhan Sirhan, an Arab nationalist who had been incensed by Kennedy's support of Israel. In effect, Kennedy's death assured the nomination of Humphrey; most professional politicians distrusted McCarthy, who was rather diffident and aloof for a politician.

The contest for the Republican nomination was far less dramatic, though its outcome, the nomination of Richard M. Nixon, would have been hard to predict a few years earlier. After his defeat in the California gubernatorial election of 1962, Nixon joined a prominent New York law firm. He remained active in Republican affairs, making countless speeches and attending political meetings throughout the country. He announced his candidacy in February 1968, swept the Republican primaries, and won an easy first-ballot victory at the Republican National Convention.

Nixon then astounded the country and dismayed liberals by choosing Governor Spiro T. Agnew of Maryland as his running mate. Agnew was a political unknown outside Maryland, but he had spoken harshly about black radicalism. Nixon chose him primarily to attract southern votes. Placating the South seemed necessary because Governor George C. Wallace of Alabama was making a determined bid to win enough electoral votes for his American Independent Party to prevent any candidate's obtaining a majority. Wallace was flagrantly antiblack and sure to attract substantial southern and conservative support.

This Republican strategy disturbed liberals and heightened the tension surrounding the Democratic Convention, which met in Chicago in late August. Humphrey delegates controlled the convention. The vice president had a solid liberal record on domestic issues, but he had supported Johnson's Vietnam policy with equal solidity. Those who could not stomach the Nixon-Agnew ticket and who opposed the war faced a difficult choice. Hundreds of radicals and young activists descended on Chicago to put pressure on the delegates to repudiate the Johnson Vietnam policy.

In the tense atmosphere that resulted, the party hierarchy overreacted. The mayor of Chicago, Richard J. Daley, an old-fashioned political boss, ringed the convention with barricades and policemen to protect it from disruption. Inside the building, administration forces easily nominated Humphrey and adopted a war plank satisfactory to Johnson. Outside, the police, provoked by the abusive language and violent behavior of radical demonstrators, tore into the protesters, brutally beating dozens while millions watched on television in fascinated horror.

At first the mayhem at Chicago seemed to benefit Nixon. He campaigned at a deliberate, dignified pace, making relatively few public appearances, relying instead on carefully arranged television interviews and taped commercials prepared by an advertising agency. He stressed firm enforcement of the law, and his desire "to bring us together." Agnew, however, assaulted Humphrey

and left-wing dissident groups in a series of blunt, coarse speeches. Critics, remembering Nixon's political style in the heyday of Joseph McCarthy, called Agnew "Nixon's Nixon."

The Democratic campaign was badly organized. Humphrey seemed far behind in the early stages. Shortly before election day, President Johnson helped him by suspending air attacks on North Vietnam, and in the long run the Republican strategy helped too. Black voters and the urban poor had no practical choice but to vote Democratic. Gradually, Humphrey gained ground, and on election day the popular vote was close: Nixon slightly less than 31.8 million votes, Humphrey nearly 31.3 million. Nixon's electoral college margin, however, was substantial—301 to 191. The remaining 46 electoral votes went to Wallace. Despite Nixon's triumph, the Democrats retained control of both houses of Congress.

Nixon as President: "Vietnamizing" the War

When he took office in January 1969, Richard Nixon projected an image of calm and deliberate statesmanship; he introduced no startling changes, proposed no important new legislation. Indeed, he accepted more or less uncritically the New Deal approach to managing the economy. He considered the solution of the Vietnam problem his chief task. During the 1968 campaign, he suggested no policy very different from what Johnson was doing, though he insisted he would end the war on "honorable" terms if elected.

In office, Nixon proposed a phased withdrawal of all non–South Vietnamese troops, to be followed by an internationally supervised election in South Vietnam. The North Vietnamese rejected this scheme and insisted that the United States withdraw its forces unconditionally. Their intransigence left the president in a difficult position. He could not compel the foe to negotiate meaningfully, yet every passing day added to the strength of antiwar sentiment, which, as it expressed itself in ever more emphatic terms, in turn led to deeper divisions in the country.

The president responded to the dilemma by trying to build up the South Vietnamese armed forces so that American troops could pull out without the communists overrunning South Vietnam. Soon South Vietnam had the fourth-largest air force in the world. The trouble with this strategy (called Vietnamization) was that for 15 years the United States had been employing it without success. The South Vietnamese troops had seldom displayed much enthusiasm for the kind of tough jungle fighting at which the North Vietnamese and the Vietcong excelled. Nevertheless, efforts at Vietnamization were stepped up, and in June 1969 Nixon announced that he would soon reduce the number of American soldiers in Vietnam by 25,000. In September he promised that an additional 35,000 men would be withdrawn by mid-December.

These steps did not quiet American protesters. On October 15 an antiwar demonstration, Vietnam Moratorium Day, organized by students, produced an unprecedented outpouring all over the country. This massive display produced one of Vice President Agnew's most notorious blasts of adjectival invective: He said that the moratorium was an example of "national masochism" led by "an effete corps of impudent snobs who characterize themselves as intellectuals."

A second Moratorium Day brought a crowd estimated at 250,000 to Washington, but the president could not be influenced by protests. On November 3 he defended his policy in a televised speech and announced that he planned to remove all American ground forces from Vietnam. The next day, reporting a flood of telegrams and calls supporting his position, he declared that a "silent majority" of the American people approved his course.

For a season, events appeared to vindicate Nixon's position. Troop withdrawals continued in an orderly fashion. A new lottery system for drafting men for military duty eliminated some of the inequities in the selective service law. But the war continued. Early in 1970 reports that in 1968 an American unit had massacred civilians, including dozens of women and children, in a Vietnamese hamlet known as Mylai, revived the controversy over the purposes of the war and its corrosive effects on those who were fighting it. The American people, it seemed, were being torn apart by the war: one from another according to each one's interpretation of events, many within themselves as they tried to balance the war's horrors against their pride, their detestation of communism, and

their unwillingness to turn their backs on their elected leader.

Nixon's most implacable enemy could find no reason to think the president wished the war to go on. Its human, economic, and social costs could only vex his days and threaten his future reputation. When he reduced the level of the fighting, the communists merely waited for further reductions. When he raised it, many of his own people denounced him. If he pulled out of Vietnam entirely, other Americans would be outraged.

The Cambodian "Incursion"

Late in April 1970, Nixon announced that Vietnamization was proceeding more rapidly than he had hoped, that communist power was weakening, and that within a year another 150,000 American soldiers would be extracted from Vietnam. A week later he announced that military intelligence had indicated that the enemy was consolidating its "sanctuaries" in neutral Cambodia and that he was therefore dispatching thousands of American troops to destroy these bases.*

He was escalating (dread word) the war. He even resumed the bombing of targets in North Vietnam. "Let's go blow hell out of them," he told the Joint Chiefs of Staff.

To foes of the war, Nixon's decision seemed appallingly unwise. The contradictions between his confident statements about Vietnamization and his alarmist description of powerful enemy forces poised like a dagger 30-odd miles from Saigon did not seem the product of a reasoning mind. His failure to consult congressional leaders or many of his personal advisers before drastically altering his policy, the critics claimed, was unconstitutional and irresponsible. His insensitive response to the avalanche of criticism that descended on him further disturbed observers.

Students took the lead in opposing the invasion of Cambodia. Young people had been prominent in the opposition to the war from early in the conflict. Some objected to war in principle. Many more believed that this particular war was wrong

---

*William Shawcross has pointed out in his book, *Side-Show*, that American planes had been bombing Cambodia for some time, but this fact was not known to the public (or to Congress) until 1973.

because it was being fought against a small country on the other side of the globe where America's vital interests did not seem to be threatened. As the war dragged on and casualties mounted, student opposition to the draft became intense. For some the reason was obvious—they did not want to be drafted. Others (including many of the above) objected because the universal military service required was anything but universal. Thousands of students avoided the draft simply by remaining in college; poor and disadvantaged young men did most of the fighting.

Nixon's shocking announcement triggered many campus demonstrations. One college where feeling ran high was Kent State University in Ohio. For several days students there clashed with local police; they broke windows and caused other damage to property. When the governor of Ohio called out the National Guard, angry students showered the soldiers with stones. During a noontime protest on May 4, the guardsmen, who were poorly trained in crowd control, suddenly opened fire. Four students were killed, two of them women who were merely passing by on their way to class.

While the nation reeled from this shock, two black students at Jackson State University were killed by Mississippi state policemen. A wave of student strikes followed, closing down hundreds of colleges, including many that had seen no previous unrest.

Nixon pulled American ground troops out of Cambodia quickly, but he did not change his Vietnam policy, and in fact Cambodia stiffened his determination. The balance of forces remained in uneasy equilibrium through 1971.

Late in March 1972, the North Vietnamese again mounted a series of assaults throughout South Vietnam. The president responded with heavier bombing, and he ordered the approaches to Haiphong and other northern ports sown with mines to cut off the communists' supplies.

Détente

Meanwhile, Nixon and his principal foreign policy adviser, Henry Kissinger, devised a bold and (even his critics admitted it) ingenious diplomatic offensive. Abandoning a lifetime of treating communism as a single worldwide conspiracy aimed at destroying capitalism, he sent Kissinger to China and the Soviet Union to arrange summit meetings with the communist leaders. In February 1972 Nixon and Kissinger flew to Beijing to consult with Chinese officials. They agreed to support the admission of China to the United Nations and to develop economic and cultural exchanges with the Chinese. Although these results appeared small, Nixon's visit, ending more than 20 years of adamant refusal by the American government to accept the reality of the Chinese revolution, marked a dramatic reversal of policy; as such it was hailed in the United States and elsewhere in the world.

In May Nixon and Kissinger flew to Moscow. This trip also produced striking results. A Strategic Arms Limitation Treaty (SALT) was the main concrete gain. Nixon also agreed to permit large sales of American grain to the Soviets.

Nixon and Kissinger called the new policy détente, a French term meaning the relaxation of tensions between governments. Détente lowered the cost of containment for the United States because it meant being more accommodating, which would reduce conflict. SALT did not end the production of atomic weapons, but any check on American and Soviet arms production was encouraging.

That both China and the Soviet Union had been willing to work for improved relations with the United States before America withdrew from Vietnam was also significant. This fact, plus the failure of their offensive to overwhelm South Vietnam, led the North Vietnamese to make diplomatic concessions in the interest of getting the United States out of the war. By October the draft of a settlement calling for a cease-fire in place, the return of American prisoners of war, and the withdrawal of United States forces from Vietnam had been hammered out. Kissinger then announced that peace was "at hand."

Nixon in Triumph

A few days after Kissinger's announcement, President Nixon was reelected, defeating the Democratic candidate, Senator George McGovern of South Dakota, in a landslide—521 electoral votes to 17.

President and Mrs. Nixon dining with Chinese officials in Beijing in February 1972. Even Nixon's harshest critics conceded that his initiative in reopening United States–China relations was a diplomatic master stroke.

McGovern's campaign had been hampered by divisions within the Democratic Party, by his tendency to advance poorly thought out schemes, and by the discovery, shortly after the nominating convention, that his running mate, Senator Thomas Eagleton of Missouri, had in the past undergone electric shock treatments following serious psychological difficulties. After some backing and filling, which left many voters with the impression that he was indecisive, McGovern forced Eagleton to withdraw. Sargent Shriver, former head of the Peace Corps, took Eagleton's place on the ticket. The affair hurt McGovern badly.

Nixon's triumph was so convincing that he interpreted it, understandably, as an indication that the people approved of everything for which he stood. He had won over hundreds of thousands of normally Democratic voters. The "solid South" was now solidly Republican. Nixon's "southern strategy" of reducing the pressure for school desegregation also appealed to northern blue-collar

workers. Many people smarting from the repeated setbacks the country had experienced in Vietnam and resentful of what they considered the unpatriotic tactics of the doves, also approved of Nixon's refusal to pull out of Vietnam.

Suddenly Nixon loomed as one of the most powerful and successful presidents in American history. His bold attack on inflation, even his harsh Vietnamese policy suggested decisiveness and self-confidence, qualities he had often seemed to lack. His willingness to negotiate with the communist nations indicated a new flexibility and reasonableness. His landslide victory appeared to demonstrate that the people approved his way of tackling the major problems of the times.

His first reaction was to try to extract more favorable terms from the Vietnamese communists. Announcing that they were not bargaining in good faith over the remaining details of the peace treaty, he resumed the bombing of North Vietnam in December 1972, this time sending the mighty

B-52s directly over Hanoi and other cities. The attacks caused much destruction, but their effectiveness as a means of forcing concessions from the North Vietnamese was at best debatable, and they led for the first time to the loss of large numbers of the big strategic bombers.

Nevertheless, both sides had much to gain from ending the war. In January 1973 an agreement was finally reached. The North Vietnamese retained control of large sections of the South, and they agreed to release American prisoners of war within 60 days. When this was accomplished, the last American troops were pulled out of Vietnam. More than 57,000 Americans had died in the long war, and over 300,000 more had been wounded. The cost had reached $150 billion.

The Economy Under Nixon

When Nixon became president in 1969, the major economic problem facing him was inflation. It was caused primarily by the heavy military expenditures and "easy money" policies of the Johnson administration. Nixon cut federal spending and balanced the 1969 budget, while the Federal Reserve Board forced up interest rates in order to slow the expansion of the money supply. When prices continued to rise, there was mounting uneasiness. Labor unions demanded large wage increases. In 1970 Congress passed a law giving the president power to regulate prices and wages.

Nixon had opposed this legislation, but in the summer of 1971 he changed his mind and announced a 90-day price and wage freeze. Then he set up a Pay Board and a Price Commission with authority to limit wage and price increases when the freeze ended. These controls did not check inflation completely—and they angered union leaders, who felt that labor was being shortchanged. But they did slow the upward spiral. A devaluation of the dollar in December 1971 also helped the economy by making American products more competitive in foreign markets.

In handling other domestic issues, the president was less firm. He advocated shifting the burden of welfare payments to the federal government and equalizing such payments in all the states, and he came out for a "minimum income" for poor families. These measures got nowhere in Congress, despite his "southern strategy" of seeking the support of conservative southern Democrats by appointing strict constructionist judges to the federal courts.

When Chief Justice Earl Warren retired from the Court in June 1969, Nixon replaced him with a conservative judge, Warren E. Burger. But when he sought to fill the next vacancy on the Court with another conservative, the Senate rejected two of his nominees, both southern judges. The angry president then declared that "no southern conservative" could run the "liberal" Senate gauntlet successfully. To prevent the Senate from proving him wrong he nominated a liberal, Harry A. Blackmun of Minnesota, who won the unanimous approval of the Senate. Although the Burger court turned out to be less liberal than the Warren court, it was far from being as conservative as Nixon apparently wanted.

After his triumphant reelection in 1972 and the withdrawal of the last American troops from Vietnam, Nixon was determined to change the direction in which the nation had been moving for decades. He sought on the one hand to strengthen the power of the presidency vis-à-vis Congress and on the other to decentralize administration by encouraging state and local management of government programs. People should be more self-reliant, he said. Overconcern for the interests of blacks and other minorities must end. Criminals should be punished "without pity."

These aims brought Nixon into conflict with liberal congressmen of both parties, with the leaders of minority groups, and with persons concerned about the increasing power of the executive. The conflict came to a head over the president's anti-inflation policy. After his second inauguration, he ended price and wage controls and substituted voluntary "restraints." This approach did not work. Prices soared; it was the most rapid inflation since the Korean War. In an effort to check the rise, Nixon set a rigid limit on federal expenditures, cutting or abolishing many social welfare programs, and reducing federal grants in support of science and education. He even impounded (refused to spend) funds already appropriated by Congress for purposes he disapproved of.

When the Democratic Congress failed to override vetoes of bills challenging his policy, it appeared that Nixon was in total command. The White House staff, headed by H. R. Haldeman and

John Ehrlichman, dominated the Washington bureaucracy like oriental viziers and dealt with legislators as though they were dealing with lackeys or eunuchs. When asked to account for their actions, they took refuge behind the shield of executive privilege, the doctrine, never before applied so broadly, that discussions and communications within the executive branch were confidential and therefore immune from congressional scrutiny.

The Watergate Break-in

On March 19, 1973, James McCord, a former FBI agent accused of burglary, wrote a letter to the judge presiding at his trial. His act precipitated a series of disclosures that destroyed Nixon.

McCord had been employed during the 1972 presidential campaign as a security officer of the Committee to Re-Elect the President (CREEP). At about 1 A.M. on June 17, 1972, he and four other men had broken into Democratic headquarters at the Watergate, an apartment house and office building complex in Washington. The burglars had been caught rifling files and installing electronic eavesdropping devices. Two other Republican campaign officials were soon implicated.

Nixon denied responsibility for their actions. "No one on the White House staff, no one in this Administration presently employed, was involved in this very bizarre incident," he announced. Most persons took the president at his word despite his well-known deviousness. (He had won the nickname "Tricky Dick" when he first ran for Congress in 1946.) He was far ahead in the polls and seemed so sure to win reelection that it was hard to think he would stoop to burglary to discover what the Democrats were up to. In any case, the affair did not materially affect the election. When brought to trial early in 1973, most of the defendants pleaded guilty.

Before Judge John J. Sirica imposed sentences on the culprits, however, McCord wrote his letter. High Republican officials had known about the burglary in advance and had persuaded most of the defendants to keep their connection secret, McCord claimed. Perjury had been committed during the trial.

The truth of McCord's charges swiftly became apparent. The head of CREEP, Jeb Stuart Magruder, and President Nixon's lawyer, John W.

Dean III, admitted their involvement. Among the disclosures that emerged over the following months were these:

- The acting director of the FBI, L. Patrick Gray, had destroyed documents related to the case.
- Large sums of money had been paid to the burglars at the instigation of the White House to ensure their silence.
- CREEP officials had attempted to disrupt the campaigns of leading Democratic candidates during the 1972 primaries in illegal ways.
- A number of corporations had made large contributions to the Nixon reelection campaign in violation of federal law.
- The Nixon administration had placed illegal wiretaps on the telephones of some of its own officials as well as on those of newspapermen critical of its policies.

These revelations led to the discharge of John Dean and the resignations of most of Nixon's closest advisers, including Haldeman, Ehrlichman, and Attorney General Richard Kleindienst. They also raised the question of the president's personal connection with the scandals. This he steadfastly denied. He insisted that he would investigate the Watergate affair thoroughly and see that the guilty were punished. He refused, however, to allow investigators to examine White House documents, again on grounds of executive privilege.

In the face of Nixon's denials, John Dean, testifying under oath, stated flatly and in circumstantial detail that the president had been closely involved in the Watergate cover-up. (Before testifying, Dean consulted with the conservative Senator Barry Goldwater, a Nixon supporter. When he explained what he was going to say, Goldwater replied: "Hell, I'm not surprised. That goddam Nixon has been lying all of his life.") Dean had been a persuasive witness, but—unlike Goldwater—many people were reluctant to believe that a president could lie so coldbloodedly to the entire country. Therefore, when it came out during later hearings of the Senate committee investigating the Watergate scandal, that the president had systematically made secret tape recordings of White House conversations and telephone calls, it seemed obvious that these tapes would settle the question of Nixon's involvement once and for all.

When the president refused to release the tapes, calls for his resignation, even for impeachment, began to be heard. Yielding to pressure, he agreed to the appointment of an "independent" special prosecutor to investigate the Watergate affair, and he promised the appointee, Archibald Cox of the Harvard Law School, full cooperation. Cox, however, swiftly aroused the president's ire by demanding White House records, including the tapes. When Nixon refused, Cox obtained a subpoena from Judge Sirica ordering him to do so. The administration appealed and lost in the appellate court. Then, while the case was headed for the Supreme Court, Nixon ordered the new attorney general, Elliot Richardson, to dismiss Cox. Both Richardson and his chief assistant, William Ruckelshaus, resigned rather than do so. Solicitor General Robert Bork, third-ranking officer of the Justice Department, carried out Nixon's order.

These events, which occurred on Saturday, October 20, were promptly dubbed the Saturday Night Massacre. They caused an outburst of public indignation. Congress was bombarded by thousands of letters and telegrams demanding the president's impeachment. The House Judiciary Committee began an investigation to see if enough evidence for impeachment existed.

Once again Nixon backed down. He agreed to turn over the tapes to Judge Sirica with the understanding that although relevant materials would be presented to the grand jury investigating the Watergate affair, nothing would be revealed to the public. He then named a new special prosecutor, Leon Jaworski, and promised him access to whatever White House documents he needed. However, it soon came out that some of the tapes were missing and that an important section of another had been deliberately erased.

More Troubles

The nation had never before experienced such a series of morale-shattering crises. While the seemingly unending complications of Watergate were unfolding during 1973, a number of unrelated disasters struck. First, pushed by a shortage of grains resulting from massive Soviet purchases authorized by the administration as part of its détente policy, food prices shot up—wheat from $1.45 a bushel to over $5.

Then Vice President Agnew (defender of law and order, foe of permissiveness) was accused of income tax fraud and of having accepted bribes while county executive of Baltimore and governor of Maryland. After vehemently denying all the charges for two months, Agnew (to escape a jail term) admitted in October that he had been guilty of tax evasion and resigned as vice president.

Under the new Twenty-fifth Amendment, President Nixon nominated Gerald R. Ford of Michigan as vice president, and he was confirmed by Congress. Ford had served continuously in Congress since 1949, as minority leader since 1964. His positions on public issues were close to Nixon's.

Not long after the Agnew fiasco, Nixon, responding to charges that he had paid almost no income taxes during his presidency, published his 1969 to 1972 returns. They showed that he had indeed paid very, little—only about $1,600 in two years during which his income had exceeded half a million dollars. Although Nixon claimed that his tax returns had been perfectly legal—he had taken huge deductions for the gift of some of his vice presidential papers to the National Archives—the legality and the propriety of his deductions were so questionable that he felt obliged, during a televised press conference, to assure the audience: "I am not a crook."

The Oil Crisis

Still another disaster followed as a result of the new war that broke out in October 1973 between Israel and the Arab states. The fighting, although bloody, was brief and inconclusive; a truce was soon arranged under the auspices of the United States and the Soviet Union. But in an effort to force Western nations to compel Israel to withdraw from lands held since the "Six-Day" War of 1967, the Arabs cut off oil shipments to the United States, Japan, and most of Western Europe. A worldwide energy crisis ensued.

The immediate shortage resulting from the Arab oil boycott was ended by the patient diplomacy of Henry Kissinger, whom Nixon had made secretary of state at the beginning of his second administration. After weeks of negotiating in the spring of 1974, Kissinger obtained a tentative agreement that involved the withdrawal of Israel from some of the territory it had occupied in 1967. The Arab nations then lifted the boycott.

A revolution had taken place. From the middle of the 19th century until after World War II, the United States had produced far more oil than it could use. However, the phenomenal expansion of oil consumption that occurred after the war soon absorbed the surplus. By the late 1960s, American car owners were driving more than a trillion miles a year. Petroleum was also being used to manufacture nylon and other synthetic fibers as well as paints, insecticides, fertilizers, and many plastic products. Oil and natural gas became the principal fuels for home heating. Natural gas in particular was used increasingly in factories and electric utility plants because it was less polluting than coal and most other fuels. The Clean Air Act of 1965 speeded the process of conversion from coal to gas by countless industrial consumers. Because of these developments, at the outbreak of the 1973 Arab-Israeli war, the United States was importing one-third of its oil.

In 1960 the principal oil exporters, Venezuela, Saudi Arabia, Kuwait, Iraq, and Iran, had formed a cartel, the Organization of Petroleum Exporting Countries (OPEC). For many years OPEC had been unable to control the world price of oil, which, on the eve of the 1973 war, was about $3 a barrel. The success of the Arab oil boycott served to unite the members of OPEC, and when the boycott was lifted, they boldly announced that the price was going up to $11.65 a barrel.

The announcement caused consternation throughout the industrial world. Soaring prices for oil meant soaring prices for everything made from petroleum or with petroleum-powered machinery. In the United States gasoline prices doubled overnight and the trend of all prices rose at a rate of more than 10 percent a year. This "double digit" inflation, which afficted nearly all the countries of the world, added considerably to President Nixon's woes.

The Judgment: Expletive Deleted

Meanwhile, special prosecutor Jaworski continued his investigation of the Watergate scandals. In March 1974 a grand jury indicted Haldeman, Ehrlichman, former Attorney General John Mitchell, who had been head of CREEP at the time of the break-in, and four other White House aides for conspiring to block the Watergate investigation. The jurors also named Nixon an "unindicted co-conspirator," Jaworski having informed them that their power to indict a president was constitutionally questionable. Judge Sirica thereupon turned over the jury's evidence against Nixon to the House Judiciary Committee. Then both the Internal Revenue Service and a joint congressional committee, having separately audited the president's income tax returns, announced that most of his deductions had been unjustified. The IRS assessed him nearly half a million dollars in taxes and interest, which he agreed to pay.

In an effort to check the mounting criticism, Nixon late in April released edited transcripts of the tapes he had turned over to the court the previous November. In addition to much incriminating evidence, the transcripts provided the public with a fascinating view of how the president conducted himself in private. His repeated use of foul language, so out of keeping with his public image, offended millions. The phrase "expletive deleted," inserted in place of words considered too vulgar for publication in family newspapers, became a catchword. In conversations Nixon seemed indecisive and lacking in any concern for the public interest. The publication of the transcripts led some of his strongest supporters to demand that he resign. And once the Judiciary Committee obtained the actual tapes, it came out that much material prejudicial to the president's case had been suppressed.

Yet impeaching a president seemed so drastic a step many people felt more direct proof of Nixon's involvement in the cover-up was necessary. Nixon insisted that all the relevant information was contained in these tapes; he adamantly refused to turn over others to the special prosecutor or the Judiciary Committee. Nevertheless prosecutor Jaworski subpoenaed 64 additional tapes. Nixon refused to obey the subpoena. Swiftly the case of *United States* v. *Richard M. Nixon* went to the Supreme Court.

In the summer of 1974—after so many months of alarms and crises—the Watergate drama reached its climax. The Judiciary Committee, following months of study of the evidence behind closed doors, decided to conduct its deliberations in open session. While millions watched on television, 38 members of the House of Representatives debated the charges. The discussions revealed both the thoroughness of the investigation and the soul-searching efforts of the representatives to render an impartial judgment. Three articles of impeachment were adopted. They charged the president with obstructing justice, misusing the powers of his office, and failing to obey the committee's subpoenas. Except in the case of the last article, many of the Republicans on the committee joined with the Democrats in voting aye, a clear indication that the full House would vote to impeach.

On the eve of the debates, the Supreme Court had ruled unanimously that the president must turn over the 64 subpoenaed tapes to the special prosecutor. Executive privilege had its place, the Court stated, but no person, not even a president, could "withhold evidence that is demonstrably relevant in a criminal trial." For reasons that soon became obvious, Nixon seriously considered defying the Court. Only when convinced that to do so would make his impeachment and conviction certain did he agree to comply.

He would not, however, resign. Even if the House impeached him, he was counting on his ability to hold the support of one-third plus one of the Senate to escape conviction. But events were passing beyond his control. When the 64 subpoenaed tapes were transcribed and analyzed, Nixon's fate was sealed. Three recorded conversations between the president and H. R. Haldeman on June 23, 1972 (less than a week after the break-in and only one day after Nixon had assured the nation that no one in the White House had been involved in the affair), proved conclusively that Nixon had tried to get the CIA to persuade the FBI not to follow up leads in the case on the spurious ground that national security was involved.

The president's defenders had insisted not so much that he was innocent as that solid proof of his guilt had not been demonstrated. Where, in the metaphor of the moment, was the "smoking gun"? That weapon had now been found, and it bore the fingerprints of Richard M. Nixon.

The president's chief advisers then pressed him to release the material at once and to admit he had erred in holding it back. This he did on August 5. When they read the new transcripts, all the Republican members of the Judiciary Committee who had voted against the impeachment articles reversed themselves. Republican congressional leaders told Nixon that the House would impeach him and that no more than a handful of the senators would vote to acquit him.

The Meaning of Watergate

On August 8 Nixon announced his resignation, and at noon on August 9 Gerald Ford was sworn in as president. The meaning of "Watergate" became immediately the subject of much speculation and shall no doubt so remain for many years. Whether Nixon's crude efforts to dominate Congress, to crush or inhibit dissent, and to subvert the electoral process would have permanently altered the American political system had they succeeded, is probably beyond knowing. However, the orderly way in which these efforts were checked suggests that the system would have survived in any case.

Nixon's own drama is and must remain one of the most fascinating and enigmatic episodes in American history. Despite his fall from the heights because of personal flaws, his was not a tragedy in the Greek sense. Even when he finally yielded power, he seemed without remorse or even awareness of his transgressions. He was devoid of the classic hero's pride. Did he really intend to smash all opposition and rule like a tyrant, or was he driven by lack of confidence in himself? His stubborn aggressiveness and his overblown view of executive privilege may have reflected a need for constant reassurance that he was a mighty leader. One element in his downfall, preserved for posterity in videotapes of his television appearances, was that even while he was assuring the country of his innocence most vehemently, he did not look like a victim of the machinations of overzealous supporters. Perhaps at some profound level he did not want to be believed.

This explanation of Richard Nixon makes him appear less menacing. If it is correct, Americans can deplore the injuries he inflicted on society and still feel for him a certain compassion.

Whether Nixon's disgrace marked the end of

one era or the beginning of another is a difficult question. Like most critical moments in human history, it seems in retrospect to have been both. Nixon's détent with the Soviet Union and Red China was surely an early sign of the easing of Cold War tensions that followed. Yet the failure of Nixon's interventionist domestic policies, coming just as public disillusionment with the workings of many of the ambitious Great Society programs set in motion under Lyndon Johnson was mounting, put a quietus to the liberal era that had begun with the reforms of the New Deal.

Milestones

1942	Congress of Racial Equality (CORE) founded		American troop strength in Vietnam reaches 538,000
1954	Supreme Court orders school desegregation (*Brown* v. *Board of Education*)		Lyndon Johnson withdraws as presidential candidate
1956	Founding of Southern Christian Leadership Conference (SCLC)	1969	Nixon announces "Vietnamization" of the war
1957	National Guard used to desegregate Little Rock High School	1970	Nixon announces "incursion" into Cambodia
	Establishment of Civil Rights Commission		Antiwar students killed at Kent State and Jackson State
	Montgomery, Alabama, bus boycott		Last American troops withdrawn from South Vietnam
1960	Founding of Student Nonviolent Coordinating Committee (SNCC)		Nixon fires special prosecutor Archibald Cox (Saturday Night Massacre)
1961	Bay of Pigs affair		
	Freedom riders "invade" South	1971	Nixon freezes prices
1962	Cuban missile crisis	1972	Break-in at Democratic headquarters in Washington, D.C.
1963	Assassination of President Ngo Dihn Diem of South Vietnam		Nixon and Kissinger visit China and the Soviet Union
	Martin Luther King, Jr., "Letter from Birmingham Jail"		Strategic Arms Limitation Treaty (SALT)
	President Kennedy assassinated.	1973	House Judiciary Committee begins impeachment hearings
1964	Gulf of Tonkin Resolution leads to escalation of Vietnam War		Resignation of Vice President Spiro Agnew
	Civil Rights Act		
	Economic Opportunity Act	1973–1974	Arab oil boycott
1965	Immigration Act ending national origins system	1974	Supreme Court orders release of Nixon's White House tapes
	Medicare Act		
	Elementary and Secondary Education Act		President Nixon resigns
	Clean Air Act		Gerald R. Ford becomes president
1968	Communist Tet offensive in South Vietnam		

Supplementary Reading

On Kennedy, consult H. S. Parmet, **Jack: The Struggles of John F. Kennedy** (1980) and **JFK: The Presidency of John F. Kennedy** (1983), together a fair-minded account. A. M. Schlesinger, Jr., **A Thousand Days*** (1965), and Theodore Sorensen, **Kennedy*** (1965), are rich in eyewitness detail but extremely pro-Kennedy. Peter Wyden, **Bay of Pigs** (1979), and Elie Abel, **The Missile Crisis** (1966), describe the most important foreign policy crises of the era.

On Lyndon Johnson and the Johnson era, see J. F. Heath, **Decade of Disillusionment** (1980), and A. J. Matusow, **The Unraveling of America*** (1984). W. M. O'Neill, **Coming Apart: An Informal History of the 1960s*** (1971), and Geoffrey Hodgson, **America in Our Time** (1976), deal more broadly with the period. E. F. Goldman, **The Tragedy of Lyndon Johnson*** (1969), Doris Kearns, **Lyndon Johnson and the American Dream*** (1976), George Reedy, **Lyndon Johnson** (1982), and R. N. Goodwin, **Remembering America** (1988), are valuable memoirs.

For the civil rights developments, consult Taylor Branch, **Parting the Waters*** (1988), David Garrow, **Bearing the Cross** (1981), Richard Kluger, **Simple Justice** (1975), M. L. King, Jr., **Stride Toward Freedom*** (1958), and Malcolm X, **Autobiography** (1966).

On the election of 1968, T. H. White's **The Making of the President, 1968*** (1969) is lively and entertaining, while Joe McGinniss, **The Selling of the President, 1968*** (1969), is a fascinating account of the Republican advertising and television campaign. The best biography of Nixon is Stephen Ambrose, **Nixon** (1987–1989). Garry Wills, **Nixon Agonistes*** (1970), is a thoughtful though unfriendly analysis. See also R. S. Litwak, **Détente and the Nixon Doctrine** (1984), William Safire, **Before the Fall** (1975), and Rowland Evans, Jr., and R. D. Novak, **Nixon in the White House*** (1971). White's **The Making of the President, 1972*** (1973) and **Breach of Faith: the Fall of Richard Nixon** (1975), are less satisfactory than his earlier volumes.

The literature on the war in Vietnam is already enormous. Stanley Karnow, **Vietnam: A History** (1983), is a straightforward narrative account, but see also A. J. Rotter, **The Path to Vietnam** (1987), Melvin Small, **Johnson, Nixon, and the Doves** (1988), Neil Sheehan, **A Bright and Shining Lie** (1988), Guenter Lewy, **America in Vietnam*** (1980), Frances FitzGerald, **Fire in the Lake*** (1972), and David Halberstam, **The Best and the Brightest*** (1972), which contains a mass of detail on the evolution of American policy, based on extensive interviews. William Shawcross, **Side-Show: Kissinger, Nixon, and the Destruction of Cambodia*** (1979), is extremely critical, and Norman Mailer, **The Armies of the Night*** (1968), is a vivid account of an antiwar demonstration in Washington.

R. S. Litwak, **Détente and the Nixon Doctrine** (1984), is a useful study of United States–Soviet relations in the Nixon era, and Henry Kissinger's memoirs, **White House Years** (1979) and **Years of Upheaval** (1982), are important though, like most such works, self-serving.

A convenient summary of the almost infinite complexities of the Watergate affair is **New York Times**, ed., **The End of a Presidency*** (1974), but see also Carl Bernstein and Robert Woodward, **All the President's Men*** (1974) and **Final Days*** (1976), J. W. Dean, **Blind Ambition*** (1976), and Leon Jaworski, **The Right and the Power*** (1976).

*Available in paperback.

CHAPTER 31

Society in Flux

A Changing Society

Television

"A Nation of Sheep"

Religion in Changing Times

Literature and Art

Two Dilemmas

The Costs of Prosperity

New Racial Turmoil

Native-born Ethnics

Rethinking Public Education

Students in Revolt

The Counterculture

The Sexual Revolution

Women's Liberation

*D*espite Lyndon Johnson's extravagant style and his landslide defeat of Barry Goldwater in the 1964 presidential election, the tone of his inaugural address in January 1965 was uncharacteristically restrained. The nation was "prosperous, great, and mighty," he said, but "we have no promise from God that our greatness will endure." He was obviously thinking of the enormous changes that were occurring in the country. He spoke of "this fragile existence," and he warned the people that they lived "in a world where change and growth seem to tower beyond the control, and even the judgment of men."

A Changing Society

The population was expanding rapidly, reaching 131 million in 1940. It passed 200 million in the 1960s and touched 250 million in the late 1980s. Experts observed startling shifts within this expanding mass. The westward movement had by no means ended with the closing of the frontier in the 1890s. One indication of this was the admission of Hawaii and Alaska to the Union in 1959. More significant was the growth of the "sun belt"—Florida and the states of the Southwest. California added more than 5 million to its numbers between 1950 and 1960, and in 1963 it passed New York to become the most populous state in the Union. Nevada and Arizona were expanding at an even more rapid rate.

The climate of the Southwest was particularly attractive to older people, and the population growth reflected the prosperity that enabled pensioners and other retired persons to settle there. At the same time, the area attracted millions of young workers, for it became the center of the aircraft and electronics industries and the government's atomic energy and space programs. These industries displayed the best side of modern capitalism: high wages, comfortable working conditions, complex and efficient machinery, and the marriage of scientific technology and commercial utility.

Advances in transportation and communication added to geographical mobility. In the postwar decades the automobile appeared to enter its golden age. In the booming 1920s, when the car became an instrument of mass transportation, about 31 million autos were produced by American factories. During the 1960s, 77 million rolled off the assembly lines.

Gasoline use rose sharply. The more mobile population drove further in more reliable and more comfortable vehicles over smoother and less congested highways. And the new cars were heavier and more powerful than their predecessors. Gasoline consumption first touched 15 billion gallons in 1931; it soared to 92 billion in 1970. A new business, the motel industry (the word, typically American, was a combination of *motor* and *hotel*), developed to service the millions of tourists and businessmen who burned all this fuel on their travels.

The development of the Interstate Highway System, begun under Eisenhower in 1956, was a major cause of increased mobility. The new roads did far more than facilitate long-distance travel; they accelerated the shift of population to the suburbs and the consequent decline of inner-city districts.

Despite the speeds that cars maintained on them, the new highways were much safer than the old roads. The traffic death rate per mile driven fell steadily, almost entirely because of the interstates. On the other hand, the environmental impact of the system was frequently severe. Elevated roads cut ugly swaths through cities, and the cars they carried released tons of noxious exhaust fumes into urban air. Hillsides were gashed, marshes filled in, forests felled—all in the name of speed and efficiency.

Although commercial air travel had existed in the thirties, it truly came of age when the first jetliner—the Boeing 707—went into service in 1958. Almost immediately jets came to dominate long-distance travel, while railroad passenger service and transatlantic liners declined in importance.

Television

Another important postwar change was the advent of television as a means of mass communication. By 1961 there were 55 million sets in operation, and by the sixties there were both government and commercial satellites in orbit that could relay pictures from one continent to another instantly.

Television combined the immediacy of radio with the visual impact of films, and displayed most of the strengths and weaknesses of both in exaggerated form. It swiftly became indispensable to the political system, both for its coverage of public events and as a vehicle for political advertising.

Some excellent drama was presented, especially on the National Educational Television network, along with many filmed documentaries. But the lion's share of television time was devoted to uninspired and vulgar serials, routine variety shows, giveaway and quiz programs designed to reveal and revel in the ignorance of the average citizen, and reruns of old movies cut to fit rigid time periods and repeatedly interrupted at climactic points by "commercials."

Another defect of television's virtues was its capacity for influencing the opinions and feelings of viewers. The insistent and strident claims of advertisers punctuated every program with monotonous regularity. Politicians discovered that no other device or method approached television as a means of reaching large numbers of voters with an illusion of intimacy. Since television time was expensive, candidates had to raise huge sums in order to be able to use the medium—a dangerous state of affairs in a democracy. In time Congress clamped a lid on campaign expenditures, but this action did not necessarily reduce the amounts spent on television, with its capacity to reach so many people.*

"A Nation of Sheep"

Another postwar change was the marked broadening of the middle class. In 1947 only 5.7 million American families had what might be considered middle-class incomes—enough to provide something for leisure, entertainment, and cultural activities as well as for life's necessities. By the early 1960s, more than 12 million families, about a third of the population, had such incomes.

The percentage of immigrants in the population declined steadily; in 1965, more than 95 percent of all Americans were native born. This trend contributed to social and cultural uniformity. So did the rising incomes of industrial workers and the changing character of their labor. Blue-collar workers invaded the middle class by the tens of thousands. They moved to suburbs previously reserved for junior executives, shopkeepers, and the like. They shed their work clothes for business suits. They took up golf. In sum, they adopted values and attitudes commensurate with their new status—which helps explain the growing conservatism of labor unions.

Religion in Changing Times

Sociologists and other commentators found in the expansion of the middle class another explanation of the tendency of the country to glorify the conformist. They attributed to this expansion the national obsession with "moderation" and "consensus," and the complacency of so many Americans,

---

*The government now provides substantial public funds to major candidates in presidential elections.

their tendency, for example, to be at once more interested in the social aspects of churchgoing than in the philosophic aspects of religion.

Organized religion deals with eternal values, but it is influenced by social, cultural, and economic developments. After World War II all the major faiths, despite their differences, were affected. The prosperity and buoyant optimism of the period led to an expansion of religious activity. The Catholic Church alone built over a thousand new schools and more than a hundred hospitals along with countless new churches. By 1950 the Southern Baptists had enrolled nearly 300,000 new members and built some 500 churches for them to worship in, and between 1945 and 1965, Jews spent at least $1 billion building synagogues.

But while most faiths prospered materially, the faithful tended to accept the world as it was. In *Catholic, Protestant, Jew* (1955), Will Herberg argued that in America religious toleration had become routine. According to a Gallup Poll nearly everyone in America believed in God. However, another poll revealed that large numbers of Christians were unable to tell pollsters the name of any of the four gospels.

Church and state were by law and the Constitution separate institutions, yet acts of Congress and state legislatures frequently had indirect effects on organized religion. New Deal welfare legislation took on a large part of a burden previously borne by church groups. On the one hand, the expansion of higher education appeared to make people somewhat more tolerant of the beliefs of others, religious beliefs included. On the other hand, however, studies showed that better educated people tended to be less involved in the formal aspects of organized religion. An "education gap" separated religious liberals from religious conservatives.

Unlike prewar critics who had attacked "rugged individualism," many post–New Deal social critics, alarmed by the conformity of the 1950s, urged people to be more individualistic. In *The Lonely Crowd* (1950), David Riesman drew a distinction between old-fashioned "inner-directed" people and a new type of "other-directed" conformists who were group-centered, materialistic, and accommodating.

The civil rights movement also had important religious implications. So did the Vietnam war.

Many militant blacks (Malcolm X was an early example) were converted to the Moslem faith by its lack of racial bias. Among those in the public eye who became Moslems were the heavyweight champion boxer Cassius Clay, who changed his name to Mohammed Ali, and Lew Alcindor, a basketball star who became Kareem Abdul Jabbar.

Nearly all the denominations played significant roles in the fight for racial justice that erupted after the Supreme Court outlawed segregation. Priests, ministers, ansd rabbis joined in antiwar demonstrations. Shocking photographs of police dogs being used to "subdue" demonstrating Catholic nuns in the deep South converted uncounted thousands to the struggle. The controversy over America's role in the Vietnam war had similar effects.

All the social changes of the period had religious ramifications. Feminists objected to male domination of most Christian churches and called for the ordination of female ministers and priests. Every aspect of the sexual revolution, from the practice of couples living together openly outside marriage to the tolerance of homosexuality and pornography to the legalization of contraception and abortion, caused shock waves in the religious community. The Roman Catholic insistence that the clergy remain celebate resulted in a decline in the number of young Catholics becoming priests and nuns. This dealt a crippling blow to the parochial school system, which depended heavily on the clergy for teachers.

Scientific and technological developments also affected both religious values and the way people worshipped. The social effects of Darwin's theory of evolution were to some extent still unresolved. Many religious groups still believed in the Biblical explanation of creation and sought to have "creation theory" taught in the schools.

On another level, the prestige of secular science gave Darwin's theory a kind of religious aspect disturbing to some church leaders. Medical advances that some people marveled at, such as in-vitro fertiliziation of human eggs, organ transplants, and the development of machines capable of keeping terminally ill people alive indefinitely, seemed to others "against nature" and indeed sacrilegious. Controversies over the use of atomic energy in peace and war and over the conservation of natural resources had religious aspects.

Radio and television had more direct effects on organized religion. The airwaves enabled rhetorically skilled preachers to reach millions with emotionally charged messages on religious topics and also on political and social questions. The most successful were the leaders of evangelical protestant sects.

These radio evangelists often became television preachers. They tended to found churches and educational institutions of their own and to use the airwaves to raise money to support them. Between 40 and 50 million Americans belonged to one or another evangelical sect. Most postwar revivalists, the most famous being Billy Graham, stressed interdenominational cooperation, but in the 1970s more militant fundamentalists were emerging. They were extremely conservative in their political and social views and some reached huge audiences—Jimmy Swaggert of the Assemblies of God claimed 2.2 million followers, Robert Schuller nearly as many, and Oral Roberts more than a million. They all used television to raise money to build churches and educational institutions, and many of them were phenomenally successful.

However, in the mid-1980s a number of scandals caused disillusionment and widespread defections among their followers. Both Swaggert and Jim Bakker, another popular television preacher, were caught in sex scandals and forced from their pulpits. Bakker was also convicted and jailed for fraud. By 1990 the national television congregation had shrunk drastically.

Literature and Art

For a time after World War II, the nation seemed on the verge of a literary outburst comparable to that which followed World War I. A number of excellent novels based on the military experiences of young writers appeared, the most notable being Norman Mailer's *The Naked and the Dead* (1948) and James Jones's *From Here to Eternity* (1951). Unfortunately, a new renaissance did not develop. The most talented younger writers rejected materialist values but preferred to bewail their fate rather than rebel against it. Jack Kerouac, founder of the "beat" (for beatific) school, reveled in the chaotic description of violence, perversion, and madness. At the other extreme, J. D. Salinger, perhaps the most popular writer of the 1950s and the particular favorite of college students—*The Catcher in the Rye* (1951) sold nearly 2 million copies in hardcover and paperback editions—was an impeccable stylist, witty, contemptuous of all pretense; but he too wrote about people entirely wrapped up in themselves.

In *Catch-22* (1955), the book that replaced *Catcher in the Rye* in the hearts of college students, Joseph Heller produced a war novel at once farcical and an indignant denunciation of the stupidity and waste of warfare. In *The Victim* (1947), *The Adventures of Augie March* (1953), *Herzog* (1964), and many other novels, Saul Bellow described characters possessed of their full share of eccentricities and weaknesses without losing sight of the positive side of modern life. Bellow won many literary awards, including a Nobel Prize.

All these novelists and a number of others whose books were of lesser quality were widely read. Year after year, sales of books increased, despite much talk about how television and other diversions were undermining the public's interest in reading. Sales of paperbacks, first introduced in the United States in 1939 by Pocket Books, reached enormous proportions: By 1965 about 25,000 titles were in print, and sales were approaching 1 million copies a day.

Cheapness and portability only partly accounted for the popularity of paperbacks. Readers could purchase them in drugstores, bus terminals, and supermarkets as well as in bookstores. Teachers, delighted to find out-of-print volumes easily available, assigned hundreds of them in their classes. And there was a psychological factor at work: The paperback became fashionable. People who rarely bought hardcover books purchased weighty volumes of literary criticism, translations of the works of obscure foreign novelists, specialized historical monographs, and difficult philosophical treatises now that they were available in paper covers.

The expansion of the book market, like so many other changes, was not an unalloyed benefit even for writers. It remained difficult for unknown authors to earn a decent living. Publishers tended to concentrate their interest and their money on authors already popular and on books aimed at a mass audience. Even among successful writers of unquestioned ability, the temptations involved in large advances and in book club contracts and movie rights diverted many from making the best use of their talents.

American painters were affected by the same forces that influenced writers. In the past the greatest American artists had been shaped by European influences. This situation changed dramatically after World War II with the emergence of abstract expressionism, or action painting. This "New York school" was led by Jackson Pollock (1912–1956), who composed huge abstract designs by laying his canvas on the floor of his studio and squeezing paint on it directly from tube or pot in a wild tangle of color. The abstract expressionists were utterly subjective in their approach to art. "The source of my painting is the Unconscious," Pollock explained. "I am not much aware of what is taking place; it is only after that I see what I have done." Pollock tried to produce not the representation of a landscape but, as the critic Harold Rosenberg put it, "an inner landscape that is part of himself."

Untutored observers found the abstract expressionists crude, chaotic, devoid of interest. The swirling, dripping chaos of the followers of Pollock, the vaguely defined planes of color favored by Mark Rothko and his disciples, and the sharp spatial confrontations composed by the painters Franz Kline, Robert Motherwell, and Adolph Gottlieb required too much verbal explanation to communicate their meaning to the average observer. On the other hand, viewed in its social context, abstract expressionism reflected, like so much of modern literature, the estrangement of the artist from the world of the atomic bomb and the computer, a revolt against contemporary mass culture with its unthinking acceptance of novelty for its own sake.

The experimental spirit released by the abstract expressionists led to "op" art, which employed the physical impact of pure complementary colors to produce dynamic optical effects. Even within the rigid limitations of severely formal designs composed of concentric circles, stripes, squares, and rectangles, such paintings appeared to be constantly in motion, almost alive.

"Op" was devoid of social connotations; another variant, "pop" art, playfully yet often with acid incisiveness, satirized many aspects of American culture in all its vapidity, its crudeness, and its violence. The painters Jasper Johns, Roy Lichtenstein, and Andy Warhol created portraits of mundane objects such as flags, comic strips, soup cans, and packing cases. "Op" and "pop" art reflected the mechanized aspects of life; the painters made use of technology in their work—for example, they enhanced the shock of vibrating complementary colors by using fluorescent paints. Some artists imitated newspaper-photograph techniques by fashioning their images of sharply defined dots of color. Others borrowed from contemporary commercial art, employing spray guns, stencils, and masking tape to produce flat, "hard-edge" effects. The line between "op" and "pop" was frequently crossed, as in Robert Indiana's *Love,* which was reproduced and imitated on posters, Christmas cards, book jackets, buttons, rings, and a postage stamp.

The pace of change in artistic fashion was dizzying—far more rapid than changes in literature. Aware that their generation was leading European artists instead of following them gave both artists and art lovers a sense of participating in events of historic importance.

As with literature, the effects of such success were not all healthy. Successful artists became national personalities, a few of them becoming enormously rich. For these, each new work was exposed to the glare of publicity, sometimes with unfortunate results. Too much attention, like too much money, could be distracting, even corrupting, especially for young artists who needed time and obscurity to develop their talents.

Two Dilemmas

The many changes of the era help to explain why President Johnson expressed so much uncertainty in his inaugural address. Looking at American society more broadly, two dilemmas seem to have emerged. One was that progress was often self-defeating. Reforms and innovations instituted with the best of motives often made things worse rather than better. Instances of this dilemma, large and small, are so numerous as to defy summary. DDT, a powerful chemical developed to kill insects that were spreading disease and destroying valuable food crops, proved to have lethal effects on birds and fish—and perhaps indirectly on human beings. Goods manufactured to make life fuller and happier (automobiles, detergents, electric power) produced waste products that disfigured the land and polluted air and water. Cities built in order to bring culture and comfort to millions became pestholes of crime, poverty, and depravity.

Change occurred so fast that experience (the recollection of how things had been) tended to become less useful and sometimes even counterproductive as a guide for dealing with current problems. Foreign policies designed to prevent wars, devised on the basis of knowledge of the causes of past wars, led, because the circumstances were different, to new wars. Parents who sought to transmit to their children the accumulated wisdom of their years found their advice rejected, often with good reason, because that "wisdom" had little application to the problems their children had to face.

The second dilemma was that modern industrial society placed an enormous premium on social cooperation, at the same time undermining the individual citizen's sense of being essential to the proper functioning of society. The economy was as complicated as a fine watch; a breakdown in any one sector had ramifications that spread swiftly to other sectors. Yet specialization had progressed so far that individual workers had little sense of the importance of their personal contributions and thus felt little responsibility for the smooth functioning of the whole. Effective democratic government required that all voters be knowledgeable and concerned, but few could feel that their individual voices had any effect on elections or public policies.

People tried to deal with this dilemma by joining organizations dedicated to achieving particular goals, such as the American Association of Retired People (AARP), the environmentalist Sierra Club, and the National Association for the Advancement of Colored People. But such groups became so large that members felt almost as incapable of influencing them as they did of influencing the larger society. The groups were so numer-

ous and had so many conflicting objectives that instead of making citizens more socially minded they often made them more self-centered.

These dilemmas produced a paradox. The United States was the most powerful nation in the world, its people the best educated, richest, and probably the most energetic. American society was technologically advanced and dynamic, American traditional values idealistic, humane, democratic. Yet the nation seemed incapable of mobilizing its resources to confront the most obvious challenges, its citizens unable to achieve much personal happiness or identification with their fellows, the society helpless in trying to live up to its most universally accepted ideals.

In part the paradox was a product of the strengths of the society and the individuals who made it up. The populace as a whole was more sophisticated. People were more aware of their immediate interests, less willing to suspend judgment and follow leaders or to look on others as better qualified to decide what they should do. They belonged to the "me generation"; they knew that they lived in a society and that their lives were profoundly affected by that society, but they had trouble feeling that they were part of a society.

President Johnson recognized the problem. He hoped to solve it by establishing a "consensus" and building his Great Society. No real consensus emerged; American society remained fragmented, its members divided against themselves and often within themselves.

The Costs of Prosperity

The vexing character of modern conditions could be seen in every aspect of life. The gross national product approached, and then swiftly passed, $1 trillion, but inflation was becoming increasingly serious. Workers were under constant pressure to demand raises—which only served to drive prices still higher. Socially, the effect was devastating; it became impossible to expect workers to see inflation as a national problem and to restrain their personal demands. Putting their individual interests before those of the whole, they were prepared to disrupt the economy whatever the social cost.

Economic expansion resulted in large measure from technological advances, and these too proved to be mixed blessings. As we have seen,

The 1960s saw the emergence of environmentalism as individuals rallied to reduce pollution and preserve nature. One thorny problem was dealing with the country's overflowing landfills.

World War II needs stimulated the development of plastics like nylon, of synthetic rubber, and of radar, television, and other electronic devices.

In the 1950s public utility companies began to manufacture electricity from nuclear fuels. The electricity was cheaper than that produced in conventional plants, but the possibility of catastrophic accidents and the problem of disposing of lethal radioactive waste products soon dampened public enthusiasm for nuclear power. Scientists insisted that the danger from radiation was insignificant, but the possibility of accidents could not be eliminated entirely. Equally significant was the perfection of the electronic computer, which revolutionized the collection and storage of records, solved mathematical problems beyond the scope of the most brilliant human minds, and speeded the work of bank tellers, librarians, billing clerks, statisticians—and income tax collectors.

Computers lay at the heart of industrial automation, for they could control the integration and adjustment of the most complex machines. In automobile factories they made it possible to produce entire engine blocks automatically. In steel mills molten metal could be poured into molds, cooled, rolled, and cut into slabs without the intervention of a human hand, with computers locating defects and adjusting the machinery to correct them far more accurately than the most skilled steelworker, and in a matter of seconds. But the "computerization" of record keeping and manufac-

turing raised the problem of how displaced clerks and automobile and steel workers were to find new jobs.

The material benefits of technology commonly had what the microbiologist René Dubos described as "disastrous secondary effects, many of which are probably unpredictable." The consumption of petroleum necessary to produce power began to outstrip supplies, threatening shortages that would disrupt the entire economy. The burning of this fuel released unmeasurable tons of smoke and other polluting gases into the atmosphere, endangering the health of millions. "Life is enriched by one million automobiles," Dubos noted, "but can be made into a nightmare by one hundred million."

The vast outpouring of flimsy plastic products and the increased use of paper, metal foil, and other "disposable" packaging materials seemed about to bury the country beneath mountains of trash. Even an apparently ideal form of scientific advance, the use of commercial fertilizers to boost food output, had unfortunate side effects: Phosphates washed from farmlands into streams sometimes upset the ecological balance and turned the streams into malodorous death traps for aquatic life. Above all, technology increased the capacity of the earth to support people. As population increased, production and consumption increased, exhausting supplies of raw materials and speeding the pollution of air and water resources. And where would the process end? Viewed from a world perspective, it was obvious that the population explosion must be checked or it would check itself by pestilence, war, starvation, or some combination of these scourges. Yet how to check it?

New Racial Turmoil

President Johnson and most of those who supported his policies expected that the 1964 Civil Rights Act, the Economic Opportunity Act, Medicare and Medicaid, and the other elements in the war on poverty would produce an era of racial peace and genuine social harmony—the Great Society that everyone wanted. In fact, official recognition of past injustices made blacks more insistent that all discrimination be ended. The very process of righting some past wrongs gave them the strength to fight more vigorously. Black militancy burst forth so powerfully that the most smug and obtuse white citizens had to accept its existence.

The Student Nonviolent Coordinating Committee (SNCC), which had been born out of the struggle for racial integration, had become by the mid-sixties a radical organization openly scornful of interracial cooperation. Many students had been radicalized by the violence they had experienced while trying to register rural blacks and organize schools for black children inthe South. The slogan of the radicals was "Black Power," an expression that was given national currency by Stokely Carmichael, chairman of SNCC. Carmichael was adamantly opposed to cooperating with whites. "The time for white involvement in the fight for equality is ended," he said in 1966. The movement "should be black-staffed, black-controlled, and black financed." On another occasion he said: "integration is a subterfuge for . . . white supremacy." Black Power caught on swiftly among militants. This troubled white liberals because they feared that Black Power would antagonize white conservatives.

Meanwhile, black anger erupted in a series of destructive urban riots. The most important occurred in Watts, a ghetto of Los Angeles, in August 1965. A trivial incident—police officers halted a motorist who seemed to be drunk and attempted to give him a sobriety test—brought thousands

into the streets. The neighborhood almost literally exploded: For six days Watts was swept by fire, looting, and bloody fighting. The following summer saw similar outbursts in New York, Chicago, and other cities. In 1967 further riots broke out, the most serious in Newark, where 25 were killed, and Detroit, where the death toll reached 43.

Then, in April 1968, the revered Martin Luther King, Jr. was murdered in Memphis, Tennessee, by a white man, James Earl Ray. Blacks in more than 100 cities unleashed their anger in paroxysms of burning and looting. White opinion was shocked and profoundly depressed: The death of King appeared to destroy the hope that his doctrine of pacific appeal to reason and right could solve the racial problem.

The rioters were expressing frustration and despair; their resentment was directed more at the social system than at individuals. The basic cause was an attitude of mind, the "white racism" that deprived blacks of access to good jobs, crowded them into slums, and, for the young in particular, eroded all hope of escape from such misery. Ghettos bred crime and depravity, as slums always have, and the complacent refusal of whites to adequately invest money and energy in helping ghetto residents—or even to acknowledge that the black poor deserved help—made the modern slum unbearable. While the ghettos expanded, middle-class whites tended more and more to "flee" to the suburbs or to call on the police "to maintain law and order," a euphemism for cracking down hard on deviant black behavior no matter how obvious the connection between that behavior and the slum environment.

The victims of racism employed violence not so much to force change as to obtain psychic release; it was a way of getting rid of what they could not stomach, a kind of vomiting. When fires broke out in black districts, the firefighters who tried to extinguish them were often showered with bottles and bricks and sometimes shot at, while above the roar of the flames and the hiss of steam rose the apocalyptic chant "Burn, baby, burn!"

The most frightening aspect of the riots was their tendency to polarize society on racial lines. Advocates of Black Power became more determined to separate themselves from white influence. They exasperated white supporters of school desegregation by demanding schools of their own. Extremists formed the Black Panther Party and collected weapons to resist the police.

Middle-class city residents often resented what seemed the "favoritism" of the federal government and of state and local administrations, which sought through "affirmative action" to provide blacks with economic opportunities and social benefits. Efforts to desegregate ghetto schools by "busing" children out of their local neighborhoods was a particularly bitter cause of conflict. Persons already subjected to the pressures caused by inflation, specialization, and rapid change, and worried by rising urban crime rates and welfare costs, found black radicalism infuriating.

Native-Born Ethnics

Mexican Americans responded to discrimination in much the same manner as the blacks. After World War I, thousands of immigrants from Mexico flocked into the Southwest. When the Great Depression struck, about half a million of those who had not become American citizens were either deported or "persuaded" to return to Mexico, but during World War II and again between 1948 and 1965, federal legislation encouraged the importation of temporary farm workers called *braceros.* Other Mexicans entered the country illegally. Many of them, and other Spanish-speaking people from Puerto Rico who could immigrate to the mainland legally, settled in the great cities, where low-paying but usually steady work was available. They lived in slums called *barrios,* as segregated, crowded, and crime ridden as the ghettoes of the blacks.

Spanish-speaking newcomers were for a time largely apolitical; they tended to mind their own business and not "make trouble." But in the early 1960s a new spirit of resistance arose. Leaders of the new movement called themselves Chicanos. They demanded better education for their children and urged their fellows to take pride in their traditions, demand their rights, and organize politically.

One Chicano nationalist group, the Crusade for Justice, focused on achieving social reforms and setting up political action groups. Its slogan, *Venceremos,* was Spanish for Martin Luther King's pledge: We shall overcome.

The Mexican-American founder of the National Farm Workers Association and later head of the United Farm Workers Organizing Committee, César Chávez, successfully organized migrant workers throughout California in the early 1960s and later led a nationwide boycott against California grape producers.

The Chicano leader with the widest influence was César Chávez, who concentrated on what superficially was a more limited goal—organizing migrant farm workers into unions. After serving in the navy during World War II, Chávez became general director of the Community Service Organization (CSO), a group seeking to raise the political consciousness of the poor and develop self-help programs among them. But he resigned in 1962 because he believed it was not devoting enough attention to the plight of migrant workers. He then founded the National Farm Workers' Association, later known as the United Farm Workers' Organizing Committee.

In 1965 Chávez turned a strike of grape pickers in Delano, California into a countrywide crusade against the whole migrant labor system. Avoiding violence, he enlisted the support of church leaders and organized sit-ins, a march on the state capital, and then a national consumer boycott of grapes. He proved that migrant workers could be unionized and that the militant demands of minorities for equal treatment did not necessarily lead to separatism and class or racial antagonism.

The struggles of blacks radicalized many American Indians, who used the term "Red Power" the way blacks spoke of Black Power and referred to more conservative colleagues as "Uncle Tomahawks." The National Indian Youth Council and later the American Indian Movement (AIM) demanded the return of lands taken illegally from their ancestors. They called for a concerted effort to revive tribal cultures, even the use of the the mind-altering controlled substance, peyote, in religious ceremonies.*

Some AIM leaders sought total separation from the United States; they envisaged setting up states within states such as the Cherokees had established in Georgia in Jacksonian days. In 1973 radicals occupied the town of Wounded Knee, South Dakota (site of one of the most disgraceful massacres of Indians in the 19th century), and held it at gunpoint for weeks.

While traditionalists resisted the militants, liberal white opinion proved to be generally sympathetic. In 1975 Congress passed the Indian Self-Determination Act, which gave individual tribes much greater control over such matters as education, welfare programs, and law enforcement.

Militant ethnic pride characterized the behavior of many white Americans too. Blacks donned African garments and wore their hair in natural "Afro" styles. Italian Americans, Polish Americans, and descendants of other "new immigrant" groups eagerly studied their histories in order to preserve their culture. The American "melting pot," some historians now argued, had not amalgamated the immigrant strains as completely as had been thought.

For all "ethnics" the concern for origins was in part nostalgic and romantic. As the number of, say, Greek Americans who had never seen Greece declined, the appeal of Greek culture increased. But for blacks, whose particular origins were obscured by the cataclysm of slavery, awareness of their distinctiveness was more important. Racial pride was a reflection of the achievements that blacks had made in the postwar period. There was a black on the Supreme Court (Thurgood Marshall, tactician of the fight for school desegregation). President Johnson had named the first black to a Cabinet post (Robert Weaver, secretary of housing and urban development). The first black since reconstruction (Edward W. Brooke of

Massachusetts) was elected to the United States Senate in 1966. A number of large cities elected black mayors.

The color line was broken in major league baseball in 1947, and soon all professional sports were open to black athletes. Where the reign of black heavyweight boxing champion Jack Johnson (1908–1915) had inspired an open search for a "white hope" to depose him, and where the next black champion, Joe Louis (1937–1949), was accepted by whites because he "knew his place" and was "well behaved," it was possible for champion Muhammed Ali to be a hero to both white and black boxing fans despite his often bizarre behavior and his militant advocacy of racial equality and adoption of the Muslim religion.

Their achievements and advances aside, black Americans had found real self-awareness. The attitude of mind that ran from the lonely Denmark Vesey to Frederick Douglass to W. E. B. Du Bois had become the black consensus.

Rethinking Public Education

Young people were in the forefront in both the fight for the rights of blacks and the women's liberation movement. In a time of uncertainty and discontent, full of conflict and dilemma, youth was affected more strongly than the older generations, and it reacted more forcefully. No established institution escaped its criticisms, not even the vaunted educational system, which, youth discovered, poorly suited their needs. This was still another paradox of modern life, for American public education was probably the best (it was certainly the most comprehensive) in the world.

After World War I, under the impact of Freudian psychology, the emphasis in elementary education shifted from using the schools as instruments of social change, as John Dewey had recommended, to using them to promote the emotional development of the students. "Child-centered" educators played down academic achievement in favor of "adjustment." It probably stimulated the students' imaginations and may possibly have improved their psychological well-being, but observers soon noted that the system produced poor work habits and fuzzy thinking and plain ignorance.

---

*The California Supreme Court upheld the right to use peyote in this way in *People* v. *Woody* (1964).

The demands of society for rigorous intellectual achievement made this distortion of progressive education increasingly less satisfactory. Following World War II, critics began a concerted assault on the system. The leader of the attack was James B. Conant, former president of Harvard. His book *The American High School Today* (1959) sold nearly half a million copies. Conant flayed the schools for their failure to teach English grammar and composition effectively, for neglecting foreign languages, and for ignoring the needs of both the brightest and the slowest of their students.

The success of the Soviet Union in launching the first *Sputnik* in 1957 increased the influence of critics like Conant. To match the Russian achievement, the United States needed thousands of engineers and scientists, and the schools were not turning out enough graduates prepared to study science and engineering at the college level. Suddenly the schools were under enormous pressure, for with more and more young people wanting to go to college, the colleges were raising their admission standards. The "traditionalists" thus gained the initiative, academic subjects a revived prestige. The National Defense Education Act of 1958 supplied a powerful stimulus by allocating funds for upgrading work in the sciences, foreign languages, and other subjects and for expanding guidance services and experimenting with television and other new teaching devices.

Concern for improving the training of the children of disadvantaged minority groups (Mexican Americans, Puerto Ricans, Indians, blacks), pulled the system in a different direction. Many of these children lived in horrible slums, often in broken homes. They lacked the incentives and training that middle-class children received in the family. Many did poorly in school, in part because they were poorly motivated, in part because the system was poorly adapted to their needs. But catering to the needs of such children threatened to undermine the standards being set for other children. Added to the strains imposed by racial conflicts, the effect was to create the most serious crisis American public education had ever faced.

The post-*Sputnik* stress on academic achievement profoundly affected higher education too. Prestige institutions such as Harvard, Yale, Columbia, Stanford, and dozen of other colleges and universities raised their entrance requirements. Then, by the mid-1960s, the children of the baby boom generation were flocking to the nation's high schools and colleges. Population growth and the the demands of society for specialized intellectual skills were causing educational institutions to burst at the seams. Enrollments had risen rapidly after World War II, mostly because of the G. I. Bill; by 1950 there were 2.6 million students in American colleges and universities. Yet 20 years later the total had risen to 8.6 million, a decade after that to about 12 million. To bridge the gap between high school and college, the two-year junior college proliferated. Almost unknown before 1920, there were 1,300-odd junior colleges in the late 1980s.

The federal and state governments, together with private philanthropic institutions such as the Carnegie Corporation and the Ford Foundation, poured millions of dollars into preschool programs like Head Start, into dormitory and classroom construction, into teacher education, and into scholarship funds. At the graduate level, the federal government's research and development program, administered by the National Science Foundation, provided billions for laboratories, equipment, professors' salaries, and student fellowships.

Students in Revolt

For a time after the war, the expansion of higher education took place with remarkable smoothness. Veterans, eager to make up for lost time, concentrated on their studies and most younger students followed their lead. But in the 1960s the mood changed. This college generation had grown up during the postwar prosperity and had been trained by teachers who were, by and large, New Deal liberals. They had been told that the government was supposed to regulate the economy and help the weak against the strong. But many did not think it was performing these functions adequately. Modern industrial society with its "soulless" corporations, its computers, and its almost equally unfeeling human bureaucracies made them feel insignificant and powerless. Their "advantages" also made them feel guilty when they thought about the millions of Americans who did not have them. The existence of poverty in a country as rich as the United States seemed intolerable, race prejudice both stupid and evil. The response of their elders to McCarthyism appeared craven cowardice of the worst sort.

All these influences were encapsulated in a manifesto put forth at a meeting of Students for a Democratic Society (SDS) held at Port Huron, Michigan, in 1962. "We are the people of this generation . . . looking uncomfortably to the world we inherit," their Port Huron Statement began. How to reconcile the contradictions between the idea that "all men are created equal" with "the facts of Negro life?" The government says it is for peace yet makes huge "economic and military investments in the Cold War." "We would replace power rooted in possession," the SDS manifesto ran, by power "rooted in love."

SDS grew rapidly, powered by the war in Vietnam and a seemingly unending list of local campus issues. Radical students generally had little tolerance for injustice and their dissatisfaction often found expression in public protests. The first great outburst convulsed the University of California at Berkeley in the fall of 1964. Angry students staged sit-down strikes to protest the prohibition of political canvassing on the campus. Hundreds were arrested; the state legislature threatened reprisals; the faculty became involved in the controversy.

On campus after campus in the late sixties, students organized sit-ins and employed other disruptive tactics. Frequently professors and administrators played into the radicals' hands, being so offended by their methods and manners that they refused to recognize the legitimacy of some of their demands.

At Columbia in 1968, SDS and black students occupied university buildings and issued "non-negotiable" demands concerning the university's involvement in secret military research and its relations with neighborhood minority groups. When, after long delays, the police were called to clear the buildings, dozens of students, some of them innocent bystanders, were clubbed and beaten.

Equally significant in altering the student mood was the frustration that so many of them felt with traditional aspects of college life. Dissidents denounced rules that restricted their personal lives, such as prohibitions on the use of alcohol and the banning of members of the opposite sex

from dormitories; they complained that required courses inhibited their intellectual development; and they demanded a share in the government of their institutions, long the private preserve of administrators and professors.

Beyond their specific complaints, the radicals refused to put up with anything they considered wrong. The knotty social problems that made their elders gravitate toward moderation led these students to become intransigent absolutists. Racial prejudice was evil: it must be eradicated. War in a nuclear age was insane: Armies must be disbanded. Poverty amid plenty was an abomination: End poverty now. To the counsel that evil can be eliminated only gradually, they responded with scorn. Extremists adopted a nihilistic position—the only way to deal with a "rotten" society was to destroy it; reform was impossible, constructive compromise corrupting.

Critics found the radical students infantile because they refused to tolerate frustration or delay, old-fashioned because their absolutist ideas had been exploded by several generations of philosophers and scientists, and authoritarian because they rejected majority rule. As time passed, SDS was plagued by factional disputes. Radical women claimed that it was run by male chauvinists; women who sought some say in policy matters, were met with "indifference, ridicule, and anger," one woman wrote.

By the end of the 1960s, SDS had lost much of its influence with the general student body. Nevertheless, it had succeeded in focusing attention on genuine social and political weaknesses both on the campuses and in the larger world.

Black students influenced the academic world in a variety of ways. Most colleges tried to increase black enrollments by their use of scholarship funds and by lowering academic entrance requirements when necessary to compensate for the poor preparation many black students had received. But most black students were dissatisfied with college life. They tended to keep to themselves, and usually had little to do with the somewhat elitist SDS. But they demanded more control over all aspects of their education than did the typical white. They wanted Black Studies programs taught and administered by blacks. Achievement of these goals was difficult because of the shortage of black teachers and because professors—including most black professors—considered student control of appointments and curricula unwise and in violation of the principles of academic freedom.

Unlike white radical students, blacks tended to confine their demands to matters directly related to local conditions. Although generalization is difficult, probably the majority of academics drew a distinction between black radicals, whose actions they found understandable even when they disapproved of them, and white radicals, many of whom they thought self-indulgent or emotionally disturbed.

The Counterculture

Some young people, generally known as hippies, were so "turned off" by the modern world that they retreated from it, finding refuge in communes, drugs, and mystical religions. Groups could be found in every big city in the United States and Europe. Some hippies, like the poet Allen Ginsberg and the novelist Ken Kesey, were genuinely creative people. Ginsberg's dark, desperate masterpiece, *Howl*, written in 1955, is perhaps the most widely read poem of the postwar era, certainly a work of major literary significance. *Howl* begins: "I saw the best minds of my generation destroyed by madness, starving hysterical naked," and goes on to describe the wanderings and searchings of these "angelheaded hipsters . . . seeking jazz or sex or soup" in Houston, "whoring in Colorado," and "investigating the F.B.I. in beards and shorts" in California, all the while denouncing "the narcotic tobacco haze of Capitalism." Others, however, such as the "Yippies" Abbie Hoffman and Jerry Rubin, are best described as professional iconoclasts. (In 1968 yippies went through the motions of nominating a pig named Pigassus for president.)

The hippies developed a "counterculture" so directly opposite to the way of life of their parents' generation as to suggest to critics that they were still dominated by the culture they rejected. They wore old blue jeans and (it seemed) any nondescript garments they happened to find at hand. Male hippies wore their hair long and grew beards. Females avoided make up, bras, and other devices more conventional women used to make themselves attractive to men. Both sexes rejected the old Protestant ethic; being part of the hippie

world meant not caring about money, or material goods, or power over other people. Love was more important than money or influence, feelings more significant than thought, natural things superior to anything manufactured.

Most hippies resembled the radicals in their political and social opinions, but they rejected activism. Theirs was a world of folk songs and blaring acid rock music, of "be-ins," casual sex, and drugs. Their slogan, "make love, not war," was more a general pacifist pronouncement than a specific criticism of events in Vietnam. Indeed, passivity was with them a philosophy, almost a principle. At rock concerts they listened where earlier generations had danced. Hallucinogenic drugs heightened users' "experiences" while they were in fact in a stupor; witness "tune in, turn on, drop out." Another hippie slogan, "do your own thing," would only work in social situations if no one did anything. Their communes were a far cry from the busy centers of social experimentation of the pre–Civil War age of reform.

Charles Reich, a professor at Yale, dignified the hippie view of the world in *The Greening of America* (1970) with the title, "Consciousness III." Reich's Consciousness I was the do-it-yourself, laissez-faire approach to life—having "more faith in winning than in love," while Consciousness II was the psychology of "liberal intellectuals"—marked by faith in institutional solutions to problems. Reich taught a course on "Individualism in America." One semester he had over 500 students, not one of whom failed. According to the *Yale Course Guide,* published by students, Professor Reich "thinks kids are neat and what can be bad about someone telling you how the system and the older generation have warped and destroyed things for us?"

The Sexual Revolution

Young people made the most striking contribution to the revolution that took place in the late 1960s in public attitudes toward sexual relationships. Almost overnight (it seemed in retrospect), conventional ideas about premarital sex, contraception and abortion, homosexuality, pornography, and a host of related matters were openly challenged. Probably the behavior of the majority of Americans did not alter radically. But the majority's beliefs and practices were no longer automatically acknowledged to be the only valid ones. It became possible for individuals to espouse different values and to behave differently with at least relative impunity.

The causes of this revolution were complex and interrelated; one change led to others. More efficient methods of birth control and antibiotics that cured venereal disease removed the two principal practical arguments against sex outside marriage; with these barriers down, many found their moral attitudes changing. Almost concurrently, Alfred C. Kinsey's *Sexual Behavior in the Human Male* (1948), which was based on thousands of confidential interviews, revealed that where sex was concerned, large numbers of Americans did not practice what they preached. Premarital sex, marital infidelity, homosexuality, and various forms of perversion were, Kinsey's figures showed, far more common than most persons had suspected.

Sexual Behavior in the Human Male shocked many people and when he published *Sexual Behavior in the Human Female* in 1958, which demonstrated that the sexual practices of women were as varied as those of men, he was subjected to a storm of abuse and deprived of the foundation support that had financed his research.

Kinsey has been called "the Marx of the sexual revolution." Once it became possible to accept the idea that one's own urges might not be as uncommon as one had been led to believe, it became much more difficult to object to any sexual activity practiced in private by consenting adults. Homosexuals, for example, demanded that the heterosexual society cease to harass and discriminate against them.

The sexual revolution in its many aspects served useful functions. Reducing inhibitions was liberating for many persons of both sexes, and it tended to help young people form permanent associations on the basis of deeper feelings than their sexual drives. Women surely profited from the new freedom, just as a greater sharing of family duties by husbands and fathers opened men's lives to many new satisfactions.

But like other changes, the revolution produced new problems. For young people, sexual freedom could be very unsettling; sometimes it generated social pressures that propelled them into relationships they were not yet prepared to handle. Equally perplexing was the rise in the number of illegitimate births. Easy cures did not eliminate venereal disease; on the contrary, the relaxation of sexual taboos produced an epidemic of gonorrhea, a frightening increase in the incidence of syphilis, and the emergence of a deadly new disease, acquired immune deficiency syndrome (AIDS).

Exercising the right to advocate and practice previously forbidden activities involved subjecting people who found those activities offensive—still a large proportion of the population—to embarrassment and even to acute emotional distress. To some people pornography seemed ethically wrong, and to most feminists it seemed degrading to women. Abortion raised difficult legal and moral questions. Such questions exacerbated already serious social conflicts. Clearly, however, the sexual revolution was not about to end, the direction of change not to be reversed.

Women's Liberation

Sexual freedom also contributed to the revival of the women's rights movement. For one thing, freedom involved a more drastic revolution for women than for men. Effective methods of contraception obviously affected women more directly than men, and the new attitudes heightened women's awareness of the way the old sexual standards had restricted their entire existence. In fact, the two movements interacted with each other. Concern for better job opportunities and for equal pay for equal work, for example, fed the demand for day-care centers for children.

Still another cause of the new drive for women's rights was concern for improving the treatment of minorities. Participation in the civil rights movement encouraged women to speak out more forcefully for their own rights. Feminists argued that they were being demeaned and dominated by a male-dominated society and must fight back.

When World War II ended, women who had taken jobs because of the labor shortage were expected to surrender them to veterans and return to their "traditional" roles as housewives and mothers. Some did; in 1940 about 15 percent of American women in their early thirties were unmarried, in 1965 only 5 percent. Many, however, did not meekly return to the home and many of those who did, continued to hold down jobs. Other women went to work to counterbalance the onslaughts of inflation, still others simply because they enjoyed the money and the independence that jobs made possible. Between 1940 and 1960 the proportion of women workers doubled. The rise was particularly swift among married women, and the difficulties faced by anyone trying to work while having to perform household duties increased the resentment of these workers.

Women workers still faced job discrimination of many kinds. In nearly every occupation they were paid less than men. Many interesting jobs were either closed to them entirely or doled out on the basis of some illogical and often unwritten quota system. Many women objected to this state of affairs even in the 1950s; in the 1960s their protest erupted into an organized and vociferous demand for change.

One of the leaders of the new women's movement was Betty Friedan. In *The Feminine Mystique* (1963), Friedan argued that advertisers, popular magazines, and other opinion-shaping forces were undermining the capacity of women to use their intelligence and their talents creatively by a pervasive and not very subtle form of brainwashing designed to convince them of the virtues of domesticity. She argued that without understanding why, thousands of women living supposedly happy lives were experiencing vague but persisting feelings of anger and discomfort. "The only way for a woman . . . to know herself as a person is by creative work of her own," she wrote. A "problem that had no name" was stifling women's potential.

The Feminine Mystique was what later came to be known as "consciousness raising." Over a million copies were quickly sold. After her book came out, Friedan was deluged by hundreds of letters from women who had thought their feelings of unease and depression despite their "happy" family life to be both unique to themselves and unreasonable.

Friedan had assumed that if able women acted with determination, employers would stop discriminating against them. This did not happen. In 1966 she and other feminists founded the National Organization for Women (NOW). Copying the tactics of black activists, NOW called for

Betty Friedan, author of *The Feminine Mystique,* spearheaded women's rights demonstrations like the National Women's Strike in August 1970. The strike called on women to boycott four consumer products whose advertising the protesters considered insulting to women.

equal employment opportunities and equal pay as civil rights. "The time has come for a new movement toward true equality for all women in America and toward a fully equal partnership of the sexes," the leaders announced. In 1967 NOW came out for an equal rights amendment to the Constitution, for changes in the divorce laws, and for the legalization of abortion, the right of "control of one's body."

By 1967 some feminists were arguing that NOW was not radical enough. They deplored its hierarchical structure and its imitation of conventional pressure-group tactics. Equality of the two sexes smacked of "separate but equal" to these women.

Typical was Kate Millett, whose *Sexual Politics* (1970) called for "a sexual revolution" to do away with "traditional inhibitions and taboos." Millett denounced male supremacy and drew a distinction between the immutable biological differences between men and women, and gender, how men and women relate to one another socially and culturally, which are learned ways of behaving and thus capable of change. For example, people must stop thinking of words like *violent* and *efficiency* as male characteristics and *passive* and *tenderness* as female.

The radicals gathered in small consciousness-raising groups to discuss subjects as varied as the need for government child-care centers, how best to denounce the annual Miss America contests, and lesbianism. They held conferences and seminars and published magazines, the most widely known being *Ms*, edited by Gloria Steinem. Academics among them organized women's studies programs at dozens of colleges.

Some radical feminists advocated raising children in communal centers and doing away with marriage as a legal institution. "The family unit is a decadent, energy-absorbing, destructive, wasteful institution," one prominent feminist declared. Others described marriage as "legalized rape."

The militants attacked the standard image of the female sex. Avoiding the error of the Progressive Era reformers who had fought for the vote by stressing differences between the sexes, they insisted on total equality. Cliches such as "the weaker sex" made them see red. They insisted that the separation of "Help Wanted—Male" and "Help Wanted—Female" classified ads in newspapers violated the Civil Rights Act of 1964 and they demanded that men bear more of the burden of caring for their children, cooking, and housework. They took courses in self-defense in order to be able to protect themselves from muggers, rapists,

Milestones

1948	Alfred C. Kinsey, *Sexual Behavior in the Human Male*	**1968**	Student strike at Columbia University broken by police
1950	David Riesman, *The Lonely Crowd*		Martin Luther King, Jr., murdered
1954	Launching of USS *Nautilus*, first atomic-powered ship	**1962**	Students for a Democratic Society's Port Huron Statement
1955	Allen Ginsberg, "Howl"	**1963**	Betty Friedan, *The Feminine Mystique*
	AFL and CIO merge		Supreme Court guarantees free legal counsel for indigents accused of crimes (*Gideon* v. *Wainright*)
1956	William Whyte, *The Organization Man*		
1957	Russians launch first *Sputnik*	**1964**	Free speech movement at University of California
	Supreme Court reinstates "clear and present danger" standard in First Amendment cases	**1965**	Malcolm X murdered
			César Chávez organizes boycott to support grape pickers
	(*Yates* v. *U.S.*)	**1969**	American astronauts land on the moon
1958	National Defense Education Act		
1965–1967	Riots in black ghettos	**1970**	Kate Millet, *Sexual Politics*
1966	National Organization for Women (NOW) founded	**1973**	Supreme Court guarantees right of abortion in early stages of pregnancy (*Roe* v. *Wade*)
		1975	Indian Self-Determination Act

and casual mashers. They denounced the use of masculine words like *chairman* (favoring *chairperson)* and of such terms as *mankind* and *men* to designate people in general.[†] They substituted *Ms.* for both *Miss* and *Mrs.* on the ground that the language drew no such distinction between unmarried and married men.

The most radical of the feminists went still further. As Todd Gitlin put it in *The Sixties: Years of Hope, Days of Rage,* they attacked "not just capitalism, but men."

At the other extreme, many women rejected the position even of moderate feminists like Betty Friedan. Conservatives campaigned against the Equal Rights Amendment. After the Supreme Court declared in *Roe* v. *Wade* (1973) that women had a constitutional right to have an abortion during the early stages of pregnancy, a right-to-life movement dedicated to the overturn of the decision sprang up. But few people escaped being affected by the women's movement. Even the most unregenerate male seemed to recognize that the balance of power and influence between the sexes had been altered. Clearly, the sexual revolution was not about to end, the direction of change in gender relationships not to be reversed.

Supplementary Reading

J. F. Heath, **Decade of Disillusionment: The Kennedy-Johnson Years** (1980), and A. J. Matusow, **The Unravelling of America** (1984), are good surveys of the period. On Kennedy, consult H. S. Parmet, **Jack** (1980) and **JFK** (1983), and also A. M. Schlesinger, Jr., **A Thousand Days*** (1965). On Johnson, see Rowland Evans and Robert Novak, **Lyndon B. Johnson*** (1966), E. F. Goldman, **The Tragedy of Lyndon Johnson*** (1969), and Doris Kearns, **Lyndon Johnson and the American Dream*** (1976).

On the changes of the period, see J. K. Galbraith, **The Affluent Society*** (1958) and **The**
New Industrial State*** (1967), Paul Goodman, **Growing Up Absurd*** (1960), and C. A. Reich, **The Greening of America*** (1970).

For television, see G. A. Steiner, **The People Look at Television** (1963). Daniel Hoffman, ed., **Harvard Guide to Contemporary American Writing** (1979), contains convenient discussions of postwar literature. Morris Dickstein, **Gates of Eden: American Culture in the Sixties** (1977), is part history, part literary criticism, part memoir. Modern art is discussed in Barbara Rose, **American Art Since 1900*** (1967).

For poverty and urban problems, see Michael Harrington, **The Other America*** (1962), Oscar Lewis, **La Vida: A Puerto Rican Family in the Culture of Poverty*** (1966), and Mitchell Gordon, **Sick Cities: Psychology and Pathology of American Urban Life*** (1963). On race relations, see James Baldwin, **The Fire Next Time*** (1963), M. L. King, Jr., **Stride Toward Freedom*** (1958), Malcolm X, **Autobiography*** (1966), C. E. Silberman, **Crisis in Black and White*** (1964), K. B. Clark, **Youth in the Ghetto** (1964), and David Lewis, **King: A Critical Biography** (1970). M. S. Meier and Feliciano Rivera, **The Chicanos*** (1972), provides a sympathetic discussion of the problems and aspirations of Mexican Americans, but see also Joan London and Henry Anderson, **So Shall Ye Reap: The Story of César Chávez & the Farm Workers' Movement*** (1970), and J. R. Garcia, **Operation Wetback** (1980). The revived interest in ethnicity is discussed in Michael Novak, **The Rise of the Unmeltable Ethnics** (1972), and Thomas Sowell, **Ethnic America** (1981).

The literature on the women's movement is voluminous. See W. H. Chafe, **The American Woman*** (1972) and **Women and Equality*** (1977), Betty Friedan, **The Feminine Mystique*** (1963), and C. N. Degler, **At Odds*** (1981).

Educational trends are discussed in R. N. Sanford, ed., **The American College** (1962), Martin Mayer, **The Schools*** (1961), and Robert Coles, **Children of Crisis*** (1967). On militancy among college students, see Kenneth Keniston, **Young Radicals** (1968), and Theodore Roszak, **The Making of a Counter-Culture** (1969).

[†]The difficulty here was that this form of discrimination was built into the structure of the language. Even the word *woman* derives from the Anglo-Saxon *wif-mann,* "wife of a man." Efforts to avoid the use of masculine words in general references led to such awkward expressions as *his/her* and *(s)he.*

*Available in paperback.

CHAPTER 32

Our Times

Ford as President
The Carter Presidency
Cold War or Détente?
A Time of Troubles
Double-Digit Inflation
The Carter Recession
The Iranian Crisis: Origins
The Iranian Crisis: Carter's Dilemma
The Election of 1980
Reagan as President
Four More Years
The "Reagan Revolution"
Change and Uncertainty
The Merger Movement
The Iran-Contra Arms Deal
The Election of 1988
The End of the Cold War
Domestic Problems and Possibilities
The War in the Persian Gulf
Things Go Wrong
The Election of 1992
A New Start
The Imponderable Future

*T*he country greeted the accession of Gerald Ford to the presidency with a collective sigh of relief. Most observers considered Ford unimaginative, but his record was untouched by scandal. He was Nixon's opposite as a person, be-

ing gregarious and open, and he stated repeatedly that he took a dim view of Nixon's high-handed way of dealing with Congress. The president and Congress must work together in the nation's interest, he insisted.

Ford as President

Ford obviously desired to live up to public expectations, yet he was soon embroiled in controversy. At the outset, he roused widespread resentment by pardoning Nixon for whatever crimes, known or unknown, he had committed in office. Not many Americans wanted to see the ex-president lodged in jail, but pardoning him seemed incomprehensible when he had admitted no guilt and had not yet been officially charged with any crime. Ugly rumors of a deal worked out before Nixon resigned were soon circulating, for the pardon seemed grossly unfair. Why should Nixon go scot-free when his chief underlings, Mitchell, Haldeman, and Ehrlichman, were being brought to trial for their part in the Watergate scandal? (All three were eventually convicted and jailed.)

Ford displayed inconsistency and apparent incompetence in managing the economy. He announced that inflation was the major problem and called on patriotic citizens to signify their willingness to fight it by wearing buttons inscribed "Whip Inflation Now." Almost immediately the economy entered a precipitous slump. Production fell and the unemployment rate rose above 9 percent. The president was forced to ask for tax cuts and other measures aimed at stimulating business activity. While pressing for them, he continued to fulminate against spending money on social programs designed to help the urban poor.

That Ford would never act rashly proved to be an incorrect assumption. Ford had always taken a hawkish position on the Vietnam War. As the military situation deteriorated in the spring of 1975, he tried to persuade Congress to pour more arms into the South to stem the North Vietnamese advance. The legislators flatly refused to do so, and late in April, Saigon fell. The long Vietnam War was finally over.

Two weeks earlier local communists of a particularly radical persuasion had overturned the pro-American regime in Cambodia. On May 12,

Cambodian naval forces seized the American merchant ship *Mayaguez* in the Gulf of Siam. Without allowing the new regime time to respond to his perfectly proper demand that the *Mayaguez* and its crew be freed, Ford ordered Marine units to attack Tang Island, where the captured vessel had been taken. The assault succeeded in that the Cambodians released the *Mayaguez* and its crew of 39, but 38 Marines died in the operation. Since the Cambodians had released the ship before the Marines struck, Ford's reflexive response was probably unnecessary.

After some hesitation, Ford decided to seek the Republican presidential nomination in 1976. He was opposed by Ronald Reagan, ex-governor of California, a movie actor turned politician who was the darling of the Republican right wing. Reagan's campaign was well organized and well financed. He was an excellent speaker, where Ford proved somewhat bumbling on the stump. The contest was close, both candidates winning important primaries and gathering substantial blocs of delegates in nonprimary states. At the convention in August, Ford obtained a slim majority. The Democrats chose James Earl Carter, a former governor of Georgia, as their candidate. Carter had been a naval officer and a substantial peanut farmer and warehouse owner before entering politics. He was elected governor of Georgia in 1970. While governor, he won something of a reputation as a southern public official who treated black citizens fairly. (He hung a portrait of Martin Luther King, Jr., in his office.)

Carter's political style was informal—he insisted on being called Jimmy. During the campaign he turned his inexperience in national politics to his advantage, emphasizing his lack of connection with the Washington establishment rather than apologizing for it. He repeatedly called attention to his integrity and his deep religious faith. "I'll never lie to you," he promised voters, a pledge that no candidate would have bothered to make before Nixon's disgrace.

In the election campaign Ford stressed controling inflation, Carter high unemployment. After a close but uninspiring contest, Carter was elected, 297 electoral votes to 241, having carried most of the South and a few large industrial states. A key element in his victory was the fact that he got an overwhelming majority of the black vote (partly on his record in Georgia, partly because Ford had been unsympathetic toward the demands of the urban poor). He also ran well in districts where labor unions were influential.

The Carter Presidency

Carter shone brightly in comparison with Nixon, and he seemed more forward-looking and imaginative than Ford. He tried to give a tone of democratic simplicity and moral fervor to his administration. He enrolled his daughter Amy, a fourth grader, in a largely black Washington public school. Soon after taking office he held a "call-in," for two hours answering questions phoned in by people from all over the country.

As an administrator, Carter fared poorly. He submitted many complicated proposals to Congress, but failed in most instances to follow them up. This tendency led to frequent changes in policy. After campaigning on the need to restrain inflation, he came out for a $50 income tax rebate that would surely have caused prices to rise if Congress had passed it.

He also tended to blame others when his plans went awry. In an important television address, he described a national malaise that was sapping people's energies and undermining civic pride. Although there was some truth to this observation, it made the president seem ineffective and petulant.

Cold War or Détente?

In foreign affairs Carter displayed the same indecision and inconsistency. He announced that he would put defense of "basic human rights" before all other concerns. He cut off aid to Chile and Argentina because of human rights violations and negotiated treaties gradually transferring control of the Panama Canal to Panama. He also sought to continue the Nixon-Kissinger policy of détente.

In 1979 he agreed to exchange ambassadors with the People's Republic of China. However, maintaining good relations with the Soviet Union was more difficult. He negotiated another Strategic Arms Limitation Treaty (SALT II) with the Soviet Union in the summer of 1979, but when the Soviets sent troops into Afgh.anistan to overthrow a government they disapproved of, Carter denounced the invasion and threatened to use force if they invaded any country bordering on the Persian Gulf. Carter also stopped shipments of grain and technologically advanced products to the Soviet Union and withdrew the new SALT treaty.

Carter's one striking diplomatic achievement was the so-called Camp David Agreement between Israel and Egypt. Avoiding war in the Middle East was crucial because war in that part of the world was likely to result in a cutoff of oil supplies from the Arab nations. In September 1978 the president of Egypt, Anwar Sadat, and Prime Minister Menachem Begin of Israel came to the United States at Carter's invitation to negotiate a peace treaty ending the state of war that had existed between their countries for many years. For two weeks they conferred at Camp David, the presidential retreat outside the capital, and Carter's mediation had much to do with their successful negotiations. In the treaty Israel promised to withdraw from territory captured from Egypt during the Six-Day War of 1967. Egypt in turn recognized Israel as a nation, the first Arab country to do so.

A Time of Troubles

Carter had promised to fight inflation by reducing government spending and balancing the budget,

and to stimulate the economy by cutting taxes. He advanced an admirable, if complicated, plan for conserving energy and reducing the dependence of the United States on OPEC oil. It involved raising the tax on gasoline and imposing a new tax on "gas guzzlers," cars that got relatively few miles per gallon. But in typical fashion he did not press for these measures.

For reasons that were not entirely Carter's fault, national self-confidence was at a low ebb. The United States had lost considerable international prestige. To a degree this was unavoidable. The very success of American policies after World War II had something to do with the decline of American influence in the world. The Marshall Plan, for example, enabled the nations of Western Europe to rebuild their economies; thereafter they were less dependent on outside aid, and in the course of pursuing their own interests they sometimes adopted policies that did not seem to be in the best interests of the United States. Under American occupation, Japan rebuilt its shattered economy. By the 1960s and 1970s, it had become one of the world's leading manufacturing nations, its exporters providing fierce competition in markets previously dominated by Americans.

At home the decay of the inner sections of many cities was a continuing cause of concern. The older cities seemed almost beyond repair.

Egypt's President Anwar Sadat, Jimmy Carter, and Israeli Prime Minister Menachem Begin clasp hands after the signing of the Camp David Agreement in 1978. Carter's active role in the peace negotiations showed his hands-on approach to the presidency.

Crime rates were high, public transportation was dilapidated and expensive, other city services were understaffed and inefficient, the schools were crowded, and student performance was poor. Blacks, Hispanics, and other minorities made up a large percentage of the population in decaying urban areas. That they had to live in such surroundings made a mockery of the commitment of the civil rights legislation of the 1960s and Lyndon Johnson's Great Society program to treat all people equally, and improve the lives of the poor.

Double-Digit Inflation

The most vexing problem in the Carter years was soaring inflation. Prices had been rising for an unprecedentedly long period and in recent years at an unusually rapid pace. In 1971 an inflation rate of 5 percent had so alarmed President Nixon that he had imposed a price freeze. In 1979 a 5 percent rate would have seemed almost deflationary—the actual rate was nearly 13 percent.

Double-digit inflation had a devastating effect on the poor, the retired, and others who were living on fixed incomes. However, the squeeze that price increases put on these unfortunates was only part of the damage done. People began to anticipate inflation. They bought goods they did not really need, on the assumption that whatever today's price, tomorrow's would be higher still. This behavior increased demand and pushed prices up still more. At another level, a kind of "flight from money" began. Well-to-do individuals transferred their assets from cash to durable goods such as land and houses, gold, works of art, jewelry, rare postage stamps, and other "collectibles." Interest rates rose rapidly as lenders demanded higher returns to compensate for expected future inflation.

Congress raised the minimum wage to help low-paid workers cope with inflation. It pegged Social Security payments to the cost of living index in an effort to protect retirees. The poor and the pensioners got some immediate relief because of these laws, but their increased spending power caused further upward pressure on prices. The price spiral seemed unstoppable.

The federal government made matters worse in several ways. People's wages and salaries rose in response to inflation, but their taxes went up more because larger dollar incomes put them in higher tax brackets. This "bracket creep" caused resentment and frustration among middle-class families. There were "taxpayer revolts" as many people turned against government programs for aiding the poor. Inflation also increased the government's need for money. Year after year, it spent more than it received in taxes. By thus unbalancing the budget it pumped billions of dollars into the economy, and by borrowing to meet the deficits it pushed up interest rates, increasing costs to businesses that had to borrow.

The Carter Recession

Carter had little to suggest that was different from the policies of Nixon and Ford. In 1978 he named a conservative banker, Paul A. Volcker, as chairman of the Federal Reserve Board. Volcker believed that the way to check inflation was to limit the growth of the money supply. Under his direction, the Board adopted a tight-money policy, which caused already high interest rates to soar. High interest rates hurt all borrowers, but they were especially damaging to the automobile and housing industries, because car and home buyers tended to borrow a large portion of the purchase price. High interest charges caused tens of thousands of automobile workers, carpenters, bricklayers and other skilled workers to lose their jobs. Savings and loan institutions were especially hard hit because they were saddled with countless mortgages made when rates were as low as 4 and 5 percent. Now they had to pay much more than that to hold deposits and offer even higher rates to attract new money.

The Iranian Crisis: Origins

By the autumn of 1979 Carter's standing in public opinion polls was extremely low and his chances of being elected to a second term seemed dim. But at this point a dramatic upheaval in the Middle East revived his prospects. On November 4, 1979, about 400 armed Moslem militants broke into the American Embassy compound in Teheran, Iran, and took everyone within the walls captive.

The seizure had roots that ran far back in Iranian history. During World War II, Great

Britain, the Soviet Union, and later the United States occupied Iran and forced its pro-German shah into exile, replacing him with his 22-year-old son, Muhammad Reza Pahlavi. In the early 1950s, when liberal and nationalist elements in Iran, led by Premier Muhammad Musaddig, sought to reduce the power of the Anglo-Iranian Oil Company, American mediators engineered a compromise that increased the price Iran received for its petroleum. Musaddig was a liberal by Iranian standards but by Western standards somewhat eccentric. He went about in pink pajamas and broke into tears at the slightest provocation. In 1953 a CIA coup, presumably designed to prevent the nationalization of Iranian petroleum resouces and the abolition of the monarchy, resulted in his overthrow. His fall helped the international oil industry to export billions of barrels of cheap oil, but it turned most Iranians against the United States and Shah Resa Pahlavi. His unpopularity led the shah to purchase enormous amounts of American arms. He loaded up on sophisticated F-14 and F-15 fighters and other weapons. Over the years, Iran became the most powerful military force in the region.

Although Iran was an enthusiastic member of the OPEC cartel, the shah was for obvious reasons a firm friend of the United States. Iran seemed, as President Carter said in 1977, "an island of stability" in the troubled Middle East. The appearance of stability was deceptive because of the shah's unpopularity. He suppressed liberal opponents brutally and his attempts to introduce Western ideas and technology angered conservatives. Moslem religious leaders were particularly offended by such "radical" policies as the shah's tentative efforts to improve the position of women in Iranian society. Because of his American-supplied army and his American-trained secret police, his opponents hated the United States almost as much as they hated their ruler.

Throughout 1977, riots and demonstrations convulsed Iran. When soldiers fired on protesters, the bloodshed caused more unrest. The whole country seemed to rise against the shah. In January 1979, he was forced to flee. A revolutionary government headed by a revered religious leader, the Ayatollah Ruhollah Khomeini, assumed power.

Khomeini denounced the United States, the "Great Satan" whose support of the shah, he said, had caused the Iranian people untold suffering. When President Carter allowed the shah to come to the United States for medical treatment, the seizure of the Teheran embassy resulted.

The Iranian Crisis: Carter's Dilemma

The militants announced that the captive Americans would be held as hostages until the United States returned the shah to Iran for trial as a traitor. They also demanded that the shah's vast wealth be confiscated and surrendered to the Iranian government. President Carter naturally rejected these demands. Deporting the shah, who had entered the United States legally, and confiscating his property, were not possible under American law. Instead, Carter froze Iranian assets in the United States and banned trade with Iran until the hostages were freed.

A stalemate developed. Months passed. Even after the shah, who was terminally ill with cancer, left the United States for Panama, the Iranians remained adamant. The crisis provoked a remarkable emotional response in the United States. For once the entire country agreed on something. One result of this was a revival of Carter's political fortunes. Before the attack, Senator Edward M. Kennedy of Massachusetts, youngest brother of John F. Kennedy, had decided to seek the Democratic presidential nomination. He seemed a likely winner until the seizure of the hostages, which caused the public to rally round the president.

Nevertheless, the hostages languished in Iran and an intense debate raged within the administration about whether or not to attempt to rescue them. In April 1980 Carter finally ordered a team of marine commandos flown into Iran in helicopters in a desperate attempt to free them. The raid was a fiasco. Several helicopters broke down. While the others were gathered at a desert rendezvous south of Teheran, Carter called off the attempt and the Iranians made political capital of the incident, gleefully displaying on television the wrecked aircraft and captured American equipment. The stalemate continued. And when the shah died in July 1980, it made no difference to the Iranians.

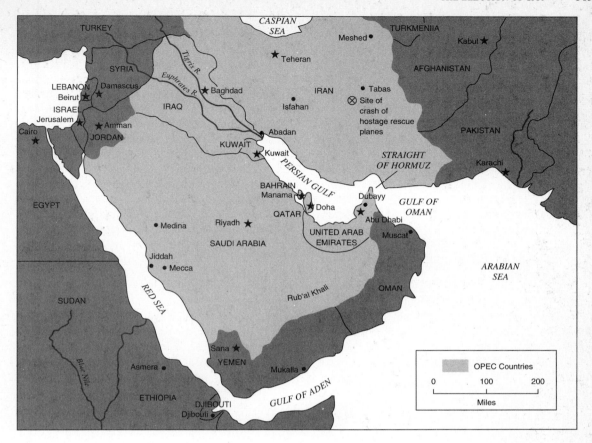

The Middle East

The Election of 1980

Despite the failure of the raid, Carter had more than enough delegates at the Democratic convention to win nomination on the first ballot. His Republican opponent in the campaign that followed was Ronald Reagan, the candidate who had almost defeated Gerald Ford for the nomination in 1976. Reagan had been a New Deal Democrat, but after World War II he became disillusioned with liberalism. When his movie career ended, he did publicity for General Electric and worked for various conservative causes. In 1966 he was elected governor of California.

The 1980 presidential campaign ranks among the most curious in American history. One of Reagan's opponents at the Republican convention,

Congressman John Anderson of Illinois, ran for president as an independent. Both Carter and Reagan spent much time explaining why the other was unsuited to be president. Carter defended his record, though without much conviction. Reagan denounced criminals, drug addicts, and all varieties of immorality and spoke favorably of patriotism, religion, and family life. He also called for rejection of the SALT II treaty and increased spending on defense, and he promised to reduce spending and cut taxes, at the same time insisting that the budget could be balanced and inflation sharply reduced.

Reagan's tendency to depend on popular magazine articles, half-remembered conversations, and other informal sources for his economic "facts" reflected a mental imprecision that alarmed his critics. But his sunny disposition and his reassuring relaxed style compared favorably with Carter's personality. The president seemed tight-lipped and tense even when flashing his habitual toothy smile. A television debate between Carter and Reagan pointed up their personal differences but Reagan's question to the audience—"Are you better off now than you were four years ago?"—had more effect on the election than any statement on policy.

On election day, voter turnout was light, but lopsided, Reagan garnering over 43 million votes to Carter's 35 million and Anderson's 5.6 million. Dissatisfaction with the Carter administration seems to have accounted for the result. The Republicans also won control of the Senate and cut deeply into the Democratic majority in the House of Representatives.

Carter devoted his last weeks in office to the continuing hostage crisis. War had broken out between Iran and Iraq. The additional strain on an Iranian economy already shattered by revolution raised hopes that the Ayatollah Khomeini would release the captive Americans. With Algeria acting as intermediary, American and Iranian diplomats worked out an agreement. Perhaps for fear that the new president might take some drastic action, Iran at last agreed to free the hostages in return for the release of its assets in the United States. After 444 days in captivity, the 52 hostages were set free on January 20, the day Reagan was inaugurated.

Reagan as President

Despite his amiable, unaggressive style, Reagan acted rapidly and with determination once in office. He hoped to change the direction in which the country was moving by turning many functions of the federal government over to the states and relying more on individual initiative. The marketplace, not bureaucratic regulations, should govern most economic decisions. Yet he also set out to increase military spending and defend American interests more vigorously in order to check what he saw as a steadily increasing gap between the strength and influence of the United States and that of the Soviet Union.

In August 1981, Reagan displayed his determination in convincing fashion when the nation's air traffic controllers went on strike. The law forbade them to do so, and Reagan ordered them to return to work. When more than 11,000 controllers refused to obey this order, Reagan discharged them and began a crash program to train replacements. Even after the strike collapsed, Reagan refused to rehire the strikers. The air controllers' union was destroyed.

Reagan made cutting taxes his first priority. He persuaded Congress to lower income taxes by 25 percent over three years and to check the growth of federal spending on social services such as welfare payments and food stamps. He insisted that in the long run the poor and everyone else would benefit more from his program.

His reasoning was based on what was known as "supply-side economics." He claimed that people would have more money to invest because of the tax cut, that they would invest the money in productive ways rather than spend it on consumer goods (because they would be able to keep a larger share of their profits), and that the investments would lead to increased production, more jobs, prosperity, and therefore more tax income for the government despite the lower tax rates.

"Reaganomics," as administration policy was called, was not a new theory. Carter had advocated tax cuts, reduced federal spending, and tight money, and during his term the airlines were freed from control by the Civil Aeronautics Board. But supply-side economics was old-fashioned to the point of being antique. It differed little from the policy Herbert Hoover had favored in the Great Depression, which his critics had derided as the "trickle-down" theory.

Most economists did not think that Reaganomics would work. By December 1982 the economy was in a full-scale recession. More than 10 percent of the work force was unemployed. Lower tax rates, soaring military expenditures without a corresponding reduction in domestic spending, and a slumping economy were further unbalancing the budget. In 1983 the deficit topped $195 billion, up from $59 billion only three years earlier, and it continued to expand thereafter. The Treasury was forced to borrow billions, which kept interest rates high. Only the fact that inflation was slowing brightened the gloomy picture.

Then, however, the economy began to pick up. With inflation down from more than 12 percent to less than 4 percent, the Federal Reserve

Board relaxed its tight-money policy. Interest rates then declined, making it easier for people to finance the purchase of homes and automobiles. Unemployment, while still high, fell below 8 percent in 1984.

But the recovery did not lead to much new business investment. People seemed to be spending their additional income on consumer goods. Together with the federal deficits caused by the increase in military expenditures, this spending prevented interest rates from going down as far as economists had hoped.

Many of Reagan's advisers urged him to reduce the military budget and seek some kind of tax increase in order to bring the government's income more nearly in line with its outlays. However, the president insisted that the military buildup was necessary because of the threat posed by the Soviet Union, which he called an "evil empire." Claiming that the communists were sending arms and supplies to the leftist government of Nicaragua and encouraging communist rebels in El Salvador, Reagan sought to undermine the Nicaraguan regime and bolster the conservative government of El Salvador. He used American troops to overthrow a Cuban-backed regime on the Caribbean island of Grenada. With the reluctant support of the Western democracies, he installed new nuclear missiles in Europe.

Four More Years

Although some Americans considered both his domestic and foreign policies wrong-headed, Reagan's standing in public opinion polls remained high. At the 1984 Republican Convention he was nominated for a second terrn without opposition. The Democrats nominated Walter Mondale of Minnesota, who had been vice president under Carter. Mondale electrified the country by choosing a woman, Representative Geraldine Ferraro of New York, as his running mate. The Democrats expected that she would win the votes of many Republican women and that her selection would counter the claims of Mondale's critics that he was unimaginative and overly cautious. On the stump, she drew large crowds and proved to be an excellent campaign orator.

Reagan began the campaign with several important advantages. He was especially popular among religious fundamentalists and other social conservatives. Many fundamentalist television preachers campaigned in his behalf. "Americans are sick and tired of . . . amoral liberals," the Reverend Jerry Falwell, founder of the Moral Majority movement, declared. Falwell was against drugs, the "coddling" of criminals, homosexuality, communism, and abortion, all views that Reagan shared. Though not openly antiblack, Falwell disapproved of forced busing and a number of other government policies designed to help blacks and other minorities. Of course, Walter Mondale was also against many of the things that Falwell and his followers denounced, but Reagan was against them all.

But Moral Majority, despite its name, was far from an actual majority. Reagan's support was much more broadly based. Thousands of working people and an enormous percentage of white southerners, types that had been solidly Democratic during the New Deal and beyond, now voted Republican. The president's personality was another important plus. Voters continued to admire his informal yet firm style and his stress on patriotism and other old-fashioned virtues.

Mondale emphasized the difficulties that he saw ahead for the nation. He blamed Reagan for the huge increase in the federal deficit and accused him of misleading the public by saying that he would not raise taxes if reelected. He stated frankly that he *would* raise taxes if elected. This admission, most unusual for a person running for office, was another attempt to counter his reputation for political caution.

All the president's economic policies, Mondale insisted, hurt the poor, women, and minorities. He pointed out, correctly, that the number of people living below the poverty line had grown in the Reagan years to over 35 million, 15.2 percent of the population.

Most polls showed Reagan far in the lead when the campaign began, and this remained true throughout the contest. Optimism and opportunity were his catchwords. Mondale argued his case forcefully, but the nature of that case sometimes made him seem gloomy, complaining, and mean spirited. Reagan avoided specifics, promising only that if he was elected, prosperity would continue and the future would be bright. Reagan's advanced age (73) was a legitimate issue, but when asked by a reporter whether he thought "the age question" important, he responded with a quip—he would not make an issue of his opponent's youth. On election day the president swept the nation, gathering nearly 60 percent of the popular vote and losing only in Mondale's Minnesota and the District of Columbia. His margin in the Electoral College was 525 to 13.

Of all the elements in the New Deal coalition, only the blacks, who voted overwhelmingly Democratic, remained loyal. The Democratic strategy of nominating a woman for vice president failed. Far more women voted for Reagan than for the Mondale-Ferraro ticket. Reagan's victory, like the Eisenhower landslides of the 1950s, was a personal one. The Republicans made only minor gains in the House of Representatives and actually lost two seats in the Senate.

The "Reagan Revolution"

Reagan's agenda for his second term closely resembled that of his first. In foreign affairs his anti-Soviet policies, and particularly his belligerent rhetoric, attracted no better than lukewarm support. This was particularly true after Mikhail S. Gorbachev became the Soviet premier in March 1985. Gorbachev was far more moderate and flexible than his predecessors, and much more concerned about public opinion in the Western democracies. He encouraged political debate and criticism in the Soviet Union—the policy known as *glasnost*—and sought to stimulate its stagnant economy by decentralizing administration and rewarding individual enterprise (*perestroika*).

Gorbachev also announced that he would continue to honor the unratified SALT II agreement, whereas Reagan seemed bent on pushing ahead with the expansion of America's nuclear arsenal. He wished to develop a computer-controlled strategic defense initiative (SDI) that would supposedly be capable of destroying enemy missiles in outer space where they could do no damage. Despite his insistence that SDI would be a defensive system, the Soviets objected to it vociferously.

But after he realized that the Soviet leader was eager to limit nuclear weapons, Reagan met with Gorbachev in October 1986 in Iceland to negotiate an arms control agreement. This summit

The arms cuts made at the 1988 Moscow Summit showed how Ronald Reagan's ideas about the "evil empire" had changed. Yet Reagan was surprised to find that Mikhail Gorbachev believed "the communist propaganda he's grown up hearing about our country"—above all, that business dominates the government.

got nowhere, partly beause Reagan was determined to push SDI and partly because he apparently did not understand that the Europeans, fearing Soviet superiority in conventional weapons, were horrified by the thought of total nuclear disarmament. The Iceland setback, however, proved temporary and in 1988 at a second summit, Reagan and Gorbachev signed a treaty eliminating medium-range nuclear missiles.

Reagan nevertheless persisted in pressing his SDI scheme. After the spectacular Apollo program, which sent six expeditions to the moon between 1969 and 1972, NASA's prestige was beyond measurement. Its Skylab orbiting space station program (1973–1974) was equally successful. Early in 1981 the manned space shuttle *Columbia,* after orbiting for several days, returned to earth intact, gliding on its stubby, swept-back wings to an appointed landing strip. *Columbia* and other shuttles were soon transporting satellites into space for the government and private companies, and its astronauts were conducting military and scientific experiments of great importance.

Congress, however, boggled both at the enormous estimated cost of SDI and the idea of relying for national defense on the complex technology involved. The entire space program suffered a further setback in 1986, when the space shuttle *Challenger* exploded shortly after takeoff, killing its seven-member crew. This disaster put a stop to the program while complex engineering changes were made. Finally, however, in 1989 the shuttles began flying again.

The president was more successful in winning public support for his get-tough-with-terrorists policy. In October 1985, four Arabs seized control of a cruise ship in the Mediterranean. After killing an elderly American tourist, they surrendered to Egyptian authorities on condition that they be provided with safe passage to Libya on an Egyptian airliner.

The terrorists chose Libya because its president, Muammar al-Qaddafi, was a bitter enemy of Israel and the United States. On Reagan's orders Navy F-14 jets forced the Egyptian pilot to land in Italy instead of Libya and the terrorists were taken into custody.

Then, after a Libyan-planned bombing of a West German club frequented by American servicemen, Reagan launched an air strike against Libyan bases from airfields in Great Britain. This attack greatly alarmed Europeans, but in America the president's popularity reached an all-time high.

Reagan's basic domestic objectives—to reduce the scope of federal activity, particularly in the social welfare area; to lower income taxes; and to increase the strength of the armed forces—did not change either. Despite the tax cuts already made, congressional leaders agreed to the Income Tax Act of 1986, which reduced the top levy on personal incomes from 50 percent to 28 percent and the tax on corporate profits from 46 percent to 34 percent.

Liberal members of Congress had found it politically difficult to oppose the measure. The old tax system was full of "loopholes" benefiting particular interests, and the new law did away with most tax shelters that had enabled high-income citizens to reduce their tax bills sharply. The law also relieved 6 million low-income people from paying any federal income tax at all. The objective of the law was to require people with similar incomes to pay roughly equal taxes.

But the law undermined the principle of progressive taxation—the practice, dating back to the first income tax enacted after the adoption of the

Sixteenth Amendment in 1913, of requiring high-income people to pay a larger *percentage* of their income than those with smaller incomes. The new law set only two rates: 15 percent on taxable incomes below $29,750 for families, and 28 percent on incomes above this limit. A family with a taxable income of $30,000 would pay at the same rate as one with $300 million.

Reagan advanced another of his objectives by appointing conservatives to federal judgeships. In 1981 he named Sandra Day O'Connor to the Supreme Court. Justice O'Connor was the first woman to be appointed to the Court, but she was nevertheless conservative on most constitutional questions. When Chief Justice Warren C. Burger resigned in 1986 Reagan replaced him with Associate Justice William H. Rehnquist, probably the most conservative member of the Court, and he filled the vacancy with Antonin Scalia, an even more conservative judge. After the resignation of Associate Justice Lewis F. Powell in 1987, the president nominated the extremely conservative Robert Bork, the man who, while Nixon's solicitor general, had discharged the Watergate special prosecutor, Archibald Cox. But the Senate refused to confirm Bork, and eventually the appointment went to a less controversial but by no means liberal judge, David Kennedy. By 1988 Reagan had appointed well over half of all the members of the federal bench.

Change and Uncertainty

But if the "Reagan Revolution" seemed to have triumphed, powerful forces were at work that no individual or party could effectively control. For one thing, the makeup of the American people, always in a state of flux, was changing at a rate approaching that of the early 1900s when the "new immigration" was at its peak. In the 1970s, after the Immigration Act of 1965 had put an end to the national origins system, more than 4 million immigrants entered the country, the vast majority from Asia and Latin America. This trend continued; of the 643,000 who arrived in 1986, more than 550,000 were from these regions. More than 111,000 of the immigrants came from three East Asian countries, the Philippines, Korea, and Vietnam. In addition, uncounted thousands entered the United States illegally, most crossing the long, sparsely settled border with Mexico.

Some of the immigrants were refugees fleeing from repressive regimes in Vietnam, Cuba, Haiti, and Central America, and nearly all were poor. Most tended, like their predecessors, to crowd together in ethnic neighborhoods. Spanish could be heard more often than English in sections of Los Angeles, New York, Miami, and many other cities.

No strong demand for immigration restriction developed, perhaps because so many Americans were themselves the children of immigrants. However, conservatives found it appalling that so many people could enter the country illegally, and even Americans sympathetic to the undocumented aliens agreed that control was desirable. Finally, in 1986, Congress passed a law offering amnesty to illegal immigrants long resident in the country but penalizing employers who hired illegal immigrants in the future. Many persons legalized their status under the new law, but the influx of illegal immigrants continued. Problems developed because some employers refused to hire anyone with a foreign accent on the ground that they might be "illegals" bearing false papers.

There were other disturbing trends. The postwar population explosion and the subsequent decline in the birth rate made pressure on the Social Security system inevitable when the baby boomers reached retirement age in the early 21st century. More immediately, the traditional family, consisting of a husband and wife and their children, with the man the breadwinner and the woman the housewife, seemed in danger of ceasing to be the norm. An ever-larger number of families were headed by single parents, in most cases by women, often black and nearly always poor.

Year after year more than a million marriages ended in divorce. The tendency of couples to live together without getting married also continued, helping to explain why the number of illegitimate births rose steadily. So did the number of abortions—from 763,000 in 1974 after abortion was legalized to an annual average of 1.3 million in the 1980s. Conversely to the increase in abortions, many young women, married and unmarried, who had chosen careers over motherhood were having second thoughts as they approached the age when having children would no longer be possible.

The Reagan administration devoted much effort to fighting crime, but despite the fact that the number of prison inmates reached an all-time high, little progress was made. A campaign against illegal drugs resulted in many arrests, but the drugs remained widely available. Cocaine became, in a cheap, smokeable, and especially addictive form called "crack," a problem of epidemic proportion.

The drug problem was part of a larger and still more threatening one, the spread of the deadly new disease, AIDS. AIDS was caused by a virus that destroyed the body's immune system, exposing the victim to a host of deadly diseases. It was inevitably fatal. Since it was transmitted by the exchange of bodily fluids, intravenous drug users (who frequently shared needles) and homosexuals were its chief victims in the United States. But since it was a venereal disease, the possibility of its spreading through the general population was a constant danger.

AIDS had enormous effects on public policy and private behavior. On balance it led to a deeper understanding of homosexuality. It resulted in the expenditure of large sums on research aimed at finding a cure for the disease and to a new emphasis on contraception, especially on the use of condoms, which by 1990 were being distributed free in many high schools.

Other social and economic changes that were difficult to control included the continuing shift of employment opportunities from the production of goods to the production of services—from raising wheat and manufacturing steel to advertising, banking, and record keeping. This meant a shift from blue to white collar work, which called for more better-educated workers and increasing joblessness for the unskilled. Union membership had been falling since long before Reagan became president, but by 1985 it was down to about 19 percent of the work force, in large part because white-collar workers were difficult to organize.

These trends were magnified by the technological revolution created by computers. Computers created thousands of jobs, but they also made other thousands of workers superfluous. Combined with the changes in the tax structure and

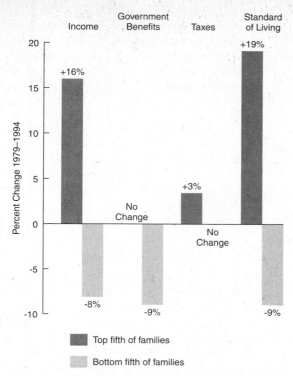

Changing Living Standards, 1979–1994

the sluggish economy of the period, these factors undermined the confidence in the future that wage earners had experienced in the 1950s and 1960s.

The Merger Movement

Another worrisome trend was the merger movement, which saw often unrelated companies swallowing up one another in unprecedented fashion. The movement began while Carter was president, and Reagan's abandonment of strict enforcement of the antitrust laws strengthened the trend. The merger movement was also encouraged by the federal tax structure; corporations had to pay taxes on stock dividends, which were treated as profits. But the interest paid on corporate bonds was a business expense and thus a tax deduction. In 1989 Time Inc. borrowed $13.9 billion to purchase Warner Communications, thus forming one of the world's largest publishing concerns. This combination would have been financially unprofitable if Time had had to raise the money by issuing new stock.

Piratical corporate "raiders" raised cash by issuing high-interest bonds secured by the assets of the company purchased. A shrewd broker, Michael Milkin of the firm of Drexel Burnham Lambert, emerged as the "king" of this "junk bond" business. The system enabled a small company or even a single entrepreneur to buy a giant corporation. One deal often led to another. In 1985 the R. J. Reynolds Tobacco Company purchased the food conglomerate Nabisco for $4.9 billion. Three years later this new giant, RJR Nabisco, was itself taken over by Kohlberg, Kravis, Roberts and Company for $24.9 billion.

Still another economic condition that defied national control was the falling world price of petroleum. This eased inflationary pressures and helped speed recovery in the United States, but cheaper oil dealt a devastating blow to the economy of the Southwest, a region where support of Reagan's policies was particularly strong. Lower oil prices also forced oil producing countries in and out of OPEC to cut back on their imports of manufactured goods. Many American banks suffered heavy losses when domestic and foreign oil-related loans went sour.

But by that time inflation had slowed to a crawl because of the tight money policy, and world agricultural prices were falling. Between 1982 and 1986, the value of American wheat exports fell from $8 billion to less than half that amount. For many debt-ridden farmers, this meant bankruptcy. More generally, the Reagan tax reductions and the president's refusal to consider any change in course on this subject meant that the federal government continued to run ever-larger deficits. The shortfall rose from $179 billion in 1985 to more than $350 billion in 1992.

The Iran-Contra Arms Deal

All these matters were partly beyond human control, or at least beyond what seemed practicable under the American political system. They diminished the effectiveness of the Reagan administration. But the administration suffered most from two self-inflicted wounds, these involving American policy in Central America and the Middle East.

The Central American problem resulted from a revolution in Nicaragua, where in 1979 leftist rebels had overthrown the dictatorial regime of Anastasio Somoza. Because the victorious "Sandinista" government was supported by both Cuba and the Soviet Union, President Reagan was determined to force it from power. He backed anti-Sandinista elements in Nicaragua known as the Contras and in 1981 persuaded Congress to provide these "freedom fighters" with arms.

But the Contras made little progress and many Americans feared that aiding them would lead, as it had in Vietnam, to the use of American troops in the fighting. In October 1984, Congress banned further military aid to the rebels. The president then sought to persuade other countries and private American groups to help the Contras (as he put it) to keep "body and soul together."

In the Middle East, war had been raging between Iran and Iraq since 1980. The chief interest of the United States in the conflict was to make sure that it did not cause the flow of Middle Eastern oil to be cut off. But public opinion in the country was particularly incensed against the Iranians. Memories of the hostage crisis of the Carter years did not fade, and Iran was widely believed to be responsible for the fact that a number of Americans were being held hostage by terrorists in Lebanon. Reagan was known to oppose any bargaining with terrorists. Nevertheless, he was eager to find some way to free the captive Americans. During 1985 he made the fateful decision to allow the indirect shipment of arms to Iran by way of Israel. He hoped that this would result in the hostages' release. When it had no effect, he went further. In January 1986 he authorized the secret sale of American weapons directly to the Iranians.

The arms sale was arranged by Marine Colonel Oliver North, an aide of Reagan's national security adviser, Admiral John Poindexter. North, who was already in charge of the administration's effort to supply the Nicaraguan Contras indirectly, used $12 million of the profit from the Iranian sales to provide weapons for the Contras, in plain violation of the congressional ban on such aid.

News of the sales to Iran and of the use of the profits to supply the Contras came to light in November 1986 and of course they caused a sensation.

Admiral Poindexter resigned; Colonel North was fired from his job with the Security Council; a special prosecutor was appointed to investigate the affair; and both a presidential committee and a joint congressional committee began investigations. Reagan insisted that he knew nothing about the aid to the Contras, but according to polls, a majority of the people did not believe him, and critics pointed out that if he was telling the truth it was almost as bad, since that meant that he had not been in control of his own administration. Although he remained personally popular, his influence with Congress and his reputation as a political leader plummeted.

The Election of 1988

The decline of Reagan's influence was also related to his status as a lame-duck president entering the last year of his tenure. In both the major political parties, attention turned to the choice of presidential candidates.

After a shaky start, Reagan's vice president, George Bush, ran away with the Republican primaries and won the nomination easily. The Democratic race was more complicated by far. So many candidates entered the field that the average citizen found it hard to tell them apart. Wits began to call the Democratic hopefuls the "seven dwarfs," suggesting both their lack of distinguishing qualities and their lack of distinction. Gradually, however, the field shrank and the race settled down to a contest between Governor Michael S. Dukakis of Massachusetts and the black leader Jesse Jackson. Jackson proposed to reduce military spending sharply and invest the savings in improving education, health care, and other social services. Jackson had the support of most blacks, but he also attracted a substantial percentage of white Democrats.

Dukakis stressed his record as an efficient manager—the Massachusetts economy was booming. His campaign was well organized and well financed. By the end of the primary season, he had a solid majority of convention delegates. He selected a conservative senator, Lloyd Bentzen of Texas, as his running mate.

In his capacity as vice president, Bush had been accused by critics of being a "wimp"—a weak, bloodless person who fawningly accepted every

Reagan policy. As candidate for president, he set out to destroy this impression without rejecting the conservative Reagan philosophy. He attacked Dukakis savagely, charging him with coddling criminals because of a Massachusetts law granting furloughs to prisoners serving life sentences for murder.

Dukakis conducted a curiously lifeless campaign. He stressed his supposed leadership qualities and his administrative abilities, but he avoided speaking out strongly for the liberal social policies that every Democratic presidential candidate since Franklin Roosevelt had supported. Consequently he found himself more often than not on the defensive against Bush's emotion-charged attacks.

Bush's choice of Senator Dan Quayle of Indiana as his running mate, proved politically damaging to the Republicans. Although Quayle was an ardent supporter of military preparedness, it came out that he had avoided the Vietnam draft by enrolling in the Indiana National Guard. More seriously, he proved slow -witted in political debate.

As the campaign progressed, neither presidential candidate aroused much enthusiasm among voters, but most polls indicated that Bush was gradually pulling away from his Democratic opponent. On election day he won handily, garnering 54 percent of the popular vote and carying the Electoral College, 426 to 112.

The End of the Cold War

Once in office, President Bush softened his tough tone, saying that he hoped to "make kinder the face of the nation and gentler the face of the world." He also displayed a more traditional command of the workings of government than his predecessor, which was reassuring to persons put off by Reagan's lack of interest in the details of government. He pleased "Reagan loyalists" by his opposition to abortion and gun control and by calling for a constitutional amendment prohibiting the burning of the American flag. His standing in the polls soared.

One important reason for this was the flood of good news from abroad. In Moscow, President Michail Gorbachev announced that the Soviet Union would not use force to keep communist governments in power in the satellite nations of Eastern Europe. Swiftly the people of Poland, Hungary, Czechoslovakia, Bulgaria, Romania, and East Germany did away with the repressive regimes that had ruled them throughout the postwar era and moved toward more democratic forms of govenment. Except in Romania, where the dictator Nicolae Ceausescu was executed by revolutionary leaders, all these fundamental changes were carried out peacefully.

Almost overnight the international political climate changed. Soviet-style communism had been discreditied. The Warsaw Pact was no longer a significant force in European international politics. The Cold War was over at last. With prodemocratic forces in power in East Germany, demand for union with West Germany quickly emerged. The infamous Berlin Wall was torn down, and talks were begun that led quickly to unification.

The United States had nothing to do with the Eastern European upheavals, but President Bush profited from them immensely. He expressed moral support for the new governments (and provided some with modest amounts of financial assistance) but refrained from trying to embarrass the Soviets. At a summit meeting in Washington in June 1990, Bush and Gorbachev signed agreements reducing American and Russian stockpiles of long-range nuclear missiles by 30 percent and eliminating chemical weapons. They also announced plans for still further cuts in weaponry, and President Bush agreed to the relaxation of barriers on trade with the Soviet Union.

More controversial was the president's decision to send troops into Panama to overthrow General Manuel Noriega, who had refused to yield power even when his figurehead presidential candidate was defeated in a national election. Noriega was under indictment in the United States for drug trafficking, and after temporarily seeking refuge in the Vatican Embassy in Panama, he surrendered to the American forces and was taken to the United States, put on trial, and convicted. Bush thus accomplished the objective of the invasion. Latin Americans were alarmed at the United States' use of force in the region, but the president's popularity was not seriously affected.

The president also benefited from the ending of the conflict between the Sandinistas and the Contras in Nicaragua, although he did not contribute much to its solution. For the first time in that nation's history, a free presidential election was held. The result was a victory for middle-of-the-road forces.

Domestic Problems and Possibilities

Bush's approach to domestic issues aroused a great deal of criticism even among Republicans. In general, like Reagan, he urged voluntarism rather than new legislation for dealing with problems. During the presidential campaign he promised not to raise taxes if elected, prefacing his statement with a phrase made famous by the actor Clint Eastwood: "Read my lips." In office he recommitted himself to that objective; in fact, he proposed reducing the tax on capital gains, a measure that would increase revenues briefly but cost the government billions in the long run. No one enjoys paying taxes; however, the national debt was huge and rapidly increasing. Dealing with it by reducing nonmilitary expenditures was extremely difficult.

Moreover, unforeseen needs for *more* expenditures were constantly arising. Nearly everyone favored extending aid to Poland and other Eastern European countries struggling to revive their stagnant economies. The invasion of Panama had been expensive, and the cost of repairing the damage and helping the new government get on its feet was also substantial.

Larger still were the sums needed to bail out the bankrupt savings and loan industry. The combination of Reagan-inspired bank deregulation, inflation, and rising interest rates had led many savings and loan institutions to lend money recklessly. A large number invested huge sums in risky junk bonds and in questionable real estate ventures. In booming states like Texas, Florida, and California such policies led to disaster when the economy cooled. In some cases the bankers had been no better than thieves, but their depositors were innocent victims, and in any case their deposits were insured. The government (meaning the general public) had to make good, and the cost was enormous. Shortly after his inauguration, Bush estimated the cost as $30 billion. Within months estimates had risen to $130 billion.

Logic would suggest that if the tax burden had been roughly proportional to the needs of society when President Bush was elected, these unplanned but legitimate new expenses justified and indeed required a tax increase. But Bush refused to be influenced by such logic, and the Democrats were unwilling to press for new revenues unless he would agree. One indirect result of the no-new-taxes policy was to strain the resources of state governments, which had to assume burdens previously borne by Washington.

Another result was the tendency of the Bush administration to settle for half-measures even when considering matters the president considered important. Bush professed to be concerned about Japanese domination of the electronics industry, yet he cut back support of research on high-definition television, semiconductors, and similar projects. He called himself the "education president," and he recognized the government's obligation to tackle the drug problem, to protect the environment, and to support efforts to discover a cure for AIDS. In all these areas, however, the sums budgeted by the administration were relatively small.

When the economy slowed in 1990, the resulting increase in the federal budget deficit finally forced the president to capitulate to reality and agree to the raising of the top income tax rate from 28 percent to 31 percent and to higher taxes on gasoline, liquor, and certain expensive luxuries. Since he had sworn not to raise taxes, this damaged his credibility and particularly angered conservative Republicans. By midsummer the nation was heading into a serious recession and Bush's standing in the polls suffered a substantial decline.

The War in the Persian Gulf

Early in August 1990, President Saddam Hussein of Iraq suddenly launched an all-out attack on Iraq's tiny neighbor, the oil-rich sheikdom of Kuwait. His pretext was Kuwait's supposed draining off of oil from the Rumalia oil field, much of which lay on the Iraqi side of their border. Saddam hoped to swallow up Kuwait, thus increasing Iraq's already large oil reserves to about 25 percent of the world total, and then to force up the world price of petroleum in order to replenish his treasury, badly depleted during his war with Iran.

His soldiers overran Kuwait swiftly, then began systematically to carry off everything of value they could transport back to Iraq. Within a week Saddam formally annexed Kuwait and he also massed troops along the border of neighboring Saudi Arabia. His army greatly outnumbered Saudi forces, and if he got control of Saudi Arabia's vast oil fields he would be able to dictate world oil prices.

The Saudis and the Kuwaitis turned at once to the United States and other nations for help, and it was quickly given. In a matter of days, the UN had applied trade sanctions against Iraq and, at the invitation of Saudi Arabia, the United States (along with Great Britain, France, Italy, Egypt, and Syria) began to move troops to Saudi bases.

The anti-Iraq buildup took time, for aside from troops, planes, tanks, ammunition, and all sorts of other military equipment had to be transported by sea and air nearly half way across the globe. But the buildup deterred the Iraqis from invading Saudi Arabia. Instead, they concentrated their forces in strong defensive positions in Kuwait and southern Iraq. This led President Bush to increase the American force in the area from 180,000 to more than 500,000, an army deemed capable of driving the Iraqis from their defenses and liberating Kuwait. In late November the UN took the fateful step of authorizing the use of this force if Saddam Hussein did not withdraw from Kuwait by January 15, 1991. Saddam flatly refused to do so.

American opinion was divided between those who hoped to starve Saddam into submission by means of sanctions and those who favored the use of force. A solid majority of Congress finally voted for the latter course as the UN deadline approached, and on January 17, the Americans unleashed an enormous air attack, directed by General Norman Schwartzkopf.

This air assault went on for nearly a month and it reduced a good deal of Iraq to rubble. The Iraqi forces, aside from firing a number of Scud missiles at Israel and Saudi Arabia, and setting fire to hundreds of Kuwaiti oil wells, simply endured the rain of destruction that fell on them daily.

On February 23 Bush issued an ultimatum to Saddam: Pull out of Kuwait or face an invasion. When Saddam ignored the deadline, UN troops, more than 200,000 strong, struck. Between February 24 and February 27, they retook Kuwait, killing tens of thousands of Iraqis in the process

and capturing still larger numbers. Some 4,000 tanks and enormous quantities of other military equipment were destroyed.

President Bush then ordered an end to the attack and Saddam agreed to UN terms that included paying reparations to Kuwait. Polls indicated that about 90 percent of the American people approved both the president's management of the war and his overall performance as chief executive. These were the highest presidential approval ratings ever recorded.

Things Go Wrong

President Bush and indeed most observers expected Saddam to be driven from power in disgrace by his own people. Indeed, Bush publicly urged the Iraqis to do so. The Kurds in northern Iraq and pro-Iranian Moslems in the south then took up arms, but Saddam used the remnants of his army to crush them. He also refused repeatedly to carry out the terms of the peace agreement, which included destruction of his capacity for manufacturing missiles and developing atomic weapons. This led critics to argue that Bush should not have stopped the fighting until Baghdad, the Iraqi capital, had been captured and Saddam's army totally crushed.

To make matters worse, the American economy continued sluggish. Production lagged and unemployment rose to 7 percent in June 1991. Automobile sales slumped to new lows despite steep cuts in interest rates. Hard times made people feel insecure and thus reluctant to spend, further dampening economic activity. All these developments caused President Bush's popularity to fall steeply from its heady level at the end of the Gulf War.

Meanwhile, political and economic conditions in Eastern Europe and the Soviet Union continued to deteriorate. In the summer of 1991, civil war broke out in Yugoslavia. Throughout the Soviet Union, nationalist and anticommunist groups demanded more local control of their affairs. President Gorbachev, who opposed the breakup of the Union, sought compromise, backing a draft treaty that would increase local autonomy and further "privatize" the Soviet economy.

In August, however, hard line communists attempted a coup. They arrested Gorbachev, who was vacationing in the Crimea and attempted to cow resistance by pouring tanks into Moscow. But Boris Yeltsin, the anticommunist president of the Russian Republic, defied the rebels and roused the people of Moscow. The coup then swiftly collapsed. Its leaders were arrested, the Communist Party was officially disbanded, and the Soviet Union itself was replaced by a federation of states, of which Russia, led by Yeltsin, was the most important. Gorbachev, who had begun the process of liberation, thus found himself without a job.

These events further shook the world economy and did little to check the decline in public support for President Bush, who seemed unable to make up his mind how to deal with the new situation.

The Election of 1992

Bush was opposed for the Republican presidential nomination by Patrick Buchanan, an outspoken conservative who had written speeches for presidents Nixon and Reagan. Buchanan did well enough in the early primaries to alarm White House strategists. Then Ross Perot, a billionaire Texan, announced his independent candidacy. He promised to spend $100 million of his own money on his campaign and to "take the shackles off of American business," and cut government spending by "getting rid of waste." He also strongly supported gun control, backed a woman's right to have an abortion, and called for an all-out effort to "restructure" the health care system.

Perot was popular in California, Texas, and other key states that Bush was counting on easily winning. But when his often-contradictory proposals were attacked in detail, he withdrew his candidacy. At the Republican Convention in August, Bush was nominated without opposition.

Meanwhile the Democrats had nominated Governor Bill Clinton of Arkansas for president. Bush's popularity immediately after the Gulf War had discouraged many well-known Democrats from seeking the office. Of the relatively obscure men who announced their candidacies, Clinton had by far the most impressive command of the details of public issues. He won most of the primaries and had a solid majority of the delegates at the Democratic Convention.

In the campaign Clinton accused Bush of failing to deal effectively with the lingering economic recession. He promised to undertake public works projects and to encourage private investment and to reform the nation's education and health insurance systems. Bush played down the seriousness of the recession and emphasized the need to reduce the national deficit and balance the budget.

Early polls showed Clinton well ahead, but then Ross Perot reentered the race. On election day, more than 100 million citizens voted, a record. About 44 million voted for Clinton, 38 million for Bush, and 20 million for Perot. Clinton was elected with 370 electoral votes to Bush's 168. Despite his substantial popular vote, Perot did not win any electoral college votes.

A New Start

One major reason for Clinton's success was his expressed intention to effect changes in the way such important issues as health insurance and the government's skyrocketing budget deficits were dealt with. Another was his apparent reasonableness, his willingness to reconcile differences. "Cooperation is better than conflict," he said on more than one occasion.

But, however valuable during a campaign, reasonableness was sometimes a disadvantage once the power of the presidency was at Clinton's command. He set out to reverse many of the policies of the Reagan–Bush era, but when opposition developed, circumstances often led him to back down. He lacked Lyndon Johnson's ability to overwhelm opposition with the aura surrounding the presidency and the sheer force of his personality. He had promised to end the ban on gays and lesbians in the armed services, but when the Joint Chiefs and a number of important congressmen objected, he settled for a policy known as "don't ask, don't tell," meaning that such persons would be allowed to enlist only if they did not openly proclaim their sexual preferences. When relatively minor objections were raised to a number of his important appointments, he tended to back down rather than stand behind his choices.

Clinton did succeed in using his executive authority to reverse the adamant Reagan–Bush opposition to abortion. When Justice Byron White resigned from the court in July 1993, Clin-

At his 1993 inauguration, President Bill Clinton announced, "A new season of
American renewal has begun."

ton appointed Ruth Bader Ginsberg, a judge
known to believe that abortion was constitutional. By also indicating that he would veto any
congressional bill making free choice illegal,
Clinton effectively took the abortion question out
of national politics.

The first major test of the president's will
came when he submitted his first budget to Congress. He hoped to reduce the deficit by spending
cuts and new taxes. The ending of the Cold War
made steep cuts in military spending politically acceptable (though doing so further weakened the
economy), but Clinton's major proposal for raising
new revenue included a levy on the energy content of all fuels, a scheme estimated to produce
more than $70 billion. A number of congressional
Democrats refused to go along with this tax, and
since the Republicans in Congress voted solidly
against any increase in taxes, the president was
forced to accept an increase of only 4.3 cents a gallon in the federal gasoline tax.

The most important Clinton initiative was his
attempt to reform the nation's health insurance
system. The cost of Medicare, Medicaid, and also
of private health insurance was rising rapidly. A

committee headed by his wife, Hillary Rodham
Clinton, worked for months, but the plan it produced seemed even more complex than the existing system. It found few supporters in the medical
profession, the insurance industry, and among the
general public.

As a result of the ineffectiveness of the Clinton administration, the Republicans swept the
1994 congressional elections, winning majorities
in both the House and Senate. The jubilant new
Speaker of the House of Representatives, Newt
Gingrich, announced that his party had made a
"Contract with America," which he promised to
put into effect quickly.

The Imponderable Future

If historians can locate suitable records and other
sources about a past event, they are able to explain, or at least make plausible guesses about,
what it was and why it happened. But historians
are no better than anyone else at predicting the future. They can rarely anticipate accurately what
the future will bring.

Milestones

1974	President Ford issues blanket pardon to Richard Nixon		President Reagan proposes Strategic Defense Initiative ("Star Wars")
1978	Camp David Agreement between Israel and Egypt	**1986**	Reagan-Gorbachev summit meeting in Iceland
	Paul A. Volcker named chairman of Federal Reserve Board		Immigration Act grants amnesty to long-term illegal aliens
1979	Sandinistas overthrow Somosa government in Nicaragua		Secret Iran-Contra arms deal exposed
	The Reverend Jerry Falwell founds Moral Majority	**1988**	American-Soviet treaty bans medium-range missiles
	American interest rates exceed 10 percent	**1989**	Gorbachev allows Eastern European nations to establish independent democratic governments
	United States recognizes People's Republic of China	**1990**	Iraq invades Kuwait; UN applies sanctions and authorizes use of force if Iraq does not evacuate Kuwait
	Shah forced to flee Iran; radical students seize United States Embassy in Iran and hold occupants as hostages	**1991**	UN force, led by the United States, drives Iraq from Kuwait
1981	American hostages in Iran released		Soviet Union disbanded; Boris Yeltsin becomes president of Russia
	Reagan appoints Sandra Day O'Connor to Supreme Court	**1992**	Ross Perot makes strong independent run for president
	Tax Reform Act lowers rates and eliminates loopholes	**1993**	Ruth Bader Ginsburg becomes second woman associate justice of the Supreme Court
1984	Boland Amendment bans military aid to Nicaraguan Contras		
1985	Mikhail Gorbachev becomes premier of Soviet Union		

Supplementary Reading

Authoritative works on recent history are hard to find. On Gerald Ford, see Clark Mollenhoff, **The Man Who Pardoned Nixon** (1976), Richard Reeves, **A Ford, Not a Lincoln** (1975), and Ford's autobiography, **A Time to Heal** (1979). Betty Ford's frank **The Times of My Life** (1978) is a cut above most such memoirs.

For the Carter years, see Betty Glad, **Jimmy Carter in Search of the Great White House** (1980), which is critical of Carter's style and actions. Zbigniew Brzezinski, **Power and Principle** (1983), discusses the foreign policy of the ad-

ministration, while James A. Bill, **The Eagle and the Lion** (1988), and Michael Ledeen and William Lewis, **Debacle** (1981), cover the Iranian hostage crisis.

Books dealing with Reagan and his administration include Hedrick Smith, **Reagan, the Man, the President** (1980), Robert Dallek, **Ronald Reagan: The Politics of Symbolism** (1984), and Rowland Evans and Robert Novak, **The Reagan Revolution** (1981). D. A. Stockman, **The Triumph of Politics** (1986), contains a frank discussion of administration fiscal policies. Of the memoirs by insiders, Martin Anderson, **Revolution** (1988), is favorable to Reagan; D. T.

Regan, **For the Record** (1988), is critical. Peggy Noonan, **What I Saw at the Revolution** (1990), is both insightful and amusing. For the Reagan foreign policy, see J. J. Girkpatrick, **Dictatorships and Double Standards** (1982), and Strobe Talbott, **The Russians and Reagan** (1984). W. S. Cohen and G. J. Mitchell, **Men of Zeal** (1988), describe the congressional Iran-Contra hearings.

Contrasting views of recent conservative trends are provided by Alan Crawford, **Thunder on the Right** (1980), and Richard Viguerie, **The New Right** (1981). See also, John Kater, **Christians on the Right** (1982).

When in the Course of human events, it becomes necessary for one people to dissolve the political bands which have connected them with another, and to assume among the Powers of the earth, the separate and equal station to which the Laws of Nature and of Nature's God entitle them, a decent respect to the opinions of mankind requires that they should declare the causes which impel them to the separation.

We hold these truths to be self-evident, that all men are created equal, that they are endowed by their Creator with certain unalienable Rights, that among these are Life, Liberty and the pursuit of Happiness. That to secure these rights, Governments are instituted among Men, deriving their just powers from the consent of the governed, That whenever any Form of Government becomes destructive of these ends, it is the Right of the People to alter or to abolish it, and to institute new Government, laying its foundation on such principles and organizing its powers in such form, as to them shall seem most likely to effect their Safety and Happiness. Prudence, indeed, will dictate that Governments long established should not be changed for light and transient causes; and accordingly all experience hath shown, that mankind are more disposed to suffer, while evils are sufferable, than to right themselves by abolishing the forms to which they are accustomed. But when a long train of abuses and usurpations, pursuing invariably the same Object evinces a design to reduce them under absolute Despotism, it is their right, it is their duty, to throw off such Government, and to provide new Guards for their future security.—Such has been the patient sufferance of these Colonies; and such is now the necessity which constrains them to alter their former Systems of Government. The history of the present King of Great Britain is a history of repeated injuries and usurpations, all having in direct object the establishment of an absolute Tyranny over these States. To prove this, let Facts be submitted to a candid world.

He has refused his Assent to Laws, the most wholesome and necessary for the public good.

He has forbidden his Governors to pass Laws of immediate and pressing importance, unless suspended in their operation till his Assent should be obtained; and when so suspended, he has utterly neglected to attend to them.

He has refused to pass other Laws for the accommodation of large districts of people, unless those people would relinquish the right of Representation in the Legislature, a right inestimable to them and formidable to tyrants only.

He has called together legislative bodies at places unusual, uncomfortable, and distant from the depository of their Public Records, for the sole purpose of fatiguing them into compliance with his measures.

He has dissolved Representative Houses repeatedly, for opposing with manly firmness his invasions on the rights of the people.

He has refused for a long time, after such dissolutions, to cause others to be elected; whereby the Legislative Powers, incapable of Annihilation, have returned to the People at large for their exercise; the State remaining in the mean time exposed to all the dangers of invasion from without, and convulsions within.

He has endeavoured to prevent the population of these States; for that purpose obstructing the Laws of Naturalization of Foreigners; refusing to pass others to encourage their migration hither, and raising the conditions of new Appropriations of Lands.

He has obstructed the Administration of Justice, by refusing his Assent to Laws for establishing Judiciary Powers.

He has made Judges dependent on his Will alone, for the tenure of their offices, and the amount and payment of their salaries.

He has erected a multitude of New Offices, and sent hither swarms of Officers to harass our People, and eat out their substance.

He has kept among us, in times of peace, Standing Armies without the Consent of our legislature.

He has affected to render the Military independent of and superior to the Civil Power.

He has combined with others to subject us to a jurisdiction foreign to our constitution, and unacknowledged by our laws; giving his Assent to their acts of pretended legislation:

For quartering large bodies of armed troops among us:

For protecting them, by a mock Trial, from Punishment for any Murders which they should commit on the Inhabitants of these States:

For cutting off our Trade with all parts of the world:

For imposing taxes on us without our Consent:

For depriving us in many cases, of the benefits of Trial by Jury:

For transporting us beyond Seas to be tried for pretended offences:

For abolishing the free System of English Laws in a neighbouring Province, establishing therein an Arbitrary government, and enlarging its Boundaries so as to render it at once an example and fit instrument for introducing the same absolute rule into these Colonies:

For taking away our Charters, abolishing our most valuable Laws, and altering fundamentally the Forms of our Governments:

For suspending our own Legislature, and declaring themselves invested with Power to legislate for us in all cases whatsoever.

He has abdicated Government here, by declaring us out of his Protection and waging War against us.

He has plundered our seas, ravaged our Coasts, burnt our towns, and destroyed the lives of our people.

He is at this time transporting large armies of foreign mercenaries to compleat the works of death, desolation and tyranny, already begun with circumstances of Cruelty & perfidy scarcely paralleled in the most barbarous ages, and totally unworthy the Head of a civilized nation.

He has constrained our fellow Citizens taken Captive on the high Seas to bear Arms against their Country, to become the executioners of their friends and Brethren, or to fall themselves by their Hands.

He has excited domestic insurrections amongst us, and has endeavoured to bring on the inhabitants of our frontiers, the merciless Indian Savages, whose known rule of warfare, is an undistinguished destruction of all ages, sexes and conditions.

In every stage of these Oppressions We have Petitioned for Redress in the most humble terms: Our repeated Petitions have been answered only by repeated injury. A Prince, whose character is thus marked by every act which may define a Tyrant, is unfit to be the ruler of a free People.

Nor have We been wanting in attention to our British brethren. We have warned them from time to time of attempts by their legislature to extend an unwarrantable jurisdiction over us. We have reminded them of the circumstances of our emigration and settlement here. We have appealed to their native justice and magnanimity, and we have conjured them by the ties of our common kindred to disavow these usurpations, which, would inevitably interrupt our connections and correspondence. They too have been deaf to the voice of justice and of consanguinity. We must, therefore, acquiesce in the necessity, which denounces our Separation, and hold them, as we hold the rest of mankind, Enemies in War, in Peace Friends.

We, therefore, the Representatives of the united States of America, in General Congress, Assembled, appealing to the Supreme Judge of the world for the rectitude of our intentions, do, in the Name, and by Authority of the good People of these Colonies, solemnly publish and declare, That these United Colonies are, and of Right ought to be Free and Independent States; that they are Absolved from all Allegiance to the British Crown, and that all political connection between them and the State of Great Britain, is and ought to be totally dissolved; and that as Free and Independent States, they have full Power to levy War, conclude Peace, contract Alliances, establish Commerce, and to do all other Acts and Things which Independent States may of right do. And for the support of this Declaration, with a firm reliance on the Protection of Divine Providence, we mutually pledge to each other our Lives, our Fortunes and our sacred Honor.

John Hancock, Josiah Bartlett, Wm Whipple, Saml Adams, John Adams, Robt Treat Paine, Elbridge Gerry, Steph. Hopkins, William Ellery, Roger Sherman, Samel Huntington, Wm Williams, Oliver Wolcott, Matthew Thornton, Wm Floyd, Phil Livingston, Frans Lewis, Lewis Morris, Richd Stockton, Jno Witherspoon, Fras Hopkinson, John Hart, Abra Clark, Robt Morris, Benjamin Rush, Benja Franklin, John Morton, Geo Clymer, Jas Smith, Geo. Taylor, James Wilson, Geo. Ross, Caesar Rodney, Geo Read, Thos M:Kean, Samuel Chase, Wm Paca, Thos Stone, Charles Carroll of Carrollton, George Wythe, Richard Henry Lee, Th. Jefferson, Benja Harrison, Thos Nelson, Jr., Francis Lightfoot Lee, Carter Braxton, Wm Hooper, Joseph Hewes, John Penn, Edward Rutledge, Thos Heyward, Junr., Thomas Lynch, Junor., Arthur Middleton, Button Gwinnett, Lyman Hall, Geo Walton.

We the people of the United States, in Order to form a more perfect Union, establish Justice, insure domestic Tranquility, provide for the common defence, promote the general Welfare, and secure the Blessings of Liberty to ourselves and our Posterity, do ordain and establish this Constitution for the United States of America.

Article I

Section 1. All legislative Powers herein granted shall be vested in a Congress of the United States, which shall consist of a Senate and House of Representatives.

Section 2. The House of Representatives shall be composed of Members chosen every second Year by the People of the several States, and the Electors in each State shall have the Qualifications requisite for Electors of the most numerous Branch of the State Legislature.

No Person shall be a Representative who shall not have attained to the Age of twenty-five Years, and been seven Years a Citizen of the United States, and who shall not, when elected, be an Inhabitant of that State in which he shall be chosen.

Representatives and direct Taxes shall be apportioned among the several States which may be included within this Union, according to their respective Numbers, which shall be determined by adding to the whole Number of free Persons, including those bound to Service for a Term of Years, and excluding Indians not taxed, three fifths of all other Persons. The actual Enumeration shall be made within three Years after the first Meeting of the Congress of the United States, and within every subsequent Term of ten Years, in such Manner as they shall by Law direct. The Number of Representatives shall not exceed one for every thirty Thousand, but each State shall have at Least one Representative; and until such enumeration shall be made, the State of New Hampshire shall be entitled to chuse three, Massachusetts eight, Rhode-Island and Providence Plantations one, Connecticut five, New-York six, New Jersey four, Pennsylvania eight, Delaware one, Maryland six, Virginia ten, North Carolina five, South Carolina five, and Georgia three.

When vacancies happen in the Representation from any State, the Executive Authority thereof shall issue Writs of Election to fill such Vacancies.

The House of Representatives shall chuse their Speaker and other Officers; and shall have the sole Power of Impeachment.

Section 3. The Senate of the United States shall be composed of two Senators from each State, chosen by the Legislature thereof, for six Years; and each Senator shall have one Vote.

Immediately after they shall be assembled in Consequence of the first Election, they shall be divided as equally as may be into three Classes. The Seats of the Senators of the first Class shall be vacated at the Expiration of the second Year, of the second Class at the Expiration of the fourth Year, and of the third Class at the Expiration of the sixth Year, so that one-third may be chosen every second Year; and if Vacancies happen by Resignation, or otherwise, during the Recess of the Legislature of any State, the Executive thereof may make temporary Appointments until the next Meeting of the Legislature, which shall then fill such Vacancies.

No Person shall be a Senator who shall not have attained to the Age of thirty Years, and been nine Years a Citizen of the United States, and who shall not, when elected, be an Inhabitant of that State in which he shall be chosen.

The Vice President of the United States shall be President of the Senate, but shall have no vote, unless they be equally divided.

The Senate shall chuse their other Officers, and also a President pro tempore, in the absence of the Vice President, or when he shall exercise the Office of the President of the United States.

The Senate shall have the sole Power to try all Impeachments. When sitting for that purpose, they shall be on Oath or Affirmation. When the President of the United States is tried, the Chief Justice shall preside: And no person shall be convicted without the Concurrence of two thirds of the Members present.

Judgment in Cases of Impeachment shall not extend further than to removal from Office, and disqualification to hold and enjoy any Office of honor, Trust, or Profit under the United States: but the Party convicted shall nevertheless be liable and subject to Indictment, Trial, Judgment, and Punishment, according to Law.

Section 4. The Times, Places and Manner of holding Elections for Senators and Representatives, shall be prescribed in each state by the Legislature thereof; but the Congress may at any time by Law make or alter such Regulations, except as to the Places of Chusing Senators.

The Congress shall assemble at least once in every Year, and such Meeting shall be on the first Monday in December, unless they shall by Law appoint a different Day.

Section 5. Each House shall be the Judge of the Elections, Returns and Qualifications of its own Members, and a Majority of each shall constitute a Quorum to do Business; but a smaller number may adjourn from day to day, and may be authorized to compel the Attendance of absent Members, in such Manner, and under such Penalties, as each House may provide.

Each House may determine the Rules of its Proceedings, punish its Members for disorderly Behavior, and, with the Concurrence of two thirds, expel a Member.

Each House shall keep a Journal of its Proceedings, and from time to time publish the same, excepting such Parts as may in their Judgment require Secrecy; and the Yeas and Nays of the Members of either House on any question shall, at the Desire of one fifth of those Present, be entered on the Journal.

Neither House, during the Session of Congress, shall, without the Consent of the other, adjourn for more than three days, nor to any other Place than that in which the two Houses shall be sitting.

Section 6. The Senators and Representatives shall receive a Compensation for their Services, to be ascertained by Law, and paid out of the Treasury of the United States. They shall in all Cases, except Treason, Felony, and Breach of the Peace, be privileged from arrest during their Attendance at the Session of their respective Houses, and in going to and returning from the same; and for any Speech or Debate in either House, they shall not be questioned in any other Place.

No Senator or Representative shall, during the Time for which he was elected, be appointed to any civil Office under the Authority of the United States, which shall have been created, or the Emoluments whereof shall have been increased, during such time; and no Person holding any Office under the United States shall be a Member of either House during his continuance in Office.

Section 7. All Bills for raising Revenue shall originate in the House of Representatives; but the Senate may propose or concur with Amendments as on other bills.

Every Bill which shall have passed the House of Representatives and the Senate, shall, before it become a Law, be presented to the President of the United States; If he approve he shall sign it, but if not he shall return it, with his Objections, to that House in which it shall have originated, who shall enter the Objections at large on their Journal, and proceed to reconsider it. If after such Reconsideration two thirds of that House shall agree to pass the bill, it shall be sent, together with the objections, to the other House, by which it shall likewise be reconsidered, and if approved by two thirds of that House, it shall become a Law. But in all such Cases the Votes of both Houses shall be determined by Yeas and Nays, and the Names of the Persons voting for and against the Bill shall be entered on the Journal of each House respectively. If any Bill shall not be returned by the President within ten Days (Sundays excepted) after it shall have been presented to him, the Same shall be a Law, in like Manner as if he had signed it, unless the Congress by their Adjournment prevent its Return, in which Case it shall not be a Law.

Every Order, Resolution, or Vote to which the Concurrence of the Senate and House of Representatives may be necessary (except on a question of Adjournment) shall be presented to the President of the United States; and before the Same shall take Effect, shall be approved by him, or being disapproved by him, shall be repassed by two thirds of the Senate and House of Representatives, according to the Rules and Limitations prescribed in the Case of a Bill.

Section 8. The Congress shall have Power To lay and collect Taxes, Duties, Imposts and Excises, to pay the Debts and provide for the common Defence and general Welfare of the United States; but all Duties, Imposts and Excises shall be uniform throughout the United States;

To borrow money on the credit of the United States;

To regulate Commerce with foreign Nations, and among the several States, and with the Indian Tribes;

To establish an uniform Rule of Naturalization, and uniform Laws on the subject of Bankruptcies throughout the United States;

To coin Money, regulate the Value thereof, and of foreign Coin, and fix the Standard of Weights and Measures;

To provide for the Punishment of counterfeiting the Securities and current Coin of the United States;

To establish Post Offices and post Roads;

To promote the Progress of Science and useful Arts, by securing for limited Times to Authors and Inventors the exclusive Right to their respective Writings and Discoveries;

To constitute Tribunals inferior to the Supreme Court;

To define and punish Piracies and Felonies committed on the high Seas, and Offences against the Law of Nations;

To declare War, grant Letters of Marque and Reprisal, and make Rules concerning Captures on Land and Water;

To raise and support Armies, but no Appropriation of Money to that Use shall be for a longer Term than two Years;

To provide and maintain a Navy;

To make Rules for the Government and Regulation of the land and naval forces;

To provide for calling forth the Militia to execute the Laws of the Union, suppress Insurrections and repel Invasions;

To provide for organizing, arming, and disciplining the Militia, and for governing such Part of them as may be employed in the Service of the United States, reserving to the States respectively, the Appointment of the Officers, and the Authority of training the Militia according to the discipline prescribed by Congress;

To exercise exclusive Legislation in all Cases whatsoever, over such District (not exceeding ten Miles square) as may, by Cession of particular States, and the acceptance of Congress, become the Seat of Government of the United States, and to exercise like Authority over all Places purchased by the Consent of the Legislature of the State in which the Same shall be, for the Erection of Forts, Magazines, Arsenals, dock-Yards, and other needful Buildings;—And

To make all Laws which shall be necessary and proper for carrying into Execution the foregoing Powers, and all other Powers vested by this Constitution in the government of the United States, or in any Department or Officer thereof.

Section 9. The Migration or Importation of such Persons as any of the States now existing shall think proper to admit, shall not be prohibited by the Congress prior to the Year one thousand eight hundred and eight, but a tax or duty may be imposed on such Importation, not exceeding ten dollars for each Person.

The privilege of the Writ of Habeas Corpus shall not be suspended, unless when in Cases of Rebellion or Invasion the public Safety may require it.

No Bill of Attainder or ex post facto Law shall be passed.

No capitation, or other direct, Tax shall be laid unless in Proportion to the Census or Enumeration herein before directed to be taken.

No Tax or Duty shall be laid on Articles exported from any State.

No Preference shall be given by any Regulation of Revenue to the Ports of one State over those of another: nor shall Vessels bound to, or from, one State, be obliged to enter, clear, or pay Duties in another.

No Money shall be drawn from the Treasury, but in Consequence of Appropriations made by Law; and a regular Statement and Account of the Receipts and Expenditures of all public Money shall be published from time to time.

No Title of Nobility shall be granted by the United States: And no Person holding any Office of Profit or Trust under them, shall, without the Consent of the Congress, accept of any present, Emolument, Office, or Title, of any kind whatever, from any King, Prince, or foreign State.

Section 10. No State shall enter into any Treaty, Alliance, or Confederation; grant Letters of Marque and Reprisal; coin Money; emit Bills of Credit; make any Thing but gold and silver Coin a Tender in Payment of Debts; pass any Bill of Attainder, ex post facto Law, or Law impairing the Obligation of Contracts, or grant any Title of Nobility.

No State shall, without the Consent of the Congress, lay any Imposts or Duties on Imports or Exports, except what may be absolutely necessary for executing its inspection Laws: and the net Produce of all Duties and Imposts, laid by any State on Imports or Exports, shall be for the Use of the Treasury of the United States; and all such Laws shall be subject to the Revision and Control of the Congress.

No State shall, without the Consent of Congress, lay any duty of Tonnage, keep Troops, or Ships of War in time of Peace, enter into any Agreement or Compact with another State, or with a foreign Power, or engage in War, unless actually invaded, or in such imminent Danger as will not admit of delay.

Article II

Section 1. The executive Power shall be vested in a President of the United States of America. He shall hold his Office during the Term of four years, and, together with the Vice President, chosen for the same Term, be elected, as follows:

Each State shall appoint, in such Manner as the Legislature thereof may direct, a Number of Electors, equal to the whole Number of Senators and Representatives to which the State may be entitled in the Congress; but no Senator or Representative, or Person holding an Office of Trust or Profit under the United States, shall be appointed an Elector.

The Electors shall meet in their respective States, and vote by Ballot for two persons, of whom one at least shall not be an Inhabitant of the same State with themselves. And they shall make a List of all the Persons voted for, and of the Number of Votes for each; which List they shall sign and certify, and transmit sealed to the Seat of the Government of the United States, directed to the President of the Senate. The President of the Senate shall, in the Presence of the Senate and House of Representatives, open all the Certificates, and the Votes shall then be counted. The Person having the greatest Number of Votes shall be the President, if such Number be a Majority of the whole Number of Electors appointed; and if there be more than one who have such Majority, and have an equal Number of Votes, then the House of Representatives shall immediately chuse by Ballot one of them for President; and if no Person have a Majority, then from the five highest on the List the said House shall in like Manner chuse the President. But in chusing the President, the votes shall be taken by States, the Representation from each State having one Vote; a quorum for this Purpose shall consist of a Member or Members from two-thirds of the States, and a Majority of all the States shall be necessary to a Choice. In every Case, after the Choice of the President, the Person having the greatest Number of Votes of the Electors shall be the Vice President. But if there should remain two or more who have equal votes, the Senate shall chuse from them by Ballot the Vice President.

The Congress may determine the time of chusing the Electors, and the Day on which they shall give their Votes; which Day shall be the same throughout the United States.

No person except a natural-born Citizen, or a Citizen of the United States, at the time of the Adoption of this Constitution, shall be eligible to the Office of President; neither shall any Person be eligible to that Office who shall not have attained to the Age of thirty-five years, and been fourteen Years a Resident within the United States.

In Case of the Removal of the President from Office, or of his Death, Resignation, or Inability to discharge the Powers and Duties of the said Office, the same shall devolve on the Vice President, and the Congress may by Law provide for the Case of Removal, Death, Resignation, or Inability, both of the President and Vice President, declaring what Officer shall then act as President, and such Officer shall act accordingly, until the disability be removed, or a President shall be elected.

The President shall, at stated Times, receive for his Services a Compensation, which shall neither be increased nor diminished during the Period for which he shall have been elected, and he shall not receive within that Period any other Emolument from the United States, or any of them.

Before he enter on the execution of his Office, he shall take the following Oath or Affirmation:—"I do solemnly swear (or affirm) that I will faithfully execute the Office of President of the United States, and will, to the best of my Ability, preserve, protect, and defend the Constitution of the United States."

Section 2. The President shall be Commander in Chief of the Army and Navy of the United States, and of the Militia of the several States, when called into the actual Service of the United States; he may require the Opinion, in writing, of the principal Officer in each of the executive Departments, upon any subject relating to the Duties of their respective Offices, and he shall have Power to Grant Reprieves and Pardons for Offences against the United States, except in Cases of Impeachment.

He shall have Power, by and with the Advice and Consent of the Senate, to make Treaties, provided two thirds of the Senators present concur; and he shall nominate, and by and with the Advice and Consent of the Senate, shall appoint Ambassadors, other public Ministers and Consuls, Judges of the supreme Court, and all other Officers of the United States, whose Appointments are not herein otherwise provided for, and which shall be established by Law: but the Congress may by Law vest the Appointment of such inferior Officers, as they think proper, in the President alone, in the Courts of Law, or in the Heads of Departments.

The President shall have Power to fill up all Vacancies that may happen during the Recess of the Senate, by granting Commissions which shall expire at the End of their next Session.

Section 3. He shall from time to time give to the Congress Information of the State of the Union, and recommend to their Consideration such Measures as he shall judge necessary and expedient; he may, on extraordinary occasions, convene both Houses, or either of them, and in Case of Disagreement between them, with respect to the Time of Adjournment, he may adjourn them to such Time as he shall think proper; he shall receive Ambassadors and other public Ministers; he shall take Care that the Laws be faithfully executed, and shall Commission all the Officers of the United States.

Section 4. The President, Vice President and all civil Officers of the United States, shall be removed from Office on Impeachment for, and Conviction of, Treason, Bribery, or other high Crimes and Misdemeanors.

Article III

Section 1. The judicial Power of the United States, shall be vested in one supreme Court, and in such inferior Courts as the Congress may from time to time ordain and establish. The Judges, both of the supreme and inferior Courts, shall hold their Offices during good Behaviour, and shall, at stated Times, receive for their Services, a Compensation, which shall not be diminished during their Continuance in Office.

Section 2. The judicial Power shall extend to all Cases, in Law and Equity, arising under this Constitution, the Laws of the United States, and treaties made, or which shall be made, under their Authority;—to all Cases affecting ambassadors, other public ministers and consuls;—to all cases of admiralty and maritime Jurisdiction;—to Controversies to which the United States shall be a Party;—to Controversies between two or more States;—between a State and Citizen of another State;—between Citizens of different States,—between Citizens of the same State claiming Lands under Grants of different States, and between a State, or the Citizens thereof, and foreign States, Citizens or Subjects.

In all Cases affecting Ambassadors, other public Ministers and Consuls, and those in which a State shall be Party, the supreme Court shall have original Jurisdiction. In all the other Cases before mentioned, the supreme Court shall have appellate Jurisdiction, both as to Law and Fact, with such Exceptions, and under such Regulations as the Congress shall make.

The trial of all Crimes, except in Cases of Impeachment, shall be by Jury; and such Trial shall be held in the State where the said Crimes shall have been committed; but when not committed within any State, the Trial shall be at such Place or Places as the Congress may by Law have directed.

Section 3. Treason against the United States, shall consist only in levying War against them, or in adhering to their Enemies, giving them Aid and Comfort. No Person shall be convicted of Treason unless on the testimony of two Witnesses to the same overt Act, or on Confession in open Court.

The Congress shall have power to declare the Punishment of Treason, but no Attainder of Treason shall work Corruption of Blood, or Forfeiture except during the Life of the Person attained.

Article IV

Section 1. Full Faith and Credit shall be given in each State of the public Acts, Records, and judicial Proceedings of every other State. And the Congress may by general Laws prescribe the Manner in which such Acts, Records and Proceedings shall be proved, and the Effect thereof.

Section 2. The Citizens of each State shall be entitled to all Privileges and Immunities of Citizens in the several States.

A Person charged in any State with Treason, Felony, or other Crime, who shall flee from Justice, and be found in another State, shall on demand of the executive Authority of the State from which he fled, be delivered up, to be removed to the State having Jurisdiction of the crime.

No Person held to Service or Labour in one State, under the Laws thereof, escaping into another, shall, in Consequence of any Law or Regulation therein, be discharged from such Service or Labour, but shall be delivered up on Claim of the Party to whom such Service or Labour may be due.

Section 3. New States may be admitted by the Congress into this Union; but no new State shall be formed or erected within the Jurisdiction of any other State; nor any State be formed by the Junction of two or more States, or parts of States, without the Consent of the Legislatures of the States concerned as well as of the Congress.

The Congress shall have Power to dispose of and make all needful Rules and Regulations respecting the Territory or other Property belonging to the United States; and nothing in this Constitution shall be so construed as to Prejudice any Claims of the United States, or of any particular State.

Section 4. The United States shall guarantee to every State in this Union a Republican Form of Government, and shall protect each of them against Invasion; and on Application of the Legislature, or the Executive (when the Legislature cannot be convened) against domestic Violence.

Article V

The Congress, whenever two-thirds of both Houses shall deem it necessary, shall propose Amendments to this Constitution, or, on the Application of the Legislatures of two-thirds of the several States, shall call a Convention for proposing Amendments, which, in either Case, shall be valid to all Intents and Purposes, as part of this Constitution, when ratified by the Legislatures of three-fourths of the several States, or by Conventions in three-fourths thereof, as the one or the other Mode of Ratification may be proposed by the Congress; Provided that no Amendment which may be made prior to the Year One thousand eight hundred and eight shall in any Manner affect the first and fourth Clauses in the Ninth Section of the first Article; and that no State, without its Consent, shall be deprived of its equal Suffrage in the Senate.

Article VI

All Debts contracted and Engagements entered into, before the Adoption of this Constitution, shall be as valid against the United States under this Constitution, as under the Confederation.

This Constitution, and the Laws of the United States which shall be made in Pursuance thereof; and all Treaties made, or which shall be made, under the Authority of the United States, shall be the supreme Law of the Land; and the Judges in every State shall be bound thereby, any Thing in the Constitution or Laws of any State to the Contrary notwithstanding.

The Senators and Representatives before mentioned, and the Members of the several State Legislatures, and all executive and judicial Officers, both of the United States and of the several States, shall be bound by Oath or Affirmation to support this Constitution; but no religious Test shall ever be required as a qualification to any Office or public Trust under the United States.

Article VII

The Ratification of the Conventions of nine States shall be sufficient for the Establishment of this Constitution between the States so ratifying the same. Done in Convention by the Unanimous Consent of the States present the Seventeenth Day of September in the Year of our Lord one thousand seven hundred and Eighty seven, and of the Independence of the United States of America the Twelfth. In Witness whereof We have hereunto subscribed our Names.

Go. Washington, President and deputy from Virginia;

Attest William Jackson, Secretary; Delaware: Geo. Read,* Gunning Bedford, Jr., John Dickinson, Richard Bassett, Jaco. Broom; Maryland: James McHenry, Daniel of St. Thomas' Jenifer, Danl. Carroll; Virginia: John Blair, James Madison, Jr.; North Carolina: Wm. Blout, Richd. Dobbs Spaight, Hu Williamson; South Carolina: J. Rutledge, Charles Cotesworth Pinckney, Charles Pinckney, Pierce Butler; Georgia: William Few, Abr. Baldwin; New Hampshire: John Langdon, Nicholas Gilman; Massachusetts: Nathaniel Gorham, Rufus King; Connecticut: Wm. Saml. Johnson, Roger Sherman;* New York: Alexander Hamilton; New Jersey: Wil. Livingston, David Brearley, Wm. Paterson, Jona. Dayton; Pennsylvania: B. Franklin,* Thomas Mifflin, Robt. Morris,* Geo. Clymer,* Thos. FitzSimons, Jared Ingersoll, James Wilson, Gouv. Morris.

Articles in Addition to, and Amendment of, the Constitution of the United States of America, Proposed by Congress, and Ratified by the Legislatures of the Several States, Pursuant to the Fifth Article of the Original Constitution.

Amendment I [1791]

Congress shall make no law respecting an establishment of religion, or prohibiting the free exercise thereof; or abridging the freedom of speech, or of the press; or the right of the people peaceably to assemble, and to petition the Government for a redress of grievances.

Amendment II [1791]

A well regulated Militia, being necessary to the security of a free State, the right of the people to keep and bear Arms shall not be infringed.

Amendment III [1791]

No Soldier shall, in time of peace, be quartered in any house, without the consent of the Owner, nor in time of war, but in a manner to be prescribed by law.

Amendment IV [1791]

The right of the people to be secure in their persons, houses, papers, and effects, against unreasonable searches and seizures, shall not be violated, and no Warrants shall issue, but upon probable cause, supported by Oath or affirmation, and particularly describing the place to be searched, and the persons or things to be seized.

Amendment V [1791]

No person shall be held to answer for a capital or otherwise infamous crime, unless on a presentment or indictment of a Grand Jury, except in cases arising in the land or naval forces, or in the Militia, when in actual service in time of War or public danger; nor shall any person be subject for the same offence to be twice put in jeopardy of life or limb; nor shall be compelled in any criminal case to be a witness against himself, nor be deprived of life, liberty, or property, without due process of law; nor shall private property be taken for public use, without just compensation.

Amendment VI [1791]

In all criminal prosecutions, the accused shall enjoy the right to a speedy and public trial, by an impartial jury of the State and district wherein the crime shall have been committed, which district shall have been previously ascertained by law, and to be informed of the nature and cause of the accusation; to be confronted with the witnesses against him; to have compulsory process for obtaining witnesses in his favor, and to have the Assistance of Counsel for his defence.

Amendment VII [1791]

In suits at common law, where the value in controversy shall exceed twenty dollars, the right of trial by jury shall be preserved, and no fact tried by a jury, shall be otherwise reexamined in any Court of the United States, than according to the rules of the common law.

Amendment VIII [1791]

Excessive bail shall not be required, nor excessive fines imposed, nor cruel and unusual punishments inflicted.

Amendment IX [1791]

The enumeration in the Constitution, of certain rights, shall not be construed to deny or disparage others retained by the people.

Amendment X [1791]

The powers not delegated to the United States by the Constitution, nor prohibited by it to the States, are reserved to the States respectively, or to the people.

Amendment XI [1798]

The Judicial power of the United States shall not be construed to extend to any suit in law or equity, commenced or prosecuted against one of the United States by Citizens of another State, or by Citizens or Subjects of any Foreign State.

Amendment XII [1804]

The Electors shall meet in their respective States and vote by ballot for President and Vice-President, one of whom, at least, shall not be an inhabitant of the same State with themselves; they shall name in their ballots the person voted for as President, and in distinct ballots the person voted for as Vice-President, and they shall make distinct lists of all persons voted for as President, and of all persons voted for as Vice-President, and of the number of votes for each, which lists they shall sign and certify, and transmit sealed to the seat of the government of the United States, directed to the President of the Senate;—The President of the Senate shall, in the presence of the Senate and House of Representatives, open all the certificates and the votes shall then be counted;—The person having the greatest number of votes for President, shall be the President, if such number be a majority of the whole number of Electors appointed; and if no person have such majority, then from the persons having the highest numbers not exceeding three on the list of those voted for as President, the House of Representatives shall choose immediately, by ballot, the President. But in choosing the President, the votes shall be taken by states, the representation from each state having one vote; a quorum for this purpose shall consist of a member or members from two-thirds of the states, and a majority of all the states shall be necessary to a choice. And if the House of Representatives shall not choose a President whenever the right of choice shall devolve upon them, before the fourth day of March next following, then the Vice-President shall act as President, as in the case of the death or other constitutional disability of the President.—The person having the greatest number of votes as Vice-President, shall be the Vice-President, if such number be a majority of the whole number of Electors appointed, and if no person have a majority, then from the two highest numbers on the list, the Senate shall choose the Vice-President; a quorum for the purpose shall consist of two-thirds of the whole number of Senators, and a majority of the whole number shall be necessary to a choice. But no person constitutionally ineligible to the office of President shall be eligible to that of Vice-President of the United States.

Amendment XIII [1865]

Section 1. Neither slavery nor involuntary servitude, except as a punishment for crime whereof the party shall have been duly convicted, shall exist within the United States, or any place subject to their jurisdiction.

Section 2. Congress shall have power to enforce this article by appropriate legislation.

Amendment XIV [1868]

Section 1. All persons born or naturalized in the United States, and subject to the jurisdiction thereof, are citizens of the United States and of the State wherein they reside. No State shall make or enforce any law which shall abridge the privileges or immunities of citizens of the United States; nor shall any State deprive any person of life, liberty, or property, without due process of law; nor deny to any person within its jurisdiction the equal protection of the laws.

Section 2. Representatives shall be apportioned among the several States according to their respective numbers, counting the whole number of persons in each State, excluding Indians not taxed. But when the right to vote at any election for the choice of electors for President and Vice-President of the United States, Representatives in Congress, the Executive and Judicial officers of a State, or the members of the Legislature thereof, is denied to any of the male inhabitants of such State, being twenty-one years of age, and citizens of the United States, or in any way abridged, except for participation in rebellion, or other crime, the basis of representation therein shall be reduced in the proportion which the number of such male citizens shall bear to the whole number of male citizens twenty-one years of age in such State.

Section 3. No person shall be a Senator or Representative in Congress, or elector of President and Vice-President, or hold any office, civil or military, under the United States, or under any State, who, having previously taken an oath, as a member of Congress, or as an officer of the United States, or as a member of any State legislature, or as an executive or judicial officer of any State, to support the Constitution of the United States, shall have engaged in insurrection or rebellion against the same, or given aid or comfort to the enemies thereof. But Congress may by a vote of two-thirds of each House, remove such disability.

Section 4. The validity of the public debt of the United States, authorized by law, including debts incurred for payment of pensions and bounties for services in suppressing insurrection or rebellion, shall not be questioned. But neither the United States nor any State shall assume or pay any debt or obligation incurred in aid of insurrection or rebellion against the United States, or any claim for the loss or emancipation of any slave; but all such debts, obligations, and claims shall be held illegal and void.

Section 5. The Congress shall have the power to enforce, by appropriate legislation, the provisions of this article.

Amendment XV [1870]

Section 1. The right of citizens of the United States to vote shall not be denied or abridged by the United States or by any State on account of race, color, or previous condition of servitude—

Section 2. The Congress shall have power to enforce this article by appropriate legislation.

Amendment XVI [1913]

The Congress shall have power to lay and collect taxes on incomes, from whatever source derived, without apportionment among the several States, and without regard to any census or enumeration.

Amendment XVII [1913]

The Senate of the United States shall be composed of two Senators from each State, elected by the people thereof, for six years; and each Senator shall have one vote. The electors in each State shall have the qualifications requisite for electors of the most numerous branch of the State legislatures.

When vacancies happen in the representation of any State in the Senate, the executive authority of such State shall issue writs of election to fill such vacancies: Provided, That the legislature of any State may empower the executive thereof to make temporary appointments until the people fill the vacancies by election as the legislature may direct. This amendment shall not be so construed as to affect the election or term of any Senator chosen before it becomes valid as part of the Constitution.

Amendment XVIII [1919]

Section 1. After one year from the ratification of this article the manufacture, sale, or transportation of intoxicating liquors within, the importation thereof into, or the exportation thereof from the United States and all territory subject to the jurisdiction thereof for beverage purposes is hereby prohibited.

Section 2. The Congress and the several States shall have concurrent power to enforce this article by appropriate legislation.

Section 3. This article shall be inoperative unless it shall have been ratified as an amendment to the Constitution by the legislatures of the several States, as provided in the Constitution, within seven years from the date of the submission hereof to the States by the Congress.

Amendment XIX [1920]

The right of citizens of the United States to vote shall not be denied or abridged by the United States or by any State on account of sex.

Congress shall have power to enforce this article by appropriate legislation.

Amendment XX [1933]

Section 1. The terms of the President and Vice-President shall end at noon on the 20th day of January, and the terms of Senators and Representatives at noon on the 3d day of January, of the years in which such terms would have ended if this article had not been ratified; and the terms of their successors shall then begin.

Section 2. The Congress shall assemble at least once in every year, and such meeting shall begin at noon on the 3d day of January, unless they shall by law appoint a different day.

Section 3. If, at the time fixed for the beginning of the term of the President, the President elect shall have died, the Vice-President elect shall become President. If a President shall not have been chosen before the time fixed for the beginning of his term, or if the President elect shall have failed to qualify, then the Vice-President elect shall act as President until a President shall have qualified; and the Congress may by law provide for the case wherein neither a President elect nor a Vice-President elect shall have qualified, declaring who shall then act as President, or the manner in which one who is to act shall be selected, and such person shall act accordingly until a President or Vice-President shall have qualified.

Section 4. The Congress may by law provide for the case of the death of any of the persons from whom the House of Representatives may choose a President whenever the right of choice shall have devolved upon them and for the case of the death of any of the persons from whom the Senate may choose a Vice-President whenever the right of choice shall have devolved upon them.

Section 5. Sections 1 and 2 shall take effect on the 15th day of October following the ratification of this article.

Section 6. This article shall be inoperative unless it shall have been ratified as an amendment to the Constitution by the legislatures of three-fourths of the several States within seven years from the date of its submission.

Amendment XXI [1933]

Section 1. The eighteenth article of amendment to the Constitution of the United States is hereby repealed.

Section 2. The transportation or importation into any State, Territory, or possession of the United States for delivery or use therein of intoxicating liquors, in violation of the laws thereof, is hereby prohibited.

Section 3. This article shall be inoperative unless it shall have been ratified as an amendment to the Constitution by conventions in the several States, as provided in the Constitution, within seven years from the date of the submission hereof to the States by the Congress.

Amendment XXII [1951]

No person shall be elected to the office of the President more than twice, and no person who has held the office of President, or acted as President, for more than two years of a term to which some other person was elected President shall be elected to the office of the President more than once.

But this Article shall not apply to any person holding the office of President when this Article was proposed by the Congress, and shall not prevent any person who may be holding the office of President, or acting as President, during the term within which this Article becomes operative from holding the office of President or acting as President during the remainder of such term.

Amendment XXIII [1961]

Section 1. The District constituting the seat of Government of the United States shall appoint in such manner as the Congress may direct:

A number of electors of President and Vice President equal to the whole number of Senators and Representatives in Congress to which the District would be entitled if it were a State, but in no event more than the least populous State; they shall be in addition to those appointed by the States, but they shall be considered, for the purposes of the election of President and Vice President, to be electors appointed by a State; and they shall meet in the District and perform such duties as provided by the twelfth article of amendment.

Section 2. The Congress shall have power to enforce this article by appropriate legislation.

Amendment XXIV [1964]

Section 1. The right of citizens of the United States to vote in any primary or other election for President or Vice President, for electors for President or Vice President, or for Senator or Representative in Congress, shall not be denied or abridged by the United States or any State by reason of failure to pay any poll tax or other tax.

Section 2. The Congress shall have the power to enforce this article by appropriate legislation.

Amendment XXV [1967]

Section 1. In case of the removal of the President from office or his death or resignation, the Vice President shall become President.

Section 2. Whenever there is a vacancy in the office of the Vice President, the President shall nominate a Vice President who shall take the office upon confirmation by a majority vote of both houses of Congress.

Section 3. Whenever the President transmits to the President pro tempore of the Senate and the Speaker of the House of Representatives his written declaration that he is unable to discharge the powers and duties of his office, and until he transmits to them a written declaration to the contrary, such powers and duties shall be discharged by the Vice President as Acting President.

Section 4. Whenever the Vice President and a majority of either the principal officers of the executive departments, or of such other body as Congress may by law provide, transmit to the President pro tempore of the Senate and the Speaker of the House of Representatives their written declaration that the President is unable to discharge the powers and duties of his office, the Vice President shall immediately assume the powers and duties of the office as Acting President.

Thereafter, when the President transmits to the President pro tempore of the Senate and the Speaker of the House of Representatives his written declaration that no inability exists, he shall resume the powers and duties of his office unless the Vice President and a majority of either the principal officers of the executive departments, or of such other body as Congress may by law provide, transmit within four days to the President pro tempore of the Senate and the Speaker of the House of Representatives their written declaration that the President is unable to discharge the powers and duties of his office. Thereupon Congress shall decide the issue, assembling within 48 hours for that purpose if not in session. If the Congress, within 21 days after receipt of the latter written declaration, or, if Congress is not in session, within 21 days after Congress is required to assemble, determines by two-thirds vote of both houses that the President is unable to discharge the powers and duties of his office, the Vice President shall continue to discharge the same as Acting President; otherwise, the President shall resume the powers and duties of his office.

Amendment XXVI [1971]

Section 1. The right of citizens of the United States, who are 18 years of age or older, to vote shall not be denied or abridged by the United States or any state on account of age.

Section 2. The Congress shall have the power to enforce this article by appropriate legislation.

Amendment XXVII [1992]

No law, varying the compensation for the services of the Senators and Representatives shall take effect, until an election of Representatives shall have intervened.

12 Dover Publications   *15* Courtesy, Plymouth Plantation, Plymouth, MA   *20* Mary Evans Picture Library/Photo Researchers   *30* Library Company of Philadelphia   *31* Peabody and Essex Museum, Salem, MA   *53* Yale University Art Gallery, Bequest of Eugene Phelps Edwards   *65* American Antiquarian Society   *72* Chicago Historical Society   *73* Copyright Yale University Art Gallery   *82* Anne S. K. Brown, Brown University Library, Military Collection   *84* New York State Historical Association, Cooperstown   *86* Courtesy, Brooklyn Museum   *92* Corbis/Bettmann Archive   *93* Bowdoin Museum of Fine Arts, Bowdoin College, Brunswick, ME   *97* Stokes Collection/New York Public Library, Astor Lenox & Tilden Foundations   *98* National Portrait Gallery, Washington, D. C.   *111* Library Company of Philadelphia   *118* Library of Congress   *125* Library Company of Philadelphia   *130* Peale Museum, Baltimore, MD   *135* Collection of Davenport West, Jr./The Picture Collection/New York Public Library   *138* Chicago Historical Society   *154* St. Louis Museum of Art, Collection of Arthur Ziern, Jr.   *158* Stokes Collection/New York Public Library, Astor, Lenox and Tilden Foundations   *159* Boston Athenaeum   *171* "Trail of Tears" by Robert Lindneaux, Woolaroc Museum, Bartesville, Oklahoma   *176* Library of Congress   *182* Abby Aldrich Rockefeller Folk Art Center/Colonial Williamsburg Foundation   *184* Brown Brothers   *188, 195* New-York Historical Society, New York City   *196* National Archives   *198* New-York Historical Society   *199* Courtesy, Museum of Fine Arts Boston   *208* Western History Collection/Denver Public Library   *212* Yale University Library, Beinecke Rare Book and Manuscript Library   *223* Granger Collection   *230* Historic New Orleans Collection   *232* Library of Congress   *238* Granger Collection, New York   *243* Missouri Historical Society   *246*(R) Library of Congress   *246*(L) Chicago Historical Society, Neg. #ICHi-20265, photo by Alexander Hesler   *254* Courtesy, Museum of the Confederacy, Richmond, VA   *260* Library of Congress   *263* Chicago Historical Society   *275* *Harper's Weekly,* November 16, 1867   *277* New-York Historical Society   *279* Culver Pictures Inc.   *286* By permission of the Darwin Museum, Down House, Courtesy of Mr. G. P. Darwin.   *290* Brown Brothers   *293* National Archives   *306* Brown Brothers   *308* Carnegie Museum of Art   *310* Puck   *321* Library of Congress   *327* *New York Sun*   *328* New-York Historical Society   *336* Courtesty, Joseph Pulitzer, Jr.   *341* Brown Brothers   *343* Corbis/Bettmann Archive   *345* Metropolitan Museum of Art, New York   *358* Granger Collection   *366* New York Public Library, Astor, Lenox & Tilden Foundations   *369* Keystone-Mast Collection/California Museum of Photography, Riverside   *370* Culver Pictures Inc.   *379* Library of Congress   *387* Granger Collection   *395* Corbis/Bettmann Archive   *405* Courtesy, American Legion   *413* Granger Collection   *423* Corbis/Bettmann Archive   *427*(B) John Fitzgerald Kennedy Library   *427*(T) Brown Brothers   *432, 438* Library of Congress   *443* Corbis/UPI/Bettmann Archive   *447* National Archives   *451, 457* Corbis/ Bettmann Archive   *471* Superstock, Inc.   *479* Culver Pictures Inc.   *484* Granger Collection   *488* Elliott Erwitt/Magnum Photos   *492* Corbis/Bettmann Archive   *502* Corbis/UPI/Bettmann   *511*(B) Corbis/Bettmann Archive   *511*(T) Elliott Erwitt/Magnum Photos   *521* Magnum Photos   *536* Russ Zimmerman/Black Star   *537* Bob Fitch/Black Star   *543* Corbis/UPI/Bettmann   *548* Dennis Brack/Black Star   *554* Larry Downing/Woodfin Camp & Associates   *563* Ira Wymass/Sygma

Abolitionists, 187
Abortion rights, 542
Abstract impressionism, 531
Acculturation, 30–31
Acquired immune deficiency syndrome, 540, 554
Adams, Abigail, 83
Adams, John, 63, 67, 79, 97, 107, 109
Adams, John Quincy, 132–133, 138, 142–143, 164–165
Adams, Samuel, 65, 96
Adamson Act, 402
Addams, Jane, 332
African colonization movement, 290
African-Americans. *See* Blacks
Afro-American League (1887), 290
Age of Reason, 54
Agency for International Development, 507
Agnew, Spiro T., 516
resigns vice-presidency, 522
Agricultural Adjustment Act (AAA), 452, 460
declared unconstitutional, 459
Agriculture, 442
colonial, 25–26
Aguinaldo, Emilio, 388, 390
AIDS, 540, 554
Air brake, 305
Air travel, commercial, 528
Airplane industry, 431–432
Alabama claims, 383
Alamo, 206
Alaska, 133
purchased by United States, 384
Albany Plan (1754), 59
Albany Regency, 139
Albemarle settlement, 19
Alcott, Bronson, 181
Alexander IV (Pope), 4
Alien and Sedition Acts, 106
Alliance movement, 355–356
Amana Community, 184
Amendments to the Constitution.
See Constitution
America
in the British Empire, 47–69

discovery of, 1–22
government of. *See* American government
as modern world power, 546
American, origins of, 23–24, 51
American Art-Union, 198
American Association of Retired People (AARP), 532
American Birth Control League, 420
American Board of Commissioners of Foreign Missions, 183
American Civil Liberties Union, 424
American Expeditionary Forces (AEF), 408
American Federation of Labor (AFL), 315–316, 452
American government
checks and balances, 95
early years, 97–98
formation of, 80
regulation
Big Business, 313–314
railroads, 312–313
The American High School Today (1959) (Conant), 537
American Independent Party, 516
American Indian Movement (AIM), 536
American Museum of Natural History, 329
American Party, 241, 248
American Philosophical Society, 55
American Railway Union, 316, 317
American Revolution
financing of, 80
origins of, 67–68
American Sugar Refining Company, 314
American System, 140, 144, 235
American Telephone and Telegraph Company, 306
American Tobacco Company, 372
American Women's Suffrage Association, 370
Americans for Democratic Action (ADA), 491
"Anaconda Plan," 254

Anderson, Marian, 462
Anderson, Mary, 421
Anderson, Robert, 252
Andros, Edmund, 37
Anglican Church, 13
Anglo-American relations, 103–104, 132
Annapolis convention, 92
Anthony, Susan B., 190, 370
Antietam, 260
Antifederalists, 95–96
Anti-Imperialists, 389–390
Antinomianism, 17
Anti-Saloon League, 425, 426
Antitrust laws, enforcement of, 555
A&P food chain, 442
Applied Christianity (Gladden), 332
Appomattox Court House, 266
Architecture, 329
American, 197–198
Arizona, 296
Arms embargo law, 464
Arms race, 507
Arnold, Benedict, 76–77, 78
Art
American painters, 344
in post World War America, 531
progressive: "ashcan school," 365
Arthur, Chester A., 289
and "Stalwart" faction, 351
Articles of Confederation, 80, 89
Assembly line, 430
Aswan Dam project, 498
Atlanta Compromise, 290–291
Atlantic Monthly, 197
Atom Bomb
development, 466, 481–482
first use, 481
Atomic Energy Commission, 489
Autocracy *vs.* Socialism, 311
Automobile industry, 430–431
Axis Powers, declation of war on United States, 471
Aztecs, 7

Babcock, Orville E., 281
Baby Boom, 487–488

Bache, Benjamin, 106
Bacon's Rebellion, 29–30
Badoglio, Pietro, 477
Baker v. *Carr* (1962), 502
Bakker, Jim, 530
Balance of trade, 49
Balboa, Vasco Núñze de, 4
Ballinger, Richard A., 376
Baltimore and Ohio Railroad, 231
Bancroft, George, *History of the United States,* 197
Bank deregulation, 558
Bank notes, 172
Bank of United States, 99–100, 136–137, 146, 159, 166–168, 172, 205
"Bank War," 166–168
"Bankers' conspiracy," 356
Bao Dai, 498
Baptists, Southern, 529
Barbados, 49
Barbary pirates, 113–114
Barbed wire, 301
Barnard, Henry, 199
"Barnburners," 216
Bartram, John, 55
Baruch, Bernard M., 404
    Baruch Plan, 489
Batista, Fulgencio, 500
Battle of Leyte, 480
Battle of Seven Pines, 258
Battle of the Bulge, 477
Battle of the Coral Sea, 479
Battle of the Philippine Sea, 480
Bay of Pigs, 506
Beauregard, Pierre G.T., 254
Beecher, Catherine, *Treatise on Domestic Economy for the Use of Women,* 181
Belknap, William W., 281
Bell, Alexander Graham, 306
Bell, John, 248
Bellamy, Edward, *Looking Backward 2000–1887,* 312
Bellow, Saul, 530
Belmont, Alva, 371
Benton, Thomas Hart, 166
Bering, Vitus, 133
Berkeley, Lord John, 19
Berkeley, Sir William, 29
Berkeley, University of California at, 538
Berkman, Alexander, 316
Berlin airlift, 490, 491
Berlin Wall, 507

Bessemer, Henry, 306
Bethune, Mary McLeod, 463
Bethune-Cookman College, 463
Beverly, Robert, *The History and Present State of Virginia,* 25
Biddle, Nicholas, 166–168
Bill of Rights, 98, 244
Bingham, George Caleb, 198
Birney, James G., 188, 210
Birth control, 420, 502
Black Death, effect on trade, 2–3
Black militancy, 533
    beginnings of, 379–380
Black Muslim movement, 510
Black nationalism, 510
Black Power, 534
Black students, influence of, 538
Black Studies programs, 538–539
Blackmun, Harry A., 520
Blacks. *See also* Slavery
    and California Gold Rush, 217
    colonization to Africa, 152
    and the Compromise of 1877, 284
    containment of after Emancipation Proclamation, 261
    curtailment of rights after Civil War, 289
    and Federal Elections Bill, 353
    free, 276–277
    migration to northern cities, 407
    during New Deal, 462–463
    and organized labor, 428
    and prejudice, 341
    and Republican Party in Gilded Age, 287
    as soldiers in Civil War, 262
    in sports, 536
    in World War I, 407–408
    in World War II, 473
Blackstone, Sir William, 64
Blackwell, Elizabeth, 265
Blaine, James G., 352, 353–354
Bland-Allison Act, 357
"Bleeding Kansas," 242
Blennerhassett Island, 119
Bliss, William D.P., 332
Blitzkrieg, 466
Board of Trade, 48
Boeing, William E., 433
"Bonus Army," 446
Booth, John Wilkes, 270
Borah, William E., 413
"Border Ruffians," 242
Boston, 41

Boston Associates, 147, 148–149
Boston Gazette, 40
Boston Massacre, 65–66
Boston Museum of Fine Arts, 329–330
Boston Port Act, 67
Boston Symphony, 330
Boston "Tea Party," 67
Bounties, 91
Bowditch, Nathaniel, 202
Boxer Rebellion, 393
Braceros, 535
Braddock, Gen. Edward, 58
Bradford, William, 14
Bradley, Omar N., 493
Bradstreet, Anne, 34
Brandeis, Louis D., 369, 401
Breckenridge, John C., 248
Brewster, William, 14
British Colonial System, 47–48
British East India Company, 66
Brock, Gen. Issac, 127
Brooklyn Bridge, 329
Brooks, Preston S., 242
Brown, John, 242, 247
Brown, Moses, 147
Brown University, 53, 201
Brown v. *Board of Education of Topeka,* 501
Bryan, William Jennings, 358–360, 398
    and election of 1908, 375
    and Fundamentalism, 424–425
    and Spanish treaty allowing purchase of Phillipines, 390
Bryan-Chamorro Treaty (1914), 398
Bryce, James, 289
    The American Commonwealth (1888), 311
Bryn Mawr College, 338
Buchanan, James, 243–244, 250
Buchanan, Patrick, 560
Buffalo, destruction of, 294
Bull Run, 254–255
    Second, 259
Bullfinch, Charles, 197
Bulwer, Henry Lytton, 239
Bunker Hill, 71–72
Bureau of Corporations, 372, 373, 378
Burger, Warren, 520, 553
Burgoyne, Gen. John, 76–77
Burlingame Treaty of 1868, 291
Burnside, Ambrose E., 262
Burr, Aaron, 19, 109, 116

Bush, George, 556–559
  domestic problems, 558
  fall from favor, 560
Business, regulation of, 435
Butler, Andrew P., 242
Butler, Benjamin F., 354
Byrd, William (II), 33
Byrnes, James F., 472

Cabot, John, 8
Cacafuego, 9
Caesar's Column (Donnelly), 356
Calhoun, John C., 139–140, 142,
    143, 168–169, 170–171, 216
California, 209, 213, 216–217
  gold discovery, 214
Calvert, George (Lord Baltimore),
    18, 32
Calvin, John, 9
Cambodian "Incursion," 517–518
Camp, Walter, 331
Camp David Agreement, 546
Canada, border agreement with
    U.S., 132
Canals, 155–157, 233–234
Capitalism, 312
Capone, Alphonse "Scarface Al,"
    425
Caribbean, United States' role as
    protector, 392
Carmichael, Stokley, 533
Carnegie, Andrew, 308–309, 311,
    316
Carnegie Endowment for Interna-
    tional Peace, 439
Carolina Charter, 19
Carolinas, 18–19
Carpetbaggers, 275–276
Carranza, Venustiano, 399
Carroll, Father John, 87
Carter, James Earl, 545–550
  as president, 545
Carteret, Sir George, 19
Cash-and-carry, 466
Cass, Lewis, 216
Cassatt, Mary, 345
Castro, Cipriano, 392
Castro, Fidel, 500, 506
Catch-22 (Heller), 530
The Catcher in the Rye (Salinger),
    530
Catherine of Aragon, 9
Catholic, Protestant, Jew (1955)
    (Herberg), 529
Catholic Church, 331, 529

Catlin, George, 198
Catt, Carrie Chapman, 370
Cattle, 299–300
  drives, 299
Cattlemen's associations, 301
Ceausescu, Nicolae, 557
Census. *See* population
Central Intelligence Agency (CIA),
    490, 506, 524
  and coup in Iran, 548
Central Pacific, 298
Central Powers, 400, 408, 416
Cervera, Pascual, 388
Chambers, Whitaker, 494
Champlain, Samuel de, 17
Champlain Canal, 156
Chancellorsville, 262
Chaplin, Charlie, 422
Charles I, 15, 18
Charles II, 20, 38
Charles River Bridge Case, 160
Charleston, 30, 170
Charleston colony, 19
Chase, Salmon P., 219, 255, 274
Chase, Samuel, 113
Chattanooga, 263
Chautauqua movement, 335
Chávez, César, 535
Checks and balances, 95
Cherokee Indians, 169
Cherokee Nation v. *Georgia,* 169
Chesapeake, 121
Chesapeake Bay region, 24
Chiang Kai-shek, 440, 490–491, 492
Chicago, 326
Chicago Democratic Convention
    (1968), 516
Chicanos, 535
Child, Lydia Maria, *The Mother's
    Book,* 181
Child labor, 228, 363, 368, 452
Children, in colonial times, 34–35
China
  becomes communist, 492
  commercial privileges with U.S.,
    384
  included in Open Door policy,
    394
  relations with, 545
China trade, 1–3
Chinese, immigration of, to U.S.,
    291
Chivington, J.M. (Chivington Mas-
    sacre), 292
Choctaw Indians, 169

Church of England, 13
Churchill, Winston, 466, 467, 482
CIA. *See* Central Intelligence
    Agency
Cigarette-rolling machine, 303
Circular Letter, 65
Civil rights, 500–502
Civil Rights Act (1866), 272
Civil Rights Act of 1875, 289
Civil Rights Act of 1957, 501
Civil Rights Cases (1883), 289
Civil Service Commission, 352
Civil War
  casualties in, 267
  causes, 190
  costs of, 267–268
  funding for, 255
Civil Works Administration (CWA),
    454
Civilian Conservation Corps, 463
Clark, William, 116–117
Clark Memorandum (1930), 440
Clay, Henry, 127, 140, 142, 167, 173,
    205, 209, 217–218, 235
Clayton, John M., 239
Clayton Antitrust Act, 378
Clayton-Bulwer Treaty (1850), 385
Clayton-Bulwer Treaty, renegoti-
    ated, 394
Clean Air Act of 1965, 525
Clemenceau, Georges, 411
Clement VII (Pope), 9
Cleveland, 309
Cleveland, Grover, 287, 316,
    352–353
  and Latin American policy, 386
Clinton, Bill, 560–562
Clinton, De Witt, 156
Clinton, Gen. Henry, 77
Cocaine, 554
Coercive Acts, 67
Cohn, Roy M., 497
Coinage Act of 1873, 357
Cold Harbor, 265
Cold War, 488–490
  end of, 557–558
College enrollment, 537
Colonial policy, following Spanish-
    American War, 389
Colonies, Middle, 19–20, 41–43
  farming, 44
Colorado, 296
Colored Alliance, 356
Columbia, South Carolina, capture
    of, 266

Columbia space shuttle disaster, 552–553
Columbia University (formerly King's College), 54, 538
Columbus, Christopher, 1–4
  death of, 4
Committee for Industrial Organization (CIO), 452, 460, 487
Committee on Civil Rights, 491, 501
Committee to Re-Elect the President (CREEP), 521
Commodity Credit Corporation, 460
Common school movement, 198–200
Common Sense (Paine), 72
Commonwealth v. *Hunt,* 229
Communism
  and American diplomacy during World War II, 482
  and American security, 494–495
  during Great Depression, 446
  Red Scare after World War I, 415–416
Communitarianism, 185–186
Community Service Organization (CSO), 535
The Companionate Marriage (1927) (Lindsey), 419
Compromise of 1850, 217–219, 237
Compromise of 1877, 283–284, 351
Computers, 533, 554
Conant, James B., *The American High School Today* (1959), 537
Concessions and Agreements (1677), 20
Concord, 70
Confederacy, 248, 253–254
  defeat of, 264–266
Congregationalists, 13
Congress for Racial Equality (CORE), 509
Congressional Union, 371
Conkling, Roscoe, 351, 354
Connecticut, 35–36
Conquistadores, 4–6
Conscription, 261, 468
Constitution
  Amendment, 12th, 110
  Amendment, 13th, 271
  Amendment, 14th, 272–273, 368
  Amendment, 15th, 274–275
  Amendment, 16th, 371, 553
  Amendment, 17th, 371
  Amendment, 18th, 425
  Amendment, 19th, 371

  Amendment, 21st, 450
  Amendment, 25th, 522
  equal rights amendment, 541
  ratification of, 95–97
USS *Constitution,* 127
Constitutional Convention (Philadelphia), 93–94
Constitutional Union party, 248
Consumers' League, 369
Continental Congress, 80
  First, 67–68
  Second, 71
Contraception, 420
"Contract with America," 561
Contras, 556, 557
Convention of 1818, 132
Cook, William, *The Corporation Problem* (1891), 311
Coolidge, Calvin, 415, 436
Cooper, James Fenimore, 192
Cooper, Peter, 288
Copley, John Singleton, 192
"Copperhead" Democrats, 255–256
Corn, 40
Corning, Erastus, 231, 232–233
Cornwallis, Gen. George, 77–79
Coronado, Francisco Vasquez de, 4
The Corporation Problem (1891) (Cook), 311
Corporations, 150, 158–159, 363–364
Cortés, Hernan, 4
Cosby, William, 45
Cost of living, 405
Cotton, 150–152, 221–222, 235
Cotton, Reverend John, 35
Cotton gin, 146, 151
"Cotton Whigs," 240
Coughlin, Charles E., 456, 458
Council for New England, 15
Counterculture, 539
Cowpens, Battle of, 78
Cox, Archibald, 522
Cox, James M., 416
Coxey, Jacob S., Coxey's "army," 357
Crane, Stephen, *The Red Badge of Courage,* 344
Crawford, William H., 139, 142
Crédit Mobilier, 298
Crèvecoeur, Hector St. John de, 44
Crittenden Compromise, 250
Croghan, George, 56–57
Croker, Richard, 350
Croly, Herbert, *The Promise of American Life,* 377

Cromwell, Oliver, 18, 37
Crop-lien system, 278–279, 322
"Cross of Gold" speech, 358
Crown Point, 71
Crusade for Justice, 535
Crusades, 2
Cuba, 4, 239, 500
  crises, 506–507
  establishment of independent government, 390–391
  independence, 388
  United States investment in, 396
Cuban missile crisis, 507
Cuban Revolution, 386–388
Cuban-American relations, 391
Cuffe, Paul, 152
Currency reform, 288
Currier and Ives, 198
Custer, George A., "Last Stand," 294
Cutler, Timothy, 52
Czechoslovakia, seized by Soviet Union, 492
Czolgosz, Leon, 371

Daley, Richard J., 504, 516
Dallas, George M., 209
Dana, Richard Henry, *Two Years Before the Mast,* 208
Darrow, Clarence, 424–425
Dartmouth, 67
Dartmouth College v. *Woodward,* 159
Darwin, Charles, 286
Daugherty, Harry M., 435, 436
Daughters of the American Revolution (DAR), 462
Davis, Jefferson, 219, 240, 250, 254, 270–271
Dawes Plan, 441
Dawes Severalty Act of 1887, 294–295, 379, 463
D-Day, 477
DDT, 532
De Leon, Daniel, 312
De Leon, Ponce, 4
de Lesseps, Ferdinand, 385
de Lome, Depuy, 388
De Mendoza, Pedro, 4
de Onís, Luis, 132–133
de Tocqueville, Alexis, *Democracy in America,* 178–179
de Triana, Roderigo, 1
Dean, John W., 521
Deane, Silas, 77

Debs, Eugene V., 316, 317, 358
  imprisonment of, 406
Debts, to foreign countries, 99
Declaration of Independence, 72–74
  influence on Anti-Imperialism, 389
  military implications, 74
Declaration of the Causes and Necessity of Taking Up Arms, 72
Declaratory Act, 64
Dedham, Massachusetts, 37
Deere, John, 233
Deficit spending, 458, 460
Deflation, 307
Democracy
  Jeffersonian, 117–118
  in New England Colonies, 36–37
Democracy in America (de Tocqueville), 178–179
Democratic Party, 164, 173, 216, 240, 248, 261, 281, 286–287, 350–351, 353, 359, 441–442
  "Bourbon," 288
  Greenbackers, 288
  "Peace Democrats" (Copperheads), 255
Dempsey, Jack, 423
Denby, Edwin, 436
Department of Commerce and Labor, 372
Department of Health, Education, and Welfare, 496
Depression
  of 1811, 126
  of 1819, 136
  of 1838–1843, 174
  of 1857, 235
  of 1861, 264
  agricultural, 167
  agricultural (1890's), 355
  Great, 441, 443–446
Détente, 518
Devaluation of the dollar, 520
Dewey, George, 388
Dewey, John, 340, 346
Dewey, Thomas E., 467, 481
Dewson, Molly, 462
Dias, Bartholomeu, 4
Dias, Dinis, 3
Diaz, Adolfo, 398
Díaz, Porfirio, 398
Dickens, Charles, 149
Dickinson, John, 65, 80
Diem, Ngo Dinh, assassination, 513
Dien Bien Phu, 498, 513

Dinwiddie, Gov. Robert, 57
Discovery, 11
Disney, Walt, 422
Distribution Act, 205
Divorce, 421, 554
Dix, Dorothea, 186
Dixicrat. See States' Rights Party
Dodd, Samuel C.T., 310
Doheny, Edward L., Pan-American Petroleum Company, 436
"Dollar diplomacy," 395–396
Domestic Manners of Americans (Trollope), 178–179
Dominican Republic, 392
  United States investment in, 396
"Domino theory," 513
Donnelly, Ignatius, Caesar's Column, 356
Dos Passos, John, 454
Douglas, Stephen A., 218–219, 239–240, 244, 248
Douglass, Frederick, 261
  Narrative of the Life of Frederick Douglass, 188
Downes v. Bidwell (1901), 391
Draft. See Conscription
  lottery system, 517
Draft Riots, 261
Drake, Edwin L., 306
Drake, Francis, 9
Dred Scott decision, 243–244, 246–247
Dreiser, Theodore, Sister Carrie, 344
Du Bois, William E.B., 429
  The Crisis, 381
  early life, 379
  and World War I, 407–408
Dukakis, Michael S., 556–557
Dulles, John Foster, 496–497, 499
Duncan, Isadora, 366
Dunkirk, 466
Dutch, 49–50
Dynamic Sociology,The Psychic Factors of Civilization (Ward), 340

e pluribus unum, 418
Eakins, Thomas, 344
Economic Opportunity Act of 1964, 511
Economics, 339–340, 348, 472
Economy, post-World War II, 486–487
Eden, Anthony, 482, 499
Ederle, Gertrude, 423

Edison, Thomas A., 306
Education, 323–324
  higher, 337–339
  progressive, 340–341
  public, 335–336
Edwards, Jonathan, 53–54
Ehrlichman, John, 521
Eight-hour day, 315, 402
Eisenhower, Dwight D., 495
  and civil rights, 500–502
  as General in World War II, 476–477
  and Latin America, 500
  and Soviet Union, 499
  style as president, 496
  Suez Canal incident, 499
Eisenhower Doctrine, 499
El Dorado, 49
Elections, presidential
  1789, 97
  1796, 105
  1800, 109–110
  1808, 124
  1816, 135–136
  1824, 142–143, 165
  1828, 162, 163, 165
  1832, 165, 171
  1836, 171
  1840, 165–176, 174
  1844, 209–211
  1848, 216
  1852, 240
  1856, 243
  1860, 247–248
  1868, 274–275
  1872, 281–282
  1876, 281–282, 351
  1880, 350–351
  1884, 352
  1888, 353
  1892, 287, 353, 356
  1896, 358–360
  1900, 366
  1904, 373–374
  1912, 376
  1916, 401–402
  1920, 416
  1924, 436–437
  1928, 441–442
  1932, 447–448
  1936, 458–459
  1940, 467
  1944, 481
  1948, 491–492
  1952, 495–496

Elections, presidential, *cont.*
  1956, 499
  1960, 502–503
  1964, 511–512
  1968, 515–516
  1972, 518–520
  1976, 545
  1980, 549–550
  1984, 553–554
  1988, 556–557
  1992, 560
  disputed (1876), 281–282
  at end of nineteenth century, 350
Electoral College (vote tallies), 95,
    109, 142, 163, 165, 248, 274,
    353, 356, 359, 375, 377, 402,
    437, 441, 448, 467, 491, 495,
    504, 516, 545, 552, 557, 560
Electric light bulb, 306–307
Elementary and Secondary Educa-
    tion Act, 512
Eliot, Charles W., 337
Elizabeth I, 9, 10, 11, 13
Elkins Railroad Act of 1903, 372, 374
Ellis, Havelock, 420
Ely, Richard T., 339, 348
Emancipation, voluntary, 82
Emancipation Proclamation, 260–262
Embargo Act of 1807, 121–122
Emerson, Ralph Waldo, 193–194
Energy conservation, 546
English, in America, 9–10
The Enlightenment, in America,
    54–55
Enola Gay, 481
Entail, 81
Episcopal Church, 87
Equal rights, 112
Equal Rights Amendment, 541
Equitable (life insurance company),
    310
Era of Good Feelings, 135–136
Erie Canal, 156, 157, 231
Eriksson, Leif, 1
Espionage Act (1917), 406
Essex Junto, 116
Ethnic issues, 348–349
Evangelism, on television and radio,
    530
Evans, Oliver, 146
Evolution, theory of, 286, 345–346,
    531
Excise taxes, 101
Exclusion Act of 1882, 326
Executive privilege, 521

Factors, 30
Factory system, 147–148, 181
Fair Deal, 491–492
Fair Employment Practices Com-
    mission, 491, 501
Fair Employment Practices Com-
    mittee, 474
Fair Labor Standards Act, 461
Fall, Albert B., 436
Family structure, 419
Farm Bloc, 435, 442
Farm Loan Act, 402
The Farmers Alliance, 355
Farming, 297, 321–322
  colonial, 40
  equipment, 146, 151, 233
  use of fertilizer, 221
Farouk (King of Egypt), 499
Farrell, James T., 454
Faulkner, William, 454–455
Federal Communications Commis-
    sion (FCC), 313, 422
Federal Deposit Insurance Corpora-
    tion (FDIC), 451
Federal Elections Bill ("Force"
    Bill), 353
Federal Emergency Relief Adminis-
    tration (FERA), 454
Federal employees, size of work
    force, 288
Federal Farm Board, 444
Federal Reserve Act, 377–378
Federal Reserve Banks, 378
Federal Reserve Board, 378, 430,
    435, 443, 451, 547
Federal system, 93
Federal Trade Commission (FTC),
    378
Federalism, 115–116
Federalists, 95–96, 110, 130, 131
Female Missionary Society, 183
The Feminine Mystique (1963)
    (Friedan), 541
Feminism, 542. *See also* Women
Feminism, radical, 421
Ferarro, Geraldine, 551
Ferdinand, Archduke Franz, assas-
    sination of, 400
Fessenden, William P., 272
Fetterman, W.J., 293
Fillmore, Millard, 218
Finney, Charles Grandison, 182,
    186
Fiske, John, 384
Fitch, John, 146

Fitzgerald, F. Scott, 427
Five-Power Treaty, 437
Flanders, 2
Fletcher v. *Peck,* 118–119
Florida, 114
Foot, Samuel A., 166
Football, 423
Foraker Act, 391
Foran Contract Labor Act, 334
Forbes, Charles R., 436
Ford, Gerald R.
  becomes president, 524
  becomes vice-president, 522
  incompetence of, 544
  as president, 544–545
Ford, Henry, 430, 431
Fordney-McCumber Tariff (1922),
    435
Foreign policy, 532
  as non-colonial imperial expan-
    sion, 396–397
Foreign relations, 437–439
Fort Duquesne (Pittsburgh), 58
Fort Mandan, 116
Fort McHenry, 128
Fort Orange, 17
Fort Sumpter, 252–253
Fort Ticonderoga, 71
Fortune, T. Thomas, 290
Fourier, Charles, Fourierism, 185
Four-Power Treaty, 437
France
  establishment of protectorate
    over Mexico, 383–384
  and Suez Canal, 498–499
  in Vietnam, 498
Franco, Francisco, 465
Franklin, Benjamin, 40, 45, 48, 55,
    64, 71, 79, 86
  in Paris, 77
Franklin, James, 40
Frasch, Herman, 306
Free Silver, 358, 390
Free Soil Party, 216
Freedmen's Bureau, 272, 276–277
"Freedom ride," 509
Freeport Doctrine, 247
Frelinghuysen, Theodore, 51–52
Frémont, John C., 213, 243
French Alliance, in American Revo-
    lution, 76–77
French and Indian War, 58
French Revolution, 101, 102
Freneau, Philip, 87, 102
Frick, Henry Clay, 316

Friedan, Betty, *The Feminine Mystique* (1963), 541
Frobisher, Martin, 9
From Here to Eternity (Jones), 530
Fuchs, Klaus, 494
Fugitive Slave Act, 219, 237
Fulton, Robert, 155
Fundamental Constitutions, 19
Fundamental Orders, 17
Fundamentalism, 424
Fur trade, 20, 42, 56, 89

Gage, Gen. Thomas, 70
Galloway, Joseph, 67
Garbage, disposal of, 533
Garcia, Calixto, 391
Garfield, James A., 351
Garrison, William Lloyd, 187, 188–189
Garvey, Marcus, 429
Gary, Elbert H., 372–373
Gaspee, 66
Gates, Horatio, 76
Geddes, Sir Eric, 410
General Electric, 310
General Motors, 431
Genet, Edmond Charles, 101
"Gentleman's Agreement" (1907), 394
George, Davis Lloyd, 411
George, Henry, *Progress and Poverty,* 311–312
George II, 58
George III, 70, 73
Georgia, 33–34, 266
German Americans, treatment of, 475
Germany
    attacks Poland, 466
    blockade of Venezuelan ports, 392
    conquests in World War II, 477
    division into occupation zones, 482
    expansionist aims, 465
    reparations for World War I, 412
    seizes Czechoslovakia, 466
    signs non-agression pact with Russia, 466
    surrenders at end of World War I, 478
Gettysburg, 262–263
Ghettos, 329, 428–429, 534–535
Gibbons v. *Ogden,* 159–160
Gibbs, Josiah Willard, 339

GI Bill of Rights, 487
Gilbert, Sir Humphrey, 10
Gilded Age, 287
Gilman, Daniel Coit, 337
Gingrich, Newt, 561
Ginsberg, Allen, *Howl* (1955), 539
Ginsberg, Ruth Bader, 561
Girard, Stephen, 200
Gitlin, Todd, *The Sixties: Years of Hope, Days of Rage,* 542
Gladden, Washington, *Applied Christianity,* 332
Glasnost, 552
Glass-Stegal Banking Act (1932), 445
Glorieta Pass, battle of, 258
Glorious Revolution (England), 38
Godspeed, 11
Gold, 48–49, 295–296, 360
    in Black Hills, 294
Gold Rush, 216–217
Gold standard, 357, 464
Goldman, Emma, 366
Goldmark, Josephine, 369
Goldwater, Barry M., 511–512
Gompers, Samuel, 315
Good Neighbor Policy, 439–440
Gorbachev, Michail S., 552, 557
Gottlieb, Adolph, 531
Gould, Jay, 304, 336
Government. *See* American government
Graham, Billy, 530
Grain shortage, 522
The Grange, 313
Grange, Harold "Red," 423
Grant, Ulysses S., 257, 263, 265, 274, 280–281
Gray, L. Patrick, 521
Great Awakening, 51–53
Great Awakening, Second, 182–183
Great Britain
    blockade of Venezuelan ports, 392
    Civil War involvement, 253, 256
    and Civil War reparations, 383
    control of colonies, 60–61
    and Oregon, 211
    during post-Revolutionary period, 89–90
    sovereignty of, 64
    and Suez Canal, 498–499
    taxation of colonies, 61–65
    and Venezuela, 386
    in War of 1812, 126–128

Great Compromise, 94
Great Northern Railroad, 304
Great Society, 511–512
    achievements of, 512
Great War. *See* World War I
Greeley, Horace, 179, 281
Green Spring faction, 29
Greenback Labor Party, 288
Greenback Party, 288
Greenbacks, 255
Greene, Gen. Nathaniel, 78
The Greening of America (Reich), 539
Greenwich Village, 366
Greer incident, 468
Grenville, George, 61
Griffith, David W., 422
Grimké, Sarah and Angelina, 189
Griswold v. *Connecticut* (1965), 502
Guadalcanal, 480
Guadaloupe, 17
HMS *Guerrière,* 127
Guiteau, Charles J., 351

Haiphong harbor mining, 518
Haiti, 114
    United States investment in, 396
Hakluyt, Richard, *Discourse on Western Planting,* 10
Haldeman, H.R., 520–521, 523
Hale, Sarah, 181
Half-Way Covenant, 36
Halleck, Henry W., 258–259
Hamilton, Alexander, 92–93, 96, 98–100, 105, 107, 116
Hammar v. *Dagenhart* (1918), 368
Hancock, John, 71
Hanna, Marcus Alonzo, 359–360
Harding, Warren G., 416
    character, 435
    death in office, 436
    scandals while president, 435–437
Harlan, John Marshall, 289
Harlem, 429
Harmar, Gen. Josiah, 100
Harper, William Rainey, 338
Harpers Ferry, 259
Harris, Townsend, 239
Harrison, Benjamin, 287, 353
Harrison, William Henry, 125, 127, 140, 175–176
Hartford Convention, 130
Harvard, 201, 337
Harvard, John, 39

Hawaiian Islands, 239, 384–385
  annexation by U.S., 385
Hawley-Smoot Tariff Act, 445
Hawthorne, Nathaniel, 195
Hay, John, 393–394
Hayes, Rutherford B., 281–282, 288, 316, 351
Haymarket bombing, 315
Hayne, Robert Y., 166
Haywood, William "Big Bill," 366
Head Start, 537
Headright system, 26
Health insurance reform, 561
Hearst, George, 296, 336
Hearst, William Randolph, 336
  and Cuba, 387
Heller, Joseph, *Catch-22,* 530
Heller, Walter, 504
Hemingway, Ernest, 427
Henry, Patrick, 62, 96
Henry VIII, 9
Hepburn Bill, 374
Herbart, Johann Friedrich, 340
Herberg, Will, *Catholic, Protestant, Jew* (1955), 529
Hessian soldiers, 72, 76
Highway System, Interstate, 527–528
Hill, James J., 304
Hippies, 539
Hiroshima, 481
Hiss, Alger, 494
Historians, 341
The History and Present State of Virginia (Beverly), 25
History of the United States (Bancroft), 197
Ho Chi Minh, 498, 513
Hoar, George Frisbie, 349
  as an Anti-Imperialist, 349
Hoe, Richard, 335
Hoffman, Abby, 539
Holden v. *Hardy* (1898), 368
Holmes, Jr., Oliver Wendell, 415
  The Common Law, 341
Home life, colonial, 32–34
Home Owners Loan Corporation, 451
Homer, Winslow, 344
Homestead Act of 1862, 264, 296
Homestead affair, 316
Homestead law, 248
Homeward Bound: American Families in the Cold War (May), 488
Homosexuality, policy in Armed Services, 560–561

Hooker, Joseph, 262
Hooker, Thomas, 17
Hoover, Herbert, 404, 435
  elected president, 441
  and Great Depression, 444
  and Kellogg-Briand Pact, 440
Hoover, J. Edgar, General Intelligence Division, 415
Hostages, in Lebanon, 556
House, Edward M., 402, 411
House Committee on Manufactures, 143
House on Henry Street (1915) (Wald), 332
Housing, colonial, 32–34
Houston, Sam, 206
How the Other Half Lives (1890) (Riis), 327–328
How to Make our Ideas Clear (Pierce), 346
Howe, Dr. Samuel Gridley, 185
Howe, Elias, 227
Howe, Gen. William, 72, 74, 75, 76
Howells, William Dean
  Atlantic Monthly, 343–344
  Harpers, 343
  A Hazard of New Fortunes, 343
Howl (1955) (Ginsberg), 539
Hudson River School, 198
Hudson's Bay Company, 211
Huerta, Victoriano, 399
Hughes, Charles Evans, 402, 435
Hughes, Langston, 429
Hull, Captain Issac, 127
Hull, Cordell, 470, 482
Hull, Gen. William, 127
Hull House, 332–333
Hunter, Robert, 45
Hussein, Sadam, 559
Hutchinson, Anne, 17
Hydrogen bomb, 497

Iceland summit, 552
Ickes, Harold L., 463
Idaho, 296
Illinois Central Railroad, 232, 233, 240, 297
Immigrants, 326–327, 349
  Catholic, 241, 325–326
  English, 324
  Germans, 228, 325
  Greek, 324, 325
  Irish, 228, 291, 325
  Italian, 325
  Polish, 325

Immigration, 149, 227–228, 291, 303, 324–326, 553
  quota system, 418
  Russian, 324–325
Immigration Act of 1965, 553
Immigration Restriction League, 326
Impeachment
  of Johnson, Andrew, 274
  of judges, 113
Imperial economy, British, 50–51
Imperialism, 396
Implied powers, doctrine of, 100
Impressment, 120–121
Incas, 7
Income tax, 357–358, 371, 374, 435
  graduated, 285, 378, 547, 553
Income Tax Act of 1986, 553
Indentured servant system, 27
Independent Treasury Act (1840), 174
Board of Indian Commissioners, 294
Indian Reorganization Act, 463
"Indian Ring," 294
Indian Self-Determination Act, 536
Indian Wars, 292–294
Indiana, Robert, 531
Indians, 20–21, 208, 217, 291–292
  civilizations, 6–8
  cultures, 6
  languages, 6
  and Progressive racial attitudes, 379
  "Red Power," 535–536
  religion, 7
Indigo, 30, 50, 151
Indulgences, 9
Industrial age, 319–334
Industrial Revolution in America, 146–148
Industrial Workers of the World (IWW), 366
Industry, mergers, 363
Infant mortality, 328
Inflation, 520, 532, 547, 550–551, 555
  in post-Revolutionary period, 91
Ingersoll, Jared, 63
Interest rates, 547, 551
International Harvester Company, 373
Interstate Commerce Act, 313, 314
  failure to end railroad abuses, 363
Interstate Commerce Commission (ICC), 313, 372, 375, 435

Intolerable Acts, 67
Iran-Contra Arms Deal, 555–556
Iranian Crisis, hostage situation, 548
   origins, 547–548
   resolution, 550
   stalemate, 548
Iraq, defeat of, by U.S., 559
Iron, 50
   Bessemer process, 305–306
Iron Curtain, 489
Iroquois, 56
"Irreconcilables," 413
Irving, Washington, 192
Queen Isabella, 4
Isolationism, 383, 464–465
Israel, 498–499
Italian Americans, treatment of, 475
Italy, expansionist aims, 465

Jackson, Andrew, 85, 131, 140,
   162–177
   in Florida, 132
Jackson, Thomas J. "Stonewall,"
   258, 262
Jackson State University, and Mississippi State Police killings,
   518
James, Duke of York, 19
James, Henry, 344
James, William, 346
James I, 11–12, 13
James II, 38
Jamestown, 11, 29
Japan, 239, 437
   attacks China, 465
   attacks Pearl Harbor, 470–471
   attacks Russia, 394
   conquests in World War II, 476
   defeat of China (1884–1885),
     392–393
   expansionist aims, 465
   in Manchuria, 440
   surrenders in World War II, 481
   treaty with (1858), 384
   Twenty-one Demands, 398
Japanese Americans, treatment of,
   475
Java, 127
Jaworski, Leon, 522, 523
Jay, John, 79, 101, 103–104
Jay Treaty, 103
Jazz, 429
"Jazz Age," 419–420
Jefferson, Thomas, 55, 71, 79, 82,
   106–107

Declaration of Independence,
   73–74
   as president, 109–112
Johns, Jasper, 531
Johns Hopkins University, 337–338
Johnson, Andrew, 271
   impeachment of, 274
Johnson, Lyndon B., 502, 508
Johnson, Sir William, 60–61
Johnson, Tom L., 367
Johnston, Albert Sidney, 257
Johnston, Joseph E., 258, 265–266
Jones, James, *From Here to Eter-
nity,* 530
Jones, May Harris "Mother," 366
Jones, Robert T. "Bobby," 423
Jones, Samuel M. "Golden Rule," 367
Jordan, Winthrop, 27
Journalism, magazine, 335–336
J.P. Morgan and Company, 316
Judiciary Act, 112–113
The Jungle (Sinclair), 374
The Junto, 55

Kalakaua, King (of Hawaii), 385
Kamikazes, 481
Kansas, 241–242, 244
Kansas-Nebraska Act, 240–241
Kearny, Gen. Stephen Watts, 213
Keating-Owen Child Labor Act, 402
Keayne, Robert, 40
Kelley, Abbey, 189
Kelley, Florence, 369
Kellogg-Briand Pact (1928), 439
Kelly, Oliver H., 313
Kelly, William, 306
Kennan, George F., 489, 493
   and containment, 492
Kennedy, David, 553
Kennedy, John F., 503–506, 506–507
   assassination of, 508
   domestic programs, 507–508
Kennedy, John Pendleton, 197
Kennedy, Robert, 506
Kennesaw Mountain, 265–266
Kent State University, and National
   Guard killings, 518
Kentucky Resolves, 106–107
Kerouac, Jack, 530
Key, David M., 284
Key, Francis Scott, 128–129
Keynes, John Maynard, 458
Khomeini, Ruhollah, 548
Khrushchev, Nikita, 497, 499, 500,
   507

King, Martin Luther, Jr., 509–510
   "I have a dream" address, 510
   "Letter from a Birmingham Jail,"
     510
   murdered, 534
King James Bible (1611), 14
Kinsey, Alfred C.
   *Sexual Behavior in the Human
     Female* (1958), 540
   *Sexual Behavior in the Human
     Male* (1948), 540
Kissinger, Henry, 518, 522–523
Kline, Franz, 531
Knights of Labor, 314–315, 356
Knights of Reliance, 355
Knights of the White Camelia, 279
"Know Nothing" Party, 241
   and Nativism, 325
Knox, Frank, 466
Knox, Philander C., 372
Korean War, 492–494
   ends, 496
Ku Klux Klan, 279–280
   revived, 426
Kuhn, Loeb Company, 308
Kuwait, 558–559

La Follette, Robert M., 367–368,
   436–437
Labor, 314, 320, 326
   eight-hour day, 315, 402
   "free," 280
   militancy, 315–316
   strike breaking, 316
   strikes, 315–316
   unions, 229
   during World War I, 405
Ladies' Home Journal, 488
Laissez-faire, 285–286, 313, 329, 348,
   365, 377, 435, 436
Land Ordinance of 1785, 85
Land tenure, communal, 7–8
Land-grants system, 297–298
Landon, Alfred M., 458
Latin America
   and extension of American influ-
     ence, 385–386
   and OAS, 500
Laud, William, 15
Laurens, Henry, 79
League of Nations, 412, 482
League of Women Voters, 421
Lecompton Constitution, 244
Lee, Ann, 183
Lee, Arthur, 77

Lee, Higginson Company, 308
Lee, Richard Henry, 73, 96
Lee, Robert E., 258–260, 262
Leet-men, 19
Legislatures, colonial, 48
Leisler, Jacob, 45
Leisler's Rebellion, 45
Leisure activities, 329–330
Lemke, William, 458
Lend-lease, 467
Leo XIII (Pope), *Rerum novarum,* 331
HMS *Leopard,* 121
Lever Act (1917), 404, 425
Lewis, John L., 452
Lewis, Meriwether, 116–117
Lewis, Sinclair, 428
Lexington, 479
Liberia, Republic of, 152
Liberty Party, 188, 210, 216
Lichtenstein, Roy, 531
Liliuokalani, Queen, 385
Lincoln, Abraham, 244–245, 252–254
  assassination, 270
  and Emancipation Proclamation, 260
Lincoln-Douglas debates, 245–247
Lindbergh, Charles A., 432
Lindsey, Benjamin B., *The Companionate Marriage* (1927), 419
Linotype machine, 336
Literacy, in Colonial New England, 39
Literacy tests, 289
Literacy-test bill, 326
Literary groups, 192
Literature
  in Great Depression, 454–455
  in post World War America, 530–531
  religious, 200
  in early 20th century, 426–428
  19th century trends, 342
Little Bighorn, 294
Little Turtle (Miami Indians), 100–101
Livingston, Robert R., 114
Lloyd, Henry Demarest, *Wealth Against Commonwealth* (1894), 312
Lochner v. *New York,* 368
Locke, Alain, *The New Negro,* 430
Locke, John, 19
  Second Treatise on Government, 61

Lockheed, Malcolm and Haines, 431–432
Lodge, Henry Cabot, 412–414, 435, 482
Lodge, Henry Cabot, Jr., 503
Lodge Reservations, 413
London Company, 11–13
The Lonely Crowd (1950) (Riesman), 529
Long, Huey, 456, 458
Longfellow, Henry Wadsworth, 197
Looking Backward 2000–1887 (Bellamy), 312
Lord Baltimore (George Calvert), 18, 32
Lords of Trade, 48
Loudoun, Lord John, 60
Louis XVI, 77
Louisiana purchase, 114–115
L'Ouverture, Toussaint, 114
Lovejoy, Elijah, 187
Lowell, Francis Cabot, 147
Lowell, James Russell, 197
Lowell System, 149–150
Loyalists, 74–75
Loyalty oath, 270–271
Loyalty Review Board, 494
Lucas, Eliza, 30, 32
Lucas v. *Colorado* (1964), 502
Lucayans, 6
Lusitania, 401
Lundy, Benjamin, 187
Luther, Martin, 9

MacArthur, Douglas, 479–480
  in Korea, 493
  removed from command, 493
Macdonough, Capt. Thomas, 130
HMS *Macedonia,* 127
Macomb, Gen. Alexander, 129
Macon's Bill No. 2, 124
Madero, Francisco, 399
Madison, James, 94, 124
Magazine journalism, 335–336
Magellan, Ferdinand, 4
Magon, Ricardo Flores, 406
Magruder, Jeb Stuart, 521
Mahan, Alfred Thayer, 384
Mailer, Norman, *The Naked and the Dead,* 530
Main, Gloria T., *Tobacco Colony: Life in Early Maryland,* 25
Maine, 17, 206
Maine, 387–388
Mainline Canal, 157

Malcolm X, 510
Manifest destiny, 207, 209, 238–239
Manila Bay, Battle of, 388
Mann, Horace, 199
Mann-Elkins act of 1910, 375
Manufacturing, 225–226
  post-Civil War, 303–304
Mao Tsetung, 490–491, 492
Marbury v. *Madison,* 113
Marcy, William L., 163, 240
Marshall, George C., 491
  Marshall Plan, 489–490
Marshall, John, 84–85, 113, 118, 158–160
Marshall, Thomas R., 371
Martinique, 17
Marxism, 229, 312
Marxist Social Labor Party, 312
Maryland, 18–19
Maryland Charter, 18
Massachusetts, 15–16, 35–36
Massachusetts Bay Company, 15–16
Massachusetts Government Act, 67
Massachusetts Patriots, 70
Massachusetts 54th regiment, 262
Mather, Increase & Cotton, 39
Maximilian, Archduke, 383
May, Elaine Tyler, *Homeward Bound: American Families in the Cold War,* 488
Mayaguez, 544–545
Mayflower, 14
Mayflower Compact, 14
McAdoo, William G., 404, 436
McCarran Internal Security Act, 500
McCarthy, Eugene, 515
McCarthy, Joseph R.
  Army-McCarthy hearings, 497
  McCarthyism, 495, 501
McClellan, George B., 255, 257–260
McClure, S.S., 364–365
McClure's, 364
McCord, James, 521
McCormick, Cyrus Hall, 233
McCulloch v. *Maryland,* 159, 166, 167–168
McDowell, Irvin, 254
McGovern, George, 518–519
McKinley, William, 287, 354, 358–360
  assassination of, 371
  and conquest of Philippines, 388–391
  and Cuban Revolution, 387–388
  independence in foreign affairs, 390–391

McKinley Tariff Act, 385
McNary-Haugen Bill (1927), 443
Meade, George G., 263
Measles, 7
Medicare, 512
Mellon, Andrew, 435, 436, 444
Melville, Herman, 195–196
Mencken, H. L., 428
Mental illness, care of, 186
Mercantilism, 48–49
   effects of, 50–51
Mergenthaler, Otto, 335–336
Mergers, in American industry, 363
Merry, Anthony, 119
Metropolitan Health Board, 327
Metropolitan Museum of Art, 329
Mexican Americans, 535
Mexico, 398–399, 440
   United States investment in, 396
   war with, 211–212
Michaelson, Albert A., 339
Middle class, 319, 528
   majority, 354
Middle East, 498–499
Midway Island, Battle of, 479
Midway Islands, purchased by
   United States, 384
Milan Decree (1807), 120
Miles, Nelson A., 292–293
Milkin, Michael, 555
Miller, Lewis, 335
Millett, Kate, *Sexual Politics,*
   541–542
Mills Bill, 353
Minimum wage, 459, 460, 461, 547
Minuit, Peter, 17
Minute Men, 70
Miró Esteban, 90
Missionary diplomacy, 398–399
Mississippi, 280
Mississippi River, 153
Missouri Compromise, 140–142,
   216, 240, 244
Missouri Enabling Act, 141
Mitchell, John, 373, 523
Mobility, geographical, 323–324,
   527
Modern era, 544–562
Molasses Act of 1733, 51
Molotov, V. M., 482
Mondale, Walter, 553–554
Money
   paper, distrust of, 167
   supply, 307, 361
Monkey Trial, 424–425

Monopolies, 307–308, 310, 333
   Progressive attack on, 369
   trend towards, 312
Monroe, James, 135–136
Monroe Doctrine, 133–135, 385,
   386, 500
   Roosevelt Corollary, 392, 440
Montezuma, 7
Montgomery bus boycott, 509
Moody, Dwight L., 331
Morgan, J. Pierpont, 308, 309, 358
Mormons, 184
Morrill Land Grant Act of 1862, 264,
   337, 338
Morris, Lewis, 45
Morrow, Dwight W., 440
Morse, Jedidiah, 87
Morse, Samuel F.B., 209
The Mother's Book (Child), 181
Motherwell, Robert, 531
Motion pictures, 422
Motley, Lothrop, 197
Mott, Lucretia, 189, 190
Mount, William Sidney, 198
Mount Holyoke, 338
Movies, 422
Ms. magazine, 542
Muckrakers, 364–365
Mugwumps, 352
"Mulligan letters," 352
Munn v. *Illinois,* 313
Muscovy Company, 9, 10
Mussaddig, Muhammad, 548
Mussolini, 465, 476–477
Mutual Life, 310
Mylai massacre, 517

Nagasaki, 481
Naismith, James, and basketball,
   330
The Naked and the Dead (Mailer),
   530
Napoleon, 119–120
NASA, 552
Nasser, Gamal Abdel, 499
National American Women's Suf-
   frage Association (NAWSA),
   370
National Association for the Ad-
   vancement of Colored People
   (NAACP), 381, 532
National Child Labor Committee,
   368
National Conservation Conference,
   374–375

National Defense Education Act of
   1958, 537
National government, 94–95
National Industrial Recovery Act
   (NIRA), 451–452, 462
   declared unconstitutional, 457
National Labor Relations Act (Wag-
   ner Act), 457
National Labor Relations Board
   (NLRB), 457
National Labor Union, 314
National Organization for Women
   (NOW), 541
National Origins Act (1924), 438,
   553
National Progressive Republican
   League, 376
National Recovery Administration
   (NRA), 451–452
National Republican Party, 173
National Science Foundation, 537
National War Labor Board, 405, 472
National Women's Suffrage Associ-
   ation (NWSA), 370
National Youth Administration
   (NYA), 463
Nationalism, 84, 235, 280
Nativism, American Protective As-
   sociation, 326
Natural resources, 295
Naturalism, 343
Naturalization Act, 112
Nauvoo, 184
Navigation, 3
Navigation Acts, 49–50
Nazi
   anti-Semitism, 466
   concentration camps, 477
Neutrality Act of 1935, 465
Nevada, 296
New Amsterdam, 17, 56
New Deal, 449, 450–469
   credit for, 464
   ends, 460–461
   second, 457–458
   significance of, 461–464
New England
   colonial, 17, 34–41
   Dominion of, 37–38
New England Courant, 40
New England Immigrant Aid Soci-
   ety, 242
New Freedom, 377–378
New Hampshire, 17
New Jersey, 19

New Mexico, 218
The New Negro (Locke), 430
New Orleans, 114
New Orleans, Battle of, 130–131
New Sweden, 18
New York, 19, 44, 228, 326, 327
    Washington's defeat at, 75–76
New York Central Railroad, 231, 304
New York City riots (1863), 327
New York Life, 310
"New York school" (of art), 531
New York Stock Exchange, crash (1929), 443
New York Weekly Journal, 45
Newlands Act (1902), 372
Newspapers
    technology, 336
    tycoons, 336
Ngo Dinh Diem, 498
Niagara Movement, 380
Nicaragua, 556
Nimitz, Chester W., 480
Niña, 4
Nine-Power Treaty, 437, 438
Nixon, Richard M., 499, 502, 515–516
    articles of impeachment against, 524
    cover-up of Watergate break-in, 523–524
    economy under, 520–521
    explanation for Watergate related actions, 524
    IRS problems, 522, 523
    landslide victory of 1972, 518–520
    resignation, 524
    and subpoena of White House tapes, 523–524
    unindicted co-conspiracy, 523
    White House tape recordings, 521–522
Nomura, Kichisaburo, 470
Non-Intercourse Act, 122
Noriega, Manuel, 557
"Normalcy," 416, 434–435
Norris, George W., 371
North, Lord Frederick, 66
North, Oliver, 556
North Atlantic Treaty, 492
North Atlantic Treaty Organization (NATO), 492
North Carolina, 34
Northern Pacific Railroad, 304
Northern Securities Company, 372

Northwest Ordinance of 1787, 85
Noyes, John Humphrey, 184
Nuclear power, 533
Nullification, 168–169, 170–172
Nye, Gerald P., 465

Oberlin, 201
O'Connor, Sandra Day, 553
Office of Strategic Services, 490
Office of War Mobilization, 472
Ogden, Aaron, 160
Oglethorpe, James, 33
Ohio, 100–101
Ohio Company, 57
Ohio Gang, 434, 435–436
Oil, 306, 309, 555
Oil Crisis, 522–523
Older, Fremont, 367
Olive Branch Petition, 71
Olney, Richard, 386
Oneida Community, 184
O'Neill, Eugene, 366
"Op" art, 531
Open Door policy, 392–394, 437
    tested by Boxer Rebellion, 393
Oregon, 208–209, 211
Organization of American States (OAS), 500
Organization of Petroleum Exporting Countries (OPEC), 523, 546, 548
Orlando, Vittorio, 411
Ostend Manifesto, 239
O'Sullivan, John L., 207
Oswald, Lee Harvey, 508
Oswald, Richard, 79
Otis, James, 60, 61
Owen, Robert, 185

Pacific Railway Act of 1862, 264, 298
Padrone system, 324
Pahlavi, Muhammad Reza. *See* Shah of Iran
Paine, Thomas, *Common Sense,* 72
Pale Faces, 279
Palmer, John M., 359
Palmer, Mitchell, 415–416
Palo Alto, 212
Panama, 557
    French control of, 394
    revolution, 395
Panama Canal
    built, 395
    negotiations to construct, 394–395

Panic of 1837, 174–175
Panic of 1857, 235
Paredes, Gen. Mariano, 212
Paris Peace Conference (WWI), 411–412
Parkenham, Maj. Gen. Sir Edward, 131
Parker, Alton B., 373–374
Parkman, Francis, 59, 197
Parks, Rosa, 509
Parris, Samuel, 38–39
Patent Office, U.S., 158
Patroons, 17
Patton, George S., 477
Paul, Alice, 371, 421
Paxton Boys, 45
Pay Board, 520
Payne-Aldrich bill, 375
Peace Corps, 507
Peace Movement, 439
Peace of Paris, 79–80
Peale, Charles Wilson, 193
Pearl Harbor, 470–471
Peffer, William A., 356
Pemberton, John C., 263
Pendleton Act, 352
Penn, William, 20, 44
Pennsylvania, 44–45
Pennsylvania "Dutch," 20, 45
Pennsylvania Railroad, 231
Perestroika, 552
Perkins, Francis, 462
Perkins Institution, 185
Perot, Ross, 560
Perry, Capt. Oliver Hazard, 127
Perry, Matthew C., 239
Pershing, John J., 399, 408
Persian Gulf War, 558–559
Petersburg, 265
Petroleum industry, 306
    falling prices in, 555
    refining, 309
Philadelphia, 44
Philip II, 8
Philippine Islands, 388
    purchased by U.S., 390
    in World War II, 480
Philosophy
    pragmatism, 345–346
    relativism, 346
Pickering, John, 113
Pickering, Timothy, 116
Pickett, George E., 263
Pierce, Charles S., *How to Make our Ideas Clear,* 346

Pierce, Franklin, 239, 240
Pike, James S., *The Prostrate South,* 276
Pinchot, Gifford, 376
Pinckney's Treaty, 104
Pinta, 4
Pirenne, Henri, 2
Pitt, William, 58, 59
Pizarro, Francisco, 4
Plantations, 222–223
Planter society, 32
Platt Amendment, 391, 392
Plattsburg, 129
Plessy v. *Ferguson,* 289, 501
Plymouth Company, 14–15
Plymouth Plantation, 14
Poe, Edgar Allan, 194
Poindexter, John, 556
Poland, 484
Political Parties, rise of, 102
Political reform
    in cities, 367
    in the states, 367–368
Polk, James K., 209–213
Poll taxes, 289
Pollack, Jackson, 531
Pollock v. *Farmers' Loan and Trust,* 357–358
Pollution, 533
Pontiac's Rebellion, 60
"Pop" art, 531
Popular culture, 421–423
Popular sovereignty, 216
Population, of U.S., 136, 149, 179, 253, 418–419, 473, 527
Populist movement, 355–356
Populist Party, 356, 361
    coinage of silver, 358
Portsmouth, New Hampshire, conference with Japan and Russia, 394
Portugal, 3
Potsdam, 483–484
Pottawatomie Creek, 242
Pound, Ezra, 366
Poverty, 229, 551
Powderly, Terrence V., 314
Powell, Lewis F., 553
Powhatan Indians, 12
Preemption Act of 1841, 205
Presbyterians, 13
Prescott, William Hickling, 197
Prevost, Gen. Sir George, 129
Price and wage freeze, under President Nixon, 520

Price Commission, 520
Primogeniture, 81
Prince Henry the Navigator, 3
Princeton University (formerly College of New Jersey), 53
Princip, Gavrilo, 399–400
Printing, 200
Prison system, 185–186
    population, 328
Privy Council, 48
Proclamation of 1763, 61
Progress and Poverty (George), 311–312
Progressive Era, 363–382
    and World War I, 406–407
Progressive Party, 376, 437
Prohibition, 186–187, 425–426
The Promise of American Life (Croly), 377
The Prophet (Tenskwatawa), 125–126
The Prostrate South (Pike), 276
Protectionism, 287
Protestants, 13
Providence Plantations, 16
The Psychological Care of Infant and Child (Watson), 419
Public Education, 536–537
Public Utility Holding Company Act, 458
Public Works Administration, 451
Pulitzer, Joseph, 336
    and Cuba, 387
Pullman, George, 305
Pullman strike, 316, 317
Pure Food and Drug Act, 374
Puritanism, 34
Puritans, 15–16

Qaddafi, Muammar al-, 553
Quakers, 19
Quartering Act, 63, 67
Quayle, Dan, 557
Quebec, 17
Quebec Act, 67
Quincy, Josiah, 126
Quitrent, 26, 44, 81

Racial discrimination, 508–510
Racial purity, 325
Radical feminism, 542
Radio, 422
Railroads, 231–235, 304–305
    building, 297–299
    governmental regulation, 312–313

rebates, 307
    sleeping car, 305
Raleigh, Sir Walter, 10
Ranching
    cattle, 300
    open-range, 300–301
    use of barbed wire, 301
Randolph, A. Philip, 474
Randolph, John, 118
Rapp, George, 183
Raynell, John, 65
Reagan, Ronald, 549–553
    as president, 550–551
    second term, 552–553
Realism, 342
Reaper, 233
Reconstruction, 270–272, 279
Reconstruction Act, First, 273
Reconstruction Finance Corporation, 445
The Red Badge of Courage (Crane), 344
Red Cloud, 293
Red Scare. *See* Communism
Reed, Thomas B., 354
Reformation, Protestant, 9
Regulators, 33
Rehnquist, William C., 553
Reich, Charles, *The Greening of America,* 539
Religion, 528–530
    divisions of, in Colonial America, 52–53
    in industrial society, 331
    and politics, 348–349
Religious enthusiasm, 51–53, 53–54
Republican Party, 241, 286–287
    breakup of (1910), 376
    Liberal, 281
    Mugwumps, 352
    Radical, 277
    "Radical" faction, 255
    Radicals, 271–272, 275
    "Stalwarts" and "Half-Breeds," 350–351
Rerum novarum (Pope Leo XIII), 331
Resaca de Palma, 212
Retailing, 310
Reuben James, 468
Revenue Act of 1921, 435
R. J. Reynolds Tobacco Company, 555
Rhode Island, 16
Rice, 30, 151

Richardson, Elliot, 522
Richmond, 265
    in Civil War, 258
Rickenbacker, Eddie, 404
Riesman, David, *The Lonely
    Crowd* (1950), 529
Riis, Jacob, *How the Other Half
    Lives* (1890), 327–328
Riots, urban, 534
Rittenhouse, David, 55
Roanoke, 10
Roberts, Oral, 530
Robinson, John, 14
Rockefeller, John D., 311, 338, 415
Roe v. *Wade*, 542
Roebling, John A., 329
Romantic movement, 193
Roosevelt, Eleanor, 462
Roosevelt, Franklin D., 441,
    447–448
    and concentration camps, 477
    death, 481
    election of 1936, 458–459
    fireside chats, 451, 464, 467
    "Four Freedoms," 467
    "Hundred Days," 450–451
    and isolationism, 465
    as post-war negotiator, 483
    and the Supreme Court, 459–460
    as war leader, 471–472
Roosevelt, Theodore, 288, 350, 353,
    361
    becomes president, 371
    and big business, 372–373
    and conservation of natural re-
        sources, 374–375
    involvement in Panamanian revo-
        lution, 395
    and San Juan Hill, 388
    and "square deal," 373
"Roosevelt recession," 460
"Roosevelt's Panic," 375
Root, Elihu, 395
Rosenberg, Julius and Ethel,
    494–495
Ross, Gen. Robert, 128
Rothko, Mark, 531
Royal African Company (1672), 28
Rubin, Jerry, 539
Ruckelshaus, William, 522
Ruef, Abe, 367
Rule of War (1756), 120
Ruml, Beardsley, 473
Rural Electrification Administration
    (REA), 458

Rush-Bagot Agreement of 1817, 132
Russia, non-agression pact with
    Germany, 466
Russian immigrants, 324–325
Russian Revolution, 403
Rutgers University (formerly
    Queen's College), 53
Ruth, George Herman "Babe," 423

Sac and Fox Indians, 169
Sacagawea, 116
Sacco-Vanzetti case, 426
Salem, 38
Salinger, J. D., *The Catcher in the
    Rye,* 530
Salvation Army, 331
Sampson, William T., 389
San Salvador, 1
Sandinistas, 556, 557
Sandys, Sir Edwin, 13, 14
Sanger, Margaret, 366, 420
Santa Anna, Antonio Lopez de, 206
Santa Maria, 4
Saratoga, 77–78
Saudi Arabia, 559
Savannah, 77
Savings and loan crisis, 558
Savings and loan institutions, 547
Scalawags, 275–276
Scalia, Antonin, 553
Scandinavians, 228
Schecter v. *United States* (1935), 457
Schley, Winfield Scott, 389
Schuller, Robert, 530
Schuyler, Philip, 76
Schwartzkopf, Norman, 559
Scientific advances, 339
    in Colonial America, 55
Scopes, John T., 424
Scott, Dred, 243–244
Scott, Sir Walter, 192
Scott, Thomas A., 304
Scott, Winfield, 212–213, 240, 253
Secession, 248–250, 252–253
Sectionalism, 166, 235
Sedition Act (1918), 406
Segregation, 289–290, 429
    in armed services, 473
    of Oriental children in San Fran-
        cisco, 394
    under "Progressive" government,
        379
Seminole Indians, 132, 169
Senate, U.S., and League of Na-
    tions, 412–414

Seneca Falls Convention (1848),
    190
Settlement houses, 332, 363
Settlement workers, 332
Seven Years' War, 58
Seward, William H., 383–384
Sewing machine, 227
Sexual mores, 419–420
Sexual Politics (Millett), 541–542
Sexual Revolution, 539–540
Sexually transmitted disease, 540
Seymour, Horatio, 274
Shafter, William, 388
Shah of Iran (Muhammad Resa
    Paahlavi), 548
Shakers, 183–184
Share tenancy, 278
Sharecropping, 278
Shay's Rebellion, 91–92
Sherman, John, 354
Sherman, William Tecumseh,
    265–266, 293–294
Sherman Antitrust Act, 313–314,
    353, 372
    failure to check growth of monop-
        olies, 363
    and the Pullman strike, 317
Sherman Silver Purchase Act, 357
Shiloh, 258
Shipbuilding, 119
Shipping industry, 230
Sierra Leone, 152
Silver, 48–49, 295–296, 361
    and bi-metallic standard, 357
    coinage of, 288
Silver Purchase Act, 353
Simmons, William J., 426
Simpson, "Sockless Jerry," 356
Sinclair, Harry F., Mammoth Oil
    Company, 436
Sinclair, Upton, *The Jungle*, 374
Single Tax, 312
Sioux, Oglala, 292–294
Sirica, John J., 521
Sister Carrie (Dreiser), 344
"Six-Day" War of 1967, 522
*The Sixties: Years of Hope, Days of
    Rage* (Gitlin), 542
Skylab, 552
Slater, Samuel, 146–147, 227
Slave trade, beginning of, 6
Slave trade, ending of, 223
Slavery. *See also* Blacks
    and abolition, 187–189
    and the Bill of Rights, 243–244

in the Colonial South, 27–31
and the Compromise of 1850, 217–219
as a Constitutional issue, 94
and cotton production, 152–153
and deportation to Africa, 152
and the District of Columbia, 219
and the *Dred Scott* case, 243–244, 247
economics of, 221–222
and Emancipation Proclamation, 260–261
and the Emancipation Proclamation, 260
end of, 267
first steps towards abolition, 81–82
and the fugitive slave laws, 219, 237
and John Brown, 242, 247
and the Kansas-Nebraska Act, 240–241
and Liberia, 152
and the Lincoln-Douglas debates, 246
and Mexico, 213, 215–216
and the Missouri Compromise, 140–142, 241
and New Mexico, 218
psychological effects of, 224–225
as a sectional issue, 137–138
sociology of, 223–224
and Stephen A. Douglas, 239–240
and Texas, 206–207, 215
and *Uncle Tom's Cabin,* 237–238
and Utah, 218
and the Wilmot Proviso, 215–216
Slidell, John, 212
Sloat, John D., 213
Slums, 228, 328–329, 349, 363
Smallpox, 7
Smith, Adam, *The Wealth of Nations,* 90
Smith, Al, 441
Smith, Gerald L. K., 458
Smith, Jesse, 435–436
Smith, John, 11
Smith, Joseph, 184
Smith Act (1940), 500, 502
Smith College, 338
Smithsonian Institution, 202
Smythe, Thomas, 13
Social cooperation, 532
Social Darwinism, 286, 325
Social Security Act (1935), 457
impact of, 462, 463

Social Security System, 496, 554
Socialism, 317
Socialist Party, 366
Sociology, in the 1880's, 339–340
Soil Conservation and Domestic Allotment Act, 459
Somoza, Anastasio, 556
Sons of Liberty, 62–63
Soulé, Pierre, 239
South Carolina, 248
South Carolina Exposition and Protest, 143–144
South Carolina Negro Act (1740), 30
Southeast Asia Treaty Organization, 498
Southern Alliance, 355
Southern Christian Leadership Conference (SCLC), 509
Soviet System, 483
Soviet Union, 482
collapse of, 560
Space shuttle, 552
Spain, 90
decline in New World, 8
sale of Florida to U.S., 133
surrender of Cuba, Puerto Rico and Guam, 389
Spanish Armada, 10
Spanish-American War, 388
Specie Circular, 172
Specie payments, 288
Spencer, Herbert, 340
Spock, Benjamin, 488
Spoils system, 163, 165
Sports, Golden Age of, 423
Spreckels, Rudolph, 367
Sputnik, 497, 537
Squanto, 14
Squatters' rights, 27
St. Christopher, 17
St. Clair, Gen. Arthur, 101
St. Leger, Col. Barry, 76
St. Mary's (Maryland), 18
Stalin, Joseph, 482, 483
Stamp Act, 62–63
Standard of living, 319
Standard Oil Company, 309–310, 311
Standard Oil Trust, 372–373
Stanton, Edwin M., 274
Stanton, Elizabeth Cady, 189–190, 370
State governments, 80–81
States rights, 118, 250, 282

States Rights party, 491
Steamboat, 146, 155
Steamships, 230
Steel, 306, 308–309
Steel Strike (1919), 415
Steffens, Lincoln, 364, 367
Steiglitz, Alfred, 366
Steinem, Gloria, 542
Steinbeck, John, 454–455
Stephens, Alexander H., 272
Stephens, Uriah S., 314
Stephenson, David C., 426
Stevens, John, 155
Stevens, John L., 385
Stevens, Thaddeus, 255, 277
Stevenson, Adlai E., 495
Stimson, Henry L., 440, 464, 466
Stimson Doctrine, 440
Stoddard, Solomon, 53
Stowe, Harriet Beecher, *Uncle Tom's Cabin,* 148, 237–238
Strasser, Adolph, 315
Strategic Arms Limitation Agreement (SALT II), 545–546, 549, 554
Strategic Arms Limitation Treaty (SALT), 518
Strategic Defense Initiative (SDI), 552
Streetcars, 328–329
Strong, Josiah, 384
Stuart, Gilbert, 193
Student Nonviolent Coordinating Committee (SNCC), 533
Student unrest, 537–539
Students for a Democratic Society (SDS), 538
Sturges v. *Crowninshield,* 159
Subtreasury plan, 358
Suez Canal, 498–499
Sugar Act, 61, 62
Sullivan, "Big Tim," 349–350
Sullivan, John L., 329–330
Sullivan, Louis H., 329
Sumner, Charles, 242, 255, 271–272
Sumner, William Graham, 289
Social Darwinism, 286
"Supply-side" economics (Reganomics), 550
Supreme Court, 158–160, 243–244
and the Sherman Antitrust Act, 314
Susan Constant, 11
Sussex pledge, 401, 402
Swaggert, Jimmy, 530

Taft, Robert A., 467, 495
Taft, William Howard, 395
    defeated as incumbent, 377
    elected president, 375–376
    and Phillipines, 390
Taft-Hartley Act, 487
Talleyrand, 106, 114–115
Tallmadge, James, 141
Tammany Hall organization, 350
Taney, Roger B., 160, 168, 172, 244
Tappan, Lewis, 187
Tarbell, Ida, 364
Tariff, 136–137, 142–143, 166, 171,
    205, 211, 248, 264, 287–288,
    303, 311, 350, 353, 354, 375,
    391, 402, 435, 442
Tariff Act of 1842, 205
Taxation without representation,
    61–62
Taylor, Zachary, 211, 212, 216, 219
Tea Act, 55–56
Teapot Dome scandal, 436
Technological advances, 532
Tecumseh, 125–126, 127
Teheran embassy seizure, 548
Telephone, 306
Television, 528
Television debates, 504
Teller, Henry M., 388
Temperance movement, 425
Temperance Union, 186
10 Percent Plan, 270–271
Tenement house law (1867), 327
Tennent, William, 51–52
Tennessee Valley Authority (TVA),
    452–453, 462
Tenure of Office Act of 1867, 274
Tet offensive, 515
Texas, 206–207, 209
Textiles, 225–226
Thanksgiving, first, 14
Thayer, Webster, 426
Thomas, Jesse B., 142
Thoreau, Henry David, 194
Thorpe, Jim, 423
Thurmond, J. Strom, 491
Tilden, Samuel J., 281, 308
Tilden, William "Big Bull," 423
Timber and Stone Act of 1878, 297
Timber Culture Act of 1863, 296–297
Time Inc., 555
Tippecanoe, Battle of, 125–126
Tobacco, 11, 24, 28–29, 49–50
Tobacco Colony: Life in Early Mary-
    land (Main), 25

Toleration Act (1649), 18, 33
Tories, 75
Townsend, Francis E., 456, 458
Townshend Duties, 64–65
Township system, 85
Trade, 119, 137, 229–230
    foreign, 384
    post-Revolutionary period, 90–91
    triangular, 41
    during World War I, 400
Trade associations, 442
Trafalgar, Battle of, 120
Trail of Tears, 169
Transcendentalism, 193
Transcontinental Treaty, 132–133
Transportation, in early 19th Cen-
    tury, 153–155
Travis, William B., 206
Treasury, independent, 211
Treatise on Domestic Economy for
    the Use of Women (Beecher),
    181
Treaty of Ghent, 130–132
Treaty of Greenville, 104
Treaty of Guadaloupe Hidalgo,
    213–214
Treaty of Paris, 58–59
Treaty of San Ildefonso (1800), 114
Treaty of San Lorenzo, 104
Treaty of Tordesillas, 4
Treaty of Versailles, 412
    defeat in U.S. senate, 414
Treaty of Washington (1871), 383
Trenton, 76
Trist, Nicholas P., 213–214
Trollope, Frances, Domestic Man-
    ners of Americans, 178–179
Trotter, William Monroe, 381
Truman, Harry S., 481, 483–484,
    486
    and China, 490–491
    containment policy, 490, 491
    and Japan, 490–491
    and Korea, 492–493
Trusts, 309–310
Tucker, Richard, 335
Turner, Frederick Jackson,
    341–342, 384
Turner, Nat, 170, 224
Twain, Mark (Samuel L. Clemens),
    342–343
Tweed, William Marcy, 350
Tweed Ring, 276, 350
Two Years Before the Mast (Dana),
    208

Tydings, Millard, 495
Tyler, John, 176, 205
Typewriter, 303

U-2 reconnaissance plane, 499
U-boats, 401
Uncle Tom's Cabin (Stowe), 148,
    237–238
Underwood Tariff, 377
Unemployment
    during Great Depression,
    453–454
    during World War II, 453–454
Union League of America, 279
Union movement, 314–315
Union Pacific, 298
Union Party, 458
Unions, 229, 252–253
United Fruit Company, 396
United Mine Workers, 373
United Nations, 481–482, 499
USS United States, 127
United States Steel, 309
United States v. Butler 1936, 459
United States v. E.C. Knight Com-
    pany (1895), 314, 357
Universal Negro Improvement As-
    sociation, 429
Universities, land grant, 337–338
University of Chicago, 338
University of Michigan, 338
University of Pennsylvania (for-
    merly College of Philadelphia),
    54
Upshur, Abel P., 207
Urban modernization, 328
U.S. Steel, 442, 460
Usury, 40
Utah, 218–219
Utah Territory, 184
Utica and Schenectady Railroad, 232
Utopian communities, 183–185

Vallandigham, Clement L., 256
Van Buren, Martin, 139, 174–175,
    209, 216
Van Hise, Charles R., 369
Vandenberg, Arthur H., 490
Vanderbilt, Cornelius, 160, 304
Vassar College, 338
Venezuela, boundary dispute with
    British Guiana, 386
Venice, trade with, 2
Veracruz, Mexico, United States in-
    vasion of, 213

Verdun, 408
Comte de Vergennes, 77, 79
Verrazano, Giovanni da, 8
Vesey, Denmark, 170, 224–225
Veterans, Civil War, 287
Vichy government, 476–477
Vicksburg, 263
Vietcong, 515
Vietnam, 497–498
Vietnam Moratorium Day, 517
Vietnam War, 512–515
    American casualties in, 520
    bombing of North Vietnam, 519–520
    cost of, 520
    end of, 544
    Nixon's escalation of, 517
    size of American force, 513
    and student unrest, 538
    support for and opposition to, 513–514
    Vietnamization of, 516–517
    withdrawal of American troops from, 520
Villa, Francisco "Pancho," 399
Villard, Henry, 304
Vincent, John H., 335
Virginia, settlement of, 11–13
Virginia Company, 14
Virginia Plan, 94
Virginia Resolves, 106–107
Virtual representation, 62
Visible Saints, 35–36
Volcker, Paul A., 547

Wabash Canal, 157
Wabash case, 313
Wade, Benjamin, 255
Wade-Davis Bill, 271
Wage freeze, under President Nixon, 520
Wagner Act, 457
Wald, Lillian, House on Henry Street (1915), 332
Walden, 194
Walker, Robert J., 244
Walker, William, 238–239
Wallace, George C., 516
Wallace, Henry, 435, 467, 481, 482, 491
Walpole, Sir Robert, policy of salutary neglect, 51
Waltham System, 148–149
War Hawks, 126–127, 139–140
War Industries Board (WIB), 404

War Labor Policies Board (WLPB), 405
War of 1812, 126–130
War on poverty, 511
Ward, Lester Frank, Dynamic Sociology, The Psychic Factors of Civilization, 340
Warhol, Andy, 531
Warner Communications, 555
Warren, Earl, 501, 520
Warsaw Pact, 557
Washington, Booker T., 290–291, 379
Washington, D.C., burning of, 129
Washington, George, 57–58, 86
    appointed commander in chief, 71
    chosen first president, 97
    "Farewell Address," 105
    as general, 74–78
Watergate scandals, 521–522, 523–524
Watson, John B., The Psychological Care of Infant and Child, 419
Watson, Tom, 356
Wealth Against Commonwealth (1894) (Lloyd), 312
The Wealth of Nations (Smith), 90
Weaver, James B., 356
Webster, Daniel, 139, 166, 167
Webster, Noah, 87
Webster-Ashburton Treaty, 206
Weld, Theodore Dwight, 187–188
Welfare state, 332
Wellesley College, 338
West, Benjamin, 192
Western migration, post-Civil War, 291
Westinghouse, 310
Westinghouse, George, 305
Westmoreland, William C., 515
Weyler, Valeriano, 386, 387
Wheat, 42, 233–234, 354, 522
Whigs, 173, 212–213, 216, 240, 241, 248
Whiskey Rebellion, 102–103
Whiskey Ring affair, 281
Whiskey Tax, 112
Whistler, James A. McNeill, 344–345
Whitefield, Reverend George, 52
Whitman, Walt, 333
    Leaves of Grass, 196
Whitney, Eli, 146, 151
Battle of the Wilderness, 265

Wilhelm II, Kaiser, 411
Wilkie, Wendell L., 453, 467
    One World, 482
Wilkins, Roy, 474
William of Orange, 38
Williams, Roger, 16
Williams, William Appleman, 396
Wills, Helen, 423
Wilmot Proviso, 216
Wilson, Woodrow, 369–370, 398–417
    and big business, 378
    Congressional Government, 340
    and dollar diplomacy, 398
    elected president, 376–377
    and Fourteen Points, 409–410
    and League of Nations, 412
    and Mexico, 398–399
    and New Freedom, 376–377
    and Open Door policy, 398
    and Panama Canal, 398
    and "peace without victory," 402
    physical collapse, 414
    religious influence on, 403
    and United States Peace Commission, 411
    and World War I, 400–401
Winthrop, John, 16, 41, 55
Wirz, Henry, 270–271
Wisconsin Idea, 368
Witchcraft, 38
Wolfe, James, 58
Women. See also Feminism
    after World War II, 540–541
    and the American Revolution, 83–84
    and athletics, 331
    in Civil War, 264–265
    colleges, 338
    in colonial times, 35
    in the Democratic party, 462
    in higher education, 421
    job discrimination, 541
    right to vote, 275
    and settlement houses, 332
    voting patterns, 421
    wage standards, 368
    in work force, 421
    as workers in World War II, 475–476
    working hours, 368
    in World War I, 407
Women's Bureau, 421
Women's Christian Temperance Union, 425
Women's Home Companion, 488

Women's liberation, 540
Women's Party, 421
Women's rights, 181, 189–190
Women's suffrage, 370
Wood, Leonard, 391
Woodrow Wilson Foundation, 439
The Wool Act of 1699, 50
Woolworth chain, 442
Worcester v. *Georgia,* 169
Working class, 148
  attitudes, 322–323
  family life, 322
Working hours, 181, 315, 319–320,
  368, 402, 461
Works Progress Administration
  (WPA), 454, 462
World Anti-Slavery Convention
  (1840), 189
World War I
  Allied shipping losses, 408
  American casualties, 408

and American neutrality, 400
causes, 399–400
demobilization after, 414
financing, 405–406
peace process, 408–411
propaganda and civil liberties
  during, 406
rationing during, 404–405
reparations for, 441
U.S. entry into, 403
U.S. financing of, 400–401
World War II, 470–485
  Allied strategy, 476–477
  diplomacy during, 482
  economy, 472–473
  and Hispanics, 464
  and Indians, 474
  Japanese surrender, 481
  in the Pacific, 470–480
  social change, 473
Wright, Orville and Wilbur, 431

XYZ Affair, 106

Yale, Elihu, 40
Yale University, 52, 201, 331
Yalta Conference, 483–484
Yamamoto, Isoroku, 479
Yazoo land frauds, 118
Yellow fever, 114
"Yellow Peril," 394
Yeltsin, Boris, 560
"Yippies," 539
Yorktown, 78–79
Yorktown, 479
Young, Brigham, 184
Young Men's Christian Association,
  331
Young Plan, 441
Youth culture, 419–420

Zenger, John Peter, 45
Zimmermann Telegram, 403